ACCOUNTING PRINCIPLES

SIXTH CANADIAN EDITION

→ Jerry J. Weygandt *Ph.D., CPA*
University of Wisconsin—Madison

→ Donald E. Kieso *Ph.D., CPA*
Northern Illinois University

→ Paul D. Kimmel *Ph.D., CPA*
University of Wisconsin—Milwaukee

→ Barbara Trenholm *MBA, FCA*
University of New Brunswick—Fredericton

→ Valerie A. Kinnear *M.Sc. (Bus. Admin.), CA*
Mount Royal University

→ Joan E. Barlow *B.Comm., CA*
Mount Royal University

WILEY

To our students—past, present, and future

Library and Archives Canada Cataloguing in Publication
Accounting principles / Jerry Weygandt ... [et al.]. — 6th Canadian ed.

Includes index.
Issued also in a 3 part set.
Includes indexes.
ISBN 978-1-118-55730-3 (v. 1).—ISBN 978-1-118-55732-7 (v. 2)

1. Accounting--Textbooks.   I. Weygandt, Jerry J

HF5636.A33 2012a   657.044   C2012-906551-X

Production Credits

Acquisitions Editor: Zoë Craig
Vice President and Publisher: Veronica Visentin
Vice President, Marketing, Global Education: Carolyn Wells
Marketing Manager: Anita Osborne
Editorial Manager: Karen Staudinger
Production Manager: Tegan Wallace
Developmental Editor: Daleara Jamasji Hirjikaka
Media Editor: Channade Fenandoe
Editorial Assistant: Luisa Begani
Design: Interrobang Graphic Design, Inc.
Typesetting: Aptara
Cover Design: Sean Goodchild
Cover Photo: ©Bong Grit 2010/Flickr/Getty, ©ooyoo/Vetta/Getty,
          ©John Foxx/Stockbyte/Getty
Printing and Binding: Friesens Corporation

Printed and bound in Canada
2 3 4 5 FP 17 16 15 14

John Wiley & Sons Canada, Ltd.
6045 Freemont Blvd.
Mississauga, Ontario L5R 4J3
Visit our website at: www.wiley.ca

WileyPLUS

WileyPLUS is a research-based, online environment for effective teaching and learning.

The market-leading homework experience in *WileyPLUS* offers:

A Blank Sheet of Paper Effect

The *WileyPLUS* homework experience, which includes type-ahead for account title entry, imitates a blank sheet of paper format so that students use recall memory when doing homework and will do better in class, on exams, and in their professions.

A Professional Worksheet Style

The professional, worksheet-style problem layouts help students master accounting skills while doing homework that directly applies to the classroom and the real world.

The Opportunity to Catch Mistakes Earlier

Multi-part problems further help students focus by providing feedback at the part-level. Students can catch their mistakes earlier and access content-specific resources at the point of learning.

WileyPLUS includes a full ebook, interactive tutorials, assessment capabilities, and Blackboard integration.

STARR COMPANY
Trial Balance
June 30, 2014

	Debit	Credit
cal	$	
Cash		
Owner's Capital		

Type-ahead feature for account title entry replaces drop-down menus.

WileyPLUS

ALL THE HELP, RESOURCES, AND PERSONAL SUPPORT YOU AND YOUR STUDENTS NEED!

www.wileyplus.com/resources

2-Minute Tutorials and all of the resources you and your students need to get started

WileyPLUS

Student Partner Program

Student support from an experienced student user

Wiley Faculty Network

Collaborate with your colleagues, find a mentor, attend virtual and live events, and view resources
www.WhereFacultyConnect.com

WileyPLUS

Quick Start

Pre-loaded, ready-to-use assignments and presentations created by subject matter experts

Technical Support 24/7
FAQs, online chat, and phone support
www.wileyplus.com/support

Your *WileyPLUS* Account Manager, providing personal training and support

Sixth Canadian Edition

Barbara Trenholm, MBA, FCA, is a professor emerita at the University of New Brunswick, for which she continues to teach locally and internationally on a part-time basis. Her teaching and educational leadership has been widely recognized. She is a recipient of the Leaders in Management Education Award, the Global Teaching Excellence Award, and the University of New Brunswick's Merit Award and Dr. Allan P. Stuart Award for Excellence in Teaching.

Professor Trenholm is an active member of the boards of several organizations, including Atomic Energy of Canada Limited and Plazacorp Retail Properties Ltd. She is a member of the Institute of Corporate Directors, and a past board member of the Canadian Institute of Chartered Accountants and the Atlantic School of Chartered Accountancy and past president of the New Brunswick Institute of Chartered Accountants. She has also served as a chair of the Canadian Institute of Chartered Accountants Academic Research Committee, Interprovincial Education Committee, and Canadian Institute of Chartered Accountants/ Canadian Academic Accounting Association Liaison Committee. She has served as a member of the Canadian Institute of Chartered Accountants Qualification Committee, International Qualifications Appraisal Board, and Education Reeingineering Task Force and the American Accounting Association's Globalization Initiatives Task Force, in addition to numerous other committees at the international, national, and provincial levels of the profession.

She has presented at many conferences and published widely in the field of accounting education and standard setting in journals including *Accounting Horizons*, *Journal of the Academy of Business Education*, *CAmagazine*, *CGA Magazine*, and *CMA Magazine*. She is also the Canadian author of Kimmel, Weygandt, Kieso, and Trenholm, *Financial Accounting: Tools for Business Decision-Making*, published by John Wiley & Sons Canada, Ltd.

Valerie Kinnear, M.Sc. (Bus. Admin.), CA, is an associate professor of accounting and a Nexen Scholar of teaching and learning at Mount Royal University in Calgary, Alberta. She has a wide range of teaching experience and is a recipient of the Chartered Accountants Education Foundation Teaching Award for her work on team-based learning in accounting. Professor Kinnear has held a variety of administrative positions at Mount Royal, including acting dean of the School of Business and acting director of Business Education in the Faculty of Continuing Education and academic chair of a variety of business programs, including Accounting, Financial Services, Supply Chain Management, Marketing, Human Resources, and Insurance. She has been nominated for both the Distinguished Faculty Award and the Distinguished Managers Award at Mount Royal.

She has also been active in the accounting profession. She participated in the Institute of Chartered Accountants of Alberta student education program in a variety of roles, including as an instructor, marker, author, and member of the Alberta Institute's Examinations Committee. She has also served as a member of the Professional Services Policy Board of the Canadian Institute of Chartered Accountants, as a board member of the Canadian Accounting Academic Association, and as treasurer for many volunteer community organizations in Calgary.

Professor Kinnear has a Bachelor of Social Work from the University of Calgary, a Master of Science in Business Administration from the University of British Columbia, and professional accounting experience with PricewaterhouseCoopers, Farvolden and Company Chartered Accountants, and Kinnear & Smistad Chartered Accountants.

Joan Barlow, BComm, CA, is an associate professor of accounting at Mount Royal University, in Calgary, Alberta. She has a wide range of teaching experience in financial and management accounting and is a recipient of the Chartered Accountants Education Foundation Teaching Award for her work on team-based learning in accounting.

Professor Barlow has a Bachelor of Commerce from the University of Calgary and professional accounting experience from Deloitte and Stephen Johnson Chartered Accountants. She was the recipient of the Alberta Silver Medal the year she wrote the uniform final examination for her CA designation. She has also served as treasurer on a number of not-for-profit organizations.

U.S. Edition

Jerry J. Weygandt, Ph.D., CPA, is the Arthur Andersen Alumni Professor of Accounting at the University of Wisconsin—Madison. He holds a Ph.D. in accounting from the University of Illinois. His articles have appeared in *Accounting Review, Journal of Accounting Research, Accounting Horizons, Journal of Accountancy,* and other academic and professional journals. Professor Weygandt is the author of other accounting and financial reporting books and is a member of the American Accounting Association, the American Institute of Certified Public Accountants, and the Wisconsin Society of Certified Public Accountants. He has been actively involved with the American Institute of Certified Public Accountants and has been a member of the Accounting Standards Executive Committee of that organization. He served on the FASB task force that examined the reporting issues related to accounting for income taxes and as a trustee of the Financial Accounting Foundation. Professor Weygandt has received the Chancellor's Award for Excellence in Teaching and the Beta Gamma Sigma Dean's Teaching Award. He is the recipient of the Wisconsin Institute of CPAs' Outstanding Educator's Award and the Lifetime Achievement Award. In 2001 he received the American Accounting Association's Outstanding Accounting Educator Award.

Donald E. Kieso, Ph.D., CPA, received his bachelor's degree from Aurora University and his doctorate in accounting from the University of Illinois. He has served as chairman of the Department of Accountancy and is currently the KPMG Emeritus Professor of Accounting at Northern Illinois University. He has public accounting experience with PricewaterhouseCoopers (San Francisco and Chicago) and Arthur Andersen & Co. (Chicago) and research experience with the Research Division of the American Institute of Certified Public Accountants (New York). He has done post-doctoral work as a Visiting Scholar at the University of California at Berkeley and is a recipient of NIU's Teaching Excellence Award and four Golden Apple Teaching Awards. Professor Kieso is the author of other accounting and business books and is a member of the American Accounting Association, the American Institute of Certified Public Accountants, and the Illinois CPA Society. He has served as a member of the board of directors of the Illinois CPA Society, the AACSB's Accounting Accreditation Committees, and the State of Illinois Comptroller's Commission; as secretary-treasurer of the Federation of Schools of Accountancy; and as secretary-treasurer of the American Accounting Association. He is the recipient of the Outstanding Accounting Educator Award from the Illinois CPA Society, the FSA's Joseph A. Silvoso Award of Merit, the NIU Foundation's Humanitarian Award for Service to Higher Education, the Distinguished Service Award from the Illinois CPA Society, and in 2003 an honorary doctorate from Aurora University.

Paul D. Kimmel, Ph.D., CPA, received his bachelor's degree from the University of Minnesota and his doctorate in accounting from the University of Wisconsin. He is an Associate Professor at the University of Wisconsin—Milwaukee, and has public accounting experience with Deloitte & Touche (Minneapolis). He was the recipient of the UWM School of Business Advisory Council Teaching Award and the Reggie Taite Excellence in Teaching Award, and is a three-time winner of the Outstanding Teaching Assistant Award at the University of Wisconsin. He is also a recipient of the Elijah Watts Sells Award for Honorary Distinction for his results on the CPA exam. Professor Kimmel is the author of other accounting and business books and is a member of the American Accounting Association and the Institute of Management Accountants and has published articles in *Accounting Review, Accounting Horizons, Advances in Management Accounting, Managerial Finance, Issues in Accounting Education,* and *Journal of Accounting Education,* as well as other journals. His research interests include accounting for financial instruments and innovation in accounting education. He has published papers and given numerous talks on incorporating critical thinking into accounting education, and helped prepare a catalogue of critical thinking resources for the Federated Schools of Accountancy.

How to Use the Study Aids in This Book

CHAPTER THREE
ADJUSTING THE ACCOUNTS

The Navigator is a learning system designed to guide you through each chapter and help you succeed in learning the material. It consists of (1) a checklist at the beginning of each chapter, which outlines text features and study skills you will need, and (2) a series of check boxes that prompts you to use the learning aids in the chapter and set priorities as you study.

Concepts for Review, listed at the beginning of each chapter, are the accounting concepts you learned in the previous chapters that you will need to know in order to understand the topics you are about to cover. Page references are provided for your review before reading the chapter.

THE NAVIGATOR

☐ Understand *Concepts for Review*
☐ Read *Feature Story*
☐ Scan *Study Objectives*
☐ Read *Chapter Preview*
☐ Read text and answer *Before You Go On*
☐ Review *Comparing IFRS and ASPE*
☐ Work *Demonstration Problem*
☐ Review *Summary of Study Objectives*
☐ Answer *Self-Study Questions*
☐ Complete assignments
☐ Go to *WileyPLUS* for practice and tutorials

CONCEPTS FOR REVIEW

Before studying this chapter, you should understand or, if necessary, review:

a. The double-entry accounting system. (Ch. 2, p. 61)
b. How to increase and decrease assets, liabilities, and owner's equity accounts using debit and credit procedures. (Ch. 2, pp. 58–61)
c. How to journalize transactions. (Ch. 2, pp. 64–65)
d. How to post transactions to the general ledger. (
e. How to prepare a trial balance. (Ch. 2, pp. 75–77)

CHAPTER THREE

ADJUSTING THE BOOKS AFTER HITTING THE BOOKS

TORONTO, ON—You probably pay your tuition just before classes start in September, but how does your college or university account for your money after that?

In Ontario, all colleges have a fiscal year that ends on March 31, which is also the provincial government's fiscal year end. "All the colleges' financial information is fully consolidated onto the province's books," explains Jeanette Dias D'Souza, former Vice President of Finance and Administration at Seneca College of Applied Arts & Technology, with 10 locations in the Greater Toronto area.

Many academic years end in late April, however. According to what's called accrual accounting, any revenues for services performed after March 31 have to be recognized in the following fiscal year, even though the money was collected earlier. So if a study term ends in late April, a small portion of the tuition for that semester will be recognized as revenue by the college in the next fiscal year.

The same revenue recognition criteria applies for students who study in the summer term: if they pay tuition before March 31, it can't be recognized as revenue until the teaching services are performed in the summer. That term is important

for Seneca. "We have a very large summer program," says Ms. Dias D'Souza.

Seneca's main sources of operating funding are provincial grants and student tuition fees. It also receives revenue from private and corporate training. As with tuition fees, revenue from this training is recognized in the period in which the training is provided.

The college also receives revenue from renting space for private functions, including Eaton Hall, a former estate of the famed Eaton retailing family that is located on one of Seneca's campuses. If an engaged couple puts down a deposit in February for their July wedding, that revenue is not recognized until the wedding takes place in the next fiscal year, Ms. Dias D'Souza says.

Expenses, too, must be recorded in the year when they are incurred. For example, Seneca's invoices for utilities and legal fees for the last month of the fiscal year tend to come in after the year end, so the college uses estimates to accrue for these expenses at the year end.

Recording revenues and expenses in the correct period is a challenge, but one that must be met to properly reflect the school's activity in each period.

THE NAVIGATOR

The Feature Story helps you picture how the chapter topic relates to the real world of accounting and business. Throughout the chapter, references to the Feature Story will help you put new ideas in context, organize them, and remember them.

Study Objectives at the beginning of each chapter provide you with a framework for learning the specific concepts and procedures covered in the chapter. Each study objective reappears at the point within the chapter where the concept is discussed. You can review all the study objectives in the **Summary of Study Objectives** at the end of the chapter. End-of-chapter material is keyed to study objectives.

 STUDY **OBJECTIVES**

After studying this chapter, you should be able to:

1. Explain accrual basis accounting, and when to recognize revenues and expenses.
2. Prepare adjusting entries for prepayments.
3. Prepare adjusting entries for accruals.
4. Describe the nature and purpose of an adjusted trial balance, and prepare one.
5. Prepare adjusting entries for the alternative treatment of prepayments (Appendix 3A).

THE NAVIGATOR

PREVIEW OF CHAPTER THREE

In Chapter 2, we learned the accounting cycle up to and including the preparation of the trial balance. In this chapter, we will learn that additional steps are usually needed before preparing the financial statements. These steps adjust accounts for timing mismatches, like the ones Seneca College has with the tuition it receives for its summer classes and the costs it incurs to offer these classes. In this chapter, we introduce the accrual accounting concepts that guide the adjustment process.

The chapter is organized as follows:

Adjusting the Accounts

Timing Issues	The Basics of Adjusting Entries	The Adjusted Trial Balance and Financial Statements
➤ Accrual versus cash basis accounting ➤ Revenue and expense recognition	➤ Adjusting entries for prepayments ➤ Adjusting entries for accruals	➤ Preparing the adjusted trial balance ➤ Preparing financial statements

The **Preview** graphically outlines the major topics and subtopics that will be discussed. This narrative and visual preview gives you a mental framework upon which to arrange the new information you are about to learn.

Timing Issues

STUDY OBJECTIVE 1

Explain accrual basis accounting, and when to recognize revenues and expenses.

Accounting would be simple if we could wait until a company ended its operations before preparing its financial statements. As the following anecdote shows, if we waited until then we could easily determine the amount of lifetime profit earned:

A grocery store owner from the old country kept his accounts payable on a wire memo spike, accounts receivable on a notepad, and cash in a shoebox. His daughter, a CGA, chided her father: "I don't understand how you can run your business this way. How do you know what you've earned?"

"Well," her father replied, "when I arrived in Canada 40 years ago, I had nothing but the pants I was wearing. Today, your brother is a doctor, your sister is a teacher, and you are a CGA. Your mother and I have a nice car, a well-furnished house, and a home by the lake. We have a good business and everything is paid for. So, you add all that together, subtract the pants, and there's your profit."

Although the grocer may be correct in his evaluation about how to calculate his profit over his lifetime, most companies need more immediate feedback on how they are doing. For example, management usually wants monthly financial statements. Investors want to view the results of publicly traded companies at least quarterly. The Canada Revenue Agency requires financial statements to be filed with annual income tax returns.

Consequently, accountants divide the life of a business into specific time periods, such as a month, a three-month quarter, or a year. An accounting time period that is one year long is called a fiscal year. Time periods of less than one year are called interim periods.

The fiscal year used by many businesses is the same as the calendar y[...]
However, it can be different. Seneca College's fiscal year is April 1 throug[...]
many colleges, universities, and governments. Some retail companies u[...]
exactly one year, for their fiscal year. Reitmans (Canada) Limited does t[...]
urday in January as the end of its fiscal year. But because 52 weeks [...]
some years Reitmans has to use a 53-week period with the first Saturday i[...]

Because the life of a business is divided into accounting time [...]
record transactions is important. Many business transactions affect n[...]
period. For example, equipment is used over several years. We also saw [...]
times Seneca College collects tuition fees in one fiscal year and then [...]
fiscal year. In the following section, we will see that deciding when to r[...]
will have a significant impact on the usefulness of financial statements [...]

▶ **ADJUSTMENT** 5
Accrued Revenue—
Accounts Receivable

Basic Analysis	The asset account Accounts Receivable is increased by $200 for the revenue earned and the revenue account Service Revenue is increased by $200.		
Equation Analysis	Assets Accounts Receivable +200	= Liabilities	+ Owner's Equity Service Revenue +200
Debit-Credit Analysis	Debits increase assets: Debit Accounts Receivable $200. Credits increase revenues: Credit Service Revenue $200.		

Adjusting Journal Entry	Oct. 31	Accounts Receivable Service Revenue To accrue revenue earned but not billed or collected.	200	200

Posting	Accounts Receivable	Service Revenue
	Oct. 21 10,000 Oct. 31 9,000 31 **Adj. 200** Oct. 31 Bal. 1,200	Oct. 21 10,000 25 800 31 Adj. 400 31 **Adj. 200** Oct. 31 Adj. 11,400

The asset Accounts Receivable shows that $1,200 is owed by clients at the balance sheet date. The balance of $11,400 in Service Revenue represents the total revenue earned during the month. If the adjusting entry is not made, assets and owner's equity on the balance sheet, and revenues and profit on the income statement, will all be understated.

On November 10, Pioneer receives $200 cash for the services performed in October. The following entry is made:

A = L + OE
+200
−200
⬆ Cash flows: +200

Nov. 10	Cash Accounts Receivable To record cash collected on account.	200	200

The **Accounting Equation** has been inserted in the margin next to journal entries throughout the text. This feature helps you understand the impact of each accounting transaction on the financial position and cash flows.

Alternative Terminology familiarizes you with other commonly used terms.

Alternative terminology Accrued expenses are also called *accrued liabilities.*

Accrued Expenses

Expenses incurred but not yet paid or recorded at the statement date are called accrued expenses. Interest, rent, property taxes, and salaries can be accrued expenses. As we saw in our feature story, Seneca College uses estimates to accrue for legal and utility expenses because the actual invoices are received after its year end. Accrued expenses result from the same causes as accrued revenues. In fact, an accrued expense on the books of one company is an accrued revenue for another company. For example, the $200 accrual of revenue by Pioneer is an accrued expense for the client that received the service.

Adjustments for accrued expenses are needed for two purposes: (1) to record the obligations that exist at the balance sheet date, and (2) to recognize the expenses that apply to the current accounting period. Before adjustment, both liabilities and expenses are understated. Profit and owner's equity are overstated. An adjusting entry for accrued expenses results in an increase (debit) to an expense account and an increase (credit) to a liability account, as follows:

Accrued Expenses

Expense	Liability
Debit Adjusting Entry (+)	Credit Adjusting Entry (+)

ACCOUNTING IN ACTION
ALL ABOUT YOU INSIGHT

We all know the importance of literacy. But what about financial literacy—the ability to understand and manage your finances? It seems Canadians don't place the same importance on financial literacy—but with rising household debt levels, falling savings levels, increasing personal bankruptcies, and continuing economic uncertainty, they should. According to Statistics Canada research, in 2009 only half of Canadians had a household budget and one in three were struggling to pay their bills. On a scale of 1 to 100, Canadians scored an average of 66 in terms of their ability to keep track of their finances and 61 out of 100 in terms of planning for life goals such as buying a house or retiring. To improve the situation the federal government launched a Task Force on Financial

Literacy. The task force recommended that financial literacy be taught at a young age and that Canadians continue learning about finances throughout their lives. Making the right financial decisions can have a major impact on an individual's financial well-being, health, and happiness.

Learning the basics of accounting will help you make the right financial decisions. Accounting will help you make investment decisions, determine how much interest you are paying on your student loan or credit cards, and prepare your personal budget. To demonstrate the value of accounting to you, included in each chapter is an "All About You" feature and a related activity (BYP–6) that links accounting to your life as a student or to a situation you are likely to face.

Sources: Task Force on Financial Literacy, Canadians and Their Money: Building a Brighter Financial Future, December 2010; Financial Consumer Agency of Canada, The Future of Financial Education: Report on the 2011 FCAC-OECD Conference on Financial Literacy, 2011; Robin Taub and Mary Teresa Bitt, "It Pays to Know," CA Magazine, October 2011.

How might learning accounting help you make sure that your employer or bank hasn't made an error with your paycheque or bank account?

USING ACCOUNTING INFORMATION

There are two broad groups of users of accounting information: internal users and external users.

Internal Users

Internal users of accounting information plan, organize, and run companies. They work for the company. This includes finance directors, marketing managers, human resources personnel, production supervisors, and company officers. In running a business, internal users must answer many important questions, as shown in Illustration 1-1.

Accounting in Action insights give examples of accounting situations from different perspectives: all about you, across the organization, and in terms of business and ethics. At the end of the chapter, you will find answers to the questions that are asked after each insight.

▶ ILLUSTRATION 1-1
Questions asked by

Finance
Is there enough cash to pay the bills?

Marketing
What price should we sell smart phones for to maximize profits?

Human Resources
How many employees can we afford to hire this year?

Production
Which product line is the most profitable?

Accounting in Action insight boxes give you glimpses into how companies make decisions using accounting information. These high-interest boxes are classified by three different points of view—Across the Organization, Business Insight, and All About You. Each ends with a question to show the relevance of the box. Suggested answers appear at the end of the chapter.

Colour illustrations, such as this infographic, help you visualize and apply the information as you study. They summarize and reinforce important concepts.

---

10 | CHAPTER 1   Accounting in Action

International Financial Reporting Standards and Accounting Standards for Private Enterprises

The AcSB recognizes that "one size does not necessarily fit all" and has developed and adopted separate standards for publicly accountable enterprises and for private enterprises. Canadian public enterprises must follow International Financial Reporting Standards (IFRS), a set of global standards developed by the International Accounting Standards Board (IASB). Publicly accountable enterprises include publicly traded corporations, as well as securities brokers and dealers, banks, and credit unions whose role is to hold assets for the public as part of their primary business. Reitmans is a public company and therefore is required to follow IFRS.

Traditionally, accounting standards differed from country to country, making it difficult for investors, creditors, and others to make informed decisions about companies doing business in today's increasingly global environment. The IASB has worked, and continues to do so, with accounting standard setters across the globe to harmonize accounting standards where possible. IFRS are used as the main basis of financial reporting in more than 100 countries, including Australia, Brazil, Russia, members of the European Union, China, India, Japan, Mexico, and Canada. Although the United States does not use IFRS, its standard setters are working on a joint project with the IASB to develop and revise accounting standards so that they are consistent between U.S. GAAP and IFRS.

Following IFRS enhances Canadian public companies' ability to compete in an increasingly global marketplace. When IFRS are used, the financial statements of Canadian public companies are understood by investors and creditors throughout the world. Using IFRS also helps Canadian companies that operate in multiple countries, by allowing them to produce one set of financial statements rather than multiple sets with different accounting principles.

On the other hand, the users of a private company's financial statements generally have the ability to obtain additional information from the company if required. Because these users typically require less information in the financial statements, the AcSB developed Accounting Standards for Private Enterprises (ASPE). ASPE requires considerably less information in financial statements than is required by IFRS. While public companies have to follow IFRS, Canadian private companies, including private corporations such as McCain Foods and EllisDon Inc., have the choice to report under ASPE or IFRS. As proprietorships and partnerships are private companies, these companies will generally follow ASPE for financial reporting.

Given the differences between IFRS and ASPE, and the fact that private companies have a choice, financial statement users will need to know which standards the company is following. Companies are required to report this in their financial statements. In this textbook, as we proceed through the material, we will point out where there are differences in the two sets of standards. However, the two sets of standards have a great deal in common in the type of material covered in an introductory accounting textbook.

Both IFRS and ASPE are considered "principles-based" as opposed to "rules-based" standards. Principles-based standards are designed to encourage the use of professional judgement in applying basic accounting principles. As you learn more about accounting, you will see that we will frequently refer to basic principles, as opposed to detailed rules, when deciding how to account for specific events. In this chapter, we introduce a few of these basic principles and concepts.

It is important to understand that GAAP is not static and that it changes over time. The AcSB and IASB continue to create new standards and modify GAAP. AcSB and IASB use a process that involves consultation with organizations and individuals that are interested in, or affected by, the standards. This process can take a long time but it ensures that the main purpose of financial statements—providing information that is relevant to decision-making—continues to be met.

The length of time involved in adding new or changing existing accounting standards can make it difficult to determine what information we should include in this textbook—should it be the currently approved standard or the proposed new standard? Sometimes the proposals are modified or dropped altogether before being approved. Normally the textbook will cover only the currently approved standards. But where we believe it is important to do so, we will introduce new standards that were proposed at the time the textbook was written.

Helpful hint Accounting standards use the word "enterprise" as it is a broader term than "company" or "business." The word "enterprise" means that the accounting standard applies to the different forms of business organizations, as well as specific projects. Throughout this text, instead of using the word "enterprise," we will frequently use the words "company" or "business," as they are more common terms.

The ASPE Icon indicates where differences between IFRS and ASPE are explained. These differences are also summarized at the end of each chapter.

Helpful Hints in the margins help clarify concepts being discussed.

Key Terms that represent essential concepts are printed in blue where they are first explained in the text. They are defined again in the end-of-chapter **Glossary**.

ASPE icons in the margin highlight differences between International Financial Reporting Standards (IFRS) and Accounting Standards for Private Enterprises (ASPE).

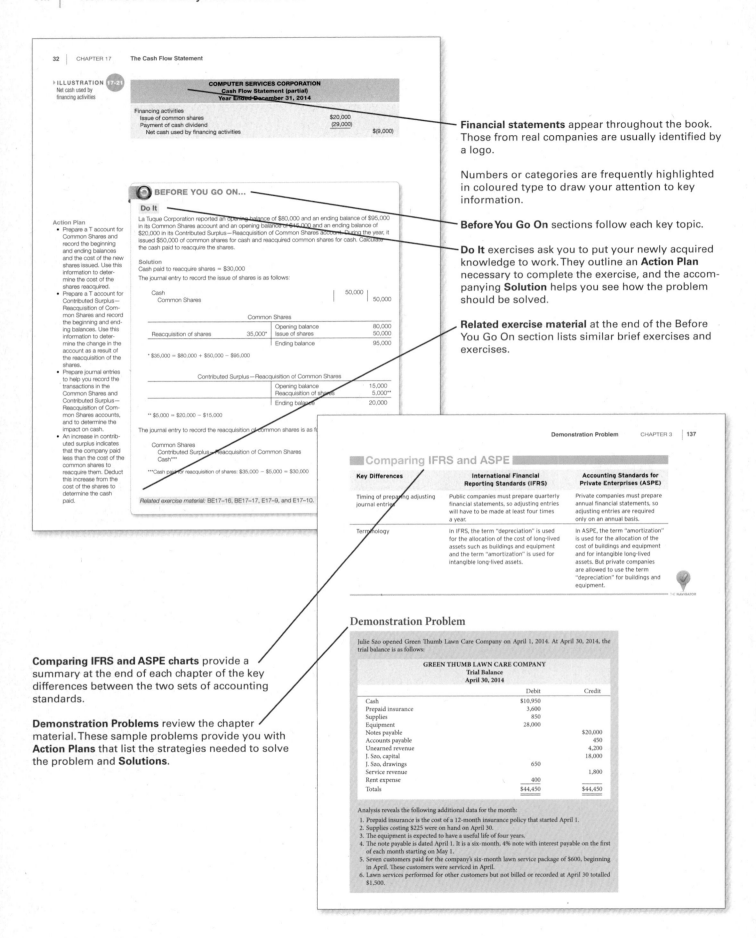

32   CHAPTER 17   The Cash Flow Statement

▶ILLUSTRATION 17-21
Net cash used by
financing activities

COMPUTER SERVICES CORPORATION
Cash Flow Statement (partial)
Year Ended December 31, 2014

Financing activities		
Issue of common shares	$20,000	
Payment of cash dividend	(29,000)	
Net cash used by financing activities		$(9,000)

Financial statements appear throughout the book. Those from real companies are usually identified by a logo.

Numbers or categories are frequently highlighted in coloured type to draw your attention to key information.

BEFORE YOU GO ON...

Do It

La Tuque Corporation reported an opening balance of $80,000 and an ending balance of $95,000 in its Common Shares account and an opening balance of $15,000 and an ending balance of $20,000 in its Contributed Surplus—Reacquisition of Common Shares account. During the year, it issued $50,000 of common shares for cash and reacquired common shares for cash. Calculate the cash paid to reacquire the shares.

Solution

Cash paid to reacquire shares = $30,000

The journal entry to record the issue of shares is as follows:

Cash	50,000	
Common Shares		50,000

Common Shares		
	Opening balance	80,000
Reacquisition of shares 35,000*	Issue of shares	50,000
	Ending balance	95,000

* $35,000 = $80,000 + $50,000 − $95,000

Contributed Surplus—Reacquisition of Common Shares		
	Opening balance	15,000
	Reacquisition of shares	5,000**
	Ending balance	20,000

** $5,000 = $20,000 − $15,000

The journal entry to record the reacquisition of common shares is as f...

Common Shares		
Contributed Surplus—Reacquisition of Common Shares		
Cash***		

*** Cash paid for reacquisition of shares: $35,000 − $5,000 = $30,000

Related exercise material: BE17–16, BE17–17, E17–9, and E17–10.

Action Plan
- Prepare a T account for Common Shares and record the beginning and ending balances of the new shares issued. Use this information to determine the cost of the shares reacquired.
- Prepare a T account for Contributed Surplus—Reacquisition of Common Shares and record the beginning and ending balances. Use this information to determine the change in the account as a result of the reacquisition of the shares.
- Prepare journal entries to help you record the transactions in the Common Shares and Contributed Surplus—Reacquisition of Common Shares accounts, and to determine the impact on cash.
- An increase in contributed surplus indicates that the company paid less than the cost of the common shares to reacquire them. Deduct this increase from the cost of the shares to determine the cash paid.

Before You Go On sections follow each key topic.

Do It exercises ask you to put your newly acquired knowledge to work. They outline an **Action Plan** necessary to complete the exercise, and the accompanying **Solution** helps you see how the problem should be solved.

Related exercise material at the end of the Before You Go On section lists similar brief exercises and exercises.

Demonstration Problem   CHAPTER 3   137

Comparing IFRS and ASPE

Key Differences	International Financial Reporting Standards (IFRS)	Accounting Standards for Private Enterprises (ASPE)
Timing of preparing adjusting journal entries	Public companies must prepare quarterly financial statements, so adjusting entries will have to be made at least four times a year.	Private companies must prepare annual financial statements, so adjusting entries are required only on an annual basis.
Terminology	In IFRS, the term "depreciation" is used for the allocation of the cost of long-lived assets such as buildings and equipment and the term "amortization" is used for intangible long-lived assets.	In ASPE, the term "amortization" is used for the allocation of the cost of buildings and equipment and for intangible long-lived assets. But private companies are allowed to use the term "depreciation" for buildings and equipment.

THE NAVIGATOR

Demonstration Problem

Julie Szo opened Green Thumb Lawn Care Company on April 1, 2014. At April 30, 2014, the trial balance is as follows:

GREEN THUMB LAWN CARE COMPANY
Trial Balance
April 30, 2014

	Debit	Credit
Cash	$10,950	
Prepaid insurance	3,600	
Supplies	850	
Equipment	28,000	
Notes payable		$20,000
Accounts payable		450
Unearned revenue		4,200
J. Szo, capital		18,000
J. Szo, drawings	650	
Service revenue		1,800
Rent expense	400	
Totals	$44,450	$44,450

Analysis reveals the following additional data for the month:

1. Prepaid insurance is the cost of a 12-month insurance policy that started April 1.
2. Supplies costing $225 were on hand on April 30.
3. The equipment is expected to have a useful life of four years.
4. The note payable is dated April 1. It is a six-month, 4% note with interest payable on the first of each month starting on May 1.
5. Seven customers paid for the company's six-month lawn service package of $600, beginning in April. These customers were serviced in April.
6. Lawn services performed for other customers but not billed or recorded at April 30 totalled $1,500.

Comparing IFRS and ASPE charts provide a summary at the end of each chapter of the key differences between the two sets of accounting standards.

Demonstration Problems review the chapter material. These sample problems provide you with **Action Plans** that list the strategies needed to solve the problem and **Solutions**.

82 CHAPTER 2 The Recording Process

Summary of Study Objectives

1. **Define debits and credits and illustrate how they are used to record transactions.** Debit means left and credit means right. The normal balance of an asset is a debit because assets are on the left side of the accounting equation. Assets are increased by debits and decreased by credits. The normal balance of liabilities and owner's capital is a credit because they are on the right side of the accounting equation. Liabilities and owner's capital are increased by credits and decreased by debits. Revenues increase owner's equity and therefore are recorded as credits because increase owner's equity. Credits increase revenues and debits decrease revenues. Expenses and drawings decrease owner's equity and therefore are recorded as debits because debits decrease owner's equity. Expenses and drawings are increased by debits and decreased by credits.

2. **Explain the recording process and analyze, journalize, and post transactions.** The steps in the recording process are the first three steps in the accounting cycle. These steps are: (a) analyze each transaction for its effect on the accounts, (b) record the transaction in a journal, and (c) transfer the journal information to the correct accounts in the ledger.

A journal (a) discloses the complete effect of a transaction in one place, (b) provides a chronological record of transactions, (c) helps to prevent and locate errors because the debit and credit amounts for each entry can be easily compared, and (d) explains the transaction and, if there is one, identifies the source document.

The entire group of accounts maintained by a company is called the ledger. The ledger keeps in one place all the information about changes in each of the specific account balances. Posting is the procedure of transferring journal entries to the ledger accounts. After the journal entries have been posted, the ledger will show all of the increases and decreases that have been made to each account.

3. **Explain the purpose of a trial balance, and prepare one.** A trial balance is a list of the accounts in the ledger and the account balances at a specific time. Its main purpose is to prove that debits and credits are equal after posting. A trial balance uncovers certain types of errors in journalizing and posting, and is useful in preparing financial statements. Preparing a trial balance is the fourth step in the accounting cycle.

Flash cards

Glossary

Account A record of increases and decreases in a specific asset, liability, or owner's equity item. (p. 58)

Accounting cycle A series of steps followed by accountants in preparing financial statements. (p. 62)

Chart of accounts A list of accounts and the account numbers that identify where the accounts are in the ledger. (p. 67)

Compound entry A journal entry that affects three or more accounts. (p. 65)

Credit The right side of an account. (p. 58)

Debit The left side of an account. (p. 58)

Double-entry accounting system A system that records the dual (two-sided) effect of each transaction in appropriate accounts. (p. 61)

General journal The most basic form of journal in which transactions are recorded when they are not recorded in other specialized journals. (p. 64)

General ledger A ledger that contains accounts for all assets, liabilities, equities, revenues, and expenses. (p. 65)

Journal An accounting record where transactions are recorded in chronological (date) order. It shows the debit and credit effect of each transaction on specific accounts. (p. 64)

Journalizing The entering of transaction data in the journal. (p. 64)

Ledger A record that contains all of a company's accounts. It keeps all the information about changes in each account in one place. (p. 65)

Posting The procedure of transferring journal entries to the ledger accounts. (p. 66)

Recording process The first [...] cycle. (p. 62)

T account A form of accou[...] has the title above the horizon[...] left of the vertical line, credits [...]

Three-column form of accou[...] umns for debit, credit, and balan[...]

Trial balance A list of the [...] account balances at a specific [...] accounting period. (p. 75)

The **Summary of Study Objectives** relates the study objectives to the key points in the chapter. It gives you another opportunity to review, as well as to see how all the key topics within the chapter are related.

The **Glossary** defines all the terms and concepts introduced in the chapter. Page references help you find any terms you need to study further. QR codes appear throughout this text. Scanning the code will lead to additional resources related to the text content. You can scan using your smart phone and a QR code scanning app. Many free QR scanning apps can be found by searching your app store.

Self-Study Questions

Answers are at the end of the chapter.

(SO 1) K 1. Which of the following statements about an account is true?
(a) The left side of an account is the credit or decrease side.
(b) An account is an individual accounting record of increases and decreases in specific asset, liability, and owner's equity items.
(c) There are separate accounts for specific assets and liabilities but only one account for owner's equity items.
(d) The right side of an account is the debit or increase side.

(SO 1) K 2. Credits:
(a) increase both assets and liabilities.
(b) decrease both assets and liabilities.
(c) increase assets and decrease liabilities.
(d) decrease assets and increase liabilities.

(SO 1) K 3. An expense account:
(a) is increased by debits.
(b) has a normal balance of a credit.
(c) is decreased by debits.
(d) is increased by credits.

(SO 1) K 4. Accounts that normally have debit balances are:
(a) assets, expenses, and revenues.
(b) assets, expenses, and owner's capital.
(c) assets, liabilities, and drawings.
(d) assets, expenses, and drawings.

(SO 2) K 5. What is the correct sequence of steps in the recording process?
(a) Analyzing transactions; preparing a trial balance
(b) Analyzing transactions; entering transactions in a journal; posting transactions
(c) Entering transactions in a journal; posting transactions; preparing a trial balance
(d) Entering transactions in a journal; posting transactions; analyzing transactions

(SO 2) AP 6. Performing services for a customer on account should result in:
(a) a decrease in the liability account Accounts Payable and an increase in the revenue account Service Revenue.
(b) an increase in the asset account Cash and a decrease in the asset account Accounts Receivable.
(c) an increase to the asset account Accounts Receivable and an increase to the liability account Unearned Revenue.

(d) an increase to the asset account Accounts Receivable and an increase to the revenue account Service Revenue.

(SO 2) AP 7. The purchase of equipment on account should result in:
(a) a debit to Equipment and a credit to Accounts Payable.
(b) a debit to Equipment Expense and a credit to Accounts Payable.
(c) a debit to Equipment and a credit to Cash.
(d) a debit to Accounts Receivable and a credit to Equipment.

(SO 2) K 8. Which of these statements about a journal is false?
(a) It is not a book of original entry.
(b) It provides a chronological record of transactions.
(c) It helps to locate errors because the debit and credit amounts for each entry can be easily compared.
(d) It shows in one place the complete effect of a transaction.

(SO 2) K 9. A ledger:
(a) contains only asset and liability accounts.
(b) should show accounts in alphabetical order.
(c) is a collection of the entire group of accounts maintained by a company.
(d) is a book of original entry.

(SO 2) K 10. Posting:
(a) is normally done before journalizing.
(b) transfers ledger transaction data to the journal.
(c) is an optional step in the recording process.
(d) transfers journal entries to ledger accounts.

(SO 3) K 11. A trial balance:
(a) is a list of accounts with their balances at a specific time.
(b) proves that journalized transactions are accurate.
(c) will not balance if a correct journal entry is posted twice.
(d) proves that all transactions have been recorded.

(SO 3) AP 12. A trial balance will not balance if:
(a) the collection of an account receivable is posted twice.
(b) the purchase of supplies on account is debited to Supplies and credited to Cash.
(c) a $100 cash drawing by the owner is debited to Drawings for $1,000 and credited to Cash for $100.
(d) a $450 payment on account is debited to Accounts Payable for $45 and credited to Cash for $45.

Questions

(SO 1) C 1. What is an account? Will a company need more than one account? Explain.

(SO 1) K 2. What is debiting an account? What is crediting an account?

(SO 1) K 3. Explain the relationship between the normal balance in each type of account and the accounting equation.

Self-Study Questions form a practice test that gives you an opportunity to check your knowledge of important topics. Answers appear on the last page of the chapter.

Self-study questions are keyed to study objectives. In addition, the level of cognitive skill required to solve the question has been classified with a letter code following Bloom's Taxonomy. You will find more information about Bloom's Taxonomy and this coding system on page XIII of this Preface.

Questions allow you to explain your understanding of concepts and relationships covered in the chapter. (These are keyed to study objectives and Bloom's Taxonomy.)

Brief Exercises

BE6–1 Helgeson Company has identified the following items to include or exclude when it takes its physical inventory. Indicate whether each item should be included or excluded.

(a) Goods shipped on consignment by Helgeson to another company
(b) Goods in transit to Helgeson from a supplier, shipped FOB destination
(c) Goods sold to a customer but being held for delivery
(d) Goods from another company held on consignment by Helgeson
(e) Goods in transit to a customer, shipped FOB shipping point

Identify items in inventory. (SO 1) K

BE6–2 The merchandise inventory in Carla's Clothing Store was counted after the close of business on December 31, 2014, the company's year end. It was determined that the total cost of this inventory was $55,500. Carla wants to know if this is the correct amount that should be reported on the company's December 31, 2014, balance sheet or if an adjustment needs to be made for any of the following items:

(a) The count included merchandise "on hold" for customers. These items cost $950 and will be held until noon on January 2, 2015. Carla expects at least one-half of the customers will return to purchase the items.
(b) The count also included items costing $1,200 that had been sold but are being held for alterations. The customers have paid in full for these items.
(c) Carla's Clothing Store has $4,250 of merchandise held on consignment for a local designer. These items were included in the inventory count.
(d) A shipment of inventory costing $2,875 was received on January 2, 2015. It had been shipped by the seller on December 30, FOB shipping point. Freight charges are $310. These items were not included in the inventory count.
(e) A second shipment of inventory costing $4,350 was received on January 3, 2015. It had been shipped by the seller on December 31, FOB destination. Freight charges are $390. These items were also not included in the inventory count.

Determine the correct amount of Carla's Clothing Store's merchandise inventory at December 31, 2014.

Calculate inventory balance. (SO 1) AP

BE6–3 In October, Claire's Gallery purchased four original paintings for resale for the following amounts: Painting 1, $1,000; Painting 2, $2,000; Painting 3, $3,000; and Painting 4, $4,000. Paintings 3 and 4 were sold during October for $6,500 each. Calculate the cost of goods sold for the month and the ending inventory balance on October 31 using specific identification.

Apply specific identification cost determination method. (SO 2) AP

BE6–4 The following are three inventory cost determination methods:

1. Specific identification
2. FIFO
3. Average

Below is a list of different types of companies and their main inventory item. Beside each one, insert the number of the inventory cost determination method above that the company would most likely use.

(a) _____ Grocery store (food)
(b) _____ Coffee shop (coffee beans)
(c) _____ Car dealership (automobiles)
(d) _____ Clothing store (clothing)
(e) _____ Car dealership (parts)
(f) _____ Gas station (fuel)
(g) _____ Jewellery store (custom-made jewellery)
(h) _____ Consignment clothing store (clothing)

Recommend cost determination method. (SO 2) AP

BE6–5 First Choice Company uses the FIFO cost formula in a perpetual inventory system. Fill in the missing amounts for items (a) through (k) in the following perpetual inventory schedule:

Apply perpetual FIFO.

Date	PURCHASES			COST OF GOODS SOLD			BALANCE		
	Units	Cost	Total	Units	Cost	Total	Units	Cost	To
June 1							200	$25.00	$5,0
7	400	$22.00	$8,800.00				(a)	(b)	
18				350	(d)	(e)	(f)	(g)	
26	350	$20.00	7,000.00				(i)	(j)	

BE6–6 Average Joe Company uses the average cost formula in a perpetual inventory system. Fill in the amounts for items (a) through (k) in the following perpetual inventory schedule:

Brief Exercises generally focus on one study objective at a time. They help you build confidence in your basic skills and knowledge. (These are keyed to study objectives and Bloom's Taxonomy.)

E3–13 The adjusted trial balance for Lane Company is given in E3–12.

Instructions
Prepare Lane Company's income statement, statement of owner's equity, and balance sheet.

Prepare financial statements from adjusted trial balance. (SO 4) AP

*E3–14 Refer to the transaction information provided in E3–4 for Action Quest Games. Assume that prepaid expenses are initially recorded as expenses (not as assets as in E3–4). Assume that revenues collected in advance of the work are initially recorded as revenue (not as liabilities as in E3–4).

Instructions
(a) For each transaction: (1) prepare the journal entry to record the initial transaction, and (2) prepare the adjusting journal entry required on December 31, 2014.
(b) Post each of these entries to T accounts and calculate the final balance in each account. (*Note*: Posting to the Cash account is not necessary.)
(c) Compare your balances in (b) above with those obtained in E3–4, part (b). Comment on your findings.

Prepare and post transaction and adjusting entries for prepayments. (SO 5) AP

*E3–15 At Richmond Company, the following select transactions occurred in January, the company's first month of operations:

Jan. 1 Paid rent of $1,000 for January.
      2 Paid $1,920 for a one-year insurance policy.
      5 Paid $1,700 for supplies.
    19 Received $6,100 cash for services to be performed in the future.
    31 Paid rent of $1,000 for February.

Additional information:

1. On January 31, it is determined that $2,500 of the service revenue has been earned.
2. On January 31, a count of supplies shows that there is $650 of supplies on hand.

Instructions
(a) Assume Richmond records all prepaid costs as expenses, and all revenue collected in advance as revenue. Journalize the January transactions and post to T accounts. (*Note*: Posting to the Cash account is not necessary.)
(b) Journalize and post the January 31 adjustments.
(c) Determine the ending balances in each of the accounts.

Prepare and post transaction and adjusting entries for prepayments. (SO 2, 5) AP

Problems: Set A

P3–1A Your examination of the records of Southlake Co. shows the company collected $85,500 cash from customers and paid $48,400 cash for operating costs during 2014. If Southlake followed the accrual basis of accounting, it would report the following year-end balances:

	2014	2013
Accounts payable	$ 1,500	$ 2,250
Accounts receivable	4,200	2,700
Accumulated depreciation	11,300	10,000
Prepaid insurance	1,500	1,300
Supplies	750	400
Unearned revenues	1,200	1,500

Instructions
(a) Determine Southlake's profit on a cash basis for 2014.
(b) Determine Southlake's profit on an accrual basis for 2014.

TAKING IT FURTHER   Which method do you recommend Southlake use? Why?

Determine profit on cash and accrual bases; recommend method. (SO 1) AP

P3–2A Ouellette & Associates began operations on January 1, 2014. Its fiscal year end is December 31 and it prepares financial statements and adjusts its accounts annually. Selected transactions for 2014 follow:

1. On January 10, bought office supplies for $3,400 cash. A physical count at December 31, 2014, revealed $925 of supplies still on hand.
2. Paid cash for a $3,780, one-year insurance policy on February 1, 2014. The policy came into effect on this date.
3. On March 31, purchased equipment for $21,240 cash. The equipment has an estimated six-year useful life.

Prepare and post prepayment transaction entries. Prepare basic analysis, debit/credit analysis, and journal entry, and post adjustments for the prepayments. (SO 2) AP

Exercises that gradually increase in difficulty help you to build your confidence in your ability to use the material learned in the chapter. (These are keyed to study objectives and Bloom's Taxonomy.)

Each **Problem** helps you pull together and apply several concepts of the chapter. Two sets of problems—Set A and Set B—are usually keyed to the same study objectives and cognitive level. These provide additional opportunities to apply concepts learned in the chapter.

Taking It Further is an extra question at the end of each problem designed to challenge you to think beyond the basic concepts covered in the problem, and to provide written explanations. Your instructor may assign problems with or without this extra element.

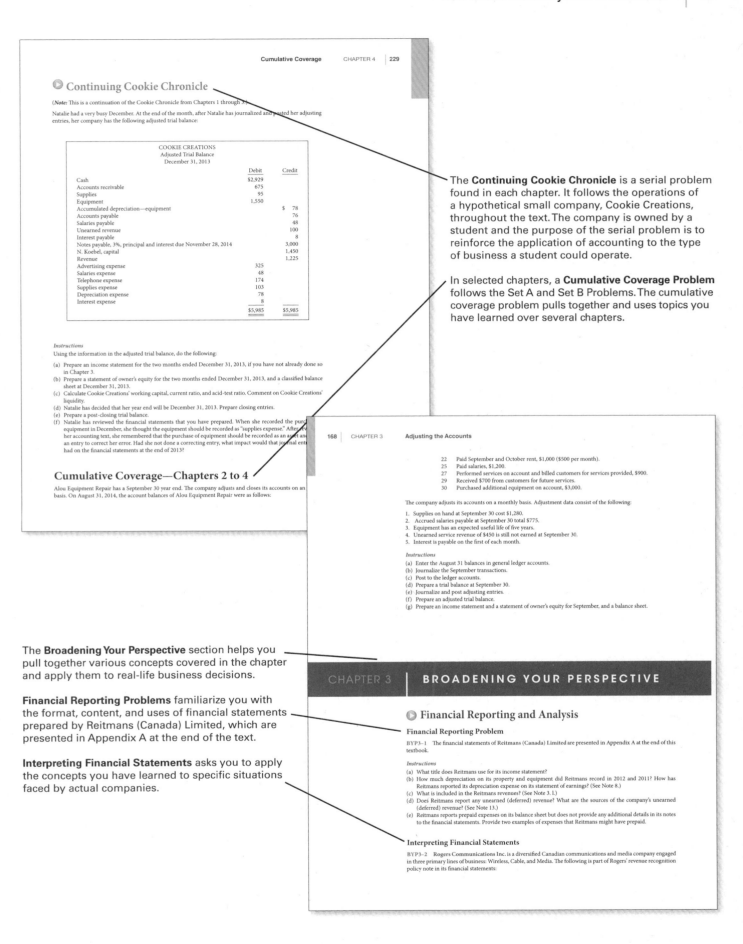

Continuing Cookie Chronicle

(*Note:* This is a continuation of the Cookie Chronicle from Chapters 1 through 3.)

Natalie had a very busy December. At the end of the month, after Natalie has journalized and posted her adjusting entries, her company has the following adjusted trial balance:

COOKIE CREATIONS
Adjusted Trial Balance
December 31, 2013

	Debit	Credit
Cash	$2,929	
Accounts receivable	675	
Supplies	95	
Equipment	1,550	
Accumulated depreciation—equipment		$ 78
Accounts payable		76
Salaries payable		48
Unearned revenue		100
Interest payable		8
Notes payable, 3%, principal and interest due November 28, 2014		3,000
N. Koebel, capital		1,450
Revenue		1,225
Advertising expense	325	
Salaries expense	48	
Telephone expense	174	
Supplies expense	103	
Depreciation expense	78	
Interest expense	8	
	$5,985	$5,985

Instructions

Using the information in the adjusted trial balance, do the following:

(a) Prepare an income statement for the two months ended December 31, 2013, if you have not already done so in Chapter 3.

(b) Prepare a statement of owner's equity for the two months ended December 31, 2013, and a classified balance sheet at December 31, 2013.

(c) Calculate Cookie Creations' working capital, current ratio, and acid-test ratio. Comment on Cookie Creations' liquidity.

(d) Natalie has decided that her year end will be December 31, 2013. Prepare closing entries.

(e) Prepare a post-closing trial balance.

(f) Natalie has reviewed the financial statements that you have prepared. When she recorded the purchase of equipment in December, she thought the equipment should be recorded as "supplies expense." After reviewing her accounting text, she remembered that the purchase of equipment should be recorded as an asset and prepared an entry to correct her error. Had she not done a correcting entry, what impact would that journal entry had on the financial statements at the end of 2013?

Cumulative Coverage—Chapters 2 to 4

Alou Equipment Repair has a September 30 year end. The company adjusts and closes its accounts on an basis. On August 31, 2014, the account balances of Alou Equipment Repair were as follows:

The **Continuing Cookie Chronicle** is a serial problem found in each chapter. It follows the operations of a hypothetical small company, Cookie Creations, throughout the text. The company is owned by a student and the purpose of the serial problem is to reinforce the application of accounting to the type of business a student could operate.

In selected chapters, a **Cumulative Coverage Problem** follows the Set A and Set B Problems. The cumulative coverage problem pulls together and uses topics you have learned over several chapters.

22	Paid September and October rent, $1,000 ($500 per month).
25	Paid salaries, $1,200.
27	Performed services on account and billed customers for services provided, $900.
29	Received $700 from customers for future services.
30	Purchased additional equipment on account, $3,000.

The company adjusts its accounts on a monthly basis. Adjustment data consist of the following:

1. Supplies on hand at September 30 cost $1,280.
2. Accrued salaries payable at September 30 total $775.
3. Equipment has an expected useful life of five years.
4. Unearned service revenue of $450 is still not earned at September 30.
5. Interest is payable on the first of each month.

Instructions

(a) Enter the August 31 balances in general ledger accounts.

(b) Journalize the September transactions.

(c) Post to the ledger accounts.

(d) Prepare a trial balance at September 30.

(e) Journalize and post adjusting entries.

(f) Prepare an adjusted trial balance.

(g) Prepare an income statement and a statement of owner's equity for September, and a balance sheet.

The **Broadening Your Perspective** section helps you pull together various concepts covered in the chapter and apply them to real-life business decisions.

Financial Reporting Problems familiarize you with the format, content, and uses of financial statements prepared by Reitmans (Canada) Limited, which are presented in Appendix A at the end of the text.

Interpreting Financial Statements asks you to apply the concepts you have learned to specific situations faced by actual companies.

CHAPTER 3 | BROADENING YOUR PERSPECTIVE

Financial Reporting and Analysis

Financial Reporting Problem

BYP3–1 The financial statements of Reitmans (Canada) Limited are presented in Appendix A at the end of this textbook.

Instructions

(a) What title does Reitmans use for its income statement?

(b) How much depreciation on its property and equipment did Reitmans record in 2012 and 2011? How has Reitmans reported its depreciation expense on its statement of earnings? (See Note 8.)

(c) What is included in the Reitmans revenues? (See Note 3.1.)

(d) Does Reitmans report any unearned (deferred) revenue? What are the sources of the company's unearned (deferred) revenue? (See Note 13.)

(e) Reitmans reports prepaid expenses on its balance sheet but does not provide any additional details in its notes to the financial statements. Provide two examples of expenses that Reitmans might have prepaid.

Interpreting Financial Statements

BYP3–2 Rogers Communications Inc. is a diversified Canadian communications and media company engaged in three primary lines of business: Wireless, Cable, and Media. The following is part of Rogers' revenue recognition policy note in its financial statements:

● Critical Thinking

Collaborative Learning Activity

Note to instructor: Additional instructions and material for this group activity can be found on the Instructor Resource Site and in *WileyPLUS.*

BYP2–3   In this group activity, students will be given a trial balance and will be asked to work backwards to create a set of journal entries that would result in the trial balance.

Communication Activity

BYP2–4   White Glove Company offers home cleaning services. Three common transactions for the company are signing contracts with new customers, billing customers for services performed, and paying employee salaries. For example, on March 15 the company did the following:

1. Signed a contract with a new customer for $125 per week starting the first week in April.
2. Sent bills that totalled $6,000 to customers.
3. Paid $2,000 in salaries to employees.

Instructions
Write an e-mail to your instructor that explains if and how these transactions are recorded in the double-entry system. Include in your e-mail (a) whether, and why, the transaction should or should not be recorded, and (b) how the debit and credit rules are applied if the transaction is recorded.

Ethics Case

BYP2–5   Vu Hung is the assistant chief accountant at Lin Company, a manufacturer of computer chips and cellular phones. The company currently has total sales of $20 million. It is the end of the first quarter. Vu is hurriedly trying to prepare a general ledger trial balance so that quarterly financial statements can be prepared and released to management and regulatory agencies. The credits on the trial balance add up to $1,000 more than the debits.
    In order to meet the 4:00 p.m. deadline, Vu decides to force the debits and credits into balance by adding the amount of the difference to the Equipment account. She chose Equipment because it is one of the larger account balances. Proportionally, it will be the least misstated. She believes that the difference will not affect anyone's decisions. She wishes that she had more time to find the error, but realizes that the financial statements are already late.

Instructions
(a) Who are the stakeholders in this situation?
(b) What are the ethical issues involved?
(c) What are Vu's alternatives?

"All About You" Activity

BYP2–6   The "All About You" feature indicates that Luca Pacioli, who described the double-entry accounting system used over 500 years ago, wrote "a person should not go to sleep at night until the debits equalled the credits."
    In the double-entry system, debits and credits are used to record the dual effect of each transaction on appropriate accounts and to keep the basic accounting equation in balance. For each transaction, the debits equal the credits; therefore, the total debits and credits for all of the accounts should be equal. If the total debits do not equal the credits, there is an error in the accounting records.
    You are a first-year university student and very excited about moving away from home to go to university. Your parents have given you $4,000 and you have a $14,000 student loan. Your parents have told you that $4,000 is all you get for the school year and you are not to phone home for more money.
    At September 1, you had $18,000 cash ($4,000 + $14,000), $1,000 worth of clothes, and a cell phone that cost $200. You have kept all of the receipts for all of your expenditures between September 1 and December 31. The following is a complete list of your receipts.

Collaborative Learning Activities prepare you for the business world, where you will be working with many people, by giving you practice in solving problems with colleagues. They also allow you to learn from fellow students.

Communication Activities ask you to engage in real-life business situations using your writing, speaking, or presentation skills.

Through **Ethics Cases**, you will reflect on ethical situations an accountant typically confronts.

All About You Activities ask you questions about the All About You feature in the chapter, helping you apply accounting principles to your personal finances.

ANSWERS TO CHAPTER QUESTIONS

ANSWERS TO ACCOUNTING IN ACTION INSIGHT QUESTIONS

All About You Insight, p. 114

Q: How should you account for the cost of your post-secondary education? Should you be recognizing the cost as an expense each year or should you recognize it as an asset?
A: Expenses are recognized when there has been a decrease in an asset or an increase in a liability. Paying for an education will reduce assets such as cash and may also increase liabilities if you have to take out student loans. Therefore, most accountants would tell you that you should record the cost of your education as an expense as you incur those costs. On the other hand, it could be argued that your education is creating an asset—your increased future earning power. But then you would have to estimate the value of this asset. As with many situations in accounting, it is not easy to determine the correct answer.

Business Insight, p. 122

Q: If a business collects cash when the gift card is sold, how can gift card sales in December result in revenues in January?
A: Gift cards sales are simply another example of unearned revenues. At the time the gift card is sold, the business must record unearned revenue, which is a liability. When a customer redeems the gift card by making a purchase, then the company will reduce the liability and record revenue.

ANSWERS TO SELF-STUDY QUESTION

1. b   2. d   3. d   4. b   5. c   6. d   7. a   8. a   9. b   10. a   11. a   *12. a   *13. c

Answers to Chapter Questions offer suggested answers for questions that appear in the chapter's **Accounting in Action** insight boxes and the **Self-Study Questions**.

After you complete your assignments, it's a good idea to go back to **The Navigator** checklist at the start of the chapter to see if you have used all the study aids of the chapter.

Remember to go back to the beginning of the chapter to check off your completed work!

The Use of Bloom's Taxonomy

Bloom's Taxonomy is a classification framework that you can use to develop your skills from the most basic to the most advanced competence levels: knowledge, comprehension, application, analysis, synthesis, and evaluation. These levels are in a hierarchy. In order to perform at each level, you must have mastered all prior levels.

Questions, exercises, and problems at the end of each chapter of this text have been classified by the knowledge level required in answering each one. Below you will learn what your role is in each of the six skill levels and how you can demonstrate mastery at each level. Key word clues will help you recognize the skill level required for a particular question.

(K) Knowledge (Remembering)

Student's role: "I read, listen, watch, or observe; I take notes and am able to recall information; ask and respond to questions."
Student demonstrates knowledge by stating who, what, when, why, and how in the same form in which they learned it.
Key word clues: define, identify, label, name, etc.

(C) Comprehension (Understanding)

Student's role: "I understand the information or skill. I can recognize it in other forms and I can explain it to others and make use of it."
Student demonstrates comprehension by giving an example of how the information would be used.
Key word clues: describe, distinguish, give example, compare, differentiate, explain, etc.

(AP) Application (Solving the Problem)

Student's role: "I can apply my prior knowledge and understanding to new situations."
Student demonstrates knowledge by solving problems independently, recognizing when the information or skill is needed and using it to solve new problems or complete tasks.
Key word clues: calculate, illustrate, prepare, complete, use, produce, etc.

(AN) Analysis (Detecting)

Student's role: "I can break down the information into simpler parts and understand how these parts are related."
Student demonstrates knowledge by recognizing patterns and hidden meanings, filling in missing information, correcting errors, and identifying components and effects.
Key word clues: analyze, break down, compare, contrast, deduce, differentiate, etc.

(S) Synthesis (Creating)

Student's role: "I use all knowledge, understanding, and skills to create alternatives. I can convey this information to others effectively."
Student demonstrates knowledge by acting as a guide to others, designing, and creating.
Key word clues: relate, tell, write, categorize, devise, formulate, generalize, create, design, etc.

(E) Evaluation (Appraisal)

Student's role: "I am open to and appreciative of the value of ideas, procedures, and methods and can make well-supported judgements, backed up by knowledge, understanding, and skills."
Student demonstrates knowledge by formulating and presenting well-supported judgement, displaying consideration of others, examining personal options, and making wise choices.
Key word clues: appraise, assess, criticize, critique, decide, evaluate, judge, justify, recommend, etc.

Learning Styles Chart

Everybody has a preferred learning style. One part of that learning style is your preference for the intake and the output of ideas and information. This textbook contains features to help you learn best, whatever your learning style. Look at this page for how you can apply an understanding of your learning style to this course. Then read the Student Owner's Manual to view the features of this textbook and to understand their purpose.

Visual

WHAT TO DO IN CLASS	WHAT TO DO WHEN STUDYING	TEXT FEATURES THAT MAY HELP YOU	WHAT TO DO PRIOR TO EXAMS
• Pay close attention to charts, drawings, and handouts your instructor uses. • Underline and highlight. • Use different colours. • Use symbols, flow charts, graphs, different arrangements on the page, white space.	Convert your lecture notes into "page pictures." To do this: • Use the "What to do in class" strategies. • Reconstruct images in different ways. • Redraw pages from memory. • Replace words with symbols and initials. • Look at your pages.	• The Navigator • Feature Story • Preview • Infographics/Illustrations • Photos • Accounting in Action insight boxes • Accounting Equation Analyses in margins • Key Terms in blue • Words in bold or italics • Demonstration Problem/Action Plan • Questions/Exercises/Problems • Financial Reporting and Analysis	• Recall your "page pictures." • Draw diagrams where appropriate. • Practise turning your visuals back into words.

Aural

WHAT TO DO IN CLASS	WHAT TO DO WHEN STUDYING	TEXT FEATURES THAT MAY HELP YOU	WHAT TO DO PRIOR TO EXAMS
• Attend lectures and tutorials. • Discuss topics with students and instructors. • Explain new ideas to other people. • Leave spaces in your lecture notes for later recall. • Describe overheads, pictures, and visuals to somebody who was not in class.	You may take poor notes because you prefer to listen. Therefore: • Expand your notes by talking with others and with information from your textbook. • Record summarized notes and listen. • Read summarized notes out loud. • Explain your notes to another "aural" person.	• Preview • Infographics/Illustrations • Accounting in Action insight boxes • Do It/Action Plan • Summary of Study Objectives • Glossary • Demonstration Problem/Action Plan • Self-Study Questions • Questions/Exercises/Problems • Financial Reporting and Analysis • Critical Thinking, particularly the Collaborative Learning Activities	• Talk with the instructor. • Spend time in quiet places recalling the ideas. • Practise writing answers to old exam questions. • Say your answers out loud.

Reading/Writing

WHAT TO DO IN CLASS	WHAT TO DO WHEN STUDYING	TEXT FEATURES THAT MAY HELP YOU	WHAT TO DO PRIOR TO EXAMS
• Use lists and headings. • Use dictionaries, glossaries, and definitions. • Read handouts, textbooks, and supplemental library readings. • Use lecture notes.	• Write out words again and again. • Reread notes silently. • Rewrite ideas and principles into other words. • Turn charts, diagrams, and other illustrations into statements.	• The Navigator • Feature Story • Study Objectives • Preview • Accounting Equation Analysis in margins • Do It/Action Plan • Summary of Study Objectives • Glossary • Self-Study Questions • Questions/Exercises/Problems/ Taking It Further • Writing Problems • Financial Reporting and Analysis • Critical Thinking, particularly the Communication activities and the Collaborative Learning activities	• Write exam answers. • Practise with multiple-choice questions. • Write paragraphs, beginnings, and endings. • Write your lists in outline form. • Arrange your words into hierarchies and points.

Kinesthetic

WHAT TO DO IN CLASS	WHAT TO DO WHEN STUDYING	TEXT FEATURES THAT MAY HELP YOU	WHAT TO DO PRIOR TO EXAMS
• Use all your senses. • Go to labs, take field trips. • Listen to real-life examples. • Pay attention to applications. • Use hands-on approaches. • Use trial-and-error methods.	You may take poor notes because topics do not seem concrete or relevant. Therefore: • Put examples in your summaries. • Use case studies and applications to help with principles and abstract concepts. • Talk about your notes with another "kinesthetic" person. • Use pictures and photographs that illustrate an idea.	• The Navigator • Feature Story • Preview • Infographics/Illustrations • Do It/Action Plan • Summary of Study Objectives • Demonstration Problem/Action Plan • Self-Study Questions • Questions/Exercises/Problems • Financial Reporting and Analysis • Critical Thinking, particularly the All About You activities and the Collaborative Learning a ctivities	• Write practice answers. • Role-play the exam situation.

For all learning styles: Be sure to use the learning aids on the companion website and in *WileyPLUS* to enhance your understanding of the text's concepts and procedures. In particular, use the tutorials, study aids (including the searchable glossary, PowerPoint® presentations, and problem-solving techniques), and practice tools (including additional demonstration problems, key term matching activities, and quizzes).

To the Instructor

Student-Focused and Instructor-Friendly—
The Solution for Your Accounting Principles Class!

In the previous editions of *Accounting Principles*, we sought to create a book about accounting that makes the subject clear and fascinating to students. And that is still our passion: to empower students to succeed by giving them the tools and the motivation they need to excel in their accounting courses and their future careers. We are confident that this new edition, with its strong pedagogical foundations, continuing currency and accuracy of the material, and exciting new features, is the best edition yet.

Preparing the Sixth Canadian Edition

This revision of *Accounting Principles* provided us with an opportunity to improve a textbook that had already set high standards for quality. In the fifth edition, we began the process of incorporating the new world of multiple GAAP while new standards for private enterprises were being created and implemented. In this edition, we have furthered our incorporation of International Financial Reporting Standards (IFRS) and Accounting Standards for Private Enterprises (ASPE) into the text material. Differences between IFRS and ASPE are highlighted throughout each chapter with an ASPE logo (ASPE) where applicable. Each chapter concludes with a *Comparing IFRS and ASPE* table to provide a quick summary of key differences between the two sets of standards.

While the implementation of these new accounting standards represents a significant change, from an introductory accounting point of view, much is still the same. The basic accounting cycle remains unchanged and the focus for introductory students continues to be the fundamental principles. We have undertaken to reduce unnecessary complexities where possible and have decreased the number of account titles used in the textbook and the on-line homework system. Our goal is to keep students focused on the concepts that really matter.

WileyPLUS is an innovative, research-based on-line environment for effective teaching and learning.

WileyPLUS builds students' confidence because it takes the guesswork out of studying by providing students with a clear roadmap: **what to do, how to do it, if they did it right.** This interactive approach focuses on:

CONFIDENCE: Research shows that students experience a great deal of anxiety over studying. That's why we provide a structured learning environment that helps students focus on **what to do,** along with the support of immediate resources.

MOTIVATION: To increase and sustain motivation throughout the semester, *WileyPLUS* helps students learn **how to do it** at a pace that's right for them. Our integrated resources—available 2/47—function like a personal tutor, directly addressing each student's demonstrated needs with specific problem-solving techniques.

SUCCESS: *WileyPLUS* helps to assure that each study session has a positive outcome by putting students in control. Through instant feedback and study objective reports, students know **if they did it right,** and where to focus next, so they achieve the strongest results.

With *WileyPLUS*, our efficacy research shows that students improve their outcomes by as much as one letter grade. *WileyPLUS* helps students take more initiative, so you'll have a greater impact on their achievement in the classroom and beyond.

What do students receive with *WileyPLUS*?
- The complete digital textbook, saving students up to 60% off the cost of a printed text.
- Question assistance, including links to relevant sections in the on-line digital textbook.
- Immediate feedback and proof of progress, 24/7.
- Integrated multimedia resources—including MP3 downloads, visual exhibits, animations, demonstration problems, simulations, and much more—that provide multiple study paths and encourage more active learning.

What do instructors receive with *WileyPLUS*?
- Reliable resources that reinforce course goals inside and outside of the classroom.
- Media-rich course materials and assessment content, including Instructor's Manual, Test Bank, PowerPoint® Slides, Learning Objectives, Solutions Manual, Study Guide, Computerized Test Bank, Practice Quizzes, and much more.
- The ability to easily identify those students who are falling behind.

Relevance for Users

It has always been our goal to motivate both accounting and non-accounting majors to learn accounting. In order to illustrate the importance of financial accounting to non-accounting majors, we started Chapter 1 with a section about why accounting is important to everyone, not just accountants. We consistently emphasize this point throughout the text and have an Accounting in Action insight box in each chapter called All About You. These boxes demonstrate how learning accounting is useful for students in managing their own financial affairs. We also have many Across the Organization Accounting in Action insight boxes. These clearly demonstrate how accounting is used to address issues in marketing, finance, management, and other functions. It is our sincere hope that non-accounting majors have the opportunity to appreciate accounting both personally and professionally.

This edition continues, and expands, the inclusion of user-oriented material to demonstrate the relevance of accounting to all students, no matter what their area of study is. We have a new focus company this edition—Reitmans (Canada) Limited—Canada's largest women's specialty retailer. Reitmans was chosen because its stores have high name recognition with students, it operates in a single industry, and it has relatively simple financial statements. References to Reitmans have been included throughout the chapter, including ratio analysis, end-of-chapter assignments, and in Reitmans' financial statements in Appendix A at the end of the textbook.

This edition was also subject to a comprehensive updating to ensure that it continues to be relevant and fresh. All real-world examples were updated, or replaced, in the text as appropriate, including the chapter-opening feature stories, the Accounting in Action insight boxes, and references to real-world examples in the text and end-of-chapter material. Our textbook includes references to over 200 real companies. In addition, 55% of the chapter-opening feature stories were replaced with new stories, and a large percentage of the Accounting in Action insight boxes are new.

We continue to feature problem material that allows students to tie the concepts they are learning together and place them in context. Central to this is the Continuing Cookie Chronicle. This serial problem allows students to apply chapter topics in an ongoing scenario where a young entrepreneur builds her small business.

Expanded Topical Coverage

Additional topical coverage was requested by instructors to help them better prepare students for the complexities of today's world of accounting. As always, these topics had to pass a strict test to warrant their inclusion: they were added only if they represented a major concept, issue, or procedure that a beginning student should understand. Some of the more significant additions include the following:

- Chapter 1: Accounting in Action introduced the objective of financial reporting (the financial statements) to enhance students' understanding of each of the financial statements. The transaction analysis has been supplemented by including a basic analysis of each transaction before the effect on the balance sheet equation is illustrated.
- Chapter 2: The Recording Process has been supplemented by adding a partial diagram of the accounting cycle to the trial balance material to more clearly demonstrate that the trial balance builds on the first three steps in the accounting cycle introduced earlier in the chapter.
- Chapter 3: Adjusting the Accounts includes an enhanced explanation of adjusting journal entries. A basic analysis and debit-credit analysis have been added to walk students through the thinking process and to emphasize the similarities to basic transaction journal entries introduced in Chapter 2.
- Chapter 4: Completion of the Accounting Cycle has illustrations of the formula used in calculating cost of goods sold and its components under a periodic system. An example of calculating the working capital, current, and acid-test ratios was added in a new "Do It" exercise and to the end-of-chapter Demonstration Problem.
- Chapter 5: Accounting for Merchandising Operations includes a side-by-side comparison of the journal entries for the buyer and seller in the end-of-chapter Demonstration Problem. A "Do It" exercise on the gross profit margin and profit margin

ratios, and illustrations of the formulas to calculate cost of goods sold in the periodic inventory system, were added.

- Chapter 6: Inventory Costing has a diagram of the impact of an ending inventory error on the Merchandise Inventory account over a two-year period. "Do It" exercises were added on the financial statement impact of inventory cost formulas, and on the inventory turnover and days sales in inventory ratios. Journal entries were added to the "Do It" and Demonstration Problem material on the inventory cost determination methods.
- Chapter 7: Internal Control and Cash now includes an explanation of fraud using the "fraud triangle" and a "Do It" on reporting cash.
- Chapter 8: Accounting for Receivables now has illustrations that show the calculation of bad debt expense if there is a credit or debit balance in the allowance for doubtful accounts prior to the adjustment.
- Chapter 9: Long-Lived Assets now includes T accounts of the long-lived asset and accumulated depreciation accounts for each of the disposal examples in order to clarify how those numbers are determined. A "Do It" on the asset turnover and return on assets ratios has been added. More explicit information was included on the differences between ASPE and IFRS.
- Chapter 10: Current Liabilities and Payroll has a "Do It" on preparing the current liabilities section of the balance sheet.
- Chapter 11: Financial Reporting Concepts includes an explanation of how revenue should be recognized if a sales transaction includes both the sale of a product and a service component. The chapter includes a discussion on common ways that the recognition and measurement concepts are violated either by error or by intentional misstatement.
- Chapter 13: Introduction to Corporations was substantially rewritten to focus on topics that affect private corporations following ASPE. It explains the different economic and accounting issues for private and public companies when issuing shares. An illustration of the closing process for a corporation was added.
- Chapter 14: Corporations: Additional Topics and IFRS was also substantially rewritten and builds on the material introduced in Chapter 13. The material moved into this chapter from Chapter 13 includes reacquisition of shares, which was expanded to show an example of a reacquisition of shares above cost with and without a balance in the Contributed Surplus account.
- Chapter 16: Investments now includes the effective-interest method to amortize the discount and premium on long-term investment in bonds. The effective-interest method for the investment in bonds is illustrated using the Candlestick example that is used to illustrate bonds payable in Chapter 15 so that students can compare the accounting for the investment with the accounting for the bonds payable.
- Chapter 17: The Cash Flow Statement includes a new illustration comparing the cash from operating activities section prepared under the indirect and direct methods before these methods are explained. Journal entries have been included to support

the account analysis and to walk students through the thinking process used to determine the cash impact of transactions.

- Chapter 18: Financial Statement Analysis now includes expanded "Do It" examples for more comprehensive coverage of the material in the chapter.

Organizational Changes

Changes to the text's organization were made to simplify chapters or to provide instructors with greater flexibility of coverage. Some of the areas most affected are as follows:

- Chapter 1: Accounting in Action includes more emphasis on the objective of financial reporting. The objective of financial reporting is introduced before the concept of financial statements to enhance students' understanding of the purpose of each of the statements. The introduction to the financial statements and the elements reported in each statement has been combined with the explanation of the accounting model before the transaction analysis. Recognition and measurement concepts are explained in the section on transaction analysis to help students connect these concepts to the recording of transactions.
- Chapter 2: The Recording Process moved the material on the double-entry system to the end of the section on debit and credit procedures to allow students to focus on learning the effects of debits and credits before starting to think about the need to record the dual effect of a transaction.
- Chapter 6: Inventory Costing moved material on inventory errors and lower of cost and net realizable value into separate study objectives. Journal entries illustrated for the first-in, first-out and average cost formulas allow students to better understand the relationship of the material in Chapter 6 with that in Chapter 5.
- Chapter 7: Internal Control and Cash combined the material on control features of a bank account and preparing a bank reconciliation into one study objective as it is interrelated material.
- Chapter 8: Accounting for Receivables focuses on the percentage of receivables approach to estimating the allowance for doubtful accounts and bad debt expense because of the increasing emphasis in GAAP on proper balance sheet valuations.
- Chapter 10: Current Liabilities and Payroll has simplified the material on contingencies and removed contingent assets.
- Chapter 13: Introduction to Corporations was substantially revised to shift material between Chapters 13 and 14 to provide better flexibility for instructors to teach only ASPE. Chapter 13 now includes all of the basic material on corporations and focuses on ASPE. Material on income taxes and a simple corporate income statement, cash dividends, and the statement of retained earnings was moved from Chapter 14 to 13. More complex material, such as reacquisition of shares, was moved from Chapter 13 to 14.
- Chapter 14: Corporations: Additional Topics and IFRS was substantially revised as described in the explanation of the

changes to Chapter 13. The material on correction of prior period errors has been repositioned under the topic of accounting changes.

- Chapter 15: Non-Current Liabilities now includes the effective-interest method of amortizing discounts and premiums on bonds payable in the chapter and not in a separate appendix because of the requirements under IFRS to use this method.
- Chapter 18: Financial Statement Analysis separates the material on ratio analysis into the three types of ratios: liquidity, solvency, and profitability. The summary of each type of ratio was moved to that section.

Unparalleled End-of-Chapter Material

The sixth Canadian edition continues to have a complete range of end-of-chapter material to satisfy all courses. This material guides students through the basic levels of cognitive understanding—knowledge, comprehension, application, analysis, synthesis, and evaluation—in a step-by-step process, starting first with questions, followed by brief exercises, exercises, problems, and finally, integrative cases to broaden a student's perspective.

Instructors told us they wanted more breadth and depth within each of these groupings to give them more flexibility in assigning end-of-chapter material. Using Bloom's Taxonomy of Learning, all of the end-of-chapter material was carefully reviewed. Topical gaps were identified and material added as required to facilitate progressive learning. Complexities were added to the Before You Go On, Self-Study Questions, and selected end-of-chapter material to increase the range and difficulty level of material available to test critical problem-solving skills.

A Taking It Further question is included at the end of every problem. These questions are designed to help you determine how far your students have taken their understanding of the material. To ensure maximum flexibility, problems can also be assigned with or without the Taking It Further question. They also make excellent classroom discussion questions.

The Continuing Cookie Chronicle, a serial problem in each chapter, follows the life of a simulated student-owned company. This edition has been revised to include moving the business into a family-owned corporation. The conceptual material in each problem attempts to integrate real-life experience and examples with the changing demands of financial accounting and reporting requirements.

The Collaborative Learning Activities address several major concerns related to improving student learning. They provide an effective method of actively engaging students that cannot be accomplished through traditional lecture and large group discussion. Students benefit from the opportunity to hear multiple perspectives from their group members and enhance their learning through explaining ideas to other students. These activities have been substantially updated and revised in this edition and include a variety of collaborative activities. Instructor resource material includes information on how to use these in class as well as suggestions for modifying them depending on the amount of time available for the activity.

The All About You boxes mentioned earlier are mirrored in the Broadening Your Perspective section. The All About You activities have been designed to help students appreciate that learning accounting is helpful for everyone, regardless of their current and future career plans.

In total, we have over 1,750 end-of-chapter items for students to test their understanding of accounting. We have added more than 580 new questions, brief exercises, exercises, problems, and cases to the end-of-chapter material. That means that over one-third of the end-of-chapter material is new! The remaining material was substantially updated and revised, as required.

Special Student Supplements

Accounting Principles is accompanied by special student supplements to help students master the material and achieve success in their studies.

The **City Cycle Practice Set** exposes students to a real-world simulation of maintaining a complete set of accounting records for a business.

Acknowledgements

During the course of developing *Accounting Principles*, Sixth Canadian Edition, the authors benefited from the feedback from instructors and students of accounting principles courses throughout the country, including many users of the previous editions of this text. The constructive suggestions and innovative ideas helped focus this revision on motivating students to want to learn accounting. In addition, the input and advice of the ancillary authors, contributors, and proofreaders provided valuable feedback throughout the development of this edition.

Workshop Participants

Workshops were set up to allow instructors to meet, discuss, and share ideas. They allowed us to better understand your challenges as you endeavour to bring accounting to life for your students. Participants in workshops held for the current edition include:

Alym Amlani, *Kwantlen Polytechnic University*
Anita Braaksma, *Kwantlen Polytechnic University*
Amy Hoggard, *Camosun College*
Alison Feirerband, *Sheridan College*
Gordon Fisher, *Kwantlen Polytechnic University*
Tom Lewis, *Red Deer College*
Pina Salvaggio, *Dawson College*
Helen Vallee, *Kwantlen Polytechnic University*

Reviewers

Peter Alpaugh, *George Brown College*
Alym Amlani, *Kwantlen Polytechnic University*
Karen Baker, *Loyalist College*
Vida Barker, *Centennial College*
Mike Bozzo, *Mohawk College*
Leelah Dawson, *Camosun College*
Dennis Dober, *College of the North Atlantic*
Denise Dodson, *Nova Scotia Community College*
Dave Fleming, *George Brown College*
John Harris, *Centennial College*
Robert Holland, *Nova Scotia Community College*
Jeremy Jarvis, *Kwantlen Polytechnic University*
Sepand Jazzi, *Kwantlen Polytechnic University*
Marc Kampschuur, *Kwantlen Polytechnic University*

Barbara Katz, *Kwantlen Polytechnic University*
Steven Konvalinka, *George Brown College*
Douglas Leatherdale, *Georgian College*
Barb Lee, *College of New Caledonia*
Cynthia Lone, *Red River College*
Ferne MacLennan, *Nova Scotia Community College*
Pat Margeson, *New Brunswick Community College, Moncton*
Debbie Musil, *Kwantlen Polytechnic University*
Michelle Nicholson, *Okanagan College*
Pamela Quon, *Athabasca University*
Pina Salvaggio, *Dawson College*
Don Smith, *Georgian College*
Jessica Sottosanti, *Lambton College*
Bruce Takeno, *Centennial College*
Rod Tilley, *Mount Saint Vincent University*
John Varga, *George Brown College*
Leanne Vig, *Red Deer College*
Jeanine Wall, *Red River College*
Joan Wallwork, *Kwantlen Polytechnic University*
Valerie Warren, *Kwantlen Polytechnic University*

Textbook Contributors

Sally Anderson, *Mount Royal University*
Cécile Laurin, *Algonquin College*
Dal Pirot, *Grant MacEwan University*

Supplement Contributors

Vida Barker, *Centennial College*
Maria Belanger, *Algonquin College*
Angela Davis, *Booth University College*
Robert Ducharme, *University of Waterloo*
Ilene Gilborn, *Mount Royal University*
Rosalie Harms, *University of Winnipeg*
Amy Hoggard, *Camosun College*
Cécile Laurin, *Algonquin College*
Kayla Levesque, *Cambrian College*
Richard Michalski, *McMaster University*
Debbie Musil, *Kwantlen Polytechnic University*
Marie Sinnott, *College of New Caledonia*
Traven Reed, *Canadore College*

Ruth Ann Strickland, *Western University*
Brian Trenholm
Jerry P. Zdril, *Grant MacEwan University*
Patricia Zima, *Mohawk College*

Through their editorial contributions, Laurel Hyatt and Zofia Laubitz added to the real-world flavour of the text and its clarity.

Accuracy

We have made every effort to ensure that this text is error-free. *Accounting Principles* has been extensively reviewed and proofed at more than five different production stages prior to publication. In addition, the end-of-chapter material has been independently solved and then checked by at least three individuals, in addition to the authors, prior to publication of the text. We would like to express our sincere gratitude to everyone who spent countless hours ensuring the accuracy of this text and the solutions to the end-of-chapter material.

Publications

We would like to thank Reitmans (Canada) Limited for allowing us to reproduce its 2012 financial statements in Appendix A. We would also like to acknowledge the co-operation of the many Canadian and international companies that allowed us to include extracts from their financial statements in the text and end-of-chapter material.

A Final Note of Thanks

We appreciate the exemplary support and professional commitment given us by the talented team in the Wiley Canada higher education division, including Luisa Begani, Editorial Assistant; Zoë Craig, Acquisitions Editor; Deanna Durnford, Supplements Coordinator; Channade Fenandoe, Media Editor; Daleara Hirjikaka, Developmental Editor; Anita Osborne, Marketing Manager; Karen Staudinger, Editorial Manager; Maureen Talty, General Manager, Higher Education; Veronica Visentin, Vice-President and Publisher; Tegan Wallace, Production Manager; and Carolyn Wells, Vice-President, Marketing. We wish to also thank Wiley's dedicated sales representatives who work tirelessly to serve your needs.

It would not have been possible to write this text without the understanding of our employer, colleagues, students, family, and friends. Together, they provided a creative and supportive environment for our work.

We have tried our best to produce a text and supplement package that is error-free and meets your specific needs. Suggestions and comments from all users—instructors and students alike—are encouraged and appreciated.

Valerie Kinnear
vkinnear@mtroyal.ca
Calgary, Alberta

Joan Barlow
jbarlow@mtroyal.ca
Calgary, Alberta

November 2012

BRIEF CONTENTS

Part One

Part Two

Part Three

Part Four

CONTENTS – VOLUME ONE

ACCOUNTING IN ACTION

The Navigator learning system encourages you to use the learning aids in the chapter and set priorities as you study.

Concepts for Review highlight concepts from your earlier reading that you need to understand before starting the new chapter.

 THE **NAVIGATOR**

☐ Understand *Concepts for Review*

☐ Read *Feature Story*

☐ Scan *Study Objectives*

☐ Read *Chapter Preview*

☐ Read text and answer *Before You Go On*

☐ Review *Comparing IFRS and ASPE*

☐ Work *Demonstration Problem*

☐ Review *Summary of Study Objectives*

☐ Answer *Self-Study Questions*

☐ Complete assignments

☐ Go to *WileyPLUS* for practice and tutorials

CONCEPTS FOR **REVIEW**

Before studying this chapter, you should understand or, if necessary, review:

a. How to use the study aids in this book. (pp. v–xii)

b. What the Bloom's Taxonomy classifications (K, C, AP, AN, S, and E) mean. (p. xiii)

c. The learning styles chart. (pp. xiv–xv)

d. The student supplements that accompany this text. (p. xix)

The Feature Story helps you see how the chapter topic fits with the real world of accounting and business. The story will be mentioned frequently throughout the chapter.

DRESSED FOR SUCCESS

MONTREAL, Que.—When Herman and Sarah Reitman opened a small department store in Montreal in the early 1900s, they likely would never have predicted that it would grow into Canada's largest women's specialty clothing retailer. The couple's department store was so popular, they opened a second store in 1926, selling only women's clothing. That remains the company's focus as the Reitmans' children and grandchildren carry on the family tradition.

Today, Reitmans (Canada) Limited operates more than 950 stores in every province and territory, under several names (or "banners"): Reitmans, Smart Set, RW&CO., Penningtons, Addition-Elle, and Thyme Maternity. Each banner focuses on affordable women's clothing, catering to a particular niche, such as age or size. And in 2010, Reitmans joined the e-commerce trend by selling Reitmans, Penningtons, and Addition-Elle merchandise on-line. In total, the company brings in more than $1 billion in sales every year.

How did Reitmans go from one store to a billion-dollar company? By using accounting to keep a close eye on all its numbers. Reitmans, like all successful companies, makes decisions by analyzing the costs and rewards of each move to determine if they make financial sense. The company partially credits its solid performance in a tough retail environment to keeping costs low, such as the cost of merchandise, foreign exchange, and distribution—something only possible by maintaining reliable cost information.

The company says it "continues to grow all areas of its business by investing in stores, technology and people." On an ongoing basis, Reitmans assesses the viability of each store by constantly monitoring its profitability. These strategic decisions require good accounting information to decide on where to make those investments.

Not only do Reitmans' managers rely on accounting information, but external users want to know how the company is faring as well. As a company whose shares trade on the Toronto Stock Exchange (under the ticker symbol RET), Reitmans makes its financial information available to the public through its annual report. Reitmans has thousands of owners in the form of shareholders. Potential and existing shareholders are interested in the company's consistent issuing of dividends and its continuing ability to grow and be profitable. Other external users are banks and other lenders that provide loans to Reitmans, which want to know about the company's cash flow and whether it can pay its obligations. In its most recent annual report, for the year ended January 28, 2012, Reitmans' revenues were $1.02 billion, with profits of $47.5 million.

Equipped with solid accounting numbers, Reitmans is dressed for success.

SOURCES: "Announcing Reitmans.com: The Canadian Company That Dresses Everybody and Every Body Has Taken Its Unique Proposition Online," company news release, December 16, 2010; Reitmans Annual Report 2012; Simon Avery, "Reitmans' Dominance Helps it Take on Retail Sector's Hurdles," *Globe and Mail*, March 29, 2011; John Heinzl, "Why Investors Should Try Reitmans on for Size," *Globe and Mail*, June 9, 2011.

Study Objectives show what you should be able to do after learning the specific concepts presented in the chapter.

THE **NAVIGATOR**

» STUDY **OBJECTIVES**

After studying this chapter, you should be able to:

1. Identify the use and users of accounting and the objective of financial reporting.

2. Compare different forms of business organizations and explain how Canadian accounting standards apply to these organizations.

3. Describe the components of the financial statements and explain the accounting equation.

4. Determine what events are recognized in the financial statements and how the events are measured.

5. Analyze the effects of business transactions on the accounting equation.

6. Prepare financial statements.

THE **NAVIGATOR**

The Chapter Preview outlines the major topics and subtopics you will see in the chapter.

The feature story about Reitmans highlights the importance of having good financial information to make good business decisions. This applies not just to companies but also to individuals. You cannot earn a living, spend money, buy on credit, make an investment, or pay taxes without receiving, using, or giving financial information. Good decision-making for companies and individuals depends on good information.

This chapter shows you that accounting is the system that produces useful financial information for decision-making. The chapter is organized as follows:

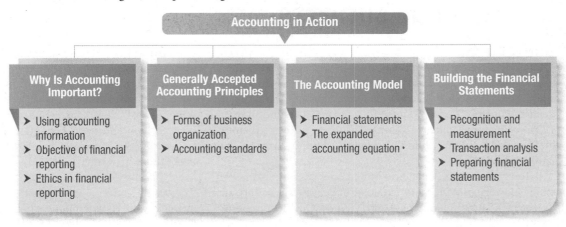

Why Is Accounting Important?

> **STUDY OBJECTIVE 1**
>
> Identify the use and users of accounting and the objective of financial reporting.

Essential (key) terms are printed in blue when they first appear, and are defined in the end-of-chapter glossary.

Accounting is the information system that identifies, records, and communicates the economic events of an organization to a wide variety of interested users. The world's economic systems depend on highly transparent and relevant financial reporting that provides a true representation of the economic events. When that does not happen, it can have disastrous results. Lehman Brothers, a major United States bank, used misleading accounting practices to reduce its debt and make its financial position healthier than it was. Not only were Lehman Brothers' investors and lenders unaware of the bank's financial difficulties when the company went into bankruptcy, but economists believe the bankruptcy was a major contributor to the worldwide economic crises that began in 2008.

A vital part of communicating economic events is the accountant's ability and responsibility to analyze and interpret the reported information. In analysis, accountants use ratios, percentages, graphs, and charts to highlight significant financial trends and relationships. In interpretation, they explain the uses, meaning, and limitations of the reported data. Accounting has long been labelled the "language of business" and has consistently ranked as one of the top career opportunities in business.

You might think this is all well and good for students who want to become accountants, but what about someone who has plans to be anything *but* an accountant?

Understanding the basics of accounting is helpful for almost every endeavour you can think of. By studying accounting, you will learn how the world of business—large and small—actually works. Whether you plan to own your own business in the future, work for someone else in their business, or invest in a business, learning how to read and interpret financial information is a valuable set of skills.

When you study accounting, you will also learn a lot about management, finance, and marketing, which will give you a solid foundation for your future studies. For example, you will learn how making a sale is meaningless unless it is a profitable sale and the money can eventually be collected from the customer. Marketing managers must also be able to decide pricing strategies based on costs. Accounting is what quantifies these costs and explains why a product or service costs what it does. So think of this textbook as your introduction to accounting across the organization.

It doesn't matter if you plan to become a doctor, lawyer, social worker, teacher, engineer, architect, or entrepreneur—whatever you choose, a working knowledge of accounting will be relevant and useful. Accounting is all about you. Make the most of this course—it will serve you for a lifetime in ways you cannot now imagine.

ACCOUNTING IN ACTION
ALL ABOUT YOU INSIGHT

We all know the importance of literacy. But what about financial literacy—the ability to understand and manage your finances? It seems Canadians don't place the same importance on financial literacy—but with rising household debt levels, falling savings levels, increasing personal bankruptcies, and continuing economic uncertainty, they should. According to Statistics Canada research, in 2009 only half of Canadians had a household budget and one in three were struggling to pay their bills. On a scale of 1 to 100, Canadians scored an average of 66 in terms of their ability to keep track of their finances and 61 out of 100 in terms of planning for life goals such as buying a house or retiring. To improve the situation the federal government launched a Task Force on Financial

Literacy. The task force recommended that financial literacy be taught at a young age and that Canadians continue learning about finances throughout their lives. Making the right financial decisions can have a major impact on an individual's financial well-being, health, and happiness.

Learning the basics of accounting will help you make the right financial decisions. Accounting will help you make investment decisions, determine how much interest you are paying on your student loan or credit cards, and prepare your personal budget. To demonstrate the value of accounting to you, included in each chapter is an "All About You" feature and a related activity (BYP–6) that links accounting to your life as a student or to a situation you are likely to face.

Sources: Task Force on Financial Literacy, *Canadians and Their Money: Building a Brighter Financial Future*, December 2010; Financial Consumer Agency of Canada, *The Future of Financial Education: Report on the 2011 FCAC-OECD Conference on Financial Literacy*, 2011; Robin Taub and Mary Teresa Bitt, "It Pays to Know," *CA Magazine*, October 2011.

How might learning accounting help you make sure that your employer or bank hasn't made an error with your paycheque or bank account?

USING ACCOUNTING INFORMATION

There are two broad groups of users of accounting information: internal users and external users.

Internal Users

Internal users of accounting information plan, organize, and run companies. They work for the company. This includes finance directors, marketing managers, human resources personnel, production supervisors, and company officers. In running a business, internal users must answer many important questions, as shown in Illustration 1-1.

Accounting in Action insights give examples of accounting situations from different perspectives: all about you, across the organization, and in terms of business and ethics. At the end of the chapter, you will find answers to the questions that are asked after each insight.

Finance
Is there enough cash to pay the bills?

Marketing
What price should we sell smart phones for to maximize profits?

▶ILLUSTRATION 1-1
Questions asked by internal users

Human Resources
How many employees can we afford to hire this year?

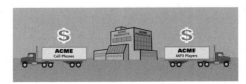

Production
Which product line is the most profitable?

To answer these and other questions, users need detailed information on a timely basis; that is, it must be available when needed. Some examples of information that internal users need include forecasts of cash flows for the next year, projections of profit from new sales campaigns, financial comparisons of operating alternatives, analyses of salary costs, and budgeted financial statements. Internal users generally have direct access to the business's accounting information and are able to request a wide variety of custom reports designed for their specific needs.

External Users

There are several types of external users of accounting information. Investors, who are owners—or potential owners—of the business, use accounting information to make decisions to buy, hold, or sell their ownership interest. Creditors—persons or other businesses that are owed money by the business, such as suppliers and bankers—use accounting information to evaluate the risks of granting credit or lending money. Investors and creditors are the main external users of accounting information, but there are also many other external users with a large variety of information needs and questions.

For example, labour unions want to know whether the owners can afford to pay increased salaries and benefits. Customers are interested in whether a company will continue to honour its product warranties and support its product lines. Taxing authorities, such as Canada Revenue Agency, want to know whether the company respects the tax laws. Regulatory agencies, such as provincial securities commissions that regulate companies that sell shares to the public, want to know whether the company is respecting established rules. And economic planners use accounting information to forecast economic activity.

Some questions that external users may ask about a company are shown in Illustration 1-2.

▶ **ILLUSTRATION 1-2**
Questions asked by external users

Investors
Is the company earning enough to give me a return on my investment?

Creditors
Will the company be able to pay its debts as they come due?

Labour Unions
Can the company afford the pay raise we are asking for?

Customers
Will the company stay in business long enough to service the products I buy from it?

Unlike internal users, external users have access to only the accounting information provided to them by the business. Because external users are not able to request specific information, there are many rules about what information must be provided. Determining what information should be provided to external users, and how, is the focus of financial accounting.

OBJECTIVE OF FINANCIAL REPORTING

Accounting information is communicated in financial reports, and the most common reports are financial statements. The main objective of financial statements is to provide useful information to investors and creditors (external users) to make decisions about a business. To make the decision to invest in a business or to lend to a business, users need information about the business's ability to earn a profit and generate cash. Consequently, financial statements must give information about the following:

1. The business's economic resources. What resources does the business have that it can use to carry out its business activities?

2. The claims to the business's economic resources. What are the amounts owed by the business and the owner's rights to the business's resources?

3. Economic performance. Is the business generating a profit and sufficient cash to pay its debts, and provide a return to its owners?

We will learn more about financial statements in the following sections.

ETHICS IN FINANCIAL REPORTING

In order for financial information to have value for its users, whether internal or external, it must be prepared by individuals with high standards of ethical behaviour. Ethics in accounting is of the utmost importance to accountants and decision makers who rely on the financial information they produce.

Fortunately, most individuals in business are ethical. Their actions are both legal and responsible. They consider the organization's interests when they make decisions. Accountants and other professionals have extensive rules of conduct to guide their behaviour with each other and the public. In addition, many companies today have codes of conduct, or statements of corporate values, that outline their commitment to ethical behaviour in their internal and external relationships. The behaviour of management is critical for creating the appropriate tone from the top of the organization.

Throughout this textbook, ethical considerations will be presented to highlight the importance of ethics in financial reporting. Every chapter includes an Ethics Case in the end-of-chapter material that simulates a business situation and asks you to put yourself in the position of a key decision maker. When you analyze these ethical situations, you should follow the steps outlined in Illustration 1-3.

▶ **ILLUSTRATION** 1-3
Steps used to analyze ethics cases and situations

1. Recognize an ethical situation and the ethical issues involved.

Use your personal ethics or an organization's code of ethics to identify ethical situations and issues. Some business and professional organizations provide written codes of ethics for guidance in common business situations.

2. Identify and analyze the main elements in the situation.

Identify the *stakeholders*— persons or groups who may be harmed or benefited. Ask the question: What are the responsibilities and obligations of the parties involved?

3. Identify the alternatives, and weigh the impact of each alternative on various stakeholders.

Select the most ethical alternative, considering all the consequences. Sometimes there will be one right answer. Other situations involve more than one possible solution. These situations require an evaluation of each alternative and the selection of the best one.

The companion website to this text includes a discussion of ethics and ethical issues that involve accounting and financial reporting.

 BEFORE YOU GO ON...

Do It

The following is a list of some users of accounting information. For each user indicate:

(a) whether they are an internal or external user and

(b) an example of a question that might be asked by that user.

1. Creditor
2. Canada Revenue Agency
3. Investor
4. Production department
5. Human resources department

Before You Go On Do It exercises like the one here ask you to put your new knowledge to work. They also outline an Action Plan you need to follow to do the exercise. *Related exercise material* tells you which Brief Exercises (BE) and Exercises (E) at the end of the chapter have similar study objectives.

Action Plan

• Understand that internal users work for the company and have direct access to the business's accounting information.

Action Plan (cont'd)
- Understand that external users are users that do not work for the company and have access to only the accounting information provided to them by the company.
- Understand that users require information to make decisions.

THE **NAVIGATOR**

BEFORE YOU GO ON continued...

Solution

User	(a) Internal or External	(b) Question
1. Creditor	External	Will the business be able to pay back the loan?
2. Canada Revenue Agency	External	Is the company following the tax laws?
3. Investor	External	Should I invest money in the company?
4. Production department	Internal	How much will it cost to produce the product?
5. Human resources department	Internal	Can the company afford to give the employees raises?

Related exercise material: BE1–1, BE1–2, and E1–1.

Generally Accepted Accounting Principles

STUDY OBJECTIVE 2

Compare different forms of business organizations and explain how Canadian accounting standards apply to these organizations.

Businesses can be organized in different ways. The specific financial statements prepared, and the accounting standards followed, differ depending on the form and nature of the business organization.

FORMS OF BUSINESS ORGANIZATION

The most common forms of business organizations are the proprietorship, partnership, and corporation. Illustration 1-4 compares some of the characteristics of these forms.

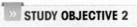

ILLUSTRATION 1-4
Characteristics of business organizations

	Proprietorship	Partnership	Corporation
Owners	Proprietor: one	Partners: two or more	Shareholders: one or more
Owner's liability	Unlimited	Unlimited	Limited
Private or public	Private	Usually private	Private or public
Taxation of profits	Paid by the owner	Paid by the partners	Paid by the corporation
Life of organization	Limited	Limited	Indefinite

Proprietorship

A business owned by one person is a **proprietorship**. The owner is usually the operator of the business. Small service businesses (hair stylists, plumbers, and mechanics), farms, and small retail stores (antique shops, corner grocery stores, and independent bookstores) are often proprietorships.

Often only a relatively small amount of money (capital) is needed to start in business as a proprietorship. The owner (the proprietor) receives any profits, suffers any losses, and is personally liable (responsible) for all debts of the business. This is known as **unlimited liability**.

There is no legal distinction between the business as an economic unit and the owner. Thus the life of a proprietorship is limited to the life of the owner. This also means that the profits of the business are reported and taxed on the owner's personal income tax return. However, for accounting purposes, the records of the proprietorship's business activities are kept separate from the personal records and activities of the owner.

Many businesses in Canada are proprietorships, but they earn only a small percentage of the revenue earned by Canadian businesses as a whole. In this textbook, we start with proprietorships because many students organize their first business this way.

Partnership

A business owned by two or more persons who are associated as partners is a partnership. In most aspects, a partnership is similar to a proprietorship, except that there is more than one owner. Partnerships are often used to organize service-type businesses, including professional practices (lawyers, doctors, architects, and accountants).

Typically, a partnership agreement (written or oral) defines the initial investments of each partner, the duties of each partner, how profit (or loss) will be divided, and what the settlement will be if a partner dies or withdraws. As in a proprietorship, for accounting purposes a partnership's business activities must be kept separate from the personal activities of each partner. The partners' share of the profit must be reported and taxed on the partners' income tax returns.

Each partner generally has unlimited liability for all debts of the partnership, even if one of the other partners created the debt. This means that any of the partners can be forced to give up his or her personal assets in order to repay the partnership debt, just as can happen to an owner in a proprietorship. We will learn more about partnerships in Chapter 12.

Corporation

A business that is organized (incorporated) as a separate legal entity under federal or provincial corporate law is a corporation. A corporation is responsible for its debts and paying taxes on its profit. A corporation's ownership is divided into transferable shares. The corporation's separate legal status provides the owners of the shares (shareholders) with limited liability as they risk losing only the amount that they have invested in the company's shares. They are not personally liable for the debts of the corporate entity. Shareholders may sell all or part of their shares to other investors at any time. Easy changes of ownership are part of what makes it attractive to invest in a corporation. Because ownership can be transferred through the sale of shares and without dissolving the corporation, the corporation enjoys an unlimited life.

Although there are many more proprietorships and partnerships than corporations in Canada, the revenue produced by corporations is far greater. Most of the largest companies in Canada—for example, Royal Bank of Canada, Suncor Energy, Research In Motion, and Barrick Gold—are corporations.

Corporations such as these are publicly traded. That is, their shares are listed on Canadian stock exchanges. Public corporations commonly distribute their financial statements to shareholders, creditors, other interested parties, and the general public upon request. Reitmans is a public corporation, whose shares are traded on the Toronto Stock Exchange. You can access its financial statements on its website, which is given in Appendix A at the back of this textbook.

Other companies are private corporations, as they do not issue publicly traded shares. Some of the largest private companies in Canada include Bombardier Aerospace, McCain Foods, and EllisDon Inc. Like proprietorships and partnerships, these companies almost never distribute their financial statements publicly. We will discuss the corporate form of organization in Chapters 13 and 14.

ACCOUNTING STANDARDS

To make the information in financial statements meaningful, accountants have to prepare the reports in a standardized way. Every profession develops a body of theory based on principles and assumptions. Accounting is no exception.

The accounting profession has developed a set of standards that are generally accepted and universally practised. This common set of standards, called generally accepted accounting principles (GAAP), includes broad principles and practices, as well as rules and procedures. These standards indicate how to report economic events.

In Canada, the Accounting Standards Board (AcSB), an independent standard-setting body created by the Canadian Institute of Chartered Accountants (CICA), has the main responsibility for developing GAAP. The AcSB's most important criterion for accounting standards is this: the standard should lead to external users having the most useful financial information possible when they are making business decisions.

Helpful hints help clarify concepts or items that are being discussed.

Helpful hint You can usually tell if a company is a corporation by looking at its name. The words *Limited (Ltd.), Incorporated (Inc.),* or *Corporation (Corp.)* usually follow its name.

Alternative terminology notes give synonyms that you may hear or see in the workplace, in companies' financial statements, and occasionally in this textbook.

Alternative terminology The terms *standard* and *principle* mean the same thing in accounting.

International Financial Reporting Standards and Accounting Standards for Private Enterprises

Helpful hint Accounting standards use the word "enterprise" as it is a broader term than "company" or "business." The word "enterprise" means that the accounting standard applies to the different forms of business organizations, as well as specific projects. Throughout this text, instead of using the word "enterprise," we will frequently use the words "company" or "business," as they are more common terms.

The AcSB recognizes that "one size does not necessarily fit all" and has developed and adopted separate standards for publicly accountable enterprises and for private enterprises. Canadian public enterprises must follow **International Financial Reporting Standards (IFRS)**, a set of global standards developed by the International Accounting Standards Board (IASB). **Publicly accountable enterprises** include publicly traded corporations, as well as securities brokers and dealers, banks, and credit unions whose role is to hold assets for the public as part of their primary business. Reitmans is a public company and therefore is required to follow IFRS.

Traditionally, accounting standards differed from country to country, making it difficult for investors, creditors, and others to make informed decisions about companies doing business in today's increasingly global environment. The IASB has worked, and continues to do so, with accounting standard setters across the globe to harmonize accounting standards where possible. IFRS are used as the main basis of financial reporting in more than 100 countries, including Australia, Brazil, Russia, members of the European Union, China, India, Japan, Mexico, and Canada. Although the United States does not use IFRS, its standard setters are working on a joint project with the IASB to develop and revise accounting standards so that they are consistent between U.S. GAAP and IFRS.

Following IFRS enhances Canadian public companies' ability to compete in an increasingly global marketplace. When IFRS are used, the financial statements of Canadian public companies are understood by investors and creditors throughout the world. Using IFRS also helps Canadian companies that operate in multiple countries, by allowing them to produce one set of financial statements rather than multiple sets with different accounting principles.

On the other hand, the users of a private company's financial statements generally have the ability to obtain additional information from the company if required. Because these users typically require less information in the financial statements, the AcSB developed **Accounting Standards for Private Enterprises (ASPE)**. ASPE requires considerably less information in financial statements than is required by IFRS. While public companies have to follow IFRS, Canadian private companies, including private corporations such as McCain Foods and EllisDon Inc., have the choice to report under ASPE or IFRS. As proprietorships and partnerships are private companies, these companies will generally follow ASPE for financial reporting.

The ASPE Icon indicates where differences between IFRS and ASPE are explained. These differences are also summarized at the end of each chapter.

Given the differences between IFRS and ASPE, and the fact that private companies have a choice, financial statement users will need to know which standards the company is following. Companies are required to report this in their financial statements. In this textbook, as we proceed through the material, we will point out where there are differences in the two sets of standards. However, the two sets of standards have a great deal in common in the type of material covered in an introductory accounting textbook.

Both IFRS and ASPE are considered "principles-based" as opposed to "rules-based" standards. Principles-based standards are designed to encourage the use of professional judgement in applying basic accounting principles. As you learn more about accounting, you will see that we will frequently refer to basic principles, as opposed to detailed rules, when deciding how to account for specific events. In this chapter, we introduce a few of these basic principles and concepts.

It is important to understand that GAAP is not static and that it changes over time. The AcSB and IASB continue to create new standards and modify GAAP. AcSB and IASB use a process that involves consultation with organizations and individuals that are interested in, or affected by, the standards. This process can take a long time but it ensures that the main purpose of financial statements—providing information that is relevant to decision-making—continues to be met.

The length of time involved in adding new or changing existing accounting standards can make it difficult to determine what information we should include in this textbook—should it be the currently approved standard or the proposed new standard? Sometimes the proposals are modified or dropped altogether before being approved. Normally the textbook will cover only the currently approved standards. But where we believe it is important to do so, we will introduce new standards that were proposed at the time the textbook was written.

Economic Entity Concept

Financial statements are prepared for a business or economic unit. This is referred to as the **economic entity concept**. The concept requires that the accounting for an economic entity's activities be kept separate and distinct from the accounting for the activities of its owner and all other economic entities. An economic entity can be any organization or unit in society. You will recall that proprietorships' and partnerships' records of their business activities are kept separate from the personal records of their owners. That is because proprietorships and partnerships are considered economic entities for financial reporting purposes. Similarly, a corporation (such as Reitmans) is considered an economic entity for financial reporting purposes. If one corporation owns another corporation, the two corporations combined may be considered an economic entity for financial reporting purposes. Other examples of economic entities are a governmental unit (such as the Province of Manitoba), a municipality (such as the Ville de Montréal), a native band council (such as the Kingsclear Indian Band), a school board (such as the Burnaby School Board), and a club (such as the Melfort Rotary Club).

It is important to understand that an economic entity may not necessarily be a separate legal entity. For example, proprietorships and partnerships are not a separate legal entity from their owners. Regardless, the economic entity concept requires separate financial reporting.

Going Concern Assumption

The **going concern assumption** is the assumption that the economic entity will continue to operate in the foreseeable future. Although some businesses fail, most companies continue operating for a long time. The going concern assumption presumes that the company will operate long enough to use its resources for their intended purpose and to complete the company's commitments.

This assumption is one of the most important assumptions in GAAP as it has implications regarding what information is useful for decision makers and affects many of the accounting standards you will learn. If a company is a going concern, then financial statement users will find it useful for the company to report certain resources, such as land, at their cost. Land is acquired so a company can use it, not so it can be resold. Therefore, what matters is the amount the company gave up to acquire the land, not an estimate of its current worth. If a company is not a going concern, and the land is going to be sold, then financial statement users will be more interested in the land's current value.

If a company is not regarded as a going concern, or if there are significant doubts about its ability to continue as a going concern, then this must be stated in the financial statements, along with the reason why the company is not regarded as a going concern. Otherwise, you can assume that the company is a going concern—even though this is not explicitly stated. Since it is not necessary to include in the financial statements that the company is a going concern, this assumption is considered an underlying assumption.

 BEFORE YOU GO ON...

Do It

For each type of organization (proprietorship, partnership, and corporation) indicate:

1. Number and type of owners.
2. If it has limited or unlimited liability.
3. If it is a separate legal entity from its owners.

Action Plan
- Understand the characteristics of the most common forms of business organizations.

Solution

	Proprietorship	Partnership	Corporation
1.	Proprietor: one	Partners: two or more	Shareholders: one or more
2.	Unlimited	Unlimited	Limited
3.	Not a separate legal entity from its owners	Not a separate legal entity from its owners	Separate legal entity from the shareholders

Related exercise material: BE1–3, BE1–4, and E1–2.

THE **NAVIGATOR**

The Accounting Model

FINANCIAL STATEMENTS

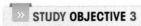

STUDY OBJECTIVE 3

Describe the components of the financial statements and explain the accounting equation.

You will recall that the main objective of the financial statements is to provide information about the business's resources, claims to its resources, and its ability to earn a profit and generate cash to allow investors and creditors (external users) to make decisions about a business. Here we will introduce four basic financial statements and show how this information is included in these statements. Later in the chapter, we will illustrate how to prepare these statements.

The specific financial statements prepared differ depending on the nature of the business organization; however, all businesses prepare a balance sheet and income statement. As you go through this section, we recommend you refer to Reitmans' financial statements for the year ended January 28, 2012, in Appendix A of this textbook, for an example. We will refer to these statements often throughout the textbook.

Balance Sheet

Alternative terminology The balance sheet is sometimes called the statement of financial position.

Users need information on the economic resources that the business can use to carry out its business activities to earn a profit and the claims to these economic resources. In accounting, economic resources that are owned or controlled by a business are called "assets." Claims on the economic resources are the amounts owed by the business and the owner's rights to the resources. In accounting, amounts owed by the business are called "liabilities" and the owner's right to these resources is called "owner's equity." **Assets, liabilities, and owner's equity are reported in the** balance sheet.

The balance sheet is like a snapshot of the company's financial condition at a specific moment in time (usually the end of a month, quarter, or year). The heading of a balance sheet must identify the company, statement, and date. To indicate that the balance sheet is at a specific point in time, the date only mentions the point in time (there is no indication of a time period). Let's look at the categories in the balance sheet in more detail.

Assets. **Assets** are the resources owned or controlled by a business that are expected to provide future services or economic benefits. In a company, that future service potential or economic benefit eventually results in cash inflows (receipts).

Assets are used to carry out activities such as the production and distribution of merchandise. For example, imagine that a local pizza parlour, called Campus Pizza, owns a delivery truck. The truck provides economic benefits because it is used to deliver pizzas. Campus Pizza also owns other assets, such as tables, chairs, a sound system, a cash register, an oven, dishes, supplies, and, of course, cash.

Other common assets include merchandise held for resale (inventory), investments, land, buildings, patents, and copyrights. **Accounts receivable** is the asset created when a company sells services or products to customers who promise to pay cash for the service or product in the future. **Prepaid expense**, another common asset, is the asset created when a business pays cash for costs incurred in advance of being used or consumed. Common types of prepaid expenses are insurance, rent, and supplies.

Liabilities. **Liabilities** are current obligations, arising from past events, to make a future payment of assets or services. That is, liabilities are present debts and obligations. For example, businesses of all sizes usually borrow money and purchase merchandise inventory on credit. If a business borrows money to do such things as purchase equipment, it usually has a note payable for the amount borrowed. A **note payable** is supported by a written promise to pay a specific amount, at a specific time, in the future. Obligations to pay cash to suppliers in the future are called **accounts payable**.

Sometimes customers might pay a business in advance of being provided a service or product. This advance by the customer is a liability, **unearned revenue**, as the business has an obligation to provide the service or product in the future. Businesses may also have salaries payable to employees, Goods and Services Tax (GST/HST) payable and Provincial Sales Tax (PST) payable to the federal and provincial governments, and property taxes payable to the municipality.

Recall that persons or other businesses that are owed money by the business, such as suppliers and bankers, are called "creditors." A creditor who is not paid after a certain length of time has the legal right to force the liquidation of a business. In that case, the law requires that creditor claims be paid before ownership claims are paid.

Owner's Equity. The owner's claim on the assets of the company is known as **owner's equity**. It is equal to total assets minus total liabilities. Since the claims of creditors must be paid before ownership claims, the owner's equity is often called "residual equity." If the equity is negative—that is, if total liabilities are more than total assets—the term "owner's deficiency" (or deficit) describes the shortage. Owner's equity is a general accounting term that could be used for any type of organization. It is used most frequently for proprietorships. Partnerships use the term "partners' equity"; corporations, such as Reitmans, use "shareholders' equity."

The Accounting Equation. The relationship between assets, liabilities, and owner's equity is expressed as an equation, called the **accounting equation**. Assets must equal the sum of liabilities and owner's equity. Liabilities are shown before owner's equity in the accounting equation because creditors' claims are paid before ownership claims if a business is liquidated. Illustration 1-5 shows the accounting equation for Reitmans at January 28, 2012.

Alternative terminology The accounting equation is sometimes referred to as the *balance sheet equation*.

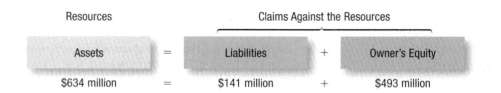

▶ **ILLUSTRATION** **1-5**
Accounting equation

The accounting equation is the same for all economic entities regardless of their size, nature of business, or form of business organization. It applies to a small proprietorship such as a corner grocery store as much as it does to a large corporation such as Reitmans. Not only is the balance sheet based on the equation, but as we will see, the equation is the basis for recording and summarizing the economic events of a company.

Because the balance sheet is based on the accounting equation, you should never see a balance sheet where assets are not equal to liabilities plus owner's equity. If you do, it contains one or more errors. In that situation, we would say that the balance sheet is not balanced.

Income Statement

Investors and creditors want to know if the business is generating a profit from its business activities. The main purpose of the **income statement** is to report the profitability of the business's operations over a specified period of time (a month, quarter, or year). **Profit** is measured by the difference between revenues and expenses. Profit results when revenues are greater than expenses and conversely a **loss** results when expenses are greater than revenues.

Alternative terminology The income statement is sometimes called the *statement of earnings* or *statement of operations*.

Revenues. **Revenues** result from business activities that are done to earn profit, such as performing services, selling merchandise inventory, renting property, and lending money. Revenues result in an increase in an asset (or a decrease in a liability when a customer has paid in advance) and an increase in owner's equity. They come from different sources and are given different names, depending on the type of business. Campus Pizza, for instance, has two categories of revenue: food sales and beverage sales. Common sources of revenue include sales, fees, services, commissions, interest, and rent.

Alternative terminology Profit is sometimes called *net income* or *earnings* or *net earnings*.

Expenses. **Expenses** are the costs of assets that are consumed and services that are used in a company's business activities. Expenses are decreases in assets or increases in liabilities, excluding withdrawals made by the owners, and result in a decrease to owner's equity. Like revenues, there are many kinds of expenses and they are identified by various names, depending on the type of asset consumed or service used. For example, Campus Pizza recognizes (records) the following expenses: cost of ingredients (such as meat, flour, cheese, tomato paste, and mushrooms), cost of beverages, salaries expense, utilities expense (electric, gas, and water expense), telephone expense, delivery expense (such as gasoline, repairs, and licences), supplies expense (such as napkins, detergents, and aprons), rent expense, insurance expense, and interest expense.

Statement of Owner's Equity

The **statement of owner's equity** shows the changes in owner's equity for the same period of time as the income statement. In a proprietorship, owner's equity is increased by investments made by the owner and decreased by withdrawals made by the owner. Owner's equity is also increased when a business generates a profit from business activities or decreased if the business has a loss. Let's look at each of these equity components in more detail.

Investments. **Investments by the owner** are contributions of cash or other assets (e.g., a vehicle or computer) made by the owners to the business. In a proprietorship, investments are recorded as increases to what is known as the owner's capital account. Accordingly, investments by owners result in an increase in an asset and an increase in owner's equity.

Drawings. An owner may withdraw cash (or other assets) for personal use. In a proprietorship, these withdrawals could be recorded as a direct decrease to the owner's capital account. However, it is generally considered better to use a separate account classification called **drawings** so that the total withdrawals for the accounting period can be determined. Drawings result in a decrease in an asset and a decrease in owner's equity.

Profit. As previously explained, revenues increase owner's equity and expenses decrease owner's equity. We also learned that profit results from revenues being greater than expenses and a loss results if expenses are greater than revenues. Therefore, profit increases owner's equity and losses decrease owner's equity.

Illustration 1-6 summarizes the transactions that change owner's equity.

▶**ILLUSTRATION 1-6**
Transactions that increase and decrease owner's equity

Increases in owner's equity	Decreases in owner's equity
Investments by the owner	Drawings by the owner
Revenues	Expenses

We will see later in the chapter how this information is shown in the statement of owner's equity.

Cash Flow Statement

Alternative terminology The cash flow statement is sometimes called the *statement of cash flows*.

Investors and creditors need information on the business's ability to generate cash from its business activities and how the business uses cash. The **cash flow statement** gives information about the cash receipts and cash payments for a specific period of time. The cash flow statement gives answers to the following simple but important questions:

1. Where did the cash come from during the period?
2. What was the cash used for during the period?
3. What was the change in the cash balance during the period?

To help investors, creditors, and others analyze a company's cash, the cash flow statement reports the following: (1) the cash effects of the company's operating activities during a period; (2) the cash inflows and outflows from investing transactions (e.g., the purchase and sale of land, buildings, and equipment); (3) the cash inflows and outflows from financing transactions (e.g., borrowing and repayments of debt, and investments and withdrawals by the owner); (4) the net increase or decrease in cash during the period; and (5) the cash amount at the end of the period.

Accounting Differences by Type of Business Organization

Previously, you were introduced to different forms of business organizations: the proprietorship, partnership, and corporation. Basically, accounting for assets, liabilities, revenues, expenses, and cash flows is the same, regardless of the form of business organization. The main distinction between the forms of organizations is found in (1) the terminology that is used to name the equity section, (2) the accounting for the owner's investments and withdrawals, and (3) the name of the statement showing the changes in owner's equity. In Illustration 1-7, we summarize these differences.

	Proprietorship	Partnership	Corporation
Equity section called:	Owner's equity	Partners' equity	Shareholders' equity
Investments by owners added to:	Owner's capital	Partners' capital	Share capital
Profits added to:	Owner's capital	Partners' capital	Retained earnings
Withdrawals by owners called:	Drawings	Drawings	Dividends
Withdrawals deducted from:	Owner's capital	Partners' capital	Retained earnings
Name of statement:	Statement of Owner's Equity	Statement of Partners' Equity	Statement of Retained Earnings (ASPE)
Statement of Comprehensive Income	Not allowed	Not allowed	Statement of Shareholders' Equity (IFRS) Not allowed under ASPE Required under IFRS

▶ ILLUSTRATION 1-7
Accounting differences by type of business organization

In a proprietorship, equity is summarized and reported in a one-line capital account. In a partnership, equity is summarized and reported in separate one-line capital accounts for each partner. In a corporation, investments by all of the shareholders are grouped together and called "share capital." In a corporation, regardless of the number of shareholders, one account called Retained Earnings is used to record the accumulated profit (or earnings) of the company that has been retained (i.e., not paid out to shareholders) in the company.

A close examination of Reitmans' financial statements in Appendix A shows that, in addition to these statements, it has also prepared a Statement of Comprehensive Income. That is because Reitmans follows IFRS, not simply because it is a corporation. You will learn more about that statement in Chapter 14. For companies following ASPE, there is no such thing as a statement of comprehensive income.

THE EXPANDED ACCOUNTING EQUATION

The basic accounting equation in Illustration 1-5 simply shows that assets are equal to liabilities plus owner's equity. Recall that the basic equation is a summary of the information shown on the balance sheet. But we also know that it is necessary to report on revenues, expenses, and other changes in owner's equity. In Illustration 1-8, we have expanded the basic accounting equation to show the different parts of owner's equity and the relationship between revenues, expenses, profit (or loss), and owner's equity.

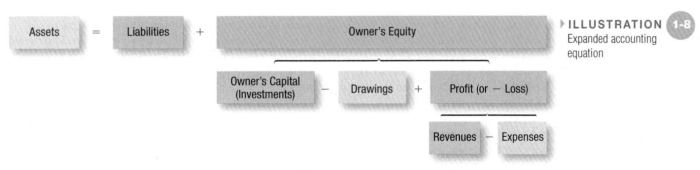

▶ ILLUSTRATION 1-8
Expanded accounting equation

By expanding the equation, we have created a framework that can be used to report the information required in the income statement and the statement of owner's equity, as well as the balance sheet. The components in the expanded accounting equation are known as the **elements of the financial statements**.

Remember that the equation must always balance. Assets must equal liabilities plus owner's equity. From the expanded equation we can see that if revenue increases, owner's equity increases and therefore either assets increase or liabilities decrease to keep the equation balanced. Conversely, if expenses increase, owner's equity decreases and therefore either assets decrease or liabilities increase to keep the equation balanced.

Action Plan

- Understand that assets are resources that are capable of providing future service or benefit that are owned or controlled by a business.
- Understand that liabilities are amounts owed by a business.
- Review which transactions affect owner's equity.
- Recall what information is included in each of the financial statements.

THE **NAVIGATOR**

BEFORE YOU GO ON...

Do It

The following are a few of the items that are reported in financial statements: (1) cash, (2) service revenue, (3) drawings, (4) accounts receivable, (5) accounts payable, and (6) salaries expense.

(a) Classify the items as assets, liabilities, or owner's equity: For the owner's equity items, indicate whether these items increase or decrease equity.

(b) Indicate which financial statement the item is reported in.

Solution

	(a) Type of Item	(b) Financial Statement
1. Cash	Asset	Balance Sheet
2. Service Revenue	Owner's equity—increase	Income Statement
3. Drawings	Owner's equity—decrease	Statement of Owner's Equity
4. Accounts Receivable	Asset	Balance Sheet
5. Accounts Payable	Liability	Balance Sheet
6. Salaries Expense	Owner's equity—decrease	Income Statement

Related exercise material: BE1–5, BE1–6, BE1–7, BE1–8, BE1–9, E1–3, E1–4, E1–5, and E1–6.

Building the Financial Statements

RECOGNITION AND MEASUREMENT

» **STUDY OBJECTIVE 4**

Determine what events are recognized in the financial statements and how the events are measured.

The first step in preparing financial statements is to determine what the company should record. Not all events are recorded and reported in the financial statements. For example, suppose a new employee is hired. Should this event be recorded in the company's accounting records? The answer is no. Why? Only events that cause changes in assets, liabilities, or owner's equity should be recorded. These events are called **accounting transactions**. While the hiring of an employee will lead to future accounting transactions (e.g., the payment of a salary after the work has been completed), an accounting transaction has not occurred at the time of hiring.

Recognition is the process of recording an asset, liability, revenue, or expense in the accounting records. Once a transaction has been recognized or recorded, it will be included in the financial statements. **Measurement** is the process of determining the amount that should be recognized. At the time something is acquired, the transaction is first measured at the amount of cash that was paid or at the value exchanged. For example, if the Gjoa Company purchased land for $100,000, the land is recorded in Gjoa's records at its cost of $100,000. This amount is referred to as the asset's historical cost.

Alternative terminology The *cost principle* is also known as the *historical cost principle*.

But what should Gjoa Company do if, by the end of the next year, the land's fair value has increased to $120,000? Under both IFRS and ASPE, historical cost is the primary basis used in financial statements, which means that Gjoa Company would continue to report the land at its historical cost of $100,000. This is often called the **cost principle**.

Cost has an important advantage over other valuations. Cost is definite and verifiable. The values exchanged at the time something is acquired can be objectively measured. Users can therefore rely on the information that is supplied, as they know it is based on fact. Cost is relevant if a business is a going concern and the asset is going to continue to be used in the business. What is relevant is, what did the business give up to acquire the asset to use in the business?

However, cost may not always be the most relevant measure of certain types of assets. Fair values may provide more useful information. For example, with an investment purchased for the purpose of trading to make a gain, the fair value of the investment provides more relevant information to the user. **Fair value** generally would be the amount the asset could be sold for in the market.

Fundamental to this discussion is that only transactions that can be reliably expressed as an amount of money can be included in the accounting records. This has been known as the **monetary unit assumption**. This assumption makes it possible for accounting to quantify (measure) economic events. In Canada, we mainly use the Canadian dollar to record these transactions. However, some companies report their results in U.S. dollars. In Europe, the euro (€) is used; in China, the yuan (CNY) is used; and so on.

The monetary unit assumption allows us to ignore the impact of inflation. Although inflation can be a significant accounting issue in some countries, Canada's inflation policy—set out by the federal government and the Bank of Canada—is to keep inflation at between 1% and 3% per year. Consequently, inflation is not considered an issue for accounting in Canada.

The monetary unit assumption does prevent some relevant information from being included in the accounting records. For example, the health of the owner, the quality of service, and the morale of employees would not be included, because they cannot be reliably quantified in monetary amounts.

In summary, a transaction is recognized in the accounting records if there is a change in assets, liabilities, or owner's equity and the change can be reliably measured in monetary terms.

Illustration 1-9 summarizes the process that is used to decide whether or not to record an event.

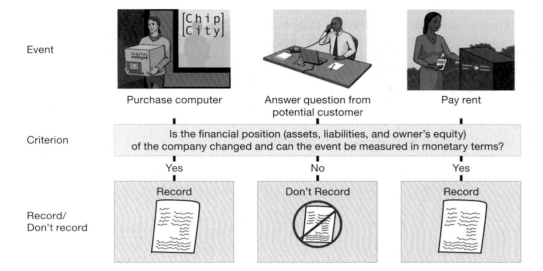

▶ **ILLUSTRATION 1-9**
Transaction identification process

 BEFORE YOU GO ON...

Do It

For each of the following events, indicate if it should be recognized (recorded) in the accounting records. Explain your reason.

1. An auto repair shop received $10,000 cash from the bank, to be repaid in a year.
2. A consulting company paid $20,000 cash to purchase equipment.
3. A hockey team recruits a talented new player.

Solution

1. The transaction will be recorded. There is a change in assets and liabilities and the amount can be reliably measured. The asset cash increased by $10,000. A liability increased because $10,000 is owed to the bank.
2. The transaction will be recorded. There is a change in two assets and the amount can be reliably measured. The asset cash decreased by $20,000 and the asset equipment increased by $20,000.
3. The event will not be recorded. The financial position of the business may have improved as the result of hiring this new hockey player; however, the team does not control the player and the change cannot be reliably measured.

Related exercise material: BE1–10, E1–7, and E1–8.

Action Plan
- Recall that only events that change an asset, liability, or owner's equity are recorded as accounting transactions.
- Determine if the event can be reliably quantified in monetary terms before recognizing it in the accounting records.

THE **NAVIGATOR**

TRANSACTION ANALYSIS

Once it has been determined that an event or transaction should be recognized, it must be analyzed for its effect on the components of the accounting equation before it can be recorded. This analysis must identify the specific items that are affected and the amount of change in each item.

» STUDY OBJECTIVE 5

Analyze the effects of business transactions on the accounting equation.

Each transaction must have a dual effect on the equation for the two sides of the accounting equation to remain equal. For example, if an asset is increased, there must be a corresponding

1. decrease in another asset, or
2. increase in a liability, or
3. increase in owner's equity.

Two or more items could be affected by a transaction. For example, an asset (equipment) could increase by $10,000, a different asset (cash) could decrease by $6,000, and a liability (notes payable) could increase by $4,000.

As a general example, we will now look at transactions incurred by Softbyte, a computer programming business, during its first month of operations. You should study these transactions until you are sure you understand them. They are not difficult, but they are important to your success in this course. Being able to analyze how transactions affect the accounting equation is essential for understanding accounting.

To keep it simple, we will not include cents in the dollar amounts we record in the following analysis of Softbyte's transaction. In reality, it is important to understand that cents should be, and are, used when transactions are recorded in a company's internal accounting records.

Transaction (1): Investment by Owner. Marc Doucet decides to open a computer programming business, which he names Softbyte. On September 1, 2014, he invests $15,000 cash in the business, which he deposits in a bank account opened under the name of Softbyte. This transaction results in an equal increase in both assets and owner's equity for Softbyte.

Basic Analysis	The asset Cash is increased by $15,000 and the owner's equity account, M. Doucet, Capital, is increased by $15,000.

		Assets	=	Liabilities	+	Owner's Equity
Equation Analysis						M. Doucet,
		Cash	=			Capital
	(1)	+$15,000	=			+$15,000

Notice that the two sides of the basic equation remain equal. Note also that investments by an owner are **not** revenues and are not included in calculating profit. The increase therefore has to be recorded as an investment in the owner's capital account rather than as revenue from operations.

Transaction (2): Purchase of Equipment for Cash. Softbyte purchases computer equipment for $7,000 cash. This transaction results in an equal increase and decrease in total assets, though the composition of assets changes. The specific effect of this transaction and the cumulative effect of the first two transactions are:

Basic Analysis	The asset Cash is decreased by $7,000 and the asset Equipment is increased by $7,000.

		Assets			=	Liabilities	+	Owner's Equity
		Cash	+	Equipment	=			M. Doucet, Capital
Equation Analysis	Old Balances	$15,000			=			$15,000
	(2)	−7,000		+$7,000				
	New Balances	$ 8,000 +		$7,000	=			$15,000
			$15,000					$15,000

Notice that total assets are still $15,000, and that Doucet's equity also remains at $15,000, the amount of his original investment.

Transaction (3): Purchase of Supplies on Credit. Softbyte purchases $1,600 of computer paper and other supplies that are expected to last several months from the Chuah Supply Company. Chuah Supply agrees to allow Softbyte to pay this bill next month (in October). This transaction is referred to as a purchase on account, or a credit purchase. Assets are increased because of the expected future benefits of using the paper and supplies. Liabilities are increased by the amount that is due to Chuah Supply Company.

Basic Analysis	The asset Supplies is increased by $1,600 and the liability Accounts Payable is increased by the same amount.

Equation Analysis

		Assets			=	Liabilities	+	Owner's Equity
		Cash	+ Supplies	+ Equipment	=	Accounts Payable	+	M. Doucet, Capital
	Old Balances	$8,000 +		+ $7,000	=			$15,000
(3)			+$1,600			+$1,600		
	New Balances	$8,000 +	$1,600 +	$7,000	=	$1,600	+	$15,000
			$16,600				$16,600	

Total assets are now $16,600. This total is matched by a $1,600 creditor's claim and a $15,000 ownership claim.

Transaction (4): Services Provided for Cash. Softbyte receives $1,200 cash from customers for programming services it has provided. This transaction is Softbyte's main revenue-producing activity. Remember that revenue increases profit, which then increases owner's equity.

Basic Analysis	The asset Cash is increased by $1,200 and the owner's equity account Service Revenue is increased by $1,200.

Equation Analysis

		Assets			=	Liabilities	+	Owner's Equity		
		Cash	+ Supplies	+ Equipment	=	Accounts Payable	+	M. Doucet, Capital	+	Revenues
	Old Balances	$8,000 +	$1,600 +	$7,000	=	$1,600	+	$15,000		
(4)		+1,200								+$1,200
	New Balances	$9,200 +	$1,600 +	$7,000	=	$1,600	+	$15,000	+	$1,200
			$17,800					$17,800		

The two sides of the equation still balance at $17,800.

We don't have room to give details for each revenue and expense account in this illustration, so revenues (and expenses when we get to them) will be summarized under one column heading for Revenues and one for Expenses. However, it is important to keep track of the account titles that are affected (e.g., Service Revenue), as they will be needed when the income statement is prepared in the next section.

Transaction (5): Purchase of Advertising on Credit. Softbyte receives a bill for $250 from the local newspaper for advertising the opening of its business. It postpones payment of the bill until a later date. The cost of advertising is an expense, and not an asset, because the benefits have already been used. Owner's equity decreases because an expense is incurred. Expenses reduce profit and owner's equity.

Basic Analysis	The liability Accounts Payable is increased by $250 and the owner's equity account Advertising Expense is increased by $250.

Equation Analysis

		Assets			=	Liabilities	+	Owner's Equity			
		Cash	+ Supplies	+ Equipment	=	Accounts Payable	+	M. Doucet, Capital	+ Revenues	−	Expenses
	Old Balances	$9,200 +	$1,600 +	$7,000	=	$1,600	+	$15,000	+ $1,200		
(5)						+$250					−$250
	New Balances	$9,200 +	$1,600 +	$7,000	=	$1,850	+	$15,000	+ $1,200	−	$250
			$17,800					$17,800			

The two sides of the equation still balance at $17,800. Note that, although the expense increases, this is shown as a negative number because expenses reduce owner's equity.

Expenses do not have to be paid in cash at the time they are incurred. When payment is made on the later date, the liability Accounts Payable will be decreased and the asset Cash will also be decreased [see transaction (8)].

Transaction (6): Services Provided for Cash and Credit. Softbyte provides $3,500 of programming services for customers. Cash of $1,500 is received from customers, and the balance of $2,000 is billed to customers on account. This transaction results in an equal increase in assets and owner's equity.

Basic Analysis	Three specific items are affected: the asset Cash is increased by $1,500; the asset Accounts Receivable is increased by $2,000; and the owner's equity account Service Revenue is increased by $3,500.

Equation Analysis

		Cash	+	Accounts Receivable	+	Supplies	+	Equipment	=	Accounts Payable	+	M. Doucet, Capital	+	Revenues	−	Expenses
				Assets					=	**Liabilities** +			**Owner's Equity**			
Old Balances		$ 9,200			+	$1,600	+	$7,000	=	$1,850	+	$15,000	+	$1,200	−	$250
(6)		+1,500		+$2,000										+3,500		
New Balances		$10,700 +		$2,000	+	$1,600	+	$7,000	=	$1,850	+	$15,000	+	$4,700	−	$250
				$21,300									$21,300			

You might wonder why owner's equity is increased by $3,500 when only $1,500 has been collected. The reason is that the assets from earning revenues do not have to be in cash. Owner's equity is increased when revenues are earned. In Softbyte's case, revenues are earned when the service is provided. When collections on account are received at a later date, Cash will be increased and Accounts Receivable will be decreased [see transaction (9)].

Transaction (7): Payment of Expenses. The expenses paid in cash for September are store rent, $600; salaries of employees, $900; and utilities, $200. These payments result in an equal decrease in assets and owner's equity.

Basic Analysis	The asset Cash is decreased by $1,700 in total ($600 + $900 + $200) and owner's equity expense accounts are increased by the same amount, which then decreases owner's equity.

Equation Analysis

		Cash	+	Accounts Receivable	+	Supplies	+	Equipment	=	Accounts Payable	+	M. Doucet, Capital	+	Revenues	−	Expenses
				Assets					=	**Liabilities** +			**Owner's Equity**			
Old Balances		$10,700 +		$2,000	+	$1,600	+	$7,000	=	$1,850	+	$15,000	+	$4,700	−	$ 250
(7)		−600														−600
		−900														−900
		−200														−200
New Balances		$ 9,000 +		$2,000	+	$1,600	+	$7,000	=	$1,850	+	$15,000	+	$4,700	−	$1,950
				$19,600									$19,600			

The two sides of the equation now balance at $19,600. Three lines are needed in the analysis in order to show the different types of expenses that have been paid. Note that total expenses increase but, as explained in transaction (5), it is shown as a negative number because expenses decrease owner's equity.

Transaction (8): Payment of Accounts Payable. Softbyte pays its $250 advertising bill in cash. Remember that the bill was previously recorded in transaction (5) as an increase in Accounts Payable and a decrease in owner's equity.

Basic Analysis	The asset Cash is decreased by $250 and the liability Accounts Payable is decreased by $250.

Equation Analysis

		Assets				=	Liabilities +		Owner's Equity		
	Cash +	Accounts Receivable +	Supplies +	Equipment =		Accounts Payable +	M. Doucet, Capital	+ Revenues	− Expenses		
Old Balances	$9,000 +	$2,000 +	$1,600 +	$7,000 =		$1,850 +	$15,000	+ $4,700	− $1,950		
(8)	−250					−250					
New Balances	$8,750 +	$2,000 +	$1,600 +	$7,000 =		$1,600 +	$15,000	+ $4,700	− $1,950		
		$19,350						$19,350			

Notice that the payment of a liability for an expense that has previously been recorded does not affect owner's equity. The expense was recorded in transaction (5) and should not be recorded again.

Transaction (9): Receipt of Cash on Account. The sum of $600 in cash is received from some customers who were billed for services in transaction (6). This transaction does not change total assets, but it does change the composition of those assets.

Basic Analysis	The asset Cash is increased by $600 and the asset Accounts Receivable is decreased by $600.

Equation Analysis

		Assets				=	Liabilities +		Owner's Equity		
	Cash +	Accounts Receivable +	Supplies +	Equipment =		Accounts Payable +	M. Doucet, Capital	+ Revenues	− Expenses		
Old Balances	$8,750 +	$2,000 +	$1,600 +	$7,000 =		$1,600 +	$15,000	+ $4,700	− $1,950		
(9)	+600	−600									
New Balances	$9,350 +	$1,400 +	$1,600 +	$7,000 =		$1,600 +	$15,000	+ $4,700	− $1,950		
		$19,350						$19,350			

Note that a collection of an account receivable for services that were billed and recorded earlier does not affect owner's equity. Revenue was already recorded in transaction (6) and should not be recorded again.

Transaction (10): Signed Contract to Rent Equipment in October. Marc Doucet and an equipment supplier sign a contract for Softbyte to rent equipment for the months of October and November at the rate of $250 per month. Softbyte is to pay each month's rent at the start of the month. There is no effect on the accounting equation because the assets, liabilities, and owner's equity have not been changed by the signing of the contract. An accounting transaction has not occurred. At this point, Softbyte has not paid for anything, nor has it used the equipment, and therefore it has not incurred any expenses.

		Assets				=	Liabilities +		Owner's Equity		
	Cash +	Accounts Receivable +	Supplies +	Equipment =		Accounts Payable +	M. Doucet, Capital	+ Revenues	− Expenses		
Old Balances	$9,350 +	$1,400 +	$1,600 +	$7,000 =		$1,600 +	$15,000	+ $4,700	− $1,950		
(10) No entry											
New Balances	$9,350 +	$1,400 +	$1,600 +	$7,000 =		$1,600 +	$15,000	+ $4,700	− $1,950		
		$19,350						$19,350			

Note that the new balances are all identical to the old balances as nothing has changed.

Transaction (11): Withdrawal of Cash by Owner. Marc Doucet withdraws $1,300 in cash from the business for his personal use. This transaction results in an equal decrease in assets and owner's equity.

Basic Analysis	The asset Cash is decreased by $1,300, and the owner's equity account Drawings is increased by $1,300, which then decreases owner's equity, as follows:

Equation Analysis

	Assets				=	Liabilities +		Owner's Equity			
	Cash	+ Accounts Receivable	+ Supplies	+ Equipment	=	Accounts Payable	+ M. Doucet, Capital	− M. Doucet, Drawings	+ Revenues	− Expenses
Old Balances	$9,350 +	$1,400	+ $1,600	+ $7,000	=	$1,600	+ $15,000		+ $4,700	− $1,950
(11)	−1,300							−$1,300		
New Balances	$8,050 +	$1,400	+ $1,600	+ $7,000	=	$1,600	+ $15,000	− $1,300	+ $4,700	− $1,950
	$18,050						$18,050			

Note that both drawings and expenses reduce owner's equity, as shown in the accounting equation above. However, **owner's drawings are not expenses**. Expenses are incurred for the purpose of earning revenue and are reported in the income statement. Drawings do not generate revenue. They are a *disinvestment*; that is, the effect of an owner's cash withdrawal is the opposite of the effect of an owner's investment. Like owner's investments, drawings are not included in the determination of profit.

Summary of Transactions

Softbyte's transactions are summarized in Illustration 1-10 to show their cumulative effect on the accounting equation. The transaction number and the specific effects of each transaction are indicated.

▶ **ILLUSTRATION 1-10**
Tabular summary of Softbyte transactions

	Assets				=	Liabilities +		Owner's Equity			
	Cash	+ Accounts Receivable	+ Supplies	+ Equipment	=	Accounts Payable	+ M. Doucet, Capital	− M. Doucet, Drawings	+ Revenues	− Expenses
(1)	+$15,000						+$15,000			
(2)	−7,000			+$7,000						
(3)			+$1,600			+$1,600				
(4)	+1,200								+$1,200	
(5)						+250				−$ 250
(6)	+1,500	+$2,000							+3,500	
(7)	−600									−600
	−900									−900
	−200									−200
(8)	−250					−250				
(9)	+600	−600								
(10)	No entry									
(11)	−1,300							−$1,300		
	$ 8,050 +	$1,400	+ $1,600	+ $7,000	=	$1,600	+ $15,000	− $1,300	+ $4,700	− $1,950
	$18,050						$18,050			

The illustration demonstrates some significant facts.

1. Each transaction must be analyzed for its effects on:
   (a) the three components (assets, liabilities, and owner's equity) of the accounting equation, and
   (b) specific items within each component.
2. The two sides of the equation must always be equal.

This section on transaction analysis does not show the formal method of recording transactions. We will start illustrating that in Chapter 2. But understanding how transactions change assets, liabilities, and owner's equity is fundamental to understanding accounting and also business in general.

BEFORE YOU GO ON...

Do It

Transactions for the month of August by Verma & Co., a public accounting firm, are shown below. Make a table that shows the effects of these transactions on the accounting equation, like the tabular analysis shown in Illustration 1-10.

1. The owner, Anil Verma, invested $25,000 of cash in the business.
2. Equipment was purchased on credit, $7,000.
3. Services were performed for customers for $8,000. Of this amount, $2,000 was received in cash and $6,000 is due on account.
4. Rent of $850 was paid for the month.
5. Customers on account paid $4,000 (see transaction 3).
6. The owner withdrew $1,000 of cash for personal use.

Solution

	Cash	+	Accounts Receivable	+	Office Equipment	=	Accounts Payable	+	A. Verma, Capital	−	A. Verma, Drawings	+	Revenues	−	Expenses
					Assets					Liabilities +		Owner's Equity			
1.	+$25,000								+$25,000						
2.					+$7,000		+$7,000								
3.	+2,000		+$6,000										+$8,000		
4.	−850														−$850
5.	+4,000		−4,000												
6.	−1,000										−$1,000				
	$29,150	+	$2,000	+	$7,000	=	$7,000	+	$25,000	−	$1,000	+	$8,000	−	$850
			$38,150								$38,150				

Related exercise material: BE1–11, BE1–12, BE1–13, E1–9, E1–10, E1–11, and E1–12.

Action Plan
- Analyze the effects of each transaction on the accounting equation.
- Use appropriate account names for the account titles (not descriptions).
- Keep the accounting equation in balance.

THE NAVIGATOR

PREPARING FINANCIAL STATEMENTS

The next step in accounting is to prepare the financial statements. You will recall that these include the balance sheet, income statement, statement of owner's equity, and cash flow statement.

Illustration 1-11 shows Softbyte's statements prepared from the transaction analysis in Illustration 1-10 and how the statements are interrelated. It is important to note that because of the interrelationships of the financial statements, they are always prepared in the following order: (1) income statement, (2) statement of owner's equity, (3) balance sheet, and (4) cash flow statement.

The essential features of Softbyte's four financial statements, and their interrelationships, are briefly described in the following sections.

Income Statement

The income statement is prepared from the data in the owner's equity columns (specifically the Revenues and Expenses columns) of Illustration 1-10. The statement's heading names the company and type of statement, and to indicate that it applies to a period of time, the income statement date names the time period. For Softbyte, this appears as Month Ended September 30, 2014, which means the statement is for a one-month period—September 1 to 30, 2014.

 STUDY OBJECTIVE 6
Prepare financial statements.

Helpful hint The income statement, statement of owner's equity, and cash flow statement all report information for a period of time. The balance sheet reports information at a point in time.

▶ **ILLUSTRATION 1-11**
Financial statements
and their interrelationships

SOFTBYTE
Income Statement
Month Ended September 30, 2014

Revenues		
Service revenue		$4,700
Expenses		
Advertising expense	$250	
Rent expense	600	
Salaries expense	900	
Utilities expense	200	
Total expenses		1,950
Profit		$2,750

SOFTBYTE
Statement of Owner's Equity
Month Ended September 30, 2014

M. Doucet, capital, September 1, 2014		$ 0
Add: Investments	$15,000	
Profit	2,750	17,750
		17,750
Less: Drawings		1,300
M. Doucet, capital, September 30, 2014		$16,450

Helpful hint The arrows in this
illustration show the relationships
between the four statements.

SOFTBYTE
Balance Sheet
September 30, 2014

Assets	
Cash	$ 8,050
Accounts receivable	1,400
Supplies	1,600
Equipment	7,000
Total assets	$18,050
Liabilities and Owner's Equity	
Liabilities	
Accounts payable	$ 1,600
Owner's equity	
M. Doucet, capital	16,450
Total liabilities and owner's equity	$18,050

SOFTBYTE
Cash Flow Statement
Month Ended September 30, 2014

Operating activities		
Cash receipts from customers	$ 3,300	
Cash payments for operating expenses	(1,950)	
Net cash provided by operating activities		$ 1,350
Investing activities		
Purchase of equipment	$ (7,000)	
Net cash used by investing activities		(7,000)
Financing activities		
Investments by owner	$ 15,000	
Drawings by owner	(1,300)	
Net cash provided by financing activities		13,700
Net increase in cash		8,050
Cash, September 1, 2014		0
Cash, September 30, 2014		$ 8,050

On the income statement, revenues of $4,700 appear first, followed by a list of the expenses totalling $1,950. Finally, profit of $2,750 is determined. The income statement is always prepared first in order to determine the amount of profit or loss used in the Statement of Owner's Equity.

Statement of Owner's Equity

Data for preparing the statement of owner's equity are taken from the owner's equity columns (specifically the Capital and Drawings columns) of the tabular summary (Illustration 1-10) and from the income statement. The heading of this statement names the company and type of statement, and shows the time period covered by the statement. As the time period is the same as it is for the income statement, it is also dated Month Ended September 30, 2014.

The beginning owner's equity amount is shown on the first line of the statement. In this example, it is a zero balance because it is Softbyte's first period of operations. For a company that is continuing its operations, the beginning balance is equal to the ending balance from the previous period. Then the owner's investments of $15,000 and profit $2,750, from the income statement, are added to the beginning balance. Then drawings of $1,300 are deducted to calculate the ending balance of $16,450 in owner's equity.

What if Softbyte reported a loss in its first month? The loss would reduce owner's capital. Instead of adding profit, the loss would be deducted in the same section as owner's drawings.

Balance Sheet

The balance sheet is prepared from the Assets and Liabilities column headings and the month-end data shown in the last line of the tabular summary (Illustration 1-10), and from the statement of owner's equity. Owner's capital of $16,450 at the end of the reporting period in the statement of owner's equity is reported on the balance sheet.

The heading of a balance sheet must identify the company, statement, and date. To indicate that the balance sheet is at a specific point in time, the date only mentions the point in time (there is no indication of a time period). For Softbyte, the date is September 30, 2014. Sometimes, the words "as at" precede the balance sheet date. Notice that the assets are listed at the top, followed by liabilities and owner's equity. Total assets must equal total liabilities and owner's equity. In other words, the balance sheet must balance.

Cash Flow Statement

Softbyte's cash flow statement, shown in Illustration 1-11, is for the same period of time as the income statement and the statement of owner's equity. Note that the positive numbers indicate cash inflows or increases. Numbers in parentheses indicate cash outflows or decreases. Parentheses are often used in financial statements to indicate negative, or opposite, numbers. At this time, you do not need to know how these amounts are determined. In Chapter 17, we will look at the cash flow statement in detail. But you should note that Cash of $8,050 on the September 30, 2014, balance sheet is also reported at the bottom of the cash flow statement.

Using the Information in the Financial Statements

Illustration 1-11 showed the financial statements for Softbyte. Every set of financial statements also has explanatory notes and supporting schedules that are an essential part of the statements. For example, as previously mentioned, at the very least a company will have to indicate if it is following IFRS or ASPE.

Public corporations issue their financial statements and supplementary materials in an annual report. The **annual report** is a document that includes useful non-financial information about the company, as well as financial information.

Non-financial information may include a management discussion of the company's mission, goals, and objectives; market position; and the people involved in the company. Financial information may include a review of current operations and a historical summary of key financial figures and ratios, in addition to comparative financial statements. Public company financial statements are audited and include the auditors' report. There is also a statement of management responsibility for the statements.

Now is a good time to look again at Reitmans' financial statements in Appendix A. Carefully examine the format and content of each financial statement and compare them with Softbyte's financial statements in Illustration 1-11. What similarities can you find between Softbyte's financial statements and the more complicated financial statements for Reitmans?

You will see that Reitmans' transactions have been accumulated for the year ended January 28, 2012, and grouped together in categories. When similar transactions are grouped together, they are being reported in aggregate. By presenting recorded data in aggregate, the accounting information system simplifies a large number of transactions. As a result, the company's activities are easier to understand and are more meaningful. This simplification does mean less detail, however. Reitmans' financial statements are highly condensed and some critics might argue that the statements are too simple. Still, Reitmans is not the only organization that reports in this way. Most companies report condensed information for two reasons: it's simpler, and it also avoids revealing significant details to competitors.

You should note that financial statement amounts are normally rounded to the nearest dollar, thousand dollars, or million dollars, depending on the size of the company. Reitmans rounds its numbers to the nearest thousand dollars. This is done to remove unimportant detail and make the information easier for the reader to understand.

ACCOUNTING IN ACTION
ETHICS INSIGHT

What would you do if you suspected a co-worker was stealing? Would you confront them or tell your employer or the authorities? Would you keep quiet if you feared losing your job? What to do about suspected fraud is an ethical question facing not just those working in the accounting field, but employees in any role. Workplace fraud can take many forms. It could be an employee forging a cheque or stealing inventory. But it could also be an executive who "cooks the books" to make their department's sales figure look better, to meet company targets and collect a bonus or keep their job. Organizations need to send a strong message that they won't tolerate fraud. One way of doing that is to protect and encourage "whistleblowers"— employees who suspect fraud and report it to their employers. As an example, in 2007, the federal government passed the *Public Servants Disclosure Protection Act* to protect whistleblowers working in federal departments and agencies. The Ontario Securities Commission has proposed legislation to protect employees of public companies who blow the whistle to the regulator. Another way to discourage fraud is to set up an internal crime hotline for employees to report suspected wrongdoing. Alerting an employer to a possible fraud is not tattling—it could save employers millions of dollars and assure shareholders and the public that a company's financial statements are accurate.

Sources: Marjo Johne, "Don't Fall Victim to an Inside Job," *Globe and Mail*, December 14, 2011; David Malamed, "Whistle Where You Work?", *CA Magazine*, January/February 2012; Michael McKiernan, "Regulator at a Crossroads," *Canadian Lawyer*, April 2012.

What risks might you face as an employee and individual if you don't blow the whistle on fraud?

 BEFORE YOU GO ON...

Do It

Listed below, in alphabetical order, are the financial statement items for Park Accounting Services. Prepare an income statement, statement of owner's equity, and balance sheet for the month ended January 31, 2014.

Accounts payable	$ 5,000	M. Park, capital, January 1, 2014	$10,350
Accounts receivable	2,500	M. Park, drawings	3,000
Advertising expense	500	Prepaid rent	1,300
Cash	8,200	Rent expense	850
Equipment	10,000	Service revenue	11,000

Solution

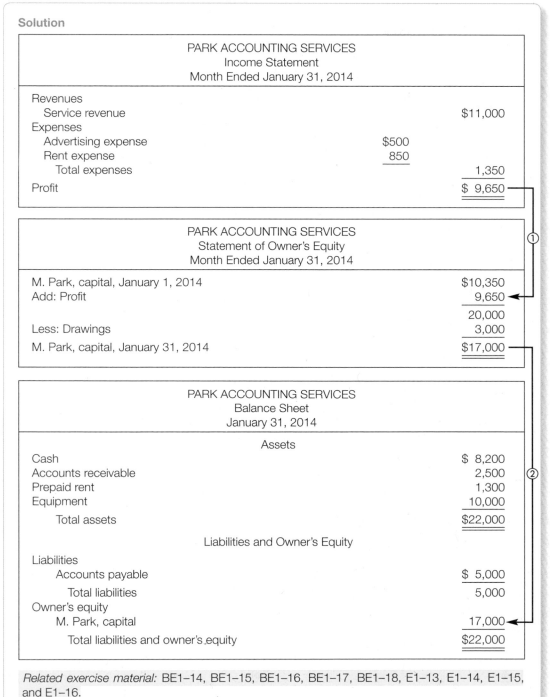

PARK ACCOUNTING SERVICES
Income Statement
Month Ended January 31, 2014

Revenues		
Service revenue		$11,000
Expenses		
Advertising expense	$500	
Rent expense	850	
Total expenses		1,350
Profit		$ 9,650

PARK ACCOUNTING SERVICES
Statement of Owner's Equity
Month Ended January 31, 2014

M. Park, capital, January 1, 2014	$10,350
Add: Profit	9,650
	20,000
Less: Drawings	3,000
M. Park, capital, January 31, 2014	$17,000

PARK ACCOUNTING SERVICES
Balance Sheet
January 31, 2014

Assets	
Cash	$ 8,200
Accounts receivable	2,500
Prepaid rent	1,300
Equipment	10,000
Total assets	$22,000
Liabilities and Owner's Equity	
Liabilities	
Accounts payable	$ 5,000
Total liabilities	5,000
Owner's equity	
M. Park, capital	17,000
Total liabilities and owner's equity	$22,000

Related exercise material: BE1–14, BE1–15, BE1–16, BE1–17, BE1–18, E1–13, E1–14, E1–15, and E1–16.

Action Plan

- Understand what components are reported in the income statement, statement of owner's equity and balance sheet.
- Each statement's heading includes the company name, the name of the statement, and a date line. The date line for the income statement and statement of owner's equity covers a specified period of time and the date line for the balance sheet is at a specific point in time.
- Understand that the profit reported in the income statement is added to the owner's capital in the statement of owner's equity.
- Understand that the owner's capital at the end of period reported in the statement of owner's equity is reported in the owner's equity section of the balance sheet.

THE NAVIGATOR

Comparing IFRS and ASPE

Key Differences	International Financial Reporting Standards (IFRS)	Accounting Standards for Private Enterprises (ASPE)
Accounting standards	Required for publicly accountable enterprises and optional for private enterprises	Private enterprises only

(continued)

Key Differences	International Financial Reporting Standards (IFRS)	Accounting Standards for Private Enterprises (ASPE)
Level of accounting information required	Users require extensive detailed information	Users require less information
Equity reporting	Statement of Shareholders' Equity	• Proprietorships: Statement of Owner's Equity • Partnerships: Statement of Partners' Equity • Corporation: Statement of Retained Earnings
Income reporting	Income Statement and Statement of Comprehensive Income	Income Statement

The Demonstration Problem is a final review before you work on the assignment material. The problem-solving strategies in the margins give you tips about how to approach the problem. The solutions show both the form and the content of complete answers.

ACTION PLAN

• Make sure that assets equal liabilities plus owner's equity in each transaction.

• Investments and revenues increase owner's equity. Withdrawals and expenses decrease owner's equity.

• Prepare the financial statements in the order listed.

• The income statement shows revenues and expenses for a period of time.

Demonstration Problem

Raman Balakra opens his own law office on July 1, 2014. During the first month of operations, the following transactions occurred:

1. Invested $11,000 in cash in the law practice.
2. Hired a legal assistant to work part-time for $500 per month.
3. Paid $800 for July rent on office space.
4. Purchased equipment on account, $3,000.
5. Provided legal services to clients for cash, $1,500.
6. Borrowed $700 cash from a bank on a note payable.
7. Provided legal services to a client on account, $2,000.
8. Collected $500 of the amount owed by a client on account (see transaction 7).
9. Paid monthly expenses: salaries, $500; telephone, $100; and utilities, $300.
10. Withdrew $1,000 cash for personal use.

Instructions

(a) Prepare a tabular analysis of the transactions.

(b) Prepare the income statement, statement of owner's equity, and balance sheet for Raman Balakra, Barrister & Solicitor.

Solution to Demonstration Problem

(a)

Transaction	Cash	+ Accounts Receivable	+ Equipment	= Notes Payable	+ Accounts Payable	+ R. Balakra Capital	− R. Balakra, Drawing	+ Revenues	− Expenses
(1)	+$11,000					+$11,000			
(2) No Entry									
(3)	−800								−$800
(4)			+$3,000		+$3,000				
(5)	+1,500							+$1,500	
(6)	+700			+$700					
(7)		+$2,000						+2,000	
(8)	+500	−500							
(9)	−500								−500
	−100								−100
	−300								−300
	−1,000						−$1,000		
	$11,000	+ $1,500	+ $3,000	= $700	+ $3,000	+ $11,000	− $1,000	+ $3,500	− $1,700

Assets $15,500

Liabilities + Owner's Equity $15,500

(b)

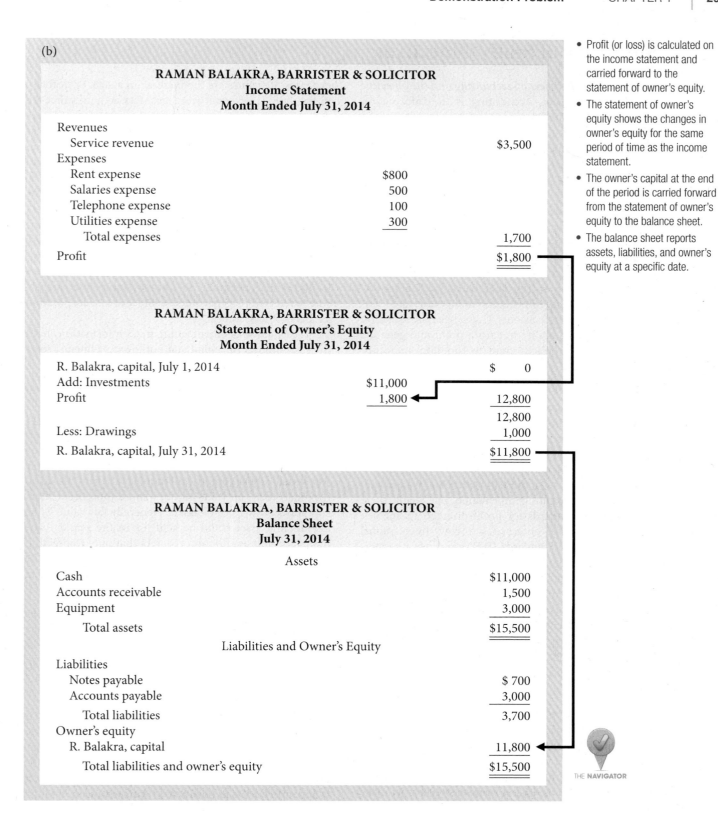

RAMAN BALAKRA, BARRISTER & SOLICITOR
Income Statement
Month Ended July 31, 2014

Revenues		
Service revenue		$3,500
Expenses		
Rent expense	$800	
Salaries expense	500	
Telephone expense	100	
Utilities expense	300	
Total expenses		1,700
Profit		$1,800

RAMAN BALAKRA, BARRISTER & SOLICITOR
Statement of Owner's Equity
Month Ended July 31, 2014

R. Balakra, capital, July 1, 2014		$ 0
Add: Investments	$11,000	
Profit	1,800	12,800
		12,800
Less: Drawings		1,000
R. Balakra, capital, July 31, 2014		$11,800

RAMAN BALAKRA, BARRISTER & SOLICITOR
Balance Sheet
July 31, 2014

Assets	
Cash	$11,000
Accounts receivable	1,500
Equipment	3,000
Total assets	$15,500
Liabilities and Owner's Equity	
Liabilities	
Notes payable	$ 700
Accounts payable	3,000
Total liabilities	3,700
Owner's equity	
R. Balakra, capital	11,800
Total liabilities and owner's equity	$15,500

- Profit (or loss) is calculated on the income statement and carried forward to the statement of owner's equity.
- The statement of owner's equity shows the changes in owner's equity for the same period of time as the income statement.
- The owner's capital at the end of the period is carried forward from the statement of owner's equity to the balance sheet.
- The balance sheet reports assets, liabilities, and owner's equity at a specific date.

THE NAVIGATOR

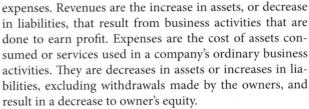

Summary of Study Objectives

1. *Identify the use and users of accounting and the objective of financial reporting.* Accounting is the information system that identifies, records, and communicates the economic events of an organization to a wide variety of interested users. Good accounting is important to people both inside and outside the organization. Internal users, such as management, use accounting information to plan, control, and evaluate business operations. External users include investors and creditors, among others. Accounting data are used by investors (owners or potential owners) to decide whether to buy, hold, or sell their financial interests. Creditors (suppliers and bankers) evaluate the risks of granting credit or lending money based on the accounting information. The objective of financial reporting is to provide useful information to investors and creditors to make these decisions. Users need information about the business's ability to earn a profit and generate cash. For our economic system to function smoothly, reliable and ethical accounting and financial reporting are critical.

2. *Compare different forms of business organizations and explain how Canadian accounting standards apply to these organizations.* The most common examples of business organizations are proprietorships, partnerships, and corporations. Generally accepted accounting principles are a common set of guidelines that are used to prepare and report accounting information. In Canada, there are two sets of standards for profit-oriented businesses. Publicly accountable enterprises follow International Financial Reporting Standards (IFRS) and private enterprises have the choice of following IFRS or Accounting Standards for Private Enterprises (ASPE).

   The economic entity concept requires the business activities of each economic entity to be kept separate from the activities of its owner and other economic entities. The going concern assumption presumes that a business will continue operations for enough time to use its assets for their intended purpose and to fulfill its commitments.

3. *Describe the components of the financial statements and explain the accounting equation.* Assets, liabilities, and owner's equity are reported in the balance sheet. Assets are resources owned or controlled by a business that are expected to provide future services or benefits. Liabilities are current obligations arising from past events to make future payments of assets or services. Owner's equity is the owner's claim on the company's assets and is equal to total assets minus total liabilities. The balance sheet is based on the accounting equation: Assets = Liabilities + Owner's Equity.

   The income statement reports the profit or loss for a specified period of time. Profit is equal to revenues minus

expenses. Revenues are the increase in assets, or decrease in liabilities, that result from business activities that are done to earn profit. Expenses are the cost of assets consumed or services used in a company's ordinary business activities. They are decreases in assets or increases in liabilities, excluding withdrawals made by the owners, and result in a decrease to owner's equity.

The statement of owner's equity summarizes the changes in owner's equity during the period. Owner's equity is increased by investments by the owner and profits. It is decreased by drawings and losses. Investments are contributions of cash or other assets by owners. Drawings are withdrawals of cash or other assets from the business for the owner's personal use. Owner's equity in a partnership is referred to as partners' equity and in a corporation as shareholders' equity.

A cash flow statement summarizes information about the cash inflows (receipts) and outflows (payments) for a specific period of time.

4. *Determine what events are recognized in the financial statements and how the events are measured.* Only events that cause changes in assets, liabilities, or owner's equity are recorded. Recognition is the process of recording items and measurement is the process of determining the amount that should be recognized. The cost principle states that assets should be recorded at their historical (original) cost. Fair value may be a more appropriate measure for certain types of assets. Generally fair value is the amount the asset could be sold for in the market. The monetary unit assumption requires that only transaction data that can be expressed as an amount of money be included in the accounting records, and it assumes that the monetary unit is stable.

5. *Analyze the effects of business transactions on the accounting equation.* Each business transaction must have a dual effect on the accounting equation. For example, if an individual asset is increased, there must be a corresponding (1) decrease in another asset, (2) increase in a liability, and/or (3) increase in owner's equity.

6. *Prepare financial statements.* The income statement is prepared first. Expenses are deducted from revenues to calculate the profit or loss for a specific period of time. Then the statement of owner's equity is prepared using the profit or loss reported in the income statement. The profit is added to (losses are deducted from) the owner's equity at the beginning of the period. Drawings are then deducted to calculate owner's equity at the end of the period. A balance sheet reports the assets, liabilities, and owner's equity of a business as at the end of the accounting period. The owner's equity at the end of period, as calculated in the statement of owner's equity, is reported in the balance sheet in the owner's equity section.

THE NAVIGATOR

▶ Glossary

Accounting   The information system that identifies, records, and communicates the economic events of an organization to a wide variety of interested users. (p. 4)

Accounting equation   Assets = Liabilities + Owner's Equity. (p. 13)

Accounting Standards for Private Enterprises (ASPE)   A set of standards developed by the Accounting Standards Board (AcSB) that may be used for financial reporting by private enterprises in Canada. (p. 10)

Accounting transaction   An economic event that is recorded in the accounting records because it changes the assets, liabilities, or owner's equity items of the organization. (p. 16)

Accounts payable   A liability created by buying services or products on credit. It is an obligation to pay cash to a supplier in the future. (p. 12)

Accounts receivable   An asset created when selling services or products to customers who promise to pay cash in the future. (p. 12)

Annual report   Information that a company gives each year to its shareholders and other interested parties about its operations and financial position. It includes the financial statements and auditors' report, in addition to information and reports by management. (p. 25)

Assets   Resources owned or controlled by a business that are expected to provide future services or benefits. (p. 12)

Balance sheet   A financial statement that reports the assets, liabilities, and owner's equity at a specific date. (p. 12)

Cash flow statement   A financial statement that provides information about the cash receipts and cash payments for a specific period of time. (p. 14)

Corporation   A business organized as a separate legal entity under corporation law, with ownership divided into transferable shares. (p. 9)

Cost principle   An accounting principle that states that assets should be recorded at their historical (original) cost. (p. 16)

Creditors   All of the persons or entities that a company owes money to. (p. 6)

Drawings   Withdrawals of cash or other assets from an unincorporated business for the owner's personal use. Drawings result in a decrease in an asset and a decrease in owner's equity. (p. 14)

Economic entity concept   The concept that the accounting for an economic entity's activities be kept separate and distinct from the accounting for the activities of its owner and all other economic entities. (p. 11)

Elements of the financial statements   The components in the financial statements. Assets, liabilities, owner's equity, revenues, and expenses. (p. 15)

Expenses   The cost of assets consumed or services used in a company's ordinary business activities. Expenses are decreases in assets or increases in liabilities, excluding withdrawals made by the owners, and result in a decrease to owner's equity. (p. 13)

Fair value   Generally the amount the asset could be sold for in the market assuming the company is a going concern, not the amount that a company would receive in an involuntary liquidation or distress sale. (p. 16)

Generally accepted accounting principles (GAAP)   An accepted set of accounting standards that includes broad principles and practices, as well as rules and procedures. These standards indicate how to report economic events. (p. 9)

Going concern assumption   An assumption that a company will continue to operate in the foreseeable future. (p. 11)

Income statement   A financial statement that presents the revenues and expenses and resulting profit (or loss) for a specific period of time. (p. 13)

International Financial Reporting Standards (IFRS)   A set of global standards developed by the International Accounting Standards Board (IASB) used for financial reporting by publicly accountable enterprises. (p. 10)

Investments by the owner   The increase in owner's equity that results from assets put into the business by the owner. (p. 14)

Investors   Owners or potential owners of a business. (p. 6)

Liabilities   Current obligations, arising from past events, to make future payments of assets or services. (p. 12)

Limited liability   The legal principle that the owners' liability for the debts of the business is limited to the amount they invested in the business. (p. 9)

Loss   The amount by which expenses are greater than revenues. A loss decreases owner's equity. (p. 13)

Measurement   The process of determining the amount that should be recognized. (p. 16)

Monetary unit assumption   An assumption that states that only transaction data that can be expressed as an amount of money may be included in the accounting records. It is also assumed that the monetary unit is stable. (p. 16)

Note payable   A liability supported by a written promise to pay a specific amount, at a specific time, in the future. (p. 12)

Owner's equity   The owner's claim on the assets of the company, which is equal to total assets minus total liabilities. (p. 13)

Partnership   An association of two or more persons to carry on as co-owners of a business for profit. (p. 9)

Prepaid expense   The asset created when a business pays cash for costs incurred in advance of being used or consumed. (p. 12)

Profit The amount by which revenues are greater than expenses. Profit increases owner's equity. (p. 13)

Proprietorship A small business owned by one person. (p. 8)

Publicly accountable enterprises Publicly traded companies, as well as securities brokers and dealers, banks, and credit unions whose role is to hold assets for the public as part of their primary business. (p. 10)

Recognition The process of recording a transaction in the accounting records. (p. 16)

Revenues The increase in assets, or decrease in liabilities, that result from business activities that are done to earn profit; result in an increase in owner's equity. (p. 13)

Statement of owner's equity A financial statement that summarizes the changes in owner's equity for a specific period of time. (p. 14)

Unearned revenue The liability created when a customer pays in advance of being provided a service or product. (p. 12)

Unlimited liability The principle that the owners of a business are personally liable (responsible) for all debts of the business. (p. 8)

Flash cards

▶ Self-Study Questions
Answers are at the end of the chapter.

(SO 1) K 1. The main objective of the financial statements is to provide useful information to
    (a) government in deciding if the company is respecting tax laws
    (b) increase the value of the company
    (c) investors and creditors that is useful when they are making decisions about the business
    (d) management that is useful when they are making decisions about the business

(SO 2) K 2. Which of the following characteristics are related to corporations as opposed to partnerships and proprietorships?
    (a) Simple to form, unlimited legal liability, limited life
    (b) Limited legal liability, limited life, income taxes on profit paid by the organization
    (c) More than one owner, income taxes on profit paid by the owners, unlimited legal liability
    (d) Income taxes paid by the organization, limited legal liability, indefinite life

(SO 2) K 3. Which of the following statements about International Financial Reporting Standards (IFRS) is correct?
    (a) All Canadian enterprises must follow IFRS.
    (b) Under IFRS, companies that operate in more than one country must produce separate financial statements for each of those countries.
    (c) All Canadian publicly accountable enterprises must use IFRS.
    (d) Canadian private enterprises are not allowed to use IFRS. They must use ASPE.

(SO 2) C 4. Which of the following statements about the going concern assumption is correct?
    (a) The going concern assumption is the assumption that the economic entity will continue to operate in the future.
    (b) Under the going concern assumption, all of the business's assets must be reported at their fair value.
    (c) The financial statements must report whether or not a company is a going concern.
    (d) The going concern assumption is not followed under ASPE.

(SO 3) C 5. Which of the following items is not reported on the statement of owner's equity?
    (a) Investments by the owner
    (b) Drawings
    (c) Profit
    (d) Revenues

(SO 3) AP 6. As at December 31, after its first year of operations, Stoneland Company has assets of $8,500; revenues of $6,000; expenses of $3,500; owner's capital of $5,000; and drawings of $500. What are the liabilities for Stoneland Company as at December 31?
    (a) $1,500
    (b) $2,500
    (c) $500
    (d) $3,500

(SO 4) K 7. Which of the following best describes when an event should be recognized in the accounting records?
    (a) An event should be recognized in the accounting records if there is a change in assets, liabilities, or owner's equity and the change can be measured in monetary terms.
    (b) An event should be recognized in the accounting records if it involves an interaction between the company and another external entity.
    (c) Where there is uncertainty about a future event occurring or not, it should not be recognized.
    (d) Accountants use tradition to determine which events to recognize.

(SO 5) AP 8. Genesis Company buys a $10,000 machine on credit. Initially, this transaction will only affect the:
    (a) income statement.
    (b) balance sheet.
    (c) income statement and statement of owner's equity.
    (d) income statement, statement of owner's equity, and balance sheet.

(SO 5) AP 9. Bing Company pays $700 for store rent for the month. The basic analysis of this transaction on the accounting records is:

(a) the asset Cash is increased by $700 and the expense Rent Expense is increased by $700.

(b) the asset Cash is decreased by $700 and the expense Rent Expense is increased by $700.

(c) the asset Cash is decreased by $700 and the liability Rent Payable is increased by $700.

(d) the asset Cash is increased by $700 and the liability Rent Payable is decreased by $700.

(SO 6) C   10. Which of the following statements about the income statement and balance sheet is correct?
(a) The income statement and the balance sheet both show information as at a specific point in time.
(b) The income statement shows information as at a specific point in time; the balance sheet shows information for a specified time period.
(c) The income statement and the balance sheet both show information for a specified time period.
(d) The income statement shows information for a specified time period; the balance sheet shows information as at a specific point in time.

THE NAVIGATOR

▶ Questions

(SO 1) C   1. "Accounting is ingrained in our society and it is vital to our economic system." Do you agree? Explain.

(SO 1) C   2. Why should everyone study accounting whether they are going to be an accountant or not?

(SO 1) C   3. Distinguish between internal and external users of accounting data. Include in your answer what kinds of questions both internal and external users might want answered.

(SO 1) K   4. What is the main objective of financial reporting?

(SO 1) C   5. Why is ethics important to the accounting profession? To statement users?

(SO 2) C   6. Explain the differences between the following forms of business organization: (a) proprietorship, (b) partnership, (c) public corporation, and (d) private corporation.

(SO 2) C   7. Veronica argues that all Canadian companies should follow the same set of generally accepted accounting principles. Explain to Veronica why there are two sets of standards for profit-oriented enterprises in Canada and how she can tell what standards the company is using.

(SO 2) K   8. What is the economic entity concept?

(SO 2) C   9. Explain the going concern assumption and how it supports the use of the cost principle.

(SO 3) K   10. What is the accounting equation and what is its purpose?

(SO 3) K   11. (a) Define assets, liabilities, and owner's equity. (b) What items increase and decrease owner's equity?

(SO 3) K   12. What is the difference between Accounts Payable and Accounts Receivable?

(SO 3) K   13. What are revenues and expenses and how do they affect profit?

(SO 3) K   14. Amal can never remember which accounts belong on the balance sheet and which accounts belong on the income statement. Provide Amal with an explanation that will help her remember what to do.

(SO 4) C   15. Wayne thinks that all events must be recognized in the accounting records. He argues that, if they aren't recognized, the records will be incomplete. Explain to Wayne why he is incorrect and provide him with two examples of events that are not recorded.

(SO 4) C   16. What is the monetary unit assumption? What type of information is not included in the financial statements because of this assumption?

(SO 5) C   17. Can a business have a transaction in which only the left (assets) side of the accounting equation is affected? If yes, give an example.

(SO 5) AP   18. Paul Dumas withdrew $10,000 from his business, Dumas Pharmacy, which is organized as a proprietorship. Dumas' accountant recorded this withdrawal as an increase in an expense and a decrease in cash. Is this treatment correct? Why or why not?

(SO 6) C   19. A company's profit appears directly on the income statement and the statement of owner's equity. It is also included indirectly in the company's balance sheet. Do you agree or disagree? Explain.

(SO 6) C   20. André is puzzled as he reads **Reitmans'** financial statements. He notices that the numbers have all been rounded to the nearest thousand. He thought financial statements were supposed to be accurate and he is now wondering what happened to the rest of the money. Respond to André's concern.

▶ Brief Exercises

BE1–1   A list of decisions made by different users of accounting information follows:

1. Decide whether the company pays fair salaries.
2. Decide whether the company can pay its obligations.
3. Decide whether a marketing proposal will be cost-effective.
4. Decide whether the company's profit will permit an increase in drawings.
5. Decide how the company should finance its operations.

When the financial results of real companies are used in the end-of-chapter material, the company's name is shown in red.

Identify users of accounting information. (SO 1) K

The different users are identified in the table that follows. (a) Insert the number (1–5) of the kind of decision described above that each user would likely make. (b) Indicate whether the user is internal or external.

User	(a) Kind of Decision	(b) Internal or External User
Owner		
Marketing manager		
Creditor		
Chief financial officer		
Labour union		

Discuss ethical issues.
(SO 1) AN

BE1–2 Describe an ethical dilemma that each of the following individuals might encounter:

(a) A student in an introductory accounting course
(b) A production supervisor
(c) A salesperson
(d) A banker
(e) The prime minister of Canada

Identify forms of business organization. (SO 2) C

BE1–3 Match each of the following forms of business organization with the correct set of characteristics: proprietorship (PP), partnership (P), and corporation (C).

(a) _____ Shared control; combined skills and resources
(b) _____ Easier to transfer ownership and raise funds; no personal liability; entity pays income tax
(c) _____ Simple to set up; founder keeps control

Identify application of IFRS and ASPE. (SO 2) C

BE1–4 For each of the following statements, indicate whether the statement is true or false by placing a T or an F in the blank at the start of each statement.

(a) _____ Canadian publicly accountable enterprises have the choice to report under IFRS or ASPE.
(b) _____ All private enterprises must follow ASPE.
(c) _____ There are more requirements to provide information in the financial statements under ASPE than under IFRS.
(d) _____ Companies are required to include a note in their financial statements stating if they are using IFRS or ASPE.
(e) _____ Using IFRS may help Canadian public companies attract investors from around the globe.

Identify the components of the financial statements. (SO 3) (C)

BE1–5 Match the following components with the best description below and indicate if the component is reported on the balance sheet (BS) or income statement (IS).

1. Assets
2. Liabilities
3. Owner's Equity
4. Revenues
5. Expenses
6. Profit

Description	Component	Balance Sheet or Income Statement
(a) The increase in assets, or decrease in liabilities, resulting from business activities done to earn profit.		
(b) Resources owned or controlled by a business that are expected to provide future benefits.		
(c) The owner's claim on the resources of the company.		
(d) Current obligations to make future payments of assets or services.		
(e) The cost of resources consumed or services used in the company's business activities.		

Solve accounting equation.
(SO 3) AP

BE1–6 Presented below is the accounting equation. Determine the missing amounts:

Assets	=	Liabilities	+	Owner's Equity
$75,000		$24,000		(a)
(b)		$150,000		$91,000
$89,000		(c)		$52,000

BE1-7 Use the accounting equation to answer each of the following questions:

(a) Greenway Co. has total assets of $600,000 and its owner's equity is equal to one third of its total assets. What is the amount of Greenway Co.'s liabilities?

(b) May Company has liabilities of $280,000. The balance in C. May, Capital, is $130,000; in drawings, $40,000; revenues, $440,000; and expenses, $330,000. What is the amount of May Company's total assets?

(c) Fereira Company has total assets of $90,000. The balance in Sharon Fereira's Capital is $35,000; in drawings, $7,000; revenues, $55,000; and expenses, $45,000. What is the amount of the company's total liabilities?

Solve accounting equation. (SO 3) AP

BE1-8 Butler Company is owned by Rachel Butler. The company had total assets of $850,000 and total liabilities of $550,000 at the beginning of the year. Answer each of the following independent questions:

(a) During the year, total assets increased by $130,000 and total liabilities decreased by $80,000. What is the amount of owner's equity at the end of the year?

(b) Total liabilities decreased by $95,000 during the year. The company incurred a loss of $40,000. R. Butler made an additional investment of $100,000 and made no withdrawals. What is the amount of total assets at the end of the year?

(c) During the year, total assets increased by $100,000. Profit was $185,000. There were no additional owner's investments, but R. Butler withdrew $50,000. What is the amount of total liabilities at the end of the year?

(d) Total assets increased by $45,000, and total liabilities decreased by $50,000. There were no additional owner's investments, and R. Butler withdrew $40,000. What is the amount of profit or loss for the year?

Solve accounting equation. (SO 3) AP

BE1-9 Below are some items found in the financial statements of Stefan Knoler, MD. Indicate (a) whether each of the following items is an asset (A), liability (L), or part of owner's equity (OE); and (b) which financial statement—income statement (IS), statement of owner's equity (OE), or balance sheet (BS)—it would be reported on. The first one has been done for you as an example.

Identify assets, liabilities, and owner's equity. (SO 3) AP

	(a)	(b)
1. Accounts receivable	A	BS
2. Salaries payable		
3. Salaries expense		
4. Supplies		
5. Supplies expense		
6. S. Knoler, capital		
7. Service revenue		
8. Equipment		
9. Notes payable		
10. Cash		
11. Prepaid expense		
12. S. Knoler, drawings		

BE1-10 Match each of the following terms with the best description below:

1. Cost principle
2. Generally accepted accounting principles
3. Going concern assumption
4. Economic entity concept
5. Monetary unit assumption

   (a) _____ Transactions are recorded in terms of units of money.

   (b) _____ Transactions are recorded based on the actual amount received or paid.

   (c) _____ Accounting for a business excludes any personal transactions of the owner and the transactions of any other entity.

   (d) _____ The broad principles and practices, as well as rules and procedures, that indicate how to report economic events.

   (e) _____ Businesses are expected to continue operating indefinitely.

Identify GAAP concepts. (SO 2, 4) C

BE1-11 Presented below are eight business transactions. Indicate whether the transactions increased (+), decreased (−), or had no effect (NE) on each element of the accounting equation.

(a) Purchased $250 of supplies on account.

(b) Performed $500 of services on account.

(c) Paid $300 of operating expenses.

(d) Paid $250 cash on account for the supplies purchased in item 1 above.

(e) Invested $1,000 cash in the business.

Determine effects of transactions on accounting equation. (SO 5) AP

(f) Owner withdrew $400 cash.
(g) Hired an employee to start working the following month.
(h) Received $500 from a customer who had been billed previously in item (b) above.
(i) Purchased $450 of equipment in exchange for a note payable.

Use the following format, in which the first one has been done for you as an example:

			Owner's Equity			
Transaction	Assets	Liabilities	Capital	Drawings	Revenues	Expenses
1	+$250	+$250	NE	NE	NE	NE

Match basic transaction analysis with transaction description. (SO 5) AP

BE1–12 Match the following basic transaction analysis with the best description of the economic event.

1. Cash increased by $10,000 and the owner's equity account, D. Morris, Capital, is increased by $10,000.
2. Cash is decreased by $2,500 and the asset account Prepaid Insurance is increased.
3. Supplies is increased by $1,000 and the liability account Accounts Payable is increased by $1,000.
4. Accounts receivable is increased by $500 and the revenue account Service Revenue is increased by $500.
5. Cash is decreased by $1,000 and the liability account Accounts Payable is decreased by $1,000.
6. Cash is increased by $500 and the account Accounts Receivable is decreased by $500.

Description	Transaction Analysis
(a) Cash collected on account.	_____
(b) Owner invests cash in the business.	_____
(c) Supplies are purchased on account.	_____
(d) Company provides service on account.	_____
(e) Payment on account made to supplier.	_____
(f) Company purchases an insurance policy.	_____

Determine effects of transactions on owner's equity. (SO 3, 5) AP

BE1–13 Classify each of the following items as owner's investments (I), drawings (D), revenue (R), expenses (E), or as having no effect on owner's equity (NE):

(a) _____ Costs incurred for advertising
(b) _____ Commission earnings
(c) _____ Equipment received from the company owner
(d) _____ Amounts paid to employees
(e) _____ Cash paid to purchase equipment
(f) _____ Services performed on account
(g) _____ Rent received
(h) _____ Utilities incurred
(i) _____ Cash distributed to company owner
(j) _____ Collection of an account receivable
(k) _____ Cash collected in advance of providing service

Determine missing items in owner's equity. (SO 3, 6) AP

BE1–14 Presented below is information from the statements of owner's equity for Kerkan Consulting for the first three years of operation. Determine the missing amounts:

	2013	2014	2015
J. Kerkan, capital, January 1	$0	$68,000	(c)
Investment in the year	50,000	0	20,000
Profit (loss) for the year	25,000	(b)	17,000
Drawings in the year	(a)	33,000	12,000
J. Kerkan, capital, December 31	68,000	65,000	(d)

Calculate profit from information on the statement of owner's equity. (SO 6) AP

BE1–15 Clinton Enterprises' statement of owner's equity showed the following balances for the owner's capital account:

1. Beginning of the year: $225,000
2. End of the year: $260,000
   (a) If the owner made no additional investments or withdrawals, what is the profit for the year?
   (b) Assume instead the owner made an additional investment of $10,000 but no withdrawals during the year. What is the profit for the year?
   (c) Assume instead the owner made an additional investment of $5,000 and a withdrawal of $7,000. What is the profit for the year?

BE1–16 Prairie Company is owned and operated by Natasha Woods. In alphabetical order below are the financial statement items for Prairie Company. Using the appropriate items, prepare an income statement for the month ended October 31, 2014.

Accounts payable	$90,000	N. Woods, capital, October 1, 2014	$36,000
Accounts receivable	77,500	N. Woods, drawings	6,000
Advertising expense	3,600	Rent expense	2,600
Cash	59,300	Service revenue	23,000

BE1–17 Refer to the data in BE1–16. Using these data and the information from Prairie's income statement, prepare a statement of owner's equity.

BE1–18 Refer to the data in BE1–16. Using these data and the information from Prairie's statement of owner's equity prepared in BE1–17, prepare a balance sheet for Prairie Company.

▶ Exercises

E1–1 **Roots Canada Ltd.**, a private company, is known around the world for its clothing and accessories. It has more than 120 stores in Canada and the United States, and more than 40 locations in Asia.

Instructions

(a) Identify two internal users of Roots' accounting information. Write a question that each user might try to answer by using accounting information.
(b) Identify two external users of Roots' accounting information. Write a question that each user might try to answer by using accounting information.

E1–2 Listed below are several statements regarding different forms of business organization.

Instructions

For each statement, indicate if that statement is true or false for each of the forms of business organizations by placing a T or an F in each column.

	Proprietorship	Partnership	Publicly Traded Corporation
(a) Owners have limited liability.	___	___	___
(b) Records of the business are combined with the personal records of the owner or owners.	___	___	___
(c) Required to follow IFRS.	___	___	___
(d) Entity pays income taxes on its profits.	___	___	___
(e) Owners are called "shareholders."	___	___	___
(f) Will have more than one owner.	___	___	___
(g) Entity has a limited life.	___	___	___
(h) The entity has a separate legal existence from its owners.	___	___	___

E1–3 Here are some terms from the chapter:

1. Accounts payable	7. Assets
2. Expenses	8. Corporation
3. Creditor	9. Unearned revenue
4. International Financial Reporting Standards (IFRS)	10. Generally accepted accounting principles
5. Prepaid expense	11. Accounts receivable
6. Profit	12. Owner's equity

Instructions

Match each term with the best description that follows:

(a) _____ A company that raises money by issuing shares
(b) _____ An accepted set of accounting standards that includes broad principles, practices, rules, and procedures
(c) _____ Obligations to suppliers of goods
(d) _____ Amounts due from customers
(e) _____ Owner's claims against the company's resources
(f) _____ Payment of cash for costs incurred in advance of being used
(g) _____ A party that a company owes money to
(h) _____ Resources owned by a business that have the ability to provide a future benefit

(i) _____ The set of accounting standards that all publicly accountable enterprises in Canada have to follow
(j) _____ Results when revenues exceed expenses
(k) _____ The cost of assets consumed or services used in a company's ordinary business activities
(l) _____ A liability arising when a customer pays in advance of receiving service

Determine missing items.
(SO 3) AP

E1-4 Summaries of selected data for three companies follow. Three items are missing from each summary.

	Midway Company	Ferris Company	Wheel Company
Beginning of year			
Total assets	$ 95,000	$162,000	(g)
Total liabilities	72,000	(d)	30,000
Total owner's equity	(a)	85,000	33,000
End of year:			
Total assets	110,000	(e)	79,000
Total liabilities	(b)	61,000	42,000
Total owner's equity	37,000	98,000	(h)
Changes during year in owner's equity:			
Investments by owner	(c)	0	5,000
Drawings	22,000	(f)	25,000
Total revenues	179,000	99,000	85,000
Total expenses	150,000	48,000	(i)

Instructions

Determine the missing amounts.

Calculate profit (or loss).
(SO 3) AP

E1-5 Shane Cooke began a business, Cooke Company, on January 1, 2012, with an investment of $100,000. The company had the following assets and liabilities on the dates indicated:

December 31	Total Assets	Total Liabilities
2012	$370,000	$210,000
2013	440,000	290,000
2014	525,000	355,000

Instructions

Use the accounting equation and the change in owner's equity during the year to calculate the profit (or loss) for:

(a) 2012, assuming Shane Cooke's drawings were $50,000 for the year.
(b) 2013, assuming Shane Cooke made an additional investment of $40,000 and had no drawings in 2013.
(c) 2014, assuming Shane Cooke made an additional investment of $10,000 and his drawings were $60,000 for the year.

Classify accounts. (SO 3) C

E1-6 Below are some items found in the financial statements of Peter Zizler, Orthodontist.

	(a)	(b)
1. Accounts payable	L	BS
2. Accounts receivable		
3. Cash		
4. Equipment		
5. Interest payable		
6. Interest revenue		
7. Interest expense		
8. Investment by the owner		
9. Service revenue		
10. Prepaid rent		
11. P. Zizler, capital (opening balance)		
12. P. Zizler, drawings		
13. Salaries expense		
14. Supplies		
15. Supplies expense		
16. Unearned revenue		

Instructions

Indicate (a) whether each of the above items is an asset (A), liability (L), or part of owner's equity (OE); and (b) which financial statement—income statement (IS), statement of owner's equity (OE), or balance sheet (BS)—it would be reported on. The first one has been done for you as an example.

E1-7 Stanley Company, a proprietorship, had the following selected business transactions during the year: Identify GAAP (SO 2, 4) C

1. Land with a cost of $208,000 was reported at its fair value of $260,000.
2. A lease agreement to rent equipment from an equipment supplier starting next year was signed. The rent is $500 per month and the lease is for two years. Payments are due at the start of each month. Nothing was recorded in Stanley Company's accounting records when the lease was signed.
3. Stanley paid the rent for an apartment for the owner's personal use and charged it to Rent Expense.
4. Stanley wanted to make its profit look worse than it really was, so it adjusted its expenses upward to include the effects of inflation.
5. Stanley included a note in its financial statements stating the company is a going concern and is following ASPE.

Instructions

(a) In each situation, identify whether the accounting treatment is correct or not, and why.
(b) If it is incorrect, state what should have been done.

E1-8 The following is a list of independent events: Determine events to be recognized. (SO 4) C

1. A company pays $10,000 cash to purchase equipment at a bankruptcy sale. The equipment's fair value is $15,000.
2. A Canadian company purchases equipment from a company in the United States and pays $5,000 US cash. It cost the company $5,200 Canadian to purchase the U.S. dollars from its bank.
3. A company provides $4,000 of services to a new customer on account.
4. A company hires a new chief executive officer, who will bring significant economic benefit to the company. The company agrees to pay the new executive officer $500,000 per year.
5. A company signs a contract to provide $10,000 of services to a customer. The customer pays the company $4,000 cash at the time the contract is signed.

Instructions

(a) Should the transaction be recorded in the accounting records? Explain why or why not.
(b) If the transaction should be recorded, indicate the amount. Explain.

E1-9 A list of effects on the accounting equation follows.   Give examples of transactions. (SO 5) C

1. Increases an asset and increases a liability.
2. Increases an asset and increases owner's equity.
3. Decreases an asset and decreases a liability.
4. Decreases owner's equity and decreases an asset.
5. Increases a liability and decreases owner's equity.
6. Increases one asset and decreases another asset.

Instructions

For each effect, give an example of a transaction that would cause it.

E1-10 Here are the transactions for Great Gardens during August, its first month, of operations: Analyze effects of transactions for new company. (SO 5) AP

1. Holly Sevigny, the owner, made a $25,000 cash investment to start business.
2. Purchased equipment for $7,000. Paid $2,000 cash and signed a note for the balance.
3. Incurred $250 of advertising expense on account.
4. Billed customers for services performed, $3,200.
5. Holly Sevigny withdrew cash for her personal use, $2,000.
6. Received $2,100 from customers billed in transaction 4.
7. Received $3,000 cash from customers for work to be performed in September.
8. Received $1,000 cash from customers for services performed.
9. Paid $250 for advertising expense incurred in transaction 3.
10. Paid $700 for a 12-month insurance policy starting September 1.

Instructions

Prepare a tabular analysis of the above transactions, as shown in Illustration 1-10 in the text.

E1-11 At the beginning of March, Brister Software Company had Cash of $12,000, Accounts Receivable of   Analyze effects of transactions for existing company. (SO 5) AP
$18,000, Accounts Payable of $4,000, and G. Brister, Capital of $26,000. During the month of March, the following transactions occurred:

1. Purchased equipment for $23,000 from Digital Equipment. Paid $3,000 cash and signed a note payable for the balance.
2. Received $12,000 from customers for contracts billed in February.

3. Paid $3,000 for March rent of office space.
4. Paid $2,500 of the amounts owing to suppliers at the beginning of March.
5. Provided software services to Brie Construction Company for $7,000 cash.
6. Paid BC Hydro $1,000 for energy used in March.
7. G. Brister withdrew $5,000 cash from the business.
8. Paid Digital Equipment $2,100 on account of the note payable issued for the equipment purchased in transaction 1. Of this, $100 was for interest expense.
9. Hired an employee to start working in April.
10. Incurred advertising expense on account for March, $1,500.

Instructions

Prepare a tabular analysis of the above transactions, as shown in Illustration 1-10 in the text. The first row contains the amounts the company had at the beginning of March.

Analyze transactions. Calculate profit and increase in owner's equity. (SO 5) AP

E1–12 A tabular summary of the transactions for Star & Co., an accounting firm, for its first month of operations, July 2014, follows:

	Cash	+	Accounts Receivable	+	Prepaid Insurance	+	Equipment	=	Accounts Payable	+	B. Star, Capital	−	B. Star, Drawings	+	Revenues	−	Expenses
1	$18,000						$6,000				$24,000						
2	−4,000						8,000		$4,000								
3	−750				$750												
4	3,500		$4,800												$8,300		
5	−2,000								−2,000								
6	−3,300												−$3,300				
7	−800																−800 Rent
8	1,350		−1,350														
9	−2,700																−2,700 Salaries
10									420								−420 Utilities

Instructions

(a) Describe each transaction that occurred in the month.
(b) Calculate the amount of profit for the month.
(c) Calculate the increase in owner's equity for the month.

Prepare financial statements. (SO 6) AP

E1–13 An analysis of transactions for Star & Co. for July 2014 was presented in E1–12.

Instructions

Prepare an income statement and statement of owner's equity for July and a balance sheet at July 31.

Prepare income statement and statement of owner's equity. (SO 6) AP

E1–14 Atlantic Cruise Co. is owned by Irina Temelkova. The following information is an alphabetical listing of financial statement items for the company for the year ended May 31, 2014:

Accounts payable	$ 49,000	Interest expense	$ 20,000
Accounts receivable	42,000	Investments by owner	6,000
Advertising expense	3,500	Maintenance expense	83,000
Cash	19,400	Notes payable	400,000
Equipment	120,000	Prepaid insurance	1,200
Food, fuel, and other expenses	65,500	Salaries expense	128,000
I. Temelkova, capital, June 1, 2013	275,000	Ships	550,000
I. Temelkova, drawings	35,000	Supplies	15,000
Insurance expense	2,400	Ticket revenue	355,000

Instructions

Prepare an income statement and a statement of owner's equity for the year.

Prepare balance sheet. (SO 6) AP

E1–15 Refer to the financial information in E1–14 for the Atlantic Cruise Co. at May 31, 2014.

Instructions

Prepare the balance sheet.

E1–16 Judy Cumby is the sole owner of Deer Park, a public camping ground near Gros Morne National Park. Judy has gathered the following financial information for the year ended March 31, 2014:

Revenues—camping fees	$150,000	Revenues—general store	$ 40,000
Operating expenses	150,000	Cash on hand	9,400
Supplies on hand	2,500	Original cost of equipment	110,000
Fair value of equipment	125,000	Notes payable	70,000
Accounts payable	11,500	J. Cumby, capital, April 1, 2013	17,000
Accounts receivable	21,000	J. Cumby, drawings	5,000
Camping fees collected for April	10,000	Insurance paid for in advance for April to June, 2014	600

Calculate profit and owner's equity and prepare balance sheet. (SO 6) AP

Instructions

(a) Calculate Deer Park's profit for the year.
(b) Calculate Judy's owner's equity at March 31.
(c) Prepare a balance sheet at March 31.

⏵ Problems: Set A

P1–1A Specific financial decisions often depend more on one type of accounting information than another. Consider the following independent, hypothetical situations:

1. Pierson Industries is thinking about extending credit to a new customer. The terms of credit would require the customer to pay within 45 days of receipt of the goods.
2. An investor is considering purchasing a company called Organic Food Solutions Ltd. The investor plans on owning the company for at least five years.
3. The president of Hi-tech Adventure Limited is trying to determine whether the company is generating enough cash to increase the amount of dividends paid to shareholders and still have enough cash to buy additional equipment when needed.
4. Standen Bank is thinking about extending a loan to a small company. The company would be required to make interest payments at the end of each year for five years, and to repay the loan at the end of the fifth year.

Identify users and uses of accounting information. (SO 1) S

Instructions

(a) Identify types of user(s) of accounting information in each situation and indicate if they are external or internal.
(b) For each situation, state whether the user making the decision would depend mostly on information about (1) the business's economic resources and claims to the resources, or (2) the economic performance of the business. Justify your choice.

TAKING IT FURTHER   Why is it important to users of financial statements to know that the statements have been prepared by individuals who have high standards of ethical behaviour?

Taking It Further is an extra question at the end of each problem designed to challenge students to think beyond the basic concepts covered in the problem, and to provide written explanations. Your instructor may assign problems with or without this extra element.

P1–2A Five independent situations follow:

1. Tom Courtney, a student looking for summer employment, started a dog-walking service. He picks up the dog while its owner is at work and returns it after a walk.
2. Joseph Counsell and Sabra Surkis each own a bike shop. They have decided to combine their businesses and try to expand their operations to include snowboards. They expect that in the coming year they will need funds to expand their operations.
3. Three chemistry professors have formed a business that uses bacteria to clean up toxic waste sites. Each has contributed an equal amount of cash and knowledge to the venture. The use of bacteria in this situation is experimental, and legal obligations could result.
4. Abdur Rahim has run a successful but small organic food store for over five years. The increased sales at his store have made him believe the time is right to open a chain of organic food stores across the country. Of course, this will require a substantial investment for inventory and equipment, as well as for employees and other resources. Abdur has minimal personal savings.
5. Evelyn Church, Amaan Abu, and Brenda Gorny have recently passed their professional accounting exams. They have decided to start an accounting practice in their hometown.

Determine forms of business organization and type of accounting standards. (SO 2) AP

Instructions

(a) In each case, explain what form of organization the business is likely to take: proprietorship, partnership, or corporation. Give reasons for your choice.
(b) In each case indicate what accounting standards, IFRS or ASPE, the business is likely to use in its financial statements. Give reasons for your choice.

TAKING IT FURTHER   Frequently, individuals start a business as a proprietorship and later incorporate the business. What are some of the advantages of doing this?

Determine missing items.
(SO 3) AP

P1-3A The following selected data are for Perron Importers Limited for its first three years of operations:

January 1:	2013	2014	2015
Total assets	$ 40,000	$ (f)	(j)
Total liabilities	0	50,000	(k)
Total owner's equity	(a)	75,000	(l)
December 31:			
Total assets	(b)	140,000	172,000
Total liabilities	50,000	(g)	65,000
Total owner's equity	(c)	97,000	(m)
Changes during year in owner's equity:			
Investments by owner during the year	7,000	0	(n)
Drawings by owner during the year	15,000	(h)	36,000
Profit or loss for the year	(d)	40,000	(o)
Total revenues for the year	132,000	(i)	157,000
Total expenses for the year	(e)	95,000	126,000

Instructions

Determine the missing amounts.

TAKING IT FURTHER What information does the owner of a company need in order to decide whether he or she is able to withdraw cash from the business?

Classify accounts and prepare accounting equation.
(SO 3) AP

P1-4A Listed in alphabetical order, the following selected items (in thousands) were taken from Sunrise Cruise Ltd.'s December 31 financial statements:

1.	L BS	Accounts payable	$ 2,598	12.	___ ___	Other assets	$ 905
2.	___ ___	Accounts receivable	869	13.	___ ___	Other expenses	4,650
3.	___ ___	Cash	1,700	14.	___ ___	Other liabilities	1,735
4.	___ ___	Equipment	26,785	15.	___ ___	Other revenue	230
5.	___ ___	Food service revenues	5,500	16.	___ ___	Passenger revenues	19,765
6.	___ ___	Fuel expense	1,750	17.	___ ___	Port fee expense	429
7.	___ ___	G. Hirsch, capital, Jan. 1	2,738	18.	___ ___	Salaries expense	5,675
8.	___ ___	G. Hirsch, drawings	2,500	19.	___ ___	Supplies	550
9.	___ ___	Interest expense	675	20.	___ ___	Unearned passenger	
10.	___ ___	Maintenance expense	1,578			revenues	2,000
11.	___ ___	Notes payable	13,500				

Instructions

(a) In each case, identify on the blank line in the first column whether the item is an asset (A), liability (L), capital (C), drawings (D), revenue (R), or expense (E) item. The first one has been done for you as an example.
(b) Indicate on the blank line in the second column which financial statement—income statement (IS), statement of owner's equity (OE), or balance sheet (BS)—each item would be reported on. The first one has been done for you as an example.
(c) Show the amounts in Sunset Cruise's accounting equation by calculating the value of total assets, total liabilities, and total owner's equity at December 31.

TAKING IT FURTHER Is it important for Sunset Cruise to keep track of its different types of revenues as separate items? Explain.

Assess accounting treatment.
(SO 2, 4) C

P1-5A Five independent situations follow:

1. Human Solutions Incorporated believes its people are its most significant asset. It estimates and records their value on its balance sheet.
2. Sharon Barton, president and owner of Barton Industries, has instructed the accountant to report the company's land and buildings at its current value of $500,000 instead of its cost of $350,000. "Reporting the land and buildings at $500,000 will make it easier to get a loan from the bank next month," Sharon states.
3. Will Viceira, owner of the Music To You Company, bought an electric guitar for his personal use. He paid for the guitar with company funds and debited the equipment account.
4. West Spirit Oil Corp. is a very small oil and gas company that is listed on the Alberta Stock Exchange. The president asked each of the shareholders to approve using ASPE instead of IFRS to reduce expenses for accounting services. He received 100% approval and has advised the company accountant to prepare the 2014 financial statements accordingly.

5. Colour Photo Company is potentially on the verge of bankruptcy and the accountant is preparing its financial statements. The accountant advises the owner that it will be necessary to include a note to this effect in the financial statements.

Instructions

(a) For each of the above situations, determine if the accounting treatment of the situation is correct or incorrect. Explain why.

(b) If the accounting treatment is incorrect, explain what should be done.

TAKING IT FURTHER   Why is it important for companies to follow generally accepted accounting principles when preparing their financial statements?

P1-6A   On June 1, Leanne Aiken established Leanne's Travel Agency. The following transactions are for her first month of operations:

> *Analyze transactions and calculate owner's equity. (SO 3, 5) AP*

June	1	Deposited $23,000 in the agency's bank account at the Scotiabank.
	2	Purchased equipment for $6,800, paying $3,000 cash and signing a note payable for the balance.
	3	Paid rent for the month, $2,500.
	7	Paid $675 for supplies.
	8	Incurred $300 of advertising expense, on account.
	15	Earned $11,000 for services provided, with $3,500 paid in cash and the remainder on account.
	22	Withdrew $1,500 for personal use.
	25	Paid the amount due in the June 8 transaction.
	30	Paid employee salaries, $5,750.
	30	Received a bill for utilities for the month, $300.
	30	Received $6,000 from customers who were billed in the June 15 transaction.
	30	Paid $2,400 for a one-year insurance policy, starting July 1.

Instructions

(a) Prepare a tabular analysis of the effects of the above transactions on the accounting equation.

(b) From an analysis of the owner's equity, calculate the account balance in L. Aiken, Capital, at June 30.

TAKING IT FURTHER   Assume on June 30 there is $300 of supplies on hand and that $375 of supplies had been used during June. What amount should be reported as an asset, Supplies, on the June 30 balance sheet? What amount should be reported as an expense?

P1-7A   The following events concern Anita LeTourneau, a Manitoba law school graduate, for March 2014:

> *Analyze transactions and prepare balance sheet. (SO 3, 4, 5, 6) AP*

1. On March 4, she spent $20 on a lottery ticket.
2. On March 7, she won $250,000 in the lottery and immediately quit her job as a junior lawyer.
3. On March 10, she decided to open her own law practice, and deposited $50,000 of her winnings in a business chequing account, LeTourneau Legal Services.
4. On March 14, she purchased a new luxury condominium with a down payment of $150,000 from her personal funds plus a home mortgage of $200,000.
5. On March 15, Ms. LeTourneau signed a rental agreement for her law office space for $2,500 a month, starting March 15. She paid the first month's rent, as it is due on the 15th of each month.
6. On March 19, she hired a receptionist. He will be paid $500 a week and will begin working on March 24.
7. On March 20, she purchased equipment for her law practice from a company that had just declared bankruptcy. The equipment was worth at least $15,000 but Anita was able to buy it for only $10,000.
8. On March 21, she purchased $400 of supplies on account.
9. On March 24, she purchased an additional $6,500 of equipment for her law practice for $3,000 plus a $3,500 note payable due in six months.
10. On March 31, she performed $3,500 of legal services on account.
11. On March 31, she received $2,500 cash for legal services to be provided in April.
12. On March 31, she paid her receptionist $500 for the week.
13. On March 31, she paid $400 for the supplies purchased on account on March 21.

Instructions

(a) Prepare a tabular analysis of the effects of the above transactions on the accounting equation.

(b) Calculate profit and owner's equity for the month ended March 31.

(c) Prepare a balance sheet at March 31.

TAKING IT FURTHER   How should Anita determine which transactions should be recorded and which ones should not be recorded?

Analyze transactions and prepare financial statements. (SO 4, 5, 6) AP

P1-8A Lise Anderson opened a medical office under the name Lise Anderson, MD, on August 1, 2014. On August 31, the balance sheet showed Cash $3,000; Accounts Receivable $1,500; Supplies $600; Equipment $7,500; Accounts Payable $5,500; Note Payable $3,000; and L. Anderson, Capital, $4,100. During September, the following transactions occurred:

Sept.	4	Collected $800 of accounts receivable.
	5	Provided services of $10,500, of which $7,700 was collected from patients and the remainder was on account.
	7	Paid $2,900 on accounts payable.
	12	Purchased additional equipment for $2,300, paying $800 cash and leaving the balance on account.
	15	Paid salaries, $2,800; rent for August, $1,900; and advertising expenses, $275.
	18	Collected the balance of the accounts receivable from August 31.
	20	Withdrew $1,000 for personal use.
	26	Borrowed $3,000 from the Bank of Montreal on a note payable.
	28	Signed a contract to provide medical services, not covered under the government health plan, to employees of CRS Corp. in October for $5,700. CRS Corp. will pay the amount owing after the medical services have been provided.
	29	Received the telephone bill for September, $325.
	30	Billed the government $10,000 for services provided to patients in September.

Instructions

(a) Beginning with the August 31 balances, prepare a tabular analysis of the effects of the September transactions on the accounting equation.
(b) Prepare an income statement and statement of owner's equity for September, and a balance sheet at September 30.

TAKING IT FURTHER What are the differences between purchasing an item on account and signing a note payable for the amount owing?

Prepare financial statements. (SO 6) AP

P1-9A Bennett's Home Renovations was started in 2008 by Jim Bennett. Jim operates the business from an office in his home. Listed below, in alphabetical order, are the company's assets and liabilities as at December 31, 2014, and the revenues, expenses, and drawings for the year ended December 31, 2014:

Accounts payable	$ 7,850	Prepaid insurance	$ 1,685
Accounts receivable	10,080	Service revenue	153,750
Cash	8,250	Supplies	595
Equipment	29,400	Supplies expense	20,095
Insurance expense	3,375	Salaries expense	88,230
Interest expense	1,195	Unearned revenue	15,000
J. Bennett, drawings	44,800	Vehicles	42,000
Notes payable	30,800	Vehicle operating expenses	3,545

Jim's capital at the beginning of 2014 was $45,850. He made no investments during the year.

Instructions

Prepare an income statement, statement of owner's equity, and balance sheet.

TAKING IT FURTHER Why is it necessary to prepare the income statement first, then the statement of owner's equity, and the balance sheet last?

Determine missing amounts, and comment. (SO 6) AN

P1-10A Here are incomplete financial statements for Lee Company:

LEE COMPANY
Balance Sheet
February 28, 2014

Assets		Liabilities and Owner's Equity	
Cash	$ 9,500	Liabilities	
Accounts receivable	5,300	Notes payable	$26,000
Land	(i)	Accounts payable	(iii)
Building and equipment	41,500	Total liabilities	43,800
Total assets	$ (ii)	M. Lee, Capital	(iv)
		Total liabilities and owner's equity	$91,300

```
                              LEE COMPANY
                             Income Statement
                        Year Ended February 28, 2014

Revenues
   Service revenues                                              $95,000
Expenses
   Salaries expense               $32,000
   Other expenses                    (v)
   Supplies expense                1,500
      Total expenses                                             59,500
Profit                                                             (vi)
```

```
                              LEE COMPANY
                       Statement of Owner's Equity
                        Year Ended February 28, 2014

M. Lee, capital, March 1, 2013                                  $22,000
Add: Investments                                                  (vii)
     Profit                                                      (viii)
                                                                 62,500
Less: M. Lee, drawings                                             (ix)
M. Lee, capital, February 28, 2014                                 (x)
```

Instructions

(a) Calculate the missing amounts (i) to (x).
(b) Write a memo explaining (1) the sequence for preparing the financial statements, and (2) the interrelationships between the income statement, statement of owner's equity, and balance sheet.

TAKING IT FURTHER   Why isn't the balance sheet dated the same way as the income statement and statement of owner's equity: "Year Ended February 28, 2014"?

P1-11A   The balance sheet of Confucius Book Shop at April 30, 2014, is as follows:

Discuss errors and prepare corrected balance sheet.
(SO 3, 4, 5, 6) AP

```
                          CONFUCIUS BOOK SHOP
                               Balance Sheet
                              April 30, 2014

         Assets                        Liabilities and Owner's Equity

Building        $110,000        Accounts payable        $ 15,000
C. Cai, capital    85,000       Accounts receivable       37,000
Cash               10,000       Equipment                 58,000
Land               50,000       Supplies                   1,000
Notes payable     120,000       "Plug"                   264,000
                 --------                                --------
                 $375,000                                $375,000
```

Cenhai Cai, the owner of the book shop, admits that he is not an accountant. In fact, he couldn't get the balance sheet to balance without "plugging" the numbers (making up numbers to give the desired result). He gives you the following additional information:

1. A professional real estate appraiser estimated the value of the land at $50,000. The actual cost of the land was $36,000.
2. Accounts receivable includes amounts due from customers in China for 35,000 yuan, which is about $5,000 Canadian. Cenhai didn't know how to convert the currency for reporting purposes so he added the 35,000 yuan to the $2,000 due from Canadian customers. He thought it more important to know how much he was owed by each customer in the currency they would likely pay him with anyway. Cenhai also believes that Accounts Receivable is a liability. He sees it as bad for the business that he doesn't have the cash from his customers yet.

3. Cenhai reasons that equipment is a liability because it will cost him money in the future to maintain these items.
4. Cenhai reasons that the note payable must be an asset because getting the loan was good for the business. If he had not obtained the loan, he would not have been able to purchase the land and buildings.
5. Cenhai believes that his capital account is also an asset. He has invested in the business, and investments are assets; therefore his capital account is an asset.
6. The book shop owns 650 books that are for sale. The books cost $15,000. Cenhai knows that most book stores call their books "merchandise inventory," but he doesn't know if this should be reported on the balance sheet.

Instructions

(a) Identify any corrections that should be made to the balance sheet, and explain why by referring to the appropriate accounting concept.
(b) Prepare a corrected balance sheet for Confucius Book Shop at April 30. (*Hint:* The capital account may need to be adjusted in order to balance.)

TAKING IT FURTHER   Explain to Cenhai why all transactions affect at least two financial statement items.

▶ Problems: Set B

Identify users and uses of accounting information.
(SO 1) S

P1–1B   Specific financial decisions often depend more on one type of accounting information than another. Consider the following independent, hypothetical situations:

1. A B.C. investor is considering purchasing a company called Organics To You, which operates a chain of 20 organic food stores across Canada. The investor plans on owning the company for a minimum of five years.
2. The Backroads Company is considering extending credit to a new customer. The terms of credit would require the customer to pay within 45 days of receipt of the goods.
3. The senior partner of Accountants R Us is trying to determine if the partnership is generating enough cash to increase the partners' drawings and still ensure the partnership has enough cash to expand its operations.
4. Shields Bank is thinking about extending a loan to a small company. The company would be required to make interest payments at the end of each year for three years, and to repay the loan at the end of the third year.

Instructions

(a) Identify types of user(s) of accounting information in each situation and indicate if they are external or internal.
(b) For each situation, state whether the user making the decision would depend mostly on information about (1) the business's economic resources and claims to the resources, or (2) the economic performance of the business. Justify your choice.

TAKING IT FURTHER   Why is it important to users of financial statements to know that the statements have been prepared by individuals who have high standards of ethical behaviour?

Determine forms of business organization and types of accounting standards.
(SO 2) AP

P1–2B   Five independent situations follow:

1. Three computer science students have formed a business to develop a new social media application (app) for the Internet. Each has contributed an equal amount of cash and knowledge to the venture. While their app looks promising, they are concerned about the legal liabilities that their business might confront.
2. Shamira Hatami, a student looking for summer employment, opened a small cupcake shop out of her summer vacation home.
3. Robert Steven and Tom Cheng each own a snowboard manufacturing business and have now decided to combine their businesses. They expect that in the next year they will need funds to expand their operations.
4. Darcy Becker, Ellen Leboeuf, and Meg Dwyer recently graduated with marketing degrees. Friends since childhood, they have decided to start a consulting business that focuses on branding strategies for small and medium-sized businesses.
5. Leisha Pimienta wants to rent baby strollers at major Canadian airports. Travellers will rent out a stroller when they arrive at an airport, use it during their vacation, and return it to the airport when they depart.

Of course, this will require a substantial investment for strollers, as well as employees and space in each airport.

Instructions

(a) In each case, explain what form of organization the business is likely to take: proprietorship, partnership, or corporation. Give reasons for your choice.
(b) In each case indicate what accounting standards, IFRS or ASPE, the business is likely to use in its financial statements. Give reasons for your choice.

TAKING IT FURTHER   What are the advantages of two individuals first forming a partnership to run a business, and later incorporating?

P1–3B   The following selected data are for Alexei Imports Limited for its first three years of operations.

Determine missing items.
(SO 3) AP

January 1:	2013	2014	2015
Total assets	(a)	$75,000	$127,000
Total liabilities	0	(e)	(k)
Total owner's equity	60,000	(f)	(l)
December 31:			
Total assets	75,000	(g)	170,000
Total liabilities	(b)	45,000	(m)
Total owner's equity	45,000	(h)	100,000
Changes during year in owner's equity:			
Investments by owner during the year	5,000	(i)	0
Drawings by owner during the year	0	10,000	(n)
Profit or loss for the year	(c)	35,000	30,000
Total revenues for the year	(d)	(j)	160,000
Total expenses for the year	120,000	95,000	(o)

Instructions

Determine the missing amounts.

TAKING IT FURTHER   What information does the owner of a company need in order to decide whether he or she needs to invest additional cash in the business?

P1–4B   Listed in alphabetical order, the following selected items (in thousands) were taken from Paradise Mountain Family Resort's December 31 financial statements:

Classify accounts and prepare accounting equation.
(SO 3) AP

1.	L	BS	Accounts payable	$ 195	10.	Operating expenses	$ 871
2.			Accounts receivable	160	11.	Other assets	615
3.			Cash	120	12.	Other liabilities	396
4.			Equipment	600	13.	Other revenue	52
5.			Interest expense	45	14.	Rent revenues	1,295
6.			Insurance expense	15	15.	Salaries payable	125
7.			Land and buildings	1,495	16.	T. Yuen, capital, January 1	934
8.			Notes payable	950	17.	T. Yuen, drawings	20
9.			Prepaid insurance	30	18.	Unearned rent revenue	24

Instructions

(a) In each case, identify on the blank line, in the first column, whether the item is an asset (A), liability (L), capital (C), drawings (D), revenue (R), or expense (E) item. The first one has been done for you as an example.
(b) Indicate on the blank line, in the second column, which financial statement—income statement (IS), statement of owner's equity (OE), or balance sheet (BS)—each item would be reported on. The first one has been done for you as an example.
(c) Show the amounts in Paradise Mountain Family Resort's accounting equation by calculating the value of total assets, total liabilities, and total owner's equity at December 31.

TAKING IT FURTHER   Is it important for Paradise Mountain Family Resort to keep track of its different types of expenses as separate items? Explain.

Assess accounting treatment.
(SO 2, 4) C

P1–5B   Five independent situations follow:

1. In preparing its financial statements, Karim Company estimated and recorded the impact of the recent death of its president.
2. Power Drilling Company recently purchased a fishing boat. It plans on inviting clients for outings occasionally, so the boat was paid for with company funds and recorded in the company's records. Dave Power's family will use the boat whenever it is not being used to entertain clients. It is estimated that the boat will be used by the family about 85% of the time.
3. Because of a "flood sale," equipment worth $300,000 was purchased by Montigny Company for only $200,000. The equipment was recorded at $300,000 on Montigny's books.
4. Vertical Lines Company was on the verge of filing for bankruptcy, but a turnaround in the economy has resulted in the company being very healthy financially. The company president insists that the accountant put a note in the financial statements that states the company is a real going concern now.
5. Harjinder and Jamal operate two oil wells as a partnership. The partners are planning on expanding. They plan on incorporating and going public in three years. They agree that the company should use International Financial Reporting Standards (IFRS) and also agree that they do not need to put that information in the financial statements as they are currently a private company.

Instructions
(a) For each of the above situations, determine if the accounting treatment of the situation is correct or incorrect. Explain why.
(b) If the accounting treatment is incorrect, explain what should be done.

TAKING IT FURTHER   Why is it important for private and public companies to follow generally accepted accounting principles when preparing their financial statements?

Analyze transactions and calculate owner's equity.
(SO 3, 5) AP

P1–6B   Kensington Bike Repair Shop was started on April 1 by L. Depres. A summary of the April transactions follows:

April   1   Invested $21,000 to start the repair shop.
     2   Purchased equipment for $9,000, paying $3,000 cash and signing a note payable for the balance.
     5   Paid rent for the month, $1,050.
     7   Purchased $975 of supplies on account.
     9   Received $3,200 in cash from customers for repair services.
     16 Provided repair services on account to customers, $2,900.
     26 Collected $1,200 on account for services billed on April 16.
     27 Paid for supplies purchased on April 7.
     28 Paid $290 for advertising.
     29 Withdrew $1,300 for personal use.
     30 Received April utility bill, $200.
     30 Paid part-time employee salaries, $1,400.
     30 Billed a customer $750 for repair services.
     30 Received an advance from a customer for repairs to be performed in May, $2,100.

Instructions
(a) Prepare a tabular analysis of the effects of the above transactions on the accounting equation.
(b) From an analysis of the owner's equity, calculate the account balance in L. Depres, Capital at April 30.

TAKING IT FURTHER   Assume on April 30 there is $500 of supplies on hand and that $475 of supplies had been used during April. What amount should be reported as an asset, Supplies, on the April 30 balance sheet? What amount should be reported as an expense?

Analyze transactions and prepare balance sheet.
(SO 3, 4, 5, 6) AP

P1–7B   Lynn Barry started her own consulting firm, Barry Consulting, on June 1, 2014. The following transactions occurred during the month of June:

June   1   Sold her shares in Big Country Airlines for $7,000, which she deposited in her personal bank account.
     1   Transferred $6,000 from her personal account to a business account in the name of Barry Consulting.
     2   Paid $900 for office rent for the month.
     3   Purchased $545 of supplies on account.
     5   Paid $95 to advertise in the *County News*.
     9   Received $3,275 for services provided.
     12 Withdrew $600 for personal use.

15 Performed $5,000 of services on account.
17 Paid $1,800 for employee salaries.
21 Received $3,000 for services provided on account on June 15.
22 Paid for the supplies purchased on account on June 3.
25 Signed a contract to provide consulting services to a client for $5,500. Services will be performed and paid for in July.
26 Borrowed $5,500 from the bank and signed a note payable.
29 Used part of the cash borrowed from the bank on June 26 to purchase equipment for $2,150.
30 Paid $150 for telephone service for the month.
30 Received $2,500 from client for consulting to be provided in July.

Instructions

(a) Prepare a tabular analysis of the effects of the above transactions on the accounting equation.
(b) Calculate profit and owner's equity for the month ended June 30.
(c) Prepare a balance sheet at June 30.

TAKING IT FURTHER   How should Lynn determine which transactions should be recorded and which ones should not be recorded?

P1–8B   Fraser Baker opened Baker's Accounting Service in Winnipeg on September 1, 2014. On September 30, the balance sheet showed Cash $5,700; Accounts Receivable $2,100; Supplies $350; Equipment $7,600; Accounts Payable $4,300; and F. Baker, Capital $11,450. During October, the following transactions occurred:

Analyze transactions and prepare financial statements. (SO 4, 5, 6) AP

Oct. 1 Paid $3,800 of the accounts payable.
1 Paid $900 rent for October.
4 Collected $1,550 of the accounts receivable.
5 Hired a part-time office assistant at $80 per day to start work the following week.
8 Purchased additional equipment for $4,000, paying $500 cash and signing a note payable for the balance.
14 Performed $900 of accounting services on account.
15 Paid $300 for advertising.
18 Collected $400 from customers who received services on October 14.
20 Paid $500 for family dinner celebrating Fraser's son's university graduation.
25 Borrowed $8,000 from the Manitoba Bank on a note payable.
26 Sent a statement reminding a customer that he still owed the company money from September.
28 Earned revenue of $5,400, of which $3,100 was paid in cash and the balance was due in November.
29 Paid the part-time office assistant $720 for working nine days in October.
29 Received $2,800 cash for accounting services to be performed in November.
30 Received the telephone bill for the month, $205.
30 Withdrew $1,200 cash for personal expenses.

Instructions

(a) Beginning with the September 30 balances, prepare a tabular analysis of the effects of the October transactions on the accounting equation.
(b) Prepare an income statement and statement of owner's equity for October, and a balance sheet at October 31.

TAKING IT FURTHER   Explain the correct accounting treatment of the transaction on October 20.

P1–9B   Judy Johansen operates an interior design business, Johansen Designs. Listed below, in alphabetical order, are the company's assets and liabilities as at December 31, 2014, and the revenues, expenses, and drawings for the year ended December 31, 2014:

Prepare financial statements. (SO 6) AP

Accounts payable	$ 6,590	Prepaid insurance	$ 600
Accounts receivable	6,745	Rent expense	18,000
Cash	11,895	Salaries expense	70,500
Equipment	9,850	Service revenue	132,900
Furniture	15,750	Supplies	675
Interest expense	350	Supplies expense	3,225
Insurance expense	1,800	Telephone expense	3,000
J. Johansen drawings	40,000	Unearned revenue	2,500
Notes payable	7,000	Utilities expense	2,400

Judy's capital at the beginning of 2014 was $35,800. She made no investments during the year.

Instructions

Prepare an income statement, statement of owner's equity, and balance sheet.

TAKING IT FURTHER   Why is the balance sheet prepared after the statement of owner's equity?

Determine missing amounts, and comment. (SO 6) AN

P1–10B   Here are incomplete financial statements for Deol Company:

DEOL COMPANY
Balance Sheet
October 31, 2014

Assets		Liabilities and Owner's Equity	
Cash	$ 5,000	Liabilities	
Accounts receivable	10,000	Notes payable	$59,600
Land	(i)	Accounts payable	(ii)
Building and equipment	45,000	Total liabilities	66,500
Total assets	$110,000	Owner's equity	
		B. Deol, capital	(iii)
		Total liabilities and owner's equity	$ (iv)

DEOL COMPANY
Income Statement
Year Ended October 31, 2014

Revenues		
Service revenue		$80,000
Expenses		
Salaries expense	$37,500	
Other expenses	(v)	
Supplies expense	6,000	
Total expenses		62,500
Profit		$ (vi)

DEOL COMPANY
Statement of Owner's Equity
Year Ended October 31, 2014

B. Deol, capital, November 1, 2013	$35,000
Add: Investments	(vii)
Profit	(viii)
	57,500
Less: B. Deol, drawings	(ix)
B. Deol, capital, October 31, 2014	$ (x)

Instructions

(a) Calculate the missing amounts (i) to (x).

(b) Write a memo explaining (1) the sequence for preparing the financial statements, and (2) the interrelationships between the income statement, statement of owner's equity, and balance sheet.

TAKING IT FURTHER   Why aren't the income statement and the statement of owner's equity dated the same way as the balance sheet: "October 31, 2014"?

P1-11B   GG Company was formed on January 1, 2014. On December 31, Guy Gélinas, the owner, prepared a balance sheet:

Discuss errors and prepare corrected balance sheet. (SO 2, 3, 5, 6) AP

GG COMPANY			
Balance Sheet			
December 31, 2014			
Assets		Liabilities and Owner's Equity	
Cash	$ 15,000	Accounts and notes payable	$ 45,000
Accounts receivable	55,000	Boat loan payable	13,000
Supplies	20,000	G. Gélinas, capital	25,000
Boat	18,000	Profit for 2014	25,000
	$108,000		$108,000

Guy willingly admits that he is not an accountant. He is concerned that his balance sheet might not be correct. He gives you the following additional information:

1. The boat actually belongs to Guy Gélinas, not to GG Company. However, because he thinks he might take customers out on the boat occasionally, he decided to list it as an asset of the company. To be consistent, he also listed as a liability of the company the personal bank loan that he took out to buy the boat.
2. Guy spent $15,000 to purchase more supplies than he usually does, because he heard that the price of the supplies was expected to increase. It did, and the supplies are now worth $20,000. He thought it best to record the supplies at $20,000, as that is what it would have cost him to buy them today.
3. Guy has signed a contract to purchase equipment in January 2015. The company will have to pay $5,000 cash for the equipment when it arrives and the balance will be payable in 30 days. Guy has already reduced Cash by $5,000 because he is committed to paying this amount.
4. The balance in G. Gélinas, Capital is equal to the amount Guy originally invested in the company when he started it on January 1, 2014.
5. Guy combined notes payable of $15,000 with accounts payable of $30,000 as he thought this was more efficient.
6. Guy paid $1,200 for a one-year insurance policy on December 31. He did not include it in the balance sheet because the insurance is for 2015 and not 2014.
7. Guy knows that a balance sheet needs to balance but on his first attempt he had $108,000 of assets and $83,000 of liabilities and owner's equity. He reasoned that the difference was the amount of profit the company earned this year and added that to the balance sheet as part of owner's equity.

Instructions

(a) Identify any corrections that should be made to the balance sheet, and explain why by referring to the appropriate accounting concepts, assumption, or principle.
(b) Prepare a corrected balance sheet for GG Company. (*Hint:* To get the balance sheet to balance, adjust owner's equity.)

TAKING IT FURTHER   Assume that Guy did not make any withdrawals from the company in 2014, nor any investments other than his initial investment of $25,000. What was the actual profit for the year?

⊙ Continuing Cookie Chronicle

Natalie Koebel spent much of her childhood learning the art of cookie-making from her grandmother. They passed many happy hours mastering every type of cookie imaginable and later creating new recipes that were both healthy and delicious. Now at the start of her second year in college, Natalie is investigating various possibilities for starting her own business as part of the requirements of the Entrepreneurship program she is taking. A long-time friend insists that Natalie has to somehow include cookies in her business plan and, after a series of brainstorming sessions, Natalie settles on the idea of operating a cookie-making school. She will start on a part-time basis and offer her services in peoples' homes. Now that she has started thinking about it,

The Continuing Cookie Chronicle starts in this chapter and continues in every chapter throughout the book. This feature chronicles the growth of a hypothetical small business to show how the concepts you learn in each chapter can be applied in the real world.

the possibilities seem endless. During the fall, she will concentrate on Christmas cookies. She will offer group sessions (which will probably be more entertainment than education for the participants) and individual lessons. Natalie also decides to include children in her target market. The first difficult decision is coming up with the perfect name for her business. In the end, she settles on "Cookie Creations" and then moves on to more important issues.

Instructions

(a) What form of business organization—proprietorship, partnership, or corporation—do you recommend that Natalie use for her business? Discuss the benefits and weaknesses of each form and give the reasons for your choice.

(b) Will Natalie need accounting information? If yes, what information will she need and why? How often will she need this information?

(c) In addition to Natalie, who do you anticipate to be the users of Natalie's accounting information? What information will these identified users need and why?

(d) Which set of accounting standards will Natalie likely adopt when compiling her accounting information? Why?

(e) Identify specific asset, liability, and equity accounts that Cookie Creations will likely use to record its business transactions.

(f) Should Natalie open a separate bank account for the business? Why or why not?

CHAPTER 1 | BROADENING YOUR PERSPECTIVE

▶ Financial Reporting and Analysis

Financial Reporting Problem

BYP1-1 **Reitmans (Canada) Limited's** financial statements have been reproduced in Appendix A at the back of the textbook.

Instructions

(a) How many notes to the financial statements are presented for Reitmans? How many pages of the financial statement package do these notes use? How many pages do the financial statements themselves use?

(b) Many companies use a calendar year for their financial statements. What does Reitmans use?

(c) Where in the financial statements does it indicate that Reitmans' statements have been prepared using IFRS?

(d) What five financial statements has Reitmans presented for the year ended January 28, 2012?

(e) Where in the financial statements does it indicate that Reitmans reports the financial amounts in thousands of Canadian dollars?

(f) What were Reitmans' total assets as at January 28, 2012? As at January 29, 2011?

(g) What were Reitmans' total liabilities as at January 28, 2012? As at January 29, 2011?

(h) What is the amount of change in Reitmans' profit (Reitmans calls this "net earnings") from 2012 to 2011?

Interpreting Financial Statements

BYP1-2 **Apple Inc.** is an international corporation that designs, manufactures, and markets a range of mobile communication and media devices, personal computing products, and portable digital music players, as well as a variety of related software, networking solutions and hardware products. Apple is known for the Mac computer products, iPhones, iPads, and iPods. In the assets section of its 2011 balance sheet, the following data were presented:

APPLE INC. Balance Sheets (partial) (in U.S. millions)		
Assets	September 24, 2011	September 25, 2010
Cash and cash equivalents	$ 9,815	$11,261
Short term marketable securities	16,137	14,359
Accounts receivable, less allowance	5,369	5,510
Inventories	776	1,051
Deferred tax assets	2,014	1,636
Vendor non-trade receivables	6,348	4,414
Other current assets	4,529	3,447
Long term marketable securities	55,618	25,391
Property, plant and equipment, net	7,777	4,768
Goodwill	896	741
Acquired intangible assets, net	3,536	342
Other assets	3,556	2,263
Total assets	$116,371	$75,183

Instructions

(a) For a company such as Apple, what do you think its most important economic resource is? Where is this recorded on the balance sheet? At what value (if any) should it be shown?

(b) Do the assets reported on the balance sheet above tell you what Apple is worth? What information does the balance sheet give you about the company's value?

▶ Critical Thinking

Collaborative Learning Activity

Note to instructor: Additional instructions and material for this group activity can be found on the Instructor Resource Site and in *WileyPLUS*.

BYP1–3   In this group activity, students will be asked to identify (or determine) the information they would require if they were making a decision whether or not to lend money or to invest in a company.

Communication Activity

BYP1–4   Robert Joote is the owner of Peak Company. Robert has prepared the following balance sheet:

PEAK COMPANY Balance Sheet Month Ended December 31, 2014	
Assets	
Equipment	$20,500
Cash	10,500
Supplies	2,000
Accounts payable	(5,000)
Total assets	$28,000
Liabilities and Owner's Equity	
R. Joote, capital	$23,500
Accounts receivable	(3,000)
R. Joote, drawings	(2,000)
Prepaid insurance	(2,500)
Notes payable	12,000
Total liabilities and owner's equity	$28,000

Robert didn't know how to determine the balance for his capital account so he just "plugged" the number (he made up a number that would give him the result that he wanted). He had heard somewhere that assets had to equal the total of liabilities and owner's equity so he made up a number for capital so that these would be equal.

Instructions

In a memo, explain to Robert (a) how to determine the balance for his capital account, (b) why his balance sheet is incorrect, and (c) what he should do to correct it. Include in your explanation how the financial statements are interrelated, and why the order of preparation is important.

Ethics Case

BYP1–5   Chief executive officers (CEOs) and chief financial officers (CFOs) of publicly traded companies must personally certify that their companies' financial statements and other financial information contain no untrue statements and do not leave out any important facts. After many corporate scandals, the certification requirement was introduced as a way to hold top executives personally responsible for the integrity of their company's financial information.

Khan Corporation just hired a new management team, and its members say they are too new to the company to know whether the most recent financial reports are accurate or not. They refuse to sign the certification.

Instructions

(a) Who are the stakeholders in this situation?
(b) Should the CEO and CFO sign the certification? Explain why or why not.
(c) What are the CEO's and CFO's alternatives?

"All About You" Activity

BYP1–6   In the "All About You" feature, we introduced the idea that being financially literate has a major impact on our ability to meet our financial goals and even on our health and happiness. We all face financial decisions each day. Some of these decisions are small and others are critical. Making the right financial decisions is important to your well-being. Following are three financial decisions that you as a student will likely have to make.

1. You have to pay for your tuition, books, and spending money during college. You are trying to decide what kind of summer job you should apply for and whether or not you need to work part-time during the school year.
2. You need to have transportation to get back and forth to college each day. You are trying to decide if you can afford to buy a second-hand car and pay for parking or whether you should use public transit. You will have to borrow money to purchase the car.
3. You will be graduating this year and have received job offers from two different companies. You are deciding which company you should work for, and you want to accept a position in a company that is financially stable and has growth potential.

Instructions

(a) For each decision, indicate what financial information you would want to have in order to make an optimal decision.
(b) Based on what you have learned in Chapter 1, how will learning about accounting help you with the above decisions?

ANSWERS TO CHAPTER QUESTIONS

ANSWERS TO ACCOUNTING IN ACTION INSIGHT QUESTIONS

All About You Insight, p. 5

Q: How might learning accounting help you make sure that your employer or bank hasn't made an error with your paycheque or bank account?

A: Learning accounting will provide you with tools that will help you track your transactions and ensure that the bank balance is correct. You will learn how to calculate how much your paycheque should be. You will learn how to calculate interest on loans and the total cost of borrowing. Examining your potential employer's financial statements will help you predict if the company will have enough cash to pay you now and if the company has growth potential. Stay tuned to the "All About You" features and related activities for more!

Ethics Insight, p. 26

Q. What risks might you face as an employee and individual if you don't blow the whistle on fraud?

A: If you do not blow the whistle on fraud, you risk your personal reputation. For example, if you are working for a company whose management purposely misstates the financial statements and shareholders and other stakeholders are hurt, will you want that company's name on your resumé when the misstatement is discovered and made public?

　What if you are aware that another employee is stealing from the company and you do not report it? Your boss may question your integrity when it is later discovered that you were aware of the theft.

ANSWERS TO SELF-STUDY QUESTIONS

1. c   2. b   3. c   4. a   5. d   6. a   7. a   8. b   9. b   10. d

Remember to go back to the beginning of the chapter to check off your completed work!

THE RECORDING PROCESS

 THE **NAVIGATOR**

- ☐ Understand *Concepts for Review*
- ☐ Read *Feature Story*
- ☐ Scan *Study Objectives*
- ☐ Read *Chapter Preview*
- ☐ Read text and answer *Before You Go On*
- ☐ Review *Comparing IFRS and ASPE*
- ☐ Work *Demonstration Problem*
- ☐ Review *Summary of Study Objectives*
- ☐ Answer *Self-Study Questions*
- ☐ Complete assignments
- ☐ Go to *WileyPLUS* for practice and tutorials

CONCEPTS FOR **REVIEW**

Before studying this chapter, you should understand or, if necessary, review:

a. Why assets equal liabilities plus owner's equity. (Ch. 1, p. 13).

b. What assets, liabilities, owner's capital, drawings, revenues, and expenses are. (Ch. 1, pp. 12–13).

c. What transactions are, and how they affect the basic accounting equation. (Ch. 1, pp. 17–23).

DANCING TO HER OWN BUSINESS TUNE

CALGARY, AB—At the Prestige Dance Academy, tiny pink ballerinas admire themselves before the mirrors. Their energetic teacher, Amanda Hunsley, dances along with them, encouraging them to express themselves through music.

Even when she was a young child taking dance lessons, Ms. Hunsley knew she wanted to run her own business. At just 19, while in her second year of studies at Mount Royal College (now Mount Royal University), she opened her own dance school. Ten years later, the Prestige Dance Academy has a part-time staff of 11 teaching some 850 students tap, jazz, ballet, creative performing arts, lyrical, preschool, mom and me, hip-hop, and competitive dance.

"I combined my love for kids and for business," Ms. Hunsley says. She takes care of hiring and scheduling the staff, registrations and any other administrative work, and advertising and marketing.

While the dance academy provides birthday parties and summer camps, the bulk of the business is weekly dance lessons that run from September to June. Parents register their children in the fall, providing postdated cheques or a lump-sum payment for the entire year.

Ms. Hunsley uses QuickBooks accounting software. As the business has grown, so has the number of items in her chart of accounts—the list of account names for revenues and expenses, and assets and liabilities. Under revenues, she has accounts for student fees for regular classes and birthday parties, as well as

sales of promotional dancewear bearing the Prestige logo. Her expense accounts include dance studio expenses, advertising and promotion, lease payments, bank service charges, business taxes and permits, insurance, meals and entertainment, and mileage. Other expense accounts are salaries, employer deductions, professional fees such as legal fees, and repairs and maintenance.

Prestige's asset accounts include long-lived assets such as computers, video camera (to record recitals), and leasehold improvements. "Even though I lease the building, we expanded a couple of years ago and we had to do all the renovations inside," Ms. Hunsley explains. The cost of those renovations, called leasehold improvements, is considered an asset and is included in the other assets account.

In terms of liabilities, Prestige's accounts include GST payable, and federal and provincial income tax payable for the business. Finally, the owner's equity account shows the amount that Ms. Hunsley, as Prestige's single owner, has invested and retained in the business.

It may seem like a lot of accounts, but Ms. Hunsley doesn't require as many as a larger business does. "I try to keep things as simple as possible" to easily keep track of the business, she says.

She also has an additional priority in her life: a baby boy, her second child. While her family responsibilities have reduced her teaching to three hours a week, she still keeps an eye on the accounting. "I don't think you could run a business properly without being so on top of the finances."

THE **NAVIGATOR**

STUDY **OBJECTIVES**

After studying this chapter, you should be able to:

1. Define debits and credits and illustrate how they are used to record transactions.

2. Explain the recording process and analyze, journalize, and post transactions.

3. Explain the purpose of a trial balance, and prepare one.

THE **NAVIGATOR**

In Chapter 1, we used the accounting equation to analyze transactions. The combined effects of these transactions were presented in a tabular form. This method could work for small companies like Softbyte (the fictitious company discussed in Chapter 1) because they have relatively few transactions. But imagine Prestige Dance in the feature story using the same tabular format as Softbyte. With 850 students, the dance academy has too many transactions to record each one this way. Instead, a set of procedures and records are used to keep track of transaction data more easily.

This chapter introduces and illustrates the basic procedures and records. It is organized as follows:

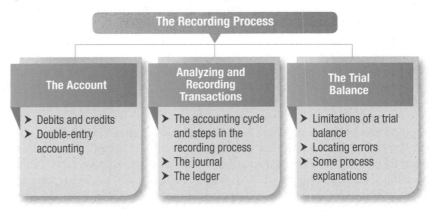

The Account

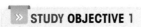

An **account** is an individual accounting record of increases and decreases in a specific asset, liability, or owner's equity item. For example, Softbyte has separate accounts called Cash, Accounts Receivable, Accounts Payable, Service Revenue, Salaries Expense, and so on.

In its simplest form, an account has three parts: (1) the title of the account, (2) a left or a debit side, and (3) a right or a credit side. Because these parts of an account are positioned like the letter T, it is called a **T account**. The basic form of an account is shown in Illustration 2-1.

ILLUSTRATION 2-1
Basic form of T account

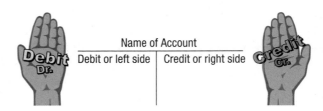

The actual format that is used in real life is more complex than the above T, and will be explained later in the chapter. The T account format is a learning tool that will be used throughout the book to explain basic accounting relationships. It is also a format used by professional accountants for analytical purposes.

DEBITS AND CREDITS

The term **debit** means left. The term **credit** means right. These terms are often abbreviated Dr. for debit and Cr. for credit. Debit and credit are simply directional signals that describe where entries are made in the accounts. Entering an amount on the left side of an account is called debiting the account. Entering an amount on the right side is called crediting the account.

When the totals of the two sides are compared, an account will have a debit balance if the total of the debit amounts exceeds the credits. On the other hand, an account will have a credit balance if the credit amounts are more than the debits.

The recording of debits and credits in an account is shown in Illustration 2-2 for Softbyte's cash transactions. The data are taken from the Cash column of the tabular summary in Illustration 1-10.

▶ ILLUSTRATION 2-2
Tabular summary and
account form comparison

Tabular Summary Cash		
+$15,000		
−7,000		
+1,200		
+1,500		
−600		
−900		
−200		
−250		
+600		
−1,300		
$ 8,050		

Account Form Cash		
(Debits)		(Credits)
15,000		7,000
1,200		600
1,500		900
600		200
		250
		1,300
Balance	8,050	

In the tabular summary, every positive item is a receipt of cash. Every negative amount is a payment of cash. Notice that in the account format the increases in cash are recorded as debits, and the decreases in cash are recorded as credits. The account balance, a debit of $8,050, indicates that Softbyte had $8,050 more increases than decreases in cash. We will learn in the next section why debits and credits are used in this way.

Debit and Credit Procedure

It is very important to understand that debit does not mean increase nor does it mean decrease. Sometimes we use a debit to increase an account and sometimes we use a debit to decrease an account. Credits are the same—sometimes a credit is used to increase an account and sometimes a credit is used to decrease an account. The system of using debits and credits is based on the accounting equation, introduced in Chapter 1, and the definitions of debit and credit, as shown in the following diagram:

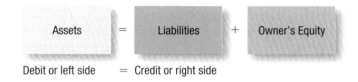

Assets = Liabilities + Owner's Equity

Debit or left side = Credit or right side

We will use this diagram to apply debit and credit procedures to each part of the accounting equation—assets, liabilities, and owner's equity—in the following sections.

Assets and Liabilities. As assets are on the left or debit side of the accounting equation, the normal balance of an asset is also on the left or debit side of the account. Logically, then, for the balance in an asset account to be on the debit side, increases also need to be recorded on the debit side and decreases in assets must be entered on the right or credit side. This is why in Illustration 2-2, the Softbyte illustration, increases in Cash—an asset account—were entered on the debit side, and decreases in Cash were entered on the credit side.

Similarly, because liabilities are on the right or credit side of the accounting equation, liability accounts normally show credit balances. That means increases in liabilities must be entered on the right or credit side, and decreases in liabilities must be entered on the left or debit side.

To summarize, because assets are on the opposite side of the accounting equation from liabilities, increases and decreases in assets are recorded opposite from increases and decreases in liabilities. The effects that debits and credits have on assets and liabilities and the normal balances are as follows:

Helpful hint Increases in accounts are always on the same side as the normal balance for that account.

Assets		Liabilities	
Debit for increase	Credit for decrease	Debit for decrease	Credit for increase
Normal balance			Normal balance

Knowing the normal balance in an account may also help you find errors. In automated systems, the software is programmed to find these normal balance exceptions and to print out error or exception reports. In manual systems, a careful inspection of the accounts has to be done to find balances that are not normal. For example, a credit balance in an asset account such as Land or a debit balance in a liability account such as Wages Payable probably means there was a recording error. Occasionally, an abnormal balance may be correct. The Cash account, for example, will have a credit balance when a company has overdrawn its bank balance.

Owner's Equity. As liabilities and owner's equity are on the same side of the accounting equation, the rules of debit and credit are the same for these two types of accounts. Credits increase owner's equity and debits decrease owner's equity. And as explained in Chapter 1, owner's equity is increased by owner's investments and revenues. It is decreased by owner's drawings and expenses. Separate accounts are kept for each of these types of transactions.

Owner's Capital. Investments by owners are credited to the owner's capital account because they increase owner's equity. For example, when cash is invested in the business, the Cash account is debited and Owner's Capital is credited.

The rules of debit and credit for the Owner's Capital account and the normal balance are as follows:

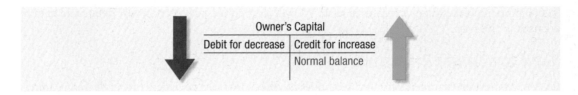

Owner's Drawings. An owner may withdraw cash or other assets for personal use. Withdrawals are recorded as debits because withdrawals decrease owner's equity. Withdrawals could be debited directly to Owner's Capital. However, it is better to have a separate account, called Drawings, as we did in Chapter 1. The separate account makes it easier to add up the total withdrawals for the accounting period and to prepare the statement of owner's equity.

Because withdrawals decrease owner's equity, the drawings account has a normal debit balance. Credits to an owner's drawings account are unusual, but might be used, for example, to correct a withdrawal recorded in error.

The rules of debit and credit for the Drawings account and the normal balance are as follows:

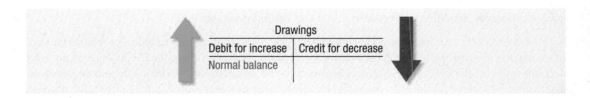

Note that increases and decreases to the drawings account are recorded opposite to increases and decreases in Owner's Capital. That is because investments, which increase owner's equity, are recorded in Owner's Capital, and withdrawals, which decrease owner's equity, are recorded in Drawings.

Revenues and Expenses. When revenues are earned, owner's equity is increased. As credits increase owner's equity, revenues are recorded as credits. Thus, Revenue accounts normally show credit balances. Similar to the Owner's Capital account, Revenue accounts are increased by credits and decreased by debits. Credits to revenue accounts should exceed the debits.

Expenses have the opposite effect: expenses decrease owner's equity. As a result, expenses are recorded as debits because debits decrease owner's equity. Thus, Expense accounts normally show debit balances. Similar to the Owner's Drawings account, expense accounts are increased by debits and decreased by credits. Debits to expense accounts should exceed the credits.

Since revenues are the positive factor in calculating profit, and expenses are the negative factor, it is logical that the increase and decrease sides of revenue accounts should be the reverse of expense accounts.

The effect of debits and credits on revenues and expenses and the normal balances are as follows:

Summary of Debit and Credit Effects

Illustration 2-3 shows the expanded accounting equation and a summary of the debit/credit rules on each type of account.

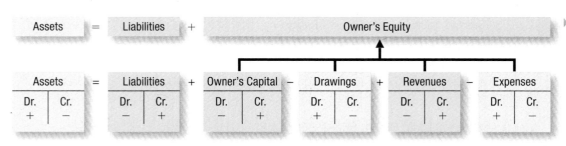

▶ **ILLUSTRATION 2-3**
Summary of debit/credit rules and effects for the expanded accounting equation

Remember, the normal balance of each account is on its increase side. So assets, drawings, and expense accounts have a normal debit balance, while liabilities, owner's capital, and revenue accounts have a normal credit balance.

DOUBLE-ENTRY ACCOUNTING

In Chapter 1, you learned that each transaction must affect two or more accounts to keep the basic accounting equation in balance. This is known as the **double-entry accounting system** in which the dual (two-sided) effect of each transaction is recorded in the appropriate accounts. This system provides a logical method for recording transactions and ensuring the amounts are recorded accurately.

Helpful hint Debits must equal credits for each transaction.

Now that you have learned the debit and credit procedure of recording transactions, you should also see that, for each transaction, debits must equal credits. The equality of debits and credits is the basis for the double-entry accounting system of recording transactions.

If every transaction is recorded with equal debits and credits, then the sum of all the debits to the accounts must equal the sum of all the credits. And, if the debit and credit procedures are correctly applied, the total amount of debits will always equal the total amount of credits and the accounting equation stays in balance.

Carefully reviewing Illustration 2-3, previously shown, will also help you to understand the basics of the double-entry accounting system.

 BEFORE YOU GO ON...

Do It

Eszter Schwenke has just rented space in a shopping mall where she will open a beauty salon called Hair It Is. Eszter has determined that the company will need the following accounts:

1. Accounts Payable
2. Cash
3. E. Schwenke, Capital
4. E. Schwenke, Drawings

Action Plan
- Use the expanded accounting equation to determine the type of account.
- Remember that the normal balance of an account is on its increase side.
- Remember that assets are increased by debits, and that liabilities and owner's equity are increased by credits.

THE **NAVIGATOR**

5. Rent Expense
6. Equipment
7. Service Revenue
8. Supplies
   (a) Indicate whether each of these accounts is an asset, liability, or owner's equity account. If it is an owner's equity account, indicate what type it is (e.g., owner's capital, drawings, revenue, or expense).
   (b) What is the normal balance of these accounts?
   (c) Will a debit increase or decrease these accounts?

Solution

Account	(a) Type of Account	(b) Normal Balance	(c) Debit Effect
1. Accounts Payable	Liability	Credit	Decrease
2. Cash	Asset	Debit	Increase
3. E. Schwenke, Capital	Owner's Equity	Credit	Decrease
4. E. Schwenke, Drawings	Owner's Equity (drawing)	Debit	Increase
5. Rent Expense	Owner's Equity (expense)	Debit	Increase
6. Equipment	Asset	Debit	Increase
7. Service Revenue	Owner's Equity (revenue)	Credit	Decrease
8. Supplies	Asset	Debit	Increase

Related exercise material: BE2–1, BE2–2, BE2–3, BE2–4, BE2–5, BE2–6, E2–2, and E2–3.

Analyzing and Recording Transactions

THE ACCOUNTING CYCLE AND STEPS IN THE RECORDING PROCESS

» STUDY OBJECTIVE 2

Explain the recording process and analyze, journalize, and post transactions.

▶ **ILLUSTRATION 2-4**
The accounting cycle —Steps 1 to 3

The **accounting cycle** is a series of steps followed by accountants in preparing financial statements. We will learn about the first four steps of the accounting cycle in this chapter and the remaining steps in Chapters 3 and 4. The procedures used in analyzing and recording transaction information are the first three steps, shown in Illustration 2-4. These three steps are also known as the **recording process**.

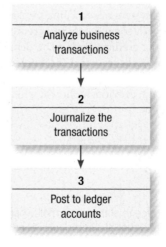

Analyzing Business Transactions

As shown in Illustration 2-4, the recording process begins with analyzing the transaction. Evidence of a transaction comes from a **source document**, such as a sales slip, cheque, bill, cash register tape, or bank statement.

We started to learn how to analyze transactions in Chapter 1. Deciding what to record is the most critical point in the accounting cycle. Recall from Chapter 1 that a transaction is recorded only if it causes the company's financial position (assets, liabilities, and owner's equity) to change.

Recall also from Chapter 1 that, once it had been determined that a transaction should be recorded, it was analyzed for its specific effect on the elements of the accounting equation. We saw in the transaction analysis process that it is necessary to identify the accounts that were changed and to determine if these accounts had increased or decreased and by how much. Remember that if the amount cannot be measured, it cannot be recorded. This is often referred to as the **basic analysis** of the transaction.

After the basic analysis is complete, then the debit and credit procedures you learned in the previous section of this chapter are applied to determine which account or accounts should be debited and which account or accounts should be credited. This is often referred to as the **debit/credit analysis** of the transaction.

Analyzing transactions is the most difficult part of the accounting cycle because there are so many different types of transactions. Throughout this textbook, and in later accounting courses, you will continue to be introduced to different transactions. As you learn about new transactions, remember to first do your basic analysis and then the debit/credit analysis. If you follow this system, your ability to correctly analyze and record transactions will improve.

After the transaction has been analyzed, then it can be entered in the accounting records—steps 2 and 3 of the accounting cycle. We will explain how this is done in the following sections on the journal and the ledger.

The Recording Process in Computerized and Manual Accounting Systems

The first two steps in the recording process—analyzing and journalizing transactions—must be done by a person even when a computerized system is used. The major difference between a computerized and a manual accounting system is in Step 3—transferring information from the journal to the ledger. In computerized systems, this is done automatically by the computer, which substantially reduces the possibility of making mistakes.

ACCOUNTING IN ACTION
BUSINESS INSIGHT

Does hiring a great employee add value for a company? In the case of sports teams, owners, players, and fans all agree that having the most talented players makes a huge difference. But how does a team attract and keep those players? Is simply offering the player a contract sufficient to attract talent? Not these days. And accountants would agree that simply having a player sign a contract doesn't change the team's assets, liabilities, or owner's equity. This isn't a transaction that would get recorded in the team's accounting records even if it does bring value to the team.

Signing bonuses are different because they affect cash. And they are used partly to deal with the league's salary caps, which restrict how much can be included in individual players' and the whole team's salaries in each year. A signing bonus can be paid in one year but be included in the team's salary cap in a year that's financially advantageous to the team. To make matters even more interesting, there was a new twist in Buffalo Sabres defenceman Andrej Sekera's four-year, $11-million deal signed in July 2011. The contract wasn't just front-loaded: it was heavily so, with $6 million, or 55% of the contract, due in the first 11.5 months. As one agent put it after seeing the figures: "It's a new world order in Buffalo!" The accounting question as to whether these bonuses should be considered assets or expenses may become more complicated than ever.

Sources: James Mirtle, "Big Signing Bonuses Becoming NHL's New Norm," *Globe and Mail* blog, July 20, 2011, http://www.theglobeandmail.com/sports/hockey/globe-on-hockey/big-signing-bonuses-becoming-nhls-new-norm/article2103658/, accessed on January 18, 2012; Darren Dreger, "Leagues Disciplined by NHL for Handling of Frogen Contract," TSN.ca, April 1, 2009; Collective Bargaining Agreement FAQs, NHL.com, http://www.nhl.com/ice/page.htm?id=26366, accessed on February 9, 2012.

What are the issues involved in determining if a signing bonus is an asset or an expense?

THE JOURNAL

Transactions are first recorded in chronological (date) order in a **journal**. For this reason, the journal is referred to as the book of original entry. For each transaction, the journal shows the debit and credit effects on specific accounts. Companies can use various kinds of specialized journals, but every company has the most basic form of journal, a **general journal**. Whenever we use the term "journal" in this textbook without a description of it, we mean the general journal.

The journal makes some important contributions to the recording process:

- It discloses the complete effect of a transaction in one place.
- It provides a chronological record of transactions.
- It helps to prevent and locate errors, because the debit and credit amounts for each entry can be easily compared.
- It gives an explanation of the transaction and, if there is one, identifies the source document.

Journalizing

The second step in the accounting cycle, entering transaction data in the journal, is known as **journalizing**. A separate journal entry is made for each transaction. A complete entry consists of the following: (1) the date of the transaction, (2) the accounts and amounts to be debited and credited, and (3) a brief explanation of the transaction.

To illustrate the technique of journalizing, let's look at the first two transactions of Softbyte from Chapter 1. These transactions were (1) September 1, Marc Doucet invested $15,000 cash in the business, and (2) computer equipment was purchased for $7,000 cash (we will assume that this transaction also occurred on September 1). In tabular form, as shown in Chapter 1, these transactions appeared as follows:

	Assets			=	Liabilities	+	Owner's Equity
	Cash	+	Equipment				M. Doucet, Capital
(1)	+$15,000						+$15,000
(2)	−7,000		+$7,000				

In journal form, these transactions would appear as follows:

	GENERAL JOURNAL			J1
Date	**Account Titles and Explanation**	**Ref**	**Debit**	**Credit**
2014				
Sept. 1	Cash		15,000	
	M. Doucet, Capital			15,000
	Invested cash in business.			
1	Equipment		7,000	
	Cash			7,000
	Purchased equipment for cash.			

A	=	L	+	OE
+15,000				+15,000

⬆Cash flows: +15,000

A	=	L	+	OE
+7,000				
−7,000				

⬇Cash flows: −7,000

In the margins next to journal entries are **equation analyses** that show the effect of the transaction on the accounting equation (A = L + OE) and on cash flows. You should think of these as part of Step 1 of the accounting cycle.

Since this is the first page of Softbyte's general journal, it is numbered J1. You should note the following features of journal entries:

1. The date of the transaction is entered in the Date column.
2. The account to be debited is entered first at the left margin of the column headed Account Titles and Explanation. The account to be credited is then entered on the next line and indented from the left margin. The indentation visually separates the accounts to be debited and credited, so there is less chance of switching the debits and credits.
3. The amounts for the debits are recorded in the Debit (left) column and the amounts for the credits are recorded in the Credit (right) column.

4. A brief explanation of the transaction is given on the line below the credit account title. To simplify the illustrations in this textbook, journal entry explanations are often left out. Remember, however, that in real life, explanations are essential for every journal entry.
5. The column titled Ref. (which stands for "reference") is left blank when the journal entry is made. This column is used later, when the journal entries are transferred to the ledger accounts.

It is important to use correct and specific account titles in journal entries. While there is some flexibility in creating accounting names, **each title has to accurately describe the account's content**. For example, the account title used for the computer equipment purchased by Softbyte may be Equipment, Computer Equipment, Computers, or Office Equipment. However, once a company chooses the specific title to use, all transactions for the account should be recorded with the same title.

When you complete the assignments in this text, if specific account titles are given, you should use those. If account titles are not given, you should create account titles that identify the nature and content of each account. **Account titles used in journalizing should not contain explanations (such as Cash Paid or Cash Received).**

If an entry affects only two accounts, it will have one debit and one credit. This is considered a simple journal entry. Some transactions, however, involve more than two accounts. When three or more accounts are required in one journal entry, the entry is called a compound entry. To illustrate, recall from Chapter 1 that Softbyte provided $3,500 of programming services to customers (assume this was on September 9). It received $1,500 cash from the customers for these services. The balance, $2,000, was owed on account. The compound entry to record this transaction is as follows:

GENERAL JOURNAL					J1
Date	Account Titles and Explanation	Ref	Debit		Credit
2014					
Sept. 9	Cash		1,500		
	Accounts Receivable		2,000		
	Service Revenue				3,500
	Performed services for cash and credit.				

A   =   L   +   OE
+1,500   +3,500
+2,000
↑Cash flows: +1,500

In a compound entry, just as in a simple entry, the total debit and credit amounts must be equal. Also, all of the debits are listed before the credits are listed.

THE LEDGER

The entire group of accounts maintained by a company is called the ledger. The ledger keeps all the information about changes in each account in one place.

Companies can use different kinds of ledgers, but every company has a general ledger. A general ledger contains accounts for all the assets, liabilities, equities, revenues, and expenses. Whenever we use the term "ledger" on its own in this textbook, we mean the general ledger.

A business can use a loose-leaf binder or card file for the ledger, with each account kept on a separate sheet or card. However, most companies use a computerized accounting system that keeps each account in a separate file. In a computerized system, such as the QuickBooks accounting software used by Prestige Dance Academy in the feature story, each account is numbered so that it is easier to identify.

The accounts in the ledger should be arranged in the same order that is used to present the accounts in the financial statements, beginning with the balance sheet accounts. The asset accounts come first, followed by liability accounts, owner's capital, drawings, revenues, and expenses. The ledger gives the balance in each account. The ledger will also show all of the increases and decreases that have been made to each account.

Standard Form of Account

The simple T account form used in accounting textbooks is often very useful for analyzing illustrations, and for learning accounting. However, in practice, the account forms that are used in ledgers are designed to include additional information. A very popular form in both manual and computerized systems, using the data (and assumed dates) from Softbyte's Cash account in Illustration 2-2, follows:

GENERAL LEDGER					
CASH					
Date	**Explanation**	**Ref**	**Debit**	**Credit**	**Balance**
2014					
Sept. 1			15,000		15,000
1				7,000	8,000
3			1,200		9,200
9			1,500		10,700
17				600	10,100
17				900	9,200
20				200	9,000
25				250	8,750
30			600		9,350
30				1,300	8,050

This form is often called the **three-column form of account** because it has three money columns: debit, credit, and balance. The balance in the account is determined after each transaction. The explanation and reference columns make it possible to give more information about the transaction than can be included in the T account form. In manual accounting systems, the explanation column is usually left blank because it is too time-consuming to copy explanations from the general journal. Computerized accounting systems will automatically copy the explanation that was originally recorded in the journal entry into the ledger.

Posting

The procedure of transferring journal entries to the ledger accounts is called **posting**. It is the third step in the accounting cycle. Posting has the following steps:

1. General Ledger. In the ledger, enter the date, journal page, and debit or credit amount shown in the journal in the correct columns of each affected account.
2. General Journal. In the reference column of the journal, write the account numbers to which the debit and credit amounts were posted in the ledger.

These steps are shown in Illustration 2-5 using Softbyte's first journal entry.

▶ **ILLUSTRATION 2-5**
Posting a journal entry

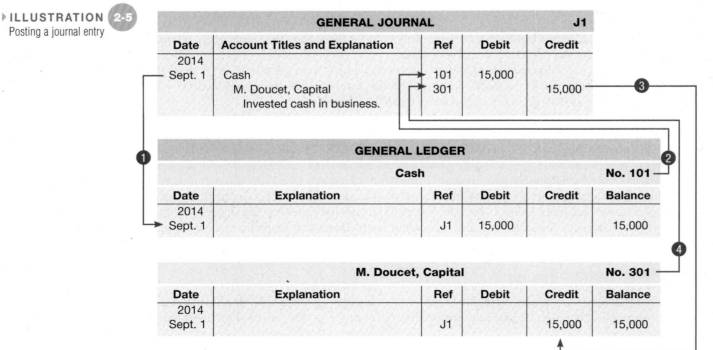

1. Post to debit account: enter date, journal page number, and amount.
2. Enter debit account number in journal reference column.
3. Post to credit account: enter date, journal page number, and amount.
4. Enter credit account number in journal reference column.

The reference column in the journal shows the entries that have been posted. The references also show the account numbers to which the amounts have been posted. The reference column of a ledger account indicates the journal page where the transaction was posted from.

Posting should be done in chronological order. That is, all the debits and credits of one journal entry should be posted before going to the next journal entry. Postings should be made on a timely basis to keep the ledger up to date. In a computerized accounting system, posting is done automatically, usually right after each journal entry is prepared.

Chart of Accounts

The first step in designing an accounting system—whether computerized or manual—is to create a chart of accounts. The chart of accounts is a list of the accounts and account numbers that identify where the accounts are in the ledger. It is the framework for the entire database of accounting information. The numbering system that is used to identify the accounts usually starts with the balance sheet accounts. The income statement accounts come next.

Because each company is different, the types of accounts they have and how many they have are also different. The number of accounts depends on the amount of detail that management wants. The management of one company may want one account for all types of utility expense. Another company may keep separate expense accounts for each type of utility expense, such as gas, electricity, and water. Many companies, such as Prestige Dance Academy, in our feature story, use different revenue accounts for difference sources of revenue.

The chart of accounts for Pioneer Advertising Agency, a proprietorship owned by Clarence Byrd, is shown in Illustration 2-6. Accounts 100–199 indicate asset accounts; 200–299 indicate liabilities; 300–399 indicate owner's equity accounts; 400–499, revenues; and 500–999, expenses. There are gaps in the numbering system to permit the insertion of new accounts as needed during the life of the business.

▶ ILLUSTRATION 2-6
Chart of accounts

PIONEER ADVERTISING AGENCY
Chart of Accounts

Assets		Owner's Equity	
101	Cash	301	C. Byrd, Capital
112	Accounts Receivable	306	C. Byrd, Drawings
129	Supplies	350	Income Summary
130	Prepaid Insurance		
151	Equipment	**Revenues**	
152	Accumulated Depreciation— Equipment	400	Service Revenue
		Expenses	
Liabilities		711	Depreciation Expense
200	Notes Payable	722	Insurance Expense
201	Accounts Payable	726	Rent Expense
209	Unearned Revenue	729	Salaries Expense
212	Salaries Payable	740	Supplies Expense
230	Interest Payable	905	Interest Expense

In this and the next two chapters, we will show the accounting cycle for Pioneer Advertising Agency—a service company. Accounts shown in red are used in this chapter; accounts shown in black are explained in later chapters.

The Recording Process Illustrated

In the following section, we show the three steps in the recording process—analyze, journalize, and post—using the October 2014 transactions of Pioneer Advertising Agency. The agency's accounting period is one month. As Pioneer Advertising Agency is started on October 1, 2014, there are no balances in its accounts from prior transactions.

Study these transactions carefully. Remember that in Step 1 of the recording process the transaction is analyzed to identify (1) the type of accounts involved, (2) whether the accounts are increased or decreased, and (3) whether the accounts need to be debited or credited. This is shown in the basic analysis and the debit/credit analysis for each transaction in the illustrations before journalizing and posting. For simplicity, the illustrations use the T account form to show posting instead of the standard account form.

▶ **TRANSACTION 1**
Investment of cash by owner

Transaction	October 1, Clarence Byrd invests $10,000 cash in an advertising venture to be known as the Pioneer Advertising Agency.
Basic Analysis	The asset Cash is increased by $10,000, and the owner's equity account C. Byrd, Capital, is increased by $10,000.
Debit/Credit Analysis	Debits increase assets: debit Cash $10,000. Credits increase owner's equity: credit C. Byrd, Capital, $10,000.

Journal Entry				
Oct. 1	Cash	101	10,000	
	C. Byrd, Capital	301		10,000
	Invested cash in business.			

Posting

Cash	101		C. Byrd, Capital	301
Oct. 1 10,000			Oct. 1 10,000	

▶ **TRANSACTION 2**
Purchase of office equipment

Transaction	October 2, office equipment costing $5,000 is purchased by signing a $5,000, 6% note payable, due in three months on January 2, 2015.
Basic Analysis	The asset account Equipment is increased by $5,000, and the liability account Notes Payable is increased by $5,000.
Debit/Credit Analysis	Debits increase assets: debit Equipment $5,000. Credits increase liabilities: credit Notes Payable $5,000.

Journal Entry				
Oct. 2	Equipment	151	5,000	
	Notes Payable	200		5,000
	Issued a three-month, 6% note for equipment.			

Posting

Equipment	151		Notes Payable	200
Oct. 2 5,000			Oct. 2 5,000	

▶ **TRANSACTION 3**
Receipt of cash in advance from customer

Transaction	October 3, a $1,200 cash advance is received from R. Knox, a client, for advertising services that are expected to be completed by December 31.
Basic Analysis	The asset account Cash is increased by $1,200; the liability account Unearned Revenue is increased by $1,200 because the service has not been provided yet. That is, when an advance payment is received, unearned revenue (a liability) should be recorded in order to recognize the obligation that exists. Note also that unearned revenue is not a revenue account and does not increase owner's equity even though the word "revenue" is used.
Debit/Credit Analysis	Debits increase assets: debit Cash $1,200. Credits increase liabilities: credit Unearned Revenue $1,200.

Journal Entry				
Oct. 3	Cash	101	1,200	
	Unearned Revenue	209		1,200
	Received advance from R. Knox for future services.			

Posting

Cash		101		Unearned Revenue	209
Oct. 1	10,000			Oct. 3 1,200	
3	1,200				

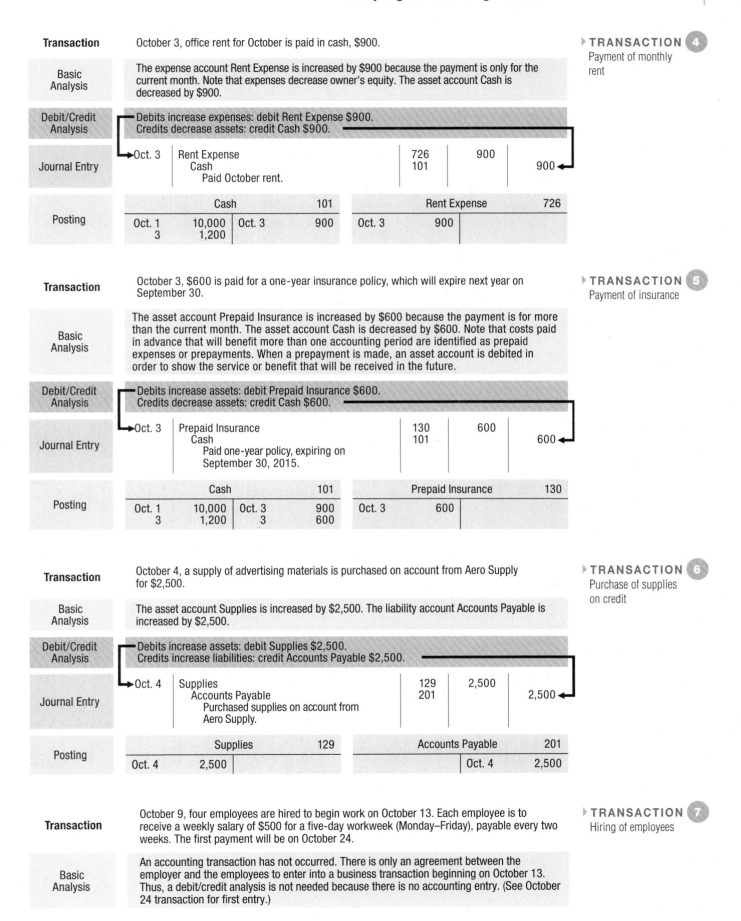

| Transaction | October 3, office rent for October is paid in cash, $900. | ▶ TRANSACTION ④ Payment of monthly rent |

Transaction — October 3, office rent for October is paid in cash, $900.

Basic Analysis — The expense account Rent Expense is increased by $900 because the payment is only for the current month. Note that expenses decrease owner's equity. The asset account Cash is decreased by $900.

Debit/Credit Analysis — Debits increase expenses: debit Rent Expense $900. Credits decrease assets: credit Cash $900.

Journal Entry

Oct. 3	Rent Expense	726	900	
	Cash	101		900
	Paid October rent.			

Posting

Cash			101	Rent Expense		726
Oct. 1	10,000	Oct. 3	900	Oct. 3	900	
3	1,200					

Transaction — October 3, $600 is paid for a one-year insurance policy, which will expire next year on September 30.

▶ TRANSACTION ⑤ Payment of insurance

Basic Analysis — The asset account Prepaid Insurance is increased by $600 because the payment is for more than the current month. The asset account Cash is decreased by $600. Note that costs paid in advance that will benefit more than one accounting period are identified as prepaid expenses or prepayments. When a prepayment is made, an asset account is debited in order to show the service or benefit that will be received in the future.

Debit/Credit Analysis — Debits increase assets: debit Prepaid Insurance $600. Credits decrease assets: credit Cash $600.

Journal Entry

Oct. 3	Prepaid Insurance	130	600	
	Cash	101		600
	Paid one-year policy, expiring on September 30, 2015.			

Posting

Cash			101	Prepaid Insurance		130
Oct. 1	10,000	Oct. 3	900	Oct. 3	600	
3	1,200	3	600			

Transaction — October 4, a supply of advertising materials is purchased on account from Aero Supply for $2,500.

▶ TRANSACTION ⑥ Purchase of supplies on credit

Basic Analysis — The asset account Supplies is increased by $2,500. The liability account Accounts Payable is increased by $2,500.

Debit/Credit Analysis — Debits increase assets: debit Supplies $2,500. Credits increase liabilities: credit Accounts Payable $2,500.

Journal Entry

Oct. 4	Supplies	129	2,500	
	Accounts Payable	201		2,500
	Purchased supplies on account from Aero Supply.			

Posting

| Supplies | | 129 | Accounts Payable | | 201 |
| Oct. 4 | 2,500 | | | Oct. 4 | 2,500 |

Transaction — October 9, four employees are hired to begin work on October 13. Each employee is to receive a weekly salary of $500 for a five-day workweek (Monday–Friday), payable every two weeks. The first payment will be on October 24.

▶ TRANSACTION ⑦ Hiring of employees

Basic Analysis — An accounting transaction has not occurred. There is only an agreement between the employer and the employees to enter into a business transaction beginning on October 13. Thus, a debit/credit analysis is not needed because there is no accounting entry. (See October 24 transaction for first entry.)

▶ **TRANSACTION** ⑧
Withdrawal of cash by
owner

Transaction	October 20, Clarence Byrd withdraws $500 cash for personal use.
Basic Analysis	The owner's equity account C. Byrd, Drawings is increased by $500. Note that drawings decrease owner's equity. The asset account Cash is decreased by $500.
Debit/Credit Analysis	Debits increase drawings: debit C. Byrd, Drawings, $500. Credits decrease assets: credit Cash $500.

Journal Entry

Oct. 20	C. Byrd, Drawings	306	500	
	Cash	101		500
	Withdrew cash for personal use.			

Posting

Cash				101
Oct. 1	10,000	Oct. 3		900
3	1,200	3		600
		20		500

C. Byrd, Drawings		306
Oct. 20	500	

▶ **TRANSACTION** ⑨
Service performed on
account

Transaction	October 21, a customer, Copa Company, is billed $10,000 for advertising services performed to date.
Basic Analysis	The asset account Accounts Receivable is increased by $10,000. The revenue account Service Revenue is increased by $10,000. Note that revenue is recorded when the service is performed, regardless of when the cash is received. Accounts Receivable is an asset because Pioneer Advertising expects a future benefit—the cash payment by Copa Company.
Debit/Credit Analysis	Debits increase assets: debit Accounts Receivable $10,000. Credits increase revenues: credit Service Revenue $10,000.

Journal Entry

Oct. 21	Accounts Receivable	112	10,000	
	Service Revenue	400		10,000
	Performed services on account for Copa Company.			

Posting

Accounts Receivable		112
Oct. 21	10,000	

Service Revenue		400
	Oct. 21	10,000

▶ **TRANSACTION** ⑩
Payment of salaries

Transaction	October 24, employee salaries of $4,000 (4 × $500 × 2) are owed and paid. (See October 9 transaction.)
Basic Analysis	The expense account Salaries Expense is increased by $4,000. The asset account Cash is decreased by $4,000.
Debit/Credit Analysis	Debits increase expenses: debit Salaries Expense $4,000. Credits decrease assets: credit Cash $4,000.

Journal Entry

Oct. 24	Salaries Expense	729	4,000	
	Cash	101		4,000
	Paid biweekly salaries.			

Posting

Cash				101
Oct. 1	10,000	Oct. 3		900
3	1,200	3		600
		20		500
		24		4,000

Salaries Expense		729
Oct. 24	4,000	

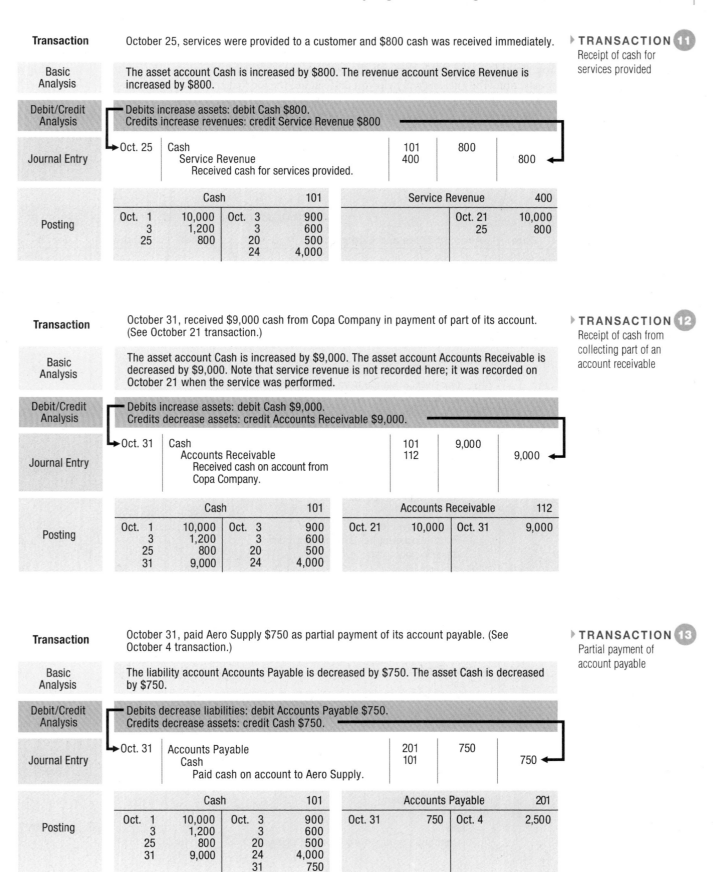

Transaction	October 25, services were provided to a customer and $800 cash was received immediately.	▶ **TRANSACTION** ⑪ Receipt of cash for services provided

Basic Analysis

The asset account Cash is increased by $800. The revenue account Service Revenue is increased by $800.

Debit/Credit Analysis

Debits increase assets: debit Cash $800.
Credits increase revenues: credit Service Revenue $800

Journal Entry

Oct. 25	Cash	101	800	
	Service Revenue	400		800
	Received cash for services provided.			

Posting

Cash			101		Service Revenue		400
Oct. 1	10,000	Oct. 3	900			Oct. 21	10,000
3	1,200	3	600			25	800
25	800	20	500				
		24	4,000				

Transaction	October 31, received $9,000 cash from Copa Company in payment of part of its account. (See October 21 transaction.)	▶ **TRANSACTION** ⑫ Receipt of cash from collecting part of an account receivable

Basic Analysis

The asset account Cash is increased by $9,000. The asset account Accounts Receivable is decreased by $9,000. Note that service revenue is not recorded here; it was recorded on October 21 when the service was performed.

Debit/Credit Analysis

Debits increase assets: debit Cash $9,000.
Credits decrease assets: credit Accounts Receivable $9,000.

Journal Entry

Oct. 31	Cash	101	9,000	
	Accounts Receivable	112		9,000
	Received cash on account from Copa Company.			

Posting

Cash			101	Accounts Receivable			112
Oct. 1	10,000	Oct. 3	900	Oct. 21	10,000	Oct. 31	9,000
3	1,200	3	600				
25	800	20	500				
31	9,000	24	4,000				

Transaction	October 31, paid Aero Supply $750 as partial payment of its account payable. (See October 4 transaction.)	▶ **TRANSACTION** ⑬ Partial payment of account payable

Basic Analysis

The liability account Accounts Payable is decreased by $750. The asset Cash is decreased by $750.

Debit/Credit Analysis

Debits decrease liabilities: debit Accounts Payable $750.
Credits decrease assets: credit Cash $750.

Journal Entry

Oct. 31	Accounts Payable	201	750	
	Cash	101		750
	Paid cash on account to Aero Supply.			

Posting

Cash			101	Accounts Payable			201
Oct. 1	10,000	Oct. 3	900	Oct. 31	750	Oct. 4	2,500
3	1,200	3	600				
25	800	20	500				
31	9,000	24	4,000				
		31	750				

Summary Illustration of Journalizing and Posting

You should always think through the basic analysis and debit/credit analysis before journalizing a transaction. The analysis will help you understand the journal entries discussed in this chapter, as well as more complex journal entries in later chapters.

However, the actual accounting records will not show this analysis for each transaction. Instead the accounting records will show a chronological list of the transactions in the journal, and a ledger showing the effect on each account of posting all of the transactions.

The general journal for Pioneer Advertising Agency for October 2014 is summarized as follows:

	GENERAL JOURNAL			J1
Date	Account Titles and Explanation	Ref	Debit	Credit
2014 Oct. 1	Cash	101	10,000	
	C. Byrd, Capital	301		10,000
	Invested cash in business.			
2	Equipment	151	5,000	
	Notes Payable	200		5,000
	Issued three-month, 6% note for equipment.			
3	Cash	101	1,200	
	Unearned Revenue	209		1,200
	Received advance from R. Knox for future services.			
3	Rent Expense	726	900	
	Cash	101		900
	Paid October rent.			
3	Prepaid Insurance	130	600	
	Cash	101		600
	Paid one-year policy, expiring on September 30, 2015.			
4	Supplies	129	2,500	
	Accounts Payable	201		2,500
	Purchased supplies on account from Aero Supply.			
20	C. Byrd, Drawings	306	500	
	Cash	101		500
	Withdrew cash for personal use.			
21	Accounts Receivable	112	10,000	
	Service Revenue	400		10,000
	Performed services on account for Copa Company.			
24	Salaries Expense	729	4,000	
	Cash	101		4,000
	Paid biweekly salaries.			
25	Cash	101	800	
	Service Revenue	400		800
	Received cash for services provided.			
31	Cash	101	9,000	
	Accounts Receivable	112		9,000
	Received cash on account from Copa Company.			
31	Accounts Payable	201	750	
	Cash	101		750
	Paid cash on account to Aero Supply.			

The general ledger, with all account balances highlighted in red, for Pioneer Advertising Agency follows:

GENERAL LEDGER

Cash   101

Date	Debit	Date	Credit
Oct. 1	10,000	Oct. 3	900
3	1,200	3	600
25	800	20	500
31	9,000	24	4,000
		31	750
Bal.	14,250		

Accounts Receivable   112

Date	Debit	Date	Credit
Oct. 21	10,000	Oct. 31	9,000
Bal.	1,000		

Supplies   129

Date	Debit	Date	Credit
Oct. 4	2,500		
Bal.	2,500		

Prepaid Insurance   130

Date	Debit	Date	Credit
Oct. 3	600		
Bal.	600		

Equipment   151

Date	Debit	Date	Credit
Oct. 2	5,000		
Bal.	5,000		

Notes Payable   200

Date	Debit	Date	Credit
		Oct. 2	5,000
		Bal.	5,000

Accounts Payable   201

Date	Debit	Date	Credit
Oct. 31	750	Oct. 4	2,500
		Bal.	1,750

Unearned Revenue   209

Date	Debit	Date	Credit
		Oct. 3	1,200
		Bal.	1,200

C. Byrd, Capital   301

Date	Debit	Date	Credit
		Oct. 1	10,000
		Bal.	10,000

C. Byrd, Drawings   306

Date	Debit	Date	Credit
Oct. 20	500		
Bal.	500		

Service Revenue   400

Date	Debit	Date	Credit
		Oct. 21	10,000
		25	800
		Bal.	10,800

Rent Expense   726

Date	Debit	Date	Credit
Oct. 23	900		
Bal.	900		

Salaries Expense   729

Date	Debit	Date	Credit
Oct. 24	4,000		
Bal.	4,000		

BEFORE YOU GO ON...

Do It

Selected transactions from the first two weeks of business for Hair It Is, a hair salon owned by Eszter Schwenke, follow:

1. On May 1, Eszter Schwenke opened a bank account in the name of Hair It Is and deposited $20,000 of her own money in this account as her initial investment.
2. On May 3, Hair It Is purchased equipment on account (to be paid in 30 days), for a total cost of $4,800.
3. Hired a stylist who started working on May 7 and agreed to pay her $500 per week.
4. During the first two weeks, performed $1,280 of hairstyling services, all collected in cash. (Note: Date this May 14.)
5. On May 15, paid the employee, hired on May 7, her $500 weekly salary.
   (a) For each of the transactions, prepare a basic analysis, a debit/credit analysis, and a journal entry.
   (b) Post the journal entries to the general ledger.

Action Plan

- Understand which activities need to be recorded and which do not.
- Analyze the transactions. Determine the accounts affected and whether the transaction increases or decreases the account.
- Apply the debit and credit rules.
- Record the transactions in the general journal following the formatting rules. Remember that the name of the account to be credited is indented and the amount is recorded in the right-hand column.
- Posting involves transferring the journalized debits and credits to specific accounts in the ledger.
- Determine the ending balances by netting (calculating the difference between) the total debits and credits.

⊘ BEFORE YOU GO ON continued...

Solution

(a)

Transaction 1:

Basic Analysis	The asset account Cash is increased by $20,000. The owner's equity account E. Schwenke, Capital is increased by $20,000.
Debit/Credit Analysis	Debits increase assets: debit Cash $20,000. Credits increase owner's equity: credit E. Schwenke, Capital $20,000.

Journal Entry	May 1 Cash 20,000
	             E. Schwenke, Capital 20,000
	                Invested cash in business.

Transaction 2:

Basic Analysis	The asset account Equipment is increased by $4,800. The liability account Accounts Payable is increased by $4,800.
Debit/Credit Analysis	Debits increase assets: debit Equipment $4,800. Credits increase liabilities: credit Accounts Payable $4,800.

Journal Entry	May 3 Equipment 4,800
	             Accounts Payable 4,800
	                Purchased equipment on account.

Transaction 3:

Basic Analysis	An accounting transaction has not occurred.

Transaction 4:

Basic Analysis	The asset account Cash is increased by $1,280. The revenue account Service Revenue is increased by $1,280.
Debit/Credit Analysis	Debits increase assets: debit Cash $1,280. Credits increase revenues: credit Service Revenue $1,280.

Journal Entry	May 14 Cash 1,280
	             Service Revenue 1,280
	                Performed services for cash.

Transaction 5:

Basic Analysis	The expense account Salaries Expense is increased by $500. The asset account Cash is decreased by $500.
Debit/Credit Analysis	Debits increase expenses: debit Salaries Expense $500. Credits decrease assets: credit Cash $500.

Journal Entry	May 14 Salaries Expense 500
	          Cash 500
	                Paid salary for a week.

(b)

Cash		Equipment	Accounts Payable	E. Schwenke, Capital
20,000		4,800	4,800	20,000
1,280	500			
20,780				

		Service Revenue	Salaries Expense	
		1,280	500	

Related exercise material: BE2–7, BE2–8, BE2–9, BE2–10, BE2–11, BE2–12, E2–4, E2–5, E2–6, E2–7, and E2–8.

THE NAVIGATOR

The Trial Balance

As discussed earlier in the chapter, the steps in the recording process are the first three steps in the accounting cycle. The fourth step in the accounting cycle, as shown in Illustration 2-7, is to prepare a trial balance.

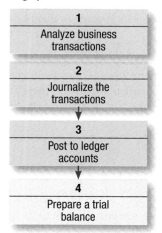

» **STUDY OBJECTIVE 3**

Explain the purpose of a trial balance, and prepare one.

▶ **ILLUSTRATION** 2-7
The accounting cycle
—Steps 1 to 4

A **trial balance** is a list of the accounts in the ledger and the account balances at a specific time. If any accounts have a zero balance, they can be omitted from the trial balance. It is prepared at the end of an accounting period. In the trial balance, the accounts are listed in the same order as they are in the ledger, with debit balances in the left column and credit balances in the right column.

The main purpose of a trial balance is to prove (check) that the debits equal the credits after posting. That is, the sum of the debit account balances must equal the sum of the credit account balances. If the totals are not the same, this means an error was made in journalizing or posting the transactions, or in preparing the trial balance. For example, the trial balance will not balance if an incorrect amount is posted in the ledger. If the trial balance does not balance, then the error must be located and corrected before proceeding.

Helpful hint When the totals of the two columns are equal, the trial balance is considered "balanced."

A trial balance is also useful in preparing financial statements, as will be explained in the next two chapters. The procedure for preparing a trial balance is as follows:

1. List the account titles and their balances in the same order as in the chart of accounts. Debit balances are entered in the debit column and credit balances are entered in the credit column.
2. Total the debit and credit columns.
3. Ensure that the totals of the two columns are equal.

To illustrate how a trial balance is prepared, we will continue with the Pioneer Travel Agency illustration in the previous section of this chapter. We use the information in Pioneer Travel Agency's general ledger to prepare its trial balance shown in Illustration 2-8.

▶ **ILLUSTRATION** 2-8
Pioneer Advertising Agency's trial balance

PIONEER ADVERTISING AGENCY Trial Balance October 31, 2014		
	Debit	**Credit**
Cash	$14,250	
Accounts receivable	1,000	
Supplies	2,500	
Prepaid insurance	600	
Equipment	5,000	
Notes payable		$ 5,000
Accounts payable		1,750
Unearned revenue		1,200
C. Byrd, capital		10,000
C. Byrd, drawings	500	
Service revenue		10,800
Rent expense	900	
Salaries expense	4,000	
Totals	$28,750	$28,750

You should note the following:

1. The accounts are listed in the same order they were in the general ledger (and chart of accounts in Illustration 2-6).
2. The balance at October 31, 2014, of each account in the general ledger is included in the correct debit or credit column.
3. The total of the debit accounts, $28,750, is equal to the total of the credit accounts, $28,750.

LIMITATIONS OF A TRIAL BALANCE

Although a trial balance can reveal many types of bookkeeping errors, it does not prove that all transactions have been recorded or that the ledger is correct. There can be many errors even when the trial balance columns agree. For example, the trial balance may balance even when:

1. a transaction is not journalized,
2. a correct journal entry is not posted,
3. a journal entry is posted twice,
4. incorrect accounts are used in journalizing or posting, or
5. offsetting errors (errors that hide each other) are made in recording the amount of a transaction.

As long as equal debits and credits are posted, even to the wrong account or in the wrong amount, the total debits will equal the total credits when the trial balance is prepared.

LOCATING ERRORS

Errors generally result from mathematical mistakes, incorrect postings, or simply recopying data incorrectly. In a computerized system, the trial balance is usually balanced because most computerized systems will not let you enter an unbalanced journal entry, and because there are rarely software errors in posting or in the preparation of the trial balance.

What do you do if you have a manual trial balance that does not balance? First determine the amount of the difference between the two columns of the trial balance. After you know this amount, try the following steps:

1. If the error is an amount such as $1, $100, or $1,000, re-add the trial balance columns and recalculate the account balances.
2. If the error can be evenly divided by two, scan the trial balance to see if a balance equal to half the error has been entered in the wrong column.

ACCOUNTING IN ACTION
ALL ABOUT YOU INSIGHT

The double-entry accounting system used by many businesses today is in fact more than 500 years old. An Italian friar, Luca Pacioli, is considered to be the "Father of Accounting." His book, *Summa de Arithmetica, Geometria, Proportioniet Proportionalita* (Everything about Arithmetic, Geometry, and Proportions), published in 1494, included a section on accounting. However, Pacioli didn't invent double-entry accounting; he simply described a method that Venetian merchants used during the Italian Renaissance. Pacioli's chapters on accounting, entitled "De Computis et Scripturis" (Of Reckonings and Writings), included most of the accounting cycle known today. They described journals and ledgers, assets (including receivables and inventories), liabilities, capital, revenue, and expense accounts. The book demonstrated year-end closing entries and proposed using a trial balance to prove a balanced ledger. The details of the bookkeeping method Pacioli presented have been followed in accounting texts and the profession for centuries and are just as appropriate for individuals to use as for businesses.

Sources: L. Murphy Smith, "Luca Pacioli: The Father of Accounting" (revised 2011), <http://aaahq.org/southwest/pacioli.htm> (accessed July 31, 2012).

Pacioli also wrote "a person should not go to sleep at night until the debits equalled the credits." Is this still good advice over 500 years later?

3. If the error can be evenly divided by nine, retrace the account balances on the trial balance to see whether they are incorrectly copied from the ledger. For example, if a balance was $12 but was listed as $21, a $9 error has been made. Reversing the order of numbers is called a transposition error.

4. If the error cannot be evenly divided by two or nine, scan the ledger to see whether an account balance in the amount of the error has been omitted from the trial balance. Scan the journal to see whether a posting in the amount of the error has been omitted.

SOME PROCESS EXPLANATIONS

Use of Dollars and Cents

In this textbook, in order to simplify the process, we have not included cents in the amounts we record in journal entries, general ledger accounts, and trial balances. In reality, cents are used in the formal accounting records. When a transaction is recorded in the journal and then posted to the ledger, cents are always used. But when the financial statements are prepared, the account balances are normally rounded to the nearest dollar, and in larger companies, they may be rounded to the nearest thousand or even million. Even though the Canadian government is eliminating the penny for cash transactions, cheques will still be written to the nearest cent.

Use of Dollar Signs and Underlining

Both in practice and in accounting textbooks, dollar signs are not used in the journals or ledgers. Dollar signs are used only in the trial balance and the financial statements. Generally, a dollar sign is shown only for the first item in the column, and for the total of that column.

A single line is placed under a column of figures to be added or subtracted. Total amounts are double-underlined to indicate they are the final sum. In other words, a double underline under a number means that no further amounts will be added to, or subtracted from, that amount.

Account Numbers

As previously mentioned, in practice companies use both account names and account numbers. In this textbook, we have included account numbers in some of our examples and in some of the end-of-chapter exercises and problems. But in most of the examples throughout the textbook, we will use only account names, not account numbers, to simplify the process.

 BEFORE YOU GO ON...

Do It

Koizumi Kollections has the following alphabetical list of accounts and balances at July 31, 2014:

Account	Amount	Account	Amount
Accounts payable	$33,700	Land	$ 51,000
Accounts receivable	71,200	Notes payable	49,500
Building	86,500	Operating expenses	102,000
Cash	3,200	Prepaid insurance	3,100
Equipment	35,700	Service revenue	171,100
J. Koizumi, capital	99,400	Unearned revenue	3,000
J. Koizumi, drawings	4,000		

Each of the above accounts has a normal balance. Prepare a trial balance with the accounts in the same order as they would be in the ledger (in other words, in financial statement order).

Action Plan

- Reorder the accounts as they would normally be in the general ledger: balance sheet accounts are listed first (assets, liabilities, and equity) followed by income statement accounts (revenues and expenses).
- Determine whether each account has a normal debit or credit balance.
- List the amounts in the appropriate debit or credit column.
- Total the trial balance columns. Total debits must equal total credits or a mistake has been made.

BEFORE YOU GO ON continued...

Solution

KOIZUMI KOLLECTIONS
Trial Balance
July 31, 2014

	Debit	Credit
Cash	$ 3,200	
Accounts receivable	71,200	
Prepaid insurance	3,100	
Land	51,000	
Building	86,500	
Equipment	35,700	
Accounts payable		$ 33,700
Unearned revenue		3,000
Notes payable		49,500
J. Koizumi, capital		99,400
J. Koizumi, drawings	4,000	
Service revenue		171,100
Operating expenses	102,000	
Totals	$356,700	$356,700

THE NAVIGATOR

Related exercise material: BE2–13, BE2–14, BE2–15, E2–1, E2–9, E2–10, E2–11, E2–12, E2–13, and E2–14.

Comparing IFRS and ASPE

THE NAVIGATOR

Key Differences	International Financial Reporting Standards (IFRS)	Accounting Standards for Private Enterprises (ASPE)
No significant differences		

Demonstration Problem

Nge Aung opened the Campus Laundromat on September 1, 2014. During the first month of operations, the following transactions occurred:

Sept. 1   Invested $15,000 cash and laundry equipment worth $5,000 in the business.
      2   Paid $1,000 cash for store rent for the month of September.
      3   Borrowed $15,000 cash from the bank and signed a $15,000, 6-month, 5% note payable.
      3   Purchased washers and dryers for $20,000 cash.
      6   Paid $1,200 for a one-year insurance policy.
    10   Received a bill from *The Daily News* for advertising the opening of the laundromat, $300.
    15   Billed a nearby restaurant $500 for laundry services performed on account.
    20   Withdrew $700 cash for personal use.
    25   Received $300 cash from the restaurant billed on September 15. The balance of the account will be collected in October.
    29   Received $400 cash advance from the college residence for services to be performed in October.
    30   Cash receipts for laundry services performed for the month were $6,200.
    30   Paid employee salaries of $1,600.
    30   Paid *The Daily News* $200 of the amount owed from the bill received September 10.

The chart of accounts for the company is the same as the one for Pioneer Advertising Agency in Illustration 2-6 except for the following: No. 610 Advertising Expense.

Instructions

(a) Journalize the September transactions.
(b) Open ledger accounts and post the September transactions.
(c) Prepare a trial balance at September 30, 2014.
(d) Prepare an income statement, statement of owner's equity, and balance sheet for Campus Laundromat.

Solution to Demonstration Problem

(a)

Date	Account Titles and Explanation	Ref	Debit	Credit
GENERAL JOURNAL				**J1**
2014				
Sept. 1	Cash	101	15,000	
	Equipment	151	5,000	
	N. Aung, Capital	301		20,000
	Invested cash and equipment in business.			
2	Rent Expense	726	1,000	
	Cash	101		1,000
	Paid September rent.			
3	Cash	101	15,000	
	Notes Payable	200		15,000
	Borrowed from bank and signed a 6-month, 5% note payable.			
3	Equipment	151	20,000	
	Cash	101		20,000
	Purchased laundry equipment for cash.			
6	Prepaid Insurance	130	1,200	
	Cash	101		1,200
	Paid for a one-year insurance policy.			
10	Advertising Expense	610	300	
	Accounts Payable	201		300
	Received bill from *The Daily News* for advertising.			
15	Accounts Receivable	112	500	
	Service Revenue	400		500
	Performed laundry services on account.			
20	N. Aung, Drawings	306	700	
	Cash	101		700
	Withdrew cash for personal use.			
25	Cash	101	300	
	Accounts Receivable	112		300
	Received cash on account.			
29	Cash	101	400	
	Unearned Revenue	209		400
	Received cash in advance from customer.			
30	Cash	101	6,200	
	Service Revenue	400		6,200
	Received cash for laundry services.			
30	Salaries Expense	729	1,600	
	Cash	101		1,600
	Paid employee salaries.			
30	Accounts Payable	201	200	
	Cash	101		200
	Made a partial payment to *The Daily News*.			

ACTION PLAN

- Determine if the transaction should be recorded or not.
- Do a basic analysis of the transaction. Identify the accounts that were changed and determine if these accounts increased or decreased and by how much.
- Do a debit/credit analysis of the transaction. Determine which account or accounts should be debited and which account or accounts should be credited and make sure debits equal credits.
- In the journal entry, use specific account titles taken from the chart of accounts.
- Include an appropriate description of each journal entry.
- Arrange the ledger in statement order, beginning with the balance sheet accounts.
- Post in chronological order.
- Put account numbers in the reference column of the journal to indicate the amount has been posted.
- In the trial balance, list the accounts in the same order as in the ledger (financial statement order).
- List debit balances in the left column of the trial balance and credit balances in the right column.
- Prepare the income statement first, then the statement of owner's equity, then the balance sheet.
- Use the profit from the income statement when preparing the statement of owner's equity.
- Use the owner's capital balance at September 30, 2014, in the statement of owner's capital when preparing the balance sheet.
- Remember that an income statement and a statement of owner's equity are for a period of time. A balance sheet is at a point in time.

Solution to Demonstration Problem *continued*

(b)

GENERAL LEDGER

Cash				101
Sept. 1	15,000	Sept. 2	1,000	
3	15,000	3	20,000	
25	300	6	1,200	
29	400	20	700	
30	6,200	30	1,600	
		30	200	
Bal.	12,200			

Accounts Receivable				112
Sept. 15	500	Sept. 25	300	
Bal.	200			

Prepaid Insurance				130
Sept. 6	1,200			
Bal.	1,200			

Equipment				151
Sept. 1	5,000			
3	20,000			
Bal.	25,000			

Notes Payable				200
		Sept. 3	15,000	
		Bal.	15,000	

Accounts Payable				201
Sept. 30	200	Sept. 10	300	
		Bal.	100	

Unearned Revenue				209
		Sept. 29	400	
		Bal.	400	

N. Aung, Capital				301
		Sept. 1	20,000	
		Bal.	20,000	

N. Aung, Drawings				306
Sept. 20	700			
Bal.	700			

Service Revenue				400
		Sept. 15	500	
		30	6,200	
		Bal.	6,700	

Advertising Expense				610
Sept. 10	300			
Bal.	300			

Rent Expense				726
Sept. 2	1,000			
Bal.	1,000			

Salaries Expense				729
Sept. 30	1,600			
Bal.	1,600			

(c)

CAMPUS LAUNDROMAT
Trial Balance
September 30, 2014

	Debit	Credit
Cash	$12,200	
Accounts receivable	200	
Prepaid insurance	1,200	
Equipment	25,000	
Notes payable		$15,000
Accounts payable		100
Unearned revenue		400
N. Aung, capital		20,000
N. Aung, drawings	700	
Service revenue		6,700
Advertising expense	300	
Rent expense	1,000	
Salaries expense	1,600	
Totals	$42,200	$42,200

(d)

CAMPUS LAUNDROMAT
Income Statement
Month Ended September 30, 2014

Revenues		
Service revenue		$6,700
Expenses		
Advertising expense	$ 300	
Rent expense	1,000	
Salaries expense	1,600	2,900
Profit		$3,800

CAMPUS LAUNDROMAT
Statement of Owner's Equity
Month Ended September 30, 2014

N. Aung, capital, September 1		$ 0
Add: Investments	$20,000	
Profit	3,800	23,800
Less: Drawings		700
N. Aung, capital, September 30		$23,100

CAMPUS LAUNDROMAT
Balance Sheet
September 30, 2014

Assets

Cash	$12,200
Accounts receivable	200
Prepaid insurance	1,200
Equipment	25,000
Total assets	$38,600

Liabilities and Owner's Equity

Liabilities	
Notes payable	$15,000
Accounts payable	100
Unearned revenue	400
Total liabilities	15,500
Owner's equity	
N. Aung, capital	23,100
Total liabilities and owner's equity	$38,600

THE **NAVIGATOR**

▶ Summary of Study Objectives

THE **NAVIGATOR**

1. *Define debits and credits and illustrate how they are used to record transactions* Debit means left and credit means right. The normal balance of an asset is a debit because assets are on the left side of the accounting equation. Assets are increased by debits and decreased by credits. The normal balance of liabilities and owner's capital is a credit because they are on the right side of the accounting equation. Liabilities and owner's capital are increased by credits and decreased by debits. Revenues increase owner's equity and therefore are recorded as credits because credits increase owner's equity. Credits increase revenues and debits decrease revenues. Expenses and drawings decrease owner's equity and therefore are recorded as debits because debits decrease owner's equity. Expenses and drawings are increased by debits and decreased by credits.

2. *Explain the recording process and analyze, journalize, and post transactions.* The steps in the recording process are the first three steps in the accounting cycle. These steps are: (a) analyze each transaction for its effect on the accounts, (b) record the transaction in a journal, and (c) transfer the journal information to the correct accounts in the ledger.

A journal (a) discloses the complete effect of a transaction in one place, (b) provides a chronological record of transactions, (c) helps to prevent and locate errors because the debit and credit amounts for each entry can be easily compared, and (d) explains the transaction and, if there is one, identifies the source document.

The entire group of accounts maintained by a company is called the ledger. The ledger keeps in one place all the information about changes in each of the specific account balances. Posting is the procedure of transferring journal entries to the ledger accounts. After the journal entries have been posted, the ledger will show all of the increases and decreases that have been made to each account.

3. *Explain the purpose of a trial balance, and prepare one.* A trial balance is a list of the accounts in the ledger and the account balances at a specific time. Its main purpose is to prove that debits and credits are equal after posting. A trial balance uncovers certain types of errors in journalizing and posting, and is useful in preparing financial statements. Preparing a trial balance is the fourth step in the accounting cycle.

Flash cards

▶ Glossary

Account A record of increases and decreases in a specific asset, liability, or owner's equity item. (p. 58)

Accounting cycle A series of steps followed by accountants in preparing financial statements. (p. 62)

Chart of accounts A list of accounts and the account numbers that identify where the accounts are in the ledger. (p. 67)

Compound entry A journal entry that affects three or more accounts. (p. 65)

Credit The right side of an account. (p. 58)

Debit The left side of an account. (p. 58)

Double-entry accounting system A system that records the dual (two-sided) effect of each transaction in appropriate accounts. (p. 61)

General journal The most basic form of journal in which transactions are recorded when they are not recorded in other specialized journals. (p. 64)

General ledger A ledger that contains accounts for all assets, liabilities, equities, revenues, and expenses. (p. 65)

Journal An accounting record where transactions are recorded in chronological (date) order. It shows the debit and credit effect of each transaction on specific accounts. (p. 64)

Journalizing The entering of transaction data in the journal. (p. 64)

Ledger A record that contains all of a company's accounts. It keeps all the information about changes in each account in one place. (p. 65)

Posting The procedure of transferring journal entries to the ledger accounts. (p. 66)

Recording process The first three steps of the accounting cycle. (p. 62)

T account A form of account that looks like the letter T. It has the title above the horizontal line. Debits are shown to the left of the vertical line, credits to the right. (p. 58)

Three-column form of account An account form with columns for debit, credit, and balance amounts in an account. (p. 66)

Trial balance A list of the accounts in the ledger and the account balances at a specific time, usually at the end of the accounting period. (p. 75)

⯈ Self-Study Questions

Answers are at the end of the chapter.

(SO 1) K   1. Which of the following statements about an account is true?
  (a) The left side of an account is the credit or decrease side.
  (b) An account is an individual accounting record of increases and decreases in specific asset, liability, and owner's equity items.
  (c) There are separate accounts for specific assets and liabilities but only one account for owner's equity items.
  (d) The right side of an account is the debit or increase side.

(SO 1) K   2. Credits:
  (a) increase both assets and liabilities.
  (b) decrease both assets and liabilities.
  (c) increase assets and decrease liabilities.
  (d) decrease assets and increase liabilities.

(SO 1) K   3. An expense account:
  (a) is increased by debits.
  (b) has a normal balance of a credit.
  (c) is decreased by debits.
  (d) is increased by credits.

(SO 1) K   4. Accounts that normally have debit balances are:
  (a) assets, expenses, and revenues.
  (b) assets, expenses, and owner's capital.
  (c) assets, liabilities, and drawings.
  (d) assets, expenses, and drawings.

(SO 2) K   5. What is the correct sequence of steps in the recording process?
  (a) Analyzing transactions; preparing a trial balance
  (b) Analyzing transactions; entering transactions in a journal; posting transactions
  (c) Entering transactions in a journal; posting transactions; preparing a trial balance
  (d) Entering transactions in a journal; posting transactions; analyzing transactions

(SO 2) AP   6. Performing services for a customer on account should result in:
  (a) a decrease in the liability account Accounts Payable and an increase in the revenue account Service Revenue.
  (b) an increase in the asset account Cash and a decrease in the asset account Accounts Receivable.
  (c) an increase to the asset account Accounts Receivable and an increase to the liability account Unearned Revenue.
  (d) an increase to the asset account Accounts Receivable and an increase to the revenue account Service Revenue.

(SO 2) AP   7. The purchase of equipment on account should result in:
  (a) a debit to Equipment and a credit to Accounts Payable.
  (b) a debit to Equipment Expense and a credit to Accounts Payable.
  (c) a debit to Equipment and a credit to Cash.
  (d) a debit to Accounts Receivable and a credit to Equipment.

(SO 2) K   8. Which of these statements about a journal is false?
  (a) It is not a book of original entry.
  (b) It provides a chronological record of transactions.
  (c) It helps to locate errors because the debit and credit amounts for each entry can be easily compared.
  (d) It shows in one place the complete effect of a transaction.

(SO 2) K   9. A ledger:
  (a) contains only asset and liability accounts.
  (b) should show accounts in alphabetical order.
  (c) is a collection of the entire group of accounts maintained by a company.
  (d) is a book of original entry.

(SO 2) K   10. Posting:
  (a) is normally done before journalizing.
  (b) transfers ledger transaction data to the journal.
  (c) is an optional step in the recording process.
  (d) transfers journal entries to ledger accounts.

(SO 3) K   11. A trial balance:
  (a) is a list of accounts with their balances at a specific time.
  (b) proves that journalized transactions are accurate.
  (c) will not balance if a correct journal entry is posted twice.
  (d) proves that all transactions have been recorded.

(SO 3) AP 12. A trial balance will not balance if:
  (a) the collection of an account receivable is posted twice.
  (b) the purchase of supplies on account is debited to Supplies and credited to Cash.
  (c) a $100 cash drawing by the owner is debited to Drawings for $1,000 and credited to Cash for $100.
  (d) a $450 payment on account is debited to Accounts Payable for $45 and credited to Cash for $45.

THE NAVIGATOR

⯈ Questions

(SO 1) C   1. What is an account? Will a company need more than one account? Explain.

(SO 1) K   2. What is debiting an account? What is crediting an account?

(SO 1) K   3. Explain the relationship between the normal balance in each type of account and the accounting equation.

(SO 1) C   4. Kim Nguyen, a beginning accounting student, believes credit balances are favourable and debit balances are unfavourable. Is Kim correct? Discuss.

(SO 1) C   5. Dmitri Karpov doesn't understand how a debit increases Equipment and a credit increases Accounts Payable. He believes that debits and credits cannot both increase account balances. Explain to Dmitri why he is wrong.

(SO 1) C   6. Why are increases to drawings and expenses recorded as debits?

(SO 1) C   7. Jermyn Orsen, an introductory accounting student, thinks that a double-entry accounting system means that each transaction is recorded twice. Is Jermyn correct? Explain.

(SO 2) C   8. Jennifer Halford doesn't understand why some events are recorded as accounting transactions but others are not. Explain.

(SO 2) C   9. What is involved in analyzing a business transaction?

(SO 2) K   10. What is the difference between a simple and a compound journal entry? What rule must be followed when recording a compound entry so the accounting equation remains balanced?

(SO 2) K   11. Hiroshi Benoit, a fellow student, is unclear about similarities and differences between using a manual system or a computerized system in the recording process. Briefly explain, including the benefit of a computerized system.

(SO 2) C   12. A company receives cash from a customer. List three different accounts that could be credited and the circumstances under which each of these accounts would be credited.

(SO 2) C   13. Amber Rose believes that accounting would be more efficient if transactions were recorded directly in the ledger accounts. Explain to Amber the advantages of first recording transactions in the journal, and then posting them to the ledger.

(SO 2) C   14. Explain the differences between the format of a T account and the standard form of accounts. In your explanation, include the benefits of each format, and when each format is typically used.

(SO 2) C   15. What are the differences between a ledger and a chart of accounts?

(SO 3) K   16. What is a trial balance? What are its purposes?

(SO 3) C   17. Does it matter in what order the accounts are listed on a trial balance? Explain.

(SO 3) C   18. Yue Shin thinks it doesn't matter in what order the first four steps in the accounting cycle are completed, as long as they are all done before moving on to remaining steps. Do you agree or disagree with Yue? Explain.

(SO 3) C   19. Jamal Nazari is doing the accounting for a company that has a December 31 year end. He is wondering if the heading on its trial balance should read "Year Ended December 31" or just "December 31." Which one is correct? Explain why.

(SO 3) AN   20. Two students are discussing the use of a trial balance. They wonder if the following errors in different companies would prevent a trial balance from balancing. For each error, what would you tell the students?
(a) The bookkeeper debited Supplies for $750 and debited Accounts Payable for $750 for the purchase of supplies on account.
(b) Cash collected on account was debited to Cash for $1,000 and credited to Service Revenue for $1,000.
(c) A journal entry recording the payment of rent expense was posted to the general ledger as a $650 debit to Rent Expense and a $560 credit to Cash.

(SO 3) AP   21. Maureen Melnyk has just prepared a trial balance for a company and found that the total debits were $450 higher than the total credits. Assuming that the account balances in the ledger are correct, give Maureen three examples of things that she might have done incorrectly when preparing the trial balance.

▶ Brief Exercises

Calculate missing amounts and account balances. (SO 1) AP

BE2–1   For the three accounts that follow, fill in the missing amounts (a) through (f):

Accounts Receivable		Supplies		Notes Payable	
7,500		6,400			100,000
16,700		(c)		24,000	
	15,400		6,800		45,000
Bal. (a)		Bal. 3,800		Bal. (e)	
13,100		7,700			(f)
	(b)		5,900	27,000	
Bal. 4,700		Bal. (d)			Bal. 149,000

Indicate type of account and normal balance. (SO 1) K

BE2–2   For each the following accounts, indicate (a) if the account is an asset, liability, or owner's equity account; and (b) whether the account would have a normal debit or credit balance.

1. Accounts Receivable
2. Accounts Payable
3. Equipment
4. Rent Expense
5. B. Damji, Drawings
6. Supplies
7. Unearned Revenue
8. Cash
9. Service Revenue
10. Prepaid Insurance
11. Utilities Expense
12. Notes Payable

BE2-3 For each of the following accounts, indicate (a) the normal balance, (b) the effect of a debit on the account, and (c) the effect of a credit on the account:

1. Accounts Payable
2. Accounts Receivable
3. Cash
4. Supplies
5. J. Takamoto, Capital
6. J. Takamoto, Drawings
7. Prepaid Rent
8. Rent Expense
9. Service Revenue
10. Unearned Revenue

Indicate normal balance and debit and credit effects. (SO 1) K

BE2-4 For each of the following, indicate (a) if the account is an asset, liability, or owner's equity account; and (b) whether you would use a debit or credit to record the change:

1. Increase in D. Parmelee, Capital
2. Decrease in Cash
3. Decrease in Notes Payable
4. Increase in Rent Expense
5. Increase in D. Parmelee, Drawings
6. Increase in Equipment
7. Increase in Accounts Payable
8. Increase in Service Revenue

Indicate type of account and when to use debits and credits (SO 1) K

BE2-5 Levine Legal Services had the following transactions:

1. Cash is paid for the purchase of $445 of office supplies.
2. Customer is billed $1,500 for services provided that day.
3. Equipment with a cost of $2,500 is purchased on account.
4. The current month's utility bill of $225 is paid in cash.
5. Cash of $500 is received for services provided that day.
6. Ruben Levine, the company's owner, withdraws $800 cash from the company's bank account for personal use.
7. Cash of $2,200 is paid to employees for the current month's wages.
8. Cash of $750 is received for services to be provided in the next month.

Prepare basic analysis and debit/credit analysis for transactions. (SO 1) C

For each transaction, prepare a basic analysis and a debit/credit analysis. Use the following format, in which the first one has been done for you as an example:

Transaction 1:

Basic Analysis	The asset Cash is decreased by $445. The asset Supplies is increased by $445.
Debit/Credit Analysis	Debits increase assets: debit Supplies $445. Credits decrease assets: credit Cash $445.

BE2-6 Fleming's Logistics Consulting has the following transactions during August.

Aug. 1	Received $16,750 cash from the company's owner, Barbara Fleming.
4	Paid rent in advance for three months, $3,900.
5	Purchased $645 of office supplies on account.
6	Received $950 from clients for services provided.
17	Billed clients $1,500 for services provided.
27	Paid secretary $875 salary.
29	Paid the company's owner, Barbara Fleming, $700 cash for personal use.

Identify accounts and debit/credit analysis. (SO 1) C

For each transaction, indicate (a) the basic type of account to be debited and credited (asset, liability, owner's equity); (b) the specific accounts to debit and credit (for example, Cash, Service Revenue, Accounts Payable); and (c) whether each account is increased (+) or decreased (−), and by what amount. Use the following format, in which the first one has been done for you as an example:

	Account Debited			Account Credited		
	(a)	(b)	(c)	(a)	(b)	(c)
Transaction	Basic Type	Specific Account	Effect	Basic Type	Specific Account	Effect
Aug. 1	Asset	Cash	+$16,750	Owner's Equity	B. Fleming, Capital	+$16,750

BE2-7 Princess Printing Company had the following transactions with a customer during January: (1) performed services, such as printing flyers, and billed the customer; (2) collected cash on account from the customer; and (3) sent a statement at the end of the month, showing the balance owing, to the customer. Analyze each of these transactions and determine if they should be recorded or not. Explain why or why not for each transaction.

Analyze transactions. (SO 2) AP

Prepare basic analysis, debit/ credit analysis, and journal entry. (SO 1, 2) AP

BE2-8 Pridham Welding Company had the following transactions for June.

June 1   Tyler Pridham invested $9,500 cash in a small welding business.
      2   Bought used welding equipment on account for $3,000.
      5   Hired an employee to start work on July 15. Agreed on a salary of $3,600 per month.
    17   Billed R. Windl $1,975 for welding work done.
    27   Received $1,000 cash from R. Windl for work billed on June 17.
    29   Paid for equipment purchased on June 2.
    30   Paid employee $1,800 for one-half of a month's work.

For each transaction, prepare a basic analysis, a debit/credit analysis, and journalize the transaction. Use the following format, in which the first one has been done for you as an example:

June 1 transaction:

Basic Analysis	The asset account Cash is increased by $9,500. The owner's equity account T. Pridham, Capital is increased by $9,500.		
Debit/Credit Analysis	Debits increase assets: debit Cash $9,500. Credits increase owner's equity: credit T. Pridham, Capital $9,500.		

Journal Entry	June 1 Cash
	         T. Pridham, Capital
	            Invested cash in business.
		9,500	9,500

Record transactions. (SO 2) AP

BE2-9 Using the data in BE2–5 for Levine Legal Services, journalize the transactions. Assume all of the transactions occurred on August 31.

Record transactions. (SO 2) AP

BE2-10 Using the data in BE2–6 for Fleming's Logistics Consulting, journalize the transactions.

Post journal entries. (SO 2) AP

BE2-11 Using T accounts, post the journal entries from BE2–10 to the general ledger.

Post journal entries. (SO 2) AP

BE2-12 Using T accounts, post the following journal entries to the general ledger.

GENERAL JOURNAL			
Date	Account title and explanation	Debit	Credit
Sept. 2	Accounts Receivable	2,275	
	Service Revenue		2,275
4	Supplies	750	
	Accounts Payable		750
10	Cash	1,050	
	Service Revenue		1,050
14	Utilities Expense	95	
	Cash		95
15	Salaries Expense	850	
	Cash		850
28	Cash	1,325	
	Accounts Receivable		1,325
30	Accounts Payable	450	
	Cash		450

Prepare trial balance. (SO 3) AP

BE2-13 Use the ledger balances that follow to prepare a trial balance for the Pettipas Company at April 30, 2014. All account balances are normal.

Accounts payable	$ 3,300	Prepaid rent	$ 800
Accounts receivable	5,000	Rent expense	4,500
C. Pettipas, capital	22,500	Salaries expense	1,000
C. Pettipas, drawings	1,100	Service revenue	8,000
Cash	6,400	Supplies	650
Equipment	14,600	Unearned revenue	250

BE2–14 There are two errors in the following trial balance: (1) one account has been placed in the wrong column, and (2) there is a transposition error in the balance of the L. Bourque, Capital account. Explain the two errors.

Explain errors in trial balance.
(SO 3) AP

BOURQUE COMPANY
Trial Balance
December 31, 2014

	Debit	Credit
Cash	$15,000	
Accounts receivable	1,800	
Prepaid insurance		$ 3,500
Accounts payable		2,000
Unearned revenue		2,200
L. Bourque, capital		15,400
L. Bourque, drawings	4,900	
Service revenue		27,500
Rent	2,400	
Salaries	18,600	
Totals	$42,700	$50,600

▶ Exercises

E2–1 Here are some of the concepts discussed in the chapter:

Match concepts with descriptions. (SO 1, 2, 3) K

1. Account
2. Analyzing transactions
3. Chart of accounts
4. Credit
5. Debit
6. Journal
7. Journalizing
8. Ledger
9. Posting
10. Trial balance

Instructions

Match each concept with the best description below. Each concept may be used more than once, or may not be used at all.

(a) _____ The normal balance for liabilities
(b) _____ The first step in the recording process
(c) _____ The procedure of transferring journal entries to the ledger accounts
(d) _____ A record of increases and decreases in a specific asset, liability, or owner's equity item
(e) _____ The left side of an account
(f) _____ The entering of transaction data in the journal
(g) _____ A list of accounts and their balances at a specific time
(h) _____ Used to decrease the balance in an asset account
(i) _____ A list of all of a company's accounts
(j) _____ An accounting record where transactions are recorded in chronological (date) order

E2–2 Kobayashi Company has the following accounts:

Identify type of account, financial statement, and normal balance. Explain normal balances. (SO 1) C

Account	(1) Type of Account	(2) Financial Statement	(3) Normal Balance
Cash	Asset	Balance Sheet	Debit
M. Kobayashi, Capital			
Accounts Payable			
Building			
Fees Earned			
Insurance Expense			
Interest Revenue			
M. Kobayashi, Drawings			
Notes Receivable			
Prepaid Insurance			
Rent Expense			
Supplies			

Instructions

(a) Complete the table. Identify (1) the type of account as asset, liability, or owner's equity (for owner's equity accounts, also identify if it is a capital, drawings, revenue, or expense account); (2) what financial statement it is presented on; and (3) the normal balance of the account. The first one has been done for you as an example.

(b) Explain why the normal balance for each of the different types of accounts is either a debit or credit. Refer to the accounting equation in your explanation.

Identify accounts and determine debits and credits. (SO 1) C

E2-3 In the first month of business, Jakmak Interior Design Company had the following transactions:

Mar.	3	The owner, Jackie MacKenzie, invested $10,000 cash in the business.
	4	Borrowed $10,000 from the bank and signed a note payable.
	6	Purchased a used car for $9,500 cash, for use in the business.
	7	Purchased supplies on account for $1,500.
	12	Billed customers $2,100 for services performed.
	21	Paid $525 cash for advertising the launch of the business.
	25	Received $1,200 cash from customers billed on March 12.
	28	Paid for the supplies purchased on March 7.
	30	Received $750 cash from a customer for services to be performed in April.
	31	Paid Jackie MacKenzie $1,400 cash for her personal use.

Instructions

For each transaction, indicate:

(a) The basic type of account debited and credited (asset, liability, owner's equity)
(b) The specific account debited and credited (Cash, Rent Expense, Service Revenue, etc.)
(c) Whether each account is increased (+) or decreased (−), and by what amount.

Use the following format, in which the first transaction is given as an example:

	Account Debited			Account Credited		
	(a)	(b)	(c)	(a)	(b)	(c)
Transaction	Basic Type	Specific Account	Effect	Basic Type	Specific Account	Effect
Mar. 3	Asset	Cash	+$10,000	Owner's Equity	J. MacKenzie, Capital	+ $10,000

Prepare basic analysis, debit/ credit analysis, and journal entry. (SO 1, 2) AP

E2-4 Bratt Plumbing Company had the following transactions for June.

June	1	Paid $550 for rent for the month of June.
	2	Paid $175 for one month of insurance.
	5	Collected an account of $1,255 for plumbing services provided in May. This account was billed and correctly recorded in May.
	9	Provided Jeff Dupuis, a potential customer, with an estimate of $5,000 for plumbing work that will be performed in July if the customer hires Bratt Plumbing.
	14	Paid $675 for supplies purchased on account in May. The purchase in May had been correctly recorded.
	17	Billed Rudy Holland $1,420 for plumbing work done.
	19	Jeff Dupuis agreed to hire Bratt Plumbing (see the June 9 transaction) and gave Bratt Plumbing a down payment of $1,000.
	29	Purchased $1,575 of equipment on account.
	30	Paid an employee $850.
	30	Paid D. Bratt, the company owner, $1,250.

Instructions

For each transaction, prepare a basic analysis and a debit/credit analysis, and journalize the transaction. Use the format shown in BE2-8.

Record transactions. (SO 2) AP

E2-5 Data for Jakmak Interior Design Company are presented in E2-3.

Instructions

Journalize the transactions.

Record transactions and identify impact on owner's equity. (SO 2) AP

E2-6 At the end of March 2014, total owner's equity for Beaulieu Group Company was $8,050. During April, the following transactions occurred:

1. Provided services to a client and received $1,785 cash.
2. Paid $965 for April's rent.
3. Purchased $480 of supplies on account.

4. Provided services to a client and billed the client $2,160.
5. Collected $1,000 from the client billed in transaction 4.
6. Received $5,000 cash from the bank and signed a one-year, 5% note payable.
7. Used the cash received in transaction 6 to purchase equipment.
8. Received $800 cash from a client for services to be provided in May.
9. Paid $850 cash for radio advertising that will be aired in May.
10. Paid for the supplies purchased on account in transaction 3.
11. Shehla Beaulieu, the owner, withdrew $1,565 cash for personal use.

Instructions

(a) Journalize the transactions.
(b) For each transaction, identify if it increased, decreased, or had no effect on owner's equity and explain why.
(c) Calculate total owner's equity as at April 30.

E2–7   Selected transactions for Polland Real Estate Agency during its first month of business follow:

Record transactions.
(SO 2) AP

Oct.	1	Samantha Polland opened Polland Real Estate Agency with an investment of $14,000 cash and $3,000 of equipment.
	2	Paid $1,200 for a one-year insurance policy.
	3	Purchased additional equipment for $4,450, paying $850 cash and signing a note payable for the balance.
	10	Received $350 cash as a fee for renting an apartment.
	16	Sold a house and lot to B. Rollins. The commission due from Rollins is $7,500 (it is not paid by Rollins at this time).
	27	Paid $700 for advertising costs during October.
	29	Received a $95 bill for telephone service during the month of October (the bill is paid in November).
	30	Paid an administrative assistant $2,000 in salary for October.
	31	Received $7,500 cash from B. Rollins for the October 16 transaction.

Instructions

Journalize the transactions.

E2–8   Journal entries for Polland Real Estate Agency's transactions were prepared in E2–7.

Post journal entries.
(SO 2) AP

Instructions

Post the journal entries to the general ledger, using T accounts.

E2–9   Fortin Co.'s ledger is as follows:

Record transactions and
prepare trial balance.
(SO 2, 3) AP

Cash

Oct.	1	1,200	Oct.	3	400
	10	650		12	500
	15	3,000		30	600
	20	800		31	250
	25	2,000		31	500

Accounts Receivable

Oct.	6	1,000	Oct.	20	800
	20	940			

Supplies

Oct.	4	800	

Equipment

Oct.	3	5,400	

Notes Payable

			Oct.	3	5,000

Accounts Payable

Oct.	12	500	Oct	4	800
				28	400

A. Fortin, Capital

			Oct.	1	1,200
				25	2,000

A. Fortin, Drawings

Oct.	30	600	

Service Revenue

			Oct.	6	1,000
				10	650
				15	3,000
				20	940

Advertising Expense

Oct.	28	400	

Rent Expense

Oct.	31	250	

Salaries Expense

Oct.	31	500	

Instructions

(a) Journalize the October transactions, and give explanations for each entry.
(b) Determine the October 31, 2014, balance for each account. Prepare a trial balance at October 31, 2014.

Post journal entries and prepare trial balance.
(SO 2, 3) AP

E2–10 On July 31, 2014, Lee Meche, MD, had the following balances in the ledger for his medical practice: Cash $8,800; Accounts Receivable $2,750; Supplies $585; Equipment $15,550; Notes Payable $10,000; Accounts Payable $850; L. Meche, Capital $15,000; L. Meche, Drawings $5,125; Fees Earned $10,410; Rent Expense $1,200; and Salaries Expense $2,250. Selected transactions during August 2014 follow:

GENERAL JOURNAL				
Date	Account title and explanation	Ref	Debit	Credit
2014				
Aug. 1	Rent Expense		1,200	
	Cash			1,200
10	Accounts Payable		420	
	Cash			420
12	Cash		2,400	
	Accounts Receivable			2,400
25	Salaries Expense		2,250	
	Cash			2,250
30	Notes Payable		500	
	Interest Expense		40	
	Cash			540
31	Cash		5,910	
	Accounts Receivable		2,550	
	Fees Earned			8,460
31	L. Meche, Drawings		4,770	
	Cash			4,770

Instructions

(a) Create T accounts and enter the July 31 balances.
(b) Post the transactions to the T accounts. Create new T accounts if needed.
(c) Prepare a trial balance at August 31.

Prepare and post journal entries. Prepare trial balance and financial statements.
(SO 2, 3) AP

E2–11 Ahuja Dental Services' general ledger at April 30, 2014, included the following: Cash, $6,000; Supplies, $1,000; Equipment, $65,000; Notes Payable, $50,000; Accounts Payable, $800; and S. Ahuja, Capital, $21,200. During May 2014, the following transactions occurred:

May 2 Paid May's rent of $1,200.
4 Purchased $700 supplies on account.
15 Paid the accounts payable owing from April 30, 2014.
31 Paid the dental assistant's salary of $1,800.
31 Earned revenue of $10,000 for dental services during May. Collected $9,500 of this in cash.

Instructions

(a) Journalize May's transactions.
(b) Using T accounts, enter the balances as at April 30, 2014, then post May's journal entries.
(c) Prepare a trial balance.
(d) Prepare financial statements for May.

Prepare trial balance and financial statements.
(SO 3) AP

E2–12 A list of accounts and their balances of O'Neill's Psychological Services, at its year end July 31, 2014, is presented below.

Supplies	$ 790	Notes Payable	$22,960
Unearned Revenue	1,350	Salaries Expense	45,540
Supplies Expense	5,960	T. O'Neill, Drawings	57,980
Cash	6,470	Equipment	58,900
Accounts Receivable	7,340	T. O'Neill, Capital	64,340
Accounts Payable	9,030	Service Revenue	96,180
Rent Expense	10,880		

Instructions

(a) Prepare a trial balance in financial statement order.
(b) Prepare an income statement, statement of owner's equity, and balance sheet.

E2–13   The accountant for Smistad Guitar Repair Company made a number of errors in journalizing and posting, as described below:

1. A credit posting of $400 to Accounts Payable was omitted.
2. A debit posting of $750 for Rent Expense was debited to Prepaid Rent.
3. A collection on account of $100 was journalized and posted as a $100 debit to Cash and a $100 credit to Service Revenue.
4. A credit posting of $500 to Accounts Payable was made twice.
5. A cash purchase of supplies for $250 was journalized and posted as a $25 debit to Supplies and a $25 credit to cash.
6. A debit of $475 to Advertising Expense was posted as $457.
7. A journal entry for the payment of $1,200 of salaries expense was posted twice.

Analyze errors and their effect on the trial balance. (SO 3) AN

Instructions

Considering each error separately, indicate the following using the format below, where error number 1 is given as an example.

(a) Will the trial balance be in balance?
(b) What is the amount of the error if the trial balance will not balance?
(c) Which trial balance column will have the larger total?
(d) Which account or accounts have an incorrect balance? If the balance in all of the accounts is correct, write "all correct."

Error	(a) In Balance	(b) Difference	(c) Larger Column	(d) Incorrect Accounts
1	No	$400	Debit	Accounts Payable

E2–14   Terry Zelinski, the owner of Royal Mountain Tours, prepared the following trial balance at March 31, 2014.

Prepare corrected trial balance. (SO 3) AP

Cash	$12,800	
Accounts receivable	4,090	
Supplies	840	
Equipment	7,350	
Accounts payable		$ 2,500
T. Zelinski, capital		24,000
T. Zelinski, drawings		3,650
Service revenue	6,750	
Advertising expense	3,700	
Salaries expense	400	
Totals	$35,930	$30,150

A review shows that Terry made the following errors in the accounting records:

1. A purchase of $400 of supplies on account was recorded as a credit to cash. The debit entry was correct.
2. A $100 credit to accounts receivable was posted as $1,000.
3. A journal entry to record service revenue of $770 earned on account was not prepared or posted.
4. A journal entry to record the payment of $240 for an advertising expense was correctly prepared but the credit to cash was posted as a debit. The debit to advertising expense was properly posted.

Instructions

Prepare the correct trial balance at March 31, 2014, using the format shown in the chapter. (*Hint*: You should also make sure that the account balances are recorded in the correct columns on the trial balance.)

▶ Problems: Set A

Identify type of account, financial statement, normal balances, and debits and credits. (SO 1) K

P2–1A   Miranda Brock, Lawyer, has the following accounts:

Accounts Payable	Land	Rent Revenue
Accounts Receivable	Fees Earned	Salaries Expense
Building	M. Brock, Capital	Salaries Payable
Cash	M. Brock, Drawings	Supplies
Equipment	Notes Receivable	Supplies Expense
Insurance Expense	Prepaid Insurance	Unearned Revenue
Interest Revenue	Rent Expense	

Instructions

For each of these accounts, identify (a) the type of account (e.g., asset, liability, owner's capital, drawings, revenue, expense); (b) what financial statement it is presented on; (c) the normal balance of the account; (d) whether the account is increased by a debit or credit; and (e) whether the account is decreased by a debit or credit. Use the following format, in which the first one has been done for you as an example.

	(a)	(b)	(c)	(d)	(e)
Account	Type of Account	Financial Statement	Normal Balance	Increase	Decrease
Accounts Payable	Liability	Balance sheet	Credit	Credit	Debit

TAKING IT FURTHER   Explain the relationship between the normal balance in each type of account and the basic accounting equation.

Perform transaction analysis and journalize transactions. (SO 1, 2) AP

P2–2A   JB Paint Designs began operations on April 1, 2014. The company completed the following transactions in its first month:

Apr. 1   The owner, Jay Barr, invested $13,500 cash in the company.
  2   Purchased a one-year insurance policy effective April 1, and paid the first month's premium of $115.
  2   Purchased equipment for $5,000 on account.
  3   Paid for $435 of supplies.
  7   Paid cash for $870 of advertising expenses.
  8   Finished a painting project for Maya Angelina and collected $750 cash.
  10   Received a $1,500 contract from a customer, SUB Terrain Inc., to paint its new office space. SUB Terrain will pay when the project is complete.
  25   Completed the contract with SUB Terrain Inc. from April 10 and collected the amount owing.
  28   The owner, Jay Barr, withdrew $975 cash for his personal use.
  29   Received $1,250 cash from Memphis Shek for a painting project that JB Paint Designs will start on May 5.
  30   Paid for the equipment purchased on account on April 2.

Instructions

(a) For each transaction, indicate: (1) the basic type of account debited and credited (asset, liability, or owner's equity); (2) the specific account debited and credited (Cash, Rent Expense, Service Revenue, etc.); and (3) whether each account is increased (+) or decreased (−), and by what amount. Use the following format, in which the first transaction is given as an example:

	Account Debited			Account Credited		
	(1)	(2)	(3)	(1)	(2)	(3)
Transaction	Basic Type	Specific Account	Effect	Basic Type	Specific Account	Effect
Apr. 1	Asset	Cash	+$13,500	Owner's Equity	J. Barr, Capital	+$13,500

(b) Prepare a journal entry for each transaction.

TAKING IT FURTHER   Jay doesn't understand why a debit increases the cash account and yet a credit to J. Barr, Capital increases that account. He reasons that debits and credits cannot both increase account balances. Explain to Jay why he is wrong.

P2–3A   Bucket Club Miniature Golf and Driving Range was opened on May 1. The following events and transactions are for May:

Journalize transactions.
(SO 2) AP

May	1	Amin Mawani, the owner, invested $75,000 cash in the business.
	2	Purchased Lee's Golf Land for $250,000. The price consists of land, $120,000; building, $80,000; and equipment, $50,000. Paid $60,000 cash and signed a note payable for the balance.
	4	Purchased golf clubs and other equipment for $16,000 from Woods Company on account.
	5	Hired a golf pro to teach lessons at the golf range at a rate of $40 per hour.
	6	Paid $2,760 cash for a one-year insurance policy.
	15	Collected $2,000 golf fees earned in cash from customers.
	19	Paid Woods Company $5,000 for the items purchased on May 4.
	20	Billed a customer, Deer Fern Inc., $1,500 for golf fees earned. Deer Fern Inc. paid $500 and agreed to pay the remaining amount owing in 10 days.
	30	Received $1,000 from Deer Fern Inc. for the May 20 transaction.
	31	Collected $4,000 cash from customers for golf fees earned.
	31	Paid salaries of $2,480.
	31	Paid $715 of interest on the note payable.
	31	Paid Amin Mawani $1,750 for his personal use.

The company's chart of accounts includes the following accounts: Cash; Accounts Receivable; Prepaid Insurance; Land; Buildings; Equipment; Accounts Payable; Notes Payable; A. Mawani, Capital; A. Mawani, Drawings; Fees Earned; Salaries Expense; and Interest Expense.

Instructions

Journalize the May transactions.

TAKING IT FURTHER   After Amin has reviewed the journal entries, he complains that they don't seem to be very useful. Explain to Amin the purpose of the journal entries and the next step in the accounting cycle. Include in your answer whether or not Amin will find any useful information after the next step is completed.

P2–4A   Grete Rodewald formed a dog grooming and training business called Grete Kanines on September 1, 2014. After consulting with a friend who had taken introductory accounting, Grete created a chart of accounts for the business as follows: No. 101 Cash; No. 112 Accounts Receivable; No. 130 Prepaid Insurance; No. 151 Equipment; No. 201 Accounts Payable; No. 209 Unearned Revenue; No. 301 G. Rodewald, Capital; No. 306 G. Rodewald, Drawings; No. 400 Service Revenue; No. 610 Advertising Expense; No. 726 Rent Expense; and No. 737 Utilities Expense. During September, the following events and transactions occurred:

Journalize transactions, post, and prepare trial balance.
(SO 2, 3) AP

Sept.	1	Grete transferred $9,000 from her personal bank account to a bank account under the company name, Grete Kanines.
	1	Signed a one-year rental agreement for $650 per month. Paid the first month's rent.
	2	Paid $720 for a one-year insurance policy effective September 1, 2014.
	3	Purchased $2,500 of equipment on credit.
	6	Paid $450 for advertising in several community newsletters in September.
	15	Collected $500 cash for providing dog grooming services.
	19	Attended a dog show and provided $700 of dog grooming services for one of the major kennel owners. The kennel owner will pay the amount owing within two weeks.
	24	Collected $500 from the kennel owner for the services provided on September 19. The kennel owner promised to pay the rest on October 2.
	25	Paid $175 for utilities for the month of September.
	26	Paid $1,500 of the amount owed from the September 3 equipment purchase.
	29	Received $850 cash for dog training lessons that will start on October 7.
	30	Collected $975 cash for providing dog grooming services.
	30	Paid the owner, Grete Rodewald, $1,350 for her personal use.

Instructions

(a) Journalize the transactions.
(b) Post to the ledger accounts. Use the standard form of account.
(c) Prepare a trial balance as at September 30, 2014.

TAKING IT FURTHER   Grete thinks she needs only one account for investments, drawings, revenues, and expense because these are all owners' equity accounts. Explain to her why she needs separate accounts.

Journalize transactions, post, and prepare trial balance. (SO 2, 3) AP

P2–5A Abramson Financial Services was formed on May 1, 2014. The following events and transactions are from its first month:

May	1	Jacob Abramson invested $40,000 cash and equipment worth $10,000 in the company.
	1	Hired one employee to work in the office for a salary of $2,475 per month.
	2	Paid $3,300 cash for a one-year insurance policy.
	5	Signed a two-year rental agreement on an office and paid $4,800 cash. Half was for the May 2014 rent and the other half was for the final month's rent. (*Hint:* The portion for the final month is considered prepaid rent.)
	8	Purchased additional equipment costing $17,000. A cash payment of $7,000 was made immediately. Signed a note payable for the balance.
	9	Purchased supplies for $500 cash.
	15	Purchased more supplies for $750 on account.
	17	Completed a contract for a client for $3,000 on account.
	22	Paid $250 for May's telephone bill.
	25	Completed services for a client and immediately collected $1,100.
	26	Paid Jacob Abramson $1,600 cash for his personal use.
	28	Collected $2,500 from the client billed on May 17.
	30	Paid for the supplies purchased on account on May 15.
	30	Paid $50 interest expense on the note payable.
	31	Received a cash advance of $500 for services to be completed in June.
	31	Paid the employee's monthly salary, $2,475.

Instructions

(a) Prepare journal entries to record the transactions.
(b) Post the journal entries to ledger accounts. Use T accounts.
(c) Prepare a trial balance as at May 31, 2014.

TAKING IT FURTHER   Jacob asks if the change in his cash account balance, from the beginning to the end of the month, is equal to his profit or loss for the month. Explain to Jacob whether or not this is true and why.

Journalize transactions, post, and prepare trial balance. (SO 2, 3) AP

P2–6A Sequel Theatre, owned by Nadia Fedkovych, is unique as it shows only movies that are part of a theme with sequels. As at June 30, 2014, the ledger of Sequel Theatre showed the following: Cash, $17,000; Land, $80,000; Buildings, $70,000; Equipment, $20,000; Accounts Payable, $5,000; Mortgage Payable, $118,000; and N. Fedkovych, Capital, $64,000. In July, the following events and transactions occurred:

July	1	Rented the first four *Harry Potter* movies, to be shown in the first two weeks of July. The film rental was $25,000. Of that amount, $10,000 was paid in cash and the balance will be paid on July 15.
	2	Hired M. Brewer to operate the concession stand. Brewer agreed to pay Sequel Theatre 15% of gross concession receipts, on the last day of each month, for the right to operate the concession stand.
	3	Paid advertising expenses, $1,150.
	14	Received $35,600 cash from customers for admissions.
	15	Paid the balance due from the July 1 movie rental transaction.
	16	Received the final four *Harry Potter* movies to be shown in the last two weeks of July. The film rental cost was $30,000. Paid $15,000 cash and the balance will be paid on August 1.
	27	Paid the accounts payable owing at the end of June.
	30	Paid salaries of $6,200.
	31	Received statement from Brewer showing gross receipts from concessions of $27,300 and the balance due to Sequel Theatre of $4,095 ($27,300 × 15%) for July. Brewer paid $2,500 of the balance due and will pay the rest on August 5.
	31	Received $42,400 cash from admissions.
	31	Made a $1,725 mortgage payment. Of this amount, $1,250 is a principal payment, and $475 is interest on the mortgage.

In addition to the accounts identified above, Sequel Theatre's ledger includes the following: Accounts Receivable; Admission Revenue; Concession Revenue; Advertising Expense; Film Rental Expense; Interest Expense; and Salaries Expense.

Instructions

(a) Journalize the July transactions.
(b) Enter the beginning balances in the ledger as at July 1. Use the standard form of account.
(c) Post the July journal entries to the ledger.
(d) Prepare a trial balance at the end of July.

TAKING IT FURTHER   A friend of yours is considering buying Sequel Theatre from the current owner. Using the information in the trial balance, comment on whether or not this may be a sound company for your friend to purchase.

P2–7A   Aduke Zhawaki is a talented musician who runs a business teaching music and playing in gigs with a variety of other musicians. Her business is operated as a proprietorship, under the name A to Z Music, which has a December 31 year end. On November 30, 2014, the company's general ledger included the following accounts (all accounts have normal balances):

Journalize transactions, post, and prepare trial balance.
(SO 2, 3) AP

Cash	$ 2,965	A. Zhawaki, drawings	$31,350
Accounts receivable	2,200	Fees earned	47,075
Supplies	1,450	Insurance expense	3,410
Equipment	17,500	Rent expense	5,225
Accounts payable	4,235	Telephone expense	1,485
Unearned revenue	825	Travel expense	6,050
A. Zhawaki, capital	19,500		

December transactions were as follows:

Dec. 1   Paid December rent on her studio space, $475.
    1   Purchased additional sound equipment for $3,500 from a friend who was going back to school to study accounting. The equipment was probably worth $5,000, but the friend needed the cash for tuition and was anxious to sell it. Paid $1,500 cash and promised to pay the remaining amount by December 5.
    3   Borrowed $2,500 cash from her parents and signed a note payable.
    4   Paid her friend the remaining amount owing on the December 1 transaction.
    4   Collected $1,800 from customers in payment of their accounts.
    7   Paid the $310 monthly insurance premium.
    8   Paid for $150 of supplies.
    10   Paid $2,130 of the accounts payable from November.
    15   Gave musical performances at two recitals and earned $825. The customers had paid her in November. (*Hint:* In November Aduke had recorded the $825 received in advance as a liability, Unearned Revenue. By performing at the recitals, she has "paid" this obligation.)
    20   Received $3,300 cash from students for music lessons provided in December.
    21   Paid her monthly telephone bill of $135.
    22   Billed customers $2,250 for providing music at several holiday parties.
    24   Withdrew $3,000 for personal use.
    29   Received $525 cash advance from a customer for a performance in January.
    30   Travel expenses of $695 for December paid in cash.
    31   Paid her parents $210. Of this amount, $10 is interest and the remainder is a principal payment on the note payable.

Instructions

(a) Enter the November 30 balances in ledger accounts. Use T accounts.
(b) Journalize the December transactions.
(c) Post the December journal entries to the T accounts. Add new accounts if needed.
(d) Prepare a trial balance at December 31, 2014.

TAKING IT FURTHER   Comment on A to Z Music's cash balance at December 31, 2014. What concerns or suggestions do you have for Aduke to consider in January?

P2–8A   Refer to the trial balance for Abramson Financial Services prepared in P2–5A, part (c).

Prepare financial statements.
(SO 3) AP

Instructions

(a) Prepare an income statement for May.
(b) Prepare a statement of owner's equity for May.
(c) Prepare a balance sheet at the end of May 2014.

TAKING IT FURTHER   Discuss how well the company performed in its first month of operations.

P2–9A   Derek Scoffin owns and operates YH Curling School on evenings and weekends. The company had the following balances in its general ledger at January 31, 2014: Cash, $2,100; Accounts Receivable, $720; Equipment, $12,400; Accounts Payable, $1,470; and D. Scoffin, Capital, $13,750. The following events and transactions occurred during February 2014.

Journalize transactions, post, and prepare trial balance.
(SO 2, 3) AP

Feb.	1	Received and paid a $430 advertising bill.
	2	Paid the YH Curling Club $1,050 rent for use of the ice for lessons during the first two weeks of February.
	3	Collected $4,240 cash for February's curling lessons.
	4	Collected all of the accounts receivable at January 31 in cash.
	6	Paid $970 of the accounts payable at January 31.
	14	Paid his part-time assistant $400.
	15	Paid the YH Curling Club $1,050 rent for use of the ice for lessons during the last two weeks of February.
	23	Provided $1,475 of coaching services to curlers preparing for a tournament. The curlers will pay him on March 2.
	26	Paid $185 cash for his Internet bill for February. This is a business, not a personal, expense.
	27	Received $2,830 cash for curling lessons in March.
	27	Withdrew $575 cash. Used the cash to pay his Visa bill.
	28	Paid his part-time assistant $400.
	28	Paid the YH Curling Club $1,050 rent for use of the ice for lessons during the first two weeks of March.

Instructions

(a) Prepare journal entries to record each of YH Curling School's February transactions. (*Hint:* use the revenue account Fees Earned, for all revenue earned in February.)

(b) Open ledger accounts for each of the accounts listed in the trial balance, and enter the January 31, 2014, balances. Use T accounts.

(c) Post the journal entries to the accounts in the ledger.

(d) Prepare a trial balance as at February 28, 2014.

TAKING IT FURTHER   Are the February payments to YH Curling Club for ice rental an asset, a reduction of a liability, or an expense? Explain.

Prepare financial statements.
(SO 3) AP

P2–10A   Refer to the trial balance prepared in part (d) of P2–9A for YH Curling School.

Instructions

Use the trial balance to do the following:

(a) Prepare an income statement for YH Curling School.

(b) Prepare a statement of owner's equity.

(c) Prepare a balance sheet.

TAKING IT FURTHER   Derek has reviewed the financial statements. He does not understand why the company's revenue is not equal to the cash he collected from customers. Explain.

Prepare trial balance and
financial statements.
(SO 3) AP

P2–11A   The ledger of Super Delivery Service has the following account balances at the company's year end, August 31, 2014:

Accounts Payable	$ 3,235		Repairs Expense	$ 1,580
Accounts Receivable	4,275		Salaries Expense	5,665
Cash	?		Salaries Payable	925
Equipment	49,720		Service Revenue	37,780
Fuel Expense	12,145		Supplies	265
Insurance Expense	2,020		Supplies Expense	2,650
Interest Expense	975		T. Rowe, Capital	48,750
Notes Payable	19,500		T. Rowe, Drawings	24,400
Prepaid Insurance	405		Unearned Revenue	675

Instructions

(a) Prepare a trial balance, with the accounts arranged in ledger (financial statement) order, as illustrated in the chapter, and determine the missing amount for Cash.

(b) Prepare an income statement, statement of owner's equity, and balance sheet.

TAKING IT FURTHER   The owner, Tom Rowe, is not sure how much cash he can withdraw from the company each year. After reviewing the financial statements, comment on the amount he withdrew this year.

P2–12A   A co-op student, working for Insidz Co., recorded the company's transactions for the month. At the end of the month, the owner of Insidz Co. reviewed the student's work and had some questions about the following transactions:

Analyze errors and effects on trial balance.
(SO 3) AN

1. Insidz Co. received $425 cash from a customer on account, which was recorded as a debit to Cash of $425 and a credit to Accounts Receivable of $425.
2. A service provided for cash was posted as a debit to Cash of $2,000 and a credit to Service Revenue of $2,000.
3. A credit of $750 for interest earned was neither recorded nor posted. The debit was recorded and posted correctly.
4. The debit to record $1,000 of drawings was posted to the Salary Expense account. The credit was posted correctly.
5. Services of $325 were provided to a customer on account. The co-op student debited Accounts Receivable $325 and credited Unearned Revenue $325.
6. A purchase of supplies for $770 on account was recorded as a credit to Supplies and a credit to Accounts Payable.
7. Insidz Co. received a cash advance of $500 from a customer for work to be done next month. Cash was debited $500 but there was no credit because the co-op student was not sure what to credit.
8. A cash payment of $495 for salaries was recorded as a debit to Salaries Expense and a credit to Salaries Payable.
9. Insidz Co. purchased $2,600 of equipment on account and made a $6,200 debit to Equipment and a $2,600 credit to Accounts Payable.
10. A $650 utility bill for the month was received at the end of the month. It was not recorded because it had not been paid.

Instructions
(a) Indicate which transactions are correct and which are incorrect.
(b) For each error identified in (a), answer the following:
   1. Will the trial balance be in balance?
   2. Which account(s) will be incorrectly stated because of the error?
   3. For each account you identified in (2) as being incorrect, is the account overstated or understated? By how much?
   4. Is the debit column total of the trial balance stated correctly? If not, does correcting the errors increase or decrease the total and by how much?
   5. Is the credit column total of the trial balance stated correctly? If not, does correcting the errors increase or decrease the total and by how much?

TAKING IT FURTHER   Your best friend thinks it is a waste of time to correct all of the above errors. Your friend reasons that as long as the trial balance is balanced, then there is no need to correct an error. Do you agree or disagree with your friend? Explain, using at least two of the above errors to make your points.

P2–13A   The trial balance of Winter Co. does not balance:

Prepare correct trial balance.
(SO 3) AN

WINTER CO.
Trial Balance
June 30, 2014

	Debit	Credit
Cash	$ 2,835	
Accounts receivable	1,861	
Supplies	500	
Equipment		$ 7,900
Accounts payable		2,695
Unearned revenue	1,855	
F. Winter, capital		11,231
F. Winter, drawings	800	
Service revenue		3,460
Office expense	1,010	
Salaries expense	3,000	
	$11,861	$25,286

Your review of the ledger reveals that each account has a normal balance. You also discover the following errors:

1. Cash received from a customer on account was debited to Cash for $750 and Accounts Receivable was credited for the same amount. The actual collection was $570.
2. The purchase of supplies on account for $360 was recorded as a debit to Equipment for $360 and a credit to Accounts Payable for $360.
3. Services of $980 were performed on account for a client. Accounts Receivable was debited for $98 and Fees Earned was credited for $980.
4. A debit posting to Office Expense of $500 was not done.
5. A payment on account for $806 was credited to Cash for $806 and debited to Accounts Payable for $608.
6. The withdrawal of $400 cash for Winter's personal use was debited to Salaries Expense for $400 and credited to Cash for $400.
7. A transposition error (reversal of digits) was made when copying the balance in Service Revenue to the trial balance. The correct balance recorded in the account was $4,360.
8. The general ledger contained a Prepaid Insurance account with a debit balance of $655.

Instructions
Prepare a correct trial balance.

TAKING IT FURTHER   After the trial balance is corrected for the above errors, could there still be errors in any of the account balances? Explain why or why not.

▶ Problems: Set B

Identify type of account, financial statement, normal balances, and debits and credits. (SO 1) K

P2–1B   Walter Isaacson, Medical Practice, has the following accounts:

Salaries Payable	Equipment
Salaries Expense	Notes Payable
W. Isaacson, Drawings	Fees Earned
W. Isaacson, Capital	Interest Expense
Unearned Revenue	Insurance Expense
Rent Revenue	Land
Rent Expense	Building
Prepaid Rent	Cash
Supplies Expense	Accounts Receivable
Supplies	Accounts Payable

Instructions
For each of these accounts, identify (a) the type of account (e.g., asset, liability, owner's capital, drawings, revenue, expense); (b) what financial statement it is presented on; (c) the normal balance of the account; (d) whether the account is increased by a debit or credit; and (e) whether the account is decreased by a debit or credit. Use the following format, in which the first one has been done for you as an example.

	(a)	(b)	(c)	(d)	(e)
Account	Type of Account	Financial Statement	Normal Balance	Increase	Decrease
Salaries Payable	Liability	Balance Sheet	Credit	Credit	Debit

TAKING IT FURTHER   Explain the relationship between the normal balance in each type of account and the basic accounting equation.

Perform transaction analysis and journalize transactions. (SO 1, 2) AP

P2–2B   Battistella Couture & Design Co. began operations in 2012. During January 2014, the company had the following transactions:

Jan. 2   Paid January rent, $475.
    4   Finished sewing a suit, delivered it to the customer, and collected $975 cash.
    5   Purchased supplies for $250 on account.
    7   Received an order from another customer to design and sew a leather jacket for $885.
    10   Agreed to sew a wedding dress for a customer for $1,000. Received $500 cash from the customer as a down payment.

12   The owner, Karen Battistella, withdrew $700 cash for personal use.
18   Finished sewing the leather jacket (see January 7 transaction), and delivered it to the customer. The customer, a friend of Karen's, asked if she could pay at the end of the month. Karen agreed.
25   Paid for the supplies purchased on January 5.
27   The customer billed on January 18 paid the amount owing.
28   Borrowed $2,000 cash from the bank and signed a one-year, 5% note payable.
29   Used $1,950 of the bank loan to purchase a new pressing machine.

Instructions

(a) For each transaction, indicate: (1) the basic type of account debited and credited (asset, liability, or owner's equity); (2) the specific account debited and credited (Cash, Rent Expense, Service Revenue, etc.); and (3) whether each account is increased (+) or decreased (−), and by what amount. Use the following format, in which the first transaction is given as an example:

	Account Debited			Account Credited		
Transaction	Basic Type	Specific Account	Effect	Basic Type	Specific Account	Effect
Jan. 2	Owner's Equity	Rent Expense	+$475	Asset	Cash	−$475

(b) Prepare a journal entry for each transaction.

TAKING IT FURTHER   Karen is confused about why credits are used to decrease cash. She tells you that when she gets her bank statements, the bank uses credits when the balance in her bank account is increased. Explain.

P2–3B   Mountain Adventure Biking Park was started on May 1 by Dustin Tanner. The following events and transactions are for May:

Journalize transactions. (SO 2) AP

May 1   Tanner invested $50,000 cash in the business.
     3   Purchased an out-of-use ski hill for $355,000, paying $35,000 cash and signing a five-year, 4.5% note payable for the balance. The $355,000 purchase price consisted of land, $225,000; building, $75,000; and equipment, $55,000.
     3   Purchased a one-year insurance policy effective May 1 for $5,496. Paid the first month's premium of $458.
     8   Paid $1,950 for advertising expenses.
    15   Received $2,200 cash from customers for admission fees.
    16   Paid salaries to employees, $1,800.
    20   Billed a customer, Celtic Fern Ltd., $1,500 for admission fees for exclusive use of the park that day. Celtic Fern Ltd. paid $500 cash and agreed to pay the amount owing within 10 days.
    22   Hired a park manager to start June 1 at a salary of $4,000 per month.
    29   Received the balance owing cash from Celtic Fern Ltd. for the May 20 transaction.
    30   Received $4,800 cash for admission fees.
    31   Paid $3,800 on the note payable, of which $1,300 is interest expense.
    31   Dustin Tanner, the owner, withdrew $800 cash for his personal use.
    31   Paid salaries to employees, $1,800.

The company's chart of accounts includes the following accounts: Cash; Accounts Receivable; Prepaid Insurance; Land; Building; Equipment; Accounts Payable; Notes Payable; D. Tanner, Capital; D. Tanner, Drawings; Admissions Revenue; Advertising Expense; Salaries Expense; and Interest Expense.

Instructions

Journalize the May transactions.

TAKING IT FURTHER   After Dustin has reviewed the journal entries, he complains that they don't seem to be very useful. Explain to Dustin the purpose of the journal entries and the next step in the accounting cycle. Include in your answer whether or not Dustin will find any useful information after the next step is completed.

P2–4B   Thanh Nguyen started a business, Nguyen Import Services, on August 1, 2014. After consulting with a friend who had taken introductory accounting, Thanh created a chart of accounts for the business as follows: No. 101 Cash; No. 112 Accounts Receivable; No. 126 Supplies; No. 151 Equipment; No. 201 Accounts Payable; No. 209

Journalize transactions, post, and prepare trial balance. (SO 2, 3) AP

Unearned Revenue; No. 301 T. Nguyen, Capital; No. 306 T. Nguyen, Drawings; No. 400 Service Revenue; No. 610 Advertising Expense; No. 726 Rent Expense; and No. 737 Utilities Expense. During August, the following events and transactions occurred:

Aug. 1   Thanh transferred $25,000 cash from his personal bank account to a bank account under the company name, Nguyen Import Services.
      1   Signed a one-year rental agreement for $750 per month. Paid the first month's rent.
      2   Paid $250 for utilities for August.
      3   Purchased equipment for $5,250 cash.
      5   Purchased $675 of supplies on account.
      8   Provided services to a client and billed them $1,270.
      12   Paid $945 for advertising the opening of the company.
      20   Provided services to a client and collected $1,320 cash.
      24   Received a $2,500 cash advance for a consulting engagement to be started in September.
      25   Paid the balance due for the purchase of supplies on August 5.
      28   Received $970 cash from the client billed in the August 8 transaction.
      29   Paid Thanh, the owner, $1,225 cash for his personal use.
      31   Received a $225 utility bill for August. It will be paid on September 1.

Instructions

(a) Journalize the transactions.
(b) Post to the ledger accounts. Use the standard form of account.
(c) Prepare a trial balance at August 31, 2014.

TAKING IT FURTHER   Thanh asks why separate drawings, revenue, and expense accounts are necessary since all of these accounts are owner's equity accounts. Thanh thinks he should be able to use one account. Explain if he is correct or not.

Journalize transactions, post, and prepare trial balance.
(SO 2, 3) AP

P2–5B   Kiersted Financial Services was formed on November 1, 2014. During the month of November, the following events and transactions occurred:

Nov. 1   Haakon Kiersted, the owner, invested $35,000 cash in the company. He also invested equipment that had originally cost Haakon $25,000 but was currently worth $12,000.
      2   Hired one employee to work in the office for a monthly salary of $2,825.
      3   Signed a three-year contract to lease office space for $2,140 per month. Paid the first and last month's rent in cash. (*Hint:* The payment for the final month's rent should be considered an asset and be recorded in Prepaid Rent.)
      4   Purchased a one-year insurance policy for $4,740 to be paid in monthly instalments on the fourth day of each month. Paid the first month's premium.
      5   Purchased additional equipment for $18,000. Paid $6,000 cash and signed a note payable for the balance.
      6   Purchased supplies for $1,550 on account.
      7   Purchased additional supplies for $475 cash.
      16   Completed services for a customer and immediately collected $990.
      20   Completed services for two customers and billed them a total of $4,500.
      26   Paid $1,000 for the supplies purchased on account on November 6.
      27   The telephone bill for November was $220. It will be paid in December.
      27   Received a $750 cash advance from a customer for services to be provided in December.
      29   Collected $2,800 from one of the customers billed on November 20.
      30   Paid $60 interest on the note payable.
      30   Paid the employee's monthly salary, $2,825.
      30   Paid Haakon Kiersted $700 for his personal use.
      30   Paid Sony Ltd. for a new sound system for Haakon's home, $1,150 cash.

Instructions

(a) Prepare journal entries to record the transactions.
(b) Post the journal entries to T accounts.
(c) Prepare a trial balance as at November 30, 2014.

TAKING IT FURTHER   Haakon asks if the change in his cash account balance from the beginning to the end of the month is equal to his profit or loss for the month. Explain to Haakon whether or not this is true and why.

P2-6B Highland Theatre is owned by Finnean Ferguson. At June 30, 2014, the ledger showed the following: Cash, $6,000; Land, $100,000; Buildings, $80,000; Equipment, $25,000; Accounts Payable, $5,000; Mortgage Payable, $125,000; and F. Ferguson, Capital, $81,000. During July, the following events and transactions occurred:

Journalize transactions, post, and prepare trial balance.
(SO 2, 3) AP

July 2   Paid film rental of $800 on first movie to run in July.
2   Paid advertising expenses, $620.
3   Ordered two additional films at $750 each.
5   Highland Theatre contracted with Seibert Company to operate a concession stand. Seibert agreed to pay Highland Theatre 20% of gross concession receipts, payable monthly, for the right to operate the concession stand.
10   Received $1,950 cash from admissions.
11   Paid $2,000 of the mortgage principal. Also paid $500 interest on the mortgage.
12   Paid $350 cash to have the projection equipment repaired.
16   Paid $2,800 of the accounts payable.
19   Received one of the films ordered on July 3 and was billed $750. The film will be shown in July.
29   Received $3,500 cash from customers for admissions.
30   Paid Finnean Ferguson $1,200 for his personal use.
30   Prepaid a $700 rental on a special film to be shown in August.
31   Paid salaries, $1,900.
31   Received a statement from Seibert. It shows gross concession receipts of $2,600 and a balance due to Highland Theatre of $520 ($2,600 × 20%) for July. Seibert paid one half of the balance due and will pay the rest on August 5.

In addition to the accounts identified above, Highland Theatre's ledger includes the following: Accounts Receivable; Prepaid Film Rental; F. Ferguson, Drawings; Admission Revenue; Concession Revenue; Advertising Expense; Film Rental Expense; Repairs Expense; Salaries Expense; and Interest Expense.

Instructions

(a) Journalize the July transactions.
(b) Enter the beginning balances in the ledger as at June 30. Use the standard form of account.
(c) Post the July journal entries to the ledger.
(d) Prepare a trial balance at the end of July 2014.

TAKING IT FURTHER A friend of yours is considering buying Highland Theatre from the current owner. Using the information in the trial balance, comment on whether or not this may be a sound company for your friend to purchase.

P2-7B Lena Kuznetsova provides coaching and mentoring services to individuals and companies. She operates the business as a proprietorship, under the name LVK Coaching Services, which has a December 31 year end. On November 30, 2014, the company's general ledger included the following accounts (all accounts have normal balances):

Journalize transactions, post, and prepare trial balance.
(SO 2, 3) AP

Cash	$ 7,315	L. Kuznetsova, Drawings	$34,200
Accounts Receivable	4,020	Service Revenue	55,175
Supplies	1,805	Advertising Expense	3,550
Equipment	21,500	Insurance Expense	3,135
Accounts Payable	8,660	Rent Expense	8,250
Unearned Revenue	1,370	Salaries Expense	10,560
L. Kuznetsova, Capital	29,130		

December transactions were as follows:

Dec. 1   Paid December rent on her office space, $750.
1   Purchased additional equipment with a manufacturer's suggested price of $4,000. After negotiations with the retailer, paid $1,500 cash and signed a note payable for $2,000.
4   Collected $2,850 from customers in payment of their accounts.
7   Paid the $285 monthly insurance premium.
8   Purchased $315 of supplies on account.
10   Paid $5,660 of the accounts payable from November.
12   Finished a coaching contract with a client and earned $1,370. The client had paid her in November. (*Hint:* In November, Lena had recorded the $1,370 as a liability, Unearned Revenue. By finishing the coaching contract, she has "paid" this obligation.)

20	Received $3,055 cash from clients for services provided in December.
21	Paid monthly charges for maintaining a website advertising her services, $325.
24	Withdrew $2,650 for personal use.
28	Billed clients $2,250 for coaching services provided in December. These clients will pay in January.
29	Received $925 cash advance from a client for a coaching contract that will start in January.
30	Paid part-time office assistant, $960.
31	Made a $170 payment on the note payable. Of this amount, $10 is interest and the remainder is a principal payment on the note payable.

Instructions

(a) Enter the November 30 balances in ledger accounts. Use T accounts.
(b) Journalize the December transactions.
(c) Post the December journal entries to the T accounts. Add new accounts if needed.
(d) Prepare a trial balance at December 31, 2014.

TAKING IT FURTHER   Comment on the company's cash balance. What concerns and suggestions do you have for the company to consider in January?

Prepare financial statements.
(SO 3) AP

P2–8B   Refer to the trial balance prepared for Kiersted Financial Services in P2–5B, part (c).

Instructions

(a) Prepare an income statement.
(b) Prepare a statement of owner's equity.
(c) Prepare a balance sheet.

TAKING IT FURTHER   Discuss how well the company did in its first month of operations.

Journalize transactions, post, and prepare trial balance.
(SO 2, 3) AP

P2–9B   Hobson Nolan is a human resources professional who operates a consulting practice under the name HN HR Consulting. The company had the following balances in its general ledger at February 28, 2014: Cash, $3,500; Accounts Receivable, $14,450; Equipment, $15,100; Accounts Payable, $18,750; and H. Nolan, Capital, $14,300. The following events and transactions occurred during March 2014.

Mar.	1	Borrowed $12,000 cash from the bank, signing a note payable.
	2	Paid $13,000 to creditors on account.
	3	Paid the monthly insurance premium of $145.
	10	Paid the monthly charge of $550 for keeping the company's website up to date. The company uses the website to advertise its services.
	16	Collected accounts receivable of $8,000.
	18	Paid an additional $5,000 to creditors on account.
	30	Miscellaneous expenses were paid in cash, $580.
	31	Consulting services provided in March were for $2,000 cash and $5,000 on account.
	31	Paid salaries, $1,650.
	31	Paid the bank $555 on the note payable, of which $55 is interest and $500 is a partial payment of the note.
	31	Paid March and April's rent, which totalled $1,900 ($950 per month).
	31	Withdrew $1,000 cash for personal use.

Instructions

(a) Prepare journal entries to record each of the March transactions.
(b) Open ledger accounts for each of the accounts listed in the trial balance, and enter the February 28, 2014, balances. Use T accounts.
(c) Post the journal entries to the accounts in the ledger.
(d) Prepare a trial balance as at the end of March.

TAKING IT FURTHER   Is the March 31 rent payment an asset or an expense? Explain.

Prepare financial statements.
(SO 3) AP

P2–10B   Refer to the trial balance prepared in part (d) of P2–9B for HN HR Consulting.

Instructions

Use the trial balance to do the following:

(a) Prepare an income statement.
(b) Prepare a statement of owner's equity.
(c) Prepare a balance sheet.

TAKING IT FURTHER Hobson would like to close the business and retire. He has reviewed the financial statements, and thinks he will be able to take out cash equal to the balance in his capital account. Do you agree? Why or why not?

P2–11B   The ledger of Lazdowski Marketing Services has the following account balances at the company's year end, October 31, 2014:

Prepare trial balance and financial statements.
(SO 3) AP

Accounts payable	$ 4,430	Insurance expense	$ 2,020
Accounts receivable	6,010	Interest expense	2,445
Advertising expense	14,970	Notes payable	48,850
Cash	4,930	Prepaid rent	975
Equipment	25,970	Rent expense	11,700
Fees earned	?	Salaries expense	20,545
Furniture	56,685	Supplies	1,240
I. Lazdowski, capital	57,410	Supplies expense	5,000
I. Lazdowski, drawings	75,775	Unearned revenue	3,555

Instructions

(a) Prepare a trial balance, with the accounts arranged in ledger (financial statement) order, as illustrated in the chapter, and determine the missing amount for fees earned.
(b) Prepare an income statement, statement of owner's equity, and balance sheet.

TAKING IT FURTHER The owner, Inga Lazdowski, is not sure how much cash she can withdraw from the company each year. After reviewing the financial statements, comment on the amount she withdrew this year.

P2–12B   The bookkeeper for Shigeru's Dance Studio did the following in journalizing and posting:

Analyze errors and effects on trial balance.
(SO 3) AN

1. A debit posting to Prepaid Insurance of $3,600 was not done.
2. A debit posting of $500 to Accounts Receivable was debited to Accounts Payable.
3. A purchase of supplies on account of $850 was debited to Supplies for $850 and credited to Accounts Payable for $850.
4. A credit to Salaries Payable for $1,200 was posted as a credit to Cash.
5. A credit posting of $250 to Cash was posted twice.
6. A debit side of the entry to record the payment of $1,200 for drawings was posted to Salaries Expense.
7. A credit to Unearned Revenue for $400 was posted as a credit to Service Revenue.
8. A credit to Accounts Payable of $375 was posted as a debit to Accounts Payable.
9. A purchase of equipment on account for $6,800 was posted as an $8,600 debit to Equipment and an $8,600 debit to Cash.
10. The provision of $950 of services on account was not recorded because the customer did not pay cash until the following month.

Instructions

(a) Indicate which of the above transactions are correct and which are incorrect.
(b) For each error identified in (a), answer the following:
   1. Will the trial balance be in balance?
   2. Which account(s) will be incorrectly stated because of the error?
   3. For each account identified in (2) as being incorrect, is the account overstated or understated and by how much?
   4. Is the debit column total of the trial balance stated correctly? If not, does correcting the errors increase or decrease the total and by how much?
   5. Is the credit column total of the trial balance stated correctly? If not, does correcting the errors increase or decrease the total and by how much?

TAKING IT FURTHER Your best friend thinks it is a waste of time to correct all of the above errors. Your friend reasons that as long as the trial balance is balanced, then there is no need to correct an error. Do you agree or disagree with your friend? Explain using at least two of the above errors to make your points.

Prepare correct trial balance.
(SO 3) AN

P2–13B   The trial balance that follows for Shawnee Slopes Company does not balance:

SHAWNEE SLOPES COMPANY
Trial Balance
June 30, 2014

	Debit	Credit
Cash	$ 5,875	
Accounts receivable		$ 3,620
Equipment	14,020	
Accounts payable	5,290	
Property taxes payable		500
A. Shawnee, capital		17,900
Service revenue	7,027	
Advertising expense		1,132
Property tax expense	1,100	
Salaries expense	4,150	
Totals	$37,462	$23,152

Your review of the ledger reveals that each account has a normal balance. You also discover the following errors:

1. Property Tax Expense was understated by $500 and Property Tax Payable was overstated by $500.
2. A $650 credit to Service Revenue was incorrectly posted as a $560 credit.
3. A debit posting to Salaries Expense of $350 was not done.
4. A $750 cash withdrawal by the owner was debited to A. Shawnee, Capital, for $750 and credited to Cash for $750.
5. A $650 purchase of supplies on account was debited to Equipment for $650 and credited to Cash for $650.
6. A cash payment of $120 for advertising was debited to Advertising Expense for $210 and credited to Cash for $210.
7. A $385 collection from a customer was debited to Cash for $385 and debited to Accounts Receivable for $385.
8. A cash payment on account for $165 was recorded as a $165 credit to Cash and a $165 credit to Accounts Payable.
9. A $2,000 note payable was issued to purchase equipment. The transaction was neither journalized nor posted.

Instructions

Prepare a correct trial balance. (*Note:* You may need to add new accounts.)

TAKING IT FURTHER   After the trial balance is corrected for the above errors, could there still be errors? Explain why or why not.

▶ Continuing Cookie Chronicle

(**Note:** The Continuing Cookie Chronicle began in Chapter 1 and will continue in each chapter.)

After researching the different forms of business organization, Natalie Koebel decides to operate Cookie Creations as a proprietorship. She then starts the process of getting the business running. During the months of November and December 2013, the following activities take place:

Nov. 12   Natalie cashes her Canada Savings Bonds and receives $980, which she deposits in her personal bank account.

   12   She opens a bank account under the name "Cookie Creations" and transfers $900 from her personal account to the new account.

   18   Natalie pays $325 to advertise in the November 29 issue of her community newspaper. Natalie hopes that this ad will generate revenue during the months of November and December.

20 She buys supplies, such as flour, sugar, butter, and chocolate chips, for $198 cash.

25 Natalie starts to gather some equipment to take with her when teaching the cookie classes. She has an excellent top-of-the-line food processor and mixer that originally cost her $825. Natalie decides to start using it only in her new business. She estimates that the equipment is currently worth $550.

26 Natalie teaches her first class, a group of Grade 2 students, how to make sugar cookies. At the end of the class, Natalie leaves an invoice for $300 with the school principal. The principal says that she will pass the invoice along to the school board and the invoice will be paid sometime in December.

27 A $98 invoice is received for the use of Natalie's cell phone. The cell phone is used exclusively for Cookie Creations' business. The invoice is for services provided in November and is due on December 13.

29 Natalie realizes that her initial cash investment is not enough. Her grandmother lends her $3,000 cash, for which Natalie signs a one-year, 3% note payable in the name of the business. Natalie deposits the money in the business bank account.

Dec. 2 Natalie teaches a class and collects $250 cash.

3 Natalie buys more equipment for $1,000 cash.

9 The school where Natalie taught her first class is in touch and wishes for Natalie to teach all of the Grade 3 and 4 students how to make sugar cookies. Natalie is thrilled! She anticipates teaching at least five classes at the school. She receives $125 in advance as a down payment.

13 Natalie pays the amount outstanding on her cell phone bill.

16 Natalie receives and deposits the amount outstanding from the November 26 transaction.

17 Natalie receives an unexpected invitation to teach a cookie-making class at a children's Christmas party. At the end of the class, she prepares an invoice for $500 and leaves it with the organization's corporate controller. The controller indicates that the invoice will likely be paid in the next 30 days.

30 A $76 invoice is received for the use of Natalie's cell phone. The invoice is for services provided in December and is due on January 15, 2014.

Instructions

(a) Prepare journal entries to record the transactions.
(b) Post the journal entries to ledger accounts. Use T accounts.
(c) Prepare a trial balance as at December 31, 2013.

BROADENING YOUR PERSPECTIVE | CHAPTER 2

Financial Reporting and Analysis

Financial Reporting Problem

BYP2–1 The financial statements of **Reitmans (Canada) Limited** for 2012 are shown in Appendix A at the back of this textbook. They contain the following selected accounts:

Administrative expenses	Long-term debt
Cash and cash equivalents	Prepaid expenses
Finance costs	Sales
Inventories	Trade and other payables

Instructions

(a) Answer the following questions:
   1. In which financial statement is the account included?
   2. Is it an asset, liability, revenue, or expense?

3. What is the normal balance (debit or credit) for each of these accounts?
4. What are the increase side and decrease side (debit or credit) for each of these accounts?
(b) Identify the probable other account(s) in the transaction, and the effect on that account(s), when:
  1. Trade and other payables are decreased.   4. Inventory is increased.
  2. Long-term debt is increased.   5. Prepaid expenses are increased.
  3. Sales are increased.

Interpreting Financial Statements

BYP2–2   WestJet Airlines Ltd. is one of the most profitable airlines in North America. The following list of accounts and amounts was taken from its December 31, 2011, financial statements (in thousands):

Accounts payable and accrued liabilities	$ 307,279
Accounts receivable	34,122
Advance ticket sale liability	432,186
Aircraft fuel, leasing, and maintenance expense	1,227,709
Airport operations expense	421,561
Cash	1,291,946
Deferred income tax liability	326,456
Depreciation and amortization expense	174,751
Employee profit share expense	23,804
Flight operations and navigational charges	483,920
Guest revenues	2,790,299
Income tax expense	59,304
Intangible and other assets	137,752
Inventory	31,695
Long-term debt	828,712
Maintenance provisions liability	151,645
Marketing, general, and administration expense	209,880
Non-operating expenses	48,545
Non-refundable guest credits liability	43,485
Other liabilities	13,698
Other revenues	281,241
Prepaid expenses and deposits	66,936
Property and equipment	1,911,227
Sales and distribution expense	273,364
Shareholders' (owners) "drawings"	82,718
Shareholders' (owners) equity, January 1, 2011	1,304,233

Instructions

(a) WestJet Airlines Ltd. is a corporation. Which of the items listed above are used only in corporations?
(b) Prepare a trial balance for WestJet with the accounts in financial statement order.
(c) WestJet has grouped several items together in its financial statements. For example, marketing, general, and administration expenses are shown as one amount. What are some possible reasons for doing this?
(d) In Chapter 2, you learned about unearned revenue. Would you expect a company like WestJet to have unearned revenue? If so, what account name has WestJet used for its unearned revenue?

⏵ Critical Thinking

Collaborative Learning Activity

Note to instructor: Additional instructions and material for this group activity can be found on the Instructor Resource Site and in *WileyPLUS.*

BYP2–3   In this group activity, students will be given a trial balance and will be asked to work backwards to create a set of journal entries that would result in the trial balance.

Communication Activity

BYP2–4   White Glove Company offers home cleaning services. Three common transactions for the company are signing contracts with new customers, billing customers for services performed, and paying employee salaries. For example, on March 15 the company did the following:

1. Signed a contract with a new customer for $125 per week starting the first week in April.
2. Sent bills that totalled $6,000 to customers.
3. Paid $2,000 in salaries to employees.

Instructions

Write an e-mail to your instructor that explains if and how these transactions are recorded in the double-entry system. Include in your e-mail (a) whether, and why, the transaction should or should not be recorded, and (b) how the debit and credit rules are applied if the transaction is recorded.

Ethics Case

BYP2–5   Vu Hung is the assistant chief accountant at Lim Company, a manufacturer of computer chips and cellular phones. The company currently has total sales of $20 million. It is the end of the first quarter. Vu is hurriedly trying to prepare a general ledger trial balance so that quarterly financial statements can be prepared and released to management and regulatory agencies. The credits on the trial balance add up to $1,000 more than the debits.

In order to meet the 4:00 p.m. deadline, Vu decides to force the debits and credits into balance by adding the amount of the difference to the Equipment account. She chose Equipment because it is one of the larger account balances. Proportionally, it will be the least misstated. She believes that the difference will not affect anyone's decisions. She wishes that she had more time to find the error, but realizes that the financial statements are already late.

Instructions

(a) Who are the stakeholders in this situation?
(b) What are the ethical issues involved?
(c) What are Vu's alternatives?

"All About You" Activity

BYP2–6   The "All About You" feature indicates that Luca Pacioli, who described the double-entry accounting system used over 500 years ago, wrote "a person should not go to sleep at night until the debits equalled the credits."

In the double-entry system, debits and credits are used to record the dual effect of each transaction in the appropriate accounts and to keep the basic accounting equation in balance. For each transaction, the debits must equal the credits; therefore, the total debits and credits for all of the accounts should be equal. If the total debits do not equal the credits, there is an error in the accounting records.

You are a first-year university student and very excited about moving away from home to go to university. Your parents have given you $4,000 and you have a $14,000 student loan. Your parents have told you that $4,000 is all you get for the school year and you are not to phone home for more money.

At September 1, you had $18,000 cash ($4,000 + $14,000), $1,000 worth of clothes, and a cell phone that cost $200. You have kept all of the receipts for all of your expenditures between September 1 and December 15. The following is a complete list of your receipts.

Receipts	Amount
Rent on furnished apartment ($400 per month)	$1,600
Damage deposit on apartment	400
Groceries	1,200
Tuition for September to December	2,800
Textbooks	600
Entertainment (movies, beverages, restaurants)	1,500
New clothes	1,500
Cell phone charges	250
Cable TV and Internet bill	200
Computer	1,000
Eight-month bus pass (September to April)	500
Airfare to go home at Christmas	450

PERSONAL TRIAL BALANCE
December 15, 2014

Account	Debit	Credit
Cash	$ 6,500	
Clothes	2,500	
Cell phone	200	
Computer	100	
Student loan		$14,000
Personal equity		5,200
Rent expense	2,000	
Groceries		1,200
Tuition for September to December	2,800	
Textbooks for September to December	600	
Entertainment expense	1,500	
Cell phone expense	250	
Cable TV and Internet expense	200	
Bus pass expense	500	
Airfare	540	
	$17,690	$20,400

On December 15, you checked the balance in your bank account and you only have $6,000 cash. You can't sleep, because you know there are some errors in your accounting records and that you will probably have to ask your parents for more money for the next semester.

Instructions

(a) Calculate your personal equity (deficit) at September 1, 2014.
(b) Prepare a corrected trial balance at December 15, 2014. For each error identified, describe the error.
(c) Calculate your total expenses for the semester and your personal equity (deficit) at December 15, 2014.
(d) Prepare a personal balance sheet at December 15, 2014.
(e) Assuming you will have the same expenses in the second semester, will you have enough cash to pay for them?
(f) Are there any expenses you might be able to avoid in the second semester to save cash?
(g) Are there any additional cash expenditures that will need to be made in the second semester?
(h) Will it be necessary for you to ask your parents for more money for the next semester? Explain.

ANSWERS TO CHAPTER QUESTIONS

ANSWERS TO ACCOUNTING IN ACTION INSIGHT QUESTIONS

Business Insight, p. 63

Q: What are the issues involved in determining if a signing bonus is an asset or an expense?

A: Signing bonuses are paid because a company expects to benefit in the future from hiring the individual. Bonuses could be recorded as an asset at the time they are paid. A decision would be made by the team's management to treat the bonus as an expense once the benefit represented by this asset was used up. In the NHL, they would have to consider such things as the length of the contract, how well the player is performing, and whether or not the player is injured in order to decide when to record the bonus as an expense.

All About You Insight, p. 76

Q: Pacioli also wrote "a person should not go to sleep at night until the debits equalled the credits." Is this still good advice over 500 years later?

A: Perseverance can be a very useful attribute for an accounting student. Sometimes it can be difficult and time-consuming to find an error and correct it. Many students find this very frustrating and give up too soon and thus miss the opportunity to learn and increase their confidence. On the other hand, sleep is very important and can provide you with a fresh perspective the next day.

ANSWERS TO SELF-STUDY QUESTIONS

1. b   2. d   3. a   4. d   5. b   6. d   7. a   8. a   9. c   10. d   11. a   12. c

Remember to go back to the beginning of the chapter to check off your completed work!

←

CHAPTER THREE

ADJUSTING THE ACCOUNTS

 THE **NAVIGATOR**

- ☐ Understand *Concepts for Review*
- ☐ Read *Feature Story*
- ☐ Scan *Study Objectives*
- ☐ Read *Chapter Preview*
- ☐ Read text and answer *Before You Go On*
- ☐ Review *Comparing IFRS and ASPE*
- ☐ Work *Demonstration Problem*
- ☐ Review *Summary of Study Objectives*
- ☐ Answer *Self-Study Questions*
- ☐ Complete assignments
- ☐ Go to *WileyPLUS* for practice and tutorials

CONCEPTS FOR **REVIEW**

Before studying this chapter, you should understand or, if necessary, review:

a. The double-entry accounting system. (Ch. 2, p. 61)

b. How to increase and decrease assets, liabilities, and owner's equity accounts using debit and credit procedures. (Ch. 2, pp. 58–61)

c. How to journalize transactions. (Ch. 2, pp. 64–65)

d. How to post transactions to the general ledger. (Ch. 2, pp. 65–67)

e. How to prepare a trial balance. (Ch. 2, pp. 75–77)

ADJUSTING THE BOOKS AFTER HITTING THE BOOKS

TORONTO, ON—You probably pay your tuition just before classes start in September, but how does your college or university account for your money after that?

In Ontario, all colleges have a fiscal year that ends on March 31, which is also the provincial government's fiscal year end. "All the colleges' financial information is fully consolidated onto the province's books," explains Jeanette Dias D'Souza, former Vice President of Finance and Administration at Seneca College of Applied Arts & Technology, with 10 locations in the Greater Toronto area.

Many academic years end in late April, however. According to what's called accrual accounting, any revenues for services performed after March 31 have to be recognized in the following fiscal year, even though the money was collected earlier. So if a study term ends in late April, a small portion of the tuition for that semester will be recognized as revenue by the college in the next fiscal year.

The same revenue recognition criteria applies for students who study in the summer term: if they pay tuition before March 31, it can't be recognized as revenue until the teaching services are performed in the summer. That term is important

for Seneca. "We have a very large summer program," says Ms. Dias D'Souza.

Seneca's main sources of operating funding are provincial grants and student tuition fees. It also receives revenue from private and corporate training. As with tuition fees, revenue from this training is recognized in the period in which the training is provided.

The college also receives revenue from renting space for private functions, including Eaton Hall, a former estate of the famed Eaton retailing family that is located on one of Seneca's campuses. If an engaged couple puts down a deposit in February for their July wedding, that revenue is not recognized until the wedding takes place in the next fiscal year, Ms. Dias D'Souza says.

Expenses, too, must be recorded in the year when they are incurred. For example, Seneca's invoices for utilities and legal fees for the last month of the fiscal year tend to come in after the year end, so the college uses estimates to accrue for these expenses at the year end.

Recording revenues and expenses in the correct period is a challenge, but one that must be met to properly reflect the school's activity in each period.

THE **NAVIGATOR**

>> STUDY **OBJECTIVES**

After studying this chapter, you should be able to:

1. Explain accrual basis accounting, and when to recognize revenues and expenses.

2. Prepare adjusting entries for prepayments.

3. Prepare adjusting entries for accruals.

4. Describe the nature and purpose of an adjusted trial balance, and prepare one.

5. Prepare adjusting entries for the alternative treatment of prepayments (Appendix 3A).

THE **NAVIGATOR**

In Chapter 2, we learned the accounting cycle up to and including the preparation of the trial balance. In this chapter, we will learn that additional steps are usually needed before preparing the financial statements. These steps adjust accounts for timing mismatches, like the ones Seneca College has with the tuition it receives for its summer classes and the costs it incurs to offer these classes. In this chapter, we introduce the accrual accounting concepts that guide the adjustment process.

The chapter is organized as follows:

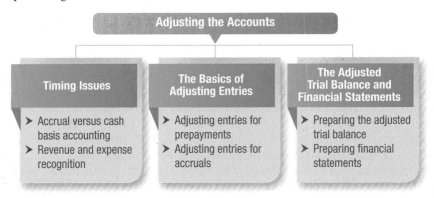

Timing Issues

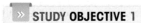

STUDY OBJECTIVE 1

Explain accrual basis accounting, and when to recognize revenues and expenses.

Accounting would be simple if we could wait until a company ended its operations before preparing its financial statements. As the following anecdote shows, if we waited until then we could easily determine the amount of lifetime profit earned:

> A grocery store owner from the old country kept his accounts payable on a wire memo spike, accounts receivable on a notepad, and cash in a shoebox. His daughter, a CGA, chided her father: "I don't understand how you can run your business this way. How do you know what you've earned?"
>
> "Well," her father replied, "when I arrived in Canada 40 years ago, I had nothing but the pants I was wearing. Today, your brother is a doctor, your sister is a teacher, and you are a CGA. Your mother and I have a nice car, a well-furnished house, and a home by the lake. We have a good business and everything is paid for. So, you add all that together, subtract the pants, and there's your profit."

Although the grocer may be correct in his evaluation about how to calculate his profit over his lifetime, most companies need more immediate feedback on how they are doing. For example, management usually wants monthly financial statements. Investors want to view the results of publicly traded companies at least quarterly. The Canada Revenue Agency requires financial statements to be filed with annual income tax returns.

Consequently, accountants divide the life of a business into specific time periods, such as a month, a three-month quarter, or a year. An accounting time period that is one year long is called a fiscal year. Time periods of less than one year are called interim periods.

The fiscal year used by many businesses is the same as the calendar year (January 1 to December 31). However, it can be different. Seneca College's fiscal year is April 1 through March 31, which is typical of many colleges, universities, and governments. Some retail companies use a 52-week period, instead of exactly one year, for their fiscal year. Reitmans (Canada) Limited does this, and has chosen the last Saturday in January as the end of its fiscal year. But because 52 weeks isn't exactly equal to one year, some years Reitmans has to use a 53-week period with the first Saturday in February as its fiscal year end.

Because the life of a business is divided into accounting time periods, determining when to record transactions is important. Many business transactions affect more than one accounting time period. For example, equipment is used over several years. We also saw in the feature story that sometimes Seneca College collects tuition fees in one fiscal year and then teaches the course in the next fiscal year. In the following section, we will see that deciding when to recognize revenues and expenses will have a significant impact on the usefulness of financial statements.

ACCRUAL VERSUS CASH BASIS ACCOUNTING

There are two ways of deciding when to recognize or record revenues and expenses:

1. **Accrual basis accounting** means that transactions and other **events are recorded in the period when they occur, and not when the cash is paid or received.** For example, service revenue is recognized when it is earned, rather than when the cash is received. Expenses are recognized when services (e.g., salaries) or goods (e.g., supplies) are used or consumed, rather than when the cash is paid.
2. Under **cash basis accounting**, revenue is recorded when cash is received, and expenses are recorded when cash is paid.

Which one provides better information for users when they make decisions about companies? To answer that question, consider this simple example. Suppose you own a painting company and you paint a large building during year 1. In year 1, you pay $50,000 cash for the cost of the paint and your employees' salaries. Assume that you bill your customer $80,000 at the end of year 1, and that you receive the cash from your customer in year 2.

On an accrual basis, the revenue is reported during the period when the service is performed—year 1. Expenses, such as employees' salaries and the paint used, are recorded in the period in which the employees provide their services and the paint is used—year 1. Thus, your profit for year 1 is $30,000. No revenue or expense from this project is reported in year 2.

If, instead, you were reporting on a cash basis, you would report expenses of $50,000 in year 1 because you paid for them in year 1. Revenues of $80,000 would be recorded in year 2 because you received cash from the customer in year 2. For year 1, you would report a loss of $50,000. For year 2, you would report a profit of $80,000.

Illustration 3-1 summarizes this information and shows the differences between the accrual-based numbers and cash-based numbers.

	Year 1		Year 2	
Activity				
	Purchased paint, painted building, paid employees		Received payment for work done in year 1	
Accrual basis	Revenue	$ 80,000	Revenue	$ 0
	Expenses	50,000	Expenses	0
	Profit	$ 30,000	Profit	$ 0
Cash basis	Revenue	$ 0	Revenue	$80,000
	Expenses	50,000	Expenses	0
	Loss	$(50,000)	Profit	$80,000

▶ **ILLUSTRATION 3-1**
Accrual versus cash basis accounting

Note that the total profit for years 1 and 2 is $30,000 for both the accrual and cash bases. However, the difference in when the revenue and expense are recognized causes a difference in the amount of profit or loss each year. Which basis provides better information about how profitable your efforts were each year? It's the accrual basis, because it shows the profit earned on the job in the same year as when the work was performed.

Thus, accrual basis accounting is widely recognized as being significantly more useful for decision-making than cash basis accounting. In fact, it is assumed that all financial statements are prepared using accrual basis accounting. This means there is no need to report that the accrual basis has been used.

While accrual basis accounting provides better information, it is more complex than cash basis accounting. It is easy to determine when to recognize revenues or expenses if the only determining factor is when the cash is received or paid. But when using the accrual basis, it is necessary to have standards about when to record revenues and expenses.

REVENUE AND EXPENSE RECOGNITION

Recall that revenue is an increase in assets—or a decrease in liabilities—as the result of the company's business activities with its customers. Revenue recognition criteria provide guidance about when this increase in assets (or decrease in liabilities) has happened and thus when revenue is to be recognized. In general, revenue is recognized when the service has been performed or the goods have been sold and delivered. We also need to ensure that revenue can be reliably measured, and collection is reasonably certain, when recognizing revenue.

Revenue recognition criteria follow accrual basis accounting—revenue is recognized in the period when it is earned. Recall that in the painting example shown in Illustration 3-1, revenue was recorded in year 1 when the service was performed. At that point, there was an increase in the painting businesses assets—specifically Accounts Receivable—as the result of doing the work. At the end of year 1, the painting business would report the receivable on its balance sheet and revenue on its income statement for the service performed. In year 2, when the cash is received, the painting business records a reduction of its receivables, not revenue.

Expense recognition criteria provide guidance about when to record expenses. Recall that expenses are a decrease in assets—or an increase in liabilities—excluding transactions with the owner. Expenses are the costs of assets that are consumed and services that are used in a company's business activities. Expense recognition is tied to revenue recognition when there is a direct association between costs incurred and the earning of revenue. For example, as we saw with the painting business, under accrual basis accounting the salaries and cost of the paint for the painting in year 1 are reported in the income statement for the same period in which the service revenue is recognized. This process is commonly referred to as matching.

Sometimes, however, there is no direct relationship between expenses and revenue. For example, we will see in the next section that long-lived assets may be used to help generate revenue over many years, but the use of the asset is not directly related to earning specific revenue. In these cases, we will see that expenses are recognized in the income statement over the life of the asset.

In other cases, the benefit from the expenditure is fully used in the current period, or there is a great deal of uncertainty about whether or not there is a future benefit. In these situations, the costs are reported as expenses in the period in which they occur.

ACCOUNTING IN ACTION
ALL ABOUT YOU INSIGHT

You are probably paying a lot for your education. According to Statistics Canada, in 2011–12, the average undergraduate tuition fee for Canadian full-time university students was $5,366. If the cost of books, supplies, student fees, transportation, housing, and other expenses is factored in, that amount can rise substantially. In 2009, it was estimated that the average four-year undergraduate degree in Canada costs about $55,000 for those living at home and $84,000 for students living away from home.

That is the cost, but what is the future value of your education? According to the TD Bank, "Investment in post-secondary education remains the single best investment that one can make." Post-secondary graduates are more likely to be employed, and typically earn more money over their lifetimes. The 2006 Census found that university graduates in Canada earned an average of $35,168 a year after taxes, compared with $27,741 for college graduates, $19,744 for high school graduates, and $15,523 for those who did not graduate from high school.

There are also indirect benefits of post-secondary education. Graduates tend to have higher literacy and financial management skills, manage their health better, are more active in their community, and are more likely to pursue continuing education and therefore adapt better to the information economy.

When you consider all these benefits, the money you're spending now on your education should be a significant advantage to you in the future.

Sources: CanLearn.ca, www.canlearn.ca/eng/postsec/cost/index.shtml; TD Economics, "Post-Secondary Education Is the Best Investment You Can Make," Special Report, September 12, 2011; Statistics Canada, "University Tuition Fees 2011/2012," *The Daily*, September 16, 2011.

How should you account for the cost of your post-secondary education? Should you be recognizing the cost as an expense each year or should you recognize it as an asset?

BEFORE YOU GO ON...

Do It

On January 1, 2014, customers owed Jomerans $30,000 for services provided in 2013. During 2014, Jomerans Co. received $125,000 cash from customers. On December 31, 2014, customers owed Jomerans $19,500 for services provided in 2014. Calculate revenue for 2014 using (a) cash basis accounting, and (b) accrual basis accounting.

Solution

(a) Revenue for 2014, using cash basis accounting $125,000

(b) Cash received from customers in 2014 $125,000
    Deduct: Collection of 2013 receivables   (30,000)
    Add: Amounts receivable at December 31, 2014   19,500

    Revenue for 2014, using accrual basis accounting $114,500

Related exercise material: BE3–1, E3–1, and E3–2.

THE NAVIGATOR

Action Plan
- For cash basis accounting, revenue is equal to the cash received.
- For accrual basis accounting, revenue is recognized in the period in which it is earned, not when it is collected.
- Under accrual basis accounting, cash collected in 2014 for revenue earned in 2013 should not be included in the 2014 revenue.
- Under accrual basis accounting, amounts receivable at the end of 2014 for services provided in 2014 should be included in the 2014 revenue.

The Basics of Adjusting Entries

For revenues and expenses to be recorded in the correct period, adjusting entries are made at the end of the accounting period. **Adjusting entries** are needed to ensure that revenue and expense recognition criteria are followed and that the correct amounts for assets, liabilities, and owner's equity are reported on the balance sheet.

Adjusting entries are needed every time financial statements are prepared. Companies reporting under IFRS must prepare quarterly financial statements and thus adjusting entries are required every quarter. Companies following ASPE must prepare annual financial statements and thus need only annual adjusting entries. For both public and private companies, if management wants monthly statements, then adjustments are prepared every month end.

You will recall that we learned the first four steps of the accounting cycle in Chapter 2. Adjusting entries are Step 5 of the accounting cycle, as shown in Illustration 3-2.

ASPE

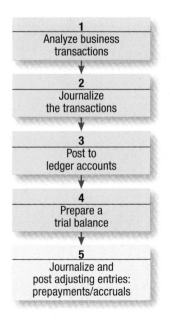

▶ ILLUSTRATION 3-2
The accounting cycle—Steps 1 to 5

There are some common reasons why the trial balance—from Step 4 in the accounting cycle—may not contain complete and up-to-date data.

1. Some events are not recorded daily because it would not be efficient to do so. For example, companies do not record the daily use of supplies or the earning of wages by employees.
2. Some costs are not recorded during the accounting period because they expire with the passage of time rather than through daily transactions. Examples are rent and insurance.
3. Some items may be unrecorded. An example is a utility bill for services in the current accounting period that will not be received until the next accounting period.

Therefore, we must analyze each account in the trial balance to see if it is complete and up to date. The analysis requires a full understanding of the company's operations and the interrelationship of accounts. Preparing adjusting entries is often a long process. For example, to accumulate the adjustment data, a company may need to count its remaining supplies. It may also need to prepare supporting schedules of insurance policies, rental agreements, and other contractual commitments.

Adjustment data are often not available until after the end of the period; for example, telephone and other bills received after the month end or year end. In such cases, the data are gathered as soon as possible after the end of the period and adjusting entries are made but they are still dated as at the balance sheet date.

Adjusting entries can be classified as prepayments or accruals, as follows:

PREPAYMENTS	ACCRUALS
1. **Prepaid Expenses** Expenses paid in cash and recorded as assets before they are used or consumed.	1. **Accrued Expenses** Expenses incurred but not yet paid in cash or recorded.
2. **Unearned Revenues** Cash received and recorded as a liability before revenue is earned.	2. **Accrued Revenues** Revenues earned but not yet received in cash or recorded.

Examples and explanations of each type of adjustment are given on the following pages. Each example is based on the October 31 trial balance of Pioneer Advertising Agency from Chapter 2, reproduced here in Illustration 3-3.

▶ILLUSTRATION 3-3
Trial balance

PIONEER ADVERTISING AGENCY
Trial Balance
October 31, 2014

	Debit	Credit
Cash	$14,250	
Accounts receivable	1,000	
Supplies	2,500	
Prepaid insurance	600	
Equipment	5,000	
Notes payable		$ 5,000
Accounts payable		1,750
Unearned revenue		1,200
C. Byrd, capital		10,000
C. Byrd, drawings	500	
Service revenue		10,800
Rent expense	900	
Salaries expense	4,000	
Totals	$28,750	$28,750

For illustration purposes, we assume that Pioneer Advertising uses an accounting period of one month. Thus, monthly adjusting entries will be made and they will be dated October 31.

ADJUSTING ENTRIES FOR PREPAYMENTS

Prepayments are either prepaid expenses or unearned revenues. Adjusting entries are used to record the portion of the prepayment consumed in the current accounting period and to reduce the asset account where the prepaid expense was originally recorded. This type of adjustment is necessary because the prepayment no longer has future benefit and consequently is no longer an asset—it has been used.

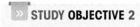

STUDY OBJECTIVE 2

Prepare adjusting entries for prepayments.

For unearned revenues, the adjusting entry records the revenue earned in the current period and reduces the liability account where the unearned revenue was originally recorded. This type of adjustment is necessary because the unearned revenue is no longer owed and so is no longer a liability—the service has been provided and the revenue earned.

Prepaid Expenses

Recall from Chapter 1 that costs paid in cash before they are used are called prepaid expenses. When such a cost is incurred, an asset (prepaid) account is debited to show the service or benefit that will be received in the future and cash is credited.

Helpful hint A cost can be an asset or an expense. If it has future benefits, it is an asset. If the benefits have expired or been used, it is an expense.

Prepaid expenses are assets that expire either with the passage of time (e.g., rent and insurance) or as the asset is used up (e.g., supplies). It is not practical to record the expiration of these assets daily. Instead, they are recorded when financial statements are prepared. At each statement date, companies make adjusting entries: (1) to record an expense for the cost of the asset that has been used up that period, and (2) to show an asset for the remaining amount (unexpired costs).

Before the prepaid expenses are adjusted, assets are overstated and expenses are understated. Therefore, as shown below, **an adjusting entry for prepaid expenses results in an increase (debit) to an expense account and a decrease (credit) to an asset account.**

In the following section, we will look at three examples of adjusting prepaid expenses: supplies, insurance, and depreciation.

Supplies. The purchase of supplies, such as pens and paper, generally results in an increase (debit) to an asset account. During daily operations, supplies are used up. Rather than recording journal entries as the supplies are used, supplies expense is recorded at the end of the accounting period as an adjustment. At that point, the remaining supplies are counted (a physical inventory of supplies is taken). The difference between the balance in the supplies (asset) account and the cost of supplies actually remaining gives the supplies used (the expense) for the period.

Recall from Chapter 2 that Pioneer Advertising Agency purchased supplies costing $2,500 on October 4. A debit (increase) was made to the asset account Supplies. This account shows a balance of $2,500 in the October 31 trial balance. An inventory count at the close of business on October 31 reveals that only $1,000 of supplies remains. That means $1,500 ($2,500 − $1,000) of the supplies have been used.

The following illustration outlines the analysis used to determine the adjusting journal entry to record and post. Note that the debit-credit rules you learned in Chapter 2 are also used for adjusting journal entries.

▸**ADJUSTMENT 1**
Prepaid Expenses—
Supplies

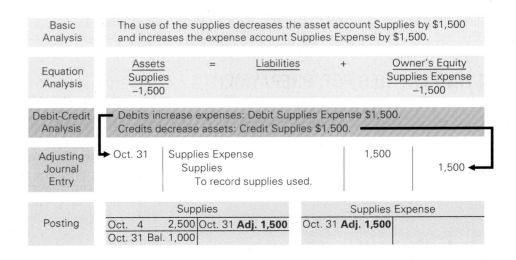

After the adjustment, the asset account Supplies now shows a balance of $1,000, which is equal to the cost of supplies remaining at the statement date. Supplies Expense shows a balance of $1,500, which is the cost of supplies used in October. If the adjusting entry is not made, October expenses will be understated and profit overstated by $1,500. Also, both assets and owner's equity will be overstated by $1,500 on the October 31 balance sheet.

Insurance. Companies purchase insurance to protect themselves from losses caused by fire, theft, and unforeseen accidents. Insurance must be paid in advance and the term of coverage is usually one year. Insurance payments (premiums) made in advance are normally charged to the asset account Prepaid Insurance when they are paid. At the financial statement date, it is necessary to make an adjustment to debit (increase) Insurance Expense and credit (decrease) Prepaid Insurance for the cost that has expired during the period.

On October 3, Pioneer Advertising Agency paid $600 for a one-year fire insurance policy. The starting date for the coverage was October 1. The premium was charged to Prepaid Insurance when it was paid. This account shows a balance of $600 in the October 31 trial balance. An analysis of the policy reveals that $50 ($600 ÷ 12 months) of insurance expires each month. The adjusting entry for prepaid insurance is made as follows:

▸**ADJUSTMENT 2**
Prepaid Expenses—
Insurance

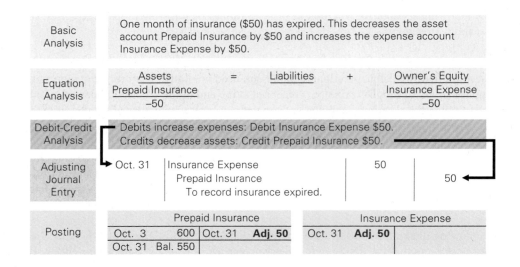

After the adjustment, the asset Prepaid Insurance shows a balance of $550. This amount represents the unexpired cost for the remaining 11 months of coverage (11 × $50). The $50 balance in Insurance Expense is equal to the insurance cost that has expired in October. If this adjustment is not made, October expenses will be understated by $50 and profit overstated by $50. Also, both assets and owner's equity will be overstated by $50 on the October 31 balance sheet.

Depreciation. A business usually owns a variety of assets that have long lives such as land, buildings, and equipment. These long-lived assets provide service for a number of years. The length of service is called the **useful life**.

From an accounting perspective, the purchase of a long-lived asset is basically a long-term prepayment for services. Similar to other prepaid expenses, it is necessary to recognize the cost that has been used up (the expense) during the period, and report the unused cost (the asset) at the end of the period. **Depreciation** is the process of allocating the cost of long-lived assets to expense over their useful lives in a systematic and rational manner. Only assets with limited useful lives are depreciated. We call them depreciable assets. When an asset, such as land, has an unlimited useful life, it is not depreciated.

It is important to note that depreciation is an allocation concept. The portion of the long-lived asset that is used up in each period is reported as depreciation expense. Depreciation is not an attempt to recognize the change in the value of the long-lived asset.

Some companies use the term "amortization" instead of "depreciation," especially private companies following ASPE. The two terms mean the same thing—allocation of the cost of a long-lived asset to expense over its useful life. In Chapter 9, we will learn that the term "amortization" is also used under both ASPE and IFRS for the allocation of cost to expense for certain intangible long-lived assets.

Calculation of Depreciation. A common method of calculating depreciation expense is to divide the cost of the asset by its useful life. This is called the **straight-line depreciation method**. The useful life must be estimated because, at the time an asset is acquired, the company does not know exactly how long the asset will be used. Thus, depreciation is an estimate rather than a factual measurement of the expired cost.

Pioneer Advertising purchased equipment that cost $5,000 on October 2. If its useful life is expected to be five years, annual depreciation is $1,000 ($5,000 ÷ 5). Illustration 3-4 shows the formula to calculate annual depreciation expense in its simplest form.

| Cost | ÷ | Useful Life (in years) | = | Annual Depreciation Expense |

▶ **ILLUSTRATION 3-4**
Formula for straight-line depreciation

Of course, if you are calculating depreciation for partial periods, the annual expense amount must be adjusted for the relevant portion of the year. For example, if we want to determine the depreciation for one month, we would multiply the annual expense by $\frac{1}{12}$ as there are 12 months in a year.

Adjustments of prepayments involve decreasing (or crediting) an asset by the amount that has been used or consumed. Therefore, it would be logical to expect we should credit Equipment when recording depreciation. But in the financial statements we must report both the original cost of long-lived assets and the total cost that has been used. We therefore use an account called **Accumulated Depreciation** to show the cumulative sum of the depreciation expense since the asset was purchased. This account is a **contra asset account** because it has the opposite (credit) balance to its related asset Equipment, which has a debit balance.

For Pioneer Advertising, depreciation on the equipment is estimated to be $83 per month ($1,000 × $\frac{1}{12}$). Because depreciation is an estimate, we can ignore the fact that Pioneer Advertising bought the equipment on October 2, not October 1. The adjusting entry to record the depreciation on the equipment for the month of October is made as follows:

Helpful hint To make the depreciation calculation easier to understand, we have assumed the asset has no value at the end of its useful life. In Chapter 9, we will show how to calculate depreciation when there is an estimated value at the end of the asset's useful life.

▸**ADJUSTMENT** ③
Prepaid Expenses—
Depreciation

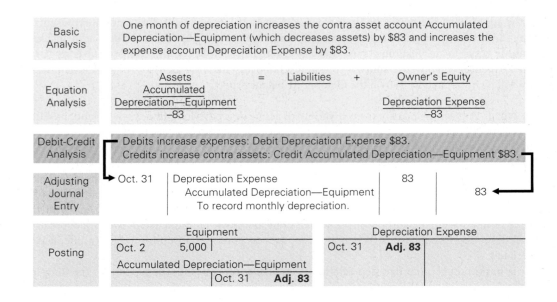

Basic Analysis	One month of depreciation increases the contra asset account Accumulated Depreciation—Equipment (which decreases assets) by $83 and increases the expense account Depreciation Expense by $83.

Equation Analysis

Assets	=	Liabilities	+	Owner's Equity
Accumulated Depreciation—Equipment −83				Depreciation Expense −83

Debit-Credit Analysis — Debits increase expenses: Debit Depreciation Expense $83.
Credits increase contra assets: Credit Accumulated Depreciation—Equipment $83.

Adjusting Journal Entry

Oct. 31	Depreciation Expense	83	
	Accumulated Depreciation—Equipment		83
	To record monthly depreciation.		

Posting

Equipment		Depreciation Expense
Oct. 2 5,000		Oct. 31 **Adj. 83**
Accumulated Depreciation—Equipment		
Oct. 31 **Adj. 83**		

Helpful hint Increases, decreases, and normal balances of contra accounts are the opposite of the accounts they relate to.

The balance in the Accumulated Depreciation account will increase by $83 each month and the balance in the Equipment account will remain unchanged until the asset is sold. We will learn in Chapter 9 that both the accumulated depreciation and the equipment accounts are reduced when the asset is sold.

As in the case of other prepaid expenses, if this adjusting entry is not made, total assets, owner's equity, and profit will be overstated and expenses will be understated.

Statement Presentation. Accumulated Depreciation—Equipment, a contra asset account, has the opposite balance from its related asset account Equipment. In the financial statements, **a contra account is always offset against (deducted from) its related account.** Thus, on the balance sheet, Accumulated Depreciation—Equipment is deducted from Equipment, as follows:

Equipment	$5,000
Less: Accumulated depreciation—equipment	83
Carrying amount	$4,917

Alternative terminology An asset's carrying amount is also called its *carrying value, net book value,* or *book value.*

The difference between the cost of any depreciable asset and its accumulated depreciation is called the **carrying amount** of that asset. In the above diagram, the carrying amount of the equipment at October 31, 2014, is $4,917. Remember, depreciation does not attempt to show what an asset is worth. The carrying amount and the fair value of the equipment (the price at which it could be sold) are generally two different amounts.

If a company owns both equipment and buildings, it calculates and records depreciation expense on each category. It can use one depreciation expense account but it must create separate accumulated depreciation accounts for each category.

Unearned Revenues

Alternative terminology Unearned revenues are sometimes referred to *as deferred revenues* or *future revenues.*

Cash received before revenue is earned is recorded by increasing (crediting) a liability account for unearned revenues. Examples are rent, magazine subscriptions, and customer deposits for future services. Airlines such as Air Canada treat receipts from the sale of tickets as unearned revenue until the flight service is provided. Similarly, tuition fees that are received prior to the start of an academic session, as in the feature story about the summer session at Seneca College, are considered unearned revenue.

Unearned revenues are the opposite of prepaid expenses. Indeed, unearned revenue on the books of one company is likely to be a prepayment on the books of the company that has made the advance payment. For example, your landlord will have unearned rent revenue when you (the tenant) have prepaid rent.

Recall that, when a payment is received for services that will be provided in a future accounting period, Cash is debited (increased) and an unearned revenue account (a liability) should be credited (increased) to recognize the obligation that exists. Unearned revenues become earned when the service is provided to the customer.

It may not be practical to make daily journal entries as the revenue is earned. Instead, recognition of earned revenue is normally delayed until the end of the accounting period. Then an adjusting entry is made to record the revenue that has been earned and to show the liability that remains at the end of the accounting period. Before adjustment, liabilities are overstated and revenues are understated. If revenues are understated, then profit and owner's equity will also be understated. As shown below, the adjusting entry for unearned revenues results in a decrease (debit) to a liability account and an increase (credit) to a revenue account.

Unearned Revenue

Liability		Revenue	
Debit Adjusting Entry (−)	Unadjusted Balance		Credit Adjusting Entry (+)

In our Pioneer Advertising Agency example, the company received $1,200 on October 3 from R. Knox for advertising services that will be completed by December 31. The payment was originally credited to Unearned Revenue, and this account shows a balance of $1,200 in the October 31 trial balance. An evaluation of work performed by Pioneer for Knox during October shows that $400 of work was done. The following adjusting entry is used to record earning this revenue:

▶ **ADJUSTMENT** 4
Unearned Revenues

Basic Analysis	The liability account Unearned Revenue is decreased by $400 for the revenue earned and the revenue account Service Revenue is increased by $400.

Equation Analysis	Assets	=	Liabilities Unearned Revenue −400	+	Owner's Equity Service Revenue +400

Debit-Credit Analysis	Debits decrease liabilities: Debit Unearned Revenue $400. Credits increase revenues: Credit Service Revenue $400.

Adjusting Journal Entry	Oct. 31	Unearned Revenue	400	
		Service Revenue		400
		To record revenue for services provided in October.		

Posting

Unearned Revenue					Service Revenue		
Oct. 31	**Adj. 400**	Oct. 4	1,200		Oct. 21		10,000
		Oct. 31	Bal. 800		25		800
					31		**Adj. 400**
					Oct. 31		Bal. 11,200

The liability Unearned Revenue now shows a balance of $800. This amount represents the remaining advertising services that will be performed in the future. At the same time, Service Revenue shows additional revenue of $400 earned in October. If this adjustment is not made, revenues and profit will be understated by $400 in the income statement. As well, liabilities will be overstated by $400 and owner's equity understated by that amount on the October 31 balance sheet.

ACCOUNTING IN ACTION
BUSINESS INSIGHT

Gift cards have become more popular in Canada. And with recent legislation in Ontario, Alberta, British Columbia, Nova Scotia, and other provinces eliminating the use of expiry dates on the cards, their benefits to the consumer have increased. But what is the benefit to businesses? Many have discovered that gift card sales in December give their revenues in the new year a boost. Many gift cards sold in December are used in January or February. In fact, Statistics Canada has found that the usual drop in sales from December to January has started to moderate, which it attributes in part to the redemption of gift cards early in the new year. Businesses must recognize revenue from gift cards when they're redeemed, which boosts revenues in traditionally slower times.

Sources: "Nova Scotia to Ban Gift Card Expiry Dates," CBC News online, December 3, 2009; "B.C. Government Bans Gift Cards with Fees or Expiry Dates," CanWest MediaWorks, October 18, 2008; Daniel Bahta, Rhoda Tsang, and Monica Weise, "Gift Cards: The Gift of Choice," Statistics Canada analytical paper, 2006.

If a business collects cash when the gift card is sold, how can gift card sales in December result in revenues in January?

BEFORE YOU GO ON...

Do It

The trial balance of Panos Co. on March 31, 2014, includes the following selected accounts before adjusting entries:

	Debit	Credit
Prepaid insurance	$ 1,200	
Supplies	2,800	
Equipment	24,000	
Accumulated depreciation—equipment		$2,200
Unearned revenue		9,300

An analysis of the accounts shows the following:

1. A one-year insurance policy for $1,200 was purchased on March 1, 2014.
2. Supplies on hand at March 31, 2014, total $800.
3. Equipment was purchased on April 1, 2013, and has an estimated useful life of 10 years.
4. One third of the unearned revenue was earned in March 2014.

Prepare the adjusting entries for the month of March.

Action Plan

- Make sure you prepare adjustments for the correct time period.
- Adjusting entries for prepaid expenses require a debit to an expense account and a credit to an asset or contra asset account.
- Adjusting entries for unearned revenues require a debit to a liability account and a credit to a revenue account.

Solution

1.	Mar. 31	Insurance Expense		100	
		Prepaid Insurance			100
		To record insurance expired: $1,200 ÷ 12.			
2.	31	Supplies Expense		2,000	
		Supplies			2,000
		To record supplies used: $2,800 previously			
		on hand − $800 currently on hand = $2,000 used.			

3.	31	Depreciation Expense	200	
		Accumulated Depreciation—Equipment		200
		To record monthly depreciation: $24,000 \div 10 \times \frac{1}{12}$.		
4.	31	Unearned Revenue	3,100	
		Service Revenue		3,100
		To record revenue earned: $9,300 \times \frac{1}{3} = \$3,100$ earned.		

Related exercise material: BE3–2, BE3–3, BE3–4, BE3–5, BE3–6, E3–4, and E3–5.

THE NAVIGATOR

ADJUSTING ENTRIES FOR ACCRUALS

The second category of adjusting entries is accruals. Unlike prepayments, which have already been recorded in the accounts, accruals are not recognized through transaction journal entries and thus are not included in the accounts. Accruals are required in situations where cash will be paid or received after the end of the accounting period.

Until an accrual adjustment is made, the revenue account (and the related asset account) is understated for accrued revenues. Similarly, the expense account (and the related liability account) is understated for accrued expenses. Thus, adjusting entries for accruals increase both a balance sheet account and an income statement account. We now look at each type of adjusting entry for accruals—accrued revenues and accrued expenses—in more detail.

>> **STUDY OBJECTIVE 3**

Prepare adjusting entries for accruals.

Accrued Revenues

Revenues earned but not yet received in cash or recorded at the statement date are **accrued revenues**. Accrued revenues may accumulate (accrue) with the passage of time, as happens with interest revenue and rent revenue. Or they may result when services have been performed but the payment has not been billed or received, as can happen with commissions and fees. The former are unrecorded because the earning of interest and rent does not involve daily transactions. The latter may be unrecorded because only a portion of the total service has been provided or the bill has not been prepared.

Alternative terminology Accrued revenues are also called *accrued receivables.*

An adjusting entry is required for two purposes: (1) to show the receivable that exists at the balance sheet date, and (2) to record the revenue that has been earned during the period. Before the adjustment is recorded, both assets and revenues are understated. Accordingly, as shown below, an adjusting entry for accrued revenues results in an increase (debit) to an asset account and an increase (credit) to a revenue account.

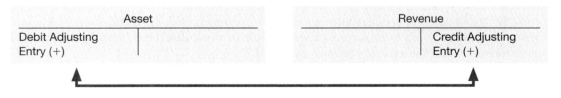

In October, Pioneer Advertising Agency earned $200 in fees for advertising services that were not billed to clients until November. Because these services have not been billed, they have not been recorded. An adjusting entry on October 31 is required as follows:

▶ADJUSTMENT 5
Accrued Revenue—
Accounts Receivable

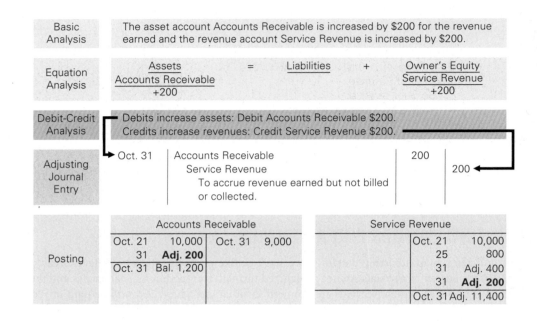

The asset Accounts Receivable shows that $1,200 is owed by clients at the balance sheet date. The balance of $11,400 in Service Revenue represents the total revenue earned during the month. If the adjusting entry is not made, assets and owner's equity on the balance sheet, and revenues and profit on the income statement, will all be understated.

On November 10, Pioneer receives $200 cash for the services performed in October. The following entry is made:

A	=	L	+	OE
+200				
−200				

↑ Cash flows: +200

Nov. 10	Cash	200	
	Accounts Receivable		200
	To record cash collected on account.		

Accrued Expenses

Alternative terminology Accrued expenses are also called *accrued liabilities*.

Expenses incurred but not yet paid or recorded at the statement date are called **accrued expenses**. Interest, rent, property taxes, and salaries can be accrued expenses. As we saw in our feature story, Seneca College uses estimates to accrue for legal and utility expenses because the actual invoices are received after its year end. Accrued expenses result from the same causes as accrued revenues. In fact, an accrued expense on the books of one company is an accrued revenue for another company. For example, the $200 accrual of revenue by Pioneer is an accrued expense for the client that received the service.

Adjustments for accrued expenses are needed for two purposes: (1) to record the obligations that exist at the balance sheet date, and (2) to recognize the expenses that apply to the current accounting period. Before adjustment, both liabilities and expenses are understated. Profit and owner's equity are overstated. An adjusting entry for accrued expenses results in an increase (debit) to an expense account and an increase (credit) to a liability account, as follows.

Accrued Expenses

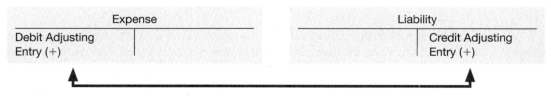

There are many types of expenses that might need to be accrued at the end of an accounting period. Two of the most common are interest and salaries.

Interest. On October 2, Pioneer Advertising Agency signed a $5,000, three-month note payable, due January 2, 2015. The note requires interest to be paid at an annual rate of 6%. The amount of interest that has accumulated is determined by three factors: (1) the principal amount of the note; (2) the interest rate, which is always expressed as an annual rate; and (3) the length of time that the note is outstanding (unpaid). The **principal** amount is the amount borrowed or the amount still owed on a loan, separate from interest.

Interest is sometimes due monthly, and sometimes when the principal is due. For Pioneer, the total interest due on the $5,000 note at its due date three months later is $75 ($5,000 × 6% × $\frac{3}{12}$ months). Interest rates are always expressed as an annual rate. Because the interest rate is for one year, the time period must be adjusted for the fraction of the year that the note is outstanding.

The formula for calculating interest and how it applies to Pioneer Advertising Agency for the month of October are shown in Illustration 3-5.

Helpful hint To make the illustration easier to understand, a simplified method for calculating interest is used. In reality, interest is calculated using the exact number of days in the interest period and year.

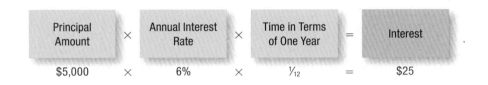

▶ILLUSTRATION 3-5
Formula for calculating interest

The accrued interest expense adjusting entry at October 31 follows:

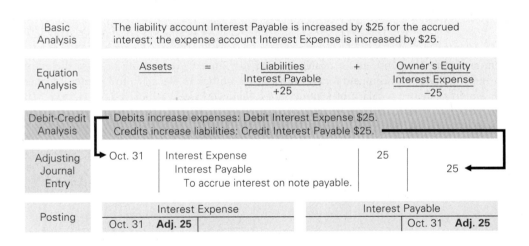

▶ADJUSTMENT 6
Accrued Expenses—Interest

Interest Expense shows the interest charges for the month of October. The amount of interest owed at the statement date is shown in Interest Payable. It will not be paid until the note comes due, on January 2, 2015. The Interest Payable account is used instead of crediting Notes Payable in order to show the two types of obligations (interest and principal) in the accounts and statements. If this adjusting entry is not made, liabilities and expenses will be understated, and profit and owner's equity will be overstated.

Since this is a three-month note, Pioneer Advertising will also need to make identical adjustments at the end of November and at the end of December to accrue for interest expense incurred in each of these months. After the three adjusting entries have been posted, the balance in Interest Payable is $75 ($25 × 3). The following entry is made on January 2, 2015, when the note and interest are paid:

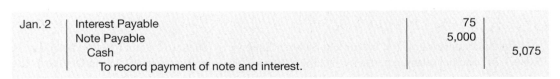

This entry does two things: (1) it eliminates the liability for Interest Payable that was recorded in the October 31, November 30, and December 31 adjusting entries; and (2) it eliminates the note payable. Notice also that the Interest Expense account is not included in this entry, because the full amount of interest incurred was accrued in previous months.

Salaries. Some types of expenses, such as employee salaries and commissions, are paid after the work has been performed. At Pioneer Advertising, employees began work on October 13. They are paid every two weeks and were last paid on October 24. The next payment of salaries will not occur until November 7. As shown on the calendar, in Illustration 3-6, there are five working days that remain unpaid at October 31 (October 27–31).

▶ **ILLUSTRATION 3-6**
Calendar showing Pioneer Advertising's pay periods

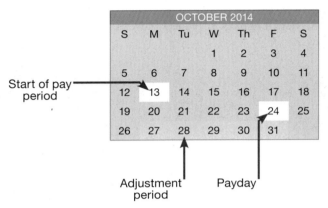

Helpful hint Recognition of an accrued expense does not mean that a company is slow or bad at paying its debts. The accrued liability may not be payable until after the balance sheet date.

At October 31, the salaries for the last five working days (Monday, October 27, to Friday, October 31) represent an accrued expense and a related liability for Pioneer Advertising because the employees have worked but have not been paid for this work as at October 31. Recall from Chapter 2 that each of the four employees earns a salary of $500 for a five-day workweek, which is $100 per day. Thus, at October 31 the accrued salaries are $2,000 (4 employees × $100/day × 5 days). Pioneer's accrued salaries expense adjusting entry follows:

▶ **ADJUSTMENT 7**
Accrued Expenses— Salaries

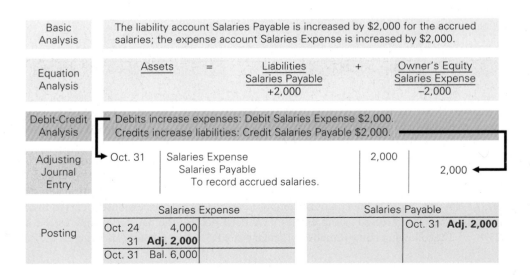

After this adjustment, the balance in Salaries Expense of $6,000 (4 employees × $100/day × 15 days) is the actual salary expense for October (the employees have worked 15 days in October). The balance in Salaries Payable of $2,000 is the amount of the liability for salaries owed as at October 31. If the $2,000 adjustment for salaries is not recorded, Pioneer's expenses and liabilities will be understated by $2,000. Profit and owner's equity will be overstated by $2,000.

At Pioneer Advertising, salaries are payable every two weeks. The next payday is November 7, when total salaries of $4,000 will again be paid. The November 7 payment consists of $2,000 of salaries payable at October 31 plus $2,000 of salaries expense for November (4 employees $\times$ $100/day $\times$ 5 working days [for the period November 3–7]). The following entry is therefore made on November 7:

Nov. 7	Salaries Payable	2,000	
	Salaries Expense	2,000	
	Cash		4,000
	To record November 7 payroll.		

A	=	L	+	OE
−4,000		−2,000		−2,000

↓ Cash flows: −4,000

This entry does two things: (1) it eliminates the liability for salaries payable that was recorded in the October 31 adjusting entry, and (2) it records the proper amount of salaries expense for the five-day period from Monday, November 3, to Friday, November 7.

BEFORE YOU GO ON...

Do It

Alvin Hobbs is the owner of the new company Micro Computer Services. At the end of August 2014, the first month of business, Alvin is trying to prepare monthly financial statements. The following information is for August:

1. At August 31, Micro Computer Services owed its employees $800 in salaries that will be paid on September 2.
2. On August 1, Micro Computer Services borrowed $30,000 from a local bank on a five-year term loan. The annual interest rate is 5% and interest is paid monthly on the first of each month.
3. Service revenue earned in August but not yet billed or recorded at August 31 totalled $1,100.

Prepare the adjusting entries needed at August 31, 2014.

Solution

1.	Aug. 31	Salaries Expense	800	
		Salaries Payable		800
		To record accrued salaries.		
2.	31	Interest Expense	125	
		Interest Payable		125
		To record accrued interest: $30,000 $\times$ 5% $\times$ $\frac{1}{12}$		
3.	31	Accounts Receivable	1,100	
		Service Revenue		1,100
		To accrue revenue earned but not billed or collected.		

Related exercise material: BE3–7, BE3–8, BE3–9, BE3–10, BE3–11, BE3–12, E3–3, E3–6, E3–7, E3–8, E3–9, and E3–10.

Action Plan
- Remember that accruals are adjusting entries for revenues earned or expenses incurred that have not been recorded. The cash is received or paid after the end of the accounting period.
- Adjusting entries for accrued revenues increase a receivable account (an asset) and increase a revenue account.
- Remember that debits increase assets and credits increase revenues.
- Adjusting entries for accrued expenses increase a payable account (a liability) and increase an expense account.
- Remember that debits increase expenses and credits increase liabilities.

THE **NAVIGATOR**

Summary of Basic Relationships

The two basic types of adjusting entries are summarized below. Take some time to study and analyze the adjusting entries in the summary. Be sure to note that **each adjusting entry affects one balance sheet account and one income statement account.**

	Type of Adjustment	Reason for Adjustment	Accounts before Adjustment	Adjusting Entry
Prepayments	Prepaid expenses	Prepaid expenses, originally recorded in asset accounts, have been used.	Assets overstated; expenses understated	Dr. Expense Cr. Asset
	Unearned revenues	Unearned revenues, originally recorded in liability accounts, have been earned.	Liabilities overstated; revenues understated	Dr. Liability Cr. Revenue
Accruals	Accrued revenues	Revenues have been earned but not yet received in cash or recorded.	Assets understated; revenues understated	Dr. Asset Cr. Revenue
	Accrued expenses	Expenses have been incurred but not yet paid in cash or recorded.	Expenses understated; liabilities understated	Dr. Expense Cr. Liability

Note that adjusting entries never involve the Cash account (except for bank reconciliations, which we will study in Chapter 7). In the case of prepayments, cash has already been received or paid, and was already recorded in the original journal entry. The adjusting entry reallocates or adjusts amounts between a balance sheet account (e.g., prepaid assets or unearned revenues) and an income statement account (e.g., expenses or revenues). In the case of accruals, cash will be received or paid in the future and recorded then. The adjusting entry records the receivable or payable and the related revenue or expense.

Pioneer Advertising Agency Illustration

The journalizing and posting of adjusting entries for Pioneer Advertising Agency on October 31 are shown below and on the following two pages. The title "Adjusting Entries" may be inserted in the general journal between the last transaction entry from Chapter 2 and the first adjusting entry so that the adjusting entries are clearly identified. As you review the general ledger, note that the adjustments are highlighted in colour.

GENERAL JOURNAL					J2
Date	**Account Titles and Explanation**	**Ref**	**Debit**	**Credit**	
2014	Adjusting Entries				
Oct. 31	Supplies Expense	740	1,500		
	Supplies	129		1,500	
	To record supplies used.				
31	Insurance Expense	722	50		
	Prepaid Insurance	130		50	
	To record insurance expired.				
31	Depreciation Expense	711	83		
	Accumulated Depreciation—Equipment	152		83	
	To record monthly depreciation.				
31	Unearned Revenue	209	400		
	Service Revenue	400		400	
	To record revenue for services provided in October.				
31	Accounts Receivable	112	200		
	Service Revenue	400		200	
	To accrue revenue earned but not billed or collected.				
31	Interest Expense	905	25		
	Interest Payable	230		25	
	To accrue interest on note payable.				

31	Salaries Expense			729	2,000	
	Salaries Payable			212		2,000
	To record accrued salaries.					

GENERAL LEDGER

Cash			101
Oct. 1	10,000	Oct. 3	900
3	1,200	3	600
25	800	20	500
31	9,000	24	4,000
		31	750
Bal.	14,250		

Accounts Receivable			112
Oct. 21	10,000	Oct. 31	9,000
31 Adj.	200		
Bal.	1,200		

Supplies			129
Oct. 4	2,500	Oct. 31 Adj.	1,500
Bal.	1,000		

Prepaid Insurance			130
Oct. 3	600	Oct. 31 Adj.	50
Bal.	550		

Equipment			151
Oct. 2	5,000		
Bal.	5,000		

Accumulated Depreciation—Equipment			152
		Oct. 31 Adj.	83
		Bal.	83

Notes Payable			200
		Oct. 2	5,000
		Bal.	5,000

Accounts Payable			201
Oct. 31	750	Oct. 4	2,500
		Bal.	1,750

Unearned Revenue			209
Oct. 31 Adj.	400	Oct. 3	1,200
		Bal.	800

Salaries Payable			212
		Oct. 31 Adj.	2,000
		Bal.	2,000

Interest Payable			230
		Oct. 31 Adj.	25
		Bal.	25

C. Byrd, Capital			301
		Oct. 1	10,000
		Bal.	10,000

C. Byrd, Drawings			306
Oct. 20	500		
Bal.	500		

Service Revenue			400
		Oct. 21	10,000
		25	800
		31 Adj.	400
		31 Adj.	200
		Bal.	11,400

Depreciation Expense			711
Oct. 31 Adj.	83		
Bal.	83		

Insurance Expense			722
Oct. 31 Adj.	50		
Bal.	50		

Rent Expense			726
Oct. 3	900		
Bal.	900		

Salaries Expense			729
Oct. 24	4,000		
31 Adj.	2,000		
Bal.	6,000		

Supplies Expense			740
Oct. 31 Adj.	1,500		
Bal.	1,500		

Interest Expense			905
Oct. 31 Adj.	25		
Bal.	25		

The Adjusted Trial Balance and Financial Statements

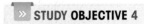
▶ **ILLUSTRATION 3-7**
The accounting cycle—Steps 1 to 7

After all adjusting entries have been journalized and posted, another trial balance is prepared from the general ledger accounts. This is called an **adjusted trial balance**. Financial statements are then prepared from the adjusted trial balance. Preparation of the adjusted trial balance and the financial statements are steps 6 and 7 of the accounting cycle, as shown in Illustration 3-7.

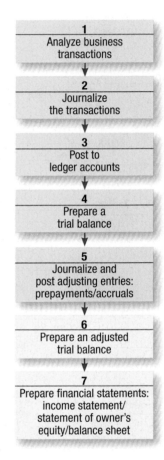

PREPARING THE ADJUSTED TRIAL BALANCE

The procedures for preparing an adjusted trial balance are the same as those described in Chapter 2 for preparing a trial balance. An adjusted trial balance, like a trial balance, only proves that the ledger is mathematically accurate. As discussed in Chapter 2, it does not prove that there are no mistakes in the ledger.

An adjusted trial balance proves that the total of the debit and credit balances in the ledger are equal after all adjustments have been posted. The adjusted trial balance gives all data that are needed for preparing financial statements.

The adjusted trial balance for Pioneer Advertising Agency is presented in Illustration 3-8. It has been prepared from the ledger accounts shown in the previous section. The amounts affected by the adjusting entries are highlighted in colour in the adjusted trial balance columns. Compare these amounts with those in the trial balance in Illustration 3-3.

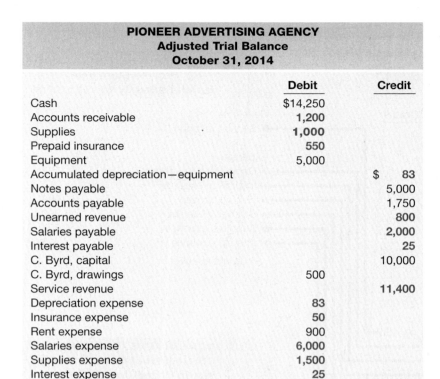

▶ ILLUSTRATION 3-8
Adjusted trial balance

PIONEER ADVERTISING AGENCY
Adjusted Trial Balance
October 31, 2014

	Debit	Credit
Cash	$14,250	
Accounts receivable	1,200	
Supplies	1,000	
Prepaid insurance	550	
Equipment	5,000	
Accumulated depreciation—equipment		$ 83
Notes payable		5,000
Accounts payable		1,750
Unearned revenue		800
Salaries payable		2,000
Interest payable		25
C. Byrd, capital		10,000
C. Byrd, drawings	500	
Service revenue		11,400
Depreciation expense	83	
Insurance expense	50	
Rent expense	900	
Salaries expense	6,000	
Supplies expense	1,500	
Interest expense	25	
	$31,058	$31,058

PREPARING FINANCIAL STATEMENTS

As shown in Illustration 3-7, preparing financial statements is the seventh step in the accounting cycle. In Chapter 2, you saw examples of preparing financial statements from a trial balance, without adjusting entries. Those examples were included to provide you with opportunities to practise preparing financial statements. But in reality, adjusting entries are almost always necessary to prepare financial statements on an accrual basis. Therefore, you should always prepare financial statements from an adjusted trial balance, never from trial balances prepared before adjusting entries (also known as unadjusted trial balances).

The preparation of financial statements from the adjusted trial balance of Pioneer Advertising Agency and the interrelationships of the data are shown in Illustrations 3-9 and 3-10. As Illustration 3-9 shows, companies first prepare the income statement from the revenue and expense accounts. Next, the statement of owner's equity is prepared from the owner's capital and drawings accounts, and from the profit (or loss) shown in the income statement. As Illustration 3-10 shows, companies then prepare the balance sheet from the asset and liability accounts and the ending owner's capital balance that is reported in the statement of owner's equity.

▶ILLUSTRATION 3-9

Preparation of the income statement and statement of owner's equity from the adjusted trial balance

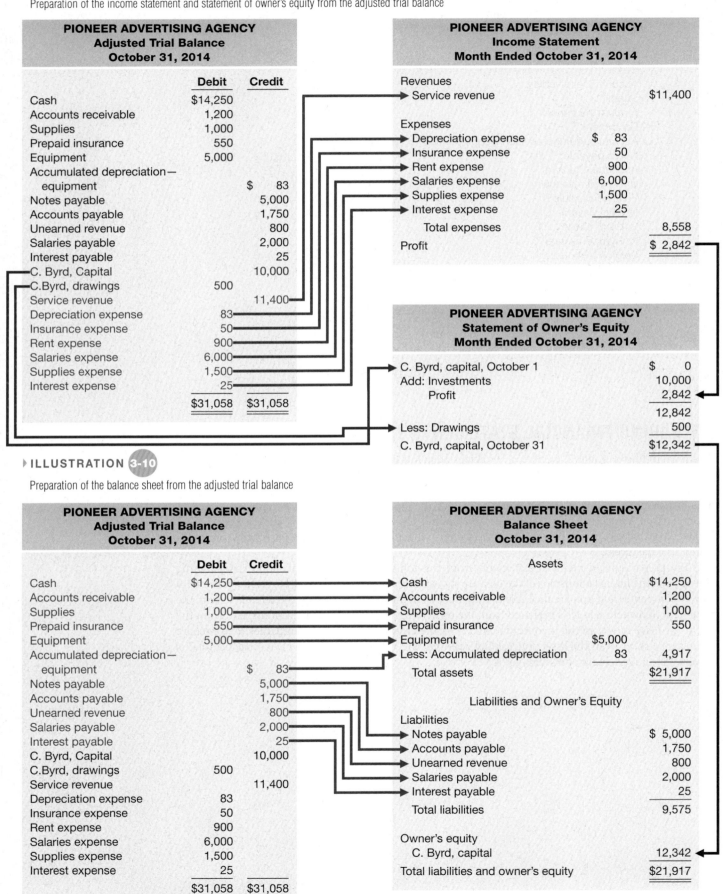

PIONEER ADVERTISING AGENCY Adjusted Trial Balance October 31, 2014		
	Debit	**Credit**
Cash	$14,250	
Accounts receivable	1,200	
Supplies	1,000	
Prepaid insurance	550	
Equipment	5,000	
Accumulated depreciation— equipment		$ 83
Notes payable		5,000
Accounts payable		1,750
Unearned revenue		800
Salaries payable		2,000
Interest payable		25
C. Byrd, Capital		10,000
C.Byrd, drawings	500	
Service revenue		11,400
Depreciation expense	83	
Insurance expense	50	
Rent expense	900	
Salaries expense	6,000	
Supplies expense	1,500	
Interest expense	25	
	$31,058	$31,058

PIONEER ADVERTISING AGENCY Income Statement Month Ended October 31, 2014		
Revenues		
Service revenue		$11,400
Expenses		
Depreciation expense	$ 83	
Insurance expense	50	
Rent expense	900	
Salaries expense	6,000	
Supplies expense	1,500	
Interest expense	25	
Total expenses		8,558
Profit		$ 2,842

PIONEER ADVERTISING AGENCY Statement of Owner's Equity Month Ended October 31, 2014	
C. Byrd, capital, October 1	$ 0
Add: Investments	10,000
Profit	2,842
	12,842
Less: Drawings	500
C. Byrd, capital, October 31	$12,342

▶ILLUSTRATION 3-10

Preparation of the balance sheet from the adjusted trial balance

PIONEER ADVERTISING AGENCY Adjusted Trial Balance October 31, 2014		
	Debit	**Credit**
Cash	$14,250	
Accounts receivable	1,200	
Supplies	1,000	
Prepaid insurance	550	
Equipment	5,000	
Accumulated depreciation— equipment		$ 83
Notes payable		5,000
Accounts payable		1,750
Unearned revenue		800
Salaries payable		2,000
Interest payable		25
C. Byrd, Capital		10,000
C.Byrd, drawings	500	
Service revenue		11,400
Depreciation expense	83	
Insurance expense	50	
Rent expense	900	
Salaries expense	6,000	
Supplies expense	1,500	
Interest expense	25	
	$31,058	$31,058

PIONEER ADVERTISING AGENCY Balance Sheet October 31, 2014		
Assets		
Cash		$14,250
Accounts receivable		1,200
Supplies		1,000
Prepaid insurance		550
Equipment	$5,000	
Less: Accumulated depreciation	83	4,917
Total assets		$21,917
Liabilities and Owner's Equity		
Liabilities		
Notes payable		$ 5,000
Accounts payable		1,750
Unearned revenue		800
Salaries payable		2,000
Interest payable		25
Total liabilities		9,575
Owner's equity		
C. Byrd, capital		12,342
Total liabilities and owner's equity		$21,917

BEFORE YOU GO ON...

Do It

Listed below, in alphabetical order, are the account balances (after adjustments) from the general ledger of KS Service Company at December 31, 2014. All accounts have normal balances.

Accounts payable	$4,660	K. Samji, drawings	$11,700
Accounts receivable	9,584	Note payable	1,000
Accumulated depreciation—equipment	1,764	Rent expense	20,762
Cash	1,100	Salaries expense	30,714
Depreciation expense	588	Salaries payable	310
Equipment	8,820	Service revenue	67,200
Interest expense	524	Supplies	180
K. Samji, capital	8,700	Supplies expense	672
		Unearned service revenue	1,010

Prepare the adjusted trial balance. Beside each account, identify if it should be included on the income statement (IS), statement of owner's equity (OE), or balance sheet (BS).

Solution

KS SERVICE COMPANY			
Adjusted Trial Balance			
December 31, 2014			
	Debit	Credit	Statement
Cash	$ 1,100		BS
Accounts receivable	9,584		BS
Supplies	180		BS
Equipment	8,820		BS
Accumulated depreciation—equipment		$ 1,764	BS
Note payable		1,000	BS
Accounts payable		4,660	BS
Salaries payable		310	BS
Unearned service revenue		1,010	BS
K. Samji, capital		8,700	OE & BS
K. Samji, drawings	11,700		OE
Service revenue		67,200	IS
Depreciation expense	588		IS
Rent expense	20,762		IS
Salaries expense	30,714		IS
Supplies expense	672		IS
Interest expense	524		IS
	$84,644	$84,644	

Action Plan
- The trial balance title includes the name of the company, the type of trial balance, and the date.
- Accounts are listed in financial statement order: assets, liabilities, owner's equity, revenues, and expenses.
- Apply the normal balance rules and list the account balances in the correct columns.
- Ensure that the totals of the two columns are equal.
- Recall that assets, liabilities, and capital belong on the balance sheet; revenues and expenses belong on the income statement; and capital and drawings belong on the statement of owner's equity.

Related exercise material: BE3–13, E3–11, E3–12, and E3–13.

THE **NAVIGATOR**

ALTERNATIVE TREATMENT OF PREPAID EXPENSES AND UNEARNED REVENUES | APPENDIX 3A

In our discussion of adjusting entries for prepaid expenses and unearned revenues, we illustrated transactions for which the company had previously made entries in balance sheet accounts. In the case of prepaid expenses, the prepayment was debited to an asset account. In the case of unearned revenue, the cash received was credited to a liability account. Recording transactions in a balance sheet account improves internal control over assets and liabilities and imitates the real flow of costs (i.e., from asset to expense).

» STUDY OBJECTIVE 5

Prepare adjusting entries for the alternative treatment of prepayments.

Some businesses use an alternative treatment: (1) When a company prepays an expense, it debits that amount to an expense account instead of an asset. (2) When it receives cash for future services, it credits a revenue account instead of a liability account. The following sections describe the circumstances that justify such entries and the different adjusting entries that may be needed.

PREPAID EXPENSES

Prepaid expenses become expired costs either as time passes, as with insurance, or as they are used up, as with supplies. If, when it makes a purchase, the company expects to consume the supplies before the next financial statement date, it may be more convenient to first debit (increase) an expense account rather than an asset account.

Assume that Pioneer Advertising expects that all of the supplies purchased on October 4 will be used before the end of the month. A debit of $2,500 to Supplies Expense on October 4, rather than to the asset account Supplies, will eliminate the need for an adjusting entry on October 31, if all the supplies are used. At October 31, the Supplies Expense account will show a balance of $2,500, which is the cost of supplies purchased between October 4 and October 31.

But what if the company does not use all the supplies? What if an inventory of $1,000 of supplies remains on October 31? Obviously, an adjusting entry is needed. Pioneer will need to decrease its Supplies Expense account because it didn't use all of the supplies purchased. And it will need to increase an asset account, Supplies, to show it has supplies on hand. The following adjusting entry is then made:

A = L + OE			
+1,000 +1,000			
Cash flows: no effect			

Oct. 31 | Supplies ... 1,000
Supplies Expense ... 1,000
To record supply inventory.

After posting of the adjusting entry, the accounts show the following:

Supplies		Supplies Expense	
Oct. 31 **Adj.** 1,000		Oct. 4 2,500	Oct. 31 **Adj.** 1,000
		Bal. 1,500	

After adjustment, the asset account Supplies shows a balance of $1,000, which is equal to the cost of supplies on hand at October 31. In addition, Supplies Expense shows a balance of $1,500, which is equal to the cost of supplies used between October 4 and October 31 ($2,500 − $1,000). If the adjusting entry is not made, expenses will be overstated and profit will be understated by $1,000 in the October income statement. Also, both assets and owner's equity will be understated by $1,000 on the October 31 balance sheet.

A comparison of the entries and accounts for supplies in the chapter and here in the appendix follows:

Prepayment Debited to Asset Account (as in chapter)			**Prepayment Debited to Expense Account (as in appendix)**		
Oct. 4	Supplies	2,500	Oct. 4	Supplies Expense	2,500
	Accounts Payable	2,500		Accounts Payable	2,500
31	Supplies Expense	1,500	31	Supplies	1,000
	Supplies	1,500		Supplies Expense	1,000

After posting of the entries, the accounts appear as follows:

Prepayment Debited to Asset Account (as in chapter)		
Supplies		
Oct. 4	2,500	Oct. 31 Adj. 1,500
Bal.	1,000	
Supplies Expense		
Oct. 31 Adj.	1,500	

Prepayment Debited to Expense Account (as in appendix)		
Supplies		
Oct. 31 Adj.	1,000	
Supplies Expense		
Oct. 4	2,500	Oct. 31 Adj. 1,000
Bal.	1,500	

Note that the account balances under each alternative are the same at October 31 (Supplies $1,000, and Supplies Expense $1,500).

UNEARNED REVENUES

Unearned revenues are earned either as time passes, as with unearned rent, or by providing the service, as with unearned fees. Rather than first crediting (increasing) an unearned revenue (liability) account, a revenue account may be credited (increased) when cash is received for future services. Then a different adjusting entry may be necessary.

To illustrate, assume that when Pioneer Advertising received $1,200 for future services on October 3, the services were expected to be performed before October 31. In such a case, Service Revenue would be credited. If all the revenue is in fact earned before October 31, no adjustment is needed. However, if at the statement date $800 of the services have not been provided, an adjusting entry is needed to reduce revenue and increase liabilities by $800. The following adjusting entry is made:

Oct. 31	Service Revenue	800	
	Unearned Revenue		800
	To record unearned revenue.		

$A = L + OE$
$+800 \quad -800$
Cash flows: no effect

After posting of the adjusting entry, the accounts show:

Unearned Revenue			Service Revenue		
	Oct. 31 Adj. 800		Oct. 31 Adj. 800	Oct. 3	1,200
				Bal.	400

The liability account Unearned Revenue shows a balance of $800, which is equal to the services that will be provided in the future. In addition, the $400 balance in Service Revenue is equal to the services provided in October ($1,200 − $800). If the adjusting entry is not made, both revenues and profit will be overstated by $800 in the October income statement. On the October 31 balance sheet, liabilities will also be understated by $800, and owner's equity will be overstated by $800.

A comparison of the entries and accounts for service revenue and unearned revenue in the chapter and here in the appendix follows:

Unearned Revenue Credited to Liability Account (as in chapter)		
Oct. 3 Cash	1,200	
Unearned Revenue		1,200
31 Unearned Revenue	400	
Service Revenue		400

Unearned Revenue Credited to Revenue Account (as in appendix)		
Oct. 3 Cash	1,200	
Service Revenue		1,200
31 Service Revenue	800	
Unearned Revenue		800

After posting the entries, the accounts will show:

Unearned Revenue Credited to Liability Account (as in chapter)		Unearned Revenue Credited to Revenue Account (as in appendix)	
Unearned Revenue		**Unearned Revenue**	
Oct. 31 **Adj.** 400 | Oct. 3 1,200		| Oct. 31 **Adj.** 800	
| Oct. 31 **Bal.** 800			
Service Revenue		**Service Revenue**	
| Oct. 31 **Adj.** 400		Oct. 31 **Adj.** 800 | Oct. 3 1,200	
		| Oct. 31 **Bal.** 400	

Note that the balances in the accounts are the same under the two alternatives (Unearned Revenue $800, and Service Revenue $400).

As companies always record long-lived assets as assets, there isn't an alternative method of making an adjusting entry for depreciation. And there isn't an alternative method of making adjusting entries for accruals, because no entries occur before accrual adjusting entries are made. Remember, with an accrual, cash is paid or received after the end of the accounting period.

BEFORE YOU GO ON...

Do It

Mansell Consulting records prepayments as expenses and cash received in advance of providing services as revenue. During February, the following transactions occurred:

> Feb. 4 Paid $950 for supplies.
>   10 Received $2,350 from a client for services to be performed in the future.

On February 28, Mansell determined that $1,750 of the service revenue had been earned and that there was $750 of supplies on hand.

1. Journalize the February transactions.
2. Journalize the adjusting entries at February 28.

Solution

1.	Feb. 4	Supplies Expense	950	
		Cash		950
		To record purchase of supplies.		
	10	Cash	2,350	
		Service Revenue		2,350
		To record cash received for services to be provided.		
2.	28	Supplies	750	
		Supplies Expense		750
		To record supplies on hand as an asset.		
	28	Service Revenue	600	
		Unearned Revenue		600
		To record the obligation to provide services in the future ($2,350 − $1,750).		

Action Plan

- Expenses are recorded as debits and revenues as credits.
- If a prepayment is recorded as an expense, an adjustment will be required at the end of the period if an asset exists.
- If cash received in advance of providing services is recorded as revenue, an adjustment will be required at the end of the period if part of the revenue is still unearned.

THE **NAVIGATOR**

Related exercise material: *BE3–14, *BE3–15, *E3–14, and *E3–15.

Comparing IFRS and ASPE

Key Differences	International Financial Reporting Standards (IFRS)	Accounting Standards for Private Enterprises (ASPE)
Timing of preparing adjusting journal entries	Public companies must prepare quarterly financial statements, so adjusting entries will have to be made at least four times a year.	Private companies must prepare annual financial statements, so adjusting entries are required only on an annual basis.
Terminology	In IFRS, the term "depreciation" is used for the allocation of the cost of long-lived assets such as buildings and equipment and the term "amortization" is used for intangible long-lived assets.	In ASPE, the term "amortization" is used for the allocation of the cost of buildings and equipment and for intangible long-lived assets. But private companies are allowed to use the term "depreciation" for buildings and equipment.

THE NAVIGATOR

Demonstration Problem

Julie Szo opened Green Thumb Lawn Care Company on April 1, 2014. At April 30, 2014, the trial balance is as follows:

GREEN THUMB LAWN CARE COMPANY
Trial Balance
April 30, 2014

	Debit	Credit
Cash	$10,950	
Prepaid insurance	3,600	
Supplies	850	
Equipment	28,000	
Notes payable		$20,000
Accounts payable		450
Unearned revenue		4,200
J. Szo, capital		18,000
J. Szo, drawings	650	
Service revenue		1,800
Rent expense	400	
Totals	$44,450	$44,450

Analysis reveals the following additional data for the month:

1. Prepaid insurance is the cost of a 12-month insurance policy that started April 1.
2. Supplies costing $225 were on hand on April 30.
3. The equipment is expected to have a useful life of four years.
4. The note payable is dated April 1. It is a six-month, 4% note with interest payable on the first of each month starting on May 1.
5. Seven customers paid for the company's six-month lawn service package of $600, beginning in April. These customers were serviced in April.
6. Lawn services performed for other customers but not billed or recorded at April 30 totalled $1,500.

Instructions

(a) Prepare the adjusting entries for the month of April. Show calculations.

(b) Prepare T accounts for the accounts affected by the adjusting entries. Post the adjusting entries to the T accounts.

(c) Prepare an adjusted trial balance at April 30, 2014.

(d) Prepare an income statement, statement of owner's equity, and balance sheet.

Solution to Demonstration Problem

(a)

GENERAL JOURNAL

Date	Account Titles and Explanation	Debit	Credit
	Adjusting Entries		
Apr. 30	Insurance Expense	300	
	Prepaid Insurance		300
	To record insurance expired:		
	$3,600 ÷ 12 = $300 per month.		
30	Supplies Expense	625	
	Supplies		625
	To record supplies used: $850 − $225 = $625		
30	Depreciation Expense	583	
	Accumulated Depreciation—Equipment		583
	To record monthly depreciation:		
	$28,000 ÷ 4 = $7,000 × $\frac{1}{12}$ = $583 per month.		
30	Interest Expense	67	
	Interest Payable		67
	To accrue interest on note payable:		
	$20,000 × 4% × $\frac{1}{12}$ = $67.		
30	Unearned Revenue	700	
	Service Revenue		700
	To record service revenue:		
	$600 ÷ 6 months = $100 per month;		
	$100 per month × 7 customers = $700.		
30	Accounts Receivable	1,500	
	Service Revenue		1,500
	To accrue revenue earned but not billed		
	or collected.		

(b)

GENERAL LEDGER

Accounts Receivable				Accumulated Depreciation—Equipment	
Apr. 30 Adj.	1,500			Apr. 30 Adj.	583
Bal.	1,500			Bal.	583

Prepaid Insurance				Interest Payable	
Apr. 30 Bal.	3,600	Apr. 30 Adj. 300		Apr. 30 Adj.	67
Bal.	3,300			Bal.	67

Supplies				Unearned Revenue	
Apr. 30 Bal.	850	Apr. 30 Adj. 625	Apr. 30 Adj. 700	Apr. 30 Bal.	4,200
Bal.	225			Bal.	3,500

Service Revenue		
	Apr. 30 Bal.	1,800
	30 Adj.	700
	30 Adj.	1,500
	Bal.	4,000

Depreciation Expense		
Apr. 30 Adj.	583	
Bal.	583	

Insurance Expense		
Apr. 30 Adj.	300	
Bal.	300	

Supplies Expense		
Apr. 30 Adj.	625	
Bal.	625	

Interest Expense		
Apr. 30 Adj.	67	
Bal.	67	

(c)

GREEN THUMB LAWN CARE COMPANY
Adjusted Trial Balance
April 30, 2014

	Debit	Credit
Cash	$10,950	
Accounts receivable	1,500	
Prepaid insurance	3,300	
Supplies	225	
Equipment	28,000	
Accumulated depreciation—equipment		$ 583
Notes payable		20,000
Accounts payable		450
Interest payable		67
Unearned revenue		3,500
J. Szo, capital		18,000
J. Szo, drawings	650	
Service revenue		4,000
Depreciation expense	583	
Insurance expense	300	
Interest expense	67	
Rent expense	400	
Supplies expense	625	
Totals	$46,600	$46,600

Solution to Demonstration Problem *continued*
(d)

GREEN THUMB LAWN CARE COMPANY
Income Statement
Month Ended April 30, 2014

Revenues		
Service revenue		$4,000
Expenses		
Depreciation expense	$583	
Insurance expense	300	
Interest expense	67	
Rent expense	400	
Supplies expense	625	1,975
Profit		$2,025

GREEN THUMB LAWN CARE COMPANY
Statement of Owner's Equity
Month Ended April 30, 2014

J. Szo, capital, April 1		$ 0
Add: Investments	$18,000	
Profit	2,025	20,025
Less: Drawings		650
J. Szo, capital, April 30		$19,375

GREEN THUMB LAWN CARE COMPANY
Balance Sheet
April 30, 2014

Assets		
Cash		$10,950
Accounts receivable		1,500
Prepaid insurance		3,300
Supplies		225
Equipment	$28,000	
Less: Accumulated depreciation	583	27,417
Total assets		$43,392

Liabilities and Owner's Equity		
Liabilities		
Notes payable		$20,000
Accounts payable		450
Interest payable		67
Unearned revenue		3,500
Total liabilities		24,017
Owner's equity		
J. Szo, capital		19,375
Total liabilities and owner's equity		$43,392

THE NAVIGATOR

▶ Summary of Study Objectives

1. **Explain accrual basis accounting, and when to recognize revenues and expenses.** In order to provide timely information, accountants divide the life of a business into specific time periods. Therefore it is important to record transactions in the correct time period. Under accrual basis accounting, events that change a company's financial statements are recorded in the periods in which the events occur, rather than in the periods in which the company receives or pays cash. Revenue and expense recognition criteria provide guidance about when to recognize revenues and expenses. Revenue is recognized when the service has been performed or the goods have been sold and delivered, as long as the revenue can be reliably measured and collection is reasonably certain. Expenses are recorded in the same period as revenue is recognized, if there is a direct association between the revenues and expenses. If there is no association between revenues and expenses, expenses are recorded in the period they are incurred.

2. **Prepare adjusting entries for prepayments.** Prepayments are either prepaid expenses or unearned revenues. Adjusting entries for prepayments record the portion of the prepayment that applies to the expense or revenue of the current accounting period. The adjusting entry for prepaid expenses debits (increases) an expense account and credits (decreases) an asset account. For a long-lived asset, the contra asset account Accumulated Depreciation is used instead of crediting the asset account directly. The adjusting entry for unearned revenues debits (decreases) a liability account and credits (increases) a revenue account.

3. **Prepare adjusting entries for accruals.** Accruals are either accrued revenues or accrued expenses. Adjusting entries for accruals record revenues and expenses that apply to the current accounting period and that have not yet been recognized through daily journal entries. The adjusting entry for accrued revenue debits (increases) a receivable account and credits (increases) a revenue account. The adjusting entry for an accrued expense debits (increases) an expense account and credits (increases) a liability account.

4. **Describe the nature and purpose of an adjusted trial balance, and prepare one.** An adjusted trial balance shows the balances of all accounts, including those that have been adjusted, at the end of an accounting period. It proves that the total of the accounts with debit balances is still equal to the total of the accounts with credit balances after the adjustments have been posted. Financial statements are prepared from an adjusted trial balance in the following order: (1) income statement, (2) statement of owner's equity, and (3) balance sheet.

5. **Prepare adjusting entries for the alternative treatment of prepayments (Appendix 3A).** Prepayments may initially be debited (increased) to an expense account. Unearned revenues may initially be credited (increased) to a revenue account. At the end of the period, these revenue or expense accounts may be overstated. The adjusting entries for prepaid expenses are a debit (increase) to an asset account and a credit (decrease) to an expense account. Adjusting entries for unearned revenues are a debit (decrease) to a revenue account and a credit (increase) to a liability account. It does not matter which alternative is used to record and adjust prepayments, as the ending account balances should be the same with both methods.

THE NAVIGATOR

Flash cards

▶ Glossary

Accrual basis accounting A basis for accounting in which revenues are recorded when earned and expenses are recorded when incurred. (p. 113)

Accrued expenses Expenses incurred but not yet paid in cash or recorded. (p. 124)

Accrued revenues Revenues earned but not yet received in cash or recorded. (p. 123)

Accumulated depreciation The cumulative sum of the depreciation expense since the asset was purchased. (p. 119)

Adjusted trial balance A list of accounts and their balances after all adjustments have been posted. (p. 130)

Adjusting entries Entries made at the end of an accounting period to ensure that the revenue and expense recognition criteria are followed. (p. 115)

Carrying amount The difference between the cost of a depreciable asset and its accumulated depreciation; in other words, it is the unallocated or unexpired portion of the depreciable asset's cost. (p. 120)

Cash basis accounting A basis for accounting in which revenue is recorded when cash is received and an expense is recorded when cash is paid. (p. 113)

Contra asset account An account with the opposite balance (credit) compared with its related asset account, which has a debit balance. A contra asset is deducted from the related asset on the balance sheet. (p. 119)

Depreciation The allocation of the cost of a long-lived asset to expense over its useful life in a rational and systematic manner. (p. 119)

Expense recognition criteria Criteria that provide guidance about when to record expenses. Tied to revenue recognition when there is a direct association between costs incurred and the earning of revenue (matching). (p. 114)

Fiscal year An accounting period that is one year long. It does not need to start and end on the same days as the calendar year. (p. 112)

Interim periods Accounting time periods that are less than one year long such as a month or a quarter of a year. (p. 112)

Principal The amount borrowed or the amount still owed on a loan, separate from interest. (p. 125)

Revenue recognition criteria Criteria that provide guidance about when to record revenue. In general, it is recorded when the service has been performed or the goods sold and delivered, as long as the revenue can be reliably measured and collection is reasonably certain. (p. 114)

Straight-line depreciation method A depreciation method in which depreciation expense is calculated as the cost divided by the useful life. (p. 119)

Useful life The length of service of a depreciable asset. (p. 119)

Note: All questions, exercises, and problems below with an asterisk (*) relate to material in Appendix 3A.

▶ Self-Study Questions
Answers are at the end of the chapter.

(SO 1) C 1. The accrual basis of accounting is considered superior to the cash basis of accounting because it:
  (a) is easier to use.
  (b) provides better information about the activities of the business.
  (c) records events in the period in which the cash is paid.
  (d) is used by most businesses.

(SO 1) K 2. Revenue should be recognized when:
  (a) it is earned.
  (b) there is an increase in assets or decrease in liabilities as the result of the company's business activities with its customers.
  (c) the service is provided or the goods are sold and delivered.
  (d) All of the above.

(SO 1) K 3. Adjusting entries are made to ensure that:
  (a) revenues and expenses are recorded in the correct accounting period.
  (b) the accrual basis of accounting is used.
  (c) assets and liabilities have up-to-date balances at the end of an accounting period.
  (d) All of the above.

(SO 2) AP 4. A company pays $1,140 for a one-year insurance policy effective April 1, 2014. The payment is recorded as Prepaid Insurance. On April 30, 2014, an adjusting entry is required to:
  (a) increase the asset Prepaid Insurance by $95 and increase the expense Insurance Expense by $95.
  (b) decrease the asset Prepaid Insurance by $95 and increase the expense Insurance Expense by $95.
  (c) decrease the asset Prepaid Insurance by $1,045 and increase the expense Insurance Expense by $1,045.
  (d) increase the asset Prepaid Insurance by $1,045 and increase the expense Insurance Expense by $1,045.

(SO 2) AP 5. The trial balance shows Supplies $1,350 and Supplies Expense $0. If $600 of supplies are on hand at the end of the period, the adjusting entry is:

(a) Supplies	600	
Supplies Expense		600
(b) Supplies	750	
Supplies Expense		750
(c) Supplies Expense	750	
Supplies		750
(d) Supplies Expense	600	
Supplies		600

(SO 2) K 6. Accumulated Depreciation is:
  (a) an expense account.
  (b) an owner's equity account.
  (c) a liability account.
  (d) a contra asset account.

(SO 2) AP 7. Queenan Company calculates depreciation on its equipment of $1,000 for the month of June. The adjusting journal entry to record this depreciation expense is:

(a) Depreciation Expense	1,000	
Accumulated Depreciation—Equipment		1,000
(b) Depreciation Expense	1,000	
Equipment		1,000
(c) Equipment Expense	1,000	
Equipment		1,000
(d) Accumulated Depreciation—Equipment	1,000	
Equipment		1,000

(SO 2) K 8. A company records all cash received in advance of providing a service as a liability. At the end of the accounting period, an adjustment for unearned revenues is required to:

(a) decrease liabilities and increase revenues.
(b) increase assets and increase revenues.
(c) decrease revenues and increase liabilities.
(d) decrease revenues and decrease assets.

(SO 3) AP 9. A bank has a three-month, 4%, $6,000 note receivable, issued on November 1. Interest is due at maturity. What adjusting entry should the bank record on November 30?

(a) Cash	20	
Interest Revenue		20
(b) Interest Receivable	20	
Interest Revenue		20
(c) Interest Receivable	60	
Unearned Interest Revenue		60
(d) Interest Receivable	60	
Interest Revenue		60

(SO 3) AP 10. Kathy Kiska earned a salary of $400 in the last week of September. She will be paid for this in October. The adjusting entry for Kathy's employer at September 30 is:

(a) Salaries Expense	400	
Salaries Payable		400
(b) Salaries Expense	400	
Cash		400
(c) Salaries Payable	400	
Cash		400
(d) No entry is required		

(SO 4) C 11. Which of the following statements about the adjusted trial balance is *correct*?
(a) An adjusted trial balance proves that the total debit balances and the total credit balances in the ledger are equal after all adjustments are made.

(b) The adjusted trial balance is prepared after preparing financial statements.
(c) The adjusted trial balance lists the account balances divided into assets and liabilities.
(d) The adjusted trial balance proves that the total debits in the adjusting journal entries are equal to the total credits in the adjusting journal entries.

(SO 5) AP *12. The trial balance shows Supplies $0 and Supplies Expense $1,350. If $600 of supplies are on hand at the end of the period, the adjusting entry is:

(a) Supplies	600	
Supplies Expense		600
(b) Supplies Expense	750	
Supplies		750
(c) Supplies	750	
Supplies Expense		750
(d) Supplies Expense	600	
Supplies		600

(SO 5) AP*13. On February 1, Mag City received $6,000 for services to be provided in the future and credited the Service Revenue account. As at February 28, $3,200 of the services have been provided. How should this be reported in the February 28 financial statements?

	Balance Sheet	Income Statement
(a)	Unearned revenue $3,200	Service revenue $2,800
(b)	Service revenue $2,800	Unearned revenue $3,200
(c)	Unearned revenue $2,800	Service revenue $3,200
(d)	Service revenue $3,200	Unearned revenue $2,800

▶ Questions

(SO 1) K 1. (a) Why do accountants divide the life of a business into specific time periods? (b) What is the difference between a fiscal year and a calendar year?

(SO 1) C 2. Why is an accrual basis income statement more useful than a cash basis income statement?

(SO 1) C 3. Pierce Dussault, a lawyer, accepts a legal engagement in March, does the work in April, and is paid in May. If Dussault's law firm prepares monthly financial statements, when should it recognize revenue from this engagement? Why?

(SO 1) C 4. In completing the engagement in question 3, Dussault incurred $500 of salary expenses in March that are specifically related to this engagement, $2,500 in April, and none in May. How much expense should be deducted from revenue in the month(s) when the revenue is recognized? Why?

(SO 1) C 5. The Higher Education College collects tuition for the fall term in August. The fall term runs from September to December. In what month(s) should the college recognize the revenue earned from tuition fees? Explain your reasoning.

(SO 2) C 6. The name Prepaid Expense suggests that this account is an expense and belongs on an income statement. Instead the account appears on the balance sheet as an asset. Explain why this is appropriate and why prepaid expenses may need to be adjusted at the end of each period.

(SO 2) C 7. Roger is a business student at a college. He forgot to keep track of how much of his school supplies he used during the semester. Explain to Roger how he can still determine his supply expense for the semester even though he didn't keep detailed records of what he used.

(SO 2) C 8. "Depreciation is a process of valuation that results in the reporting of the fair value of the asset." Do you agree? Explain.

(SO 2) K 9. Explain the difference between (a) depreciation expense and accumulated depreciation, and (b) cost and carrying amount.

(SO 2) C 10. Why do we credit the contra asset account Accumulated Depreciation—Equipment when recording depreciation instead of crediting Equipment? How is it presented in the financial statements?

(SO 2) C 11. The name Unearned Revenue suggests that this type of account is a revenue account and belongs on the income statement. Instead the account appears on the balance sheet as a liability. Explain why this is appropriate and why unearned revenues may need to be adjusted at the end of the period.

(SO 3) C 12. Waiparous General Store has a note receivable from a customer. The customer pays the interest for the previous month on the first day of each month. Assuming Waiparous prepares monthly financial statements, will it need to accrue for interest revenue on the note at the end of each month? Why or why not? When the interest payment is received each month, what accounts will Waiparous increase and/ or decrease?

(SO 3) C 13. On February 4, ARU Company receives and pays a utility bill for the month of January. Is it necessary to make an adjusting entry for January? Why or why not? If yes, specify the name and type of accounts that need to be adjusted and whether the accounts should be increased or decreased.

(SO 3) AP 14. Sophie has been reading about a recent accounting scandal where the company overstated its revenue on purpose. She then argues that it is never appropriate to make adjusting entries to accrue for revenue. Do you agree or disagree? Why?

(SO 3) AP 15. A company makes an accrued expense adjusting entry for $600. Which financial statement items were overstated or understated before this entry? Explain.

(SO 2, 3) C 16. For each of the following items, indicate (a) the type of adjusting entry required (prepaid expense, unearned revenue, accrued revenue, or accrued expense), and (b) the name of the other account included in the adjusting entry and whether that account is over- or understated prior to the adjustment.
  1. Accounts Receivable is understated.
  2. Unearned Revenue is overstated.
  3. Interest Payable is understated.

  4. Supplies Expense is understated.
  5. Prepaid Insurance is overstated.
  6. Interest Revenue is understated.

(SO 2, 3) K 17. Adjusting entries for accruals always involve the Cash account, and adjusting entries for prepayments never include the Cash account. Do you agree or disagree? Why?

(SO 2, 3) C 18. "An adjusting entry may affect two balance sheet or two income statement accounts." Do you agree? Why or why not?

(SO 4) C 19. Identify the similarities and differences between a trial balance and an adjusted trial balance. What is the purpose of each one?

(SO 4) C 20. "The amount included in an adjusted trial balance for a specific account will always be more than the amount that was included in the trial balance for the same account." Do you agree or disagree? Why?

(SO 4) C 21. On Silver Company's trial balance, Accounts Payable is $4,250. After the adjusting entries have been posted, the balance in this account is still $4,250. Since there is no change, it is not necessary to include Accounts Payable on the adjusted trial balance. Do you agree or disagree? Why?

(SO 4) C 22. Jeremiah is preparing a balance sheet. He includes the amount shown in the adjusted trial balance for the owner's capital account on the balance sheet. Will the balance sheet balance? Why or why not?

(SO 5) C *23. Some companies debit an expense account at the time an expense is prepaid instead of debiting an asset account. The problem with this approach is that expenses will always be overstated, and assets understated. Do you agree or disagree? Why?

(SO 5) C *24. If a company credits a revenue account when cash is received in advance of providing a service, then the adjusting entry is the same as if the company had debited a liability account when it received the cash. Is this correct? Why or why not?

▶ Brief Exercises

Determine profit using cash and accrual bases. (SO 1) AP

BE3–1 AA Lawn Care had the following transactions in May, its first month of business:

1. Collected $500 cash from customers for services provided in May.
2. Billed customers $600 for services provided in May.
3. Received $100 from customers for services to be provided in June.
4. Purchased $250 of supplies on account. All of the supplies were used in May but were paid for in June.
    (a) Calculate profit for May using cash basis accounting.
    (b) Calculate profit for May using accrual basis accounting.

Calculate missing data for supplies. (SO 2) AP

BE3–2 Calculate the missing information in each of the following independent situations:

	Red Co.	Blue Co.
Supplies on hand, May 31, 2013	$ 795	$ 985
Supplies purchased during the year	3,830	3,070
Supplies on hand, May 31, 2014	665	?
Supplies used during the year	?	2,750

BE3–3 Hahn Consulting Company's general ledger showed $825 in the Supplies account on January 1, 2014. On May 31, 2014, the company paid $3,165 for additional supplies. A count on December 31, 2014, showed $1,015 of supplies on hand.

(a) Using T accounts, enter the January 1, 2014, balance in the Supplies and Supplies Expense accounts.
(b) Prepare the journal entry to record the purchase of supplies on May 31, 2014. Post the part of the journal entry that affects only the Supplies or Supplies Expense accounts.
(c) Calculate the amount of supplies used in 2014.
(d) Determine what amounts should appear on the 2014 financial statements for Supplies and Supplies Expense.
(e) Prepare and post the adjusting entry required at December 31, 2014.

Prepare and post transaction and adjusting entries for supplies. (SO 2) AP

BE3–4 On March 1, 2014, Eire Co. paid $4,800 to Big North Insurance for a one-year insurance policy. Eire Co. has a December 31 fiscal year end and adjusts accounts annually. Complete the following for Eire Co.

(a) Prepare the March 1, 2014, journal entry.
(b) Calculate the amount of insurance that expired during 2014 and the unexpired cost at December 31, 2014.
(c) Prepare the adjusting entry required at December 31, 2014.
(d) Using T accounts, post the journal entries in (a) and (c) above, and indicate the adjusted balance in each account.

Prepare and post transaction and adjusting entries for insurance. (SO 2) AP

BE3–5 Reed Company paid $18,000 to purchase equipment on January 1, 2013. Reed Company has a December 31 fiscal year end and uses straight-line depreciation. The company estimates the equipment will have a six-year useful life.

(a) Prepare the journal entry to record the purchase of the equipment on January 1, 2013.
(b) Prepare the adjusting entries required on December 31, 2013 and 2014.
(c) Show the balance sheet presentation of the equipment at December 31, 2013 and 2014.
(d) What amount of depreciation expense will be included in the 2013 and 2014 income statements?

Prepare transaction and adjusting entries for depreciation; show statement presentation. (SO 2) AP

BE3–6 On March 1, 2014, Big North Insurance received $4,800 cash from Eire Co. for a one-year insurance policy. Big North Insurance has an October 31 fiscal year end and adjusts accounts annually. Complete the following for Big North Insurance.

(a) Prepare the March 1, 2014, journal entry.
(b) Calculate the amount of revenue earned during 2014 and the amount unearned at October 31, 2014.
(c) Prepare the adjusting entry required on October 31, 2014.
(d) Using T accounts, post the entries for (a) and (c) above and indicate the adjusted balance in each account.

Prepare and post transaction and adjusting entries for unearned revenue. (SO 2) AP

BE3–7 Ullmann Maintenance Co. has a $455 monthly contract with the sports store Rackets Plus for general maintenance services. Ullmann invoices Rackets Plus on the first of the month for the previous month's services provided. Rackets Plus must then pay for the previous month's services by the 10th of the following month.

(a) Ullmann has a November 30 fiscal year end. Why will it need to prepare an adjusting entry on November 30?
(b) Prepare Ullmann's November 30 adjusting entry.
(c) Will Ullmann need to record a journal entry on December 1 when it invoices Rackets Plus? Why or why not?
(d) Ullmann receives $455 from Rackets Plus on December 9 for services provided in November. Prepare Ullmann's journal entry.

Prepare adjusting and transaction entries for accrued revenue. (SO 3) AP

BE3–8 Refer to BE3–7. Assume that Rackets Plus adjusts its accounts on a monthly basis.

(a) Will Rackets Plus need to prepare an adjusting entry on November 30? If so, prepare the entry.
(b) Will Rackets Plus need to record a journal entry on December 1 when it receives the invoice from Ullmann Maintenance for November's services? If so, prepare the journal entry.
(c) Prepare Racket Plus's journal entry on December 9 when it pays Ullmann $455.

Prepare adjusting and transaction entries for accrued expenses. (SO 3) AP

BE3–9 Vintage Clothing Co. is open for business six days a week. Weekly total salaries of $6,000 are paid every Monday morning to employees for salary earned during the previous six-day workweek (Monday through Saturday). The company has a July 31 fiscal year end, which falls on Thursday this year. Salaries were last paid on Monday, July 28 (for July 21 to 26). The next payday is Monday, August 4 (for July 28 to August 2). Prepare the journal entries to record the following:

(a) The payment of salaries on July 28
(b) The adjusting journal entry to accrue salaries at July 31
(c) The payment of salaries on August 4

Prepare transaction and adjusting entries for salaries. (SO 3) AP

BE3–10 Butternut Squash Company has the following two notes receivable at May 31, 2014, its fiscal year end:

1. $40,000 six-month, 5% note issued January 1, 2014
2. $10,000 three-month, 6% note issued April 30, 2014

Calculate and record accrued interest. (SO 3) AP

Interest is payable at maturity for both notes.

(a) Calculate the accrued interest on both notes at May 31, 2014.
(b) Prepare one adjusting journal entry to record the accrued interest on both notes.

Prepare adjusting and transaction entries for interest. (SO 3) AP

BE3–11 On July 31, 2013, a company purchased equipment for use in the business for $50,000, paying $14,000 cash and signing a 4.5% note payable for the remainder. The interest and principal of the note are due on January 31, 2014. Prepare the journal entry to record the following:

(a) The purchase of the equipment on July 31, 2013
(b) The accrual of the interest at year end, November 30, 2013, assuming interest has not previously been accrued
(c) The repayment of the interest and note on January 31, 2014

Identify effect of adjustment on elements of financial statements. (SO 2, 3) C

BE3–12 In Chapter 3, you learned about four types of adjustments: (1) prepaid expenses; (2) unearned revenues; (3) accrued revenues; and (4) accrued expenses. For each type of adjustment, indicate the following:

(a) The reason the adjustment is required.
(b) The effect of the balance sheet and income statement if the adjustment is not recorded.

Prepare adjusted trial balance and identify financial statement. (SO 4) AP

BE3–13 The account balances (after adjustments) from the general ledger of Winterholt Company at September 30, 2014, follow in alphabetical order. All accounts have normal balances.

Accounts payable	$ 2,890	Rent expense	$ 1,560
Accounts receivable	6,050	Salaries expense	12,215
Accumulated depreciation—equipment	6,400	Salaries payable	875
Cash	1,100	Service revenue	48,450
Depreciation expense	3,100	Unearned service revenue	840
Equipment	29,800	W. Winterholt, capital	16,150
Prepaid rent	780	W. Winterholt, drawings	21,000

(a) Prepare an adjusted trial balance.
(b) Beside each account, identify whether it is an asset (A), liability (L), capital (C), drawing (D), revenue (R), or expense (E).
(c) Beside each account, identify whether it should be included on the income statement (IS), statement of owner's equity (OE), or balance sheet (BS).

Prepare and post adjusting entry for supplies. (SO 5) AP

*BE3–14 Refer to BE3–3. Assume that instead of debiting an asset account for the purchases of supplies, Hahn Consulting Company debits an expense account. Recall that (1) on January 1, 2014, the company had supplies of $825 on hand; (2) the company purchased $3,165 of supplies on May 31, 2014; and that (3) on December 31, 2014, a count showed there was $1,015 of supplies on hand.

(a) Using T accounts, enter the January 1, 2014, balance in the Supplies and Supplies Expense accounts.
(b) Prepare the journal entry to record the purchase of supplies on May 31, 2014. Post the part of the journal entry that affects only the Supplies or Supplies Expense accounts.
(c) Determine what amounts should appear on the 2014 financial statements for Supplies and Supplies Expense.
(d) Prepare and post the adjusting entry required at December 31, 2014.
(e) Compare part (c) above with part (c) in BE3–3. Does it matter whether an original entry is recorded to an asset account or an expense account? Explain.

Prepare and post adjusting entry for unearned revenue. (SO 5) AP

*BE3–15 Refer to BE3–6. Assume that instead of crediting a liability account for the $4,800, one-year insurance policy, Big North Insurance credits a revenue account on March 1, 2014.

(a) Prepare the adjusting entry at October 31, 2014. Using T accounts, enter the balances in the accounts, post the adjusting entry, and indicate the adjusted balance in each account.
(b) Compare the adjusted balances in BE3–6, where a liability account was originally credited, with the adjusted balances you determined here in (a), where a revenue account was originally credited. Does it matter whether an original entry is recorded to a liability account or a revenue account? Explain.

▶ Exercises

Determine profit using cash and accrual bases. Comment on usefulness. (SO 1) AP

E3–1 Cassist Enterprises began operations on January 1, 2013. During 2013 and 2014, the company entered into the following transactions:

	2013	2014
1. Cash collected from customers during the year for services provided that year.	$50,000	$55,000
2. Accounts receivable at year end for services provided on account during the year.	12,000	18,000
3. Cash collected from customers for services provided on account the previous year.	0	12,000

	2013	2014
4. Cash collected from customers for services to be provided the following year.	4,500	2,000
5. Services provided to customers who had paid cash in advance the previous year.	0	4,500
6. Cash paid for operating expenses incurred during the year.	17,250	19,750
7. Accounts payable at year end for operating expenses incurred on account during the year.	2,400	3,100
8. Cash paid to creditors for operating expenses incurred on account during the previous year.	0	2,400

Instructions

(a) Calculate revenue, operating expenses, and profit for 2013 and 2014 using cash basis accounting.

(b) Calculate revenue, operating expenses, and profit for 2013 and 2014 using accrual basis accounting.

(c) Which basis of accounting (cash or accrual) gives more useful information for decision-makers? Explain.

E3–2   For the following independent situations, use professional judgement to determine when the company should recognize revenue from the transactions:

Identify when revenue is recognized. (SO 1) AP

(a) **WestJet Airlines** sells you a nonrefundable airline ticket in September for your flight home at Christmas.

(b) **Leon's Furniture** sells you a home theatre in January on a "no money down, no interest, and no payments for one year" promotional deal.

(c) The **Toronto Blue Jays** sell season tickets to games in the Rogers Centre on-line. Fans can purchase the tickets at any time, although the season does not officially begin until April. It runs from April through October.

(d) The **RBC Financial Group** loans you money at the beginning of August. The loan and the interest are repayable in full at the end of November.

(e) In August, you order a sweater from **Sears** using its on-line catalogue. Sears ships the sweater to you in September and you charge it to your Sears credit card. In October, you receive your Sears bill and pay it.

(f) You pay for a one-year subscription to *Canadian Business* magazine in May.

(g) You purchase a gift card in December from **iTunes** to give to your friend for Christmas. Your friend uses the gift card in January.

Instructions

Identify when revenue should be recognized in each of the above situations.

E3–3   Havanese Services Company records adjusting entries on an annual basis. The following information is available to be used in recording adjusting entries for the year ended December 31, 2014.

Prepare basic analysis, debit/credit analysis, and adjusting journal entry. (SO 2, 3) AP

1. Prepaid insurance totalling $350 has expired.
2. Supplies of $300 have been used.
3. Annual depreciation on equipment is $1,140.
4. Unearned service revenue of $260 has been earned.
5. Salaries of $800 are unpaid.
6. Utility expenses for 2014 of $225 are unrecorded and unpaid.
7. Services provided but not collected in cash or recorded total $1,000.
8. Interest of $125 on a note payable has accrued.

Instructions

For each adjustment, prepare a basic analysis, a debit/credit analysis, and the adjusting journal entry. Use the following format, in which the first one has been done for you as an example:

Adjustment 1:

Basic Analysis	The asset Prepaid Insurance is decreased by $350. The expense Insurance Expense is increased by $350.
Debit/Credit Analysis	Debits increase expenses: debit Insurance Expense $350. Credits decrease assets: credit Prepaid Insurance $350.

Adjusting Journal Entry	Dec. 31 Insurance Expense 350
	                  Prepaid Insurance 350
	                      To record insurance expired.

E3–4   Action Quest Games adjusts its accounts annually. Assume that any prepaid expenses are initially recorded in asset accounts. Assume that any revenue collected in advance is initially recorded as liabilities. The following information is available for the year ended December 31, 2014:

Prepare and post transaction and adjusting entries for prepayments. (SO 2) AP

1. A $4,020 one-year insurance policy was purchased on April 1, 2014.
2. Paid $6,500 on August 31, 2014, for five months' rent in advance.

3. On September 27, 2014, received $3,600 cash from a corporation that sponsors games for the most improved students attending a nearby school. The $3,600 was for 10 games, worth $360 each, that are played on the first Friday of each month starting in October. (Use the Unearned Revenue account.)
4. Signed a contract for cleaning services starting December 1, 2014, for $500 per month. Paid for the first three months on November 30, 2014.
5. On December 15, 2014, sold $935 of gift certificates to a local game club. On December 31, 2014, determined that $545 of these gift certificates had not yet been redeemed. (Use the account Unearned Gift Certificate Revenue.)

Instructions

(a) For each transaction: (1) prepare the journal entry to record the initial transaction, then (2) prepare the adjusting journal entry required on December 31, 2014. Do both for each transaction before doing the next transaction.
(b) Post each of these entries to T accounts and calculate the final balance in each account. (*Note:* Posting to the Cash account is not necessary.)

Prepare adjusting entries for depreciation; calculate accumulated depreciation and carrying amount. (SO 2) AP

E3–5   Action Quest Games owns the following long-lived assets:

Asset	Date Purchased	Cost	Estimated Useful Life
Building	January 1, 2010	$68,000	25 years
Vehicles	December 31, 2013	28,000	7 years
Equipment	July 1, 2012	12,600	4 years

Instructions

(a) Prepare depreciation adjusting entries for Action Quest Games for the year ended December 31, 2014.
(b) For each asset, calculate its accumulated depreciation and carrying amount at December 31, 2014.

Prepare adjusting and related transaction entries for accruals. (SO 3) AP

E3–6   Action Quest Games records adjusting entries on an annual basis. The company has the following information available on accruals that must be recorded for the year ended December 31, 2014:

1. Action Quest has a 4% note payable with its bank for $48,000. Interest is payable on a monthly basis on the first of the month.
2. Action Quest is open seven days a week and employees are paid a total of $3,500 every Monday for a seven-day (Monday–Sunday) workweek. December 31, 2014, is a Wednesday, so employees will have worked three days (Monday–Wednesday) before the year end that they have not been paid for as at December 31. Employees will be paid next on Monday, January 5, 2015.
3. Action Quest receives a commission from Pizza Shop next door for all pizzas sold to customers using Action Quest's facility. The amount owing for December is $520, which Pizza Shop will pay on January 7, 2015.
4. The December utility bill for $425 was unrecorded on December 31. Action Quest paid the bill on January 9, 2015.
5. Action Quest sold some equipment on October 1, 2014, in exchange for a $6,000, 6% note receivable. The principal and interest are due on February 1, 2015.

Instructions

(a) For each of the above items, prepare the adjusting entry required at December 31, 2014.
(b) For each of the above items, prepare the journal entry to record the related cash transaction in 2015. Assume all payments and receipts are made as indicated.

Prepare transaction and adjusting entries. (SO 2, 3) AP

E3–7   Nile Company had the following trial balance at June 30, 2014 (its year end):

	Debit	Credit
Cash	$ 5,840	
Accounts receivable	850	
Supplies	1,100	
Equipment	9,360	
Accumulated depreciation—equipment		$ 3,900
Unearned service revenue		1,500
R. Nile, capital		11,750
Totals	$17,150	$17,150

During the month of July, the following selected transactions took place:

July	2	Paid $750 cash for rent for July, August, and September.
	10	Purchased $200 of supplies for cash.
	14	Collected the full balance of accounts receivable.
	20	Received $700 cash from a customer for services to be provided in August.
	25	Provided $1,300 of services for a customer and immediately collected cash.

Additional information:

1. At July 31, the company had provided $800 of services for a client that it had not billed or recorded.
2. Supplies on hand at July 31 were $800.
3. The equipment has a six-year useful life.
4. As at July 31, the company had earned $900 of revenue that had been paid in advance.

Instructions

(a) Record the July transactions.
(b) Prepare monthly adjusting entries at July 31.

E3–8 The ledger of Bourque Rental Agency on March 31, 2014, includes the following selected accounts before preparing quarterly adjusting entries:

Prepare adjusting entries.
(SO 2, 3) AP

	Debit	Credit
Supplies	$14,400	
Prepaid insurance	3,600	
Equipment	37,800	
Accumulated depreciation—equipment		$ 9,450
Unearned rent revenue		9,300
Notes payable		30,000
Rent revenue		30,000
Wages expense	14,000	

An analysis of the accounts shows the following:

1. The equipment has a four-year useful life.
2. One-quarter of the unearned rent is still unearned on March 31, 2014.
3. The note payable has an interest rate of 6%. Interest is paid every June 30 and December 31.
4. Supplies on hand at March 31 total $850.
5. The one-year insurance policy was purchased on January 1, 2014.
6. As at March 31, a tenant owed Bourque $700 for the month of March.

Instructions

Prepare the quarterly adjusting entries required at March 31, 2014.

E3–9 During 2014, Aubergine Co. borrowed cash from Chartreuse Company by issuing notes payable as follows:

Prepare transaction and adjusting entries for notes and interest. (SO 3) AP

1. July 1, 2014, issued an eight-month, 4% note for $75,000. Interest and principal are payable at maturity.
2. November 1, 2014, issued a three-month, 5% note for $42,000. Interest is payable monthly on the first day of the month. Principal is payable at maturity.

Aubergine has a December 31 fiscal year end and prepares adjusting entries on an annual basis.

Instructions

Prepare all necessary journal entries for Aubergine in 2014 and 2015 regarding the notes and interest including adjusting entries. Prepare separate adjusting entries for each note.

E3–10 Refer to the information provided in E3–9 for Aubergine Co. and Chartreuse Company. Chartreuse has a November 30 fiscal year end and prepares adjusting entries on an annual basis.

Prepare transaction and adjusting entries for notes and interest. (SO 3) AP

Instructions

Prepare all necessary journal entries for Chartreuse in 2014 and 2015 regarding the notes and interest, including adjusting entries. Prepare separate adjusting entries for each note.

E3–11 Trenton Company's fiscal year end is December 31. On January 31, 2014, the company's partial adjusted trial balance shows the following:

Analyze adjusted data.
(SO 2, 3, 4) AN

TRENTON COMPANY
Adjusted Trial Balance (Partial)
January 31, 2014

	Debit	Credit
Supplies	$ 700	
Prepaid insurance	1,600	
Equipment	7,200	
Accumulated depreciation—equipment		$3,660
Salaries payable		800
Unearned revenue		750
Service revenue		2,000
Depreciation expense	60	
Insurance expense	400	
Salaries expense	1,800	
Supplies expense	950	

Instructions

(a) If $1,600 was received in January for services performed in January, what was the balance in Unearned Revenue at December 31, 2013?

(b) If the amount in Depreciation Expense is the depreciation for one month, when was the equipment purchased?

(c) If the amount in Insurance Expense is the January 31 adjusting entry, and the original insurance premium was for one year, what was the total premium, and when was the policy purchased? (Hint: Assume the policy was purchased on the first day of the month.)

(d) If the amount in Supplies Expense is the January 31 adjusting entry, and the balance in Supplies on January 1 was $800, what was the amount of supplies purchased in January?

(e) If the balance in Salaries Payable on January 1, 2014, was $1,200, what was the amount of salaries paid in cash during January?

Prepare adjusting entries from analysis of trial balances. (SO 2, 3, 4) AP

E3-12 The trial balances before and after adjustment for Lane Company at October 31, 2014, which is the end of its fiscal year are as follows:

	Before Adjustment Debit	Before Adjustment Credit	After Adjustment Debit	After Adjustment Credit
Cash	$ 9,100		$ 9,100	
Accounts receivable	8,700		9,230	
Supplies	2,450		710	
Prepaid insurance	3,775		2,525	
Equipment	34,100		34,100	
Accumulated depreciation—equipment		$ 3,525		$ 5,800
Accounts payable		5,900		5,900
Notes payable		40,000		40,000
Salaries payable		0		1,125
Interest payable		0		500
Unearned service revenue		1,600		900
E. Lane, capital		5,600		5,600
E. Lane, drawings	10,000		10,000	
Service revenue		45,000		46,230
Depreciation expense	0		2,275	
Insurance expense	0		1,250	
Interest expense	1,500		2,000	
Rent expense	15,000		15,000	
Salaries expense	17,000		18,125	
Supplies expense	0		1,740	
Totals	$101,625	$101,625	$106,055	$106,055

Instructions

Prepare the adjusting entries that were made.

E3–13   The adjusted trial balance for Lane Company is given in E3–12.

Instructions

Prepare Lane Company's income statement, statement of owner's equity, and balance sheet.

Prepare financial statements from adjusted trial balance. (SO 4) AP

E3–14   Refer to the transaction information provided in E3–4 for Action Quest Games. Assume that prepaid expenses are initially recorded as expenses (not as assets as in E3–4). Assume that revenues collected in advance of the work are initially recorded as revenue (not as liabilities as in E3–4).

Prepare and post transaction and adjusting entries for prepayments. (SO 5) AP

Instructions

(a) For each transaction: (1) prepare the journal entry to record the initial transaction, and (2) prepare the adjusting journal entry required on December 31, 2014.
(b) Post each of these entries to T accounts and calculate the final balance in each account. (*Note:* Posting to the Cash account is not necessary.)
(c) Compare your balances in (b) above with those obtained in E3–4, part (b). Comment on your findings.

E3–15   At Richmond Company, the following select transactions occurred in January, the company's first month of operations:

Prepare and post transaction and adjusting entries for prepayments. (SO 2, 5) AP

Jan.	1	Paid rent of $1,000 for January.
	2	Paid $1,920 for a one-year insurance policy.
	5	Paid $1,700 for supplies.
	19	Received $6,100 cash for services to be performed in the future.
	31	Paid rent of $1,000 for February.

Additional information:

1. On January 31, it is determined that $2,500 of the service revenue has been earned.
2. On January 31, a count of supplies shows that there is $650 of supplies on hand.

Instructions

(a) Assume Richmond records all prepaid costs as expenses, and all revenue collected in advance as revenue. Journalize the January transactions and post to T accounts. (*Note:* Posting to the Cash account is not necessary.)
(b) Journalize and post the January 31 adjustments.
(c) Determine the ending balances in each of the accounts.

▶ Problems: Set A

P3–1A   Your examination of the records of Southlake Co. shows the company collected $85,500 cash from customers and paid $48,400 cash for operating costs during 2014. If Southlake followed the accrual basis of accounting, it would report the following year-end balances:

Determine profit on cash and accrual bases; recommend method. (SO 1) AP

	2014	2013
Accounts payable	$ 1,500	$ 2,250
Accounts receivable	4,200	2,700
Accumulated depreciation	11,300	10,000
Prepaid insurance	1,500	1,300
Supplies	750	400
Unearned revenues	1,200	1,500

Instructions

(a) Determine Southlake's profit on a cash basis for 2014.
(b) Determine Southlake's profit on an accrual basis for 2014.

TAKING IT FURTHER   Which method do you recommend Southlake use? Why?

P3–2A   Ouellette & Associates began operations on January 1, 2014. Its fiscal year end is December 31 and it prepares financial statements and adjusts its accounts annually. Selected transactions for 2014 follow:

Prepare and post prepayment transaction entries. Prepare basic analysis, debit/credit analysis, and journal entry, and post adjustments for the prepayments. (SO 2) AP

1. On January 10, bought office supplies for $3,400 cash. A physical count at December 31, 2014, revealed $925 of supplies still on hand.
2. Paid cash for a $3,780, one-year insurance policy on February 1, 2014. The policy came into effect on this date.
3. On March 31, purchased equipment for $21,240 cash. The equipment has an estimated six-year useful life.

4. Leased a truck on September 1 for a one-year period for $500 per month. Paid the full lease cost of $6,000 in cash.
5. On October 15, received a $1,800 advance cash payment from a client for accounting services expected to be provided in the future. As at December 31, one-third of these services had not been performed.
6. On November 1, rented out unneeded office space for a six-month period starting on this date, and received a $1,725 cheque for the first three months' rent.

Instructions

(a) Prepare a journal entry to record transactions 1 to 6. All prepaid costs should be recorded in asset accounts. All revenue collected in advance of providing services should be recorded as liabilities.
(b) An adjusting entry at December 31, 2014, is required for each of these transactions. Using the format shown in E3–3, prepare the following:
   1. A basic analysis and a debit-credit analysis of the required adjustment.
   2. The adjusting journal entry.
(c) Post the transactions and adjusting entries to T accounts and calculate the final balance in each account. (*Note:* Posting to the Cash account is not necessary.)

TAKING IT FURTHER   Could Ouellette & Associates avoid the need to record adjusting entries by originally recording items 1 through 4 as expenses, and items 5 and 6 as revenues? Explain.

Prepare entries for accrual adjustments and subsequent cash transactions. (SO 3) AP

P3–3A   Ouellette & Associates records adjusting entries on an annual basis. The company has the following information available on accruals that must be recorded for the year ended December 31, 2014:

1. Ouellette has a $10,000, 8% note receivable with a customer. The customer pays the interest on a monthly basis on the first of the month. Assume the customer pays the correct amount each month.
2. Ouellette pays its employees a total of $6,500 every second Tuesday. Employees work a five-day week, Monday to Friday, and are paid for all statutory holidays. December 31, 2014, is a Wednesday. Employees were paid on Tuesday, December 23, 2014 (for the pay period starting Wednesday, December 10, and ending Tuesday, December 23) and will be paid again on Tuesday, January 6, 2015 (for the pay period starting on Wednesday, December 24, and ending on Tuesday, January 6).
3. Ouellette has a contract with a customer where it provides services prior to billing the customer. On December 31, 2014, this customer owed Ouellette $3,375. Ouellette billed the customer on January 7, 2015, and collected the full amount on January 18, 2015.
4. Ouellette received the $485 December utility bill on January 10, 2015. The bill was paid on its due date, January 22, 2015.
5. Ouellette has a $25,000, 5% note payable. Interest is paid every six months, on October 31 and April 30. Assume that Ouellette made the correct interest payment on October 31, 2014, and April 30, 2015.

Instructions

For each of the above items, do the following:

(a) Prepare the adjusting journal entries required on December 31, 2014.
(b) Prepare the journal entry to record the related cash transaction in 2015. Assume all payments and receipts are made as indicated.

TAKING IT FURTHER   Indicate which elements in the financial statements (assets, liabilities, owner's equity, revenue, expenses, and profit) would be either understated or overstated at December 31, 2014, if the accounts were not adjusted.

Prepare transaction and adjusting entries. (SO 2, 3) AP

P3–4A   The following independent items for Last Planet Theatre during the year ended December 31, 2014, may require a transaction journal entry, an adjusting entry, or both. The company records all prepaid costs as assets and all unearned revenues as liabilities and adjusts accounts annually.

1. Supplies on hand amounted to $535 on December 31, 2013. On February 10, 2014, additional supplies were purchased for $1,085 cash. On December 31, 2014, a physical count showed that supplies on hand amounted to $370.
2. Purchased equipment on September 2, 2014, for $23,500 cash. The equipment was estimated to have a useful life of 10 years.
3. Last Planet Theatre puts on seven plays each season. Season tickets sell for $200 each and 250 sold in October for the upcoming 2014–2015 season, which begins in November 2014 and ends in May 2015 (one play per month). Last Planet Theatre credited Unearned Revenue for the full amount received.
4. Every Tuesday, the total payroll is $4,200 for wages earned during the previous six-day workweek (Tuesday to Sunday). Wages were last paid on Tuesday, December 30. This year, December 31 falls on a Wednesday.

5. Last Planet Theatre rents the theatre to a local children's choir, which uses the space for rehearsals twice a week at a rate of $500 per month. The choir was short of cash at the beginning of December and sent Last Planet Theatre a cheque for $350 on December 5, and a promise to pay the balance in January. On January 7, 2015, Last Planet Theatre received a cheque for the balance owing from December plus all of January's rent.

6. On June 1, 2014, the theatre borrowed $25,100 from its bank at an annual interest rate of 4.25%. The principal and interest are to be repaid on March 1, 2015.

7. Upon reviewing its accounting records on December 31, 2014, the theatre noted that the telephone bill for the month of December had not yet been received. A call to the phone company determined that the December telephone bill was $325. The bill was paid on January 10, 2015.

Instructions

(a) Prepare the journal entries to record the 2014 transactions for items 1 though 6.
(b) Prepare the year-end adjusting entry for items 1 through 7.
(c) Prepare the journal entries to record:
　　1. the payment of wages on Tuesday, January 6 (item 4).
　　2. the receipt of the cheque from the children's choir on January 7 (item 5)
　　3. the payment of the telephone bill on January 10 (item 7)
　　4. the payment of the note and interest on March 1, 2015 (item 6)

TAKING IT FURTHER　There are three basic reasons why an unadjusted trial balance may not contain complete or up-to-date data. List these reasons and provide examples of each one using items 1 to 7 to illustrate your explanation.

P3–5A　Melody Lane Co. provides music lessons to many clients across the city. The following information is available to be used in recording annual adjusting entries at the company's September 30, 2014, year end: *Prepare adjusting entries. (SO 2, 3) AP*

1. On October 1, 2013, the company had a balance of $2,000 in its supplies account. Additional supplies were purchased during the year totalling $1,800. The supplies inventory on September 30, 2014, amounts to $750.
2. On November 1, 2013, Melody Lane purchased a one-year insurance policy for $3,200.
3. On February 28, 2014, Melody Lane borrowed $20,000 from the bank and signed a 10-month, 6% note payable. Interest and principal are to be paid at maturity.
4. On March 1, 2014, Melody Lane purchased a grand piano (to be used in music lessons) for $24,000. The piano's estimated useful life is 15 years.
5. On June 1, 2014, a client paid $1,500 for six months of lessons starting June 1, 2014. Melody Lane recorded this cash receipt as Unearned Revenue.
6. On July 15, 2014, the company paid $9,000 to Pinnacle Holdings to rent additional studio space for nine months starting August 1. Melody Lane recorded the full payment as Prepaid Rent.
7. On September 1, 2014, Melody Lane signed a contract with a neighbourhood school to provide weekly piano lessons to some of its students for a fee of $2,000 per month. The contract calls for lessons to start on October 1, 2014.
8. Music lessons were provided to a local church group for $1,500 on September 28, 2014. Melody Lane has not yet invoiced the group or recorded the transaction.
9. Melody Lane's instructors have earned wages of $2,900 for the last week of September, 2014. This amount will be paid to the instructors on the next payday: October 2, 2014.
10. In early October 2014, Melody Lane received an invoice for $475 from the utility company for September utilities. The amount has not yet been recorded or paid.

Instructions
Prepare the adjusting journal entries.

TAKING IT FURTHER　Is it better to prepare monthly adjusting entries or annual adjusting entries as Melody Lane does? Why?

P3–6A　A review of the ledger of Greenberg Company at December 31, 2014, produces the following important data for the preparation of annual adjusting entries: *Prepare adjusting entries. (SO 2, 3) AP*

1. Prepaid Advertising, December 31, 2014, unadjusted balance, $15,600. This balance consists of payments on two advertising contracts for monthly advertising in two trade magazines. The terms of the contracts are as follows:

Contract	First Month	Amount	Number of Magazine Issues
A650	May 2014	$ 6,000	12
B974	October 2014	9,600	24
		$15,600	

2. Vehicles, December 31, 2014, unadjusted balance, $70,000. The company owns two vehicles used for delivery purposes. The first, purchased for $30,000 on January 2, 2012, has an estimated five-year useful life. The second, purchased for $40,000 on June 1, 2014, has an estimated six-year useful life.

3. Prepaid Insurance, December 31, 2014, unadjusted balance, $17,250. This balance consists of two insurance policies: a two-year policy effective July 1, 2013, to June 30, 2015, that cost $12,360 and a one-year policy effective May 1, 2014, to April 30, 2015, that cost $7,980. (*Hint:* Appropriate adjusting entries were made at December 31, 2013.)

4. Notes Payable, December 31, 2014, unadjusted balance, $85,000. This consists of an eight-month, 6.5% note, dated August 1. Interest is payable at maturity.

5. Salaries Payable, December 31, 2014, unadjusted balance, $0. There are nine salaried employees. Salaries are paid every Saturday for a six-day workweek (Monday–Saturday). Six employees receive a salary of $750 per week, and three employees earn $600 per week. December 31, 2014, is a Wednesday.

6. Unearned Revenue, December 31, 2014, unadjusted balance, $270,000. Greenberg began renting office space to tenants in its new building on November 1. At December 31, Greenberg had the following rental contracts that were paid in full for the entire term of the lease:

Rental Term	Monthly Rent	Number of Tenants	Total Rent Paid
Nov. 1, 2014, to Apr. 30, 2015	$4,000	6	$144,000
Dec. 1, 2014, to May 31, 2015	7,000	3	126,000
			$270,000

Instructions

(a) Prepare the adjusting entries at December 31, 2014. Show all your calculations.

(b) For item 2, calculate the accumulated depreciation and carrying amount of each vehicle on December 31, 2014.

TAKING IT FURTHER   What is the purpose of recording depreciation? Why is land not depreciated?

Prepare transaction and adjusting entries for notes and interest. (SO 3) AP

P3–7A   During 2014, Cobalt Co. borrowed cash from Azores Enterprises by issuing notes payable as follows:

1. March 31, 2014, issued a one-year, 4% note for $100,000. Interest is payable quarterly, on June 30, September 30, and December 31, 2014, and March 31, 2015. Principal is payable at maturity.

2. June 1, 2014, issued a nine-month, 4.5% note for $60,000. Interest and principal are payable at maturity.

3. September 1, 2014, issued a three-month, 5% note for $25,000. Interest is payable monthly on the first day of the month. Principal is payable at maturity.

Both Cobalt and Azores prepare adjusting entries on an annual basis. Cobalt has a September 30 fiscal year end. Azores' fiscal year end is October 31.

Instructions

(a) Prepare all necessary journal entries for Cobalt in 2014 and 2015 regarding the notes and interest including adjusting entries. Prepare separate adjusting entries for each note if an adjustment is required.

(b) Prepare all necessary journal entries for Azores in 2014 and 2015 regarding the notes and interest including adjusting entries. Prepare separate adjusting entries for each note if an adjustment is required.

TAKING IT FURTHER   Is it appropriate for Cobalt to have interest payable on its September 30, 2014, balance sheet if the interest isn't payable until some point after the year end? Explain.

Prepare and post adjusting entries, and prepare adjusted trial balance. (SO 2, 3, 4) AP

P3–8A   Reyes Rides is owned by Jason Reyes. The company has an August 31 fiscal year end and prepares adjustments on an annual basis. The following is an alphabetical list of its accounts at August 31, 2014, before adjustments. All accounts have normal balances.

Accounts payable	$ 5,700	J. Reyes, drawings	$141,000
Accounts receivable	7,080	Notes payable	162,000
Accumulated depreciation—equipment	25,200	Prepaid insurance	12,660
Accumulated depreciation—vehicles	175,500	Rent expense	22,810
Cash	9,000	Salaries expense	140,625
Equipment	40,320	Service revenue	334,300
Fuel expense	23,972	Supplies	4,455
Interest expense	9,653	Unearned revenue	25,000
J. Reyes, capital	105,075	Vehicles	421,200

Additional information:

1. On August 31, a physical count shows $630 of supplies on hand.
2. The insurance policy has a one-year term that began on November 1, 2013.
3. The equipment has an estimated useful life of eight years. The vehicles have an estimated useful life of 10 years.
4. The company collects cash in advance for any special services requested by customers. As at August 31, the company has provided all but $4,500 of these services.
5. The note payable has an annual interest rate of 6.5%. Interest is paid on the first day of each month.
6. Employees are paid a combined total of $545 per day. At August 31, 2014, three days of salaries are unpaid.
7. On August 31, the company provided $1,350 of services for a senior citizens' group. The group was not billed for the services until September 2. They paid on September 3.
8. Additional fuel costs of $620 have been incurred but not recorded. (Use the Accounts Payable account.)

Instructions

(a) Journalize the annual adjusting entries at August 31, 2014.
(b) Prepare a ledger. Enter the trial balance amounts and post the adjusting entries.
(c) Prepare an adjusted trial balance at August 31, 2014.

TAKING IT FURTHER   As at August 31, 2014, approximately how old are the equipment and vehicles?

P3–9A   The Highland Cove Resort has an August 31 fiscal year end and prepares adjusting entries on a monthly basis. The following trial balance was prepared before recording the August 31 month-end adjustments:

Prepare and post adjusting entries, and prepare adjusted trial balance and financial statements. (SO 2, 3, 4) AP

HIGHLAND COVE RESORT Trial Balance August 31, 2014		
	Debit	Credit
Cash	$ 17,520	
Prepaid insurance	4,240	
Supplies	995	
Land	35,000	
Buildings	150,000	
Accumulated depreciation—buildings		$ 47,750
Furniture	33,000	
Accumulated depreciation—furniture		12,925
Accounts payable		8,500
Unearned revenue		15,000
Mortgage payable		96,000
K. MacPhail, capital		85,000
K. MacPhail, drawings	42,735	
Rent revenue		246,150
Depreciation expense	5,775	
Insurance expense	6,890	
Interest expense	5,720	
Repairs expense	14,400	
Salaries expense	153,000	
Supplies expense	4,450	
Utilities expense	37,600	
	$511,325	$511,325

Additional information:

1. The company pays $6,360 for its annual insurance policy on March 31 of each year.
2. A count shows $560 of supplies on hand on August 31, 2014.
3. The buildings have an estimated useful life of 50 years.
4. The furniture has an estimated useful life of 10 years.
5. Customers must pay a $100 deposit if they want to book a room during peak times. An analysis of these bookings indicates that 150 deposits were received (all credited to Unearned Revenue) and only 40 of the deposits have not yet been earned by August 31, 2014.

6. The mortgage interest rate is 6.5% per year. Interest has been paid to August 1, 2014.
7. Salaries accrued to the end of August were $1,450.
8. The August utility bill of $3,420 is unrecorded and unpaid.
9. On August 31, Highland Cove has earned $1,350 of rent revenue from customers who are currently renting rooms but will not pay the amount owing until they check out in September. This amount is in addition to any deposits earned in item (5) above.

Instructions

(a) Prepare the monthly adjusting journal entries on August 31.
(b) Prepare a ledger, enter the trial balance amounts, and post the adjusting entries.
(c) Prepare an adjusted trial balance at August 31.
(d) Prepare an income statement and a statement of owner's equity for the year ended August 31, and a balance sheet as at August 31, 2014.

TAKING IT FURTHER Is the owner's capital account on the August 31, 2014, adjusted trial balance the same amount as shown in the August 31, 2014, balance sheet? Why or why not?

Prepare adjusting entries and financial statements.
(SO 2, 3, 4) AP

P3–10A The unadjusted and adjusted trial balances of the Queen Street Advertising Agency as at November 30, 2014, follow:

QUEEN STREET ADVERTISING AGENCY
Trial Balance
November 30, 2014

	Unadjusted		Adjusted	
	Debit	Credit	Debit	Credit
Accounts payable		$ 4,200		$ 4,800
Accounts receivable	$ 13,650		$ 14,750	
Accumulated depreciation—equipment		28,500		34,000
Cash	9,000		9,000	
Depreciation expense	0		5,500	
Equipment	66,000		66,000	
Insurance expense	0		1,600	
Interest expense	875		1,000	
Interest payable		0		125
Note payable		30,000		30,000
Prepaid insurance	2,400		800	
Rent expense	7,150		7,750	
S. Dufferin, capital		17,800		17,800
S. Dufferin, drawings	27,200		27,200	
Salaries expense	12,875		14,350	
Salaries payable		0		1,475
Service revenue		58,750		60,750
Supplies	7,200		1,265	
Supplies expense	0		5,935	
Unearned revenue		7,100		6,200
	$146,350	$146,350	$155,150	$155,150

Instructions

(a) Prepare the adjusting entries that were made.
(b) Prepare an income statement and a statement of owner's equity for the year ended November 30, 2014, and a balance sheet at November 30, 2014.
(c) Calculate the annual interest rate on the note. The note payable has been outstanding for eight months. Interest is paid on a monthly basis at the beginning of each month.
(d) Determine the balance in Salaries Payable on November 30, 2013. The company paid $15,250 in salaries in 2014.

TAKING IT FURTHER A friend of yours is considering purchasing the company from Sally Dufferin and asks you to comment on the company's results of operations and its financial position. Is the company performing well or not? Does the financial position appear healthy or weak? Use specific information from the financial statements to support your answer.

P3–11A Agopian Enterprises is owned by Edmund Agopian and has a January 31 fiscal year end. The company prepares adjusting entries on an annual basis. The following trial balance was prepared before adjustments:

Prepare adjusting entries, adjusted trial balance, and financial statements. (SO 2, 3, 4) AP

AGOPIAN ENTERPRISES
Trial Balance
January 31, 2014

	Debit	Credit
Cash	$ 4,970	
Accounts receivable	14,540	
Prepaid insurance	3,960	
Supplies	6,580	
Equipment	32,350	
Accumulated depreciation—equipment		$ 12,940
Accounts payable		7,760
Note payable		11,000
Unearned revenue		7,480
E. Agopian, capital		18,320
E. Agopian, drawings	119,000	
Service revenue		214,500
Rent expense	20,750	
Salaries expense	66,950	
Telephone expense	2,900	
	$272,000	$272,000

Additional information:

1. A one-year insurance policy was purchased on July 1, 2013.
2. A count of supplies on January 31, 2014, shows $920 of supplies on hand.
3. The equipment has an estimated useful life of five years.
4. An analysis of the Unearned Revenue account shows that $5,230 has been earned by January 31, 2014.
5. The eight-month, 6% note was issued on November 1, 2013. Interest and principal are due on the maturity date.
6. Salaries accrued to January 31, 2014, were $1,315.
7. On January 31, 2014, the company had earned but not billed or recorded consulting revenue of $2,675.
8. The telephone bill for January 2014 was $170. It has not been recorded or paid. (Use the Accounts Payable account.)

Instructions

(a) Prepare adjusting journal entries for the year ended January 31, 2014, as required.
(b) Prepare an adjusted trial balance at January 31, 2014.
(c) Prepare an income statement and statement of owner's equity for the year ended January 31, 2014, and a balance sheet at January 31, 2014.

TAKING IT FURTHER Comment on the company's results of operations and its financial position. In your analysis, refer to specific items in the financial statements.

*P3–12A Horowitz Piano Co. began operations on January 1, 2014. Its fiscal year end is December 31. It prepares financial statements and adjusts its accounts annually. Selected transactions for 2014 follow:

Prepare and post transaction and adjusting entries for prepayments. (SO 2, 5) AP

1. On January 15, 2014, bought supplies for $960 cash. A physical count on December 31, 2014, revealed $245 of supplies still on hand.
2. Bought a $3,090, one-year insurance policy for cash on April 1, 2014. The policy came into effect on this date.
3. On November 1, 2014, received a $1,750 advance cash payment from five clients ($350 each) for services expected to be provided in the future. As at December 31, 2014, services had still not been performed for two of the clients.

Instructions

(a) Assume that Horowitz Piano Co. records all prepaid costs as assets and all revenues collected in advance as liabilities.
1. Prepare the journal entries for the original transactions.
2. Prepare the adjusting journal entries at December 31, 2014.
3. Post these journal entries to T accounts and calculate the balance in each account after adjustments. You do not need to post to the Cash account.
(b) Assume instead that Horowitz Piano Co. records all prepaid costs as expenses and all revenues collected in advance as revenues.
1. Prepare the journal entries for the original transactions.
2. Prepare the adjusting journal entries at December 31, 2014.
3. Post these journal entries to T accounts and calculate the balance in each account after adjustments. You do not need to post to the Cash account.

TAKING IT FURTHER Compare the balance in each account calculated under (a) above with the balances calculated in (b). Comment on your findings.

Prepare adjusting entries and adjusted trial balance using the alternative treatment of prepayments. (SO 3, 4, 5) AP

*P3–13A Winter Designs was organized on January 1, 2014, by Katie Brownsey. Winter Designs records all prepaid costs as expenses and revenue received in advance as revenue. At the end of the first year of operations, the trial balance had the following accounts:

	WINTER DESIGNS Trial Balance December 31, 2014	
	Debit	Credit
Cash	$ 16,600	
Accounts receivable	26,000	
Equipment	80,000	
Accounts payable		$ 14,820
Note payable		44,000
K. Brownsey, capital		60,000
K. Brownsey, drawings	40,000	
Service revenue		121,400
Insurance expense	4,020	
Rent expense	7,800	
Salaries expense	59,900	
Supplies expense	5,900	
	$240,220	$240,220

Analysis reveals the following additional data:

1. On February 1, 2014, the company purchased a one-year insurance policy.
2. The one-year, 5% note payable was issued on March 1, 2014. Interest and principal are payable on the maturity date.
3. The equipment was purchased on March 2, 2014, and has an estimated useful life of eight years.
4. At December 31, 2014, there was $785 of supplies on hand.
5. At December 31, 2014, service revenue of $2,550 was unearned.
6. Service revenue earned but unbilled and unrecorded at December 31, 2014, totalled $1,275.
7. January 2015 rent of $600 was paid on December 31, 2014, and is included in Rent Expense.

Instructions

(a) Journalize the adjusting entries at December 31, 2014. (Adjustments are recorded annually.)
(b) Prepare an adjusted trial balance.

TAKING IT FURTHER If Winter Designs initially recorded all prepaid costs as assets and all revenue received in advance as a liability, would this result in different numbers in the adjusted trial balance than in (b)? Explain.

Problems: Set B

P3–1B   Your examination of the records of Northland Co. shows the company collected $136,200 cash from customers and paid $108,700 cash for operating costs in 2014. If Northland followed the accrual basis of accounting, it would report the following year-end balances:

Determine profit on cash and accrual bases; recommend method. (SO 1) AP

	2014	2013
Accounts payable	$ 3,990	$ 1,460
Accounts receivable	6,100	13,200
Accumulated depreciation	18,250	15,000
Prepaid insurance	620	1,530
Supplies	550	2,350
Unearned revenues	7,400	1,560

Instructions

(a) Determine Northland's profit on a cash basis for 2014.
(b) Determine Northland's profit on an accrual basis for 2014.

TAKING IT FURTHER   Which method do you recommend Northland use? Why?

P3–2B   Burke Bros. began operations on January 1, 2014. Its fiscal year end is December 31 and it prepares financial statements and adjusts its accounts annually. Selected transactions from 2014 follow:

Prepare and post prepayment transaction entries. Prepare basic analysis, debit/credit analysis, and journal entry, and post adjustments for the prepayments. (SO 2) AP

1. On January 9, bought office supplies for $2,950 cash. A physical count on December 31, 2014, revealed $715 of supplies still on hand.
2. Purchased a $4,920, one-year insurance policy for cash on March 1. The policy came into effect on this date.
3. On June 1, purchased equipment for $31,200 cash. The equipment has an estimated eight-year useful life.
4. Rented equipment from Abe's Rentals for a six-month period effective September 1, 2014, for $275 per month and paid cash for the full amount.
5. Rented unused office space to Negaar Madhany for an eight-month period effective October 1, 2014, for $325 per month and collected cash from Negaar for the full amount.
6. On November 15, received a $500 cash payment from each of five clients for services to be provided in the future (total = $2,500). As at December 31, services had been performed for three of the clients.

Instructions

(a) Prepare a journal entry to record transactions 1 to 6. All prepaid costs should be recorded in asset accounts. All revenue collected in advance of providing services should be recorded as liabilities.
(b) An adjusting entry is required for each of these transactions at December 31, 2014. Using the format shown in E3–3, prepare the following:
   1. A basic analysis and a debit-credit analysis of the required adjustment.
   2. The adjusting journal entry.
(c) Post the transactions and adjusting entries to T accounts and calculate the final balance in each account. (*Note:* Posting to the Cash account is not necessary.)

TAKING IT FURTHER   Could Burke Bros. avoid the need to record adjusting entries by originally recording items 1 through 4 as expenses, and items 5 and 6 as revenues? Explain.

P3–3B   Burke Bros. records adjusting entries on an annual basis. The company has the following information available on accruals that must be recorded for the year ended December 31, 2014:

Prepare entries for accrual adjustments and subsequent cash transactions. (SO 3) AP

1. Burke Bros. has a $40,000, 5.5% note payable. Interest is payable on a monthly basis on the first of the month. Assume that Burke Bros. made the correct interest payment on December 1, 2014, and January 1, 2015.
2. Burke Bros. owns drilling equipment, which it rents to customers for $1,200 per day. On December 31, 2014, a customer has had the equipment for 10 days. Burke Bros. billed the customer for 15 days when the equipment was returned on January 5, 2015. The customer paid the full amount that day.
3. Burke Bros. received the $290 December telephone bill on January 5, 2015. The bill was paid on January 9, 2015.
4. Burke Bros. pays its employees a total of $7,500 every second Monday for work completed the two preceding weeks. Employees work a five-day week, Monday to Friday, and are paid for all statutory holidays. December 31, 2014, is a Wednesday. Employees were paid on Monday, December 29, 2014, and will be paid again on Monday, January 12, 2015.

5. Burke Bros. has a $10,000, 7% note receivable with a customer. Interest is receivable every six months on October 31 and April 30. Assume the customer makes the correct payment to Burke Bros. on October 31, 2014, and April 30, 2015.

Instructions

For each of the above items, do the following:

(a) Prepare the adjusting journal entry required on December 31, 2014.
(b) Prepare the journal entry to record the related cash transaction in 2015. Assume all payments and receipts are made as indicated.

TAKING IT FURTHER Indicate which elements in the financial statements (assets, liabilities, owner's equity, revenue, expenses, and profit) would be either understated or overstated at December 31, 2014, if the accounts were not adjusted.

Prepare transaction and adjusting entries.
(SO 2, 3) AP

P3–4B The following independent items for Théâtre Dupuis during the year ended November 30, 2014, may require a transaction journal entry, an adjusting entry, or both. The company records all prepaid costs as assets and all unearned revenues as liabilities and adjusts accounts annually.

1. Supplies on hand amounted to $650 on November 30, 2013. On January 31, 2014, additional supplies were purchased for $1,975 cash. On November 30, 2014, a physical count showed that supplies on hand amounted to $440.
2. Théâtre Dupuis puts on 10 plays each season. Season tickets sell for $210 each and 245 were sold in August for the upcoming 2014–2015 season, which starts in September 2014 and ends in June 2015 (one play per month). Théâtre Dupuis credited Unearned Revenue for the full amount received.
3. The total payroll for the theatre is $4,500 every Wednesday for employee salaries earned during the previous five-day week (Wednesday through Sunday). Salaries were last paid (and recorded) on Wednesday, November 26. In 2014, November 30 falls on a Sunday. The next payday is Wednesday, December 3, 2014.
4. Théâtre Dupuis rents the theatre to a local seniors' choir, which uses the space for rehearsals twice a week at a rate of $425 per month. The new treasurer of the choir accidentally sent a cheque for $245 on November 1. The treasurer promised to send a cheque in December for the balance when she returns from her vacation. On December 4, Théâtre Dupuis received a cheque for the balance owing from November plus all of December's rent.
5. On June 1, 2014, borrowed $14,000 from La caisse populaire Desjardins at an annual interest rate of 5.5%. The principal and interest are to be repaid on February 1, 2015.
6. Upon reviewing the books on November 30, 2014, it was noted that the utility bill for the month of November had not yet been received. A call to Hydro-Québec determined that the utility bill was for $935. The bill was paid on December 10.
7. Owned a truck during the year that had originally been purchased on December 1, 2010, for $37,975. The truck's estimated useful life is seven years.

Instructions

(a) Prepare the journal entries to record the original transactions for items 1 through 5.
(b) Prepare the year-end adjusting entry for items 1 through 7.
(c) Prepare the journal entry to record:
   1. the payment of wages on Wednesday, December 3 (item 3)
   2. the receipt of the cheque from the seniors' choir on December 4 (item 4)
   3. the payment of the utility bill on December 10 (item 6)
   4. the payment of the note and interest on February 1, 2015 (item 5)

TAKING IT FURTHER There are three basic reasons why an unadjusted trial balance may not contain complete or up-to-date data. List these reasons and provide examples of each one using items 1 to 7 to illustrate your explanation.

Prepare adjusting entries.
(SO 2, 3) AP

P3–5B Best First Aid offers first aid training to individuals and groups across the city. The following information is available to be used in recording annual adjusting entries for the company's October 31, 2014, year end:

1. Best First Aid purchased equipment on November 1, 2009, for $9,000. The equipment was estimated to have a useful life of six years.
2. On November 1, 2013, the company had a balance of $1,000 in its supplies account. Additional supplies were purchased during the year totalling $2,500. The supplies inventory on October 31, 2014, amounts to $980.
3. The company paid a premium of $3,600 for a one-year insurance policy starting on May 31, 2014. Best First Aid recorded the payment as prepaid insurance.

4. On July 1, 2014, Best First Aid borrowed $28,000 and signed a nine-month, 6% note payable. Interest and principal are payable at maturity.

5. On October 1, 2014, Best First Aid moved to new offices. Rent is $800 per month. Best First Aid paid the first three months' rent that day.

6. Best First Aid requires a $200 deposit from clients as an advance payment for first aid training courses when they are booked. As at October 31, 2014, Best First Aid has deposits for 15 training courses recorded as unearned revenue. A review of the company's records shows that the company has provided all but five of the 15 training courses.

7. On October 1, 2014, Best First Aid signed a contract with UC Company to provide seven days of first aid training to UC employees, starting in November, at a rate of $1,500 per day. The contract calls for UC to pay the amount owed by December 31, 2014.

8. On October 28, 2014, Best First Aid provided a first aid training course to MRC employees. Best First Aid was too busy to invoice MRC that day. Instead, it prepared the $1,550 invoice on November 2, 2014. MRC agreed to pay this amount on November 15, 2014.

9. Best First Aid has two employees, who are each paid $125 per day. On October 31, 2014, these employees had each worked three days since they were last paid.

10. In early November, Best First Aid received an invoice for $360 from BellTel for October telephone charges. The amount has not yet been recorded or paid.

Instructions
Prepare the adjusting journal entries.

TAKING IT FURTHER   Is it better to prepare monthly adjusting entries or annual adjusting entries as Best First Aid does? Why?

P3–6B   A review of the ledger of Hashmi Company at December 31, 2014, produces the following data for the preparation of annual adjusting entries:

Prepare adjusting entries.
(SO 2, 3) AP

1. Notes Receivable, December 31, 2014, unadjusted balance, $25,000. Hashmi has a 7% note receivable issued on October 1, 2014, maturing on June 1, 2015. Interest and principal are to be paid in full on the maturity date.

2. Prepaid Insurance, December 31, 2014, unadjusted balance, $14,100. The company has separate insurance policies on its buildings and its motor vehicles. Policy B4564 on the buildings was purchased on September 1, 2013, for $10,440. The policy has a term of two years. Policy A2958 on the vehicles was purchased on March 1, 2014, for $5,400. This policy also has a term of one year.

3. Prepaid Rent, December 31, 2014, unadjusted balance, $3,135. The company has prepaid rental agreements for two pieces of equipment. The first one costs $335 per month and is for September 30, 2014, to March 31, 2015. The other costs $375 per month and is for December 1, 2014, to March 1, 2015. The company paid the full amount for each rental agreement at the start of the rental period.

4. Buildings, December 31, 2014, unadjusted balance, $291,960. The first, purchased for $127,800 on September 1, 2001, has an estimated 30-year useful life. The second, purchased for $164,160 on May 1, 2003, has an estimated 40-year useful life.

5. Unearned Revenue, December 31, 2014, unadjusted balance, $46,550. The company began selling magazine subscriptions in 2014. The selling price of a subscription is $35 for 12 monthly issues. Customers start receiving the magazine in the month the subscription is purchased. A review of subscription contracts that customers have paid for prior to December 31 reveals the following:

Subscription Date	Number of Subscriptions
October 1	325
November 1	450
December 1	555

6. Salaries Payable, December 31, 2014, unadjusted balance, $0. There are nine salaried employees, each of whom is paid every Monday for the previous week (Monday to Friday). Six employees receive a salary of $650 each per week, and three employees earn $850 each per week. December 31 is a Wednesday.

Instructions
(a) Prepare calculations to show why the balance (before adjustments) in the Prepaid Insurance account is $14,100 and why the balance (before adjustments) in the Unearned Subscription Revenue account is $46,550.

(b) Prepare the adjusting entries at December 31, 2014. Show all your calculations.

(c) For item 4, calculate the accumulated depreciation and carrying amount of each building on December 31, 2014.

TAKING IT FURTHER   What is the purpose of recording depreciation? Why is land not depreciated?

Prepare transaction and adjusting entries for notes and interest. (SO 3) AP

P3–7B   During 2014, Alabaster Co. borrowed cash from Fuchsia Enterprises by issuing notes payable as follows:

1. June 1, 2014, issued a seven-month, 4% note for $50,000. Interest and principal are payable at maturity.
2. September 30, 2014, issued a one-year, 3.5% note for $80,000. Interest is payable quarterly, on December 31, 2014, and March 31, June 30, and September 30, 2015. Principal is payable at maturity.
3. October 1, 2014, issued a three-month, 5.5% note for $45,000. Interest is payable monthly on the first day of the month. Principal is payable at maturity.

Both Alabaster and Fuchsia prepare adjusting entries on an annual basis. Alabaster has an October 31 fiscal year end. Fuchsia's fiscal year end is November 30.

Instructions

(a) Prepare all necessary journal entries for Alabaster in 2014 and 2015 regarding the notes and interest including adjusting entries. Prepare separate adjusting entries for each note if an adjustment is required.

(b) Prepare all necessary journal entries for Fuchsia in 2014 and 2015 regarding the notes and interest including adjusting entries. Prepare separate adjusting entries for each note if an adjustment is required.

TAKING IT FURTHER   Is it appropriate for Fuchsia to have interest receivable on its November 30, 2014, balance sheet if the interest isn't due until some point after the year end? Explain.

Prepare and post adjusting entries, and prepare adjusted trial balance. (SO 2, 3, 4) AP

P3–8B   Red Bridges Towing is owned by Ken Cordial. The company has a June 30 fiscal year end and prepares adjustments on an annual basis. The following is an alphabetical list of its accounts at June 30, 2014, before adjustments. All accounts have normal balances.

Accounts payable	$ 5,075	K. Cordial, drawings	$ 91,650
Accounts receivable	5,310	Notes payable	120,000
Accumulated depreciation—equipment	5,040	Prepaid insurance	9,480
Accumulated depreciation—vehicles	26,325	Rent expense	17,095
Cash	9,810	Salaries expense	101,400
Equipment	30,240	Service revenue	252,795
Fuel expense	17,980	Supplies	4,470
Interest expense	4,950	Unearned revenue	18,750
K. Cordial, capital	75,000	Vehicles	210,600

Additional information:

1. On June 30, a physical count of supplies shows $715 of supplies on hand.
2. The insurance policy has a one-year term that began on October 1, 2013.
3. The equipment has an estimated useful life of six years. The vehicles have an estimated useful life of eight years.
4. The company collects cash in advance for any special services requested by customers. As at June 30, the company has provided all but $2,250 of these services.
5. The note payable has an annual interest rate of 4.5%. Interest is paid on the first day of each month.
6. Employees are paid a combined total of $390 per day. At June 30, 2014, six days of salaries are unpaid.
7. On June 30, the company provided $1,100 of services at a local boat show. The group organizing the show was not billed for the services until July 2. They paid on July 5.

Instructions

(a) Journalize the annual adjusting entries at June 30, 2014.

(b) Prepare a ledger. Enter the trial balance amounts and post the adjusting entries.

(c) Prepare an adjusted trial balance at June 30.

TAKING IT FURTHER   As at June 30, 2014, approximately how old are the equipment and vehicles?

P3–9B Mountain Best Lodge has a May 31 fiscal year end and prepares adjusting entries on a monthly basis. The following trial balance was prepared before recording the May 31 month-end adjustments:

Prepare and post adjusting entries, and prepare adjusted trial balance and financial statements. (SO 2, 3, 4) AP

MOUNTAIN BEST LODGE
Trial Balance
May 31, 2014

	Debit	Credit
Cash	$ 12,365	
Prepaid insurance	3,080	
Supplies	1,050	
Land	80,000	
Buildings	180,000	
Accumulated depreciation—buildings		$ 76,125
Furniture	21,000	
Accumulated depreciation—furniture		12,250
Accounts payable		4,780
Unearned revenue		8,500
Mortgage payable		146,400
M. Rundle, capital		54,800
M. Rundle, drawings	18,750	
Rent revenue		102,100
Advertising expense	500	
Depreciation expense	7,975	
Salaries expense	49,304	
Supplies expense	5,410	
Interest expense	7,381	
Insurance expense	4,840	
Utilities expense	13,300	
	$404,955	$404,955

Additional information:

1. The company pays $5,280 for its annual insurance policy on November 30 of each year.
2. A count of supplies on May 31 shows $760 of supplies on hand.
3. The buildings were purchased on May 31, 1997, and have an estimated useful life of 40 years.
4. The furniture was purchased on June 1, 2011, and has an estimated useful life of five years.
5. Customers must pay a $50 deposit if they want to book a room in advance during peak times. An analysis of these bookings indicates that 170 deposits were received (all credited to Unearned Revenue) and 40 of the deposits have been earned by May 31, 2014.
6. The mortgage interest rate is 5.5% per year. Interest has been paid to May 1, 2014. The next payment is due on June 1.
7. Salaries accrued to the end of May were $1,025.
8. The May utility bill of $1,250 is unrecorded and unpaid.
9. On May 31, Mountain Best Lodge has earned $950 of rent revenue from customers who are currently using the rooms but will not pay the amount owing until they check out in June. This amount is in addition to any deposits earned in item (5) above.

Instructions

(a) Journalize the monthly adjusting entries on May 31.
(b) Prepare a ledger. Enter the trial balance amounts and post the adjusting entries.
(c) Prepare an adjusted trial balance at May 31.
(d) Prepare an income statement and statement of owner's equity for the year ended May 31, and a balance sheet at May 31.

TAKING IT FURTHER Is the owner's capital account on the May 31, 2014, adjusted trial balance the same amount as shown in the May 31, 2014, balance sheet? Why or why not?

Prepare adjusting entries and financial statements.
(SO 2, 3, 4) AP

P3–10B The unadjusted and adjusted trial balances of Sainte-Catherine Interior Design Co. as at September 30, 2014, follow:

	Unadjusted		Adjusted	
SAINTE-CATHERINE INTERIOR DESIGN CO. Trial Balance September 30, 2014	Debit	Credit	Debit	Credit
Accounts payable		$ 4,350		$ 4,660
Accounts receivable	$ 6,335		$ 7,435	
Accumulated depreciation—equipment		4,500		5,000
C. Larocque, capital		10,000		10,000
C. Larocque, drawings	2,700		2,700	
Cash	3,250		3,250	
Depreciation expense	0		500	
Equipment	16,000		16,000	
Interest expense	50		100	
Interest payable		0		50
Notes payable		12,000		12,000
Prepaid rent	2,400		1,050	
Rent expense	0		1,350	
Service revenue		14,420		15,845
Salaries expense	13,050		13,990	
Salaries payable		0		940
Supplies	1,750		1,075	
Supplies expense	0		675	
Unearned revenue		875		550
Utilities expense	610		920	
	$46,145	$46,145	$49,045	$49,045

Instructions

(a) Prepare the adjusting journal entries that were made for the quarter.
(b) Prepare an income statement and a statement of owner's equity for the three months ending September 30 and a balance sheet at September 30.
(c) If the note bears interest at 5%, how many months has it been outstanding? Interest is payable at the beginning of the month.

TAKING IT FURTHER A friend of yours is considering purchasing the company from Catherine Larocque and asks you to comment on the company's results of operations and its financial position. Is the company performing well or not? Does the financial position appear healthy or weak? Use specific information from the financial statements to support your answer.

Prepare adjusting entries, adjusted trial balance, and financial statements.
(SO 2, 3, 4) AP

P3–11B Shek Enterprises is owned by Memphis Shek and has a December 31 fiscal year end. The company prepares adjusting entries on an annual basis. Some additional information follows:

1. A one-year insurance policy was purchased on May 1, 2014.
2. A count of supplies on December 31, 2014, shows $1,290 of supplies on hand.
3. The equipment has an estimated useful life of six years.
4. An analysis of the Unearned Revenue account shows that $4,000 has been earned by December 31, 2014.
5. The three-year, 5% note payable was issued on April 1, 2014. Interest is payable every six months on April 1 and October 1 each year. The principal is payable at maturity.
6. Salaries accrued to December 31, 2014, were $915.
7. On December 31, 2014, the company had earned but not billed or recorded consulting revenue of $2,000.
8. The telephone bill for December 2014 was $210. It has not been recorded or paid. (Use the Accounts Payable account.)

The following trial balance was prepared before adjustments:

SHEK ENTERPRISES
Trial Balance
December 31, 2014

	Debit	Credit
Cash	$ 6,725	
Accounts receivable	10,915	
Prepaid insurance	5,940	
Supplies	8,680	
Equipment	24,240	
Accumulated depreciation—equipment		$ 10,100
Accounts payable		5,765
Note payable		14,000
Unearned revenue		5,550
M. Shek, capital		13,750
M. Shek, drawings	85,000	
Service revenue		160,875
Interest expense	350	
Rent expense	15,600	
Salaries expense	50,225	
Telephone expense	2,365	
	$210,040	$210,040

Instructions

(a) Prepare adjusting journal entries for the year ended December 31, 2014, as required.
(b) Prepare an adjusted trial balance at December 31, 2014.
(c) Prepare an income statement and statement of owner's equity for the year ended December 31, 2014, and a balance sheet at December 31, 2014.

TAKING IT FURTHER Comment on the company's results of operations and its financial position. In your analysis, refer to specific items in the financial statements.

*P3–12B Garrett Bass Co. began operations on January 1, 2014. Its fiscal year end is December 31. It prepares financial statements and adjusts its accounts annually. Selected transactions for 2014 follow:

1. On January 1, 2014, bought supplies for $1,250 cash. A physical count at December 31, 2014, revealed $375 of supplies still on hand.
2. Bought a $2,820, one-year insurance policy for cash on February 1, 2014. The policy came into effect on this date.
3. On December 1, Garrett received a $1,200 advance cash payment from four clients ($300 each) for services expected to be provided in the future. As at December 31, services had been performed for only one of the clients.

Instructions

(a) Assume that Garrett Bass Co. records all prepaid costs as assets and all revenues collected in advance as liabilities.
   1. Prepare the journal entries for the original transactions.
   2. Prepare the adjusting journal entries at December 31, 2014.
   3. Post these journal entries to T accounts and calculate the balance in each account after adjustments. You do not need to post to the Cash account.
(b) Assume instead that Garrett Bass Co. records all prepaid costs as expenses and all revenues collected in advance as revenues.
   1. Prepare the journal entries for the original transactions.
   2. Prepare the adjusting journal entries at December 31, 2014.
   3. Post these journal entries to T accounts and calculate the balance in each account after adjustments. You do not need to post to the Cash account.

Prepare and post transaction and adjusting entries for prepayments. (SO 2, 5) AP

TAKING IT FURTHER   Compare the balances in each account calculated under (a) above with those calculated in (b). Comment on your findings.

Prepare adjusting entries, and adjusted trial balance using the alternative treatment of prepayments. (SO 3, 4, 5) AP

*P3–13B   Summer Design Company was organized on January 1, 2014, by Corine Burian. Summer Design records all prepaid costs as expenses and all revenues received in advance as revenue. At the end of the first year of operations, the trial balance had the following accounts:

SUMMER DESIGN COMPANY
Trial Balance
December 31, 2014

	Debit	Credit
Cash	$ 8,790	
Accounts receivable	12,970	
Equipment	45,900	
Accounts payable		$ 5,500
Note payable		32,400
C. Burian, capital		28,000
C. Burian, drawings	16,800	
Service revenue		64,300
Insurance expense	1,980	
Interest expense	1,485	
Rent expense	8,125	
Salaries expense	28,800	
Supplies expense	5,350	
	$130,200	$130,200

Analysis reveals the following additional information:

1. A one-year, 5% note payable was issued January 2, 2014. Interest is payable monthly on the first of the month. Principal is payable at maturity.
2. Equipment was purchased on January 3, 2014, and has an estimated useful life of 12 years.
3. On April 1, 2014, the company purchased a one-year insurance policy.
4. During the year, Summer Designs collected $6,000 cash from customers before providing services to them. At December 31, 2014, $4,500 of this amount has been earned.
5. A count at December 31, 2014, showed $445 of supplies on hand.
6. Salaries of $850 are owed at December 31, 2014.
7. January 2015 rent of $625 was paid on December 31, 2014, and is included in Rent Expense.

Instructions

(a) Journalize the adjusting entries at December 31. (Adjustments are recorded annually.)
(b) Prepare an adjusted trial balance.

TAKING IT FURTHER   If Summer Designs recorded all prepaid costs as assets and all revenue received in advance as a liability, would this result in different numbers in the adjusted trial balance than in (b)?

▶ Continuing Cookie Chronicle

(*Note:* This is a continuation of the Cookie Chronicle from Chapters 1 and 2. Use the information from the previous chapters and follow the instructions below using the ledger accounts you have already prepared.)

It is the end of December and Natalie has been in touch with her grandmother. Her grandmother is curious to know if Natalie has been profitable and if Natalie requires another loan to help finance her business. Natalie too would like to know if she has been profitable during her first two months of operation. Natalie realizes that, in order to determine Cookie Creations' income, she must first make adjustments. Natalie puts together the following

additional information:

1. A count reveals that $95 of supplies remain at the end of December.
2. Natalie was invited to teach a cookie-making class at a children's New Year's Eve function at her local community centre. At the end of the class, she left an invoice for $175 with the program director. Natalie had not had time to record this invoice in her accounting records. Because there were so many children expected to attend, she asked a friend to help with the class and promised to pay her $12 an hour. The payment to her friend was made on January 4, 2014, for four hours of work.
3. Natalie estimates that all of her equipment will have a useful life of three years or 36 months. (Assume Natalie decides to record a full month's worth of depreciation, regardless of when the equipment was acquired by the business.)
4. Recall that Natalie's grandmother is charging 3% interest on the note payable extended on November 29. The loan plus interest is to be repaid in 12 months. (Calculate interest to the nearest month.)

Instructions

Using the information that you have gathered through Chapter 2, and based on the new information above, do and answer the following:

(a) Prepare and post the adjusting journal entries. Round all amounts to the nearest dollar.
(b) Prepare an adjusted trial balance.
(c) Prepare an income statement for the two-month period ended December 31, 2013.
(d) Was Cookie Creations profitable during these first two months of operation? Why is it better for Cookie Creations to measure profitability after adjusting journal entries have been prepared and posted instead of before?
(e) How much cash is available to Natalie to operate her business? Why is the amount of cash different than the amount of profit that Cookie Creations has earned? What is the most likely reason that Natalie may need to borrow additional money from her grandmother?

Cumulative Coverage—Chapters 1 to 3

On August 31, 2014, the account balances of Pitre Equipment Repair were as follows:

PITRE EQUIPMENT REPAIR
Trial Balance
August 31, 2014

	Debit	Credit
Cash	$ 1,880	
Accounts receivable	3,720	
Supplies	800	
Equipment	15,000	
Accumulated depreciation—equipment		$ 1,500
Accounts payable		3,100
Unearned revenue		400
Salaries payable		700
R. Pitre, capital		15,700
	$21,400	$21,400

During September, the following transactions were completed:

Sept. 1   Borrowed $10,000 from the bank and signed a two-year, 5% note payable.
     8   Paid $1,100 for employees' salaries, of which $400 is for September and $700 for August.
     10   Received $1,200 cash from customers on account.
     12   Received $3,400 cash for services performed in September.
     17   Purchased additional supplies on account, $1,500.
     20   Paid creditors $4,500 on account.

22   Paid September and October rent, $1,000 ($500 per month).
25   Paid salaries, $1,200.
27   Performed services on account and billed customers for services provided, $900.
29   Received $700 from customers for future services.
30   Purchased additional equipment on account, $3,000.

The company adjusts its accounts on a monthly basis. Adjustment data consist of the following:

1. Supplies on hand at September 30 cost $1,280.
2. Accrued salaries payable at September 30 total $775.
3. Equipment has an expected useful life of five years.
4. Unearned service revenue of $450 is still not earned at September 30.
5. Interest is payable on the first of each month.

Instructions

(a) Enter the August 31 balances in general ledger accounts.
(b) Journalize the September transactions.
(c) Post to the ledger accounts.
(d) Prepare a trial balance at September 30.
(e) Journalize and post adjusting entries.
(f) Prepare an adjusted trial balance.
(g) Prepare an income statement and a statement of owner's equity for September, and a balance sheet.

CHAPTER 3 | BROADENING YOUR PERSPECTIVE

▶ Financial Reporting and Analysis

Financial Reporting Problem

BYP3–1   The financial statements of **Reitmans (Canada) Limited** are presented in Appendix A at the end of this textbook.

Instructions

(a) What title does Reitmans use for its income statement?
(b) How much depreciation on its property and equipment did Reitmans record in 2012 and 2011? How has Reitmans reported its depreciation expense on its statement of earnings? (See Note 8.)
(c) What is included in the Reitmans revenues? (See Note 3. l.)
(d) Does Reitmans report any unearned (deferred) revenue? What are the sources of the company's unearned (deferred) revenue? (See Note 13.)
(e) Reitmans reports prepaid expenses on its balance sheet but does not provide any additional details in its notes to the financial statements. Provide two examples of expenses that Reitmans might have prepaid.

Interpreting Financial Statements

BYP3–2   Rogers Communications Inc. is a diversified Canadian communications and media company engaged in three primary lines of business: Wireless, Cable, and Media. The following is part of Rogers' revenue recognition policy note in its financial statements:

ROGERS COMMUNICATIONS INC.
Notes to the Financial Statements
December 31, 2011

Note 2 (d): Significant accounting policies—Revenue recognition

The Company's principal sources of revenue and recognition of these revenues for financial statement purposes are as follows:

- Monthly subscriber fees in connection with wireless and wireline services, cable, telephony, Internet services, rental of equipment, network services, and media subscriptions are recorded as revenue on a pro rata basis as the service is provided;
- Installation fees and activation fees charged to subscribers are recorded in Wireless as part of equipment revenue and, in Cable, are deferred and amortized over the related service period. The related service period for Cable ranges from 26 to 48 months, based on subscriber disconnects, transfers of service and moves. . . . New connect installation costs are capitalized [added] to PP&E [long-lived assets] and depreciated over the useful lives of the related assets;
- Advertising revenue is recorded in the period the advertising airs on the Company's radio or television stations; is featured in the Company's publications; or is displayed on the Company's digital properties.
- The Toronto Blue Jays Baseball Club's revenue from home game admission and concessions is recognized as the related games are played during the baseball season. Revenue from radio and television agreements is recorded at the time the related games are aired.

Rogers' balance sheet included a current liability of $335 million at December 31, 2011, called Unearned Revenue. Unearned revenue includes subscriber deposits, cable installation fees, and amounts received from subscribers related to services and subscriptions to be provided in future periods.

Instructions

(a) When does Rogers recognize its revenue from monthly subscriber fees?

(b) When should Rogers record unearned revenue from its subscription services? When should it record unearned revenue for its Blue Jays home game admission revenue?

(c) If Rogers (inappropriately) recorded these unearned revenues as revenue when the cash was received in advance, what would be the effect on the company's financial position? (Use the basic accounting equation and explain what elements would be overstated or understated.)

(d) According to this note, Rogers' new installation costs are depreciated over the useful life of the related assets. Is this an appropriate method of expense recognition for these costs? Explain.

⊙ Critical Thinking

Collaborative Learning Activity

Note to instructor: Additional instructions and material for this group activity can be found on the Instructor Resource Site and in *WileyPLUS*.

BYP3–3   In this group activity, you will work in two different groups to improve your understanding of adjusting entries. First you will work in "expert" groups in which you will ensure that each group member thoroughly understands one type of adjusting journal entry. Then you will move to a second group consisting of one student from each of the different expert groups, and take turns teaching the different types of adjusting entries.

Communication Activity

BYP3–4   Some people believe that cash basis accounting is better than accrual basis accounting in predicting a company's future success. This idea became more popular after many reports of corporate financial scandals where management manipulated the timing of recognizing expenses and revenues in accrual accounting to influence profit. Others argue it is easier to manipulate profit using cash basis accounting.

Write a memo discussing the following issues:

(a) What is the difference in calculating profit using accrual basis accounting versus cash basis accounting?
(b) Identify one way that management might be able to increase profit by manipulating the timing of revenue or expense recognition under accrual accounting.
(c) Identify one way that management might be able to increase profit using cash basis accounting.
(d) Which basis do you believe is more reliable for measuring performance and why?

Ethics Case

BYP3–5 Die Hard Company is a pesticide manufacturer. Its sales dropped a lot this year because of new legislation that outlawed the sale of many of Die Hard's chemical pesticides. In the coming year, Die Hard will have new, environmentally safe chemicals to replace these discontinued products. Sales in the next year are expected to be much higher than sales of any previous year. The drop in sales and profits appears to be a one-year exception.

Still, the company president is afraid that a large drop in the current year's profits could cause a significant drop in the market price of Die Hard's shares, and could make the company a takeover target. To avoid this possibility, the company president urges Carole Chiasson, the controller, to accrue all possible revenues and to defer as many expenses as possible when preparing this period's December 31 year-end adjusting entries. He says to Carole, "We need the revenues this year, and next year we can easily absorb expenses deferred from this year." Carole did not record the adjusting entries until January 17, but she dated the entries December 31 as if they were recorded then. Carole also did everything possible to follow the president's request.

Instructions

(a) Who are the stakeholders in this situation?
(b) What are the ethical considerations of (1) the president's request, and (2) Carole's decision to date the adjusting entries December 31?
(c) Can Carole aggressively accrue revenues and defer expenses and still be ethical?

"All About You" Activity

BYP3–6 A critical issue for accountants is the decision whether an expenditure should be recorded as an asset or an expense. The distinction between asset and expense is not always clear. In certain instances, businesses have been forced to restate their financial statements because management has recorded an asset when an expense should be recorded. The "All About You" feature indicates that post-secondary education results in higher earnings over an adult's working life and thus the money you are spending on your education today should be of significant future benefit. The question then is whether your education would meet the accounting definition of an asset or an expense.

Instructions

(a) Consider the nature of the cost of your education. What factors suggest that it should be considered an asset? What factors suggest that it should be considered an expense?
(b) Do you think the nature of the program you're taking should affect whether the cost of your education should be considered an asset or an expense? Explain.
(c) Economic theory suggests that people will always consider the benefit and cost of any expenditure and only incur the cost if the expected benefit is greater. Wouldn't this mean that every expenditure would meet the definition of an asset? Would you consider the cost of a vacation to Hawaii to be as valuable as a year of college? Would you record them both as assets on a personal balance sheet? Why or why not?
(d) If you were applying for a loan, what might the potential effect be on the success of your application if you understated your assets? What might be the potential effect on the bank if your assets are overstated and expenses understated?

ANSWERS TO CHAPTER QUESTIONS

ANSWERS TO ACCOUNTING IN ACTION INSIGHT QUESTIONS

All About You Insight, p. 114

Q: How should you account for the cost of your post-secondary education? Should you be recognizing the cost as an expense each year or should you recognize it as an asset?

A: Expenses are recognized when there has been a decrease in an asset or an increase in a liability. Paying for an education will reduce assets such as cash and may also increase liabilities if you have to take out student loans. Therefore, most accountants would tell you that you should record the cost of your education as an expense as you incur those costs. On the other hand, it could be argued that your education is creating an asset—your increased future earning power. But then you would have to estimate the value of this asset. As with many situations in accounting, it is not easy to determine the correct answer.

Business Insight, p. 122

Q: If a business collects cash when the gift card is sold, how can gift card sales in December result in revenues in January?

A: Gift cards sales are simply another example of unearned revenues. At the time the gift card is sold, the business must record unearned revenue, which is a liability. When a customer redeems the gift card by making a purchase, then the company will reduce the liability and record revenue.

ANSWERS TO SELF-STUDY QUESTION

1. b   2. d   3. d   4. b   5. c   6. d   7. a   8. a   9. b   10. a   11. a   *12. a   *13. c

Remember to go back to the beginning of the chapter to check off your completed work!

←

 THE **NAVIGATOR**

- ☐ Understand *Concepts for Review*
- ☐ Read *Feature Story*
- ☐ Scan *Study Objectives*
- ☐ Read *Chapter Preview*
- ☐ Read text and answer *Before You Go On*
- ☐ Review *Comparing IFRS and ASPE*
- ☐ Work *Demonstration Problem*
- ☐ Review *Summary of Study Objectives*
- ☐ Answer *Self-Study Questions*
- ☐ Complete assignments
- ☐ Go to *WileyPLUS* for practice and tutorials

CONCEPTS FOR **REVIEW**

Before studying this chapter, you should understand or, if necessary, review:

a. How to increase and decrease assets, liabilities, and owner's equity accounts using debit and credit procedures. (Ch. 2, pp. 58–62)

b. When to recognize revenues and expenses. (Ch. 3, p. 114)

c. How to make adjusting entries. (Ch. 3, pp. 115–129)

d. How to prepare an adjusted trial balance. (Ch. 3, pp. 130–133)

e. How the balance sheet, income statement, and statement of owner's equity are connected. (Ch. 3, p. 132)

NO "SHORT CUTS" IN ACCOUNTING

OTTAWA, Ont.—Before launching a career as a hair stylist, Nelson Hickey studied accounting in high school and university. That's why he's so involved in the bookkeeping of Character Salon, which he opened in 2004 in a trendy Ottawa neighbourhood.

Mr. Hickey closes his books at year end. "We all know that everything has to balance—left and right, debit and credit—at the end of the year. If you are out by pennies, it's going to cause problems," he says.

If he does find any discrepancies at year end, he looks for the error. "That's one of the hardest things at the end of the year, if I'm out $4," Mr. Hickey says. Often, he will uncover a transposition error, where numbers were reversed when entered, such as $94 instead of $49. He still appreciates the tip he learned in school that if the discrepancy is divisible by 9 (in this case, $45), it can indicate a transposition error. When he finds the error, he makes a correcting entry in his Simply Accounting software. Mr. Hickey also makes adjusting entries to estimate final expenses for the year, such as an electricity bill that he hasn't received yet for the last month of the year.

Closing the books at year end became easier when Mr. Hickey recently installed another software program, Salonware, to track his revenues, which he used to compile manually at the end of every day in a spreadsheet program. Salonware is also his point-of-sale system when customers pay for their hair services and products. By tracking the sales of his five stylists, the software makes it easier to pay their salaries and commissions. All of this means he now can make general journal entries for sales weekly instead of daily, with far fewer errors that need to be corrected at year end. "It's definitely simplified the amount of data entry," he says.

When all the correcting and adjusting entries are made, Mr. Hickey makes closing entries and then Simply Accounting automatically generates an income statement and balance sheet that he gives to his accountant to prepare his annual income tax return. While today's technology makes bookkeeping much easier, he's glad he learned accounting principles on paper. "That's basically the only way to understand bookkeeping," he says.

In other words, there are no "short cuts" in accounting.

THE **NAVIGATOR**

STUDY **OBJECTIVES**

After studying this chapter, you should be able to:

1. Prepare closing entries and a post-closing trial balance.

2. Explain the steps in the accounting cycle including optional steps.

3. Prepare correcting entries.

4. Prepare a classified balance sheet.

5. Illustrate measures used to evaluate liquidity.

6. Prepare a work sheet (Appendix 4A).

7. Prepare reversing entries (Appendix 4B).

THE **NAVIGATOR**

In Chapter 3, we learned about the adjusting process and how to prepare financial statements from the adjusted trial balance. In this chapter, we will explain the remaining steps in the accounting cycle—the closing process. Once again, we will use the Pioneer Advertising Agency as an example.

After that, we will look at correcting entries. As Nelson Hickey of Character Salon notes in the feature story, locating and correcting errors is very important. We end by discussing the classification and use of balance sheets. The chapter is organized as follows:

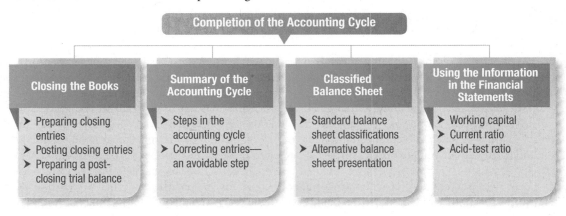

Completion of the Accounting Cycle

Closing the Books	Summary of the Accounting Cycle	Classified Balance Sheet	Using the Information in the Financial Statements
➤ Preparing closing entries ➤ Posting closing entries ➤ Preparing a post-closing trial balance	➤ Steps in the accounting cycle ➤ Correcting entries—an avoidable step	➤ Standard balance sheet classifications ➤ Alternative balance sheet presentation	➤ Working capital ➤ Current ratio ➤ Acid-test ratio

Closing the Books

» STUDY OBJECTIVE 1

Prepare closing entries and a post-closing trial balance.

At the end of the accounting period, after the adjusting entries have been posted and the financial statements prepared, it is necessary to get the accounts in the general ledger ready for the next period. This is the next step in the accounting cycle and is called **closing the books**. This step involves bringing the balances in all revenue, expense, and drawings accounts to zero, and updating the balance in the owner's capital account.

Why is this necessary? Recall from Illustration 1-6 in Chapter 1 that revenues and investments by the owner increase owner's equity, and expenses and drawings decrease owner's equity. Also recall from Chapters 1 and 2 that investments by the owner are directly recorded in the owner's capital account, but that revenues, expenses, and drawings are all recorded in separate accounts. We use separate accounts for revenues, expenses, and drawings in order to create the information needed to prepare an income statement and a statement of owner's equity for the accounting period.

At the start of the next accounting period, we need to begin that period with zero in the revenue, expense, and drawings accounts. This will allow us to create the information to prepare the income statement and statement of owner's equity for the next accounting period. Thus all revenue, expense, and drawings accounts are considered **temporary accounts** because they contain data for only a single accounting period and are closed at the end of the period. The journal entries to close the temporary accounts also update the balance in the owner's capital account.

In contrast, balance sheet accounts are considered **permanent accounts** because their balances are carried forward into the next accounting period. It is important to know the difference between temporary and permanent accounts. Temporary accounts are closed; permanent accounts are not closed. Illustration 4-1 summarizes temporary versus permanent accounts.

▶ **ILLUSTRATION 4-1**
Temporary versus permanent accounts

TEMPORARY These accounts are closed.	PERMANENT These accounts are not closed.
All revenue accounts	All asset accounts
All expense accounts	All liability accounts
Owner's drawings account	Owner's capital account

PREPARING CLOSING ENTRIES

The journal entries used to close the temporary accounts are called **closing entries**. Closing entries reduce the balance in the temporary accounts (revenues, expenses, and drawings) to zero and transfer the balances of these accounts to the permanent owner's capital account. The temporary accounts are then ready to collect data in the next accounting period.

After the closing entries are prepared and posted, the balance in the owner's capital account is equal to the end-of-period balance shown on the statement of owner's equity and the balance sheet. The **statement of owner's equity shows users of financial statements** the effect of that period's profit (or loss)—revenues minus expenses—and drawings on the owner's capital account. **Closing entries record in the ledger the effect of that period's profit (or loss) and the owner's drawings on the owner's capital account.**

When closing entries are prepared, each income statement account could be closed directly to the owner's capital account. However, to do so would result in an excessive amount of detail in the owner's capital account. Instead, companies first close the revenue and expense accounts to another temporary account, **Income Summary**. The balance in the income summary account after closing revenues and expenses is equal to that period's profit or loss. Then the profit or loss is transferred from the income summary account to owner's capital.

The closing entry process is based on the expanded accounting equation shown in Illustration 1-8. Recall that the expanded accounting equation shows the relationship between revenues, expenses, profit (or loss), and owner's equity. Similarly, Illustration 4-2 shows the impact of the steps in the closing process on the owner's capital account. It also shows that the closing process does not affect the asset and liability accounts.

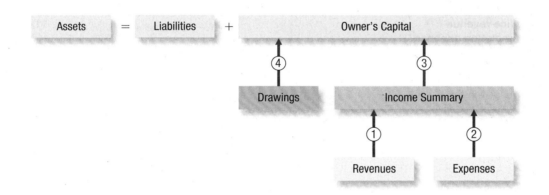

▶ **ILLUSTRATION 4-2**
Closing process

The four steps in Illustration 4-2 represent four closing entries:

1. **Close revenue accounts.** Debit each individual revenue account for its balance, and credit Income Summary for total revenues.
2. **Close expense accounts.** Debit Income Summary for total expenses, and credit each individual expense account for its balance.
3. **Close Income Summary account.** Debit Income Summary for its balance (or credit it if there is a loss) and credit (debit) the owner's capital account.
4. **Close drawings.** Debit the owner's capital account and credit the owner's drawings account for the balance in drawings.

Companies record closing entries in the general journal. The heading "Closing Entries," inserted in the journal between the last adjusting entry and the first closing entry, identifies these entries. Then the company posts the closing entries to the ledger accounts.

Closing Entries Illustrated

To illustrate the journalizing and posting of closing entries, we will continue using the example of Pioneer Advertising Agency introduced in Chapters 2 and 3. In practice, companies generally prepare closing entries only at the end of the annual accounting period. Most companies, including Character

Salon, introduced in the feature story, close their books once a year. However, to illustrate the process, we will assume that Pioneer Advertising Agency closes its books monthly.

Pioneer Advertising's adjusted trial balance on October 31, 2014, first shown in Chapter 3 (Illustration 3-8), is shown again here in Illustration 4-3. The temporary accounts have been highlighted in red. C. Byrd, Capital is a permanent account. It is highlighted in blue because it is used in the closing process, but it is not a temporary account.

▶ **ILLUSTRATION**  **4-3**
Adjusted trial balance

PIONEER ADVERTISING AGENCY Adjusted Trial Balance October 31, 2014		
	Debit	**Credit**
Cash	$14,250	
Accounts receivable	1,200	
Supplies	1,000	
Prepaid insurance	550	
Equipment	5,000	
Accumulated depreciation—equipment		$ 83
Notes payable		5,000
Accounts payable		1,750
Unearned revenue		800
Salaries payable		2,000
Interest payable		25
C. Byrd, capital		10,000
C. Byrd, drawings	500	
Service revenue		11,400
Depreciation expense	83	
Insurance expense	50	
Rent expense	900	
Salaries expense	6,000	
Supplies expense	1,500	
Interest expense	25	
	$31,058	$31,058

Notice that the C. Byrd, Capital account balance of $10,000 in the adjusted trial balance is the opening balance of $0 plus the $10,000 investment made by C. Byrd during the period—it is not the ending balance of $12,342 that appears in the statement of owner's equity and balance sheet in Illustrations 3-9 and 3-10. This permanent account is updated to its ending balance by the closing entries as follows:

▶ **CLOSING ENTRY ①**
Revenues to income summary

Basic Analysis	The revenue account Service Revenue is decreased by $11,400 to bring the balance to zero and the Income Summary account is increased by $11,400.		
Debit-Credit Analysis	Debits decrease revenues: Debit Service Revenue $11,400. Credits increase Income Summary: Credit Income Summary $11,400.		
Closing Journal Entry	Oct. 31	Service Revenue	11,400	
		Income Summary		11,400
		To close revenue account.		

This closing entry transfers revenue to the Income Summary account. If there are two or more revenue accounts, they are all closed in one entry with a separate debit to each revenue account and one credit to Income Summary for the total amount.

▸ CLOSING ENTRY ②
Expenses to income summary

Basic Analysis	The expense accounts are decreased to bring the balance in each account to zero and the Income Summary account is decreased by the total of the expenses of $8,558.
Debit-Credit Analysis	Debits decrease Income Summary: Debit Income Summary $8,558. Credits decrease expenses: Credit each expense account by the balance in that account; the total of the credits is $8,558.

Closing Journal Entry	Oct. 31	Income Summary	8,558	
		Depreciation Expense		83
		Insurance Expense		50
		Rent Expense		900
		Salaries Expense		6,000
		Supplies Expense		1,500
		Interest Expense		25
		To close expense accounts.		

This closing entry transfers the expenses to the Income Summary account. Notice that the closing entry includes **a separate credit to each of the expense accounts** but only one debit for the total amount to Income Summary.

As a result of these two closing entries, there is a credit balance of $2,842 ($11,400 − $8,558) in the Income Summary account. There is a credit balance because revenues were greater than expenses. The credit balance is equal to Pioneer's profit for October as shown in Illustration 3-9. If expenses were greater than revenues, Pioneer would have a loss and this would result in a debit balance in the Income Summary account after closing revenues and expenses.

▸ CLOSING ENTRY ③
Income summary to owner's capital

Basic Analysis	The Income Summary account is decreased by the balance in the account of $2,842 to bring it to zero and the owner's equity account C. Byrd, Capital is increased by $2,842 because profit increases owner's equity.
Debit-Credit Analysis	Debits decrease Income Summary: Debit Income Summary $2,842. Credits increase owner's equity: Credit C. Byrd, Capital $2,842.

Closing Journal Entry	Oct. 31	Income Summary	2,842	
		C. Byrd, Capital		2,842
		To close profit to capital.		

This closing entry transfers the profit to the capital account. If Pioneer had a loss then it would have been necessary to credit the Income Summary account to bring it to zero and debit the owner's capital account. Since losses decrease owner's equity, it makes sense to debit the capital account when there is a loss.

▸ CLOSING ENTRY ④
Drawings to owner's capital

Basic Analysis	The drawings account C. Byrd, Drawings is decreased by $500 to bring the balance to zero and the owner's equity account C. Byrd, Capital is decreased by $500 because drawings decrease owner's equity.
Debit-Credit Analysis	Debits decrease owner's equity: Debit C. Byrd, Capital $500. Credits decrease drawings: Credit C. Byrd, Drawings $500.

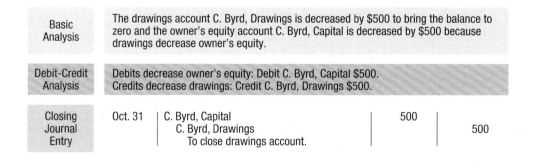

Closing Journal Entry	Oct. 31	C. Byrd, Capital	500	
		C. Byrd, Drawings		500
		To close drawings account.		

This closing entry transfers the drawings to the capital account. Always close drawings separately from revenues and expenses. Drawings are not used to determine profit. Remember, drawings are shown on the statement of owner's equity as a separate item and thus are also closed in a separate entry.

The closing entries are recorded in the general journal for Pioneer Advertising Agency as follows:

	GENERAL JOURNAL			J3
Date	Account Titles and Explanation	Ref.	Debit	Credit
	Closing Entries			
2014	(1)			
Oct. 31	Service Revenue	400	11,400	
	Income Summary	350		11,400
	To close revenue account.			
	(2)			
31	Income Summary	350	8,558	
	Depreciation Expense	711		83
	Insurance Expense	722		50
	Rent Expense	726		900
	Salaries Expense	729		6,000
	Supplies Expense	740		1,500
	Interest Expense	905		25
	To close expense accounts.			
	(3)			
31	Income Summary	350	2,842	
	C. Byrd, Capital	301		2,842
	To close profit to capital.			
	(4)			
31	C. Byrd, Capital	301	500	
	C. Byrd, Drawings	306		500
	To close drawings account.			

Be careful when you prepare closing entries. Remember that the reason for making closing entries is to bring the temporary accounts to zero balances. Do not make the mistake of doubling the revenue, expense, drawings, and income summary account balances, rather than bringing them to zero.

POSTING CLOSING ENTRIES

The asset and liability accounts are never affected by the closing process. Thus we have not included them in the following diagram. The only accounts that will change are the temporary accounts and the owner's capital account.

After the closing entries have been posted, all of the increases and decreases to owner's equity during the period are recorded in the owner's capital account. The posting of the closing entries ("Clos.") and the updated balances ("Bal.") are as follows:

	GENERAL LEDGER		

C. Byrd, Capital 301

				Oct. 1		10,000
Oct. 31	Clos.	500		31	Clos.	2,842
				Oct. 31	Bal.	12,342

Service Revenue 400

				Oct. 21		10,000
				25		800
				31	Adj.	400
Oct. 31	Clos.	11,400		31	Adj.	200
				Oct. 31	Bal.	0

C. Byrd, Drawings 306

Oct. 20		500	Oct. 31 Clos.	500
Oct. 31	Bal.	0		

Depreciation Expense 711

Oct. 31 Adj.		83	Oct. 31 Clos.	83
Oct. 31 Bal.		0		

Income Summary 350

			Oct. 31 Clos.	11,400
Oct. 31 Clos.	8,558			
			Oct. 31 Bal.	2,842
Oct. 31 Clos.	2,842			
			Oct. 31 Bal.	0

Insurance Expense 722

Oct. 31 Adj.		50	Oct. 31 Clos.	50
Oct. 31 Bal.		0		

Rent Expense		726		Supplies Expense		740
Oct. 3	900	Oct. 31 Clos. 900	Oct. 31 Adj.	1,500	Oct. 31 Clos.	1,500
Oct. 31 Bal.	0		Oct. 31 Bal.	0		

Salaries Expense		729		Interest Expense		905
Oct. 24	4,000		Oct. 31 Adj.	25	Oct. 31 Clos.	25
31 Adj.	2,000	Oct. 31 Clos. 6,000	Oct. 31 Bal.	0		
Oct. 31 Bal.	0					

Stop and check your work after the closing entries are posted:

1. The balance in Income Summary, immediately before the final closing entry to transfer the balance to the owner's capital account, should equal the profit (or loss) reported in the income statement (see Illustration 3-9 in Chapter 3).
2. All temporary accounts (revenues, expenses, owner's drawings, and Income Summary) should have zero balances.
3. The balance in the capital account should equal the ending balance reported in the statement of owner's equity and balance sheet (see Illustrations 3-9 and 3-10 in Chapter 3).

PREPARING A POST-CLOSING TRIAL BALANCE

After all closing entries have been journalized and posted, another trial balance is prepared from the ledger. It is called a **post-closing trial balance**. The post- (or after-) closing trial balance lists permanent accounts and their balances after closing entries have been journalized and posted. The purpose of this trial balance is to prove the equality of the permanent account balances that are carried forward into the next accounting period. Since all temporary accounts have zero balances after closing, the post-closing trial balance contains only permanent—balance sheet—accounts.

The post-closing trial balance for Pioneer Advertising Agency is shown in Illustration 4-4. Note that the account balances are the same as the ones in the company's balance sheet. (Pioneer Advertising's balance sheet is shown in Chapter 3, Illustration 3-10.)

Helpful hint Total debits in a post-closing trial balance will not equal total assets on the balance sheet if contra accounts, such as accumulated depreciation, are present. Accumulated depreciation is deducted from assets on the balance sheet but added to the credit column in a trial balance.

▶ **ILLUSTRATION** 4-4
Post-closing trial balance

PIONEER ADVERTISING AGENCY Post-Closing Trial Balance October 31, 2014		
	Debit	**Credit**
Cash	$14,250	
Accounts receivable	1,200	
Supplies	1,000	
Prepaid insurance	550	
Equipment	5,000	
Accumulated depreciation—equipment		$ 83
Notes payable		5,000
Accounts payable		1,750
Unearned revenue		800
Salaries payable		2,000
Interest payable		25
C. Byrd, capital		12,342
	$22,000	$22,000

A post-closing trial balance provides evidence that the journalizing and posting of closing entries has been completed properly. It also shows that the accounting equation is in balance at the end of the accounting period and the beginning of the next accounting period.

As in the case of the trial balance, the post-closing trial balance does not prove that all transactions have been recorded or that the ledger is correct. For example, the post-closing trial balance will still balance if a transaction is not journalized and posted, or if a transaction is journalized and posted twice.

Accounting software, such as Simply Accounting, used by Character Salon in our feature story, will automatically record and post closing entries when given instructions to prepare the accounting records for the next fiscal year. But it is still very important to understand what is happening in the closing process. You will find your understanding of adjusting entries is enhanced once you have mastered closing entries.

BEFORE YOU GO ON...

Do It

The adjusted trial balance for the Nguyen Company shows the following:

	Debit	Credit
Cash	$20,000	
Equipment	35,000	
Accounts payable		$10,000
H. Nguyen, capital		42,000
H. Nguyen, drawings	5,000	
Service revenue		18,000
Rent expense	2,000	
Salaries expense	7,500	
Supplies expense	500	
	$70,000	$70,000

Nguyen Company's statement of owner's equity for the year showed a profit of $8,000 and closing owner's capital of $45,000.

(a) Prepare the closing entries at December 31.
(b) Create T accounts for Income Summary and H. Nguyen, Capital, and post the closing entries to these accounts.

Solution

Dec. 31	Service Revenue	18,000	
	Income Summary		18,000
	To close revenue account.		
31	Income Summary	10,000	
	Rent Expense		2,000
	Salaries Expense		7,500
	Supplies Expense		500
	To close expense accounts.		
31	Income Summary	8,000	
	H. Nguyen, Capital		8,000
	To close Income Summary.		
31	H. Nguyen, Capital	5,000	
	H. Nguyen, Drawings		5,000
	To close drawings.		

Income Summary

Clos.	10,000	Clos.	18,000
		Bal.	8,000*
Clos.	8,000		
		Bal.	0

*Check if this equals profit.

H. Nguyen, Capital

		Bal.	42,000
Clos.	5,000	Clos.	8,000
		Bal.	45,000**

**Check if this equals closing owner's capital.

Related exercise material: BE4–1, BE4–2, BE4–3, BE4–4, E4–1, E4–2, E4–3, and E4–4.

Action Plan
- Debit each individual revenue account for its balance and credit the total to Income Summary.
- Credit each individual expense account for its balance and debit the total to Income Summary.
- Stop and check your work: Does the balance in Income Summary equal the reported profit?
- Debit the balance in Income Summary and credit the amount to the owner's capital account. (Do the opposite if the company had a loss.)
- Credit the balance in the drawings account and debit the amount to the owner's capital account. Do not close drawings with the expenses.
- Stop and check your work: Will your closing entries result in the temporary accounts having zero balances? Does the ending balance in the owner's capital account equal the closing owner's capital reported on the statement of owner's equity?

THE NAVIGATOR

Summary of the Accounting Cycle

In Chapter 2, we introduced the accounting cycle as series of steps that accountants take to prepare financial statements. You have now learned all of the steps. In the following section, we review the cycle and discuss optional steps.

STEPS IN THE ACCOUNTING CYCLE

As introduced in Chapter 2, the cycle begins with the analysis and recording of business transactions (Steps 1, 2, and 3). This is followed by the preparation of a trial balance (Step 4), as also shown in Chapter 2. Chapter 3 covered the adjustment process and the preparation of financial statements (Steps 5, 6, and 7). In the first part of Chapter 4, the final steps of the accounting cycle—the closing process (Steps 8 and 9)—were covered. The full accounting cycle is reproduced here in Illustration 4-5.

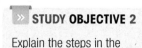

» STUDY OBJECTIVE 2

Explain the steps in the accounting cycle including optional steps.

▸ **ILLUSTRATION 4-5**
Steps in the accounting cycle

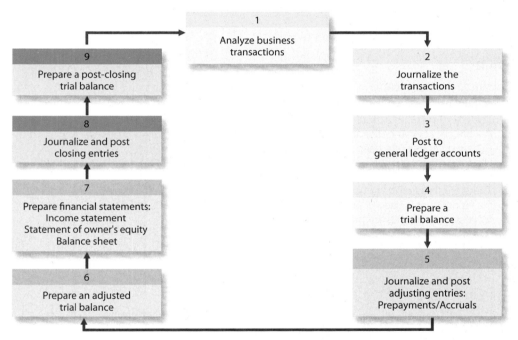

Optional steps: If a work sheet is prepared, Steps 4, 5, and 6 are done in the work sheet, and adjusting entries are journalized and posted after Step 7. If reversing entries are prepared, they occur between Steps 9 and 1.

The steps in the cycle are done in sequence (Steps 1 to 9). Once Step 9 is completed for an accounting period, the company can begin again with Step 1 in the next accounting period and repeat the steps for that accounting period and so on. Because the steps are repeated each accounting period, we show the full accounting cycle as a circle. Steps 1, 2, and 3 can occur every day during the accounting period, as explained in Chapter 2. Steps 4 through 7 are done periodically, such as monthly, quarterly, or annually. Steps 8 and 9, closing entries and a post-closing trial balance, are usually done only at the end of a company's annual accounting period.

There are also two optional steps in the accounting cycle: work sheets and reversing entries. These optional steps are explained in the following two sections.

Work Sheets—An Optional Step

Some accountants like to use an optional multiple-column form known as a **work sheet** to help them prepare adjusting entries and the financial statements. As its name suggests, the work sheet is a working tool. It is not a permanent accounting record; it is neither a journal nor a part of the general ledger. Companies generally computerize work sheets using an electronic spreadsheet program such as Excel.

Although using a work sheet is optional, it is useful. For example, a work sheet makes it easier to prepare interim (e.g., monthly or quarterly) financial information. The monthly or quarterly adjusting entries can be entered in the work sheet, and interim financial statements can then be easily developed.

As the preparation of a work sheet is optional, its basic form and the procedure for preparing it are explained in Appendix 4A at the end of the chapter.

Reversing Entries—An Optional Step

Some accountants prefer to reverse certain adjusting entries by making a reversing entry at the beginning of the next accounting period. A **reversing entry** is the exact opposite of the adjusting entry made in the previous period. Use of reversing entries is an optional bookkeeping procedure; it is not a required step in the accounting cycle. We have therefore chosen to explain this topic in Appendix 4B at the end of the chapter.

 BEFORE YOU GO ON...

Do It

Indicate which of the following statements are true and which are false with a T or F.

1. Reversing entries are an optional step in the accounting cycle.
2. The first step in the accounting cycle is journalizing transactions.
3. A work sheet is an optional step in the accounting cycle.
4. Reversing entries are used to reverse closing entries.
5. Closing entries must be prepared on a monthly basis if financial statements are prepared monthly.
6. There are three different types of trial balances used in the accounting cycle.
7. If a work sheet is used, it is not necessary to prepare adjusting entries.
8. Financial statements are prepared after the adjustment process.

Action Plan
- Review the accounting cycle.

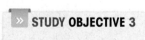
THE NAVIGATOR

Solution
1. T   5. F
2. F   6. T
3. T   7. F
4. F   8. T

Related exercise material: BE4–5, BE4–6, E4–5, E4–6, and E4–7.

CORRECTING ENTRIES—AN AVOIDABLE STEP

» **STUDY OBJECTIVE 3**

Prepare correcting entries.

Unfortunately, errors may happen in the recording process. The accounting cycle does not include a specific step for correcting errors because this step is not needed if the accounting records have no errors. But if errors exist, they should be corrected as soon as they are discovered by journalizing and posting **correcting entries**. If the accounting records have no errors, no correcting entries are needed.

You should understand several differences between correcting entries and adjusting entries. First, adjusting entries are an integral part of the accounting cycle. Correcting entries, on the other hand, are unnecessary if the records have no errors. Second, adjustments are journalized and posted only at the end of an accounting period. In contrast, correcting entries are made whenever an error is discovered. Finally, adjusting entries always affect at least one balance sheet account (not Cash) and one income statement account. In contrast, correcting entries can involve any combination of accounts that need to be corrected. Adjusting and correcting entries do have one thing in common, however: in both cases, they must be journalized and posted before closing entries.

Correcting Entries Illustrated

To determine the correcting entry, it is useful to compare the incorrect entry with the entry that should have been made. Doing this helps identify the accounts and amounts that should—and should not—be corrected. After comparison, a correcting entry is made to correct the accounts. This approach is shown in the following two cases.

Case 1. On May 10, a $50 cash collection on account from a customer is journalized and posted as a debit to Cash $50 and as a credit to Service Revenue $50. The error is discovered on May 20 when the customer pays the remaining balance in full.

Incorrect Entry (May 10)		Correct Entry (May 10)	
Cash	50	Cash	50
Service Revenue	50	Accounts Receivable	50

    Comparison of the incorrect entry with the correct entry that should have been made (but was not) reveals that the debit to Cash of $50 is correct. However, the $50 credit to Service Revenue should have been credited to Accounts Receivable. As a result, both Service Revenue and Accounts Receivable are overstated in the ledger. The following correcting entry is needed:

	Correcting Entry		
May 20	Service Revenue	50	
	Accounts Receivable		50
	To correct entry of May 10.		

A = L + OE
−50   −50
Cash flows: no effect

Case 2. On May 18, equipment that costs $450 is purchased on account. The transaction is journalized and posted as a debit to Supplies $45 and as a credit to Accounts Payable $45. The error is discovered on June 3 when the monthly statement for May is received from the creditor.

Incorrect Entry (May 18)		Correct Entry (May 18)	
Supplies	45	Equipment	450
Accounts Payable	45	Accounts Payable	450

    A comparison of the two entries shows that three accounts are incorrect. Supplies is overstated by $45; Equipment is understated by $450; and Accounts Payable is understated by $405 ($450 − $45). The correcting entry is as follows:

	Correcting Entry		
June 3	Equipment	450	
	Supplies		45
	Accounts Payable		405
	To correct May 18 entry.		

A = L + OE
+450   +450
−45
Cash flows: no effect

Alternative Approach

Instead of preparing a correcting entry, many accountants simply reverse the incorrect entry and then record the correct entry. This approach will result in more entries and postings, but it is often easier and more logical.

    Sometimes errors are not found until after the temporary accounts have been closed. A correcting entry that fixes an error from a previous accounting year is called a prior period adjustment. These correcting entries can be very complex, and will be covered in a later chapter.

BEFORE YOU GO ON...

Do It

The Chip 'N Dough Company made the following adjusting journal entry to record $5,200 of depreciation expense on a vehicle at year end:

Feb. 28	Depreciation Expense	520	
	Cash		520
	To record depreciation on a vehicle.		

Prepare the required correcting entry.

Solution

Feb. 28	Cash	520	
	Depreciation Expense ($5,200 − $520)	4,680	
	Accumulated Depreciation—Vehicles		5,200
	To correct depreciation adjustment.		

OR

Feb. 28	Cash	520	
	Depreciation Expense		520
	To reverse incorrect depreciation adjustment.		
28	Depreciation Expense	5,200	
	Accumulated Depreciation—Vehicles		5,200
	To record the correct depreciation entry.		

Related exercise material: BE4–7, BE4–8, E4–8, and E4–9.

Action Plan

- Determine the correct entry that should have been made.
- Compare it with the incorrect entry made and make the required corrections. Note that three accounts must be corrected.
- You could instead use the alternative approach of reversing the incorrect journal entry and recording the correct journal entry.

THE NAVIGATOR

Classified Balance Sheet

>> **STUDY OBJECTIVE 4**

Prepare a classified balance sheet.

The balance sheet presents a snapshot of a company's financial position at a point in time. The balance sheets that we have seen so far have all been very basic, with items classified simply as assets, liabilities, or owner's equity. To improve users' understanding of a company's financial position, companies often group similar assets and similar liabilities together.

STANDARD BALANCE SHEET CLASSIFICATIONS

Alternative terminology The balance sheet is also known as the *statement of financial position.*

A **classified balance sheet** generally has the standard classifications listed in Illustration 4-6.

▶ **ILLUSTRATION 4-6**
Standard balance sheet classifications

Assets	Liabilities and Owner's Equity
Current assets	Current liabilities
Long-term investments	Non-current liabilities
Property, plant, and equipment	Owner's (shareholders') equity
Intangible assets	
Goodwill	

These groupings help readers determine such things as (1) whether the company has enough assets to pay its debts as they come due, and (2) the claims of short- and long-term creditors on total assets. These classifications are shown in the balance sheet of MacDonald Company in Illustration 4-7. In the sections that follow, we explain each of these groupings.

MACDONALD COMPANY
Balance Sheet
November 30, 2014

Assets

Current assets		
Cash	$ 6,600	
Short-term investments	2,000	
Accounts receivable	7,000	
Inventories	4,000	
Supplies	2,100	
Prepaid insurance	400	
Total current assets		$ 22,100
Long-term investments		
Equity investment	$ 5,200	
Debt investment	2,000	
Total long-term investments		7,200
Property, plant, and equipment		
Land	$35,000	
Building	$75,000	
Less: Accumulated depreciation	15,000	60,000
Equipment	$24,000	
Less: Accumulated depreciation	5,000	19,000
Total property, plant, and equipment		114,000
Licences		5,000
Goodwill		3,100
Total assets		$151,400

Liabilities and Owner's Equity

Current liabilities		
Short-term notes payable	$11,000	
Accounts payable	2,100	
Unearned revenue	900	
Salaries payable	1,600	
Interest payable	450	
Current portion of long-term notes payable	1,000	
Total current liabilities		$ 17,050
Non-current liabilities		
Mortgage payable	$ 9,000	
Long-term notes payable	1,300	
Total non-current liabilities		10,300
Total liabilities		27,350
Owner's equity		
J. MacDonald, capital		124,050
Total liabilities and owner's equity		$151,400

Current Assets

Current assets are normally cash and other assets that will be converted to cash, sold, or used up within one year from the balance sheet date. Some companies use a period longer than one year to classify assets as current because they have an operating cycle that is longer than one year.

The **operating cycle** of a company is the time it takes to go from starting with cash to ending with cash in producing revenues. Illustration 4-8 shows the basic steps involved in an operating cycle.

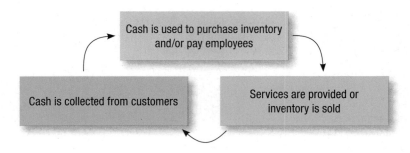

For most businesses, this cycle is less than one year, so they use the one-year cutoff. But for some businesses, such as vineyards or airplane manufacturers, this period may be longer than one year. Except where noted, we will assume companies use one year to determine whether an asset is current or non-current.

Common types of current assets are: (1) cash; (2) short-term investments, such as equity and long-term debt securities that are held for trading, or short-term debt securities; (3) receivables, such as notes receivable, accounts receivable, and interest receivable; (4) inventories or merchandise available for sale; (5) supplies; and (6) prepaid expenses, such as rent and insurance. Accounts receivable are current assets because they will be collected and converted to cash within one year. Inventory is a current asset because a company expects to sell it within one year. Supplies are a current asset because a company expects to use or consume supplies within one year. In Illustration 4-7, MacDonald Company had current assets of $22,100.

In Canada, companies generally list current assets in the order of their liquidity; that is, in the order in which they are expected to be converted into cash. Some international companies list current assets in reverse order of liquidity.

Current assets for Canada Post Corporation, one of the largest Crown corporations owned by the federal government, are shown in Illustration 4-9. Note that Canada Post lists its current assets in order of liquidity and that it calls its balance sheet "statement of financial position," as do many companies.

CANADA POST CORPORATION
Statement of Financial Position (partial)
December 31, 2011
(in millions)

Current assets	
Cash and cash equivalents	$ 271
Marketable securities	842
Trade and other receivables	662
Income taxes receivable	56
Other assets	115
Total current assets	1,946

We have already learned about most of these accounts in previous chapters except for "cash equivalents." Cash equivalents are investments in very liquid debt securities that can easily be converted into cash. Canada Post uses the term "marketable securities," which is another name for short-term investments used in the MacDonald Company example in Illustration 4-7.

The assets described in the next three sections are **non-current assets**. These are assets that will not be converted to cash, sold, or used by the business within one year of the balance sheet date or its operating cycle. Basically that means that non-current assets are everything that is not classified as a current asset.

Long-Term Investments

Long-term investments include (1) investments in long-term debt (for example, loans, notes, bonds, or mortgages) that management intends to hold to earn interest, and (2) equity securities (for example, shares) of other corporations that management plans to hold for many years for strategic reasons. These assets are classified as long-term because they are not readily marketable or expected to be converted into cash within one year. In Illustration 4-7, MacDonald Company reported long-term investments of $7,200 on its balance sheet.

Some companies have only one line on the balance sheet showing total long-term investments, and provide all of the details in the notes to the financial statements. If an item is simply called an "investment," without specifying if it is a short- or long-term investment, it is assumed to be a long-term investment.

Empire Company Limited (shown in the partial balance sheet in Illustration 4-10) has three lines for long-term investments on its balance sheet. Additional information on these investments is included in note 6. A total for long-term investments is not included in Illustration 4-10, as Empire does not show a subtotal for all of its long-term investments on the balance sheet.

EMPIRE COMPANY LIMITED Balance Sheet (partial) November 5, 2011 (in millions)	
Loans and other receivables	$ 71.9
Investments	13.6
Investments, at equity (Note 6)	261.6

▶ ILLUSTRATION **4-10**
Long-term investments section

Investments that are accounted for using the equity method must be shown separately, as Empire has done. Equity accounting is used when a company owns enough of another company to have a significant influence over its operations. This will be discussed further in Chapter 16.

Property, Plant, and Equipment

Property, plant, and equipment are long-lived, tangible assets that are used in the business and are not intended for sale. This category includes land, buildings, equipment, vehicles, and furniture. In Illustration 4-7, MacDonald Company reported property, plant, and equipment of $119,000.

Although the order of property, plant, and equipment on the balance sheet can vary among companies, in Canada these assets have traditionally been listed in their order of permanency. That is, land is usually listed first, because it has an indefinite life, and is followed by the asset with the next longest useful life (normally buildings), and so on.

Since property, plant, and equipment benefit future periods, their cost is allocated to expense over their useful lives through depreciation, as we learned in Chapter 3. Assets that are depreciated are reported at their carrying amount (cost minus accumulated depreciation).

Danier Leather Inc. reported the total carrying amount (or "net carrying value" as Danier calls it) of $15,315 thousand for its property, plant, and equipment on its balance sheet. Danier reports the cost, accumulated depreciation (or "accumulated amortization" as Danier calls it), and net carrying value of each category of property, plant, and equipment in a note to the financial statements, as shown in Illustration 4-11. This practice is very common for public companies to keep the balance sheet from looking too cluttered.

Note that, except for land (which has an unlimited useful life), all other property, plant, and equipment items are depreciated. This includes leasehold improvements, which are long-lived additions or renovations made to leased property.

Alternative terminology Property, plant, and equipment are sometimes called *capital assets* or *fixed assets*.

DANIER LEATHER INC. Notes to the Financial Statements December 24, 2011 (in thousands)			
Note 7. Property and Equipment			
	Cost	Accumulated Amortization	Net Carrying Value
Land	$ 1,000	$ —	$ 1,000
Building	6,063	2,275	3,788
Roof	308	193	115
Heating, ventilation, and air conditioning	793	554	239
Leasehold improvements	23,745	17,364	6,381
Furniture & equipment	9,277	6,369	2,908
Computer hardware	3,277	2,393	884
	$44,463	$29,148	$15,315

▶ ILLUSTRATION **4-11**
Property, plant, and equipment section

Intangible Assets and Goodwill

Intangible assets are long-lived assets that do not have physical substance. They give a company rights and privileges and include such things as patents, copyrights, franchises, trademarks, trade names, and licences.

Intangible assets are normally divided into two groups for accounting purposes: those with definite lives and those with indefinite lives. Similar to buildings and equipment, the cost of intangible assets with definite useful lives is allocated to expense over their useful lives. Similar to land, the cost of intangible assets with indefinite lives is not allocated over future periods.

As we learned in Chapter 3, the term "depreciation" is normally used for the allocation of cost over the useful lives of property, plant, and equipment; the term "amortization" is used for the allocation of the cost of intangible assets. We will learn more about intangible assets in Chapter 9.

An asset that is similar to intangible assets is goodwill. Goodwill results from the acquisition of another company when the price paid for the company is higher than the fair value of the purchased company's net assets. In Illustration 4-7, MacDonald Company reported $5,000 of an intangible asset, licences, and $3,100 of goodwill.

Illustration 4-12 shows how Research In Motion Limited reported intangible assets and goodwill in its balance sheet. The word "net" indicates accumulated amortization has been deducted from the cost of the intangible assets. The notes to the financial statements explain that the intangible assets are composed of patents, licences, and acquired technology. As required by IFRS, Research In Motion's balance sheet reports goodwill separately from intangible assets.

▶ **ILLUSTRATION 4-12**
Intangible assets and goodwill section

RESEARCH IN MOTION LIMITED Balance Sheet (partial) November 26, 2011 (in USD millions)	
Intangible assets, net	$2,472
Goodwill	659

Current Liabilities

Current liabilities are obligations that are expected to be settled within one year from the balance sheet date or in the company's operating cycle. As with current assets, companies use a period longer than one year if their operating cycle is longer than one year. In this textbook, we will always assume an operating cycle equal to, or shorter than, one year.

Common examples of current liabilities are notes payable, accounts payable, salaries payable, interest payable, sales taxes payable, unearned revenues, and current maturities of non-current liabilities (payments to be made within the next year on long-term debt). Corporations may also have income taxes payable included in the current liabilities section of the balance sheet. In Illustration 4-7, MacDonald Company reported six different types of current liabilities, for a total of $17,050.

Similar to current assets, North American companies often list current liabilities in order of liquidity. That is, the liabilities that will be due first are listed first. However, many companies simply list the items in their current liabilities section according to a company tradition. Some international companies list current liabilities in reverse order of liquidity, similar to current assets.

The current liabilities section from Tim Hortons Inc.'s balance sheet is shown in Illustration 4-13.

▶ **ILLUSTRATION 4-13**
Current liabilities section

TIM HORTONS INC. Balance Sheet (partial) January 1, 2012 (in thousands)	*Tim Hortons*
Current liabilities	
Accounts payable (note 13)	$177,918
Accrued liabilities	
Salaries and wages	23,531
Taxes	26,465
Other (note 13)	179,315
Advertising fund restricted liabilities (note 21)	59,420
Current portion of long-term obligations	10,001
	476,650

Users of financial statements look closely at the relationship between current assets and current liabilities. This relationship is important in evaluating a company's ability to pay its current liabilities. We will talk more about this later in the chapter when we learn how to use the information in the financial statements.

Non-Current Liabilities

Obligations that are expected to be paid after one year or longer are classified as **non-current liabilities**. Liabilities in this category can include bonds payable, mortgages payable, notes payable, lease liabilities, and deferred income taxes (income taxes payable after more than one year), among others. In Illustration 4-7, MacDonald Company reported non-current liabilities of $10,300.

Illustration 4-14 shows the non-current liabilities that Sears Canada Inc. reported on a recent balance sheet, or statement of financial position as Sears calls it.

Alternative terminology Non-current liabilities are sometimes called *long-term liabilities, long-term obligations,* or *long-term debt.*

SEARS CANADA INC. Statement of Financial Position (partial) January 28, 2012 (in millions)	
Non-current liabilities	
Long-term obligations (notes 14, 17, 19, and 24)	$117.6
Deferred revenue (note 13)	89.2
Retirement benefit liability (note 20.1)	144.1
Deferred tax liabilities (note 22)	48.9
Other long-term liabilities (notes 16 and 18)	75.8
	475.6

▶ **ILLUSTRATION 4-14**
Non-current liabilities section

The notes contain additional details about the liabilities, including how much must be paid during each of the next five years. The notes also contain information about restrictions placed on Sears Canada as a result of these obligations.

Equity

As introduced in Chapter 1, the name and specific accounts of the equity section vary with the form of business organization. In a proprietorship, there is one capital account under the heading "Owner's equity." In a partnership, there is a capital account for each partner under the heading "Partners' equity."

For a corporation, shareholders' equity always includes two parts: share capital and retained earnings. Amounts that are invested in the business by the shareholders are recorded as share capital. Profit that is kept for use in the business is recorded in the retained earnings account.

Some corporations may have other parts to the equity section, such as contributed surplus, which arises from the sale of shares, and accumulated other comprehensive income (or loss). We will learn more about corporation equity accounts in later chapters.

Illustration 4-15 shows how Canadian National Railway Company, a corporation, reported its shareholders' equity section in its balance sheet.

Alternative terminology Share capital is also commonly known as *capital stock* or *common shares.*

CANADIAN NATIONAL RAILWAY COMPANY Balance Sheet (partial) December 31, 2011 (in millions)	
Shareholders' equity	
Common shares	$ 4,141
Accumulated other comprehensive loss	(2,839)
Retained earnings	9,378
	10,680

▶ **ILLUSTRATION 4-15**
Shareholders' equity section

ALTERNATIVE BALANCE SHEET PRESENTATION

It is important to note that, when it comes to balance sheet presentation, both IFRS and ASPE allow for some choices. It is also interesting to note that, as different countries have adopted IFRS, where choices exist, companies have continued to follow the practices they used prior to adopting IFRS. Thus, the differences in balance sheet presentation when following IFRS, as compared with ASPE, are not necessarily that significant.

We will look at three differences that could arise.

Statement Name

IFRS uses "statement of financial position" and ASPE uses "balance sheet" in the written standards. But both sets of standards allow companies to use either of these titles. While "statement of financial position" more accurately describes the content of the statement, "balance sheet" has been much more widely used in Canada. As many Canadian companies, both public and private, continue to use "balance sheet," we also use that term in this textbook.

Classification of Assets

Both IFRS and ASPE require companies to separately present current assets; property, plant, and equipment; intangible assets; goodwill; and long-term investments in the same way as in Illustration 4-7. The standards are designed to ensure separate presentation on the face of the balance sheet for items that are different in nature or function.

In practice, companies following IFRS typically include the heading "non-current assets" on the balance sheet, and group property, plant, and equipment; intangible assets; goodwill; and long-term investments under this heading. You will note that this method is used in Reitmans' balance sheet in Appendix A.

We did not use the heading "non-current assets" in the MacDonald Company example in Illustration 4-7 because it has not been used by many Canadian companies. It has always been assumed that if an asset is not included with current assets, then it must be a non-current asset. Because of this assumption, it is not necessary to use the "non-current asset" heading under IFRS and ASPE. Therefore, we do not use it in illustrations in this textbook.

Order of Items

Illustration 4-7 uses the common Canadian practice of ordering items on the balance sheet in order of liquidity (from the most to the least liquid). Accounting standards do not lay down the order in which items are to be presented in the balance sheet. Companies are allowed to choose how to order items, depending on the nature of the company and its transactions, to provide information that is relevant to understanding the company's financial position.

As mentioned earlier, international companies often present the balance sheet in reverse order of liquidity. Some Canadian companies, particularly financial institutions and real estate companies, use the reverse-liquidity order format as well.

Statements prepared using reverse-liquidity order usually show assets first, followed by shareholders' equity, then liabilities. Non-current assets are shown before current assets and non-current liabilities before current liabilities.

Alternative Presentation Illustrated

In order to help you understand some of the potential differences in balance sheet presentation, we have created a balance sheet for a hypothetical company, International MacDonald Limited, shown in Illustration 4-16. The information is based on the balance sheet for MacDonald Company, shown earlier in Illustration 4-7.

In Illustration 4-16, we have assumed the business is an incorporated company, not a proprietorship as in Illustration 4-7, in order to show the differences in the equity section. Notice the different statement name, the different classifications, and the different order of items in the statement. But total assets, and total liabilities and equity, are still the same amounts.

INTERNATIONAL MACDONALD LIMITED Statement of Financial Position November 30, 2014			
Assets			
Non-current assets			
Goodwill			$ 3,100
Licences			5,000
Property, plant, and equipment			
Land		$35,000	
Building	$75,000		
Less: Accumulated depreciation	15,000	60,000	
Equipment	$24,000		
Less: Accumulated depreciation	5,000	19,000	
Total property, plant, and equipment			114,000
Long-term investments			
Equity investment		$ 5,200	
Debt investment		2,000	
Total long-term investments			7,200
Total non-current assets			129,300
Current assets			
Prepaid insurance		$ 400	
Supplies		2,100	
Inventories		4,000	
Accounts receivable		7,000	
Short-term investments		2,000	
Cash		6,600	
Total current assets			22,100
Total assets			$151,400
Equity and Liabilities			
Shareholders' equity			
Share capital		$74,000	
Retained earnings		50,050	
Total shareholders' equity			$124,050
Non-current liabilities			
Mortgage payable		$ 9,000	
Long-term notes payable		1,300	
Total non-current liabilities			$ 10,300
Current liabilities			
Current portion of long-term notes payable		$ 1,000	
Interest payable		450	
Salaries payable		1,600	
Unearned revenue		900	
Accounts payable		2,100	
Short-term notes payable		11,000	
Total current liabilities			17,050
Total liabilities			27,350
Total equity and liabilities			$151,400

▶ ILLUSTRATION 4-16
Classified statement of financial position in reverse order of liquidity

ACCOUNTING IN ACTION
ALL ABOUT YOU INSIGHT

Similar to a company's balance sheet, a personal balance sheet reports what you own and what you owe. What are the items of value that you own—your personal assets? Some of your assets are liquid—such as cash or short-term savings. Others, such as vehicles, real estate, and some types of investments, are less liquid. Some assets, such as real estate and investments, tend to increase in value, thereby increasing your personal equity. Other assets, such as vehicles, tend to fall in value, thereby decreasing your personal equity.

What are the amounts that you owe—your personal liabilities? Student loans, credit cards? Your equity is the difference between your total assets and total liabilities. Financial planners call this your *net worth* or *personal equity*.

Each quarter, Statistics Canada reports on the national balance sheet accounts and net worth of households in Canada. Household debt continued to rise in 2011, from $44,500 per capita to $46,700. At the same time, Canadian stock prices fell significantly, resulting in a drop in household net worth from $183,300 per capita to $182,200. You could use this information to create the average household's balance sheet at December 31, 2011, as follows:

Assets	=	Liabilities (Debt)	+	Equity (Net Worth)
$228,900	=	$46,700	+	$182,200

In more general terms this also means that the average household had 26 cents of debt for every $1 of net worth as at December 31, 2011. While this might not be a problem, it is the trend that concerns the government. At December 31, 2010, the average household had only 24 cents of debt for every $1 of net worth.

How can you increase your net worth? As a student, you may not have a lot of assets now, but by learning to control your spending and using debt wisely, you will be better able to increase your net worth when you graduate and start working full-time.

Source: Statistics Canada, "National balance sheet accounts," *The Daily*, Thursday, March 15, 2012.

How can preparing a personal balance sheet help you manage your net worth?

 BEFORE YOU GO ON...

Do It

The following selected accounts were taken from a company's balance sheet:

Accounts payable
Accounts receivable
Accumulated depreciation—buildings
Current portion of notes payable
Goodwill
Intangibles
Interest payable

Merchandise inventories
Mortgage payable (due in 10 years)
Notes receivable (due in 5 years)
Other investments
Short-term investments
Unearned revenue
Vehicles

Classify each of the above accounts as current assets, non-current assets, current liabilities, or non-current liabilities.

Solution

Account	Balance Sheet Classification
Accounts payable	Current liabilities
Accounts receivable	Current assets
Accumulated depreciation—buildings	Non-current assets
Current portion of notes payable	Current liabilities
Goodwill	Non-current assets
Intangibles	Non-current assets
Interest payable	Current liabilities
Merchandise inventories	Current assets

Action Plan
- Current assets include all assets that will be realized within one year.
- Current liabilities are obligations that are expected to be paid within one year.
- Non-current assets are all assets that will be realized in more than one year.
- Obligations that are due after more than one year are classified as non-current liabilities.

Mortgage payable (due in 10 years)	Non-current liabilities
Notes receivable (due in 5 years)	Non-current assets
Other investments	Non-current assets
Short-term investments	Current assets
Unearned revenue	Current liabilities
Vehicles	Non-current assets

Related exercise material: BE4–9, BE4–10, and E4–10.

THE NAVIGATOR

Using the Information in the Financial Statements

In Chapter 1, we briefly discussed how the financial statements give information about a company's performance and financial position. In this chapter, we will begin to learn about a tool, called ratio analysis, that can be used to analyze financial statements in order to make a more meaningful evaluation of a company. Ratio analysis expresses the relationships between selected items in the financial statements.

As you study the chapters of this book, you will learn about three general types of ratios that are used to analyze financial statements: liquidity, profitability, and solvency ratios. Liquidity ratios measure a company's liquidity—the company's ability to pay its obligations as they come due within the next year and to meet unexpected needs for cash. As the name suggests, profitability ratios measure a company's profit or operating success for a specific period of time. Solvency ratios measure a company's ability to pay its total liabilities and survive over a long period of time. In this chapter, we introduce three liquidity ratios: working capital, the current ratio, and the acid-test ratio.

>> **STUDY OBJECTIVE 5**

Illustrate measures used to evaluate liquidity.

WORKING CAPITAL

When liquidity is being evaluated, an important relationship is the one between current assets and current liabilities. The difference between current assets and current liabilities is called working capital. Working capital is important because it shows a company's ability to pay its short-term debts. When current assets are more than current liabilities at the balance sheet date, the company will likely be able to pay its liabilities. When the reverse is true, short-term creditors may not be paid.

Reitmans' working capital is $277,851 thousand, as shown in Illustration 4-17, where amounts are in thousands.

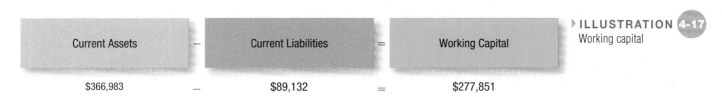

Current Assets	–	Current Liabilities	=	Working Capital
$366,983	–	$89,132	=	$277,851

▶ **ILLUSTRATION 4-17**
Working capital

CURRENT RATIO

A second measure of short-term debt-paying ability is the current ratio, which is calculated by dividing current assets by current liabilities. The current ratio is a more dependable indicator of liquidity measures than working capital. Two companies with the same amount of working capital may have very different current ratios.

Illustration 4-18 ($ in thousands) shows the current ratio for Reitmans at January 28, 2012:

▶ ILLUSTRATION 4-18
Current ratio

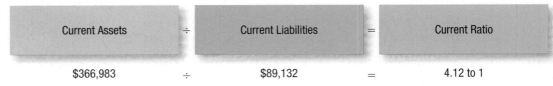

Current Assets	÷	Current Liabilities	=	Current Ratio
$366,983	÷	$89,132	=	4.12 to 1

This ratio tells us that on January 28, 2012, Reitmans had $4.12 of current assets for every dollar of current liabilities. As a general rule, a higher current ratio indicates better liquidity.

The current ratio is useful, but it does not take into account the composition of the current assets. For example, a satisfactory current ratio does not disclose the fact that a portion of current assets may be tied up in slow-moving inventory.

ACCOUNTING IN ACTION
BUSINESS INSIGHT

Generally, a higher current ratio is better as it indicates more liquidity—a company's ability to pay its short-term debts. But how high is too high? Some analysts argue that a current ratio of more than 3 or 4 is not good because it might mean that accounts receivable or inventory is building up. It could also mean that the company has too much cash and short-term investments that are not earning a greater rate of return or are not being put back into the business. But sometimes a high current ratio can be good, such as when a company is building up cash for strategic moves. For example, after Microsoft Corporation's current ratio reached 4, it paid shareholders its first dividend ever, made more acquisitions, and repurchased billions of dollars worth of shares. Afterwards, Microsoft's current ratio returned to a more moderate range of between 2 and 3. What is considered a desirable current ratio also varies by industry. For example, restaurants tend to have low current ratios because they usually have little or no accounts receivable.

Sources: "Current Ratio," Reuters Financial Glossary, retrieved from http://glossary.reuters.com/index.php/Current_Ratio; Joshua Kennon, "The Current Ratio," About.com; Bloomberg Businessweek, "Microsoft Corp.," retrieved from http://investing.businessweek.com/research/stocks/financials/ratios.asp?ticker=MSFT:US

Does a current ratio of less than one indicate the company will have problems paying its obligations?

ACID-TEST RATIO

The **acid-test ratio** is a measure of the company's immediate short-term liquidity. The ratio is calculated by dividing the sum of cash, short-term investments, and receivables by current liabilities. These assets are highly liquid compared with inventory and prepaid expenses. The inventory may not be readily saleable, and the prepaid expenses may not be transferable to others.

Alternative terminology The acid-test ratio is also known as the *quick ratio*.

Illustration 4-19 ($ in thousands) shows the acid-test ratio for Reitmans at January 28, 2012.

▶ ILLUSTRATION 4-19
Acid-test ratio

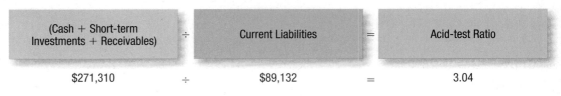

(Cash + Short-term Investments + Receivables)	÷	Current Liabilities	=	Acid-test Ratio
$271,310	÷	$89,132	=	3.04

This ratio tells us that on January 28, 2012, Reitmans had $3.04 of highly liquid assets for every dollar of current liabilities. As with the current ratio, a higher acid-test ratio generally indicates better liquidity.

Ratios should never be interpreted without considering certain factors: (1) general economic and industry conditions, (2) other specific financial information about the company over time, and (3) comparison with ratios for other companies in the same or related industries. We will have a longer discussion about how to interpret ratios in Chapter 18.

 BEFORE YOU GO ON...

Do It

Selected financial information is available at December 31 for Dominic Co.

	2014	2013
Cash	$ 5,460	$ 6,645
Accounts receivable	3,505	3,470
Current assets	18,475	19,035
Current liabilities	18,860	17,305

(a) Calculate (1) working capital, (2) the current ratio, and (3) the acid-test ratio for 2013 and 2014.
(b) Indicate whether there was an improvement or deterioration in liquidity for Dominic in 2014.

Solution

(a)

		2014	2013
(1)	Working capital	= $18,475 − $18,860	= $19,035 − $17,305
		= $(385)	= $1,730
(2)	Current ratio	= $18,475 ÷ $18,860	= $19,035 ÷ $17,305
		= 0.98 to 1	= 1.1 to 1
(3)	Acid-test ratio	= ($5,460 + $3,505)	= ($6,645 + $3,470)
		$18,860	$17,305
		= 0.48 to 1	= 0.58 to 1

(b) Working capital, the current ratio, and the acid-test ratio have all decreased in 2014 from 2013. This means that the company's liquidity has deteriorated during 2014.

Related exercise material: BE4–11, BE4–12, E4–11, and E4–12.

Action Plan
- Subtract current liabilities from current assets to calculate working capital.
- Divide current assets by current liabilities to calculate current ratio.
- Divide cash plus accounts receivable by current liabilities to calculate acid-test ratio.
- Recall if higher or lower ratios indicate if liquidity has improved or deteriorated.

THE **NAVIGATOR**

WORK SHEETS | APPENDIX 4A

As discussed in the chapter, a work sheet is a multiple-column form that may be used in the adjustment process and in preparing financial statements. The five steps for preparing a work sheet are described in the next section. They must be done in the order they are presented in.

STEPS IN PREPARING A WORK SHEET

We will use the October 31 trial balance and adjustment data for Pioneer Advertising Agency from Chapter 3 to show how to prepare a work sheet. Each step of the process is described below and is shown in Illustration 4A-1.

Step 1. Prepare a Trial Balance on the Work Sheet. Enter all ledger accounts with balances in the account title space. Debit and credit amounts from the ledger are entered in the trial balance columns.

Step 2. Enter the Adjustments in the Adjustment Columns. When a work sheet is used, all adjustments are entered in the adjustment columns. In entering the adjustments, relevant trial balance accounts should be used. If additional accounts are needed, they should be inserted on the lines immediately below the trial balance totals. A different letter identifies the debit and credit for each adjusting entry.

Year-end adjustments must still be recorded in the journal, but not until after the work sheet is completed and the financial statements have been prepared.

The adjustments on Pioneer Advertising Agency's work sheet in Illustration 4A-1 are the adjustments from the Pioneer Advertising Agency example in Chapter 3. They are recorded in the adjustment columns of the work sheet as follows:

(a) Debit Supplies Expense (an additional account) $1,500 for the cost of supplies used, and credit Supplies $1,500.

(b) Debit Insurance Expense (an additional account) $50 for the insurance that has expired, and credit Prepaid Insurance $50.

(c) Debit Unearned Revenue $400 for fees previously collected and now earned, and credit Service Revenue $400.

(d) Debit Accounts Receivable $200 for fees earned but not billed, and credit Service Revenue $200.

(e) Two additional accounts relating to interest are needed. Debit Interest Expense $25 for accrued interest, and credit Interest Payable $25.

(f) Debit Salaries Expense $2,000 for accrued salaries, and credit Salaries Payable (an additional account) $2,000.

(g) Two additional accounts are needed. Debit Depreciation Expense $83 for the month's depreciation, and credit Accumulated Depreciation—Equipment $83.

Note in the illustration that, after all the adjustments have been entered, the adjustment columns are totalled to prove the equality of the two adjustment column totals.

Step 3. Enter the Adjusted Balances in the Adjusted Trial Balance Columns. The adjusted balance of an account is calculated by combining the amounts entered in the first four columns of the work sheet for each account. For example, the Prepaid Insurance account in the trial balance columns has a $600 debit balance and a $50 credit in the adjustment columns. These two amounts combine to result in a $550 debit balance in the adjusted trial balance columns. For each account on the work sheet, the amount in the adjusted trial balance columns is equal to the account balance that will appear in the ledger after the adjusting entries have been journalized and posted. The balances in these columns are the same as those in the adjusted trial balance in Illustration 4-3.

After all account balances have been entered in the adjusted trial balance columns, the columns are totalled to prove the equality of the two columns. If these columns do not agree, the financial statement columns will not balance and the financial statements will be incorrect. The total of each of these two columns in Illustration 4A-1 is $31,058.

Step 4. Enter the Adjusted Trial Balance Amounts in the Correct Financial Statement Columns. The fourth step is to enter adjusted trial balance amounts in the income statement or balance sheet columns of the work sheet. Balance sheet accounts are entered in the correct balance sheet debit and credit columns. For instance, Cash is entered in the balance sheet debit column and Notes Payable is entered in the credit column. Accumulated Depreciation is entered in the credit column because it has a credit balance.

Because the work sheet does not have columns for the statement of owner's equity, the balance in owner's capital is entered in the balance sheet credit column. In addition, the balance in the owner's drawings account is entered in the balance sheet debit column because it is an owner's equity account with a debit balance.

The amounts in revenue and expense accounts such as Service Revenue and Salaries Expense are entered in the correct income statement columns. The last four columns of Illustration 4A-1 show where each account is entered.

Step 5. Total the Statement Columns, Calculate the Profit (or Loss), and Complete the Work Sheet. Each of the financial statement columns must be totalled. The profit or loss for the period is then found by calculating the difference between the totals of the two income statement columns. If total credits are more than total debits, profit has resulted. In such a case, as shown in Illustration 4A-1, the word "Profit" is inserted in the account title space. The amount is then entered in the income statement debit column so that the totals of the two income statement columns are equal.

Helpful hint Every adjusted trial balance amount must appear in one of the four statement columns.

▶ILLUSTRATION 4A-1

Preparing a work sheet—Steps 1 to 5

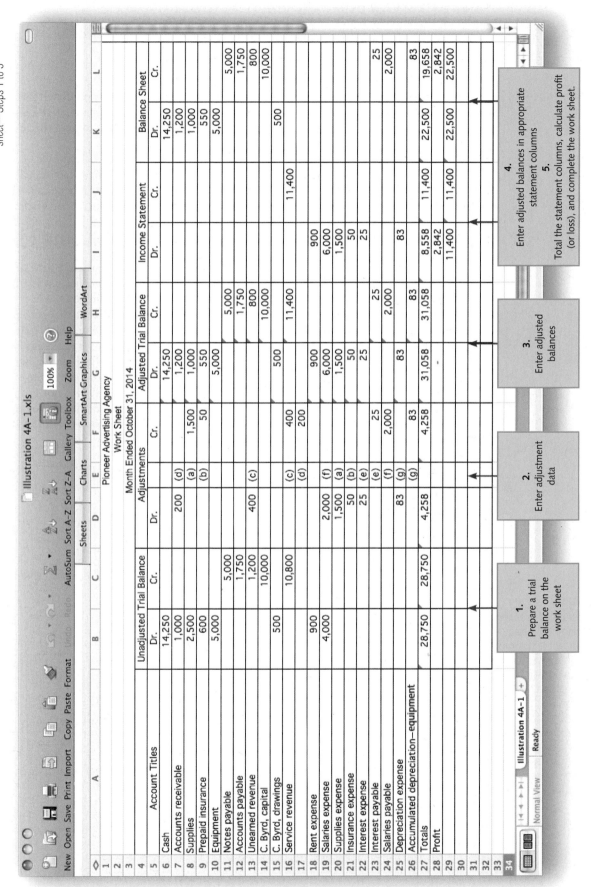

The profit or loss must also be entered in the balance sheet columns. If there is a profit, as is the case for Pioneer Agency, the amount is entered in the balance sheet credit column. The credit column is used because profit increases owner's equity. It is also necessary to enter the same amount in the credit column of the balance sheet as was entered in the debit column of the income statement so the financial statement columns will balance.

Conversely, if total debits in the income statement columns are more than total credits, a loss has occurred. In such a case, the amount of the loss is entered in the income statement credit column (to balance the income statement columns) and the balance sheet debit column (because a loss decreases owner's equity).

After the profit or loss has been entered, new column totals are determined. The totals shown in the debit and credit income statement columns will now match. The totals shown in the debit and credit balance sheet columns will also match. If either the income statement columns or the balance sheet columns are not equal after the profit or loss has been entered, there is an error in the work sheet.

PREPARING FINANCIAL STATEMENTS FROM A WORK SHEET

After a work sheet has been completed, all the data required to prepare the financial statements are at hand. The income statement is prepared from the income statement columns. The balance sheet and statement of owner's equity are prepared from the balance sheet columns.

Note that the amount shown for owner's capital in the work sheet is the account balance before considering drawings and profit (loss). When there have been no additional investments of capital by the owner during the period, this amount is the balance at the beginning of the period.

Using a work sheet, accountants can prepare financial statements before adjusting entries have been journalized and posted. However, the completed work sheet is not a substitute for formal financial statements. Data in the financial statement columns of the work sheet are not properly arranged for statement purposes. Also, as noted earlier, the financial statement presentation for some accounts differs from their statement columns on the work sheet. A work sheet is basically an accountant's working tool. It is not given to management or other parties.

 BEFORE YOU GO ON...

Do It

Susan Elbe is preparing a work sheet. Explain to Susan how she should extend the following adjusted trial balance accounts to the financial statement columns of the work sheet.

Accumulated Depreciation—Equipment
B. Sykes, Drawings
Cash
Equipment
Salaries Expense
Salaries Payable
Service Revenue

Action Plan

- Assets and drawings belong in the balance sheet debit column.
- Liabilities, capital, and contra assets belong in the balance sheet credit column.
- Revenues belong in the income statement credit column.
- Expenses belong in the income statement debit column.

Solution

Account	Work Sheet Column
Accumulated Depreciation—Equipment	Balance sheet credit column
B. Sykes, Drawings	Balance sheet debit column
Cash	Balance sheet debit column
Equipment	Balance sheet debit column
Salaries Expense	Income statement debit column
Salaries Payable	Balance sheet credit column
Service Revenue	Income statement credit column

Related exercise material: *BE4–13, *BE4–14, *E4–13, and *E4–14.

THE NAVIGATOR

REVERSING ENTRIES

APPENDIX 4B

After the financial statements are prepared and the books are closed, it can be helpful to reverse some of the adjusting entries before recording the regular transactions of the next period. Such entries are called reversing entries. A reversing entry is made at the beginning of the next accounting period and is the exact opposite of the adjusting entry that was made in the previous period. The recording of reversing entries is an optional step in the accounting cycle.

» STUDY **OBJECTIVE 7**

Prepare reversing entries.

The purpose of reversing entries is to simplify the recording of future transactions that are related to an adjusting entry. As you may recall from Chapter 3, the payment of salaries on November 7 after an adjusting entry resulted in two debits: one to Salaries Payable and the other to Salaries Expense. With reversing entries, the entire later payment can be debited to Salaries Expense. You do not have to remember what has gone on before. The use of reversing entries does not change the amounts reported in the financial statements. It simply makes it easier to record transactions in the next accounting period.

ACCOUNTING WITH AND WITHOUT REVERSING ENTRIES

Reversing entries are used to reverse two types of adjusting entries: accrued revenues and accrued expenses. To illustrate the optional use of reversing entries for accrued expenses, we will use the salaries expense transactions for Pioneer Advertising Agency shown in Chapters 2, 3, and 4. The transaction and adjustment data were as follows:

1. October 24 (initial salary entry): Salaries of $4,000 earned between October 13 and October 24 are paid.
2. October 31 (adjusting entry): Salaries earned between October 24 and October 31 are $2,000. The company will pay the employees this amount in the November 7 payroll.
3. November 7 (subsequent salary entry): Salaries paid are $4,000. Of this amount, $2,000 applies to accrued salaries payable and $2,000 was earned between November 1 and November 7.

The comparative entries with and without reversing entries are as follows.

When Reversing Entries are not Used (as in the chapter)			When Reversing Entries are Used (as in the appendix)		
Initial Salary Entry			**Initial Salary Entry**		
Oct. 24 Salaries Expense	4,000		Oct. 24 (Same Entry)		
Cash		4,000			
Adjusting Entry			**Adjusting Entry**		
31 Salaries Expense	2,000		31 (Same Entry)		
Salaries Payable		2,000			
Closing Entry			**Closing Entry**		
31 Income Summary	6,000		31 (Same Entry)		
Salaries Expense		6,000			
Reversing Entry			**Reversing Entry**		
Nov. 1 No reversing entry is made.			Nov. 1 Salaries Payable	2,000	
			Salaries Expense		2,000
Subsequent Salary Entry			**Subsequent Salary Entry**		
7 Salaries Payable	2,000		7 Salaries Expense	4,000	
Salaries Expense	2,000		Cash		4,000
Cash		4,000			

The first three entries are the same whether or not reversing entries are used. The last two entries are different. The November 1 reversing entry eliminates the $2,000 balance in Salaries Payable that was created by the October 31 adjusting entry. The reversing entry also creates a $2,000 credit balance in the Salaries Expense account. As you know, it is unusual for an expense account to have a credit balance. The balance is correct in this instance, though, because it anticipates that the entire amount of the first salary payment in the new accounting period will be debited to Salaries Expense. This debit will eliminate the credit balance, and the resulting debit balance in the expense account will equal the actual salaries expense in the new accounting period ($2,000 in this example).

When reversing entries are made, all cash payments of expenses can be debited to the expense account. This means that on November 7 (and every payday) Salaries Expense can be debited for the amount paid without regard to any accrued salaries payable. Being able to make the same entry each time simplifies the recording process: future transactions can be recorded as if the related adjusting entry had never been made.

The posting of the entries with reversing entries is as follows, using T accounts.

Salaries Expense					Salaries Payable				
Oct. 24	Paid	4,000				Nov. 1	Rev. 2,000	Oct. 31 Adj.	2,000
31	Adj.	2,000						Nov. 1 Bal.	0
Oct. 31	Bal.	6,000	Oct. 31 Clos.	6,000					
Oct. 31	Bal.	0	Nov. 1 Rev.	2,000					
Nov. 7	Paid	4,000							
Nov. 7	Bal.	2,000							

Pioneer Agency could also have used reversing entries for accrued revenues. Recall that Pioneer had accrued revenues of $200, which were recorded by a debit to Accounts Receivable and credit to Service Revenue. Thus, the reversing entry on November 1 is:

A = L + OE
−200   −200
Cash flows: no effect

Nov. 1	Service Revenue	200	
	Accounts Receivable		200
	To reverse Oct. 31 accrued revenue adjusting entry.		

Later in November, when Pioneer collects the accrued revenue, it debits Cash and credits Service Revenue for the full amount collected. There would be no need to refer back to the October 31 adjusting entries to see how much relates to the prior month. Thus, as shown in the previous example with accrued expenses, the recording process is simplified.

BEFORE YOU GO ON...

Do It

Pelican Company has a note receivable with a customer. On March 31, Pelican recorded an adjusting entry to accrue $300 of interest earned on the note. On April 30, Pelican collected $400 cash from the customer for interest earned from January 1 to April 30. Record Pelican's (a) March 31 adjusting entry, (b) April 1 reversing entry, and (c) April 30 entry.

Solution

(a) Mar. 31	Interest Receivable	300	
	Interest Revenue		300
	To record accrued interest.		
(b) Apr. 1	Interest Revenue	300	
	Interest Receivable		300
	To reverse Mar. 31 adjusting entry.		
(c) Apr. 3	Cash	400	
	Interest Revenue		400
	To record interest collected.		

Related exercise material: *BE4–15, *BE4–16, *E4–15, and *E4–16.

▮Comparing IFRS and ASPE ▮

Key Differences	International Financial Reporting Standards (IFRS)	Accounting Standards for Private Enterprises (ASPE)
Statement name	Use "statement of financial position" but "balance sheet" is allowed.	Use "balance sheet" but "statement of financial position" is allowed.
Classification of assets	May group together property, plant, and equipment; intangibles; goodwill; and long-term investments under "non-current assets."	Typically do not use the subheading "non-current assets."
Order of presentation	May present assets, liabilities, and shareholders' equity in reverse order of liquidity.	Typically present assets and liabilities in order of liquidity.

THE **NAVIGATOR**

Demonstration Problem

At the end of its first month of operations, Paquet Answering Service has the following unadjusted trial balance, with the accounts presented in alphabetical order rather than in financial statement order:

PAQUET ANSWERING SERVICE
Trial Balance
August 31, 2014

	Debit	Credit
Accounts payable		$ 2,400
Accounts receivable	$ 2,800	
Accumulated depreciation—building		500
Accumulated depreciation—equipment		1,000
Advertising expense	400	
Cash	5,400	
Building	150,000	
Depreciation expense	1,500	
Equipment	60,000	
Insurance expense	200	
Interest expense	350	
Interest payable		1,350
Land	50,000	
Long-term debt investments	15,000	
Long-term equity investments	7,000	
Mortgage payable		140,000
Prepaid insurance	2,200	
R. Paquet, capital		155,000
R. Paquet, drawings	1,000	
Rent revenue		700
Salaries expense	3,200	
Service revenue		5,000
Short-term investments	4,800	
Supplies	1,000	
Supplies expense	300	
Utilities expense	800	
Totals	$305,950	$305,950

Instructions

(a) Calculate the profit or loss for the month.
(b) Calculate owner's equity at August 31, 2014.
(c) Prepare a classified balance sheet for Paquet Answering Service at August 31, 2014. Assume that $5,000 of the mortgage payable is due over the next year.
(d) Journalize the closing entries.
(e) Create T accounts for Income Summary and R. Paquet, Capital, and post the closing entries.
(f) Prepare a post-closing trial balance.
(g) Calculate working capital, current ratio, and acid-test ratio.

Solution to Demonstration Problem

(a) Profit (loss) = Revenue − expenses
= $700 + $5,000 − $400 − $1,500 − $200 − $350 − $3,200 − $300 − $800
= $(1,050)

(b) Owner's equity at August 31, 2014 = Opening capital − loss − drawings
= $155,000 − $1,050 − $1,000
= $152,950

(c)

PAQUET ANSWERING SERVICE
Balance Sheet
August 31, 2014

Assets

Current assets			
Cash			$ 5,400
Short-term investments			4,800
Accounts receivable			2,800
Prepaid insurance			2,200
Supplies			1,000
Total current assets			16,200
Long-term investments			
Equity investments		$ 7,000	
Debt investments		15,000	
Total long-term investments			22,000
Property, plant, and equipment			
Land		$ 50,000	
Building	$150,000		
Less: Accumulated depreciation	500	149,500	
Equipment	$ 60,000		
Less: Accumulated depreciation	1,000	59,000	258,500
Total assets			$296,700

Liabilities and Owner's Equity

Current liabilities		
Accounts payable		$ 2,400
Interest payable		1,350
Current portion of mortgage payable		5,000
Total current liabilities		8,750
Non-current liabilities		
Mortgage payable		135,000
Total liabilities		143,750
Owner's equity		
R. Paquet, capital		152,950
Total liabilities and owner's equity		$296,700

(d)

Aug. 31	Service Revenue	5,000	
	Rent Revenue	700	
	Income Summary		5,700
	To close revenue account.		
	Income Summary	6,750	
	Advertising Expense		400
	Depreciation Expense		1,500
	Insurance Expense		200
	Interest Expense		350
	Salaries Expense		3,200
	Supplies Expense		300
	Utilities Expense		800
	To close expense accounts.		
31	R. Paquet, Capital	1,050	
	Income Summary		1,050
	To close Income Summary.		
31	R. Paquet, Capital	1,000	
	R. Paquet, Drawings		1,000
	To close drawings.		

(e)

Income Summary					R. Paquet, Capital		
Clos.	6,750	Clos.	5,700			Bal.	155,000
Bal.	1,050			Clos.	1,050		
		Clos.	1,050	Clos.	1,000		
		Bal.	0			Bal.	152,950

(f)

PAQUET ANSWERING SERVICE
Post-Closing Trial Balance
August 31, 2014

	Debit	Credit
Cash	$ 5,400	
Short-term investments	4,800	
Accounts receivable	2,800	
Prepaid insurance	2,200	
Supplies	1,000	
Long-term equity investments	7,000	
Long-term debt investments	15,000	
Land	50,000	
Building	150,000	
Accumulated depreciation—building		$ 500
Equipment	60,000	
Accumulated depreciation—equipment		1,000
Accounts payable		2,400
Interest payable		1,350
Mortgage payable		140,000
R. Paquet, capital		152,950
Totals	$298,200	$298,200

(g)

(1)	Working capital = Current assets − Current liabilities	= \$16,200 − \$8,750 = \$7,450
(2)	Current ratio = Current assets ÷ Current liabilities	= \$16,200 ÷ \$8,750 = 1.85 to 1
(3)	Acid-test ratio (Cash + Short-term investments + Accounts receivable) = ───────────────────────── Current liabilities	= $\dfrac{(\$5,400 + \$4,800 + \$2,800)}{\$8,750}$ = 1.49 to 1

THE NAVIGATOR

▶ Summary of Study Objectives

1. **Prepare closing entries and a post-closing trial balance.** At the end of an accounting period, the temporary account balances (revenue, expense, income summary, and owner's drawings) are transferred to the owner's capital account by journalizing and posting closing entries. Separate entries are made to close revenues and expenses to Income Summary; then Income Summary to owner's capital; and, finally, owner's drawings to owner's capital. The temporary accounts begin the new period with a zero balance and the owner's capital account is updated to show its end-of-period balance. A post-closing trial balance has the balances in permanent accounts (i.e., balance sheet accounts) that are carried forward to the next accounting period. The purpose of this balance, as with other trial balances, is to prove the equality of these account balances.

2. **Explain the steps in the accounting cycle including optional steps.** The steps in the accounting cycle are (1) analyze business transactions, (2) journalize the transactions, (3) post to ledger accounts, (4) prepare a trial balance, (5) journalize and post adjusting entries, (6) prepare an adjusted trial balance, (7) prepare financial statements, (8) journalize and post closing entries, and (9) prepare a post-closing trial balance. A work sheet may be used to help prepare adjusting entries and financial statements. Reversing entries are an optional step that may be used at the beginning of the next accounting period.

3. **Prepare correcting entries.** Correcting entries are recorded whenever an error (an incorrect journal entry) is found. A correcting entry can be determined by comparing the incorrect entry with the journal entry that should have been recorded (the correct entry). The comparison will show which accounts need to be corrected and by how much. The correcting entry will correct the accounts. An equally acceptable alternative is to reverse the incorrect entry and then record the correct entry.

4. **Prepare a classified balance sheet.** In a classified balance sheet, assets are classified as current assets; long-term investments; property, plant, and equipment; intangible assets; and goodwill. Liabilities are classified as either current or non-current. Current assets are assets that will be realized within one year of the balance sheet date. Current liabilities are liabilities that must be paid from current assets within one year of the balance sheet date. The classified balance also includes an equity section, which varies with the form of business organization.

5. **Illustrate measures used to evaluate liquidity.** One of the measures used to evaluate a company's short-term liquidity is its working capital, which is the excess of current assets over current liabilities. This can also be expressed as the current ratio (current assets ÷ current liabilities). The acid-test ratio is a measure of the company's immediate short-term liquidity and is calculated by dividing the sum of cash, short-term investments, and receivables by current liabilities.

6. **Prepare a work sheet (Appendix 4A).** A work sheet is an optional multi-column form, used to assist in preparing adjusting entries and financial statements. The steps in preparing a work sheet are (1) prepare a trial balance on the work sheet; (2) enter the adjustments in the adjustment columns; (3) enter adjusted balances in the adjusted trial balance columns; (4) enter adjusted trial balance amounts in correct financial statement columns; and (5) total the statement columns, calculate profit (or loss), and complete the work sheet.

7. **Prepare reversing entries (Appendix 4B).** Reversing entries are optional entries used to simplify bookkeeping. They are made at the beginning of the new accounting period and are the direct opposite of the adjusting entry made in the preceding period. Only accrual adjusting entries are reversed. If reversing entries are used, then subsequent cash transactions can be recorded without referring to the adjusting entries prepared at the end of the previous period.

THE NAVIGATOR

⊙ Glossary

Acid-test ratio   A measure of the company's immediate short-term liquidity. (p. 194)

Classified balance sheet   A balance sheet that has several classifications or sections. (p. 184)

Closing entries   Entries made at the end of an accounting period to transfer the balances of temporary accounts (revenues, expenses, income summary, and drawings) to the permanent owner's equity account, owner's capital. (p. 175)

Closing the books   The process of journalizing and posting closing entries to update the capital account and prepare the temporary accounts for the next period's postings. (p. 174)

Correcting entries   Entries to correct errors that were made when transactions were recorded. (p. 182)

Current assets   Cash and other assets that will be converted to cash, sold, or used up within one year from the balance sheet date or in the company's normal operating cycle. (p. 185)

Current liabilities   Obligations that are expected to be settled within one year from the balance sheet date or in the company's normal operating cycle. (p. 188)

Current ratio   A measure of short-term debt-paying ability that is determined by dividing current assets by current liabilities. (p. 193)

Income Summary   A temporary account that is used in closing revenue and expense accounts. (p. 175)

Intangible assets   Long-lived assets that do not have physical substance and are rights and privileges that result from ownership. They include patents, copyrights, trademarks, trade names, and licences. (p. 188)

Liquidity   The ability of a company to pay obligations as they come due within the next year and to meet unexpected needs for cash. (p. 193)

Long-term investments   Investments in long-term debts that management intends to hold to earn interest or in equity of other companies that management plans to hold for many years as a strategic investment. (p. 186)

Non-current assets   Assets that will not be converted to cash, sold, or used by the business within one year of the balance sheet date or its operating cycle. (p. 186)

Non-current liabilities   Obligations that are expected to be paid after one year or longer. (p. 189)

Operating cycle   The time it takes to go from starting with cash to ending with cash in producing revenues. (p. 185)

Permanent accounts   Balance sheet accounts, whose balances are carried forward to the next accounting period. (p. 174)

Post-closing trial balance   A list of debit and credit balances of the permanent (balance sheet) accounts after closing entries have been journalized and posted. (p. 179)

Property, plant, and equipment   Long-lived tangible assets that are used in the operations of the business and are not intended for sale. They include land, buildings, equipment, and furniture. (p. 187)

Reversing entry   An entry made at the beginning of the next accounting period that is the exact opposite of the adjusting entry made in the previous period. (p. 182)

Temporary accounts   Revenue, expense, income summary, and drawings accounts, whose balances are transferred to owner's capital at the end of an accounting period. (p. 174)

Working capital   The difference between current assets and current liabilities. (p. 193)

Work sheet   A multiple-column form that may be used in the adjustment process and in preparing financial statements. (p. 181)

Note: All questions, exercises, and problems below with an asterisk (*) relate to material in Appendices 4A and 4B.

Flash cards

⊙ Self-Study Questions

Answers are at the end of the chapter.

(SO 1) K   1. When a loss has occurred, the journal entry to close the Income Summary account is:
(a) debit Income Summary; credit owner's capital.
(b) debit owner's capital; credit Income Summary.
(c) debit Income Summary; credit owner's drawings.
(d) debit owner's drawings; credit Income Summary.

(SO 1) K   2. After the closing entries have been posted, the balance in the owner's capital account should equal:
(a) the profit or loss reported on the income statement.
(b) the opening capital balance reported on the statement of owner's equity.

(c) the ending capital balance reported on the statement of owner's equity and balance sheet.
(d) the opening capital balance plus any investments made by the owner during the period.

(SO 1) K   3. Which accounts will appear in the post-closing trial balance?
(a) Assets, liabilities, and owner's capital
(b) Revenues, expenses, owner's drawings, and owner's capital
(c) Assets, liabilities, revenues, and expenses
(d) All accounts

(SO 2) K   4. The proper order of the following steps in the accounting cycle is:
(a) prepare unadjusted trial balance, journalize transactions, post to ledger accounts, journalize and post adjusting entries.
(b) journalize transactions, prepare unadjusted trial balance, post to ledger accounts, journalize and post adjusting entries.
(c) journalize transactions, post to ledger accounts, prepare unadjusted trial balance, journalize and post adjusting entries.
(d) prepare unadjusted trial balance, journalize and post adjusting entries, journalize transactions, post to ledger accounts.

(SO 2) C   5. Which of the following is an optional step in the accounting cycle?
(a) Journalizing and posting closing entries
(b) Journalizing and posting adjusting entries
(c) Analyzing transactions
(d) Journalizing and posting reversing entries

(SO 3) K   6. When Zander Company purchased supplies worth $500, it incorrectly recorded a credit to Supplies for $5,000 and a debit to Cash for $5,000. Before correcting this error:
(a) Cash is overstated and Supplies is overstated.
(b) Cash is understated and Supplies is understated.
(c) Cash is understated and Supplies is overstated.
(d) Cash is overstated and Supplies is understated.

(SO 3) AP   7. Cash of $550 is received at the time a service is provided. The transaction is journalized and posted as a debit to Accounts Receivable of $550 and a credit to Service Revenue of $550. The correcting entry is:

(a) Accounts Receivable	550	
Service Revenue		550
(b) Service Revenue	550	
Accounts Receivable		550
(c) Cash	550	
Service Revenue		550
(d) Cash	550	
Accounts Receivable		550

(SO 4) K   8. Which of the following statements about classifying assets is *correct*?
(a) Supplies are not current assets and should be included as part of property, plant, and equipment on the balance sheet.
(b) Current assets normally are cash and other assets that will be converted to cash, sold, or used up within one year from the balance sheet date.
(c) Some companies use a period shorter than one year to classify assets as current because they have an operating cycle that is shorter than one year.
(d) Prepaid expenses are considered non-current assets because they are intangible assets.

(SO 4) K   9. Non-current liabilities:
(a) are obligations that are expected to be paid before one year from the balance sheet date.
(b) cannot be called long-term liabilities.
(c) are sometimes listed on the balance sheet before current liabilities, if the company is following International Financial Reporting Standards.
(d) include accounts payable, salaries payable, and interest payable.

(SO 5) AP 10. A company reports current assets of $10,000 and current liabilities of $8,000. Its current ratio is:
(a) $2,000.
(b) 80%.
(c) 1.25:1.
(d) unknown without information about the amount of cash, short-term investments, and receivables, which is needed to calculate the ratio.

(SO 6) K *11. In†a work sheet, profit is entered in the following columns:
(a) income statement (Dr.) and balance sheet (Dr.).
(b) income statement (Cr.) and balance sheet (Dr.).
(c) income statement (Dr.) and balance sheet (Cr.).
(d) income statement (Cr.) and balance sheet (Cr.).

(SO 7) AP *12. On December 31, 2014, Mott Company correctly made an adjusting entry to recognize $2,000 of accrued salaries payable. On January 8, 2015, total salaries of $3,400 were paid. Assuming the correct reversing entry was made on January 1, 2015, the entry on January 8, 2015, will result in a credit to Cash of $3,400, and the following debit(s):
(a) Salaries Expense $3,400.
(b) Salaries Payable $1,400, and Salaries Expense $2,000.
(c) Salaries Payable $2,000, and Salaries Expense $1,400.
(d) Salaries Payable $3,400.

▶ Questions

(SO 1) C   1. What are permanent and temporary accounts? What is the relationship between them?

(SO 1) C   2. What are the two reasons for recording closing entries?

(SO 1) C   3. What is the purpose of using an income summary account? If an income summary account was not used, how would the closing entries change?

(SO 1) C   4. Why is the owner's drawings account not closed with the expense accounts? Why is a separate entry required to close this account?

(SO 1) C   5. Brenda has been told that, after the closing entries have been posted, she should stop and check her work. Explain to Brenda what she should be checking for.

(SO 1, 2) C 6. Kathleen thinks that, after the financial statements have been prepared, it is necessary to prepare and post closing entries before starting to record transactions for the next accounting period. Explain to Kathleen why this is not always correct.

(SO 2) C 7. Balpreet thinks that analyzing business transactions is an optional step in the accounting cycle. Explain if this is correct or not.

(SO 2) C 8. Explain the differences between the three trial balances used in the accounting cycle and why is it important to prepare all three.

(SO 2) K 9. Which steps in the accounting cycle may be done daily? Which steps are done on a periodic basis (monthly, quarterly, or annually)? Which steps are usually done only at the company's fiscal year end?

(SO 2, 3) C 10. Eduardo argues that correcting entries and reversing entries are the same thing. Is Eduardo correct? Explain why or why not.

(SO 3) C 11. Christobal thinks that correcting entries are unnecessary. He suggests that, if an incorrect journal entry is found, it should be erased or removed and then the correct entry can be recorded in its place. Explain to Christobal why this is not the correct thing to do.

(SO 3) C 12. Describe how to determine which accounts, and what amounts, to include in a correcting entry.

(SO 4) C 13. What are current assets and current liabilities? How are they different from non-current assets and non-current liabilities?

(SO 4) C 14. What is meant by the term "operating cycle"?

(SO 4) C 15. A Canadian company has the following current assets listed in alphabetical order: accounts receivable, cash, inventory, prepaid insurance, short-term investments, and supplies. In what order will they appear on the company's balance sheet and why?

(SO 4) C 16. What are the differences between the four categories of non-current assets: long-term investments; property, plant, and equipment; intangible assets; and goodwill?

(SO 4) K 17. What alternative methods of presentation can a company follow when preparing its balance sheet? Are these choices affected by whether or not the company is using IFRS or ASPE?

(SO 5) C 18. What is liquidity? Identify one measure of liquidity.

(SO 5) C 19. What factors need to be considered when interpreting ratios?

(SO 5) C 20. What are the differences between the current ratio and the acid-test ratio?

(SO 6) C *21. How is profit or loss calculated on a work sheet? How is this number entered on the work sheet if the company has profit? How is it entered if the company has a loss?

(SO 6) C *22. Why is it necessary to journalize and post adjusting entries if they have already been entered on the work sheet?

(SO 6) C *23. Although using a work sheet is optional, it is useful. Do you agree? Explain.

(SO 7) C *24. What are reversing entries and how are they related to adjusting entries? When are they prepared?

(SO 7) C *25. How is it helpful to use reversing entries? Explain if the use of reversing entries changes the amounts reported in the financial statements or not.

▶ Brief Exercises

BE4–1 The following accounts were included on a company's adjusted trial balance. In the blank space, identify which accounts should be closed (C) or not closed (NC) at the year end.

Identify accounts to be closed. (SO 1) K

_____ Accounts payable
_____ Accounts receivable
_____ Depreciation expense
_____ Operating expenses
_____ Unearned revenue
_____ Interest expense
_____ S. Young, capital

_____ Notes payable
_____ Rent revenue
_____ Prepaid expenses
_____ Equipment
_____ S. Young, drawings
_____ Accumulated depreciation
_____ Supplies

BE4–2 Rizzo Company has the following year-end account balances on November 30, 2014: Service Revenue $38,500; Insurance Expense $2,750; Rent Expense $8,000; Supplies Expense $1,500; L. Wilfrid, Capital $42,000; and L. Wilfrid, Drawings $29,000.

Calculate profit, prepare closing entries, and calculate capital account balance. (SO 1) AP

(a) Calculate profit or loss for the year.
(b) Prepare the closing entries.
(c) Calculate the balance in L. Wilfrid, Capital after the closing entries are posted.

Prepare and post closing entries. (SO 1) AP

BE4–3 The adjusted trial balance for Mosquera Golf Club at its October 31, 2014, year end included the following:

	Debit	Credit
Cash	$ 7,500	
Prepaid expenses	3,000	
Equipment	65,000	
Accumulated depreciation—equipment		$ 15,000
Accounts payable		14,000
Unearned revenue		1,500
N. Mosquera, capital		65,000
N. Mosquera, drawings	45,000	
Service revenue		130,000
Maintenance expense	23,000	
Rent expense	10,000	
Salaries expense	72,000	

(a) Prepare closing entries.
(b) Using T accounts, post the closing entries and calculate the balance in each account.

Prepare post-closing trial balance. (SO 1) AP

BE4–4 Refer to the information in BE4–3 for Mosquera Golf Club. Prepare a post-closing trial balance.

List steps in accounting cycle. (SO 2) K

BE4–5 The required steps in the accounting cycle are listed below in random order. List the steps in the correct order by writing the numbers 1 to 9 in the blank spaces.

(a) _____ Prepare a post-closing trial balance.　(f) _____ Journalize and post the closing entries.
(b) _____ Prepare an adjusted trial balance.　(g) _____ Prepare the financial statements.
(c) _____ Analyze business transactions.　(h) _____ Journalize and post the adjusting entries.
(d) _____ Prepare a trial balance.　(i) _____ Post to the ledger accounts.
(e) _____ Journalize the transactions.

Apply the steps in the accounting cycle to the purchase and use of supplies. (SO 1, 2) AP

BE4–6 Flamingo Company opened for business on April 1, 2013, and purchased supplies on April 15, 2013, for $1,850 cash. On March 31, 2014, the company's year end, it had $400 of supplies on hand. Complete the following steps in the accounting cycle with regard to the supplies:

(a) Journalize the April 15, 2013, transaction.
(b) Post to the ledger accounts. (Use T accounts; ignore the Cash account.)
(c) Journalize and post any required adjusting entries at March 31, 2014.
(d) Journalize and post required closing entries.

Identify impact of error. (SO 3) AP

BE4–7 At Hébert Company, the following errors were discovered after the transactions had been journalized and posted:

1. A collection of cash on account from a customer for $750 was recorded as a debit to Cash of $750 and a credit to Service Revenue of $750.
2. An invoice to a customer for $600 of services on account was recorded as a $600 debit to Accounts Receivable and a $600 credit to Unearned Revenue.
3. A $500 cash payment to the owner, Roch Hébert, was recorded as a debit to Salary Expense of $500 and a credit to Cash of $500.
4. The payment of cash to a creditor of $280 was recorded as a $280 credit to Accounts Payable and a $280 debit to Cash.

Indicate the impact of each error on the balance sheet and income statement by stating whether assets, liabilities, owner's equity, revenues, expenses, and profit are understated (U), overstated (O), or if there is no effect (NE). Use the following format, in which the answer for the first error is given as an example:

	Balance Sheet			Income Statement		
Error	Assets	Liabilities	Owner's Equity	Revenues	Expenses	Profit
1	O	NE	O	O	NE	O

Prepare correcting entries. (SO 3) AP

BE4–8 Refer to the information in BE4–7 for Hébert Company. Prepare the correcting journal entries.

BE4–9   The December 31, 2014, adjusted trial balance of Darius Company includes the following accounts:

Prepare current assets section of balance sheet and classify other accounts. (SO 4) AP

Accounts receivable	$14,500	Patents	$ 3,900
Prepaid insurance	1,600	Unearned revenue	2,900
Goodwill	9,250	Cash	16,400
Supplies	4,200	Short-term investments	8,200
Vehicles	22,500	Merchandise inventory	9,000
Notes receivable (due February 1, 2016)	5,500		

(a) Determine which accounts are current assets and prepare the current assets section of the balance sheet as at December 31, 2014, with the accounts in order of decreasing liquidity.

(b) For each account that is not classified as a current asset, indicate how it would be classified on the balance sheet.

BE4–10   The December 31, 2014, adjusted trial balance of Odom Company includes the following accounts:

Classify balance sheet accounts. (SO 4) AP

Supplies	$ 2,900	Land	$ 85,000
Notes payable (due March 1, 2017)	28,000	Buildings	125,000
Accumulated depreciation—equipment	25,800	Patents	12,300
Equipment	43,000	Goodwill	5,520
Accumulated depreciation—building	37,400	Merchandise inventory	14,000
Notes receivable (due April 1, 2015)	7,800		

(a) Determine which accounts are non-current assets and prepare the non-current assets section of the balance sheet as at December 31, 2014.

(b) For each item that is not classified as a non-current asset, indicate how it would be classified on the balance sheet.

BE4–11   On December 31, 2014, Big River Company had $1 million of current assets and $900,000 of current liabilities. On the same day, Small Fry Company had $200,000 of current assets and $100,000 of current liabilities. Calculate the working capital and current ratio for both companies and compare the results. Which liquidity measure is more relevant?

Calculate working capital and current ratio and compare liquidity ratio measures. (SO 5) K

BE4–12   Selected financial information is available at July 31 for Drew Co.

Calculate working capital, current ratio, and acid-test ratio, and comment on liquidity. (SO 5) AP

	2014	2013
Cash and accounts receivable	$22,680	$20,430
Current assets	35,100	33,510
Current liabilities	24,460	24,800

(a) Calculate (1) working capital, (2) the current ratio, and (3) the acid-test ratio for 2013 and 2014.

(b) Indicate whether there was an improvement or deterioration in liquidity for Drew in 2014.

*****BE4–13**   The accountant for Coulombe Company is almost finished preparing the work sheet for the year ended July 31, 2014. The totals of the accounts in the income statement and balance sheet columns are presented below. Calculate the profit or loss, write this number in the proper columns, and calculate the final totals for these columns. Clearly indicate whether the company had a profit or a loss.

Complete work sheet. (SO 6) AP

	Income Statement		Balance Sheet	
	Dr.	Cr.	Dr.	Cr.
Totals	75,000	95,500	191,000	170,500
Profit or loss				
Totals				

*****BE4–14**   The accountant for Orange Line Company is almost finished preparing the work sheet for the year ended August 31, 2014. The totals of the accounts in the income statement and balance sheet columns are presented below. Calculate the profit or loss, write this in the proper columns, and calculate the final totals for these columns. Clearly indicate whether the company had a profit or loss.

Complete work sheet. (SO 6) AP

	Income Statement		Balance Sheet	
	Dr.	Cr.	Dr.	Cr.
Totals	53,875	43,425	55,550	66,000
Profit or loss				
Totals				

Prepare and post adjusting, closing, reversing, and subsequent entries. (SO 7) AP

*BE4–15   At December 31, 2014, Giselle Company made an accrued expense adjusting entry of $1,700 for salaries. On January 4, 2015, it paid salaries of $3,000: $1,700 for December salaries and $1,300 for January salaries. (a) Prepare the December 31 adjusting entry. (b) Prepare the December 31 closing entry for salaries. (c) Prepare the January 1 reversing entry and the January 4 journal entry to record the payment of salaries. (d) Indicate the balances in Salaries Payable and Salaries Expense after posting these entries.

Prepare adjusting, reversing, and subsequent entries. (SO 7) AP

*BE4–16   At December 31, 2014, Giselle Company had a five-month, 5%, $90,000 note receivable that was issued on October 1, 2014. Interest and principal are payable at maturity on March 1, 2015. (a) Prepare the December 31, 2014, adjusting entry for accrued interest. (b) Prepare the January 1, 2015, reversing entry. (c) Prepare the March 1, 2015, entry to record the receipt of cash at maturity for the note.

▶ Exercises

Prepare closing entries. (SO 1) AP

E4–1   Selected T accounts for Welker Training Services follow. The May 31 postings include both adjusting and closing entries.

L. Welker, Capital

		May 1 Bal.	11,000
May 31	2,500	31	3,700
		May 31 Bal.	12,200

Advertising Expense

May 1	600		
31	700	May 31	1,300
May 31 Bal.	0		

L. Welker, Drawings

May 13	1,000	May 31	2,500
25	1,500		
May 31 Bal.	0		

Rent Expense

May 1	3,000	May 31	3,000
May 31 Bal.	0		

Service Revenue

		May 15	14,500
May 31	16,800	31	2,300
		May 31 Bal.	0

Salaries Expense

May 1	7,200		
31	1,600	May 31	8,800
May 31 Bal.	0		

Instructions

(a) Using the above information, and without doing any calculations, what was the company's profit or loss for May? Indicate how you determined this amount.
(b) What is total owner's equity at May 31?
(c) Prepare the closing entries that were made.
(d) Post the closing entries to the Income Summary.

Prepare a statement of owner's equity and closing entries. (SO 1) AP

E4–2   Selected T accounts for Victoire Esthetics to August 31, 2014, follow.

B. Victoire, Capital

		Aug. 1 Bal.	9,000
		10	2,000
		Aug. 31 Bal.	11,000

B. Victoire, Drawings

Aug. 15	2,200		
25	2,500		
Aug. 31 Bal.	4,700		

Income Summary

Aug. 31	8,000	Aug. 31	15,000
		Aug. 31 Bal.	7,000

Instructions

(a) Prepare a statement of owner's equity for August 2014.
(b) Prepare entries to close the income summary and drawings accounts. Post these entries.

E4–3 At the end of its fiscal year, the adjusted trial balance of Donatello Company is as follows:

Prepare and post closing entries and prepare post-closing trial balance. (SO 1) AP

DONATELLO COMPANY
Adjusted Trial Balance
July 31, 2014

	Debit	Credit
Cash	$ 4,650	
Accounts receivable	11,400	
Prepaid rent	500	
Supplies	750	
Debt investments	8,000	
Equipment	19,950	
Accumulated depreciation—equipment		$ 5,700
Patents	18,300	
Accounts payable		4,245
Interest payable		750
Unearned revenue		2,050
Notes payable (due on July 1, 2016)		45,000
B. Donatello, capital		28,285
B. Donatello, drawings	16,500	
Service revenue		75,000
Interest revenue		320
Depreciation expense	2,850	
Interest expense	3,000	
Rent expense	18,550	
Salaries expense	36,050	
Supplies expense	20,850	
	$161,350	$161,350

Instructions

(a) Prepare the closing entries and post them to the correct accounts.
(b) Prepare a post-closing trial balance at July 31, 2014.

E4–4 An alphabetical list of the adjusted account balances (all accounts have normal balances) at August 31, 2014, for Alpine Bowling Lanes is as follows:

Prepare and post closing entries and prepare post-closing trial balance. (SO 1) AP

Accounts payable	$ 8,200	Interest revenue	$ 400
Accounts receivable	10,980	Notes payable	25,000
Accumulated depreciation—equipment	18,600	Prepaid insurance	820
Cash	17,940	Service revenue	35,900
Debt investments	10,000	Supplies	740
Depreciation expense	9,300	Supplies expense	7,845
Equipment	93,000	T. Williams, capital	85,500
Insurance expense	4,100	T. Williams, drawings	18,500
Interest expense	1,500	Unearned revenue	980
Interest payable	145		

Instructions

(a) Prepare the closing entries at August 31.
(b) Prepare T accounts for the accounts affected by the closing entries. Post the closing entries.
(c) Prepare a post-closing trial balance at August 31, 2014.

E4–5 Tim Sasse started Sasse Roof Repairs on April 2, 2014, by investing $4,000 cash in the business. During April, the following transactions occurred:

Apply the steps in the accounting cycle. (SO 1, 2) AP

Apr. 6 Purchased supplies for $1,500 cash.
   15 Repaired a roof for a customer and collected $600 cash.
   25 Received $2,200 cash in advance from a customer for roof repairs to his house and garage.

On April 30, 2014, the following information was available:

1. Earned but unbilled revenue at April 30 was $600.
2. There is $800 of supplies on hand.
3. Of the $2,200 received on April 25, the company has earned $800 by completing repairs to the garage roof.

Instructions

(a) Journalize the transactions.
(b) Post to the ledger accounts. (Use T accounts.)
(c) Journalize and post any required adjusting entries.
(d) Prepare an adjusted trial balance.
(e) Assuming the company closes its books on a monthly basis, journalize and post closing entries.

Prepare adjusting and closing entries. (SO 1, 2) AP

E4–6 The unadjusted trial balance for Garden Designs at its month end, April 30, 2014, is as follows:

GARDEN DESIGNS Trial Balance April 30, 2014	Debit	Credit
Cash	$14,840	
Accounts receivable	8,780	
Prepaid rent	4,875	
Equipment	24,000	
Accumulated depreciation—equipment		$ 6,000
Accounts payable		5,650
Notes payable		12,000
Unearned revenue		1,500
T. Muzyka, capital		25,960
T. Muzyka, drawings	4,150	
Service revenue		15,400
Salaries expense	9,865	
	$66,510	$66,510

Additional information:

1. $500 of the unearned revenue has been earned by April 30, 2014.
2. On April 1, the company paid $4,875 rent in advance for April 1 to August 31.
3. The equipment has an estimated useful life of eight years.
4. Interest on the note payable is due on the first day of each month for the previous month's interest. The note payable has a 6% annual interest rate.

Instructions

(a) Prepare adjusting entries for the month ended April 30, 2014.
(b) Prepare closing entries.

Prepare adjusting and closing entries. (SO 1, 2) AP

E4–7 The unadjusted trial balance for Swift Creek Engineering at its year end, December 31, 2014, is as follows:

SWIFT CREEK ENGINEERING Trial Balance December 31, 2014	Debit	Credit
Cash	$ 8,450	
Accounts receivable	6,250	
Supplies	5,260	
Prepaid insurance	7,440	
Notes receivable	12,000	
Equipment	27,800	
Accumulated depreciation—equipment		$ 8,340
Accounts payable		4,560
H. Duguay, capital		34,900
H. Duguay, drawings	53,500	
Service revenue		112,300
Salaries expense	39,400	
	$160,100	$160,100

Additional information:

1. Revenue of $1,440 was earned but unrecorded as at December 31, 2014.
2. On June 1, the company purchased a one-year insurance policy.
3. Depreciation on the equipment for 2014 is $2,780.
4. A count on December 31, 2014, showed $750 of supplies on hand.
5. The four-month, 4% note receivable was issued on October 1, 2014. Interest and principal are payable on the maturity date.

Instructions

(a) Prepare adjusting entries for the year ended December 31, 2014.
(b) Prepare closing entries.

E4–8 Choi Company has an inexperienced accountant. During the first two weeks on the job, the accountant made the following errors in journalizing transactions. All incorrect entries were posted.

Prepare correcting entries and analyze impact of error. (SO 3) AP

1. A payment on account of $1,750 to a creditor was debited $750 to Accounts Payable and credited $750 to Cash.
2. The purchase of supplies on account for $860 was not recorded.
3. A $400 withdrawal of cash for L. Choi's personal use was debited $400 to Salaries Expense and credited $400 to Cash.
4. Received $700 cash from a customer on account. Cash was debited $700 and Service Revenue was credited $700.
5. A customer was billed $350 for services provided. Accounts Receivable was debited $350 and Unearned Revenue was credited $350.

Instructions

(a) Prepare the correcting entries.
(b) Indicate the impact of each error on the balance sheet and income statement by stating whether total assets, liabilities, owner's equity, revenues, expenses, and profit are understated (U), overstated (O), or if there is no effect (NE). Use the following format, in which the answer for the first error is given as an example:

	Balance Sheet			Income Statement		
Error	Assets	Liabilities	Owner's Equity	Revenues	Expenses	Profit
1	O	O	NE	NE	NE	NE

E4–9 The owner of D'Addario Company has been doing all of the company's bookkeeping. When the accountant arrived to do the year-end adjusting entries, she found the following errors:

Prepare correcting entries. (SO 3) AP

1. A payment of salaries of $625 was debited to Supplies and credited to Cash, both for $625.
2. The investment of cash of $2,000 by the owner, Toni D'Addario, was debited to Short-Term Investments and credited to Cash, both for $2,000.
3. The collection of an account receivable of $780 was debited to Cash and credited to Accounts Receivable, both for $870.
4. The company had purchased $440 of supplies on account. This entry was correctly recorded. When the account was paid, Supplies was debited $440 and Cash was credited $440.
5. Equipment costing $3,500 was purchased by signing a six-month note payable. Equipment Expense was debited and Accounts Payable was credited, both for $3,500.

Instructions

(a) Correct the errors by reversing the incorrect entry and preparing the correct entry.
(b) Correct the errors without reversing the incorrect entry.

E4–10 The adjusted trial balance for Donatello Company is presented in E4–3.

Prepare financial statements. (SO 4) AP

Instructions

(a) Prepare an income statement and statement of owner's equity for the year. Mr. Donatello invested $5,000 cash in the business during the year.
(b) Prepare a classified balance sheet at July 31, 2014.

E4–11 Selected financial information for JPC Enterprises as of December 31, 2014, follows:

Prepare classified balance sheet and comment on liquidity. (SO 4, 5) AN

Accounts payable	$210,100	Land	$105,600
Accounts receivable	197,000	Licences	58,300
Accumulated depreciation—building	79,900	Merchandise inventory	173,200
Accumulated depreciation—equipment	71,100	Mortgage payable	230,000
Building	256,300	Notes payable	55,000
Cash	16,500	Notes receivable (due in 2016)	34,700
Debt investments	62,600	Prepaid expenses	6,900
Equipment	92,100	Salaries payable	28,700
Equity investments	45,800	Supplies	10,100
Goodwill	36,000	Unearned revenue	27,400
Interest payable	16,500		
J. Chrowder, capital	376,400		

Additional information:

1. All accounts have normal balances.
2. $17,250 of the mortgage payable will be paid before December 31, 2015.
3. The company intends to keep its investment in bonds (a debt instrument) until the bonds mature in 2020.
4. The notes payable are payable on May 17, 2015.

Instructions

(a) Prepare a classified balance sheet.
(b) Calculate working capital, the current ratio, and the acid-test ratio.
(c) Comment on the company's liquidity.

Calculate working capital, current ratio, and acid-test ratio, and comment on liquidity. (SO 5) AN

E4–12 **Shoppers Drug Mart Corporation** is Canada's largest retail pharmacy, with stores in each province (including Pharmaprix in Quebec) and two territories. The following data (in thousands) were taken from Shoppers' financial statements:

	Dec. 31, 2011	Jan. 1, 2011	Jan. 2, 2010
Cash	$ 118,566	$ 64,354	$ 44,391
Accounts receivable	493,338	432,089	470,935
Inventory	2,042,302	1,957,525	1,852,441
Current assets	2,695,647	2,542,820	2,441,973
Current liabilities	1,776,238	1,527,567	1,706,541

Instructions

(a) Calculate the working capital, current ratio, and acid-test ratio for each year.
(b) Discuss Shoppers Drug Mart's liquidity on December 31, 2011, compared with the two previous years.

Prepare work sheet. (SO 6) AP

*E4–13** The unadjusted trial balance at April 30, 2014, and adjustment data for the month of April 2014 for Garden Designs is presented in E4–6.

Instructions

Prepare the work sheet for the month ended April 30, 2014.

Prepare work sheet. (SO 6) AP

*E4–14** The unadjusted trial balance at December 31, 2014, and the year-end adjustment data for Swift Creek Engineering is presented in E4–7.

Instructions

Prepare the work sheet for the year ended December 31, 2014.

Prepare and post adjusting, closing, reversing, and subsequent entries. (SO 1, 7) AP

*E4–15** On December 31, the unadjusted trial balance of Masterson Employment Agency shows the following selected data:

Accounts receivable	$24,000	Cash	$ 7,600
Interest expense	7,800	Service revenue	92,000
I. Masterson, capital	48,000	Interest payable	0

Analysis shows that adjusting entries are required to (1) accrue $4,400 of service revenue, and (2) accrue $1,500 of interest expense.

Instructions

(a) Prepare and post (1) the adjusting entries and (2) the closing entries for the temporary accounts at December 31.
(b) Prepare and post reversing entries on January 1.
(c) Prepare and post the entries to record (1) the collection of $6,200 of service revenue (including the accrued service revenue from December 31) on January 10, and (2) the payment of $2,235 interest on January 31 (consisting of the accrued interest from December 31 plus January's interest).

Prepare adjusting, reversing, and subsequent entries. (SO 7) AP

*E4–16** Rosborough Company provides property management services to a variety of companies. At its fiscal year end on April 30, 2014, adjustments were required for the following items:

1. Service revenue of $600 was earned but not recorded.
2. Of the balance in the Unearned Revenue account, $250 had been earned.
3. Depreciation expense for the year ended April 30, 2014, was $4,850.
4. Interest of $545 on a note payable had accrued.
5. Prepaid insurance of $385 had expired.
6. Property taxes for the calendar year are payable every year on June 30. The company estimated property taxes for 2014 to be $3,912.

Instructions

(a) Identify the adjustments for which it could be useful to prepare reversing entries.

(b) Prepare these reversing entries on May 1, 2014.

(c) Explain why and how the reversing entries are useful for these adjustments but not for the other adjustments.

▶ Problems: Set A

P4–1A   The adjusted trial balance for Marine Fishing Centre is as follows:

Prepare financial statements, closing entries, and post-closing trial balance.
(SO 1, 4) AP

MARINE FISHING CENTRE Adjusted Trial Balance March 31, 2014		
	Debit	Credit
Cash	$ 7,720	
Interest receivable	750	
Supplies	1,425	
Debt investments	30,000	
Land	46,800	
Building	186,900	
Accumulated depreciation—building		$ 31,150
Equipment	36,200	
Accumulated depreciation—equipment		18,100
Accounts payable		5,875
Interest payable		990
Unearned revenue		2,190
Notes payable ($6,000 must be paid in 2015)		66,000
R. Falkner, capital		165,300
R. Falkner, drawings	46,200	
Service revenue		124,300
Interest revenue		1,500
Depreciation expense	9,850	
Interest expense	3,960	
Insurance expense	4,500	
Salaries expense	30,000	
Supplies expense	5,700	
Utilities expense	5,400	
	$415,405	$415,405

Instructions

(a) Calculate profit or loss for the year. (*Note:* It is not necessary to prepare an income statement.)

(b) Prepare a statement of owner's equity. The owner, Rachael Falkner, invested $2,300 cash in the business during the year. (*Note:* This transaction has been correctly recorded.)

(c) Prepare a classified balance sheet.

(d) Prepare closing entries.

(e) Use T accounts to post the closing entries and calculate the balance in each account. (Ignore the accounts not affected by the closing entries.)

(f) Prepare a post-closing trial balance and compare the balance in the R. Falkner, Capital account with the information in the statement of owner's equity.

TAKING IT FURTHER   What alternatives should be considered when deciding on the presentation of information in the classified balance sheet?

Prepare adjusting entries, adjusted trial balance, financial statements, and closing entries. (SO 1, 4) AP

P4-2A   The following is Elbow Cycle Repair Shop's trial balance at January 31, 2014, the company's fiscal year end:

	Debit	Credit
ELBOW CYCLE REPAIR SHOP		
Trial Balance		
January 31, 2014		
Cash	$ 3,200	
Accounts receivable	6,630	
Prepaid insurance	6,420	
Supplies	5,240	
Land	50,000	
Building	90,000	
Accumulated depreciation—building		$ 11,000
Equipment	27,000	
Accumulated depreciation—equipment		4,500
Accounts payable		6,400
Unearned revenue		1,950
Mortgage payable		102,000
H. Dude, capital		61,000
H. Dude, drawings	101,100	
Service revenue		235,550
Salaries expense	115,200	
Utilities expense	12,000	
Interest expense	5,610	
	$422,400	$422,400

Additional information:

1. Service revenue earned but not recorded at January 31, 2014, was $1,550.
2. The 12-month insurance policy was purchased on March 1, 2013.
3. A physical count of supplies shows $580 on hand on January 31, 2014.
4. The building has an estimated useful life of 45 years. The equipment has an estimated useful life of 15 years.
5. Salaries of $1,520 are accrued and unpaid at January 31, 2014.
6. The mortgage payable has a 6% interest rate. Interest is paid on the first day of each month for the previous month's interest.
7. By January 31, 2014, $850 of the unearned revenue has been earned.
8. During the next fiscal year, $4,500 of the mortgage payable is to be paid.

Instructions

(a) Prepare the adjusting entries.
(b) Prepare an adjusted trial balance.
(c) Prepare an income statement, statement of owner's equity, and classified balance sheet. The owner, Henry Dude, invested $5,000 cash in the business on November 17, 2013.
(d) Prepare the closing entries.

TAKING IT FURTHER   Henry Dude is concerned that he had to invest cash in the business this year. Based on the information in the financial statements, what do you suggest to Henry?

Complete all steps in the accounting cycle. (SO 1, 2, 4) AP

P4-3A   Lee Chang opened Lee's Window Washing on July 1, 2014. In July, the following transactions were completed:

July	1	Lee invested $20,000 cash in the business.
	1	Purchased a used truck for $25,000, paying $5,000 cash and signing a note payable for the balance.
	3	Purchased supplies for $2,100 on account.
	5	Paid $1,800 on a one-year insurance policy, effective July 1.
	12	Billed customers $4,500 for cleaning services.
	18	Paid $1,400 of amount owed on supplies.
	20	Paid $2,000 for employee salaries.
	21	Collected $3,400 from customers billed on July 12.
	25	Billed customers $9,000 for cleaning services.
	31	Paid $550 for fuel for the month on the truck.
	31	Withdrew $1,600 cash for personal use.

Instructions

(a) Journalize and post the July transactions.
(b) Prepare a trial balance at July 31.
(c) Journalize and post the following adjustments:
   1. Earned but unbilled fees at July 31 were $1,500.
   2. The truck has an estimated useful life of four years.
   3. One-twelfth of the insurance expired.
   4. An inventory count shows $700 of supplies on hand at July 31.
   5. Accrued but unpaid employee salaries were $800.
   6. The note payable has a 5.5% annual interest rate.
(d) Prepare an adjusted trial balance.
(e) Prepare the income statement and statement of owner's equity for July, and a classified balance sheet at July 31, 2014. Of the note payable, $5,000 must be paid by July 1, 2015.
(f) Journalize and post the closing entries.
(g) Prepare a post-closing trial balance at July 31.

TAKING IT FURTHER   Do companies need to make adjusting and closing entries at the end of every month?

P4–4A   Silver Ridge Plumbing's year end is October 31. The company's trial balance prior to adjustments follows:

Prepare adjusting entries, adjusted trial balance, financial statements, and closing entries.
(SO 1, 2, 4) AP

SILVER RIDGE PLUMBING Trial Balance October 31, 2014		
	Debit	Credit
Cash	$ 15,420	
Supplies	26,000	
Debt investments	20,000	
Equipment	120,000	
Accumulated depreciation—equipment		$ 42,000
Vehicles	110,000	
Accumulated depreciation—vehicles		48,125
Accounts payable		7,950
Unearned revenue		5,000
Notes payable		55,000
H. Burke, capital		75,750
H. Burke, drawings	36,000	
Service revenue		200,125
Interest revenue		400
Fuel expense	28,038	
Insurance expense	9,500	
Interest expense	3,392	
Rent expense	21,000	
Salaries expense	45,000	
	$434,350	$434,350

Additional information:

1. The equipment has an expected useful life of 10 years. The vehicles' expected useful life is eight years.
2. A physical count showed $2,000 of supplies on hand at October 31, 2014.
3. As at October 31, 2014, there was $1,000 of revenue received in advance that was still unearned.
4. Silver Ridge has a debt investment (in bonds) that it intends to hold to earn interest until the bonds mature in 15 years. The bonds have an interest rate of 4% and pay interest on May 1 and November 1 each year.
5. Accrued salaries payable at October 31, 2014, were $2,550.
6. Interest on the 5.5% note payable is payable at the end of each month and $10,000 of the principal must be paid on December 31 each year. Interest payments are up to date as at October 31, 2014.
7. The owner, H. Burke, invested $2,000 cash in the business on December 28, 2013. (*Note:* This has been correctly recorded.)

Instructions

(a) Prepare the adjusting entries and an adjusted trial balance.

(b) Calculate profit or loss for the year.

(c) Prepare a statement of owner's equity and a classified balance sheet.

(d) Prepare the closing entries. Using T accounts, post to the income summary, and owner's drawings and capital accounts. Compare the ending balance in the owner's capital account with the information in the statement of owner's equity.

TAKING IT FURTHER   Why do you need to know the amount the owner invested in the business this year if it has been correctly recorded?

Analyze errors and prepare corrections. (SO 3) AP

P4–5A   Bob Hibberd, CGA, was hired by Edgemont Entertainment Installations to prepare its financial statements for April 2014. Using all the ledger balances in the owner's records, Bob put together the following trial balance:

EDGEMONT ENTERTAINMENT INSTALLATIONS Trial Balance April 30, 2014		
	Debit	Credit
Cash	$ 4,010	
Accounts receivable	3,225	
Supplies	3,800	
Equipment	11,460	
Accumulated depreciation—equipment		$ 2,200
Accounts payable		2,275
Salaries payable		650
Rent payable	950	
Unearned revenue		1,250
S. Morris, capital		17,700
Service revenue		7,950
Salaries expense	7,400	
Advertising expense	585	
Miscellaneous expense	595	
Totals	$32,025	$32,025

Bob reviewed the records and found the following errors:

1. The first salary payment made in April was for $1,900, which included $650 of salaries payable on March 31. The payment was recorded as a debit to Salaries Expense of $2,100 and a credit to Cash of $2,100. (No reversing entries were made on April 1.)

2. The owner, Stuart Morris, paid himself $2,400 and recorded this as salary expense.

3. April rent of $950 was paid on April 26. It was recorded as a debit to rent payable and a credit to cash, both for $950.

4. Cash paid on account was recorded as $740 instead of $470.

5. A payment of $195 for an advertising expense was entered as a debit to Miscellaneous Expense of $95 and a credit to Cash of $95.

6. A cash payment for a repair expense on equipment of $460 was recorded as a debit to Equipment of $460 and a credit to Accounts Payable of $460.

7. Services of $1,250 were provided to a customer on account. Accounts receivable was debited $1,250 and Unearned Revenue was credited the same amount.

8. The depreciation expense for the month of April has not been recorded. All of the company's equipment is expected to have a five-year useful life.

Instructions

(a) Prepare an analysis of each error that shows (1) the incorrect entry, (2) the correct entry, and (3) the correcting entry.

(b) Prepare a correct trial balance.

TAKING IT FURTHER   Explain how the company's financial statements would be incorrect if error 2 was not corrected and why it is important to correct this error.

P4-6A   The following accounting errors were found in the journal of Crossé Company:

1. The payment of the current month's rent for $500 was recorded as a debit to Rent Payable and a credit to Cash, both for $500. (*Note:* This had not been previously accrued.)
2. The collection of an account receivable for $400 was debited to Cash and credited to Service Revenue, both for $400.
3. A payment for Utilities Expense of $230 was recorded as a debit to Utilities Expense and a credit to Cash, both for $320.
4. A customer was billed $850 for services provided on account. Accounts Receivable was debited and Unearned Revenue was credited, both for $850.
5. A $600 accrual of Interest Revenue was recorded as a debit to Interest Expense and a credit to Interest Receivable, both for $600.
6. A payment of a $250 account payable was recorded as a debit to Accounts Payable and a credit to Cash, both for $250.
7. A $300 advance from a customer was recorded as a debit to Cash and a credit to Service Revenue, both for $300.
8. The purchase of $2,000 of equipment on account was recorded as a debit to Repair Expense and a credit to Accounts Payable, both for $2,000.

Instructions

(a) For each item, indicate the effect and amount of the error—understatement (U), overstatement (O), or no effect (NE)—on the income statement and balance sheet components. Use the following format, where the first one has been done for you as an example.

	Income Statement			Balance Sheet		
Item	Revenue	Expenses	Profit	Assets	Liabilities	Owner's Equity
1.	NE	U $500	O $500	NE	U $500	O $500

(b) Correct each error by reversing the incorrect entry and then recording the correct entry.

TAKING IT FURTHER   Explain why it is incorrect to record billing a customer for services provided on account, as described in error 4.

P4-7A   Below is an alphabetical list of the adjusted accounts of Dunder Tour Company at its year end, December 31, 2014. All accounts have normal balances.

Accounts payable	$ 7,300	Interest receivable	$ 100
Accounts receivable	3,500	Interest revenue	1,100
Accumulated depreciation—equipment	15,000	Notes payable	40,000
Cash	4,500	Notes receivable	18,400
Depreciation expense	10,000	Patents	15,000
Equipment	50,000	Prepaid insurance	2,900
F. Dunder, capital	17,300	Service revenue	65,000
F. Dunder, drawings	33,000	Short-term investments	2,700
Insurance expense	1,500	Supplies	3,100
Interest expense	2,800	Supplies expense	2,400
Interest payable	700	Unearned revenue	3,500

Additional information:

1. In 2015, $3,000 of the notes payable becomes due.
2. The note receivable is due in 2016.
3. On July 18, 2014, Fred Dunder invested $3,200 cash in the business.

Instructions

(a) Calculate the post-closing balance in F. Dunder, Capital on December 31, 2014.
(b) Prepare a classified balance sheet.
(c) On December 31, 2013, Dunder Tour Company had current assets of $17,400 and current liabilities of $22,300. Calculate the company's working capital and current ratio on December 31, 2013, and December 31, 2014.
(d) On December 31, 2013, the total of Dunder Tour Company's cash, short-term investments, and current receivables was $15,600. Calculate the company's acid-test ratio on December 31, 2013, and December 31, 2014.

TAKING IT FURTHER   Has the company's ability to pay its debts improved or weakened over the year?

Determine impact of errors on financial statements, and correct. (SO 3) AP

Calculate capital account balance; prepare classified balance sheet and liquidity ratios. (SO 1, 4, 5) AP

Calculate current assets and liabilities, working capital, current ratio, and acid-test ratio; comment on liquidity. (SO 5) AN

P4–8A **Danier Leather Inc.** is one of the largest publicly traded specialty apparel leather retailers in the world. The following information (all amounts in thousands) can be found on its recent balance sheets (or statements of financial position, as Danier Leather calls them):

	Dec. 24, 2011	June 25, 2011	Dec. 25, 2010
Cash and cash equivalents	$31,803	$28,698	$25,406
Accounts receivable	1,686	391	385
Inventories	36,789	28,964	41,163
Prepaid expenses	426	901	381
Property and equipment	15,315	14,404	15,808
Other long-term assets	2,677	2,732	2,943
Payables and accruals	16,010	11,024	19,650
Income taxes payable	583	278	1,097
Other current liabilities	3,586	1,536	3,659
Non-current liabilities	1,392	1,318	1,414
Shareholders' equity	67,125	60,272	61,928

Instructions

(a) Calculate Danier Leather's current assets and current liabilities for each period.
(b) Calculate Danier Leather's working capital, current ratio, and acid-test ratio for each period.
(c) What does each of the measures calculated in (b) show? Comment on Danier's liquidity.

TAKING IT FURTHER   The three balance sheet dates given in the problem are at two different points in the year (December and June). How, if at all, might that affect the comparability of the ratios?

Prepare work sheet. (SO 6) AP

P4–9A   The unadjusted trial balance and adjustment data for Elbow Cycle Repair Shop are presented in P4–2A.

Instructions

Prepare a work sheet for the year ended January 31, 2014.

TAKING IT FURTHER   Is it still necessary to record the adjusting entries in the journal and post them to the ledger accounts when using a work sheet?

Prepare work sheet. (SO 6) AP

P4–10A   The unadjusted trial balance and adjustment data for Silver Ridge Plumbing are presented in P4–4A.

Instructions

Prepare a work sheet for the year ended October 31, 2014.

TAKING IT FURTHER   Explain why preparing a work sheet is an optional step in the accounting cycle.

Prepare and post adjusting, closing, reversing, and cash transaction entries. (SO 1, 7) AP

P4–11A   Bugatti Company has a September 30 fiscal year end and prepares adjusting entries on an annual basis. The trial balance included the following selected accounts:

Accumulated depreciation	$ 4,250
Depreciation expense	0
Interest expense	3,333
Interest payable	0
Interest receivable	0
Interest revenue	0
Salaries expense	153,000
Salaries payable	0

Additional information for its September 30, 2014, year-end adjustments:

1. Bugatti has a two-year, 3.5% note receivable for $50,000 that was issued on April 1, 2014. Interest is payable every six months, on October 1 and April 1. Principal is payable at maturity. Bugatti collected the correct amount on October 1, 2014.

2. Accrued salaries as at September 30, 2014, were $2,400. Payroll totalling $3,000 was paid on October 2, 2014.
3. Bugatti has a five-year, 5% note payable for $80,000 issued in 2012. Interest is payable quarterly on January 31, April 30, July 31, and October 31 each year. Bugatti paid the correct amounts in 2014.
4. Depreciation expense for the year ended September 30, 2014, was $4,250.

Instructions

(a) Prepare T accounts and record the September 30, 2014, balances.
(b) Prepare and post adjusting journal entries for items 1 to 4 above.
(c) Prepare entries to close these revenue and expense accounts. Post to the T accounts. *Note:* Do not post to the income summary account.
(d) Prepare and post reversing journal entries on October 1, 2014, as appropriate.
(e) Prepare and post the journal entry to record the cash transactions that occurred in October 2014.

TAKING IT FURTHER   Comment on the usefulness of reversing entries.

*P4–12A   The unadjusted trial balance for Veda's Video Arcade at its fiscal year end of May 31, 2014, is as follows:

Prepare adjusting, reversing, and subsequent cash entries. (SO 7) AP

> **VEDA'S VIDEO ARCADE**
> Trial Balance
> May 31, 2014
>
> | | Debit | Credit |
> |---|---|---|
> | Cash | $ 5,940 | |
> | Supplies | 2,910 | |
> | Equipment | 115,000 | |
> | Accumulated depreciation—equipment | | $ 46,000 |
> | Notes payable | | 60,000 |
> | Unearned revenue | | 1,500 |
> | V. Gupta, capital | | 32,200 |
> | V. Gupta, drawings | 35,400 | |
> | Service revenue | | 81,250 |
> | Rent expense | 12,600 | |
> | Salaries expense | 45,800 | |
> | Interest expense | 3,300 | |
> | | $220,950 | $220,950 |

Additional information:

1. On May 31, 2014, Veda's Video Arcade had earned but not collected or recorded $750 of revenue. On June 19, it collected this amount plus an additional $1,150 for revenue earned in June.
2. There was $765 of supplies on hand on May 31, 2014.
3. The equipment has an estimated useful life of 10 years.
4. Accrued salaries to May 31 were $1,390. The next payday is June 3 and the employees will be paid a total of $1,980 that day.
5. The note payable has a 6% annual interest rate. Interest is paid monthly on the first day of the month.
6. As at May 31, 2014, there was $700 of unearned revenue.

Instructions

(a) Prepare adjusting journal entries for the year ended May 31, 2014, as required.
(b) Prepare reversing entries where appropriate.
(c) Prepare journal entries to record the June 2014 cash transactions.
(d) Now assume reversing entries were not prepared as in (b) above. Prepare journal entries to record the June 2014 cash transactions.

TAKING IT FURTHER   Why is it not appropriate to use reversing entries for all of the adjusting entries?

▶ Problems: Set B

Prepare financial statements, closing entries, and post-closing trial balance. (SO 1, 4) AP

P4–1B   The adjusted trial balance for Boreal Rock Climbing Centre is as follows:

BOREAL ROCK CLIMBING CENTRE
Adjusted Trial Balance
January 31, 2014

	Debit	Credit
Cash	$ 9,650	
Short-term investment	9,375	
Supplies	1,780	
Equity investments (long-term)	20,000	
Land	58,500	
Building	165,000	
Accumulated depreciation—building		$ 27,500
Equipment	45,250	
Accumulated depreciation—equipment		22,625
Accounts payable		7,355
Salaries payable		1,250
Notes payable ($5,500 must be paid on May 1, 2014)		110,000
L. Massak, capital		150,700
L. Massak, drawings	52,500	
Service revenue		114,300
Depreciation expense	10,025	
Interest expense	4,950	
Insurance expense	5,625	
Salaries expense	37,200	
Supplies expense	7,125	
Utilities expense	6,750	
	$433,730	$433,730

Instructions

(a) Calculate profit or loss for the year. (*Note:* It is not necessary to prepare an income statement.)

(b) Prepare a statement of owner's equity. The owner, Lil Massak, invested $3,700 cash in the business during the year. (*Note:* This transaction has been correctly recorded.)

(c) Prepare a classified balance sheet.

(d) Prepare closing entries.

(e) Use T accounts to post the closing entries and calculate the balance in each account. (Ignore the accounts not affected by the closing entries.)

(f) Prepare a post-closing trial balance and compare the balance in the L. Massak, Capital account with the information in the statement of owner's equity.

TAKING IT FURTHER   What alternatives should be considered when deciding on the presentation of information in the classified balance sheet?

P4–2B The following is Edge Sports Repair Shop's trial balance at September 30, 2014, the company's fiscal year end:

EDGE SPORTS REPAIR SHOP
Trial Balance
September 30, 2014

	Debit	Credit
Cash	$ 6,750	
Accounts receivable	11,540	
Prepaid insurance	4,140	
Supplies	3,780	
Land	55,000	
Building	98,000	
Accumulated depreciation—building		$ 17,150
Equipment	38,000	
Accumulated depreciation—equipment		9,500
Accounts payable		8,850
Unearned revenue		3,300
Mortgage payable		125,000
R. Brachman, capital		60,000
R. Brachman, drawings	103,525	
Service revenue		189,250
Interest expense	6,302	
Salaries expense	75,900	
Utilities expense	10,113	
	$413,050	$413,050

Additional information:

1. Service revenue earned but not recorded at September 30, 2014, was $1,150.
2. The 12-month insurance policy was purchased on December 1, 2013.
3. A physical count of supplies shows $960 on hand on September 30, 2014.
4. The building has an estimated useful life of 40 years. The equipment has an estimated useful life of eight years.
5. Salaries of $975 are accrued and unpaid at September 30, 2014.
6. The mortgage payable has a 5.5% interest rate. Interest is paid on the first day of each month for the previous month's interest.
7. On September 30, 2014, one-quarter of the unearned revenue was still unearned.
8. During the next fiscal year, $5,400 of the mortgage payable is to be paid.

Instructions

(a) Prepare the adjusting entries.
(b) Prepare an adjusted trial balance.
(c) Prepare an income statement, statement of owner's equity, and classified balance sheet. The owner, Ralph Brachman, invested $4,000 cash in the business on November 21, 2013.
(d) Prepare the closing entries.

TAKING IT FURTHER Ralph Brachman is concerned that he had to invest $4,000 cash in the business this year. Based on the information in the financial statements, what are your recommendations to Ralph?

P4–3B Laura Eddy opened Eddy's Carpet Cleaners on March 1, 2014. In March, the following transactions were completed:

Mar. 1	Laura invested $10,000 cash in the business.
1	Purchased a used truck for $6,500, paying $1,500 cash and signing a note payable for the balance.
3	Purchased supplies for $1,200 on account.
5	Paid $1,200 on a one-year insurance policy, effective March 1.
12	Billed customers $4,800 for cleaning services.
18	Paid $500 of amount owed on supplies.
20	Paid $1,800 for employee salaries.
21	Collected $1,400 from customers billed on March 12.
25	Billed customers $2,500 for cleaning services.
31	Paid $375 for fuel for the month on the truck.
31	Withdrew $900 cash for personal use.

Instructions

(a) Journalize and post the March transactions.

(b) Prepare a trial balance at March 31.

(c) Journalize and post the following adjustments:

    1. The truck has an estimated useful life of five years.

    2. One-twelfth of the insurance expired.

    3. An inventory count shows $400 of supplies on hand at March 31.

    4. Accrued but unpaid employee salaries were $500.

    5. The note payable has a 4.5% annual interest rate.

    6. Earned but unbilled fees at March 31 were $500.

(d) Prepare an adjusted trial balance.

(e) Prepare the income statement and statement of owner's equity for March, and a classified balance sheet at March 31, 2014. Of the note payable, $2,000 must be paid by March 1, 2015.

(f) Journalize and post the closing entries.

(g) Prepare a post-closing trial balance at March 31.

TAKING IT FURTHER Do companies need to make adjusting and closing entries at the end of every month?

Prepare adjusting entries, adjusted trial balance, financial statements, and closing entries. (SO 1, 2, 4) AP

P4–4B Nazari Electrical Services has an August 31 fiscal year end. The company's trial balance prior to adjustments follows:

NAZARI ELECTRICAL SERVICES
Trial Balance
August 31, 2014

	Debit	Credit
Cash	$ 13,870	
Supplies	23,400	
Debt investments	18,000	
Equipment	108,000	
Accumulated depreciation—equipment		$ 38,250
Vehicles	98,000	
Accumulated depreciation—vehicles		42,875
Accounts payable		7,115
Unearned revenue		4,500
Notes payable		48,000
A. Nazari, capital		68,175
A. Nazari, drawings	32,400	
Service revenue		180,115
Interest revenue		360
Fuel expense	25,235	
Insurance expense	8,550	
Interest expense	2,535	
Rent expense	18,900	
Salaries expense	40,500	
	$389,390	$389,390

Additional information:

1. The equipment has an expected useful life of 12 years. The vehicles' expected useful life is eight years.

2. A physical count showed $1,500 of supplies on hand at August 31, 2014.

3. As at August 31, 2014, there was $2,500 of revenue received in advance that was still unearned.

4. Nazari Electrical Services has an investment in bonds that it intends to hold to earn interest until the bonds mature in 10 years. The bonds have an interest rate of 4% and pay interest on March 1 and September 1 each year.

5. Accrued salaries payable at August 31, 2014, were $1,850.

6. Interest on the 5% note payable is payable at the end of each month and $8,000 of the principal must be paid on December 31 each year. Interest payments are up to date as at August 31, 2014.

7. The owner, A. Nazari, invested $3,000 cash in the business on December 29, 2013. (*Note:* This has been correctly recorded.)

Instructions

(a) Prepare the adjusting entries and an adjusted trial balance.
(b) Calculate profit or loss for the year.
(c) Prepare a statement of owner's equity and a classified balance sheet.
(d) Prepare the closing entries. Using T accounts, post to the income summary, and owner's drawings and capital accounts. Compare the ending balance in the owner's capital account with the information in the statement of owner's equity.

TAKING IT FURTHER   Why do you need to know the amount the owner invested in the business this year if it has been correctly recorded?

P4–5B   Ilana Mathers, CGA, was hired by Interactive Computer Installations to prepare its financial statements for March 2014. Using all the ledger balances in the owner's records, Ilana put together the following trial balance: *Analyze errors and prepare corrections. (SO 3) AP*

INTERACTIVE COMPUTER INSTALLATIONS Trial Balance March 31,2014		
	Debit	Credit
Cash	$ 6,680	
Accounts receivable	3,850	
Supplies	3,900	
Equipment	12,620	
Accumulated depreciation—equipment		$ 6,000
Accounts payable		5,330
Salaries payable	2,250	
Unearned revenue		955
M. Hubert, capital		15,375
Service revenue		7,800
Miscellaneous expense	1,360	
Salaries expense	4,800	
Totals	$35,460	$35,460

Ilana then reviewed the records and found the following errors:

1. The purchase on account of equipment for $2,100 on March 1 was recorded as a debit to Supplies and a credit to Accounts Payable, both for $1,200.
2. March rent of $1,150 was paid on March 2. The company recorded this as a debit to miscellaneous expense and a credit to cash, both for $1,150.
3. Cash of $955 was received from a customer on account. It was recorded as a debit to Cash and a credit to Service Revenue, both for $955.
4. A payment of a $575 account payable was entered as a debit to Cash and a credit to Accounts Receivable, both for $575.
5. The first salary payment made in March was for $3,000, which included $750 of salaries payable on February 28. The payment was recorded as a debit to Salaries Payable of $3,000 and a credit to Cash of $3,000. (No reversing entries were made on March 1.)
6. Equipment repairs of $260 on account were recorded as a debit to Equipment and a credit to Cash, both for $620.
7. The owner, Maurice Hubert, paid himself $1,800 and recorded this as salary expense.
8. The depreciation expense for the month of March has not been recorded. All of the company's equipment is expected to have a five-year useful life.

Instructions

(a) Prepare an analysis of each error that shows (1) the incorrect entry, (2) the correct entry, and (3) the correcting entry.
(b) Prepare a correct trial balance.

TAKING IT FURTHER   Explain how the company's financial statements would be incorrect if error 6 was not corrected and why it is important to correct this error.

Determine impact of errors on financial statements, and correct. (SO 3) AP

P4–6B Fu Company is owned and operated by Jeremy Fu. The following errors were found in the company's journal:

1. The purchase of $700 of supplies on account was recorded as a debit to Supplies Expense and a credit to accounts payable, both for $700. (*Note:* The company records prepayments as assets.)
2. A $600 payment of an account payable was recorded as a debit to Cash and a credit to Accounts Payable, both for $600.
3. A cash advance of $575 from a customer was recorded as a debit to Service Revenue and a credit to Unearned Revenue, both for $350.
4. The depreciation adjusting entry was incorrectly recorded as $1,280. The amount should have been $1,820.
5. A customer was billed $650 for services provided on account. Unearned Revenue was debited and Service Revenue was credited, both for $650.
6. The accrual of $750 of interest expense was recorded as a debit to Interest Receivable and a credit to Interest Payable, both for $750.
7. A $500 collection of cash from a customer on account was recorded as a debit to Accounts Receivable and a credit to cash, both for $500.
8. A $950 payment for rent for Jeremy Fu's (the company's owner) apartment was debited to Rent Expense and credited to Cash, both for $950.

Instructions

(a) For each item, indicate the effect and amount of the error—understatement (U), overstatement (O), or no effect (NE)—on the income statement and balance sheet components. Use the following format, where the first one has been done for you as an example.

	Income Statement			Balance Sheet		
Item	Revenue	Expenses	Profit	Assets	Liabilities	Owner's Equity
1.	NE	O $700	U $700	U $700	NE	U $700

(b) Correct each error by reversing the incorrect entry and then recording the correct entry.

TAKING IT FURTHER Why it is incorrect to record the payment of the company owner's apartment rent as an expense, as described in error 8?

Calculate capital account balance; prepare classified balance sheet and liquidity ratios. (SO 1, 4, 5) AP

P4–7B Below is an alphabetical list of the adjusted accounts of Matrix Consulting Services at its year end, March 31, 2014. All accounts have normal balances.

Accounts payable	$11,650	Interest revenue	$ 400
Accounts receivable	4,700	N. Anderson, capital	36,500
Accumulated depreciation—equipment	20,000	N. Anderson, drawings	57,700
Advertising expense	12,000	Notes payable	30,000
Cash	3,900	Notes receivable	10,000
Depreciation expense	8,000	Patents	16,000
Equipment	48,000	Prepaid insurance	4,400
Insurance expense	4,000	Service revenue	79,800
Interest expense	1,800	Short-term investments	3,000
Interest payable	150	Supplies	2,300
Interest receivable	200	Supplies expense	3,700
		Unearned revenue	1,200

Additional information:

1. Of the notes payable, $10,000 becomes due on July 1, 2014, and the rest on July 1, 2015.
2. The note receivable is due on June 1, 2016.
3. On September 20, 2013, Neil Anderson, the owner, invested $3,800 cash in the business.

Instructions

(a) Calculate the post-closing balance in N. Anderson, Capital, on March 31, 2014.
(b) Prepare a classified balance sheet.
(c) On March 31, 2013, Matrix Consulting Services had current assets of $30,700 and current liabilities of $15,950. Calculate the company's working capital and current ratio on March 31, 2013, and March 31, 2014.
(d) On March 31, 2013, the total of Matrix Consulting Services' cash, short-term investments, and current receivables was $25,500. Calculate the company's acid-test ratio on March 31, 2013, and March 31, 2014.

TAKING IT FURTHER Has the company's short-term ability to pay its debts improved or weakened over the year?

P4–8B **Big Rock Brewery Inc.** creates and sells premium natural unpasteurized beer. The following information (all amounts in thousands) can be found on its recent balance sheets (or statements of financial position, as Big Rock calls them):

Calculate current assets and liabilities, working capital, current ratio, and acid-test ratio; comment on liquidity. (SO 5) AN

	December 30, 2011	December 31, 2010	January 1, 2010
Property, plant and equipment	$36,874	$38,595	$40,889
Intangible assets	207	286	344
Inventories	4,429	3,951	3,333
Accounts receivable	2,788	1,789	3,617
Prepaid expense	217	397	305
Cash	655	769	728
Accounts payable and accrued liabilities	3,663	3,016	4,725
Dividends payable	1,212	606	0
Current portion of long-term debt	700	700	0
Long-term liabilities and shareholders' equity	39,595	41,465	44,491

Instructions

(a) Calculate Big Rock's current assets and current liabilities for each year.
(b) Calculate Big Rock's working capital, current ratio, and acid-test ratio for each year.
(c) What does each of the measures calculated in (b) show? Comment on Big Rock's liquidity.

TAKING IT FURTHER At a specific point in time, a company will always have a larger current ratio than its acid-test ratio. Why? Would you expect this difference to be larger in a company like Big Rock Brewery than in a company like **WestJet Airlines**? Why or why not?

*P4–9B The unadjusted trial balance and adjustment data for Edge Sports Repair Shop are presented in P4–2B.

Prepare work sheet. (SO 6) AP

Instructions

Prepare a work sheet for the year ended September 30, 2014.

TAKING IT FURTHER Is it still necessary to record the adjusting entries in the journal and post them to the ledger accounts?

*P4–10B The unadjusted trial balance and adjustment data for Nazari Electrical Services are presented in P4–4B.

Prepare work sheet. (SO 6) AP

Instructions

Prepare a work sheet for the year ended August 31, 2014.

TAKING IT FURTHER Explain why preparing a work sheet is an optional step in the accounting cycle.

*P4–11B Cypress Company has an October 31 fiscal year end and prepares adjusting entries on an annual basis. The October 31, 2014, trial balance included the following selected accounts:

Prepare and post adjusting, closing, reversing, and cash transaction entries. (SO 1, 7) AP

Accumulated depreciation	$ 16,500
Depreciation expense	0
Interest expense	3,750
Interest payable	0
Interest receivable	0
Interest revenue	0
Salaries expense	156,000
Salaries payable	0

Additional information for its October 31, 2014, year-end adjustments:

1. Cypress has a two-year, 3.75% note receivable for $60,000 that was issued on May 1, 2014. Interest is payable every six months, on November 1 and May 1. Principal is payable at maturity. Cypress collected the correct amount on November 1, 2014.
2. Accrued salaries as at October 31, 2014, were $3,200. Payroll totalling $6,000 was paid on November 6, 2014.

3. Cypress has a five-year, 5% note payable for $90,000 issued in 2012. Interest is payable quarterly on March 1, June 1, September 1, and December 1 each year. Cypress paid the correct amounts during 2014.
4. Depreciation expense for the year ended October 31, 2014, was $5,500.

Instructions

(a) Prepare T accounts and record the October 31, 2014, balances.
(b) Prepare and post adjusting journal entries for items 1 to 4 above.
(c) Prepare entries to close these revenue and expense accounts.. Post to the T accounts. *Note:* Do not post to the income summary account.
(d) Prepare and post reversing journal entries on November 1, 2014, as appropriate.
(e) Prepare and post the journal entry to record the cash receipts or payments that occurred in November and December 2014.

TAKING IT FURTHER   Comment on the usefulness of reversing entries.

Prepare adjusting, reversing, and subsequent cash entries. (SO 7) AP

*P4–12B   The unadjusted trial balance for Laurie's Laser Games at its fiscal year end of April 30, 2014, is as follows:

		Debit	Credit
LAURIE'S LASER GAMES Trial Balance April 30, 2014			
Cash		$ 3,800	
Supplies		4,270	
Equipment		130,000	
Accumulated depreciation—equipment			$ 39,000
Notes payable			90,000
Unearned revenue			1,965
L. Glans, capital			33,100
L. Glans, drawings		25,000	
Fees Earned			70,180
Rent expense		13,200	
Salaries expense		53,850	
Interest expense		4,125	
		$234,245	$234,245

Additional information:

1. On April 30, 2014, Laurie's Laser Games had earned but not collected or recorded $550 of fees earned. On May 21, 2014, Laurie's Laser Games collected this amount plus an additional $1,250 for fees earned in May.
2. There was $480 of supplies on hand on April 30, 2014.
3. The equipment has an estimated useful life of 10 years.
4. On April 30, salaries earned but not paid or recorded were $1,150. The next payday is May 8 and the employees will be paid a total of $2,290 that day.
5. The note payable has a 5% annual interest rate. Interest is paid monthly on the first of the month. The next payment is due on May 1, 2014.
6. On April 30, $1,165 of the unearned revenue had been earned.

Instructions

(a) Prepare adjusting journal entries for the year ended April 30, 2014, as required.
(b) Prepare reversing entries where appropriate.
(c) Prepare journal entries to record the May 2014 cash transactions.
(d) Now assume reversing entries were not prepared as in (b) above. Prepare journal entries to record the May 2014 cash transactions.

TAKING IT FURTHER   Why is it not appropriate to use reversing entries for all of the adjusting entries?

Continuing Cookie Chronicle

(*Note:* This is a continuation of the Cookie Chronicle from Chapters 1 through 3.)

Natalie had a very busy December. At the end of the month, after Natalie has journalized and posted her adjusting entries, her company has the following adjusted trial balance:

COOKIE CREATIONS
Adjusted Trial Balance
December 31, 2013

	Debit	Credit
Cash	$2,929	
Accounts receivable	675	
Supplies	95	
Equipment	1,550	
Accumulated depreciation—equipment		$ 78
Accounts payable		76
Salaries payable		48
Unearned revenue		100
Interest payable		8
Notes payable, 3%, principal and interest due November 28, 2014		3,000
N. Koebel, capital		1,450
Revenue		1,225
Advertising expense	325	
Salaries expense	48	
Telephone expense	174	
Supplies expense	103	
Depreciation expense	78	
Interest expense	8	
	$5,985	$5,985

Instructions

Using the information in the adjusted trial balance, do the following:

(a) Prepare an income statement for the two months ended December 31, 2013, if you have not already done so in Chapter 3.
(b) Prepare a statement of owner's equity for the two months ended December 31, 2013, and a classified balance sheet at December 31, 2013.
(c) Calculate Cookie Creations' working capital, current ratio, and acid-test ratio. Comment on Cookie Creations' liquidity.
(d) Natalie has decided that her year end will be December 31, 2013. Prepare closing entries.
(e) Prepare a post-closing trial balance.
(f) Natalie has reviewed the financial statements that you have prepared. When she recorded the purchase of equipment in December, she thought the equipment should be recorded as "supplies expense." After reviewing her accounting text, she remembered that the purchase of equipment should be recorded as an asset and made an entry to correct her error. Had she not done a correcting entry, what impact would that journal entry have had on the financial statements at the end of 2013?

Cumulative Coverage—Chapters 2 to 4

Alou Equipment Repair has a September 30 year end. The company adjusts and closes its accounts on an annual basis. On August 31, 2014, the account balances of Alou Equipment Repair were as follows:

ALOU EQUIPMENT REPAIR
Trial Balance
August 31, 2014

	Debit	Credit
Cash	$ 2,790	
Accounts receivable	7,910	
Supplies	8,500	
Equipment	9,000	
Accumulated depreciation—equipment		$ 1,800
Accounts payable		3,100
Unearned revenue		400
J. Alou, capital		21,200
J. Alou, drawings	15,600	
Service revenue		49,600
Rent expense	5,500	
Salaries expense	24,570	
Telephone expense	2,230	
	$76,100	$76,100

During September, the following transactions were completed:

Sept.	1	Borrowed $10,000 from the bank and signed a two-year, 5% note payable.
	2	Paid September rent, $500.
	8	Paid employee salaries, $1,050.
	12	Received $1,500 cash from customers on account.
	15	Received $5,700 cash for services performed in September.
	17	Purchased additional supplies on account, $1,300.
	20	Paid creditors $2,300 on account.
	21	Paid September telephone bill, $200.
	22	Paid employee salaries, $1,050.
	27	Performed services on account and billed customers for services provided, $900.
	29	Received $550 from customers for services to be provided in the future.
	30	Paid J. Alou $800 cash for personal use.

Adjustment data consist of the following:

1. Supplies on hand at September 30 cost $1,000.
2. Accrued salaries payable at September 30 total $630.
3. The equipment has an expected useful life of five years.
4. Unearned revenue of $450 is still not earned at September 30.
5. Interest is payable on the first of each month.

Instructions

(a) Prepare T accounts and enter the August 31 balances.
(b) Journalize the September transactions.
(c) Post to T accounts.
(d) Prepare a trial balance at September 30.
(e) Journalize and post adjusting entries.
(f) Prepare an adjusted trial balance at September 30.
(g) Prepare an income statement and a statement of owner's equity, and a classified balance sheet.
(h) Prepare and post closing entries.
(i) Prepare post-closing trial balance at September 30.

▶ Financial Reporting and Analysis

BYP4–1   The financial statements and accompanying notes of **Reitmans (Canada) Limited** are presented in Appendix A at the end of this book.

Instructions

(a) What classifications does Reitmans use in its balance sheet?

(b) In what order are Reitmans' current assets listed? Its non-current assets?

(c) Under IFRS, what other alternatives does Reitmans have for ordering its assets and liabilities in the balance sheet?

(d) Reitmans' working capital, current ratio, and acid-test ratio for the fiscal year 2012 are calculated in the chapter. Calculate its working capital, current ratio, and acid-test ratio for the fiscal year 2011. Compare the 2012 figures with the 2011 results and comment on the differences.

Interpreting Financial Statements

BYP4–2   The Gap, Inc. reports its financial results for 52-week fiscal periods ending on a Saturday around the end of January each year. The following information (in US$ millions) was included in recent annual reports:

	Jan. 28, 2012	Jan. 29, 2011	Jan. 30, 2010	Jan. 31, 2009	Feb. 2, 2008
Total assets	$7,422	$7,065	$7,985	$7,564	$7,838
Working capital	$2,181	$1,831	$2,533	$1,847	$1,653
Current ratio	2.02:1	1.87:1	2.19:1	1.86:1	1.68:1
Acid-test ratio	0.89:1	0.79:1	1.21:1	0.79:1	0.78:1
Cash & cash equivalents	$1,885	$1,561	$2,348	$1,715	$1,724
Current liabilities	$2,128	$2,095	$2,131	$2,158	$2,433

Instructions

(a) By what percentage did The Gap's total assets increase or decrease overall from 2008 to 2012? What was the change in each year?

(b) Comment on the changes in The Gap's liquidity over the five-year period. Which measure seems to give a better indication of its liquidity: working capital or the current ratio? Suggest a reason for the changes in The Gap's liquidity during the period.

(c) Do you believe that The Gap's creditors should be concerned about its liquidity?

▶ Critical Thinking

Collaborative Learning Activity

Note to instructor: Additional instructions and material for this group activity can be found on the Instructor Resource Site and in *WileyPLUS.*

BYP4–3   In this group activity, you will create a classified balance sheet by piecing together the information, and using the clues, given to you by your instructor.

Communication Activity

BYP4–4   Your best friend is thinking about opening a business. He has never studied accounting and has no idea about the steps that must be followed in order to produce financial statements for his business.

Instructions

Write a memo to your friend that lists and explains each of the steps in the accounting cycle in the order in which they should be completed. Include information on when each of these steps should be done and explain the purpose of the different types of journal entries and trial balances. Your memo should also discuss the optional steps in the accounting cycle.

Ethics Case

BYP4–5   As the controller of Select Cleaning Services, you discover a significant error in the previous year's financial statements. Two journal entries for services provided on account were recognized in the previous fiscal year but should have been recognized this fiscal year. The incorrect financial statements were issued to banks and other creditors less than a month ago.

After much thought about the consequences of telling the president, Eddy Lieman, about this misstatement, you gather your courage to inform him. Eddy says, "Hey! What they don't know won't hurt them. We have earned that revenue by now so it doesn't really matter when it was recorded. We can afford to have lower revenues this year than last year anyway! Just don't make that kind of mistake again."

Instructions

(a) Assuming the error is not corrected, how, if at all, does this error affect last year-end's balance sheet and current ratio? This year-end's balance sheet and current ratio?
(b) Who are the stakeholders in this situation and what are the ethical issues?
(c) As the controller, what would you do in this situation?

"All About You" Activity

BYP4–6   As discussed in the "All About You" feature, in order to evaluate your personal financial position, you need to prepare a personal balance sheet. Assume that you have gathered the following information about your current personal finances.

Amount owed on student loan (long-term)	$10,000
Balance in chequing account	1,200
Automobile	8,000
Balance on automobile loan (short-term)	2,400
Balance on automobile loan (long-term)	3,600
Computer and accessories	1,200
Clothes and furniture	4,000
Balance owed on credit cards	1,000

Instructions

(a) Prepare a personal balance sheet using the format you have learned for a balance sheet for a proprietorship. For the Capital account, use Personal Equity (Deficit).
(b) Assume that you borrow an additional $5,000 in student loans to cover the cost of tuition for the upcoming school year. What is the impact on your Personal Equity (Deficit) if the cost of tuition is considered an expense? What is the impact on your Personal Equity (Deficit) if the cost of tuition is considered an asset?
(c) Assume that, instead of borrowing to cover the cost of tuition, you earn $8,000 working during the summer and that after paying for your tuition you have $2,000 in your chequing account. What is the impact on your Personal Equity (Deficit) if the cost of the tuition is considered an expense?
(d) Assume that you make a $600 payment from your chequing account on your automobile loan. What is the impact on your Personal Equity (Deficit)?

ANSWERS TO CHAPTER QUESTIONS

ANSWERS TO ACCOUNTING IN ACTION INSIGHT QUESTIONS

All About You Insight, p. 192

Q: How can preparing a personal balance sheet help you manage your net worth?

A: In order to attain your financial objectives, you need to set goals early. A personal balance sheet provides a benchmark that allows you to measure your progress toward your financial goals.

Business Insight, p. 194

Q: Does a current ratio of less than one indicate that the company will have problems paying its obligations?

A: Not necessarily. A current ratio of less than one only indicates that at the balance sheet date the company would not have been able to pay off all of its current liabilities. But current liabilities don't have to be paid on the balance sheet date; a current liability is an obligation to pay an amount at some point over the following year. Therefore, as long as a company is able to generate cash quickly enough through its sales, it will have the cash available to pay the obligations as they come due.

ANSWERS TO SELF-STUDY QUESTIONS

1. b   2. c   3. a   4. c   5. d   6. d   7. d   8. b   9. c   10. c   *11. c   *12. a

Remember to go
back to the beginning
of the chapter to
check off your
completed work!

←

CHAPTER FIVE

ACCOUNTING FOR MERCHANDISING OPERATIONS

THE NAVIGATOR

- ☐ Understand *Concepts for Review*
- ☐ Read *Feature Story*
- ☐ Scan *Study Objectives*
- ☐ Read *Chapter Preview*
- ☐ Read text and answer Before *You Go On*
- ☐ Review *Comparing IFRS and ASPE*
- ☐ Work *Demonstration Problems*
- ☐ Review *Summary of Study Objectives*
- ☐ Answer *Self-Study Questions*
- ☐ Complete assignments
- ☐ Go to *WileyPLUS* for practice and tutorials

CONCEPTS FOR REVIEW

Before studying this chapter, you should understand or, if necessary, review:

a. How to increase and decrease assets, liabilities, and owner's equity accounts using debit and credit procedures. (Ch. 2, pp. 58–62)

b. When to recognize revenues and expenses. (Ch. 3, p. 114)

c. How to close revenue, expense, and drawings accounts. (Ch. 4, pp. 174–180)

d. The steps in the accounting cycle. (Ch. 4, p. 181)

e. How to prepare an income statement. (Ch. 3, p. 132)

f. How to prepare a classified balance sheet. (Ch. 4, pp. 184–193)

TRACKING FASHION AND INVENTORY TRENDS

WINNIPEG, Man.—Style knows no borders, but an international retailer does.

Moulé operates four boutiques in Winnipeg, Vancouver, and Portland, Oregon, selling women's and men's fashions and gifts. Its buying office is in Vancouver, where buyers issue purchase orders to various distributors. Goods from American distributors destined for the Portland store are shipped directly there, while U.S. goods bound for the Canadian stores are sent to the central warehouse in Winnipeg. "We try to minimize shipping costs," says Chief Operations Officer Laurie Gorenstein, whose family owns Moulé.

In both cases, staff receiving the goods ensure they got what they ordered and are billed for. "Our purchase orders are always checked against invoices," Mr. Gorenstein says. If there's any discrepancy in price, colour, style, or quantity, he will phone the distributor to rectify it. The items are coded with a barcode and entered into Moulé's point-of-sale (POS) computerized inventory system. In Winnipeg, goods are then packed into smaller shipments and sent to the two Vancouver stores, where the managers scan the barcodes and enter the items into their stores' own inventory as they stock the shelves and racks.

Even though the stores are boutiques, they still carry a total of 24,000 stock-keeping units, or individual items. In addition to clothes, these items range from rock memorabilia to a $1,500

table, Mr. Gorenstein says. The Winnipeg warehouse receives at least one shipment a day, getting up to five a day in the pre-holiday rush in October and November. The POS system allows Moulé to use a perpetual inventory system, so it constantly knows what it has in stock and its value.

Moulé recently opened an online store with selected merchandise. The items come from whichever store has an item in stock, so when filling an online order, the company checks its POS system to see where an item will be shipped from.

Retailers that carry the same items year-round worry about stockouts—running out of a particular item. But because Moulé sells seasonal trendy fashions, it constantly has to rejuvenate its inventory, ordering six months in advance. When quantities get low, "sometimes we can reorder an item, but most of the time we can't. With fashion, it comes in for the season and it goes out," Mr. Gorenstein says. Although it can't keep a particular item in stock, the retailer still wants to maintain a certain inventory level in a particular category, such as women's jeans. It does this by tracking past sales to determine how much to order. For example, "We know how much denim we've sold in the last 10 years."

While Moulé uses the QuickBooks software for its accounting, its POS system is used to generate inventory-related reports such as the stores' gross profit margin and profit margin so managers can keep an eye on trends of the financial kind.

THE **NAVIGATOR**

STUDY **OBJECTIVES**

After studying this chapter, you should be able to:

1. Describe the differences between service and merchandising companies.

2. Prepare entries for purchases under a perpetual inventory system.

3. Prepare entries for sales under a perpetual inventory system.

4. Perform the steps in the accounting cycle for a merchandising company.

5. Prepare single-step and multiple-step income statements.

6. Calculate the gross profit margin and profit margin.

7. Prepare the entries for purchases and sales under a periodic inventory system and calculate cost of goods sold (Appendix 5A).

THE **NAVIGATOR**

The first four chapters of this text focused mostly on service companies, like the fictional Pioneer Advertising Agency. Other examples of service companies include Air Canada, Canada Post, College Pro Painters, and Scotiabank. Moulé, as indicated in the feature story, buys and sells goods instead of performing services to earn a profit. Merchandising companies that purchase and sell directly to consumers—such as Moulé, Reitmans, Canadian Tire, Mountain Equipment Co-op, and Toys "R" Us—are called retailers.

The chapter is organized as follows:

Merchandising Operations

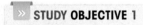
STUDY OBJECTIVE 1

Describe the differences between service and merchandising companies.

Merchandising involves purchasing products—also called merchandise inventory or just inventory—to resell to customers. The steps in the accounting cycle for a merchandising company are the same as the steps for a service company. However, merchandising companies need additional accounts and entries in order to record merchandising transactions.

Measuring profit for a merchandising company is basically the same as for a service company. That is, profit (or loss) is equal to revenues less expenses. In a merchandising company, the main source of revenues is the sale of merchandise. These revenues are called **sales revenue**, or simply sales. Expenses for a merchandising company are divided into two categories: (1) cost of goods sold, and (2) operating expenses. A service company does not have a cost of goods sold because it provides services, not goods.

The **cost of goods sold** is the total cost of merchandise sold during the period. This expense is directly related to the revenue earned from the sale of the goods. Sales revenue less cost of goods sold is called **gross profit**. For example, when a calculator that costs $15 is sold for $25, the gross profit is $10. Merchandisers report gross profit earned on sales in the income statement.

After gross profit is calculated, operating expenses are deducted to determine profit (or loss). **Operating expenses** are expenses that are incurred in the process of earning sales revenue or service revenue. The operating expenses of a merchandising company include the same basic expenses found in a service company, such as salaries, advertising, insurance, rent, and depreciation.

The calculations of profit for both a service and a merchandising company are shown in Illustration 5-1. As you can see, the items in the two blue boxes are used only by a merchandising company because service companies do not sell goods.

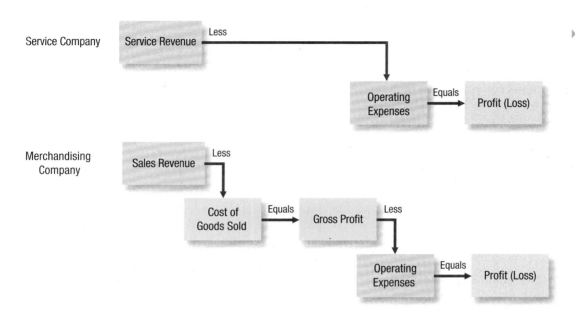

▶ **ILLUSTRATION 5-1**
Earnings measurement
process for a service and
a merchandising company

In addition, you will recall from Chapter 4 that the operating cycle—the time it takes to go from cash to cash in producing revenues—is usually longer in a merchandising company than in a service company. The purchase of merchandise inventory and the lapse of time until it is sold lengthen the cycle. We will learn more about measuring the length of the operating cycle in later chapters.

INVENTORY SYSTEMS

A merchandising company must keep track of its inventory to determine what is available for sale (inventory) and what has been sold (cost of goods sold). The flow of costs for a merchandising company is as follows: Beginning inventory (inventory on hand at the beginning of the period) plus the cost of goods purchased is the cost of goods available for sale. As goods are sold, the cost of these goods becomes an expense (cost of goods sold). Those goods not sold by the end of the accounting period represent ending inventory. The ending inventory is reported as a current asset on the balance sheet. The cost of goods sold is an expense on the income statement. Illustration 5-2 describes these relationships.

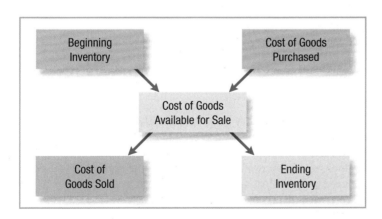

▶ **ILLUSTRATION 5-2**
Flow of inventory costs
for a merchandising company

Companies use one of two kinds of systems to account for inventory: a perpetual inventory system or a periodic inventory system.

Perpetual Inventory System

In a **perpetual inventory system**, the company keeps detailed records of each inventory purchase and sale. This system continuously—perpetually—shows the quantity and cost of the inventory that should be on hand for every item. With the use of bar codes, optical scanners, and point-of-sale software, a store can keep a running record of every item that it buys and sells. Moulé in our feature story uses its perpetual inventory system so it constantly knows what it has in stock and its value.

When inventory is purchased under a perpetual system, the purchase is recorded by increasing (debiting) the Merchandise Inventory account. When inventory items are sold under a perpetual inventory system, the cost of the goods sold (the original purchase cost of the merchandise) is transferred from the Merchandise Inventory account (an asset) to the Cost of Goods Sold account (an expense). Under a perpetual inventory system, the company determines and records the cost of goods sold and the reduction in inventory **each time a sale occurs**.

Periodic Inventory System

In a **periodic inventory system**, companies do not keep detailed inventory records of the goods on hand throughout the period. Instead, the cost of goods sold is determined **only at the end of the accounting period**; that is, periodically. At that point, the company takes a physical inventory count to determine the quantity and cost of the goods on hand.

To determine the cost of goods sold in a periodic inventory system, the following steps are necessary:

1. Determine the beginning inventory—the cost of goods on hand at the beginning of the accounting period. (This is the same amount as the previous period's ending inventory.)
2. Add the cost of goods purchased during the period.
3. Subtract the ending inventory—the cost of goods on hand at the end of the accounting period as determined from the physical inventory count.

Illustration 5-3 compares when each activity is done and the timing of the cost of goods sold calculation under the two inventory systems.

▶**ILLUSTRATION 5-3**
Comparing perpetual and periodic inventory systems

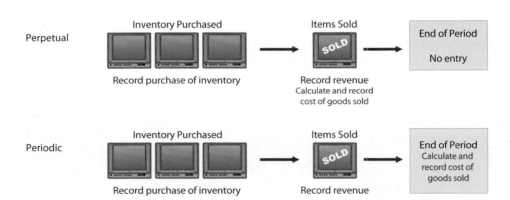

Choosing an Inventory System

How do companies decide which inventory system to use? They compare the cost of the detailed record keeping that is required for a perpetual inventory system with the benefits of having the additional information about, and control over, their inventory. Traditionally, only companies that sold merchandise with high unit values—such as automobiles or major home appliances—used the perpetual inventory system. However, the reduced cost of computers and electronic scanners has enabled many more companies to install perpetual inventory systems.

A perpetual inventory system gives better control over inventories. Since the inventory records show the quantities that should be on hand, the goods can be counted at any time to see whether the amount of goods actually on hand agrees with the inventory records. Any shortages that are uncovered can be immediately investigated.

A perpetual inventory system also makes it easier to answer questions from customers about merchandise availability. Management can also maintain optimum inventory levels and avoid running out of stock. As discussed in the feature story, Moulé likes to keep a certain inventory level in particular categories and uses its perpetual inventory system to track past sales. This helps the buyers to determine how much to buy and stock at each store.

Some businesses find it unnecessary or uneconomical to invest in a computerized perpetual inventory system. Many small businesses, in particular, find that a perpetual inventory system costs more than it is worth. Managers of these businesses can control merchandise and manage day-to-day operations using a periodic inventory system.

A complete physical inventory count is always taken at least once a year under both the perpetual and periodic inventory systems. Companies using a periodic inventory system must count their merchandise to determine quantities on hand and establish the cost of the goods sold and the ending inventory for accounting purposes. In a perpetual inventory system, they must count their merchandise to verify that the accounting records are correct. We will learn more about how to determine the quantity and cost of inventory later in this chapter and in the next chapter.

Because the perpetual inventory system is widely used, we illustrate it in this chapter. The periodic system is described in Appendix 5A.

 BEFORE YOU GO ON...

Do It

Snowflake Company began the year with $15,000 of inventory. During the year, it purchased an additional $75,000 of inventory and earned $120,000 in sales revenue. At its year end, Snowflake had to count its inventory to determine that it had $20,000 of inventory on hand.

(a) What kind of an inventory system does the company appear to be using?
(b) Determine the following: (1) cost of good available for sale; (2) cost of goods sold.
(c) With regard to its inventory, what will appear on Snowflake's income statement and the balance sheet?

Solution

(a) It appears the company is using the periodic system because it had to count its inventory in order to know how much was on hand. And there was no specific information given about the cost of goods sold during the year. From the information provided, cost of goods sold can only be calculated after counting the ending inventory.
(b) (1) Cost of Goods Available for Sale = $15,000 + $75,000 = $90,000
    (2) Cost of Goods Sold = $90,000 − $20,000 = $70,000
(c) Income statement: Balance Sheet:

| Sales | $120,000 | Current assets | |
| Cost of goods sold | 70,000 | Inventory | $20,000 |

Related exercise material: BE5–1.

Action Plan
- Recall that in a perpetual system the cost of goods sold is determined with each sale, and in the periodic system it is determined at the end of the year.
- Remember that beginning inventory + cost of goods purchased = cost of goods available for sale.
- Cost of goods available for sale − cost of inventory on hand = cost of goods sold.
- Expenses go on an income statement; assets on the balance sheet.

THE **NAVIGATOR**

Recording Purchases of Merchandise

Companies purchase inventory using either cash or credit (on account). They normally record purchases when the goods are received from the seller. Every purchase should be supported by a document that provides written evidence of the transaction.

For example, there should be a cash receipt that indicates the items purchased and the amounts paid for each cash purchase. Cash purchases are recorded by an increase in Merchandise Inventory and a decrease in Cash.

Credit purchases should be supported by a purchase invoice showing the total purchase price and other relevant information. The purchaser uses a copy of the sales invoice sent by the seller as a purchase invoice. For example, in Illustration 5-4, Chelsea Electronics (the buyer) uses as a purchase invoice the sales invoice prepared by Highpoint Audio & TV Supply (the seller).

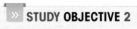

》 STUDY OBJECTIVE 2

Prepare entries for purchases under a perpetual inventory system.

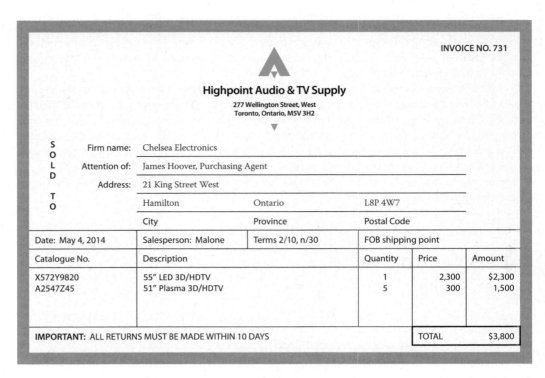

The buyer, Chelsea Electronics, makes the following entry to record the purchase of merchandise from Highpoint Audio & TV Supply. The entry increases (debits) Merchandise Inventory and increases (credits) Accounts Payable.

A	=	L	+	OE
+3,800		+3,800		

Cash flows: no effect

May 4	Merchandise Inventory	3,800	
	Accounts Payable		3,800
	To record goods purchased on account per invoice #731, terms 2/10, n/30.		

Only the goods purchased to sell to customers are recorded in the Merchandise Inventory account. As we learned in Chapter 2, purchases of assets to use in the business—such as supplies or equipment—should be debited to the specific asset accounts.

SUBSIDIARY INVENTORY RECORDS

Imagine an organization like Moulé recording purchases and sales of its 24,000 inventory items in only one general ledger account—Merchandise Inventory. It would be almost impossible to determine the balance remaining of any particular inventory item at any specific time.

Instead, under a perpetual inventory system, a subsidiary ledger is used to organize and track individual inventory items. A **subsidiary ledger** is a group of accounts that share a common characteristic (for example, all inventory accounts). The subsidiary ledger frees the general ledger from the details of individual balances. In addition to having one for inventory, it is very common to have subsidiary ledgers for accounts receivable (to track individual customer balances), accounts payable (to track individual creditor balances), and payroll (to track individual employee pay records).

A subsidiary ledger is an addition to, and an expansion of, the general ledger, as Illustration 5-5 shows.

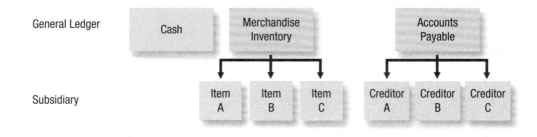

The general ledger account that summarizes the subsidiary ledger data is called a **control account**. In this illustration, the general ledger accounts Merchandise Inventory and Accounts Payable are control accounts with subsidiary ledgers. Cash is not a control account because there is no subsidiary ledger for this account.

Purchases and sales of each item of merchandise are recorded and posted to the individual inventory subsidiary ledger account. At any point in time, the inventory subsidiary ledger shows detailed information about the quantity and cost of each inventory item.

The detailed individual data from the inventory subsidiary ledger are summarized in the Merchandise Inventory control account in the general ledger. At all times, the control account balance must equal the total of all the individual inventory account balances.

Additional information about how to record and balance subsidiary and control account transactions can be found in Appendix C at the end of this textbook.

SALES TAXES

Sales taxes include the federal Goods and Services Tax (GST), the Provincial Sales Tax (PST), and in several provinces, the Harmonized Sales Tax (HST), which is a combination of GST and PST. GST or HST are paid by merchandising companies on the goods they purchase for resale. However, this cost is rarely part of the cost of the merchandise, because in most businesses companies can get back any GST or HST they pay on purchases by offsetting it against the GST or HST they collect from customers or by filing a claim with the government.

PST is not paid by a merchandiser—it is paid only by the final consumer. Therefore, retail businesses do not have to pay PST on any merchandise they purchase for resale.

As mentioned in Chapter 2, the accounting transactions described in this textbook are presented without the added complexity of sales taxes. That is why Invoice No. 731 shown in Illustration 5-4 did not include HST, which would normally be added to the invoice price for a business operating in Ontario. Sales taxes are discussed in more detail in Appendix B at the end of this textbook.

FREIGHT COSTS

The sales/purchase invoice should indicate when ownership of the goods transfers from the seller to the buyer. The company that owns the goods while they are being transported to the buyer's place of business pays the transportation charges and is responsible for any damage to the merchandise during transit. The point where ownership is transferred is called the FOB point and may be expressed as either "FOB destination" or "FOB shipping point." The letters FOB mean "free on board."

> Alternative terminology Other common shipping terms include *FCA* (free carrier), *CIF* (cost, insurance, freight), *FAS* (free alongside), and *CPT* (carriage paid to).

FOB shipping point means:

1. Ownership changes from the seller to the buyer when the goods are placed on the carrier by the seller—the "shipping point."
2. The buyer pays the freight costs and is responsible for damages.

FOB destination means:

1. Ownership changes from the seller to the buyer when the goods are delivered by the carrier to the buyer's place of business—the "destination."
2. The seller pays the freight and is responsible for damages.

For example, the purchase invoice in Illustration 5-4 indicates that freight is FOB shipping point. The buyer (Chelsea Electronics) therefore pays the freight charges. Illustration 5-6 demonstrates these shipping terms.

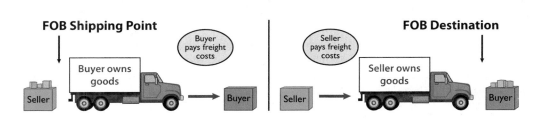

FOB Shipping Point — Buyer owns goods — Buyer pays freight costs — Seller → Buyer

FOB Destination — Seller owns goods — Seller pays freight costs — Seller → Buyer

▶ ILLUSTRATION 5-6
Terms of shipping

When the buyer pays for the freight costs, Merchandise Inventory is debited for the cost of the transportation. Why? Freight is just another part of the cost of purchasing the goods.

For example, if upon delivery of the goods to Chelsea Electronics on May 4, Chelsea pays Public Carrier Co. $150 for freight charges, the entry on Chelsea Electronics' books is:

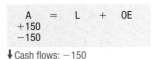

May 4	Merchandise Inventory	150	
	Cash		150
	To record payment of freight on goods purchased.		

Thus, any freight costs incurred by the buyer are included in the cost of the merchandise.

PURCHASE RETURNS AND ALLOWANCES

A purchaser may be dissatisfied with the merchandise received if the goods are damaged or defective or of inferior quality, or if the goods do not meet the purchaser's specifications. In such cases, the purchaser may return the goods to the seller. This transaction is known as a **purchase return**. Alternatively, the purchaser may choose to keep the merchandise if the seller is willing to grant an allowance (deduction) from the purchase price. This transaction is known as a **purchase allowance**.

Assume that Chelsea Electronics returned goods costing $300 to Highpoint Audio & TV Supply on May 9. Highpoint will issue Chelsea a credit, which allows Chelsea to reduce its accounts payable. The entry by Chelsea Electronics for the returned merchandise is as follows:

May 9	Accounts Payable	300	
	Merchandise Inventory		300
	To record return of goods to Highpoint Audio & TV Supply.		

Because Chelsea Electronics increased Merchandise Inventory when the goods were purchased, Merchandise Inventory is decreased when Chelsea Electronics returns the goods (or when it is granted an allowance).

DISCOUNTS

Some events do not require a separate journal entry. For example, the terms of a credit purchase may include an offer of a **quantity discount** for a bulk purchase. A quantity discount gives a reduction in price according to the volume of the purchase—in other words, the larger the number of items purchased, the better the discount. Quantity discounts are not recorded or accounted for separately.

Quantity discounts are not the same as **purchase discounts**, which are offered to customers for early payment of the balance due. This incentive offers advantages to both parties: the purchaser saves money and the seller shortens its operating cycle by more quickly converting accounts receivable to cash.

Purchase discounts are noted on the invoice by the use of credit terms that specify the amount and time period for the purchase discount. They also indicate the length of time the buyer has to pay the full invoice price. In the sales invoice in Illustration 5-4, credit terms are 2/10, n/30 (read "two ten, net thirty"). This means that a 2% cash discount may be taken on the invoice price (less any returns or allowances) if payment is made within 10 days of the invoice date (the discount period). Otherwise, the invoice price, less any returns or allowances, is due 30 days from the invoice date.

Although purchase discounts are common in certain industries, not every seller offers them. When the seller chooses not to offer a discount for early payment, credit terms will specify only the maximum time period for paying the balance due. For example, the time period may be stated as n/30, meaning that the net amount must be paid in 30 days.

In contrast to quantity discounts, purchase discounts are recorded separately. When an invoice is paid within the discount period, the Merchandise Inventory account will be reduced by the amount of the discount because inventory is recorded at cost. By paying within the discount period, a company reduces the cost of its inventory.

To illustrate, assume that Chelsea Electronics pays the balance owing to Highpoint Audio & TV Supply of $3,500 (gross invoice price of $3,800 less purchase returns and allowances of $300) on May 14, the last day of the discount period. The discount is $70 ($3,500 × 2%), and the amount of cash paid by Chelsea Electronics to Highpoint Audio & TV Supply is $3,430 ($3,500 − $70). Chelsea Electronics' entry to record its May 14 payment to Highpoint Audio & TV Supply is:

May 14	Accounts Payable	3,500	
	Merchandise Inventory		70
	Cash		3,430
	To record payment of invoice #731 within discount period.		

A = L + OE
−70 −3,500
−3,430

↓ Cash flows: −3,430

As a general rule, a company should usually take all available discounts. Not taking a discount is viewed as paying interest for use of the money not yet paid to the seller. For example, if Chelsea Electronics passed up the discount, it would have paid 2% for the use of $3,500 for 20 days. This equals an annual interest rate of 36.5% (2% × 365 ÷ 20). Obviously, it would be better for Chelsea Electronics to borrow at bank interest rates than to lose the purchase discount.

If, contrary to best practices, Chelsea Electronics did not take advantage of the purchase discount and instead made full payment of $3,500 on June 3, the journal entry to record this payment would be:

June 3	Accounts Payable	3,500	
	Cash		3,500
	To record payment of invoice #731 with no discount taken.		

A = L + OE
−3,500 −3,500

↓ Cash flows: −3,500

SUMMARY OF PURCHASE TRANSACTIONS

The following T account (with transaction descriptions in parentheses) gives a summary of the effects of the transactions on Merchandise Inventory. Chelsea Electronics originally purchased $3,800 worth of inventory for resale. It paid $150 in freight charges. It then returned $300 worth of goods. And Chelsea Electronics received a discount of $70 by paying Highpoint Audio & TV Supply in the discount period. This results in a balance in Merchandise Inventory of $3,580.

		Merchandise Inventory			
Purchase	May 4	3,800	May 9	300	Purchase return
Freight	4	150	14	70	Purchase discount
	Bal.	3,580			

BEFORE YOU GO ON...

Do It

New Idea Company had the following transactions in September:

Sept. 4   Bought merchandise on account from Junot Company for $1,500, terms 2/10, n/30, FOB destination.
5   The correct company paid freight charges of $75.
8   Returned $200 of the merchandise to Junot Company.
14   Paid the total amount owing.

(a) Record the transactions on New Idea Company's books and (b) post the transactions to the inventory account.

Action Plan

- Purchases of goods for resale are recorded in the asset account Merchandise Inventory.
- Freight costs are paid by the seller when the freight terms are FOB destination.
- Freight charges paid by the purchaser increase the cost of the merchandise inventory.
- The Merchandise Inventory account is reduced by the cost of merchandise returned.
- Calculate purchase discounts using the net amount owing.
- Reduce the Merchandise Inventory account by the amount of the purchase discount.

Solution

(a)

New Idea Company (buyer)

Sept. 4	Merchandise Inventory		1,500	
	Accounts Payable			1,500
	To record goods purchased on account.			
5	No journal entry. Terms FOB destination, therefore			
	seller pays the freight.			
8	Accounts Payable		200	
	Merchandise Inventory			200
	To record return of goods.			
14	Accounts Payable ($1,500 − $200)		1,300	
	Merchandise Inventory ($1,300 × 2%)			26
	Cash ($1,300 − $26)			1,274
	To record cash payment within the discount period.			

(b)

Merchandise Inventory

Sept. 4		1,500	Sept. 8		200
			14		26
Sept. 30	Bal.	1,274			

Related exercise material: BE5–2, BE5–3, BE5–4, BE5–5, BE5–6, and E5–2.

THE NAVIGATOR

Recording Sales of Merchandise

» STUDY **OBJECTIVE 3**

Prepare entries for sales under a perpetual inventory system.

Sales revenue, like service revenue, is recorded when there is an increase in assets (typically cash or accounts receivable) resulting from the company's business activities with its customers. For merchandising companies, this means that sales revenue is recorded (recognized) when the ownership of the goods is transferred from the seller to the buyer. This is typically when the goods have been sold and delivered. At this point, the sales transaction is completed and the sale price has been established. Alternatively, if the customer has paid in advance, a merchandiser may decrease a liability (unearned sales revenue) when the sales transaction is completed.

Sales of merchandise may be made on credit or for cash. Every sales transaction should be supported by a business document that gives written evidence of the sale. Cash register tapes provide evidence of cash sales. A sales invoice, like the one shown in Illustration 5-4, provides support for a credit or cash sale. The seller prepares the invoice and gives a copy to the buyer.

Two entries are made for each sale in a perpetual inventory system:

1. The first entry records the sales revenue: Cash (or Accounts Receivable, if it is a credit sale) is increased by a debit, and the revenue account Sales is increased by a credit for the selling (invoice) price of the goods.
2. The second entry records the cost of the merchandise sold: the expense account Cost of Goods Sold is increased by a debit, and the asset account Merchandise Inventory is decreased by a credit for the cost of the goods. This entry ensures that the Merchandise Inventory account will always show the amount of inventory that should be on hand.

To illustrate a credit sales transaction, we will use the sales invoice shown in Illustration 5-4. Assuming that the merchandise cost Highpoint $2,400 when purchased, Highpoint Audio & TV Supply's $3,800 sale to Chelsea Electronics on May 4 is recorded as follows:

A	=	L	+	OE
+3,800				+3,800

Cash flows: no effect

May 4	Accounts Receivable		3,800	
	Sales			3,800
	To record credit sale to Chelsea Electronics per			
	invoice #731.			

A	=	L	+	OE
−2,400				−2,400

Cash flows: no effect

4	Cost of Goods Sold		2,400	
	Merchandise Inventory			2,400
	To record cost of merchandise sold to Chelsea			
	Electronics per invoice #731.			

For internal decision-making purposes, merchandisers may use more than one sales account, just as they use more than one inventory account. For example, Highpoint Audio & TV Supply may keep separate sales accounts for its televisions, DVD players/recorders, and home theatre systems. By using separate sales accounts for major product lines, company management can monitor sales trends more closely and respond more strategically to changes in sales patterns. For example, if home theatre system sales are increasing while DVD player/recorder sales are decreasing, the company can re-evaluate its advertising and pricing policies on each of these items.

On the income statement shown to outside investors, a merchandiser would normally give only a single sales figure—the sum of all of its individual sales accounts. This is done for two reasons. First, giving details on individual sales accounts would add too much length to the income statement and possibly make it less understandable. Second, companies do not want their competitors to know the details of their operating results.

SALES TAXES

Sales taxes are collected by merchandising companies on the goods that they sell. When a company collects sales taxes on the sale of a good or service, these sales taxes are not recorded as revenue. The sales taxes are collected for the federal and provincial governments, and are owed to these collecting authorities. Sales taxes that are collected on the sale of a good or service are recorded as a liability until they are paid to the governments. As stated earlier, accounting for sales taxes is complicated and is explained in Appendix B at the end of this textbook.

FREIGHT COSTS

As discussed earlier in the chapter, freight terms—FOB destination and FOB shipping point—on the sales invoice indicate when ownership is transferred, and they therefore indicate who is responsible for shipping costs. As explained earlier, if the term is FOB destination, the seller is responsible for getting the goods to their intended destination.

In Highpoint Audio & TV Supply's sale of electronic equipment to Chelsea Electronics, the freight terms (FOB shipping point) indicate that the purchaser, Chelsea Electronics, must pay the cost of shipping the goods from Highpoint Audio & TV Supply's location in Toronto to Chelsea Electronics' location in Hamilton. **Highpoint Audio & TV Supply, the seller, makes no journal entry to record the cost of shipping, since this is Chelsea's cost.**

If the freight terms on the invoice in Illustration 5-4 had been FOB destination, then Highpoint Audio & TV Supply would have paid the delivery charge. Freight costs paid by the seller on merchandise sold are an operating expense to the seller and are debited to a Freight Out account. Costs incurred to earn revenue are recorded as expenses. **The following journal entry shows how Highpoint would have recorded the freight transaction if the terms had been FOB destination:**

Alternative terminology The *Freight Out* account is also called *Delivery Expense* by some companies.

May 4	Freight Out	150	
	Cash		150
	To record payment of freight on goods sold.		

A = L + OE
−150   −150
↓Cash flows: −150

When the seller pays the freight charges, it will usually establish a higher invoice price for the goods to cover the shipping expense.

SALES RETURNS AND ALLOWANCES

We now look at the "flip side" of purchase returns and allowances, which the seller records as **sales returns and allowances**. When customers (purchasers) return goods, or are given price reductions, the seller will either return cash to the buyer, or reduce the buyer's account receivable if the goods were originally purchased on credit.

The seller will need to record the reduction in cash or accounts receivable as well as the reduction in sales. But it is important for management to know about the amount of sales returns and allowances. If there is a large amount of returns and allowances, this suggests that there is inferior merchandise, inefficiencies in filling orders, errors in billing customers, and/or mistakes in the delivery or shipment

Helpful hint Remember that the increases, decreases, and normal balances of contra accounts are the opposite of the accounts they correspond to.

of goods. In order to provide information on sales returns and allowances to management, a **contra revenue account** called Sales Returns and Allowances is used. Recall that a contra account is deducted from its related account in the financial statements. By using a contra account, management can keep track of both the original sales and the amount of sales returns and allowances.

To illustrate, Highpoint Audio & TV Supply will make the following entry to record the goods returned on May 9 by Chelsea Electronics for a credit of $300:

A = L + OE			
−300 −300			

Cash flows: no effect

May 9	Sales Returns and Allowances	300	
	Accounts Receivable		300
	To record credit granted to Chelsea Electronics for returned goods.		

If the merchandise is not damaged and can be sold again, the seller will also need to record a second entry when goods are returned. Assuming this is the case with the goods returned by Chelsea, and assuming that the goods originally cost Highpoint $140, Highpoint Audio & TV Supply will record a second entry as follows:

A = L + OE			
+140 +140			

Cash flows: no effect

May 9	Merchandise Inventory	140	
	Cost of Goods Sold		140
	To record cost of returned goods.		

Notice that these two entries are basically the reverse of the entries recorded when the sale was originally made. Since the customer is reversing the original sale, it should make sense that the journal entries reflect this reversal.

If the goods are damaged or defective and can no longer be sold, the second entry is not prepared. The second entry is also not required when the seller gives the buyer an allowance. If the goods have not been returned, or are defective and cannot be resold, the seller cannot increase its Merchandise Inventory and the original cost of goods sold recorded is still the correct amount. Giving a customer a sales allowance, or letting it return defective goods, does not change the original cost of the goods sold.

ACCOUNTING IN ACTION
BUSINESS INSIGHT

Returned goods can put a dent in a business's profits. When a customer returns a product, the business has to decide whether to scrap, liquidate, refurbish, return to seller, or return to stock. Mississauga-based XS Cargo, one of the largest close-out retailers in Canada, has made a successful venture out of offering companies an opportunity to get some value out of unwanted products by liquidating them. It buys returned, refurbished, and excess merchandise from retailers, wholesalers, and manufacturers and sells it in outlets across Canada at deep discounts. It's essentially a win-win situation for businesses and consumers: consumers get good value on a variety of quality goods, while manufacturers, wholesalers, and retailers have a place to dispose of unwanted merchandise.

Source: "Duncan Reith Named President and CEO of XS Cargo," company news release, January 11, 2012; "Glitches Hurt XS Cargo," *Edmonton Journal*, May 10, 2007; XS Cargo website, www.shopxscargo.com.

What accounting information would help a manager decide what to do with returned goods?

DISCOUNTS

Sales are recorded at invoice price—whether it is the full retail price, a sales price, or a volume discount price. No separate entry is made to record a quantity discount, or to show that the goods were sold at a special sales price.

Another type of discount, as discussed earlier in the chapter, is a cash discount for the early payment of the balance due. A seller may offer this to a customer to provide an incentive to pay early. From the seller's point of view, this is called a **sales discount**.

Basically, a sales discount is a reduction in the selling price that a customer may or may not take advantage of. At the point of sale, it is not known if the customer will use the discount, so the revenue recorded at the point of sale is the full invoice price. If the customer subsequently decides to take advantage of the discount, then the seller must record the fact that revenue has been reduced.

As with sales returns and allowances, management will want to monitor if customers are taking advantage of the sales discounts. Thus, a second contra revenue account, Sales Discounts, is used instead of directly reducing the Sales account. The entry by Highpoint Audio & TV Supply to record the cash receipt from Chelsea Electronics on May 14 (within the discount period) is:

May 14	Cash	3,430	
	Sales Discounts	70	
	Accounts Receivable		3,500
	To record collection of invoice #731 within discount period.		

A = L + OE
+3,430   −70
−3,500

↑ Cash flows: +3,430

If the discount is not taken, and Chelsea Electronics instead pays the full amount on June 3, Highpoint Audio & TV Supply increases Cash and decreases Accounts Receivable by $3,500 at the date of collection, as shown below:

June 3	Cash	3,500	
	Accounts Receivable		3,500
	To record collection of invoice #731 with no discount taken.		

A = L + OE
+3,500
−3,500

↑ Cash flows: +3,500

SUMMARY OF SALES TRANSACTIONS

Highpoint Audio & TV Supply sold merchandise for $3,800, with $300 of it later returned. A sales discount of $70 was given because the invoice was paid within the discount period. In contrast to the purchase transactions shown earlier in the chapter, which affected only one account, Merchandise Inventory, sales transactions are recorded in different accounts. A summary of these transactions is provided in the following T accounts:

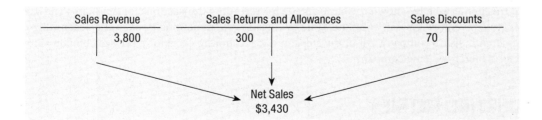

These three accounts are combined to determine net sales. **Net sales** is the balance in the Sales account (a credit) minus the balances in Sales Discounts and in Sales Returns and Allowances (both debits). Total sales, before deducting the contra revenue accounts, is also known as **gross sales**.

BEFORE YOU GO ON...

Do It

Record the following transactions for Junot Company:

Sept. 4 Sold merchandise for $1,500 on account to New Idea Company, terms 2/10, n/30, FOB destination. The original cost of the merchandise to Junot Company was $800.
5 The correct company pays freight charges of $75.
8 New Idea Company returned goods with a selling price of $200 and a cost of $80. The goods are restored to inventory.
14 Received the correct payment from New Idea Company.

Solution

Junot Company (seller)

Sept. 4	Accounts Receivable		1,500	
	Sales			1,500
	To record credit sale.			
4	Cost of Goods Sold		800	
	Merchandise Inventory			800
	To record cost of goods sold.			
5	Freight Out		75	
	Cash			75
	To record freight paid on goods sold.			
8	Sales Returns and Allowances		200	
	Accounts Receivable			200
	To record credit given for receipt of returned goods.			
8	Merchandise Inventory		80	
	Cost of Goods Sold			80
	To record cost of goods returned.			
14	Cash ($1,300 − $26)		1,274	
	Sales Discounts ($1,300 × 2%)		26	
	Accounts Receivable ($1,500 − $200)			1,300
	To record cash receipt within the discount period.			

Action Plan
- Record both the sale and the cost of goods sold at the time of the sale.
- Freight costs are paid by the seller when the freight terms are FOB destination.
- Record sales returns in the contra account Sales Returns and Allowances and reduce Cost of Goods Sold when merchandise is returned to inventory.
- Calculate sales discounts using the net amount owing.
- Record sales discounts in the contra account Sales Discounts.

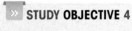

Related exercise material: BE5–7, BE5–8, BE5–9, E5–3, E5–4, and E5–5.

Completing the Accounting Cycle

Up to this point, we have shown the basic entries for recording transactions for purchases and sales in a perpetual inventory system. Now, it is time to consider the remaining steps in the accounting cycle for a merchandising company. All of the steps in the accounting cycle for a service company are also used for a merchandising company.

ADJUSTING ENTRIES

A merchandising company generally has the same types of adjusting entries as a service company. But a merchandiser that uses a perpetual inventory system may need one additional adjustment to make the accounting inventory records the same as the actual inventory on hand. This is necessary if errors in the accounting records have occurred, or if inventory has been stolen or damaged. Even though the Merchandise Inventory account gives a record of the inventory on hand, it only indicates what *should* be there, not necessarily what actually *is* there.

How does a company know if an adjustment is needed? The company will need to do a physical count of inventory on hand. As mentioned earlier in the chapter, a company must do a physical inventory count at least once a year.

If Highpoint Audio & TV Supply's accounting records show an ending inventory balance of $40,500 at the end of May and a physical inventory count indicates only $40,000 on hand, the following adjusting journal entry should be prepared.

May 31	Cost of Goods Sold	500	
	Merchandise Inventory		500
	To record difference between inventory records and physical units on hand.		

A = L + OE
−500   −500

Cash flows: no effect

The procedures involved in doing a physical count, and arriving at the total cost of the items counted, are covered in Chapter 6.

ACCOUNTING IN ACTION
ALL ABOUT YOU INSIGHT

Retailers around the world lost an estimated US$119 billion in 2011 to shrinkage—inventory loss due to theft and other reasons. In Canada, shrinkage amounted to US$3.6 billion, or 1.49% of total sales. Globally, the causes of shrinkage were shoplifters (thought to be responsible for about 43% of inventory loss), employee theft (35%), internal errors including mispricing (16%), and dishonest suppliers/vendors (6%). Retailers are fighting back, spending more than US$28.3 billion on loss prevention measures in 2011. In Canada, for example, women's clothing chain Le Château became the

first retailer to implement technology called Fitting Room Central, which allows staff to scan and keep track of items as they go in and out of the fitting rooms—one of the most popular places for shoplifting to occur. Within eight months, Le Château's largest Montreal store, with 20 change rooms, reduced shrinkage by $30,000. Other loss prevention technology measures used by stores are radio frequency identification tags, magnetic tags, and surveillance cameras. Retailers also use low-tech methods to protect inventory, such as employing security guards; counting the number of items customers bring in and out of fitting rooms; publicizing anti-theft policies to customers, employees, and suppliers; and prosecuting those caught in the act of stealing to send a strong signal that theft will not be tolerated.

Sources: Centre for Retail Research, "Global Retail Theft Barometer 2011," accessed on April 30, 2012, at http://www.retailresearch.org/grtb_currentsurvey.php; PricewaterhouseCoopers Canada, "Q&A: Canadian Retail Security Survey 2008," accessed on April 30, 2012, at http://www.pwc.com/ca/en/retail-consumer/security-survey-2008-q-a.jhtml; Denise Deveau, "Out of Fitting Rooms, into the Profits," *Canadian Retailer*, September/October 2007.

Are there advantages to you as a customer when retailers increase theft prevention measures?

CLOSING ENTRIES

Using assumed data, an adjusted trial balance follows in Illustration 5-7 for Highpoint Audio & TV Supply at May 31, the company's year end. The accounts that are used only by a merchandising company are highlighted in red.

▶ILLUSTRATION **5-7**
Adjusted trial balance

HIGHPOINT AUDIO & TV SUPPLY Adjusted Trial Balance May 31, 2014		
	Debit	**Credit**
Cash	$ 9,500	
Notes receivable	20,000	
Accounts receivable	7,900	
Merchandise inventory	**40,000**	
Equipment	70,000	
Accumulated depreciation—equipment		$ 24,000
Accounts payable		25,800
Notes payable		36,000
R. Lamb, capital		45,000
R. Lamb, drawings	15,000	
Sales		480,000
Sales returns and allowances	**16,700**	
Sales discounts	**4,300**	
Cost of goods sold	**315,000**	
Salaries expense	45,000	
Rent expense	19,000	
Utilities expense	17,000	
Advertising expense	16,000	
Depreciation expense	8,000	
Freight out	**7,000**	
Insurance expense	2,000	
Interest revenue		1,000
Rent revenue		2,400
Interest expense	1,800	
Totals	$614,200	$614,200

A merchandising company, like a service company, closes all accounts that affect profit to Income Summary. In journalizing, the company credits all temporary accounts with debit balances, and debits all temporary accounts with credit balances, as shown below for Highpoint Audio & TV Supply.

Helpful hint A merchandising company has more temporary accounts than a service company. Remember that Sales Returns and Allowances, Sales Discounts, Cost of Goods Sold, and Freight Out are temporary accounts with debit balances and must be closed to Income Summary.

May 31	Sales	480,000	
	Interest Revenue	1,000	
	Rent Revenue	2,400	
	Income Summary		483,400
	To close income statement accounts with credit balances.		
31	Income Summary	451,800	
	Sales Returns and Allowances		**16,700**
	Sales Discounts		**4,300**
	Cost of Goods Sold		**315,000**
	Salaries Expense		45,000
	Rent Expense		19,000
	Utilities Expense		17,000
	Advertising Expense		16,000
	Depreciation Expense		8,000
	Freight Out		**7,000**
	Insurance Expense		2,000
	Interest Expense		1,800
	To close income statement accounts with debit balances.		
31	Income Summary	31,600	
	R. Lamb, Capital		31,600
	To close income summary to capital.		
	R. Lamb, Capital	15,000	
	R. Lamb, Drawings		15,000
	To close drawings to capital.		

POST-CLOSING TRIAL BALANCE

After the closing entries are posted, all temporary accounts have zero balances. The R. Lamb, Capital account will have the same balance as is reported on the statement of owner's equity and balance sheet, and will be carried over to the next period. As with a service company, the final step in the accounting cycle is to prepare a post-closing trial balance. You will recall that the purpose of this trial balance is to ensure that debits equal credits in the permanent (balance sheet) accounts after all temporary accounts have been closed.

The only new account in the post-closing trial balance of a merchandising company is the current asset account Merchandise Inventory. The post-closing trial balance is prepared in the same way as described in Chapter 4 and is not shown again here.

SUMMARY OF MERCHANDISING ENTRIES

Illustration 5-8 summarizes the entries for the merchandising accounts using a perpetual inventory system.

	Transactions	Daily Recurring Entries	Debit	Credit
Purchases	Purchasing merchandise for resale.	Merchandise Inventory Cash or Accounts Payable	XX	 XX
	Paying freight costs on merchandise purchases, FOB shipping point.	Merchandise Inventory Cash	XX	 XX
	Receiving purchase returns or allowances from suppliers.	Cash or Accounts Payable Merchandise Inventory	XX	 XX

	Paying creditors on account within discount period.	Accounts Payable
		    Merchandise Inventory
		    Cash
			XX	
				XX
				XX

	Paying creditors on account after the discount period.	Accounts Payable Cash	XX	 XX

Sales	Selling merchandise to customers.	Cash or Accounts Receivable
		    Sales
		Cost of Goods Sold
		    Merchandise Inventory
			XX
			
			XX
				
				XX
				
				XX

	Giving sales returns or allowances to customers.	Sales Returns and Allowances
		    Cash or Accounts Receivable
		Merchandise Inventory
		    Cost of Goods Sold
			XX
			
			XX
				
				XX
				
				XX

	Paying freight costs on sales, FOB destination	Freight Out Cash	XX	 XX
	Receiving payment on account from customers within discount period.	Cash Sales Discounts Accounts Receivable	XX XX	 XX
	Receiving payment on account from customers after discount period.	Cash Accounts Receivable	XX	 XX

▶ **ILLUSTRATION 5-8**
Daily recurring, adjusting, and closing entries

▶**ILLUSTRATION 5-8**
(*continued*)

Events		Adjusting and Closing Entries	Debit	Credit
Adjusting Entries	Determining, after a physical count, that inventory in general ledger is higher than inventory actually on hand.	Cost of Goods Sold Merchandise Inventory	XX	XX
Closing Entries	Closing temporary accounts with credit balances.	Sales Other Revenues Income Summary	XX XX	XX
	Closing temporary accounts with debit balances.	Income Summary Sales Returns and Allowances Sales Discounts Cost of Goods Sold Freight Out Other expenses	XX	XX XX XX XX XX

Action Plan

- Debit each temporary account with a credit balance and credit the total to the Income Summary account.
- Credit each temporary account with a debit balance and debit the total to the Income Summary account.
- Stop and check your work: Does the balance in the Income Summary account equal the reported profit?
- Debit the balance in the Income Summary account and credit the amount to the owner's capital account. (Do the opposite if the company had a loss.)
- Credit the balance in the drawings account and debit the amount to the owner's capital account. Do not close drawings with expenses.
- Stop and check your work: Does the balance in the owner's capital account equal the ending balance reported in the statement of owner's equity?

BEFORE YOU GO ON...

Do It

The trial balance of Yee Clothing Company at December 31 shows Merchandise Inventory $25,000; J. Yee, Capital $12,000; Sales $162,400; Sales Returns and Allowances $4,800; Sales Discounts $950; Cost of Goods Sold $110,000; Rental Revenue $6,000; Freight Out $1,800; Rent Expense $8,800; Salaries Expense $22,000; and J. Yee, Drawings $3,600. Yee Clothing Company's statement of owner's equity for the year showed profit of $20,050 and closing owner's capital of $28,450. (a) Prepare the closing entries for the above accounts. (b) Create T accounts for Income Summary and J. Yee, Capital, and post the closing entries to these accounts.

Solution

Dec. 31	Sales	162,400	
	Rental Revenue	6,000	
	Income Summary		168,400
	To close income statement accounts with		
	credit balances.		
31	Income Summary	148,350	
	Sales Returns and Allowances		4,800
	Sales Discounts		950
	Cost of Goods Sold		110,000
	Freight Out		1,800
	Rent Expense		8,800
	Salaries Expense		22,000
	To close income statement accounts with		
	debit balances.		
31	Income Summary	20,050	
	J. Yee, Capital		20,050
	To close Income Summary account.		
31	J. Yee, Capital	3,600	
	J. Yee, Drawings		3,600
	To close drawings account.		

Income Summary			
Clos.	148,350	Clos.	168,400
		Bal.	20,050*
Clos.	20,050		
		Bal.	0

*Check = Profit

J. Yee, Capital			
		Bal.	12,000
Clos.	3,600	Clos.	20,050
		Bal.	28,450**

**Check = Closing owner's capital

THE NAVIGATOR

Related exercise material: BE5–10, BE5–11, E5–6, and E5–7.

Merchandising Financial Statements

Merchandisers widely use the classified balance sheet introduced in Chapter 4 and one of two forms of income statements. This section explains the use of these financial statements by merchandisers.

SINGLE-STEP INCOME STATEMENT

» STUDY **OBJECTIVE 5**

Prepare single-step and multiple-step income statements.

The income statement form used in previous chapters of this textbook is the **single-step income statement**. The statement is so named because only one step—subtracting total expenses from total revenues—is required in determining profit.

In a single-step income statement, all data are classified under two categories: (1) revenues and (2) expenses. A single-step income statement for Highpoint Audio & TV Supply, using the data from the adjusted trial balance in Illustration 5-7, is shown in Illustration 5-9.

▸ **ILLUSTRATION** **5-9**
Single-step income statement

HIGHPOINT AUDIO & TV SUPPLY Income Statement Year Ended May 31, 2014		
Revenues		
Net sales		$459,000
Interest revenue		1,000
Rent revenue		2,400
Total revenues		462,400
Expenses		
Cost of goods sold	$315,000	
Salaries expense	45,000	
Rent expense	19,000	
Utilities expense	17,000	
Advertising expense	16,000	
Depreciation expense	8,000	
Freight out	7,000	
Insurance expense	2,000	
Interest expense	1,800	
Total expenses		430,800
Profit		$ 31,600

Note that net sales was calculated by deducting sales returns and allowances and sales discounts from sales ($459,000 = $480,000 − $16,700 − $4,300). Revenue from investments, such as interest revenue, must be shown separately from other revenue. Cost of goods sold and interest expense (also income tax expense for corporations) must be reported separately on the income statement. Expenses that are not significant in themselves can be included separately in the income statement as shown above, or grouped with other similar items, with additional details in the notes to the financial statements.

Under ASPE, companies do not have to list their expenses in any particular order. Under IFRS, companies must classify operating and other expenses based on either the **nature** of the expenses or their **function** within the company. Classifying expenses by nature means that expenses are reported based on what the resources were spent on (e.g., depreciation, employee costs, transportation, and advertising). Classifying expenses by function means that expenses are reported based on which business function the resources were spent on (e.g., costs of sales, administration, and selling).

Companies select the method, either nature or function, that provides the most relevant information. It should also be noted that if a company chooses to classify expenses according to function on the income statement, it has to report additional information about the nature of the expenses in the notes to the financial statements.

There are two main reasons for using the single-step format: (1) a company does not realize any profit until total revenues exceed total expenses, so it makes sense to divide the statement into these two categories; and (2) the single-step format is simple and easy to read.

MULTIPLE-STEP INCOME STATEMENT

The **multiple-step income statement** is so named because it shows several steps in determining profit (or loss). This form is often considered more useful than a single-step income statement because the steps give additional information about a company's profitability and distinguish between the company's operating and non-operating activities. The multiple-step income statement shows several steps, as explained below.

Net Sales

The multiple-step income statement for a merchandising company begins by presenting sales revenue. The contra revenue accounts Sales Returns and Allowances and Sales Discounts are deducted from Sales to arrive at **net sales**. The sales revenue section for Highpoint Audio & TV Supply (using data from the adjusted trial balance in Illustration 5-7) is as follows:

Sales revenue		
Sales		$480,000
Less: Sales returns and allowances	$16,700	
Sales discounts	4,300	21,000
Net sales		**459,000**

Many companies condense this information and report only the net sales figure in their income statement. This alternative was shown in the single-step income statement in Illustration 5-9.

Gross Profit

The next step is the calculation of gross profit. In Illustration 5-1, you learned that cost of goods sold is deducted from sales revenue to determine **gross profit**. For this calculation, companies use net sales as the amount of sales revenue. Based on the sales data above and the cost of goods sold in the adjusted trial balance in Illustration 5-7, the gross profit for Highpoint Audio & TV Supply is $144,000, calculated as follows:

Net sales	$459,000
Cost of goods sold	315,000
Gross profit	**144,000**

Operating Expenses

Operating expenses are the next component in measuring profit for a merchandising company. They are the recurring expenses associated with the central operations of the company—other than cost of goods sold—that are incurred in the process of earning sales revenue. These expenses are similar in service and merchandising companies.

Highpoint Audio & TV Supply would classify the following items in its adjusted trial balance (as shown in Illustration 5-7) as operating expenses: Salaries Expense, $45,000; Rent Expense, $19,000; Utilities Expense, $17,000; Advertising Expense, $16,000; Depreciation Expense, $8,000; Freight Out, $7,000; and Insurance Expense, $2,000. This results in total operating expenses of $114,000.

Recall our discussion in the single-step income statement section about classifying expenses by nature or function. Subdividing the operating expenses into selling expenses and administrative expenses is an example of classifying expenses by function. Selling expenses are associated with making sales. They include expenses for sales promotion, as well as the expenses of completing the sale (e.g., freight costs). Administrative expenses relate to general operating activities such as management, accounting, and legal costs. This classification method can be used in both multiple and single-step income statements.

Profit from Operations

Profit from operations, or the results of the company's normal operating activities, is determined by subtracting operating expenses from gross profit. Based on the gross profit and operating expenses data determined above, Highpoint Audio & TV Supply's profit from operations is $30,000, calculated as follows:

Gross profit	$144,000
Operating expenses	114,000
Profit from operations	**30,000**

The purpose of showing profit from operations as a separate number from overall profit is to assist users of financial statements in understanding the company's main operations. The additional information helps users in making projections of future financial performance.

Non-Operating Activities

Non-operating activities are other revenues and expenses not related to the company's main operations. Examples of other revenues include interest revenue, rental revenue (if earned from renting assets not needed for operations), and investment income. Examples of other expenses include interest expense.

Distinguishing between operating and non-operating activities is important to external users of financial statements. Non-operating activities are often short-term activities and are not expected to continue into the future as the company's main operating activities are. Separating the two in the income statement increases the predictive value of the statement.

Based on the data in Highpoint Audio & TV Supply's adjusted trial balance shown in Illustration 5-7, the company will show its non-operating activities as follows in its multiple-step income statement:

Other revenues	
Interest revenue	$1,000
Rent revenue	2,400
Total non-operating revenues	3,400
Other expenses	
Interest expense	1,800
Net non-operating revenues	**1,600**

It is also common for companies to combine the two non-operating sections—other revenues and other expenses—into a single "Other Revenues and Expenses" section.

Profit

Profit is the final outcome of all the company's operating and non-operating activities. Highpoint's profit is $31,600 after adding its net non-operating revenues of $1,600 to profit from operations as follows:

Profit from operations	$30,000
Net non-operating revenues	1,600
Profit	**$31,600**

If there are no non-operating activities, the company's profit from operations becomes its profit—or "bottom line."

Corporations, unlike proprietorships and partnerships, also have income tax expense. You will learn about how income tax expense is calculated and shown in an income statement in Chapter 13.

In Illustration 5-10, we bring together all of these steps in a comprehensive multiple-step income statement for Highpoint Audio & TV Supply.

Note that the profit amounts in Illustrations 5-9 (single-step) and 5-10 (multiple-step) are the same. The only differences between the two forms of income statements are the amount of detail shown and the order of presentation.

HIGHPOINT AUDIO & TV SUPPLY Income Statement Year Ended May 31, 2014			
Calculation of net sales and gross profit	Sales revenue		
	Sales		$480,000
	Less: Sales returns and allowances	$16,700	
	Sales discounts	4,300	21,000
	Net sales		459,000
	Cost of goods sold		315,000
	Gross profit		144,000
Calculation of operating expenses and profit from operations	Operating expenses		
	Salaries expense	$45,000	
	Rent expense	19,000	
	Utilities expense	17,000	
	Advertising expense	16,000	
	Depreciation expense	8,000	
	Freight out	7,000	
	Insurance expense	2,000	
	Total operating expenses		114,000
	Profit from operations		30,000
Calculation of non-operating activities and profit	Other revenues		
	Interest revenue	$ 1,000	
	Rent revenue	2,400	
	Total non-operating revenues	3,400	
	Other expenses		
	Interest expense	1,800	
	Net non-operating revenues		1,600
	Profit		$ 31,600

CLASSIFIED BALANCE SHEET

Recall from Chapter 4 that merchandise inventory is a current asset because we expect to sell it within one year of the balance sheet date. Also recall from Chapter 4 that items are typically listed under current assets in their order of liquidity. Merchandise inventory is less liquid than accounts receivable and short-term notes receivable because the goods must first be sold before revenue can be collected from the customer. Thus, in the balance sheet, merchandise inventory is reported as a current asset immediately below accounts receivable. Illustration 5-11 presents the assets section of a classified balance sheet for Highpoint Audio & TV Supply.

▶ ILLUSTRATION 5-11
Assets section of a
merchandising company's
classified balance sheet

Helpful hint The $40,000 is the cost of the inventory on hand, not its expected selling price.

HIGHPOINT AUDIO & TV SUPPLY Balance Sheet (partial) May 31, 2014		
Assets		
Current assets		
Cash		$ 9,500
Notes receivable		20,000
Accounts receivable		7,900
Merchandise inventory		**40,000**
Total current assets		77,400
Property, plant, and equipment		
Equipment	$70,000	
Less: Accumulated depreciation	24,000	46,000
Total assets		$123,400

The remaining two financial statements, the statement of owner's equity and cash flow statement (to be discussed in Chapter 17), are the same as those of a service company. They are not shown in this chapter.

BEFORE YOU GO ON...

Do It

Silver Store reported the following information: Sales $620,000; Sales Returns and Allowances $32,000; Sales Discounts $10,200; Cost of Goods Sold $422,000; Depreciation Expense $10,000; Freight Out $5,000; Interest Expense $1,700; Rent Expense $15,000; and Salaries Expense $80,000. Calculate the following amounts: (a) net sales, (b) gross profit, (c) total operating expenses, (d) profit from operations, and (e) profit.

Solution

(a) Net sales: $620,000 − $32,000 − $10,200 = $577,800
(b) Gross profit: $577,800 − $422,000 = $155,800
(c) Total operating expenses: $10,000 + $5,000 + $15,000 + $80,000 = $110,000
(d) Profit from operations: $155,800 − $110,000 = $45,800
(e) Profit: $45,800 − $1,700 = $44,100

Related exercise material: BE5–12, BE5–13, E5–8, and E5–9.

THE NAVIGATOR

Action Plan
- Deduct Sales Returns and Allowances and Sales Discounts from Sales to arrive at net sales.
- Deduct Cost of Goods Sold from net sales to arrive at gross profit.
- Identify which expenses are operating expenses and which are non-operating expenses.
- Deduct operating expenses from gross profit to arrive at profit from operations.
- Deduct any non-operating expenses from (and add any non-operating revenues to) profit from operations to arrive at profit.

Using the Information in the Financial Statements

In Chapter 4, we introduced a tool called ratio analysis that investors and creditors use to determine additional information about how a company is performing. In this chapter, we introduce two profitability ratios: gross profit margin and profit margin. **Profitability ratios** measure a company's operating success for a specific period of time.

 STUDY OBJECTIVE 6

Calculate the gross profit margin and profit margin.

GROSS PROFIT MARGIN

A company's gross profit may be expressed as a percentage, called the **gross profit margin**. This is calculated by dividing the amount of gross profit by net sales. Illustration 5-12 shows the gross profit margin for Reitmans for the year ended January 28, 2012 (dollars in thousands).

Gross Profit	÷	Net Sales	=	Gross Profit Margin
$656,064	÷	$1,019,397	=	64.4%

▶ **ILLUSTRATION 5-12**
Gross profit margin

The gross profit *margin* is generally considered to be more useful than the gross profit *amount* because the margin shows the relative relationship between net sales and gross profit. For example, a gross profit amount of $1 million may sound impressive. But, if it is the result of net sales of $50 million, then the gross profit margin is only 2%, which is not so impressive.

The amount and trend of gross profit are closely watched by management and other interested parties. They compare current gross profit margin with past periods' gross profit margin. They also compare the company's gross profit margin with the margin of competitors and with industry averages.

Such comparisons give information about the effectiveness of a company's purchasing and the soundness of its pricing policies. In general, a higher gross profit margin is seen as being more favourable than a lower gross profit margin.

Gross profit is important because inventory has a significant effect on a company's profitability. Cost of goods sold is usually the largest expense on the income statement. Gross profit represents a company's merchandising profit. It is not a measure of the overall profitability, because operating expenses have not been deducted.

PROFIT MARGIN

Overall profitability is measured by examining profit. Profit is often expressed as a percentage of sales, similar to the gross profit margin. The **profit margin** measures the percentage of each dollar of sales that results in profit. It is calculated by dividing profit by net sales. Illustration 5-13 shows the profit margin for Reitmans for the year ended January 28, 2012 (dollars in thousands).

▶ **ILLUSTRATION 5-13**
Profit margin

Profit	÷	Net Sales	=	Profit Margin
$47,539	÷	$1,019,397	=	4.7%

How do the gross profit margin and profit margin differ? The gross profit margin measures how much more the selling price is than the cost of goods sold. The profit margin measures by how much the selling price covers all expenses (including the cost of goods sold). A company can improve its profit margin by increasing its gross profit margin, or by controlling its operating expenses (and non-operating activities), or by doing both.

⟳ BEFORE YOU GO ON...

Do It

Selected financial information is available for two recent fiscal years for Antonia Co.

	2014	2013
Net sales	$550,000	$600,000
Cost of goods sold	300,000	350,000
Profit	50,000	25,000

(a) Calculate (1) gross profit, (2) gross profit margin, and (3) profit margin for 2013 and 2014.
(b) Comment on any changes in profitability.

Solution

(a)

	2014	2013
(1) Gross profit	= $550,000 − $300,000 = $250,000	= $600,000 − $350,000 = $250,000
(2) Gross profit margin	= $250,000 ÷ $550,000 = 45.5%	= $250,000 ÷ $600,000 = 41.7%
(3) Profit margin	= $50,000 ÷ $550,000 = 9.1%	= $25,000 ÷ $600,000 = 4.2%

(b) The gross profit margin and profit margin have both increased in 2014 from 2013. In general, higher ratios indicate that the company's profitability has improved during 2014.

Related exercise material: BE5–14, E5–1, E5–10, and E5–11.

Action Plan
- Gross profit is net sales minus cost of goods sold.
- Divide gross profit by net sales to calculate gross profit margin.
- Divide profit by net sales to calculate profit margin.
- Recall whether higher or lower ratios indicate improvement or deterioration in profitability.

THE **NAVIGATOR**

PERIODIC INVENTORY SYSTEM | APPENDIX 5A

As described in this chapter, there are two basic systems of accounting for inventories: (1) the perpetual inventory system, and (2) the periodic inventory system. In the chapter, we focused on the characteristics of the perpetual inventory system. In this appendix, we discuss and illustrate the periodic inventory system.

One key difference between the two inventory systems is the timing for calculating the cost of goods sold. In a periodic inventory system, the cost of the merchandise sold is not recorded on the date of sale. Instead, the cost of goods sold during the period is calculated by taking a physical inventory count at the end of the period and deducting the cost of this inventory from the cost of the merchandise available for sale during the period, as shown in Illustration 5A-1.

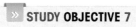
» STUDY **OBJECTIVE 7**

Prepare the entries for purchases and sales under a periodic inventory system and calculate cost of goods sold.

▶ ILLUSTRATION 5A-1
Basic formula for cost of goods sold

There are other differences between the perpetual and periodic inventory systems. Under a periodic inventory system, purchases of merchandise are recorded in the Purchases expense account, rather than the Merchandise Inventory asset account. Also, under a periodic system, it is customary to record in separate accounts purchase returns and allowances, purchase discounts, and freight in. That way, accumulated amounts are known for each.

To illustrate the recording of merchandise transactions under a periodic inventory system, we will use the purchase/sale transactions between Highpoint Audio & TV Supply (the seller) and Chelsea Electronics (the buyer) from earlier in this chapter.

RECORDING PURCHASES OF MERCHANDISE

Based on the sales invoice (Illustration 5-4) and receipt of the merchandise ordered from Highpoint Audio & TV Supply, Chelsea Electronics records the $3,800 purchase as follows:

May 4	Purchases	3,800	
	Accounts Payable		3,800
	To record goods purchased on account per invoice #731, terms 2/10, n/30.		

A = L + OE
+3,800 −3,800
Cash flows: no effect

Purchases is a temporary account whose normal balance is a debit.

Freight Costs

When the buyer pays for the freight costs, the account Freight In is debited. For example, Chelsea pays Public Carrier Co. $150 for freight charges on its purchase from Highpoint Audio & TV Supply. The entry on Chelsea's books is as follows:

May 4	Freight In	150	
	Cash		150
	To record payment of freight on goods purchased.		

A = L + OE
−150 −150
↓ Cash flows: −150

Like Purchases, Freight In is a temporary account whose normal balance is a debit. Just as freight was a part of the cost of the merchandise inventory in a perpetual inventory system, freight in is part of the cost of goods purchased in a periodic inventory system. The cost of goods purchased should include any freight charges for transporting the goods to the buyer.

Purchase Returns and Allowances

Chelsea Electronics returns $300 worth of goods and prepares the following entry to recognize the return:

A = L + OE			
−300 +300			

Cash flows: no effect

May 9	Accounts Payable	300	
	Purchase Returns and Allowances		300
	To record return of goods to Highpoint Audio & TV Supply.		

Purchase Returns and Allowances is a temporary account whose normal balance is a credit. It is a contra account subtracted from the Purchases account.

Purchase Discounts

Recall that the invoice terms were 2/10, n/30. On May 14, Chelsea Electronics pays the balance owing to Highpoint Audio & TV Supply of $3,500 ($3,800 less return of $300) less the 2% discount for payment within 10 days. Chelsea Electronics records the following entry:

A = L + OE			
−3,430 −3,500 +70			

↓ Cash flows: −3,430

May 14	Accounts Payable ($3,800 − $300)	3,500	
	Purchase Discounts ($3,500 × 2%)		70
	Cash ($3,500 − $70)		3,430
	To record payment of invoice #731 within discount period.		

Purchase Discounts is a temporary account whose normal balance is a credit. It is a contra account subtracted from the Purchases account.

In each of the above transactions, a temporary expense account was used to record the transactions related to purchases of merchandise rather than the Merchandise Inventory account that is used in a perpetual inventory system. A comparison of purchase transactions under the two inventory systems is shown later in the appendix.

RECORDING SALES OF MERCHANDISE

The seller, Highpoint Audio & TV Supply, records the sale of $3,800 of merchandise to Chelsea Electronics on May 4 (sales invoice in Illustration 5-4) as follows:

A = L + OE			
+3,800 +3,800			

Cash flows: no effect

May 4	Accounts Receivable	3,800	
	Sales		3,800
	To record credit sale to Chelsea Electronics per invoice #731.		

As previously explained, in a periodic inventory system, there is no entry to record the cost of goods sold and reduction of inventory at the point of sale.

Freight Costs

There is no difference between the accounting for freight costs by the seller in a perpetual and a periodic inventory system. In both systems, freight costs paid by the seller are debited to Freight Out, an operating expense account. Recall that in this example the freight terms were FOB shipping point, so Highpoint did not incur freight costs.

Sales Returns and Allowances

The $300 return of goods on May 9 is recorded by Highpoint Audio & TV Supply as follows:

A = L + OE			
−300 −300			

Cash flows: no effect

May 9	Sales Returns and Allowances	300	
	Accounts Receivable		300
	To record credit given to Chelsea Electronics for returned goods.		

Just as there is only one entry needed when sales are recorded in a periodic inventory system, one entry is also all that is needed to record a return. Different from the perpetual system, it doesn't matter if the inventory is damaged and discarded, or returned to inventory; no entry is needed in the periodic inventory system.

Sales Discounts

On May 14, Highpoint Audio & TV Supply receives a payment of $3,430 on account from Chelsea Electronics. Highpoint records this payment as follows:

May 14	Cash ($3,500 − $70)	3,430	
	Sales Discounts ($3,500 × 2%)	70	
	Accounts Receivable ($3,800 − $300)		3,500
	To record collection of invoice #731 within discount period.		

A	=	L	+	OE
+3,430				−70
−3,500				

↑ Cash flows: +3,430

COMPARISON OF ENTRIES—PERPETUAL VS. PERIODIC

Illustration 5A-2 summarizes the periodic inventory entries shown in this appendix and compares them with the perpetual inventory entries shown earlier in the chapter. Entries that are different in the two systems are shown in colour.

▶ **ILLUSTRATION 5A-2**
Comparison of journal entries under perpetual and periodic inventory systems

ENTRIES ON CHELSEA ELECTRONICS' BOOKS (BUYER)

	Transaction	Perpetual Inventory System			Periodic Inventory System		
May 4	Purchase of merchandise on credit.	Merchandise Inventory	3,800		Purchases	3,800	
		Accounts Payable		3,800	Accounts Payable		3,800
4	Freight cost on purchases.	Merchandise Inventory	150		Freight In	150	
		Cash		150	Cash		150
9	Purchase returns and allowances.	Accounts Payable	300		Accounts Payable	300	
		Merchandise Inventory		300	Purchase Returns and Allowances		300
14	Payment on account with a discount.	Accounts Payable	3,500		Accounts Payable	3,500	
		Merchandise Inventory		70	Purchase Discounts		70
		Cash		3,430	Cash		3,430

ENTRIES ON HIGHPOINT AUDIO & TV SUPPLY'S BOOKS (SELLER)

	Transaction	Perpetual Inventory System			Periodic Inventory System		
May 4	Sale of merchandise on credit.	Accounts Receivable	3,800		Accounts Receivable	3,800	
		Sales		3,800	Sales		3,800
		Cost of Goods Sold	2,400		No entry for cost of goods sold		
		Merchandise Inventory		2,400			
9	Return of merchandise sold.	Sales Returns and Allowances	300		Sales Returns and Allowances	300	
		Accounts Receivable		300	Accounts Receivable		300
		Merchandise Inventory	140		No entry for cost of goods sold		
		Cost of Goods Sold		140			
14	Cash received on account with a discount.	Cash	3,430		Cash	3,430	
		Sales Discounts	70		Sales Discounts	70	
		Accounts Receivable		3,500	Accounts Receivable		3,500

CALCULATING COST OF GOODS SOLD

In a periodic inventory system, the Merchandise Inventory account is not continuously updated for each purchase and sale. As we saw in the entries above, temporary accounts are used instead to accumulate the cost of the goods purchased throughout the period, and no entries are made to accumulate the cost of goods sold. Thus, the dollar amount of merchandise on hand at the end of the period and the cost of goods sold for the period are not known by looking at the general ledger accounts.

Instead, these amounts will have to be determined at the end of the accounting period in a periodic inventory system. Recall from Illustration 5A-1 that the basic equation to calculate cost of goods sold is: Beginning Inventory + Cost of Goods Purchased = Cost of Goods Available for Sale − Ending Inventory = Cost of Goods Sold.

To illustrate the calculation of cost of goods sold, we will use assumed data for Highpoint Audio & TV Supply so we can compare the results with its cost of goods sold under the perpetual inventory system shown in the chapter. Assume that Highpoint Audio & TV Supply's general ledger, under the periodic inventory system, shows the following balances at its year end on May 31, 2014:

- Merchandise Inventory $ 35,000
- Purchases   325,000
- Purchase Returns and Allowances   10,400
- Purchase Discounts   6,800
- Freight In   12,200

Beginning Inventory

If Highpoint Audio & TV Supply uses the periodic inventory system, it will not record any transactions in the Merchandise Inventory account during the period, and the balance in this account will not have changed since the beginning of the year. Thus **the $35,000 balance in the general ledger—as shown above—is equal to beginning inventory.**

Cost of Goods Purchased

In a periodic inventory system, four accounts—Purchases, Purchase Returns and Allowances, Purchase Discounts, and Freight In—are used to record the purchase of inventory. These four accounts are combined to calculate the cost of goods purchased.

First, **net purchases** is calculated by subtracting purchase returns and allowances and purchase discounts (both credit balances) from purchases (a debit balance). This calculation for Highpoint for the year ended May 31, 2014, is $307,800 as shown in Illustration 5A-3.

▶ **ILLUSTRATION 5A-3**
Formula for net purchases

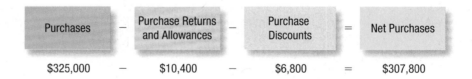

Then the **cost of goods purchased** is calculated by adding the balance in the Freight In account to net purchases. Highpoint's cost of goods purchased for the year ended May 31, 2104, is $320,000, as shown in Illustration 5A-4.

▶ **ILLUSTRATION 5A-4**
Formula for cost of goods purchased

Cost of Goods Available for Sale

As shown in Illustration 5A-1, the **cost of goods available for sale** is equal to the cost of the goods on hand at the beginning of the period (beginning inventory) plus the cost of goods purchased during the period. This is the total amount that the company could have sold during the period. Highpoint's cost of goods available for sale for the year ended May 31, 2014, is $355,000 ($35,000 + $320,000).

Ending Inventory

To determine the cost of the inventory on hand on May 31, 2014, Highpoint Audio & TV Supply must take a physical inventory. You will recall from earlier in this chapter that Highpoint determined that its cost of goods on hand on May 31, 2014 (ending inventory) is $40,000. The inventory on hand is the same regardless of the inventory system used. But with a periodic inventory system, Highpoint will have no way of knowing if there are inventory shortages or not.

You will learn later in this appendix that the balance in the Merchandise Inventory account is adjusted from the beginning balance of $35,000 to the ending balance of $40,000 as part of the closing process.

Cost of Goods Sold

As shown in Illustration 5A-1, once the ending inventory is determined, the cost of goods sold is calculated by subtracting the ending inventory from the cost of goods available for sale. Highpoint's cost of goods sold is $315,000 ($355,000 − $40,000).

MULTIPLE-STEP INCOME STATEMENT—PERIODIC

The only reporting difference in a multiple-step income statement is that the cost of goods sold section has more detail in a periodic inventory system—as shown in Illustration 5A-5—than in a perpetual inventory system, where only one line is reported for the cost of goods sold. Note that cost of goods sold, gross profit, and profit are the same amounts as shown in Illustration 5-10 in the chapter.

ILLUSTRATION 5A-5
Multiple-step income statement—periodic inventory system

HIGHPOINT AUDIO & TV SUPPLY
Income Statement
Year Ended May 31, 2014

Sales revenue				
Sales				$480,000
Less: Sales returns and allowances			$ 16,700	
Sales discounts			4,300	21,000
Net sales				459,000
Cost of goods sold				
Inventory, June 1, 2013			$ 35,000	
Purchases		$325,000		
Less: Purchase returns and allowances	$10,400			
Purchase discounts	6,800	17,200		
Net purchases		307,800		
Add: Freight in		12,200		
Cost of goods purchased		320,000		
Cost of goods available for sale		355,000		
Inventory, May 31, 2014		40,000		
Cost of goods sold				315,000
Gross profit				144,000
Operating expenses				
Salaries expense			$ 45,000	
Rent expense			19,000	
Utilities expense			17,000	
Advertising expense			16,000	
Depreciation expense			8,000	
Freight out			7,000	
Insurance expense			2,000	
Total operating expenses				114,000
Profit from operations				30,000
Other revenues				
Interest revenue			$ 1,000	
Rent revenue			2,400	
Total non-operating revenues			3,400	
Other expenses				
Interest expense			1,800	
Net non-operating revenues				1,600
Profit				$ 31,600

Using the periodic inventory system does not affect the content of the balance sheet. As in the perpetual system, merchandise inventory is reported in the current assets section, and at the same amount.

COMPLETING THE ACCOUNTING CYCLE

After preparing the financial statements, closing entries and a post-closing trial balance complete the accounting cycle. For a merchandising company, as for a service company, all accounts that affect the determination of profit are closed to the owner's capital account.

It is also necessary to update the balance of the Merchandise Inventory account as part of the closing process in a periodic inventory system. During the year, no entries are made to this account when inventory is purchased or sold. Therefore, the merchandise inventory balance in the adjusted trial balance is its beginning balance, not its ending balance.

Two closing journal entries are used to update the Merchandise Inventory account from the beginning balance of $35,000 to the ending balance of $40,000. These two entries for Highpoint Audio & TV Supply are as follows:

A = L + OE
−35,000 −35,000
Cash flows: no effect
	May 31	Income Summary
		    Merchandise Inventory
		        To close beginning inventory.
			35,000
			
			     35,000

A = L + OE
+40,000 +40,000
Cash flows: no effect
	31	Merchandise Inventory
		    Income Summary
		        To record ending inventory.
			40,000
			
			     40,000

The income summary account is used because beginning and ending inventory are used in the cost of goods sold calculation, which is then used to determine profit or loss for the period. After the closing entries are posted, the Merchandise Inventory account will show the following:

Merchandise Inventory					
June 1, 2013	Bal.	35,000	May 31, 2014	Clos.	35,000
May 31, 2014	Clos.	40,000			
May 31, 2014	Bal.	40,000			

The effect of the two closing journal entries on the Merchandise Inventory account is similar to the effect that the closing process has on the owner's capital account. The ending inventory and capital balances must be updated to agree with the balance sheet at the end of the period. The balance sheet reports these ending balances, not the amounts in the adjusted trial balance. The ending balance in Merchandise Inventory now becomes the beginning inventory amount for the next period.

The remaining closing entries are the same as those as we saw in prior chapters and are not shown here. The only difference between a merchandising company using the periodic inventory system and a service company is that there are several additional temporary accounts that must be closed.

Temporary accounts with credit balances include the Sales, Purchase Returns and Allowances, and Purchase Discounts accounts. These will need to be debited for their individual account balances and the total is credited to the Income Summary account. Temporary accounts with debit balances include the Sales Returns and Allowances, Sales Discounts, Purchases, and Freight In accounts. These will need to be credited for their individual account balances and the total is debited to the Income Summary account.

After the closing entries are posted, a post-closing trial balance is prepared. The post-closing trial balance is prepared in the same way as described in earlier chapters and is not explained again here.

BEFORE YOU GO ON...

Do It

The following transactions occurred in August:

Aug. 1 White Company buys merchandise on account from Red Company for $1,000, terms 2/10, n/30, FOB destination.
   1 The correct company pays freight charges of $70.
   3 White Company returns $150 of the merchandise to Red Company. Red returns the goods to its inventory.
   10 White Company pays the total amount owing.

Both companies use a periodic inventory system.

(a) Record White Company's transactions.
(b) Record Red Company's transactions.

Solution

(a) White Company (buyer)

Aug. 1	Purchases	1,000	
	Accounts Payable		1,000
	Goods purchased on account.		
1	No entry; seller pays for freight		
3	Accounts Payable	150	
	Purchase Returns and Allowances		150
	Returned goods.		
10	Accounts Payable ($1,000 − $150)	850	
	Purchase Discounts ($850 × 2%)		17
	Cash ($850 − $17)		833
	Cash payment within discount period.		

(b) Red Company (seller)

Aug. 1	Accounts Receivable	1,000	
	Sales		1,000
	Credit sale of merchandise.		
1	Freight Out	70	
	Cash		70
	Payment of freight costs.		
3	Sales Returns and Allowances	150	
	Accounts Receivable		150
	Customer returned goods.		
10	Cash ($850 − $17)	833	
	Sales Discounts ($850 × 2%)	17	
	Accounts Receivable		850
	Cash receipt within discount period.		

Related exercise material: *BE5–15, *BE5–16, *BE5–17, *E5–12, *E5–13, *E5–14, *E5–15, and *E5–16

Action Plan
- In a periodic system, purchases of inventory are recorded in the Purchases account.
- Examine freight terms to determine which company pays the freight charges.
- Calculate purchase discounts using the net amount owing and record in a Purchase Discounts account.
- In a periodic system, the cost of goods sold is not recorded at the time of the sale.
- In a periodic system, inventory is not adjusted for returned merchandise.
- Calculate purchase/ sales discounts using the net amount owing and record in a Purchase/Sales Discounts account.

THE **NAVIGATOR**

▬Comparing IFRS and ASPE▬

Key Differences	International Financial Reporting Standards (IFRS)	Accounting Standards for Private Enterprises (ASPE)
Classification of expense in the income statement	Expenses must be classified by either nature or function.	Expenses can be classified in any manner the company finds useful.

THE **NAVIGATOR**

Demonstration Problem 1

Cappelio Retailers and AP Distributors had the following transactions in June. Both companies use a perpetual inventory system.

June 1 Cappelio Retailers purchased merchandise inventory for resale from AP Distributors for $7,000. Terms of purchase were 2/10, n/30, FOB shipping point.
   2 The correct company paid $225 cash for freight charges.
   3 Cappelio noted that some of the goods were not exactly as ordered and returned the goods to AP Distributors. AP Distributors granted Cappelio a $500 purchase return.
   10 Cappelio paid AP Distributors the amount owing.

Additional information for AP Distributors:

1. The cost of the merchandise sold on June 1 was $4,200.
2. The cost of the merchandise returned on June 3 was $300. The goods were returned to inventory.

ACTION PLAN

- Merchandise Inventory account is used for all transactions that affect the cost of the goods purchased.
- Cost of goods sold must be calculated and recorded at point of sale in a perpetual inventory system.
- A contra revenue account is used for sales allowances given to customers.
- A contra revenue account is used for sales discounts taken by customers.

Instructions

(a) Journalize the June transactions for Cappelio Retailers.
(b) Journalize the June transactions for AP Distributors.

Solution to Demonstration Problem 1

(a) Cappelio Retailers (buyer)

Date	Account Titles and Explanation	Debit	Credit
June 1	Merchandise Inventory	7,000	
	Accounts Payable		7,000
	Purchased merchandise on account.		
2	Merchandise Inventory	225	
	Cash		225
	Paid freight charges on goods purchased.		
3	Accounts Payable	500	
	Merchandise Inventory		500
	Returned merchandise		
10	Accounts Payable ($7,000 − $500)	6,500	
	Merchandise Inventory ($6,500 × 2%)		130
	Cash ($6,500 − $130)		6,370
	Paid for merchandise in discount period.		

(b) AP Distributors (seller)

Date	Account Titles and Explanation	Debit	Credit
June 1	Accounts Receivable	7,000	
	Sales		7,000
	Sold merchandise on account		
	Cost of goods sold	4,200	
	Merchandise Inventory		4,200
	Record cost of goods sold.		
2	No entry. Purchaser pays freight.		
3	Sales Returns and Allowances	500	
	Accounts Receivable		500
	Customer returned merchandise.		
	Merchandise Inventory	300	
	Cost of Goods Sold		300
	Cost of goods returned.		
10	Cash	6,370	
	Sales Discount	130	
	Accounts Receivable		6,500
	Received payment in discount period.		

Demonstration Problem 2

The adjusted trial balance data for the year ended December 31, 2014, for Dykstra Company are as follows:

DYKSTRA COMPANY
Adjusted Trial Balance
December 31, 2014

	Debit	Credit
Cash	$ 14,500	
Accounts receivable	15,100	
Merchandise inventory	29,000	
Prepaid insurance	2,500	
Land	150,000	
Building	500,000	
Accumulated depreciation—building		$ 40,000
Equipment	95,000	
Accumulated depreciation—equipment		18,000
Accounts payable		10,600
Property taxes payable		4,000
Mortgage payable—due before December 31, 2015		25,000
Mortgage payable—long-term		530,000
G. Dykstra, capital		81,000
G. Dykstra, drawings	12,000	
Sales		627,200
Sales returns and allowances	5,700	
Sales discounts	1,000	
Cost of goods sold	353,800	
Advertising expense	12,000	
Depreciation expense	29,000	
Freight out	7,600	
Insurance expense	4,500	
Property tax expense	24,000	
Salaries expense	61,000	
Utilities expense	18,000	
Interest revenue		2,500
Interest expense	3,600	
Totals	$1,338,300	$1,338,300

Instructions

(a) Prepare a single-step income statement for the year ended December 31, 2014.
(b) Prepare a multiple-step income statement for the year ended December 31, 2014.
(c) Prepare a statement of owner's equity for Dykstra Company for the year ended December 31, 2014. No additional investments were made by Mr. Dykstra during the year.
(d) Prepare a classified balance sheet as at December 31, 2014.
(e) Prepare closing entries.

ACTION PLAN

- Recall that in a single-step income statement all revenues are together, then all of the expenses. Profit is the difference between the two subtotals.
- Remember that the major subtotal headings in the multiple-step income statement are net sales, gross profit, profit from operations, and profit (loss).
- Prepare the multiple-step income statement in steps:
  1. Sales less sales returns and allowances and sales discounts equals net sales.
  2. Net sales less cost of goods sold equals gross profit.
  3. Gross profit less operating expenses equals profit from operations.
  4. Profit from operations plus (minus) non-operating revenue (expense) items equals profit.
- Merchandise Inventory is a current asset in the classified balance sheet.
- Sales Returns and Allowances, Sales Discounts, and Cost of Goods Sold are temporary accounts with debit balances that must be closed.

Solution to Demonstration Problem 2

(a)

DYKSTRA COMPANY
Income Statement
Year Ended December 31, 2014

Revenues		
Net sales		$620,500
Interest revenue		2,500
Total revenues		623,000
Expenses		
Cost of goods sold	$353,800	
Advertising expense	12,000	
Depreciation expense	29,000	
Freight out	7,600	
Insurance expense	4,500	
Interest expense	3,600	
Property tax expense	24,000	
Salaries expense	61,000	
Utilities expense	18,000	
Total expenses		513,500
Profit		$109,500

(b)

DYKSTRA COMPANY
Income Statement
Year Ended December 31, 2014

Sales revenue		
Sales		$627,200
Less: Sales returns and allowances	$ 5,700	
Sales discounts	1,000	6,700
Net sales		620,500
Cost of goods sold		353,800
Gross profit		266,700
Operating expenses		
Advertising expense	$12,000	
Depreciation expense	29,000	
Freight out	7,600	
Insurance expense	4,500	
Property tax expense	24,000	
Salaries expense	61,000	
Utilities expense	18,000	
Total operating expenses		156,100
Profit from operations		110,600
Other revenues and expenses		
Interest revenue	$ 2,500	
Interest expense	(3,600)	(1,100)
Profit		$109,500

(c)

DYKSTRA COMPANY
Statement of Owner's Equity
Year Ended December 31, 2014

G. Dykstra, capital, January 1, 2014	$ 81,000
Add: Profit	109,500
	190,500
Deduct: Drawings	12,000
G. Dykstra, capital, December 31, 2014	$178,500

(d)

DYKSTRA COMPANY
Balance Sheet
December 31, 2014

Assets

Current assets		
Cash		$ 14,500
Accounts receivable		15,100
Merchandise inventory		29,000
Prepaid insurance		2,500
Total current assets		61,100
Property, plant, and equipment		
Land		150,000
Building	$500,000	
Less: Accumulated depreciation	40,000	460,000
Equipment	$ 95,000	
Less: Accumulated depreciation	18,000	77,000
Total property, plant, and equipment		687,000
Total assets		$748,100

Liabilities and Owner's Equity

Current liabilities	
Accounts payable	$ 10,600
Property taxes payable	4,000
Current portion of mortgage payable	25,000
Total current liabilities	39,600
Non-current liabilities	
Mortgage payable	530,000
Total liabilities	569,600
Owner's equity	
G. Dykstra, capital	178,500
Total liabilities and owner's equity	$748,100

(e)

Dec. 31	Sales	627,200	
	Interest Revenue	2,500	
	Income Summary		629,700
	To close revenue accounts.		
31	Income Summary	520,200	
	Sales Returns and Allowances		5,700
	Sales Discounts		1,000
	Cost of Goods Sold		353,800
	Advertising Expense		12,000
	Depreciation Expense		29,000
	Freight Out		7,600
	Insurance Expense		4,500
	Property Tax Expense		24,000
	Salaries Expense		61,000
	Utilities Expense		18,000
	Interest Expense		3,600
	To close expense accounts.		
31	Income Summary (629,700 − 520,200)	109,500	
	G. Dykstra, Capital		109,500
	To close Income Summary.		
31	G. Dykstra, Capital	12,000	
	G. Dykstra, Drawings		12,000
	To close drawings.		

THE NAVIGATOR

▶ Summary of Study Objectives

1. **Describe the differences between service and merchandising companies.** A service company performs services. It has service or fee revenue and operating expenses. A merchandising company sells goods. It has sales revenue, cost of goods sold, gross profit, and operating expenses. Merchandising companies must decide if they want to spend the extra resources to use a perpetual inventory system in which inventory records are updated with each purchase and sale. The benefit of the perpetual system is that it provides better information and control over inventory than a periodic system in which inventory records are updated only at the end of the accounting period.

2. **Prepare entries for purchases under a perpetual inventory system.** The Merchandise Inventory account is debited (increased) for all purchases of merchandise and freight, if freight is paid by the buyer. It is credited (decreased) for purchase returns and allowances and purchase discounts. Purchase discounts are cash reductions to the net invoice price for early payment.

3. **Prepare entries for sales under a perpetual inventory system.** When inventory is sold, two entries are required: (1) Accounts Receivable (or Cash) is debited and Sales is credited for the selling price of the merchandise. (2) Cost of Goods Sold (an expense) is debited (increased) and Merchandise Inventory (a current asset) is credited (decreased) for the cost of the inventory items sold. Contra revenue accounts are used to record sales returns and allowances and sales discounts. Two entries are also required to record sales returns when the returned merchandise can be sold again in the future. Freight costs paid by the seller are recorded as an operating expense.

4. **Perform the steps in the accounting cycle for a merchandising company.** Each of the required steps in the accounting cycle for a service company is also done for a merchandising company. An additional adjusting journal entry may be required under a perpetual inventory system. The Merchandise Inventory account must be adjusted to agree with the physical inventory count if there is a difference in the amounts. Merchandising companies have additional temporary accounts that must also be closed at the end of the accounting year.

5. **Prepare single-step and multiple-step income statements.** In a single-step income statement, all data are classified under two categories (revenues or expenses), and profit is determined by one step. A multiple-step income statement shows several steps in determining profit. Net sales is calculated by deducting sales returns and allowances and sales discounts from sales. Next, gross profit is calculated

by deducting the cost of goods sold from net sales. Profit (loss) from operations is then calculated by deducting operating expenses from gross profit. Total non-operating activities are added to (or deducted from) profit from operations to determine profit.

6. *Calculate the gross profit margin and profit margin.* The gross profit margin, calculated by dividing gross profit by net sales, measures the gross profit earned for each dollar of sales. The profit margin, calculated by dividing profit by net sales, measures the profit (total profit) earned for each dollar of sales. Both are measures of profitability that are closely watched by management and other interested parties.

7. *Prepare the entries for purchases and sales under a periodic inventory system and calculate cost of goods sold*

(Appendix 5A). In a periodic inventory system, separate temporary accounts are used to record (a) purchases, (b) purchase returns and allowances, (c) purchase discounts, and (d) freight costs paid by the buyer. Purchases − purchase returns and allowances − purchase discounts = net purchases. Net purchases + freight in = cost of goods purchased.

In a periodic inventory system, only one journal entry is made to record a sale of merchandise. Cost of goods sold is not recorded at the time of the sale. Instead, it is calculated as follows at the end of the period after the ending inventory has been counted: Beginning inventory + cost of goods purchased = cost of goods available for sale. Cost of goods available for sale − ending inventory = cost of goods sold.

Flash cards

▶ Glossary

Contra revenue account   An account with the opposite balance (debit) compared with its related revenue account, which has a credit balance. The contra revenue account is deducted from the revenue account on the income statement. (p. 246)

Control account   An account in the general ledger that summarizes the detail for a subsidiary ledger and controls it. (p. 241)

Cost of goods available for sale   The cost of the goods on hand at the beginning of the period (beginning inventory) plus the cost of goods purchased during the period. (p. 262)

Cost of goods purchased   Net purchases (purchases minus purchase returns and allowances and purchase discounts) plus freight in. (p. 262)

Cost of goods sold   The total cost of merchandise sold during the period. In a perpetual inventory system, it is calculated and recorded for each sale. In a periodic inventory system, the total cost of goods sold for the period is calculated at the end of the accounting period by deducting ending inventory from the cost of goods available for sale. (p. 236)

FOB destination   A freight term indicating that the buyer accepts ownership when the goods are delivered to the buyer's place of business. The seller pays the shipping costs and is responsible for damages to the goods during transit. (p. 241)

FOB shipping point   A freight term indicating that the buyer accepts ownership when the goods are placed on the carrier by the seller. The buyer pays freight costs from the shipping point to the destination and is responsible for damages. (p. 241)

Function   A method of classifying expenses on the income statement based on which business function the resources were spent on (e.g., costs of sales, administration, and selling). (p. 253)

Gross profit   Sales revenue (net sales) less cost of goods sold. (p. 236)

Gross profit margin   Gross profit expressed as a percentage of net sales. It is calculated by dividing gross profit by net sales. (p. 257)

Gross sales   Total sales before deducting the contra revenue accounts. (p. 247)

Multiple-step income statement   An income statement that shows several steps to determine profit or loss. (p. 254)

Nature   A method of classifying expenses on the income statement based on what the resources were spent on (e.g., depreciation, employee costs, transportation, and advertising). (p. 253)

Net purchases   Purchases minus purchase returns and allowances and purchase discounts. (p. 262)

Net sales   Sales less sales returns and allowances and sales discounts. (p. 247)

Non-operating activities   Other revenues and expenses that are unrelated to the company's main operations. (p. 255)

Operating expenses   Expenses incurred in the process of earning sales revenues. They are deducted from gross profit in the income statement. (p. 236)

Periodic inventory system   An inventory system where detailed inventory records are not updated whenever a transaction occurs. The cost of goods sold is determined only at the end of the accounting period. (p. 238)

Perpetual inventory system   An inventory system where detailed records, showing the quantity and cost of each inventory item, are updated whenever a transaction occurs. The records continuously show the inventory that should be on hand. (p. 237)

Profit from operations   Profit from a company's main operating activity, determined by subtracting operating expenses from gross profit. (p. 255)

Profit margin Profit expressed as a percentage of net sales. It is calculated by dividing profit by net sales. (p. 258)

Profitability ratios Measures of a company's profit or operating success (or shortcomings) for a specific period of time. (p. 257)

Purchase discount A discount, based on the invoice price less any returns and allowances, given to a buyer for early payment of a balance due. (p. 242)

Purchase returns (allowances) The return, or reduction in price, of unsatisfactory merchandise that was purchased. It results in a debit to Cash or Accounts Payable. (p. 242)

Quantity discount A cash discount that reduces the invoice price and is given to the buyer for volume purchases. (p. 242)

Sales discount A reduction, based on the invoice price less any returns and allowances, given by a seller for early payment of a credit sale. (p. 247)

Sales returns (allowances) The return, or reduction in price, of unsatisfactory merchandise that was sold. It results in a credit to Cash or Accounts Receivable. (p. 245)

Sales revenue The main source of revenue in a merchandising company. (p. 236)

Single-step income statement An income statement that shows only one step (revenues less expenses) in determining profit (or loss). (p. 253)

Subsidiary ledger A group of accounts that give details for a control account in the general ledger. (p. 240)

Note: All questions, exercises, and problems below with an asterisk (*) relate to material in Appendix 5A.

▶ Self-Study Questions
Answers are at the end of the chapter.

(SO 1) C 1. Which of the following statements is an advantage of a perpetual inventory system?
  (a) It is not necessary to calculate and record the cost of goods sold with each sale with a perpetual inventory system.
  (b) The perpetual inventory system provides better control over inventory because inventory shortages can be more easily identified.
  (c) It is not necessary to do a physical count of the inventory in a perpetual inventory system.
  (d) A perpetual inventory system results in less clerical work and is less costly than a periodic inventory system.

(SO 2) K 2. Which of the following statements is correct?
  (a) If an inventory subsidiary ledger is used then it is not necessary to have a merchandise inventory account in the general ledger.
  (b) An inventory subsidiary ledger is used to track the quantity of each inventory item; the merchandise inventory account in the general ledger is used to track the cost of each inventory item.
  (c) It is common for companies to have a separate subsidiary ledger for each of their current assets.
  (d) An inventory subsidiary ledger is used in a perpetual inventory system to organize and track the quantity and cost of individual inventory items.

(SO 2) AP 3. A $750 purchase of merchandise inventory is made on June 13, terms 2/10, n/30. On June 16, merchandise costing $50 is returned. What amount will be paid as payment in full on June 22?
  (a) $686
  (b) $700
  (c) $735
  (d) $750

(SO 2, 3) K 4. When goods are shipped with the freight terms FOB shipping point:
  (a) the buyer pays the freight costs and debits Merchandise Inventory.
  (b) the buyer pays the freight costs and debits Freight Expense.
  (c) the seller pays the freight costs and debits Freight Out.
  (d) the seller pays the freight costs and debits Cost of Goods Sold.

(SO 2, 3) C 5. Discounts offered to customers for early payment of the balance due:
  (a) will reduce the cost of the merchandise for the purchaser and increase the cost of goods sold for the seller.
  (b) reduce the cash paid by the purchaser, and the cash received by the seller, by the same amount.
  (c) are required by provincial law.
  (d) benefit the seller but generally do not benefit the purchaser.

(SO 3) K 6. To record the sale of goods for cash in a perpetual inventory system:
  (a) only one journal entry is necessary to record the cost of goods sold and reduction of inventory.
  (b) only one journal entry is necessary to record the receipt of cash and the sales revenue.
  (c) two journal entries are necessary: one to record the receipt of cash and sales revenue, and one to record the cost of the goods sold and reduction of inventory.
  (d) two journal entries are necessary: one to record the receipt of cash and reduction of inventory, and one to record the cost of the goods sold and sales revenue.

(SO 3) K 7. Which of the following is a contra revenue account that normally has a debit balance?
(a) Sales Returns and Allowances
(b) Sales
(c) Freight Out
(d) Cost of Goods Sold

(SO 4, 5) K 8. The steps in the accounting cycle for a merchandising company using the perpetual inventory system are the same as those for a service company *except*:
(a) closing journal entries are not required for a merchandising company.
(b) a post-closing trial balance is not required for a merchandising company.
(c) an additional adjusting journal entry for inventory may be needed in a merchandising company.
(d) a multiple-step income statement is required for a merchandising company.

(SO 5) K 9. Which of the following appears on both a single-step and a multiple-step income statement for a merchandising company?
(a) Merchandise inventory
(b) Gross profit
(c) Profit from operations
(d) Cost of goods sold

(SO 6) AP 10. Net sales are $400,000, cost of goods sold is $310,000, operating expenses are $60,000, and other revenues are $5,000. What are the gross profit margin and profit margin?
(a) 7.5% and 8.8%
(b) 22.5% and 7.4%
(c) 22.5% and 8.8%
(d) 77.5% and 8.8%

(SO 7) K *11. When goods are sold by a company using a periodic inventory system:
(a) the Sales account is credited with the selling price of the goods and the cost of the goods sold is not recorded.
(b) sales discounts are deducted from purchases on the income statement.
(c) sales returns are credited to Sales Returns and Allowances.
(d) freight costs are debited to cost of goods sold.

(SO 7) AP *12. If beginning inventory is $60,000, purchases are $400,000, purchase returns and allowances are $25,000, freight in is $5,000, and ending inventory is $50,000, what is the cost of goods sold?
(a) $385,000
(b) $390,000
(c) $410,000
(d) $430,000

▶ Questions

(SO 1) C 1. What is the difference in determining profit for a merchandising company in comparison with a service company?

(SO 1) C 2. Explain the differences between a perpetual and a periodic inventory system. Include in your explanation why the words "perpetual" and "periodic" are used for the two systems.

(SO 1) C 3. Song Yee wonders why a physical inventory count is necessary in a perpetual inventory system. After all, the accounting records show how much inventory is on hand. Explain why a physical inventory count is required in a perpetual inventory system.

(SO 1) C 4. Describe the costs and the benefits of a perpetual inventory system compared with a periodic inventory system.

(SO 2) C 5. Jermyn argues that if the balance in the inventory subsidiary ledger must equal the balance in the Merchandise Inventory control account in the general ledger, then there is no reason for using a subsidiary ledger. Do you agree or disagree? Explain.

(SO 2) C 6. Rosalee tells a friend in her introductory accounting class that they don't have to worry about how to account for sales taxes on inventory purchases because merchandising companies don't pay sales tax. Do you agree or disagree? Explain.

(SO 2, 3) C 7. What are the differences between FOB shipping point and FOB destination? Explain the differences between how freight costs are recorded for inventory purchases as opposed to inventory sales.

(SO 2) C 8. Willow Ridge Company uses a perpetual inventory system. The company recently purchased merchandise for resale from one of its suppliers. Several of the items were not exactly what had been ordered. The supplier gave Willow Ridge a purchase allowance and it was agreed that Willow Ridge should keep the items. Willow Ridge's accountant does not want to credit the merchandise inventory account because the merchandise was not returned. Is this correct or not? Why?

(SO 2) C 9. Fukushima Company received an invoice for $16,000, terms 1/10, n/30. It will have to borrow from its bank in order to pay the invoice in 10 days. The interest rate Fukushima pays on its bank loans is 7.25%. Should Fukushima take advantage of the cash discount offered or not? Support your answer with calculations.

(SO 3) C 10. Shapiro Book Company sells a book that cost $50 for $75 cash. The accountant prepares a journal entry with a debit to Cash for $75, a credit to Inventory for $50, and a credit to Gross Profit for $25. What part of this is incorrect and why is it important to use the correct accounts? The company uses a perpetual inventory system.

(SO 2, 3) C 11. Explain the difference between a quantity discount, a purchase discount, and a sales discount. Explain how each of them is recorded.

(SO 3) C 12. Chandler Retail has a December 31 fiscal year end and the company sells more merchandise in November and December than in any other month. The company has a "no questions asked" policy in terms of accepting sales returns up to six months after the initial sale. What uncertainties does the company face in terms of recognizing sales revenue?

(SO 3) C 13. Raymond is the accountant at an electronics retail store. He is friends with one of the sales people, Geoff. Geoff tells Raymond to simply debit sales whenever a customer returns an item that Geoff originally sold. Why might Geoff suggest this and what should Raymond do?

(SO 3) C 14. When the seller records a sales return or a sales allowance, sometimes they also adjust cost of goods sold and inventory, and sometimes they do not. Explain when it is necessary to also record an entry in the cost of goods sold and inventory accounts, what is debited and credited, and what amount is used.

(SO 4) C 15. "The steps in the accounting cycle for a merchandising company are different from those in the accounting cycle for a service company." Do you agree or disagree? Explain.

(SO 4) C 16. Neptune Stores uses a perpetual inventory system and has just completed its annual physical inventory count. The accountant determines that the physical inventory count is higher than the accounting records. How could this be possible and what adjustment should be recorded, if any?

(SO 4) K 17. Compared with a service company, what additional accounts must be closed for a merchandising company using a perpetual inventory system? Include in your answer if the account should be debited or credited to close it.

(SO 5) K 18. Explain the differences between a single-step and a multiple-step income statement.

(SO 5) K 19. Explain the terms "net sales," "gross profit," "profit from operations," and "profit." Are these terms used only by merchandising companies or are they used by service companies also?

(SO 5) C 20. Why is interest expense reported as a non-operating expense instead of as an operating expense on a multiple-step income statement?

(SO 5) C 21. Is it possible for a company's profit from operations and its profit to be the same amount? If so, should any company bother to calculate both numbers?

(SO 6) C 22. What is the difference between gross profit and gross profit margin? Why is it useful to calculate a company's gross profit margin?

(SO 6) C 23. SnowCo monitors its gross profit margin on a regular basis. Is there any need for it to also monitor its profit margin?

(SO 7) K *24. Explain the differences between how inventory purchases are recorded in a periodic system and in a perpetual system. Also explain the differences in recording sales between a periodic system and a perpetual system.

(SO 7) K *25. Renata purchases merchandise at garage sales and later sells these goods at a flea market. Assuming Renata uses a periodic inventory system, how would she calculate her cost of goods sold and gross profit?

(SO 7) C *26. In a periodic inventory system, closing entries are posted to the Merchandise Inventory account. What is the purpose of these entries?

▶ Brief Exercises

Calculate missing amounts in determining profit or loss.
(SO 1) AP

BE5–1 The components in the income statements of companies A, B, C, and D follow. Determine the missing amounts.

	Sales	Cost of Goods Sold	Gross Profit	Operating Expenses	Profit/(Loss)
Company A	$250,000	$170,000	$ (a)	$ 50,000	$ (b)
Company B	108,000	70,000	(c)	(d)	29,500
Company C	75,000	(e)	30,000	(f)	10,800
Company D	(g)	75,000	95,000	115,000	(h)

Calculate balance in inventory control account.
(SO 2) AP

BE5–2 Old Fashioned Candy Company sells three types of candies. The company uses a perpetual inventory system and a subsidiary ledger to keep track of its inventory. Determine the balance in the inventory control account in the general ledger if the company had the following items on hand on March 31:

Inventory Item	Packages on Hand	Cost per Package
Bubble gum	600	$0.95
Jelly beans	400	1.25
Lollipops	350	1.60

BE5–3 Old Fashioned Candy Company (see BE5–2) has decided to expand its sales to include Canada Mints. It purchases 500 packages from its supplier at a cost of $5.50 per package, terms 2/10, n/30, FOB shipping point. The freight charges are $75. Old Fashioned Candy Company pays for the merchandise within the discount period. What are the total cost and cost per package of this inventory item, and the balance in the Merchandise Inventory control account in the general ledger after these transactions?

Calculate inventory balances (SO 2) AP

BE5–4 Fresh Look Paint Store uses a perpetual inventory system. The company had the following transactions in March.

Mar. 16 Purchased $15,000 of merchandise from Central Paint Distributors, terms 2/10, n/30, FOB destination.
    18 Fresh Look Paint Store received an allowance of $750 for the merchandise purchased on March 16 because of minor damage to the goods.
    25 Paid the balance due to Central Paint Distributors.

For each transaction, (a) prepare a journal entry to record the transaction and (b) indicate the amount that the transaction increased or decreased total assets, total liabilities, and owner's equity. Indicate NE (no effect) if the transaction neither increased nor decreased any of these items.

Record purchase transactions and indicate impact on assets, liabilities, and owner's equity. (SO 2) C

BE5–5 Prepare the journal entries to record the following purchase transactions in Xiaoyan Company's books. Xiaoyan uses a perpetual inventory system.

Jan. 2 Xiaoyan purchased $20,000 of merchandise from Feng Company, terms n/30, FOB shipping point.
    4 The correct company paid freight costs of $215.
    6 Xiaoyan returned $1,500 of the merchandise purchased on January 2 because it was not needed.
Feb. 1 Xiaoyan paid the balance owing to Feng.

Record purchase transactions—perpetual system. (SO 2) AP

BE5–6 Prepare the journal entries to record the following purchase transactions in Jarek Company's books. Jarek uses a perpetual inventory system.

Mar. 12 Jarek purchased $25,000 of merchandise from Dalibor Company, terms 2/10, n/30, FOB destination.
    13 The correct company paid freight costs of $265.
    14 Jarek returned $2,000 of the merchandise purchased on March 12 because it was damaged.
    21 Jarek paid the balance owing to Dalibor.

Record purchase transactions with a purchase discount—perpetual system. (SO 2) AP

BE5–7 Central Paint Distributors uses a perpetual inventory system. The company had the following transactions in March.

Mar. 16 Sold $15,000 of merchandise to Fresh Look Paint Stores, terms 2/10, n/30, FOB destination. The merchandise had cost Central Paint Distributors $8,700.
    17 Paid freight costs of $170 for the March 16 sale.
    18 Gave Fresh Look Paint Stores an allowance of $750 for the March 16 sale. There was some minor damage to the goods.
    25 Collected the balance due from Fresh Paint Stores.

For each transaction, (a) prepare a journal entry to record the transaction and (b) indicate the amount that the transaction increased or decreased total assets, total liabilities, and owner's equity. Indicate NE (no effect) if the transaction neither increased nor decreased any of these items.

Record sales transactions and indicate impact on assets, liabilities, and owner's equity. (SO 3) C

BE5–8 Prepare journal entries to record the following sales transactions in Feng Company's books. Feng uses a perpetual inventory system.

Jan. 2 Feng sold $20,000 of merchandise to Xiaoyan Company, terms n/30, FOB shipping point. The cost of the merchandise sold was $7,900.
    4 The correct company paid freight costs of $215.
    6 Xiaoyan returned $1,500 of the merchandise purchased on January 2 because it was not needed. The cost of the merchandise returned was $590, and it was restored to inventory.
Feb. 1 Feng received the balance due from Xiaoyan.

Record sales transactions with a sales discount—perpetual system. (SO 3) AP

BE5–9 Prepare journal entries to record the following sales transactions in Dalibor Company's books. Dalibor uses a perpetual inventory system.

Mar. 12 Dalibor sold $25,000 of merchandise to Jarek Company, terms 2/10, n/30, FOB destination. The cost of the merchandise sold was $13,250.
    13 The correct company paid freight costs of $265.
    14 Jarek returned $2,000 of the merchandise purchased on March 12 because it was damaged. The cost of the merchandise returned was $1,060. Dalibor examined the merchandise, decided it was no longer saleable, and discarded it.
    22 Dalibor received the balance due from Jarek.

Record sales transactions—perpetual system. (SO 3) AP

Prepare adjusting entry.
(SO 4) AP

BE5–10 At its June 30 year end, the inventory records of Pajewski Company showed merchandise inventory of $89,000. Through a physical count, the company determined that its actual inventory on hand was $86,500. Record the necessary adjusting entry.

Prepare closing entries.
(SO 4) AP

BE5–11 Home Goods Retail Company has the following merchandise account balances at its September 30 year end:

Cost of goods sold	$125,000	Sales	$218,750
Freight out	1,900	Sales discounts	950
Merchandise inventory	22,000	Sales returns and allowances	3,150
Salaries expense	40,000	Supplies	2,500

Prepare the entries to close the appropriate accounts to the Income Summary account.

Calculate net sales, gross profit, operating expenses, profit from operations, and profit. (SO 5) AP

BE5–12 Chocolate Treats has the following account balances:

Cost of goods sold	$385,000	Rent expense	$ 44,000
Depreciation expense	13,200	Salaries expense	55,000
Insurance expense	3,300	Sales	561,000
Interest expense	11,000	Sales discounts	5,500
Interest revenue	8,800	Sales returns and allowances	16,500

Assuming Chocolate Treats uses a multiple-step income statement, calculate the following: (a) net sales, (b) gross profit, (c) operating expenses, (d) profit from operations, and (e) profit.

Identify placement of items on income statements.
(SO 5) AP

BE5–13 Explain where each of the following items would appear on (a) a single-step income statement and (b) a multiple-step income statement: cost of goods sold, depreciation expense, freight out, insurance expense, interest expense, interest revenue, rent revenue, rent expense, sales revenue, and sales returns and allowances.

Calculate profitability ratios and comment. (SO 6) AP

BE5–14 Gabalon Retail reported the following for the past two fiscal years:

	2014	2013
Net sales	$950,000	$800,000
Cost of goods sold	600,000	500,000
Profit	70,000	65,000

(a) Calculate the gross profit margin and profit margin for both years. (b) Comment on any changes in profitability.

Record purchase transactions—periodic system. (SO 7) AP

*BE5–15 Prepare the journal entries to record these transactions on Allied Company's books. Allied Company uses a periodic inventory system.

Feb. 5   Allied purchased $12,000 of merchandise from NW Wholesale Company, terms 2/10, n/30, FOB shipping point.
     6   The correct company paid freight costs of $110.
     8   Allied returned $1,000 of the merchandise purchased on February 5.
    11   Allied paid the balance due to NW Wholesale.

Record sales transactions—periodic system. (SO 7) AP

*BE5–16 Prepare the journal entries to record these transactions on NW Wholesale Company's books. NW Wholesale Company uses a periodic inventory system.

Feb. 5   NW Wholesale sells $12,000 of merchandise to Allied, terms 2/10, n/30, FOB shipping point.
     6   The correct company paid freight costs of $110.
     8   Allied returned $1,000 of the merchandise purchased on February 5.
        The inventory is not damaged and can be resold. NW Wholesale restores it to inventory.
    11   NW Wholesale collects the balance due from Allied.

Calculate net purchases, cost of goods purchased, cost of goods sold, and gross profit. (SO 7) AP

*BE5–17 Clef Stores uses a periodic inventory system and reports the following information for 2014:

Beginning inventory	$51,000	Net sales	$531,250
Ending inventory	68,000	Purchase discounts	6,800
Freight in	13,600	Purchase returns and allowances	9,350
Freight out	10,625	Purchases	340,000

Calculate (a) net purchases, (b) cost of goods purchased, (c) cost of goods available for sale, (d) cost of goods sold, and (e) gross profit.

▶ Exercises

E5-1 The following are some of the terms discussed in the chapter:

1. Gross profit
2. Perpetual inventory system
3. Cost of goods sold
4. Purchase returns
5. Freight out
6. FOB shipping point
7. Periodic inventory system
8. Subsidiary ledger

9. Sales discounts
10. FOB destination
11. Sales allowance
12. Non-operating activities
13. Profit margin
14. Contra revenue account
15. Merchandise inventory
16. Purchase discounts

Match concepts with descriptions.
(SO 1, 2, 3, 4, 5, 6) K

Instructions

Match each term with the best description below. Each term may be used more than once, or may not be used at all.

(a) _____ An expense account that shows the cost of merchandise sold
(b) _____ A group of accounts that share a common characteristic, such as all inventory accounts
(c) _____ An account, such as Sales Discounts, that is deducted from a revenue account on the income statement
(d) _____ The return of unsatisfactory purchased merchandise
(e) _____ Freight terms where the seller will pay for the cost of shipping the goods
(f) _____ An inventory system where the inventory records need to be updated at year end to show the inventory on hand
(g) _____ A reduction in price given for unsatisfactory inventory
(h) _____ Sales revenue less cost of goods sold
(i) _____ Revenues, expenses, gains, and losses that are not part of the company's main operations
(j) _____ Freight terms where the buyer will pay for the cost of shipping the goods
(k) _____ An inventory system where the cost of goods sold is calculated and recorded with every sales transaction
(l) _____ An asset that shows the cost of goods purchased for resale
(m) _____ Profit divided by net sales
(n) _____ A price reduction given by a seller for early payment on a credit sale

E5-2 Stellar Stores is a new company that started operations on March 1, 2014. The company has decided to use a perpetual inventory system. The following purchase transactions occurred in March:

Record purchase transactions.
(SO 2) AP

Mar. 1 Stellar Stores purchases $9,000 of merchandise for resale from Octagon Wholesalers terms 2/10, n/30, FOB shipping point.
2 The correct company pays $155 for the shipping charges.
3 Stellar returns $1,000 of the merchandise purchased on March 1 because it was the wrong colour. Octagon gives Stellar a $1,000 credit on its account.
21 Stellar Stores purchases an additional $13,000 of merchandise for resale from Octagon Wholesalers terms 2/10, n/30, FOB destination.
22 The correct company pays $170 for freight charges.
23 Stellar returns $400 of the merchandise purchased on March 21 because it was damaged. Octagon gives Stellar a $400 credit on its account.
30 Stellar paid Octagon the amount owing for the merchandise purchased on March 1.
31 Stellar paid Octagon the amount owing for the merchandise purchased on March 21.

Instructions

(a) Prepare Stellar Stores' journal entries to record the above transactions.
(b) Post the transactions to the merchandise inventory account. Compare the total in this account with the total of the cash paid during March by Stellar for the purchase of inventory. (*Note:* assume there were no sales of inventory in March.)

E5-3 Octagon Wholesalers uses a perpetual inventory system. Refer to the data in E5–2 regarding sales transactions with Stellar Stores and to the additional information below for Octagon.

Record sales transactions.
(SO 3) AP

Mar. 1 Octagon's cost of the merchandise sold to Stellar was $3,960.
3 Octagon's cost of the merchandise returned by Stellar was $440. As the merchandise was not damaged it was returned to Octagon's inventory.

21   Octagon's cost of the additional merchandise sold to Stellar Stores was $5,720.
23   Octagon's cost of the merchandise returned by Stellar was $176. As the merchandise was damaged, it was put in the recycling bin.

Instructions

(a) Prepare Octagon Wholesalers' journal entries to record the sale transactions with Stellar. Remember to record the freight and cash receipt transactions as appropriate.
(b) Calculate Octagon's net sales, cost of goods sold, and gross profit for these sales.

Record purchase and sales transactions—perpetual system. (SO 1, 2, 3) AP

E5–4   The following transactions occurred in April and May. Both companies use a perpetual inventory system.

Apr. 5   Olaf Company purchased merchandise from DeVito Company for $12,000, terms 2/10, n/30, FOB shipping point. DeVito had paid $8,500 for the merchandise.
    6   The correct company paid freight costs of $300.
    8   Olaf Company returned damaged merchandise to DeVito Company and was given a purchase allowance of $1,800. DeVito determined the merchandise could not be repaired and sent it to the recyclers. The merchandise had cost DeVito $1,275.
May 4   Olaf paid the amount due to DeVito Company in full.

Instructions

(a) Prepare the journal entries to record the above transactions for Olaf Company.
(b) Prepare the journal entries to record the above transactions for DeVito Company.
(c) Calculate the gross profit earned by DeVito on these transactions.

Record purchase and sales transactions—perpetual system. (SO 1, 2, 3) AP

E5–5   The following merchandise transactions occurred in December. Both companies use a perpetual inventory system.

Dec. 3   Pippen Company sold merchandise to Thomas Co. for $32,000, terms 2/10, n/30, FOB destination. This merchandise cost Pippen Company $18,000.
    4   The correct company paid freight charges of $650.
    8   Thomas Co. returned unwanted merchandise to Pippen. The returned merchandise had a sales price of $1,800 and a cost of $990. It was restored to inventory.
    13   Pippen Company received the balance due from Thomas Co.

Instructions

(a) Prepare the journal entries to record these transactions on the books of Pippen Company.
(b) Prepare the journal entries to record these transactions on the books of Thomas Co.
(c) Calculate the gross profit earned by Pippen on the above transactions.

Record inventory transactions and closing entries—perpetual system. (SO 2, 3, 4) AP

E5–6   The following transactions occurred in June and July. Pele Company uses a perpetual inventory system.

June 10   Pele Company purchased $4,000 of merchandise from Duvall Company, terms 2/10, n/30, FOB shipping point.
    11   The correct company paid $375 of freight costs to Hoyt Movers.
    12   Damaged goods totalling $200 were returned to Duvall for credit.
    20   Pele paid Duvall Company in full.
July 15   Pele sold all of the remaining merchandise purchased from Duvall for $9,275 cash.
    15   Pele paid $350 of freight costs to AAA Transit to deliver the goods to the customer.
    17   Pele gave its customer a $500 cash sales allowance for damaged goods. Pele uses a perpetual inventory system.

Instructions

(a) Record each of the above transactions on the books of Pele Company.
(b) Prepare closing entries on July 31 for the temporary accounts.

Calculate cost of goods available for sale, ending inventory, cost of goods sold, net sales, and gross profit. Record adjusting entries—perpetual system. (SO 1, 2, 3, 4) AP

E5–7   Delta Furniture Supply sells various furniture items and uses a perpetual inventory system. On November 1 it had no tables in stock. The following transactions occurred during November:

Nov. 3   Delta purchased 150 tables from Burnaby Manufacturing Ltd. for $13,500, terms n/30, FOB shipping point.
    3   Delta paid $450 to Freight Forward Company for the delivery of the tables.
    19   Delta sold 45 tables to Hobby Horse Inc. for $170 each on credit, terms 2/10, n/30, FOB destination.
    19   Delta paid $135 cash to Freight Forward Company for the delivery of the tables to Hobby Horse Inc.

21 Hobby Horse Inc. returned five tables. Delta credited Hobby Horse's account and the tables were returned to inventory.

29 Delta received the amount owing from Hobby Horse Inc.

30 Paid Burnaby Manufacturing Ltd. for the tables purchased on November 3.

On November 30, Delta did an inventory count and found that there were 109 tables on hand.

Instructions

(a) Calculate the total cost of the tables purchased during the month and the average cost per table.

(b) Calculate the number of tables that the company should have on hand according to its subsidiary ledger and determine if an adjustment is required. If so, prepare the adjusting journal entry. Calculate the correct dollar amount for the tables in the subsidiary ledger after any required adjustments.

(c) Calculate cost of goods sold after recording any required adjustments.

(d) Calculate the net sales and gross profit that Delta earned on its tables during November.

E5–8 Financial information follows for three different companies:

Calculate missing amounts.
(SO 5) AP

	Natural Cosmetics	Mattar Grocery	SE Footware
Sales	$215,000	$ (e)	$275,000
Sales returns and allowances	(a)	25,000	20,000
Net sales	201,000	335,000	(i)
Cost of goods sold	99,000	(f)	(j)
Gross profit	(b)	195,000	150,000
Operating expenses	45,000	(g)	95,000
Profit from operations	(c)	(h)	(k)
Other expenses	5,000	10,000	(l)
Profit	(d)	63,000	41,000

Instructions

Determine the missing amounts.

E5–9 The following is information from Lefebvre Company's adjusted trial balance at December 31, 2014:

Prepare single-step and multiple-step income statements, closing entries, and post-closing trial balance—perpetual system.
(SO 4, 5) AP

	Debit	Credit
Cash	$ 75,700	
Notes receivable	100,000	
Merchandise inventory	70,000	
Equipment	450,000	
Accumulated depreciation—equipment		$ 135,000
Unearned revenue		8,000
Notes payable		175,000
C. Lefebvre, capital		235,000
C. Lefebvre, drawings	150,000	
Interest revenue		10,000
Rent revenue		24,000
Sales		1,980,000
Advertising expense	55,000	
Cost of goods sold	851,500	
Depreciation expense	45,000	
Freight out	25,000	
Insurance expense	15,000	
Interest expense	10,500	
Salaries expense	650,000	
Sales discounts	9,900	
Sales returns and allowances	59,400	
	$2,567,000	$2,567,000

Instructions

(a) Prepare a single-step income statement.

(b) Prepare a multiple-step income statement.

(c) Prepare closing entries and a post-closing trial balance.

Prepare financial statements
and calculate ratios—
perpetual system.
(SO 5, 6) AP

E5–10   An alphabetical list of Rikard's adjusted accounts at its fiscal year end, August 31, 2014, follows. All accounts have normal balances.

Accounts payable	$ 15,500	Notes payable	$ 42,000
Accumulated depreciation—equipment	14,000	Prepaid insurance	575
Accumulated depreciation—furniture	17,500	R. Smistad, capital	65,750
Cash	15,450	R. Smistad, drawings	80,000
Cost of goods sold	271,500	Rent expense	24,000
Depreciation expense	7,000	Salaries expense	50,000
Equipment	35,000	Salaries payable	2,250
Furniture	42,000	Sales	465,000
Insurance expense	3,575	Sales returns and allowances	16,300
Interest expense	2,100	Supplies	950
Interest payable	525	Supplies expense	6,325
Merchandise inventory	70,350	Unearned sales revenue	2,600

Additional information:

1. Of the notes payable, $6,000 becomes due on February 17, 2015. The balance is due in 2016.
2. On July 18, 2014, Rikard invested $3,500 cash in the business.

Instructions

(a) Prepare a multiple-step income statement, statement of owner's equity, and classified balance sheet.
(b) Calculate the gross profit margin and profit margin.

Calculate profitability ratios.
(SO 6) AN

E5–11   **Toys "R" Us, Inc.** reported the following information (in U.S. millions) for the three fiscal years ended:

	Jan. 28, 2012	Jan. 29, 2011	Jan. 30, 2010
Net sales	$13,909	$13,864	$13,568
Cost of goods sold	8,939	8,939	8,790
Profit from operations	582	646	784
Profit	149	168	312

Instructions

(a) Calculate the gross profit margin and profit margin for Toys "R" Us for each of the three years.
(b) Recalculate profit margin using profit from operations as opposed to profit.
(c) Comment on whether the ratios improved or weakened over the three years.

Record purchase and sales
transaction entries—periodic
system. (SO 7) AP

E5–12   Data for Olaf Company and DeVito Company are presented in E5–4.

Instructions

(a) Prepare the journal entries to record these transactions on the books of Olaf Company using a periodic inventory system instead of a perpetual system.
(b) Prepare the journal entries to record these transactions on the books of DeVito Company using a periodic inventory system instead of a perpetual system.

Record purchase and sales
transaction entries—periodic
system. (SO 7) AP

E5–13   Data for Pippen Company and Thomas Co. are presented in E5–5.

Instructions

(a) Prepare the journal entries to record these transactions on the books of Pippen Company assuming a periodic inventory system is used instead of a perpetual system.
(b) Prepare the journal entries to record these transactions on the books of Thomas Co. assuming a periodic inventory system is used instead of a perpetual system.

Record inventory transactions
and calculate gross profit—
periodic system. (SO 7) AP

E5–14   Memories Company commenced operations on July 1. Memories Company uses a periodic inventory system. During July, Memories Company was involved in the following transactions and events:

July	2	Purchased $15,000 of merchandise from Suppliers Inc. on account, terms 2/10, n/30, FOB shipping point.
	3	Returned $1,200 of merchandise to Suppliers Inc. as it was damaged. Received a credit on account from Suppliers.
	4	Paid $500 of freight costs on July 2 shipment.
	8	Sold merchandise for $2,000 cash.
	11	Paid Suppliers Inc. the full amount owing.
	15	Sold merchandise for $6,000 on account, 1/10, n/30, FOB shipping point.
	25	Received full payment for the merchandise sold on July 15.
	31	Memories did a physical count and determined there was $10,500 of inventory on hand.

Instructions

(a) Record the transactions in Memories Company's books.

(b) What was Memories' gross profit for July?

*E5–15   Below are the cost of goods sold sections for the two most recent years for two companies using a periodic inventory system:

	Company 1		Company 2	
	Year 1	Year 2	Year 1	Year 2
Beginning inventory	$ 250	$ (e)	$1,000	$ (n)
Purchases	1,500	(f)	(j)	9,550
Purchase returns and allowances	50	100	300	400
Purchase discounts	30	50	150	100
Net purchases	(a)	1,850	7,210	(o)
Freight in	110	(g)	(k)	550
Cost of goods purchased	(b)	(h)	7,900	(p)
Cost of goods available for sale	(c)	2,300	(l)	(q)
Ending inventory	(d)	400	1,450	1,250
Cost of goods sold	1,480	(i)	(m)	(r)

Determine missing amounts for cost of goods sold section—periodic system. (SO 7) AP

Instructions

Fill in the missing amounts to complete the cost of goods sold sections.

*E5–16   The following selected information is for Okanagan Company for the year ended January 31, 2014:

Freight in	$ 6,500	Purchase discounts	$ 12,000
Freight out	7,000	Purchase returns and allowances	16,000
Insurance expense	12,000	Rent expense	20,000
Interest expense	6,000	Salaries expense	61,000
Merchandise inventory, beginning	61,000	Salaries payable	2,500
Merchandise inventory, ending	42,000	Sales	325,000
O. G. Pogo, capital	105,000	Sales discounts	14,000
O. G. Pogo, drawings	42,000	Sales returns and allowances	20,000
Purchases	210,000	Unearned sales revenue	4,500

Prepare multiple-step income statement and closing entries—periodic system. (SO 7) AP

Instructions

(a) Prepare a multiple-step income statement.

(b) Prepare closing entries.

▶ Problems: Set A

P5–1A   AAA Dog 'n Cat Shop sells a variety of merchandise for the pet owner, including pet food, grooming supplies, toys, and kennels. Most customers use the option to purchase on account and take 60 days, on average, to pay their accounts. The owner of AAA Dog 'n Cat Shop, Adam Fleming, has decided the company needs a bank loan because the accounts payable need to be paid in 30 days. Adam estimates that it takes 45 days, on average, to sell merchandise from the time it arrives at his store. Since the company earns a good profit every year, the bank manager is willing to give AAA Dog 'n Cat Shop a loan but wants monthly financial statements.

Identify problems and recommend inventory system. (SO 1) C

Adam has also noticed that, while some of the merchandise sells very quickly, other items do not. Sometimes he wonders just how long he has had some of those older items. He has also noticed that he regularly seems to run out of some merchandise items. Adam is also concerned about preparing monthly financial statements. The company uses a periodic inventory system and Adam counts inventory once a year. He is wondering how he is going to calculate the cost of goods sold for the month without counting the inventory at the end of every month. He has come to you for help.

Instructions

(a) Explain to Adam what an operating cycle is and why he is having problems paying the bills.

(b) Explain to Adam how the periodic inventory system is contributing to his problems.

TAKING IT FURTHER   Make a recommendation about what inventory system the company should use and why.

Record and post inventory transactions—perpetual system. Calculate net sales and gross profit.
(SO 1, 2, 3) AP

P5–2A At the beginning of the current tennis season, on April 1, 2014, Kicked-Back Tennis Shop's inventory consisted of 50 tennis racquets at a cost of $40 each. Kicked-Back uses a perpetual inventory system. The following transactions occurred in April:

Apr. 2   Purchased 160 additional racquets from Roberts Inc. for $6,400, terms n/30.
     4   Determined that five of the racquets purchased on April 2 were damaged and returned them to Roberts Inc. Roberts Inc. credited Kicked-Back's account.
     5   Sold 45 racquets to Tennis Dome for $90 each, terms n/30.
     6   Tennis Dome returned 15 of the racquets after determining it had purchased more racquets than it needed. Kicked-Back gave Tennis Dome a credit on its account and returned the racquets to inventory.
    10   Sold 40 racquets at $90 each to cash customers.
    12   Ten of these racquets were returned for cash. The customers claimed they never play tennis and had no idea how they had been talked into purchasing the racquets. Refunded cash to these customers and returned the racquets to inventory.
    17   An additional 10 of the racquets sold on April 10 were returned because the racquets were damaged. The customers were refunded cash and the racquets were sent to a local children's club as a gift.
    25   Sold 60 racquets to the Summer Club for $90 each, terms n/30.
    29   Summer Club returned 25 of the racquets after the tennis pro had examined them and determined that these racquets were of inferior quality. Kicked-Back gave Summer Club a credit and decided to return the racquets to inventory with plans to sell them for the reduced price of $75 each.

Instructions

(a) Record the transactions for the month of April for Kicked-Back.
(b) Create T accounts for sales, sales returns, cost of goods sold, and merchandise inventory. Post the opening balance and April's transactions, and calculate the April 30 balances.
(c) Calculate net sales and gross profit.

TAKING IT FURTHER   Assume that the owner of Kicked-Back hired an employee to run the store and is not involved in operating the business. The owner wants to know the amount of net sales and gross profit for the month. Will the owner be missing any important information by requesting only these two numbers? Explain.

Record inventory transactions—perpetual system. (SO 2, 3) AP

P5–3A Presented below are selected transactions for Norlan Company during September and October of the current year. Norlan uses a perpetual inventory system.

Sept. 1   Purchased merchandise on account from Hillary Company at a cost of $45,000, FOB destination, terms 1/15, n/30.
     2   The correct company paid $2,000 of freight charges to Trucking Company on the September 1 merchandise purchase.
     5   Returned for credit $3,000 of damaged goods purchased from Hillary Company on September 1.
    15   Sold the remaining merchandise purchased from Hillary Company to Irvine Company for $70,000, terms 2/10, n/30, FOB destination.
    16   The correct company paid $1,800 of freight charges on the September 15 sale of merchandise.
    17   Issued Irvine Company a credit of $5,000 for returned goods. These goods had cost Norlan Company $3,000 and were returned to inventory.
    25   Received the balance owing from Irvine Company for the September 15 sale.
    30   Paid Hillary Company the balance owing for the September 1 purchase.
Oct. 1   Purchased merchandise on account from Kimmel Company at a cost of $52,000, terms 2/10, n/30, FOB shipping point.
     2   The correct company paid freight costs of $1,100 on the October 1 purchase.
     3   Obtained a purchase allowance of $2,000 from Kimmel Company to compensate for some minor damage to goods purchased on October 1.
    10   Paid Kimmel Company the amount owing on the October 1 purchase.
    11   Sold all of the merchandise purchased from Kimmel Company to Kieso Company for $83,500, terms 2/10, n/30, FOB shipping point.
    12   The correct company paid $800 freight costs on the October 11 sale.
    17   Issued Kieso Company a sales allowance of $1,500 because some of the goods did not meet Kieso's exact specifications.
    31   Received a cheque from Kieso Company for the balance owing on the October 11 sale.

Instructions

Prepare journal entries to record the above transactions for Norlan Company.

TAKING IT FURTHER   Explain why companies should always take advantage of purchase discounts even if they have to borrow from the bank. Refer to the two purchases made by Norlan Company in your answer.

P5–4A   Travel Warehouse distributes suitcases to retail stores and extends credit terms of n/30 to all of its customers. Travel Warehouse uses a perpetual inventory system and at the end of June its inventory consisted of 25 suitcases purchased at $30 each. During the month of July, the following merchandising transactions occurred:

Record inventory transactions and post to inventory account—perpetual system.
(SO 2, 3) AP

July	1	Purchased 50 suitcases on account for $30 each from Trunk Manufacturers, terms n/30, FOB destination.
	2	The correct company paid $125 freight on the July 1 purchase.
	4	Received $150 credit for five suitcases returned to Trunk Manufacturers because they were damaged.
	10	Sold 45 suitcases on account to Satchel World for $55 each.
	12	Issued a $275 credit for five suitcases returned by Satchel World because they were the wrong colour. The suitcases were returned to inventory.
	15	Purchased 60 additional suitcases from Trunk Manufacturers for $27.50 each, terms n/30, FOB shipping point.
	18	Paid $150 freight to AA Trucking Company for merchandise purchased from Trunk Manufacturers.
	21	Sold 54 suitcases on account to Fly-By-Night for $55 each.
	23	Gave Fly-By-Night a $110 credit for two returned suitcases. The suitcases had been damaged and were sent to the recyclers.
	30	Paid Trunk Manufacturers for the July 1 purchase.
	31	Received balance owing from Satchel World.

Instructions

(a) Record the transactions for the month of July for Travel Warehouse.
(b) Create a T account for Merchandise Inventory. Post the opening balance and July's transactions, and calculate the July 31 balance.
(c) Determine the number of suitcases on hand at the end of the month and calculate the average cost per suitcase of the inventory on hand.

TAKING IT FURTHER   Explain how freight terms can affect the selling price, and the cost, of merchandise. Use the transactions on July 1 and 15 between Travel Warehouse and Trunk Manufacturer as part of your explanation.

P5–5A   At the beginning of June 2014, Willingham Distributing Company's ledger showed Cash $18,000, Merchandise Inventory $5,000, and D. Willingham, Capital, $23,000. During the month of June, the company had the following selected transactions:

Record and post inventory transactions—perpetual system. Prepare partial income statement.
(SO 2, 3, 5) AP

June	1	Purchased $9,000 of merchandise inventory from Sun Supply Co., terms 1/15, n/30, FOB destination.
	2	The correct company paid $225 cash for freight charges on the June 1 purchase.
	5	Sold merchandise inventory to Moose Jaw Retailers for $12,000. The cost of the merchandise was $7,540 and the terms were 2/10, n/30, FOB destination.
	6	Issued a $950 credit for merchandise returned by Moose Jaw Retailers. The merchandise originally cost $595 and was returned to inventory.
	6	The correct company paid $290 freight on the June 5 sale.
	7	Purchased $800 of supplies for cash.
	10	Purchased $4,300 of merchandise inventory from Fey Wholesalers, terms 2/10, n/30, FOB shipping point.
	10	The correct company paid $100 freight costs on the purchase from Fey Wholesalers.
	12	Received a $300 credit from Fey Wholesalers for returned merchandise.
	14	Paid Sun Supply Co. the amount due.
	15	Collected the balance owing from Moose Jaw Retailers.
	19	Sold merchandise for $7,250 cash. The cost of this merchandise was $4,570.
	20	Paid Fey Wholesalers the balance owing from the June 10 purchase.
	25	Made a $500 cash refund to a cash customer for merchandise returned. The returned merchandise had a cost of $315. The merchandise was damaged and could not be resold.
	30	Sold merchandise to Bauer & Company for $4,280, terms n/30, FOB shipping point. Willingham's cost for this merchandise was $2,700.

Instructions

(a) Record the transactions assuming Willingham uses a perpetual inventory system.
(b) Set up general ledger accounts for Merchandise Inventory, Sales, Sales Returns and Allowances, Sales Discounts, and Cost of Goods Sold. Enter the beginning merchandise inventory balance, and post the transactions.
(c) Prepare a partial multiple-step income statement, up to gross profit, for the month of June 2014.

TAKING IT FURTHER   Assume that Willingham has a "no questions asked" policy in terms of accepting sales returns up to six months after the initial sale. What uncertainties does the company face in terms of calculating its gross profit for June?

Prepare adjusting and closing entries, and single-step and multiple-step income statements—perpetual system. Calculate ratios. (SO 4, 5, 6) AP

P5–6A Wolcott Warehouse Store has an August 31 fiscal year end and uses a perpetual inventory system. An alphabetical list of its account balances at August 31, 2014, follows. All accounts have normal balances.

Accounts payable	$ 30,000	Interest revenue	$ 960
Accounts receivable	20,000	Merchandise inventory	57,440
Accumulated depreciation—		Notes payable	36,000
equipment	26,720	Notes receivable	32,000
Cash	12,525	Rent expense	16,000
Cost of goods sold	569,680	Sales	703,360
Depreciation expense	6,680	Sales discounts	3,700
Equipment	66,800	Sales returns and allowances	14,440
Freight out	4,720	Supplies expense	5,840
Insurance expense	2,895	Unearned revenue	6,040
Interest expense	2,160	V. Wolcott, capital	72,680
Interest receivable	240	V. Wolcott, drawings	60,640

Additional information:

1. All adjustments have been recorded and posted except for the inventory adjustment. According to the inventory count, the company has $55,000 of merchandise on hand.
2. Last year Wolcott Warehouse Store had a gross profit margin of 20% and a profit margin of 10%.

Instructions

(a) Prepare any additional required adjusting entries.
(b) Prepare a single-step income statement.
(c) Prepare a multiple-step income statement.
(d) Calculate gross profit margin and profit margin. Compare with last year's margins and comment on the results.
(e) Prepare the closing entries. Post to the Income Summary account. Before closing the Income Summary account, check that the balance is equal to profit.

TAKING IT FURTHER Compare the two income statements and comment on the usefulness of each one.

Prepare adjusting and closing entries and financial statements—perpetual system. Calculate ratios. (SO 4, 5, 6) AP

P5–7A The unadjusted trial balance of World Enterprises for the year ending December 31, 2014, follows:

WORLD ENTERPRISES
Trial Balance
December 31, 2014

	Debit	Credit
Cash	$ 15,000	
Accounts receivable	19,200	
Merchandise inventory	37,050	
Prepaid insurance	3,000	
Supplies	2,950	
Equipment	150,000	
Accumulated depreciation—equipment		$ 35,000
Furniture	45,000	
Accumulated depreciation—furniture		18,000
Accounts payable		33,200
Unearned revenue		4,000
Mortgage payable		125,000
S. Kim, capital		46,200
S. Kim, drawings	48,000	
Sales		265,000
Sales returns and allowances	2,500	
Sales discounts	3,275	
Cost of goods sold	153,000	
Interest expense	6,875	
Salaries expense	35,450	
Utilities expense	5,100	
	$526,400	$526,400

Additional information:

1. There is $750 of supplies on hand on December 31, 2014.
2. The one-year insurance policy was purchased on March 1, 2014.
3. Depreciation expense for the year is $10,000 for the equipment and $4,500 for the furniture.
4. Accrued interest expense at December 31, 2014, is $675.
5. Unearned revenue of $975 is still unearned at December 31, 2014. On the sales that were earned, cost of goods sold was $1,750.
6. A physical count of merchandise inventory indicates $32,750 on hand on December 31, 2014.
7. Of the mortgage payable, $8,500 is to be paid in 2015.
8. Seok Kim invested $5,000 cash in the business on July 19, 2014.
9. Last year, the company had a gross profit margin of 35%, and profit margin of 10%.

Instructions

(a) Prepare the adjusting journal entries assuming they are prepared annually.
(b) Prepare a multiple-step income statement, statement of owner's equity, and classified balance sheet.
(c) Prepare the closing entries.
(d) Calculate the gross profit margin and profit margin for 2014. Compare with the 2013 ratios and comment on any trends.

TAKING IT FURTHER   Compare the presentation of information in a multiple-step income statement for a service company with one for merchandising company. How would they be similar and how would they be different?

P5–8A   **Magna International Inc.** is a leading global supplier of technologically advanced automotive components, systems, and modules. Selected financial information (in U.S. millions) follows:

Calculate ratios and comment. (SO 6) AN

	2011	2010	2009
Sales	$28,748	$23,465	$16,876
Cost of goods sold	25,401	20,456	15,387
Profit (loss)	1,018	1,003	(453)
Current assets	8,146	7,485	6,233
Current liabilities	5,724	4,968	4,232

Instructions

(a) Calculate the gross profit margin, profit margin, and current ratio for each year.
(b) Comment on whether the ratios have improved or deteriorated over the three years.

TAKING IT FURTHER   Assume you are thinking about investing in Magna International Inc. What other information would be useful in assessing these ratios?

P5–9A   Data for Norlan Company are presented in P5–3A.

Record inventory transactions—periodic system. (SO 7) AP

Instructions

Record the September and October transactions for Norlan Company, assuming a periodic inventory system is used instead of a perpetual inventory system.

TAKING IT FURTHER   Why might a periodic system be better than a perpetual system for Norlan Company?

P5–10A   Data for Travel Warehouse are presented in P5–4A.

Record inventory transactions—periodic system. (SO 7) AP

Instructions

Record the July transactions for Travel Warehouse, assuming a periodic inventory system is used instead of a perpetual inventory system.

TAKING IT FURTHER   What are the costs and benefits for Travel Warehouse of using a perpetual, as opposed to a periodic, system?

P5–11A   Data for Willingham Distributing Company are presented in P5–5A. A physical inventory count shows $3,715 of inventory on hand on June 30, 2014.

Record and post inventory transactions—periodic system. Prepare partial income statement. (SO 7) AP

Instructions

(a) Record the transactions assuming Willingham uses a periodic inventory system.
(b) Set up general ledger accounts for merchandise inventory and all of the temporary accounts used in the merchandising transactions. Enter beginning balances, and post the transactions.
(c) Prepare a partial multiple-step income statement, up to gross profit, for the month of June 2014.

TAKING IT FURTHER   Will gross profit be higher, lower, or the same amount, if using a periodic inventory system instead of a perpetual inventory system? Explain.

Prepare correct multiple-step income statement, statement of owner's equity, and classified balance sheet—periodic system. (SO 7) AP

*P5–12A New West Company recently hired a new accountant whose first task was to prepare the financial statements for the year ended December 31, 2014. The following is what he produced:

NEW WEST COMPANY
Income Statement
December 31, 2014

Sales			$395,000
Less: Unearned revenue		$ 5,500	
Purchase discounts		3,480	8,980
Total revenue			386,020
Cost of goods sold			
Purchases		$232,000	
Less: Purchase returns and allowances		4,000	
Net purchases		236,000	
Add: Sales returns and allowances		7,500	
Cost of goods available for sale		243,500	
Add: Freight out		9,500	
Cost of selling merchandise			253,000
Gross profit margin			133,020
Operating expenses			
Freight in		$ 4,500	
Insurance expense		10,500	
Interest expense		2,500	
Rent expense		18,000	
Salaries expense		42,000	
Total operating expenses			77,500
Profit margin			55,520
Other revenues			
Interest revenue	$ 1,500		
Investment by owner	3,500	5,000	
Other expenses			
Depreciation expense	7,000		
Drawings by owner	48,000	55,000	(50,000)
Profit from operations			$ 5,520

NEW WEST COMPANY
Balance Sheet
Year Ended December 31, 2014

Assets

Cash		$16,780
Accounts receivable		7,800
Merchandise inventory, January 1, 2014		30,000
Merchandise inventory, December 31, 2014		24,000
Equipment	$70,000	
Less: loan payable (for equipment purchase)	50,000	20,000
Total assets		$98,580

Liabilities and Owner's Equity

Long-term debt investment	$50,000
Accumulated depreciation—equipment	21,000
Sales discounts	2,900
Total liabilities	73,900
Owner's equity	24,680
Total liabilities and owner's equity	$98,580

The owner of the company, Lily Oliver, is confused by the statements and has asked you for your help. She doesn't understand how, if her owner's capital account was $75,000 at December 31, 2013, owner's equity is now only $24,680. The accountant tells you that $24,680 must be correct because the balance sheet is balanced. The accountant also tells you that he didn't prepare a statement of owner's equity because it is an optional statement. You are relieved to find out that, even though there are errors in the statements, the amounts used from the accounts in the general ledger are the correct amounts.

Instructions

Prepare the correct multiple-step income statement, statement of owner's equity, and classified balance sheet. You determine that $5,000 of the loan payable on the equipment must be paid during 2015.

TAKING IT FURTHER   If a company uses a periodic inventory system, does it have to show on its income statement all of the details as to how cost of goods sold was calculated? Why or why not?

*P5–13A   The following is an alphabetical list of Bud's Bakery's adjusted account balances at the end of the company's fiscal year on November 30, 2014:

(margin note) Prepare financial statements and closing entries—periodic system. (SO 7) AP

Accounts payable	$ 32,310	Merchandise inventory	$ 34,360
Accounts receivable	13,770	Mortgage payable	106,000
Accumulated depreciation—building	61,200	Prepaid insurance	4,500
Accumulated depreciation—equipment	19,880	Property tax expense	3,500
Building	175,000	Purchases	634,700
B. Hachey, capital	104,480	Purchase discounts	6,300
B. Hachey, drawings	12,000	Purchase returns and allowances	13,315
Cash	8,500	Rent revenue	2,800
Depreciation expense	14,000	Salaries expense	122,000
Equipment	57,000	Salaries payable	8,500
Freight in	5,060	Sales	872,000
Freight out	8,200	Sales discounts	8,250
Insurance expense	9,000	Sales returns and allowances	9,845
Interest expense	5,300	Unearned revenue	3,000
Land	85,000	Utilities expense	19,800

Additional facts:

1. Bud's Bakery uses a periodic inventory system.
2. Of the mortgage payable, $8,500 is due in the next year.
3. A physical count determined that merchandise inventory on hand at November 30, 2014, was $37,350.

Instructions

(a) Prepare a multiple-step income statement, statement of owner's equity, and classified balance sheet.
(b) Prepare the closing journal entries.
(c) Post closing entries to the merchandise inventory and capital accounts. Check that the balances in these accounts are the same as the amounts on the balance sheet.

TAKING IT FURTHER   If you had not been told that Bud's Bakery uses a periodic inventory system, how could you have determined that? What information is available in a periodic inventory system that is not available in a perpetual inventory system?

▶ Problems: Set B

P5–1B   Home Décor Company sells a variety of home decorating merchandise, including pictures, small furniture items, dishes, candles, and area rugs. The company uses a periodic inventory system and counts inventory once a year. Most customers use the option to purchase on account and many take more than a month to pay. The owner of Home Décor, Rebecca Sherstabetoff, has decided that the company needs a bank loan because the accounts payable need to be paid long before the accounts receivable are collected. The bank manager is willing to give Home Décor a loan but wants monthly financial statements.

(margin note) Identify problems and recommend inventory system. (SO 1) C

Rebecca has also noticed that, while some of her merchandise sells very quickly, other items do not. Sometimes she wonders just how long she has had some of those older items. She has also noticed that she regularly seems to run out of some merchandise. And she is wondering how she is going to find time to count the inventory every month so she can prepare the monthly financial statements for the bank. She has come to you for help.

Instructions

(a) Explain to Rebecca what an operating cycle is and why she is having problems paying her bills.

(b) Explain to Rebecca how her inventory system is contributing to her problems.

TAKING IT FURTHER   Make a recommendation about what inventory system she should use and why.

Record and post inventory transactions—perpetual system. Calculate net sales and gross profit.
(SO 1, 2, 3) AP

P5–2B   At the beginning of the current golf season, on April 1, 2014, Swing-Town Golf Shop's merchandise inventory included 20 specialty hybrid golf clubs at a cost of $160 each. Swing-Town uses a perpetual inventory system. The following transactions occurred in April:

Apr.	2	Purchased 100 additional clubs from Weir Inc. for $16,000, terms n/30.
	4	Received credit from Weir for five returned damaged clubs purchased on April 2.
	5	Sold 20 clubs to Big Golf Practice Range for $265 each, terms n/30.
	6	Big Golf Practice Range returned eight of the clubs after determining it had purchased more clubs than it needed. Swing-Town gave Big Golf Practice Range a credit on its account and returned the clubs to inventory.
	10	Sold 30 clubs at $265 each to cash customers.
	12	Ten of these clubs were returned for cash. The customers claimed they never play golf and had no idea how they had been talked into purchasing the clubs. Refunded cash to these customers and returned the clubs to inventory.
	17	An additional 10 of the clubs sold on April 10 were returned because the clubs were damaged. The customers were refunded cash and the clubs were sent to a local seniors' club as a gift.
	25	Sold 45 clubs to Pro-Shop for $265 each, terms n/30.
	29	Pro-Shop returned 25 of the clubs after the golf pro had examined them and determined that these clubs were of inferior quality. Swing-Town gave Pro-Shop a credit and decided to return the clubs to inventory with plans to sell them for the reduced price of $185 each.

Instructions

(a) Record the transactions for the month of April for Swing-Town Golf.

(b) Create T accounts for sales, sales returns, cost of goods sold, and merchandise inventory. Post the opening balance and April's transactions, and calculate the April 30 balances.

(c) Calculate net sales and gross profit.

TAKING IT FURTHER   Swing-Town's owner thinks that it is a waste of time and effort for the bookkeeper to use a sales returns and allowances account and thinks that the bookkeeper should just reduce the sales account for any sales returns or allowances. Explain to Swing-Town's owner how he would benefit from using a sales returns and allowances account.

Record inventory transactions—perpetual system. (SO 2, 3) AP

P5–3B   Transactions follow for Leeland Company during October and November of the current year. Leeland uses a perpetual inventory system.

Oct.	2	Purchased merchandise on account from Gregory Company at a cost of $35,000, terms 2/10, n/30, FOB destination.
	4	The correct company paid freight charges of $900 to Rail Company for shipping the merchandise purchased on October 2.
	5	Returned damaged goods having a gross invoice cost of $6,000 to Gregory Company. Received a credit for this.
	11	Paid Gregory Company the balance owing for the October 2 purchase.
	17	Sold the remaining merchandise purchased from Gregory Company to Kurji Company for $62,500, terms 2/10, n/30, FOB shipping point.
	18	The correct company paid Intermodal Co. $800 freight costs for the October 17 sale.
	19	Issued Kurji Company a sales allowance of $2,500 because some of the goods did not meet Kurji's exact specifications.
	27	Received the balance owing from Kurji Company for the October 17 sale.

Nov. 1 Purchased merchandise on account from Romeo Company at a cost of $60,000, terms 1/15, n/30, FOB shipping point.
2 The correct company paid freight charges of $4,000.
5 Sold the merchandise purchased from Romeo Company to Bear Company for $110,500, terms 2/10, n/30, FOB destination.
6 The correct company paid freight charges of $2,600.
7 Issued Bear Company a credit of $7,000 for returned goods. These goods had cost Leeland $4,050 and were returned to inventory.
29 Received a cheque from Bear Company for the balance owing on the November 5 sale.
30 Paid Romeo Company the amount owing on the November 1 purchase.

Instructions

Prepare journal entries to record the above transactions for Leeland Company.

TAKING IT FURTHER   Explain why companies should always take advantage of purchase discounts even if they have to borrow from the bank. Refer to the two purchases made by Leeland Company in your answer.

P5–4B   Phantom Book Warehouse distributes hardcover books to retail stores and extends credit terms of n/30 to all of its customers. Phantom uses a perpetual inventory system and at the end of May had an inventory of 230 books purchased at $7 each. During the month of June, the following merchandise transactions occurred:

Record inventory transactions and post to inventory account—perpetual system. (SO 2, 3) AP

June 1 Purchased 170 books on account for $7 each from Reader's World Publishers, terms n/30, FOB destination.
2 The correct company paid $85 freight on the June 1 purchase.
3 Sold 190 books on account to Book Nook for $12 each.
6 Received $70 credit for 10 books returned to Reader's World Publishers.
18 Issued a $48 credit to Book Nook for the return of four damaged books. The books were determined to be no longer saleable and were destroyed.
20 Purchased 140 books on account for $6.50 each from Reader's World Publishers, terms n/30, FOB shipping point.
21 The correct company paid $70 freight for the July 20 purchase.
27 Sold 100 books on account to Readers Bookstore for $12 each.
28 Granted Readers Bookstore a $180 credit for 15 returned books. These books were restored to inventory.
30 Paid Reader's World Publishers for the June 1 purchase.
30 Received the balance owing from Book Nook.

Instructions

(a) Record the transactions for the month of June for Phantom Book Warehouse.
(b) Create a T account for Merchandise Inventory. Post the opening balance and June's transactions, and calculate the June 30 balance.
(c) Determine the number of books on hand at the end of the month and calculate the average cost per book of the inventory on hand at June 30.

TAKING IT FURTHER   Explain how freight terms can affect the selling price, and the cost, of merchandise. Use the transactions on June 1 and 20 between Phantom Book Warehouse and Reader's World Publishers as part of your explanation.

P5–5B   At the beginning of September 2014, Stojanovic Distributing Company's ledger showed Cash $12,500, Merchandise Inventory $7,500, and D. Stojanovic, Capital, $20,000. During the month of September, the company had the following selected transactions:

Record and post inventory transactions—perpetual system. Prepare partial income statement. (SO 2, 3, 5) AP

Sept. 2 Purchased $13,500 of merchandise inventory from Moon Supply Co., terms 1/15, n/30, FOB destination.
4 The correct company paid $325 cash for freight charges on the September 2 purchase.
5 Sold merchandise inventory to Brandon Retailers for $18,000. The cost of the merchandise was $11,310 and the terms were 2/10, n/30, FOB destination.
6 Issued a $1,425 credit for merchandise returned by Brandon Retailers. The merchandise originally cost $890 and was returned to inventory.
6 The correct company paid $420 freight on the September 5 sale.
8 Purchased $900 of supplies for cash.
10 Purchased $6,450 of merchandise inventory from Tina Wholesalers, terms 2/10, n/30, FOB shipping point.
10 The correct company paid $150 freight costs on the purchase from Tina Wholesalers.

12	Received a $450 credit from Tina Wholesalers for returned merchandise.
15	Paid Moon Supply Co. the amount due.
15	Collected the balance owing from Brandon Retailers.
19	Sold merchandise for $10,875 cash. The cost of this merchandise was $6,855.
20	Paid Tina Wholesalers the balance owing from the September 10 purchase.
25	Made a $750 cash refund to a cash customer for merchandise returned. The returned merchandise had a cost of $470. The merchandise was damaged and could not be resold.
30	Sold merchandise to Dragen & Company for $6,420, terms n/30, FOB shipping point. Stojanovic's cost for this merchandise was $4,050.

Instructions

(a) Record the transactions assuming Stojanovic uses a perpetual inventory system.

(b) Set up general ledger accounts for Merchandise Inventory, Sales, Sales Returns and Allowances, Sales Discounts, and Cost of Goods Sold. Enter the beginning merchandise inventory balance, and post the transactions.

(c) Prepare a partial multiple-step income statement, up to gross profit, for the month of September 2014.

TAKING IT FURTHER   Assume that Stojanovic has a "no questions asked" policy in terms of accepting sales returns up to six months after the initial sale. What uncertainties does the company face in terms of calculating its gross profit for September?

Prepare adjusting and closing entries, and single-step and multiple-step income statements—perpetual system. Calculate ratios. (SO 4, 5, 6) AP

P5-6B   Western Lighting Warehouse has a July 31 fiscal year end and uses a perpetual inventory system. An alphabetical list of its account balances at July 31, 2014, follows. All accounts have normal balances.

A. Jamal, capital	$166,500	Interest expense	$ 2,300
A. Jamal, drawings	39,600	Interest revenue	3,000
Accounts payable	7,600	Merchandise inventory	41,250
Accounts receivable	38,900	Note payable	46,000
Accumulated depreciation—equipment	33,400	Notes receivable	75,000
Cash	30,875	Rent expense	62,000
Cost of goods sold	247,500	Salaries expense	45,000
Depreciation expense	8,350	Sales	450,000
Equipment	83,500	Sales discounts	4,500
Freight out	6,055	Sales returns and allowances	11,250
Insurance expense	3,195	Unearned revenue	4,800
Interest payable	575	Utilities expense	12,600

Additional information:

1. All adjustments have been recorded and posted except for the inventory adjustment. According to the inventory count, the company has $40,000 of merchandise on hand.
2. Last year Western Lighting Warehouse had a gross profit margin of 40% and a profit margin of 10%.

Instructions

(a) Prepare any additional required adjusting entries.

(b) Prepare a single-step income statement.

(c) Prepare a multiple-step income statement.

(d) Calculate gross profit margin and profit margin. Compare with last year's margins and comment on the results.

(e) Prepare the closing entries. Post to the Income Summary account. Check that the balance in the Income Summary account before closing it is equal to profit.

TAKING IT FURTHER   Compare the two income statements and comment on the usefulness of each one.

P5–7B The unadjusted trial balance of Global Enterprises for the year ending December 31, 2014, follows:

Prepare adjusting and closing entries and financial statements—perpetual system. Calculate ratios. (SO 4, 5, 6) AP

GLOBAL ENTERPRISES Trial Balance December 31, 2014		
	Debit	Credit
Cash	$ 16,400	
Short-term investments	18,000	
Accounts receivable	15,700	
Merchandise inventory	37,500	
Supplies	1,650	
Furniture	26,800	
Accumulated depreciation—furniture		$ 10,720
Equipment	42,000	
Accumulated depreciation—equipment		8,400
Accounts payable		26,850
Unearned revenue		3,000
Notes payable		35,000
I. Rochefort, capital		45,500
I. Rochefort, drawings	35,500	
Sales		245,000
Sales returns and allowances	6,670	
Sales discounts	2,450	
Cost of goods sold	132,300	
Insurance expense	1,800	
Rent expense	9,300	
Salaries expense	28,400	
	$374,470	$374,470

Additional information:

1. There was $700 of supplies on hand on December 31, 2014.
2. Depreciation expense for the year is $5,360 on the furniture, and $4,200 on the equipment.
3. Accrued interest expense at December 31, 2014, is $1,750.
4. Accrued interest revenue at December 31, 2014, is $720.
5. Of the unearned revenue, $1,600 is still unearned at December 31, 2014. On the sales that were earned, the cost of goods sold was $755.
6. A physical count of merchandise inventory indicates $35,275 on hand on December 31, 2014.
7. Of the note payable, $5,000 is to be paid in 2015.
8. Ingrid Rochefort invested $5,500 cash in the business on May 21, 2014.
9. Last year, the company had a gross profit margin of 40%, and profit margin of 25%.

Instructions

(a) Prepare the adjusting journal entries assuming they are prepared annually.
(b) Prepare a multiple-step income statement, statement of owner's equity, and classified balance sheet.
(c) Prepare the closing entries.
(d) Calculate the gross profit margin and profit margin for 2014. Compare with the 2013 ratios and comment on any trends.

TAKING IT FURTHER Compare the presentation of information in a multiple-step income statement for a service company with one for merchandising company. How would they be similar and how would they be different?

Calculate ratios and comment. (SO 6) AN

P5–8B The following information (in thousands) is for **Danier Leather Inc.**:

	2011	2010	2009
Current assets	$ 59,370	$ 55,241	$ 48,056
Current liabilities	12,495	17,905	10,967
Net sales	157,621	164,217	162,106
Cost of goods sold	71,333	77,438	88,589
Profit (loss)	7,638	7,219	(2,309)

Instructions

(a) Calculate the gross profit margin, profit margin, and current ratio for Danier Leather for 2011, 2010, and 2009.
(b) Comment on whether the ratios have improved or deteriorated over the three years.

TAKING IT FURTHER What other information would be useful when evaluating these ratios over the three-year period?

Record inventory transactions—periodic system. (SO 7) AP

*P5–9B Data for Leeland Company are presented in P5–3B.

Instructions

Record the October and November transactions for Leeland Company, assuming a periodic inventory system is used instead of a perpetual inventory system.

TAKING IT FURTHER Why might a periodic system be better than a perpetual system for Leeland Company?

Record inventory transactions—periodic system. (SO 7) AP

*P5–10B Data for Phantom Book Warehouse are presented in P5–4B.

Instructions

Record the June transactions for Phantom Book Warehouse, assuming a periodic inventory system is used instead of a perpetual inventory system.

TAKING IT FURTHER What are the costs and benefits for Phantom Book Warehouse of using a perpetual, as opposed to a periodic, inventory system?

Prepare financial statements and closing entries—periodic system. (SO 7) AP

*P5–11B Data for Stojanovic Distributing Company are presented in P5–5B. A physical inventory count shows the company has $5,570 of inventory on hand at September 30, 2014.

Instructions

(a) Record the transactions assuming Stojanovic Distributing Company uses a periodic inventory system.
(b) Set up general ledger accounts for merchandise inventory and all of the temporary accounts used in the merchandising transactions. Enter beginning balances, and post the transactions.
(c) Prepare a partial multiple-step income statement, up to gross profit, for the month of September 2014.

TAKING IT FURTHER Will Stojanovic Distributing Company's gross profit be higher, lower, or the same amount, if it uses a periodic inventory system instead of a perpetual inventory system? Explain.

*P5–12B   Up North Company recently hired a new accountant whose first task was to prepare the financial statements for the year ended December 31, 2014. The following is what she produced:

Prepare correct multiple-step income statement, statement of owner's equity, and classified balance sheet—periodic system. (SO 7) AP

UP NORTH COMPANY
Income Statement
December 31, 2014

Sales			$474,000
Less: Unearned revenue		$ 6,600	
Purchase discounts		4,175	10,775
Total revenue			463,225
Cost of goods sold			
Purchases		$278,400	
Less: Purchase returns and allowances		4,800	
Net purchases		283,200	
Add: Sales returns and allowances		9,000	
Cost of goods available for sale		292,200	
Add: Freight out		11,400	
Cost of selling merchandise			303,600
Gross profit margin			159,625
Operating expenses			
Freight in		$ 5,400	
Insurance expense		12,600	
Interest expense		3,000	
Rent expense		21,600	
Salaries expense		50,400	
Total operating expenses			93,000
Profit margin			66,625
Other revenues			
Interest revenue	$ 1,800		
Investment by owner	4,200	6,000	
Other expenses			
Depreciation expense	8,400		
Drawings by owner	57,600	66,000	(60,000)
Profit from operations			$ 6,625

UP NORTH COMPANY
Balance Sheet
Year Ended December 31, 2014

Assets

Cash		$ 20,135
Accounts receivable		9,360
Merchandise inventory, January 1, 2014		36,000
Merchandise inventory, December 31, 2014		28,800
Equipment	$84,000	
Less: loan payable (for equipment purchase)	60,000	24,000
Total assets		$118,295

Liabilities and Owner's Equity

Long-term debt investment		$ 60,000
Accumulated depreciation—equipment		25,200
Sales discounts		3,480
Total liabilities		88,680
Owner's equity		29,615
Total liabilities and owner's equity		$118,295

The owner of the company, James Prideaux, is confused by the statements and has asked you for your help. He doesn't understand how, if his owner's capital account was $90,000 at December 31, 2013, owner's equity is now only $29,615. The accountant tells you that $29,615 must be correct because the balance sheet is balanced. The accountant also tells you that she didn't prepare a statement of owner's equity because it is an optional statement. You are relieved to find out that, even though there are errors in the statements, the amounts used from the accounts in the general ledger are the correct amounts.

Instructions

Prepare the correct multiple-step income statement, statement of owner's equity, and classified balance sheet. You determine that $6,000 of the loan payable on the equipment must be paid during 2015.

TAKING IT FURTHER   Why do we not include both the beginning and the ending merchandise inventory amounts on the balance sheet?

Prepare financial statements and closing entries—periodic system. (SO 7) AP

*P5–13B   The following is an alphabetical list of Tse's Tater Tots' adjusted account balances at the end of the company's fiscal year on December 31, 2014:

Accounts payable	$ 86,300	Interest revenue	$ 1,050
Accounts receivable	44,200	Land	75,000
Accumulated depreciation—building	51,800	Merchandise inventory	40,500
Accumulated depreciation—equipment	42,900	Mortgage payable	155,000
Building	190,000	Property tax expense	4,800
Cash	17,000	Purchases	441,600
Depreciation expense	23,400	Purchase discounts	8,830
Equipment	110,000	Purchase returns and allowances	20,070
Freight in	5,600	Salaries expense	127,500
Freight out	7,500	Salaries payable	3,500
H. Tse, capital	143,600	Sales	642,800
H. Tse, drawings	14,450	Sales discounts	12,700
Insurance expense	9,600	Sales returns and allowances	11,900
Interest expense	11,345	Unearned revenue	8,300
Interest payable	945	Utilities expense	18,000

Additional information:

1. Tse's Tater Tots uses a periodic inventory system.
2. A physical inventory count determined that merchandise inventory on December 31, 2014, was $34,600.
3. Of the mortgage payable, $17,000 is to be paid during the next year.

Instructions

(a) Prepare a multiple-step income statement, a statement of owner's equity, and a classified balance sheet.
(b) Prepare the closing journal entries.
(c) Post the closing entries to the inventory and capital accounts. Check that the balances in these accounts are the same as the amounts on the balance sheet.

TAKING IT FURTHER   If you had not been told that Tse's Tater Tots uses a periodic inventory system, how could you have determined that? What information is available in a periodic inventory system that is not available in a perpetual inventory system?

▶ Continuing Cookie Chronicle

(*Note:* This is a continuation of the Cookie Chronicle from Chapters 1 through 4. From the information gathered in the previous chapters, follow the instructions below using the ledger account balances from Chapter 4.)

Because Natalie has had such a successful first few months, she is considering other opportunities to develop her business. One opportunity is the sale of fine European mixers. The owner of Kzinski Supply Co. has approached Natalie to become the exclusive Canadian distributor of these fine mixers. The current cost of a mixer is approximately $525 Canadian, and Natalie would sell each one for $1,050. Natalie comes to you for advice on how to account for these mixers. Each appliance has a serial number and can be easily identified.

Natalie asks you the following questions:

1. "Would you consider these mixers to be inventory? Or should they be classified as supplies or equipment?"
2. "I've learned a little about keeping track of inventory using both the perpetual and the periodic systems of accounting for inventory. Which system do you think is better? Which one would you recommend for the type of inventory that I want to sell?"
3. "How often do I need to count inventory if I maintain it using the perpetual system? Do I need to count inventory at all?"

   In the end, Natalie decides to use the perpetual inventory system. The following transactions happen during the month of January 2014:

Jan. 6   Purchased and received three deluxe mixers on account from Kzinski Supply Co. for $1,575, FOB shipping point, terms n/30.
  7   Paid $60 freight on the January 6 purchase.
  8   Returned one of the mixers to Kzinski because it was damaged during shipping. Kzinski issued Cookie Creations a credit note for the cost of the mixer plus $20 for the cost of freight that was paid on January 6 for one mixer.
  9   Collected $500 of the accounts receivable from December 2013.
  13   Two deluxe mixers were sold on account for $2,100, FOB destination, terms n/30. The mixers were sold to Koebel's Family Bakery, the bakery that is owned and operated by Natalie's mom and dad. Natalie expects that the mixers will be paid for in early February.
  14   Paid the $75 of delivery charges for the two mixers that were sold on January 13.
  14   Purchased and received four deluxe mixers on account from Kzinski Supply Co. for $2,100, FOB shipping point, terms n/30.
  15   Received a deposit of $125 from another school in Natalie's area to teach a class during the month of February.
  20   Natalie was concerned that there was not enough cash available to pay for all of the mixers purchased. She invested an additional $1,000 cash in Cookie Creations.
  21   Paid $80 freight on the January 14 purchase.
  21   Sold two deluxe mixers for $2,100 cash.
  28   Natalie issued a cheque to her assistant for all the help the assistant has given her during the month. Her assistant worked 20 hours in January and was also paid the $48 owing at December 31, 2013. (Natalie's assistant earns $12 an hour.)
  29   Paid a $154 cell phone bill ($76 for the December 2013 account payable and $78 for the month of January). (Recall that the cell phone is only used for business purposes.)
  29   Paid Kzinski all amounts due.

As at January 31, the following adjusting entry data are available:

1. A count of baking supplies reveals that none were used in January.
2. Another month's worth of depreciation needs to be recorded on the baking equipment bought in November and December. (Recall that the equipment cost $1,550 and has a useful life of three years or 36 months.)
3. An additional month's worth of interest on her grandmother's loan needs to be accrued. (Recall that Cookie Creations borrowed $3,000 and the interest rate is 3%.)
4. An analysis of the unearned revenue account reveals that no lessons have been taught during the month of January. As a result, the opening balance in Unearned Revenue is still unearned. Natalie has been in contact with the schools that have provided deposits and lessons have been booked for early February.
5. An inventory count of mixers at the end of January reveals that Natalie has two mixers remaining.

Instructions

Using the information from previous chapters and the new information above, do the following:

(a) Answer Natalie's questions.
(b) Prepare and post the January 2014 transactions.
(c) Prepare a trial balance.
(d) Prepare and post the adjusting journal entries required.
(e) Prepare an adjusted trial balance.
(f) Prepare a multiple-step income statement for the month ended January 31, 2014.
(g) Calculate gross profit margin and profit margin.

Cumulative Coverage—Chapters 2 to 5

The Board Shop, owned by Andrew John, sells skateboards in the summer and snowboards in the winter. The shop has an August 31 fiscal year end and uses a perpetual inventory system. On August 1, 2014, the company had the following balances in its general ledger:

Cash	$21,385	A. John, drawings	$ 52,800
Merchandise inventory	64,125	Sales	485,500
Supplies	3,750	Rent revenue	1,200
Equipment	70,800	Sales returns and allowances	11,420
Accumulated depreciation—equipment	13,275	Cost of goods sold	301,010
Accounts payable	12,650	Salaries expense	68,200
Unearned revenue	4,680	Rent expense	18,150
Notes payable	42,000	Insurance expense	4,140
A. John, capital	58,400	Interest expense	1,925

During August, the last month of the fiscal year, the company had the following transactions:

Aug. 1 Paid $1,650 for August's rent.
   2 Paid $6,500 on account.
   4 Sold merchandise costing $7,900 for $12,260 cash.
   5 Purchased merchandise on account from Orange Line Co., FOB shipping point, for $24,500.
   5 Paid freight charges of $500 on merchandise purchased from Orange Line Co.
   8 Purchased supplies on account for $345.
   9 Refunded a customer $425 cash for returned merchandise. The merchandise had cost $265 and was returned to inventory.
   10 Sold merchandise on account to Spider Company for $15,750, terms 2/10, n/30, FOB shipping point. The merchandise had a cost of $9,765.
   11 Paid Orange Line Co. for half of the merchandise purchased on August 5.
   12 Spider Company returned $750 of the merchandise it purchased. Board Shop issued Spider a credit memo. The merchandise had a cost of $465 and was returned to inventory.
   15 Paid salaries, $3,100.
   19 Spider Company paid the amount owing.
   21 Purchased $9,900 of merchandise from Rainbow Option Co. on account, terms 2/10, n/30, FOB destination.
   23 Returned $800 of the merchandise to Rainbow Option Co. and received a credit memo.
   24 Received $525 cash in advance from customers for merchandise to be delivered in September.
   30 Paid salaries, $3,100.
   30 Paid Rainbow Option Co. the amount owing.
   31 Andrew John withdrew $4,800 cash.

Adjustment and additional data:

1. A count of supplies on August 31 shows $755 on hand.
2. The equipment has an estimated eight-year useful life.
3. Of the notes payable, $6,000 must be paid on September 1 each year.
4. An analysis of the Unearned Revenue account shows that $3,750 has been earned by August 31. A corresponding $2,325 for Cost of Goods Sold will also need to be recorded for these sales.
5. Interest accrued on the note payable to August 31 was $175.
6. A count of the merchandise inventory on August 31 shows $76,560 of inventory on hand.

Instructions

(a) Create a general ledger account for each of the above accounts and enter the August 1 balances.
(b) Record and post the August transactions.
(c) Prepare a trial balance at August 31, 2014.
(d) Record and post the adjustments required at August 31, 2014.
(e) Prepare an adjusted trial balance at August 31, 2014.
(f) Prepare a multiple-step income statement, statement of owner's equity, and classified balance sheet.
(g) Record and post closing entries.
(h) Prepare a post-closing trial balance at August 31, 2014.

BROADENING YOUR PERSPECTIVE | CHAPTER 5

⏵ Financial Reporting and Analysis

Financial Reporting Problem

BYP5–1   The financial statements for Reitmans (Canada) Limited are reproduced in Appendix A at the end of this text.

Instructions

(a) Is Reitmans a service company or a merchandising company?

(b) Reitmans does not disclose in its financial statements or notes if it uses a periodic or perpetual inventory system. Why do you think that readers of the financial statements do not need to know that information? What inventory system do you think it uses and why?

(c) Does Reitmans use a single-step or multiple-step income statement format?

(d) What non-operating revenues and non-operating expenses are included in Reitmans' income statement?

(e) Does Reitmans show the amount of sales returns? Why do you think it does this?

(f) Read the parts of Note 2 (d) and Note 3 (l) related to sales returns. Why do you think Reitmans needs to record estimated possible returns? Is it appropriate to use an estimate in financial statements?

(g) Also read Note 12. What is Reitmans' estimated amount of sales returns at January 28, 2012? What journal entry do you think the company used to record that amount?

(h) Read Note 3 (h). How does Reitmans account for the cost of freight on purchases of inventory? Is this consistent with what you learned in this chapter?

Interpreting Financial Statements

BYP5–2   Selected information from **Big Rock Brewery Inc.**'s income statements for three recent years follows (in thousands):

	2011	2010	2009
Net revenue	$45,183	$ 45,130	$46,232
Cost of goods sold	21,385	20,735	20,216
Operating expense	20,455	20,262	19,180
Non-operating income (expenses)	147	(12,989)	304
Income tax expense (recovery)	957	(658)	(289)

Instructions

(a) Calculate gross profit, profit from operations, and profit for each of the three years.

(b) Calculate the percentage change in net revenue and profit from operations, from 2009 to 2011.

(c) Calculate the gross profit margin for each of the three years. Comment on any trend in this percentage.

(d) Calculate the profit margin for each of the three years. Comment on any trend in this percentage.

(e) Calculate profit margin again using profit from operations instead of profit. Comment on any trend in this percentage.

(f) In Big Rock Brewery's 2011 annual report management states that they believe profit from operations is a more meaningful basis of comparison than profit. Based on your findings in (d) and (e) above, do you agree or disagree with this statement? Explain.

⏵ Critical Thinking

Collaborative Learning Activity

Note to instructor: Additional instructions and material for this group activity can be found on the Instructor Resource Site and in *WileyPLUS*.

BYP5–3   The purpose of this group activity is to improve your understanding of merchandising journal entries. You will be given a merchandising company's general ledger in T account format with missing transaction data. With your group you will analyze these T accounts to determine the underlying journal entries and balance the general ledger.

Communication Activity

BYP5–4   Consider the following events listed in chronological order:

1. Dexter Maersk decides to buy a custom-made snowboard. He calls Great Canadian Snowboards and asks it to manufacture one for him.
2. The company e-mails Dexter a purchase order to fill out, which he immediately completes, signs, and sends back with the required 25% down payment.
3. Great Canadian Snowboards receives Dexter's purchase order and down payment, and begins working on the board.
4. Great Canadian Snowboards has its fiscal year end. At this time, Dexter's board is 75% completed.
5. The company completes the snowboard for Dexter and notifies him.
6. Dexter picks up his snowboard from the company and takes it home.
7. Dexter tries the snowboard out and likes it so much that he carves his initials in it.
8. Great Canadian Snowboards bills Dexter for the cost of the snowboard, less the 25% down payment.
9. The company receives partial payment (another 25%) from Dexter.
10. The company receives payment of the balance due from Dexter.

Instructions

In a memo to the president of Great Canadian Snowboards, answer these questions:

(a) When should Great Canadian Snowboards record the revenue and cost of goods sold related to the snowboard? Refer to the revenue and expense recognition criteria in your answer.
(b) Suppose that, with his purchase order, Dexter was required to pay for 100% of the board. Would that change your answer to part (a)?

Ethics Case

BYP5–5   Rita Pelzer was just hired as the assistant controller of Liu Stores. The company is a specialty chain store with nine retail stores concentrated in one metropolitan area. Among other things, the payment of all invoices is centralized in one of the departments Rita will manage. Her main responsibilities are to maintain the company's high credit rating by paying all bills when they are due and to take advantage of all cash discounts.

Jamie Caterino, the former assistant controller, who has now been promoted to controller, is training Rita in her new duties. He instructs Rita to continue the practice of preparing all cheques for the amount due less the discount and to date the cheques the last day of the discount period. "But," Jamie continues, "we always hold the cheques at least four days beyond the discount period before mailing them. That way we get another four days of interest on our money. Most of our creditors need our business and don't complain. And, if they scream about our missing the discount period, we blame it on Canada Post. I think everybody does it. By the way, welcome to our team!"

Instructions

(a) What are the ethical considerations in this case?
(b) Which stakeholders are harmed or benefited?
(c) Should Rita continue the practice started by Jamie? Does she have any choice?

"All About You" Activity

BYP5–6   In the "All About You" feature, you learned about inventory theft and a relatively new technology to help prevent theft. You have recently accepted a part-time sales position at a clothing store called College Fashions. The owner-manager of the store knows that you are enrolled in a business program and seeks your advice on preventing inventory shrinkage due to theft. The owner-manager is aware that the industry average shrinkage rates are 1.49% of revenues but does not know College Fashions' shrinkage rate.

Instructions

(a) Assume the store uses a perpetual inventory system. Explain to the owner-manager how she can determine the amount of inventory shrinkage.
(b) The owner-manager wants to know if she should implement some type of technology to prevent theft. What would you advise her to consider before making an expenditure on technology to prevent theft?
(c) Assume that College Fashions' sales revenues are $400,000 and the shrinkage rate is 4%. What is the dollar amount that College Fashions loses due to shrinkage?
(d) Some believe that great customer service is the best defence against shoplifting. Discuss why great customer service may help prevent shoplifting.

(e) You also learned in the All About You feature that employee inventory theft is a significant problem. What procedures might management implement to prevent or reduce employee theft of inventory?

(f) In your part-time sales position, you have observed a fellow employee that you are friendly with provide unauthorized sales discounts to her friends when they purchase merchandise from the store. Is it appropriate for this employee to give her friend unauthorized sales discounts? Explain. What might be a consequence for you as an employee if you fail to inform management of these unauthorized sales discounts?

ANSWERS TO CHAPTER QUESTIONS

ANSWERS TO ACCOUNTING IN ACTION INSIGHT QUESTIONS

Business Insight, p. 246

Q: What accounting information would help a manager decide what to do with returned goods?

A: The manager would need to know the potential revenues and expenses for each alternative. For example, returning goods to stock and selling them again may provide the highest revenue but the cost of getting the goods ready for resale may also be high. The revenue earned from liquidating the returned goods may be much lower but the cost of doing this may also be very low. The manager should compare the estimated profit—not just the revenue earned—of each alternative when deciding what to do.

All About You Insight, p. 249

Q: Are there advantages to you as a customer when retailers increase theft prevention measures?

A: Many customers see theft prevention measures, such as locked fitting rooms, or having a store employee track the items they are taking into a fitting room, as a very annoying personal inconvenience. But there are benefits to the customers as well as the stores. Retailers have to be able to pass all of their costs on to customers in order to remain in business. When inventory theft increases, the selling price will also have to increase or the store will not be profitable. If customers are not willing to pay the increased prices, then the store may have to go out of business, resulting in less choice for consumers and fewer jobs. Inconveniences in using the fitting rooms may be a far smaller price to pay than the alternatives.

ANSWERS TO SELF-STUDY QUESTIONS

1. b   2. d   3. a   4. a   5. b   6. c   7. a   8. c   9. d   10. c   *11. a   *12. b

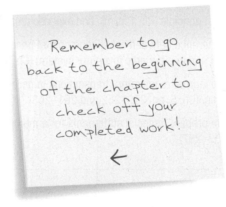

INVENTORY COSTING

 THE **NAVIGATOR**

- ☐ Understand *Concepts for Review*
- ☐ Read *Feature Story*
- ☐ Scan *Study Objectives*
- ☐ Read *Chapter Preview*
- ☐ Read text and answer *Before You Go On*
- ☐ Review *Comparing IFRS and ASPE*
- ☐ Work *Demonstration Problems*
- ☐ Review *Summary of Study Objectives*
- ☐ Answer *Self-Study Questions*
- ☐ Complete assignments
- ☐ Go to *WileyPLUS* for practice and tutorials

CONCEPTS FOR **REVIEW**

Before studying this chapter, you should understand or, if necessary, review:

a. The cost principle (Ch. 1, p. 16) and expense recognition criteria (Ch. 3, p. 114).

b. The difference between calculating cost of goods sold in a perpetual inventory system and in a periodic inventory system. (Ch. 5, pp. 245–248 and 261–263)

c. How to journalize inventory transactions in perpetual and periodic inventory systems. (Ch. 5, pp. 239–252 and 261–263)

d. How to prepare financial statements for a merchandising company. (Ch. 5, pp. 253–257)

COUNTING INVENTORY IS NOT A "SHOE"-IN

EDMONTON, AB.—With between 150 and 200 brands and more than 73,000 stock-keeping units (SKUs), counting inventory at gravitypope is an intensive process. The women's and men's footwear and clothing retailer does a physical count of all inventory once a year, close to its fiscal year end, with smaller counts throughout the year of pricier items.

"We have a lot of inventory to deal with," says CEO and founder Louise Dirks, who started with a shoe store in 1990 in Edmonton's trendy Whyte Avenue neighbourhood and now has three shoe stores and two gravitypope Tailored Goods clothing stores in Edmonton, Vancouver, and Calgary. "If you see something on the shelf, we've got anywhere from 8 to 30 units of it in the back."

Over approximately a three-week period, inventory is counted in each of the stores, its two warehouses, and the third floor of the Edmonton shoe store that coordinates sales from its website. The counts are generally done after the stores close, and the inventory records are "frozen" before the count starts—no sales can take place during inventory counting so that the counts are accurate.

Each location is divided into batches of between 40 and 60 items. A team of three employees does the count of each batch. "I like to hold my people accountable and it's also much easier having employees do inventory because they know best where the product is located," Ms. Dirks says in explaining why she doesn't use a third party to count inventory. Employees use por-

table data transmitter (PDT) guns to scan the barcode of each item, while two other independent manual counts are done to ensure an unbiased count. When their counts all match, the team moves on to the next batch. If the counts don't match, they can quickly see where they went wrong. This is the reason that inventory is divided into small quantities. Sometimes it's a simple error of scanning a barcode incorrectly, Ms. Dirks says.

The data from the PDT guns are uploaded to and compared with the stores' point-of-sale (POS) system, which allows for a perpetual inventory system. Any discrepancies between the PDT and POS data are investigated. Sometimes a clerk may have sold an item under the wrong SKU or an inventory counter scanned the wrong barcode. If an item genuinely cannot be accounted for, it's written off with a journal entry as shrinkage due to loss or theft, says Ms. Dirks.

Gravitypope uses the first-in, first-out method to determine the cost of its inventory and calculate its cost of goods sold. For items that remain past a season, the company writes them down to their net realizable value. Because it imports more than half of its goods, the retailer's cost of goods sold includes the exchange rate for foreign currencies it uses to buy items, usually euros, British pounds, U.S. dollars, and Japanese yen—all part of selling fashions from around the globe.

THE **NAVIGATOR**

≫ STUDY **OBJECTIVES**

After studying this chapter, you should be able to:

1. Describe the steps in determining inventory quantities.

2. Calculate cost of goods sold and ending inventory in a perpetual inventory system using the specific identification, FIFO, and average methods of cost determination.

3. Explain the financial statement effects of inventory cost determination methods.

4. Determine the financial statement effects of inventory errors.

5. Value inventory at the lower of cost and net realizable value.

6. Demonstrate the presentation and analysis of inventory.

7. Calculate ending inventory and cost of goods sold in a periodic inventory system using FIFO and average inventory cost formulas (Appendix 6A).

8. Estimate ending inventory using the gross profit and retail inventory methods (Appendix 6B).

THE **NAVIGATOR**

In the previous chapter, we discussed accounting for merchandise transactions. In this chapter, we first explain the procedures for determining inventory quantities. We then discuss the three methods for determining the cost of goods sold and the cost of inventory on hand: the specific identification method and the two cost formulas, FIFO and average. Next we see the effects of cost determination methods and inventory errors on a company's financial statements. We end by illustrating methods of reporting and analyzing inventory.

The chapter is organized as follows:

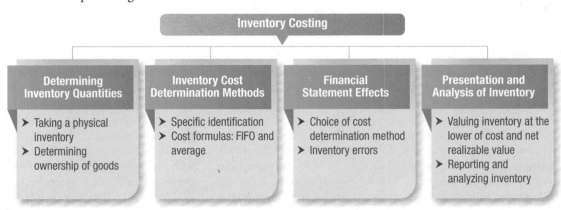

Determining Inventory Quantities

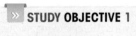

STUDY OBJECTIVE 1

Describe the steps in determining inventory quantities.

Companies count their entire inventory at least once a year, whether they are using a perpetual or a periodic inventory system. This is called taking a physical inventory. If they are using a perpetual system, like gravitypope in our feature story, they will use this information to check the accuracy of their perpetual inventory records. As we saw in Chapter 5, in a perpetual inventory system, the accounting records continuously—perpetually—show the amount of inventory that should be on hand, not necessarily the amount that actually is on hand. An adjusting entry is required if the physical inventory count does not match what was recorded in the general ledger.

In a periodic inventory system, inventory quantities are not continuously updated. Companies using a periodic inventory system must take a physical inventory to determine the amount on hand at the end of the accounting period. Once the ending inventory amount is known, this amount is then used to calculate the cost of goods sold for the period and to update the Merchandise Inventory account in the general ledger.

Inventory quantities are determined in two steps: (1) by taking a physical inventory of goods on hand, and (2) by determining the ownership of goods.

TAKING A PHYSICAL INVENTORY

Taking a physical inventory involves actually counting, weighing, or measuring each kind of inventory on hand. Taking a physical inventory can be an enormous task for many companies, especially for retail stores such as gravitypope, which has thousands of inventory items. An inventory count is generally more accurate when goods are not being sold or received during the counting. This is why companies often count their inventory when they are closed or when business is slow.

To make fewer errors in taking the inventory, a company should ensure that it has a good system of internal control. Internal control is the process designed and implemented by management to help the company achieve reliable financial reporting, effective and efficient operations, and compliance with relevant laws and regulations. Some of the internal control procedures for counting inventory are as follows:

1. The counting should be done by employees who are not responsible for either custody of the inventory or keeping inventory records.
2. Each counter should establish that each inventory item actually exists, how many there are of it, and what condition each item is in. For example, does each box actually contain what it is supposed to contain?

3. There should be a second count by another employee or auditor. Counting should be done in teams of two.
4. Prenumbered inventory tags should be used to ensure that all inventory items are counted and that no items are counted more than once.

In our feature story, we saw how gravitypope incorporates many of these controls into its inventory count. We will learn more about internal controls in Chapter 7.

After the physical inventory is taken, the quantity of each kind of inventory item is listed on inventory summary sheets. The second count by another employee or auditor helps ensure the count is accurate. Unit costs are then applied to the quantities in order to determine the total cost of the inventory; this will be explained later in the chapter, when we discuss inventory costing.

DETERMINING OWNERSHIP OF GOODS

When we take a physical inventory, we need to consider the ownership of goods. To determine ownership of the goods, two questions need to be answered: Do all of the goods included in the count belong to the company? Does the company own any goods that were not included in the count?

Goods in Transit

A complication in determining ownership is goods in transit (on board a public carrier such as a railway, airline, truck, or ship) at the end of the accounting period. The problem is determining which company should include the goods in its inventory: the purchaser or the seller.

Goods in transit should be included in the inventory of the company that has ownership (legal title) of the goods. We learned in Chapter 5 that ownership is determined by the terms of sale, as shown in Illustration 6-1 and described below:

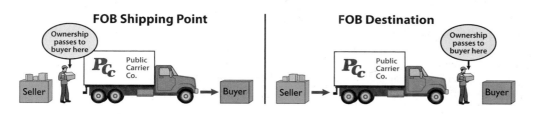

▶ **ILLUSTRATION 6-1**
Terms of sale

1. When the terms are FOB (free on board) shipping point, ownership (legal title) of the goods passes to the buyer when the public carrier accepts the goods from the seller.
2. When the terms are FOB destination, ownership (legal title) of the goods remains with the seller until the goods reach the buyer.

Inventory quantities may be seriously miscounted if goods in transit at the statement date are ignored. The company may have purchased goods that have not yet been received, or it may have sold goods that have not yet been delivered. For example, assume that Hill Company has 20,000 units of inventory in its warehouse on December 31. It also has the following goods in transit on December 31:

1. sales of 1,500 units shipped December 31, FOB destination, and,
2. purchases of 2,500 units shipped FOB shipping point by the seller on December 31.

Hill has legal title to both the units sold and the units purchased. If units in transit are ignored, inventory quantities would be understated by 4,000 units (1,500 + 2,500).

As we will see later in this chapter, inaccurate inventory quantities not only affect the inventory amount on the balance sheet, they also affect the cost of goods sold reported in the income statement.

Consigned Goods

For some businesses, it is customary to hold goods belonging to other parties and to sell them, for a fee, without ever taking ownership of the goods. These are called **consigned goods**.

For example, artists often display their paintings and other works of art on consignment at galleries. In such cases, the art gallery (the consignee) does not take ownership of the art—it still belongs to the artist (the consignor). Therefore, if an inventory count is taken, any art on consignment should not be included in the art gallery's inventory.

When a consigned good sells, the consignee then takes a commission and pays the consignor the remainder. Many craft stores, second-hand clothing and sporting goods stores, and antique dealers sell goods on consignment to keep their inventory costs down and to avoid the risk of purchasing an item they will not be able to sell.

Other Situations

Sometimes goods are not physically present at a company because they have been taken home *on approval* by a customer. Goods on approval should be added to the physical inventory count because they still belong to the seller. The customer will either return the item or decide to buy it.

In other cases, goods are sold but the seller is holding them for alteration, or until they are picked up or delivered to the customer. These goods should not be included in the physical count, because legal title to ownership has passed to the customer. Damaged or unsaleable goods should be separated from the physical count and any loss should be recorded.

ACCOUNTING IN ACTION
ALL ABOUT YOU INSIGHT

Have you ever shopped in or sold some things at a consignment store? Many students buy and sell second-hand items such as clothing and furniture to save money and help the environment. That popularity has spread throughout the general Canadian population as the economy softened. In Vancouver, for example, consignment sales rose an estimated 25% in 2011. Shoppers are attracted to lower prices for higher-quality goods and making long-term investments in designer and classic items, while sellers want to earn some cash for things they don't use anymore. The Internet has exposed people to designer brands and unique looks that consumers are eager to try out on a budget. For consignment store owners, the business model is attractive, too, because they have virtually no inventory costs. The stores only pay for an item once it's sold. Typically, stores give a commission of about 40% of the sale price to the person who brought in the item. Often, the commission will drop as time passes and the sale price is reduced.

Source: "Consignment Sales Up as Fashionistas Get Frugal," CTV News British Columbia on-line, January 26, 2012; Colin McAllister and Justin Ryan, "Consignment Stores Hold Relics to Relish," *Vancouver Sun*, November 10, 2011; Ed Stoddard and Tim Gaynor, "Second-Hand Retailers Score During Recession," Reuters, *The Globe and Mail*, October 5, 2009.

What is one disadvantage of buying items on consignment?

Action Plan

Apply the rules of ownership to goods held on consignment:

- Goods held on consignment for another company are not included in inventory.
- Goods held on consignment by another company are included in inventory.

Apply the rules of ownership to goods in transit:

 BEFORE YOU GO ON...

Do It

Too Good to Be Threw Company completed its inventory count on June 30. It arrived at a total inventory value of $200,000, counting everything currently on hand in its warehouse. You have been given the information listed below. How will the following information affect the inventory count and cost?

1. Goods costing $15,000 that are being held on consignment for another company were included in the inventory.
2. Goods purchased for $10,000 and in transit at June 30 (terms FOB shipping point) were not included in the count.
3. Inventory sold for $18,000 that cost $12,000 when purchased and was in transit at June 30 (terms FOB destination) was not included in the count.

- FOB shipping point: Goods sold or purchased and shipped FOB shipping point belong to the buyer when in transit.
- FOB destination: Goods sold or purchased and shipped FOB destination belong to the seller until they reach their destination.

Solution

Original count	$200,000
1. Goods held on consignment from another company	(15,000)
2. Goods in transit purchased FOB shipping point	10,000
3. Goods in transit sold FOB destination	12,000
Adjusted count	$207,000

Related exercise material: BE6–1, BE6–2, E6–1, and E6–2.

THE **NAVIGATOR**

Inventory Cost Determination Methods

The physical inventory count we described in the last section determines the quantities on hand, but does not determine their cost. Before comparing with the perpetual inventory records, costs will need to be assigned to the inventory items. In a perpetual inventory system, costs must also be assigned to inventory items when calculating the cost of goods sold each time a sale is recorded.

When all identical inventory items have been purchased at the same unit cost, the calculations are simple. However, when identical items have been purchased at different costs during the period, it is difficult to decide what the unit costs are of the items that have been sold and what the unit costs are of the items that remain in inventory.

In Chapter 5, you did not have this problem because you were either told the cost of goods sold, or it was assumed for simplicity that all identical inventory items had the same unit cost. In Chapter 6, we build on what you learned in Chapter 5. In this chapter, identical items will not be purchased for the same cost and you will have to determine the cost of the goods sold and the cost of the ending inventory.

In the next section, we will examine three methods of determining cost of goods sold and the cost of inventory. One method—specific identification—uses the actual physical flow of goods to determine cost. We will look at this method first.

» **STUDY OBJECTIVE 2**

Calculate cost of goods sold and ending inventory in a perpetual inventory system using the specific identification, FIFO, and average methods of cost determination.

SPECIFIC IDENTIFICATION

The **specific identification** method tracks the actual physical flow (movement) of the goods in a perpetual inventory system. Each item of inventory is marked, tagged, or coded with its specific unit cost so that, at any point in time, the cost of the goods sold and the cost of the ending inventory can be determined.

The specific identification method is used by companies that have unique or different products so that no two products are identical. For example, Demitre's Designs, a jewellery store that sells "one-of-a-kind" rings, would use specific identification. To illustrate, assume that Demitre's Designs had three rings available for sale in January with a total cost of $9,200 ($2,000 + $3,000 + $4,200).

As shown in Illustration 6-2, the cost of the two rings sold is $6,200 ($2,000 + $4,200), and the cost of the ring still on hand at the end of January is $3,000. Therefore, the cost of goods sold on the January income statement is $6,200 and the merchandise inventory on the January 31 balance sheet is $3,000. This determination is possible because it is easy to track the actual physical flow of the goods.

▶ **ILLUSTRATION** 6-2
Specific identification

Price $5,400

Cost: 3,000
FOR SALE

Price $3,600

Cost: 2,000
SOLD

Price $7,000

Cost: 4,200
SOLD

Specific identification **must be** used for goods that are not ordinarily interchangeable, or for goods that are produced for specific projects. In addition to the ring example, it would be used for any other customized products such as furniture and artistic work. Car manufacturers and dealerships also use specific identification for cars as each car has its own unique characteristics and vehicle identification number.

It may seem that specific identification is the ideal method for determining cost because it matches sales with the actual cost of the good sold. But it can be time-consuming and expensive to apply. And if it is used for identical items, then management could manipulate profit by choosing which units to sell. Therefore, it can be used **only** for inventory that is not ordinarily interchangeable.

COST FORMULAS: FIFO AND AVERAGE

Because the specific identification method is only suitable for certain kinds of inventories, other methods of cost determination, known as cost formulas, are used. The two inventory cost formulas used in Canada and internationally are:

1. First-in, first-out (FIFO), where the cost of the first item purchased is considered to be the cost of the first item sold
2. Average, where the cost is determined using an average of the cost of the items purchased

FIFO and average are known as "cost formulas" because they assume a flow of costs that may not be the same as the actual physical flow of goods, unlike the specific identification method.

While specific identification is normally used only in a perpetual inventory system, FIFO and average can be used in both the perpetual and periodic inventory systems. Recall from Chapter 5 that the two systems differ in determining when the cost of goods sold is calculated and recorded.

Under a perpetual inventory system, the cost of goods sold is determined as each item is sold. Under a periodic inventory system, the cost of goods available for sale (beginning inventory plus the cost of goods purchased) is allocated to ending inventory and to cost of goods sold at the end of the period. Recall that in a periodic system, the cost of goods sold is calculated by deducting the ending inventory from the cost of goods available for sale. How to calculate cost of goods sold and ending inventory in a periodic system using the FIFO and average cost formulas is included in Appendix 6A.

To illustrate how the FIFO and average cost formulas are applied, we will assume that Bennett Lighting has the information shown in Illustration 6-3 for one of its products, the Anti-Bug Lightbulb:

▶**ILLUSTRATION 6-3**
Inventory purchases, sales, and units on hand

	BENNETT LIGHTING **Anti-Bug Lightbulb**				
Date	**Explanation**	**Units**	**Unit Cost**	**Total Cost**	**Total Units in Inventory**
Jan. 1	Beginning inventory	100	$10	$ 1,000	100
Apr. 15	Purchase	200	11	2,200	300
May 1	Sales	(150)			150
Aug. 24	Purchase	300	12	3,600	450
Sept. 1	Sales	(400)			50
Nov. 27	Purchase	400	13	5,200	450
				$12,000	

Perpetual Inventory System—First-In, First-Out (FIFO)

The **first-in, first-out (FIFO) cost formula** assumes that the earliest (oldest) goods purchased are the first ones to be sold. This does not necessarily mean that the oldest units are in fact sold first; only that the cost of the oldest units is used first to calculate cost of goods sold. It is used by a variety of companies including gravitypope in our feature story. Although the cost formula chosen by a company does not have to match the actual physical movement of the inventory, it should correspond as closely as possible. FIFO often does match the actual physical flow of merchandise, because it generally is good business practice to sell the oldest units first.

We will use the information for Bennett Lighting's Anti-Bug Lightbulb in Illustration 6-3 to prepare a perpetual inventory schedule with the FIFO cost formula. Perpetual inventory schedules are organized to show how the cost of goods sold for each sale is calculated. They also show the cost and number of units of inventory on hand throughout the year.

A perpetual inventory schedule starts with the inventory on hand at the beginning of the year. Purchases are added and sales are deducted in the schedule in chronological order. Illustration 6-4 shows how to record the beginning inventory of 100 units costing $10 each and the April 15 purchase of 200 units costing $11 each. Notice that the $10 units are shown separately from the $11 units in the balance columns and that the total cost of $3,200 is equal to 100 units × $10/unit + 200 units × $11/unit.

	PURCHASES			COST OF GOODS SOLD			BALANCE		
Date	Units	Cost	Total	Units	Cost	Total	Units	Cost	Total
Jan. 1							100	$10	$1,000
Apr. 15	200	$11	$2,200				100	10	} 3,200
							200	11	

▶ **ILLUSTRATION 6-4**
Perpetual inventory schedule—FIFO (calculation as at April 15)

The next transaction is the May 1 sale of 150 units. Remember that in a perpetual inventory system the cost of the goods sold is calculated every time a sale is made. Therefore, on May 1, we apply FIFO to determine if the 150 units that were sold cost $10, $11, or a mix of both amounts.

Under FIFO, the cost of the oldest goods on hand before the sale is allocated to the cost of goods sold. Accordingly, we start with the beginning inventory of 100 units costing $10 each. Since 150 units were sold on May 1, this means they sold the entire beginning inventory, and 50 of the $11 units. This leaves 150 (200 – 50) of the $11 units on hand after the sale is recorded. In Illustration 6-5, we have added this information to the perpetual inventory schedule started in Illustration 6-4.

	PURCHASES			COST OF GOODS SOLD			BALANCE		
Date	Units	Cost	Total	Units	Cost	Total	Units	Cost	Total
Jan. 1							100	$10	$1,000
Apr. 15	200	$11	$2,200				100	10	} 3,200
							200	11	
May 1				100	$10	} $1,550			
				50	11		150	11	1,650

▶ **ILLUSTRATION 6-5**
Perpetual inventory schedule—FIFO (calculation as at May 1)

After additional purchases are made on August 24, the inventory on hand now consists of 150 units at $11 and 300 units at $12, which totals 450 units at $5,250, as shown in Illustration 6-6.

	PURCHASES			COST OF GOODS SOLD			BALANCE		
Date	Units	Cost	Total	Units	Cost	Total	Units	Cost	Total
Jan. 1							100	$10	$1,000
Apr. 15	200	$11	$2,200				100	10	} 3,200
							200	11	
May 1				100	$10	} $1,550			
				50	11		150	11	1,650
Aug. 24	300	12	3,600				150	11	} 5,250
							300	12	

▶ **ILLUSTRATION 6-6**
Perpetual inventory schedule—FIFO (calculation as at August 24)

On September 1, when 400 units are sold, the cost of goods sold is assumed to consist of the remaining $11 units purchased on April 15 (150 units), and 250 of the $12 units purchased on August 24. This leaves 50 of the $12 units in inventory, or $600 in total.

After a purchase of 400 units on November 27, the inventory consists of 450 units, of which there are 50 of the $12 units from the August 24 purchase and 400 of the $13 units purchased on

November 27. These two transactions are shown in Illustration 6-7, to complete the perpetual inventory schedule started in Illustration 6-4.

▶ ILLUSTRATION 6-7
Perpetual inventory schedule—FIFO (calculation as at November 27)

Date	PURCHASES			COST OF GOODS SOLD			BALANCE		
	Units	Cost	Total	Units	Cost	Total	Units	Cost	Total
Jan. 1							100	$10	$1,000
Apr. 15	200	$11	$2,200				100	10	} 3,200
							200	11	
May 1				100	$10	} $1,550			
				50	11		150	11	1,650
Aug. 24	300	12	3,600				150	11	} 5,250
							300	12	
Sept. 1				150	11	} 4,650			
				250	12		50	12	600
Nov. 27	400	13	5,200				50	12	} 5,800
							400	13	
	900		$11,000	550		$6,200			

Note that beginning inventory is $1,000, total purchases are $11,000, total cost of goods sold is $6,200, and ending inventory is $5,800. These numbers can be used to check the calculations in the perpetual inventory schedule. Remember that beginning inventory plus purchases minus cost of goods sold equals ending inventory. In this case, we see that the schedule is balanced because $1,000 + $11,000 − $6,200 = $5,800.

Perpetual Inventory System—Average

The **average cost formula** recognizes that it is not possible to measure a specific physical flow of inventory when the goods available for sale are homogeneous and non-distinguishable. It is used by a variety of companies including gravitypope in our feature story to calculate the cost of goods sold for items that remain past a season. Under this cost formula, the allocation of the cost of goods available for sale is based on the weighted average unit cost. The formula of the **weighted average unit cost** is presented in Illustration 6-8.

▶ ILLUSTRATION 6-8
Calculation of weighted average unit cost

Cost of Goods Available for Sale ÷ Total Units Available for Sale = Weighted Average Unit Cost

Note that the weighted average unit cost is **not** calculated by taking a simple average of the costs of each purchase. Rather, it is calculated by weighting the quantities purchased at each unit cost. This is done by dividing the cost of goods available for sale by the units available for sale at the date of each purchase.

We will again use the information for Bennett Lighting's Anti-Bug Lightbulb, in Illustration 6-3, to prepare a perpetual inventory schedule with the average cost formula so you can compare the similarities and differences between the average and FIFO methods. In Illustration 6-9, notice that the beginning inventory of $1,000 and the April 15 purchase of $2,200 are combined to show a total cost of goods available for sale of $3,200 and that the 100 units in beginning inventory and the 200 units purchased on April 15 are combined to show a total of 300 units. Using the formula in Illustration 6-8, the weighted average unit cost on April 15 is $10.67 per unit ($3,200 ÷ 300).

▶ ILLUSTRATION 6-9
Perpetual inventory schedule—average (calculation as at April 15)

Date	PURCHASES			COST OF GOODS SOLD			BALANCE		
	Units	Cost	Total	Units	Cost	Total	Units	Cost	Total
Jan. 1							100	$10.00	$1,000.00
Apr. 15	200	$11.00	$2,200.00				300	**10.67**	3,200.00

On May 1, the cost of goods sold is calculated using the $10.67 weighted average unit cost. The cost of the remaining 150 units of inventory on hand is also calculated using the same unit cost.

On August 24, when 300 units costing $12 each are purchased, it is necessary to calculate a new weighted average unit cost. After adding the total cost of the August 24 purchase to the May 1 ending balance, the total cost of the goods available for sale is $5,200 ($3,600 + $1,600). There are 450 total units available for sale, calculated by adding the 300 units purchased on August 24 to the 150 units in inventory. The new weighted average unit cost is $11.56 ($5,200 ÷ 450).

These two transactions have been added to the perpetual inventory schedule as shown in Illustration 6-10.

	PURCHASES			COST OF GOODS SOLD			BALANCE		
Date	Units	Cost	Total	Units	Cost	Total	Units	Cost	Total
Jan. 1							100	$10.00	$1,000.00
Apr. 15	200	$11.00	$2,200.00				300	10.67	3,200.00
May 1				150	$10.67	$1,600.00	150	10.67	1,600.00
Aug. 24	300	12.00	3,600.00				450	11.56	5,200.00

▶ILLUSTRATION 6-10
Perpetual inventory schedule—average (calculation as at August 24)

Notice that the May 1 sale did not change the average unit cost. But the August 24 purchase did change the average unit cost. This pattern is repeated with the September 1 sale and the November 27 purchase. The cost of goods sold and ending inventory on September 1 are calculated using the $11.56 average unit cost calculated on August 24. On November 27, after purchasing 400 units at $13 each, a new weighted average unit cost of $12.84 is determined ($5,777.88 ÷ 450). The August 24 and November 27 transactions are shown in Illustration 6-11, to complete the perpetual inventory schedule started in Illustration 6-9.

Helpful hint The weighted average cost per unit almost always changes when the company purchases more units. It never changes when the company sells units.

	PURCHASES			COST OF GOODS SOLD			BALANCE		
Date	Units	Cost	Total	Units	Cost	Total	Units	Cost	Total
Jan. 1							100	$10.00	$1,000.00
Apr. 15	200	$11.00	$ 2,200,00				300	10.67	3,200.00
May 1				150	$10.67	$1,600.00	150	10.67	1,600.00
Aug. 24	300	12.00	3,600.00				450	11.56	5,200.00
Sept. 1				400	11.56	4,622.22	50	11.56	577.78
Nov. 27	400	13.00	5,200.00				450	12.84	5,777.78
	900		$11,000.00	550		$6,222.22			

▶ILLUSTRATION 6-11
Perpetual inventory schedule—average (calculation as at November 27)

As with FIFO, it is important to check that beginning inventory + purchases − cost of goods sold = ending inventory. Once again we can see that the perpetual inventory schedule is balanced because $1,000.00 + $11,000.00 − $6,222.22 = $5,777.78.

In practice, these average unit costs may be rounded to the nearest cent, or even to the nearest dollar. In the calculations in Illustrations 6-9 to 6-11, the exact unit cost amounts were used, along with a computerized schedule. But for presentation purposes, the unit costs have been rounded to the nearest two digits. However, it is important to remember that this is a method of allocating costs and not a method to track actual costs. Using four digits, or even cents, may suggest a false level of accuracy but it will reduce rounding errors in the perpetual inventory schedules.

In summary, this cost formula uses the average unit cost of the goods that are available for sale to determine the cost of goods sold and ending inventory. When a perpetual inventory system is used, an updated average unit cost is determined after each purchase. This amount is then used to record the cost of goods sold on subsequent sales until another purchase is made and a new average unit cost is calculated. Because the average unit cost changes with each purchase, this cost formula is sometimes called the moving average cost formula.

BEFORE YOU GO ON...

Do It

Wynneck Sports Company uses a perpetual inventory system. All inventory items are sold for $10 per unit and all sales and purchases are on account. The company's accounting records show the following:

Date		Explanation	Units	Unit Cost	Total Cost
Mar.	1	Beginning inventory	4,000	$3	$12,000
	10	Purchase	6,000	4	24,000
	19	Sales	(8,000)		
	22	Purchase	5,000	5	25,000
	28	Sales	(5,500)		
					$61,000

(a) Assume Wynneck uses FIFO. (1) Prepare a perpetual inventory schedule and determine the cost of goods sold and ending inventory. (2) Prepare journal entries to record the March 10 purchase and the March 19 sale.

(b) Assume Wynneck uses the average cost formula. (1) Prepare a perpetual inventory schedule and determine the cost of goods sold and ending inventory. (2) Prepare journal entries to record the March 10 purchase and the March 19 sale.

Action Plan

- For FIFO, allocate the first costs to the cost of goods sold at the date of each sale. The latest costs will be allocated to the goods on hand (ending inventory).
- For average, determine the weighted average unit cost (cost of goods available for sale ÷ number of units available for sale) after each purchase. Multiply this cost by the number of units sold to determine the cost of goods sold and by the number of units on hand to determine the cost of the ending inventory.
- Prove that beginning inventory + purchases − cost of goods sold = ending inventory.
- Use the information in the perpetual inventory schedules (purchases and costs of goods sold columns) when preparing the journal entries.

Solution

(a) FIFO—Perpetual

1. Perpetual Inventory Schedule

	PURCHASES			COST OF GOODS SOLD			BALANCE		
Date	Units	Cost	Total	Units	Cost	Total	Units	Cost	Total
Mar. 1							4,000	$3	$12,000
10	6,000	$4	$24,000				4,000 6,000	3 4	} 36,000
19				4,000 4,000	$3 4	} $28,000	2,000	4	8,000
22	5,000	5	25,000				2,000 5,000	4 5	} 33,000
28				2,000 3,500	4 5	} 25,500	1,500	5	7,500
	11,000		$49,000	13,500		$53,500			

Check: $12,000 + $49,000 − $53,500 = $7,500

2. Journal Entries

Mar. 10	Merchandise Inventory	24,000	
	Accounts Payable		24,000
	To record goods purchased on account.		
19	Accounts Receivable	80,000	
	Sales		80,000
	To record credit sale ($10 × 8,000).		
	Cost of Goods Sold	28,000	
	Merchandise Inventory		28,000
	To record cost of goods.		

(b) Average—Perpetual
  1. Perpetual Inventory Schedule

Date	PURCHASES			COST OF GOODS SOLD			BALANCE		
	Units	Cost	Total	Units	Cost	Total	Units	Cost	Total
Mar. 1							4,000	$3.00	$12,000
10	6,000	$4	$24,000				10,000	3.60	36,000
19				8,000	$3.60	$28,800	2,000	3.60	7,200
22	5,000	5	25,000				7,000	4.60	32,200
28				5,500	4.60	25,300	1,500	4.60	6,900
	11,000		$49,000	13,500		$54,100			

Check: $12,000 + $49,000 − $54,100 = $6,900

  2. Journal Entries:

Mar. 10	Merchandise Inventory	24,000	
	Accounts Payable		24,000
	To record goods purchased on account.		
19	Accounts Receivable	80,000	
	Sales		80,000
	To record credit sale ($10 × 8,000).		
	Cost of Goods Sold	28,800	
	Merchandise Inventory		28,800
	To record cost of goods.		

Related exercise material: BE6–3, BE6–4, BE6–5, BE6–6, BE6–7, BE6–8, E6–3, E6–4, and E6–5.

THE NAVIGATOR

Financial Statement Effects

Inventory affects both the income statement and the balance sheet. The ending inventory is included as a current asset on the balance sheet and cost of goods sold is an expense on the income statement. Cost of goods sold will affect profit, which in turn will affect owner's equity on the balance sheet. Thus, the choice of cost determination method can have a significant impact on the financial statements.

Errors can occur when a physical inventory is being taken or when the cost of the inventory is being determined. The effects of these errors on financial statements can be significant. We will address these topics in the next two sections.

CHOICE OF COST DETERMINATION METHOD

If companies have goods that are not ordinarily interchangeable, or goods that have been produced for specific projects, they must use the specific identification method to determine the cost of their inventory. Otherwise, they must use either FIFO or average.

We learned in our feature story that gravitypope uses the FIFO cost formula. How should a company such as gravitypope choose between FIFO and average? It should consider the following objectives in determining the correct method:

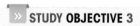

STUDY OBJECTIVE 3

Explain the financial statement effects of inventory cost determination methods.

1. Choose the method that corresponds as closely as possible to the physical flow of goods.
2. Report an inventory cost on the balance sheet that is close to the inventory's recent costs.
3. Use the same method for all inventories having a similar nature and use in the company.

After a company chooses a method of determining the cost of its inventory, this method should be used consistently from one period to the next. Consistency is what makes it possible to compare financial statements from one period to the next. Using FIFO in one year and average in the next year would make it difficult to compare the profits for the two years.

This is not to say that a company can never change from one method to another. However, a change in the method of cost determination can only occur if the physical flow of inventory changes and a different method would result in more relevant information in the financial statements. Such changes and their effect on profit should be disclosed in the notes to the financial statements. Where possible, companies must also go back and restate the prior years' financial statements using the new method. This respects the **full disclosure** requirement, in which all relevant information is to be disclosed. Full disclosure is discussed more in Chapter 11.

Income Statement Effects

To understand the impact of the FIFO and average cost formulas on the income statement, let's look at Bennett Lighting's sales, cost of goods sold, and operating expenses on the Anti-Bug Lightbulb. The condensed income statements in Illustration 6-12 assume that Bennett Lighting sold 550 Anti-Bug Lightbulbs for $11,500 and that operating expenses were $2,000. The cost of goods sold was previously calculated in Illustrations 6-7 and 6-11.

▶ **ILLUSTRATION** 6-12
Comparative effects of
inventory cost formulas

BENNETT LIGHTING Condensed Income Statements		
	FIFO	**Average**
Sales	$11,500	$11,500
Cost of goods sold	6,200	6,222
Gross profit	5,300	5,278
Operating expenses	2,000	2,000
Profit	$ 3,300	$ 3,278

The sales and the operating expenses are the same under both FIFO and average. But the cost of goods sold amounts are different. This difference is the result of how the unit costs are allocated under each cost formula. Each dollar of difference in cost of goods sold results in a corresponding dollar difference in profit. For Bennett Lighting, there is a $22 difference in cost of goods sold and in profit between FIFO and average.

In periods of changing prices, the choice of inventory cost formula can have a significant impact on profit. In a period of rising prices, as is the case here, FIFO produces a higher profit. This happens because the expenses matched against revenues are the lower unit costs of the first units purchased. As shown in Illustration 6-12, FIFO reports the higher profit ($3,300) and average the lower profit ($3,278).

If prices are decreasing, the results from the use of FIFO and average are reversed. FIFO will report the lower profit and average the higher profit. If prices are stable, both cost formulas will report the same results.

Compared with FIFO, average will result in more recent costs being reflected in cost of goods sold. This will better match current costs with current revenues and provide a better income statement valuation. But better matching is not critical in the choice of inventory cost determination methods. It is more important to use the cost formula that best approximates the physical flow of goods or represents recent costs on the balance sheet.

Balance Sheet Effects

The choice of inventory cost formula will also have an impact on the balance sheet; both merchandise inventory and owner's equity will be affected. In our Bennett Lighting example, profit is $22 higher under FIFO. Therefore, owner's equity is also $22 higher under FIFO. Bennett Lighting's inventory is also $22 higher under FIFO. As shown in Illustrations 6-7 and 6-11, it was $5,800 under FIFO and $5,778 under average.

In terms of the balance sheet, one advantage of FIFO is that the costs allocated to ending inventory will approximate the inventory item's current (replacement) cost. For example, for Bennett Lighting, 400 of the 450 units in the ending inventory are costed at the November 27 unit cost of $13. Since management needs to replace inventory after it is sold, a valuation that is closer to the replacement cost is helpful for decision-making.

By extension, a limitation of the average method is that in a period of inflation the costs allocated to inventory may be understated in terms of the current cost of the inventory. That is, the average cost formula results in older costs being included in inventory. The cost of the ending inventory includes the

$10 unit cost of the beginning inventory. This understatement becomes even larger if the inventory includes goods that were purchased in one or more prior accounting periods.

Summary of Effects

When prices are constant, the cost of goods sold and ending inventory will be the same for all three cost determination methods. In specific identification, cost of goods sold and ending inventory depend on which specific units are sold and which are on hand. Thus we cannot make any general comments about how it will compare with FIFO and average.

We have seen that both inventory on the balance sheet and profit on the income statement are higher when FIFO is used in a period of rising prices. The reverse will happen in a period of falling prices. The key differences between the two cost formulas are summarized in Illustration 6-13.

	Rising Prices		Falling Prices	
Income statement	FIFO	Average	FIFO	Average
Cost of goods sold	Lower	Higher	Higher	Lower
Gross profit and profit	Higher	Lower	Lower	Higher
Balance sheet				
Cash flow	Same	Same	Same	Same
Ending inventory	Higher	Lower	Lower	Higher
Owner's equity	Higher	Lower	Lower	Higher

▶ **ILLUSTRATION 6-13**
A comparison of the FIFO and average methods when prices are rising or falling

Notice in Illustration 6-13 that cash flow is the same with both cost formulas. In fact, all three methods of cost determination—specific identification, FIFO, and average—produce exactly the same cash flow. Sales and purchases are not affected by the methods of cost determination. The only thing that is affected is the allocation between ending inventory and cost of goods sold, which does not involve cash.

It is also worth remembering that all three cost determination methods will give exactly the same results over the life cycle of the business or its product. That is, the allocation between cost of goods sold and ending inventory may vary within a period, but will produce the same cumulative results over time.

 BEFORE YOU GO ON...

Do It

Hakim Paints reported sales of $10,000 and operating expenses of $2,000. If Hakim uses FIFO, cost of goods sold is $4,700. If the average method is used, cost of goods sold is $4,550.

(a) Prepare comparative income statements for each cost formula.
(b) Which method will result in higher owner's equity?
(c) Which method should Hakim Paints use?
(d) Are prices rising or falling? Explain.

Solution

(a)

HAKIM PAINTS
Condensed Income Statements

	FIFO	Average
Sales	$10,000	$10,000
Cost of goods sold	4,700	4,550
Gross profit	5,300	5,450
Operating expenses	2,000	2,000
Profit	$ 3,300	$ 3,450

Action Plan
- In preparing comparative income statements, note that sales and operating expenses are the same for both cost formulas. Cost of goods sold, gross profit, and profit are different.
- Recall that profit is added to owner's equity.
- Review the objectives that should be considered in determining the correct method.
- Recall that FIFO uses the oldest costs in determining costs of goods sold.

> **BEFORE YOU GO ON** continued...
>
> (b) Because profit is $150 ($3,450 − $3,300) higher using average, then owner's equity will also be $150 higher using average.
> (c) The cost formula that should be used would be the one that best matches the physical flow of goods.
> (d) Since FIFO has the higher costs of goods sold, then prices must be falling. FIFO has the oldest costs in its cost of goods sold; average will have a combination of older and more recent costs in its cost of goods sold.
>
> *Related exercise material:* BE6–9, BE6–10, E6–6, and E6–7.

THE NAVIGATOR

INVENTORY ERRORS

» **STUDY OBJECTIVE 4**

Determine the financial statement effects of inventory errors.

Some inventory errors are caused by mistakes in counting or pricing the inventory. Other inventory errors are because of mistakes in recognizing the timing of the transfer of legal title for goods in transit. These mistakes result can result in errors in determining:

- beginning inventory
- cost of goods purchased
- ending inventory

Any errors in determining these items can also cause an error in cost of goods sold. Recall that these items affect the Merchandise Inventory and Cost of Goods Sold accounts as follows:

Merchandise Inventory		Cost of Goods Sold	
Beginning inventory Cost of goods purchased	Cost of goods sold →	Cost of goods sold	
Ending inventory			

Errors in cost of goods sold will affect the income statement. If there is an error in ending inventory it will affect the balance sheet, both in ending inventory and in owner's capital. In the following sections, we will illustrate these effects.

Income Statement Effects

Cost of goods sold will be incorrect if there is an error in any one of beginning inventory, cost of goods purchased, or ending inventory, but the other two are correct. This can more easily be seen if we arrange these components, as shown in the Merchandise Inventory account above, to: Beginning Inventory + Cost of Goods Purchased − Ending Inventory = Cost of Goods Sold.

A summary of the impact of errors in these components on cost of goods sold is shown in Illustration 6-14 by using the cost of goods sold formula.

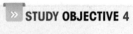

▶**ILLUSTRATION 6-14**
Effects of inventory errors on cost of goods sold

Impact on Cost of Goods Sold	Error in Beginning Inventory		Error in Cost of Goods Purchased		Error in Ending Inventory	
Beginning Inventory	Overstated	Understated				
+ Cost of Goods Purchased			Overstated	Understated		
− Ending Inventory					Overstated	Understated
= Cost of Goods Sold	Overstated	Understated	Overstated	Understated	Understated	Overstated

Notice that errors in beginning inventory and cost of goods purchased have the same impact on cost of goods sold. That is, if beginning inventory or cost of goods purchased is overstated, in both cases, cost of goods sold will be overstated (assuming that there are no other offsetting errors). And if beginning inventory or cost of goods purchased is understated, in both cases, cost of goods sold is understated. This is because beginning inventory and cost of goods purchased are both added when determining cost of goods sold.

On the other hand, an overstatement of ending inventory has the opposite impact on cost of goods sold. If ending inventory is overstated, this results in an understatement of cost of goods sold; if ending inventory is understated, this results in an overstatement of costs of goods sold. This is because ending inventory is deducted when determining cost of goods sold.

Once the impact of an error on cost of goods sold is determined, then we can determine the effect of this error on the income statement. These results are summarized below in Illustration 6-15. U stands for understatement, O for overstatement, and NE for no effect.

Nature of Error	Net Sales	–	Cost of Goods Sold	=	Gross Profit	–	Operating Expenses	=	Profit
Overstate beginning inventory or cost of goods purchased	NE		O		U		NE		U
Understate beginning inventory or cost of goods purchased	NE		U		O		NE		O
Overstate ending inventory	NE		U		O		NE		O
Understate ending inventory	NE		O		U		NE		U

▸ **ILLUSTRATION 6-15**
Effects of inventory errors on income statement

Notice that an error in cost of goods sold has the opposite impact on gross profit and profit. If cost of goods sold is overstated, then gross profit and profit are understated. If cost of goods sold is understated, the gross profit and profit are overstated. This is because cost of goods sold is deducted from net sales when calculating gross profit.

Since the ending inventory of one period becomes the beginning inventory of the next period, **an error in ending inventory of the current period will have a reverse effect on the profit of the next period**. To illustrate, assume that on December 31, 2013, inventory is overstated by $3,000. The following T accounts show the impact of this error on the Merchandise Inventory account, and thus on cost of goods sold, over two years.

Merchandise Inventory (Incorrect Dec. 31, 2013, Inventory Amount)					Merchandise Inventory (Correct Dec. 31, 2013, Inventory Amount)				
Jan. 1/13		20,000			Jan. 1/13		20,000		
Purchases		40,000	Cost of goods sold	42,000	Purchases		40,000	Cost of goods sold	45,000
Dec. 31/13 Bal.		18,000			Dec. 31/13 Bal.		15,000		
Purchases		40,000	Cost of goods sold	48,000	Purchases		40,000	Cost of goods sold	45,000
Dec. 31/14 Bal.		10,000			Dec. 31/14 Bal.		10,000		

Because ending inventory in 2013 is overstated by $3,000 ($18,000 instead of $15,000), the 2013 costs of goods sold is understated by $3,000 ($42,000 instead of $45,000). This also means that beginning inventory for 2014 is overstated by $3,000 ($18,000 instead of $15,000), and cost of goods sold for 2014 is overstated by $3,000 ($48,000 instead of $45,000).

Assuming ending inventory in 2014 is correct, there is no further impact. But over the two-year period it will impact profit, as shown in Illustration 6-16.

▶ILLUSTRATION 6-16
Effects of inventory
errors on income statements
of two successive years

	2013		2014	
	Incorrect	Correct	Incorrect	Correct
Sales	$80,000	$80,000	$80,000	$80,000
Cost of goods sold	42,000	45,000	48,000	45,000
Gross profit	38,000	35,000	32,000	35,000
Operating expenses	10,000	10,000	10,000	10,000
Profit	$28,000	$25,000	$22,000	$25,000

($3,000)
Profit overstated

$3,000
Profit understated

The combined profit for two years is correct because the
errors cancel each other out.

Note that in 2013, the $3,000 understatement of costs of goods sold results in a $3,000 overstatement of profit ($28,000 instead of $25,000). In 2014, the opposite occurs and profit is understated by $3,000 ($22,000 instead of $25,000).

Over the two years, total profit is correct. The errors offset one another. Notice that total profit using incorrect data is $50,000 ($28,000 + $22,000). This is the same as the total profit of $50,000 ($25,000 + $25,000) using correct data. Nevertheless, the distortion of the year-by-year results can have a serious impact on financial analysis and management decisions.

Note that an error in the beginning inventory does not result in a corresponding error in the ending inventory. The accuracy of the ending inventory depends entirely on correctly taking and costing the inventory at the balance sheet date.

Balance Sheet Effects

The effects of inventory errors on the balance sheet can be determined by using the basic accounting equation: assets = liabilities + owner's equity. These results are summarized in Illustration 6-17. U is for understatement, O is for overstatement, and NE is for no effect.

▶ILLUSTRATION 6-17
Effects of inventory
errors on balance sheet

Nature of Error	Assets	=	Liabilities	+	Owner's Equity
Understate ending inventory	U		NE		U
Overstate ending inventory	O		NE		O

When ending inventory is understated, total assets are understated. Understating ending inventory (assuming there are no other offsetting errors) will also overstate cost of goods sold, which will understate profit. If profit is understated, then owner's equity will also be understated, because profit is part of owner's equity.

An error in ending inventory in one period will result in an error in beginning inventory in the next period. An example of this type of error was shown in Illustration 6-16. As previously noted, total profit for the two periods is correct. Thus, total assets and owner's equity reported on the balance sheet at the end of 2014 will also be correct. In other words, errors in beginning inventory have no impact on the balance sheet if ending inventory is correctly calculated at the end of that period.

Errors in the cost of goods purchased may also have an effect on the balance sheet. For example, if a company records a purchase of inventory on account in 2014 that should have been recorded in 2015, accounts payable will be overstated at December 31, 2014. And in this situation, owner's equity at December 31, 2014, will be understated because profit for 2014 is understated. Thus, the balance sheet will still balance even though it is incorrect.

You should also note that inventory errors can occur in either a perpetual or a periodic inventory system and that the errors have the same impact on the income statement and balance sheet regardless of which system is used. But one of the major benefits of a perpetual inventory system is that many inventory mistakes are much more likely to be caught, and corrected, when the accounting records are compared with the results of the inventory count.

BEFORE YOU GO ON...

Do It

On December 31, Silas Company counted and recorded $600,000 of inventory. This count did not include $90,000 of goods in transit, shipped to Silas on December 29, FOB shipping point. Silas recorded the purchase on January 3 when the goods were received. (a) Determine the correct December 31 inventory balance. (b) Identify any accounts that are in error, and state the amount and direction (that is, overstatement or understatement) of the error.

Solution

(a) The correct inventory count should have included the goods in transit. The correct December 31 inventory balance was $690,000 ($600,000 + $90,000).

(b) *Income statement accounts:* Because the purchase had not been recorded, the cost of goods purchased is understated (U) by $90,000. And because the inventory had not been included in the inventory count, the ending inventory is also understated. Thus, as shown below, the two errors cancel each other out, and the cost of goods sold and profit will be correct.

Beginning inventory	No effect
Plus: Cost of goods purchased	U $90,000
Cost of goods available for sale	U $90,000
Less: Ending inventory	U $90,000
Cost of goods sold	No effect because the errors cancel each other out

Balance sheet accounts: Merchandise Inventory and Accounts Payable are both understated

Assets	=	Liabilities	+	Owner's equity
U $90,000	=	U $90,000	+	no effect

Related exercise material: BE6–11, BE6–12, E6–8, and E6–9.

Action Plan
- Use the cost of goods sold and income statement relationships to determine the impact of an error on the income statement.
- Use the accounting equation to determine the impact of an error on the balance sheet.

THE **NAVIGATOR**

Presentation and Analysis of Inventory

Presenting inventory on the financial statements is important because inventory is usually the largest current asset (Merchandise Inventory) on the balance sheet and the largest expense (Cost of Goods Sold) on the income statement. In addition, these reported numbers are critical for analyzing how well a company manages its inventory. In the next sections, we will discuss the presentation and analysis of inventory.

VALUING INVENTORY AT THE LOWER OF COST AND NET REALIZABLE VALUE

Before reporting inventory on the financial statements, we must first ensure that it is properly valued. The value of inventory items sometimes falls due to changes in technology or style. For example, suppose you manage a retail store that sells computers, and at the end of the year the computers' value has dropped almost 25%. Do you think inventory should be stated at cost, in accordance with the cost principle, or at its lower value?

As you probably reasoned, this situation requires an exception to following the cost basis of accounting. When the value of inventory is lower than its cost, the inventory is written down to its net realizable value at the end of the period. This is called the **lower of cost and net realizable value (LCNRV)** rule. **Net realizable value (NRV)** is the selling price less any costs required to make the goods ready for sale.

 STUDY OBJECTIVE 5

Value inventory at the lower of cost and net realizable value.

The lower of cost or NRV rule is applied to the items in inventory at the end of the accounting period. To apply this rule, four steps are followed:

1. Determine the cost of the items in ending inventory using the appropriate cost determination method: specific identification, FIFO, or average.
2. Determine the net realizable value of the items in ending inventory.
3. Compare the values determined in steps 1 and 2.
4. Use the lower value to report inventory on the balance sheet.

To illustrate, assume that on March 31, 2014, Tony's Electronics Shop has the following lines of merchandise with costs and net realizable values as indicated. The lower of cost and NRV produces the following results:

	Cost	NRV	Lower of Cost and NRV
Television sets			
LCD	$ 60,000	$ 55,000	$ 55,000
Plasma	45,000	52,000	45,000
	105,000	107,000	100,000
Car video and audio equipment			
LCD media package	48,000	45,000	45,000
Global positioning system	15,000	14,000	14,000
	63,000	59,000	59,000
Total inventory	$168,000	$166,000	$159,000

This means Tony's Electronics Shop will report $159,000 for merchandise inventory on its balance sheet. The lower of cost and net realizable value rule is applied to individual inventory items, not total inventory. In some cases, it can be applied to groups of similar items. For instance, in the above example, all of the company's different types of LCD televisions were grouped together and we compared the cost of the LCD televisions with their total net realizable value.

If Tony's Electronics Shop uses a perpetual inventory system, the entry to adjust inventory from cost to net realizable value would be the following:

A	=	L	+	OE
−9,000				−9,000

Cash flows: no effect

Mar. 31	Cost of Goods Sold	9,000	
	Merchandise Inventory		9,000
	To record decline in inventory value from original cost of $168,000 to net realizable value of $159,000.		

The Cost of Goods Sold account is debited directly for the loss because a decline in the value of inventory is considered to be part of the overall cost of buying and selling inventory. The amount of the loss must be separately reported and most companies do this in the notes to the financial statements. Thus, some companies may choose to debit a separate expense account to make it easier to keep track of the amount. Alternative methods of recording a decline in inventory value are covered in an intermediate accounting course.

When there is clear evidence of an increase in net realizable value, because of changed economic circumstances, the amount of the writedown is reversed. The evidence required for this reversal would generally be an increase in selling prices. If the item of inventory that had been previously written down has been sold, there is no need to record a reversal. If the item of inventory that was previously written down to net realizable value is still on hand, and the selling price has increased, then the reversal is recorded. The reversing entry will consist of a debit to merchandise inventory and a credit to cost of goods sold.

It is not usual for reversals to happen. Most companies will sell their inventory at a reduced price, instead of waiting for the price to recover. Thus, it is not that often that a company will still have the inventory on hand a year later, and the selling price will have increased. While reversals are relatively rare, the amount of any such reversal must be reported in the notes to the financial statements.

If there is a recovery in the value of the inventory, the write-up can never be larger than the original writedown. The lower of cost or net realizable value rule will still be applied to the inventory. This ensures that the inventory is never reported at an amount greater than its original cost.

ACCOUNTING IN ACTION
BUSINESS INSIGHT

Blockbuster Canada was placed in receivership in the spring of 2011. Competition from on-line video services had increased and Blockbuster Canada could not find a suitor. That meant that all Canadian Blockbuster stores were to be liquidated by December 31, 2011. What happens when a company is liquidated? Well, it means that a company's assets, including inventory, are sold at discounted prices. As a customer, you benefit by paying a lower price to buy a movie or game than you would normally have paid. Any money that is collected from the sale of liquidated assets is held by the receiver (Grant Thornton, in the case of Blockbuster). This money is then used to pay off the company's debt. Once a company is in receivership, it is not highly likely that money generated from selling the company's assets can pay off all of its debt.

Source: Jameson Berkow, "Blockbuster's Canadian Unit Seeks Bankruptcy Protection," *Financial Post,* May 5, 2011; The Canadian Press, "Blockbuster Canada to Close Remaining Stores," CBC News on-line, August 31, 2011; Marina Strauss and Iain Marlow, "Blockbuster to Pull Plug in Canada," *The Globe and Mail,* September 1, 2011.

When a company such as Blockbuster is placed in receivership, what would be the impact on how to account for its inventory?

BEFORE YOU GO ON...

Do It

Tanguay's Jersey Store uses a perpetual inventory system and has the following items in its inventory at December 31, 2014:

Product	Quantity	Per Unit Cost	Per Unit Net Realizable Value
Jerseys	95	$50	$45
Socks	155	5	6

(a) What amount for inventory should Tanguay's Jersey Store report on its balance sheet?
(b) Record any necessary adjustments.

Solution

(a)

	Cost		Net Realizable Value		Lower of Cost and Net Realizable Value
Jerseys	(95 × $50)	$4,750	(95 × $45)	$4,275	$4,275
Socks	(155 × $5)	775	(155 × $6)	930	775
Total inventory		$5,525		$5,205	$5,050

(b)

Dec. 31	Cost of Goods Sold ($5,525 − $5,050)	475	
	Merchandise Inventory		475
	To record decline in inventory value from its cost of $5,525 to lower of cost and net realizable value of $5,050.		

Related exercise material: BE6–13, BE6–14, and E6–10.

Action Plan
- Calculate the cost of the inventory.
- Calculate the net realizable value of the inventory.
- For each inventory item, determine which number is lower—cost or net realizable value.
- Record a journal entry to adjust the inventory account to net realizable value if required.

THE **NAVIGATOR**

REPORTING AND ANALYZING INVENTORY
Presenting Inventory in the Financial Statements

How a company classifies its inventory depends on whether the company is a merchandiser or a manufacturer. A merchandiser *buys* its inventory. A manufacturer *produces* its inventory. In a merchandising company, inventory consists of many different items. Textbooks, paper, and pens, for example, are just a few of the inventory items on hand in a bookstore. These items have two common characteristics: (1) they are owned by the company, and (2) they are in a form ready for sale to customers. Only one inventory classification, merchandise inventory, is needed to describe the many different items that make up the total inventory.

In a manufacturing company, some goods may not yet be ready for sale. As a result, inventory is usually classified into three categories: raw materials, work in process, and finished goods. For example, an automobile manufacturer classifies the steel, fibreglass, upholstery material, and other components that are on hand waiting to be used in production as raw materials. Partially completed automobiles on an assembly line are classified as work in process. Automobiles completed and ready for sale are identified as finished goods.

As discussed in the previous section, inventory is reported on the balance sheet at the lower of cost and net realizable value. Inventory is typically recorded as a current asset because management expects to sell it within the next year. But if part of the inventory will not be sold for more than a year, this inventory should be reported as a non-current asset. For example, if inventory is being stockpiled because of concerns about future prices, then it may be appropriate to classify this inventory as a non-current asset.

A company should disclose the following information in its financial statements or the notes to the statements:

1. the total amount of inventory;
2. the cost determination method (specific identification, FIFO, or average);
3. the cost of goods sold;
4. the amount of any writedown to net realizable value; and
5. the amount of any reversals of previous writedowns, including the reason why the writedown was reversed.

Publicly traded and private companies value and report inventory in a similar manner. There are no significant differences in this regard at the introductory accounting level between International Financial Reporting Standards and Accounting Standards for Private Enterprises. The few differences relate to specialized types of inventory and will not be covered in this text.

The inventory and cost of goods sold information reported in the financial statements is also used to analyze how effectively the company is managing its inventory.

Inventory Turnover

A delicate balance must be kept between having too little inventory and too much inventory. On one hand, management wants to have a variety and quantity of merchandise available so that customers will find a wide selection of items in stock. But having too much inventory on hand can cost the company money in storage costs, interest costs (on money tied up in inventory), and costs due to high-tech goods becoming obsolete, or changing fashions. On the other hand, low inventory levels can result in stockouts (item unavailability), lost sales, and unhappy customers.

How quickly a company sells its inventory, or turns it over, is one way to determine whether the company has too much or too little inventory. We can also use this information to evaluate a company's liquidity, or its ability to pay obligations that are expected to come due in the next year. In Chapter 4, we introduced the current and acid-test ratios, which are measures of liquidity. Inventory is a significant component of the current ratio and a high level of inventory will result in a high current ratio. But if the inventory is not turning over very quickly, this may be a problem. In this section, we add another liquidity ratio that is commonly used to evaluate inventory levels: the inventory turnover ratio. We also present a related measure: the average days to sell the inventory.

Inventory Turnover Ratio. The **inventory turnover** ratio measures the number of times, on average, inventory is sold (turned over) during the period. It is calculated by dividing the cost of goods sold by average inventory.

Whenever a ratio compares a balance sheet figure (e.g., inventory) with an income statement figure (e.g., cost of goods sold), the balance sheet figure must be averaged. Average balance sheet figures are determined by adding beginning and ending balances together and dividing by two. Averages are used to ensure that the balance sheet figures (which represent end-of-period amounts) cover the same period of time as the income statement figures (which represent amounts for the entire period). Illustration 6-18 shows the formula for calculating the inventory turnover ratio for Reitmans (Canada) Limited for fiscal 2012 (dollars in thousands).

Cost of Goods Sold	÷	Average Inventory	=	Inventory Turnover
$363,333	÷	$\dfrac{\$78{,}285 + \$73{,}201}{2}$	=	4.8 times

▶ **ILLUSTRATION 6-18**
Inventory turnover

Generally, the more times that inventory turns over each year, the more efficiently sales are being made.

Days Sales in Inventory. The inventory turnover ratio is complemented by the **days sales in inventory** ratio. It converts the inventory turnover ratio into a measure of the average age of the inventory on hand. This ratio is calculated by dividing 365 days by the inventory turnover ratio, as in Illustration 6-19.

Days in Year	÷	Inventory Turnover	=	Days Sales in Inventory
365 days	÷	4.8	=	76 days

▶ **ILLUSTRATION 6-19**
Days sales in inventory

This means that Reitmans' inventory, on average, is in stock for 76 days. This ratio must be interpreted carefully: it should be compared with the company's ratio in previous years, and with the industry average. However, you must recognize that this average will be different for each type of inventory item (e.g., sneakers vs. bicycles). What we see here is a total average only.

 BEFORE YOU GO ON...

Do It

The following information is available for Sanchez Company for three recent years:

	2014	2013	2012
Inventory	$ 40,000	$ 42,000	$ 46,000
Cost of goods sold	123,000	125,000	130,000

Calculate the inventory turnover ratio and days sales in inventory for Sanchez Company for 2014 and 2013 and comment on any trends.

Solution

	2014	2013
Inventory turnover	$3.00 \text{ times} = \dfrac{\$123{,}000}{[(\$40{,}000 + 42{,}000) \div 2]}$	$2.84 \text{ times} = \dfrac{\$125{,}000}{[(\$42{,}000 + 46{,}000) \div 2]}$
Days sales in inventory	$122 \text{ days} = 365 \div 3.00$	$129 \text{ days} = 365 \div 2.84$

The inventory turnover ratio has increased in 2014 and decreased the number of days sales in inventory. In general, the higher the inventory turnover and the lower the number of days sales in inventory, the better. Sanchez has improved its inventory management in 2014 compared with 2013.

Related exercise material: BE6–15, BE6–16, E6–11, and E6–12.

Action Plan
- Calculate average inventory using the inventory balance at the beginning and end of the year.
- Divide cost of goods sold by the average inventory for that year to calculate inventory turnover.
- Divide 365 by the inventory turnover to calculate days sales in inventory.
- Recall if it is better for inventory turnover to increase or decrease.

THE **NAVIGATOR**

APPENDIX 6A | INVENTORY COST FORMULAS IN PERIODIC SYSTEMS

» **STUDY OBJECTIVE 7**

Calculate ending inventory and cost of goods sold in a periodic inventory system using FIFO and average inventory cost formulas.

Both of the inventory cost formulas described in the chapter for a perpetual inventory system can be used in a periodic inventory system. To show how to use FIFO and average in a periodic system, we will use the data below for Bennett Lighting.

BENNETT LIGHTING Anti-Bug Lightbulb				
Date	Explanation	Units	Unit Cost	Total Cost
Jan. 1	Beginning inventory	100	$10	$ 1,000
Apr. 15	Purchase	200	11	2,200
Aug. 24	Purchase	300	12	3,600
Nov. 27	Purchase	400	13	5,200
Total		1,000		$12,000

These data are the same as those shown earlier in the chapter, except that the sales information has been omitted. In the periodic inventory system, we don't keep track of the number or cost of units sold during the year. Instead we wait until the end of the period to allocate the cost of goods available for sale to ending inventory and cost of goods sold.

Bennett Lighting had a total of 1,000 units available for sale during the year. The total cost of these units was $12,000. A physical inventory count at the end of the year determined that 450 units remained on hand. Using these data, Illustration 6A-1 shows the formula for calculating cost of goods sold that we first learned in Chapter 5.

▶ **ILLUSTRATION 6A-1**
Formula for cost of goods sold

Beginning Inventory	+	Cost of Goods Purchased	=	Cost of Goods Available for Sale	−	Ending Inventory	=	Cost of Goods Sold
100 units $1,000	+	900 units $11,000	=	1,000 units $12,000	−	450 units ?	=	550 units ?

If we apply this formula to the unit numbers, we can determine that 550 units must have been sold during the year. The total cost (or "pool of costs") of the 1,000 units available for sale was $12,000. We will demonstrate the allocation of this pool of costs using FIFO and average in the next sections. In a periodic system, the cost formulas are applied to the ending inventory, which is then deducted from the cost of goods available for sale to calculate the cost of goods sold.

PERIODIC SYSTEM—FIRST-IN, FIRST-OUT (FIFO)

Similar to perpetual FIFO, the cost of the oldest goods on hand is allocated to the cost of goods sold. This means that the cost of the most recent purchases is assumed to remain in ending inventory. The allocation of the cost of goods available for sale at Bennett Lighting under FIFO is shown in Illustration 6A-2.

▶ **ILLUSTRATION 6A-2**
Periodic system—FIFO

COST OF GOODS AVAILABLE FOR SALE				
Date	Explanation	Units	Unit Cost	Total Cost
Jan. 1	Beginning inventory	100	$10	$ 1,000
Apr. 15	Purchase	200	11	2,200
Aug. 24	Purchase	300	12	3,600
Nov. 27	Purchase	400	13	5,200
	Total	1,000		$12,000

Step 1: Ending Inventory				Step 2: Cost of Goods Sold	
Date	**Unit**	**Unit Cost**	**Total Cost**		
Nov. 27	400	$13	$5,200	Cost of goods available for sale	$12,000
Aug. 24	50	12	600	Less: Ending inventory	5,800
Total	450		$5,800	Cost of goods sold	$ 6,200

▶ILLUSTRATION 6A-2
(*continued*)

The cost of the ending inventory is determined by taking the unit cost of the most recent purchase and working backward until all units of inventory have been costed. In this example, the 450 units of ending inventory must be costed using the November 27 and August 24 purchase costs. The last purchase was 400 units at $13 on November 27. The remaining 50 units ($450 - 400$) are costed at the price of the second most recent purchase, $12 on August 24.

Once the cost of the ending inventory is determined, the cost of goods sold is calculated by subtracting the cost of the ending inventory (the cost of the goods not sold) from the cost of the goods available for sale (the pool of costs).

The cost of goods sold can also be separately calculated or proven as shown below. To determine the cost of goods sold using FIFO, simply start at the first item of beginning inventory and count forward until the total number of units sold (550) is reached. Note that, of the 300 units purchased on August 24, only 250 units are assumed to be sold. This agrees with our calculation of ending inventory, where 50 of these units were assumed to be unsold and included in our ending inventory.

Date	Unit	Unit Cost	Cost of Goods Sold
Jan. 1	100	$10	$1,000
Apr. 15	200	11	2,200
Aug. 24	250	12	3,000
Total	550		$6,200

It is also helpful to check that the total of the cost of goods sold and ending inventory is equal to the cost of goods available for sale ($6,200 + $5,800 = $12,000).

PERIODIC SYSTEM—AVERAGE

The weighted average unit cost is calculated in the same manner as we calculated it in a perpetual inventory system: by dividing the cost of the goods available for sale by the units available for sale. The key difference between this calculation in a periodic system and in a perpetual system is that this calculation is done after every purchase in a perpetual system. In a periodic system, it is done only at the end of the period, as shown in Illustration 6A-3.

▶ILLUSTRATION 6A-3
Calculation of
weighted average unit cost

The weighted average unit cost, $12 in this case, is then applied to the units on hand to determine the cost of the ending inventory. The allocation of the cost of goods available for sale at Bennett Lighting using the average cost formula is shown in Illustration 6A-4.

> ILLUSTRATION 6A-4
Periodic system—
average

COST OF GOODS AVAILABLE FOR SALE				
Date	Explanation	Units	Unit Cost	Total Cost
Jan. 1	Beginning inventory	100	$10	$ 1,000
Apr. 15	Purchase	200	11	2,200
Aug. 24	Purchase	300	12	3,600
Nov. 27	Purchase	400	13	5,200
	Total	1,000		$12,000

Step 1: Ending Inventory	Step 2: Cost of Goods Sold	
Calculate unit cost: $12,000 ÷ 1,000 = $12	Cost of goods available for sale	$12,000
Units × Unit cost = Total Cost	Less: Ending inventory	5,400
450 $12 $5,400	Cost of goods sold	$ 6,600

We can prove our calculation of the cost of goods sold under the average cost formula by multiplying the units sold by the weighted average unit cost (550 × $12 = $6,600). And, again, we can prove our calculations by ensuring that the total of the ending inventory and the cost of goods sold equals the cost of goods available for sale ($5,400 + $6,600 = $12,000).

Here is a comparison of FIFO and average in perpetual and periodic inventory systems. Whether a perpetual or periodic inventory system is used, FIFO will always result in the same cost of goods sold and ending inventory amounts. For example, a comparison of the results of FIFO perpetual from Illustration 6-7 with results of FIFO periodic from Illustration 6A-2 shows that in both cases, cost of goods sold is $6,200 and ending inventory is $5,800. The results are the same because under both inventory systems, the first costs are the ones assigned to cost of goods sold regardless of when the sales actually happened.

This is not the case under the average cost formula. Notice that under a periodic inventory system in Illustration 6A-4, the ending inventory of $5,400 and the cost of goods sold of $6,600 are **not** the same as the values calculated under a perpetual inventory system in Illustration 6-11, even though the average cost formula was used for both systems. This is because in a perpetual inventory system, a new (moving) average is calculated with each purchase; in a periodic inventory system, the same weighted average is used to calculate the cost of goods sold for all the units sold during the period. A summary of these results is shown in Illustration 6A-5. For ease of comparison, the information from Illustration 6-11 has been rounded to the nearest dollar.

> ILLUSTRATION 6A-5
Comparison of FIFO
and average in perpetual and
periodic inventory systems

	FIFO		Average	
	Perpetual	Periodic	Perpetual	Periodic
Cost of goods sold	$ 6,200	$ 6,200	$ 6,222	$ 6,600
Ending inventory balance	5,800	5,800	5,778	5,400
Cost of goods available for sale	$12,000	$12,000	$12,000	$12,000

As you can see, regardless of whether you use the FIFO or average cost formula using either a perpetual or periodic system, adding the cost of goods sold to the ending inventory balance will equal the goods available for sale of $12,000.

 BEFORE YOU GO ON...

Do It

Cookie Cutters Company uses the periodic inventory system. All purchases and sales are on account. The accounting records of Cookie Cutters Company show the following data:

Beginning inventory, June 1 — 4,000 units at $3
Purchases, June 13 — 6,000 units at $4
Sales, June 25 — $64,000

The physical inventory count at June 30 showed 2,000 units on hand.

(a) Determine the cost of goods available for sale and the number of units sold.

(b) Assume Cookie Cutters uses FIFO. (1) Calculate cost of goods sold and ending inventory. (2) Prepare journal entries to record the June 13 purchase and the June 25 sale.

(c) Assume Cookie Cutters uses average. (1) Calculate cost of goods sold and ending inventory. (2) Prepare journal entries to record the June 13 purchase and the June 25 sale.

Solution

(a) The cost of goods available for sale is $36,000, calculated as follows:

Beginning Inventory, June 1	4,000	units @ $3.00	$12,000
Purchases, June 13	6,000	units @ $4.00	24,000
	10,000		$36,000

Total units available for sale	10,000
Minus: units in ending inventory	2,000
Units sold	8,000

(b) FIFO—Periodic

1. Calculations:

Ending inventory:

Date	Units	Unit Cost	Total Cost
June 13	2,000	$4.00	$8,000

Cost of goods sold: $36,000 − $8,000 = $28,000

Check of cost of goods sold:

Date	Units	Unit Cost	Total Cost
June 1	4,000	$3.00	$12,000
13	4,000	4.00	16,000
	8,000		$28,000

Check: $8,000 + $28,000 = $36,000

2. Journal Entries

June 13	Purchases	24,000	
	Accounts Payable		24,000
	To record goods purchased on account.		
25	Accounts Receivable	64,000	
	Sales		64,000
	To record credit sale.		

(c) Average—Periodic

1. Calculations:

Weighted average unit cost:	$36,000 ÷ 10,000 units = $3.60 per unit
Ending inventory:	2,000 units × $3.60 = $7,200
Cost of goods sold:	$36,000 − $7,200 = $28,800
Check of cost of goods sold:	8,000 units × $3.60 = $28,800
Check:	$7,200 + $28,800 = $36,000

2. Journal Entries

June 13	Purchases	24,000	
	Accounts Payable		24,000
	To record goods purchased on account.		
25	Accounts Receivable	64,000	
	Sales		64,000
	To record credit sale.		

Related exercise material: *BE6–17, *BE6–18, *E6–13, *E6–14, *E6–15, and *E6–16.

Action Plan

- Calculate the cost of goods available for sale.
- Determine the cost of ending inventory first. Then calculate cost of goods sold by subtracting ending inventory from the cost of goods available for sale.
- For FIFO, allocate the most recent costs to the goods on hand. (The first costs will be allocated to the cost of goods sold.)
- For average, determine the weighted average unit cost (cost of goods available for sale ÷ number of units available for sale). Multiply this cost by the number of units on hand.
- Recall that in a periodic inventory system, the cost of goods sold is not recorded at the date of sale.

THE **NAVIGATOR**

APPENDIX 6B | ESTIMATING INVENTORIES

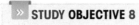

» STUDY OBJECTIVE 8

Estimate ending inventory using the gross profit and retail inventory methods.

When a company uses a periodic inventory system, it must be able to do a physical count of its inventory in order to determine the cost of its ending inventory and the cost of goods sold. But what if a company cannot do a physical count? It may be impractical or impossible to count the inventory. Fortunately, it is possible to do an estimate.

There are two reasons for sometimes needing to estimate inventories. First, management may want monthly or quarterly financial statements but does not have the time for, or want the expense of, doing a physical inventory count every month or quarter. Second, a casualty such as a fire or flood may make it impossible to take a physical inventory.

Companies that use a perpetual inventory system are less likely to need inventory estimates since the perpetual inventory system keeps detailed inventory records continuously. Inventory estimates are usually associated with the periodic system.

There are two widely used methods of estimating inventories: (1) the gross profit method, and (2) the retail inventory method.

GROSS PROFIT METHOD

The **gross profit method** estimates the cost of ending inventory by applying the gross profit margin to net sales. It is commonly used to prepare interim (e.g., monthly) financial statements in a periodic inventory system. This method is relatively simple but effective.

To use this method, a company needs to know its net sales, cost of goods available for sale (beginning inventory + cost of goods purchased), and gross profit margin. Gross profit for the period is estimated by multiplying net sales by the gross profit margin. The estimated gross profit is then used to calculate the estimated cost of goods sold and the estimated ending inventory.

The formulas for using the gross profit method are given in Illustration 6B-1.

▶ **ILLUSTRATION 6B-1**
Gross profit method formulas

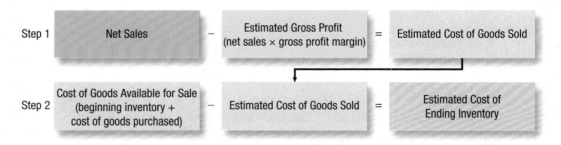

To illustrate, assume that Lalonde Company wants to prepare an income statement for the month of January. Its records show net sales of $200,000, beginning inventory of $40,000, and cost of goods purchased of $120,000. In the preceding year, the company had a 30% gross profit margin. It expects to earn the same margin this year. Given these facts and assumptions, Lalonde can calculate the estimated cost of the ending inventory at January 31 under the gross profit method as follows:

Step 1:	Net sales	$200,000
	Less: Estimated gross profit ($200,000 × 30%)	60,000
	Estimated cost of goods sold	$140,000 ⌐
Step 2:	Beginning inventory	$ 40,000
	Cost of goods purchased	120,000
	Cost of goods available for sale	160,000
	Less: Estimated cost of goods sold	140,000 ◄
	Estimated cost of ending inventory	$ 20,000

The gross profit method is based on the assumption that the gross profit margin will remain constant from one year to the next. But it may not remain constant, because of a change in merchandising policies or in market conditions. In such cases, the margin should be adjusted to reflect the current operating conditions. In some cases, a better estimate can be had by applying this method to a department or product line as a whole.

The gross profit method should not be used in preparing a company's financial statements at the end of the year. These statements should be based on a physical inventory count. Accountants and managers often use the gross profit method to test the reasonableness of the ending inventory amount, however.

RETAIL INVENTORY METHOD

A retail store, such as Reitmans, has thousands of types of merchandise. In such cases, determining the cost of each type of merchandise can be difficult and time-consuming if the company has used a periodic inventory system. For these retail companies, it can be easier to calculate the selling price, or retail price, of the total inventory than to look at the purchase invoices to find the cost of each individual inventory item. Most retail businesses can establish a relationship between cost and selling price—called the cost-to-retail percentage or ratio. The cost-to-retail percentage is then applied to the ending inventory at retail prices to determine the estimated cost of the inventory. This is called the **retail inventory method** of estimating the cost of inventory.

To use the retail inventory method, a company's records must show both the cost and the retail value of the goods available for sale. The formulas for using the retail inventory method are given in Illustration 6B-2.

Helpful hint In determining inventory at retail, selling prices on the unit are used. Tracing actual unit costs to invoices is unnecessary.

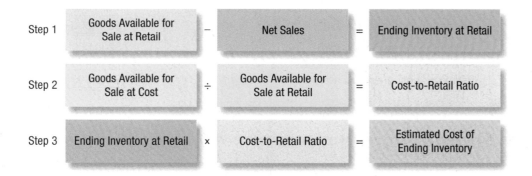

▸ **ILLUSTRATION 6B-2**
Retail inventory method formulas

The logic of the retail method can be demonstrated by using unit-cost data. Assume that 10 units purchased at $7 each ($70 in total) are priced to sell for $10 per unit ($100 in total). The cost-to-retail ratio is 70% ($70 ÷ $100). If four units remain unsold, their retail value is $40 and their cost is $28 ($40 × 70%). This amount agrees with the total cost of goods on hand on a per-unit basis (4 × $7).

The following example shows how to apply the retail method, using assumed data for Zboyovsky Co.:

	At Cost	At Retail
Beginning inventory	$14,000	$ 21,500
Goods purchased	61,000	78,500
Goods available for sale	$75,000	100,000
Net sales		70,000
Step 1: Ending inventory at retail		$ 30,000

Step 2: Cost-to-retail ratio = $75,000 ÷ $100,000 = **75%**
Step 3: Estimated cost of ending inventory $30,000 × 75% = $22,500

Using the retail inventory method also makes it easier to take a physical inventory at the end of the year. The goods on hand can be valued at the prices marked on the merchandise. The cost-to-retail ratio is then applied to the goods on hand at retail to determine the ending inventory at cost. This value can be used for reporting purposes in the year-end financial statements if the results are similar to using cost.

The retail inventory method is also useful for estimating the amount of shrinkage due to breakage, loss, or theft. For example, assume that the retail value of Zboyovsky's physical inventory count is $29,400. When this amount is compared with the estimated retail value of $30,000 that was calculated above, it reveals a $600 estimated inventory shortage at retail. The estimated inventory shortage at cost is $450 ($600 × 75%).

The major disadvantage of the retail method is that it is an averaging technique. It may produce an incorrect inventory valuation if the mix of the ending inventory is not representative of the mix in the goods available for sale. Assume, for example, that the cost-to-retail ratio of 75% in the Zboyovsky Co. illustration consists of equal proportions of inventory items that have cost-to-retail ratios of 70%, 75%, and 80%, respectively. If the ending inventory contains only items with a 70% ratio, an incorrect inventory cost will result. This problem can be lessened by applying the retail method to a department or product line as a whole.

 BEFORE YOU GO ON...

Do It

Action Plan
- Calculate the estimated cost of goods sold.
- Deduct the estimated cost of goods sold from cost of goods available for sale.

THE **NAVIGATOR**

At May 31, Purcell Company has net sales of $330,000 and cost of goods available for sale of $230,000. Last year, the company had a gross profit margin of 35%. Calculate the estimated cost of the ending inventory.

Solution

Net sales	$330,000
Less: Estimated gross profit ($330,000 × 35%)	115,500
Estimated cost of goods sold	$214,500
Cost of goods available for sale	$230,000
Less: Estimated cost of goods sold	214,500
Estimated cost of ending inventory	$ 15,500

*Related exercise material: *BE6–19, *BE6–20, *E6–17, and *E6–18.*

THE **NAVIGATOR**

Comparing IFRS and ASPE

Key Differences	International Financial Reporting Standards (IFRS)	Accounting Standards for Private Enterprises (ASPE)
No significant differences		

Demonstration Problem 1 (Perpetual Inventory System)

Englehart Company uses a perpetual inventory system. All sales and purchases are on account. The selling price is $9 per unit. The company has the following inventory data for the month of March:

Date	Explanation	Units	Unit Cost	Total Cost
Mar. 1	Beginning inventory	200	$4.30	$ 860
10	Purchase	500	4.50	2,250
15	Sales	(500)		
20	Purchase	400	4.75	1,900
25	Sales	(400)		
30	Purchase	300	5.00	1,500
		500		$6,510

Instructions

(a) Determine the cost of ending inventory at March 31 and cost of goods sold for March under (1) FIFO, and (2) average.

(b) Prepare journal entries for the March 25 sale and the March 30 purchase under (1) FIFO, and (2) average.

Solution to Demonstration Problem 1

(a) 1. FIFO—Perpetual

	PURCHASES			COST OF GOODS SOLD			BALANCE		
Date	Units	Cost	Total	Units	Cost	Total	Units	Cost	Total
Mar. 1							200	$4.30	$ 860
10	500	$4.50	$2,250				200	4.30	} 3,110
							500	4.50	
15				200	$4.30	} $2,210			
				300	4.50		200	4.50	900
20	400	4.75	1,900				200	4.50	} 2,800
							400	4.75	
25				200	4.50	} 1,850			
				200	4.75		200	4.75	950
30	300	5.00	1,500				200	4.75	} 2,450
							300	5.00	
	1,200		$5,650			$4,060			

Check: $860 + $5,650 − $4,060 = $2,450

(a) 2. Average—Perpetual

	PURCHASES			COST OF GOODS SOLD			BALANCE		
Date	Units	Cost	Total	Units	Cost	Total	Units	Cost	Total
Mar. 1							200	$4.30	$ 860
10	500	$4.50	$2,250				700	4.44	3,110
15				500	$4.44	$2,220	200	4.44	890
20	400	4.75	1,900				600	4.65	2,790
25				400	4.65	1,860	200	4.65	930
30	300	5.00	1,500				500	4.86	2,430
	1,200		$5,650	900		$4,080			

Check: $860 + $5,650 − $4,080 = $2,430

(b) 1. & 2. FIFO and average perpetual journal entries

		FIFO—Perpetual		Average—Perpetual	
Mar. 25	Accounts Receivable	3,600		3,600	
	Sales		3,600		3,600
	To record credit sale ($9 × 400).				
	Cost of Goods Sold	1,850		1,860	
	Merchandise Inventory		1,850		1,860
	To record cost of goods.				
30	Merchandise Inventory	1,500		1,500	
	Accounts Payable		1,500		1,500
	To record goods purchased on account.				

Demonstration Problem 2 (Periodic Inventory System)

Englehart Company uses a periodic inventory system. All sales and purchases are made on account. The company has the following inventory data for the month of March:

Inventory	March 1	200 units @ $4.30	$ 860
Purchases	March 10	500 units @ $4.50	2,250
	20	400 units @ $4.75	1,900
	30	300 units @ $5.00	1,500
Sales	March 15	500 units @ $9.00	4,500
	25	400 units @ $9.00	3,600

The physical inventory count on March 31 shows 500 units on hand.

Instructions
(a) Determine the cost of ending inventory at March 31 and cost of goods sold for March under (1) FIFO, and (2) average.
(b) Prepare journal entries for the March 25 sale and the March 30 purchase under (1) FIFO, and (2) average.

Solution to Demonstration Problem 2

The cost of goods available for sale is $6,510, calculated as follows:

Inventory	March 1	200	units @ $4.30	$ 860
Purchases	March 10	500	units @ $4.50	2,250
	20	400	units @ $4.75	1,900
	30	300	units @ $5.00	1,500
		1,400		$6,510

The physical inventory count on March 31 shows 500 units on hand.

The number of units sold is 900 (1,400 units available for sale − 500 units on hand).

(a) 1. FIFO—Periodic

Ending inventory:

Date	Units	Unit Cost	Total Cost
Mar. 30	300	$5.00	$1,500
20	200	4.75	950
	500		$2,450

Cost of goods sold: $6,510 − $2,450 = $4,060

Check of cost of goods sold:

Date	Units	Unit Cost	Total Cost
Mar. 1	200	$4.30	$ 860
10	500	4.50	2,250
20	200	4.75	950
	900		$4,060

Check: $4,060 + $2,450 = $6,510

2. Average—Periodic

Weighted average unit cost:	$6,510 ÷ 1,400 units = $4.65 per unit
Ending inventory:	500 units × $4.65 = $2,325
Cost of goods sold:	$6,510 − $2,325 = $4,185
Check of cost of goods sold:	900 units × $4.65 = $4,185
Check:	$4,185 + $2,325 = $6,510

ACTION PLAN

- In a periodic system, cost of ending inventory and cost of goods sold are determined at the end of the period.
- Calculate cost of goods available for sale, then allocate costs to ending inventory.
- For FIFO, allocate the latest costs to the goods on hand. (The first costs will be allocated to the cost of goods sold.)
- For average, calculate the weighted average unit cost (cost of goods available for sale divided by the total units available for sale). Multiply this cost by the number of units on hand.
- Subtract ending inventory from the cost of goods available for sale to determine the cost of goods sold for each cost formula.
- Check your work: do an independent calculation of cost of goods sold and check that cost of goods sold + ending inventory = cost of goods available for sale.
- Recall that in a periodic inventory system, cost of goods sold is not recorded at the point of sale.

(b) 1. & 2. FIFO and average periodic journal entries

		FIFO—Periodic		Average—Periodic	
Mar. 25	Accounts Receivable	3,600		3,600	
	Sales		3,600		3,600
	To record credit sale ($9 × 400).				
30	Purchases	1,500		1,500	
	Accounts Payable		1,500		1,500
	To record goods purchased on account.				

THE NAVIGATOR

▶ Summary of Study Objectives

1. **Describe the steps in determining inventory quantities.** The steps in determining inventory quantities are (1) taking a physical inventory of goods on hand, and (2) determining the ownership of goods in transit, on consignment, and in similar situations.

2. **Calculate cost of goods sold and ending inventory in a perpetual inventory system using the specific identification, FIFO, and average methods of cost determination.** Costs are allocated to the cost of goods sold account each time a sale occurs in a perpetual inventory system. The cost is determined by specific identification or by one of two cost formulas: FIFO (first-in, first-out) and average.

   Specific identification is used for goods that are not ordinarily interchangeable. This method tracks the actual physical flow of goods, allocating the exact cost of each merchandise item to cost of goods sold and ending inventory.

   The FIFO cost formula assumes a first-in, first-out cost flow for sales. Cost of goods sold consists of the cost of the earliest goods purchased. Ending inventory is determined by allocating the cost of the most recent purchases to the units on hand.

   The average cost formula is used for goods that are homogeneous or non-distinguishable. Under average, a new weighted (moving) average unit cost is calculated after each purchase and applied to the number of units sold and the number of units remaining in inventory.

3. **Explain the financial statement effects of inventory cost determination methods.** Specific identification results in the best match of costs and revenues on the income statement. When prices are rising, average results in a higher cost of goods sold and lower profit than FIFO. Average results in a better match on the income statement of more current costs with current revenues than does FIFO. On the balance sheet, FIFO results in an ending inventory that is closest to the current (replacement) value and the best balance sheet valuation. All three methods result in the same cash flow.

4. **Determine the financial statement effects of inventory errors.** An error in beginning inventory will have a reverse effect on profit in the current year (e.g., an overstatement of beginning inventory results in an overstatement of cost of goods sold and an understatement of profit). An error in the cost of goods purchased will have a reverse effect on profit (e.g., an overstatement of purchases results in an overstatement of cost of goods sold and an understatement of profit). An error in ending inventory will have a similar effect on profit (e.g., an overstatement of ending inventory results in an understatement of cost of goods sold and an overstatement of profit). If ending inventory errors are not corrected in the following period, their effect on profit for the second period is reversed and total profit for the two years will be correct. On the balance sheet, ending inventory errors will have the same effects on total assets and total owner's equity, and no effect on liabilities.

5. **Value inventory at the lower of cost and net realizable value.** The cost of the ending inventory is compared with its net realizable value. If the net realizable value is lower, a writedown is recorded, which results in an increase in cost of goods sold, and a reduction in inventory. The writedown is reversed if the net realizable value of the inventory increases, but the value of the inventory can never be higher than its original cost.

6. *Demonstrate the presentation and analysis of inventory.* Ending inventory is reported as a current asset on the balance sheet at the lower of cost and net realizable value. Cost of goods sold is reported as an expense on the income statement. Additional disclosures include the cost determination method.

    The inventory turnover ratio is a measure of liquidity. It is calculated by dividing the cost of goods sold by average inventory. It can be converted to days sales in inventory by dividing 365 days by the inventory turnover ratio.

7. *Calculate ending inventory and cost of goods sold in a periodic inventory system using FIFO and average inventory cost formulas (Appendix 6A).* Under the FIFO cost formula, the cost of the most recent goods purchased is allocated to ending inventory. The cost of the earliest goods on hand is allocated to cost of goods sold. Under the average cost formula, the total cost available for sale is divided by the total units available to calculate a weighted average unit cost. The weighted average unit cost is applied to the number of units on hand at the end of the period to determine ending inventory. Cost of goods sold is calcu-

lated by subtracting ending inventory from the cost of goods available for sale.

    The main difference between applying cost formulas in a periodic inventory system and applying cost formulas in a perpetual inventory system is the timing of the calculations. In a periodic inventory system, the cost formula is applied at the end of the period. In a perpetual inventory system, the cost formula is applied at the date of each sale to determine the cost of goods sold.

8. *Estimate ending inventory using the gross profit and retail inventory methods (Appendix 6B).* Two methods of estimating inventories are the gross profit method and the retail inventory method. Under the gross profit method, the gross profit margin is applied to net sales to determine the estimated cost of goods sold. The estimated cost of goods sold is subtracted from the cost of goods available for sale to determine the estimated cost of the ending inventory. Under the retail inventory method, a cost-to-retail ratio is calculated by dividing the cost of goods available for sale by the retail value of the goods available for sale. This ratio is then applied to the ending inventory at retail to determine the estimated cost of the ending inventory.

▶ Glossary

Flash cards

Average cost formula An inventory cost formula that assumes that the goods available for sale are homogeneous or non-distinguishable. The cost of goods sold and the ending inventory are determined using an average cost, calculated by dividing the cost of the goods available for sale by the units available for sale. (p. 308)

Consigned goods Goods held for sale that belong to another party. The party holding the goods is called the consignee, and the party that owns the goods is called the consignor. (p. 303)

Days sales in inventory A liquidity measure of the average number of days that inventory is held. It is calculated as 365 days divided by the inventory turnover ratio. (p. 321)

First-in, first-out (FIFO) cost formula An inventory cost formula that assumes that the costs of the earliest (oldest) goods purchased are the first to be recognized as the cost of goods sold. The costs of the latest goods purchased are assumed to remain in ending inventory. (p. 306)

Full disclosure The requirement that all information that is relevant for decision-making be disclosed. (p. 312)

Gross profit method A method for estimating the cost of the ending inventory by applying the gross profit margin to net sales. (p. 326)

Inventory turnover A liquidity measure of the number of times, on average, that inventory is sold during the period. It

is calculated by dividing cost of goods sold by average inventory. Average inventory is calculated by adding beginning inventory and ending inventory balances and dividing the result by two. (p. 320)

Lower of cost and net realizable value (LCNRV) A basis for stating inventory at the lower of its original cost and the net realizable value at the end of the period. (p. 317)

Net realizable value (NRV) The selling price of an inventory item, less any estimated costs required to make the item saleable. (p. 317)

Retail inventory method A method for estimating the cost of the ending inventory by applying a cost-to-retail ratio to the ending inventory at retail prices. (p. 327)

Specific identification An inventory costing method used when goods are distinguishable and not ordinarily interchangeable. It follows the actual physical flow of goods and items are specifically costed to arrive at the cost of goods sold and the cost of the ending inventory. (p. 305)

Weighted average unit cost The average cost of inventory weighted by the number of units purchased at each unit cost. It is calculated by dividing the cost of goods available for sale by the number of units available for sale. (p. 308)

Note: All questions, exercises, and problems below with an asterisk (*) relate to material in Appendices 6A and 6B.

⏵ Self-Study Questions

Answers are at the end of the chapter.

(SO 1) K **1.** Which of the following should not be included in a company's physical inventory?
(a) Goods held on consignment from another company
(b) Goods shipped on consignment to another company
(c) Goods in transit that were purchased from a supplier and shipped FOB shipping point
(d) Goods in transit that were sold to a customer and shipped FOB destination

(SO 2) C **2.** What is the most important factor in determining if specific identification can be used?
(a) Management decides to use it.
(b) The inventory consists of high-priced goods.
(c) The company has a low volume of sales.
(d) The inventory items are not interchangeable.

(SO 2) AP **3.** Fine Wine Company uses a perpetual inventory system and has the following beginning inventory, purchases, and sales of inventory in April:

	Units	Unit Cost	Total Cost
Inventory, Apr. 1	8,000	$11	$ 88,000
Purchase, Apr. 9	12,000	12	144,000
Sale, Apr. 12	(15,000)	?	
Purchase, Apr. 18	5,000	13	65,000

What was the average unit cost after the last purchase on April 18?
(a) $11.60   (c) $11.88
(b) $12.00   (d) $12.30

(SO 2) AP **4.** Using the data in question 3 above, the cost of goods sold under FIFO is:
(a) $174,000.   (c) $185,000.
(b) $172,000.   (d) $177,000.

(SO 3) C **5.** In periods of rising prices, the average cost formula will produce:
(a) higher profit than FIFO.
(b) the same inventory as FIFO.
(c) lower profit than FIFO.
(d) higher inventory than FIFO.

(SO 4) C **6.** In Fran Company, ending inventory is overstated by $4,000. The effects of this error on the current year's cost of goods sold and profit, respectively, are:
(a) understated, overstated.
(b) overstated, understated.
(c) overstated, overstated.
(d) understated, understated.

(SO 4) K **7.** Michelle Company made an error that understated ending inventory by $5,000 on December 31, 2013. It did not correct the error in 2013 or 2014. As a result, owner's equity was:
(a) overstated at December 31, 2013, and understated at December 31, 2014.

(b) overstated at December 31, 2013, and properly stated at December 31, 2014.
(c) understated at December 31, 2013, and properly stated at December 31, 2014.
(d) understated at December 31, 2013, and overstated at December 31, 2014.

(SO 5) K **8.** Rickety Company purchased 1,000 units of inventory at a cost of $91 each. There are 200 units left in ending inventory. The net realizable value of these units is $80 each. The ending inventory under the lower of cost and net realizable value rule is:
(a) $2,200.   (c) $18,200.
(b) $16,000.   (d) $80,000.

(SO 6) AP **9.** If a company's cost of goods sold is $240,000, its beginning inventory is $50,000, and its ending inventory is $30,000, what are its inventory turnover and days sales in inventory?
(a) 3 times and 122 days.
(b) 6 times and 61 days.
(c) 4.8 times and 76 days.
(d) 8 times and 46 days.

(SO 7) AP* **10.** Kam Company uses a periodic inventory system and has the following:

	Units	Unit Cost
Inventory, Jan. 1	8,000	$11
Purchase, June 19	13,000	12
Purchase, Nov. 8	5,000	13
	26,000	

If 9,000 units are on hand at December 31, what is the cost of the goods sold under average? Round cost per unit to four decimal places.
(a) $106,962.   (c) $180,000.
(b) $108,000.   (d) $202,038.

(SO 7) AP* **11.** Using the data in question 10 above, the ending inventory under FIFO is:
(a) $100,000.   (c) $113,000.
(b) $108,000.   (d) $117,000.

(SO 8) AP* **12.** Somers Company has sales of $150,000 and a cost of goods available for sale of $135,000. If the gross profit margin is 30%, the estimated cost of the ending inventory under the gross profit method is:
(a) $15,000.   (c) $40,500.
(b) $30,000.   (d) $105,000.

(SO 8) AP* **13.** Deko Company reports the following selected information: cost of goods available for sale at cost, $60,000; at retail, $100,000; and net sales at retail, $70,000. What is the estimated cost of Deko Company's ending inventory under the retail method?
(a) $18,000.   (c) $30,000.
(b) $21,000.   (d) $42,000.

▶ Questions

(SO 1) C   1. Your friend Tom Wetzel has been hired to help take the physical inventory in Kikujiro's Hardware Store. Explain to Tom what this job will involve.

(SO 1) C   2. Explain to Janine Company whether the buyer or the seller should include goods in transit in their inventory. Also explain when the seller should record the sale.

(SO 1) C   3. What are consigned goods? Which company, the consignee or the consignor, should include consigned goods in its inventory balance? Explain why.

(SO 1) C   4. Your friend, the assistant store manager at South-side Boutique, wants to know if the following items should be included in the store's inventory count: (1) items on hold for customers who promised to return and purchase the items within the next week; (2) items left for alterations by customers; and (3) items taken on approval by customers. If you need to make any assumptions to answer your friend, include that in your explanation.

(SO 2) C   5. Dave Wier believes that the allocation of the cost of goods available for sale should be based on the actual physical flow of the goods. Explain to Dave why this may be both impractical and inappropriate.

(SO 2) C   6. Explain circumstances in which the specific identification method is used.

(SO 2) C   7. Distinguish between the three methods of determining cost for inventories: specific identification, FIFO, and average. Give an example of a type of inventory for which each method might be used.

(SO 2) C   8. Sophie Yue believes that, when the perpetual system is used, the average cost per unit changes with every purchase and every sale. Explain to Sophie why this is not correct.

(SO 3) C   9. Compare the financial statement effects of using the FIFO and average cost formulas during a period of rising prices on (a) cash, (b) ending inventory, (c) cost of goods sold, and (d) profit.

(SO 3) C   10. Which inventory cost formula—FIFO or average—provides the better income statement valuation? The better balance sheet valuation? Explain.

(SO 3) C   11. What factors should a company consider when it is choosing between the two inventory cost formulas—FIFO and average?

(SO 4) C   12. Mila Company discovers in 2014 that its ending inventory at December 31, 2013, was overstated by $5,000. What effect will this error have on (a) 2013 profit, (b) 2014 profit, and (c) the combined profit for the two years?

(SO 4) C   13. If an error in ending inventory in one year will have the reverse effect in the following year, does this error need to be corrected when it is discovered?

(SO 5) C   14. Lucy Ritter is studying for the next accounting exam. What should Lucy know about (a) when not to use the cost basis of accounting for inventories, and (b) the meaning of "net realizable value" in the lower of cost and net realizable value method?

(SO 5) K   15. How is net realizable value calculated?

(SO 5) C   16. A company must record a loss (or an increase in cost of goods sold) when net realizable value is lower than cost. Should a company record a gain when net realizable value is higher than cost? Explain.

(SO 6) AN   17. What problems may occur if a company's inventory turnover ratio is too high or too low?

(SO 6) AN   18. If a company's days sales in inventory ratio decreases from one year to the next, would this be viewed as a sign that the company's inventory management has improved or deteriorated? Explain.

(SO 6) K   19. What are the differences, if any, in the valuation and reporting of inventory between companies following IFRS and companies following ASPE?

(SO 7) C *20. Why is it necessary to calculate cost of goods available for sale when applying FIFO or average in a periodic inventory system?

(SO 7) C *21. Vance is studying for his next accounting quiz. He argues that the earliest costs should be used when calculating ending inventory using FIFO in a periodic inventory system because they are the first costs. Is he correct? Why or why not?

(SO 7) C *22. Explain why ending inventory and cost of goods sold under the average cost formula are not the same amounts in a periodic inventory system as they are in a perpetual inventory system.

(SO 8) K *23. When is it necessary to estimate the cost of inventories?

(SO 8) C *24. In order to save the cost of counting inventory at year end, it is acceptable to use the gross profit method to determine ending inventory for the year-end financial statements. Do you agree or disagree? Explain.

(SO 8) C *25. Both the gross profit method and the retail inventory method are based on averages. For each method, describe the average used, how it is determined, and how it is applied.

(SO 8) C *26. Explain the major weakness of the retail method and when it is not appropriate to use it.

Brief Exercises

Identify items in inventory.
(SO 1) K

BE6–1   Helgeson Company has identified the following items to include or exclude when it takes its physical inventory. Indicate whether each item should be included or excluded.

(a) Goods shipped on consignment by Helgeson to another company
(b) Goods in transit to Helgeson from a supplier, shipped FOB destination
(c) Goods sold to a customer but being held for delivery
(d) Goods from another company held on consignment by Helgeson
(e) Goods in transit to a customer, shipped FOB shipping point

Calculate inventory balance.
(SO 1) AP

BE6–2   The merchandise inventory in Carla's Clothing Store was counted after the close of business on December 31, 2014, the company's year end. It was determined that the total cost of this inventory was $55,500. Carla wants to know if this is the correct amount that should be reported on the company's December 31, 2014, balance sheet or if an adjustment needs to be made for any of the following items:

(a) The count included merchandise "on hold" for customers. These items cost $950 and will be held until noon on January 2, 2015. Carla expects at least one-half of the customers will return to purchase the items.
(b) The count also included items costing $1,200 that had been sold but are being held for alterations. The customers have paid in full for these items.
(c) Carla's Clothing Store has $4,250 of merchandise held on consignment for a local designer. These items were included in the inventory count.
(d) A shipment of inventory costing $2,875 was received on January 2, 2015. It had been shipped by the seller on December 30, FOB shipping point. Freight charges are $310. These items were not included in the inventory count.
(e) A second shipment of inventory costing $4,350 was received on January 3, 2015. It had been shipped by the seller on December 31, FOB destination. Freight charges are $390. These items were also not included in the inventory count.

Determine the correct amount of Carla's Clothing Store's merchandise inventory at December 31, 2014.

Apply specific identification cost determination method.
(SO 2) AP

BE6–3   In October, Claire's Gallery purchased four original paintings for resale for the following amounts: Painting 1, $1,000; Painting 2, $2,000; Painting 3, $3,000; and Painting 4, $4,000. Paintings 3 and 4 were sold during October for $6,500 each. Calculate the cost of goods sold for the month and the ending inventory balance on October 31 using specific identification.

Recommend cost determination method.
(SO 2) AP

BE6–4   The following are three inventory cost determination methods:

1. Specific identification
2. FIFO
3. Average

Below is a list of different types of companies and their main inventory item. Beside each one, insert the number of the inventory cost determination method above that the company would most likely use.

(a) _____ Grocery store (food)
(b) _____ Coffee shop (coffee beans)
(c) _____ Car dealership (automobiles)
(d) _____ Clothing store (clothing)
(e) _____ Car dealership (parts)
(f) _____ Gas station (fuel)
(g) _____ Jewellery store (custom-made jewellery)
(h) _____ Consignment clothing store (clothing)

Apply perpetual FIFO.
(SO 2) AP

BE6–5   First Choice Company uses the FIFO cost formula in a perpetual inventory system. Fill in the missing amounts for items (a) through (k) in the following perpetual inventory schedule:

Date	PURCHASES			COST OF GOODS SOLD			BALANCE		
	Units	Cost	Total	Units	Cost	Total	Units	Cost	Total
June 1							200	$25.00	$5,000.00
7	400	$22.00	$8,800.00				(a)	(b)	(c)
18				350	(d)	(e)	(f)	(g)	(h)
26	350	$20.00	7,000.00				(i)	(j)	(k)

Apply perpetual average.
(SO 2) AP

BE6–6   Average Joe Company uses the average cost formula in a perpetual inventory system. Fill in the missing amounts for items (a) through (k) in the following perpetual inventory schedule:

	PURCHASES			COST OF GOODS SOLD			BALANCE		
Date	Units	Cost	Total	Units	Cost	Total	Units	Cost	Total
June 1							200	$25.00	$5,000.00
7	400	$22.00	$8,800.00				(a)	(b)	(c)
18				350	(d)	(e)	(f)	(g)	(h)
26	350	$20.00	7,000.00				(i)	(j)	(k)

Apply perpetual FIFO and average. (SO 2) AP

BE6–7 Yogi & Company uses a perpetual inventory system. The following information is available for November:

		Units	Purchase Price	Sales Price
Nov. 1	Balance	10	$5.00	
4	Purchase	20	$5.50	
7	Purchase	20	$6.00	
10	Sale	(10)		$8.00
12	Sale	(30)		$8.00

Calculate the cost of goods sold and ending inventory under (a) FIFO and (b) average. (*Hint:* Round the average cost per unit to three decimal places.)

Record journal entries using perpetual FIFO and average. (SO 2) AP

BE6–8 Refer to the data in BE6–7 for Yogi & Company. Prepare journal entries to record the November 4 purchase and the November 12 sale using (a) FIFO and (b) average. Assume all sales and purchases are on credit

Identify inventory cost formula. (SO 3) C

BE6–9 For each statement that follows, identify the inventory cost formula that best fits the description, assuming a period of rising prices:

(a) It results in a balance sheet inventory amount that is closer to the replacement cost.
(b) It does a better job of matching recent costs against revenue.
(c) It understates the value of the inventory on the balance sheet.
(d) It may overstate gross profit.

Compare impact of inventory cost formulas. (SO 3) C

BE6–10 Interactive Tech Company just started business and is trying to decide which inventory cost formula to use. Assuming prices are falling, as they often do in the information technology sector, answer the following questions for Interactive Tech:

(a) Which formula will result in the higher ending inventory? Explain.
(b) Which formula will result in the higher cost of goods sold? Explain.
(c) Which formula will result in the higher cash flow? Explain.
(d) What factors are important for Interactive Tech to consider as it tries to choose the most appropriate inventory cost formula?

Determine effect of beginning inventory error. (SO 4) AN

BE6–11 Collie Company incorrectly included $23,000 of goods held on consignment for Retriever Company in Collie's beginning inventory for the year ended December 31, 2013. The ending inventory for 2013 and 2014 was correctly counted. (a) What is the impact on the 2013 financial statements? (b) What is the impact on the 2014 financial statements?

Determine effects of inventory error over two years. (SO 4) AN

BE6–12 FirstIn Company reported profit of $90,000 in 2013. When counting its inventory on December 31, 2013, the company forgot to include items stored in a separate room in the warehouse. As a result, ending inventory was understated by $7,000.

(a) What is the correct profit for 2013?
(b) What effect, if any, will this error have on total assets and owner's equity reported on the balance sheet at December 31, 2013?
(c) Assuming the inventory is correctly counted on December 31, 2014, what effect, if any, will this error have on the 2014 financial statements?

Determine LCNRV valuation and prepare adjustment. (SO 5) AP

BE6–13 Smart-Tech Office Equipment Company has the following cost and net realizable value data at December 31, 2014:

Inventory Categories	Cost	Net Realizable Value
Computers	$24,000	$21,500
Office Equipment	19,000	19,500
Printers	14,000	10,600

(a) Calculate the lower of cost and net realizable value valuation.
(b) What adjustment should the company record if it uses a perpetual inventory system?

BE6–14 Refer to the data in BE6–13 for Smart-Tech Office Equipment Company. Prior to making the adjustment in BE6–13 (b), Smart-Tech's cost of goods sold for 2014 was $418,500. What is the correct ending inventory and cost of goods sold that should be reported in the financial statements for the year ended December 31, 2014?

Apply LCNRV. (SO 5) AP

BE6–15 Reynold's Company had net sales of $2,500,000, cost of goods sold of $1,150,000, and profit of $500,000 in 2014. The company had a January 1, 2014, inventory balance of $132,000 and a December 31, 2014, inventory balance of $143,000. Calculate the inventory turnover and days sales in inventory ratios for 2014.

Calculate inventory ratios. (SO 6) AP

BE6–16 Refer to the data in BE 6–15 for Reynold's Company. Assume for 2013 the company had an inventory turnover ratio of 9.1 and 40.1 days sales in inventory. Has the company's inventory management improved or deteriorated in 2014? Explain.

Compare inventory ratios. (SO 6) C

*BE6–17 In its first month of operations, Panther Company made three purchases of merchandise in the following sequence: 200 units at $8; 250 units at $7; and 300 units at $6. There are 400 units on hand at the end of the period. Panther uses a periodic inventory system. Calculate the cost of the ending inventory and cost of goods sold under (a) FIFO, and (b) average. (*Hint:* Round to two decimals places for the average cost per unit.)

Apply periodic cost FIFO and average. (SO 7) AP

*BE6–18 At the beginning of the year, Seller Company had 700 units with a cost of $3 per unit in its beginning inventory. The following inventory transactions occurred during the month of January:

Jan. 3   Sold 550 units on account for $6 each.
    9   Purchased 1,000 units on account for $4 per unit.
  15   Sold 850 units for cash for $7 each.

Prepare journal entries to record the January transactions assuming that Seller Company uses a periodic inventory system under (a) FIFO and (b) average.

Record transactions using periodic FIFO and average. (SO 2, 7) AP

*BE6–19 Jansen Company had beginning inventory of $60,000; net sales of $350,000; and cost of goods purchased of $250,000. In the previous year, the company had a gross profit margin of 40%. Calculate the estimated cost of the ending inventory using the gross profit method.

Apply gross profit method. (SO 8) AP

*BE6–20 On July 31, Milna's Fabric Store had the following data related to the retail inventory method: Goods available for sale at cost $25,000; at retail $40,000; and net sales of $30,000. Calculate the estimated cost of the ending inventory using the retail inventory method.

Apply retail inventory method. (SO 8) AP

▶ Exercises

E6–1 Shippers Company had the following inventory situations to consider at January 31, its year end:

Identify items in inventory. (SO 1) K

1. Goods held on consignment for MailBoxes Etc. since December 22
2. Goods shipped on consignment to Rinehart Holdings on January 5, and still on hand
3. Goods that are still in transit and were shipped to a customer, FOB destination, on January 28
4. Goods that are still in transit and were shipped to a customer, FOB shipping point, on January 27
5. Goods that are still in transit and were purchased from a supplier, FOB destination, on January 25
6. Goods that are still in transit and were purchased from a supplier, FOB shipping point, on January 29
7. Freight costs due on goods in transit from item 6 above
8. Freight costs due on goods in transit from item 3 above
9. Office supplies on hand at January 31

Instructions

Which of the above items should Shipper include in its inventory? Provide an explanation.

E6–2 First Bank is considering giving Moghul Company a loan. First, however, it decides that it would be a good idea to have further discussions with Moghul's accountant. One area of particular concern is the inventory account, which has a December 31 balance of $281,000. Discussions with the accountant reveal the following:

Determine correct inventory amount. (SO 1) AP

1. The physical count of the inventory did not include goods that cost $95,000 that were shipped to Moghul, FOB shipping point, on December 27 and were still in transit at year end.
2. Moghul sold goods that cost $35,000 to Novotna Company, FOB destination, on December 28. The goods are not expected to arrive at their destination in India until January 12. The goods were not included in the physical inventory because they were not in the warehouse.
3. Moghul sold goods that cost $49,000 to Sterling of Canada, FOB shipping point, on December 30. The goods were received by Sterling on January 8. They were not included in Moghul's physical inventory.

4. On December 31, Board Company had $30,500 of goods held on consignment for Moghul. The goods were not included in Moghul's ending inventory balance.

5. Moghul received goods that cost $28,000 on January 2. The goods were shipped FOB shipping point on December 26 by Cellar Co. The goods were not included in the physical count.

6. On January 2, Moghul received goods that cost $44,000. The goods had been shipped, FOB destination, on December 29. The shipment was a rush order that was supposed to arrive on December 31. This purchase was not included in the ending inventory of $281,000.

Instructions

Determine the correct inventory amount at December 31.

Apply specific identification. (SO 2) AP

E6–3 In December, Paul's Paintings purchased the following items:

Date Purchased	Painting	Cost
Dec. 12	1	$1,000
5	2	800
10	3	1,100
19	4	700
20	5	1,200

On December 22, paintings 1 and 5 were sold for $2,500 each.

Instructions

(a) Should Paul's Paintings use specific identification or one of the two cost formulas (FIFO or average) instead? Explain.

(b) Calculate ending inventory and cost of goods sold using specific identification.

(c) Prepare the journal entry to record the December 22 sale.

Apply perpetual FIFO, record journal entries, and calculate gross profit. (SO 2) AP

E6–4 On May 1, Black Bear Company had 400 units of inventory on hand, at a cost of $4.00 each. The company uses a perpetual inventory system. All purchases and sales are on account. A record of inventory transactions for the month of May for the company is as follows:

Purchases		Sales	
May 4	1,300 @ $4.10	May 3	300 @ $7.00
14	700 @ $4.40	16	1,000 @ 7.00
29	500 @ $4.75	18	400 @ 7.50

Instructions

(a) Calculate the cost of goods sold and ending inventory using FIFO.

(b) Prepare journal entries to record the May 4 purchase and the May 3 and 16 sales.

(c) Calculate gross profit for May.

Apply perpetual average, record journal entries, and calculate gross profit. (SO 2) AP

E6–5 Top Light Company uses a perpetual inventory system. The company began 2014 with 1,000 lamps in inventory at a cost of $12 per unit. During 2014, Top Light had the following purchases and sales of lamps:

February 15	Purchased	2,000 units @ $18 per unit
April 24	Sold	2,500 units @ $30 per unit
June 6	Purchased	3,500 units @ $23 per unit
October 18	Sold	2,000 units @ $33 per unit
December 4	Purchased	1,400 units @ $26 per unit

All purchases and sales are on account.

Instructions

(a) Calculate the cost of goods sold and ending inventory using average. (*Hint:* Round the average cost per unit to three decimal places.)

(b) Prepare journal entries to record the June 6 purchase and the October 18 sale.

(c) Calculate gross profit for the year.

Apply perpetual FIFO and average. Answer questions about results. (SO 2, 3) AP

E6–6 Dene Company uses a perpetual inventory system and reports the following inventory transactions for the month of July:

		Units	Unit Cost	Total Cost
July 1	Inventory	150	$5	$ 750
12	Purchases	230	6	1,380
15	Sale	(250)		
16	Purchases	490	7	3,430
23	Purchases	175	8	1,400
27	Sale	(570)		

Instructions

(a) Calculate the cost of goods sold and ending inventory under (1) FIFO and (2) average. (*Hint:* Round the average cost per unit to three decimal places.)

(b) Which cost formula gives the higher ending inventory? Why?

(c) Which cost formula results in the higher cost of goods sold? Why?

E6–7   Sun Care Company uses a perpetual inventory system and reports the following inventory transactions for the month of May:

Apply perpetual FIFO and average. Answer questions about results.
(SO 2, 3) AP

		Units	Unit Cost
May 1	Inventory	350	$8
4	Purchases	480	7
11	Sale	(510)	
12	Sales return	10	
17	Purchases	150	6
22	Purchases	475	5
29	Sale	(680)	

Instructions

(a) Calculate the cost of goods sold and ending inventory under (1) FIFO and (2) average. (*Hint:* Round the average cost per unit to three decimal places.)

(b) Assuming all units are sold for $15 per unit, calculate gross profit under (1) FIFO and (2) average. Comment on why gross profit is not the same under the two methods.

(c) What impact, if any, does the choice of cost formula have on cash flow? Explain.

E6–8   Glacier Fishing Gear reported the following amounts for its cost of goods sold and ending inventory:

Determine effects of inventory errors. (SO 4) AN

	2014	2013
Cost of goods sold	$170,000	$175,000
Ending inventory	30,000	30,000

Glacier made two errors: (1) 2013 ending inventory was overstated by $5,500, and (2) 2014 ending inventory was understated by $4,000.

Instructions

(a) Calculate the correct cost of goods sold and ending inventory for each year.

(b) Describe the impact of the errors on profit for 2013 and 2014 and on owner's equity at the end of 2013 and 2014.

(c) Explain why it is important that Glacier Fishing Gear correct these errors as soon as they are discovered.

E6–9   Marrakesh Company reported the following income statement data for the years ended December 31:

Correct partial income statements and calculate gross profit margin.
(SO 4) AN

	2014	2013
Sales	$500,000	$500,000
Cost of goods sold	410,000	410,000
Gross profit	$ 90,000	$ 90,000

The inventories at January 1, 2013, and December 31, 2014, are correct. However, the ending inventory at December 31, 2013, was understated by $20,000.

Instructions

(a) Prepare the correct income statement up to gross profit for the two years.

(b) What is the combined effect of the inventory error on total gross profit for the two years?

(c) Calculate the gross profit margin for each of the two years, before and after the correction.

E6–10   Tech Computing Store uses a perpetual inventory system and the FIFO cost formula for valuing inventory. The company is now in the process of comparing the cost of its inventory with its net realizable value. The following data are available at Tech Computing's year end, December 31:

Determine LCNRV valuation.
(SO 5) AP

	Units	Unit Cost	Net Realizable Value
Laptop computers	95	$710	$680
Monitors	72	275	210
External hard drives	47	55	80
Tablets	56	300	390

Instructions

(a) Determine the lower of cost and net realizable value of the ending inventory.

(b) Prepare the journal entry required, if any, to record the adjustment from cost to net realizable value.

Determine LCNRV valuation and note disclosures. (SO 5, 6) AP

E6–11 Picture Perfect Camera Shop is determining the lower of cost and net realizable value of its inventory. The following data are available at December 31:

		Units	Unit Cost	Net Realizable Value
Cameras:	Nikon	15	$675	$600
	Canon	17	400	425
Lenses:	Sony	22	135	124
	Sigma	20	215	220

Instructions

(a) Determine the lower of cost and net realizable value of the ending inventory.

(b) Prepare the journal entry required, if any, to record the adjustment from cost to net realizable value assuming Picture Perfect Camera Shop uses a perpetual inventory system.

(c) What information regarding its inventory will Picture Perfect Camera Shop need to report in the notes to its financial statements?

Calculate inventory turnover, days sales in inventory, and gross profit margin. (SO 6) AP

E6–12 Dartmouth Games reported the following information for a three-year period:

	2014	2013	2012
Ending inventory	$ 20,000	$ 30,000	$ 34,000
Sales	125,000	128,000	115,000
Cost of goods sold	50,000	51,200	46,000
Profit	30,000	42,000	40,000

Instructions

(a) Calculate the inventory turnover, days sales in inventory, and gross profit margin for 2014 and 2013.

(b) Based on this information, does the company's liquidity appear to be improving or deteriorating?

Apply periodic FIFO and average. (SO 7) AP

*E6–13 Lombart Company uses a periodic inventory system. Its records show the following for the month of April, with 25 units on hand at April 30:

			Units	Unit Cost	Total Cost
April	1	Inventory	30	$ 8	$240
	12	Purchases	45	11	495
	16	Purchases	15	12	180
		Total	90		915

Instructions

(a) Calculate the ending inventory and cost of goods sold at April 30 using the FIFO and average cost formula.

(b) Prove the cost of goods sold calculations.

Apply periodic FIFO and average. (SO 7) AP

*E6–14 Dene Company uses a periodic inventory system and its accounting records include the following inventory information for the month of July:

			Units	Unit Cost	Total Cost
July	1	Inventory on hand	150	$5	$ 750
	12	Purchase	230	6	1,380
	16	Purchase	490	7	3,430
	23	Purchase	175	8	1,400

A physical inventory count determined that 225 units were on hand at July 31.

Instructions

(a) Calculate the ending inventory and the cost of goods sold under (1) FIFO and (2) average.

(b) For part 2 of instruction (a), explain why the average unit cost is not $6.50.

(c) How do the results for instruction (a) differ from E6–6, where the same information was used in a perpetual inventory system?

Apply periodic and perpetual FIFO and average. (SO 2, 7) AP

*E6–15 Fish n'Fly sells an ultra-lightweight fishing rod that is considered to be one of the best fishing rods on the market. Information follows for Fish n'Fly's purchases and sales of the ultra-lightweight fishing rod in July:

Date	Transaction	Units	Unit Purchase Price	Unit Sales Price
July 1	Beginning inventory	25	$295	
10	Purchase	30	300	
12	Sale	(42)		$450
13	Purchase	35	305	
25	Sale	(45)		460
27	Purchase	20	310	

Instructions

(a) Calculate the cost of goods sold and the ending inventory using FIFO and average, assuming Fish n'Fly uses a perpetual inventory system. (*Hint:* Round the average cost per unit to three decimal places.)

(b) What would be the ending inventory and cost of goods sold if Fish n'Fly used FIFO and average in a periodic inventory system? (*Hint:* Round the average cost per unit to three decimal places.)

*E6–16 Refer to the data for Fish n'Fly in E6–15. Assume that all of Fish n'Fly's sales are for cash and all of its purchases are on account.

> Record transactions in perpetual and periodic inventory systems.
> (SO 2, 7) AP

Instructions

(a) Record the purchases and sales for Fish n'Fly in a perpetual inventory system under (1) FIFO and (2) average.

(b) Record the purchases and sales for Fish n'Fly in a periodic inventory system under (1) FIFO and (2) average.

*E6–17 The inventory of Marshall's Merchandise Company was destroyed by fire on June 1. From an examination of the accounting records, the following data for the first five months of the year were obtained: Sales $90,000; Sales Returns and Allowances $1,500; Sales Discounts $700; Freight Out $2,500; Purchases $51,200; Freight In $2,200; Purchase Returns and Allowances $2,400; and Purchase Discounts $1,300.

> Estimate inventory loss using gross profit method.
> (SO 8) AP

Instructions

Determine the inventory lost by fire, assuming a beginning inventory of $25,000 and a gross profit margin of 40%.

*E6–18 Zhang Shoe Store uses the retail inventory method for its two departments: men's shoes and women's shoes. The following information is obtained for each department:

> Estimate cost of ending inventory using retail method. (SO 8) AP

Item	Men's Shoes	Women's Shoes
Beginning inventory at cost	$ 36,000	$ 45,000
Beginning inventory at retail	58,050	95,750
Cost of goods purchased	216,000	315,000
Retail price of goods purchased	348,400	670,200
Net sales	365,000	635,000

Instructions

Calculate the estimated cost of the ending inventory for each shoe department under the retail inventory method.

▶ Problems: Set A

P6–1A Kananaskis Company is trying to determine the value of its ending inventory as at February 28, 2014, the company's year end. The accountant counted everything that was in the warehouse as at February 28, which resulted in an ending inventory valuation of $65,000. However, he was not sure how to treat the following transactions, so he did not include them in inventory:

> Identify items in inventory.
> (SO 1) AP

1. Kananaskis shipped $875 of inventory on consignment to Banff Company on February 20. By February 28, Banff Company had sold $365 of this inventory for Kananaskis.

2. On February 28, Kananaskis was holding merchandise that had been sold to a customer on February 25 but needed some minor alterations. The customer has paid for the goods and will pick them up on March 3 after the alterations are complete. This inventory cost $490 and was sold for $880.

3. In Kananaskis' warehouse on February 28 is $400 of inventory that Craft Producers shipped to Kananaskis on consignment.

4. On February 27, Kananaskis shipped goods costing $950 to a customer and charged the customer $1,300. The goods were shipped FOB destination and the receiving report indicates that the customer received the goods on March 3.

5. On February 26, Seller Company shipped goods to Kananaskis, FOB shipping point. The invoice price was $375 plus $30 for freight. The receiving report indicates that the goods were received by Kananaskis on March 2.

6. Kananaskis had $630 of inventory put aside in the warehouse. The inventory is for a customer who has asked that the goods be shipped on March 10.
7. On February 26, Kananaskis issued a purchase order to acquire goods costing $750. The goods were shipped FOB destination. The receiving report indicates that Kananaskis received the goods on March 2.
8. On February 26, Kananaskis shipped goods to a customer, FOB shipping point. The invoice price was $350 plus $25 for freight. The cost of the items was $280. The receiving report indicates that the goods were received by the customer on March 4.

Instructions

(a) For each of the above transactions, specify whether the item should be included in ending inventory, and if so, at what amount. Explain your reasoning.
(b) What is the revised ending inventory valuation?

TAKING IT FURTHER If the accountant of Kananaskis Company is paid a bonus based on profit, which of these errors might he consider overlooking and not correcting? Explain.

Apply specific identification.
(SO 2) AP

P6–2A EastPoint Toyota, a small dealership, has provided you with the following information with respect to its vehicle inventory for the month of November. The company uses the specific identification method.

Date	Explanation	Model	Serial #	Unit Cost	Unit Selling Price
Nov. 1	Inventory	Corolla	C63825	$15,000	
		Corolla	C81362	20,000	
		Camry	G62313	26,000	
		Venza	X3892	27,000	
		Tundra	F1883	22,000	
		Tundra	F1921	25,000	
8	Sales	Corolla	C81362		$22,000
		Camry	G62313		28,000
12	Purchases	Camry	G71811	27,000	
		Camry	G71891	25,000	
		Venza	X4212	28,000	
		Venza	X4214	31,000	
18	Sales	Camry	G71891		27,000
		Venza	X3892		31,000
		Tundra	F1921		29,000
23	Purchases	Tundra	F2182	23,000	
		Camry	G72166	30,000	

Instructions

(a) Determine the cost of goods sold and the ending inventory for the month of November.
(b) Determine the gross profit for the month of November.

TAKING IT FURTHER Should EastPoint Toyota use the specific identification cost determination method or one of the cost formulas? Explain.

Apply perpetual FIFO. Record sales and inventory adjustment, calculate gross profit, and answer questions.
(SO 2, 4) AP

P6–3A You are given the following information for Lahti Company for the month ended November 30, 2014:

Date	Description	Units	Unit Price
Nov. 1	Beginning inventory	60	$50
9	Purchase	100	46
15	Sale	(120)	
16	Sales return (Nov. 15 sale)	5	
22	Purchase	150	44
29	Sale	(160)	
30	Purchase	45	42

Lahti Company uses a perpetual inventory system. All sales and purchases are on account.

Instructions

(a) Calculate the cost of goods sold and the ending inventory using FIFO.
(b) Assume the sales price was $66 per unit for the goods sold on November 15, and $60 per unit for the sale on November 29. Prepare journal entries to record the November 22 purchase and the November 29 sale.

(c) Calculate gross profit for November.

(d) Assume that at the end of November, the company counted its inventory. There are 78 units on hand. What journal entry, if any, should the company make to record the shortage?

(e) If the company had not discovered this shortage, what would be overstated or understated on the balance sheet and income statement and by what amount?

TAKING IT FURTHER   In what respects does FIFO provide more useful information than average?

P6–4A   Information for Lahti Company is presented in P6–3A. Assume the same inventory data and that the company uses a perpetual inventory system. Ignore the inventory shortage in P6–3A (d).

Instructions

(a) Calculate the cost of goods sold and the ending inventory using average. (*Hint:* Round the average cost per unit to two decimal places.)

(b) Prepare the journal entry to record the November 15 sale and the sales return on November 16.

(c) If the company changes from average to FIFO and prices continue to fall, would you expect the cost of goods sold and ending inventory amounts to be higher or lower?

Apply perpetual average and answer questions. (SO 2, 3) AP

TAKING IT FURTHER   If Lahti Company wishes to change from average to the FIFO cost formula, what factors must it consider before making this change?

P6–5A   Fly-Buy Frisbees sells a wide variety of frisbees and uses a perpetual inventory system. On June 1, Fly-Buy Frisbees had five Fast Flying Frisbees on hand at a unit cost of $105. During June and July, the company had the following purchases and sales for this frisbee (all for cash):

Apply perpetual FIFO and average. Answer question about financial statement effects. (SO 2, 3) AP

	Purchases		Sales	
	Units	Unit Cost	Units	Unit Price
June 4			2	$210
18	5	$115		
30			6	235
July 5	5	120		
12			3	255
25			2	255

Instructions

(a) Determine the cost of goods sold and ending inventory under a perpetual inventory system using (1) FIFO and (2) average. (*Hint:* Round the average cost per unit to two decimal places.)

(b) Calculate gross profit using (1) FIFO and (2) average.

(c) What impact, if any, does the choice of cost formula have on cash flow?

TAKING IT FURTHER   What factors should the owner of Fly-Buy Frisbees consider when choosing a cost formula?

P6–6A   You are given the following information for Amelia Company. All transactions are settled in cash. Returns are usually not damaged and are restored immediately to inventory for resale. Amelia uses a perpetual inventory system and the average cost formula. Increased competition has reduced the price of the product.

Record transactions using perpetual average. Apply LCNRV. (SO 2, 5) AP

Date	Transaction	Units	Unit Price
July 1	Beginning inventory	25	$10
5	Purchase	55	9
8	Sale	(70)	15
10	Sale returns and allowances	15	15
15	Purchase	50	8
16	Purchase return	(10)	8
20	Sale	(55)	12
25	Purchase	10	7

Instructions

(a) Prepare the required journal entries for the month of July for Amelia Company. (*Hint:* Round the average cost per unit to two decimal places.)

(b) Determine the ending inventory for Amelia.

(c) On July 31, Amelia Company learns that the product has a net realizable value of $8 per unit. Prepare the journal entry, if required, to recognize the decrease in value of this product. If no entry is required, explain why.

(d) What amount should the ending inventory be valued at on the July 31 balance sheet? What amount should the cost of goods sold be valued at on the July income statement?

TAKING IT FURTHER What if Amelia had used FIFO instead of average? How would this affect the July 31 ending inventory on the balance sheet compared with average?

Determine effects of inventory errors.
(SO 1, 4) AN

P6–7A The records of Alyssa Company show the following amounts in its December 31 financial statements:

	2014	2013	2012
Total assets	$925,000	$900,000	$850,000
Owner's equity	750,000	700,000	650,000
Cost of goods sold	550,000	550,000	500,000
Profit	90,000	80,000	70,000

Alyssa Company made the following errors in determining its ending inventory:

1. The ending inventory account balance at December 31, 2012, included $20,000 of goods held on consignment for Gillies Company.
2. The ending inventory account balance at December 31, 2013, did not include goods sold and shipped on December 30, 2013, FOB destination. The selling price of these goods was $40,000 and the cost of these goods was $32,000. The goods arrived at the destination on January 4, 2014.

All purchases and sales of inventory were recorded in the correct fiscal year.

Instructions

(a) Calculate the correct amount for each of the following for 2014, 2013, and 2012:
   1. Total assets
   2. Owner's equity
   3. Cost of goods sold
   4. Profit
(b) Indicate the effect of these errors (overstated, understated, or no effect) on cash at the end of 2012, 2013, and 2014.

TAKING IT FURTHER As long as the merchandise inventory balance is correct as at December 31, 2014, is it necessary to correct the errors in the previous years' financial statements? Explain.

Determine effects of inventory errors. Calculate inventory turnover.
(SO 4, 6) AN

P6–8A Amanpreet Company has a July 31 fiscal year end and uses a perpetual inventory system. The records of Amanpreet Company show the following data:

	2014	2013	2012
Income statement:			
Sales	$350,000	$330,000	$310,000
Cost of goods sold	245,000	235,000	225,000
Operating expenses	76,000	76,000	76,000
Balance sheet:			
Merchandise inventory	55,000	45,000	35,000

After its July 31, 2014, year end, Amanpreet discovered two errors:

1. At July 31, 2013, Amanpreet had $10,000 of goods held on consignment at another company that were not included in the physical count.
2. In July 2013, Amanpreet recorded a $15,000 inventory purchase on account that should have been recorded in August 2013.

Instructions

(a) Prepare incorrect and corrected income statements for Amanpreet for the years ended July 31, 2012, 2013, and 2014.
(b) What is the impact of these errors on the owner's equity at July 31, 2014?
(c) Calculate the incorrect and correct inventory turnover ratios for 2013 and 2014.

TAKING IT FURTHER Compare the trends in the incorrectly calculated annual profits with the trends in the correctly calculated annual profits. Does it appear that management may have deliberately made these errors, or do they appear to be honest errors? Explain.

P6–9A Copperhead Company has provided you with the following information regarding its inventory of copper for September and October. Copperhead uses a perpetual inventory system.

Apply LCNRV and prepare adjustment. (SO 5) AP

	September 30	October 31
Copper Inventory (in tonnes)	2,500	2,000
Cost per tonne	$505	$535
NRV per tonne	$540	$520

Instructions

(a) Calculate the cost, the net realizable value, and the amount to be reported on the balance sheet for Copperhead's inventory at (1) September 30 and (2) October 31.

(b) Prepare any journal entries required to record the LCNRV of the copper inventory at (1) September 30 and (2) October 31.

(c) Assume that during the month of November the company did not purchase or sell any copper inventory and that the NRV per tonne was $530 on November 30. Is an adjusting entry required at November 30? Explain. If so, prepare the adjusting entry.

(d) What will have to be disclosed in Copperhead's notes to the financial statements with regard to its copper inventory?

TAKING IT FURTHER   Do all companies have to report inventory at the LCNRV on the balance sheet?

P6–10A The following financial information (in US$ millions) is for two major corporations for the three years ended December 31:

Calculate ratios. (SO 6) AN

PepsiCo Inc.	2011	2010	2009
Net sales	$66,504	$57,838	$43,232
Cost of sales	31,593	26,575	20,099
Profit	6,462	6,338	5,979
Cash and short-term investments	4,425	6,369	4,135
Accounts receivable	6,912	6,323	4,624
Inventory	3,827	3,372	2,618
Prepaid expenses and other current assets	2,277	1,505	1,194
Current liabilities	18,154	15,892	8,756

Coca-Cola Company			
Net sales	$46,542	$35,119	$30,990
Cost of sales	18,216	12,693	11,088
Profit	8,634	11,859	6,906
Cash and short-term investments	14,035	11,337	9,213
Accounts receivable	4,920	4,430	3,758
Inventory	3,092	2,650	2,354
Prepaid expenses and other current assets	3450	3,162	2,226
Current liabilities	24,283	18,508	13,721

Instructions

(a) Calculate the inventory turnover, days sales in inventory, current ratio, acid-test ratio, gross profit margin, and profit margin for each company for 2011 and 2010.

(b) Comment on each company's profitability and liquidity.

TAKING IT FURTHER   Companies are required to disclose in a significant accounting policies note how they determine the cost of their inventory. Both Pepsi and Coca-Cola state that they use average and FIFO. Under what circumstances would it make sense for a company use both cost formulas?

***P6–11A** Wolick Company had a beginning inventory on January 1 of 300 units of Product SXL at a cost of $21 per unit. During the year, the following purchases were made:

Apply periodic FIFO and average. (SO 7) AP

	Units	Unit Cost
Mar. 15	800	$20
July 20	600	19
Sept. 4	250	18
Dec. 2	100	17

At the end of the year, there were 350 units on hand. Wolick Company uses a periodic inventory system.

Instructions

(a) Determine the cost of goods available for sale.
(b) During the year, Wolick Company sold Product SXL for $33 per unit. Calculate the number of units sold during the year and total sales revenue.
(c) Determine the cost of the ending inventory and the cost of goods sold using (1) FIFO and (2) average. (*Hint:* Round the average cost per unit to two decimal places.)
(d) Calculate gross profit using (1) FIFO and (2) average.

TAKING IT FURTHER   The owner of Wolick Company would like to minimize his income taxes. Last year, prices were rising and Wolick Company used the average cost formula. This year, the owner would like to use FIFO. Should the company change? Explain.

Apply periodic and perpetual FIFO. (SO 2, 7) AP

*P6–12A   You are given the following information about Meesha Novelty's inventory for the month of July.

	Purchases			Sales	
Date	Units	Cost per unit	Date	Units	Price per unit
July 1	400	$3.00	July 2	300	$6.00
10	1,300	3.10	11	1,000	6.00
13	700	3.40	28	400	6.50
27	600	3.75			

Instructions

(a) Calculate the cost of goods available for sale and the number of units of ending inventory.
(b) Assume Meesha uses FIFO periodic. Calculate the cost of ending inventory, cost of the goods sold, and gross profit.
(c) Assume Meesha uses FIFO perpetual. Calculate the cost of ending inventory, cost of the goods sold, and gross profit.
(d) Prepare journal entries to record the July 10 purchase and the July 11 sale using (1) FIFO periodic and (2) FIFO perpetual. Assume both the sale and purchase were for cash.
(e) Compare the results of (b) and (c) above and comment.

TAKING IT FURTHER   Companies are required to disclose their cost determination method, but not the inventory system (periodic or perpetual). Provide an explanation as to why.

Apply periodic and perpetual average. (SO 2, 7) AP

*P6–13A   Aldor Corporation opened a new store on January 1, 2014. During 2014, the first year of operations, the following purchases and sales of inventory were made:

	Purchases			Sales	
Date	Units	Cost	Date	Units	Price
Jan. 5	10	$1,000	July 4	15	$2,000
June 11	10	1,200	Dec. 29	35	$2,000
Oct. 18	15	1,300			
Dec. 20	20	1,500			

Instructions

(a) Calculate the cost of goods available for sale and the number of units of ending inventory.
(b) Assume Aldor uses average periodic. Calculate the cost of ending inventory, cost of the goods sold, and gross profit.
(c) Assume Aldor uses average perpetual. Calculate the cost of ending inventory, cost of the goods sold, and gross profit.
(d) Prepare journal entries to record the December 20 purchase and the December 29 sale using (1) average periodic and (2) average perpetual.
(e) Compare the results of (b) and (c) above and comment.

TAKING IT FURTHER   If a company uses the average cost determination method, are there any benefits to using average perpetual over average periodic? Explain.

*P6–14A Westor Company lost all of its inventory in a fire on December 28, 2014. The accounting records showed the following gross profit data for November and December:

Determine inventory loss using gross profit method. (SO 8) AP

	November	December (to Dec. 28)
Sales	$674,000	$965,390
Sales returns and allowances	14,000	26,600
Purchases	441,190	621,660
Purchase returns and allowances	17,550	22,575
Freight in	6,860	12,300
Beginning inventory	34,050	39,405
Ending inventory	39,405	?

Westor is fully insured for fire losses but must prepare a report for the insurance company.

Instructions

Determine the amount of inventory lost by Westor as a result of the fire using the gross profit method.

TAKING IT FURTHER The insurance adjustor is concerned that this method of calculating the cost of the inventory destroyed might not be accurate. What factors contribute to the accuracy of the ending inventory amount when using the gross profit method?

*P6–15A Brandon Shoe Store uses the retail inventory method to estimate its monthly ending inventories. The following information is available at November 30, 2014:

Determine ending inventory using retail method. (SO 8) AP

	Women's Shoes Cost	Women's Shoes Retail	Men's Shoes Cost	Men's Shoes Retail
Beginning inventory	$ 276,000	$ 424,000	$ 191,000	$ 323,000
Purchases	1,181,000	1,801,000	1,046,000	1,772,000
Purchase returns and allowances	24,600	37,000	21,900	36,400
Freight in	6,000		7,200	
Sales		1,826,000		1,651,000
Sales returns and allowances		28,000		25,000

At November 30, Brandon Shoe Store takes a physical inventory count at retail. The actual retail values of the inventories in each department on November 30, 2014, are as follows: Women's Shoes $381,250, and Men's Shoes $426,100.

Instructions

Determine the estimated cost of the ending inventory at November 30, 2014, using the retail inventory method.

TAKING IT FURTHER Calculate the store's loss on November 30, 2014, from theft and other causes, at retail and at cost.

▶ Problems: Set B

P6–1B Banff Company is trying to determine the value of its ending inventory as at February 28, 2014, the company's year end. The accountant counted everything that was in the warehouse as at February 28, which resulted in an ending inventory cost of $56,000. However, she was not sure how to treat the following transactions, so she did not include them in inventory:

Identify items in inventory. (SO 1) AP

1. On February 20, Banff Company had received $875 of inventory on consignment from Kananaskis Company. By February 28, Banff Company had sold $365 of this inventory for Kananaskis.
2. On February 25, Banff ordered goods costing $750. The goods were shipped FOB shipping point on February 27. The receiving report indicates that Banff received the goods on March 1.
3. On February 26, Banff shipped goods costing $800 to a customer. The goods were shipped FOB shipping point. The receiving report indicates that the customer received the goods on March 1.
4. On February 27, Wah Company shipped goods to Banff, FOB destination. The invoice price was $350 plus $25 for freight. The receiving report indicates that the goods were received by Banff on March 2.

5. On February 28, Banff packaged goods and moved them to the shipping department for shipping to a customer, FOB destination. The invoice price was $425 plus $20 for freight. The cost of the items was $360. The receiving report indicates that the goods were received by the customer on March 2.

6. Banff had damaged goods set aside in the warehouse because they were not saleable. These goods originally cost $400. Banff had expected to sell these items for $600 before they were damaged.

7. On February 28, Banff was holding merchandise that had been sold to a customer on February 25 but needed some engraving done before the customer would pick it up. The customer has paid for the goods and will pick them up on March 3 after the engraving is finished. This inventory cost $940 and was sold for $1,340.

8. Banff had $620 of inventory at a customer's warehouse "on approval." The customer was going to let Banff know whether it wanted the merchandise by the end of the week, March 7.

Instructions

(a) For each of the above transactions, specify whether the item in question should be included in ending inventory, and if so, at what amount. Explain your reasoning.

(b) What is the revised ending inventory cost?

TAKING IT FURTHER   If the owner of Banff Company wants to minimize the amount of income taxes he or she will have to pay, what errors might the owner tell the accountant not to correct? Explain.

Apply specific identification. (SO 2) AP

P6–2B   EastPoint Honda, a small dealership, has provided you with the following information with respect to its vehicle inventory for the month of July. The company uses the specific identification method.

Date	Explanation	Model	Serial #	Unit Cost	Unit Selling Price
July 1	Inventory	Fit	YH6318	$26,500	
		Civic	SZ5824	26,700	
		Civic	SZ5828	26,600	
		Accord	ST0815	26,200	
		Accord	ST8411	27,600	
		Accord	ST0944	27,200	
10	Sales	Civic	SZ5828		$29,800
12	Purchases	Fit	YH4418	26,300	
		Fit	YH5632	26,600	
13	Sales	Fit	YH4418		28,900
		Accord	ST0944		28,700
		Civic	SZ5824		29,850
25	Purchases	Civic	SZ6132	26,800	
		Civic	SZ6148	26,600	
27	Sales	Civic	SZ6132		28,800
		Accord	ST0815		27,000
		Fit	YH6318		29,500

Instructions

(a) Determine the cost of goods sold and the ending inventory for the month of July.

(b) Determine the gross profit for the month of July.

TAKING IT FURTHER   Should EastPoint Honda use the specific identification cost determination method or one of the cost formulas? Explain.

Apply perpetual average. Record sales and inventory adjustment and calculate gross profit. (SO 2) AP

P6–3B   You are given the following information for Danielle Company for the month ended June 30, 2014:

Date	Description	Units	Unit Price
June 1	Beginning inventory	20	$50
4	Purchase	85	55
10	Sale	(90)	
18	Purchase	35	58
25	Sale	(30)	
26	Sales return (June 25 sale)	5	
28	Purchase	15	60

Danielle Company uses a perpetual inventory system. All sales and purchases are on account.

Instructions

(a) Calculate the cost of goods sold and the ending inventory using average. (*Hint:* Round the average cost per unit to two decimal places.)

(b) Assume the sales price was $90 per unit for the goods sold on June 10, and $95 per unit for the sale on June 25. Prepare journal entries to record the June 10 sale and the June 18 purchase.

(c) At the end of June, the company counted its inventory. There were 37 units on hand. What journal entry, if any, should the company make to record the difference?

(d) If the company had not discovered this shortage, what would be overstated or understated on the balance sheet and income statement and by what amount?

TAKING IT FURTHER   In what respects does average provide more useful information than FIFO?

P6–4B   Information for Danielle Company is presented in P6–3B. Assume the same inventory data and that the company uses a perpetual inventory system. Ignore the inventory difference from P6–3B (c).

Apply perpetual FIFO and answer questions.
(SO 2, 3) AP

Instructions

(a) Calculate the cost of goods sold and the ending inventory at June 30 using FIFO.

(b) Prepare the journal entries to record the June 25 sale and June 26 sales return.

(c) If the company changes from FIFO to average and prices continue to rise, would you expect the cost of goods sold and ending inventory amounts to be higher or lower than these amounts?

TAKING IT FURTHER   If Danielle Company wishes to change from FIFO to the average cost formula, what factors must it consider before making this change?

P6–5B   Bennett Basketball sells a variety of basketballs and accessories. Information follows for Bennett Basketball's purchases and sales during February and March for Up-Snap, one of its top brands of basketballs:

Apply perpetual FIFO and average. Answer questions about financial statement effects. (SO 2, 3) AP

	Purchases		Sales	
	Units	Unit Cost	Units	Unit Price
Feb. 7			18	$32
23	50	$20		
26			50	30
Mar. 10	24	19		
23			32	29

Bennett uses a perpetual inventory system. On February 1, Bennett had 36 units on hand at a cost of $21 each. All purchases and sales during February and March were on account.

Instructions

(a) Determine the cost of goods sold and ending inventory under a perpetual inventory system using (1) FIFO and (2) average. (*Hint:* Round the average cost per unit to three decimal places.)

(b) Calculate gross profit using (1) FIFO and (2) average.

(c) What impact, if any, does the choice of cost formula have on cash flows?

TAKING IT FURTHER   What factors should Bennett's owner consider when choosing a cost formula?

P6–6B   You are given the following information for transactions by Schwinghamer Co. All transactions are settled in cash. Returns are normally not damaged and are restored immediately to inventory for resale. Schwinghamer uses a perpetual inventory system and the FIFO cost formula.

Record transactions using perpetual FIFO. Apply LCNRV. (SO 2, 5) AP

Date	Transaction	Units	Unit Price
Oct. 1	Beginning inventory	60	$14
5	Purchase	110	13
8	Sale	(140)	20
10	Sale return	25	20
15	Purchase	35	12
16	Purchase return	(5)	12
20	Sale	(70)	16
25	Purchase	15	11

Instructions

(a) Prepare the required journal entries for the month of October for Schwinghamer Co.

(b) Determine the ending inventory for Schwinghamer.

(c) On October 31, Schwinghamer Co. determines that the product has a net realizable value of $10 per unit. What amount should the inventory be valued at on the October 31 balance sheet? Prepare any required journal entries.

(d) What amount should ending inventory be valued at on the October 31 balance sheet? What amount should cost of goods sold be valued at on the October income statement?

TAKING IT FURTHER   What if Schwinghamer had used average instead of FIFO? How would this affect the October 31 ending inventory on the balance sheet compared with FIFO?

<table>
<tr><td>Determine effects of
inventory errors.
(SO 1, 4) AN</td><td>

P6–7B   The records of Deveraux Company show the following amounts in its December 31 financial statements:

</td></tr>
</table>

	2014	2013	2012
Total assets	$600,000	$575,000	$525,000
Owner's equity	280,000	275,000	250,000
Cost of goods sold	315,000	335,000	300,000
Profit	60,000	50,000	40,000

Deveraux made the following errors in determining its ending inventory:

1. The ending inventory account balance at December 31, 2012, included $20,000 of goods held on consignment for Leblanc Company.

2. The ending inventory account balance at December 31, 2013, did not include goods that were purchased for $30,000 and shipped on December 30, 2013, FOB shipping point.

All purchases and sales of inventory were correctly recorded each year.

Instructions

(a) Calculate the correct amount for each of the following for 2012, 2013, and 2014:
   1. Total assets
   2. Owner's equity
   3. Cost of goods sold
   4. Profit

(b) Indicate the effect of these errors (overstated, understated, or no effect) on cash at the end of 2012, 2013, and 2014.

TAKING IT FURTHER   If the merchandise inventory balance is correct as at December 31, 2014, is it necessary to correct the errors in the previous years' financial statements? Explain.

<table>
<tr><td>Determine effects of
inventory errors. Calculate
inventory turnover.
(SO 4, 6) AN</td><td>

P6–8B   The records of James Company show the following data:

</td></tr>
</table>

	2014	2013	2012
Income statement:			
Sales	$648,000	$624,000	$600,000
Cost of goods sold	540,000	510,000	480,000
Operating expenses	100,000	100,000	100,000
Balance sheet:			
Merchandise inventory	40,000	60,000	70,000

After its July 31, 2014, year end, James discovered two errors:

1. In August 2012, James recorded a $30,000 inventory purchase on account for goods that had been received in July 2012. The physical inventory account correctly included this inventory, and $70,000 is the correct amount of inventory at July 31, 2012.

2. Ending inventory in 2013 was overstated by $20,000. James included goods held on consignment for another company in its physical count.

Instructions

(a) Prepare incorrect and corrected income statements for the years ended July 31, 2012, 2013, and 2014.

(b) What is the combined effect of the errors on owner's equity at July 31, 2014, before correction?

(c) Calculate the incorrect and correct inventory turnover ratios for each of the years 2013 and 2014.

TAKING IT FURTHER   Compare the trends in the incorrectly calculated annual profits with the trends in the correctly calculated annual profits. Does it appear that management may have deliberately made these errors, or do they appear to be honest errors? Explain.

P6–9B Vasquez Paper Company has provided you with the following information regarding their inventory of paper for June and July. Vasquez uses a perpetual inventory system.

	June 30	July 31
Paper Inventory (in tonnes)	4,500	6,200
Cost per tonne	$560	$680
NRV per tonne	$650	$615

Instructions

(a) Calculate the cost, the net realizable value, and the amount to be reported on the balance sheet for Vasquez Paper Company's inventory at (1) June 30 and (2) July 31.
(b) Prepare any journal entries required to record the LCNRV of the paper inventory at (1) June 30 and (2) July 31.
(c) Assume that during the month of August the company did not purchase any additional paper inventory and that on August 31 it had 5,000 tonnes in inventory and the NRV per tonne was $720. Is an adjusting entry required at August 31? Explain. If so, prepare the adjusting entry.
(d) What is Vasquez Paper Company required to disclose in its notes to the financial statements with regard to LCNRV?

TAKING IT FURTHER Why is it important to report inventory at the LCNRV on the balance sheet?

P6–10B The following financial information (in US$ millions) is for two major corporations for the three fiscal years ending as follows:

Home Depot, Inc.	January 29, 2012	January 30, 2011	January 31, 2010
Net sales	$70,395	$67,997	$66,176
Cost of sales	46,133	44,693	43,764
Profit	3,883	3,338	2,661
Cash and short-term investments	1,987	545	1,421
Accounts receivable	1,245	1,085	964
Inventory	10,325	10,625	10,188
Other current assets	963	1,224	1,327
Current liabilities	9,376	10,122	10,363

Lowe's Companies, Inc.	February 3, 2012	January 28, 2011	January 29, 2010
Net sales	$50,208	$48,815	$47,220
Cost of sales	32,858	31,663	30,757
Profit	1,839	2,010	1,783
Cash and short-term investments	1,300	1,123	1,057
Inventory	8,355	8,321	8,249
Other current assets	417	523	426
Current liabilities	7,891	7,119	7,355

Instructions

(a) Calculate the inventory turnover, days sales in inventory, current ratio, acid-test ratio, gross profit margin, and profit margin for each company for fiscal 2011 and 2010.
(b) Comment on each company's profitability and liquidity.

TAKING IT FURTHER All fiscal years shown for Home Depot are 52 weeks. Lowes' fiscal year ended February 3, 2012, is 53 weeks. Its other two fiscal years are 52 weeks. How, if at all, does the difference in the number of weeks impact our ability to compare Lowes' ratios across the two fiscal years and to Home Depot's ratios?

*P6–11B Chan Company had a beginning inventory on January 1, 2014, of 150 units of product YBB at a cost of $30 per unit. During the year, purchases were as follows:

	Units	Unit Cost
Feb. 17	700	$35
Apr. 12	400	39
July 10	300	45
Oct. 26	250	47

Chan uses a periodic inventory system. At the end of the year, there were 200 units on hand.

Instructions

(a) Determine the cost of goods available for sale.
(b) During the year, Chan Company sold product YBB for $72 per unit. Calculate the number of units sold during the year and total sales revenue.
(c) Determine the ending inventory and the cost of goods sold using (1) FIFO and (2) average.
(d) Calculate gross profit using FIFO and average.

TAKING IT FURTHER   The owner of Chan Company would like to minimize her income taxes. Last year, prices were falling and Chan Company used FIFO. This year she would like to switch to average. Do you recommend this change or not? Explain.

Apply periodic and perpetual average. (SO 2, 7) AP

*P6–12B   You are given the following information about Sasha Company's inventory for the month of April.

Purchases			Sales		
Date	Units	Cost per unit	Date	Units	Price per unit
April 1	400	$4.00	April 2	300	$7.00
10	1,300	4.10	11	1,000	7.00
25	1,200	4.50	29	1,400	7.50
27	600	4.75			

Instructions

(a) Calculate the cost of goods available for sale and the number of units of ending inventory.
(b) Assume Sasha uses average periodic. Calculate the cost of ending inventory, cost of the goods sold, and gross profit. (Note: Round the average cost per unit to three decimal places.)
(c) Assume Sasha uses average perpetual. Calculate the cost of ending inventory, cost of the goods sold, and gross profit. (Note: round the average cost per unit to three decimal places.)
(d) Prepare journal entries to record the April 25 purchase and the April 29 sale using (1) average periodic and (2) average perpetual.
(e) Compare the results of (b) and (c) above and comment.

TAKING IT FURTHER   Companies are required to disclose their cost determination method, but not the inventory system (periodic or perpetual). Provide an explanation as to why.

Apply periodic and perpetual FIFO. (SO 2, 7) AP

*P6–13B   Una Company opened a new store in February this year. During the first year of operations, the company made the following purchases and sales:

Purchases			Sales		
Date	Units	Cost	Date	Units	Price
Feb. 7	20	$100	Apr. 30	35	$120
Apr. 12	20	$120	Nov. 12	50	$160
July 18	25	$130			
Oct. 26	40	$150			

Instructions

(a) Calculate the cost of goods available for sale and the number of units of ending inventory.
(b) Assume Una uses FIFO periodic. Calculate the cost of ending inventory, cost of the goods sold, and gross profit.
(c) Assume Una uses FIFO perpetual. Calculate the cost of ending inventory, cost of the goods sold, and gross profit.
(d) Prepare journal entries to record the April 12 purchase and the April 30 sale using (1) FIFO periodic and (2) FIFO perpetual. Assume all transactions were on account.
(e) Compare the results of (b) and (c) above and comment.

TAKING IT FURTHER   If a company uses the FIFO cost determination method, are there any benefits to using FIFO perpetual over FIFO periodic? Explain.

*P6–14B   Merrett Company lost 80% of its inventory in a fire on March 23, 2014. The accounting records showed the following gross profit data for February and March:

Determine inventory loss using gross profit method. (SO 8) AP

	February	March (to Mar. 23)
Sales	$310,000	$293,500
Sales returns and allowances	7,000	6,800
Purchases	204,000	197,000
Purchase returns and allowances	5,300	4,940
Freight in	4,000	3,940
Beginning inventory	18,500	26,200
Ending inventory	26,200	?

Merrett is fully insured for fire losses but must prepare a report for the insurance company.

Instructions

Determine the amount of inventory lost by Merrett as a result of the fire using the gross profit method.

TAKING IT FURTHER   The insurance adjustor is concerned that this method of calculating the cost of the inventory destroyed might not be accurate. What factors contribute to the accuracy of the ending inventory amount when using the gross profit method?

*P6–15B   Hakim's Department Store uses the retail inventory method to estimate its monthly ending inventories. The following information is available for two of its departments at August 31, 2014:

Determine ending inventory using retail method. (SO 8) AP

	Clothing Cost	Clothing Retail	Jewellery Cost	Jewellery Retail
Sales		$1,300,000		$850,000
Sales returns and allowances		32,000		10,400
Purchases	$775,000	1,445,000	$565,000	923,000
Purchase returns and allowances	41000	71,500	17,200	25,700
Freight in	8,900		6,700	
Beginning inventory	55,600	98,000	34,000	54,000

On August 31, Hakim's Department Store takes a physical inventory count at retail. The actual retail values of the inventories in each department on August 31, 2014, are as follows: Clothing $100,750, and Jewellery $40,300.

Instructions

Determine the estimated cost of the ending inventory for each department on August 31, 2014, using the retail inventory method.

TAKING IT FURTHER   Calculate the store's loss on August 31, 2014, from theft and other causes, at retail and at cost.

▶ Continuing Cookie Chronicle

(*Note:* This is a continuation of the Cookie Chronicle from Chapters 1 through 5.)

Natalie is busy establishing both divisions of her business (cookie classes and mixer sales) and completing her business diploma. Her goals for the next 11 months are to sell one mixer per month and to give two to three classes per week.

The cost of the fine European mixers is expected to increase. Natalie has just negotiated new terms with Kzinski that include shipping costs in the negotiated purchase price. (Mixers will be shipped FOB destination.)

Recall that Natalie has two mixers in inventory: mixer #1 (serial number 12459) and mixer #2 (serial number 23568). Inventory cost for each of these units is $545.

The following mixer purchase and sale transactions occur in February and March, 2014:

Feb.   3   Natalie orders three deluxe mixers on account from Kzinski Supply Co. for $1,650 ($550 each), FOB destination, terms n/30.

      14   Natalie receives mixer #3 (serial number 49295), mixer #4 (serial number 56204), and mixer #5 (serial number 62897).

      19   Natalie sells one deluxe mixer, mixer #4, for $1,050 cash.

March   3   Natalie orders two deluxe mixers on account from Kzinski Supply Co. for $1,142, FOB destination, terms n/30.

      17   Natalie receives mixer #6 (serial number 69896) and mixer #7 (serial number 72531).

      18   Natalie returns mixer #6. It is not the one ordered.

      27   Natalie sells two deluxe mixers, mixer #2 and mixer #5, for a total of $2,100 cash.

All of the mixers Natalie has purchased and sold are identical. Natalie has accounted for all of these transactions by mixer number to ensure that she does not lose track of mixers on hand and mixers that have been sold. Natalie wonders if she is accounting for the costs of these mixers correctly.

Instructions

(a) Answer Natalie's concerns. Is Natalie accounting for these transactions correctly? Why or why not? What are the alternatives that Natalie could use in accounting for her mixer inventory?

(b) Given that Natalie has accounted for all of these transactions by mixer number, what is the total cost of goods sold for February and March, and the inventory balance at the end of March in Cookie Creations' accounting records?

(c) Using the average cost formula in a perpetual inventory system, prepare a schedule to track the purchases and sales of mixers, and the balance in the mixers inventory account. Use the format from Illustration 6-11.

(d) Prepare a journal entry to correct the March 31 inventory balance from the amount calculated in (b) to the amount determined in (c) assuming Natalie decided to use the average cost formula in a perpetual inventory system (instead of recording cost by specific mixer).

(e) Assume instead that Natalie had used the average cost formula to record all of the February and March transactions. Using the information prepared in (c) above, prepare the journal entries that would be required had Natalie used this cost formula.

CHAPTER 6 | BROADENING YOUR PERSPECTIVE

Financial Reporting and Analysis

Financial Reporting Problem

BYP6–1   Refer to the financial statements and Notes to Consolidated Financial Statements for **Reitmans (Canada) Limited** in Appendix A.

Instructions

(a) How does Reitmans value its inventory?

(b) Which inventory cost formula does Reitmans use?

(c) Would using the specific identification cost determination method be appropriate for a women's clothing retailer like Reitmans? Explain.

(d) How much did Reitmans record for inventory writedowns in fiscal 2012? Was it reported separately on the income statement or included in cost of goods sold? How much did it record for reversals of previous writedowns?

(e) For 2012 and 2011, calculate Reitmans' inventory as a percentage of current assets and its cost of sales as a percentage of total revenue. Comment on the results.

(f) Reitmans' inventory turnover and days sales in inventory were calculated for fiscal 2012 in this chapter in Illustrations 6-18 and 6-19, respectively. Calculate these same two ratios for fiscal 2011. Comment on whether Reitmans' management of its inventory improved or weakened in 2012.

Interpreting Financial Statements

BYP6–2   Headquartered in Toronto, **Indigo Books & Music Inc.** (TSX: IDG) is Canada's largest book retailer and the third largest in North America. The following information was taken from the management discussion and analysis section of the company's March 31, 2012, annual report (in thousands):

	2012	2011	2010
Cost of sales (cost of goods sold)	$600,400	$585,700	$538,500
Inventories	$229,706	$232,694	$224,406

Additional information from the company's annual report:

1. Inventories are valued at the lower of cost, determined using a moving average cost formula, and market, being net realizable value. Under this method, inventory is recorded at the level of the individual article (stock-keeping unit or SKU).
2. Costs include all direct and reasonable expenditures that are incurred in bringing inventories to their present location and condition. Vendor rebates are recorded as a reduction in the price of the products and corresponding inventory is recorded net of vendor rebates.
3. The average cost of an article is continually updated based on the cost of each purchase recorded in inventory. When the company permanently reduces the retail price of an item, there is a corresponding reduction in inventory recognized in the period if the markdown incurred brings the retail price below the cost of the item.
4. The amount of inventory writedowns as a result of net realizable value lower than cost was $10.3 million in 2012 ($7.3 million in fiscal 2011), and there were no reversals of inventory writedowns that were recognized in 2012 or in prior periods. The amount of inventory at March 31, 2012 with net realizable value equal to cost was $1.7 million ($2.3 million at March 31, 2011).

Instructions

(a) Calculate the company's inventory turnover and days sales in inventory ratios for 2012 and 2011. Comment on whether Indigo's management of its inventory improved or weakened in fiscal 2012.
(b) Does Indigo follow the lower of cost or net realizable value rule? Did the application of this rule have any effect on 2012 results? Explain.
(c) Indigo uses the average cost formula to account for its inventories. A major competitor, **Amazon.com, Inc.**, uses the FIFO cost formula to account for its inventories. What difficulties would this create in comparing Indigo's financial results with those of Amazon.com? Explain.

⦿ Critical Thinking

Collaborative Learning Activity

Note to instructor: Additional instructions and material for this group activity can be found on the Instructor Resource Site and in *WileyPLUS*.

BYP6–3   In this group activity, you will work in two different groups to improve your understanding of inventory cost determination methods using a perpetual inventory system. First, you will work in an "expert" group in which you will ensure that each group member thoroughly understands one of the inventory cost determination methods. Then you will move to a second group consisting of one student from each of the different expert groups, and take turns teaching the different inventory cost determination methods.

Communication Activity

BYP6–4   You are the controller of Small Toys Inc. Mutahir Kazmi, the president, recently mentioned to you that he found an error in the 2013 financial statements that he believes has now corrected itself. In discussions with the purchasing department, Mutahir determined that the 2013 ending inventory was understated by $1 million. However, the 2014 ending inventory is correct. Mutahir assumes that 2014 profit is correct and comments to you, "What happened has happened—there's no point in worrying about it now."

Instructions

You conclude that Mutahir is wrong. Write a brief, tactful e-mail to him that clarifies the situation.

Ethics Case

BYP6–5   Discount Diamonds carries only one brand and size of diamond—all are therefore identical. Each batch of diamonds that is purchased is carefully coded and marked with its purchase cost. You are given the following data from March:

Mar. 1   Beginning inventory was 140 diamonds at a cost of $500 per diamond.
     3   Purchased 200 diamonds at a cost of $540 each.
     5   Sold 170 diamonds for $800 each.
    10   Purchased 340 diamonds at a cost of $570 each.
    25   Sold 500 diamonds for $850 each.

Instructions
(a) Assuming that the company uses the specific identification cost determination method, do the following:
    1. Show how Discount Diamonds could *maximize* its gross profit for the month by choosing which diamonds to sell on March 5 and March 25.
    2. Show how Discount Diamonds could *minimize* its gross profit for the month by choosing which diamonds to sell on March 5 and March 25.
(b) Assume that Discount Diamonds uses the average cost formula and a perpetual inventory system. How much gross profit would Discount Diamonds report under this cost formula?
(c) Who are the stakeholders in this situation? Is there anything unethical about using the specific identification cost determination and choosing which diamonds to sell?
(d) Should Discount Diamonds choose the average or specific identification method of inventory cost determination?

"All About You" Activity

BYP6–6   In the "All About You" feature, you read about consignment shops and how they provide an alternative to paying full price for quality goods. As a student living on a tight budget, you have decided to sell some of your textbooks. You are considering two options: selling the textbooks yourself or taking them to the second-hand bookstore that sells used textbooks on consignment.

Instructions
(a) What is selling on consignment? If you sell your books on consignment, will you be the consignor or the consignee?
(b) What are the advantages and disadvantages of selling your textbooks on consignment?
(c) It is suggested that there should be a written agreement between the consignor and consignee. If you decide to sell your textbooks on consignment, what should be agreed to in writing?
(d) Assume you decide to sell your books on consignment through a second-hand bookstore. What are the risks to you of doing this?
(e) Should you keep your accounting textbook forever?

ANSWERS TO CHAPTER QUESTIONS

ANSWERS TO ACCOUNTING IN ACTION INSIGHT QUESTIONS

All About You Insight, p. 304

Q: What is one disadvantage of buying items on consignment?

A: Consignment stores do not typically allow you to return goods, so you need to be very careful when purchasing items.

Business Insight, p. 319

Q. When a company such as Blockbuster is placed in receivership, what would be the impact on how to account for its inventory?

A: As with any company, Blockbuster needs to compare the cost of its inventory with its net realizable value. But when a company is being liquidated, typically its assets will be sold for less than they would have in the normal course of business. We would therefore expect that net realizable value of Blockbuster's inventory would be considerably less than cost and a larger writeoff would be recorded. In the following period when the inventory is sold, assuming the company accurately measured the net realizable value, no further losses will be recorded but the company also won't record any profit on the sales. Thus, companies that are being liquidated must always report that there is a going concern issue.

ANSWERS TO SELF-STUDY QUESTIONS

1. a   2. d   3. d   4. b   5. c   6. a   7. c   8. b   9. b   *10. d   *11. c   *12. b   *13. a

Remember to go back to the beginning of the chapter to check off your completed work!

←

 THE **NAVIGATOR**

- ☐ Understand *Concepts for Review*
- ☐ Read *Feature Story*
- ☐ Scan *Study Objectives*
- ☐ Read *Chapter Preview*
- ☐ Read text and answer *Before You Go On*
- ☐ Review *Comparing IFRS and ASPE*
- ☐ Work *Demonstration Problem*
- ☐ Review *Summary of Study Objectives*
- ☐ Answer *Self-Study Questions*
- ☐ Complete assignments
- ☐ Go to *WileyPLUS* for practice and tutorials

CONCEPTS FOR **REVIEW**

Before studying this chapter, you should understand or, if necessary, review:

a. The role of ethics in financial reporting. (Ch. 1, p. 7)

b. How cash transactions are recorded. (Ch. 2, pp. 68–71)

c. How cash is classified on a balance sheet. (Ch. 4, pp. 185–186)

d. What internal control is. (Ch. 6, p. 302)

KEEPING TRACK OF THE CASH

CHARLOTTETOWN, P.E.I.—Located right in the heart of downtown Charlottetown, Beanz Espresso Bar is bustling with activity on weekdays. On average, 1,200 customers stop by each day for its selection of specialty coffees, homemade soups, sandwiches, and baked goods.

Lunch is the busiest time for Beanz. The two cash registers are shared by the six staff members working behind the counter on any given shift. "In an ideal situation, one or two people would be designated to ring in orders, but when we get swamped, we all have to work together to keep things running smoothly," says owner Lori Kays, who launched the business with her husband and business partner, Doug Hurry, back in 1995.

The prices of most items are preprogrammed in the machines, which reduces the chances of entry errors. Each register generates a sales report at the end of the day. Ms. Kays checks the day's cash receipts against the report to make sure they match. She also verifies the closing balances for the two floats—$250 for each till. "I tend to allow a few dollars' leeway since we round down amounts here and there when customers are short a few cents."

If the difference is larger, she goes through the register's internal tape to trace the source. "I will backtrack and try to make sure there weren't any payouts for which a receipt should have been turned in—we often make a run to the grocery store for something we need using cash from the till," she explains. For these petty cash items, staff use the Paid Out button on the till and have a receipt/invoice to match the payout. She prefers to keep track of these small purchases with the till than to have a petty cash box, which would be "just another thing that someone has to check every day to make sure it balances out," she says.

Ms. Kays deposits cash from sales in the bank at the end of the day. She does all of her bookkeeping herself using Simply Accounting software. "I post my sales totals each day and reconcile everything with my bank statements once a month," she says. "At the end of every year, I do everything except the last few adjusting entries before sending things off to the accountants." Careful cash control throughout the year helps ensure that everything adds up every time!

THE **NAVIGATOR**

>> STUDY **OBJECTIVES**

After studying this chapter, you should be able to:

1. Explain the activities that help prevent fraud and achieve internal control.

2. Apply control activities to cash receipts.

3. Apply control activities to cash payments, including petty cash.

4. Describe the control features of a bank account and prepare a bank reconciliation.

5. Report cash on the balance sheet.

THE **NAVIGATOR**

As the feature story about Beanz Espresso Bar shows, control of cash is important. Business owners and managers are responsible for safeguarding cash and other assets and for making sure that financial information is reliable. In this chapter, we explain the important features of an internal control system and describe how these controls apply to cash receipts and payments, including the use of a petty cash fund. Then we describe the use of a bank and explain how cash is reported on the balance sheet.

The chapter is organized as follows:

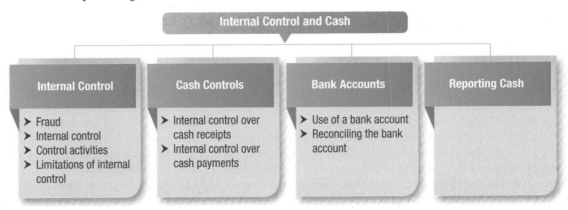

Internal Control and Cash			
Internal Control	**Cash Controls**	**Bank Accounts**	**Reporting Cash**
➤ Fraud ➤ Internal control ➤ Control activities ➤ Limitations of internal control	➤ Internal control over cash receipts ➤ Internal control over cash payments	➤ Use of a bank account ➤ Reconciling the bank account	

Internal Control

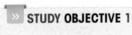
» STUDY OBJECTIVE 1

Explain the activities that help prevent fraud and achieve internal control.

Could there be dishonest employees where you work? Unfortunately, the answer is sometimes "yes". In the following sections of this chapter, we will learn about fraud and internal controls that can be put in place to help prevent and detect it.

FRAUD

Fraud is an intentional dishonest act that results in personal financial benefit by misappropriating (stealing) assets or misstating financial statements. According to a recent study by KMPG, 80% of frauds in Canada involve people inside an organization. Examples of fraud include the following real occurrences in Canada:

- A trusted bookkeeper stole almost $1 million from 21 non-profit daycare centres.
- The controller of a manufacturing company paid himself $2 million more than his normal pay level by writing unauthorized cheques on the company's payroll account. He got rid of the cancelled cheques when they were returned from the bank and then he altered the books.
- An assistant bank manager stole more than $10 million from a Toronto bank by making loans to fictitious companies.
- A liquor store employee is alleged to have pocketed $1.6 million. He was the sole order clerk for a program in which foreign diplomats could buy alcohol tax-free but payments had to be made by cash, cheque, or money order. The clerk is alleged to have either kept the cash or remitted only part of the proceeds to his employer.

Why does fraud occur in the workplace? The three main factors that contribute to fraudulent activity in the workplace are shown by the **fraud triangle** in Illustration 7-1.

▶**ILLUSTRATION 7-1**
Fraud triangle

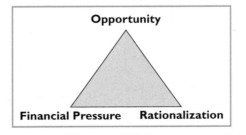

The most important element in the fraud triangle is opportunity. For an employee to commit fraud, there must be an opportunity to do so in the workplace. Opportunities occur when the workplace lacks sufficient controls to deter and detect fraud. For example, employees may be more likely to commit a fraud if they are not properly monitored and think they will not be caught.

A second factor that contributes to fraud is financial pressure. Employees sometimes commit fraud because of personal financial problems such as too much debt. Excessive lifestyles and drug or gambling addictions may also increase the likelihood that an employee will commit fraud.

The third factor that contributes to fraud is rationalization. In order to justify their fraud, employees rationalize their dishonest actions. For example, employees may believe they are underpaid and deserve to be paid more.

INTERNAL CONTROL

The risk of fraud, as well as the possibility of honest errors, emphasizes that a good system of internal control is necessary. **Internal control** consists of all of the related methods and measures that management designs and implements to help an organization achieve the following:

Helpful hint Errors are unintentional mistakes. Irregularities are intentional mistakes and misrepresentations.

1. reliable financial reporting
2. effective and efficient operations
3. compliance with relevant laws and regulations

Internal control has received increased attention in recent years. For example, the *Sarbanes-Oxley Act* governing publicly traded companies was created in the United States to help restore confidence in financial reporting. In Canada, similar legislation requires senior executives, such as CFOs and CEOs, of publicly traded companies to formally certify the effectiveness of their company's internal controls. Effective internal control systems have five basic components:

1. **Control environment:** It is the responsibility of top management to make it clear that the organization values integrity and that unethical behaviour will not be tolerated. Management must set the "tone at the top" and expect everyone to stick to the rules. This may include creating a corporate code of conduct, supporting a rigorous internal control program, establishing a hotline for anonymous reporting, and consistently disciplining employees who break the rules.
2. **Risk assessment:** Companies must identify and analyze the various factors that create risk for the business and must determine how to manage these risks.
3. **Control activities:** To reduce the occurrence of fraud and honest errors, management must design policies and procedures to address the specific risks faced by the company.
4. **Information and communication:** The internal control system must identify, collect, and communicate all relevant information to the appropriate internal and external parties.
5. **Monitoring:** Monitoring involves identifying problems and reporting them to appropriate levels of the organization where action can be taken. To be effective, problems must be communicated to the people who have the authority to act on the information, such as top management or the board of directors.

CONTROL ACTIVITIES

While each component of an internal control system is important, we will focus here on one: control activities. Control activities that apply to most companies include:

- establishment of responsibility
- segregation of duties
- documentation procedures
- physical and IT controls
- independent checks of performance
- human resource controls

Each of these control activities is explained in the following sections.

Establishment of Responsibility

An essential characteristic of internal control is assigning responsibility to specific individuals. **Control is most effective when only one person is responsible for a task.**

To illustrate, assume that the cash in the cash register at the end of the day at Beanz Espresso Bar in the feature story is $50 less than it should be according to the cash register tape. If only one person at the restaurant has operated the register, that person is probably responsible for the shortage. If two or more individuals have worked the register, however, as happens at Beanz Espresso Bar when the restaurant is busy, it may be impossible to determine who is responsible for the error.

Establishing responsibility is easier when there is a system for proper authorization of an activity. For example, computerized systems often require a passcode that keeps track of who rang up a sale, or who made a journal entry, or who entered an inventory stockroom at a particular time. Using identifying passcodes enables the company to establish responsibility by identifying the particular employee who carried out the activity.

Responsibility for authorizing and approving transactions must also be given to the correct person. For example, the vice-president of finance, not the vice-president of sales—who may be motivated to maximize sales commissions—should establish policies for making credit sales.

Segregation of Duties

Segregation of duties is essential in a system of internal control. Duties should be divided up so that one person cannot both commit a fraud and cover it up. There are two common ways of applying this control activity:

1. Different individuals should be responsible for related activities.
2. The responsibility for accounting or record keeping for an asset should be separate from the responsibility for physical custody of that asset.

Related Activities. When one person is responsible for all related activities, the potential for errors and irregularities increases. For example, companies should assign related purchasing activities to different individuals. Related purchasing activities include ordering merchandise, approving orders, receiving goods, authorizing payment, and paying for the goods or service. Various frauds are possible when one person handles related purchasing activities. For example:

- If the same person is responsible for ordering and for receiving, he can arrange to have an order sent to his home and pretend the goods were received by the company.
- If the same person is responsible for ordering and paying for the merchandise, she can place orders with friends or with suppliers who give kickbacks.
- If a purchasing agent is allowed to order goods without obtaining supervisory approval, the likelihood of the purchasing agent getting kickbacks from suppliers increases.

These abuses are less likely to occur when purchasing tasks are divided.

Similarly, related sales activities should be done by different individuals. Related selling activities include making a sale, shipping (or delivering) the goods to the customer, billing the customer, and receiving payment. Various frauds are possible when one person handles related sales transactions, as the following examples show.

- If a salesperson can make a sale without obtaining supervisory approval, he or she can make sales at unauthorized prices to increase sales commissions.
- A billing clerk who handles billing and receipt could understate the amount that is billed in sales to friends and relatives.
- A shipping clerk who has access to the accounting records could ship goods to himself.

These abuses are less likely to occur when companies divide the sales tasks: salespersons make the sale, shipping department employees ship the goods based on the sales order, and billing department employees prepare the sales invoice after comparing the sales order with the report of goods shipped.

Segregation of selling duties in a small business can be difficult, because there are fewer people. In these situations, the owner must be more involved to reduce the risk of fraud.

Custody of Assets. If the same person has physical custody of an asset and keeps the accounting records for that asset, then errors or theft could be hidden by altering the accounting records. When the employee who keeps the records of an asset is a different person from the employee who keeps the asset itself (the custodian), the employee who keeps the asset is unlikely to use it dishonestly. The separation of accounting responsibility from the custody of assets is especially important for cash and inventories because these assets are vulnerable to unauthorized use or theft.

Documentation Procedures

Documents give evidence that transactions and events have happened. At Beanz Espresso Bar, the cash register sales report is the restaurant's documentation for a sale and the amount of cash received. Similarly, a shipping document indicates that goods have been shipped, and a sales invoice indicates that the customer has been billed for the goods. By adding signatures (or initials) to a document, it also becomes possible to identify the individual(s) responsible for the transaction or event.

Procedures should be established for documents. First, whenever possible, documents should be prenumbered and all documents should be accounted for. Prenumbering helps to prevent a transaction from being recorded more than once, or not at all. Second, source documents (such as original receipts) for accounting entries should be promptly sent to the accounting department to help the transaction be recorded in a timely way. This control helps make the accounting records accurate and reliable.

Documentation as a control procedure also includes ensuring that all controls are written down and kept updated. Well-maintained documentation procedures ensure that the control activities are not forgotten and can make it easier to train new employees.

Physical and IT Controls

Physical and information technology (IT) controls include mechanical and electronic controls to safeguard (protect) assets and improve the accuracy and reliability of the accounting records. Examples of these controls are shown in Illustration 7-2.

▶ ILLUSTRATION **7-2**
Physical and IT controls

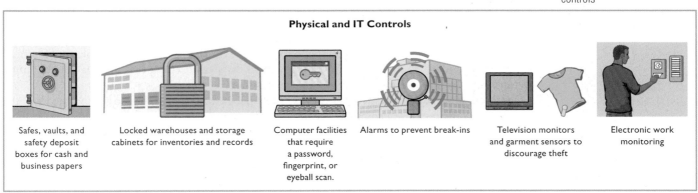

Physical and IT Controls

| Safes, vaults, and safety deposit boxes for cash and business papers | Locked warehouses and storage cabinets for inventories and records | Computer facilities that require a password, fingerprint, or eyeball scan. | Alarms to prevent break-ins | Television monitors and garment sensors to discourage theft | Electronic work monitoring |

Independent Checks of Performance

Most internal control systems include independent internal and/or external reviews of performance and records. This means having an independent person verify that the company's control activities are being correctly followed. To get the most from a performance review:

1. The review should be done periodically or by surprise.
2. The review should be done by someone who is independent of the employee who is responsible for the information.
3. Discrepancies and exceptions should be reported to a management level that can do whatever is necessary to correct the situation.

Internal Review. Segregating the physical custody of assets from accounting record keeping is not enough to ensure that nothing has been stolen. An independent review still needs to be done. In such a review, the accounting records are compared with existing assets or with external sources of information.

The reconciliation of the cash register sales report with the cash in the register by Beanz Espresso Bar owner Lori Kays in the feature story is an example of comparing records with assets. When the person who does the review works for the organization, we call this an internal review.

In large companies, control activities, including independent internal reviews, are often monitored by internal auditors. **Internal auditors** are company employees who evaluate the effectiveness of the company's system of internal control. They periodically review the activities of departments and individuals to determine whether the correct control activities are being followed.

In a publicly traded company, a management report addressed to the shareholders is included in the annual report that explains that management is responsible for the system of internal controls. Additionally, the chief executive officer and chief financial officer must certify that they have evaluated the effectiveness of the company's internal controls over financial reporting.

External Review. It is useful to contrast independent *internal* reviews with independent *external* reviews. **External auditors** are independent of the company. They are professional accountants hired by a company to report on whether or not the company's financial statements fairly present the company's financial position and results of operations.

All public companies, including Reitmans (Canada) Limited, are required to have an external audit. A copy of Reitmans' auditors' report is included in Appendix A. As you will see in the report, external auditors plan and perform an audit that will allow them to be reasonably sure that the financial statements do not contain any significant errors.

Human Resource Controls

Human resource control measures include the following:

1. **Bonding of employees who handle cash.** **Bonding** involves getting insurance protection against the theft of assets by dishonest employees. This measure also helps safeguard cash in two ways: First, the insurance company carefully screens all individuals before adding them to the policy and it may reject risky applicants. Second, bonded employees know that the insurance company will prosecute all offenders.
2. **Rotating employees' duties and requiring employees to take vacations.** These measures discourage employees from attempting any thefts since they will not be able to permanently hide their improper actions. Many banks, for example, have discovered employee thefts when the guilty employee was on vacation or assigned to a new position.
3. **Conducting thorough background checks.** Many people believe that the most important, and the least expensive, measure a company can take to reduce employee theft and fraud is to conduct thorough background checks.

LIMITATIONS OF INTERNAL CONTROL

No matter how well it is designed and operated, a company's system of internal control can only give reasonable assurance that assets are properly safeguarded and that accounting records are reliable. The concept of reasonable assurance is based on the belief that the cost of control activities should not be more than their expected benefit.

To illustrate, consider shoplifting losses in retail stores. Such losses could be eliminated by having a security guard stop and search customers as they leave the store. Store managers have concluded, however, that the negative effects of doing this cannot be justified. Instead, stores have tried to control shoplifting losses by using less costly and intrusive procedures such as posting signs that state "We reserve the right to inspect all packages" and "All shoplifters will be prosecuted," using hidden TV cameras and store detectives to watch customer activity, and using sensor equipment at exits.

The human factor is an important limit in every system of internal control. A good system can become ineffective as a result of employee fatigue, carelessness, indifference, or lack of proper training. For example, a receiving clerk may not bother to count goods received, or may alter or "fudge" the counts. Occasionally, two or more individuals may work together to get around controls, which eliminates the protection offered by segregating duties. This is often referred to as collusion.

The size of the business may also limit internal control. As mentioned earlier, in small companies it may be difficult to segregate duties or have independent checks of performance.

ACCOUNTING IN ACTION
ALL ABOUT YOU INSIGHT

Protect your identity. Personal information, such as your name, date of birth, address, credit card number, and social insurance number (SIN), can be used to steal money from your bank account, make purchases, or even get a job. Are you a victim?

According to a report by the Canadian Anti-Fraud Centre (a joint forces operation of the RCMP, Competition Bureau of Canada, and the Ontario Provincial Police), there were more than 17,000 reported cases of identity fraud in 2011. These victims reported total dollar losses of over $13.2 million. However, it's estimated that far more identity theft occurs than what is reported to police. A 2008 survey of Canadian consumers, conducted by the McMaster eBusiness Research Centre, found that almost 1.7 million Canadian adults had been the victim of some kind of identity fraud in the past year. The victims spent over 20 million hours and more than $150 million to resolve the problems associated with the frauds. More than half of these frauds involved the unauthorized use of credit cards. A key piece of information that identity thieves use to obtain personal data, to receive government benefits and tax refunds, or to get a job, is a person's SIN. To help protect Canadians, the federal government planned by March 2014 to stop issuing SIN cards, instead assigning the numbers via personal letters.

Source: Canadian Anti-Fraud Centre, "Annual Statistical Report 2011: Mass Marketing Fraud & ID Theft Activities"; Carys Mills, "Why Your SIN's Future Is No Longer in the Cards," *The Globe and Mail,* May 15, 2012; Susan Sproule and Norm Archer, "Measuring Identity Theft in Canada: 2008 Consumer Survey," Working Paper 23, McMaster eBusiness Research Centre, available at: http://www.merc-mcmaster.ca/working-papers/measuring-identity-theft-in-canada-2008-consumer-survey/

Who is responsible for losses due to unauthorized credit card use?

 BEFORE YOU GO ON...

Do It

In each of the following situations, identify the appropriate control activity and state whether it has been supported or violated.

(a) The purchasing department orders, receives, and pays for merchandise.
(b) All cheques are prenumbered and accounted for.
(c) The internal auditor performs surprise cash account checks.
(d) Extra cash is kept locked in a safe that can only be accessed by the head cashier.
(e) Each cashier has his or her own cash drawer.
(f) The company's controller received a plaque for distinguished service because he had not taken a vacation in five years.

Solution

(a) Violation of segregation of duties
(b) Support of documentation procedures
(c) Support of independent checks of performance
(d) Support of physical and IT controls
(e) Support of establishment of responsibility
(f) Violation of human resource controls (employees should take vacations)

Related exercise material: BE7–1, E7–1, and E7–2.

Action Plan
- Understand each of the control activities: establishment of responsibility, segregation of duties, documentation procedures, physical and IT controls, independent checks of performance, and human resource controls.

THE **NAVIGATOR**

Cash Controls

Cash is the one asset that is readily convertible into any other type of asset. It is also easily concealed and transported, lacks owner identification, and is highly desirable. In addition, because of the large volume of cash transactions, errors may easily happen when handling and recording cash. To safeguard cash and ensure the accuracy of the accounting records, effective internal control over cash is essential.

INTERNAL CONTROL OVER CASH RECEIPTS

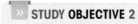

STUDY OBJECTIVE 2

Apply control activities to cash receipts.

Cash receipts come from a variety of sources: cash sales; collections on account from customers; the receipt of interest, dividends, and rents; investments by owners; bank loans; and proceeds from the sale of property, plant, and equipment. Generally, internal control over cash receipts is more effective when all cash receipts are deposited intact in the bank account every day. Illustration 7-3 shows examples of how the control activities explained earlier apply to cash receipt transactions.

Control Activities over Cash Receipts

Establishment of Responsibility

Only designated personnel (cashiers) are authorized to handle cash receipts.

Physical and IT Controls

Store cash in safes and bank vaults; limit access to storage areas; use cash registers; deposit all cash in a bank daily.

Independent Checks of Performance

Supervisors count cash receipts daily; controller's office compares total receipts with bank deposits daily.

Segregation of Duties

Different individuals receive cash, record cash receipts, and handle cash.

Human Resource Controls

Bond personnel who handle cash; require employees to take vacations; conduct background checks.

Documentation Procedures

Use remittance advices (mail receipts), cash register tapes, and deposit slips.

▶ **ILLUSTRATION 7-3**

Application of control activities to cash receipts

As might be expected, companies vary considerably in how they apply these principles. To illustrate internal control over cash receipts, we will discuss useful control activities for a retail store with over-the-counter, mail-in, and electronic receipts.

Over-the-Counter Receipts

Control of over-the-counter receipts in retail businesses is centred on cash registers that customers can see. All sales must be entered into the cash register through point-of-sale software that records the sale and updates the inventory records. Scanning bar codes on merchandise reduces the possibility of errors and fraud.

Receipts from cash sales—paid by coins and paper currency—are becoming rarer. Most customers pay by debit or bank credit card. Although banks charge retailers when these cards are used, there are many advantages for retailers that accept these forms of payment. As they are convenient for customers, the business may get more sales. They also improve internal control because employees handle less cash. The point-of-sale cash software separates daily sales according to each type of payment: cash, debit card, credit card, or cheque.

At the end of his or her shift, the cashier should count the cash in the register, record the amount, and turn over the cash and the record of the amount to either a supervisor or the person responsible for making the bank deposit. The procedures will be different in every company, but the basic principles should be the same. The person or persons who handle the cash and make the bank deposit should not be able to make changes to the sales recorded in the point-of-sale system or the accounting records. Employees must also make sure there are receipts on hand for debit or credit card sales and that these match the amounts recorded for each type of payment.

Companies with recurring cash transactions may use a special journal, called a **cash receipts journal**, to record all their receipts of cash. A **special journal** is used to record similar types of transactions. The types of special journals that are used depend largely on the types of transactions that happen frequently. Special journals are shown in Appendix C at the end of this textbook.

Debit Card Transactions. Sales using debit cards are considered cash transactions. Debit cards allow customers to spend only what is in their bank account. When a debit card sale occurs, the bank immediately deducts the cost of the purchase from the customer's bank account. The retailer has a choice about how often the proceeds from debit card transactions are electronically transferred into the retailer's bank account. Some retailers ask the bank to make one deposit at the end of each business day; other retailers wait and have several days of transactions deposited together. Banks usually charge the retailer a transaction fee for each debit card transaction and deduct this fee from the amount deposited in the retailer's bank account.

In many ways, accepting a debit card payment is similar to accepting a personal cheque from a customer. Both are ways for customers to spend the money in their bank accounts. But the major advantage of debit cards is that the retailer knows immediately if the customer has enough money in the bank to pay for the purchase. When a cheque is accepted, it takes several days for the retailer to find out whether the customer had sufficient funds. Most businesses are willing to pay a fee to the bank when customers use debit cards because there is no uncertainty about whether the customer has enough money in their bank account to pay for the purchase.

To illustrate, suppose that on March 21, ten customers use debit cards to purchase merchandise totalling $800 from Lee Company. Assuming the bank charges Lee Company $0.50 per debit card transaction, the entry made to record these transactions by Lee Company is as follows:

Mar. 21	Debit Card Expense (10 × $0.50)	5	
	Cash ($800 − $5)	795	
	Sales		800
	To record debit card sales.		

A = L + OE
+795   −5
    +800

↑ Cash flows: +795

In addition to the service charge for each transaction, Lee Company will also pay a monthly rental charge for the point-of-sale equipment that it uses for debit and credit card transactions.

Bank Credit Card Transactions. Sales using credit cards issued by banks, such as Visa and MasterCard, are considered cash sales by the retailer. A credit card gives customers access to money made available by a bank or other financial institution (essentially a short-term loan that has to be repaid). When a customer uses a bank credit card, the bank transfers the amount of the sale to the retailer's bank, less a service fee.

The rates charged by credit card companies to retailers vary greatly depending on such factors as the type of card used, the method of processing the transaction, as well as the volume of transactions. Retailers with a high number of transactions usually get a lower rate; those with a small number of transactions often have a higher rate. Similar to debit card transactions, the retailer's bank will wait until the end of the day and make one deposit for the full day's credit card transactions to the retailer's bank account; there is also the option of having one deposit every few days.

The fees for bank credit cards are generally higher than debit card fees. Why? With a debit card, the bank is charging only for transferring the customer's money to the retailer. With a credit card, the bank is taking the risk that the customer may never repay it for the loan. As we will see in Chapter 8, sometimes companies are not able to collect their receivables. Bank credit cards help retailers avoid this problem. Except for the higher bank charges, recording a bank credit card sale is very similar to recording a debit card sale.

To illustrate, suppose that on March 21, Lee Company sells $800 of merchandise to customers who use bank credit cards. The banks charge Lee Company a service fee of 3.5% for credit card sales. The entry made to record these transactions by Lee Company is:

Mar. 21	Credit Card Expense ($800 × 3.5%)	28	
	Cash ($800 − $28)	772	
	Sales		800
	To record bank credit card sales.		

A = L + OE
+772   −28
    +800

↑ Cash flows: +772

In addition to accepting bank credit cards, many large department stores and gasoline companies have their own credit cards. Sales using the retailer's own credit cards are credit sales; they result in accounts receivable, not cash, at the point of sale.

Mail-In Receipts

Helpful hint When billing customers, many companies state "Pay by cheque; do not send cash through the mail." This is done to reduce the risk of cash receipts being misappropriated when they are received.

Although the use of cheques has decreased, many companies still receive payment from their customers via cheques. In particular for high-value purchases, this reduces the service charges paid by the business as compared with credit card sales.

When a cheque is received in the mail, it is usually accompanied by a remittance slip showing the details of payment. All mail-in receipts should be opened in the presence of two mail clerks and the remittance slip compared to the cheque. The remittance slips are sent to the accounting department for recording and the cheques are stamped for deposit only and sent to the person responsible for making the bank deposits. Persons handling the cheques must not be able to alter the accounting records. An independent person should compare the deposit recorded by the bank with the amount recorded in the accounting records. In a small company, where it is not possible to have the necessary segregation of duties, the owner should be responsible for cash receipts.

Electronic Receipts

Electronic funds transfer (EFT) is the electronic exchange or transfer of money from one account to another, either within a single financial institution or across multiple institutions, through computer-based systems. Examples of transactions covered by the term "EFT" include:

- debit and credit card transactions
- pre-authorized debits
- electronic bill payments using on-line banking
- bank machine withdrawals
- prepaid smart cards

EFT transactions have grown dramatically while cheques and cash transactions have decreased. There has also been a rapid growth in the different types of EFTs. Some EFTs are initiated by the customer, such as on-line electronic bill payments. Others are initiated by the company, such as pre-authorized debits. Electronic funds transfers normally result in better internal control since no cash or cheques are handled by company employees. But it is still important to have proper authorization and segregation of duties to ensure an employee cannot divert a customer payment to a personal bank account and then cover it up through fraudulent accounting entries.

ACCOUNTING IN ACTION
ACROSS THE ORGANIZATION

Will that be cash, cheque, or smart phone? As this text went to print, Canada was on the verge of launching widescale mobile payment—the ability to swipe a mobile phone to pay for everything from a cup of coffee to bus fare. Mobile payment was expected to be a boon to consumers and business alike, as it offers unparalleled convenience, especially for purchases of low dollar value. A federal government task force on payments systems estimated that businesses could reduce invoicing costs by up to 80%. Mobile payments also cut down on transaction processing time and reduce cash handling costs. But many Canadians were sceptical of the technology. One survey found that 4 in 10 Canadians considering using their smart phone to make payments were most concerned about security, and one in three said they would never use the technology. In another survey, roughly 8 in 10 Canadian businesses thought that consumers would worry that hackers could steal their financial or other personal information from their smart phone. The government task force says the reality is quite different, because mobile payments are safer and more secure than the existing payment system.

Sources: Scott Simpson, "Canada Needs Quicker Shift to Mobile Payments, Task Force Says," *Financial Post*, March 27, 2012; Brian Jackson, "Canadians Cautious About Mobile Payment Security," ITBusiness.ca, October 6, 2011; KPMG, "Mobile Payments: Is Canada Ready? Insights from our Global Survey on Mobile Payments," October 2011.

How might an organization's marketing department assist in, and benefit from, the implementation of a mobile payments system?

BEFORE YOU GO ON...

Do It

Prepare journal entries to record the following selected debit and credit card transactions for Bulk Department Store:

July 18	A customer used her debit card to pay for a $650 purchase. Bulk Department Store was charged a $2 service fee.
22	A customer paid for a $1,200 purchase with her Visa credit card. The bank charges Bulk Department Store a service fee of 3.0%.
25	A customer paid for a $500 purchase with his Bulk Department Store credit card.

Solution

July 18	Debit Card Expense		2	
	Cash ($650 − $2)		648	
	Sales			650
	To record debit card sale.			
22	Credit Card Expense ($1,200 × 3.0%)		36	
	Cash ($1,200 − $36)		1,164	
	Sales			1,200
	To record Visa credit card sale.			
25	Accounts Receivable		500	
	Sales			500
	To record company credit card sale.			

Related exercise material: BE7–2, BE7–3, E7–3, and E7–4.

Action Plan

- Debit cards are recorded as cash sales, less the service charge.
- Bank credit cards are recorded as cash sales, less the service charge.
- Nonbank credit cards are recorded as receivables. There is no bank service charge when a customer uses a company credit card.

THE NAVIGATOR

INTERNAL CONTROL OVER CASH PAYMENTS

Cash is disbursed for a variety of reasons, such as to pay expenses and liabilities, or to purchase assets. Generally, internal control over cash payments is better when payments are made by cheque or EFT, rather than in cash. Payment by cheque should occur only after specified control procedures have been followed. The paid cheque gives proof of payment. Illustration 7-4 shows examples of how the control activities explained earlier apply to cash payments.

» STUDY OBJECTIVE 3

Apply control activities to cash payments, including petty cash.

▶ **ILLUSTRATION 7-4**
Application of control activities over cash payments

Control Activities over Cash Payments

Establishment of Responsibility

Only designated personnel are authorized to sign cheques or approve electronic payments.

Physical and IT Controls

Store cash in safes, limit access to blank cheques and signing machines, and use electronic payments when possible.

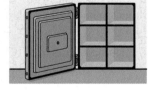

Segregation of Duties

Different individuals approve and make payments; cheque signers do not record disbursements.

Independent Checks of Performance

Compare cheques with invoices; reconcile bank statement monthly.

Documentation Procedures

Use prenumbered cheques and account for them in sequence; each cheque must have an approved invoice.

Human Resources

Bond personnel who handle cash, require employees to take vacations, and conduct background checks.

Cheques

Good control over cheques includes having them signed by at least two authorized people. The cheque signers should carefully review the supporting documentation for the payment before signing the cheque. There should be a clear segregation of duties between the cheque-signing function and the accounts payable function. Cheques should be prenumbered, and all cheque numbers must be accounted for in the payment and recording process. Cheques should never be pre-signed, and blank (unissued) cheques should be physically controlled.

Many large companies use purchase orders to improve their internal control over cash payments. A purchase order documents the details of the purchase and the fact that the purchase has been approved. The purchase order is usually prepared by the purchasing department.

When the good or service is received, the receiving report is matched with the purchase order. When the seller's invoice is later received, it is matched to the purchase order and receiving report. An authorized person in the accounts payable department then approves the invoice for payment. A cheque is sent on the due date, and the invoice is stamped "Paid."

The accounting department records the payment of the invoice. Companies that have a lot of cash payments often use a special journal, called a **cash payments journal**, to record all payments of cash. As mentioned earlier, Appendix C at the end of this textbook illustrates the use of special journals.

Electronic Payments

Just as a company may use electronic funds transfer systems to receive cash, it can also use those systems to make payments to suppliers and employees. For example, when a company pays its employees' salaries using a direct deposit option, the cash is instantly transferred from the company's bank account to each employee's bank account. Electronic pre-authorized payments are often made for things paid on a recurring basis like insurance or loans and interest.

The use of EFT for cash payments will result in better internal control as long as there is proper authorization and segregation of duties. EFT payments also reduce the extra costs of making payments by cheque, such as postage and envelope costs.

Petty Cash Fund

While making payments by EFT and cheques results in better internal control than using cash, it can be both impractical and a nuisance to use cheques or EFT to pay for small amounts. For example, a company may not want to write cheques to pay for postage, couriers, or small purchases of supplies. Beanz in our feature story uses the "Paid Out" button on its cash register to track small cash payments.

Another common way to handle such payments, while maintaining satisfactory control, is to use a **petty cash fund**. The operation of a petty cash fund, also called an imprest system, involves three steps: (1) establishing the fund, (2) making payments from the fund, and (3) replenishing the fund.

Establishing the Fund. Two essential steps are required to establish a petty cash fund: (1) appoint a petty cash custodian to be responsible for the fund, and (2) determine the size of the fund. Ordinarily, the amount is expected to be enough for likely payments in a three- to four-week period.

To establish the fund, a cheque payable to the petty cash custodian is issued for the determined amount. If Lee Company decides to establish a $100 petty cash fund on March 1, the general journal entry is as follows:

A = L + OE				
+100	Mar. 1	Petty Cash	100	
−100		Cash		100
		To establish a petty cash fund.		

Cash flows: no effect

There is no effect on cash flows because the company's total cash has not changed. There is $100 less in the bank account but $100 more cash on hand. The custodian cashes the cheque and places the proceeds in a locked petty cash box or drawer. No other entries are made to the Petty Cash account unless the size of the fund is increased or decreased. For example, if Lee Company decides on March 15 to increase the size of the fund to $250, it will debit Petty Cash and credit Cash $150 ($250 − $100).

Making Payments from the Fund. The petty cash custodian has the authority to make payments from the fund in accordance with management policies. Usually, management limits the size of expenditures that may be made. Likewise, it may not allow the fund to be used for certain types of transactions (such as making short-term loans to employees).

Each payment from the fund should be documented on a prenumbered petty cash receipt, signed by both the custodian and the person who receives the payment. If other supporting documents, such as a freight bill or invoice, are available, they should be attached to the petty cash receipt. The receipts are kept in the petty cash box until the fund runs low and the cash needs to be replenished. The sum of the petty cash receipts and money in the fund should equal the established total at all times. Surprise counts should be made by an independent person, such as a supervisor or internal auditor, to determine whether the fund is being properly administered.

An accounting entry is not recorded when a payment is made from the petty cash fund. Instead, it is recorded when the fund is replenished.

Replenishing the Fund. When the money in the petty cash fund reaches a minimum level, the company replenishes the fund. The request for reimbursement is made by the petty cash custodian. This individual prepares a schedule (or summary) of the payments that have been made and sends the schedule, supported by petty cash receipts and other documentation, to the controller's office. The receipts and supporting documents are examined in the controller's office to verify that they were proper payments from the fund. The request is approved and a cheque is issued to restore the fund to its established amount. At the same time, all supporting documentation is stamped "Paid" so that it cannot be submitted again for payment.

To illustrate, assume that on March 15, Lee's petty cash fund has $13 cash and petty cash receipts for postage $44, freight in $38 (assume a perpetual inventory system is used), and miscellaneous expenses $5. The petty cash custodian will request a cheque for $87 ($100 − $13). The entry to record the cheque is as follows:

Mar. 15	Postage Expense	44	
	Merchandise Inventory	38	
	Miscellaneous Expense	5	
	Cash		87
	To replenish petty cash.		

$A = L + OE$: +38, −87 / −44, −5; Cash flows: −87

Note that the Petty Cash account is not affected by the reimbursement entry. Replenishment changes what's in the fund by replacing the petty cash receipts with cash. It does not change the balance in the fund.

Occasionally, when replenishing a petty cash fund, the company may need to recognize a cash shortage or overage. This results when the receipts plus cash in the petty cash box do not equal the established amount of the petty cash fund. To illustrate, assume in the example above that the custodian had only $12 in cash in the fund, plus the receipts as listed. The request for reimbursement would, therefore, have been for $88 ($100 − $12). The following entry would be made:

Mar. 15	Postage Expense	44	
	Merchandise Inventory	38	
	Miscellaneous Expense	5	
	Cash Over and Short	1	
	Cash		88
	To replenish petty cash.		

$A = L + OE$: +38, −88 / −44, −5, −1; Cash flows: −88

Conversely, if the custodian had $14 in cash, the reimbursement request would have been for $86 ($100 − $14) and Cash Over and Short would have been credited for $1. A debit balance in Cash Over and Short is reported in the income statement as miscellaneous expense. A credit balance in the account is reported as miscellaneous revenue.

If the petty cash fund is not big enough, it is often increased (or decreased if the amount is too large) when the fund is replenished. Assume that Lee Company decides to increase the size of its petty cash fund from $100 to $125 on March 15 when it replenishes the fund. The entry to record the reimbursement and change in fund size is as follows:

```
A    =   L   +   OE
+25              -44
+38              -5
-113             -1
↓ Cash flows: -88
```

Mar. 15	Petty Cash	25	
	Postage Expense	44	
	Merchandise Inventory	38	
	Miscellaneous Expense	5	
	Cash Over and Short	1	
	Cash		113
	To replenish petty cash and increase the fund size by $25.		

In this entry, the Petty Cash account is affected because of the change in size of the fund. After this entry, the general ledger account shows a balance of $125 and the custodian must ensure that cash and paid-out receipts now total $125. Although a $113 cheque has been written, total cash is decreased by only $88 as $25 is added to Petty Cash.

A petty cash fund should be replenished at the end of the accounting period regardless of how much cash is in the fund. Replenishment at this time is necessary in order to recognize the effects of the petty cash payments on the financial statements.

Action Plan

- Set up a separate general ledger account when the fund is established.
- Determine how much cash is needed to replenish the fund—subtract the cash remaining from the petty cash fund balance.
- Total the petty cash receipts. Determine any cash over or short—the difference between the cash needed to replenish the fund and the total of the petty cash receipts.
- Record the expenses incurred according to the petty cash receipts when replenishing the fund.

◎ BEFORE YOU GO ON...

Do It

Bateer Company established a $50 petty cash fund on July 1. On July 30, the fund had $12 cash remaining and petty cash receipts for postage $14, supplies $10, and delivery expense $15. Prepare the journal entries to establish the fund on July 1 and replenish the fund on July 30.

Solution

July	1	Petty Cash	50	
		Cash		50
		To establish a petty cash fund.		
	30	Postage Expense	14	
		Supplies	10	
		Delivery Expense	15	
		Cash Over and Short ($39 − $38)		1
		Cash ($50 − $12)		38
		To replenish petty cash.		

Related exercise material: BE7–4, BE7–5, BE7–6, E7–5, E7–6, and E7–7.

THE **NAVIGATOR**

Bank Accounts

In the following section, we will learn about the control features of a bank account and how to prepare a bank reconciliation.

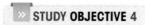

» **STUDY OBJECTIVE 4**

Describe the control features of a bank account and prepare a bank reconciliation.

USE OF A BANK ACCOUNT

Using a bank makes internal control over cash much stronger. A company can safeguard its cash by using a bank as a depository and reduce the amount of currency that must be kept on hand. In addition, using a bank increases internal control, because it creates a double record of all bank transactions—one by the business and the other by the bank. The asset account Cash, maintained by the company, should have the same balance as the bank's liability account for that company. A **bank reconciliation** compares the bank's balance with the company's balance and explains any differences.

Many companies have more than one bank account. For efficiency of operations and better control, national retailers like Sears may have local bank accounts. Similarly, a company may have a payroll bank account, as well as one or more general bank accounts. A company may also have accounts with different banks in order to have more than one source for short-term loans when needed.

Bank Deposits and Cheques

Bank deposits should be made by an authorized employee, such as the head cashier. Each deposit must be documented by a deposit slip, as shown in Illustration 7-5. Both the company and the bank will need a copy of the deposit slip.

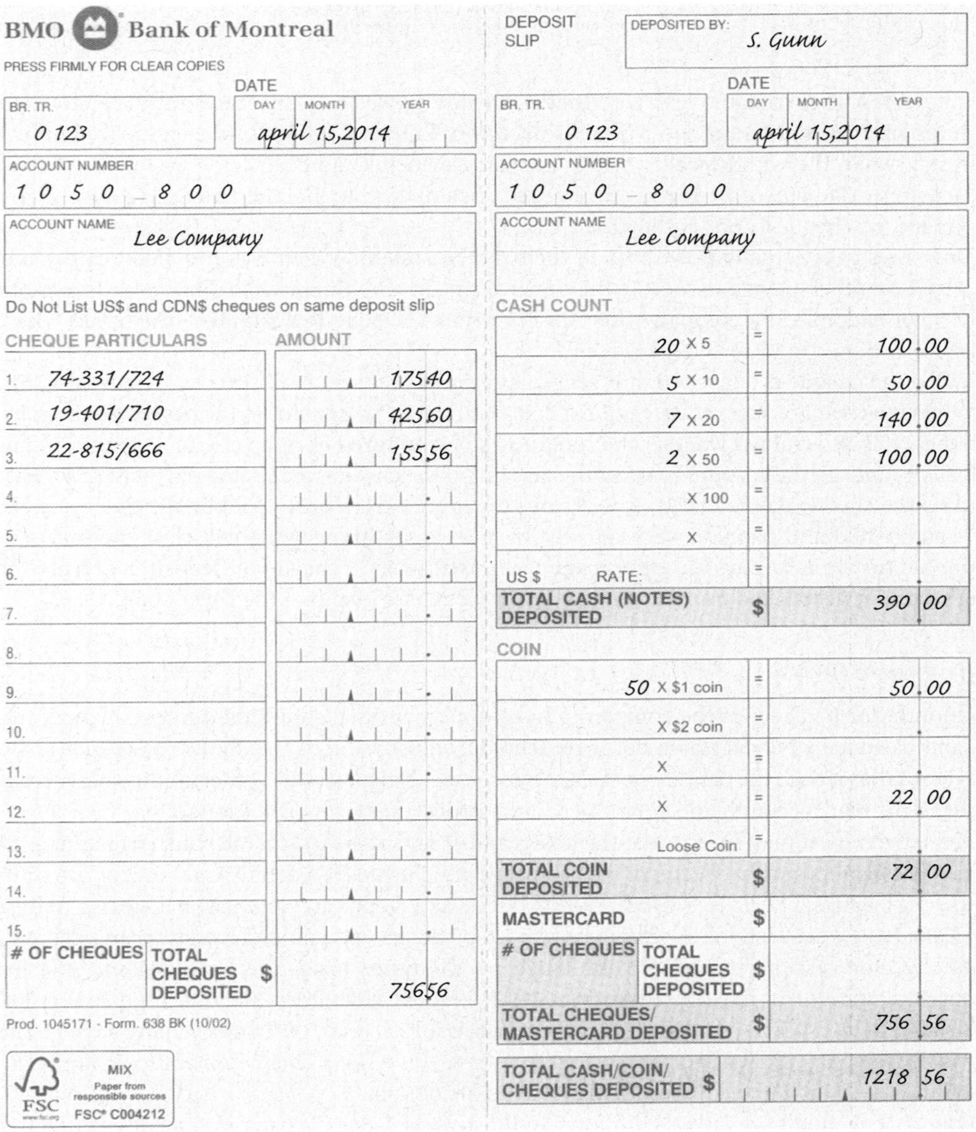

BMO Bank of Montreal

PRESS FIRMLY FOR CLEAR COPIES

BR. TR.	DATE (DAY / MONTH / YEAR)
0 123	april 15,2014

ACCOUNT NUMBER: 1 0 5 0 – 8 0 0

ACCOUNT NAME: Lee Company

Do Not List US$ and CDN$ cheques on same deposit slip

CHEQUE PARTICULARS	AMOUNT
1. 74-331/724	175.40
2. 19-401/710	425.60
3. 22-815/666	155.56
4.	
5.	
6.	
7.	
8.	
9.	
10.	
11.	
12.	
13.	
14.	
15.	
# OF CHEQUES / TOTAL CHEQUES DEPOSITED $	756.56

Prod. 1045171 - Form. 638 BK (10/02)

MIX Paper from responsible sources FSC FSC® C004212

DEPOSIT SLIP — DEPOSITED BY: S. Gunn

BR. TR.	DATE (DAY / MONTH / YEAR)
0 123	april 15,2014

ACCOUNT NUMBER: 1 0 5 0 – 8 0 0

ACCOUNT NAME: Lee Company

CASH COUNT		
20 X 5	=	100.00
5 X 10	=	50.00
7 X 20	=	140.00
2 X 50	=	100.00
X 100	=	
X	=	
US $ RATE:	=	
TOTAL CASH (NOTES) DEPOSITED	$	390.00
COIN		
50 X $1 coin	=	50.00
X $2 coin	=	
X	=	
X	=	22.00
Loose Coin	=	
TOTAL COIN DEPOSITED	$	72.00
MASTERCARD	$	
# OF CHEQUES / TOTAL CHEQUES DEPOSITED	$	
TOTAL CHEQUES/MASTERCARD DEPOSITED	$	756.56
TOTAL CASH/COIN/CHEQUES DEPOSITED	$	1218.56

ILLUSTRATION 7-5
Deposit slip
(reproduced with permission of BMO Bank of Montreal)

While bank deposits increase the bank account balance, cheques decrease it. A cheque is a written order instructing the bank to pay a specific sum of money to a designated recipient. There are three parties to a cheque: (1) the maker (or drawer) who issues the cheque, (2) the bank (or payer) on which the cheque is drawn, and (3) the payee to whom the cheque is payable. A cheque is a negotiable instrument that can be transferred to another party by endorsement.

Each cheque should clearly explain its purpose. The purpose of a cheque can be detailed on the cheque stub, as shown in Illustration 7-6. The purpose of the cheque should also be clear for the payee, either by referencing the invoice directly on the cheque—see the reference to invoice #27622 on the "For" line of the cheque in the illustration—or by attaching a copy of the invoice to the cheque.

▶ **ILLUSTRATION 7-6**
Cheque (reproduced with permission of BMO Bank of Montreal)

Automated teller machine cash withdrawals are not allowed on a business bank account where two signatures are required on cheques. There is no way of knowing if both of the authorized individuals are present when the withdrawal is made. The same principle applies to EFT payments on business bank accounts. When two signatures are required, the only way to maintain internal control is to make all payments by cheque or pre-authorized EFT.

How does cash actually flow through the banking system? When cheques, debit cards, and pre-authorized or other payments occur, they may result in one financial institution owing money to another. For example, if a company (the maker) writes a cheque to a supplier (the payee), the payee deposits the cheque in its own bank account.

When the cheque is deposited, it is sent to a regional data centre for processing, usually the same day. When the cheque arrives at the regional data centre, it is "presented" to the payee's financial institution, where it is determined whether the cheque will be honoured or returned (for example, if there are insufficient funds in the account to cover the amount of the cheque, or if a stop payment order has been placed on the cheque by the maker, which stops the money from being paid by the cheque). This process is automated and happens very quickly. In most cases, the cheque will clear the maker's bank account before the next day. **Clearing** is the term used when a cheque or deposit is accepted by the maker's bank. It results in a transfer of funds from the maker's bank to the payee's bank.

Bank Statements

Each month, the bank sends the company a **bank statement** that shows the company's bank transactions and balance. A typical statement is presented in Illustration 7-7. It shows (1) cheques paid and other debits that reduce the balance in the bank account, (2) deposits and other credits that increase the balance in the bank account, and (3) the account balance after each day's transactions.

At first glance, it may appear that the debits and credits reported on the bank statement are backward. How can amounts that decrease the balance, like a cheque, be a debit? And how can amounts that increase the balance, like a deposit, be a credit? Debits and credits are not really backward. To the company, Cash is an asset account. Assets are increased by debits (e.g., for cash receipts) and decreased by credits (e.g., for cash payments). To the bank, on the other hand, the bank account is a liability account—an amount it must repay to you upon request. Liabilities are increased by credits and decreased by debits. When you deposit money in your bank account, the bank's liability to you increases. That is why the bank shows deposits as credits. When you write a cheque on your account, the bank pays out this amount and decreases (debits) its liability to you.

Note that cheque #442 for $2,420 shown in Illustration 7-6 is the bank statement's April 8 transaction. Although the cheque was written on April 7, it did not clear the bank until April 8. You can also find the deposit slip for $1,218.56 shown in Illustration 7-5 on the bank statement's April 15 transaction. Other deposits and cheques could be found in the same way by examining the supporting documentation kept on file by the company.

Other deductions from the bank account include bank service charges. For example, on April 28, the bank charged Lee Company $30.00 as a monthly charge for operating the bank account.

Helpful hint Every deposit received by the bank is credited to the customer's account. The reverse happens when the bank "pays" a cheque issued by a company on the company's chequing account balance. Because payment reduces the bank's liability, the amount is debited to the customer's account with the bank.

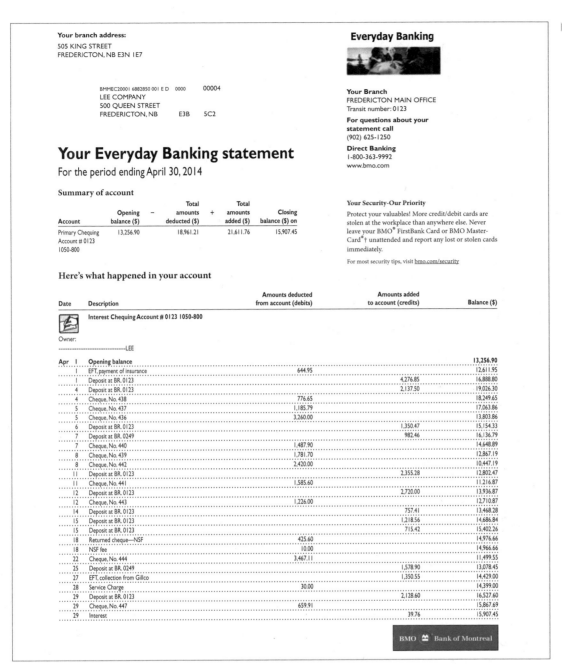

▶**ILLUSTRATION 7-7**
Bank statement
(reproduced with permission
of BMO Bank of Montreal)

The bank will include a **debit memorandum** with the bank statement when additional information is needed to explain a charge on the bank statement. The symbol DM (debit memo) is often used on the bank statement for such charges. For example, a debit memorandum is used by the bank when a deposited cheque from a customer does not clear because of insufficient funds in the customer's account. In such a case, the cheque is marked **NSF (not sufficient funds)** or RT (returned item) by the customer's bank, and is returned to the depositor's bank. (NSF cheques are sometimes referred to as "bounced" cheques.) The bank then debits the depositor's account, as shown by the April 18 entry "Returned cheque—NSF" on the bank statement in Illustration 7-7. Note that this cheque for $425.60 was originally included in the deposit made on April 15, detailed in Illustration 7-5. Because the deposit was credited (added) to the bank account on April 15 and the cheque was not honoured, it must be debited (deducted) by the bank on April 18.

The company's bank may also charge the company a service charge of $10 or more for processing the returned cheque. In Illustration 7-7 we can see that BMO writes the entry "NSF fee" on the customer's statement for these charges. The company (depositor) then advises the customer who wrote the NSF cheque that their cheque was returned NSF and that a payment is still owed on the account. The company also usually passes the bank charges on to the customer by adding them to the customer's account balance. In summary, the overall effect of an NSF cheque on the depositor is to create an account receivable, and to reduce cash in the bank account. The customer's own bank will also charge the customer an NSF fee of $40 or more for writing an NSF cheque.

Recording an account receivable assumes that the customer will honour the account due by replacing the bounced cheque with a valid cheque or with cash. This happens in most cases. In the next chapter, we will discuss how to account for uncollectible accounts receivable when customers are unable to pay their accounts.

The bank uses **credit memoranda (CM)** to identify and explain miscellaneous amounts added to the bank account for items such as interest earned on the bank account, and electronic funds transfers into the depositor's account. For example, as explained earlier in the chapter, some retailers accept electronic payments for merchandise sold on account. Funds are electronically transferred from the customer's account to the retailer's account in payment of the bill. In Illustration 7-7, Lee Company collected an electronic payment from a customer for $1,350.55 on April 27, as indicated by the symbol EFT. Also note that in Illustration 7-7, interest of $39.76 has been added to Lee Company's bank balance.

RECONCILING THE BANK ACCOUNT

You might assume that the balances you and the bank have for your account will always agree. In fact, the two balances are almost never the same at any specific time. It is necessary to make the balance per books (the balance recorded in a company's general ledger cash account) agree with the balance per bank (the balance recorded on the bank statement)—a process called reconciling the bank account.

The lack of agreement between the two balances is due to the following:

- time lags that prevent one of the parties from recording a transaction in the same period as the other or
- errors by either party in recording transactions.

Except in electronic banking applications, time lags happen often. For example, several days pass between the time a cheque is mailed to a payee and the date the cheque is presented to, and cleared (paid) by, the bank. Cheques recorded by a company that have not yet cleared the bank are called **outstanding cheques**.

Similarly, when a company uses the bank's night depository to make deposits, there will be a difference of one day (or more if it's the weekend or a holiday) between the day the receipts are recorded by the company and the day they are recorded by the bank. Deposits recorded by the company that have not yet been recorded by the bank are called **deposits in transit**.

While bank errors are less common, they can still occur. The frequency of errors by the company in its cash account depends on the effectiveness of its internal controls. For example, either party could unintentionally record a $450 cheque as $45 or $540. Or the bank might mistakenly charge a cheque to the wrong account if the proper coding is missing or if the cheque cannot be scanned.

Reconciliation Procedure

The bank reconciliation should be prepared by an employee who has no other responsibilities related to cash, or by the owner of the company. In the feature story about Beanz Espresso Bar, the owner prepares the bank reconciliation. If the control activities of segregation of duties and independent checks of performance are not followed when the reconciliation is prepared, cash embezzlements may go unnoticed. For example, a cashier who prepares the reconciliation can steal cash and conceal the theft by misstating the reconciliation. In this way, the bank accounts would appear to reconcile with the company account and the theft would not be discovered.

In reconciling the bank account, it is customary to reconcile the balance per books (found in the Cash account in the general ledger) and the balance per bank (found on the bank statement provided by the bank) to their adjusted (correct) cash balances. The starting point when preparing the reconciliation is to enter the balance per bank statement and balance per books on the schedule. Adjustments are then made to each section, as shown in Illustration 7-8.

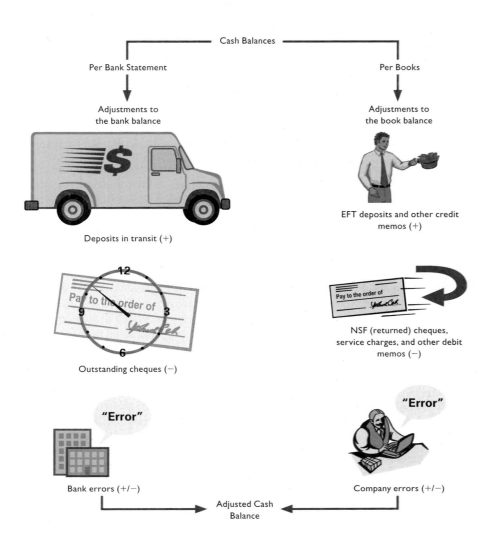

Reconciling Items per Bank. On the bank side of the reconciliation, the items to include are deposits in transit, outstanding cheques, and bank errors.

Deposits in Transit. Compare the individual deposits on the bank statement with (1) the deposits in transit from the preceding bank reconciliation, and (2) the deposits recorded in the company's books. Deposits in transit have been recorded on the company's books but have not yet been recorded by the bank. They are added to the balance per bank on the bank reconciliation.

For example, assume that Lee Company used the bank's night depository to deposit $2,201.40 on April 30. The bank will process this deposit the next day, May 1. This amount would be treated as a deposit in transit at the end of April and would be added to the balance per bank on the bank reconciliation. Note that this outstanding deposit would clear the bank in May and would no longer be a reconciling item at the end of May. As at the end of May, this amount has been recorded by both the company and the bank.

Outstanding Cheques. Compare the paid cheques shown on the bank statement or returned with the bank statement with (1) cheques that are outstanding from the preceding bank reconciliation, and (2) cheques that have been issued by the company during the month. Cheques are "outstanding" if they have been recorded on the company's books but have not cleared the bank account yet. They are deducted from the balance per bank on the bank reconciliation.

If a cheque that was outstanding in the previous period has been paid by the bank in the current period, the cheque is no longer outstanding and will **not** be included in the current month's bank reconciliation. If the cheque has still not been paid by the bank, it will continue to be outstanding and needs to be included with the outstanding cheques and deducted from the bank balance on the current month's bank reconciliation.

Bank Errors. Note any errors that are discovered in the previous steps. Errors can be made by either the bank or the company and can be in both directions (increases or decreases). Include only errors made by the bank as reconciling items when calculating the adjusted cash balance per bank. For example, if the bank processed a deposit of $1,693 as $1,639 in error, the difference of $54 is added to the balance per bank on the bank reconciliation.

Reconciling Items per Books. Reconciling items on the book side include adjustments from any unrecorded credit memoranda (amounts added) and debit memoranda (amounts deducted), and company errors.

Credit Memoranda and Other Deposits. Compare the credit memoranda and other deposits on the bank statement with the company records. Any amounts not recorded in the company's records should be added to the balance per books. For example, if the bank statement shows electronic funds transfers from customers paying their accounts on-line, these amounts will be added to the balance per books on the bank reconciliation, unless they had been previously recorded by the company. This makes the company's records agree with the bank's records.

Debit Memoranda and Other Payments. Similarly, any unrecorded debit memoranda should be deducted from the balance per books. If the bank statement shows a debit memorandum for bank service charges, this amount is deducted from the balance per books on the bank reconciliation to make the company's records agree with the bank's records. Frequently electronic payments have already been recorded by the company. If not, they must also be deducted from the balance per books on the bank reconciliation.

Company Errors. Errors discovered in the company's records must also be included in the bank reconciliation. For example, we will see below that Lee Company wrote a cheque for $1,226 and mistakenly recorded it as $1,262. The error of $36 is added to the balance per books because Lee Company reduced the balance per books by $36 too much when it recorded the cheque as $1,262 instead of $1,226. Make sure you include only errors made by the company as reconciling items when calculating the adjusted cash balance per books.

Bank Reconciliation Illustrated

The bank statement for Lee Company was shown in Illustration 7-7. It shows a balance per bank of $15,907.45 on April 30, 2014. On this date, the balance of cash per books is $11,244.14. Using the above steps, the following reconciling items are determined:

Reconciling items per bank:

1. **Deposits in transit:** After comparing the deposits recorded in the books with the deposits listed in the bank statement, it was determined that the April 30 deposit was not recorded by the bank until May 1. $2,201.40
2. **Outstanding cheques:** After comparing the cheques recorded in the books with the cheques listed on the bank statement, it was determined that three cheques were outstanding:

No. 445	$3,000.00	
No. 446	1,401.30	
No. 448	1,502.70	5,904.00

3. **Bank errors:** None

Reconciling items per books:

1. **Credit memoranda and other deposits:**
   Electronic receipt from customer on account $1,350.55
   Interest earned   39.76
2. **Debit memoranda and other payments:**
   NSF cheque from J. R. Baron   425.60
   Bank service charge for NSF cheque   10.00
   Bank service charge   30.00
3. **Company errors:** Cheque No. 443 was correctly written by Lee for $1,226.00 and was correctly paid by the bank. However, it was recorded as $1,262.00 by Lee.   36.00

The bank reconciliation follows:

LEE COMPANY Bank Reconciliation April 30, 2014		
Cash balance per bank statement		$15,907.45
Add: Deposit in transit		2,201.40
		18,108.85
Less: Outstanding cheques		
No. 445	$3,000.00	
No. 446	1,401.30	
No. 448	1,502.70	5,904.00
Adjusted cash balance per bank		$12,204.85
Cash balance per books		$11,244.14
Add: Electronic receipt from customer on account	$1,350.55	
Interest earned	39.76	
Error: cheque No. 443 for Accounts Payable		
($1,262.00 − $1,226.00)	36.00	1,426.31
		12,670.45
Less: Returned NSF cheque and bank charge		
($425.60 + $10.00)	$ 435.60	
Bank service charge	30.00	465.60
Adjusted cash balance per books		$12,204.85

The adjusted cash balances are now both equal to $12,204.85, which means the bank account has been reconciled.

Entries from Bank Reconciliation

After preparing the bank reconciliation, the company must prepare adjusting journal entries to record each reconciling item used to determine the **adjusted cash balance per books**. If these items are not journalized and posted, the Cash account will not show the correct balance. Lee Company would record the following entries on April 30:

EFT Receipt from Customer on Account. When a customer pays their account, the journal entry is the same regardless of whether the customer pays by cash, by cheque, or by EFT. The entry is:

Apr. 30	Cash	1,350.55	
	Accounts Receivable		1,350.55
	To record electronic receipt from customer on account.		

A = L + OE
+1,350.55
−1,350.55

↑Cash flows: +1,350.55

This entry is only required when the company has not already recorded the EFT receipt during the month. If that had been the case, then this item would not have been a reconciling item and would not have appeared on the bank reconciliation and thus would not have needed an adjustment.

Interest Revenue. Assuming the company had not already recorded an accrual, the interest earned is credited to the Interest Revenue account. The entry is:

Apr. 30	Cash	39.76	
	Interest Revenue		39.76
	To record interest earned.		

A = L + OE
+39.76   +39.76

↑Cash flows: 39.76

Company Error. The journal shows that cheque No. 443 had been issued to pay an account payable. The entry is:

A	=	L	+	OE
+36.00		+36.00		

↑ Cash flows: 36.00

Apr. 30	Cash	36.00	
	Accounts Payable		36.00
	To correct error in recording cheque No. 443.		

NSF Cheque. As explained earlier, a customer cheque returned for not sufficient funds and any related bank service charges become an account receivable to the depositor. The entry is:

A	=	L	+	OE
+435.60				
−435.60				

↓ Cash flows: −435.60

Apr. 30	Accounts Receivable ($425.60 + $10.00)	435.60	
	Cash		435.60
	To record NSF cheque from J. R. Baron plus bank charge.		

Bank Service Charges. Bank service charges are normally debited to Bank Charges expense. The entry is:

A	=	L	+	OE
−30.00				−30.00

↓ Cash flows: −30.00

Apr. 30	Bank Charges Expense	30.00	
	Cash		30.00
	To record bank service charge expense for April.		

The five journal entries shown above could also be combined into one compound entry. Recall that in previous chapters, the Cash account was never debited or credited in an adjusting journal entry. This was done to make learning easier, because the bank reconciliation process had not been explained. Now that you have learned about bank reconciliations, there will be times when we include adjustments to the Cash account with other adjusting entries.

After the entries above are posted, the Cash account will show the following:

		Cash		
Apr. 30	Bal.	11,244.14	Apr. 30	435.60
30		1,350.55	30	30.00
30		39.76		
30		36.00		
Apr. 30	Bal.	12,204.85		

The adjusted cash balance in the general ledger should agree with the adjusted cash balance per books in the bank reconciliation shown earlier.

What entries does the bank make? If any bank errors are discovered in preparing the reconciliation, the bank should be notified. The bank can then make the necessary corrections on its records. The bank does not correct your errors on its books, and you do not correct the bank's errors on your books. The bank does not make any entries for deposits in transit or outstanding cheques. The bank will record these items when they reach it.

 BEFORE YOU GO ON...

Do It

The Cash account of Zhizhi Company showed a balance of $16,333 on December 31, 2014. The bank statement as at that date showed a balance of $18,084. After comparing the bank statement with the cash records, the following information was determined:

1. The bank returned an NSF cheque in the amount of $239 that Zhizhi had deposited on December 20. The cheque was a payment on a customer's account.
2. Electronic receipts from customers on account totalled $2,300. These receipts have not yet been recorded by the company.

—

3. The bank issued a credit memo for $9 of interest earned on Zhizhi's account.
4. The bank issued a debit memo for bank service charges of $37. This amount included $10 for processing the NSF cheque (see #1 above).
5. The company made an error in recording a customer's deposit. The company recorded the payment on account as $209 when it should have been $290. The bank correctly recorded the deposit as $290.
6. Deposits in transit as at December 31 amounted to $3,643.
7. Outstanding cheques written in the month of December amounted to $3,000. Cheques still outstanding from the month of November totalled $280.

   Prepare a bank reconciliation and any required journal entries for Zhizhi Company at December 31, 2014.

Solution

ZHIZHI COMPANY
Bank Reconciliation
December 31, 2014

Cash balance per bank statement		$18,084
Add: Deposits in transit		3,643
		21,727
Less: Outstanding cheques ($3,000 + $280)		3,280
Adjusted cash balance per bank		$18,447
Cash balance per books		$16,333
Add:		
Electronic receipts from customers on account	$2,300	
Interest earned	9	
Error in deposit of Accounts Receivable ($290 − $209)	81	2,390
		18,723
Less: Returned NSF cheque	$ 239	
Bank service charges	37	276
Adjusted cash balance per books		$18,447

Date	Account	Debit	Credit
Dec. 31	Cash	2,300	
	Accounts Receivable		2,300
	To record electronic receipts on account.		
31	Cash	9	
	Interest Revenue		9
	To record interest earned on bank account.		
31	Cash	81	
	Accounts Receivable ($290 − $209)		81
	To correct deposit error.		
31	Accounts Receivable ($239 + $10)	249	
	Cash		249
	To re-establish accounts receivable for NSF cheque and related service charge.		
31	Bank Charges Expense ($37 − $10)	27	
	Cash		27
	To record bank service charges.		

Cash

Dec. 31	Bal.	16,333	Dec. 31		249
31		2,300	31		27
31		9			
31		81			
Dec. 31	Bal.	18,447			

Related exercise material: BE7–7, BE7–8, BE7–9, BE7–10, BE7–11, BE7–12, E7–8, E7–9, E7–10, E7–11, and E7–12.

Action Plan

- Prepare the bank reconciliation in two sections: one for the bank and one for the company.
- Determine which reconciling items each side has already recorded and adjust the other side accordingly.
- Be careful when you determine the direction of an error correction; think about how the error has affected the bank balance or the cash account balance.
- Prepare journal entries only for reconciling items to the book side, not the bank side.
- The adjusted cash balances must agree with each other when complete, and with the general ledger account after the journal entries are posted.

THE NAVIGATOR

Reporting Cash

» STUDY **OBJECTIVE 5**

Report cash on the balance sheet.

Cash consists of coins, currency (paper money), cheques, money orders, travellers' cheques, and money on deposit in a bank or similar depository. Cash does not include cheques that are postdated (payable in the future), staledated (more than six months old), or returned (NSF—not sufficient funds).

Companies report cash in two different statements: the balance sheet and the cash flow statement. The balance sheet reports the amount of cash available at a point in time (the date of the balance sheet). The cash flow statement shows the sources and uses of cash during a period of time. The cash flow statement was introduced in Chapter 1 and will be discussed in much detail in Chapter 17.

When presented on the balance sheet, cash on hand, cash in banks, and petty cash are normally combined and reported simply as Cash. Because it is the most liquid asset owned by a company, Canadian companies have traditionally listed cash first in the current assets section of the balance sheet. As explained and illustrated in Chapter 4, companies following IFRS may choose to list current assets in *increasing* order of liquidity and thus present cash as the last item in current assets. In this textbook, we will continue to follow the rule of listing current assets in *decreasing* order of liquidity as it is expected that this will continue to be the practice of Canadian companies for many years to come.

Many companies combine cash with cash equivalents. Cash equivalents are short-term, highly liquid (easily sold) investments that are not subject to significant risk of changes in value, such as term deposits, treasury bills and Guaranteed Investment Certificates (GICs). To be considered a cash equivalent they typically have maturities of three months or less from the date they are purchased.

A company may have cash that is not available for general use because it is restricted for a special purpose. An example is funds held on deposit until completion of an offer to buy real estate. Cash that has a restricted use—and is in a significant amount—should be reported separately on the balance sheet as restricted cash. If the restricted cash is expected to be used within the next year, the amount should be reported as a current asset. When restricted funds will not be used in that time, they should be reported as a non-current asset.

Illustration 7-9 shows how Tim Hortons presents its cash and cash equivalents and restricted cash on its balance sheet.

▶ ILLUSTRATION **7-9**
Presentation of cash

TIM HORTONS INC. Balance Sheet (partial) January 1, 2012 (in thousands)	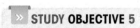

Assets	
Current assets	
Cash and cash equivalents	$126,497
Restricted cash and cash equivalents	130,613

In the notes to its financial statements, Tim Hortons states that the company considers short-term investments that are highly liquid and have original maturities of three months or less as cash equivalents. The restricted cash and cash equivalents are related to its Tim Card® quick-pay cash card program. The amount represents the net amount of cash loaded on the cards by customers, less redemptions. The balances are restricted and cannot be used for any purpose other than for settlement of obligations under the cash card program.

Some companies may be in a cash deficit or negative position at year end. This can happen when the company is in an overdraft position at the bank. A bank overdraft occurs when withdrawals or payments are more than the amount in the bank account. This becomes a short-term loan from the bank, assuming that the bank does not reject the withdrawal or payment. Most companies have overdraft protection up to a certain amount with their banks. In an overdraft situation, the Cash account shows a credit balance in the general ledger and is reported as a current liability called bank indebtedness.

BEFORE YOU GO ON...

Do It

On December 31, Ranchero Company has the following items: $12,250 in its bank chequing account; $6,400 in its bank savings account; a $250 petty cash fund; $4,300 of postdated cheques from customers; $8,800 in highly liquid short-term investments purchased with maturity dates of less than 90 days; $10,600 of short-term investments with maturity dates of 100 to 365 days; and $5,200 in a bank account restricted for use in settling advance ticket sales. How will each of these items be reported on the balance sheet?

Solution

The following items are reported as current assets on the balance sheet:

1. Cash and cash equivalents

Bank chequing account	$12,250
Bank savings account	6,400
Petty cash fund	250
Highly liquid investments < 90 days	8,800

Cash and cash equivalents	$27,700
2. Restricted cash	5,200
3. Short-term investments	10,600

The postdated cheques are not an asset and thus are not included on the balance sheet.

Related exercise material: BE7–13, BE7–14, and E7–13.

Action Plan
- Review which items are included in cash and cash equivalents.
- Determine the difference between cash equivalents and short-term investments.
- Recall that restricted cash balances must be reported separately.

THE **NAVIGATOR**

▮ Comparing IFRS and ASPE ▮

Key Differences	International Financial Reporting Standards (IFRS)	Accounting Standards for Private Enterprises (ASPE)
No significant differences		

THE **NAVIGATOR**

Demonstration Problem

On the April 30, 2014, bank reconciliation for Gurjot Imports, there were three outstanding cheques: #286 for $217, #289 for $326, and #290 for $105. There were no deposits in transit as at April 30, 2014. The bank balance at April 30 was $4,261. The adjusted cash balance was $3,613. The following is selected information from the May bank statement:

Cheques Cleared			Other Bank Account Transactions		
Date	Cheque No.	Amount	Date	Amount	Transaction
May 1	286	$ 217	May 8	$2,620+	Deposit
8	305	402	12	4,718+	Deposit
20	306	105	24	3,190+	Deposit
22	308	1,648	25	280−	NSF cheque
22	289	326	28	28−	Service charge
23	304	2,735	31	12+	Interest
31	309	175			
Total		$5,608			

The NSF cheque was originally received from a customer, R. Siddiqi, in payment of his account of $265. The bank included a $15 service charge for a total of $280. Information from the company's accounting records for May follows:

Cash Receipts			Cash Payments		
Date	Amount		Date	Cheque No.	Amount
May 5	$ 2,260		May 5	304	$2,735
12	4,718		5	305	402
23	3,190		19	306	150
31	1,004		19	307	3,266
Total	11,712		31	309	175
			31	310	2,400
			Total		$9,128

Investigation reveals that cheque #306 was issued to pay the telephone bill and cheque #308 was issued to pay rent. All deposits are for collections of accounts receivable. The bank made no errors.

Instructions

(a) Calculate the balance per bank statement at May 31 and the unadjusted Cash balance per company records at May 31.
(b) Prepare a bank reconciliation at May 31.
(c) Prepare the necessary adjusting entries at May 31.
(d) Post the adjustments to the cash account. What balance would Gurjot Imports report as cash in the current assets section of its balance sheet on May 31, 2014?

Solution to Demonstration Problem

(a) Balance per Bank Statement

Balance April 30, 2014			$ 4,261
Add: Deposits ($2,620 + $4,718 + $3,190)		$10,528	
Interest		12	10,540
			14,801
Less: Cheques cleared		$ 5,608	
NSF cheques		280	
Service charge		28	5,916
Unadjusted bank balance, May 31, 2014			$ 8,885

Cash balance per books (company records)

Adjusted cash balance at April 30, 2014	$ 3,613
Add: May cash receipts	11,172
Less: May cash payments	9,128
Unadjusted cash balance, May 31, 2014	$ 5,657

(b)

GURJOT IMPORTS
Bank Reconciliation
May 31, 2014

Unadjusted cash balance per bank balance............................		$8,885
Add: Deposits in transit...		1,004
		9,889
Less: Outstanding cheques		
No. 290	$ 105	
No. 307	3,266	
No. 310	2,400	5,771
Adjusted cash balance per bank		$4,118
Unadjusted cash balance per books		$5,657
Add: Interest	$ 12	
Error: cheque #306 ($150 − $105) [Telephone expense]	45	
Error: May 5 deposit ($2,620 − $2,260) [Accounts receivable]	360	417
		6,074
Less: NSF cheque returned	$ 280	
Error: cheque #308 not recorded [Rent expense]...........	1,648	
Bank service charges.................................	28	1,956
Adjusted cash balance		$4,118

(c)

May 31	Cash	12	
	Interest Revenue		12
	To record bank interest earned.		
31	Cash	45	
	Telephone Expense		45
	To correct error in recording cheque #306.		
31	Cash	360	
	Accounts Receivable		360
	To correct error in May 5 deposit.		
31	Accounts Receivable—R. Siddiqi	280	
	Cash		280
	To re-establish accounts receivable for NSF		
	cheque and related service charge.		
31	Bank Charges Expense	28	
	Cash		28
	To record bank service charges.		
31	Rent Expense	1,648	
	Cash		1,648
	To record cheque #308 not recorded in error.		

(d)

		Cash			
May 31	Bal.	5,657	May 31		280
	31	12	31		28
		45	31		1,648
		360			
May 31	Bal.	4,118*			

*Check that the balance is equal to the adjusted cash balance on the bank reconciliation.
The reported cash balance on the May 31, 2014, balance sheet is $4,118.

THE NAVIGATOR

▶ Summary of Study Objectives

1. ***Explain the activities that help prevent fraud and achieve internal control.*** Fraud is an intentional dishonest act that results in a personal financial benefit by misappropriating (stealing) assets or misstating financial statements. The three factors that contribute to fraud (the fraud triangle) are opportunity, financial pressure, and rationalization. Internal control consists of all the related methods and measures that management implements in order to achieve reliable financial reporting, effective and efficient operations, and compliance with relevant laws and regulations. Control activities include establishment of responsibility, segregation of duties, documentation procedures, physical and IT controls, independent checks of performance, and human resource controls.

2. ***Apply control activities to cash receipts.*** Internal controls over cash receipts include (a) designating only personnel such as cashiers to handle cash; (b) assigning the duties of handling or receiving cash, and recording cash to different individuals; (c) using remittance advices for mail receipts, cash register tapes (or point-of-sale computerized systems) for over-the-counter receipts, and deposit slips for bank deposits; (d) using company safes and bank vaults to store cash, with only authorized personnel having access, and using cash registers; (e) depositing all cash intact daily; (f) making independent daily counts of register receipts and daily comparisons of total receipts with total deposits; and (g) bonding personnel who handle cash. Debit and credit card transactions increase internal control but have related bank charges. Electronic funds transfer receipts also increase internal control over cash receipts.

3. ***Apply control activities to cash payments, including petty cash.*** Internal controls over cash payments include (a) authorizing only specified individuals such as the controller to sign cheques and authorize electronic funds transfer payments; (b) assigning the duties of approving items for payment, paying for the items, and recording the payment to different individuals; (c) using prenumbered cheques and accounting for all cheques, with each cheque supported by an approved invoice; (d) storing blank cheques and signing machines in a safe or vault, with access restricted to authorized personnel; (e) comparing each cheque with the approved invoice before issuing the cheque and making monthly reconciliations of bank and book balances; and (f) stamping each approved invoice "Paid" after payment. To operate a petty cash fund, it is necessary to establish the fund, make payments from the fund, and replenish the fund. Journal entries are only made when the fund is established and replenished.

4. ***Describe the control features of a bank account and prepare a bank reconciliation.*** A bank account contributes to good internal control by giving physical and IT controls for the storage of cash, reducing the amount of currency that must be kept on hand, and creating a double record of a depositor's bank transactions. In reconciling the bank account, the balance per books and balance per bank are reconciled to their adjusted balances. Reconciling items include deposits in transit, outstanding cheques, errors by the bank, unrecorded bank memoranda, and errors by the company. Adjusting entries must be made for any errors made by the company and unrecorded bank memoranda (e.g., interest).

5. ***Report cash on the balance sheet.*** Cash is usually listed first in the current assets section of the balance sheet. Cash may be reported together with highly liquid, very short-term investments called cash equivalents. Cash that is restricted for a special purpose is reported separately as a current asset or a non-current asset, depending on when the cash is expected to be used.

Flash cards

▶ Glossary

Bank overdraft What occurs when withdrawals are more than the amount available in the bank account. (p. 382)

Bank reconciliation A comparison of the balance in a company's bank account with the balance in the cash account at a point in time that explains any differences. (p. 373)

Bank statement A statement received monthly from the bank that shows the depositor's bank transactions and balances. (p. 374)

Bonding Obtaining insurance protection against theft by employees. (p. 364)

Cash Resources such as coins, currency (paper money), cheques, money orders, travellers' cheques, and money on deposit in a bank or similar depository. (p. 382)

Cash equivalents Highly liquid, short-term investments with maturities of three months or less that are subject to an insignificant risk of changes in value. (p. 382)

Cash payments journal A special journal used to record all cash paid. (p. 370)

Cash receipts journal A special journal used to record all cash received. (p. 367)

THE NAVIGATOR

Clearing   What occurs when a cheque or deposit is accepted by the maker's bank. Clearing results in a transfer of funds from the maker's bank to the payee's bank. (p. 374)

Credit memoranda (CM)   Supporting documentation for increases to a bank account that appear on a bank statement. (p. 376)

Debit memoranda (DM)   Supporting documentation for decreases to a bank account that appear on a bank statement. (p. 375)

Deposits in transit   Deposits recorded by the depositor that have not been recorded by the bank. (p. 376)

Electronic funds transfer (EFT)   The electronic exchange or transfer of money from one account to another, either within a single financial institution or across multiple institutions, through computer-based systems. (p. 368)

External auditors   Auditors who are independent of the organization. They report on whether or not the financial statements fairly present the financial position and performance of an organization. (p. 364)

Fraud   An intentional dishonest act that results in a personal financial benefit by misappropriating (stealing) assets or misstating financial statements. (p. 360)

Fraud triangle   The three factors that contribute to fraudulent activity by employees: opportunity, financial pressure, and rationalization. (p. 360)

Internal auditors   Company employees who evaluate the effectiveness of the company's system of internal control. (p. 364)

Internal control   The related methods and measures that management designs and implements to help an organization achieve reliable financial reporting, effective and efficient operations, and compliance with relevant laws and regulations. (p. 361)

NSF (not sufficient funds) cheque   A cheque that is not paid by the customer's bank and is returned to the depositor's bank because of insufficient funds in the customer's account. (p. 375)

Outstanding cheques   Cheques issued and recorded by a company that have not been paid by the bank. (p. 376)

Petty cash fund   A cash fund that is used for paying relatively small amounts. (p. 370)

Restricted cash   Cash that is not available for general use, but instead is restricted for a particular purpose. (p. 382)

Special journal   A journal that is used to record similar types of transactions, such as all cash receipts or all cash payments. (p. 367)

▶ Self-Study Questions

Answers are at the end of the chapter.

(SO 1) K   1. Which of the following factors does not contribute to the likelihood of fraud?
(a) Rationalization
(b) Financial pressure
(c) Segregation of duties
(d) Opportunity

(SO 1) K   2. Which of the following factors could limit a company's system of internal control?
(a) Collusion by two or more employees
(b) The cost of internal control being greater than the benefit
(c) Difficulty in segregating duties in small businesses
(d) All of the above

(SO 2) C   3. Permitting only designated personnel to handle cash receipts is an application of the concept of:
(a) segregation of duties.
(b) establishment of responsibility.
(c) independent checks of performance.
(d) human resource controls.

(SO 2) AP   4. Franks Jewellers accepted $12,000 of Visa credit card charges for merchandise sold on July 1. Visa charges Franks 5.0% for its credit card use. The entry to record this transaction by Franks Jewellers includes:

(a) a debit to Accounts Receivable of $12,000 and a credit to Sales of $12,000.
(b) a debit to Cash of $11,400 and a credit to Sales of $11,400.
(c) a debit to Accounts Receivable of $11,400, a debit to Credit Card Expense of $600, and a credit to Sales of $12,000.
(d) a debit to Cash of $11,400, a debit to Credit Card Expense of $600, and a credit to Sales of $12,000.

(SO 3) C   5. Authorizing only designated personnel to sign cheques is an application of the principle of:
(a) establishment of responsibility.
(b) segregation of duties.
(c) independent checks of performance.
(d) documentation procedures.

(SO 3) AP   6. A cheque is written to replenish a $150 petty cash fund when the fund has receipts of $148 and $7 in cash. In recording the cheque:
(a) Cash Over and Short should be debited for $5.
(b) Cash Over and Short should be credited for $5.
(c) Petty Cash should be debited for $148.
(d) Cash should be credited for $148.

(SO 4) K   7. Bank accounts improve control over cash by:
(a) safeguarding cash by using a bank as a depository.
(b) minimizing the amount of cash that must be kept on hand.
(c) giving a double record of all bank transactions.
(d) all of the above.

(SO 4) AP   8. Suzanne Terriault has a balance of $410 in her chequebook (her Cash account) at the end of the month. The balance on her bank statement is $500. Reconciling items include deposits in transit of $250, outstanding cheques of $350, and service charges of $10. What is Suzanne's adjusted cash balance?
(a) $390
(b) $400
(c) $410
(d) $500

(SO 4) AP   9. A company mistakenly recorded a $348 cheque written in payment of an account as $384. The journal entry required to correct this would be:
(a) debit Accounts Payable $36; credit Cash $36.
(b) debit Cash $36; credit Accounts Payable $36.
(c) debit Accounts Payable $348; credit Cash $348.
(d) debit Cash $384; credit Accounts Payable $384.

(SO 5) K   10. Which of the following correctly describes the reporting of cash?
(a) Petty cash must be reported separately from cash on the balance sheet.
(b) Restricted cash funds are always reported as a current asset.
(c) Cash equivalents may be combined with cash on the balance sheet.
(d) Postdated cheques from customers are included in the Cash account balance.

▶ Questions

(SO 1) K   1. Fraud experts often say there are three primary factors that contribute to employee fraud. Identify the factors and explain what is meant by each.

(SO 1) K   2. Identify and describe the five components of a good internal control system.

(SO 1) C   3. "Internal control can help organizations achieve efficiency of operations." Do you agree? Explain.

(SO 1) K   4. In the ice cream shop, all employees make change out of the same cash register drawer. Is this a violation of internal control? Why or why not?

(SO 1) C   5. Trushi Miyamura is questioning why independent checks of performance are important if the company also segregates duties. Respond to Trushi's question.

(SO 1) C   6. What are documentation procedures? Provide an example and explain how it contributes to good internal control.

(SO 1) C   7. Joan Trainer is trying to design internal control activities so that there is no possibility of errors or theft. Explain to Joan why this may be impractical, and may even be impossible.

(SO 2) C   8. What is the difference between a debit card sale and a bank credit card sale to a retailer? To the customer?

(SO 2) C   9. Over-the-counter cash receipts require special care. Explain the procedures that should be followed at the end of the day (or shift) to ensure proper internal control.

(SO 2) C   10. Best Books has just installed electronic cash registers with scanners in its stores. How do cash registers such as these improve internal control over cash receipts?

(SO 2) C   11. Describe appropriate internal control procedures for handling cheques received by mail.

(SO 2) C   12. Sanjeet argues that no special internal controls are required for electronic funds transfer (EFT) cash receipts because employees are not handling cash or cheques. Is Sanjeet correct? Explain.

(SO 3) C   13. "Use of cash for payments should be avoided. Effective internal control over cash payments can only be achieved by the use of cheques or electronic funds transfer." Is this true? Explain.

(SO 3) C   14. "EFT payments are less expensive for a company because there is a reduced need for internal control as compared with writing cheques." Is this correct? Why or why not?

(SO 3) C   15. Walter's Watches is a small retail store. Walter, the owner of the company, has recently hired a new employee, Wanda, who will be responsible for ordering merchandise, receiving the goods, and authorizing the merchandise invoices for payment. Describe the various ways Wanda could commit a fraud with this arrangement.

(SO 3) C   16. Chang Company has a petty cash fund that is used to pay for a variety of low-value items. Su Mai, the petty cash custodian, regularly borrows cash from the fund to pay for personal expenses. Su Mai has always repaid these amounts. Is this a problem for Chang Company? If it is, explain what the company could do to strengthen internal control.

(SO 4) K   17. Opening a bank account is a simple procedure. Give four examples of how a bank account improves a company's internal controls.

(SO 4) C   18. What is the purpose of a bank reconciliation? Who should prepare it? Why is it important to have the appropriate person prepare it?

(SO 4) C   19. Diablo Company wrote cheque #2375 for $1,325 on March 16. As at March 31, the cheque had not cleared the company's bank account and was correctly listed as an outstanding cheque on the March 31 bank reconciliation. The cheque has still not cleared the bank account on April 30. Astrid is doing the bank reconciliation for Diablo and thinks it is not necessary to include the cheque in the April bank reconciliation, because it was already listed as an outstanding cheque on March 31. Is she correct? Explain.

(SO 4) C 20. Paul Reimer does not keep a personal record of his bank account and does not see the need to do a bank reconciliation. He says he can always use on-line banking to look up the balance in his bank account before writing a cheque. Explain why Paul should keep his own records and do regular bank reconciliations.

(SO 4) C 21. Jayne is reviewing her June 30 bank statement and notices an entry for $32 regarding monthly interest. Jayne is not sure if she should include this in her bank reconciliation or not. If it is included, then she believes it should be in the bank section of the reconciliation because it is on the bank statement. Explain to Jayne how to handle this item.

(SO 5) C 22. "Since cash is an asset, the Cash account must always have a debit balance. If it has a credit balance, that means there is an error in the account." Do you agree? Explain.

(SO 5) C 23. What are cash equivalents? What is restricted cash? How should these be reported on the balance sheet?

▶ Brief Exercises

BE7–1   Nathan McPhail is the new owner of Liberty Parking, a parking garage. He has heard about internal control but is not clear about its importance for his business. Explain to Nathan the six types of control activities. Give him an example of how each type of activity might apply to his business.

Identify control activities. (SO 1) C

BE7–2   Miramichi Company has the following internal controls over cash receipts. Identify the control activity that is applicable to each of the following:

Identify control activities applicable to cash receipts. (SO 2) C

1. The company conducts thorough background checks on all cashiers when they are hired.
2. All sales must be entered into the cash register through a scanner and point-of-sale software.
3. Surprise cash counts are made by the department supervisors.
4. The duties of receiving cash, recording cash, and maintaining custody of cash are assigned to different individuals.
5. At the end his or her shift, the cashier ensures there are receipts on hand for all debit or credit card sales.
6. Each cashier uses a different cash register and uses a separate password.

BE7–3   Kopper Kettle Restaurant accepts Visa cards. On April 9, a customer paid for a $175 dinner using his Visa card. The bank charges a 4% fee for each transaction. Prepare the entry that Kopper Kettle must make to record this transaction. Assuming the purchase is made using a Kopper Kettle–issued credit card, would the entry change? Prepare the entry to record the purchase assuming a debit card is used for payment and that the bank charges a $2 fee for each transaction.

Record debit and credit card transactions. (SO 2) AP

BE7–4   Bujold Company has the following internal controls over cash payments. Identify the control activity that is applicable to each of the following:

Identify control activities applicable to cash payments. (SO 3) C

1. Company cheques are prenumbered.
2. Blank cheques are stored in a safe in the controller's office.
3. All employees in the accounting department are required to take vacations each year.
4. The bank statement is reconciled monthly by the assistant controller.
5. Both the controller and the treasurer are required to sign cheques or authorize EFT.
6. Cheque signers are not allowed to record cash payments.

BE7–5   On March 2, Pugh Company established a petty cash fund of $100. On March 27, the fund was replenished when it had $8 in cash and receipts for supplies $30, freight out $17, and repairs expense $43. Prepare the journal entries to establish the petty cash fund on March 2 and replenish it on March 27.

Record entries to establish and replenish a petty cash fund. (SO 3) AP

BE7–6   Carla's Snack Shop has a petty cash fund of $150. On November 21, the fund contained $10 in cash and receipts for freight out $26, and supplies $57. There is also a note from the company owner, Carla Shekk, stating that she took $60 cash for personal expenses. Make the journal entry to replenish the fund.

Record entry to replenish a petty cash fund. (SO 3) AP

BE7–7   How would each of the following items be recorded on a bank reconciliation? Next to each item, record the correct letter from this list: (a) increase to bank balance, (b) decrease to bank balance, (c) increase to company cash balance, (d) decrease to company cash balance, or (e) not included in the bank reconciliation.

Indicate location of items in bank reconciliation. (SO 4) K

1. _____ EFT payment made by a customer
2. _____ Bank debit memorandum for service charges
3. _____ Outstanding cheques from the current month
4. _____ Bank error in recording a $1,779 deposit as $1,977
5. _____ Outstanding cheques from the previous month that are still outstanding
6. _____ Outstanding cheques from the previous month that are no longer outstanding
7. _____ Bank error in recording a company cheque made out for $160 as $610
8. _____ Bank credit memorandum for interest revenue
9. _____ Company error in recording a deposit of $160 as $1,600
10. _____ Bank debit memorandum for a customer's NSF cheque
11. _____ Deposit in transit from the current month
12. _____ Company error in recording a cheque made out for $630 as $360

Identify reconciling items that require journal entries. (SO 4) C

BE7–8   Referring to BE7–7, indicate (a) the items that will result in an adjustment to the company's records, and (b) why the other items do not require an adjustment.

Prepare bank reconciliation. (SO 4) AP

BE7–9   On August 31, Howel Company had an unadjusted cash balance of $10,050. An examination of the August bank statement shows a balance of $8,370 on August 31; bank service charges $40; deposits in transit $3,005; interest earned $22; outstanding cheques $1,623; and an NSF cheque of $280. Prepare a bank reconciliation at August 31.

Prepare entries from bank reconciliation. (SO 4) AP

BE7–10   Refer to the bank reconciliation prepared in BE7–9. Prepare the adjusting journal entries for Howel Company on August 31.

Analyze errors. (SO 4) AP

BE7–11   The following errors were found when the controller at Westshore Hotel was doing the March 31 bank reconciliation:

1. On March 5, Westshore recorded a payment of an account payable as $1,720. The correct amount was $1,270. It was correctly recorded by the bank.
2. On March 19, Westshore recorded a deposit as $4,550. The correct amount was $4,250. The deposit was for the collection of an account receivable and the bank recorded it correctly.
3. On March 31, the bank recorded a deposit as $2,750. The correct amount was $5,720. This error was corrected by the bank on April 1. Westshore had correctly recorded the deposit.

For each of these errors, (a) indicate if and how it would be shown on the bank reconciliation, and (b) prepare an adjusting entry for Westshore if required.

Analyze errors. (SO 4) AP

BE7–12   The following errors were found when the controller at East Mountain Motel was doing the June 30 bank reconciliation:

1. On June 7, East Mountain recorded a payment of an account payable as $2,180. The correct amount was $2,810. It was correctly recorded by the bank.
2. On June 20, East Mountain recorded a deposit as $3,330. The correct amount was $4,440. The deposit was for the collection of an account receivable and the bank recorded it correctly.
3. On June 25, the bank posted a cheque in the amount of $825 to East Mountain's bank account. The cheque had been written by another company, East Mountainside Company.

For each of these errors, (a) indicate if and how it would be shown on the bank reconciliation, and (b) prepare an adjusting entry for East Mountain if required.

Calculate cash. (SO 5) AP

BE7–13   Sirois Company owns the following assets at the balance sheet date:

Cash in bank—savings account	$ 5,500
Cash on hand	750
Cash refund due from the Canada Revenue Agency	1,000
Cash in bank—chequing account	10,000
Staledated cheques from customers	250
Postdated cheques from customers	500
60-day treasury bill	3,500

What amount should be reported as cash and cash equivalents in the balance sheet?

Explain statement presentation. (SO 5) C

BE7–14   Dupré Company has the following items: cash in bank $17,500; payroll bank account $6,000; store cash floats $1,500; petty cash fund $250; short-term, highly liquid investments with maturity dates of less than 90 days $15,000; short-term investments with maturity dates of 100 to 365 days $40,000; and Plant Expansion Fund Cash $25,000. The plant expansion will begin in three years. Explain how each item should be reported on the balance sheet.

▶ Exercises

E7–1 Discount Toys advertises a customer-friendly return policy. The store allows returns within 30 days for any reason. The store uses a periodic inventory system. When merchandise is returned, store policy instructs employees to:

- Complete a prenumbered return form and refund cash from the cash register.
- Provide a copy of the return form to the supervisor for approval.
- Immediately return goods to the shelf.

Instructions

(a) How is it possible for a dishonest store employee to steal from Discount Toys and avoid getting caught?
(b) What changes to the policy would you recommend to the company to reduce the possibility of employee fraud?

Identify internal control weaknesses and recommend changes. (SO 1) C

E7–2 The following situations suggest either a strength or a weakness in internal control:

1. At Frederico's, Amanda and Long work alternate lunch hours. Normally Amanda works the cash register at the checkout counter, but during her lunch hour Long takes her place. They both use the same cash drawer and count cash together at the end of the day.
2. Sandeep is a very hard-working employee at Stan's Hardware. Sandeep does such a good job that he is responsible for most of the company's office and accounting tasks. The only thing the owner has to do is sign cheques.
3. At Half Pipe Skate, they are very concerned about running an efficient, low-cost business. Consequently, the manager has assigned the same individual to do the purchasing and prepare the receiving reports when the merchandise is delivered.
4. At Traction Tires, most of the tires are stored in a fenced outdoor storage area. One of the employees noticed a place where the fence needed to be repaired and reported this to the manager. The fence was fixed before the close of business that night.
5. The internal auditors at Humber Manufacturing regularly report their findings to senior management, who get the accounting department to investigate and resolve any problems.
6. All employees at Vincent Travel take vacation every year. During that time, with the exception of the controller's position, the employees' duties are assigned to another individual while they are on vacation.

Instructions

(a) State whether each situation above is a strength or a weakness in internal control.
(b) For each weakness, suggest an improvement.

Identify internal control strengths and weaknesses and suggest improvements. (SO 1) C

E7–3 The following control procedures are used in Sheridan Company for cash receipts:

1. To minimize the risk of robbery, cash in excess of $200 is stored in a locked metal box in the office manager's office until it is deposited in the bank. All employees know where the office manager keeps the key to the box.
2. The company has one cash register with a single cash drawer. Any one of three employees may operate the cash register.
3. All employees handling cash receipts are experienced and therefore are not bonded.
4. In order to increase efficiency, the assistant controller opens all of the mail, prepares the bank deposit, and prepares the journal entries to record the cash receipts.
5. Due to a lack of storage space, all remittance advices and debit or credit card sales receipts are destroyed each weekend.

Instructions

(a) For each procedure, explain the weaknesses in internal control, and identify the control activity that is violated.
(b) For each weakness, suggest a change in procedure that will result in good internal control.

Identify weaknesses in internal control over cash receipts and suggest improvements. (SO 1, 2) C

E7–4 Presented below are three independent situations:

1. On March 15, 44 customers used debit cards to purchase merchandise for a total of $5,814 from Hockey Town. Hockey Town pays a $0.25 debit card fee for each transaction.
2. On June 21, Circle Creations Gallery sells a painting to Constance Furrow for $2,400. Constance uses her Visa bank credit card to pay for the purchase. The bank charges Circle Creations a 2.75% fee for all credit card transactions. On July 17, Constance receives her Visa bill and pays for this purchase.
3. On October 7, A. Ramos uses his store credit card to purchase merchandise from The Bay for $595. On November 10, Ramos receives his credit card bill from The Bay and pays for this purchase.

Prepare entries for debit and credit card sales. (SO 2) AP

Instructions

(a) Prepare Hockey Town's journal entries for the transactions in part (1).

(b) Prepare Circle Creations' journal entries for the transactions in part (2).

(c) Prepare The Bay's journal entries for the transactions in part (3).

Identify weaknesses in internal control over cash payments, and suggest improvements. (SO 1, 3) AP

E7–5 The following control procedures are used in Centennial Bay General Merchandise for cash payments:

1. Company cheques are not prenumbered and are kept in an unlocked file cabinet in the controller's office.
2. Cheques must be signed by the controller.
3. The purchasing agent verifies that the goods have been received, verifies the accuracy of the invoice, and authorizes the controller to issue a cheque for the purchase.
4. After the controller prepares and signs the cheque, she stamps the invoice paid and files it. She then records the cheque in the journal.
5. The controller prepares the bank reconciliation on a monthly basis and gives it to the company owner. As the company owner trusts the controller, he doesn't bother checking the bank reconciliations.
6. Background checks are not conducted on personnel hired for senior positions such as the purchasing agent or controller.
7. The company owner is impressed with how hard the purchasing agent works. He hasn't taken a vacation in two years.

Instructions

(a) For each procedure, explain the weaknesses in internal control, and identify the control activity that is violated.

(b) For each weakness, suggest a change in procedure that will result in good internal control.

Record petty cash transactions. (SO 3) AP

E7–6 Bulyea Boxes uses a petty cash imprest system. The fund was established on February 14 with a balance of $150. On February 28, there were $5 cash and the following petty cash receipts in the petty cash box:

Date	Receipt No.	For	Amount
Feb. 15	1	Supplies	$15
18	2	Miscellaneous expense	10
20	3	Freight in (assume perpetual inventory system)	45
21	4	Supplies	20
22	5	Delivery charges on outgoing freight	25
27	6	Supplies	35

Instructions

(a) Record the journal entry on February 14 to establish the petty cash fund.

(b) Record the journal entry on February 28 to replenish the fund and increase the balance to $175.

Record petty cash transactions. (SO 3) AP

E7–7 Brooklyn Buttons uses a petty cash imprest system. The fund was established on September 4 with a balance of $200. On September 30, there were $50 cash and the following petty cash receipts in the petty cash box:

Date	Receipt No.	For	Amount
Sept. 5	1	Freight in (assume perpetual inventory system)	$25
9	2	Delivery charges on outgoing freight	15
14	3	Freight in	30
16	4	Supplies	10
20	5	Delivery charges on outgoing freight	20
29	6	Freight in	40

Instructions

(a) Record the journal entry on September 4 to establish the petty cash fund.

(b) Record the journal entry on September 30 to replenish the fund and decrease the balance to $150.

Prepare bank reconciliation and related entries. (SO 4) AP

E7–8 The following information is for Tindall Company in September:

1. Cash balance per bank, September 30, $7,456
2. Cash balance per books, September 30, $6,102
3. Outstanding cheques, $2,851
4. Bank service charge, $22
5. NSF cheque from customer, $206
6. Deposits in transit, $1,399
7. EFT receipts from customers in payment of their accounts, $67
8. Cheque #212 was correctly written and posted by the bank as $507. Tindall Company had recorded the cheque as $570 in error. The cheque was written for the purchase of supplies.

Instructions

(a) Prepare a bank reconciliation at September 30, 2014.
(b) Journalize the adjusting entries at September 30, 2014, on Tindall Company's books.

E7–9   On April 30, the bank reconciliation of Hidden Valley Company shows a deposit in transit of $1,437. The May bank statement and the general ledger Cash account in May show the following:

Determine deposits in transit and other reconciling items. (SO 4) AP

HIDDEN VALLEY COMPANY Bank Statement (partial) Deposits/Credits		
Date	Description	Amount
May 1	Deposit	$1,437
5	Deposit	2,255
12	Deposit	3,281
20	Deposit	945
26	Deposit	1,298
30	EFT	956
30	Interest Earned	32

HIDDEN VALLEY COMPANY Cash Account (partial) Deposits Made	
Date	Amount
May 2	$2,255
9	3,218
16	945
23	1,298
30	1,353

Additional information:

1. The bank did not make any errors in May.
2. EFT is an electronic on-line payment from a customer.

Instructions

(a) List the deposits in transit at May 31.
(b) List any other items that must be included in the bank reconciliation. Describe the impact of each item on the bank reconciliation.

E7–10   On April 30, the bank reconciliation of Hidden Valley Company shows three outstanding cheques: No. 254 for $560; No. 255 for $262; and No. 257 for $620. The May bank statement and the general ledger Cash account in May show the following:

Determine outstanding cheques and other reconciling items. (SO 4) AP

HIDDEN VALLEY COMPANY Bank Statement (partial) Cheques Paid/Debits		
Date	Cheque No.	Amount
May 2	254	$560
5	258	159
12	257	620
15	259	275
20	260	500
22	NSF	395
28	263	440
30	262	750
30	SC	54

HIDDEN VALLEY COMPANY Cash Account (partial) Cheques Written		
Date	Cheque No.	Amount
May 2	258	$159
5	259	275
9	260	50
15	261	786
22	262	750
23	263	440
29	264	680

Additional information

1. The bank did not make any errors in May.
2. NSF is a customer's cheque that was returned because the customer did not have sufficient funds.
3. SC stands for service charge.

Instructions

(a) List the outstanding cheques at May 31.
(b) List any other items that must be included in the bank reconciliation. Describe the impact of each item on the bank reconciliation.

Analyze errors. (SO 4) AP

E7–11 The following errors were found when the controller at Country Lane Camping was doing the July 31 bank reconciliation:

1. On July 9, Country Lane recorded a deposit as $2,275. The correct amount was $2,725. The deposit was for the collection of an account receivable and the bank recorded it correctly.
2. On July 14, Country Lane recorded a payment on account as $950. The correct amount was $590. It was correctly recorded by the bank.
3. On July 16, Country Lane recorded a payment for the purchase of supplies as $459. The correct amount was $549. It was correctly recorded by the bank.
4. On July 22, the bank recorded a deposit as $750. The correct amount was $720. This error was corrected by the bank on July 23. Country Lane had correctly recorded the deposit.
5. On July 31, Country Lane recorded a deposit as $778. The correct amount was $887. The deposit was for the collection of an account receivable. This deposit was correctly recorded by the bank on August 1.
6. On July 31, the bank debited Country Lane's account $282 for a cheque written by another company, Country Land, because the account number on the cheque had been damaged. The bank employee who looked up the account number made a mistake.

Instructions

(a) Describe the impact of each of these items on the bank reconciliation.
(b) Prepare any adjusting entries that Country Lane will need to record.

Prepare a bank reconciliation. (SO 4) AP

E7–12 On August 31, 2014, Claresview Company had a cash balance per its books of $26,474. The bank statement on that date showed a balance of $17,602. A comparison of the bank statement with the Cash account revealed the following:

1. The August 31 deposit of $17,127 was not included on the August bank statement.
2. The bank statement shows that Claresview received EFT deposits from customers on account totalling $2,256 in August. Claresview has not recorded any of these amounts.
3. Cheque #673 for $1,450 was outstanding on July 31. It did not clear the bank account in August. All of the cheques written in August have cleared the bank by August 31, except for cheque #710 for $2,504, and #712 for $2,600.
4. The bank statement showed on August 29 an NSF charge of $485 for a cheque issued by R. Dubai, a customer, in payment of their account. This amount included a $10 service charge by Claresview's bank.
5. Bank service charges of $25 were included on the August statement.
6. The bank recorded cheque #705 for $105 as $150. The cheque had been issued to pay for freight out on a sale. Claresview had correctly recorded the cheque.

Instructions

(a) Prepare a bank reconciliation at August 31.
(b) Prepare the necessary adjusting entries on August 31.

Calculate cash balance and report other items. (SO 5) AP

E7–13 A new accountant at Magenta Company is trying to identify which of the following amounts should be reported as the current asset Cash in the year-end balance sheet, as at June 30, 2014:

1. Currency and coins totalling $79 in a locked box used for petty cash transactions
2. A 60-day, $12,000 guaranteed investment certificate, due July 31, 2014
3. June-dated cheques worth $300 that Magenta has received from customers but not yet deposited
4. A $92 cheque received from a customer in payment of her June account, but postdated to July 1
5. A balance of $2,500 in the Royal Bank chequing account
6. A balance of $4,250 in the Royal Bank savings account
7. Prepaid postage of $70 in the postage meter
8. A $100 IOU from the company receptionist
9. Cash register floats of $300
10. Over-the-counter cash receipts for June 30 consisting of $570 of currency and coins, $130 of cheques from customers, $580 of debit card slips, and $750 of bank credit card slips. These amounts were processed by the bank and posted to the bank account on July 1.

Instructions

(a) What amount should Magenta report as its cash and cash equivalents balance at June 30, 2014?
(b) In which financial statement and in which account should the items not included as cash and cash equivalents be reported?

▶ Problems: Set A

P7–1A   Strivent Theatre's cashier's booth is located near the entrance to the theatre. Two cashiers are employed. One works from 3:00 p.m. to 7:00 p.m., the other from 7:00 p.m. to 11:00 p.m. Each cashier is bonded. The cashiers receive cash from customers and operate a machine that ejects serially numbered tickets. The rolls of tickets are inserted and locked into the machine by the theatre manager at the beginning of each cashier's shift.

Identify internal control activities related to cash receipts. (SO 1, 2) C

After purchasing a ticket, which may cost different prices depending on the customer's age group, the customer takes the ticket to an usher stationed at the entrance of the theatre lobby, about 10 metres from the cashier's booth. The usher tears the ticket in half, admits the customer, and returns the ticket stub to the customer. The other half of the ticket is dropped into a locked box by the usher.

At the end of each cashier's shift, the theatre manager removes the ticket rolls from the machine and makes a cash count. The cash count sheet is initialled by the cashier. At the end of the day, the manager deposits the receipts in total in a bank night deposit vault located in the mall. The manager also sends copies of the deposit slip and the initialled cash count sheets to the theatre company controller for verification, and to the company's accounting department. Receipts from the first shift are stored in a safe located in the manager's office.

Instructions

Identify the internal control activities and how they apply to cash receipts at Strivent Theatre.

TAKING IT FURTHER   If the usher and the cashier decide to collaborate to steal cash, how might they do this?

P7–2A   Each of the following independent situations has one or more internal control weaknesses:

Identify internal control weaknesses for cash receipts and cash payments. (SO 1, 2, 3) C

1.   Board Riders is a small snowboarding club that offers specialized coaching for teenagers who want to improve their skills. Group lessons are offered every day. Members who want a lesson pay a $15 fee directly to the teacher at the start of the lesson that day. Most members pay cash. At the end of the lesson, the teacher reports the number of students and turns over the cash to the office manager.
2.   Coloroso Agency offers parenting advice to young single mothers. Most of the agency's revenues are from government grants. The general manager is responsible for all of the accounting work, including approving invoices for payment, preparing and posting all entries into the accounting system, and preparing bank reconciliations.
3.   At Nexus Company, each salesperson is responsible for deciding on the correct credit policies for his or her customers. For example, the salesperson decides if Nexus should sell to the customer on credit and how high the credit limit should be. Salespeople receive a commission based on their sales.
4.   Algorithm Company is a software company that employs many computer programmers. The company uses accounting software that was created by one of the employees. In order to be more flexible and share the workload, all of the programmers have access to the accounting software program in case changes are needed.
5.   The warehouse manager at Orange Wing distributors is well known for running an efficient, cost-saving operation. He has eliminated the requirement for staff to create receiving reports and purchase orders because it was taking staff too long to prepare them.

Instructions

(a)   Identify the internal control weaknesses in each situation.
(b)   Explain the problems that could occur as a result of these weaknesses.

TAKING IT FURTHER   Make recommendations for correcting each situation.

P7–3A   Cedar Grove Middle School wants to raise money for a new sound system for its auditorium. The main fundraising event is a dance at which the famous disc jockey Obnoxious Al will play classic and not-so-classic dance tunes. Roger DeMaster, the music teacher, has been given the responsibility for coordinating the fundraising efforts. This is Roger's first experience with fundraising. He asks the Student Representative Council (SRC) to help him with the event.

Identify internal control weaknesses over cash receipts and cash payments and suggest improvements. (SO 1, 2, 3) C

Roger had 500 unnumbered tickets printed for the dance. He left the tickets in a box on his desk and told the SRC students to take as many tickets as they thought they could sell for $5 each. In order to ensure that no extra tickets would be floating around, he told them to dispose of any unsold tickets. When the students received payment for the tickets, they were to bring the cash back to Roger. He then put it in a locked box in his desk drawer.

Some of the students were responsible for decorating the gymnasium for the dance. Roger gave each of them a key to the cash box. He told them that if they took money out to buy materials, they should put a note in the box saying how much they took and what it was used for. After two weeks, the cash box appeared to be getting full, so

Roger asked Freda Stevens to count the money, prepare a deposit slip, and deposit the money in a bank account Roger had opened.

The day of the dance, Roger wrote a cheque from the account to pay Obnoxious Al. Al said that he accepted only cash and did not give receipts. So Roger took $200 out of the cash box and gave it to Al. At the dance, Roger had Sara Billings working at the entrance to the gymnasium. She collected tickets from students and sold tickets to those who had not prepurchased them. Roger estimated 400 students attended the dance.

The following day, Roger closed out the bank account, which had $250 in it. He gave that amount plus the $180 in the cash box to Principal Skinner. Principal Skinner seemed surprised that, after generating roughly $2,000 in sales, the dance netted only $430 in cash. Roger did not know how to respond.

Instructions

(a) Identify the weaknesses in internal control over cash receipts and cash payments.

(b) What improvements in internal control should the school consider?

TAKING IT FURTHER   Often people think internal control activities are too much work and not necessary. Explain how an improved system of internal control could help protect the individuals involved in this situation from being falsely accused of fraud.

Record debit and bank credit card and petty cash transactions, and identify internal controls.
(SO 2, 3) AP

P7–4A   Malik Retail Shop allows customers to use debit and bank credit cards as well as cash for purchases of merchandise. The company does not accept personal cheques. Malik's bank charges $0.25 for every debit card transaction and 3.0% for bank credit card transactions.

On July 1, the company established a petty cash fund. Before creating the petty cash fund, cash was taken from the cash register whenever someone needed cash to pay for a small expense.

The following transactions happened in the first two weeks of July:

July 1   Established the petty cash fund by cashing a cheque for $250.

8   Total sales for the week were $40,500. Customers paid for these purchases as follows: $14,940 in cash; $11,060 on debit cards (164 transactions); and the balance using bank credit cards.

8   Replenished the petty cash fund. On this date, the fund consisted of $75 in cash and the following petty cash receipts:

Freight out	$60
Supplies	30
Advertising in local paper	40
Personal withdrawal by owner, R. Malik	50

15   Total sales for the week were $38,459. Customers paid for these purchases as follows: $9,907 in cash; $12,252 on debit cards (156 transactions); and the balance using bank credit cards.

15   Replenished the petty cash fund and decreased the balance to $200. On this date, the fund consisted of $73 in cash and the following petty cash receipts:

Postage	$44
Advertising in local newspaper	70
Supplies	56

Instructions

(a) Record the transactions.

(b) What are the benefits of having a petty cash fund instead of paying small expenses from the cash register receipts? What policies and procedures should Malik follow to ensure there is good internal control over its petty cash fund?

TAKING IT FURTHER   What are the advantages and disadvantages of accepting debit and credit card transactions as opposed to accepting personal cheques from customers? Consider both the internal control and business reasons.

Record petty cash transactions, and identify impact on financial statements. (SO 3) AP

P7–5A   You are the accountant for Reliable Snow Removal Services. The company decided to establish a petty cash fund for small expenditures on November 1. Your responsibility is to oversee the fund, which includes collecting receipts, paying out the cash, and replenishing the fund. You completed the following transactions in November with regard to the petty cash fund:

Nov. 1   Cashed a cheque for $150 and put the cash in the petty cash box.

3   Paid $15 for windshield fluid for the company trucks.

5   Paid $28 for repairs to a tire on a company truck.

7   Paid $53 to advertise in a community newsletter.

9   Gave the company owner, Roberta Hayes, $40 cash for personal expenses. Noted this on a piece of paper and put it in the petty cash box.

14   Paid $11 for miscellaneous expenses.
15   Determined that there was $5 cash and that the fund needed to be replenished. Removed the receipts from the petty cash box for the above expenditures and filed them as documentation for the reimbursement. Cashed the cheque and put the cash in the petty cash box.
17   Paid $32 for repairs to the windshield of a company truck.
19   Paid $12 for oil for a company truck.
24   Paid $45 for supplies.
28   Gave the company owner, Roberta Hayes, $45 cash for personal expenses. Noted this on a piece of paper and put it in the petty cash box.
29   Paid $8 for miscellaneous expenses.
30   Determined that there was $4 cash and that the fund needed to be replenished. Removed the receipts from the petty cash box for the above expenditures and filed them as documentation for the reimbursement. Cashed the cheque and put the cash in the petty cash box.

Note: Use Repairs Expense for any expenditures related to the company trucks.

Instructions

(a) Record the November petty cash transactions as appropriate.
(b) Assume the company has a November 30 fiscal year end and that you did not have time to replenish the fund until early December. What impact, if any, would this have on the financial statements?

TAKING IT FURTHER   What things should the company owner check to ensure the fund is being properly administered?

P7–6A   On October 31, 2014, Lisik Company had a cash balance per books of $8,985. The bank statement on that date showed a balance of $10,173. A comparison of the statement with the Cash account revealed the following:

Prepare bank reconciliation and related entries. (SO 4) AP

1. The statement included debit memos of $40 for the printing of additional company cheques and $35 for bank service charges.
2. Cash sales of $639 on October 12 were deposited in the bank. The cash receipts journal entry and the deposit slip were incorrectly made out and recorded by Lisik as $963. The bank detected the error on the deposit slip and credited Lisik Company for the correct amount.
3. The September 30 deposit of $990 was included on the October bank statement. The deposit had been placed in the bank's night deposit vault on September 30.
4. The October 31 deposit of $965 was not included on the October bank statement. The deposit had been placed in the bank's night deposit vault on October 31.
5. Cheques #1006 for $419 and #1072 for $987 were outstanding on September 30. Of these, #1072 cleared the bank in October. All the cheques written in October except for #1278 for $555, #1284 for $646, and #1285 for $323 had cleared the bank by October 31.
6. On October 18, the company issued cheque #1181 for $568 to Helms & Co., on account. The cheque, which cleared the bank in October, was incorrectly journalized and posted by Lisik Company for $685.
7. A review of the bank statement revealed that Lisik Company received electronic payments from customers on account of $1,885 in October. The bank had also credited the account with $27 of interest revenue on October 31. Lisik had no previous notice of these amounts.
8. Included with the cancelled cheques was a cheque issued by Lasik Company for $600 that was incorrectly charged to Lisik Company by the bank.
9. On October 31, the bank statement showed an NSF charge of $820 for a cheque issued by W. Hoad, a customer, to Lisik Company on account. This amount included a $15 service charge by the bank.

Instructions

(a) Prepare the bank reconciliation at October 31.
(b) Prepare the necessary adjusting entries at October 31.

TAKING IT FURTHER   What are the risks of not performing bank reconciliations? Why not just rely on the bank records?

Prepare bank reconciliation and related entries. (SO 4) AP

P7–7A The March bank statement showed the following for Yap Co.:

	Cheques and Other Debits				
Date	Number	Amount		Deposits	Amount

	YAP CO. Bank Statement March 31, 2014				
Date	Number	Amount		Deposits	Amount
Feb. 28					$12,742
Mar. 3	3470	$1,535		$ 2,530	13,737
4	3471	845			12,892
6	3472	1,427		1,221	12,686
7	3473	275			12,411
10	NSF	595			11,816
11	3475	487		1,745	13,074
14	3477	915			12,159
17	3476	1,828		2,283	12,614
20				1,832	14,446
21	3474	2,330			12,116
26	3478	1,080		2,657	13,693
31	LN	1,125			12,568
31	3480	1,679			10,889
31	SC	49		IN 23	10,863

Additional information:

1. The bank statement contained three debit memoranda:
   - An NSF cheque of $595 that Yap had deposited was returned due to insufficient funds in the maker's bank account. This cheque was originally given to Yap by Mr. Jordan, a customer, in payment of his account. Yap believes it will be able to collect this amount from Mr. Jordan.
   - A bank loan payment (LN), which included $125 of interest and a $1,000 payment on the principal.
   - A service charge (SC) of $49 for bank services provided throughout the month.
2. The bank statement contained one credit memorandum for $23 of interest (IN) earned on the account for the month.
3. The bank made an error processing cheque #3478. No other errors were made by the bank.

   Yap's list of cash receipts and cash payments showed the following for March:

Cash Receipts			Cash Payments		
Date	Amount		Date	Cheque No.	Amount
Mar. 5	$ 1,221		Mar. 3	3472	$ 1,427
10	1,745		4	3473	725
14	2,283		6	3474	2,330
20	1,832		7	3475	487
25	2,675		13	3476	1,828
31	1,025		14	3477	915
Total	$10,781		19	3478	1,380
			21	3479	159
			28	3480	1,679
			31	3481	862
			31	3482	1,126
			Total		$12,918

The bank portion of the previous month's bank reconciliation for Yap Co. at February 28, 2014, was as follows:

YAP CO. Bank Reconciliation February 28, 2014		
Cash balance per bank		$12,742
Add: Deposits in transit		2,530
		15,272
Less: Outstanding cheques		
#3451	$2,260	
#3470	1,535	
#3471	845	4,640
Adjusted cash balance per bank		$10,632

Instructions

(a) What is Yap Co.'s unadjusted cash balance in its general ledger on March 31?
(b) Prepare a bank reconciliation at March 31.
(c) Prepare the necessary adjusting entries at March 31. (*Note:* The correction of any errors in the recording of cheques should be made to Accounts Payable. The correction of any errors in the recording of cash receipts should be made to Accounts Receivable.)

TAKING IT FURTHER   The company will prepare entries to record items found in the above bank reconciliation (see part [c] in the instructions). Describe any other follow-up actions required regarding the other reconciling items in Yap Co.'s bank reconciliation.

P7–8A   The bank portion of the bank reconciliation for Maloney Company at October 31, 2014, was as follows:

Prepare bank reconciliation and related entries. (SO 4) AP

MALONEY COMPANY Bank Reconciliation October 31, 2014		
Cash balance per bank		$11,545
Add: Deposits in transit		1,530
		13,075
Less: Outstanding cheques		
#2451	$1,260	
#2470	920	
#2471	845	
#2472	504	
#2474	1,050	4,579
Adjusted cash balance per bank		$ 8,496

The adjusted cash balance per bank agreed with the cash balance per books at October 31. The November bank statement showed the following:

MALONEY COMPANY				
Bank Statement				
November 30, 2014				

Date	Cheques and Other Debits		Deposits	Amount
	Number	Amount		
Oct. 31				$11,545
Nov. 3	2470	$ 920	$1,530	12,155
4	2471	845		11,310
5	2475	1,641	1,212	10,881
6	2474	1,050		9,831
7	2476	2,830	990	7,991
10	2477	600		7,391
13			2,575	9,966
14	2479	1,750		8,216
18	2480	1,330	1,473	8,359
21			2,966	11,325
25	NSF	260	2,567	13,632
26	2481	695		12,937
27			1,650	14,587
28	2486	900	EFT 2,479	16,166
28	2483	575	1,186	16,777
30	LN	2,250		14,527

Additional information from the bank statement:

1. The EFT of $2,479 is an electronic transfer from a customer in payment of its account. The amount includes $49 of interest that Maloney Company had not previously accrued.
2. The NSF for $260 is a $245 cheque from a customer, Pendray Holdings, in payment of its account, plus a $15 processing fee.
3. The LN is a payment of a note payable with the bank and consists of $250 interest and $2,000 principal.
4. The bank did not make any errors.

The cash records per books for November follow. Two errors were made by Maloney Company.

Cash Payments					
Date	Number	Amount	Date	Number	Amount
Nov. 3	2475	$1,641	Nov. 18	2482	$ 612
3	2476	2,380	20	2483	575
4	2477	600	21	2484	830
6	2478	538	24	2485	975
8	2479	1,750	26	2486	900
10	2480	1,330	28	2487	1,200
14	2481	695	Total		$14,026

Cash Receipts	
Date	Amount
Nov. 3	$ 1,212
7	990
12	2,575
17	1,473
20	2,699
24	2,567
27	1,650
28	1,186
30	1,338
Total	$15,690

Instructions

(a) Determine the unadjusted cash balance per books as at November 30, before reconciliation.
(b) Prepare a bank reconciliation at November 30.
(c) Prepare the necessary adjusting entries at November 30. (*Note:* The correction of any errors in the recording of cheques should be made to Accounts Payable. The correction of any errors in the recording of cash receipts should be made to Accounts Receivable.)

TAKING IT FURTHER   When there is an error, how does a company determine if it was a bank error or a company error? How would you know if the bank has made an error in your account?

P7–9A   When the accountant of Trillo Company prepared the bank reconciliation on May 31, 2014, there were three outstanding cheques: #690 for $307, #693 for $179, and #694 for $264. There were no deposits in transit as at May 31, 2014. The bank balance at May 31 was $17,690. The balance in the cash account on the May 31, 2014, adjusted trial balance was $16,940. The following is selected information from the June bank statement:

Prepare bank reconciliation and related entries. (SO 4) AP

Cheques Cleared				Other Bank Account Transactions		
Date	Cheque No.	Amount		Date	Amount	Transaction
June 1	690	$ 307		June 3	$3,325	Deposit
5	709	3,257		10	5,391	Deposit
6	693	179		17	3,180	Deposit
13	710	1,492		24	2,156	Deposit
20	712	3,266		25	−175	NSF cheque
23	7119	467		27	−500	EFT insurance payment
24	711	1,780		30	−12	Service charge
				30	35	Interest

The NSF cheque was originally received from a customer, Massif Co., in payment of its account of $165. The bank included a $10 service charge for a total of $175. Information from the company's accounting records follows:

Cash Receipts			Cash Payments		
Date	Amount		Date	Cheque No.	Amount
June 2	$3,325		June 5	708	$2,910
9	5,391		5	709	3,257
16	3,810		19	711	1,780
23	2,156		19	712	3,626
30	3,127		27	713	3,058
			27	714	3,860

Investigation reveals that cheque #712 was issued to purchase equipment and cheque #710 was issued to pay an account payable. All deposits are for collections of accounts receivable. The bank made one error: cheque #7119 for Trill Co. Ltd. was charged to Trillo's bank account.

Instructions

(a) Calculate the balance per bank statement at June 30 and the unadjusted Cash balance per company records at June 30.
(b) Prepare a bank reconciliation at June 30.
(c) Prepare the necessary adjusting entries at June 30.
(d) What balance would Trillo Company report as cash in the current assets section of its balance sheet on June 30, 2014?

TAKING IT FURTHER   Will the bank be concerned if it looks at Trillo Company's balance sheet and sees a different number than the one on the bank statement? Why or why not?

P7–10A   Sally's Sweet Shop's August 31, 2014, bank balance was $11,135. The company's cash balance at August 31 was $10,760. Other information follows:

Prepare bank reconciliation and adjusting entries. (SO 4) AP

1. Outstanding cheques were #421 for $160, #485 for $267, #492 for $175, and #494 for $1,173. Cheque #421 was also outstanding on July 31 and was included on July's bank reconciliation.
2. Included with the statement were EFT deposits totalling $1,750 during August in payment of accounts receivable. These deposits have not been recorded by the company.
3. Cheque #490 was correctly written and paid by the bank for $509. The cheque had been issued to pay accounts payable and the company had recorded it as $599.
4. The bank statement showed a cheque #4832 for $800, which did not appear on the company's books. Investigation revealed that the cheque was actually issued by Wally's Water Works and was charged to Sally's Sweet Shop's account in error.

5. The bank returned an NSF cheque from a customer for $385.
6. The bank statement showed two debit memoranda for service charges: one for $20 related to the NSF cheque (see item [5] above) and one for $40 for cheque printing charges.
7. The company's records showed the August 15 deposit as $3,680. On the bank statement, it was correctly recorded as $3,980. The deposit was for cash sales.
8. The company has a pre-authorized EFT payment for its monthly utilities for $250 scheduled for the last day of each month. As August 31 was a Sunday this year, the bank posted it on September 1. The company recorded it in August.
9. The $1,370 July 31 bank deposit was recorded on August 1 on the bank statement. The August 31 bank deposit of $2,545 was not included on the August bank statement.

Instructions

(a) Prepare a bank reconciliation.
(b) Prepare any necessary adjusting journal entries.
(c) What amount should be reported as cash in the August 31 balance sheet?

TAKING IT FURTHER   Why is it important that the person who prepares the bank reconciliation isn't also able to write and sign cheques? In what ways would that increase the opportunity for employee fraud?

Calculate cash balance and report other items. (SO 5) AP

P7–11A   A first-year co-op student is trying to determine the amount of cash and cash equivalents that should be reported on a company's balance sheet. The following information was given to the student at year end:

1. The cash float for the cash registers totals $500.
2. The balance in the Petty Cash account is $300. At year end, the fund had $125 cash and receipts totalling $175.
3. The balance in the company's chequing account is $24,500. The company also has a U.S. bank account, which contained the equivalent of $16,000 Canadian at year end.
4. The company has overdraft protection of $10,000 on its chequing account.
5. The company has a separate bank account with a balance of $4,250. This consists of cash deposits paid by tenants who lease office space from the company. The deposits will be refunded to the tenants at the end of their leases.
6. The company has $14,500 of postdated cheques from customers for payment of accounts receivable.
7. The company has the following short-term investments:
   - $25,000 in treasury bills with a maturity date of less than 90 days
   - $36,000 in shares of Reitmans (Canada) Limited
   - $12,000 in a Guaranteed Investment Certificate that matures in six months.
8. The balance in the company owner's personal bank account is $2,150.
9. The company has NSF cheques from customers totalling $875 that were returned by the bank.

Instructions

(a) Calculate the amount of cash and cash equivalents that should be reported on the year-end balance sheet as a current asset.
(b) Identify where any items that were not reported as cash and cash equivalents in (a) should be reported.

TAKING IT FURTHER   Why are restricted cash balances presented separately from cash?

▶ Problems: Set B

Identify internal control weaknesses over cash receipts and suggest improvements. (SO 1, 2) C

P7–1B   The board of trustees of a local church has asked for your help with the controls activities for the offering collections made at weekly services. At a board meeting, you learn the following:

1. The board has made the finance committee responsible for the financial management and audit of the financial records. This group prepares the annual budget and approves major payments but is not involved in collections or record keeping. No audit has been done in recent years, because the same trusted employee has kept church records and served as financial secretary for 15 years. None of the church employees, or board of trustees, are bonded.
2. The collection at the weekly service is taken by a team of ushers who volunteer to serve for one month. The ushers take the collection plates to a basement office at the rear of the church. They hand their plates to the head usher and return to the church service. After all plates have been turned in, the head usher counts the cash collected. The head usher then places the cash in the unlocked church safe and includes a note that states the amount counted. The head usher volunteers to serve for three months.
3. The next morning, the financial secretary opens the safe and recounts the collection. The secretary withholds from $150 to $200 in cash, depending on the cash expenditures expected for the week, and deposits the remainder

of the collections in the bank. To make the deposit easier, church members who contribute by cheque are asked to make their cheques payable to Cash.

4. Each month, the financial secretary reconciles the bank statement and submits a copy of the reconciliation to the board of trustees. The reconciliations have rarely contained any bank errors and have never shown any errors per books.

Instructions

(a) Indicate the weaknesses in internal control in the handling of collections.
(b) List the improvements in internal control that should be recommended with regard to (1) the ushers, (2) the head usher, and (3) the financial secretary.

TAKING IT FURTHER   Under what circumstances might these internal control weaknesses lead to fraud?

P7–2B   Seegall Supply Company recently changed its system of internal control over its purchasing operations and cash payments to make the system more efficient. One employee is now responsible for both purchasing and receiving. For each purchase, that individual matches the purchase order with the receiving report and the supplier's invoice. The invoice is approved for payment by this individual and sent to the accounting department.

Identify internal control weaknesses over cash payments and suggest improvements. (SO 1, 3, 4) C

All cheques are prenumbered and kept in a safe in the controller's office. The combination to the safe is known only by the controller, his assistant, and the company owner. Since the bank has never made a mistake with the account, the cheque numbers are not tracked.

The controller prepares all of the cheques and all of the journal entries. All cheques must be signed by the company owner, Stephanie Seegall. After the owner has signed the cheque, the controller stamps the invoice paid and has his assistant file the invoice and post the journal entry. Whenever the owner is going to be away for several days, she will leave signed blank cheques in the safe for the controller.

The controller prepares the monthly bank reconciliation. Every month he finds at least three cheques that have cleared the bank but have not been recorded by the company. These cheques are always properly signed by the owner. When the controller first started working for the company, he would ask the owner about the cheques. These cheques were always for the owner's personal expenses, so now he always records these cheques as owner's drawings when doing the bank reconciliation.

Instructions

(a) Identify the control weaknesses over cash payments.
(b) What changes should be made to improve the internal control over cash payments?

TAKING IT FURTHER   Often people think internal control activities are too much work and not necessary. Explain how an improved system of internal control could help protect the individuals working for this company from being falsely accused of fraud.

P7–3B   Each of the following independent situations has an internal control weakness:

Identify internal control weaknesses over cash receipts and cash payments. (SO 1, 2, 3) C

1. Henry's Lawn Care Service provides residential grass cutting services for a large number of clients who all pay cash. Henry collects the cash and keeps it in the glove compartment of his car until the end of the week, when he has time to count it and prepare a bank deposit.
2. Tasty Treats sells a variety of items including ice cream, pop, and other snack foods. A long-term employee is responsible for ordering all merchandise, checking all deliveries, and approving invoices for payment.
3. At Pop's Pizza, there are three sales clerks on duty during busy times. All three of them use the same cash drawer.
4. Most customers at Ultimate Definition TVs use the option to pay for their televisions in 24 equal payments over two years. These customers send the company cheques or cash each month. The office manager opens the mail each day, makes a bank deposit with the cheques received in the mail that day, and prepares and posts an entry in the accounting records.
5. Trends Incorporated manufactures celebrity posters for teenagers. Naiara Mann is the custodian of the company's $500 petty cash fund. The fund is replenished every week. Frequently people do not have a receipt for their expenses because of things like parking meter expenses. In this case, Naiara just creates a receipt for that person and gives them their cash. Naiara has been with the company for 15 years and is good friends with many of the employees. Naiara is very hard-working and never takes a vacation.

Instructions

(a) Identify the internal control weaknesses in each situation.
(b) Explain the problems that could occur as a result of these weaknesses.

TAKING IT FURTHER   Make recommendations for correcting each situation.

Record debit and bank credit card and petty cash transactions and identify internal controls. (SO 2, 3) AP

P7–4B   Ramesh & Company allows customers to use debit and bank credit cards and cash for purchases of merchandise. The company does not accept personal cheques from customers. Ramesh's bank charges $0.20 for every debit card transaction and 3% for credit card transactions.

On May 1, the company established a petty cash fund. Before creating the petty cash fund, cash was taken from the cash register whenever someone needed cash to pay for a small expense.

The following transactions happened in the first two weeks of June:

May	1	Established the petty cash fund by cashing a cheque for $150.
	8	Total sales for the week were $14,175. Customers paid for these purchases as follows: $4,550 in cash; $5,325 on debit cards (55 transactions); and the balance using bank credit cards.
	8	Replenished the petty cash fund. On this date, the fund consisted of $9 in cash and the following petty cash receipts:

Delivery of merchandise to customers	$44
Postage	30
Advertising in local paper	54
Miscellaneous expense	10

	15	Total sales for the week were $16,380. Customers paid for these purchases as follows: $3,690 in cash; $7,390 on debit cards (85 transactions); and the balance using bank credit cards.
	15	Replenished the petty cash fund and increased the balance to $250. On this date, the fund consisted of $5 in cash and the following petty cash receipts:

B. Ramesh's personal withdrawal	$60
Supplies	20
Delivery of merchandise to customers	67

Instructions

(a) Record the transactions.

(b) What are the advantages and disadvantages of accepting debit and bank credit card transactions as opposed to accepting only cash and personal cheques from customers? Consider both the internal control and business reasons.

TAKING IT FURTHER   What are the benefits of having a petty cash fund instead of paying small expenses from the cash register receipts? What policies and procedures should Ramesh & Company follow to ensure there is good internal control over its petty cash fund?

Record petty cash transactions, and identify impact on financial statements. (SO 3) AP

P7–5B   You are the accountant for Lakeside Sweetshop. The company has decided to establish a petty cash fund for small expenditures on June 1. Your responsibility is to oversee the fund, which includes collecting receipts, paying out the cash, and replenishing the fund. You completed the following transactions in September with regard to the petty cash fund:

June	1	Cashed a cheque for $200 and put the cash in the petty cash box.
	3	Paid $35 for supplies.
	5	Paid $48 for repairs to the cash register.
	7	Paid $55 to advertise in a community newsletter.
	9	Gave the company owner, Elliott Bender, $40 cash for personal expenses. Noted this on a piece of paper and put it in the petty cash box.
	14	Paid $19 for miscellaneous expenses.
	15	Determined that there was $1 cash and that the fund needed to be replenished. Removed the receipts from the petty cash box for the above expenditures and filed them as documentation for the reimbursement. Cashed the cheque and put the cash in the petty cash box.
	17	Paid $10 to one of the neighbourhood children for delivering merchandise to a customer who had a broken leg and was unable to walk to the shop.
	19	Paid $54 for supplies.
	24	Paid $48 for a sign advertising the store hours of operation.
	28	Gave the company owner, Elliott Bender, $45 cash for personal expenses. Noted this on a piece of paper and put it in the petty cash box.
	29	Paid $18 for miscellaneous expenses.
	30	Determined that there was $29 cash in the fund. Prepared a cheque to reimburse the fund. Removed the receipts from the petty cash box for the above expenditures and filed them as documentation for the reimbursement. Cashed the cheque and put the cash in the petty cash box.

Instructions

(a) Record the June petty cash transactions as appropriate.

(b) Assume the company has a June 30 fiscal year end and that you did not replenish the fund until early in July when almost all of the cash had been used. What impact, if any, would this have on the financial statements?

TAKING IT FURTHER   It was stated in the chapter that "internal control over cash payments is better when payments are made by cheque." Why, then, would a company choose to make some payments from petty cash rather than by cheque? What should a company do to maintain good internal control over the petty cash fund?

P7–6B   The Agricultural Genetics Company's Cash account in its general ledger reported a balance of $9,242 on May 31, 2014. The company's bank statement from Western Bank reported a balance of $11,890 on the same date.

A comparison of the details in the bank statement with the details in the Cash account revealed the following facts:

Prepare bank reconciliation and related entries.
(SO 4) AP

1. The bank statement included a debit memo of $50 for bank service charges.
2. Cash sales of $1,386 on May 30 were deposited in the bank. The journal entry to record the cash sales and the deposit slip to deposit the cash were correctly made out for $1,386. The bank credited Agricultural Genetics Company for $1,638. The bank found the error and corrected it on June 1.
3. The April 30 deposit of $2,190 was included on the May bank statement. The deposit had been placed in the bank's night deposit vault on April 30.
4. The May 31 deposit of $1,794 was not included on the May bank statement. The deposit had been placed in the bank's night deposit vault on May 31.
5. Cheques #928 for $180 and #1014 for $636 were outstanding on April 30. Of these, #928 cleared the bank in May. All of the cheques written in May except for #1127 for $276, #1195 for $760, and #1196 for $348 had cleared the bank by May 31.
6. On May 18, the company issued cheque #1151 for $495 to L. Kingston, on account. The cheque, which cleared the bank in May, was incorrectly journalized and posted by Agricultural Genetics Company for $945.
7. On May 28, the company issued cheque #1192 for $765 to Bow Graphics for equipment. The cheque was incorrectly recorded by Agricultural Genetics as $675. The cheque cleared the bank on May 30.
8. A review of the bank statement revealed that Agricultural Genetics Company received $2,511 of electronic payments from customers on account in May. The bank had also credited the company's account with $24 of interest revenue on May 31. Agricultural Genetics Company had no previous notice of these amounts.
9. On May 31, the bank statement showed an NSF charge of $660 for a cheque issued by Pete Dell, a customer, to Agricultural Genetics Company on account. On the same day, the bank also charged the company a $15 service charge for the returned cheque.

Instructions

(a) Prepare the bank reconciliation at May 31.

(b) Prepare the necessary adjusting entries at May 31.

TAKING IT FURTHER   What would you say to the Agricultural Genetics Company's bank manager, who is concerned that the company's May 31 Cash account balance shows a different amount than the May 31 bank statement?

P7–7B   The bank portion of the bank reconciliation for Katsaris Company at August 31, 2014, was as follows:

Prepare bank reconciliation and related entries.
(SO 4) AP

KATSARIS COMPANY
Bank Reconciliation
August 31, 2014

Cash balance per bank		$13,229
Add: Deposits in transit		2,350
		15,579
Less: Outstanding cheques		
#4451	$1,740	
#4460	549	
#4461	723	
#4462	1,840	
#4464	620	5,472
Adjusted cash balance per bank		$10,107

The adjusted cash balance per bank agreed with the cash balance per books at August 31. The September bank statement showed the following:

	KATSARIS COMPANY Bank Statement September 30, 2014			
	Cheques and Other Debits			
Date	Number	Amount	Deposits	Amount
Aug. 31				$13,229
Sept. 1	4460	$ 549	$2,350	15,030
2	4461	723		14,307
5	4465	1,459	1,212	14,060
7	4462	1,840		12,220
8	4466	1,180	2,365	13,405
9	4467	2,268		11,137
15	4468	554	3,145	13,728
16			2,673	16,401
20			1,967	18,368
23	NSF	1,027	3,126	20,467
26	4470	3,040		17,427
27	4474	1,439	1,940	17,928
27	4472	488	1,070	18,510
30	4475	535		17,975
30	SC	45		17,930

Additional information:

1. The deposit of $3,145 on September 15 is an electronic transfer from a customer in payment of its account. The amount includes $65 of interest, which Katsaris Company had not previously accrued.
2. The NSF for $1,027 is for a $1,015 cheque from a customer, Hopper Holdings, in payment of its account, plus a $12 processing fee.
3. SC represents bank service charges for the month.

The bank made one error: it recorded cheque #4475 incorrectly. Any other errors were made by Katsaris Company. The cash records per the company's books for September showed the following:

			Cash Payments				Cash Receipts	
Date	Number	Amount	Date	Number	Amount		Date	Amount
Sept. 1	4465	$1,459	Sept. 23	4474	1,439		Sept. 2	$ 1,212
2	4466	1,180	24	4475	553		7	2,365
2	4467	2,268	30	4476	1,280		15	2,763
5	4468	554	Total		$15,076		20	1,967
8	4469	600					26	3,126
12	4470	3,400					28	1,940
17	4471	621					30	1,070
20	4472	488					30	754
22	4473	1,234					Total	$15,197

Instructions

(a) Determine the unadjusted cash balance per books as at September 30 before reconciliation.
(b) Prepare a bank reconciliation at September 30.
(c) Prepare the necessary adjusting entries at September 30. (*Note:* The correction of any errors in the recording of cheques should be made to Accounts Payable. The correction of any errors in the recording of cash receipts should be made to Accounts Receivable.)

TAKING IT FURTHER   The company will prepare entries to record items found in the above bank reconciliation (see part [c] in the instructions). Describe any other follow-up actions required regarding the other reconciling items in Katsaris Company's bank reconciliation.

Prepare bank reconciliation
and related entries.
(SO 4) AP

P7-8B   You are given the following information for River Adventures Company:

RIVER ADVENTURES COMPANY
Bank Reconciliation
April 30, 2014

Cash balance per bank		$9,009
Add: Deposits in transit		846
		9,855
Less: Outstanding cheques		
#526	$1,358	
#533	279	
#541	363	
#555	79	2,079
Adjusted cash balance per bank		$7,776

The adjusted cash balance per bank agreed with the cash balance per books at April 30, 2014. The May bank statement showed the following:

RIVER ADVENTURES COMPANY
Bank Statement
May 31, 2014

	Cheques and Other Debits			
Date	Number	Amount	Deposits	Amount
Apr. 30				$9,009
May 1	526	$1,358	$ 846	8,497
2	541	363		8,134
6	556	223		7,911
6	557	1,800	1,250	7,361
9			980	8,341
12	559	1,650		6,691
13			426	7,117
13			1,650	8,767
14	561	799		7,968
16	562	2,045		5,923
20			222	6,145
21	563	2,487		3,658
22	564	603		3,055
23	565	1,033		2,022
27			980	3,002
28	NSF	440	1,771	4,333
31	SC	25		4,308

Additional information from the bank statement:

1. The deposit of $1,650 on May 13 is an electronic transfer from a customer in payment of its account. The amount includes $35 of interest, which River Adventures Company had not previously accrued.
2. The NSF for $440 is for a $425 cheque from a customer, Ralph King, in payment of his account, plus a $15 processing fee.
3. SC represents bank service charges for the month.
4. The bank made an error when processing cheque #564. The company also made two errors in the month. All cheques were written to pay accounts payable; all cash receipts were collections of accounts receivable.

The company's recorded cash payments and cash receipts for the month were as follows:

Cash Receipts			Cash Payments		
Date	Amount		Date	Cheque No.	Amount
May 5	$1,250		May 2	556	$ 223
8	980		5	557	1,800
12	426		7	558	943
18	222		7	559	1,650
25	890		8	560	890
28	1,771		12	561	799
31	1,286		15	562	2,045
Total	$6,825		16	563	2,887
			20	564	306
			23	565	1,033
			30	566	950
			Total		$13,526

Instructions

(a) Calculate the unadjusted cash balance in River Adventures' general ledger at May 31.
(b) Prepare a bank reconciliation and the necessary adjusting journal entries at May 31.

TAKING IT FURTHER When there is an error, how does a company determine if it was a bank error or a company error? How would you know if the bank has made an error in your account?

Prepare bank reconciliation and related entries.
(SO 4) AP

P7–9B In the November 30, 2014, bank reconciliation at Kiran's Kayaks, there were two outstanding cheques: #165 for $812 and #169 for $529. There was a $1,128 deposit in transit as at November 30, 2014. The bank balance at November 30 was $7,181; the adjusted cash balance was $6,968. The December bank statement had the following selected information:

Cheques Cleared			Other Bank Account Transactions		
Date	Cheque No.	Amount	Date	Amount	Transaction
Dec. 1	169	$ 529	Dec. 1	$1,128 +	Deposit
8	184	592	4	2,321 +	Deposit
17	186	3,491	11	3,991 +	Deposit
22	187	833	18	3,007 +	Deposit
23	183	2,955	23	520 −	NSF cheque
31	188	341	29	1,504 +	Deposit
			31	48 −	Service charge

The NSF cheque was originally received from a customer, M. Sevigny, in payment of her account of $500. The bank included a $20 service charge for a total of $520.

Information from the company's accounting records follows:

Cash Receipts			Cash Payments		
Date	Amount		Date	Cheque No.	Amount
Dec. 3	$2,321		Dec. 5	183	$2,955
10	3,991		5	184	592
17	3,707		12	185	1,165
24	1,504		12	186	3,941
31	2,218		16	187	833
			31	188	341
			31	189	1,721

Investigation reveals that cheque #186 was issued to buy equipment. All deposits are for collections of accounts receivable. The bank made no errors.

Instructions

(a) Calculate the balance per bank statement at December 31 and the unadjusted cash balance per company records at December 31.

(b) Prepare a bank reconciliation for Kiran's Kayaks at December 31.

(c) Prepare the necessary adjusting entries at December 31.

(d) What balance would Kiran's Kayaks report as cash in the current assets section of its balance sheet on December 31, 2014?

TAKING IT FURTHER   Explain why it is important for Kiran's Kayaks to complete the above bank reconciliation before preparing closing entries.

P7–10B   South Hampton Pool Supplies' May 31, 2014, bank balance was $7,350. The company's cash balance at May 31 was $8,210. Other information follows:

Prepare bank reconciliation and adjusting entries. (SO 4) AP

1. Outstanding cheques were #321 for $653, #371 for $238, #375 for $281, and #376 for $958. Cheque #321 was also outstanding on April 30 and was included on April's bank reconciliation.
2. Included with the statement were EFT deposits totalling $975 during May in payment of accounts receivable. These deposits have not been recorded by the company.
3. Cheque #370 was correctly written and paid by the bank for $488. The cheque had been issued to pay accounts payable and the company had recorded it as $408.
4. The bank statement showed a cheque #3723 for $600, which did not appear on the company's books. Investigation revealed that the cheque was actually issued by South Hampton Pizzeria and was charged to South Hampton Pool Supplies account in error.
5. The bank returned an NSF cheque from a customer for $249.
6. The bank statement showed two debit memoranda for service charges: one for $17 related to the NSF cheque (see item [5] above) and one for $44 for monthly bank charges.
7. The company's records showed the May 15 deposit as $2,850. On the bank statement it was correctly recorded as $2,580. The deposit was for cash sales.
8. The company has a pre-authorized EFT payment for its monthly utilities for $225 scheduled for the last day of each month. As May 31 was a Saturday this year, the bank posted it on June 2. The company recorded it in May.
9. The $1,370 April 30 bank deposit was recorded on May 1 on the bank statement. The May 31 bank deposit of $2,930 was not included on the May bank statement.

Instructions

(a) Prepare a bank reconciliation.

(b) Prepare any necessary adjusting journal entries.

(c) What amount should be reported as cash in the May 31 balance sheet?

TAKING IT FURTHER   Explain how the bank reconciliation process can strengthen internal control.

P7–11B   Sunil's Supplies has hired a new junior accountant and has given her the task of identifying what should be reported as cash as at February 28, 2014, on the company's balance sheet. The following information is available:

Calculate cash balance and report other items. (SO 5) AP

1. Cash on hand in the cash registers on February 28 totals $1,494. Of this amount, $300 is kept on hand as a cash float.
2. The balance in the petty cash fund is $175. Actual petty cash on hand at February 28 is $32. Receipts total $140. Of these receipts, $55 is for cash used by the owner for personal expenses.
3. The balance in the bank chequing account at February 28 is $7,460.
4. The company has two short-term investments: (1) $5,000 in a 60-day treasury bill, and (2) $3,000 in a six-month term deposit.
5. The company has a staledated cheque for $540 from a customer for the purchase of merchandise. The customer made a mistake on the date of the cheque and the company's bank wouldn't let it deposit the cheque. The customer has promised to fix the cheque on March 2.
6. The company has a U.S. dollar bank account. At February 28, its U.S. funds were worth the equivalent of $3,555 Canadian.
7. At February 28, the company has American Express credit card slips totalling $700 for sales made on February 27 and 28. American Express charges the company a credit card fee of 3.0%. It takes two days for American Express charges to clear the banking system and be deposited in the company's bank account.
8. The company received $1,500 of cash on February 28 as an advance deposit in trust on a property sale.
9. In order to hook up utilities, the company is required to deposit $800 in trust with Ontario Hydro. This amount must remain on deposit until a satisfactory credit history has been established. The company expects to have this deposit back within the year.

Instructions

(a) Calculate the amount of cash and cash equivalents that should be reported on the year-end balance sheet as a current asset.

(b) Identify where any items that were not reported in the balance for cash in (a) should be reported.

TAKING IT FURTHER   Under certain circumstances, cash may have to be presented as non-current. Why is this important information for users of the financial statements?

⊙ Continuing Cookie Chronicle

(*Note:* This is a continuation of the Cookie Chronicle from Chapters 1 through 6.)

Natalie is struggling to keep up with the recording of her accounting transactions. She is spending a lot of time marketing and selling mixers and giving her cookie classes. Her friend John is an accounting student who runs his own accounting service. He has asked Natalie if she would like to have him do her accounting.

    John and Natalie meet and discuss her business. John suggests that he could perform the following procedures for Natalie:

1. Take the deposits to the bank every Friday. All cheques and cash received would be kept in a locked box at Natalie's house.
2. Write and sign all of the cheques. He would review the invoices and send out cheques as soon as the invoices are received.
3. Record all of the deposits in the accounting records.
4. Record all of the cheques in the accounting records.
5. Prepare the monthly bank reconciliation.
6. Transfer Natalie's manual accounting records to his computer accounting program. John maintains the accounting information that he keeps for his clients on his laptop computer.
7. Prepare monthly financial statements for Natalie to review.
8. Write himself a cheque every month for the work he has done for Natalie.

Instructions

(a) Refer to items 1 to 8 above. Identify the procedures that Natalie should perform and explain why.

(b) Identify the procedures that John could perform.

(c) For each procedure that Natalie should perform, identify what could go wrong, in a worst-case scenario, if John were to do it.

(d) Once Natalie decides what procedures she would like John to perform, what are some of the advantages and disadvantages of having John perform these accounting services for Cookie Creations?

CHAPTER 7 | BROADENING YOUR PERSPECTIVE

⊙ Financial Reporting and Analysis

Financial Reporting Problem

BYP7–1   Two reports are attached to **Reitmans (Canada) Limited's** financial statements presented in Appendix A of this book: (1) Management's Responsibility for Financial Statements and (2) the Independent Auditors' Report.

Instructions

(a) What comments, if any, about the company's system of internal control are included in Management's Responsibility for Financial Statements? In the Independent Auditors' Report?

(b) Who is mainly responsible for the financial statements? Explain.

(c) What is the name of Reitmans' independent auditor? What is its responsibility?

(d) What is an audit committee and how does it help the external auditors with their responsibilities?

(e) What does Reitmans include in its cash and cash equivalents? By how much did cash and cash equivalents decrease during the current fiscal year? By looking at the statement of cash flows, what were the two biggest uses of cash during the current fiscal year?

Interpreting Financial Statements

BYP7-2   **Western Wind Energy Corp.** is in the business of developing, owning, and operating wind- and solar energy-generating facilities. The company is headquartered in Vancouver and has assets for both solar and wind energy in the United States, Canada, and in the Commonwealth of Puerto Rico. Selected information from Western Wind Energy's comparative balance sheet follows:

WESTERN WIND ENERGY CORP. Consolidated Balance Sheet (partial) December 31 (in US dollars)		
	2011	2010
Current assets		
Cash	$ 429,583	$ 1,119,366
Restricted cash (Note 3)	21,152,225	—
Accounts receivable	549,558	213,469
Refundable tax credits	107,199	234,873
Prepaid expenses	4,388,572	1,393,476
Deposits	89,587	—
Total current assets	$ 26,716,724	$ 2,961,184
Non-current assets		
Restricted cash (Note 3)	$ 25,863,450	$127,128,155
Power projects construction & development costs	275,102,027	12,265,529
Total current liabilities	129,198,231	26,224,629

Instructions

(a) In Note 2(d), the company explains that cash consists of cash on deposit with banks and that it doesn't have any cash equivalents. What is a cash equivalent? Provide a possible reason as to why Western Wind Energy doesn't have cash equivalents.

(b) In Note 3, the company explains that restricted cash includes cash balances held by the company for which the cash is restricted to meet specific operational, project, and debt service requirements, as required by financing arrangements. How much restricted cash in total did Western Wind Energy have at December 31, 2010 and 2011? Based on the information provided in the partial balance sheet, provide a possible explanation as to why total restricted cash decreased from 2010 to 2011.

(c) Calculate (1) working capital and (2) the current ratio for each year. Comment on your results.

(d) Should the restricted cash be included in an acid-test ratio calculation? Why or why not?

▶ Critical Thinking

Collaborative Learning Activity

Note to instructor: Additional instructions and material for this group activity can be found on the Instructor Resource Site and in *WileyPLUS*.

BYP7-3   In this group activity, you will identify the strengths and weaknesses of a small coffee shop's processes for sales or purchases and make recommendations for processes that will improve internal control.

Communication Activity

BYP7–4 Tenacity Corporation is a medium-sized private company that sells auto parts. Blake Pike has been with the company from the beginning, ordering the auto parts, taking delivery of the parts, and authorizing payments for them. Blake often signs cheques and prepares the bank reconciliation if the controller is on vacation. The company has grown in size from five employees to 25. Annual sales have increased tenfold. Blake is still performing the same tasks as he was when the company was small and he says that he does not need any help.

Instructions

Write a letter to L.S. Osman, owner of Tenacity Corporation, which outlines a plan to improve internal control within the organization given its recent increase in size. Highlight in your letter any weaknesses you are currently aware of and suggest specific recommendations.

Ethics Case

BYP7–5 Banks charge customers fees of up to $40 per cheque for writing "bounced" cheques; that is, cheques that exceed the balance in the account. It has been estimated that processing bounced cheques costs a bank roughly $5 per cheque. Thus, the profit margin on a bounced cheque is very high. Some banks process cheques from largest amount to smallest. By doing this, they maximize the number of cheques that bounce if a customer overdraws an account.

Instructions

(a) Who are the stakeholders in this situation?
(b) Antonio Freeman had a balance of $1,200 in his chequing account on a day when the bank received the following five cheques for processing against his account:

Cheque Number	Amount	Cheque Number	Amount
3150	$ 35	3165	$550
3158	1,175	3169	180
3162	400		

Assuming a $35 fee per cheque is assessed by the bank, how much fee revenue would the bank generate if it processed cheques (1) from largest to smallest, (2) from smallest to largest, and (3) in the order of the cheque numbers?
(c) Do you think that processing NSF cheques from largest to smallest is an ethical business practice for a bank?
(d) Besides ethical issues, what else should a bank consider when it decides if it should process cheques from largest to smallest?
(e) If you were managing a bank, what would be your policy on bounced cheques?

"All About You" Activity

BYP7–6 In the "All About You" feature, you learned about the dangers of identity theft. To protect yourself from identity theft, you should understand how it can happen and learn what you can do to prevent it.

Instructions

(a) Go to the Ontario Ministry of Consumer Services, Consumer Protection website at www.sse.gov.on.ca/mcs/en/pages/default.aspx and click on "Identity Theft." What is identity theft? Identify the key types of information that thieves use.
(b) On the same web page as in part (a), click on "How Can an Identity Thief Get Your Personal Information?" Identify how identity thieves can get your personal information.
(c) On the same web page as in part (a), click on "How Do I Know If My Identity Has Been Stolen?" What are some of the signs that may indicate that your identity has been stolen?
(d) Just as a business should implement internal control systems to protect its assets, an individual should also implement controls to prevent and recognize identity theft. On the same web page as in part (a), click on "How To Reduce Your Risk In the Marketplace and Online?"
   1. Identify the physical and IT controls that can be implemented to safeguard your identity.
   2. Identify the checks that you can do to recognize identity theft and prevent it from continuing.

ANSWERS TO CHAPTER QUESTIONS

ANSWERS TO ACCOUNTING IN ACTION INSIGHT QUESTIONS

All About You, p. 365

Q: Who is responsible for losses due to unauthorized credit card use?

A: Most major credit card companies offer zero liability for credit card fraud, which protects the cardholder from losses due to fraud. You should find out if your cardholder agreement for any credit cards that you have offers protection from credit card fraud so that you can avoid taking on the identity thief's debts.

Across the Organization Insight, p. 368

Q: How might an organization's marketing department assist in, and benefit from, the implementation of a mobile payments system?

A: As you read in the Accounting in Action box, many consumers are worried about security in using their cell phones to make mobile payments. The marketing department could help in creating awareness of the benefits to consumers through social media and other more traditional advertising methods. In doing so, it would also be an opportunity to promote the business.

ANSWERS TO SELF-STUDY QUESTION

1. c   2. d   3. b   4. d   5. a   6. b   7. d   8. b   9. b   10. c

Remember to go back to the beginning of the chapter to check off your completed work!

←

CHAPTER **EIGHT**

ACCOUNTING FOR RECEIVABLES

 THE **NAVIGATOR**

CONCEPTS FOR **REVIEW**

Before studying this chapter, you should understand or, if necessary, review:

a. How to record revenue. (ch. 3, pp. 123–124 and ch. 5, pp. 244–248)

b. Why adjusting entries are made. (ch. 3, pp. 115–116)

c. How to calculate interest. (ch.3, pp. 125–126)

d. What is the difference between permanent and temporary accounts. (ch. 4, p. 174)

e. What is a subsidiary ledger. (ch. 5, pp. 240–241)

f. How to record to bank credit card transactions. (ch. 7, pp. 366–368)

TRYING TO COLLECT FROM INCOMMUNICADO CLIENTS

SAINT JOHN, N.B.—Bell Aliant is the product of the 1999 merger of four Atlantic telephone service providers: New Brunswick Telephone, Maritime Tel, Island Tel, and Newfoundland Tel. The history of these four companies goes back 100 years in providing telephone service to Atlantic Canadians. In 2006, the company expanded westward with the purchase of Bell Canada's rural telephone lines in Ontario and Quebec; at the same time, it sold Bell its wireless business. In 2009, Bell Aliant became the first company in Canada to offer fibre-to-the-home technology to an entire city. Today, Bell Aliant is one of North America's largest regional communications providers, offering voice, data, Internet, and television services to customers across six provinces. With a staff of approximately 7,000, the company earns $2.8 billion a year under the brands Bell Aliant in Atlantic Canada and Bell in Ontario and Quebec, as well as Télébec, Northern Tel, and Kenora Municipal Telephone Services.

Bell Aliant's main sources of revenue are fees for local and long-distance phone services, high-speed Internet services, and television. In most areas, the company's services are bundled with wireless services from Bell Mobility. It also receives revenue from equipment rentals and value-added technology business solutions for large enterprises.

"Our total receivables balance is typically around $370 million at any one month end," says Eleanor Marshall, Vice-President and Treasurer at Bell Aliant. On the balance sheet, under IFRS, this amount includes accounts receivable the company has sold as part of its securitization program. The proceeds from the securitized receivables are reflected as short-term borrowing.

Certain of Bell Aliant's billing terms are regulated by the Canadian Radio-television and Telecommunications Commission (CRTC). The company bills monthly for services in arrears, and payments are due within 21 days of the billing date. This results in receivables being about 31 to 35 days outstanding, Ms. Marshall explains.

"The vast majority of our consumer customers pay on or slightly before the due date," she says. "We have very few accounts outstanding beyond 30 days." In contrast, businesses take longer to pay, usually 35 to 50 days.

Even though the bills are due within 21 days of the billing date, late payment charges begin to accrue at 30 days from the billing date. "Late payment charges are intended to be punitive. Since we primarily bill monthly recurring charges, we really want customers to pay on time, so they do not get behind," Ms. Marshall explains. "As such, these charges are currently set at 3% per month."

Bell Aliant classifies customers as low risk, high risk, or unknown, and this classification will determine how large and how far in arrears the company will allow the bill to get before taking action. It may also require a deposit if a customer has no or poor credit history.

If the bill does not get paid on time, Bell Aliant will start making calls, sending reminder notices and perhaps negotiating new payment terms. If there is still no payment, the company will suspend the account for 21 days, then reconnect for one day, and contact the client again. If the bill still isn't paid, it will permanently disconnect the customer. The company then sends two notices to the client, and finally the bill goes to a collection agency.

"We establish provisions for bad debts long before it gets to this point," Ms. Marshall adds. Receivables are assigned aging categories and certain percentages, which are based on experience, apply to each to estimate the amount of bad debt. The company recognizes bad debt expense, which is typically just under 1% of revenue, each month.

THE **NAVIGATOR**

>> STUDY **OBJECTIVES**

After studying this chapter, you should be able to:

1. Record accounts receivable transactions.

2. Calculate the net realizable value of accounts receivable and account for bad debts.

3. Account for notes receivable.

4. Demonstrate the presentation, analysis, and management of receivables.

THE **NAVIGATOR**

As indicated in our feature story, management of receivables is important for any company that sells on credit, as Bell Aliant does. In this chapter, we will first review the journal entries that companies make when goods and services are sold on account and when cash is collected from those sales. Next, we will learn how companies estimate, record, and then, in some cases, collect their uncollectible accounts. We will also learn about notes receivable, the statement presentation of receivables, and management of receivables.

The chapter is organized as follows:

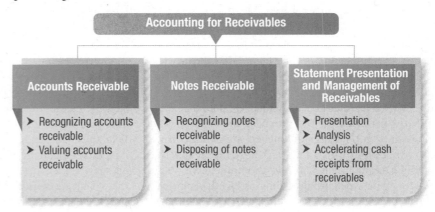

Accounts Receivable

The term "receivables" refers to amounts due to a company from individuals and other companies. They are claims that are expected to be collected in cash. The two most common types of receivables are accounts receivable and notes receivable.

Accounts receivable are amounts owed by customers on account. They result from the sale of goods and services. These receivables are generally expected to be collected within 30 days or so, and are classified as current assets. **Notes receivable** are claims for which formal instruments of credit (a written note) are issued as proof of the debt. A note normally requires the debtor to pay interest and extends for longer than the company's normal credit terms. Accounts and notes receivable that result from sale transactions are often called **trade receivables**. In this section, we will learn about accounts receivable. Notes receivable will be covered later in the chapter.

Accounts receivable are usually the most significant type of claim held by a company. Two important accounting issues—recognizing accounts receivable and valuing accounts receivable—will be discussed in this section. A third issue—accelerating cash receipts from receivables—is discussed later in the chapter.

RECOGNIZING ACCOUNTS RECEIVABLE

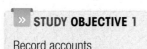

» STUDY OBJECTIVE 1

Record accounts receivable transactions.

Recognizing accounts receivable is relatively straightforward. Normally, for a service company, an asset, accounts receivable, is recorded when the service is provided on account and the revenue is recognized. The company has an asset because the company is going to receive cash from its customer in the future. For a merchandising company, a receivable is recorded at the point of sale of merchandise on account. Recall that in Chapter 5 we also saw how accounts receivable are reduced by sales returns and allowances and sales discounts. The asset is reduced because the returns and discounts will result in less cash being received from the customer.

To review, assume that Adorable Junior Garment sells merchandise on account to The Bay on July 1 for $1,000 with payment terms of 2/10, n/30. On July 4, The Bay returns merchandise worth $100 to Adorable Junior Garment. On July 10, Adorable Junior Garment receives payment from The Bay for the balance due. The journal entries to record these transactions on the books of Adorable Junior Garment are as follows:

July 1	Accounts Receivable—The Bay		1,000	
	Sales			1,000
	To record sale of merchandise on account.			
4	Sales Returns and Allowances		100	
	Accounts Receivable—The Bay			100
	To record merchandise returned.			
10	Cash [($1,000 − $100) × 98%]		882	
	Sales Discounts [($1,000 − $100) × 2%]		18	
	Accounts Receivable—The Bay ($1,000 − $100)			900
	To record collection of accounts receivable.			

A = L + OE
+1,000   +1,000
Cash flows: no effect

A = L + OE
−100   −100
Cash flows: no effect

A = L + OE
+882   −18
−900
↑ Cash flows: +882

If Adorable Junior Garment uses a perpetual inventory system, a second journal entry to record the cost of the goods sold (and the cost of the goods returned) would be required for the July 1 and July 4 transactions.

Subsidiary Accounts Receivable Ledger

Adorable Junior Garment does not have only The Bay as a customer. It has hundreds of customers. If it recorded the accounts receivable for each of these customers in only one general ledger account, as we did above in Accounts Receivable, it would be hard to determine the balance owed by a specific customer, such as The Bay, at a specific point in time. It is critical that a company knows what each customer owes so that it can collect the cash owed to it by its customers.

Most companies that sell on account use a subsidiary ledger to keep track of individual customer accounts. As we learned in Chapter 5, a subsidiary ledger gives supporting detail to the general ledger. The company's Accounts Receivable account in the general ledger is the control account that provides the balance in accounts receivable reported on the balance sheet. Illustration 8-1 shows the information

▶ ILLUSTRATION 8-1
Accounts receivable general ledger control account and subsidiary ledger

GENERAL LEDGER

Accounts Receivable is a control account.

Accounts Receivable   No. 112

Date	Explanation	Ref.	Debit	Credit	Balance
2014					
July 4				100	(100)
31			10,000		9,900
31				5,900	4,000 ←

ACCOUNTS RECEIVABLE SUBSIDIARY LEDGER

The subsidiary ledger is separate from the general ledger.

Kids Online   No. 112-203

Date	Explanation	Ref.	Debit	Credit	Balance
2014					
July 11	Invoice 1310		6,000		6,000
19	Payment			4,000	2,000 ←

Snazzy Kids Co.   No. 112-413

Date	Explanation	Ref.	Debit	Credit	Balance
2014					
July 12	Invoice 1318		3,000		3,000
21	Payment			1,000	2,000 ←

The Bay   No. 112-581

Date	Explanation	Ref.	Debit	Credit	Balance
2014					
July 1	Invoice 1215		1,000		1,000
4	Credit Memo 1222			100	900
10	Payment			900	0 ←

included in an accounts receivable subsidiary ledger and the general ledger for a simple manual accounting system, using assumed data.

Each entry that affects accounts receivable is basically posted twice: once to the subsidiary ledger and once to the general ledger. Normally, in a manual system, entries to the subsidiary ledger are posted daily, while entries to the general ledger are summarized and posted monthly. For example, the $1,000 sale to The Bay was posted to The Bay's account in the subsidiary ledger on July 1. It was also summarized with other sales entries (Kids Online $6,000 + Snazzy Kids $3,000 + The Bay $1,000 = $10,000) in a special sales journal and posted to the accounts receivable control account in the general ledger at the end of the month, on July 31.

Collections on account (Kids Online $4,000 + Snazzy Kids $1,000 + The Bay $900 = $5,900) were also posted individually to the subsidiary ledger accounts and summarized and posted in total to the general ledger account. Non-recurring entries, such as the sales return of $100, are posted to both the subsidiary and general ledgers individually.

Note that the balance of $4,000 in the control account in the general ledger agrees with the total of the balances in the individual accounts receivable accounts in the subsidiary ledger (Kids Online $2,000 + Snazzy Kids $2,000 + The Bay $0). There is more information about how subsidiary ledgers work in Appendix C at the end of this textbook.

Today, most businesses use computerized accounting systems that automatically update the subsidiary ledger and general ledger when a journal entry is recorded. Regardless of whether the accounting system is computerized or manual, the accounting records must provide accurate, up-to-date information for each customer account and the total of the customer account balances must equal the total in the general ledger control account.

Interest Revenue

At the end of each month, the company can use the subsidiary ledger to easily determine the transactions that occurred in each customer's account during the month and then send the customer a statement of transactions for the month. If the customer does not pay in full within a specified period (usually 30 days), most retailers add an interest (financing) charge to the balance due.

When financing charges are added, the seller increases the accounts receivable and recognizes interest revenue. If Kids Online still owes $2,000 at the end of the next month, August 31, and Adorable Junior Garment charges 18% on the balance due, the entry that Adorable Junior Garment will make to record interest revenue of $30 ($2,000 $\times$ 18% $\times$ $^1/_{12}$) is as follows:

A	=	L	+	OE
+30				+30

Cash flows: no effect

Aug. 31	Accounts Receivable—Kids Online	30	
	Interest Revenue		30
	To record interest on amount due.		

Bell Aliant in our feature story starts to accrue interest if payment is not received from the customer within 30 days of the billing date. The interest charges are meant to be punitive and the customer charges are 3% per month. As discussed in Chapter 5, interest revenue is included in other revenues in the non-operating section of the income statement.

Nonbank Credit Card Sales

In Chapter 7, we learned that debit and bank credit card sales are typically treated as cash sales. Sales on credit cards that are not directly associated with a bank are reported as credit sales, not cash sales. Nonbank credit card sales result in an account receivable until the credit card company pays the amount owing to the seller.

To illustrate, assume that Kerr Music accepts a nonbank credit card on October 24 for a $500 bill. An asset, accounts receivable, is recorded for the amount of cash that will be received, an expense is recorded for the service fee charged by the credit card company, and revenue is recorded for the amount of the sale. The entry for the sale by Kerr Music (assuming a 4% service fee) is:

A	=	L	+	OE
+480				−20
				+500

Cash flows: no effect

Oct. 24	Accounts Receivable—Credit Card Company	480	
	Credit Card Expense ($500 $\times$ 4%)	20	
	Sales		500
	To record nonbank credit card sale.		

When Cash is received from the credit card company, the asset cash is increased and accounts receivable is reduced for the amount collected. The entry that Kerr Music will record is as follows:

Nov. 7	Cash	480	
	Accounts Receivable—Credit Card Company		480
	To record nonbank credit card sale.		

A = L + OE
+480
−480

↑ Cash flows: +480

Advances in technology have created a rapidly changing credit card industry. Transactions and payments can be processed much more quickly, and often electronically, which reduces the time to collect cash from the credit card company. As collection time becomes shorter, credit card transactions are becoming more like cash transactions to the business.

How does a business know if it should debit Cash or Accounts Receivable when it processes a credit card transaction? Basically, it should consider how long it takes to collect the cash. If it takes longer than a few days to process the transaction and collect the cash, it should be treated as a credit sale, as shown above.

Companies that issue their own credit cards, such as Canadian Tire, always record sales paid by their cards as credit sales. When the credit card transaction results in an account receivable from the customer—as opposed to from the credit card company, as shown above—there is no service fee and the accounting treatment is the same as we have previously seen for accounts receivable.

As discussed in Chapter 7, credit card expenses, along with debit card expenses, are reported as operating expenses in the income statement.

ACCOUNTING IN ACTION
ALL ABOUT YOU INSIGHT

Interest rates on bank credit cards can vary depending on the card's various features; recently, the interest rates on Canadian bank credit cards ranged from 5.99% to 20.5%. Credit cards with lower interest rates usually have annual fees and may only be available to those with an excellent credit rating. Nonbank cards can charge significantly higher interest rates, such as retailer HBC's interest rate of 29.9%. At the same time, the Canadian banks' prime lending rate was 3.0%. The prime lending rate, the rate banks charge their best customers, changes depending on the supply and demand for money. Credit card interest rates, on the other hand, hardly budge at all. Why are credit card rates so much higher than other interest rates?

The higher rate is due to the risk involved. A bank loan, such as a mortgage, is a secured loan because the loan is backed by a tangible asset: a house. Using a credit card is essentially taking out an unsecured loan because nothing physical is used as security for the lender. In addition, credit cards are much more susceptible to fraud, and thus require a consistently high interest rate.

Sources: Credit Cards Canada website at http://www.creditcardscanada.ca; Garry Marr, "Borrowers Will Suffer After Interest Rate Hike," *National Post*, April 17, 2012; "HBC Account Agreement," available at http://financial.hbc.com/en/credit/terms.shtml.

Should you use credit cards or not?

 BEFORE YOU GO ON...

Do It

Information for Kinholm Company follows for its first month of operations:

	Credit Sales			Cash Collections	
Jan. 5	Sych Co.	$12,000	Jan.16	Sych Co.	$9,000
9	Downey Inc.	5,000	22	Downey Inc.	3,500
13	Pawlak Co.	6,000	28	Pawlak Co.	6,000

Action Plan

- Use T accounts as a simple method of calculating account balances.
- Create separate accounts for each customer and post their transactions to their accounts.
- Create one account for the Accounts Receivable general ledger (control) account.
- Post the total credit sales and the total cash collections to the general ledger.

BEFORE YOU GO ON continued...

Calculate (a) the balances that appear in the accounts receivable subsidiary ledger for each customer, and (b) the accounts receivable balance that appears in the general ledger at the end of January.

Solution

ACCOUNTS RECEIVABLE SUBSIDIARY LEDGER

Sych Co.

Jan. 5	12,000	Jan. 16	9,000
Bal.	3,000		

Downey Inc.

Jan. 9	5,000	Jan. 22	3,500
Bal.	1,500		

Pawlak Co.

Jan. 13	6,000	Jan. 28	6,000
Bal.	0		

GENERAL LEDGER

Accounts Receivable

Jan. 31	23,000[a]	Jan. 31	18,500[b]
Bal.	4,500		

[a] $12,000 + $5,000 + $6,000 = $23,000
[b] $9,000 + $3,500 + $6,000 = $18,500

Related exercise material: BE8–1, BE8–2, BE8–3, BE8–4, E8–1, and E8–2.

THE NAVIGATOR

VALUING ACCOUNTS RECEIVABLE

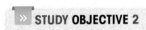

» STUDY OBJECTIVE 2

Calculate the net realizable value of accounts receivable and account for bad debts.

After receivables are recorded in the accounts, the next question is how these receivables should be reported on the balance sheet. Receivables are assets, but determining the amount to report as an asset is sometimes difficult because some receivables will become uncollectible. A receivable can only be reported as an asset if it will give a future benefit. This means that only collectible receivables can be reported as assets in the financial statements. This collectible amount is called the receivables' **net realizable value**. Reporting accounts receivable at net realizable value provides information to investors and creditors on the company's ability to generate cash.

In order to minimize the risk of uncollectible accounts, companies consider the creditworthiness of potential credit customers. But even if a customer satisfies the company's credit requirements before the credit sale was approved, inevitably, some accounts receivable still become uncollectible. For example, a usually reliable customer may suddenly not be able to pay because of an unexpected decrease in its revenues or because it is faced with unexpected bills.

Why do companies still decide to sell goods or services on credit if there is always a risk of not collecting the receivable? It is because they are expecting that the increase in revenues and profit from selling on credit will be greater than any uncollectible accounts or credit losses. Such losses are considered a normal and necessary risk of doing business on a credit basis.

When receivables are written down to their net realizable value because of expected credit losses, owner's equity must also be reduced so that assets remain equal to liabilities plus owner's equity. As we learned in Chapter 1, a decrease in an asset that results in a decrease in owner's equity (excluding withdrawals by owners) is an expense. The expense for credit losses is called **bad debt expense**.

Alternative terminology Bad debt expense is also sometimes called *uncollectible account expense.*

The key issue in valuing accounts receivable is to estimate the amount of accounts receivable that will not be collected. If the company waits until it knows for sure that a specific account will not be collected, it could end up overstating the asset accounts receivable on the balance sheet and understating expenses.

Consider the following example. Assume that in 2014, Quick Buck Computer Company decides it could increase its revenues by offering computers to students without requiring any money down and with no credit approval process. On campuses across the country, it sells 100,000 computers with a selling price of $400 each. This increases Quick Buck's receivables and revenues by $40 million. The promotion is a huge success! The 2014 balance sheet and income statement look great. Unfortunately, in 2015, nearly 40% of the student customers default on (do not pay) their accounts. This makes the 2015 balance sheet and income statement look terrible. Illustration 8-2 shows that the promotion in 2014 was not such a great success after all.

▶ILLUSTRATION 8-2
Effect of overstating
accounts receivable (AR) and
understating expenses

Year 2014

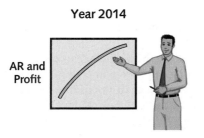

Huge sales promotion. Accounts receivable increase
dramatically. Profit increases dramatically.

Year 2015

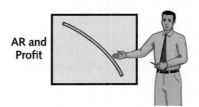

Customers default on amounts owed. Accounts receivable
drop dramatically. Bad debt expense increases and profit
decreases dramatically.

If credit losses are not recorded until they occur, the accounts receivable in the balance sheet are not reported at the amount that is actually expected to be collected. Quick Buck Computer's receivables were overstated at the end of 2014, which misrepresented the amount that should have been reported as an asset.

In addition, bad debt expense will not be matched to sales revenues in the income statement. Recall from Chapter 3 that expenses that are directly related to revenue must be recorded in the same period as the sales they helped generate. Consequently, Quick Buck Computer Company's profit was overstated in 2014 and understated in 2015 because the revenues were recorded in 2014 and the expenses directly related to the revenue were recorded in 2015.

To avoid overstating assets and profit, we cannot wait until we know exactly which receivables are uncollectible. Because we do not know which specific accounts receivable will need to be written off, we use what is known as the **allowance method** in which we estimate uncollectible accounts at the end of each accounting period. In this method, the estimated uncollectible accounts are recorded as a credit balance in a contra asset account, **Allowance for Doubtful Accounts**. The allowance is deducted from Accounts Receivable on the balance sheet to report the net realizable value of the receivables.

The allowance method also gives better matching of expenses with revenues on the income statement because credit losses that are expected to happen from sales or service revenue in that accounting period are recorded in the same accounting period as when the revenue was earned. The allowance method is required for financial reporting purposes and has three essential features:

1. **Recording estimated uncollectibles:** The amount of uncollectible accounts receivable is estimated at the end of the accounting period. An adjusting journal entry is recorded to adjust the allowance for doubtful accounts to the estimated uncollectible amount and to record bad debt expense.
2. **Writing off uncollectible accounts:** Actual uncollectibles are written off when the specific account is determined to be uncollectible.
3. **Collection of a previously written-off account:** If an account that was previously written off is later collected, the original write off is reversed and the collection is recorded.

We explain these features of the allowance method in the following sections.

1. Recording Estimated Uncollectibles

Estimating the Allowance for Doubtful Accounts. To illustrate the allowance method, assume that Adorable Junior Garment has accounts receivable of $200,000 at December 31, 2014. Not all of these receivables will be collected. As it is not known at December 31, 2014, which specific accounts are uncollectible, the amount of uncollectibles must be estimated. How is this amount estimated? The most common method used by companies is the percentage of receivables approach.

Under the **percentage of receivables approach**, management uses experience to estimate the percentage of receivables that will become uncollectible accounts. The easiest way to do this is to multiply the total amount of accounts receivable by a percentage based on an overall estimate of the total uncollectible accounts. The problem with this simple approach is that it doesn't take into consideration that the longer a receivable is past due or outstanding, the less likely it is to be collected.

Alternative terminology The percentage of receivables approach is sometimes referred to as the *balance sheet approach.*

Therefore, the more common practice is to use different percentages depending on how long the accounts receivable have been outstanding. This is more sensitive to the actual status of the accounts receivable. Bell Aliant in our feature story uses this approach.

A schedule must be prepared, called an **aging schedule**, which shows the age of each account receivable. After the age of each account receivable is determined, the loss from uncollectible accounts is estimated. This is done by applying percentages, based on experience, to the totals in each category. The estimated percentage of uncollectible accounts increases as the number of days outstanding increases. An aging schedule for Adorable Junior Garment is shown in Illustration 8-3.

▶ **ILLUSTRATION 8-3**
Aging schedule

		Number of Days Outstanding				
Customer	Total	0–30	31–60	61–90	91–120	Over 120
Bansal Garments	$ 6,000		$ 3,000	$ 3,000		
Bortz Clothing	3,000	$ 3,000				
Kids Online	4,500				$ 2,000	$ 2,500
Snazzy Kids Co.	17,000	2,000	5,000	5,000	5,000	
Tykes n' Tots	26,500	10,000	10,000	6,000	500	
The Bay	42,000	32,000	10,000			
Walmart	61,000	48,000	12,000	1,000		
Others	40,000	5,000	10,000	10,000	5,000	10,000
	$200,000	$100,000	$50,000	$25,000	$12,500	$12,500
Estimated percentage uncollectible		5%	10%	20%	30%	50%
Estimated uncollectible accounts	**$25,000**	$ 5,000	$ 5,000	$ 5,000	$ 3,750	$ 6,250

The $25,000 total for estimated uncollectible accounts is the amount of existing receivables that are expected to become uncollectible in the future. This also means that Adorable Junior Garments expects to collect the remaining accounts receivable of $175,000 ($200,000 of accounts receivable in total less the estimated uncollectible accounts of $25,000). As Adorable Junior Garment expects to collect only $175,000, this is the amount that should be shown in the balance sheet as an asset, not $200,000.

As previously explained, since Adorable Junior Garment doesn't know specifically which accounts receivable it will not collect, we do not know which specific accounts to credit in the subsidiary ledger. We cannot simply credit the Accounts Receivable control account to reduce it from $200,000 to $175,000 because the subsidiary ledger accounts must balance with Accounts Receivable, the control account.

The problem is solved by using the contra asset account, Allowance for Doubtful Accounts, instead of crediting Accounts Receivable. Remember that the balance of a contra asset account (a credit) is deducted from the related asset on the balance sheet (a debit). The difference between Adorable Junior Garment's **gross accounts receivable** and its allowance for doubtful accounts is the net realizable value (the collectible amount) of its accounts receivable. This can be represented by the formula shown in Illustration 8-4.

▶ **ILLUSTRATION 8-4**
Formula for calculating net realizable value

Gross Accounts Receivable	−	Allowance for Doubtful Accounts	=	Net Realizable Value
$200,000	−	$25,000	=	$175,000

In the current assets section of the balance sheet, Accounts Receivable, the Allowance for Doubtful Accounts, and the net realizable value are reported as follows (using assumed data for the other current asset accounts):

ADORABLE JUNIOR GARMENT
Balance Sheet (partial)
December 31, 2014

Current assets		
Cash		$ 14,800
Accounts receivable	$200,000	
Less: Allowance for doubtful accounts	25,000	175,000
Merchandise inventory		310,000
Prepaid expenses		25,000
Total current assets		$524,800

Notice that the net realizable value of the accounts receivable—$175,000—is the amount added to cash, merchandise inventory, and prepaid expenses to calculate total current assets, not the total accounts receivable ($14,800 + 175,000 + 310,000 + 25,000).

Determining Bad Debt Expense. Although the balance in the Allowance for Doubtful Accounts is $25,000, it is important to understand that this is not necessarily equal to the bad debt expense in the income statement. Why? Recall that a contra asset account is a permanent account. That means the balance in a contra asset account is carried forward to the next accounting period. We need to know the unadjusted balance in the Allowance for Doubtful Accounts in order to adjust the account to its required balance of $25,000. This adjusting entry also records the bad debt expense. Since bad debt expense is a temporary account, it starts each accounting period with a zero balance. Thus the amount in the adjusting entry will be equal to the bad debt expense reported in the income statement.

To illustrate, let us assume that Adorable Junior Garment has an unadjusted credit balance of $1,000 in its Allowance for Doubtful Accounts. Because the account already has a credit balance, it needs to be adjusted by only the difference between the required balance of $25,000 and the existing balance of $1,000. Thus the amount of the adjusting entry, which is equal to the bad debt expense, is $24,000, as shown in Illustration 8-5.

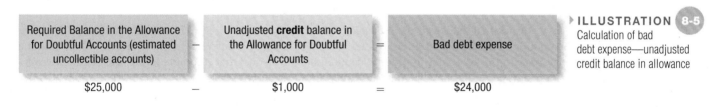

Required Balance in the Allowance for Doubtful Accounts (estimated uncollectible accounts)	−	Unadjusted **credit** balance in the Allowance for Doubtful Accounts	=	Bad debt expense
$25,000	−	$1,000	=	$24,000

▶ **ILLUSTRATION 8-5**
Calculation of bad debt expense—unadjusted credit balance in allowance

The adjusting entry for $24,000 is as follows:

Dec. 31	Bad Debt Expense	24,000	
	Allowance for Doubtful Accounts		24,000
	To record estimate of uncollectible accounts.		

A = L + OE
−24,000   −24,000
Cash flows: no effect

After the adjusting entry is posted, the balance in the Allowance for Doubtful Accounts will be equal to the estimated uncollectible accounts calculated in Illustration 8-3. This is shown in Adorable Junior Garment's accounts:

Bad Debt Expense		Allowance for Doubtful Accounts		
Dec. 31 Adj. 24,000		Dec. 31	Unadj. Bal.	1,000
		31	Adj.	24,000
		Dec. 31	Bal.	25,000

Bad debt expense of $24,000 is reported in the income statement in the period when the sales are recognized. Notice this is less than the balance in the Allowance for Doubtful Accounts. This will always be the case when there is a credit amount in the unadjusted balance of the allowance account.

Occasionally, the allowance account will have a debit balance before recording the adjusting entry. This happens when write offs in the year are higher than the previous estimates for bad debts (we will discuss write offs in the next section). If there is a debit balance prior to recording the adjusting entry, the debit balance is added to the required balance when the adjusting entry is made. For example, if there had been a $500 debit balance in the Adorable Junior Garment allowance account before adjustment, the adjusting entry would have been for $25,500, to arrive at a credit balance in the allowance account of $25,000. The calculation of the adjusting entry is shown in Illustration 8-6.

▶ **ILLUSTRATION 8-6**
Calculation of bad debt expense—unadjusted debit balance in the allowance

Required Balance in the Allowance for Doubtful Accounts (estimated uncollectible accounts)	+	Unadjusted **debit** balance in the Allowance for Doubtful Accounts	=	Bad debt expense
$25,000	+	$500	=	$25,500

In this case, the adjusting entry is for $25,500 as follows:

A	=	L	+	OE
−25,500				−25,500

Cash flows: no effect

Dec. 31	Bad Debt Expense	25,500	
	Allowance for Doubtful Accounts		25,500
	To record estimate of uncollectible accounts.		

After the adjusting entry is posted, the balance in the Allowance for Doubtful Accounts is equal to the estimated uncollectible accounts calculated in Illustration 8-3. This is shown in Adorable Junior Garment's accounts:

Bad Debt Expense	
Dec. 31 Adj. 25,500	

Allowance for Doubtful Accounts	
	Dec. 31 Unadj. Bal. 500
	31 Adj. 25,500
	Dec. 31 Bal. **25,000**

Notice that, although the adjusted balance in the Allowance for Doubtful Accounts is the same amount in the two examples shown, the Bad Debt Expense is different. In this case, it is higher than the balance in the allowance in order to compensate for the fact that Adorable Junior Garment underestimated its allowance and bad debts last year.

When preparing annual financial statements, all companies must report accounts receivable at their net realizable value, so companies must estimate the required allowance. However, when preparing monthly financial statements, some companies use a simplified approach in which bad debt expense is calculated by estimating the percent of sales that will not be collected. This approach, called the percentage of sales approach, is covered in intermediate textbooks.

2. Writing Off Uncollectible Accounts

Companies use various methods for collecting past-due accounts, including letters, calls, and legal actions. Bell Aliant, in our feature story, classifies customers by risk levels, which it uses to determine how large and how far in arrears it will allow the bill to get before taking action. Bell Aliant follows up on late accounts with letters and calls, and will cut back or suspend service if the customer does not negotiate new payment terms. If there is still no payment from the customer, service is permanently cut off. The final step involves sending the account to a collection agency.

When all the ways of collecting a past-due account have been tried and collection appears impossible, the account should be written off. To prevent premature write offs, each write off should be approved in writing by management. To keep good internal control, the authorization to write off accounts should not be given to someone who also has responsibilities related to cash or receivables.

To illustrate a receivables write off, assume that the vice-president of finance of Adorable Junior Garment authorizes the write off of a $4,500 balance owed by a delinquent customer, Kids Online, on March 1, 2015. The entry to record the write off is as follows:

Mar. 1	Allowance for Doubtful Accounts	4,500	
	Accounts Receivable—Kids Online		4,500
	Write off of uncollectible account.		

A = L + OE
+4,500
−4,500

Cash flows: no effect

Bad Debt Expense is not increased (debited) when the write off occurs. Under the allowance method, every account write off is debited to the allowance account rather than to Bad Debt Expense. A debit to Bad Debt Expense would be incorrect because the expense was already recognized when the adjusting entry was made for estimated bad debts last year.

Instead, the entry to record the write off of an uncollectible account reduces both Accounts Receivable and Allowance for Doubtful Accounts. After posting, using an assumed balance of $230,000 in Accounts Receivable on February 28, 2015, the general ledger accounts will appear as follows:

Accounts Receivable				Allowance for Doubtful Accounts			
Feb. 28 Bal.	230,000	Mar. 1	4,500	Mar. 1	4,500	Jan. 1 Bal.	25,000
Mar. 1 Bal.	225,500					Mar. 1 Bal.	20,500

A write off affects only balance sheet accounts. The write off of the account reduces both Accounts Receivable and Allowance for Doubtful Accounts. Net realizable value in the balance sheet remains the same, as shown below:

	Before Write Off	After Write Off
Accounts receivable	$230,000	$225,500
Less: Allowance for doubtful accounts	25,000	20,500
Net realizable value	$205,000	$205,000

As mentioned earlier, the allowance account can sometimes end up in a debit balance position after the write off of an uncollectible account. This can happen if the writeoffs in the period are more than the opening balance of the allowance. It means the actual credit losses were greater than the estimated credit losses. The balance in Allowance for Doubtful Accounts will be corrected when the adjusting entry for estimated uncollectible accounts is made at the end of the period.

3. Collection of a Previously Written-Off Uncollectible Account

Occasionally, a company collects cash from a customer after its account has been written off. Two entries are required to record the collection of a previously written-off account: (1) the entry previously made when the account was written off is reversed to restore the customer's account; and (2) the collection is recorded in the usual way.

To illustrate, assume that on July 1, 2015, Kids Online pays the $4,500 amount that had been written off on March 1. The entries are as follows:

	(1)		
July 1	Accounts Receivable—Kids Online	4,500	
	Allowance for Doubtful Accounts		4,500
	To reverse write off of Kids Online account.		

A = L + OE
+4,500
−4,500

Cash flows: no effect

	(2)		
July 1	Cash	4,500	
	Accounts Receivable—Kids Online		4,500
	To record collection from Kids Online.		

A = L + OE
+4,500
−4,500

Cash flows: +4,500

Note that the collection of a previously written-off account, like the write off of a bad debt, affects only balance sheet accounts. The net effect of the two entries is a debit to Cash and a credit to Allowance for Doubtful Accounts for $4,500. Accounts Receivable is debited and later credited for two reasons. First, the company must reverse the write off. Second, Kids Online did pay, so the Accounts Receivable account in the general ledger and Kids Online's account in the subsidiary ledger, if a subsidiary ledger is used, should show this payment as it will need to be considered in deciding what credit to give to Kids Online in the future.

Summary of Allowance Method

In summary, there are three types of transactions that you may need to record when valuing accounts receivable using the allowance method:

1. The estimated uncollectible accounts is determined by using the percentage of receivables approach. The estimated uncollectible accounts is the required balance in the Allowance for Doubtful Accounts, which is deducted from Accounts Receivable on the balance sheet to show the net realizable value of the receivables. The estimated uncollectible accounts receivable is recorded by using an adjusting entry at the end of the period in which Bad Debt Expense is debited and the Allowance for Doubtful Accounts is credited. The amount in the adjustment—the bad debt expense—is the difference between the required balance and the unadjusted balance in the allowance account.
2. Write offs of actual uncollectible accounts are recorded in the next accounting period by debiting Allowance for Doubtful Accounts and crediting Accounts Receivable.
3. Later collections of previously written-off accounts, if any, are recorded in two separate entries. The first reverses the write off by debiting Accounts Receivable and crediting Allowance for Doubtful Accounts. The second records the normal collection of the account by debiting Cash and crediting Accounts Receivable.

These entries are summarized in the following T accounts:

Accounts Receivable			Allowance for Doubtful Accounts	
Beginning balance	Cash collections		Write offs	Beginning balance
Credit sales	Write offs			Reverse write-off
Later recoveries				Bad debt adjusting entry
Ending balance				Ending balance

Action Plan

- Apply percentages to the receivables in each age category to determine total estimated uncollectible accounts. This is the ending balance required in the allowance account.
- Net realizable value is equal to the balance in Accounts Receivable minus the required balance in Allowance for Doubtful Accounts.
- Use the unadjusted balance in the allowance account to determine the adjusting entry. If the unadjusted balance in the allowance account is a credit, the amount of the adjustment is equal to the required balance minus the unadjusted credit balance. If the unadjusted balance is a debit, the amount of the adjustment is equal to the required balance plus the unadjusted debit balance.

BEFORE YOU GO ON...

Do It

The following information for Woo Wholesalers Co. accounts receivable is available at December 31:

Number of Days Outstanding	Accounts Receivable	Estimated Percentage Uncollectible
0–30 days	$ 85,000	5%
31–60 days	25,000	15%
Over 61 days	10,000	25%
Total	$120,000	

(a) Calculate the estimated uncollectible accounts and the net realizable value of Woo's accounts receivable at December 31.
(b) Prepare the adjusting journal entry to record bad debt expense for each of the following independent situations:
1. The Allowance for Doubtful Accounts has an unadjusted $2,000 credit balance.
2. The Allowance for Doubtful Accounts has an unadjusted $1,200 debit balance.
(c) Prepare the required journal entry if Woo learns that its $1,500 receivable from Kruger Retailers is not collectible.
(d) Prepare the required journal entries if Woo subsequently collects the $1,500 receivable from Kruger Retailers that was previously written off.

Solution

(a) Estimated uncollectible accounts = ($85,000 × 5%) + ($25,000 × 15%) + ($10,000 × 25%)
$$= \$10,500$$
Net Realizable Value = $120,000 − $10,500
$$= \$109,500$$

(b) 1. Bad Debt Expense ($10,500 − $2,000) 8,500
      Allowance for Doubtful Accounts 8,500
        To record estimate of uncollectible accounts.
    2. Bad Debt Expense ($10,500 + $1,200) 11,700
      Allowance for Doubtful Accounts 11,700
        To record estimate of uncollectible accounts.

(c) Allowance for Doubtful Accounts 1,500
     Accounts Receivable—Kruger Retailers 1,500
      To record write off of account receivable.

(d) Accounts Receivable—Kruger Retailers 1,500
     Allowance for Doubtful Accounts 1,500
      To reverse write off of Kruger Retailers' account receivable.
    Cash 1,500
     Accounts Receivable 1,500
      To record collection from Kruger Retailers.

Related exercise material: BE8–5, BE8–6, BE8–7, BE8–8, BE8–9, BE8–10, E8–4, E8–5, E8–6, and E8–7.

- Record the write offs of accounts and subsequent collection of accounts written off only in the balance sheet accounts, Accounts Receivable and Allowance for Doubtful Accounts.

THE **NAVIGATOR**

Notes Receivable

Credit may also be granted in exchange for a formal credit instrument known as a promissory note. A **promissory note** is a written promise to pay a specified amount of money on demand or at a definite time. Promissory notes may be used (1) when individuals and companies lend or borrow money, (2) when the amount of the transaction and the credit period are longer than normal limits, or (3) in the settlement of accounts receivable.

In a promissory note, the party making the promise to pay is called the **maker**. The party to whom payment is to be made is called the **payee**. In the note shown in Illustration 8-7, Higly Inc. is the maker and Wolder Company is the payee. To Wolder Company, the promissory note is a note receivable. To Higly Inc., it is a note payable.

» **STUDY OBJECTIVE 3**

Account for notes receivable.

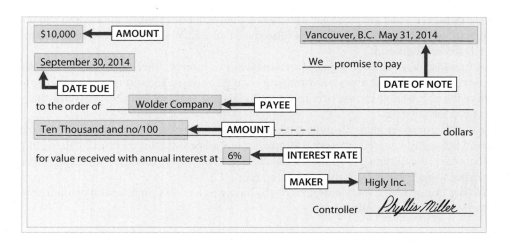

▶ **ILLUSTRATION 8-7**
Promissory note

A promissory note might also contain other details such as whether any security is pledged as collateral for the loan and what happens if the maker defaults.

A note receivable is a formal promise to pay an amount that bears interest from the time it is issued until it is due. An account receivable is an informal promise to pay that bears interest only after its due date. Because it is less formal, it does not have as strong a legal claim as a note receivable. Most accounts receivable are due within a short period of time, usually 30 days, while a note can extend over longer periods of time.

There are also similarities between notes and accounts receivable. Both are credit instruments. Both can be sold to another party. Both are valued at their net realizable values. The basic issues in accounting for notes receivable are the same as those for accounts receivable, as follows:

1. Recognizing notes receivable
2. Disposing of notes receivable

RECOGNIZING NOTES RECEIVABLE

Like accounts receivable, a note receivable is an asset, as the company will collect cash in the future. To illustrate the basic entries for notes receivable, we will use the $10,000, four-month, 6% promissory note shown in Illustration 8-7. Assuming that Higly Inc. wrote the note in settlement of an account receivable, Wolder Company makes the following entry for the receipt of the note:

A = L + OE	May 31	Notes Receivable—Higly 10,000
+10,000		Accounts Receivable—Higly 10,000
−10,000		To record acceptance of Higly note.
Cash flows: no effect		

If a note is exchanged for cash instead of an account receivable, the entry is a debit to Notes Receivable and a credit to Cash for the amount of the loan.

The note receivable is recorded at its principal amount (the value shown on the face of the note). No interest revenue is reported when the note is accepted because, according to the revenue recognition principle, revenue is not recognized until it is earned. Interest is earned (accrued) as time passes.

Recording Interest

As we learned in Chapter 3, the basic formula for calculating interest on an interest-bearing note is the following:

▶ ILLUSTRATION **8-8**
Formula for calculating interest

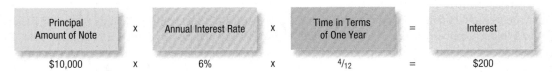

Principal Amount of Note	x	Annual Interest Rate	x	Time in Terms of One Year	=	Interest
$10,000	x	6%	x	$4/12$	=	$200

Recall from Chapter 3 that the principal amount is the amount borrowed, or the amount still outstanding on a loan, separate from interest. This is also the balance in Wolder's Notes Receivable account or Higly's Note Payable account.

The interest rate specified in a note is an annual rate of interest. There are many factors that affect the interest rate. You will learn more about that in a finance course. Interest rates may also be fixed for the term of the note or may change over the term. In this textbook, we will always assume that the rate remains fixed for the term.

The time factor in the above formula gives the fraction of the year that the note has been outstanding. As we did in past chapters, to keep it simple we will assume that interest is calculated in months rather than days. Illustration 8-8 shows the calculation of interest revenue for Wolder Company and interest expense for Higly Inc. for the term of the note.

If Wolder Company's year end was June 30, the following adjusting journal entry would be required to accrue interest for the month of June:

A = L + OE	June 30	Interest Receivable 50
+50 +50		Interest Revenue ($10,000 × 6% × $1/12$) 50
Cash flows: no effect		To accrue interest on Higly note receivable.

Notice that interest on a note receivable is not debited to the Notes Receivable account. Instead, a separate asset account for the interest receivable is used. The Note Receivable account balance must be equal to the amount still outstanding on the note, in order to correctly calculate interest.

Valuing Notes Receivable

Like accounts receivable, notes receivable are reported at their net realizable value. Each note must be analyzed to determine how likely it is to be collected. If eventual collection is doubtful, bad debt expense and an allowance for doubtful notes must be recorded in the same way as for accounts receivable. Some companies use only one allowance account for both accounts and notes, and call it Allowance for Doubtful Accounts.

DISPOSING OF NOTES RECEIVABLE

Notes are normally held to their maturity date, at which time the principal plus any unpaid interest is collected. This is known as honouring (paying) the note. Sometimes, the maker of the note defaults and an adjustment to the accounts must be made. This is known as dishonouring (not paying) the note.

Honouring of Notes Receivable

A note is honoured when it is paid in full at its maturity date. The amount due at maturity is the principal of the note plus interest for the length of time the note is outstanding (assuming interest is due at maturity rather than monthly). If Higly Inc. honours the note when it is due on September 30—the maturity date—the entry by Wolder Company to record the collection is:

Sept. 30	Cash	10,200	
	Notes Receivable—Higly		10,000
	Interest Revenue		150
	Interest Receivable		50
	To record collection of Higly note.		

A = L + OE
+10,200   +150
−10,000
−50

↑ Cash flows: +10,200

Recall that one month of interest revenue, $50 ($10,000 × 6% × $\frac{1}{12}$), was accrued on June 30, Wolder's year end. Consequently, only three months of interest revenue, $150 ($10,000 × 6% × $\frac{3}{12}$), is recorded in this period.

Dishonouring of Notes Receivable

A **dishonoured note** is a note that is not paid in full at maturity. Since a dishonoured note receivable is no longer negotiable, the Notes Receivable account must be reduced by the principal of the note. The payee still has a claim against the maker of the note for both the principal and any unpaid interest and will transfer the amount owing to an Accounts Receivable account if there is hope that the amount will eventually be collected.

To illustrate, assume that on September 30, Higly Inc. says that it cannot pay at the present time but Wolder Company expects eventual collection. Wolder would make the following entry at the time the note is dishonoured:

Sept. 30	Accounts Receivable—Higly	10,200	
	Notes Receivable—Higly		10,000
	Interest Revenue		150
	Interest Receivable		50
	To record dishonouring of Higly note where collection		
	is expected.		

A = L + OE
+10,200   +150
−10,000
−50

Cash flows: no effect

Note that the amount recorded in the accounts receivable is the total amount owed (interest and principal) by Higly.

Wolder will continue to follow up with Higly. If the amount owing is eventually collected, Wolder will simply debit Cash and credit Accounts Receivable. If Wolder decides at a later date that it will never collect this amount from Higly, Wolder will write off the account receivable in the same way we learned earlier in the chapter—debit Allowance for Doubtful Accounts, and credit Accounts Receivable.

On the other hand, Wolder could directly write the note off on September 30 if it decided there was no hope of collection. Assuming Wolder uses one allowance account for both accounts and notes, it would record the following:

A = L + OE
+10,050
−10,000
−50
Cash flows: no effect

Sept. 30	Allowance for Doubtful Accounts	10,050	
	Notes Receivable—Higly		10,000
	Interest Receivable		50
	To record dishonouring of Higly note where collection is not expected.		

No interest revenue is recorded, because collection will not occur. The interest receivable that previously had been accrued is also written off and the Allowance for Doubtful Accounts is debited for both the principal amount owed and the interest receivable.

BEFORE YOU GO ON...

Do It

Action Plan

- Calculate the accrued interest. The formula is: Principal × annual interest rate × time in terms of one year.
- Record the interest accrued on June 30 to follow revenue recognition criteria. Use Interest Receivable, not Notes Receivable, for accrued interest.
- If the note is honoured, calculate the interest accrued after June 30 and the total interest on the note. Record the interest accrued and the collection of the note and the total interest.
- If the note is dishonoured, record the transfer of the note and any interest earned to an accounts receivable account if eventual collection is expected or to an allowance account if collection is not expected.

On May 1, Gambit Stores accepts from J. Nyznyk a $3,400, three-month, 5% note in settlement of Nyznyk's overdue account. Interest is due at maturity. Gambit has a June 30 year end.

(a) Prepare the required journal entry to record the issue of the note on May 1, the adjusting journal entry on June 30, and the settlement of the note on August 1 assuming Nyznyk honours the note.

(b) Prepare the required journal entry on August 1 if Nyznyk does not pay the note and collection is not expected in the future.

Solution

(a)	May 1	Notes Receivable—J. Nyznyk	3,400	
		Accounts Receivable—J. Nyznyk		3,400
		To replace account receivable with 5% note receivable, due August 1.		
	June 30	Interest Receivable	28	
		Interest Revenue ($3,400 × 5% × $\frac{2}{12}$)		28
		To record interest earned to June 30.		
	Aug. 1	Cash	3,442	
		Interest Receivable		28
		Notes Receivable—J. Nyznyk		3,400
		Interest Revenue ($3,400 × 5% × $\frac{1}{12}$)		14
		To record collection of Nyznyk note plus interest.		
(b)	Aug. 1	Allowance for Doubtful Accounts	3,428	
		Interest Receivable		28
		Notes Receivable—J. Nyznyk		3,400
		To record dishonouring of Nyznyk note as collection is not expected.		

Related exercise material: BE8–11, BE8–12, BE8–13, E8–8, E8–9, and E8–10.

THE **NAVIGATOR**

Statement Presentation and Management of Receivables

» **STUDY OBJECTIVE 4**

Demonstrate the presentation, analysis, and management of receivables.

The way receivables are presented in the financial statements is important because receivables are directly affected by how a company recognizes its revenue and bad debt expense. In addition, these reported numbers are critical for analyzing a company's liquidity and how well it manages its receivables. In the next sections, we will discuss the presentation, analysis, and management of receivables.

PRESENTATION

Each of the major types of receivables should be identified in the balance sheet or in the notes to the financial statements. Other receivables include interest receivable, loans or advances to employees, and recoverable sales and income taxes. These receivables are generally classified and reported as separate items in the current or noncurrent sections of the balance sheet, according to their due dates. Notes receivable may also be either current assets or long-term assets, depending on their due dates.

In addition to the net realizable value of the receivables shown on the balance sheet, both the gross amount of receivables and the allowance for doubtful accounts must be disclosed in either the balance sheet or the notes to the financial statements.

Bad debt expense is reported in the operating expenses section of the income statement. At the time this textbook was being written, standard setters were proposing that bad debt expense be reported in the revenue section of the income statement as a contra revenue account—a deduction from revenues. If this change is approved, it will decrease both net sales and total operating expenses, but total profit will not change.

Illustration 8-9 shows the presentation of receivables for Shaw Communications Inc., which provides television, Internet, and other media services.

▶ ILLUSTRATION 8-9
Presentation of receivables

SHAW COMMUNICATIONS INC. Notes to the Financial Statements (partial) August 31, 2011 (in thousands)		
Note 3: Accounts Receivable	2011	2010
Subscriber and trade receivables	$424,451	$209,817
Due from officers and employees	159	148
Due from related parties	1,236	1,689
Miscellaneous receivables	45,768	3,730
	471,614	215,384
Less: Allowance for doubtful accounts	(28,797)	(18,969)
	$442,817	$196,415

Included in operating, general and administrative expenses is a provision for doubtful accounts of $33,686 (2010 − $33,746; 2009 − $19,298).

In Note 3, Shaw discloses the components of its receivables. The net realizable value of the accounts receivable of $442 million in 2011 and $196 million in 2010 was reported in the current assets section of Shaw's balance sheet. Note that subscriber and trade receivables increased from $209 million in 2010 to $424 million in 2011. This is because in October 2010, Shaw acquired $296.6 million of receivables when it purchased Canwest Global Communications Corp.

Shaw also reports in its note to the financial statements that its allowance for doubtful accounts is determined by considering the number of days the account is past due, whether or not the customer continues to receive service, the company's collection history, and changes in business circumstances.

ANALYSIS

Management of accounts receivable is critical to a business's success. Accounts receivable are generally the most important source of cash for business. If sales increase, then accounts receivable are also expected to increase. On the other hand, an increase in accounts receivable might signal trouble. Perhaps the company increased its sales by loosening its credit policy, and these receivables may be difficult or impossible to collect. The company could also end up with higher costs because of the increase in sales since it may need more cash to pay for inventory and salaries.

Recall that the ability to pay obligations as they come due is measured by a company's liquidity. How can we tell if a company's management of its receivables is helping or hurting the company's liquidity? One way of doing this is to calculate a ratio called the receivables turnover ratio. This ratio measures the number of times, on average, that receivables are collected during the period. It is calculated by dividing net credit sales by average gross receivables during the year.

Unfortunately, companies rarely report the amount of net sales made on credit in their financial statements. As a result, net sales (including both cash and credit sales) is used as a substitute. As long as net sales are used to calculate the ratio for all companies being compared, the comparison is fair.

In Illustration 8-10, the substitute figures of total sales and trade and other receivables were used to calculate Reitmans' 2012 accounts receivable turnover.

▶ **ILLUSTRATION 8-10**
Receivables turnover

Net Credit Sales	÷	Average Gross Accounts Receivable	=	Receivables Turnover
$1,019,397	÷	$\dfrac{\$3,033 + \$2,866}{2}$	=	345.6 times

The result indicates an accounts receivable turnover ratio of 345.6 times per year for Reitmans. The higher the turnover ratio, the more liquid the company's receivables are.

A popular variation of the receivables turnover ratio is to convert it into the number of days it takes the company to collect its receivables. This ratio, called the **collection period**, is calculated by dividing 365 days by the receivables turnover, as shown for Reitmans in Illustration 8-11.

▶ **ILLUSTRATION 8-11**
Collection period

Days in Year	÷	Receivables Turnover	=	Collection Period
365 days	÷	345.6	=	1.1 days

This means that in fiscal 2012, Reitmans collected its receivables, on average, in approximately 1.1 days. Reitmans does not have its own credit card. Its accounts receivable are from customers using credit cards such as MasterCard or Visa where the sales haven't been collected in cash from the credit card company prior to the year end. Reitmans' high turnover ratio and low collection period indicate that the company's receivables are highly liquid and that the company is receiving payment from the credit card companies quickly.

Bell Aliant, in our feature story, states that the vast majority of its consumer customers pay within 30 days but that it takes from 35 to 50 days to collect from businesses. The result is an overall average of between 31 and 35 days.

The collection period is often used to judge how effective a company's credit and collection policies are. The general rule is that the collection period should not be much longer than the credit term period (that is, the time allowed for payment). Accounts receivable are basically an interest-free loan to the customer, so the faster they are collected, the better.

Both the receivables turnover and the collection period are useful for judging how efficiently a company converts its credit sales to cash. Remember that these measures should also be compared with industry averages, and with previous years.

In addition, these measures should be analyzed along with other information about a company's liquidity, including the current ratio and inventory turnover. For example, low receivables may result in a low current ratio, which might make the company look like it has poor liquidity. But the receivables may be low because they are turning over quickly. In general, the faster the turnover, the more reliable the current ratio is for assessing liquidity.

The collection period can also be used to assess the length of a company's operating cycle. Recall from Chapter 4 that the operating cycle is the time it takes to go from cash to cash in producing revenues. In a merchandising company, the operating cycle may be measured by determining the average time that it takes to purchase inventory, sell it on account, and then collect cash from customers. In Chapter 6, we learned how to calculate days sales in inventory, which is the average age of the inventory on hand. The combination of the collection period and days sales in inventory is a useful way to measure the length of a company's operating cycle. Using the number of days sales in inventory calculated in Chapter 6, this calculation is shown in Illustration 8-12 for Reitmans.

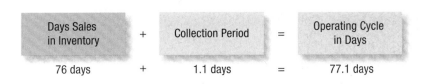

This means that in fiscal 2012, it took 77.1 days on average from the time Reitmans purchased its inventory until it collected cash.

ACCELERATING CASH RECEIPTS FROM RECEIVABLES

If a company sells on credit, it has to wait until the customer pays the receivable before it has cash available to pay for such items as inventory and operating expenses. As credit sales and receivables increase in size and significance, waiting for receivables to be collected increases costs because the company cannot use the revenue from the sale until cash is collected. If a company can collect cash more quickly from its receivables, it can shorten the cash-to-cash operating cycle discussed in the previous section. One benefit of decreasing the operating cycle is that a company can invest in additional inventory and increase sales and profit.

There are two typical ways to collect cash more quickly from receivables: using the receivables to secure a loan and selling the receivables.

Loans Secured by Receivables

One of the most common ways to speed up cash flow from accounts receivable is to go to a bank and borrow money using accounts receivable as collateral. While this does have a cost (interest has to be paid to the bank on the loan), the cash is available for the company to use earlier. The loan can then be repaid as the receivables are collected. Generally, banks are willing to give financing of up to 75% of receivables that are less than 90 days old. Quite often, these arrangements occur through an operating line of credit, which is discussed in Chapter 10.

Sale of Receivables

Companies also frequently sell their receivables to another company because it provides an immediate source of cash. There are two other reasons for the sale of receivables. The first is their size. To be competitive, sellers often give financing to purchasers of their goods to encourage the sale of the product. But the companies may not want to hold large amounts of receivables. As a result, many major companies in the automobile, truck, equipment, computer, and appliance industries have created wholly owned finance companies that accept responsibility for accounts receivable financing. An example is Ford Credit Canada, owned by the Ford Motor Company of Canada.

Another reason for selling receivables is to reduce the costs of monitoring and collecting receivables. For example, it is often more cost-effective for a retailer to sell its receivables to credit card companies, such as Visa and MasterCard, which specialize in billing and collecting accounts receivable.

Factoring. One way to accelerate receivables collection is by sale to a factor. A **factor** is a finance company or bank that buys receivables from businesses and then collects the cash directly from the customer. If the customer does not pay, the business is usually responsible for reimbursing the factor for the uncollected amounts. This is known as selling receivables on a recourse basis.

Securitization of Receivables. Another way to accelerate cash received from receivables is through a process called **securitization**. Receivables are moved to an independent trust that holds them as an investment. This converts the receivables into securities of the trust, which is why the term "securitization of receivables" is used. In some cases, the transfer is treated as a sale of receivables; in other cases, it is treated as a secured loan. For such companies as Bell Aliant, securitization of receivables is one method of using their receivables to obtain cash.

The differences between factoring and securitization are that securitization involves many investors and the cost is lower, the receivables are of higher quality, and the seller usually continues to be involved with collecting the receivables. In factoring, the sale is usually to only one company, the cost is higher, the receivables quality is lower, and the seller does not normally have any involvement with collecting the receivables.

ACCOUNTING IN ACTION
ACROSS THE ORGANIZATION

U.S. discount department store chain **Target Corp.** announced in early 2011 that it was going to get out of the credit card business and sell its credit card receivables. The retailer said it wanted to use the money from the sale to buy more inventory, pay down debt, and help pay for its planned expansion into Canada by taking over some Zellers stores from the **Hudson's Bay Company**. It also wanted to focus on merchandising instead of financial services. A year later, Target said it had not received an acceptable offer for the receivables and would hold off on selling them until late 2012 or early 2013. Some analysts thought that waiting was likely a smart move, because as the economy improves and the number of shoppers defaulting on their credit card payments declines, the value of Target's credit card receivables would increase. Others thought that the delay of the sale meant that the company was overvaluing its receivables. In the third quarter of 2011, Target's bad debts declined by 64% to $40 million, while its profit from its credit card business increased by 10%. In that period, the company's gross credit card receivables totalled $6.1 billion.

Sources: Thomas Lee, "Target Does Things Its Way—For Better or Worse," *Minneapolis StarTribune*, January 25, 2012; James Callan and Matt Townsend, "Target Suspends Efforts to Sell Credit Card Receivables," Bloomberg, January 18, 2012; Karen Talley, "Target Is Entering Canada, Selling Card Receivables," Dow Jones Newswires, January 13, 2011.

Question: What might be the advantages to Target of having its own credit card? What might be the disadvantages?

 BEFORE YOU GO ON...

Do It

Action Plan

- Calculate the average gross accounts receivable using the accounts receivable balance at the beginning and ending of the year.
- Divide net credit sales by the average accounts receivable for that year to calculate receivables turnover.
- Divide 365 by the receivables turnover to calculate collection period.
- Add the collection period to days sales in inventory to calculate operating cycle in days.

The following information is available for Jupiter Company.

	2015	2014	2013
Net credit sales	$1,500,000	$1,300,000	$1,350,000
Gross accounts receivable	127,000	124,000	118,000
Days sales in inventory	44.5 days	43 days	

Calculate the accounts receivable turnover ratio, collection period, and operating cycle in days and comment on any trends.

Solution

	2015	2014
Receivables turnover	$11.95 \text{ times} = \dfrac{\$1,500,000}{[(127,000 + 124,000) \div 2]}$	$10.74 \text{ times} = \dfrac{\$1,300,000}{[(124,000 + 118,000) \div 2]}$
Collection period	$30.54 \text{ days} = \dfrac{365 \text{ days}}{11.95 \text{ times}}$	$34 \text{ days} = \dfrac{365 \text{ days}}{10.74 \text{ times}}$
Operating cycle in days	75 days = 30.54 + 44.5	77 days = 34 + 43

The accounts receivable turnover has increased and the collection period decreased. In general, it is better to have a higher accounts receivable turnover and a lower collection period. Even though the days sales in inventory had increased, the operating cycle has decreased, which generally is better for the company.

Related exercise material: BE8–14, BE8–15, BE8–16, E8–3, E8–11, E8–12, and E8–13.

THE **NAVIGATOR**

Comparing IFRS and ASPE

Key Differences	International Financial Reporting Standards (IFRS)	Accounting Standards for Private Enterprises (ASPE)
No significant differences		

THE NAVIGATOR

Demonstration Problem

On February 28, Dylan Co. had the following balances in select accounts:

Accounts Receivable	$200,000
Allowance for Doubtful Accounts (credit)	12,500

Selected transactions for Dylan Co. follow. Dylan's year end is June 30.

Mar.	1	Sold $20,000 of merchandise to Potter Company, terms n/30.
	1	Accepted Juno Company's $16,500, six-month, 6% note for the balance due on account.
	11	Potter Company returned $600 worth of goods.
	13	Made Dylan Co. credit card sales for $13,200.
	30	Received payment in full from Potter Company.
Apr.	13	Received collections of $8,200 on Dylan Co. credit card sales. Added interest charges of 18% to the remaining balance.
May	10	Wrote off as uncollectible $15,000 of accounts receivable.
June	30	Estimated uncollectible accounts are determined to be $20,000 at June 30.
	30	Recorded the interest accrued on the Juno Company note.
July	16	Received payment in full, $4,000, on an account that was previously written off in May.
Sept.	1	Collected cash from Juno Company in payment of the March 1 note receivable.

Instructions

(a) Prepare the journal entries for the transactions. Ignore cost of goods sold entries for purposes of this question.

(b) Open T accounts for Accounts Receivable and the Allowance for Doubtful Accounts, and post the relevant journal entries to these accounts. Calculate the balance in these accounts at June 30 and at September 1.

(c) Calculate the net realizable value of the accounts receivable at June 30 and September 1.

ACTION PLAN

- Record receivables at the invoice price.
- Recognize that sales returns and allowances reduce the amount received on accounts receivable.
- Calculate interest by multiplying the principal by the interest rate by the part of the year that has passed.
- Record write offs of accounts and collection of previously written-off accounts only in balance sheet accounts.
- Consider any existing balance in the allowance account when making the adjustment for uncollectible accounts.
- Recognize any remaining interest on notes receivable when recording the collection of a note.

Solution to Demonstration Problem

(a)

Mar.	1	Accounts Receivable—Potter	20,000	
		Sales		20,000
		To record sale on account.		
	1	Notes Receivable—Juno	16,500	
		Accounts Receivable—Juno		16,500
		To record acceptance of Juno Company note.		
	11	Sales Returns and Allowances	600	
		Accounts Receivable—Potter		600
		To record return of goods.		
	13	Accounts Receivable	13,200	
		Sales		13,200
		To record company credit card sales.		
	30	Cash ($20,000 − $600)	19,400	
		Accounts Receivable—Potter		19,400
		To record collection of account receivable.		

Apr. 13	Cash			8,200	
		Accounts Receivable			8,200
		To record collection of credit card accounts receivable.			
13	Accounts Receivable [($13,200 − $8,200) × 18% × $^1/_{12}$]			75	
		Interest Revenue			75
		To record interest on amount due.			
May 10	Allowance for Doubtful Accounts			15,000	
		Accounts Receivable			15,000
		To Record write off of accounts receivable.			
June 30	Bad Debt Expense ($20,000 + $2,500)			22,500	
		Allowance for Doubtful Accounts			22,500
		To record estimate of uncollectible accounts.			
30	Interest Receivable ($16,500 × 6% × $^4/_{12}$)			330	
		Interest Revenue			330
		To record interest earned.			
July 16	Accounts Receivable			4,000	
		Allowance for Doubtful Accounts			4,000
		To reverse write off of account receivable.			
16	Cash			4,000	
		Accounts Receivable			4,000
		To record collection of account receivable.			
Sept. 1	Cash [$16,500 + ($16,500 × 6% × $^6/_{12}$)]			16,995	
		Interest Revenue ($16,500 × 6% × $^2/_{12}$)			165
		Interest Receivable			330
		Note Receivable			16,500
		To record collection of note receivable plus interest.			

(b)

Accounts Receivable

Feb. 28	Bal.	200,000		16,500
		20,000		600
		13,200		19,400
		75		8,200
				15,000
June 30	Bal.	173,575		
		4,000		4,000
Sept. 1	Bal.	173,575		

Allowance for Doubtful Accounts

		15,000	Feb. 28	Bal.	12,500
June 30	Bal.	2,500			
			June 30	Adj.	22,500
			June 30	Bal.	20,000
					4,000
			Sept. 1	Bal.	24,000

(c)

	June 30	Sept. 1
Accounts receivable	$173,575	$173,575
Less: Allowance for doubtful accounts	20,000	24,000
Net realizable value	$153,575	$149,575

THE **NAVIGATOR**

▶ Summary of Study Objectives

1. **Record accounts receivable transactions.** Accounts receivable are recorded at the invoice price. They are reduced by sales returns and allowances, and sales discounts. Accounts receivable subsidiary ledgers are used to keep track of individual account balances. When interest is charged on a past-due receivable, this interest is added to the accounts receivable balance and is recognized as interest revenue. Sales using nonbank credit cards result in a receivable, net of the credit card charges, from the credit card company; sales using company credit cards result in a receivable from the customer.

2. **Calculate the net realizable value of accounts receivable and account for bad debts.** Accounts receivable must be reported at their net realizable value on the balance sheet. The allowance method is used to record the estimated uncollectible accounts in the Allowance for Doubtful Accounts. The net realizable value of the receivables is equal to the gross accounts receivable minus the allowance. A percentage of total receivables, or an aging schedule applying different percentages to different categories of receivables, is used to estimate the allowance for doubtful accounts. The allowance method also matches bad debt expense against revenue in the period when the revenue is recognized. Bad debt expense is equal to the difference between the required balance and the unadjusted balance in the allowance for doubtful accounts.

   When a specific account receivable is determined to be uncollectible, the account is written off and the allowance is reduced. When a previously written-off account is collected, the entry previously made to write off the account is reversed and the collection is recorded.

3. **Account for notes receivable.** Notes receivable are recorded at their principal amount. Interest is earned from the date the note is issued until it matures and must be recorded in the correct accounting period. Interest receivable is recorded in a separate account from the note. Like accounts receivable, notes receivable are reported at their net realizable value.

   Notes are normally held to maturity. At that time, the principal plus any unpaid interest is due and the note is removed from the accounts. If a note is not paid at maturity, it is said to be dishonoured. If eventual collection is still expected, an account receivable replaces the note receivable and any unpaid interest. Otherwise, the note must be written off.

4. **Demonstrate the presentation, analysis, and management of receivables.** Each major type of receivable should be identified in the balance sheet or in the notes to the financial statements. Both the gross amount of receivables and the allowance for doubtful accounts/notes is required to be reported in the balance sheet or the notes to the financial statements. Bad debt expense is reported in the income statement as an operating expense.

   The liquidity of receivables can be evaluated by calculating the receivables turnover and collection period ratios. The receivables turnover is calculated by dividing net credit sales by average gross accounts receivable. This ratio measures how efficiently the company is converting its receivables into sales. The collection period converts the receivables turnover into days, dividing 365 days by the receivables turnover ratio. It shows the number of days, on average, it takes a company to collect its accounts receivable. The combination of the collection period and days sales in inventory is a useful way to measure the length of a company's operating cycle.

   Companies may accelerate the collection of cash by using the receivables to secure a loan, by selling the receivables to a factor, or by securitizing them.

Flash cards

▶ Glossary

Accounts receivable   Amounts owed by customers on account. (p. 416)

Aging schedule   A list of accounts receivable organized by the length of time they have been unpaid. (p. 422)

Allowance for Doubtful Accounts   A contra asset account that is deducted from gross account receivables to report receivables at their net realizable value. (p. 421)

Allowance method   The method of accounting for bad debts that involves estimating uncollectible accounts at the end of each period. (p. 421)

Bad debt expense   An expense account to record uncollectible receivables. (p. 420)

Collection period   The average number of days that receivables are outstanding. It is calculated by dividing 365 days by the receivables turnover. (p. 432)

Default   What happens when the maker of the note does not pay the note in full. Also referred to as dishonouring the note. (p. 420)

Dishonoured note   A note that is not paid in full at maturity. (p. 429)

Factor   A finance company or bank that buys receivables from businesses and then collects the payments directly from the customers. (p. 433)

Gross accounts receivable The total accounts receivable in the control account in the general ledger; includes both collectible and uncollectible accounts. (p. 422)

Maker The party making the promise to pay a promissory note. (p. 427)

Net realizable value The net amount of receivables expected to be collected. (p. 420)

Notes receivable Claims for which formal instruments (written instruments) of credit are issued as evidence of the debt. (p. 416)

Payee The party to whom payment is to be made. (p. 427)

Percentage of receivables approach The approach used to estimate uncollectible accounts where the allowance for

doubtful accounts is calculated as a percentage of receivables. (p. 421)

Promissory note A written promise to pay a specified amount of money on demand or at a definite time. (p. 427)

Receivables turnover ratio A measure of the liquidity of receivables, calculated by dividing net credit sales by average gross accounts receivable. (p. 431)

Securitization The transfer of receivables to a trust that holds them as an investment. This converts the receivables into securities. (p. 433)

Trade receivables Accounts and notes receivable that result from sales transactions. (p. 416)

▶ Self-Study Questions

Answers are at the end of the chapter.

(SO 1) AP **1.** On August 10, Pi Company sells merchandise on account to Murray Co. for $2,000, terms 2/10, n/30. On August 15, Murray returns merchandise worth $400 to Pi. On August 20, payment is received from Murray for the balance due. What is the amount of cash received?

(a) $1,560   (c) $1,568
(b) $1,600   (d) $1,960

(SO 1) AP **2.** Manery Company accepts a nonbank credit card on September 5 in payment of a $2,000 purchase. The credit card company charges a 2% fee. What is the amount recorded in accounts receivable on September 5?

(a) $2,000   (c) $2,040
(b) $1,960   (d) $0

(SO 2) AP **3.** Kartik Company's accounts receivable are $200,000 at the end of the year. The allowance for doubtful accounts has a credit balance of $4,000 before any adjustments have been made. The company estimates that 5% of accounts receivable will not be collected. What is the net realizable value of the accounts receivable at the end of the year?

(a) $196,000   (c) $186,000
(b) $200,000   (d) $190,000

(SO 2) AP **4.** Sanderson Company has a credit balance of $6,000 in Allowance for Doubtful Accounts before any adjustments are made. Based on an aging of its accounts receivable at the end of the period, the company estimates that $80,000 of its receivables are uncollectible. What is the amount of bad debt expense that should be reported for this accounting period?

(a) $74,000   (c) $86,000
(b) $6,000   (d) $80,000

(SO 2) AP **5.** Use the same information as in question 4, except that Sanderson Company has a debit balance of

$6,000 in Allowance for Doubtful Accounts before any adjustments are made. In this situation, what is the amount of bad debt expense that should be reported for this accounting period?

(a) $74,000   (c) $86,000
(b) $6,000   (d) $80,000

(SO 2) AP **6.** On January 1, 2014, the Allowance for Doubtful Accounts has a credit balance of $18,000. During 2014, $30,000 of uncollectible accounts receivable were written off. An aging schedule indicates that uncollectible accounts are $20,000 at the end of 2014. What is the required adjustment to the allowance for doubtful accounts at December 31, 2014?

(a) $2,000   (c) $20,000
(b) $8,000   (d) $32,000

(SO 2) AP **7.** On January 1, 2014, Allowance for Doubtful Accounts had a credit balance of $40,000. In 2014, $30,000 of uncollectible accounts receivable were written off. On December 31, 2014, the company had accounts receivable of $900,000. Experience indicates that 4% of total receivables will become uncollectible. The adjusting journal entry that would be recorded on December 31, 2014, would be:

(a) Allowance for Doubtful		
Accounts	26,000	
Accounts Receivable		26,000
(b) Bad Debt Expense	36,000	
Accounts Receivable		36,000
(c) Bad Debt Expense	26,000	
Allowance for Doubtful		
Accounts		26,000
(d) Bad Debt Expense	36,000	
Allowance for Doubtful		
Accounts		36,000

(SO 3) AP **8.** On June 1, Sorenson Co. accepts a $2,000, four-month, 6% promissory note in settlement of an account with Parton Co. Sorenson has a July 31 fiscal year end. The adjusting entry to record interest on July 31 is:

(a) Interest Receivable	20	
Interest Revenue		20
(b) Interest Receivable	120	
Interest Revenue		120
(c) Notes Receivable	120	
Unearned Interest Revenue		120
(d) Interest Receivable	40	
Interest Revenue		40

(SO 3) AP 9. Schlicht Co. holds Osgrove Inc.'s $10,000, four-month, 9% note. If no interest has been accrued, when the note is collected, the entry made by Schlicht Co. is:

(a) Cash	10,300	
Notes Receivable		10,300
(b) Cash	10,900	
Interest Revenue		900
Notes Receivable		10,000
(c) Accounts Receivable	10,300	
Notes Receivable		10,000
Interest Revenue		300
(d) Cash	10,300	
Notes Receivable		10,000
Interest Revenue		300

(SO 3) AP 10. When a note is dishonoured, an entry is made to:
(a) Reverse the interest revenue previously recognized.
(b) Record bad debt expense.
(c) Record an account receivable for the principal amount of the note and the accrued interest if the company expects to collect the amount owing.
(d) Write off the note whether or not the company expects to collect the amount owing.

(SO 4) C 11. The allowance for doubtful accounts is presented in the financial statements as:
(a) a current liability in the balance sheet.
(b) a deduction from accounts receivable in the balance sheet.
(c) a contra revenue account in the income statement.
(d) an operating expense in the income statement.

(SO 4) AP 12. Moore Company had net credit sales of $800,000 in the year and a cost of goods sold of $500,000. The balance in Accounts Receivable at the beginning of the year was $100,000 and at the end of the year it was $150,000. What were the receivables turnover and collection period ratios, respectively?
(a) 4.0 and 91 days
(b) 5.3 and 69 days
(c) 6.4 and 57 days
(d) 8.0 and 46 days

▶ Questions

(SO 1) C   1. When should a receivable be recorded for a service company? For a merchandising company?

(SO 1) K   2. Why are accounts receivable and notes receivable sometimes called trade receivables?

(SO 1) C   3. (a) What information does a company need to manage its accounts receivable? (b) How is this information tracked in an accounting system?

(SO 1) K   4. Under what circumstances is interest normally recorded for an account receivable?

(SO 1) C   5. Ernie Andrews thinks that a sale on a nonbank credit card should be recorded as a debit to cash, as cash will be received from the credit card company. Is Ernie correct? Explain.

(SO 2) C   6. Why can't a company know with certainty whether or not a customer will pay its account receivable?

(SO 2) C   7. ACCT Company has had significant bad debts in previous years. To eliminate the risk of bad debts, the accounting manager of ACCT Company has recommended to the sales manager to make only cash sales. The sales manager does not think this is the best business decision. Do you agree or disagree with the sales manager? What do you recommend the company do to reduce the risk of bad debts?

(SO 2) C   8. What is the net realizable value of accounts receivable? Why is it important that accounts receivable be reported at net realizable value?

(SO 2) K   9. Explain the allowance method of accounting for bad debts. How does this method result in (a) assets not being overstated, and (b) the matching of expenses with revenues?

(SO 2) C 10. (a) What is the purpose of the account Allowance for Doubtful Accounts? (b) Although the normal balance of this account is a credit balance, it sometimes has a debit balance. Explain how this can happen.

(SO 2) C 11. Dimitri doesn't understand why the bad debt expense reported in the income statement is usually not equal to the allowance for doubtful accounts reported in the balance sheet. Explain why this happens.

(SO 2) C 12. Zahra doesn't understand why bad debt expense is not increased when a specific customer account is determined to be uncollectible and written off. Explain.

(SO 2) C 13. What is an aging schedule? How is the aging schedule used to estimate the amount of uncollectibles?

(SO 2) C 14. When an account receivable that was written off is later collected, two journal entries are usually made. Explain why.

(SO 3) K 15. Explain how notes receivable and accounts receivable are the same and how they are different.

(SO 3) C 16. Why will a company take a note receivable from a customer in settlement of a late account receivable?

(SO 3) C 17. Danielle does not understand why a note receivable is not immediately recorded at its maturity value (principal plus interest). After all, you know you are going to collect both the principal amount and the interest and you know how much each will be. Explain to Danielle why notes are not recorded at their maturity value.

(SO 3) C 18. What does it mean if a note is dishonoured?

(SO 3) C 19. How would the entries differ if a note receivable is dishonoured and eventual collection is expected versus a note receivable where collection is not expected?

(SO 4) C 20. Mac Leonard is preparing the financial statements and has reported the Allowance for Doubtful Accounts in the current liabilities section of the balance sheet because the normal balance of the allowance is a credit. Do you agree with this treatment? Explain.

(SO 4) C 21. Saucier Company has accounts receivable, notes receivable due in three months, notes receivable due in two years, an allowance for doubtful accounts, sales taxes recoverable, and income tax receivable. How should the receivables be reported on the balance sheet?

(SO 4) C 22. The president of Unlimited Enterprises proudly announces that her company's liquidity has improved. Its current ratio increased substantially this year. Does an increase in the current ratio always indicate improved liquidity? What other ratio(s) might you review to determine whether or not the increase in the current ratio represents an improvement in the company's financial health?

(SO 4) C 23. Canadian Worldwide Communications Co.'s receivables turnover was 6.5 times in 2013 and 5.9 times in 2014. Has the company's receivables management improved or worsened?

(SO 4) C 24. Why might a company not want to have a receivables turnover that is significantly higher than that of its competitors?

(SO 4) K 25. Why do companies sometimes sell their receivables?

▶ Brief Exercises

Identify impact of transaction on receivables, total assets, liabilities, and owner's equity. (SO 1) K

BE8–1 Seven transactions follow. For each transaction, indicate if the transaction increases, decreases, or has no effect on (a) accounts receivable, (b) notes receivable, (c) total assets, (d) total liabilities, and (e) owner's equity. Use the following format, in which the first transaction is given as an example:

Transaction:	(a) Accounts Receivable	(b) Notes Receivable	(c) Total Assets	(d) Total Liabilities	(e) Owner's Equity
1. Performed services on account for a customer.	Increase	No effect	Increase	No effect	Increase
2. A customer paid cash for services to be provided next month.					
3. Performed services for a customer in exchange for a note.					
4. Collected cash from the customer in transaction 1. above.					
5. Performed services for a customer for cash.					
6. Extended a customer's account for three months by accepting a note in exchange for it.					
7. Performed services for a customer who had paid in advance.					

Record accounts receivable transactions. (SO 1) AP

BE8–2 Record the following transactions on the books of Marsh Co:

(a) On September 1, Marsh Co. sold merchandise on account to Pellerin Inc. for $20,000, terms 2/10, n/30. The cost of the merchandise sold was $12,000. Marsh Co. uses a perpetual inventory system.

(b) On September 4, Pellerin Inc. returned merchandise worth $4,000 to Marsh Co. The original cost of the merchandise was $2,400. The merchandise was returned to inventory.

(c) On September 10, Pellerin Inc. paid for the merchandise.

Record accounts receivable transactions. (SO 1) AP

BE8–3 Record the following transactions on the books of Fowler Co.:

(a) On May 1, Fowler Co. sold merchandise on account to Kaneva Inc. for $30,000, terms 2/10, n/30. Ignore any entries that affect inventory and cost of goods sold for purposes of this question.

(b) On May 6, Kaneva Inc. returned merchandise worth $6,000 to Fowler Co.

(c) On June 30, Fowler Co. charged Kaneva Inc. one month's interest for the overdue account. Fowler charges 10% on overdue accounts. (Round calculation to the nearest dollar.)

(d) On July 5, Kaneva paid the amount owing to Fowler Co.

BE8–4   Imports to You Co. accepted a credit card in payment of a $600 purchase of merchandise on August 7. For each of the following assumptions, prepare the journal entry to record the sale.

Record credit card transactions. (SO 1) AP

(a) The customer used a nonbank card and the company charges a 3% fee.

(b) The customer used a Visa card and Visa charges a 3% fee.

(c) The customer used an Imports to You Co. credit card.

BE8–5   Gourdeau Co. uses an aging schedule to determine its estimated uncollectible accounts at December 31. Complete the following schedule and determine the required balance in the allowance for doubtful accounts and the net realizable value of the accounts receivable.

Complete aging schedule and determine the allowance and net realizable value. (SO 2) AP

Number of Days Outstanding	Accounts Receivable	Estimated % Uncollectible	Estimated Uncollectible Accounts
0–30 days	$265,000	1%	
31–60 days	70,000	4%	
61–90 days	45,000	10%	
Over 90 days	20,000	20%	
Total	$400,000		

BE8–6   Refer to the data in BE8–5 for Gourdeau Co.

Determine bad debt expense. (SO 2) AP

(a) Assuming the allowance for doubtful accounts has an unadjusted credit balance of $4,500 at December 31, what is the bad debt expense for the year?

(b) Assume instead that the allowance for doubtful accounts had a debit balance of $2,500. What is the bad debt expense for the year?

BE8–7   Qinshan estimates that 4% of total accounts receivable will become uncollectible. Accounts receivable at December 31, 2014, are $250,000.

Determine the allowance and net realizable value and record bad debts. (SO 2) AP

(a) Determine the required balance in the allowance for doubtful accounts and the net realizable value of the accounts receivable.

(b) The allowance for doubtful accounts has an unadjusted debit balance of $1,500 at December 31, 2014. Prepare the adjusting entry to record bad debt expense in 2014.

(c) Assume instead that the allowance has an unadjusted credit balance of $500 at December 31, 2014. Prepare the adjusting entry to record bad debt expense.

BE8–8   Stilton Company reported the following in its general ledger. Using your knowledge of receivable transactions, match each of the transactions (a) to (f) with the best description of the economic event.

Analyze accounts receivable transactions. (SO 2) AP

Accounts Receivable			
Jan. 1	20,000	(b)	80,000
(a)	120,000	(c)	500
Dec. 31	59,500		
(e)	500	(f)	500

Service Revenue	
	120,000 (a)

Allowance for Doubtful Accounts			
		Jan. 1.	2,000
(c)	500	(d)	900
		Dec. 31	2,400
		(e)	500

Bad Debt Expense	
(d) 900	

1. Collect previously written-off account _____
2. Provide service on account _____
3. Write off uncollectible account _____
4. Collect accounts receivable _____
5. Record bad debt expense _____
6. Reverse previously written-off account _____

Record write off and compare net realizable value. (SO 2) AP

BE8–9 At the end of 2014, Perry Co. has an allowance for doubtful accounts of $28,000. On January 31, 2015, when it has accounts receivable of $575,000, Perry Co. learns that its $5,500 receivable from Young Inc. is not collectible. Management authorizes a write off.

(a) Record the write off.

(b) What is the net realizable value of the accounts receivable (1) before the write off, and (2) after the write off?

Record collection of account previously written off. (SO 2) AP

BE8–10 Assume the same information as in BE8–9. Young Inc.'s financial difficulties are over. On June 4, 2014, Perry Co. receives a payment in full of $5,500 from Young Inc. Record this transaction.

Calculate interest on notes receivable. (SO 3) AP

BE8–11 Hochelaga Co. has three outstanding notes receivable at its December 31, 2014, fiscal year end. For each note, calculate (a) total interest revenue, (b) interest revenue to be recorded in 2014, and (c) interest revenue to be recorded in 2015.

Issue Date	Term	Principal	Interest Rate
1. August 31, 2014	9 months	$15,000	6%
2. November 1, 2014	6 months	44,000	8%
3. October 1, 2014	15 months	30,000	7%

Record notes receivable transactions. (SO 3) AP

BE8–12 Alikhan Co. sold merchandise on account to Emerald Co. for $42,000, terms n/30, on April 1, 2014. Alikhan uses a perpetual inventory system and the merchandise had a cost of $25,200. On June 1, 2014, Emerald gave Alikhan a six-month, 6% promissory note in settlement of the account. Interest is to be paid at maturity. On December 1, Emerald paid the note and accrued interest. Record the above transactions for Alikhan Co. Alikhan Co. has a July 31 fiscal year end and adjusts its accounts annually.

Record notes receivable transactions. (SO 3) AP

BE8–13 Lee Company accepts a $27,000, four-month, 6% note receivable in settlement of an account receivable on June 1, 2014. Interest is to be paid at maturity. Lee Company has a December 31 year end and adjusts its accounts annually.

(a) Record (1) the issue of the note on June 1 and (2) the settlement of the note on October 1, assuming the note is honoured.

(b) Assume instead that the note is dishonoured but eventual collection is expected. Record the October 1 journal entry.

(c) Assume instead that the note is dishonoured and eventual collection is not expected. Record the October 1 journal entry.

Record notes receivable transactions and indicate statement presentation. (SO 3, 4) AP

BE8–14 Chanticlerc Co. lent Sharp Inc. $100,000 cash in exchange for a five-year, 4% note on July 1, 2014. Interest is payable quarterly on January 1, April 1, July 1, and October 1 each year. Chanticlerc Co. has a December 31 year end.

(a) Record Chanticlerc's entries related to the note to January 1, 2015.

(b) Indicate what amounts will be reported in Chanticlerc's December 31, 2014, balance sheet and where the amounts will be classified.

Prepare current assets section. (SO 4) AP

BE8–15 WAF Company's general ledger included the following accounts at November 30, 2014:

Accounts payable	$145,500
Accounts receivable	109,000
Allowance for doubtful accounts	6,950
Bad debt expense	35,970
Cash	74,000
GST recoverable	21,850
Interest receivable	2,500
Interest revenue	10,000
Merchandise inventory	110,800
Note receivable—due April 23, 2015	50,000
Note receivable—due May 21, 2018	150,000
Prepaid expenses	15,300
Short-term investments	80,500

Prepare the current assets section of the balance sheet.

Prepare current assets section. (SO 4) AN

BE8–16 The financial statements of **Maple Leaf Foods Inc.** reported the following for the years ended December 31, 2011, 2010, and 2009.

Financial Statement Data (in thousands of dollars)			
	2011	2010	2009
Sales	$4,893,624	$4,968,119	$5,221,602
Accounts receivable	133,504	108,379	372,330

(a) Calculate Maple Leaf's receivables turnover and collection period for 2011 and 2010.

(b) Has the company's liquidity improved or weakened?

▶ Exercises

E8–1 Selected transactions for Theatre Productions follow. Theatre Productions uses a perpetual inventory system.

May	8	Sold merchandise costing $5,980 to Grande Theatre for $13,000, terms 2/10, n/30.
	10	Grande returned $1,000 of the merchandise. This merchandise had originally cost Theatre $460 and was returned to inventory.
	18	Grande paid Theatre the amount owing.
	19	Sold merchandise costing $3,600 to Summer Productions for $6,000, terms 1/10, n/30.
	20	Summer Productions returned $500 of the merchandise because it was damaged. The merchandise had originally cost Theatre Productions $300. Theatre Productions scrapped the merchandise.
July	19	Added interest charges for one month to the amount owing by Summer Productions. Theatre charges 15% on outstanding receivables.
	22	Summer Productions paid the amount owing.

Identify impact and record accounts receivable transactions. (SO 1) AP

Instructions

(a) For each of these transactions, indicate if the transaction has increased (+) or decreased (−) cash, accounts receivable, inventory, and owner's equity and by how much. If the item is not changed, write NE to indicate there is no effect. Use the following format, in which the first one has been done for you as an example.

Transaction Date	Cash	Accounts Receivable	Inventory	Owner's Equity
May 8	NE	+$13,000	−$5,980	+$7,020

(b) Prepare journal entries to record the above transactions.

E8–2 Transactions follow for the Extreme Sports Ltd. store and three of its customers in the company's first month of business:

June	3	Ben Kidd used his Extreme Sports credit card to purchase $1,050 of merchandise.
	6	Biljana Pavic used her Extreme Sports credit card to purchase $840 of merchandise.
	8	Biljana Pavic returned $210 of merchandise on credit.
	9	Nicole Montpetit purchased $421 of merchandise and paid for it with Visa. Visa charges a 2% service fee.
	18	Ben Kidd used his Extreme Sports credit card to purchase an additional $348 of merchandise.
	19	Bonnie Cutcliffe used her debit card to purchase $230 of merchandise. There is a $0.50 service charge on all debit card transactions.
	20	Biljana Pavic made a $315 payment on her credit card account.
	23	Nicole Montpetit used her Extreme Sports credit card to purchase $498 of merchandise.
	25	Ben Kidd paid the amount owing on his June 3 purchase.
	30	Biljana Pavic used her Extreme Sports credit card to purchase $420 of merchandise.

Record accounts receivable transactions. Post to subsidiary and general ledgers. (SO 1) AP

Instructions

(a) Record the above transactions. Ignore any inventory or cost of goods sold entries for purposes of this question.

(b) Set up T accounts for the Accounts Receivable general ledger (control) account and for the Accounts Receivable subsidiary ledger accounts. Post the journal entries to these accounts.

(c) Prepare a list of customers and the balances of their accounts from the subsidiary ledger. Prove that the total of the subsidiary ledger is equal to the control account balance.

E8–3 Krazy Hair Salon accepts its own credit card, as well as debit cards and bank and nonbank credit cards. Krazy is charged 3.5% for all bank credit card transactions, 4.25% for all nonbank credit card transactions, and $0.50 per transaction for all debit card transactions. In October and November 2014, the following summary transactions occurred:

Record credit card transactions and indicate statement presentation. (SO 1, 4) AP

Oct.	15	Performed services totalling $15,000 for customers who used Krazy credit cards.
	20	Performed services totalling $7,500 for customers who used Visa credit cards.
	30	Performed services totalling $2,000 for customers who used nonbank credit cards.
	31	Performed services totalling $5,000 for customers who used debit cards (100 transactions).
Nov.	15	Collected $9,000 on Krazy credit cards.
	18	Collected the amount owing from the nonbank credit card companies for the October 30 transactions.
	30	Added interest charges of 24% to outstanding Krazy credit card balances. Interest is charged after 30 days from date of purchase.

Instructions

(a) Record the above transactions for Krazy Hair Salon.

(b) In addition to these transactions, Krazy Hair Salon had rent expense of $4,000, supplies expense of $500, and salary expense of $5,000 for the months of October and November. Prepare a multi-step income statement for Krazy Hair Salon for the two months ended November 30.

Calculate net realizable value and record bad debts.
(SO 2) AP

E8-4 Assen Company's general ledger at December 31, 2014, the end of the current year, shows Accounts Receivable $210,000 and Allowance for Doubtful Accounts $1,300 (credit). Uncollectible accounts are estimated to be 10% of accounts receivable.

Instructions

(a) Calculate the net realizable value of the accounts receivable.
(b) Record the adjusting journal entry at December 31, 2014.
(c) Assume instead that the Allowance for Doubtful Accounts had a debit balance of $2,800 at December 31, 2014. What is the net realizable value of the accounts receivable at December 31, 2014, and what is bad debt expense for 2014?

Prepare aging schedule and record bad debts. (SO 2) AP

E8-5 Rowen Company has accounts receivable of $241,000 at September 30, 2015. An analysis of the accounts shows the following:

Month of Sale	Balance
September	$170,000
August	35,700
July	20,000
April, May, and June	15,300
	$241,000

Credit terms are 2/10, n/30. On October 1, 2014, the Allowance for Doubtful Accounts had a credit balance of $17,600. During the year, the company wrote off accounts receivable of $19,000 as uncollectible. The company uses an aging schedule to estimate uncollectible accounts. The company's percentage estimates of bad debts are as follows:

Number of Days Outstanding	Estimated % Uncollectible
0–30	1%
31–60	10%
61–90	25%
Over 90	60%

Instructions

(a) Prepare an aging schedule to determine the total estimated uncollectible accounts at September 30, 2015.
(b) What is the net realizable value of the accounts receivable at September 30, 2015?
(c) Prepare the adjusting entry at September 30 to record bad debt expense.

Determine missing amounts and describe the accounts receivable transactions.
(SO 1, 2) AP

E8-6 Chelsea Corporation reported the following information in its general ledger at December 31.

Accounts Receivable						Sale	
Beg.	bal.	15,000		35,200			45,000
		(1)		(2)			
End.	bal.	(3)					

Allowance for Doubtful Accounts						Bad Debt Expense	
			Beg.	bal.	1,200	(4)	
		800			(4)		
			End.	bal.	(5)		

All sales were on account. At the end of the year, uncollectible accounts were estimated to be 10% of accounts receivable.

Instructions

(a) Using your knowledge of receivables transactions, determine the missing amounts. (*Hint:* You may find it helpful to reconstruct the journal entries.)
(b) Describe each transaction that has been recorded.
(c) What is the amount of cash collected?

Record bad debts, write off, and collection of previously written-off account; calculate net realizable value.
(SO 2) AP

E8-7 Accounts receivable transactions are provided below for J Looney Co.

Dec. 31, 2014   The company estimated that 5% of its accounts receivable would become uncollectible. The balances in the accounts receivable account and allowance for doubtful accounts were $650,000 and $2,300 (debit), respectively.

Mar. 5, 2015   The company determined that R. Black's $3,700 account and D. Wight's $6,900 account were uncollectible. The company's accounts receivable were $685,000 before the accounts were written off.

June 6, 2015   Wight paid his account that had been written off on March 5. The company's accounts receivable were $641,000 prior to recording the cash receipt for Wight.

Instructions

(a) Prepare the journal entries on December 31, 2014, March 5, 2015, and June 6, 2015.

(b) Post the journal entries to Allowance for Doubtful Accounts and calculate the new balance after each entry.

(c) Calculate the net realizable value of accounts receivable both before and after writing off the two accounts on March 5, 2015.

(d) Calculate the net realizable value of the accounts receivable both before and after recording the cash receipt from Wight on June 6, 2015.

E8–8   Data on three promissory notes accepted by Levin Ltd. during 2014 follow.

Calculate interest. (SO 3) AP

Date of Note	Term in Months	Principal	Interest Rate	Total Interest	Interest Revenue to Record for Year Ended December 31
Oct. 1	3	$180,000	10%	(c)	(d)
Aug. 1	6	120,000	(b)	$4,800	(e)
Nov. 1	24	(a)	6%	12,000	(f)

Instructions

Determine the missing amounts.

E8–9   Passera Supply Co. has the following transactions:

Record notes receivable transactions. (SO 3) AP

Nov.   1   Loaned $60,000 cash to A. Morgan on a one-year, 8% note.
       15   Sold goods to H. Giorgi on account for $12,000, terms n/30. The goods cost Passera $7,500. Passera uses the perpetual inventory system.
Dec.   1   Sold goods to Wrightman, Inc., receiving a $21,000, three-month, 6% note. The goods cost Passera $14,000.
       15   H. Giorgi was unable to pay her account. Giorgi gave Passera a six-month, 7% note in settlement of her account.
       31   Accrued interest revenue on all notes receivable. Interest is due at maturity.
Mar.   1   Collected the amount owing on the Wrightman note.
June   15   H. Giorgi defaults on the note. Future payment is expected.

Instructions

Record the transactions for Passera Supply Co. (Round calculations to the nearest dollar.)

E8–10   The following are notes receivable transactions for Rather Co.:

Record notes receivable transactions. (SO 3) AP

May   1   Received a $15,000, six-month, 6% note from Jioux Company in settlement of an account receivable. Interest is due at maturity.
June 30   Accrued interest on the Jioux note, at Rather's year end. Adjustments are recorded annually.
July 31   Lent $2,000 cash to an employee, Noreen Irvine, receiving a three-month, 5% note. Interest is due at the end of each month.
Aug. 31   Received the interest due from Ms. Irvine.
Sept. 30   Received the interest due from Ms. Irvine.
Oct. 31   Received payment in full for the employee note from Ms. Irvine.
Nov.   1   Jioux Company defaults on its note. Rather does not expect to collect on the note.

Instructions

Record the transactions for Rather Co. (Round calculations to the nearest dollar.)

E8–11   Ni Co. has the following notes receivable outstanding at December 31, 2014:

Record notes receivable transactions and indicate statement presentation. (SO 3, 4) AP

Issue Date	Term	Principal	Interest Rate
1. August 31, 2013	2 years	$15,000	4%
2. October 1, 2013	18 months	46,000	5%
3. February 1, 2014	1 year	32,000	4%
4. May 31, 2014	5 years	22,000	6%
5. October 31, 2014	7 months	9,000	5%

For notes with terms of one year or longer, interest is payable on the first day of each month, for interest earned the previous month. For notes with terms less than one year, interest is payable at maturity.

Instructions

(a) Calculate the interest revenue that Ni Co. will report on its income statement for the year ended December 31, 2014. Indicate where this will be presented on the income statement. (Round calculations to the nearest dollar.)

(b) Calculate the amounts related to these notes that will be reported on Ni Co.'s balance sheet at December 31, 2014. Indicate where they will be presented. Assume all required interest payments have been received on time. (Round calculations to the nearest dollar.)

Record bad debts, prepare partial balance sheet, and calculate ratios. (SO 2, 4) AP

E8-12 In its first year of operations, AJS Company had sales of $4 million (all on credit) and cost of goods sold of $1,750,000. Sales allowances of $100,000 were given on substandard merchandise. During the year, the company collected $3.2 million cash on account. At year end, December 31, 2014, the credit manager estimates that 4% of the accounts receivable will become uncollectible.

At December 31, 2014, the balances in selected other accounts were:

Accounts payable	$350,000
Cash	40,000
Interest receivable	1,125
Interest revenue	2,250
Merchandise inventory	325,000
Notes receivable, due April 10, 2017	45,000
Prepaid insurance	8,000
Short-term investments	50,000
Unearned sales revenue	25,000

Instructions

(a) Prepare the journal entry to record the bad debt expense.

(b) Prepare the current assets section of the balance sheet for AJS Company at December 31, 2014.

(c) Calculate the receivables turnover and collection period. (Remember that this is the end of the first year of business.)

Calculate ratios and comment. (SO 4) AN

E8-13 The following information (in millions) was taken from the December 31 financial statements of **Canadian National Railway Company**:

	2011	2010	2009
Accounts receivable, gross	$ 836	$ 796	$ 831
Allowance for doubtful accounts	16	21	34
Accounts receivable, net	820	775	797
Revenues	9,028	8,297	7,367
Total current assets	1,848	1,590	1,490
Total current liabilities	1,715	1,906	1,237

Instructions

(a) Calculate the 2011 and 2010 current ratios.

(b) Calculate the receivables turnover and average collection period for 2011 and 2010.

(c) Comment on any improvement or weakening in CN's liquidity and its management of accounts receivable.

▶ Problems: Set A

Record accounts receivable transactions. Post to subsidiary and general ledgers and prepare adjusting entry. (SO 1, 2) AP

P8-1A At December 31, 2014, the general ledger and subsidiary ledger for Albert's, a small auto parts store, showed the following:

General Ledger		Accounts Receivable Subsidiary Ledger	
Accounts receivable	$75,000	Best Auto Repair	$ 3,800
Allowance for doubtful accounts	3,750	Brown's Repair	23,000
		Custom Repair	0
		Jen's Auto Body	35,000
		Luxury Autos	13,200
		Total	$75,000

Jan.   3   Brown's Repair paid $18,000 on its account.
    4   Custom Repair paid $1,400 on its account that had previously been written off.
    8   Jen's Auto Body purchased $3,800 of merchandise on account.
    9   Antique Auto Repair paid cash for $1,500 of merchandise.
   18   Jen's Auto Body returned $800 of merchandise.
   19   Luxury Autos paid $13,200 on its account.
   20   Jen's Auto Body paid $25,000 on its account.
   23   Brown's Repair purchased $5,600 on account.
   25   Custom Repair purchased $10,000 of merchandise on Visa.
   26   Luxury Autos purchased $18,000 of merchandise on account.
   31   Albert's determined that the Best Auto Repair account receivable was not collectible.

Instructions

(a) Record the above transactions. Ignore credit card fees and any entries to inventory or cost of goods sold for purposes of this question.
(b) Set up T accounts for the Accounts Receivable general ledger (control) account, the Allowance for Doubtful Accounts general ledger account, and the Accounts Receivable subsidiary ledger accounts. Post the journal entries to these accounts.
(c) Albert's estimated that 10% of accounts receivable is not collectible. Record the required adjustment to the allowance for doubtful accounts.
(d) Prepare a list of customers and the balances of their accounts from the subsidiary ledger. Prove that the total of the subsidiary ledger is equal to the control account balance.

TAKING IT FURTHER   What types of errors could result in the total of the account balances in the subsidiary ledger not agreeing with the general ledger control account?

P8–2A   Silk Co. reported the following information on its December 31, 2014, balance sheet:

Accounts receivable	$760,000
Less: Allowance for doubtful accounts	76,000

Record accounts receivable and bad debt transactions; show balance sheet presentation. (SO 1, 2, 4) AP

During 2015, the company had the following transactions related to receivables:

1. Sales on account, $2,800,000
2. Sales returns and allowances, $325,000
3. Collections of accounts receivable, $2,410,000
4. Interest added to overdue accounts, $72,000
5. Write offs of accounts considered uncollectible, $58,400
6. Collection of accounts previously written off as uncollectible, $5,200

Instructions

(a) Prepare the summary journal entries to record each of these six transactions.
(b) Enter the December 31, 2014, balances in the Accounts Receivable and Allowance for Doubtful Accounts general ledger accounts, post the entries to the two accounts, and determine the balances.
(c) Calculate the net realizable value of accounts receivable at December 31, 2015. Uncollectible accounts are estimated at 10% of accounts receivable.
(d) Prepare the journal entry to record bad debt expense for 2015.
(e) Show the balance sheet presentation of the receivables as at December 31, 2015.

TAKING IT FURTHER   For several years, Silk Co. has estimated uncollectible accounts at 10% of accounts receivable. Discuss whether or not the company should continue to do this at December 31, 2015.

P8–3A   At the beginning of the current period, Huang Co. had a balance of $100,000 in Accounts Receivable and a $7,000 credit balance in Allowance for Doubtful Accounts. In the period, it had net credit sales of $400,000 and collections of $361,500. It wrote off accounts receivable of $10,500 as uncollectible. After a $1,750 account was written off as uncollectible, it was subsequently collected. This is in addition to the other cash collections. Based on an aging schedule, uncollectible accounts are estimated to be $8,000 at the end of the period.

Record accounts receivable and bad debt transactions; show financial statement presentation. (SO 1, 2, 4) AP

Instructions

(a) Record sales and collections in the period.
(b) Record the write off of uncollectible accounts in the period.
(c) Record the collection of the account previously written off as uncollectible.
(d) Record the bad debt expense adjusting entry for the period.
(e) Show the balance sheet presentation of the receivables at the end of the period.
(f) What is the amount of bad debt expense on the income statement for the period?

TAKING IT FURTHER   Why is bad debt expense not increased when an account receivable is written off because it is determined to be uncollectible?

Calculate bad debt amounts and answer questions. (SO 2) AP

P8–4A Information on Hohenberger Company for 2014 follows:

Total credit sales	$1,000,000
Accounts receivable at December 31	400,000
Uncollectible accounts written off	17,500
Amount collected on accounts previously written off (after write off but before year end)	2,500

Instructions

(a) Assume that Hohenberger Company decides to estimate its uncollectible accounts using the allowance method and an aging schedule. Uncollectible accounts are estimated to be $24,000. What amount of bad debt expense will Hohenberger Company record if Allowance for Doubtful Accounts had an opening balance of $20,000 on January 1, 2014?

(b) Assume the same facts as in (a) except that the Allowance for Doubtful Accounts had a $12,000 balance on January 1, 2014. What amount of bad debt expense will Hohenberger record on December 31, 2014?

(c) How does the amount of accounts written off during the period affect the amount of bad debt expense recorded at the end of the period?

(d) How does the collection of an account that had previously been written off affect the net realizable value of accounts receivable?

TAKING IT FURTHER Why doesn't a company sell to only those customers it knows for sure it can collect from?

Prepare aging schedule and record bad debts and explain method. (SO 2) AP

P8–5A Pearson Company uses the allowance method to estimate uncollectible accounts receivable. The company produced the following information from aging its accounts receivable at year end:

	Total	**Number of Days Outstanding**			
		0–30	31–60	61–90	91–120
Accounts receivable	$640,000	$360,000	$140,000	$100,000	$40,000
Estimated % uncollectible		2%	5%	10%	30%
Estimated uncollectible accounts					

The unadjusted balance in Allowance for Doubtful Accounts is a debit of $3,000.

Instructions

(a) Complete the aging schedule and calculate the total estimated uncollectible accounts.

(b) Record the bad debt adjusting entry using the information determined in (a).

(c) In the following year, $18,000 of the outstanding accounts receivable is determined to be uncollectible. Record the write off of the uncollectible accounts.

(d) The company collects $4,500 of the $18,000 of accounts that was determined to be uncollectible in (c). The company also expects to collect an additional $1,000. Record the journal entry (or entries) to restore the accounts receivable and the cash collected. Collection of the $1,000 is expected in the near future.

(e) Explain how using the allowance method matches expenses with revenues.

(f) Explain how using the allowance method values Accounts Receivable at net realizable value on the balance sheet.

TAKING IT FURTHER What are the advantages and disadvantages to the company of using an aging schedule to estimate uncollectible accounts, as compared with estimating uncollectible accounts as 10% of total accounts receivable?

Prepare aging schedule and record bad debts. (SO 2) AP

P8–6A An aging analysis of Hagiwara Company's accounts receivable at December 31, 2014 and 2015, showed the following:

Number of Days Outstanding	Estimated % Uncollectible	Accounts Receivable	
		2015	2014
0–30 days	3%	$115,000	$145,000
31–60 days	6%	35,000	63,000
61–90 days	12%	45,000	38,000
Over 90 days	25%	80,000	24,000
Total		$275,000	$270,000

Additional information:

1. At December 31, 2014, the unadjusted balance in Allowance for Doubtful Accounts was a credit of $6,600.
2. In 2015, $23,500 of accounts was written off as uncollectible and $2,200 of accounts previously written off was collected.

Instructions

(a) Prepare an aging schedule to calculate the estimated uncollectible accounts at December 31, 2014, and at December 31, 2015.

(b) Calculate the net realizable value of Hagiwara's accounts receivable at December 31, 2014, and December 31, 2015.

(c) Record the following:
   1. The adjusting entry on December 31, 2014
   2. The write off of uncollectible accounts in 2015
   3. The collection in 2015 of accounts previously written off
   4. The adjusting entry on December 31, 2015

TAKING IT FURTHER   What are the implications of the changes in the age of the receivables from 2014 to 2015?

P8–7A   The following information was reported in Nenshi Company's general ledger at September 30:

Determine missing amounts.
(SO 2) AN

	Accounts Receivable				Sales	
Beg.	bal.	845,000	(b)			5,370,000
		(a)	(c)			
		4,200	(f)			
End.	bal.	(d)				

	Allowance for Doubtful Accounts				Bad Debt Expense	
		Beg.	bal.	76,050	(e)	
	50,400			(e)		
				(b)		
		End.	bal.	83,475		

All sales were made on account. Uncollectible accounts are estimated to be 9% of accounts receivable.

Instructions

Determine the missing amounts in Nenshi Company's accounts. State what each of these amounts represents. You will not be able to determine the missing items in alphabetical order. (To solve this problem, it might help if you reconstruct the journal entries.)

TAKING IT FURTHER   Explain the differences between bad debt expense and the allowance for doubtful accounts.

P8–8A   Bassano Company prepares monthly financial statements and estimates its uncollectible accounts at the end of each month. Bassano Company has an October 31 fiscal year end, closes temporary accounts annually, and uses a perpetual inventory system.

Identify impact of accounts receivable and bad debt transactions; determine statement presentation.
(SO 1, 2, 4) AP

On August 31, 2014, after completing its month-end adjustments, it had accounts receivable of $74,500, a credit balance of $1,480 in Allowance for Doubtful Accounts, and bad debt expense of $9,860. In September and October, the following occurred:

September
1. Sold $56,300 of merchandise on account; the cost of the merchandise was $25,335.
2. A total of $900 of the merchandise sold on account was returned. These customers were issued credit memos. The cost of the merchandise was $400 and it was returned to inventory.
3. Collected $59,200 cash on account from customers.
4. Interest charges of $800 were charged to outstanding accounts receivable.
5. Recorded the monthly adjustment for bad debts. Uncollectible accounts were estimated to be 4% of accounts receivable.

October
1. Credit sales in the month were $66,300; the cost of the merchandise was $28,700.
2. Received $350 cash from a customer whose account had been written off in July.
3. Collected $58,500 cash, in addition to the cash collected in (2) above, from customers on account.
4. Wrote off $7,500 of accounts receivable as uncollectible.
5. Interest charges of $700 were charged to outstanding accounts receivable.
6. Recorded the year-end adjustment for bad debts. Uncollectible accounts were estimated to be 4% of accounts receivable.

Instructions

(a) For each of these transactions, indicate if the transaction has increased (+) or decreased (−) Cash, Accounts Receivable, Allowance for Doubtful Accounts, Inventory, Total Assets, and Owner's Equity and by how much. If the item is not changed, write NE to indicate there is no effect. Use the following format, in which the first one has been done for you as an example.

Transaction	Cash	Accounts Receivable	Allowance for Doubtful Accounts	Inventory	Total Assets	Owner's Equity
September:						
1.	NE	+$56,300	NE	−$25,335	+$30,965	+$30,965

(b) Show how accounts receivable will appear on the October 31, 2014, balance sheet.
(c) What amount will be reported as bad debt expense on the income statement for the year ended October 31, 2014?

TAKING IT FURTHER If Bassano's credit manager increases the amount of credit checking the company does before granting credit on all of its customers, will that eliminate the bad debts? Explain.

Record receivables transactions. (SO 1, 3) AP

P8–9A Ku Company has an April 30 fiscal year end and adjusts accounts annually. Selected transactions in the year included the following:

Jan. 2 Sold $24,000 of merchandise to Richards Company, terms n/30. The cost of the goods sold was $14,400. Ku uses the perpetual inventory system.
Feb. 1 Accepted a $24,000, four-month, 5% promissory note from Richards Company for the balance due. (See January 2 transaction.) Interest is payable at maturity.
     15 Sold $15,000 of merchandise costing $9,000 to Garrison Company and accepted Garrison's three-month, 5% note in payment. Interest is payable at maturity.
Mar. 15 Sold $12,000 of merchandise to Mantha Co., terms n/30. The cost of the merchandise sold was $7,200.
Apr. 30 Accepted a $12,000, two-month, 7% note from Mantha Co. for its balance due. Interest is payable at maturity. (See March 15 transaction.)
     30 Accrued interest at year end.
May 15 Collected the Garrison note in full. (See February 15 transaction.)
June 1 Collected the Richards Company note in full. (See February 1 transaction.)
June 30 Mantha Co. dishonours its note of April 30. Mantha Co. is bankrupt and there is no hope of future settlement.
July 13 Sold $6,000 merchandise costing $3,600 to Zorilla Inc. and accepted Zorilla's $6,000, three-month, 7% note for the amount due, with interest payable at maturity.
Oct. 13 The Zorilla Inc. note was dishonoured. (See July 13 transaction.) It is expected that Zorilla will eventually pay the amount owed.

Instructions

Record the above transactions. (Round calculations to the nearest dollar.)

TAKING IT FURTHER What are the advantages and disadvantages of Ku Company accepting notes receivable from its customers?

Record note receivable transactions; show balance sheet presentation. (SO 3, 4) AP

P8–10A Tardif Company adjusts its books monthly. On September 30, 2014, notes receivable include the following:

Issue Date	Maker	Principal	Interest	Term
Aug. 1, 2013	RJF Inc.	$19,000	4.5%	2.5 years
Mar. 31, 2014	Resolute Co.	17,000	5.0%	7 months
May 31, 2014	Imaging Ltd.	17,500	5.5%	18 months
Aug. 31, 2014	Dragon Co.	6,000	8.5%	2 months
Sept. 30, 2014	MGH Corp.	20,500	6.0%	16 months

Interest is payable on the first day of each month for notes with terms of one year or longer. Interest is payable at maturity for notes with terms less than one year. In October, the following transactions were completed:

Oct.	1	Received payment of the interest due from RJF Inc.
	1	Received payment of the interest due from Imaging Ltd.
	31	Received notice that the Dragon Co. note had been dishonoured. (Assume that Dragon is expected to pay in the future.)
	31	Collected the amount owing from Resolute Co.

Instructions

(a) Calculate the balance in the Interest Receivable and Notes Receivable accounts at September 30, 2014.
(b) Record the October transactions and the October 31 adjusting entry for accrued interest receivable.
(c) Enter the balances at October 1 in the receivables accounts, and post the entries to the receivables accounts.
(d) Show the balance sheet presentation of the interest and notes receivable accounts at October 31.
(e) How would the journal entry on October 31 be different if Dragon were not expected to pay in the future?

TAKING IT FURTHER   The interest rate for the Dragon note is higher than the other notes. Why might that have been the case?

P8–11A   Tocksfor Company's general ledger included the following selected accounts (in thousands) at September 30, 2014:

Prepare assets section of balance sheet; calculate and interpret ratios. (SO 4) AN

Accounts payable	$1,077.3
Accounts receivable	590.4
Accumulated depreciation—equipment	858.7
Allowance for doubtful accounts	35.4
Bad debt expense	91.3
Cash	395.6
Cost of goods sold	660.4
Equipment	1,732.8
Interest revenue	19.7
Merchandise inventory	630.9
Notes receivable—due May 15, 2015	96.0
Notes receivable—due in 2018	191.1
Prepaid expenses and deposits	20.1
Sales	4,565.5
Sales discounts	31.3
Short-term investments	194.9
Supplies	21.7
Unearned sales revenue	56.3

Additional information:

1. On September 30, 2013, Accounts Receivable was $611.1 thousand and the Allowance for Doubtful Accounts was $36.6 thousand.
2. The receivables turnover was 8.3 the previous year.

Instructions

(a) Prepare the assets section of the balance sheet.
(b) Calculate the receivables turnover and average collection period. Compare these results with the previous year's results and comment on any trends.

TAKING IT FURTHER   What other information should Tocksfor consider when analyzing its receivables turnover and average collection period?

P8–12A   Presented here is selected financial information (in millions) from the 2011 financial statements of Rogers Communications Inc. and Shaw Communications Inc.:

Calculate and interpret ratios. (SO 4) AN

	Rogers	Shaw
Sales	$12,428	$4,740.9
Allowance for doubtful accounts, beginning of year	138	19.0
Allowance for doubtful accounts, end of year	129	28.8
Accounts receivable balance (net), beginning of year	1,443	196.4
Accounts receivable balance (net), end of year	1,574	442.8

Instructions

(a) Calculate the receivables turnover and average collection period for both companies.
(b) Comment on the difference in their collection experiences.

TAKING IT FURTHER   Shaw acquired Canwest Global Communications Corp. in October 2010. As part of the transaction, Shaw acquired $296.6 million of receivables. What impact might this acquisition have on its 2011 receivable turnover ratio? Note that Shaw's fiscal year end was August 31, 2011. Explain.

Evaluate liquidity. (SO 4) AN   **P8–13A**   The following ratios are available for Satellite Mechanical:

	2015	2014	2013
Current ratio	2.0 to 1	1.6 to 1	1.4 to 1
Acid-test ratio	1.1 to 1	0.8 to 1	0.7 to 1
Receivables turnover	7.3 times	10.1 times	10.3 times
Inventory turnover	6.3 times	6.1 times	6.4 times

Instructions

(a) Calculate the collection period, days sales in inventory, and operating cycle in days for each year.
(b) Has Satellite Mechanical's liquidity improved or weakened over the three-year period? Explain.
(c) Do changes in turnover ratios affect profitability? Explain.
(d) Do changes in turnover ratios affect cash flow? Explain.

TAKING IT FURTHER   At the beginning of 2014, the owner of Satellite Mechanical decided to eliminate sales discounts because she thought it was costing the company too much money. The terms of credit sales were changed from 2/10, n/30 to n/30. Evaluate this decision.

▶ Problems: Set B

Record accounts receivable transactions. Post to subsidiary and general ledgers. (SO 1, 2) AP   **P8–1B**   At December 31, 2014, the general ledger and subsidiary ledger for Wow's, a small beauty supply company, showed the following:

General Ledger		Accounts Receivable Subsidiary Ledger	
Accounts receivable	$35,000	Hair Designs	$ 8,000
Allowance for doubtful accounts	3,500	Great Looks	11,000
		Ken's Salon	9,000
		Luxury Spa	7,000
		New Do	0
		Total	$35,000

Jan.	3	Hair Designs paid $8,000 on its account.
	4	New Do paid $900 on its account that had previously been written off.
	8	Great Looks purchased $3,000 of merchandise on account.
	9	Your Spa paid cash for $2,000 of merchandise.
	18	Great Looks returned $500 of merchandise.
	19	Luxury Spa paid $5,000 on its account.
	20	Great Looks paid $10,000 on is account.
	23	Hair Designs purchased $9,000 on account.
	24	Ken's Salon paid $3,000 on account.
	25	New Do purchased $5,000 of merchandise on Visa.
	26	Luxury Spa purchased $12,000 of merchandise on account.
	31	Wow determined that the Ken's Salon account receivable was not collectible.

Instructions

(a) Record the above transactions. Ignore credit card fees and inventory and cost of goods sold entries for purposes of this question.
(b) Set up T accounts for the Accounts Receivable general ledger (control) account, the Allowance for Doubtful Accounts general ledger account, and the Accounts Receivable subsidiary ledger accounts. Post the journal entries to these accounts.
(c) Wow estimated that 10% of accounts receivable is not collectible. Record the required adjustment to the allowance for doubtful accounts.

(d) Prepare a list of customers and the balances of their accounts from the subsidiary ledger. Prove that the total of the subsidiary ledger is equal to the control account balance.

TAKING IT FURTHER   What types of errors could result if the total of the account balances in the subsidiary ledger did not agree with the general ledger control account?

P8–2B   Textile Imports reported the following information on its December 31, 2014, balance sheet:

Accounts receivable	$1,580,000
Less: Allowance for doubtful accounts	94,800

During 2015, the company had the following transactions related to receivables:

1. Sales on account, $4,800,000
2. Sales returns and allowances, $120,000
3. Collections of accounts receivable, $4,700,000
4. Interest added to overdue accounts, $200,000
5. Write offs of accounts deemed uncollectible, $179,000
6. Collection of bad debts previously written off as uncollectible, $24,000

Instructions

(a) Prepare the summary journal entries to record each of these six transactions.
(b) Enter the January 1, 2015, balances in the Accounts Receivable and Allowance for Doubtful Accounts general ledger accounts, post the entries to the two accounts, and determine the balances.
(c) Record bad debt expense for 2015. Uncollectible accounts are estimated at 6% of accounts receivable.
(d) Calculate the net realizable value of accounts receivable at December 31, 2015.
(e) Show the balance sheet presentation of accounts receivable at December 31, 2015.

TAKING IT FURTHER   For several years, Textile Imports has estimated uncollectible accounts at 6% of accounts receivable. Discuss whether or not the company should continue to do this at December 31, 2015.

Record accounts receivable and bad debt transactions; show balance sheet presentation. (SO 1, 2) AP

P8–3B   At the beginning of the current period, Fassi Co. had a balance of $800,000 in Accounts Receivable and a $44,000 credit balance in Allowance for Doubtful Accounts. In the period, it had net credit sales of $1,900,000 and collections of $2,042,000. It wrote off accounts receivable of $58,000. After a $4,000 account was written off as uncollectible, it was subsequently collected. This is in addition to the other cash collections. Based on an aging schedule, uncollectible accounts are estimated to be $36,000 at the end of the period.

Record accounts receivable and bad debt transactions; show financial statement presentation. (SO 1, 2, 4) AP

Instructions

(a) Record sales and collections in the period.
(b) Record the write off of uncollectible accounts in the period.
(c) Record the collection of the account previously written off.
(d) Record the bad debt expense adjusting entry for the period.
(e) Show the balance sheet presentation of the accounts receivable at the end of the period.
(f) What is the bad debt expense on the income statement for the period?

TAKING IT FURTHER   Why is bad debt expense not reduced when a previously written-off account is collected?

P8–4B   Information for Tisipai Company in 2014 follows:

Total net credit sales	$3,300,000
Accounts receivable at December 31	1,250,000
Accounts receivable written off	48,000
Amount collected on accounts previously written off (after write off but before year end)	8,000

Calculate bad debt amounts and answer questions. (SO 2) AP

Instructions

(a) Assume that Tisipai Company decides to use the allowance method and estimates its uncollectible accounts to be $52,000 based on an aging schedule. What amount of bad debt expense will Tisipai record if Allowance for Doubtful Accounts had an opening balance of $30,000 on January 1, 2014?
(b) Assume the same facts as in (a), except that the Allowance for Doubtful Accounts had a $42,250 balance on January 1, 2014. What amount of bad debt expense will Tisipai record on December 31, 2014?
(c) How does the amount of accounts written off during the period affect the amount of bad debt expense recorded at the end of the period?
(d) How does the collection of an account that had previously been written off affect the net realizable value of accounts receivable?

Prepare aging schedule and
record bad debts and
comment. (SO 2) AP

TAKING IT FURTHER Why is a company not certain what accounts are not collectible?

P8-5B Creative Co. uses the allowance method to estimate uncollectible accounts receivable. The computer produced the following aging of the accounts receivable at year end:

| | Total | **Number of Days Outstanding** | | | |
		0–30	31–60	61–90	91–120
Accounts receivable	$210,000	$120,000	$55,000	$20,000	$15,000
Estimated % uncollectible		1%	7%	12%	25%
Estimated uncollectible accounts					

The unadjusted balance in Allowance for Doubtful Accounts is a credit of $5,000.

Instructions

(a) Complete the aging schedule and calculate the total estimated uncollectible accounts from the above information.
(b) Record the bad debt adjusting entry using the above information.
(c) In the following year, $12,200 of the outstanding accounts receivable is determined to be uncollectible. Record the write off of the uncollectible accounts.
(d) The company collects $3,400 of the $12,200 of accounts receivable that were determined to be uncollectible in (c). No further amounts are expected to be collected. Prepare the journal entry (or entries) to record the collection of this amount.
(e) Comment on how your answers to parts (a) to (d) would change if Creative Co. used a percentage of total accounts receivable of 8% instead of aging the accounts receivable.

TAKING IT FURTHER What are the advantages for the company of aging the accounts receivable rather than applying a percentage to total accounts receivable?

Prepare aging schedule and
record bad debts. (SO 2) AP

P8-6B An aging analysis of Hake Company's accounts receivable at December 31, 2014 and 2015, showed the following:

| Number of Days Outstanding | Estimated % Uncollectible | December 31 | |
		2015	2014
0–30 days	2.5%	$190,000	$220,000
31–60 days	6%	40,000	105,000
61–90 days	18%	65,000	40,000
Over 90 days	25%	75,000	25,000
Total		$370,000	$390,000

Additional information:

1. At December 31, 2014, the unadjusted balance in Allowance for Doubtful Accounts was a debit of $3,400.
2. In 2015, $22,300 of accounts was written off as uncollectible and $2,500 of accounts previously written off was collected.

Instructions

(a) Prepare an aging schedule to calculate the estimated uncollectible accounts at December 31, 2014, and at December 31, 2015.
(b) Calculate the net realizable value of Hake's accounts receivable at December 31, 2014, and December 31, 2015.
(c) Record the following:
   1. The adjusting entry on December 31, 2014
   2. The write off of uncollectible accounts in 2015
   3. The collection in 2015 of accounts previously written off
   4. The adjusting entry on December 31, 2015

TAKING IT FURTHER What are the implications of the changes in the age of accounts receivable from 2014 to 2015?

P8–7B The following information was reported in Beckford Company's general ledger at August 31:

Determine missing amounts. (SO 2) AN

Accounts Receivable

Beg.	bal.	360,000		2,545,000
		(a)		(d)
		(b)		5,520
End.	bal.	(c)		

Sales

	(a)

Allowance for Doubtful Accounts

			Beg. bal.	(e)
	28,540			(b)
				(f)
			End. bal.	29,400

Bad Debt Expense

(f)	

All sales were made on account. At the beginning of the year, uncollectible accounts were estimated to be 6% of accounts receivable. At the end of the year, uncollectible accounts were estimated to be 7% of accounts receivable.

Instructions

Determine the missing amounts in Beckford Company's accounts. State what each of these amounts represents. You will not be able to determine the missing items in alphabetical order. (To solve this problem, it might help if you reconstruct the journal entries.)

TAKING IT FURTHER   Explain the difference between bad debt expense and the allowance for doubtful accounts.

P8–8B Assiniboia Co. prepares monthly financial statements and estimates its uncollectible accounts at the end of each month. Assiniboia Co. has a May 31 fiscal year end, closes temporary accounts annually, and uses the perpetual inventory system.

Identify impact of accounts receivable and bad debt transactions; determine statement presentation. (SO 1, 2, 4) AP

On March 31, 2014, after completing its month-end adjustments, it had accounts receivable of $89,200, a credit balance of $4,930 in Allowance for Doubtful Accounts, and a debit balance in Bad Debt Expense of $17,980. In April and May, the following occurred:

April
1. Sold $65,100 of merchandise on credit. The cost of the merchandise was $35,530.
2. Accepted $800 of returns on the merchandise sold on credit. These customers were issued credit memos. The merchandise had a cost of $440 and was discarded because it was damaged.
3. Collected $69,200 cash on account from customers.
4. Interest charges of $1,700 were charged to outstanding accounts receivable.
5. Recorded the monthly adjustment for bad debts. Uncollectible accounts were estimated to be 6% of accounts receivable.

May
1. Credit sales were $76,600. The cost of the merchandise was $42,130.
2. Received $450 cash from a customer whose account had been written off in March.
3. Collected $78,500 cash, in addition to the cash collected in (2) above, from customers on account.
4. Wrote off $9,580 of accounts receivable as uncollectible.
5. Interest charges of $1,480 were charged to outstanding accounts receivable.
6. Recorded the year-end adjustment for bad debts. Uncollectible accounts were estimated to be 6% of accounts receivable.

Instructions

(a) For each of these transactions, indicate if the transaction has increased (+) or decreased (−) Cash, Accounts Receivable, Allowance for Doubtful Accounts, Inventory, Total Assets, and Owner's Equity and by how much. If the item is not changed, write NE to indicate there is no effect. Use the following format, in which the first one has been done for you as an example.

Transaction	Cash	Accounts Receivable	Allowance for Doubtful Accounts	Inventory	Total Assets	Owner's Equity
April: 1.	NE	+$65,100	NE	−$35,530	+$29,570	+$29,570

(b) Show how accounts receivable will appear on the May 31, 2014, balance sheet.
(c) What amount will be reported as bad debt expense on the income statement for the year ended May 31, 2014?

<u>TAKING IT FURTHER</u> To eliminate bad debt expense, should Assiniboia require all of its customers to pay cash? Explain.

P8–9B On January 1, 2014, Alexi Co. had a $20,000, five-month, 6% note receivable from Figaro Company dated October 31, 2012. Interest receivable of $200 was accrued on the note on December 31, 2013. Alexi Co. has a December 31 fiscal year end and adjusts its accounts annually. In 2014, the following selected transactions occurred:

Jan. 2 Sold $25,000 of merchandise costing $13,750 to Braun Company, terms 2/10, n/30. Alexi Co. uses the perpetual inventory system.
Feb. 1 Accepted Braun Company's $25,000, three-month, 6% note for the balance due. (See January 2 transaction.) Interest is due at maturity.
Mar. 31 Received payment in full from Figaro Company for the amount due.
May 1 Collected Braun Company note in full. (See February 1 transaction.)
25 Accepted Noah Inc.'s $12,000, two-month, 6% note in settlement of a past-due balance on account. Interest is payable monthly.
June 25 Received one month's interest from Noah Inc. on its note. (See May 25 transaction.)
July 25 The Noah Inc. note was dishonoured. (See May 25 transaction.) Noah Inc. is bankrupt and future payment is not expected.
Oct. 1 Loaned Martin Rowe, an employee, $4,000 on a four-month, 6% note. Interest is due at maturity.
Nov. 30 Gave UOA Corp. a $10,000 cash loan and accepted UOA's four-month, 4.5% note.
Dec. 1 Martin Rowe left for a job at another company. Alexi Co. asked him to immediately pay the note receivable. (See October 1 transaction.) Martin told the company that he does not have the money to do so.
31 Accrued interest is recorded on any outstanding notes at year end.

Instructions
Record the above transactions.

<u>TAKING IT FURTHER</u> Do you think the note receivable from Martin Rowe should be written off as at the year end? If not, do you think interest should be accrued on this note receivable at year end? What actions might the company have taken before Martin left the company to collect the note or part of it?

P8–10B Ouellette Co. adjusts its books monthly. On June 30, 2014, notes receivable include the following:

Issue Date	Maker	Principal	Term	Interest
May 1, 2013	ALD Inc.	$ 6,000	3 years	4.0%
October 31, 2013	Kabam Ltd.	10,000	15 months	5.0%
January 31, 2014	Best Foot Forward Shoe Co.	15,000	6 months	5.5%
May 31, 2014	DNR Co.	4,800	2 months	8.75%
June 30, 2014	M&J Hardware Corp.	9,000	8 months	5.0%

Interest is payable on the first day of each month for notes with terms of one year or longer. Interest is payable at maturity for notes with terms less than one year. In July, the following transactions were completed:

July 1 Received payment of the interest due from ALD Inc.
2 Received payment of the interest due from Kabam Ltd.
31 Collected the full amount on the Best Foot Forward Shoe Co. note.
31 Received notice that the DNR Co. note has been dishonoured. Assume that DNR Co. is expected to pay in the future.

Instructions
(a) Calculate the balance in the Interest Receivable and Notes Receivable accounts at June 30, 2014.
(b) Record the July transactions and the July 31 adjusting entry for accrued interest receivable.
(c) Enter the balances at July 1 in the receivables accounts. Post the entries to the receivables accounts.
(d) Show the balance sheet presentation of the receivables accounts at July 31, 2014.
(e) How would the journal entry on July 31 be different if DNR Co. were not expected to pay in the future?

Record receivables transactions. (SO 1, 2, 3) AP

Record note receivable transactions; show balance sheet presentation. (SO 3, 4) AP

TAKING IT FURTHER   The interest rate for the DNR note is higher than the other notes. Why might that be the case?

P8–11B   Norlandia Saga Company's general ledger included the following selected accounts (in thousands) at November 30, 2014:

Accounts payable	$ 546.2
Accounts receivable	311.4
Accumulated depreciation—equipment	471.7
Allowance for doubtful accounts	14.8
Bad debt expense	43.6
Cash	417.1
Cost of goods sold	353.0
Equipment	924.2
Interest revenue	10.7
Merchandise inventory	336.5
Notes receivable—due in 2015	51.2
Notes receivable—due in 2018	101.9
Prepaid expenses and deposits	19.3
Sales	2,823.8
Sales discounts	18.5
Short-term investments	224.6
Supplies	15.9
Unearned sales revenue	40.2

Prepare assets section of balance sheet; calculate and interpret ratios. (SO 4) AN

Additional information:

1. On November 30, 2013, Accounts Receivable was $271.7 thousand and the Allowance for Doubtful Accounts was $13.6 thousand.
2. The receivables turnover was 9.1 the previous year.

Instructions

(a) Prepare the assets section of the balance sheet.
(b) Calculate the receivables turnover and average collection period. Compare these results with the previous year's results and comment on any trends.

TAKING IT FURTHER   What other information should Norlandia Saga consider when analyzing its receivables turnover and average collection period?

P8–12B   Presented here is selected financial information from the 2011 financial statements of **Nike** (in U.S. millions) and **Adidas** (in euro millions):

Calculate and interpret ratios. (SO 4) AN

	Nike	Adidas
Sales	$20,862	€13,344
Allowance for doubtful accounts, Jan. 1	74	127
Allowance for doubtful accounts, Dec. 31	74	151
Accounts receivable balance (net), Jan. 1	2650	1,667
Accounts receivable balance (net), Dec. 31	3,138	1,707

Instructions

Calculate the receivables turnover and average collection period for both companies and compare the two companies. Comment on the difference in the two companies' collection experiences.

TAKING IT FURTHER   Adidas's financial statements are prepared using euros, while Nike uses U.S. dollars. How does this affect our ability to compare sales for the two companies? To compare the receivables turnover and collection period?

P8–13B   The following ratios are available for Western Roofing:

Evaluate liquidity. (SO 4) AN

	2015	2014	2013
Current ratio	1.6 to 1	2.0 to 1	1.9 to 1
Acid-test ratio	0.8 to 1	1.3 to 1	1.2 to 1
Receivables turnover	10.6 times	8.9 times	9.0 times
Inventory turnover	7.3 times	7.6 times	7.5 times

Instructions

(a) Calculate the collection period, days sales in inventory, and operating cycle for each year.
(b) Has Western Roofing's liquidity improved or weakened over the three-year period? Explain.
(c) Do changes in turnover ratios affect profitability? Explain.
(d) Do changes in turnover ratios affect cash flow? Explain.

TAKING IT FURTHER   At the beginning of 2015, the owner of Western Roofing decided to start offering customers a sales discount for early payment. The terms of credit sales were changed from n/30 to 2/10, n/30. Evaluate this decision.

Continuing Cookie Chronicle

(*Note:* This is a continuation of the Cookie Chronicle from Chapters 1 through 7.)

Natalie has been approached by one of her friends, Curtis Lesperance. Curtis runs a coffee shop where he sells specialty coffees and prepares and sells muffins and cookies. He is very anxious to buy one of Natalie's fine European mixers because he would then be able to prepare larger batches of muffins and cookies. Curtis, however, cannot afford to pay for the mixer for at least 30 days. He has asked Natalie if she would be willing to sell him the mixer on credit.

   Natalie comes to you for advice and asks the following questions.

1. Curtis has given me a set of his most recent financial statements. What calculations should I do with the data from these statements? What questions should I ask him after I have analyzed the statements? How will this information help me decide if I should extend credit to Curtis?
2. Is there another alternative to extending credit to Curtis for 30 days?
3. If, instead of extending credit to Curtis for 30 days, I have Curtis sign a promissory note and he is unable to pay at the end of the agreement term, will having that signed promissory note really make any difference?
4. I am thinking seriously about being able to have my customers use credit cards. What are some of the advantages and disadvantages of letting my customers pay by credit card? Are there differences in the types of credit cards that my customers can use?

   The following transactions occur in April and May 2014:

April	1	After much thought, Natalie sells a mixer to Curtis for $1,050 (the cost of the mixer was $553). Curtis signs a two-month, 7.5% promissory note. Curtis can repay the note at any time before the due date, with interest accruing to the date of payment.
	30	Curtis calls Natalie. He expects to pay the amount outstanding in the next week or so.
May	15	Natalie receives a cheque from Curtis in payment of his balance owing plus interest that has accrued.

Instructions

(a) Answer Natalie's questions.
(b) Prepare journal entries for the transactions that occurred in April and May.

CHAPTER 8 | BROADENING YOUR PERSPECTIVE

Financial Reporting and Analysis

Financial Reporting Problem

BYP8–1   The receivables turnover, collection period, and operating cycle for **Reitmans (Canada) Limited** were calculated in this chapter, based on the company's financial statements for the 2012 fiscal year. These financial statements are presented in Appendix A.

Instructions

(a) Calculate Reitmans' receivables turnover, collection period, and operating cycle for the 2011 fiscal year.

(b) Comment on any significant differences you observe between the ratios for 2012 (as calculated in the chapter) and 2011 (as calculated by you above).

(c) As noted earlier in the chapter, Reitmans' accounts receivable are from customers using credit cards such as MasterCard or Visa where the sales haven't been collected in cash from the credit card company prior to the year end. Are Reitmans' receivables turnover and collection period for 2012 and 2011 consistent with this information? Explain.

(d) Given that Reitmans' accounts receivable are from customers using credit cards such as MasterCard or Visa, is Reitmans at risk of having significant uncollectible accounts receivable? Explain.

Interpreting Financial Statements

BYP8–2   Shaw Communications Inc. is a diversified Canadian communications company whose core operating business is providing broadband cable television services, Internet, telecommunications services, satellite services, and programming content. Shaw reported the following information (in millions) in its financial statements for the fiscal years 2009 through 2011:

	2011	2010	2009
Operating revenues (assume all credit)	$4,741	$3,718	$3,391
Cash and cash equivalents	443	217	254
Short-term securities	0	0	199
Accounts receivable (gross)	472	215	212
Allowance for doubtful accounts	29	19	17
Inventories	97	54	52
Other current assets	279	129	58
Total current liabilities	1,131	1,019	1,377

Additional detail about Shaw's receivables includes the following:

Bad debt expense (or provision for doubtful accounts as Shaw calls it) of $33.7 (2010 − $33.7; 2009 − $19.3) is included in operating, general, and administrative expenses. Shaw writes off uncollectible accounts receivable against the allowance account based on the age of the account and payment history.

Instructions

(a) Calculate the current ratios, acid-test ratios, receivables turnover ratios, and average collection periods for fiscal 2011 and 2010. Comment on Shaw's liquidity for each of the years.

(b) Based on the information provided, calculate the amount of accounts receivable that was written off in 2011.

(c) Shaw indicates in its notes to the financial statements that it reduces the risk of uncollectible accounts by billing in advance of providing service. How does billing in advance of providing service reduce the risk of uncollectible accounts?

▶ Critical Thinking

Collaborative Learning Activity

Note to instructor: Additional instructions and material for this group activity can be found on the Instructor Resource Site and in *WileyPLUS*.

BYP8–3   In this group activity, you will prepare the year-end adjustment for bad debt expense, and finalize the financial statements, using company information given to you by your instructor. You will be required to use professional judgment to determine the amount of the adjustment and explain your rationale. Your instructor will assume the role of the company's external auditor and will judge you on the appropriateness of the amount and your rationale.

Communication Activity

BYP8–4   Toys for Big Boys sells snowmobiles, personal watercraft, ATVs, and the like. Recently, the credit manager of Toys for Big Boys retired. The sales staff threw him a big retirement party—they were glad to see him go because they felt his credit policies restricted their selling ability. The sales staff convinced management that there was no need to replace the credit manager since they could handle this responsibility in addition to their sales positions.

Management was thrilled at year end when sales doubled. However, accounts receivable quadrupled and cash flow halved. The company's average collection period increased from 30 days to 120 days.

Instructions

In a memo to management, explain the financial impact of allowing the sales staff to manage the credit function. Has the business assumed any additional credit risk? What would you recommend the company do to better manage its increasing accounts receivable?

Ethics Case

BYP8–5   The controller of Proust Company has completed draft financial statements for the year just ended and is reviewing them with the president. As part of the review, he has summarized an aging schedule showing the basis of estimating uncollectible accounts using the following percentages: 0–30 days, 5%; 31–60 days, 10%; 61–90 days, 30%; 91–120 days, 50%; and over 120 days, 80%.

The president of the company, Suzanne Bros, is nervous because the bank expects the company to sustain a growth rate for profit of at least 5% each year over the next two years—the remaining term of its bank loan. The profit growth for the past year was much more than 5% because of certain special orders with high margins, but those orders will not be repeated next year, so it will be very hard to achieve even the same profit next year, and even more difficult to grow it another 5%. It would be easier to show an increase next year if the past year's reported profit had been a little lower. President Bros recalls from her college accounting course that bad debt expense is based on certain estimates subject to judgement. She suggests that the controller increase the estimate percentages, which will increase the amount of the required bad debt expense adjustment and therefore lower profit for last year so that it will be easier to show a better growth rate next year.

Instructions

(a) Who are the stakeholders in this case?
(b) Does the president's request create an ethical dilemma for the controller?
(c) Should the controller be concerned with Proust Company's reported profit growth rate in estimating the allowance? Explain your answer.

"All About You" Activity

BYP8–6   In the "All About You" feature, you learned about interest rates charged on credit cards and some of the advantages and disadvantages of credit cards. To get the most from your credit card and to save money, you need to understand the features of your credit card and how interest is charged on credit cards.

Instructions

Go to the Financial Consumer Agency of Canada, Credit Cards at **http://www.fcac-acfc.gc.ca/eng/consumers/ creditcard/index-eng.asp** and answer the following questions:

(a) Go to the related resource, "Be Smart with Your Credit Card: 10 Tips to Help You Use Your Card Wisely." What are the 10 tips?
(b) Go to "Credit Cards: Understanding Your Rights and Responsibilities" and then go to "Understanding Your Credit Card Payment Terms." Credit cards provide interest-free loans on the purchase of goods, as long as you pay your bill in full by the end of the grace period. What is the required minimum grace period? Assume you used a credit card to purchase your textbooks on September 15, and the last date covered by your statement is October 7 and the grace period is 21 days. How many days is the interest-free period?
(c) There is no interest-free period on cash advances or balance transfers on credit cards. What is a cash advance? What is a balance transfer?
(d) Suppose you have one month left in the semester and you take a $1,000 cash advance on your credit card on April 1 to cover your living expenses until you get your first paycheque from your summer job on May 15. The interest rate on your credit card is 19%. Assuming that is the only charge on your credit card, calculate the interest you will be charged assuming you pay your bill in full on May 15. (*Hint:* Go to "How Interest Charges Are Calculated" on the website under "Credit Cards: Understanding Your Rights and Responsibilities: Understanding Your Credit Card Payment Terms.")
(e) Go to the Financial Consumer Agency of Canada's interactive tool "Credit Card Payment Calculator." (*Hint:* To find the Credit Card Payment Calculator, go to **http://www.fcac-acfc.gc.ca/eng/consumers/creditcard/ index-eng.asp** and click on "Resources," then click on "Tools and Calculators," then click on the credit card icon, and then click on the credit card payment calculator.)
   1. For option A, assume you have a credit card balance of $1,000, the interest rate is 19%, and the minimum monthly payment is $10 or 3%, whichever is greater.

2. For option B, assume the same information as in part 1, but you make an additional monthly payment of $10.

3. For option C, assume the same information as in part 1, but you make a monthly payment of $100.

For each of the options A, B, and C, calculate how long it will take to pay off the credit card, assuming there are no additional purchases made, and calculate the total amount of interest paid.

ANSWERS TO CHAPTER QUESTIONS

ANSWERS TO ACCOUNTING IN ACTION INSIGHT QUESTIONS

All About You Insight, p. 419

Q: Should you use credit cards or not?

A: Credit cards can make your life easier, as long as they are used properly. They certainly have advantages: (1) they provide interest-free loans on the purchase of goods, as long as you pay your bill in full by the end of the grace period; (2) monthly credit card statements provide detailed records of all transactions, payments, and returned merchandise; and (3) many transactions, such as Internet purchases, are difficult or impossible to carry out without a credit card.

However, credit cards also have disadvantages: (1) if you do not pay your bill in full every month, expect to pay a very high interest rate on the unpaid balance; (2) they are so easy to use that you might start buying items without thinking about whether you really need them—and can afford them; and (3) credit cards can be stolen, which might damage your credit rating.

Across the Organization Insight, p. 434

Q: What might be the advantages to Target of having its own credit card? What might be the disadvantages?

A: If customers have a Target credit card, they might be more likely to shop at Target rather than at another department store. Target can also earn interest income on any late accounts. The disadvantages might include higher administration costs to operate the credit card division and also the risk of customers defaulting on their credit card payments.

ANSWERS TO SELF-STUDY QUESTIONS

1. c   2. b   3. d   4. a   5. c   6. d   7. c   8. a   9. d   10. c   11. b   12. c

Remember to go back to the beginning of the chapter to check off your completed work!

←

LONG-LIVED ASSETS

THE **NAVIGATOR**

- ☐ Understand *Concepts for Review*
- ☐ Read *Feature Story*
- ☐ Scan *Study Objectives*
- ☐ Read *Chapter Preview*
- ☐ Read text and answer *Before You Go On*
- ☐ Review *Comparing IFRS and ASPE*
- ☐ Work *Demonstration Problems*
- ☐ Review *Summary of Study Objectives*
- ☐ Answer *Self-Study Questions*
- ☐ Complete assignment
- ☐ Go to *WileyPLUS* for practice and tutorials

CONCEPTS FOR **REVIEW**

Before studying this chapter, you should understand or, if necessary, review:

a. Expense recognition criteria (Ch. 3, pp. 114–115).

b. What depreciation is, and how to make adjustments for it. (Ch. 3, pp. 119–120).

c. Non-current assets and the classified balance sheet (Ch. 4, p. 187).

BUILDING FOR LEARNING

TORONTO, Ont.—When George Brown College in Toronto, one of the oldest colleges in Ontario, was created in 1967, its land and buildings were provided by the provincial government at nominal value. The province launched community colleges to provide vocational training for its burgeoning industries like the automotive sector and forestry. Today, however, colleges have to be much more self-sufficient when adding classrooms, labs, and other facilities.

George Brown's most recent expansion is a brand new, 380,000-square-foot (35,000-square-metre) health sciences building, the first phase of its Waterfront campus overlooking Toronto's harbour, which opened in the fall of 2012. The construction costs were estimated at about $175 million. "Out of that, there's about $92 million roughly that is funding from both the provincial and federal governments," says Controller Ric Ho. "And then we had to put in about $25 million of our own money. And we also are expected to do fundraising, up to $35 million, as part of the capital campaign." The college also expected to receive a capital contribution from Waterfront Toronto, an intergovernmental agency to develop the harbour.

How does the college determine what is a capital versus an operating expenditure and how does it account for these costs? Anything that will be used up within a fiscal year, such as office supplies, is expensed in that year. Anything that has a useful life of more than a year and is worth $5,000 or more is capitalized and depreciated. "There needs to be a threshold because we cannot capitalize every little chair or something that comes around, otherwise your capital asset list is going to be huge and doesn't serve any purpose," says Dominic Noronha, the college's Manager of Financial Services.

The college depreciates the buildings it owns using the straight-line method (partly because it's the simplest) over 40 years. While most buildings last longer than 40 years, "That's the level that's been traditionally used by other colleges," Mr. Noronha says. For space it leases, such as one floor of a building on the nearby Ryerson University campus, George Brown amortizes the leasehold improvements—considered to be assets—over the term of the lease.

Like most colleges, buildings are George Brown's most valuable long-lived assets. Its equipment and buildings have a net book value (or carrying amount) of approximately $328 million. Among its equipment are workshop benches for its programs in the trades, kitchens for its hospitality school, computers for its school of design, and costumes for its animation program. The college depreciates most equipment over five years, although its computer equipment—which can quickly become technologically obsolete—is depreciated over three years. George Brown does not recognize any intangible assets on its books. "We don't have any goodwill or intellectual property, such as patents or copyrights," says Mr. Ho.

THE **NAVIGATOR**

>> STUDY **OBJECTIVES**

After studying this chapter, you should be able to:

1. Determine the cost of property, plant, and equipment.

2. Explain and calculate depreciation.

3. Explain the factors that cause changes in periodic depreciation and calculate revisions.

4. Account for the disposal of property, plant, and equipment.

5. Calculate and record depreciation of natural resources.

6. Identify the basic accounting issues for intangible assets and goodwill.

7. Illustrate the reporting and analysis of long-lived assets.

THE **NAVIGATOR**

For organizations such as George Brown College, making the right decisions about long-lived assets is critical because these assets represent huge investments. Organizations must make decisions about what assets to acquire, how to account for them, and when to dispose of them.

In this chapter, we address these and other issues surrounding long-lived assets. Our discussions will focus on three types of long-lived assets: (1) property, plant, and equipment; (2) natural resources; and (3) intangible assets.

The chapter is organized as follows:

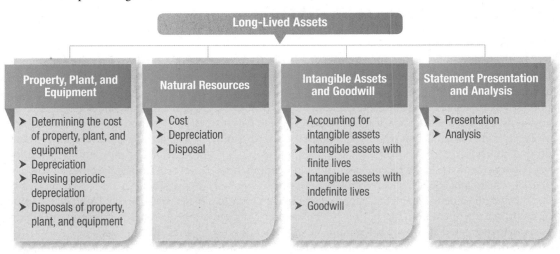

Property, Plant, and Equipment

Alternative terminology Property, plant, and equipment are also commonly known as *fixed assets*; *land, building, and equipment*; or *capital assets*.

Property, plant, and equipment are long-lived assets that the company owns and uses for the production and sale of goods or services to consumers. They have three characteristics. They (1) have a physical substance (a definite size and shape), (2) are used in the operations of the business, and (3) are not intended for sale to customers. Unlike current assets, these assets are expected to provide services to a company for a number of years.

In the following sections, we will learn more about property, plant, and equipment: determining their cost, their depreciation, and the accounting for their disposal.

DETERMINING THE COST OF PROPERTY, PLANT, AND EQUIPMENT

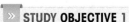

STUDY OBJECTIVE 1

Determine the cost of property, plant, and equipment.

The cost of an item of property, plant, and equipment includes the following:

1. The purchase price, plus any non-refundable taxes, less any discounts or rebates
2. The expenditures necessary to bring the asset to the required location and make it ready for its intended use

If there are obligations to dismantle, remove, or restore the asset when it is retired, an initial estimate of these costs is also included in the cost of the long-lived asset. These are known as **asset retirement costs**. Accounting for these costs can be complex and we will leave that discussion to a future accounting course. But you should be aware that the cost of some property, plant, and equipment items includes the cost of retiring the asset. For simplicity, we will assume asset retirement costs are equal to zero in the examples in this text.

Alternative terminology Asset retirement costs are also called *decommissioning costs*.

These costs are **capitalized** (recorded as property, plant, and equipment), rather than expensed, if it is probable that the company will receive an economic benefit in the future from the asset. Determining which costs to include in a long-lived asset account and which costs not to include is very important. Costs that benefit only the current period are expensed. Such costs are called **operating expenditures**. Costs that benefit future periods are included in a long-lived asset account. These costs are called **capital expenditures**.

For example, the cost to purchase equipment is recorded as a capital expenditure, because the equipment will benefit future periods. In addition, the insurance paid on the equipment as it is shipped to the company should also be capitalized because the insurance during transit benefits more than just the current period. It is considered a necessary expenditure to get the equipment to its required location and ready for use.

However, it is also important to note that companies will expense, rather than capitalize, low-cost long-lived assets. For example, George Brown College, in the feature story, capitalizes anything that has a useful life of more than a year and is worth $5,000 or more. This is an application of a concept known as materiality, which you will learn more about in Chapter 11. It allows companies to immediately record immaterial expenditures as an expense.

Subsequent to acquisition, the same distinction exists between capital and operating expenditures. For example, once the asset is in use, having an insurance policy benefits only the current period and is treated as an expense. But major expenditures that are incurred once the asset is in use that increase the life of the asset or its productivity are capitalized. We will discuss expenditures subsequent to acquisition in more depth later in the chapter.

Property, plant, and equipment are often subdivided into four classes:

1. **Land**, such as a building site
2. **Land improvements**, such as driveways, parking lots, fences, and underground sprinkler systems
3. **Buildings**, such as stores, offices, factories, and warehouses
4. **Equipment**, such as store checkout counters, cash registers, office furniture, computer equipment, factory equipment, and delivery equipment

Determining the cost of each of the major classes of property, plant, and equipment is explained in the following sections.

Land

The cost of land includes (1) the purchase price, (2) closing costs such as surveying and legal fees, and (3) the costs of preparing the land for its intended use, such as the removal of old buildings, clearing, draining, filling, and grading. All of these costs (less any proceeds from salvaged materials) are debited to the Land account.

To illustrate, assume that the Budovitch Manufacturing Company purchases real estate for $100,000 cash. The property contained an old warehouse that is removed at a net cost of $6,000 ($7,500 to remove it less $1,500 received for materials from the warehouse that were salvaged and later sold). Additional expenditures include the legal fee of $3,000. The cost of the land is $109,000, calculated as follows:

Land	
Cash price of property	$100,000
Net cost of removing warehouse ($7,500 − $1,500)	6,000
Legal fees	3,000
Cost of land	$109,000

When recording the acquisition, Land is debited for $109,000 and Cash is credited for $109,000 (assuming the costs were paid in cash). Land is a unique long-lived asset. Its cost is not depreciated—allocated over its useful life—because land has an unlimited useful life.

Land Improvements

Land improvements are structural additions made to land, such as driveways, sidewalks, fences, and parking lots. Land improvements, unlike land, decline in service potential over time, and require maintenance and replacement. Because of this, land improvements are recorded separately from land and are depreciated over their useful lives.

Many students confuse the cost to get land ready for its intended use with land improvements. They think, for example, that removing an old building or grading the land is "improving" the land, and thus incorrectly reason that these costs should be considered land improvements. When classifying costs, it is important to remember that one-time costs required for getting the land ready to use are always charged to the Land account, not the Land Improvement account.

Buildings

All costs that are directly related to the purchase or construction of a building are debited to the Buildings account. When a building is purchased, these costs include the purchase price and closing costs (such as legal fees). The costs of making a building ready to be used as intended can include expenditures for remodelling, and for replacing or repairing the roof, floors, electrical wiring, and plumbing. These costs are also debited to Buildings.

When a new building is built, its cost includes the contract price plus payments for architects' fees, building permits, and excavation costs. The interest costs of financing the construction project are also included in the asset's cost when a significant amount of time is needed to get the building ready to be used. In these circumstances, interest costs are considered to be as necessary as materials and labour are. However, only interest costs that occur during the construction period are included. After construction is finished, the company records future interest payments on funds borrowed to finance the construction as debits (increases) to Interest Expense.

Equipment

The "equipment" classification is a broad one that can include delivery equipment, office equipment, computers, machinery, vehicles, furniture and fixtures, and other similar assets. The cost of these assets includes the purchase price; freight charges and insurance during transit paid by the purchaser; and the costs of assembling, installing, and testing the equipment. These costs are treated as capital expenditures because they benefit future periods.

Annual costs such as motor vehicle licences and insurance on company trucks and cars are treated as operating expenditures because they are recurring expenditures that do not benefit future periods.

To illustrate, assume that 1 Stop Florists purchases a used delivery truck on January 1, 2014, for $24,500 cash. Related expenditures include painting and lettering, $500; a motor vehicle licence, $80; and a one-year insurance policy, $2,600. The cost of the delivery truck is $25,000, calculated as follows:

Delivery Truck	
Cash price	$24,500
Painting and lettering	500
Cost of delivery truck	$25,000

The cost of the motor vehicle licence is recorded as an expense and the cost of the insurance policy is recorded as a prepaid asset. The entry to record the purchase of the truck and related expenditures, assuming they were all paid for in cash, is as follows:

```
A    =   L   +   OE
+25,000              -80
+2,600
-27,680

↓ Cash flows: -27,680
```

Jan. 1	Vehicles	25,000	
	Licence Expense	80	
	Prepaid Insurance	2,600	
	Cash		27,680
	To record purchase of delivery truck and		
	related expenditures.		

Allocating Cost to Multiple Assets or Significant Components

Alternative terminology A basket purchase is also known as a *lump sum purchase.*

Multiple Assets. Property, plant, and equipment are often purchased together for a single price. This is known as a **basket purchase**. We need to know the cost of each individual asset in order to journalize the purchase, and later calculate the depreciation of each asset. When a basket purchase occurs, we determine individual costs by allocating the total price paid for the group of assets to each individual asset based on its relative fair value.

To illustrate, assume Sega Company purchased land, a building, and some equipment on July 31 for $400,000 cash. The land was appraised at $135,000, the building at $270,000, and the equipment at $45,000. The $400,000 cost should be allocated based on fair values (i.e., appraised values), as shown in Illustration 9-1.

Asset	Fair Value		Percent of Total Fair Value		Total Purchase Price		Cost of Each Asset
Land	$135,000	30%	($135,000 ÷ $450,000)	×	$400,000	=	$120,000
Building	270,000	60%	($270,000 ÷ $450,000)	×	$400,000	=	240,000
Equipment	45,000	10%	($ 45,000 ÷ $450,000)	×	$400,000	=	40,000
Totals	$450,000	100%					$400,000

▶ **ILLUSTRATION 9-1**
Allocating cost in a basket purchase

The journal entry to record this purchase is as follows:

July 31	Land	120,000	
	Building	240,000	
	Equipment	40,000	
	Cash		400,000
	To record purchase of land, building, and equipment with costs allocated based on appraised values of $135,000, $270,000, and $45,000, respectively.		

```
A      =   L   +   OE
+120,000
+240,000
+40,000
-400,000
```
↓ Cash flows: −400,000

Significant Components. When an item of property, plant, and equipment includes individual components that have different useful lives, the cost of the item should be allocated to each of its significant components. This allows each component to be depreciated separately over the different useful lives or possibly by using different depreciation methods. For example, an aircraft and its engine may need to be treated as separate depreciable assets if they have different useful lives.

Separating the cost of the entire asset into its significant components can be accomplished using the same process to allocate cost illustrated above for a basket purchase. The asset's total cost would be allocated to the significant components based on the components' relative fair values. The calculations would be similar to those in Illustration 9-1.

Further discussion of calculating depreciation for the different parts of an asset will be left to a later accounting course. For simplicity, we will assume in this text that all of the components of the depreciable asset have the same useful life, and we will depreciate assets as a whole.

BEFORE YOU GO ON...

Do It

Assume that factory equipment is purchased on November 6 for $10,000 cash and a $40,000 note payable. Related cash expenditures include insurance during shipping, $500; the annual insurance policy, $750; and installation and testing, $1,000. (a) What is the cost of the equipment? (b) Record these expenditures.

Solution

Factory Equipment

Purchase price	$50,000
Insurance during shipping	500
Installation and testing	1,000
Cost of equipment	$51,500

Action Plan
• Capitalize expenditures that are made to get the equipment ready for its intended use.
• Expense operating expenditures that benefit only the current period, or are recurring costs.

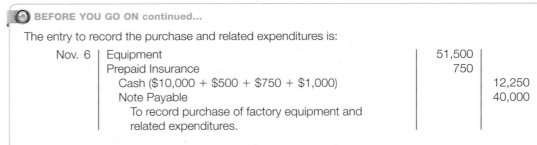

BEFORE YOU GO ON continued...

The entry to record the purchase and related expenditures is:

Nov. 6	Equipment	51,500	
	Prepaid Insurance	750	
	Cash ($10,000 + $500 + $750 + $1,000)		12,250
	Note Payable		40,000
	To record purchase of factory equipment and related expenditures.		

Related exercise material: BE9–1, BE9–2, BE9–3, BE9–4, and E9–1.

THE NAVIGATOR

DEPRECIATION

» **STUDY OBJECTIVE 2**

Explain and calculate depreciation.

ASPE

Under International Financial Reporting Standards, companies have two models they can choose between to account for their property, plant, and equipment: the cost model or the revaluation model. The cost model is the more commonly used method, and is the only model allowed under ASPE. We will cover the cost model in the following sections of the chapter and refer briefly to the revaluation model in a later section.

The **cost model** records property, plant, and equipment at cost of acquisition. After acquisition, depreciation is recorded each period and the assets are carried at cost less accumulated depreciation.

As we learned in Chapter 3, depreciation is the systematic allocation of the cost of a long-lived asset, such as property, plant, and equipment, over the asset's useful life. The cost is allocated to expense over the asset's useful life so that expenses are properly matched with the expected use of the asset.

You will recall that depreciation is recorded through an adjusting journal entry that debits Depreciation Expense and credits Accumulated Depreciation. Depreciation Expense is an operating expense on the income statement. Accumulated Depreciation appears on the balance sheet as a contra account to the related long-lived asset account. The resulting balance, cost less accumulated depreciation, is the carrying amount of the depreciable asset, as defined in Chapter 4.

Alternative terminology An asset's *carrying amount* is also called its *carrying value*, *book value*, or *net book value*.

It is important to understand that **depreciation is a process of cost allocation, not a process of determining an asset's real value.** Illustration 9-2 shows this. Under the cost model, an increase in an asset's fair value is not relevant because property, plant, and equipment are not for resale. (Fair values are only relevant if an impairment loss has occurred, which we will discuss later in the chapter.) As a result, the carrying amount of property, plant, or equipment (cost less accumulated depreciation) may be very different from its fair value.

▶ **ILLUSTRATION 9-2**

Depreciation as an allocation concept

It is also important to understand that **depreciation neither uses up nor provides cash to replace the asset**. The balance in Accumulated Depreciation only represents the total amount of the asset's cost that has been allocated to expense so far. It is not a cash fund. Cash is neither increased nor decreased by the adjusting entry to record depreciation.

During a depreciable asset's useful life, its revenue-producing ability declines because of physical factors such as wear and tear, and economic factors such as obsolescence. For example, a company may replace a truck because it is physically worn out. On the other hand, companies replace computers long before they are physically worn out because improvements in hardware and software have made the old computers obsolete.

Factors in Calculating Depreciation

In Chapter 3, we learned that depreciation expense was calculated by dividing the cost of a depreciable asset by its useful life. At that time, we assumed the asset's residual value was zero. In this chapter, we will now include a residual value when calculating depreciation. Consequently, there are now three factors that affect the calculation of depreciation:

Cost. The factors that affect the cost of a depreciable asset were explained earlier in this chapter. Remember that the cost of property, plant, and equipment includes the purchase price plus all costs necessary to get the asset ready for use. Cost includes an initial estimate of the retirement costs, if there are any.

Useful Life. **Useful life** is (a) the period of time over which an asset is expected to be available for use or (b) the number of units of production (such as machine hours) or units of output that are expected to be obtained from an asset. Useful life is an estimate based on such factors as the asset's intended use, its expected need for repair and maintenance, and how vulnerable it is to wearing out or becoming obsolete. The company's past experience with similar assets often helps in estimating the expected useful life. George Brown College, in the feature story, uses a five-year useful life for most of its equipment, but only three years for computers because computer equipment can quickly become technologically obsolete.

Residual Value. **Residual value** is the estimated amount that a company would obtain from disposing of the asset at the end of its useful life. Residual value is not depreciated, since the amount is expected to be recovered at the end of the asset's useful life.

Alternative terminology Residual value is sometimes called *salvage value*.

Illustration 9-3 summarizes these three factors in calculating depreciation.

▶ **ILLUSTRATION 9-3**
Three factors in calculating depreciation

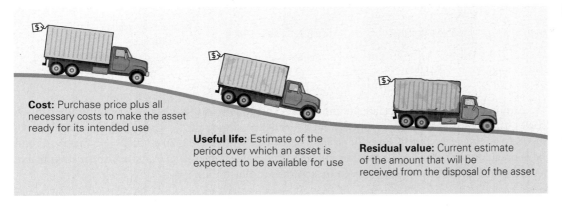

Cost: Purchase price plus all necessary costs to make the asset ready for its intended use

Useful life: Estimate of the period over which an asset is expected to be available for use

Residual value: Current estimate of the amount that will be received from the disposal of the asset

The difference between an asset's cost and its residual value is called the **depreciable amount,** which is the total amount to be depreciated over the useful life. As we learned in Chapter 3, companies reporting under ASPE may use the term "amortization" instead of "depreciation." Because of this, the depreciable amount is often called the amortizable cost.

Depreciation Methods

Depreciation is generally calculated using one of the following methods:

1. Straight-line
2. Diminishing-balance
3. Units-of-production

The straight-line method of depreciation is used by the majority of publicly traded companies. But how do companies decide which of the three depreciation methods to use? Management must choose the method that best matches the estimated pattern in which the asset's future economic benefits are expected to be consumed. The depreciation method must be reviewed at least once a year. If the expected pattern of consumption of the future economic benefits has changed, the depreciation method must be changed, and the change disclosed in the notes to the financial statements.

To learn how to calculate the three depreciation methods and to compare them, we will use the following data for the small delivery truck bought by 1 Stop Florists on January 1, 2014:

Cost (as shown earlier in the chapter)	$25,000
Estimated residual value	$2,000
Estimated useful life (in years)	5
Estimated useful life (in kilometres)	200,000

Straight-Line. The straight-line method was first defined in Chapter 3. We will define it again here, this time including the impact of a residual value on the calculation. The **straight-line method** of calculating depreciation has two steps. First, residual value is deducted from the asset's cost to determine an asset's depreciable amount. Second, the depreciable amount is divided by the asset's useful life to calculate the annual depreciation expense.

The depreciation expense will be the same for each year of the asset's useful life if the cost, the useful life, and the residual value do not change. The calculation of depreciation expense in the first year for 1 Stop Florists' delivery truck is shown in Illustration 9-4.

▶ **ILLUSTRATION 9-4**
Formula for straight-line method

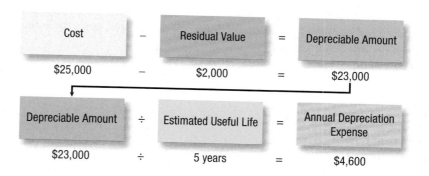

Alternatively, we can calculate an annual percentage rate to use when determining the delivery truck's straight-line depreciation expense. First, the depreciation rate is calculated by dividing 100% by the useful life in years. In this case, the straight-line depreciation rate is 20% (100% ÷ 5 years). Second, the depreciation expense is calculated by multiplying the asset's depreciable amount by the straight-line depreciation rate shown in the depreciation schedule in Illustration 9-5.

▶ **ILLUSTRATION 9-5**
Straight-line depreciation schedule

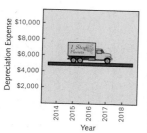

						End of Year	
Year	**Depreciable Amount**	×	**Depreciation Rate**	=	**Depreciation Expense**	**Accumulated Depreciation**	**Carrying Amount**
							$25,000
2014	$23,000		20%		$ 4,600	$ 4,600	20,400
2015	23,000		20%		4,600	9,200	15,800
2016	23,000		20%		4,600	13,800	11,200
2017	23,000		20%		4,600	18,400	6,600
2018	23,000		20%		4,600	23,000	2,000
					$23,000		

1 STOP FLORISTS
Straight-Line Depreciation Schedule

Note that the depreciation expense of $4,600 is the same each year. Also note that the column total for depreciation expense is equal to the asset's depreciable amount, and that the carrying amount at the end of the useful life is equal to the estimated $2,000 residual value.

What happens when an asset is purchased during the year, rather than on January 1 as in our example? In that case, it is necessary to **pro-rate the annual depreciation for the part of the year that the asset was used.** If 1 Stop Florists' delivery truck was ready to be used on April 1, 2014, the truck would be depreciated for nine months in 2014 (April through December). The depreciation for 2014 would be $3,450 ($23,000 × 20% × $^9/_{12}$). Note that depreciation is normally rounded to the nearest month. Since depreciation is an estimate, calculating it to the nearest day gives a false sense of accuracy.

To keep things simple, some companies establish a policy for partial-period depreciation rather than calculating depreciation monthly. Companies may choose to record a full year's depreciation in the year of acquisition and none in the year of disposal. Others may record a half year's depreciation in the year of acquisition and a half year's depreciation in the year of disposal. Whatever policy is chosen for partial-year depreciation, the impact is not significant in the long run if the policy is used consistently.

Recall that the depreciation method used must be consistent with the pattern in which the economic benefits from owning the asset are expected to be consumed. Therefore, it is appropriate to use the straight-line method when the asset is used quite uniformly throughout its useful life. Examples of assets that deliver their benefit primarily as a function of time include office furniture and fixtures, buildings, warehouses, and garages for motor vehicles. George Brown College, in the feature story, uses straight-line depreciation for its buildings.

Diminishing-Balance. The **diminishing-balance method** produces a decreasing annual depreciation expense over the asset's useful life. It is called the "diminishing-balance" method because the periodic depreciation is calculated based on the asset's carrying amount, which diminishes each year because accumulated depreciation increases. Annual depreciation expense is calculated by multiplying the carrying amount at the beginning of the year by the depreciation rate. **The depreciation rate remains constant from year to year, but the rate is applied to a carrying amount that declines each year.**

Alternative terminology The diminishing-balance method is also sometimes called the declining-balance method.

The carrying amount for the first year is the asset's cost, because the balance in Accumulated Depreciation at the beginning of the asset's useful life is zero. In the following years, the carrying amount is the difference between the cost and the accumulated depreciation at the beginning of the year. Unlike the other depreciation methods, the diminishing-balance method does not use a depreciable amount. **Residual value is not used in determining the amount that the diminishing-balance depreciation rate is applied to.** Residual value does, however, limit the total depreciation that can be taken. Depreciation stops when the asset's carrying amount equals its estimated residual value.

The diminishing-balance method can be applied using different rates, which results in varying speeds of depreciation. You will find rates such as one time (single), two times (double), and even three times (triple) the straight-line rate of depreciation. A depreciation rate that is often used is double the straight-line rate. This method is referred to as the **double diminishing-balance method.**

If 1 Stop Florists uses the double diminishing-balance method, the depreciation rate is 40% (2 × the straight-line rate of 20%). Illustration 9-6 shows the calculation of depreciation on the delivery truck for the first year.

Helpful hint The straight-line rate is determined by dividing 100% by the estimated useful life. In 1 Stop Florist's case, it is 100% ÷ 5 = 20%.

Carrying Amount at Beginning of Year	×	Straight-Line Rate × 2	=	Annual Depreciation Expense
$25,000	×	40%	=	$10,000

▶ **ILLUSTRATION 9-6**
Formula for double diminishing-balance method

The depreciation schedule under this method is given in Illustration 9-7.

When an asset is purchased during the year, it is necessary to pro-rate the diminishing-balance depreciation in the first year, based on time. For example, if 1 Stop Florists had purchased the delivery truck on April 1, 2014, the depreciation for 2014 would be $7,500 ($25,000 × 40% × $^9/_{12}$) if depreciation is calculated monthly. The carrying amount for calculating depreciation in 2015 would then become $17,500 ($25,000 − $7,500). The depreciation for 2015 would be $7,000 ($17,500 × 40%). Future calculations would follow from these amounts until the carrying amount equalled the residual value.

▸ **ILLUSTRATION 9-7**
Double diminishing-
balance depreciation schedule

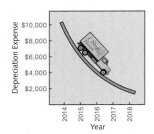

| | | | | | End of Year | |
Year	Carrying Amount Beginning Year	× Depreciation Rate	= Depreciation Expense		Accumulated Depreciation	Carrying Amount
						$25,000
2014	$25,000	40%	$10,000		$10,000	15,000
2015	15,000	40%	6,000		16,000	9,000
2016	9,000	40%	3,600		19,600	5,400
2017	5,400	40%	2,160		21,760	3,240
2018	3,240	40%	1,240*		23,000	2,000
			$23,000			

1 STOP FLORISTS
Double Diminishing-Balance Depreciation Schedule

*The calculation of $1,296 ($3,240 × 40%) is adjusted to $1,240 so that the carrying amount will equal the residual value.

Returning to Illustration 9-7, which assumes the asset was bought at the start of the year, you can see that the delivery truck is 70% depreciated ($16,000 ÷ $23,000) at the end of the second year. Under the straight-line method, it would be 40% depreciated ($9,200 ÷ $23,000) at that time. Because the diminishing-balance method produces higher depreciation expense in the early years than in the later years, it is considered an *accelerated* depreciation method. In later years its depreciation expense will be less than the straight-line depreciation expense. Regardless of the method that is used, the total amount of depreciation over the life of the delivery truck is $23,000—the depreciable amount.

Managers must choose the diminishing-balance, or another accelerated method, if the company receives more economic benefit in the early years of the asset's useful life than in the later years. That is, this method is used if the asset, for example, has higher revenue-producing ability in its early years, or if the asset is expected to become less useful over time.

Alternative terminology The units-
of-production method is often
called the *units-of-activity method*.

Units-of-Production. Useful life can be expressed in ways other than time. In the **units-of-production method**, useful life is either the estimated total units of production or total expected use from the asset, not the number of years that the asset is expected to be used. The units-of-production method is ideal for equipment whose activity can be measured in units of output, such as kilometres driven or hours in use. The units-of-production method is generally not suitable for buildings or furniture, because depreciation of these assets is more a result of time than of use.

In this method, the total units of production for the entire useful life are estimated. This amount is divided into the depreciable amount (cost − residual value) to determine the depreciable amount per unit. The depreciable amount per unit is then multiplied by the actual units of production during the year to calculate the annual depreciation expense.

To illustrate, assume that the 1 Stop Florists' delivery truck is driven 30,000 kilometres in the first year of a total estimated life of 200,000 kilometres. Illustration 9-8 shows the calculation of depreciation expense in the first year.

▸ **ILLUSTRATION 9-8**
Formula for units-of-
production method

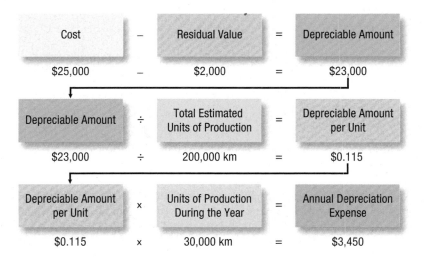

Illustration 9-9 shows the units-of-production depreciation schedule, using assumed units of production (kilometres driven) for the later years.

1 STOP FLORISTS
Units-of-Production Depreciation Schedule

| | | | | | End of Year | |
Year	Units of Production	×	Depreciable Cost/Unit	=	Depreciation Expense	Accumulated Depreciation	Carrying Amount
							$25,000
2014	30,000		$0.115		$ 3,450	$ 3,450	21,550
2015	60,000		$0.115		6,900	10,350	14,650
2016	40,000		$0.115		4,600	14,950	10,050
2017	50,000		$0.115		5,750	20,700	4,300
2018	20,000		$0.115		2,300	23,000	2,000
	200,000				$23,000		

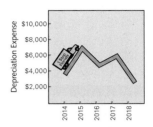

In the example in Illustration 9-9, the total actual units of production equal the original estimated total units of production of 200,000 kilometres. But in most real-life situations, the total actual units of production do not exactly equal the total estimated units of production. This means that the final year's depreciation will have to be adjusted—as we saw in the double diminishing-balance method in Illustration 9-7—so that the ending carrying amount is equal to the estimated residual value.

This method is easy to apply when assets are purchased during the year. The actual units of production already show how much the asset was used during the year. Therefore, the depreciation calculations do not need to be adjusted for partial periods as is done in the straight-line and diminishing-balance methods.

The units-of-production method is used for assets whose activity can be measured in units of output. But it can only be used if it is possible to make a reasonable estimate of total activity. Later in this chapter, we will see that this method is widely used to depreciate natural resources. The units-of-production method results in the best matching of expenses with revenues when the asset's productivity varies significantly from one period to another.

Comparison of Depreciation Methods

Illustration 9-10 presents a comparison of annual and total depreciation expense for 1 Stop Florists under each of the three depreciation methods. In addition, if we assume for simplicity that profit before deducting depreciation expense is $50,000 for each of the five years, we can clearly see the impact that the choice of method has on profit.

| | Straight-Line | | Double Diminishing-Balance | | Units-of-Production | |
Year	Depreciation Expense	Profit	Depreciation Expense	Profit	Depreciation Expense	Profit
2014	$ 4,600	$ 45,400	$10,000	$ 40,000	$ 3,450	$ 46,550
2015	4,600	45,400	6,000	44,000	6,900	43,100
2016	4,600	45,400	3,600	46,400	4,600	45,400
2017	4,600	45,400	2,160	47,840	5,750	44,250
2018	4,600	45,400	1,240	48,760	2,300	47,700
	$23,000	$227,000	$23,000	$227,000	$23,000	$227,000

Recall that straight-line depreciation results in the same amount of depreciation expense and therefore profit each year. Diminishing-balance depreciation results in a higher depreciation expense in early years, and therefore lower profit, and a lower depreciation expense and higher profit in later years. Results with the units-of-production method vary, depending on how much the asset is used each year. While the depreciation expense and profit will be different each year for each method, *total* depreciation expense and *total* profit after the five-year period are the same for all three methods.

The balance sheet is also affected by the choice of depreciation method because accumulated depreciation is increased by depreciation expense and owner's equity is increased by profit. There is no impact on cash flow because depreciation does not involve cash.

As explained earlier, management should choose the method that best matches the estimated pattern in which the asset's economic benefits are expected to be consumed. If the economic benefit of owning an asset is fairly consistent over time, the straight-line method is appropriate. The diminishing-balance method is appropriate if the company receives more economic benefit in the early years of the asset's useful life than in the later years. The units-of-production method is appropriate for assets whose usage varies over time. Because companies have more than one type of asset, they often use more than one depreciation method.

ACCOUNTING IN ACTION
BUSINESS INSIGHT

Why does **Morris Formal Wear** use the units-of-production method for its tuxedos? The reason is that the Ottawa-based family business wants to track wear and tear on each of its 5,200 tuxedos individually. Each tuxedo has its own bar code. When a tux is rented, a clerk runs its code across an electronic scanner. At year end, the computer adds up the total rentals for each of the tuxedos, then divides this number by expected total use to calculate the rate. For instance, on a two-button black tux, Morris expects a life of 30 rentals. In one year, the tux was rented 13 times. The depreciation rate for that period was 43% (13 ÷ 30) of the depreciable cost.

Is the units-of-production method the best depreciation method for Morris Formal Wear to use for its tuxedos or would you recommend another method?

Depreciation and Income Tax

The Canada Revenue Agency (CRA) allows companies to deduct a specified amount of depreciation expense when they calculate their taxable income. As we have just learned, for accounting purposes, a company must choose the depreciation method that best reflects the pattern in which the asset's future economic benefits are consumed. The CRA does not permit a choice among the three depreciation methods. Instead, it requires taxpayers to use the single diminishing-balance method on the tax return, regardless of what method is used in the financial statements.

Helpful hint Depreciation for accounting purposes is usually different from depreciation for income tax purposes.

In addition, the CRA does not allow taxpayers to estimate the useful lives of assets or depreciation rates. Assets are grouped into various classes and maximum depreciation rates for each class are specified. Depreciation allowed for income tax purposes is calculated on a class (group) basis and is called **capital cost allowance (CCA)**. Capital cost allowance is an optional deduction from taxable income, but depreciation expense is not optional in calculating profit. Consequently, you may see a company deduct depreciation on its income statement, which is required by generally accepted accounting principles, but not deduct CCA for income tax purposes.

Action Plan

- Under straight-line depreciation, annual depreciation expense is equal to the depreciable amount (cost less residual value) divided by the estimated useful life.

 BEFORE YOU GO ON...

Do It

On October 1, 2014, Iron Mountain Ski Company purchases a new snow grooming machine for $52,000. The machine is estimated to have a five-year useful life and a $4,000 residual value. It is also estimated to have a total useful life of 6,000 hours. It is used 1,000 hours in the year ended December 31, 2014, and 1,300 hours in the year ended December 31, 2015. How much depreciation expense should Iron Mountain Ski record in each of 2014 and 2015 under each depreciation method: (a) straight-line, (b) double diminishing-balance, and (c) units-of-production?

Solution

	2014	2015
Straight-line	$2,400	$ 9,600
Double diminishing-balance	5,200	18,720
Units-of-production	8,000	10,400

(a) Straight-line: ($52,000 − $4,000) ÷ 5 years = $9,600 per year
    2014: $9,600 × $^3/_{12}$ = $2,400
(b) Double diminishing-balance: 100% ÷ 5 years = 20% straight-line rate
    20% × 2 = 40% double diminishing-balance rate
    2014: $52,000 × 40% × $^3/_{12}$ = $5,200
    2015: ($52,000 − $5,200) × 40% = $18,720
(c) Units-of-production: ($52,000 − $4,000) ÷ 6,000 hours = $8.00 per hour
    2014: 1,000 × $8.00 = $8,000
    2015: 1,300 × $8.00 = $10,400

THE **NAVIGATOR**

Related exercise material: BE9–5, BE9–6, BE9–7, BE9–8, BE9–9, E9–2, E9–3, E9–4, and E9–5.

- Under double diminishing-balance depreciation, annual depreciation expense is equal to double the straight-line rate of depreciation times the asset's carrying amount at the beginning of the year. Residual values are ignored in this method.
- Under the straight-line and diminishing-balance methods, the annual depreciation expense must be pro-rated if the asset is purchased during the year.
- Under units-of-production depreciation, the depreciable amount per unit is equal to the total depreciable amount divided by the total estimated units of production. The annual depreciation expense is equal to the depreciable amount per unit times the actual usage in each year.

REVISING PERIODIC DEPRECIATION

During the useful life of a long-lived asset, the annual depreciation expense needs to be revised if there are changes to the three factors that affect the calculation of depreciation: the asset's cost, useful life, or residual value. Thus, depreciation needs to be revised if there are (1) capital expenditures during the asset's useful life, (2) impairments in the value of an asset, (3) changes in the asset's fair value when using the revaluation model, and/or (4) changes in the appropriate depreciation method, or in the asset's estimated useful life or residual value. In the following sections, we discuss each of these items and then show how to revise depreciation calculations.

» **STUDY OBJECTIVE 3**

Explain the factors that cause changes in periodic depreciation and calculate revisions.

Capital Expenditures During Useful Life

Earlier in the chapter, we learned that companies can have both operating and capital expenditures when a long-lived asset is purchased. Similarly, during the useful life of a long-lived asset, a company may incur costs for ordinary repairs, or for additions or improvements.

Ordinary repairs are costs to *maintain* the asset's operating efficiency and expected productive life. Motor tune-ups and oil changes, repainting a building, or replacing worn-out gears on equipment are examples of ordinary repairs. These costs are frequently fairly small amounts that occur regularly. They may also be larger, infrequent amounts, but if they simply restore an asset to its prior condition, they are considered an ordinary repair. Such repairs are debited to Repair (or Maintenance) Expense as they occur. Ordinary repairs are operating expenditures.

Additions and improvements are costs that are incurred to *increase* the asset's operating efficiency, productive capacity, or expected useful life. These costs are usually large and happen less often. Additions and improvements that add to the future cash flows associated with that asset are not expensed as they occur—they are capitalized. As capital expenditures, they are generally debited to the appropriate property, plant, or equipment account, or to the specific component of that asset. The capital expenditure will be depreciated over the remaining life of the original structure or the useful life of the addition. Additions and improvements can also increase the useful life of the original structure. The depreciation calculations need to be revised when a company makes an addition or improvement.

Impairments

As noted earlier in the chapter, under the cost model, the carrying amount of property, plant, and equipment is cost less any accumulated depreciation since its acquisition. And, as already discussed, the carrying amount of property, plant, and equipment is rarely the same as its fair value. Remember that the fair value is normally not relevant since property, plant, and equipment are not purchased for resale, but rather for use in operations over the long term.

While it is accepted that long-lived assets such as property, plant, and equipment may be under-valued on the balance sheet, it is not appropriate if property, plant, and equipment are overvalued. Property, plant, and equipment are considered impaired if the asset's carrying amount exceeds its **recoverable amount**. The recoverable amount is the greater of the asset's fair value less costs to sell, or the value in use, which is based on its future cash flows. When an asset is impaired, an **impairment loss** is recorded that is the amount by which the asset's carrying amount exceeds its recoverable amount. The rules for determining if an asset is impaired are somewhat different under ASPE and IFRS. While the details of these differences are left to an intermediate accounting course, it should be noted that under ASPE, impairments are recorded less often.

Companies are required to determine on a regular basis if there is any indication of impairment. If there is no such indication, it is not necessary to test the asset for impairment. If there is an indication of possible impairment, then an impairment test must be done. For example, if a machine has become obsolete, or if the market for a product made by a machine has dried up or has become very competitive, there is a strong possibility that an impairment loss exists. Management is then required to do an impairment test, which involves estimating the machine's recoverable amount.

To illustrate an impairment loss on a long-lived asset, assume that on December 31, Piniwa Company reviews its equipment for possible impairment. The equipment has a cost of $800,000 and accumulated depreciation of $200,000. The equipment's recoverable amount is currently $500,000. The amount of the impairment loss is determined by comparing the asset's carrying amount with its recoverable amount as follows:

Carrying amount ($800,000 − $200,000)	$600,000
Recoverable amount	500,000
Impairment loss	$100,000

The journal entry to record the impairment is:

A = L + OE
−100,000   −100,000

Cash flows: no effect

Dec. 31	Impairment Loss	100,000	
	Accumulated Depreciation—Equipment		100,000
	To record impairment loss on equipment.		

Assuming that the asset will continue to be used in operations, the impairment loss is reported on the income statement as part of operating profit rather than as "other expense." Often the loss is combined with depreciation expense on the income statement. The Accumulated Depreciation account, not the asset account, is credited for the impairment loss. Recording the loss this way keeps a record of the asset's original cost.

We had previously defined an asset's carrying amount as its cost less accumulated depreciation. This is still the case, but the Accumulated Depreciation account can now include more than just the depreciation recorded on the asset to date. It will also include impairment losses, if there have been any. Future depreciation calculations will need to be revised because of the reduction in the asset's carrying amount.

IFRS allow the reversal of a previously recorded impairment loss. Under IFRS, at each year end, the company must determine whether or not an impairment loss still exists by measuring the asset's recoverable amount. If this recoverable amount exceeds the current carrying amount, then a reversal is recorded. The reversal for an asset is limited to the amount required to increase the asset's carrying amount to what it would have been if the impairment loss had not been recorded. When an impairment loss is reversed, we simply credit the impairment loss account and debit the accumulated depreciation account. The reversal will result in additional revisions to depreciation calculations. As previously discussed, although impairment losses are recorded less often under ASPE, once an impairment has been recorded, it cannot be reversed later.

Cost Model Versus Revaluation Model

As previously mentioned, under IFRS, companies can choose to account for their property, plant, and equipment under either the cost model or the revaluation model. We have used the cost model in this chapter because it is used by almost all companies. Only about 3% of companies reporting under IFRS use the revaluation model. The revaluation model is allowed under IFRS mainly because it is particularly useful in countries that experience high rates of inflation or for companies in certain industries, such as investment or real estate companies, where fair values are more relevant than cost. It is not allowed under ASPE.

Under the **revaluation model**, the carrying amount of property, plant, and equipment is its fair value less any accumulated depreciation less any subsequent impairment losses. This model can be applied only to assets whose fair value can be reliably measured, and revaluations must be carried out often enough that the carrying amount is not materially different from the asset's fair value at the balance sheet date. The accounting in the revaluation model is relatively complex and will not be covered in this textbook.

Changes in Depreciation Method, Estimated Useful Life, or Residual Value

As previously explained, the depreciation method used should be consistent with the pattern in which the asset's future economic benefits are expected to be consumed by the company. The appropriateness of the depreciation method should be reviewed at least annually in case there has been a change in the expected pattern. Management must also review its estimates of the useful life and residual value of the company's depreciable assets at least at each year end. If wear and tear or obsolescence indicates that the estimates are too low or too high, estimates should be changed. If the depreciation method, estimated useful life, or residual values are changed, this will cause a revision to the depreciation calculations.

Revised Depreciation Calculations

All of the above discussed factors will result in a revision to the depreciation calculation. In each case, the revision is made for current and future years only. The revision is not made retroactively for past periods. Thus, when a change in depreciation is made, (1) there is no correction of previously recorded depreciation expense, and (2) depreciation expense for current and future years is revised. The rationale for this treatment is that the original calculation made in the past was based on the best information available at that time. The revision is based on new information that should affect only current and future periods. In addition, if past periods were often restated, users would feel less confident about financial statements.

To calculate the new annual depreciation expense, we must first calculate the asset's carrying amount at the time of the change. This is equal to the asset's original cost minus the accumulated depreciation to date, plus any capital expenditures, minus any impairment in value. We must also determine if the original depreciation method, residual value, and useful life are still appropriate. If not, we must determine which method is now appropriate, and the revised residual value and useful life.

To illustrate how to revise depreciation, assume that 1 Stop Florists decides on December 31, 2017—before recording its depreciation for 2017—to extend the estimated useful life of its truck by one more year (to December 31, 2019) because of its good condition. As a result of using the truck an extra year, the estimated residual value is expected to decline from its original estimate of $2,000 to $700. Assume that the company has been using straight-line depreciation and determines this is still the appropriate method. Recall that the truck was purchased on January 1, 2014, for $25,000 and originally had an estimated useful life of five years, with annual depreciation expense of $4,600.

The carrying amount at December 31, 2017—before recording depreciation for 2017—is $11,200 [$25,000 − (3 × $4,600)]. This is also the amount shown in Illustration 9-5 as the carrying amount at December 31, 2016. The remaining useful life of three years is calculated by taking the original useful life of five years, subtracting the three years where depreciation has already been recorded, and adding the additional estimated years of useful life—in this case one year. The new annual depreciation is $3,500, calculated as in Illustration 9-11.

▶ILLUSTRATION 9-11
Formula for revised straight-line depreciation

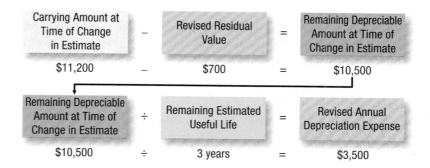

As a result of the revision to the truck's estimated useful life and residual value, 1 Stop Florists will record depreciation expense of $3,500 on December 31 of 2017, 2018, and 2019. The company will not go back and change the depreciation for 2014, 2015, and 2016. Accumulated depreciation will now equal $24,300 [($4,600 × 3) + ($3,500 × 3)] at the end of the six-year useful life instead of the $23,000 that was originally calculated. The $1,300 increase in accumulated depreciation is because the estimated residual value was revised and decreased by $1,300 ($2,000 − $700).

If the units-of-production depreciation method is used, the calculation is the same as we just saw except that the remaining useful life is expressed as units rather than years. If the diminishing-balance method is used, the revised rate would be applied to the carrying amount at the time of the change in estimate. The rate must be revised because the useful life has changed.

BEFORE YOU GO ON...

Do It

Action Plan
- Understand the difference between an operating expenditure (benefits only the current period) and a capital expenditure (benefits future periods).
- To revise annual depreciation, calculate the carrying amount (cost less accumulated depreciation) at the revision date. Note that the cost of any capital expenditure will increase the carrying amount of the asset to be depreciated.

On August 1, 1999, just after its year end, Fine Furniture Company purchased a building for $500,000. The company used straight-line depreciation to allocate the cost of this building, estimating a residual value of $50,000 and a useful life of 30 years. After 15 years of use, on August 1, 2014, the company was forced to replace the entire roof at a cost of $25,000 cash. The residual value was expected to remain at $50,000 but the total useful life was now expected to increase to 40 years. Prepare journal entries to record (a) depreciation for the year ended July 31, 2014; (b) the cost of the addition on August 1, 2014; and (c) depreciation for the year ended July 31, 2015.

Solution

(a)

July 31, 2014	Depreciation Expense [($500,000 − $50,000) ÷ 30]	15,000	
	Accumulated Depreciation—Building		15,000
	To record annual depreciation expense.		

(b)

Aug. 1, 2014	Building	25,000	
	Cash		25,000
	To record replacement of roof.		

(c) Cost: $500,000
    Less: Accumulated depreciation $15,000 per year × 15 years   225,000
    Carrying amount before replacement of roof, August 1, 2014   275,000
    Add: Capital expenditure (roof)   25,000
    Carrying amount after replacement of roof, August 1, 2014   300,000
    Less: Revised residual value   50,000
    Remaining depreciable amount   250,000
    Divide by: Remaining useful life (40 − 15)   ÷ 25 years
    Revised annual depreciation $ 10,000

July 31, 2015	Depreciation Expense	10,000	
	Accumulated Depreciation—Building		10,000
	To record revised annual depreciation expense.		

Related exercise material: BE9–10, BE9–11, E9–6, E9–7, and E9–8.

- Subtract any revised residual value from the carrying amount at the time of the change in estimate (plus the capital expenditure in this case) to determine the remaining depreciable amount.
- Allocate the revised depreciable amount over the remaining (not total) useful life.

THE NAVIGATOR

DISPOSALS OF PROPERTY, PLANT, AND EQUIPMENT

Companies dispose of property, plant, or equipment that is no longer useful to them. Illustration 9-12 shows three methods of disposal.

» **STUDY OBJECTIVE 4**

Account for the disposal of property, plant, and equipment.

Retirement

Equipment is scrapped or discarded.

Sale

Equipment is sold.

Exchange

Existing equipment is traded for new equipment.

▶ **ILLUSTRATION 9-12**
Methods of property, plant, and equipment disposal

Steps in Recording Disposals of Property, Plant, and Equipment

Whatever the disposal method, a company must take the following four steps to record the retirement, sale, or exchange of the property, plant, or equipment:

Alternative terminology Derecognition is a term used under IFRS to describe the removal of a long-lived asset from the accounts when it is disposed of or no longer provides any future benefit.

Step 1: Update Depreciation.

Depreciation must be recorded over the entire period of time an asset is available for use. Therefore, if the disposal occurs in the middle of an accounting period, depreciation must be updated for the fraction of the year since the last time adjusting entries were recorded up to the date of disposal.

Step 2: Calculate the Carrying Amount.

Calculate the carrying amount at the date of disposal after updating the accumulated depreciation for any partial year depreciation calculated in Step 1 above:

Step 3: Calculate the Gain or Loss.

Determine the amount of the gain or loss on disposal, if any, by comparing the proceeds received from the disposal with the carrying amount at the date of disposal.

If the proceeds of the sale are more than the carrying amount of the property, plant, or equipment, there is a gain on disposal. If the proceeds of the sale are less than the carrying amount of the asset sold, there is a loss on disposal.

Step 4: Record the Disposal.

The journal entry to record the disposal always involves removing the asset's cost and the accumulated depreciation from the accounts. These are the same amounts used to calculate the carrying amount in Step 2 above. The journal entry may also include recording the proceeds and the gain or loss on disposal if there are any proceeds and if there is a gain or loss. Gains on disposal are recorded as credits because credits increase owner's equity; losses on disposal are recorded as debits because debits decrease owner's equity.

> Dr. Cash (or other account)
> Dr. Accumulated Depreciation
> Dr. Loss on Disposal OR Cr. Gain on Disposal
>   Cr. Property, plant, or equipment account

Gains and losses are reported in the operating section of a multiple-step income statement. Why? Recall that depreciation expense is an estimate. A loss results when the annual depreciation expense has not been high enough so that the carrying amount at the date of disposal is equal to the proceeds. Gains are caused because annual depreciation expense has been too high, so the carrying amount at the date of disposal is less than the proceeds. Thus gains and losses are basically just adjustments to depreciation expense and should be recorded in the same section of the income statement.

Retirement of Property, Plant, and Equipment

Instead of being sold or exchanged, some assets are simply retired at the end of their useful lives. For example, some productive assets used in manufacturing may have highly specialized uses and consequently have no market when the company no longer needs the asset. In this case, the asset is simply retired.

When an asset is retired, there are no proceeds on disposal. The Accumulated Depreciation account is decreased (debited) for the full amount of depreciation taken over the life of the asset. The asset account is reduced (credited) for the asset's original cost. Even if the carrying amount equals zero, a journal entry is still required to remove the asset and its related depreciation account from the books, as shown in the following example.

To illustrate the retirement of a piece of property, plant, and equipment, assume that on December 31, 2014, Baseyev Enterprises retires equipment, which cost $31,200. At the time of purchase, on January 1, 2011, the equipment was expected to have a four-year useful life and no residual value. Baseyev used straight-line depreciation and the annual depreciation expense was $7,800 per year ($31,200 ÷ 4). The balance in the Accumulated Depreciation account at Baseyev's year end, December 31, 2013, was $23,400 ($7,800 × 3). Before recording the disposal, Baseyev must first record depreciation from the last time it was recorded—December 31, 2013—to the date of disposal—December 31, 2014. As this is one year, the amount to be recorded is $7,800, as shown in the following journal entry:

A	=	L	+	OE				
−7,800				−7,800				

Cash flows: no effect

2014	Depreciation Expense	7,800	
Dec. 31	Accumulated Depreciation—Equipment		7,800
	To record depreciation expense from last time it was recorded to date of disposal.		

After this journal entry is posted, the Equipment and Accumulated Depreciation accounts appear as follows:

Equipment				Accumulated Depreciation—Equipment	
Jan. 1, 2011	31,200			Dec. 31, 2011	7,800
				Dec. 31, 2012	7,800
				Dec. 31, 2013	7,800
				Balance	23,400
				Dec. 31, 2014	7,800
				Balance	31,200

The equipment is now fully depreciated with a carrying amount of zero (cost of $31,200 − accumulated depreciation of $31,200). As the equipment is being retired, there are zero proceeds, and since the carrying amount is equal to the proceeds and there is no gain or loss on disposal. All that is required is an entry to remove the cost and accumulated depreciation of the equipment, as follows:

2014	Accumulated Depreciation—Equipment	31,200	
Dec. 31	Equipment		31,200
	To record retirement of fully depreciated equipment.		

A = L + OE
+31,200
−31,200
Cash flows: no effect

After this entry is posted, the balance in the Equipment and Accumulated Depreciation—Equipment accounts will be zero.

What happens if a company is still using a fully depreciated asset? In this case, the asset and its accumulated depreciation continue to be reported on the balance sheet, without further depreciation, until the asset is retired. Reporting the asset and related depreciation on the balance sheet informs the reader of the financial statements that the asset is still being used by the company. Once an asset is fully depreciated, even if it is still being used, no additional depreciation should be taken. Accumulated depreciation on a piece of property, plant, and equipment can never be more than the asset's cost.

If a piece of property, plant, and equipment is retired before it is fully depreciated and no residual value is received, a loss on disposal occurs. Assume that Baseyev Enterprises retires its equipment on January 1, 2014. The loss on disposal is calculated by subtracting the asset's carrying amount from the proceeds that are received. In this case, there are no proceeds and the carrying amount is $7,800 (cost of $31,200 − accumulated depreciation of $23,400), resulting in a loss of $7,800:

Proceeds	−	Carrying amount	=	Gain (Loss)
$0	−	$7,800	=	$(7,800)
		($31,200 − $23,400)		

The entry to record the retirement of equipment is as follows:

Jan. 1	Accumulated Depreciation—Equipment	23,400	
	Loss on Disposal	7,800	
	Equipment		31,200
	To record retirement of equipment at a loss.		

A = L + OE
+23,400   −7,800
−31,200
Cash flows: no effect

You should also note that there will never be a gain when an asset is retired. The proceeds are always zero and therefore can never be greater than the carrying amount of the retired asset.

Sale of Property, Plant, and Equipment

In a disposal by sale, there are proceeds that must be recorded. Both gains and losses on disposal are common when an asset is sold. Only by coincidence will the asset's carrying amount and fair value (the proceeds) be the same when the asset is sold. We will illustrate the sale of furniture at both a gain and a loss in the following sections.

Gain on Disposal. To illustrate a gain, assume that on April 1, 2014, Baseyev Enterprises sells office furniture for $15,000 cash. The office furniture had originally been purchased on January 1, 2010, at a cost of $60,200. At that time, it was estimated that the furniture would have a residual value of $5,000 and a useful life of five years.

The first step is to update any unrecorded depreciation. Annual depreciation using the straight-line method is $11,040 [($60,200 − $5,000) ÷ 5]. The entry to record the depreciation expense and update accumulated depreciation for the first three months of 2014 is as follows:

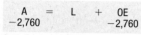

A	=	L	+	OE
−2,760				−2,760

Cash flows: no effect

2014
Apr. 1
	Depreciation Expense ($11,040 × 3/12)
	    Accumulated Depreciation—Furniture
	    To record depreciation expense for the first 3 months
	    of 2014.
		2,760	2,760

After this journal entry is posted, the Furniture and Accumulated Depreciation accounts appear as follows:

Furniture	
Jan. 1, 2010 60,200	

Accumulated Depreciation—Furniture	
	Dec. 31, 2010 11,040
	Dec. 31, 2011 11,040
	Dec. 31, 2012 11,040
	Dec. 31, 2013 11,040
	Apr. 1, 2014 2,760
	Balance 46,920

The second step is to calculate the carrying amount on April 1, 2014. Note that the balance in Accumulated Depreciation of $46,920 is equal to four years (January 1, 2010, to December 31, 2013) at $11,040/year plus $2,760 for 2014.

Cost	−	Accumulated Depreciation	=	Carrying Amount
$60,200	−	$46,920	=	$13,280

The third step is to calculate the gain or loss on disposal. A $1,720 gain on disposal is determined as follows:

Proceeds	−	Carrying Amount	=	Gain (Loss)
$15,000	−	$13,280	=	$1,720

The fourth step is the entry to record the sale of the office furniture as follows:

Apr. 1	Cash	15,000	
	Accumulated Depreciation—Furniture	46,920	
	Gain on Disposal		1,720
	Furniture		60,200
	To record the sale of office furniture at a gain.		

A = L + OE
+15,000   +1,720
+46,920
−60,200

↑ Cash flows: +15,000

Notice that the carrying amount of $13,280 does not appear in the journal entry. Instead, the asset's cost ($60,200) and the total accumulated depreciation ($46,920) are used. **Remember the carrying amount is simply a number calculated to determine the gain or loss.** It is not an account and cannot be debited or credited.

Loss on Disposal. Assume that instead of selling the furniture for $15,000, Baseyev sells it for $9,000. In this case, a loss of $4,280 is calculated as follows:

Proceeds	−	Carrying Amount	=	Gain (Loss)
$9,000	−	$13,280	=	$(4,280)

The entry to record the sale of the office furniture is as follows:

Apr. 1	Cash	9,000	
	Accumulated Depreciation—Furniture	46,920	
	Loss on Disposal	4,280	
	Furniture		60,200
	To record the sale of office furniture at a loss.		

A = L + OE
+9,000   −4,280
+46,920
−60,200

↑ Cash flows: +9,000

As previously explained, the loss on disposal is the result of not recording enough depreciation expense prior to selling the asset.

Exchanges of Property, Plant, and Equipment

An exchange of assets is recorded as the purchase of a new asset and the sale of an old asset. Typically a **trade-in allowance** on the old asset is given toward the purchase price of the new asset. An additional cash payment is usually also required for the difference between the trade-in allowance and the stated purchase price (list price) of the new asset. The trade-in allowance amount, however, is often affected by price concessions for the new asset and therefore rarely reflects the fair value of the asset that is given up. Consequently, as fair value is what matters, trade-in allowances are ignored for accounting purposes.

Instead of using the stated purchase price, the new asset is recorded at the fair value of the asset given up plus any cash paid (or less any cash received). Instead of using the trade-in allowance, the fair value of the asset given up is used to calculate the gain or loss on the asset being given up. A loss results if the carrying amount of the asset being given up is more than its fair value. A gain results if the carrying amount is less than its fair value.

Thus, the procedure to account for exchanges of assets is as follows:

Step 1: Update any unrecorded depreciation expense on the asset being given up to the date of the exchange.
Step 2: Calculate the carrying amount of the asset being given up (cost − accumulated depreciation).

Step 3: Calculate any gain or loss on disposal [fair value − carrying amount = gain (loss)].
Step 4: Record the exchange as follows:
- Remove the cost and the accumulated depreciation of the asset that is given up.
- Record any gain or loss on disposal.
- Record the new asset at the fair value of the old asset plus any cash paid (or less any cash received).
- Record the cash paid or received.

To illustrate an exchange of long-lived assets, assume that Chilko Company exchanged an old vehicle for a new vehicle on October 1, 2014. The original cost of the old vehicle was $61,000 on January 1, 2009. Depreciation was calculated using the straight-line method, over a six-year useful life, with an estimated residual value of $1,000. The fair value of the old vehicle on October 1, 2014, is $3,000.

The list price of the new vehicle was $51,000. Chilko received an $8,000 trade-in allowance from the vehicle dealership for the old vehicle and paid $43,000 cash ($51,000 − $8,000) for the new vehicle. Chilko's year end is December 31.

The first step is to update the depreciation on the old vehicle for the nine months ended October 1, 2014. Annual depreciation expense is $10,000 [($61,000 − $1,000) ÷ 6], so depreciation for nine months is $7,500 ($10,000 × $^9/_{12}$).

A	=	L	+	OE			
−7,500				−7,500			

Cash flows: no effect

Oct. 1	Depreciation Expense		7,500	
	Accumulated Depreciation—Vehicles			7,500
	To record depreciation expense for the first 9 months of 2014.			

After this journal entry is posted, the Vehicles and Accumulated Depreciation accounts appear as follows:

Vehicles	
Jan. 1, 2009 61,000	

Accumulated Depreciation—Vehicles	
	Dec. 31, 2009 10,000
	Dec. 31, 2010 10,000
	Dec. 31, 2011 10,000
	Dec. 31, 2012 10,000
	Dec. 31, 2013 10,000
	Oct. 1, 2014 7,500
	Balance 57,500

The next step is to calculate the carrying amount on October 1, 2014. Note that the balance in Accumulated Depreciation of $57,500 is equal to five years (January 1, 2009, to December 31, 2013) at $10,000/year plus $7,500 for 2014.

On October 1, 2014, the carrying amount is $3,500 (cost of $61,000 − accumulated depreciation of $57,500). The loss on disposal on the old vehicle is determined by comparing the carrying amount with the fair value, which represents the proceeds in this situation:

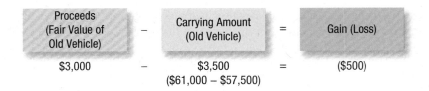

Proceeds (Fair Value of Old Vehicle)	−	Carrying Amount (Old Vehicle)	=	Gain (Loss)
$3,000	−	$3,500 ($61,000 − $57,500)	=	($500)

The cost of the new vehicle ($46,000) is determined by the fair value of the old vehicle ($3,000) plus the cash paid ($43,000). The entry to record the exchange of vehicles is as follows:

Oct. 1	Vehicles (cost of new vehicle)	46,000	
	Accumulated Depreciation—Vehicles (on the old vehicle)	57,500	
	Loss on Disposal	500	
	Vehicles (cost of old vehicle)		61,000
	Cash		43,000
	To record exchange of vehicles, plus cash.		

A	=	L	+	OE
+46,000				−500
+57,500				
−61,000				
−43,000				

Note that the exchange of vehicles is not netted. That is, it is shown as a separate increase and decrease to the general ledger account Vehicles. Also note that the list price of $51,000 and the trade-in allowance of $8,000 are ignored in determining the real cost of the new vehicle.

In some situations, the exchange lacks commercial substance or else the fair value of the asset acquired or the asset given up cannot be determined. In such cases, the new long-lived asset is recorded at the carrying amount of the old asset that was given up, plus any cash paid (or less any cash received). Carrying amount is used in these circumstances because the new asset is basically substituted or swapped for the old asset. As the carrying amount of the old asset is used for the carrying amount of the new asset, and the exchange has therefore not changed the operations of the business significantly, no gain or loss is recorded.

 BEFORE YOU GO ON...

Do It

Overland Trucking has a truck that was purchased on January 1, 2010, for $80,000. The truck had been depreciated on a straight-line basis with an estimated residual value of $5,000 and an estimated useful life of five years. Overland has a December 31 year end. Assume each of the following four independent situations:

1. On January 1, 2015, Overland retires the truck.
2. On May 1, 2014, Overland sells the truck for $9,500 cash.
3. On October 1, 2014, Overland sells the truck for $9,500 cash.
4. On November 1, 2014, Overland exchanges the old truck, plus $60,000 cash, for a new truck. The old truck has a fair value of $9,500. The new truck has a list price of $70,000, but the dealer will give Overland a $10,000 trade-in allowance on the old truck.

Prepare the journal entry to record each of these situations.

Action Plan
- Update any unrecorded depreciation for dispositions during the fiscal year.
- Compare the proceeds with the asset's carrying amount to determine if there has been a gain or loss.
- Record any proceeds received and any gain or loss. Remove both the asset and any related accumulated depreciation from the accounts.
- Determine the cash paid in an exchange situation as the difference between the list price and the trade-in allowance.
- Record the cost of the new asset in an exchange situation as the fair value of the asset given up, plus the cash paid.

Solution

$$\frac{\$80,000 - \$5,000}{5 \text{ years}} = \$15,000 \text{ annual depreciation expense}$$

$$\$15,000 \div 12 = \$1,250 \text{ per month}$$

1. Retirement of truck:

Jan. 1, 2015	Accumulated Depreciation—Vehicles ($1,250 × 60 months)	75,000	
	Loss on Disposal [$0 − ($80,000 − $75,000)]	5,000	
	Vehicles		80,000
	To record retirement of truck.		

2. Sale of truck for $9,500 on May 1, 2014:

May 1, 2014	Depreciation Expense ($1,250 × 4 months)	5,000	
	Accumulated Depreciation—Vehicles		5,000
	To record depreciation for 4 months.		
	Cash	9,500	
	Accumulated Depreciation—Vehicles ($1,250 × 52 months)	65,000	
	Loss on Disposal [$9,500 − ($80,000 − $65,000)]	5,500	
	Vehicles		80,000
	To record sale of truck at a loss.		

BEFORE YOU GO ON continued...

3. Sale of truck for $9,500 on Oct. 1, 2014:

Oct. 1, 2014	Depreciation Expense ($1,250 × 9 months)	11,250	
	Accumulated Depreciation—Vehicles		11,250
	To record depreciation for 9 months.		
	Cash	9,500	
	Accumulated Depreciation—Vehicles		
	($1,250 × 57 months)	71,250	
	Gain on Disposal [$9,500 − ($80,000 − $71,250)]		750
	Vehicles		80,000
	To record sale of truck at a gain.		

4. Exchange of truck on Nov. 1, 2014:

Nov. 1, 2014	Depreciation Expense ($1,250 × 10 months)	12,500	
	Accumulated Depreciation—Vehicles		12,500
	To record depreciation for 10 months.		
	Vehicles (cost of new) ($9,500 + $60,000)	69,500	
	Accumulated Depreciation—Vehicles		
	($1,250 × 58 months)	72,500	
	Gain on Disposal [$9,500 − ($80,000 − $72,500)]		2,000
	Vehicles (cost of old)		80,000
	Cash ($70,000 − $10,000)		60,000
	To record exchange of trucks, plus cash.		

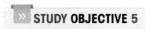

THE **NAVIGATOR**

Related exercise material: BE9–12, BE9–13, BE9–14, E9–9, and E9–10.

Natural Resources

» STUDY **OBJECTIVE 5**

Calculate and record depreciation of natural resources.

Natural resources consist of standing timber and underground deposits of oil, gas, and minerals. Canada is rich in natural resources, ranging from the towering rainforests in coastal British Columbia to one of the world's largest nickel deposits in Voisey's Bay, Labrador. These long-lived assets have two characteristics that make them different from other long-lived assets: (1) they are physically extracted in operations such as mining, cutting, or pumping; and (2) only an act of nature can replace them. Because of these characteristics, natural resources are sometimes called *wasting assets.*

Natural resources are tangible assets, similar to property, plant, and equipment. A key distinction between natural resources and property, plant, and equipment is that natural resources physically lose substance, or deplete, as they are used. For example, there is less of a tract of timberland (a natural resource) as the timber is cut and sold. When we use equipment, its physical substance remains the same regardless of the product it produces.

COST

The cost of a natural resource is determined in the same way as the cost of property, plant, and equipment and includes all expenditures necessary in acquiring the resource and preparing it for its intended use. These costs are often referred to as acquisition, exploration, and development costs. The cost of a natural resource also includes the estimated future removal and site restoration cleanup costs, which are often large. Restoration costs are usually required in order to return the resource as closely as possible to its natural state at the end of its useful life.

As discussed earlier in the chapter, accounting for asset retirement costs and the allocation of these costs over the useful life of the natural resource is complicated. Further discussion of these concepts is left to an intermediate accounting course. Accounting for exploration and development costs is also very complex. We will, however, look at how the acquisition cost of a natural resource is allocated over its useful life in the next section.

DEPRECIATION

The units-of-production method (learned earlier in the chapter) is generally used to calculate the depreciation of wasting assets. Under the units-of-production method, the total cost of the natural resource minus its residual value is divided by the number of units estimated to be in the resource. The result is a depreciable amount per unit of product. The depreciable amount per unit is then multiplied by the number of units extracted, to determine the annual depreciation expense.

Alternative terminology Depreciation for natural resources is frequently called *depletion* because the assets physically deplete as the resource is extracted.

To illustrate, assume that Rabbit Lake Company invests $5.5 million in a mine that is estimated to have 10 million tonnes (t) of uranium and a $200,000 residual value. In the first year, 800,000 tonnes of uranium are extracted. Illustration 9-13 shows the formulas and calculations.

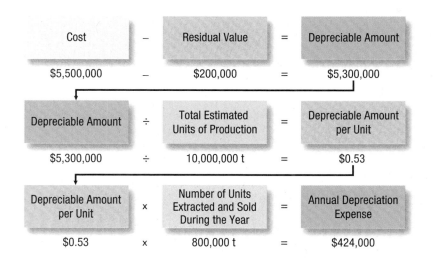

▶ **ILLUSTRATION 9-13**
Formula for units-of-production method for natural resources

The depreciation expense for the amount of the resource that has been extracted is initially charged (debited) to an inventory account, a current asset. Note that this is not the same as depreciation for property, plant, and equipment, which is recorded as an expense. Depreciation on natural resources is accounted for in this way because the resource extracted is available for sale—similar to merchandise that has been purchased or manufactured for sale, as we learned in Chapter 5.

The entry to record depreciation of the uranium mine for Rabbit Lake Company's first year of operation, ended December 31, 2014, is as follows:

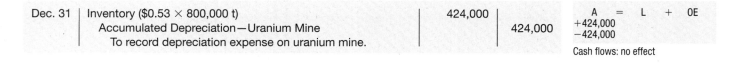

Dec. 31	Inventory ($0.53 × 800,000 t)	424,000	
	Accumulated Depreciation—Uranium Mine		424,000
	To record depreciation expense on uranium mine.		

A   =   L   +   OE
+424,000
−424,000

Cash flows: no effect

All costs of extracting the natural resource—both current production costs such as labour and depreciation of the natural resource—are recorded as inventory. When sold, the inventory costs are transferred to cost of goods sold and matched with the period's revenue. In other words, the depreciation is charged to the income statement only in the period in which the related goods are sold. Depreciation related to goods not yet sold remains in inventory and is reported as a current asset.

For example, assume that Rabbit Lake Company does not sell all of the 800,000 tonnes of uranium extracted in 2014. It sells 700,000 tonnes and stores 100,000 tonnes for later sale. In this situation, Rabbit Lake Company would include $371,000 (700,000 × $0.53) in the cost of the resource sold on its income statement. As mentioned before, the cost of labour and other production costs related to the goods sold would also be included in the cost of the resource sold on the income statement. The remaining depreciation of $53,000 ($424,000 − $371,000) is for the 100,000 tonnes kept for later sale and will be included in inventory in the current assets section of the company's balance sheet.

Like depreciation for property, plant, and equipment, the depreciation of a natural resource needs to be revised if there are capital expenditures during the useful life. Also, the depreciable amount per unit of a natural resource needs to be revised whenever the estimated total units of the resource have changed as a result of new information. Natural resources such as oil and gas deposits and some metals have provided the greatest challenges. Estimates of the total units (also called reserves) of these natural resources are mostly knowledgeable guesses and may be revised whenever more information becomes available.

Natural resources must also be reviewed and tested for impairment annually or more frequently whenever circumstances make this appropriate. For example, Rabbit Lake Company would need to test the uranium mine for impairment if there was a significant and permanent decline in the selling price of uranium. If there is impairment, the uranium mine must be written down to its fair value, an impairment loss must be recorded, and current and future depreciation needs to be revised accordingly.

DISPOSAL

At disposal, just as with property, plant, and equipment, any unrecorded depreciation of natural resources must be updated for the portion of the year up to the date of the disposal. Then proceeds are recorded, the cost and the accumulated depreciation of the natural resource are removed, and a gain or loss, if any, is recorded. As mentioned earlier, there may also be site restoration costs at this time, but we leave the accounting for these costs to a future accounting course.

Action Plan

- Use units-of-production depreciation for natural resources.
- Calculate the depreciable amount per unit by dividing the total cost minus the estimated residual value by the total estimated units.
- Multiply the depreciable amount per unit by the number of units cut to determine the total depreciation.
- Allocate the depreciation related to the units that have been cut but not yet sold to inventory.
- Allocate the depreciation related to the units that have been cut and sold to expense.

 BEFORE YOU GO ON...

Do It

High Timber Company invests $14 million in a tract of timber land. It is estimated to have 10 million cunits (1 cunit = 100 cubic feet) of timber and a $500,000 residual value. In the first year, 40,000 cunits of timber are cut, and 30,000 of these cunits are sold. Calculate depreciation for High Timber's first year of operations and allocate it between inventory and cost of goods sold.

Solution

1. Depreciable amount per unit: ($14,000,000 − 500,000) ÷ 10,000,000 cunits = $1.35 per cunit
2. Total depreciation for the year: $1.35 per cunit × 40,000 cunits cut = $54,000
3. Depreciation allocated to inventory: $1.35 per cunit × 10,000 cunits on hand = $13,500
4. Depreciation allocated to expense: $1.35 per cunit × 30,000 cunits sold = $40,500

Related exercise material: BE9–15 and E9–11.

THE NAVIGATOR

Intangible Assets and Goodwill

» **STUDY OBJECTIVE 6**

Identify the basic accounting issues for intangible assets and goodwill.

Similar to property, plant, and equipment, and natural resources, intangible assets provide economic benefits in future periods. They are used to produce products or provide services over these periods and are not intended for sale to customers. However, unlike property, plant, and equipment, and natural resources, which are **tangible assets** because they have a physical substance, **intangible assets** involve rights, privileges, and competitive advantages that have no physical substance. In other words, they are not physical things. Many companies' most valuable assets are intangible. Some widely known intangibles are Alexander Graham Bell's patent on the telephone, the franchises of Tim Hortons, the trade name of President's Choice, and the trademark CBC. On the other hand, some organizations, such as George Brown College in the feature story, do not have intangible assets or goodwill.

An intangible asset must be identifiable, which means it must meet one of the two following criteria: (1) it can be separated from the company and sold, whether or not the company intends to do so, or

(2) it is based on contractual or legal rights, regardless of whether or not it can be separated from the company. Since goodwill cannot be separated from a company and sold, there are differences in the accounting for goodwill versus other intangible assets.

ACCOUNTING FOR INTANGIBLE ASSETS

Like tangible assets (property, plant, and equipment, and natural resources), intangible assets are recorded at cost. Cost includes all the costs of acquisition and other costs that are needed to make the intangible asset ready for its intended use—including legal fees and similar charges.

As with tangible assets, companies have a choice of following the cost model or the revaluation model when accounting for intangible assets subsequent to acquisition. The majority of companies use the cost model for all long-lived assets. So we will leave further study of the revaluation model, as it applies to intangible assets, for a later accounting course.

Under the cost model, if an intangible asset has a finite (limited) life, its cost must be systematically allocated over its useful life. We called this "depreciation" when discussing tangible assets. With intangible assets, we use the term **amortization**.

For an intangible asset with a finite life, its **amortizable amount** (cost less residual value) should be allocated over the shorter of the (1) estimated useful life and (2) legal life. Intangible assets, by their nature, rarely have any residual value, so the amortizable amount is normally equal to the cost. In addition, the useful life of an intangible asset is usually shorter than its legal life, so useful life is most often used as the amortization period.

When a company estimates the useful life of an intangible asset, it must consider factors such as how long the company expects to use the asset, obsolescence, demand, and other factors that can make the intangible asset ineffective at helping to earn revenue. For example, a patent on a computer chip may have a legal life of 20 years, but with technology changing as rapidly as it does, the chip's useful life may be only four or five years maximum.

Amortization begins as soon as the asset is ready to be used as intended by management. Similar to depreciation, the company must use the amortization method that best matches the pattern with which the asset's future economic benefits are expected to be consumed. If that pattern cannot be determined reliably, the straight-line method should be used.

Just as land is considered to have an indefinite life, there are also intangible assets with an indefinite life. An intangible asset is considered to have an indefinite (unlimited) life when, based on an analysis of all of the relevant factors, there is no foreseeable limit to the period over which the intangible asset is expected to generate net cash inflows for the company. If an intangible has an indefinite life, it is not amortized.

As with tangible assets, companies must determine if there are indicators of impairment on intangible assets' definite lives. If there are indicators, an impairment test is performed. Under IFRS, intangible assets with indefinite lives must be tested for impairment at least once a year even if no indications of impairment are evident. Under ASPE, this annual test is not required unless indicators are present.

Recall from earlier in this chapter that there is impairment if the asset's recoverable amount falls below its carrying amount. If any impairment is evident, the intangible asset is written down to its recoverable amount and an impairment loss recorded. Under IFRS, an impairment loss can be reversed for intangible assets (but not goodwill), similar to property, plant, and equipment. Under ASPE, losses cannot be reversed.

Similar to tangible assets, the amortization is revised if there are changes in cost, or useful life, or an impairment loss. The revision is accounted for in the current and future periods; retroactive adjustments are not recorded.

At disposal, just as with tangible assets, the carrying amount of the intangible asset is removed, and a gain or loss, if any, is recorded.

INTANGIBLE ASSETS WITH FINITE LIVES

Examples of intangible assets with finite lives include patents and copyrights. We also include research and development costs in this section because these costs often lead to the creation of patents and copyrights.

Patents

A **patent** is an exclusive right issued by the Canadian Intellectual Property Office of Industry Canada that allows the patent holder to manufacture, sell, or otherwise control an invention for a period of 20 years from the date of the application. A patent cannot be renewed. But the legal life of a patent may be extended if the patent holder obtains new patents for improvements or other changes in the basic design.

The initial cost of a patent is the price paid to acquire it. After it has been acquired, legal costs are often incurred. Legal costs to successfully defend a patent in an infringement suit are considered necessary to prove the patent's validity. They are added to the Patent account and amortized over the patent's remaining life.

The cost of a patent should be amortized over its 20-year legal life or its useful life, whichever is shorter. As mentioned earlier, the useful life should be carefully assessed by considering whether the patent is likely to become ineffective at contributing to revenue before the end of its legal life.

Copyrights

A **copyright** is granted by the Canadian Intellectual Property Office, giving the owner an exclusive right to reproduce and sell an artistic or published work. Copyrights extend for the life of the creator plus 50 years. Generally, a copyright's useful life is significantly shorter than its legal life.

The cost of a copyright consists of the cost of acquiring and defending it. The cost may only be the fee paid to register the copyright, or it may amount to a great deal more if a copyright infringement suit is involved.

ACCOUNTING IN ACTION
ALL ABOUT YOU INSIGHT

If you copy a song from a CD to your iPod that has a "digital lock" on it to prevent unauthorized copying, you could be liable for a fine ranging from $100 to $5,000 for breaking the digital lock and copying the CD. This is one of the provisions in Canada's new *Copyright Modernization Act*, passed in 2012. The last time the copyright laws were changed was in 1997, before the first MP3 player came on the market. Since that time, the Internet and other new technologies have changed the way we produce and access copyright material. Supporters of the law argue that companies and individuals in the entertainment and creative fields need to have their songs, videos, TV shows, software, electronic books, and other works protected in order to foster creativity and innovation. But the amendments are also intended to give more flexibility to consumers such as officially legalizing the recording of television programs to watch at their convenience.

Sources: Bea Vongdouangchanh, "Parliament Passes New Copyright Law; Geist Says Feds Caved to U.S. on Digital Locks," *The Hill Times*, July 2, 2012; CBC News, "Copyright Bill Finally Clears Commons," CBC.ca, June 19, 2012; Mary Teresa Bitti, "Chambers: Copyright Lawyers Prepare for New Rules," *Financial Post*, March 26, 2012.

Why is it important that the copyrights of artists, writers, musicians, and the entertainment industry be protected?

Research and Development Costs

Research and development (R&D) costs are not intangible assets by themselves. But they may lead to patents and copyrights, new processes, and new products. Many companies spend large sums of money on research and development in an ongoing effort to develop new products or processes.

Research and development costs present two accounting problems: (1) it is sometimes difficult to determine the costs related to specific projects; (2) it is also hard to know the extent and timing of future benefits. As a result, accounting distinguishes between research costs and development costs.

Research is original, planned investigation that is done to gain new knowledge and understanding. It is not known at this stage if a future benefit will exist as a result of the research. Therefore, all research costs should be expensed when they are incurred.

Development is the use of research findings and knowledge for a plan or design before the start of commercial production. Development costs with probable future benefits should be capitalized. All of the following criteria must be met for development costs to be capitalized:

- The project is technically feasible.
- The company plans to complete the project.
- There are adequate resources to complete the project.
- A market exists for the product.

If any of these conditions are not met, the development costs must be expensed. Illustration 9-14 shows the distinction between research and development. After development is completed, the capitalized development costs are amortized over the useful life of the project developed.

Research

Examples
- Laboratory research aimed at the discovery of new knowledge
- Searching for ways to use new research findings or other knowledge
- Forming concepts and designs of possible product or process alternatives

Development

Examples
- Testing in search or evaluation of product or process alternatives
- Design, construction, and testing of pre-production prototypes and models
- Design of tools, jigs, moulds, and dies involving new technology

▶ILLUSTRATION 9-14
Distinction between research and development

INTANGIBLE ASSETS WITH INDEFINITE LIVES

An intangible asset is considered to have an indefinite life when there is no foreseeable limit to the length of time over which the asset is expected to generate cash. Examples of intangible assets with indefinite lives include trademarks and trade names, franchises, and licences. Intangible assets do not always fit perfectly in a specific category. Sometimes trademarks, trade names, franchises, or licences do have finite lives. In such cases, they would be amortized over the shorter of their legal or useful lives. It is more usual, however, for these intangible assets, along with goodwill, to have indefinite lives.

Trademarks, Trade Names, and Brands

A **trademark** or **trade name** is a word, phrase, jingle, or symbol that identifies a particular enterprise or product. Trade names like President's Choice, KFC, Nike, Tim Hortons, the Blue Jays, and TSN create immediate brand recognition and generally help the sale of a product or service. Each year, Interbrands ranks the world's best brands. In 2012, it ranked Coca-Cola as the most successful brand in the world, followed by Apple, IBM, Google, and Microsoft. In Canada, the most valuable brands in retail included lululemon and Shoppers Drug Mart.

The creator can get an exclusive legal right to the trademark or trade name by registering it with the Canadian Intellectual Property Office. This registration gives continuous protection. It may be renewed every 15 years, as long as the trademark or trade name is in use. In most cases, companies continuously renew their trademarks or trade names. In such cases, as long as the trademark or trade name continues to be marketable, it will have an indefinite useful life.

If the trademark or trade name is purchased, the cost is the purchase price. If the trademark or trade name is developed internally rather than purchased, it cannot be recognized as an intangible asset on the balance sheet. The reason is that expenditures on internally developed trademarks or brands cannot be distinguished from the cost of developing the business as a whole. The cost cannot be separately measured.

Franchises and Licences

When you purchase a Civic from a Honda dealer, fill up your gas tank at the corner Mohawk station, or buy coffee from Tim Hortons, you are dealing with franchises. A franchise is a contractual arrangement under which the franchisor grants the franchisee the right to sell certain products, to provide specific services, or to use certain trademarks or trade names, usually inside a specific geographic area.

Another type of franchise is granted by a government body that allows a company to use public property in performing its services. Examples are the use of city streets for a bus line or taxi service; the use of public land for telephone, power, and cable lines; and the use of airwaves for radio or TV broadcasting. Such operating rights are called licences.

When costs can be identified with the acquisition of the franchise or licence, an intangible asset should be recognized. These rights have indefinite lives and are not amortized. Annual payments, which are often in proportion to the franchise's total sales, are sometimes required under a franchise agreement. These payments are called royalties and are recorded as operating expenses in the period in which they are incurred.

GOODWILL

Unlike other assets, which can be sold individually in the marketplace, goodwill cannot be sold individually as it is part of the business as a whole. It cannot be separated from the company, nor is it based on legal rights. Goodwill represents the value of favourable attributes related to a business such as exceptional management, a desirable location, good customer relations, skilled employees, high-quality products, fair pricing policies, and harmonious relations with labour unions.

If goodwill can be identified only with the business as a whole, how can it be determined? An accountant could try to put a dollar value on the attributes (exceptional management, a desirable location, and so on), but the results would be very subjective. Subjective valuations would not contribute to the reliability of financial statements. For this reason, internally generated goodwill is not recognized as an asset.

Goodwill is recorded only when there is a purchase of an entire business, at which time an independent valuation can be determined. The cost of goodwill is measured by comparing the cost paid to purchase the entire business with the fair value of its net assets (assets less liabilities). If the cost is greater than these net identifiable assets, then the purchaser has paid for something that is not identifiable, that cannot be separated and sold—goodwill. In this situation, because a transaction has occurred, the cost of the purchased goodwill can be measured and therefore recorded as an asset.

Because goodwill has an indefinite life, just as the company has an indefinite life, it is not amortized. Since goodwill is measured using the company's fair value—a value that can easily change—IFRS requires goodwill to be tested annually for impairment even if there is no indication of impairment. Under ASPE, impairment tests of goodwill are only conducted if there is an indication that impairment exists.

Impairment losses on goodwill are never reversed, even if the value of the company increases after the impairment loss has been recognized. This is applicable under both IFRS and ASPE.

 BEFORE YOU GO ON...

Do It

Dummies 'R' Us Company purchased a copyright to a new book series for $15,000 cash on August 1, 2013. The books are expected to have a saleable life of three years. One year later, the company spends an additional $6,000 cash to successfully defend this copyright in court. The company's year end is July 31. Record (a) the purchase of the copyright on August 1, 2013; (b) the year-end amortization at July 31, 2014; (c) the legal costs incurred on August 1, 2014; and (d) the year-end amortization at July 31, 2015.

Solution

(a)

Aug. 1, 2013	Copyrights	15,000	
	Cash		15,000
	To record purchase of copyright.		

(b)

July 31, 2014	Amortization Expense ($15,000 ÷ 3)	5,000	
	Accumulated Amortization—Copyrights		5,000
	To record amortization expense.		

(c)

Aug. 1, 2014	Copyrights	6,000	
	Cash		6,000
	To record costs incurred to defend copyright.		

(d)

July 31, 2015	Amortization Expense	8,000*	
	Accumulated Amortization—Copyrights		8,000
	To record revised amortization expensse.		

*$15,000 − $5,000 + $6,000 = $16,000 carrying amount; $16,000 carrying amount ÷ 2 years remaining = $8,000

Related exercise material: BE9–16, E9–12, E9–13, and E9–14.

Action Plan

- Amortize intangible assets with finite lives over the shorter of their useful life and legal life (the legal life of a copyright is the life of the author plus 50 years).
- Treat costs to successfully defend an intangible asset as a capital expenditure because they benefit future periods.
- Revise amortization for additions to the cost of the asset, using the carrying amount at the time of the addition and the remaining useful life.

THE NAVIGATOR

Statement Presentation and Analysis

PRESENTATION

Long-lived assets are normally reported in the balance sheet under the headings "property, plant, and equipment," "intangible assets," and "goodwill." Some companies combine property, plant, and equipment and intangible assets under the heading "capital assets." Goodwill must be disclosed separately.

The cost and the accumulated depreciation and/or amortization for each major class of assets are disclosed in either the balance sheet or notes. In addition, the depreciation and amortization methods that are used must be described. The amount of depreciation and amortization expense for the period should also be disclosed. As previously explained, gains or losses on disposals of long-lived assets are included in operating expenses on the income statement.

Under IFRS, companies also have to disclose if they are using the cost or the revaluation model for each class of assets, and include a reconciliation of the carrying amount at the beginning and end of the period for each class of long-lived assets in the notes to the financial statements. This means they must show all of the following for each class of long-lived assets: (1) additions, (2) disposals, (3) depreciation or amortization, (4) impairment losses, and (5) reversals of impairment losses. ASPE does not require disclosure of all of these details.

Illustration 9-15 contains an excerpt from Enerflex's 2011 balance sheet (which it calls *statement of financial position*).

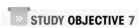

STUDY OBJECTIVE 7

Illustrate the reporting and analysis of long-lived assets.

▶ **ILLUSTRATION 9-15**
Presentation of long-lived assets

ENERFLEX LTD.
Statement of Financial Position (partial)
December 31, 2011
(in thousands)

ENERFLEX

Assets	
Property, plant, and equipment (note 10)	$123,130
Rental equipment (note 10)	101,908
Intangible assets (note 12)	31,528
Goodwill (note 13)	459,935

Enerflex provides additional details on the long-lived assets in the notes to its financial statements. For example, in note 10, Enerflex discloses the required information about all of its property, plant, and equipment, which include land, buildings, equipment, assets under construction, assets held for sale, and rental equipment.

Another note, Enerflex's summary of significant accounting policies, discloses that straight-line depreciation is used and provides information on the estimated useful lives of the company's long-lived assets. This note also states that major renewals and improvements in rental equipment and property, plant, and equipment are capitalized. It explains that significant components of property, plant, and equipment that required replacement at regular intervals are accounted for separately. The notes also include information on Enerflex's policies on testing its long-lived assets for impairment. Property, plant, and equipment, rental equipment and intangible assets are assessed for impairment whenever changes in events or changes in circumstances indicate that the asset's carrying amount may not be recovered. Goodwill is tested for impairment at least annually.

ANALYSIS

Information in the financial statements about long-lived assets allows decision makers to analyze a company's use of its total assets. We will use two ratios to analyze total assets: asset turnover and return on assets.

Asset Turnover

The **asset turnover** ratio indicates how efficiently a company uses its assets; that is, how many dollars of sales are generated by each dollar that is invested in assets. It is calculated by dividing net sales by average total assets. If a company is using its assets efficiently, each dollar of assets will create a high amount of sales. When we compare two companies in the same industry, the one with the higher asset turnover is operating more efficiently. The asset turnover ratio for fiscal 2012 for Reitmans (Canada) Limited (dollars in thousands) is calculated in Illustration 9-16.

▶ILLUSTRATION 9-16
Asset turnover

Net Sales	÷	Average Total Assets	=	Asset Turnover
$1,019,397	÷	($633,861 + $659,355) ÷ 2 =		1.58 times

The asset turnover ratio shows that each dollar invested in assets produced $1.58 in sales for Reitmans. This ratio varies greatly among different industries—from those that have a large investment in assets (e.g., utility companies) to those that have much less invested in assets (e.g., service companies). Asset turnover ratios, therefore, should only be compared for companies that are in the same industry.

Return on Assets

The **return on assets** ratio measures overall profitability. This ratio is calculated by dividing profit by average total assets. The return on assets ratio indicates the amount of profit that is generated by each dollar invested in assets. A high return on assets indicates a profitable company. Illustration 9-17 shows the return on assets for Reitmans (dollars in thousands).

▶ILLUSTRATION 9-17
Return on assets

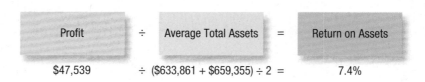

Profit	÷	Average Total Assets	=	Return on Assets
$47,539	÷	($633,861 + $659,355) ÷ 2 =		7.4%

Reitmans' return on assets was 7.4% for 2012. As with other ratios, the return on assets should be compared with previous years, with other companies in the same industry, and with industry averages, to determine how well the company has performed.

BEFORE YOU GO ON...

Do It

The following information is available for Toni's Sporting Goods for three recent years:

	2014	2013	2012
Total assets	$299,650	$259,700	$223,540
Net sales	521,180	487,150	441,280
Profit	26,390	18,210	13,540

Calculate the asset turnover and return on assets ratios for Toni's Sporting Goods for 2014 and 2013 and comment on any trends.

Solution

	2014	2013
Average total assets	($299,650 + $259,700) ÷ 2 = $279,675	($259,700 + $223,540) ÷ 2 = $241,620
Asset turnover	1.9 times = $\frac{\$521,180}{\$279,675}$	2 times = $\frac{\$487,150}{\$241,620}$
Return on assets	9.4% = $\frac{\$26,390}{\$279,675}$	7.5% = $\frac{\$18,210}{\$241,620}$

In general, it is better to have a higher asset turnover and return on assets. Toni's Sporting Goods' lower asset turnover may indicate it is not using its assets as efficiently in 2014 as compared with 2013. However, the increase in the return on assets indicates improved profitability. Given the decrease in turnover, this is a positive result.

Related exercise material: BE9–17, BE9–18, BE9–19, E9–15, and E9–16.

Action Plan
- Calculate average total assets using the total assets at the beginning and end of the year.
- Divide net sales by the average total assets for that year to calculate asset turnover.
- Divide profit by the average total assets for that year to calculate return on assets.
- Recall if it is better for asset turnover and return on assets to increase or decrease.

THE NAVIGATOR

Comparing IFRS and ASPE

Key Differences	International Financial Reporting Standards (IFRS)	Accounting Standards for Private Enterprises (ASPE)
Valuing property, plant, and equipment	Choice of cost or revaluation model.	Must use cost model.
Terminology	The term "depreciation" is used for allocating the cost of property, plant, and equipment.	The term "amortization" may be used for allocating the cost of property, plant, and equipment. The term "depreciation" is also accepted.
Impairment of property, plant, and equipment, and finite-life intangible assets	Must look for indicators of impairment annually. If exist, then must test for impairment. Allow for recoveries of previously recorded impairments.	No requirement to look for indicators of impairment annually. Perform tests only if it is apparent they exist. Impairments recorded less often, but cannot later reverse an impairment loss.
Test for impairment of indefinite-life intangible assets	Must perform impairment tests annually. Allows for recoveries of previously recorded impairments.	Same approach as for property, plant, and equipment, and intangible assets with finite lives.
Test for impairment of goodwill	Must be conducted every year.	Conducted only if there is an indication of impairment.
Disclosure	Must provide a reconciliation of the opening and closing carrying amount of each class of assets.	Reconciliation not required.

THE NAVIGATOR

Demonstration Problem 1

DuPage Company purchases a factory machine at a cost of $17,500 on June 1, 2014. The machine is expected to have a residual value of $1,500 at the end of its four-year useful life on May 31, 2018. DuPage has a December 31 year end.

During its useful life, the machine is expected to be used for 10,000 hours. Actual annual use was as follows: 1,300 hours in 2014; 2,800 hours in 2015; 3,300 hours in 2016; 1,900 hours in 2017; and 700 hours in 2018.

Instructions
Prepare depreciation schedules for the following methods: (a) straight-line, (b) units-of-production, and (c) diminishing-balance using double the straight-line rate.

ACTION PLAN

- Deduct the residual value in the straight-line and units-of-production methods, but not in the diminishing-balance method.
- In the diminishing-balance method, the depreciation rate is applied to the carrying amount (cost − accumulated depreciation). The residual value is not used in the calculations except to make sure the carrying amount is not reduced below the residual value.
- When the asset is purchased during the year, the first year's depreciation for the straight-line and diminishing-balance methods must be adjusted for the part of the year that the asset is owned. No adjustment is required for the units-of-production method. In the straight-line method, the final year must also be adjusted.
- Depreciation should never reduce the asset's carrying amount below its estimated residual value.

Solution to Demonstration Problem 1

(a) Straight-line method

| | | | | | End of Year | |
Year	Amount	×	Rate	=	Expense	Depreciation	Amount
							$17,500
2014	$16,000[a]		25%[b] × 7/12		$2,333	$ 2,333	15,167
2015	16,000		25%		4,000	6,333	11,167
2016	16,000		25%		4,000	10,333	7,167
2017	16,000		25%		4,000	14,333	3,167
2018	16,000		25% × 5/12		1,667	16,000	1,500

[a] $17,500 − $1,500 = $16,000
[b] 100% ÷ 4 years = 25%

(b) Units-of-production method

| | | | | | End of Year | |
Year	Units of Production	×	Depreciable Amount/Unit	=	Depreciation Expense	Accumulated Depreciation	Carrying Amount
							$17,500
2014	1,300		$1.60[a]		$2,080	$ 2,080	15,420
2015	2,800		1.60		4,480	6,560	10,940
2016	3,300		1.60		5,280	11,840	5,660
2017	1,900		1.60		3,040	14,880	2,620
2018	700		1.60		1,120	16,000	1,500

[a] $17,500 − $1,500 = $16,000 depreciable amount ÷ 10,000 total units = $1.60/unit

(c) Diminishing-balance method

| | | | | | End of Year | |
Year	Carrying Amount Beginning of Year	×	Depreciation Rate (25% × 2)	=	Depreciation Expense	Accumulated Depreciation	Carrying Amounts End of Year
							$17,500
2014	$17,500		50% × 7/12		$5,104	$ 5,104	12,396
2015	12,396		50%		6,198	11,302	6,198
2016	6,198		50%		3,099	14,401	3,099
2017	3,099		50%		1,549	15,950	1,550
2018	1,550		50%		50[a]	16,000	1,500

[a] Adjusted to $50 so that the carrying amount at the end of the year is not less than the residual value.

THE NAVIGATOR

Demonstration Problem 2

On January 1, 2011, Skyline Limousine Co. purchased a specialty limo for $78,000. The vehicle is being amortized by the straight-line method using a four-year service life and a $4,000 residual value. The company's fiscal year ends on December 31.

Instructions

Prepare the journal entry or entries to record the disposal of the limo, assuming that it is:

(a) retired on January 1, 2014.

(b) sold for $15,000 on July 1, 2014.

(c) traded in on a new limousine on January 1, 2014, for a trade-in allowance of $25,000 and cash of $52,000. The fair value of the old vehicle on January 1, 2014, was $20,000.

ACTION PLAN

- Calculate the annual depreciation expense and accumulated depreciation at end of previous year.
- Update the depreciation to the date of the disposal for any partial period.
- Determine the asset's carrying amount at the time of disposal.
- Calculate any gain or loss by comparing proceeds with the carrying amount.
- Remove the asset's carrying amount by debiting accumulated depreciation (for the total depreciation to the date of disposal) and crediting the asset account for the cost of the asset. Record proceeds and any gain or loss.
- Ignore trade-in allowances.
- Record the new asset in an exchange situation at the fair value of the asset given up, plus the cash paid.

Solution to Demonstration Problem 2

$$\frac{\$78,000 - \$4,000}{4 \text{ years}} = \$18,500 \text{ annual depreciation expense}$$

Accumulated Depreciation at December 31, 2013: $18,500 \times 3$ years $= \$55,500$

(a)

Jan. 1, 2014	Accumulated Depreciation—Vehicles	55,500	
	Loss on Disposal [$0 − ($78,000 − $55,500)]	22,500	
	Vehicles		78,000
	To record retirement of limo.		

(b)

July 1, 2014	Depreciation Expense ($18,500 × $^{6}/_{12}$)	9,250	
	Accumulated Depreciation—Vehicles		9,250
	To record depreciation for 6 months.		
	Cash	15,000	
	Accumulated Depreciation—Vehicles ($55,500 + $9,250)	64,750	
	Gain on Disposal [$15,000 − ($78,000 − $64,750)]		1,750
	Vehicles		78,000
	To record sale of limo.		

(c)

Jan. 1, 2014	Vehicles (cost of new) ($20,000 + $52,000)	72,000	
	Accumulated Depreciation—Vehicles	55,500	
	Loss on Disposal [$20,000 − ($78,000 − $55,500)]	2,500	
	Vehicles (cost of old)		78,000
	Cash		52,000
	To record exchange of limousines, plus cash.		

THE NAVIGATOR

▶ Summary of Study Objectives

1. ***Determine the cost of property, plant, and equipment.*** The cost of property, plant, and equipment includes all costs that are necessary to acquire the asset and make it ready for its intended use. All costs that benefit future periods (that is, capital expenditures) are included in the cost of the asset. When applicable, cost also includes asset retirement costs. When multiple assets are purchased in one transaction, or when an asset has significant components, the cost is allocated to each individual asset or component using their relative fair values.

2. *Explain and calculate depreciation.* After acquisition, assets are accounted for using the cost model or the revaluation model. Depreciation is recorded and assets are carried at cost less accumulated depreciation. Depreciation is the allocation of the cost of a long-lived asset to expense over its useful life (its service life) in a rational and systematic way. Depreciation is not a process of valuation and it does not result in an accumulation of cash. There are three commonly used depreciation methods:

Method	Effect on Annual Depreciation	Calculation
Straight-line	Constant amount	(Cost − residual value) ÷ estimated useful life (in years)
Diminishing-balance	Diminishing amount	Carrying amount at beginning of year × diminishing-balance rate
Units-of-production	Varying amount	(Cost − residual value) ÷ total estimated units of production × actual activity during the year

Each method results in the same amount of depreciation over the asset's useful life. Depreciation expense for income tax purposes is called capital cost allowance (CCA). The single diminishing-balance method is required and depreciation rates are prescribed.

3. *Explain the factors that cause changes in periodic depreciation and calculate revisions.* A revision to depreciation will be required if there are (a) capital expenditures during the asset's useful life, (b) impairments in the asset's fair value, (c) changes in the asset's fair value when using the revaluation model, and/or (d) changes in the appropriate depreciation method, estimated useful life, or residual value. An impairment loss must be recorded if the recoverable amount is less than the carrying amount. Only under IFRS can impairment losses be reversed in future periods if the recoverable amount increases. Revisions of periodic depreciation are made in present and future periods, not retroactively. The new annual depreciation is determined by using the depreciable amount (carrying amount less the revised residual value), and the remaining useful life, at the time of the revision.

4. *Account for the disposal of property, plant, and equipment.* The accounting for the disposal of a piece of property, plant, or equipment through retirement or sale is as follows:

(a) Update any unrecorded depreciation for partial periods since depreciation was last recorded.
(b) Calculate the carrying amount (cost − accumulated depreciation).
(c) Calculate any gain (proceeds > carrying amount) or loss (proceeds < carrying amount) on disposal.
(d) Remove the asset and accumulated depreciation accounts at the date of disposal. Record the proceeds received and the gain or loss, if any.

An exchange of assets is recorded as the purchase of a new asset and the sale of an old asset. The new asset is recorded at the fair value of the asset given up plus any cash paid (or less any cash received). The fair value of the asset given up is compared with its carrying amount to calculate the gain or loss. If the fair value of the new asset or the asset given up cannot be determined, the new long-lived asset is recorded at the carrying amount of the old asset that was given up, plus any cash paid (or less any cash received).

5. *Calculate and record depreciation of natural resources.* The units-of-production method of depreciation is generally used for natural resources. The depreciable amount per unit is calculated by dividing the total depreciable amount by the number of units estimated to be in the resource. The depreciable amount per unit is multiplied by the number of units that have been extracted to determine the annual depreciation. The depreciation and any other costs to extract the resource are recorded as inventory until the resource is sold. At that time, the costs are transferred to cost of resource sold on the income statement. Revisions to depreciation will be required for capital expenditures during the asset's useful life, for impairments, and for changes in the total estimated units of the resource.

6. *Identify the basic accounting issues for intangible assets and goodwill.* The accounting for tangible and intangible assets is much the same. Intangible assets are reported at cost, which includes all expenditures necessary to prepare the asset for its intended use. An intangible asset with a finite life is amortized over the shorter of its useful life or legal life, usually on a straight-line basis. The extent of the annual impairment tests depends on whether IFRS or ASPE is followed and whether the intangible asset had a finite or indefinite life. Intangible assets with indefinite lives and goodwill are not amortized and are tested at least annually for impairment. Impairment losses on goodwill are never reversed under both IFRS and ASPE. Impairment losses on intangible assets are never reversed under ASPE.

7. *Illustrate the reporting and analysis of long-lived assets.* It is common for property, plant, and equipment, and natural resources to be combined in financial statements under the heading "property, plant, and equipment." Intangible assets with finite and indefinite lives are sometimes combined under the heading "intangible assets" or are listed separately. Goodwill must be presented separately. Either on the balance sheet or in the notes, the cost of the major classes of long-lived assets is presented. Accumulated depreciation (if the asset is depreciable) and carrying amount must be disclosed either in the balance sheet or in the notes. The depreciation and amortization methods and rates, as well as the annual depreciation expense, must also be indicated. The company's impairment policy and any impairment losses should be described and reported. Under IFRS, companies must include a reconciliation of the carrying amount at the beginning and end of the period for each class of

long-lived assets and state whether the cost or revaluation model is used.

The asset turnover ratio (net sales ÷ average total assets) is one measure that is used by companies to show how efficiently they are using their assets to generate sales revenue. A second ratio, return on assets (profit ÷ average total assets), calculates how profitable the company is in terms of using its assets to generate profit.

Flash cards

Glossary

Additions and improvements   Costs that are incurred to increase the operating efficiency, productive capacity, or expected useful life of property, plant, or equipment. (p. 475)

Amortizable amount   The cost minus the residual value of a finite-life intangible asset which is amortized over its useful life. (p. 489)

Amortization   The systematic allocation of the amortizable amount of a finite-life intangible asset over its useful life. (p. 489)

Asset retirement costs   The cost to dismantle, remove, or restore an asset when it is retired. (p. 464)

Asset turnover   A measure of how efficiently a company uses its total assets to generate sales. It is calculated by dividing net sales by average total assets. (p. 494)

Basket purchase   The acquisition of a group of assets for a single price. Individual asset costs are determined by allocating relative fair values. (p. 466)

Capital cost allowance (CCA)   The depreciation of long-lived assets that is allowed by the *Income Tax Act* for income tax purposes. It is calculated on a class (group) basis and mainly uses the diminishing-balance method with maximum rates specified for each class of assets. (p. 474)

Capital expenditures   Expenditures related to long-lived assets that benefit the company over several accounting periods. (p. 464)

Copyright   An exclusive right granted by the federal government allowing the owner to reproduce and sell an artistic or published work. (p. 490)

Cost model   A model of accounting for a long-lived asset that carries the asset at its cost less accumulated depreciation or amortization and any impairment losses. (p. 468)

Depreciable amount   The cost of a depreciable asset (property, plant, and equipment, or natural resources) less its residual value. (p. 469)

Diminishing-balance method   A depreciation method that applies a constant rate to the asset's diminishing carrying amount. This method produces a decreasing annual depreciation expense over the useful life of the asset. (p. 471)

Franchise   A contractual arrangement under which the franchisor grants the franchisee the right to sell certain products, offer specific services, or use certain trademarks or trade names, usually inside a specific geographical area. (p. 492)

Goodwill   The amount paid to purchase another company that is more than the fair value of the company's net identifiable assets. (p. 492)

Impairment loss   The amount by which an asset's carrying amount exceeds its recoverable amount. (p. 476)

Intangible assets   Rights, privileges, and competitive advantages that result from owning long-lived assets that have no physical substance. (p. 488)

Land improvements   Structural additions to land that have limited useful lives, such as paving, fencing, and lighting. (p. 465)

Licences   Operating rights to use public property, granted by a government agency to a company. (p. 492)

Natural resources   Long-lived tangible assets, such as standing timber and underground deposits of oil, gas, and minerals, that are physically extracted and are only replaceable by an act of nature. (p. 486)

Operating expenditures   Expenditures that benefit only the current period. They are immediately charged against revenues as expenses. (p. 464)

Ordinary repairs   Expenditures to maintain the operating efficiency and productive life of the unit. (p. 475)

Patent   An exclusive right issued by the federal government that enables the recipient to manufacture, sell, or otherwise control an invention for a period of 20 years from the date of the application. (p. 490)

Property, plant, and equipment   Identifiable, long-lived tangible assets, such as land, land improvements, buildings, and equipment, that the company owns and uses for the production and sale of goods or services. (p. 464)

Recoverable amount   The higher of the asset's fair value, less costs to sell, and its value in use. (p. 476)

Research and development (R&D) costs   Expenditures that may lead to patents, copyrights, new processes, and new products. (p. 490)

Residual value   The estimated amount that a company would currently obtain from disposing of the asset if the asset were already as old as it will be, and in the condition it is expected to be in, at the end of its useful life. (p. 469)

Return on assets   An overall measure of profitability that indicates the amount of profit that is earned from each dollar

500 | CHAPTER 9 **Long-Lived Assets**

invested in assets. It is calculated by dividing profit by average total assets. (p. 494)

Revaluation model A model of accounting for a long-lived asset in which it is carried at its fair value less accumulated depreciation or amortization and any impairment losses. (p. 477)

Royalties Recurring payments that may be required under a franchise agreement and are paid by the franchisee to the franchisor for services provided (e.g., advertising, purchasing), and are often proportionate to sales. (p. 492)

Straight-line method A depreciation method in which an asset's depreciable amount is divided by its estimated useful life. This method produces the same periodic depreciation for each year of the asset's useful life. (p. 470)

Tangible assets Long-lived resources that have physical substance, are used in the operations of the business, and are not intended for sale to customers. Tangible assets include property, plant, and equipment, and natural resources. (p. 488)

Trade-in allowance A price reduction offered by the seller when a used asset is exchanged for a new asset as part of the deal. (p. 483)

Trademark (trade name) A word, phrase, jingle, or symbol that distinguishes or identifies a particular enterprise or product. (p. 491)

Units-of-production method A depreciation method in which useful life is expressed in terms of the total estimated units of production or use expected from the asset. Depreciation expense is calculated by multiplying the depreciable amount per unit (cost less residual value divided by total estimated activity) by the actual activity that occurs during the year. (p. 472)

Useful life The period of time over which an asset is expected to be available for use, or the number of units of production (such as machine hours) or units of output that are expected to be obtained from an asset. (p. 469)

▶ Self-Study Questions

Answers are at the end of the chapter.

(SO 1) AP **1.** Bulyea Company purchased equipment and incurred the following costs:

Cash price	$36,000
Freight – FOB shipping point	1,000
Insurance during transit	200
Annual licence fee	300
Annual insurance policy	500
Installation and testing	400
Total cost	$38,400

What amount should be recorded as the cost of the equipment?
(a) $36,000   (c) $37,600
(b) $36,200   (d) $38,400

(SO 1) AP **2.** Asura Company purchased land, a building, and equipment for a package price of $200,000. The land's fair value at the time of acquisition was $75,000. The building's fair value was $80,000. The equipment's fair value was $50,000. What costs should be debited to the three accounts Land, Building, and Equipment, respectively?
(a) $66,667, $66,667, and $66,666
(b) $73,171, $78,049, and $48,780
(c) $75,000, $80,000, and $50,000
(d) $200,000, $0, and $0

(SO 2) AP **3.** Cuso Company purchased equipment on January 1, 2013, at a cost of $40,000. The equipment has an estimated residual value of $10,000 and an estimated useful life of five years. If the straight-line method of depreciation is used, what is the amount of accumulated depreciation at December 31, 2014, the end of the second year of the asset's life?
(a) $6,000   (c) $18,000
(b) $12,000   (d) $24,000

(SO 2) AP **4.** Kant Enterprises purchases a truck for $33,000 on July 1, 2014. The truck has an estimated residual value of $3,000, and an estimated useful life of five years, or a total distance of 300,000 kilometres. If 50,000 kilometres are driven in 2014, what amount of depreciation expense would Kant record at December 31, 2014, assuming it uses the units-of-production method?
(a) $2,500   (c) $5,000
(b) $3,000   (d) $5,333

(SO 2) AP **5.** Refer to the data for Kant Enterprises in question 4. If Kant uses the double diminishing-balance method of depreciation, what amount of depreciation expense would it record at December 31, 2014?
(a) $6,000   (c) $12,000
(b) $6,600   (d) $13,200

(SO 3) K **6.** Which of the following is true regarding revising depreciation calculations?
(a) When the revision is the result of a change in management's estimation of the asset's useful life, past years should be corrected.
(b) Recording an impairment loss will result in an increase in the annual depreciation expense in future years.
(c) Capital expenditures during the asset's useful life do not result in a change in annual depreciation.
(d) Regardless of the reason for the change in depreciation, the revision is made for current and future years only.

(SO 3) AP **7.** Rubiat Company has equipment with an original cost of $200,000 and a residual value of $20,000. On December 31, 2014, the accumulated depreciation is $75,000 and the recoverable amount is $100,000.

What amount of an impairment loss should the company record?

(a) $0   (c) $25,000

(b) $5,000   (d) $80,000

(SO 4) AP 8. Oviatt Company sold equipment for $10,000. At that time, the equipment had a cost of $45,000 and accumulated depreciation of $30,000. Oviatt should record a:

(a) $5,000 loss on disposal.

(b) $5,000 gain on disposal.

(c) $15,000 loss on disposal.

(d) $15,000 gain on disposal.

(SO 4) AP 9. St. Laurent Company exchanged an old machine with a carrying amount of $10,000 and a fair value of $6,000 for a new machine. The new machine had a list price of $53,000. St. Laurent was offered a trade-in allowance of $11,000, and paid $42,000 cash in the exchange. At what amount should the new machine be recorded on St. Laurent's books?

(a) $42,000   (c) $52,000

(b) $48,000   (d) $53,000

(SO 5) AP 10. On April 1, 2013, Shady Tree Farm Company purchased a Christmas tree farm that has an estimated 100,000 harvestable Christmas trees. The purchase price was $500,000 and the tree farm is expected to have an estimated residual value of $50,000. During the first year of operations, ended January 31, 2014, Shady Tree Farm cut and sold 10,000 trees. What amount of depreciation should be included in cost of goods sold for the year ended January 31?

(a) $37,500   (c) $45,000

(b) $40,500   (d) $50,000

(SO 6) AP 11. Pierce Company incurred $150,000 of research costs in its laboratory to develop a new product in January 2014. On March 31, 2014, Pierce paid $20,000 for legal fees to register the new product. On July 31, 2014, Pierce paid $35,000 for legal fees in a successful defence of the patent. The total amount debited to Patents through July 31, 2014, should be:

(a) $20,000.   (c) $170,000.

(b) $55,000.   (d) $185,000.

(SO 7) AP 12. Cross Continental Rail Services reported net sales of $2,550 million, profit of $178 million, and average total assets of $3,132 million in 2014. What are the company's return on assets and asset turnover?

(a) 0. 81% and 5.7 times

(b) 5.7% and 1.2 times

(c) 7.0% and 5.7 times

(d) 5.7% and 0.81 times

THE NAVIGATOR

▶ Questions

(SO 1) C 1. What are the three characteristics of property, plant, and equipment? In what respect are property, plant, and equipment similar to inventory? How are they different?

(SO 1) C 2. What are the three components of the cost of property, plant, and equipment?

(SO 1) C 3. Blue Hosta Company recently purchased a new vehicle. The company also had to pay for the company's logo to be painted on the vehicle, for a safety inspection, and for an annual insurance policy on the vehicle. Explain how each of these costs should be recorded and why.

(SO 1) C 4. What are land improvements? Should the cost of clearing and grading land be recorded as a land improvement cost or not? Explain.

(SO 1) C 5. Jacques asks why the total cost in a basket purchase has to be allocated to the individual assets. For example, if we purchase land and a building for $250,000, why can we not just debit an account called Land and Building for $250,000? Answer his questions.

(SO 2) C 6. Justine argues that all companies should use the revaluation model as it provides more useful information than the cost model. She is also concerned that, if companies do have a choice, they will only use the revaluation model for assets that have increased in value. Do you agree or disagree with Justine? Why?

(SO 2) C 7. What is the relationship, if any, between depreciation and (a) cost allocation, (b) asset valuation, and (c) cash?

(SO 2) K 8. Explain the factors that are used to calculate depreciation.

(SO 2) C 9. How are annual depreciation and profit different each year over the useful life of an asset, and in total at the end of its useful life, under each of the three depreciation methods?

(SO 2, 3) C 10. What factors should be considered when choosing a depreciation method? When revising a depreciation method?

(SO 2) C 11. Ralph has a plan to reduce the amount of income taxes that will have to be paid on his company's profit. He has decided to calculate depreciation expense using very low estimated useful lives on his property, plant, and equipment. Will Ralph's plan work? Why or why not?

(SO 3) C 12. Explain the difference between operating expenditures and capital expenditures during an asset's useful life and describe the accounting treatment of each.

(SO 3) C 13. Under what circumstances will depreciation need to be revised? Should these circumstances also result in the revision of previously recorded depreciation?

(SO 3) C 14. What factors contribute to an impairment loss? In what circumstances, if any, is a company allowed to write up its property, plant, and equipment?

(SO 3) C 15. In the fourth year of an asset's five-year useful life, the company decides that the asset will have an eight-year service life. Explain how this will impact the amount of depreciation recorded each year over the asset's useful life.

(SO 4) C 16. If equipment is sold in the middle of a fiscal year, why does depreciation expense have to be recorded for the partial period? Doesn't the subsequent journal entry to record the sale remove the accumulated depreciation from the books anyway?

(SO 4) C 17. Ewing Company owns a machine that is fully depreciated but is still being used. How should Ewing account for this asset and report it in the financial statements?

(SO 4) K 18. How is a gain or loss on the sale of an item of property, plant, or equipment calculated? Is the calculation the same for an exchange of a piece of property, plant, or equipment?

(SO 4) C 19. How is the carrying amount of an item of property, plant, or equipment calculated? Why does this amount NOT appear in the journal entry to record the disposition of an item of property, plant, or equipment?

(SO 5) K 20. Describe the similarities and differences between natural resources and property, plant, and equipment.

(SO 5) C 21. Why is the units-of-production method used frequently to calculate depreciation for natural resources? Why is the term "depletion" often used instead of "depreciation"?

(SO 6) C 22. What are the similarities and differences between accounting for intangible and tangible assets?

(SO 6) C 23. Under IFRS and ASPE, what are the differences between the treatment of impairment losses for (a) finite life intangible assets, (b) indefinite life intangible assets, and (c) goodwill?

(SO 6) C 24. What is goodwill? Why can it not be sold to raise cash if a company is planning to expand?

(SO 7) K 25. How should long-lived assets be reported on the balance sheet and income statement? What information should be disclosed in the notes to the financial statements?

(SO 7) C 26. Balpreet believes that when comparing the ratios for one company over a two-year period, it is more important for a company to have an improved asset turnover than it is to have an improved return on assets. Do you agree or disagree? Why?

▶ Brief Exercises

Determine cost of land and land improvements. (SO 1) AP

BE9–1 The following costs were incurred by Shumway Company in purchasing land: cash price, $85,000; legal fees, $1,500; removal of old building, $5,000; clearing and grading, $3,500; installation of a parking lot, $5,000. (a) What is the cost of the land? (b) What is the cost of the land improvements?

Determine cost of equipment. (SO 1) AP

BE9–2 Surkis Company incurs the following costs in purchasing equipment: invoice price, $40,375; transportation-in, $625; installation and testing, $1,000; one-year insurance policy, $1,750. What is the cost of the equipment?

Identify operating and capital expenditures. (SO 1) K

BE9–3 In the space provided, indicate whether each of the following items is an operating expenditure (O) or a capital expenditure (C):

(a) _____ Repaired building roof, $1,500
(b) _____ Replaced building roof, $27,500
(c) _____ Purchased building, $480,000
(d) _____ Paid insurance on equipment in transit, $550
(e) _____ Purchased supplies, $350
(f) _____ Purchased truck, $55,000
(g) _____ Purchased oil and gas for truck, $125
(h) _____ Rebuilt engine on truck, $5,000
(i) _____ Replaced tires on truck, $600
(j) _____ Estimated retirement cost of plant, $1,000,000
(k) _____ Added new wing to building, $250,000
(l) _____ Painted interior of building, $1,500
(m) _____ Replaced an elevator, $17,500

Record basket purchase. (SO 1) AP

BE9–4 Rainbow Company purchased land, a building, and equipment on January 2, 2014, for $850,000. The company paid $170,000 cash and signed a mortgage note payable for the remainder. Management's best estimate of the value of the land was $352,000; of the building, $396,000; and of the equipment, $132,000. Record the purchase.

Calculate straight-line depreciation. (SO 2) AP

BE9–5 Surkis Company acquires equipment at a cost of $42,000 on January 3, 2014. Management estimates the equipment will have a residual value of $6,000 at the end of its four-year useful life. Assume the company uses the straight-line method of depreciation. Calculate the depreciation expense (a) for each year of the equipment's life, and (b) in total over the equipment's life. Surkis has a December 31 fiscal year end.

BE9–6   Refer to the data given for Surkis Company in BE9–5. Assume instead that the company uses the diminishing-balance method and that the diminishing-balance depreciation rate is double the straight-line rate. Calculate the depreciation expense (a) for each year of the equipment's life, and (b) in total over the equipment's life.

Calculate diminishing-balance depreciation. (SO 2) AP

BE9–7   Speedy Taxi Service uses the units-of-production method in calculating depreciation on its taxicabs. Each cab is expected to be driven 550,000 kilometres. Taxi 10 cost $38,950 and is expected to have a residual value of $4,300. Taxi 10 is driven 90,000 kilometres in 2013, and 135,000 kilometres in 2014. Calculate (a) the depreciable cost per kilometre (use three decimals), and (b) the depreciation expense for 2013 and 2014.

Calculate units-of-production depreciation. (SO 2) AP

BE9–8   Refer to the data given for Surkis Company in BE9–5. Assume the equipment was purchased on April 6, 2014, and that the company pro-rates depreciation to the nearest month. Using the straight-line method, calculate the depreciation expense (a) for each year of the equipment's life, and (b) in total over the equipment's life.

Calculate partial-year straight-line depreciation. (SO 2) AP

BE9–9   Refer to the data given for Surkis Company in BE9–5. Assume the equipment was purchased on April 6, 2014, and that the company has a policy of recording a half year's depreciation in the year of acquisition and a half year's depreciation in the year of disposal. Using the double diminishing-balance method, calculate the depreciation expense (a) for each year of the equipment's life, and (b) in total over the equipment's life.

Calculate partial-year diminishing-balance depreciation.(SO 2) AP

BE9–10   Cherry Technology purchased equipment on January 4, 2012, for $250,000. The equipment had an estimated useful life of six years and a residual value of $10,000. The company has a December 31 year end and uses straight-line depreciation. On December 31, 2014, the company tests for impairment and determines that the equipment's recoverable amount is $100,000. (a) Calculate the equipment's carrying amount at December 31, 2014 (after recording the annual depreciation). (b) Record the impairment loss.

Determine carrying amount and record impairment loss. (SO 3) AP

BE9–11   Raj Cleaning Services purchased equipment for $65,000 on January 2, 2011. Management estimated the equipment would have a useful life of seven years and a residual value of $5,500. On January 3, 2014, the equipment was upgraded at a cost of $10,200. After the upgrade, management estimates that the equipment will now have a total useful life of nine years and a residual value of $3,200. The company uses straight-line depreciation and has a December 31 fiscal year end. Calculate annual depreciation expense for 2011 through 2014.

Calculate revised depreciation. (SO 3) AP

BE9–12   On January 3, 2014, Ruiz Company retires equipment, which cost $25,700. No residual value is received. Prepare journal entries to record the transaction if (a) accumulated depreciation is also $25,700 on this equipment, and (b) the accumulated depreciation is $22,500 instead of $25,700. Ruiz has a December 31 fiscal year end.

Record disposal by retirement. (SO 4) AP

BE9–13   Wilbur Company sells equipment on March 31, 2014, for $15,000 cash. The equipment was purchased on January 5, 2009, at a cost of $86,400, and had an estimated useful life of six years and a residual value of $2,200. Adjusting journal entries are made annually at the company's year end, December 31. Prepare the journal entries to (a) update depreciation to March 31, 2014, (b) record the sale of the equipment, and (c) record the sale of the equipment if Wilbur Company received $9,000 cash for it.

Record disposal by sale. (SO 4) AP

BE9–14   Subramanian Company has equipment with an original cost of $95,000 and, as at December 31, 2013, accumulated depreciation of $78,000. On January 7, 2014, Subramanian exchanges the equipment for new equipment with a list price of $110,000. The dealer gives Subramanian a $20,000 trade-in allowance on the old equipment even though its fair value is only $15,000. Record the January 7, 2014, journal entry for the equipment exchange.

Record disposal by exchange of equipment. (SO 4) AP

BE9–15   Cuono Mining Co. purchased a mine for $6.5 million that is estimated to have 25 million tonnes of ore and a residual value of $500,000. In the first year, 5 million tonnes of ore are extracted and 3 million tonnes are sold.

(a) Record the depreciation and the cost of the ore extracted for the first year, ended August 31, 2014.
(b) Show how the mine and the ore on hand are reported on the balance sheet on August 31, 2014.

Record depreciation and show balance sheet presentation for natural resources. (SO 5) AP

BE9–16   Mabasa Company purchases a patent for $150,000 cash on January 2, 2014. Its legal life is 20 years and its estimated useful life is 8 years. On January 5, 2015, Mabasa paid $30,000 cash to successfully defend the patent in court.

(a) Record the purchase of the patent on January 2, 2014.
(b) Record amortization expense for the year ended December 31, 2014.
(c) Record the legal costs on January 5, 2015.
(d) Calculate amortization expense for 2015.

Record acquisition, legal expenditure, and amortization for patent. (SO 6) AP

BE9–17   Indicate whether each of the following items is property, plant, and equipment (write "PPE"), a natural resource ("NR"), or an intangible asset ("I"). If the item does not fit any of these categories, write "NA" (not applicable) in the space provided.

Identify and classify long-lived assets. (SO 7) K

(a)	_____ Building		(i)	_____ Mining equipment
(b)	_____ Cost of goods sold		(j)	_____ Natural gas deposit
(c)	_____ Franchise		(k)	_____ Note receivable, due in 3 years
(d)	_____ Goodwill		(l)	_____ Parking lot
(e)	_____ Inventory		(m)	_____ Patent
(f)	_____ Land		(n)	_____ Research costs
(g)	_____ Land held for resale		(o)	_____ Supplies
(h)	_____ Licence right		(p)	_____ Trademark

**Prepare partial balance sheet.
(SO 7) AP**

BE9–18 Canadian Tire Corporation, Limited reports the following selected information about long-lived assets at December 31, 2011 (in millions):

Accumulated amortization—finite-life intangibles	$ 1.5
Accumulated depreciation—assets under finance lease	138.5
Accumulated depreciation—buildings	1,014.8
Accumulated depreciation—fixtures and equipment	545.6
Accumulated depreciation—leasehold improvements	216.5
Assets under finance lease	267.4
Buildings	2,589.6
Fixtures and equipment	826.0
Construction in progress	137.0
Goodwill	377.6
Land (net of $1.4 of impairments)	748.8
Leasehold improvements	712.5
FGL Sports finite-life intangibles	22.4
FGL Sports indefinite-life intangibles	316.8
Mark's Work Wearhouse indefinite-life intangibles	64.1

FGL Sports and Mark's Work Wearhouse indefinite-life intangibles include legal trademarks such as store brands and banners, as wells as franchise agreements. Finite-life intangibles include certain brands that management has assessed to have a limited life. Prepare a partial balance sheet for Canadian Tire.

Calculate ratios. (SO 7) AP

BE9–19   Agrium Inc., a global agricultural nutrients producer that is headquartered in Calgary, Alberta, reports the following in its 2011 financial statements (in millions of US$):

	2011	2010
Net sales	$15,470	$10,743
Profit	1,375	713
Total assets	13,140	12,892

Calculate Agrium's return on assets and asset turnover for 2011.

▶ Exercises

**Classify expenditures.
(SO 1) AP**

E9–1   The following expenditures related to property, plant, and equipment were made by Pascal Company:

1. Paid $400,000 for a new plant site.
2. Paid $5,000 in legal fees on the purchase of the plant site.
3. Paid $7,500 for grading the plant site.
4. Paid $4,800 to demolish an old building on the plant site; residual materials were sold for $900.
5. Paid $54,000 for a new delivery truck.
6. Paid $200 freight to have the new delivery truck delivered.
7. Paid $450 to have the company name and advertising slogan painted on the new truck.
8. Paid the $95 motor vehicle licence fee on the new truck.
9. Paid $1,900 for a one-year accident insurance policy on the new delivery truck.
10. Paid $17,500 in architect fees for work on the new plant.
11. Paid $17,500 for paving the parking lots and driveways on the plant site.

Instructions

(a) Explain what types of costs should be included in determining the cost of property, plant, and equipment.
(b) List the numbers of the preceding transactions, and beside each number write the account title that the expenditure should be debited to.

E9-2   Hohenberger Farms purchased real estate for $1,280,000, which included $5,000 in legal fees. It paid $255,000 cash and incurred a mortgage payable for the balance. The real estate included land that was appraised at $476,000, buildings appraised at $748,000, and fences and other land improvements appraised at $136,000. The buildings have an estimated useful life of 60 years and a $50,000 residual value. Land improvements have an estimated 15-year useful life and no residual value.

Record basket purchase and calculate depreciation.
(SO 1, 2) AP

Instructions

(a) Calculate the cost that should be allocated to each asset purchased.
(b) Record the purchase of the real estate.
(c) Calculate the annual depreciation expense for the buildings and land improvements assuming Hohenberger Farms uses straight-line depreciation.

E9-3   Randell Equipment Repair purchased equipment on March 15, 2014, for $75,000. The company also paid the following amounts: $1,000 for delivery charges; $200 for insurance while the machine was in transit; $1,800 for a one-year insurance policy; and $2,800 for testing and installation. The machine was ready for use on April 1, 2014, but the company did not start using it until May 1, 2014.

Calculate cost and depreciation; recommend method.
(SO 1, 2) AP

Randell will depreciate the equipment over 10 years with no residual value. It expects to consume the equipment's future economic benefits evenly over the useful life. The company has a December 31 fiscal year end.

Instructions

(a) Calculate the cost of the equipment.
(b) When should the company begin depreciating the equipment: March 15, April 1, or May 1? Why?
(c) Which depreciation method should the company use? Why?
(d) Calculate the depreciation on the equipment for 2014 and 2015.

E9-4   On June 9, 2013, Blue Ribbon Company purchased manufacturing equipment at a cost of $345,000. Blue Ribbon estimated that the equipment will produce 600,000 units over its five-year useful life, and have a residual value of $15,000. The company has a December 31 fiscal year end and has a policy of recording a half year's depreciation in the year of acquisition.

Calculate depreciation using three methods; recommend method.
(SO 2) AP

Instructions

(a) Calculate depreciation under the straight-line method for 2013 and 2014.
(b) Calculate the depreciation expense under the diminishing-balance method using double the straight-line rate, for 2013 and 2014.
(c) Calculate the depreciation expense under the units-of-production method, assuming the actual number of units produced was 71,000 in 2013 and 118,600 in 2014.
(d) In this situation, what factors should the company consider in determining which depreciation method it should use?

E9-5   On April 22, 2013, Sandstone Enterprises purchased equipment for $129,200. The company expects to use the equipment for 12,000 working hours during its four-year life and that it will have a residual value of $14,000. Sandstone has a December 31 year end and pro-rates depreciation to the nearest month. The actual machine usage was: 1,900 hours in 2013; 2,800 hours in 2014; 3,700 hours in 2015; 2,700 hours in 2016; and 1,100 hours in 2017.

Prepare depreciation schedules and answer questions.
(SO 2) AP

Instructions

(a) Prepare a depreciation schedule for the life of the asset under each of the following methods:
    1. straight-line,
    2. diminishing-balance using double the straight-line rate, and
    3. units-of-production.
(b) Which method results in the lowest profit over the life of the asset?
(c) Which method results in the least cash used for depreciation over the life of the asset?

E9-6   Bisor Company has a December 31 year end and uses straight-line depreciation for all property, plant, and equipment. On July 1, 2010, the company purchased equipment for $500,000. The equipment had an expected useful life of 10 years and no residual value.

Record depreciation and impairment. (SO 3) AP

On December 31, 2013, after recording annual depreciation, Bisor reviewed its equipment for possible impairment. Bisor determined that the equipment has a recoverable amount of $225,000. It is not known if the recoverable amount will increase or decrease in the future.

Instructions

(a) Prepare journal entries to record the purchase of the asset on July 1, 2010, and to record depreciation expense on December 31, 2010, and December 31, 2013.
(b) Determine if there is an impairment loss at December 31, 2013, and if there is, prepare a journal entry to record it.

(c) Calculate depreciation expense for 2014 and the carrying amount of the equipment at December 31, 2014.

(d) Assume that the equipment is assessed again for impairment at December 31, 2014, and that the company determines the recoverable amount is $240,000. Should Bisor make an adjustment to reflect the increase in the recoverable amount? Why or why not?

Calculate revised depreciation. (SO 3) AP

E9-7 Lindy Weink, the new controller of Lafrenière Company, has reviewed the expected useful lives and residual values of selected depreciable assets at December 31, 2014. (Depreciation for 2014 has not been recorded yet.) Her findings are as follows:

Type of Asset	Date Acquired	Cost	Total Useful Life in Years		Residual Value	
			Current	Proposed	Current	Proposed
Building	Jan. 1, 2002	$800,000	20	30	$40,000	$60,500
Equipment	Jan. 1, 2012	125,000	5	4	5,000	4,000

After discussion, management agrees to accept Lindy's proposed changes. All assets are depreciated by the straight-line method. Lafrenière Company has a December 31 year end.

Instructions

(a) For each asset, calculate the annual depreciation expense using the original estimated useful life and residual value.

(b) Calculate the carrying amount of each asset as at January 1, 2014.

(c) For each asset, calculate the revised annual depreciation expense and the carrying amount at December 31, 2014.

(d) For each asset, calculate the total depreciation expense over the life of the asset assuming the asset is used until the end of its revised useful life.

Record asset addition and revised depreciation; show balance sheet presentation. (SO 3) AP

E9-8 On October 1, 2012, Chignecto Manufacturing Company purchased a piece of high-tech equipment for $90,000 cash. Chignecto estimated the equipment would have a six-year useful life and a residual value of $9,000. The company uses straight-line depreciation and has a September 30 fiscal year end.

On October 1, 2014, Chignecto paid $15,000 cash to upgrade the equipment. It is expected that the upgrade will significantly reduce the operating costs of the equipment. Chignecto also reviewed the equipment's expected useful life and estimated that due to changing technology, the equipment's total expected useful life will be four years and its residual value will be $5,000.

Instructions

(a) Calculate the annual depreciation expense for the first two years of the equipment's life.

(b) Calculate the carrying amount of the equipment at September 30, 2014.

(c) Record the expenditure to upgrade the equipment on October 1, 2014.

(d) Record the annual depreciation of the equipment on September 30, 2015.

(e) Show the balance sheet presentation of the equipment on September 30, 2015.

Record disposal of property, plant, and equipment. (SO 4) AP

E9-9 The following are some transactions of Surendal Company for 2014. Surendal Company uses straight-line depreciation and has a December 31 year end.

Jan. 2   Scrapped a piece of equipment that originally cost $8,000 and was fully depreciated.

Apr. 1   Retired a piece of equipment that was purchased on January 1, 2005, for $45,000. The equipment had an expected useful life of 10 years with no residual value.

July 30   Sold equipment for $1,100 cash. The equipment was purchased on January 3, 2012, for $12,600 and was depreciated over an expected useful life of three years with no residual value.

Nov. 1   Traded in an old vehicle for a new vehicle, receiving a $10,000 trade-in allowance and paying $36,000 cash. The old vehicle had been purchased on November 1, 2007, at a cost of $35,000. The estimated useful life was eight years and the estimated residual value was $5,000. The fair value of the old vehicle was $7,000 on November 1, 2014.

Instructions

(a) For each of these disposals, prepare a journal entry to record depreciation from January 1, 2014, to the date of disposal, if required.

(b) For each these disposals, indicate if the disposal has increased (+) or decreased (−) Cash, Equipment, Accumulated Depreciation, total property, plant, and equipment (PP&E), and profit, and by how much. If the item is not changed, write "NE" to indicate there is no effect. Use the following format, in which the first one has been done for you as an example.

Transaction	Cash	Equipment	Accumulated Depreciation	Total PP&E	Total Assets	Owner's Equity	Profit
Jan. 2	NE	−$8,000	−$8,000	NE	NE	NE	NE

(c) Record the disposals.

E9–10 On January 3, 2011, Hamir Company purchased equipment for $48,000. Hamir planned to keep the equipment for four years, and expected the equipment would then be sold for $4,000. On January 5, 2014, Hamir sold the computer equipment for $8,000.

Instructions

(a) Calculate the depreciation expense for 2011, 2012, and 2013 under (1) the straight-line method and (2) the double diminishing-balance method.
(b) Calculate the gain or loss on disposal if Hamir had used (1) the straight-line method and (2) the double diminishing-balance method.
(c) Explain why the gain or loss on disposal is not the same under the two depreciation methods.
(d) Calculate the total depreciation expense plus the loss or minus the gain under (1) the straight-line method and (2) the double diminishing-balance method. Comment on your findings.

Calculate gain or loss on disposal under different depreciation methods and comment. (SO 4) AP

E9–11 On July 1, 2014, Phillips Exploration Inc. invests $1.3 million in a mine that is estimated to have 800,000 tonnes of ore. The company estimates that the property will be sold for $100,000 when production at the mine has ended. During the last six months of 2014, 100,000 tonnes of ore are mined and sold. Phillips has a December 31 fiscal year end.

Instructions

(a) Explain why the units-of-production method is often used for depreciating natural resources.
(b) Record the 2014 depreciation.
(c) Show how the mine and any related accounts are reported on the December 31, 2014, income statement and balance sheet.
(d) Assume that the selling price of ore has dropped significantly after December 31, 2014. By June 30, 2015, it is $1.40 per tonne. Does this indicate that the mine may be impaired? Why or why not?

Record depreciation for natural resources; show financial statement presentation; comment on potential impairment. (SO 5) AP

E9–12 An accounting co-op student encountered the following situations at Chin Company:

1. During the year, Chin Company purchased land and paid legal fees on the purchase. The land had an old building, which was demolished. The land was then cleared and graded. Construction of a new building will start next year. All of these costs were included in the cost of land. The student decided that this was incorrect, and prepared a journal entry to put the cost of removing the building and clearing and grading the land in land improvements and the legal fees in legal fee expense.
2. The student learned that Chin is depreciating its buildings and equipment, but not its land. The student could not understand why land was not included, so she prepared journal entries to depreciate all of the company's property, plant, and equipment for the current year end.
3. The student decided that Chin's amortization policy on its intangible assets is wrong. The company is currently amortizing its patents but not its trademarks. The student fixed that for the current year end by adding trademarks to her adjusting entry for amortization. She told a fellow student that she felt she had improved the consistency of the company's accounting policies by making these changes.
4. One of the buildings that Chin uses has a zero carrying amount but a substantial fair value. The co-op student felt that leaving the carrying amount at zero did not benefit the financial information's users—especially the bank—and wrote the building up to its fair value. After all, she reasoned, you write down assets if fair values are lower. She feels that writing them up if their fair value is higher is yet another example of the improved consistency that her employment has brought to the company's accounting practices.

Instructions

Explain whether or not the co-op student's accounting treatment in each of the above situations follows generally accepted accounting principles. If it does not, explain why and what the appropriate accounting treatment should be.

Apply accounting concepts. (SO 1, 2, 6) AP

E9–13 Karsch Enterprises, a public company, has a December 31 fiscal year end and uses straight-line amortization for its finite-life intangible assets. The company has provided you with the following information related to its intangible assets and goodwill during 2013 and 2014:

2013

Jan. 9 Purchased a patent with an estimated useful life of five years and a legal life of 20 years for $45,000 cash.
May 15 Purchased another company and recorded goodwill of $450,000 as part of the purchase.
Dec. 31 Recorded adjusting entries as required for amortization.
Dec. 31 Tested assets for impairment and determined the patent and the goodwill's recoverable amounts were $40,000 and $400,000, respectively.

2014

Jan. 2 Incurred legal fees of $30,000 to successfully defend the patent.
Mar. 31 Incurred research costs of $175,000.

Record acquisition, amortization, and impairment of intangible assets. (SO 6) AP

Apr. 1 Purchased a copyright for $66,000 cash. The company expects the copyright will benefit the company for 10 years.

July 1 Purchased a trademark with an indefinite expected life for $275,000 cash.

Dec. 31 Recorded adjusting entries as required for amortization.

Dec. 31 Tested assets for impairment and determined the copyright and the trademark's recoverable amounts were in excess of their cost. The patent and the goodwill's recoverable amounts were $45,000 and $425,000, respectively.

Instructions

(a) Record the transactions and adjusting entries as required.

(b) Show the balance sheet presentation of the intangible assets and goodwill at December 31, 2014.

Determine balance sheet and income statement presentation for intangible assets and goodwill.
(SO 6) AP

E9–14 Whiteway Company has a December 31 fiscal year end. Selected information follows for Whiteway Company for three independent situations as at December 3, 2014:

1. Whiteway purchased a patent from Hopkins Inc. for $400,000 on January 1, 2011. The patent expires on January 1, 2019. Whiteway has been amortizing it over its legal life. During 2014, Whiteway determined that the patent's economic benefits would not last longer than six years from the date of acquisition.

2. Whiteway has a trademark that had been purchased in 2010 for $250,000. During 2013, the company spent $50,000 on a lawsuit that successfully defended the trademark. On December 31, 2014, it was assessed for impairment and the recoverable amount was determined to be $275,000.

3. In 2012, Whiteway purchased another business and paid $70,000 in excess of the fair value of the net identifiable assets of that business. This goodwill was assessed for impairment as at December 31, 2013, and December 31, 2014. The recoverable amount was determined to be $55,000 at December 31, 2013, and $80,000 at December 31, 2014.

Instructions

(a) For each of these assets, determine the amount that will be reported on Whiteway's December 31, 2013 and 2014, balance sheets.

(b) For each of these assets, determine what, if anything, will be recorded on Whiteway's 2014 income statement. Be specific about the account name and the amount.

Classify long-lived assets; prepare partial balance sheet.
(SO 7) AP

E9–15 **Shoppers Drug Mart Corporation** reported the following selected information as at December 31, 2011 (in thousands):

Accumulated amortization—computer software	$ 136,406
Accumulated amortization—customer relationships	13,691
Accumulated amortization—other intangible assets	6,262
Accumulated amortization—prescription files	64,372
Accumulated depreciation—assets under financing leases	16,411
Accumulated depreciation—buildings	24,325
Accumulated depreciation—equipment, fixtures, and computer equipment	792,644
Accumulated depreciation—leasehold improvements	451,481
Assets under financing leases	127,034
Depreciation and amortization expense	297,682
Buildings	214,043
Computer software	308,478
Customer relationships	50,736
Equipment, fixtures, and computer equipment	1,283,062
Goodwill	2,499,722
Finance expenses	64,038
Investment property	16,372
Land	65,478
Leasehold improvements	1,291,445
Loss on disposal of property, plant, and equipment	1,498
Other non-current assets	39,289
Other intangible assets	9,267
Prescription files	133,987
Properties under development	71,342

Prescription files and customer relationships were acquired in the process of purchasing independent drug stores and are being amortized over their estimated useful lives. Computer software includes the costs of developing the software and is being amortized over its useful life.

Instructions

(a) Identify in which financial statement (balance sheet or income statement) and which section (e.g., property, plant, and equipment) each of the above items should be reported.

(b) Prepare the non-current assets section of the balance sheet as at December 31, 2011.

E9–16 Suncor Energy Inc. reported the following information for the fiscal years ended December 31, 2011, and December 31, 2010 (in millions):

Calculate asset turnover and return on assets. (SO 7) AN

	Dec. 31, 2011	Dec. 31, 2010
Net revenues	$39,337	$32,003
Profit	4,304	3,829
Total assets, end of year	74,777	68,607
Total assets, beginning of year	68,607	67,799

Instructions

(a) Calculate Suncor's asset turnover and return on assets for the two years.

(b) Comment on what the ratios reveal about Suncor Energy Inc.'s effectiveness in using its assets to generate revenues and produce profit.

▶ Problems: Set A

P9–1A In 2014, Kadlec Company had the following transactions related to the purchase of a property. All transactions were for cash unless otherwise stated.

Record property transactions. (SO 1) AP

Jan. 12 Purchased real estate for a future plant site for $420,000, paying $95,000 cash and signing a note payable for the balance. On the site, there was an old building, and the fair values of the land and building were $400,000 and $40,000, respectively. The old building will be demolished and a new one built.

16 Paid $8,500 for legal fees on the real estate purchase.

31 Paid $25,000 to demolish the old building to make room for the new plant.

Feb. 13 Received $10,000 for residual materials from the demolished building.

28 Graded and filled the land in preparation for the construction for $9,000.

Mar. 14 Paid $38,000 in architect fees for the building plans.

31 Paid the local municipality $15,000 for building permits.

Apr. 22 Excavation costs for the new building were $17,000.

Sept. 26 The construction of the building was completed. The full cost was $750.000. Paid $150,000 cash and signed a mortgage note payable for the balance.

Sept. 30 Purchased a one-year insurance policy for the building, $4,500.

Oct. 20 Paved the parking lots, driveways, and sidewalks for $45,000.

Nov. 15 Installed a fence for $12,000.

Instructions

(a) Record the above transactions.

(b) Determine the cost of the land, land improvements, and building that will appear on Kadlec's December 31, 2014, balance sheet.

TAKING IT FURTHER When should Kadlec start to record depreciation and on which assets?

P9–2A In its first year of business, ChalkBoard purchased land, a building, and equipment on March 5, 2013, for $650,000 in total. The land was valued at $275,000, the building at $343,750, and the equipment at $68,750. Additional information on the depreciable assets follows:

Allocate cost and calculate partial period depreciation. (SO 1, 2) AP

Asset	Residual Value	Useful Life in Years	Depreciation Method
Building	$25,000	60	Straight-line
Equipment	5,000	8	Double diminishing-balance

Instructions

(a) Allocate the purchase cost of the land, building, and equipment to each of the assets.

(b) ChalkBoard has a December 31 fiscal year end and is trying to decide how to calculate depreciation for assets purchased during the year. Calculate depreciation expense for the building and equipment for 2013 and 2014 assuming:

1. depreciation is calculated to the nearest whole month.

2. a half year's depreciation is recorded in the year of acquisition.

(c) Which policy should ChalkBoard follow in the year of acquisition: recording depreciation to the nearest whole month or recording a half year of depreciation?

TAKING IT FURTHER   In the year the asset is purchased should ChalkBoard record depreciation for the exact number of days the asset is owned? Why or why not?

Determine cost; calculate and compare depreciation under different methods.
(SO 1, 2) AP

P9–3A   Payne Company purchased equipment on account on September 3, 2012, at an invoice price of $210,000. On September 4, 2012, it paid $4,400 for delivery of the equipment. A one-year, $1,975 insurance policy on the equipment was purchased on September 6, 2012. On September 20, 2012, Payne paid $5,600 for installation and testing of the equipment. The equipment was ready for use on October 1, 2012.

Payne estimates that the equipment's useful life will be four years, with a residual value of $13,000. It also estimates that, in terms of activity, the equipment's useful life will be 75,000 units. Payne has a September 30 fiscal year end. Assume that actual usage is as follows:

# of Units	Year Ended September 30
15,750	2013
23,900	2014
20,200	2015
15,350	2016

Instructions

(a) Determine the cost of the equipment.
(b) Prepare depreciation schedules for the life of the asset under the following depreciation methods:
    1. straight-line
    2. diminishing-balance at double the straight-line rate
    3. units-of-production
(c) Which method would result in the highest profit for the year ended September 30, 2013? Over the life of the asset?
(d) Which method would result in the least cash used for the year ended September 30, 2013? Over the life of the asset?

TAKING IT FURTHER   Assume instead that, when Payne purchased the equipment, it had a legal obligation to ensure that the equipment was recycled at the end of its useful life. Assume the cost of doing this is significant. Would this have had an impact on the answers to (a) and (b) above? Explain.

Account for operating and capital expenditures, and asset impairments.
(SO 1, 3) AP

P9–4A   Arnison Company has a December 31 fiscal year end and follows ASPE. The following selected transactions are related to its property, plant, and equipment in 2014:

Jan. 12	All of the company's light bulbs were converted to energy-efficient bulbs for $2,200. Arnison expects that this will save money on its utility bills in the future.
Feb. 6	Paid $5,400 to paint equipment that had started to rust.
Apr. 24	An air conditioning system in the factory was installed for $75,000.
May 17	Safety training was given to factory employees on using the equipment at a cost of $3,100.
July 19	Windows broken in a labour dispute (not covered by insurance) were replaced for $5,900.
Aug. 21	Paid $26,000 to convert the company's delivery vehicles from gasoline to propane. Arnison expects this will substantially reduce the vehicles' future operating costs, but it will not extend the vehicles' useful lives.
Sept. 20	The exhaust system in a delivery vehicle was repaired for $2,700.
Oct. 25	New parts were added to equipment for $20,000. Arnison expects this will increase the equipment's useful life by four years.
Dec. 31	After recording annual depreciation, Arnison reviewed its property, plant, and equipment for possible impairment. Arnison determined the following:

    1. Land that originally cost $200,000 had previously been written down to $175,000 in 2011 as a result of a decline in the recoverable amount. The current recoverable amount of the land is $220,000.
    2. The recoverable amount of equipment that originally cost $150,000 and has accumulated depreciation of $62,500 is $50,000.

Instructions

(a) For each of these transactions, indicate if the transaction has increased (+) or decreased (−) Land, Buildings, Equipment, Accumulated Depreciation, total property, plant, and equipment (PP&E), and profit, and by how much. If the item is not changed, write "NE" to indicate there is no effect. Use the following format, in which the first one has been done for you as an example.

Transaction	Land	Buildings	Equipment	Accumulated Depreciation	Total PP&E	Profit
Jan. 12	NE	NE	NE	NE	NE	−$2,200

(b) Prepare journal entries to record the above transactions. All transactions are paid in cash.

TAKING IT FURTHER   Assume that Arnison also purchases equipment with an expected useful life of 12 years. Assume also that the equipment's engine will need to be replaced every four years. Which useful life should Arnison use when calculating depreciation on the equipment? Explain.

P9–5A   Slope Style Snowboarding Company, a public company, purchased equipment on January 10, 2010, for $750,000. At that time, management estimated that the equipment would have a useful life of 10 years and a residual value of $50,000. Slope Style uses the straight-line method of depreciation and has a December 31 year end.

Record impairment and calculate revised depreciation. (SO 3) AP

Slope Style tested the equipment for impairment on December 31, 2014, after recording the annual depreciation expense. It was determined that the equipment's recoverable amount was $320,000, and that the total estimated useful life would be eight years instead of ten, with a residual value of $10,000 instead of $50,000.

Instructions

(a) Calculate the annual depreciation expense for the years 2010 to 2014 and the carrying amount at December 31, 2014.
(b) Record the impairment loss, if any, on December 31, 2014.
(c) What will appear on Slope Style's 2014 income statement and balance sheet with regard to this equipment?
(d) Assuming no further impairments or recoveries, calculate the annual depreciation expense for the years 2015 to 2017.
(e) Determine the equipment's accumulated depreciation and carrying amount at the end of its useful life.

TAKING IT FURTHER   Suggest some possible reasons as to why companies are allowed to record recoveries of previously recorded impairments under IFRS but not under ASPE.

P9–6A   NW Tool Supply Company purchased land and a building on May 1, 2012, for $385,000. The company paid $115,000 in cash and signed a 5% note payable for the balance. At that time, it was estimated that the land was worth $150,000 and the building, $235,000. The building was estimated to have a 25-year useful life with a $35,000 residual value. The company has a December 31 year end and uses the single diminishing-balance depreciation method for buildings. The following are related transactions and adjustments during the next three years.

Record acquisition, depreciation, impairment, and disposal of land and building. (SO 2, 3, 4) AP

2012

Dec. 31   Recorded annual depreciation.
   31   Paid the interest owing on the note payable.

2013

Feb. 17   Paid $225 to have the furnace cleaned and serviced.
Dec. 31   Recorded annual depreciation.
   31   Paid the interest owing on the note payable.
   31   The land and building were tested for impairment. The land had a recoverable amount of $120,000 and the building, $240,000.

2014

Jan. 31   Sold the land and building for $320,000 cash: $110,000 for the land and $210,000 for the building.
Feb. 1   Paid the note payable and interest owing.

Instructions

(a) Record the above transactions and adjustments, including the purchase on May 1, 2012.
(b) What factors may have been responsible for the impairment?
(c) Assume instead that the company sold the land and building on October 31, 2014, for $400,000 cash: $160,000 for the land and $240,000 for the building. Record the journal entries to record the sale.

TAKING IT FURTHER   How might management determine the recoverable amount of the land and building at each year end? Would the company need to test the assets for impairment every year?

P9–7A   On December 27, 2011, Wolcott Windows purchased a piece of equipment for $107,500. The estimated useful life of the equipment is either three years or 60,000 units, with a residual value of $10,500. The company has a December 31 fiscal year end and normally uses straight-line depreciation. Management is considering the merits

Calculate and compare depreciation and gain or loss on disposal under three methods of depreciation. (SO 2, 4) AP

of using the units-of-production or diminishing-balance method of depreciation instead of the straight-line method. The actual numbers of units produced by the equipment were 10,000 in 2012, 20,000 in 2013, and 29,000 in 2014. The equipment was sold on January 5, 2015, for $15,000.

Instructions

(a) Calculate the actual cost of owning this equipment.
(b) Calculate the depreciation for the equipment for 2012 to 2014 under (1) the straight-line method, (2) the diminishing-balance method, using a 40% rate, and (3) units-of-production. (*Hint:* Round the depreciable cost per unit to three decimal places.)
(c) Calculate the gain or loss on the sale of the equipment under each of the three methods.
(d) Calculate the total depreciation expense plus the loss on sale (or minus the gain on sale) under each of the three depreciation methods. Compare these totals with your answer in (a) above. Comment on your results.

TAKING IT FURTHER The owner of Wolcott Windows believes that having a gain or loss on sale indicates the company had made a mistake in calculating depreciation. Do you agree or disagree? Explain.

Record acquisition, depreciation, and disposal of equipment. (SO 2, 4) AP

P9–8A Express Co. purchased equipment on March 1, 2012, for $95,000 on account. The equipment had an estimated useful life of five years, with a residual value of $5,000. The equipment is disposed of on February 1, 2015. Express Co. uses the diminishing-balance method of depreciation with a 20% rate and calculates depreciation for partial periods to the nearest month. The company has an August 31 year end.

Instructions

(a) Record the acquisition of the equipment on March 1, 2012.
(b) Record depreciation at August 31, 2012, 2013, and 2014.
(c) Record the disposal on February 1, 2015, under the following assumptions:
1. It was scrapped with no residual value.
2. It was sold for $55,000.
3. It was sold for $45,000.
4. It was traded for new equipment with a list price of $97,000. Express was given a trade-in allowance of $52,000 on the old equipment and paid the balance in cash. Express determined the old equipment's fair value to be $47,000 at the date of the exchange.

TAKING IT FURTHER What are the arguments in favour of recording gains and losses on disposals of property, plant, and equipment as part of profit from operations? What are the arguments in favour of recording them as non-operating items?

Record property, plant, and equipment transactions; prepare partial financial statements. (SO 2, 4, 7) AP

P9–9A At January 1, 2014, Hamsmith Corporation reported the following property, plant, and equipment accounts:

Accumulated depreciation—buildings	$31,100,000
Accumulated depreciation—equipment	27,000,000
Buildings	48,700,000
Equipment	75,000,000
Land	10,000,000

Hamsmith uses straight-line depreciation for buildings and equipment and its fiscal year end is December 31. The buildings are estimated to have a 50-year useful life and no residual value; the equipment is estimated to have a 10-year useful life and no residual value. Interest on the notes is payable or collectible annually on the anniversary date of the issue.

During 2014, the following selected transactions occurred:

Apr. 1 Purchased land for $2.2 million. Paid $550,000 cash and issued a three-year, 6% note for the balance.
May 1 Sold equipment for $150,000 cash. The equipment cost $1.4 million when originally purchased on January 1, 2006.
June 1 Sold land for $1.8 million. Received $450,000 cash and accepted a three-year, 5% note for the balance. The land cost $700,000.
July 1 Purchased equipment for $1.1 million cash.
Dec. 31 Retired equipment that cost $500,000 when purchased on December 31, 2004.

Instructions

(a) Record the above transactions.
(b) Record any adjusting entries required at December 31, 2014.
(c) Prepare the property, plant, and equipment section of Hamsmith's balance sheet at December 31, 2014.

TAKING IT FURTHER   The owner of Hamsmith suggests the company should start using the revaluation model, not the cost model, for property, plant, and equipment now that it is following IFRS. Comment on this suggestion.

P9–10A   Due to rapid turnover in the accounting department, several transactions involving intangible assets were improperly recorded by Riley Co. in the year ended December 31, 2014:

Correct errors in recording intangible asset transactions.
(SO 6) AP

1. Riley developed a new manufacturing process early in the year, incurring research and development costs of $160,000. Of this amount, 45% was considered to be development costs that could be capitalized. Riley recorded the entire $160,000 in the Patents account and amortized it using a 15-year estimated useful life.
2. On July 1, 2014, Riley purchased a small company and, as a result of the purchase, recorded goodwill of $400,000. Riley recorded a half year's amortization on the goodwill in 2014 based on a 40-year useful life.
3. The company purchased a trademark for $47,500. Shortly thereafter, it was sued for trademark infringement. At the end of the year, Riley determined that the recoverable amount of the trademark was $35,000. Riley did not record an impairment loss because it is hopeful that the recoverable amount will rebound next year after the conclusion of a legal case defending the company's right to use this trademark.
4. Several years ago, Riley paid $70,000 for a licence to be the exclusive Canadian distributor of a Danish beer. In 2011, Riley determined there was an impairment of $40,000 in the value of the licence and recorded the loss. In 2014, because of a change in consumer tastes, the value of the licence increased to $80,000. Riley recorded the $50,000 increase in the licence's value by crediting Impairment Loss and debiting the licence account. Management felt the company should consistently record increases and decreases in value.
5. The company made an $8,000 charitable donation on December 31, 2014, which it debited to goodwill.

Instructions

Assuming that Riley reports under IFRS, prepare the journal entries that are needed to correct the errors made during 2014.

TAKING IT FURTHER   The majority of the intangible assets reported on a balance sheet have been purchased as opposed to being internally generated. Why? What happens to the cost of an internally generated intangible asset if it is not recorded as an asset?

P9–11A   The intangible assets reported by Ip Company at December 31, 2013, follow:

Record intangible asset transactions; prepare partial balance sheet. (SO 6, 7) AP

Patent #1	$80,000	
Less: Accumulated amortization	16,000	$ 64,000
Copyright #1	$48,000	
Less: Accumulated amortization	28,800	19,200
Goodwill		220,000
Total		$303,200

Patent #1 was acquired in January 2012 and has an estimated useful life of 10 years. Copyright #1 was acquired in January 2008 and also has an estimated useful life of 10 years. The following cash transactions may have affected intangible assets and goodwill during the year 2014:

Jan.   2   Paid $23,200 of legal costs to successfully defend Patent #1 against infringement by another company.
June 30   Developed a new product, incurring $180,000 in research costs and $60,000 in development costs, which were paid in cash. Patent #2 was granted for the product on July 1. Its estimated useful life is equal to its legal life of 20 years.
Sept. 1   Paid $12,000 to an Olympic athlete to appear in commercials advertising the company's products. The commercials will air in September.
Oct. 1   Acquired a second copyright for $18,000 cash. Copyright #2 has an estimated useful life of six years.
Dec. 31   Determined the recoverable amount of the goodwill to be $240,000. The company had originally paid $250,000 for the goodwill in 2011. In 2012, the company had recorded a $30,000 impairment loss on the goodwill. There is no indication that the patents and copyrights were impaired.

Instructions

(a) Record the above transactions.
(b) Prepare any adjusting journal entries required at December 31, 2014, the company's year end.
(c) Show how the intangible assets and goodwill will be reported on the balance sheet at December 31, 2014.

TAKING IT FURTHER   Since intangible assets do not have physical substance, why are they considered to be assets?

Record natural resource transactions; prepare partial financial statements.
(SO 3, 5, 7) AP

P9–12A Yount Mining Company has a December 31 fiscal year end. The following information relates to its Gough Alexander mine:

1. Yount purchased the Gough Alexander mine on March 31, 2013, for $2.6 million cash. On the same day, modernization of the mine was completed at a cash cost of $260,000. It is estimated that this mine will yield 560,000 tonnes of ore. The mine's estimated residual value is $200,000. Yount expects it will extract all the ore, and then close and sell the mine site in four years.
2. During 2013, Yount extracted and sold 120,000 tonnes of ore from the mine.
3. At the beginning of 2014, Yount reassessed its estimate of the remaining ore in the mine. Yount estimates that there is still 550,000 tonnes of ore in the mine at January 1, 2014. The estimated residual value remains at $200,000.
4. During 2014, Yount extracted and sold 100,000 tonnes of ore from the mine.

Instructions

(a) Prepare the 2013 and 2014 journal entries for the above, including any year-end adjustments.
(b) Show how the Gough Alexander mine will be reported on Yount's December 31, 2014, income statement and balance sheet.

TAKING IT FURTHER If the total estimated amount of units that will be produced (extracted) changes during the life of the natural resource, is it still appropriate to use the units-of-production method? Explain.

Calculate ratios and comment. (SO 7) AN

P9–13A Andruski Company and Brar Company both manufacture school science equipment. The following financial information is for three years ended December 31 (in thousands):

Andruski Company	2014	2013	2012
Net sales	$552.0	$515.9	$469.0
Profit	21.4	20.6	18.7
Total assets	702.5	662.8	602.5

Brar Company	2014	2013	2012
Net sales	$1,762.9	$1,588.2	$1,484.3
Profit	96.5	85.4	79.8
Total assets	1,523.5	1,410.7	1,318.4

Instructions

(a) Calculate the asset turnover and return on assets ratios for both companies for 2013 and 2014. Round your answers to two decimal points.
(b) Comment on how effective each of the companies is at using its assets to generate sales and produce profit.

TAKING IT FURTHER After reading the notes to the financial statements, you have determined that Andruski Company uses diminishing-balance depreciation and Brar uses straight-line. Does this affect your ability to compare these two companies?

▶ Problems: Set B

Record property transactions.
(SO 1) AP

P9–1B In 2014, Weisman Company had the following transactions related to the purchase of a property. All transactions are for cash unless otherwise stated.

Feb. 7 Purchased real estate for $575,000, paying $115,000 cash and signing a note payable for the balance. The site had an old building on it and the fair value of the land and building were $555,000 and $30,000, respectively. Weisman intends to demolish the old building and construct a new apartment building on the site.
9 Paid legal fees of $7,500 on the real estate purchase on February 7.
15 Paid $19,000 to demolish the old building and make the land ready for the construction of the apartment building.
17 Received $8,500 from the sale of material from the demolished building.
25 Graded and filled the land in preparation for the building construction at a cost of $10,500.
Mar. 2 Architect's fees on the apartment building were $28,000.
15 Excavation costs were $18,000. Construction began on March 20.

Aug. 31 The apartment building was completed. The full cost of construction was $850,000. Paid $170,000 cash and signed a note payable for the balance.
Sept. 3 Paid $40,000 for sidewalks and a parking lot for the building.
   10 Purchased a one-year insurance policy on the finished building for $3,750.
Oct. 31 Paid $37,750 for landscaping.

Instructions

(a) Record the above transactions.
(b) Determine the cost of the land, land improvements, and building that will appear on Weisman's December 31, 2014, balance sheet.

TAKING IT FURTHER When should Weisman begin recording depreciation on this property and on which assets?

P9–2B In its first year of business, Solinger Company purchased land, a building, and equipment on November 5, 2013, for $700,000 in total. The land was valued at $262,500, the building at $337,500, and the equipment at $150,000. Additional information on the depreciable assets follows:

Allocate cost and calculate partial period depreciation. (SO 1, 2) AP

Asset	Residual Value	Useful Life in Years	Depreciation Method
Building	$15,000	60	Straight-line
Equipment	15,000	8	Double diminishing-balance

Instructions

(a) Allocate the purchase cost of the land, building, and equipment to each of the assets.
(b) Solinger has a December 31 fiscal year end and is trying to decide how to calculate depreciation for assets purchased during the year. Calculate depreciation expense for the building and equipment for 2013 and 2014 assuming:
  1. depreciation is calculated to the nearest whole month.
  2. a half year's depreciation is recorded in the year of acquisition.
(c) Which policy should Solinger follow in the year of acquisition: recording depreciation to the nearest whole month or recording a half year of depreciation?

TAKING IT FURTHER Suppose that Solinger decided to use the units-of-production depreciation method instead of diminishing-balance for its equipment. How would this affect your answer to (c) above?

P9–3B Glans Company purchased equipment on account on April 6, 2012, at an invoice price of $442,000. On April 7, 2012, it paid $4,000 for delivery of the equipment. A one-year, $3,000 insurance policy on the equipment was purchased on April 9, 2012. On April 22, 2012, Glans paid $6,000 for installation and testing of the equipment. The equipment was ready for use on May 1, 2012.
   Glans estimates that the equipment's useful life will be four years, with a residual value of $20,000. It also estimates that, in terms of activity, the equipment's useful life will be 150,000 units. Glans has an April 30 fiscal year end. Assume that actual usage is as follows:

Determine cost; calculate and compare depreciation under different methods. (SO 1, 2) AP

# of Units	Year Ended April 30
22,600	2013
45,600	2014
49,700	2015
32,200	2016

Instructions

(a) Determine the cost of the equipment.
(b) Prepare depreciation schedules for the life of the asset under the following depreciation methods:
  1. straight-line
  2. diminishing-balance at double the straight-line rate
  3. units-of-production
(c) Which method would result in the highest profit for the year ended April 30, 2013? Over the life of the asset?
(d) Which method would result in the least cash used for the year ended April 30, 2013? Over the life of the asset?

TAKING IT FURTHER Assume instead that at the time Glans purchased the equipment, it had a legal obligation to ensure that the equipment was recycled at the end of its useful life. Assume the cost of doing this is significant. Would this have had an impact on the answers to (a) and (b) above? Explain.

Account for operating and capital expenditures and asset impairments. (SO 1, 3) AP

P9–4B Sugden Company has a December 31 fiscal year end and follows IFRS. The following selected transactions are related to its property, plant, and equipment in 2014:

Jan. 22   Performed an annual safety inspection on the equipment for $4,600.

Apr. 10   Installed a conveyor belt system in the factory for $95,000, which is expected to increase efficiency and allow the company to produce more products each year.

May 6   Painted the interior of the entire building at a cost of $30,500.

July 20   Repaired a machine for $10,000. An employee had used incorrect material in the machine, which resulted in a complete mechanical breakdown.

Aug. 7   Overhauled equipment that originally cost $100,000 for $35,000. This increased the equipment's expected useful life by three years.

    15   Trained several new employees to operate the company's equipment at a cost of $1,900.

Oct. 25   Paid $16,700 for the purchase of new equipment and $1,500 to a consultant for testing and installing the equipment.

Nov. 6   Added an elevator and ramps to a building owned by the company to make it wheelchair accessible for $120,000.

Dec. 31   After recording annual depreciation, Sugden reviewed its property, plant, and equipment for possible impairment. Sugden determined the following:
    1. The recoverable amount of equipment that originally cost $250,000 and has accumulated depreciation of $75,000 is $90,000.
    2. Land that originally cost $575,000 had previously been written down to $500,000 as a result of an impairment in 2011. Circumstances have changed, and the land's recoverable amount is now $600,000.

Instructions

(a) For each of these transactions, indicate if the transaction has increased (+) or decreased (−) Land, Buildings, Equipment, Accumulated Depreciation, total property, plant, and equipment (PP&E), and profit, and by how much. If the item is not changed, write "NE" to indicate there is no effect. Use the following format, in which the first one has been done for you as an example.

Transaction	Land	Buildings	Equipment	Accumulated Depreciation	Total PP&E	Profit
Jan. 22	NE	NE	NE	NE	NE	−$4,600

(b) Prepare journal entries to record the above transactions. All transactions are on account.

TAKING IT FURTHER   Assume that Sugden also purchased equipment with an expected useful life of 15 years and that the equipment's engine will need to be replaced every five years. Which useful life should Sugden use when calculating depreciation on the equipment? Explain.

Record impairment and calculate revised depreciation. (SO 3) AP

P9–5B Short Track Speed Skating, a public company, purchased equipment on January 10, 2010, for $600,000. At that time, management estimated that the equipment would have a useful life of 10 years and a residual value of $25,000. Short Track uses the straight-line method of depreciation and has a December 31 year end.

Short Track tested the equipment for impairment on December 31, 2014, after recording the annual depreciation expense. It was determined that the equipment's recoverable amount was $260,000, and that the total estimated useful life would be seven years instead of ten, with a residual value of $10,000 instead of $25,000.

Instructions

(a) Calculate the annual depreciation expense for the years 2010 to 2014 and the carrying amount at December 31, 2014.

(b) Record the impairment loss, if any, on December 31, 2014.

(c) What will appear on Short Track's 2014 income statement and balance sheet with regard to this equipment?

(d) Assuming no further impairments or recoveries, calculate the annual depreciation expense for the years 2015 and 2016.

(e) Determine the equipment's accumulated depreciation and carrying amount at the end of its useful life.

TAKING IT FURTHER   Suggest some possible reasons as to why the IFRS accounting standards result in recording impairments of long-lived assets more frequently than ASPE.

Record acquisition, depreciation, impairment, and disposal of land and buildings. (SO 1, 2, 3, 4) AP

P9–6B SE Parts Supply Company purchased land and a building on August 1, 2012, for $595,000. It paid $200,000 in cash and signed a 5% note payable for the balance. The company estimated the land was worth $340,000 and the building, $255,000. The building was estimated to have a 40-year useful life with a $15,000 residual value. The company has a December 31 year end and uses the straight-line depreciation method for buildings. The following are related transactions and adjustments during the next three years.

<u>2012</u>

Dec. 31 Recorded annual depreciation.
    31 Paid the interest owing on the note payable.

<u>2013</u>

May 21 Paid $2,000 to fix the roof.
Dec. 31 Recorded annual depreciation.
    31 Paid the interest owing on the note payable.
    31 The land and building were tested for impairment. The land had a recoverable amount of $280,000 and the building, $249,000.

<u>2014</u>

Mar. 31 Sold the land and building for $480,000 cash: $250,000 for the land and $230,000 for the building.
Apr. 1 Paid the note payable and interest owing.

Instructions

(a) Record the above transactions and adjustments, including the acquisition on August 1, 2012.
(b) What factors may have been responsible for the impairment?
(c) Assume instead that the company sold the land and building on November 30, 2014, for $650,000 cash: $390,000 for the land and $260,000 for the building. Record the journal entries to record the sale.

TAKING IT FURTHER   How might management determine the recoverable amount of the land and building at each year end? Does the company need to test the assets for impairment every year?

P9–7B   On January 3, 2013, Ajax Adanacs purchased a piece of equipment for $125,000. The equipment's estimated useful life is either three years or 12,000 units, with a residual value of $18,000. The company has a December 31 fiscal year end and normally uses straight-line depreciation. Management is considering the merits of using the units-of-production or diminishing-balance method of depreciation instead of the straight-line method. The actual numbers of units produced by the equipment were 6,000 in 2013, 2,000 in 2014, and 3,800 in 2015. The equipment was sold on January 5, 2016, for $21,000.

Calculate and compare depreciation and gain or loss on disposal under three methods of depreciation. (SO 2, 4) AP

Instructions

(a) Calculate the actual cost of owning this equipment.
(b) Calculate the depreciation for the equipment for 2013 to 2015 under (1) the straight-line method, (2) the diminishing-balance method, using a 45% rate, and (3) units-of-production. (*Hint:* Round the depreciable cost per unit to three decimal places.)
(c) Calculate the gain or loss on the sale of the equipment under each of the three methods.
(d) Calculate the total depreciation expense plus the loss on sale (or minus the gain on sale) under each of the three depreciation methods. Compare these totals with your answer in (a) above. Comment on your results.

TAKING IT FURTHER   The owner of Ajax Adanacs believes that having a gain or loss on sale indicates the company had made a mistake in calculating depreciation. Do you agree or disagree? Explain.

P9–8B   Walker Co. purchased furniture on February 4, 2012, for $70,000 on account. At that time, it was expected to have a useful life of five years and a $1,000 residual value. The furniture was disposed of on January 26, 2015, when the company moved to new premises. Walker Co. uses the diminishing-balance method of depreciation with a 20% rate and calculates depreciation for partial periods to the nearest month. The company has a September 30 year end.

Record acquisition, depreciation, and disposal of furniture. (SO 2, 4) AP

Instructions

(a) Record the acquisition of the furniture on February 4, 2012.
(b) Record depreciation for each of 2012, 2013, and 2014.
(c) Record the disposal on January 26, 2015, under the following assumptions:
    1. It was scrapped and has no residual value.
    2. It was sold for $30,000.
    3. It was sold for $40,000.
    4. It was traded for new furniture with a catalogue price of $115,000. Walker Co. was given a trade-in allowance of $45,000 on the old furniture and paid the balance in cash. Walker Co. determined that the old furniture's fair value was $30,000 at the date of the exchange.

TAKING IT FURTHER   What are the arguments in favour of recording gains and losses on disposals of property, plant, and equipment as part of profit from operations? What are the arguments in favour of recording them as non-operating items?

Record property, plant, and equipment transactions; prepare partial financial statements. (SO 2, 4, 7) AP

P9–9B   At January 1, 2014, Jaina Company reported the following property, plant, and equipment accounts:

Accumulated depreciation—buildings	$12,100,000
Accumulated depreciation—equipment	15,000,000
Buildings	28,500,000
Equipment	48,000,000
Land	4,000,000

Jaina uses straight-line depreciation for buildings and equipment, and its fiscal year end is December 31. The buildings are estimated to have a 50-year life and no residual value; the equipment is estimated to have a 10-year useful life and no residual value. Interest on all notes is payable or collectible at maturity on the anniversary date of the issue.

     During 2014, the following selected transactions occurred:

Apr. 1   Purchased land for $1.9 million. Paid $475,000 cash and issued a 10-year, 6% note for the balance.

May 1   Sold equipment that cost $750,000 when purchased on January 1, 2007. The equipment was sold for $350,000 cash.

June 1   Sold land purchased on June 1, 1996, for $1.2 million. Received $380,000 cash and accepted a 6% note for the balance. The land cost $300,000.

July 1   Purchased equipment for $1 million on account, terms n/60.

Dec. 31   Retired equipment that cost $470,000 when purchased on December 31, 2004.

Instructions

(a) Record the above transactions.
(b) Record any adjusting entries required at December 31, 2014.
(c) Prepare the property, plant, and equipment section of Jaina's balance sheet at December 31, 2014.

TAKING IT FURTHER   The owner of Jaina Company suggests the company should start using the revaluation model, not the cost model, for property, plant, and equipment now that it is following IFRS. Comment on this suggestion.

Correct errors in recording intangible asset transactions. (SO 6) AP

P9–10B   Due to rapid employee turnover in the accounting department, the following transactions involving intangible assets were recorded in a questionable way by Hahn Company in the year ended August 31, 2014:

1. Hahn developed an electronic monitoring device for running shoes. It incurred research costs of $70,000 and development costs with probable future benefits of $45,000. It recorded all of these costs in the Patent account.
2. The company registered the patent for the monitoring device developed in transaction 1. Legal fees and registration costs totalled $21,000. These costs were recorded in the Professional Fees Expense account.
3. The company successfully fought a competitor in court, defending its patent. It incurred $38,000 of legal fees. These costs were recorded in the Legal Fees Expense account.
4. The company recorded $5,750 of annual amortization on the patent over its legal life of 20 years [($70,000 + $45,000 = $115,000) ÷ 20 years]. The patent's expected economic life is five years. Assume that for amortization purposes, all costs occurred at the beginning of the year.
5. At the end of the year, Hahn tested the patent for impairment and found that its recoverable amount of $110,000 exceeded its carrying amount of $109,250 ($115,000 − $5,750). Since Hahn follows the cost model, it did not record an entry.

Instructions

Assuming Hahn reports under ASPE, prepare the journal entries that are needed to correct the errors made during 2014.

TAKING IT FURTHER   The majority of the intangible assets reported on a balance sheet have been purchased as opposed to being internally generated. Why? What happens to the cost of an internally generated intangible asset if it is not recorded as an asset?

Record intangible asset transactions; prepare partial balance sheet. (SO 6, 7) AP

P9–11B   The intangible assets section of Ghani Corporation's balance sheet at December 31, 2013, is as follows:

Copyright #1	$36,000	
Less: Accumulated amortization	24,000	$ 12,000
Trademark		52,000
Goodwill		150,000
Total		$214,000

The copyright was acquired in January 2012 and has an estimated useful life of three years. The trademark was acquired in January 2010 and is expected to have an indefinite useful life. The following cash transactions may have affected intangible assets during 2014:

Jan.   2   Paid $7,000 in legal costs to successfully defend the trademark against infringement by another company.

July   1   Developed a new product, incurring $275,000 in research costs and $50,000 in development costs. A patent was granted for the product on July 1, and its useful life is equal to its legal life.

Aug.   1   Paid $45,000 to a popular hockey player to appear in commercials advertising the company's products. The commercials will air in September and October.

Oct.   1   Acquired a second copyright for $168,000. The new copyright has an estimated useful life of six years.

Dec. 31   The company determined the recoverable amount of the trademark and goodwill to be $50,000 and $170,000, respectively. There was no indication that any of the patents or copyrights were impaired.

Instructions

(a) Prepare journal entries to record the transactions.
(b) Prepare any adjusting journal entries required at December 31, 2014, the company's year end.
(c) Show how the intangible assets and goodwill will be presented on the balance sheet at December 31, 2014.

TAKING IT FURTHER   Since intangible assets do not have physical substance, why are they considered to be assets?

P9–12B   Cypress Timber Company has a December 31 fiscal year end. The following information is related to its Westerlund tract of timber land:

Record equipment, note payable, and natural resource transactions; prepare partial financial statements. (SO 2, 5, 7) AP

1. Cypress purchased a 50,000-hectare tract of timber land at Westerlund on June 7, 2013, for $50 million, paying $10 million cash and signing a 7% mortgage payable for the balance. Principal payments of $8 million and the annual interest on the mortgage are due each December 31. It is estimated that this tract will yield 1 million tonnes of timber. The timber tract's estimated residual value is $2 million. Cypress expects it will cut all the trees and then sell the Westerlund site in seven years.

2. On June 26, 2013, Cypress purchased and installed equipment at the Westerlund timber site for $196,000 cash. The equipment will be amortized on a straight-line basis over an estimated useful life of seven years with no residual value. Cypress has a policy of recording depreciation for partial periods to the nearest month. The equipment will be scrapped after the Westerlund site is harvested.

3. In 2013, Cypress cut and sold 110,000 tonnes of timber.
4. In 2014, Cypress cut and sold 240,000 tonnes of timber.

Instructions

(a) Prepare the 2013 and 2014 journal entries for the above, including any year-end adjustments.
(b) Show how property, plant, and equipment, natural resources, and related accounts will be reported on Cypress's December 31, 2014, income statement and balance sheet.

TAKING IT FURTHER   If the total estimated amount of units that will be produced (extracted) changes during the life of the natural resource, is it still appropriate to use the units-of-production method? Explain.

P9–13B   Mock Orange Company and Cotoneaster Company both manufacture pruning shears. The following financial information is for three years ended December 31 (in thousands):

Calculate ratios and comment. (SO 7) AN

Mock Orange Company	2014	2013	2012
Net sales	$9,428.0	$8,894.3	$8,235.5
Profit	627.7	597.8	553.5
Total assets	5,829.1	5,771.4	5,343.9

Cotoneaster Company	2014	2013	2012
Net sales	$3,839.8	$3,656.9	$3,417.7
Profit	143.4	137.9	128.9
Total assets	2,754.5	2,504.1	2,340.3

Instructions

(a) Calculate the asset turnover and return on assets ratios for both companies for 2013 and 2014. Round your answers to two decimal points.
(b) Comment on how effective each of the companies is at using its assets to generate sales and produce profit.

TAKING IT FURTHER   After reading the notes to the financial statements, you have determined that Mock Orange Company uses straight-line depreciation and Cotoneaster uses diminishing-balance. Does this affect your ability to compare these two companies?

▶ Continuing Cookie Chronicle

(**Note:** This is a continuation of the Cookie Chronicle from Chapters 1 through 8.)

Natalie is thinking of buying a van that will be used only for business. She estimates that she can buy the van for $28,400. Natalie would spend an additional $3,000 to have the van painted. As well, she wants the back seat of the van removed so that she will have lots of room to transport her mixer inventory and baking supplies. The cost of taking out the back seat and installing shelving units is estimated at $1,600. She expects the van to last about five years and to be driven for 200,000 km. The annual cost of vehicle insurance will be $1,440. Natalie estimates that at the end of the five-year useful life, the van will sell for $5,000. Assume that she will buy the van on April 15, 2014, and it will be ready for use on May 1, 2014.

   Natalie is concerned about the impact of the van's cost and related depreciation on Cookie Creations' income statement and balance sheet.

Instructions

(a) Determine the cost of the van.
(b) Prepare depreciation schedules for the life of the van under the following depreciation methods:
   1. straight-line.
   2. diminishing-balance at double the straight-line rate.
   3. units-of-production. It is estimated that the van will be driven as follows: 30,000 km in 2014, 37,500 km in 2015, 40,000 km in 2016, 47,500 km in 2017, 35,000 km in 2018, and 10,000 km in 2019.
   Recall that Cookie Creations has a December 31 year end.
(c) Which method of depreciation would result in the highest profit for the year ended December 31, 2014? Over the life of the asset?
(d) Which method would result in the van's highest carrying amount for the year ended December 31, 2014? Over the life of the asset?
(e) Which method would result in the least cash used for the year ended December 31, 2014? Over the life of the asset?
(f) Which method of depreciation would you recommend that Natalie use? Why?

CHAPTER 9 | BROADENING YOUR PERSPECTIVE

▶ Financial Reporting and Analysis

Financial Reporting Problem

BYP9–1   Refer to the financial statements and the Notes to Consolidated Statements for **Reitmans (Canada) Limited**, which are reproduced in Appendix A.

Instructions

(a) For each type of property and equipment that Reitmans reports in note 8 to its balance sheet, identify the following amounts at January 28, 2012: (1) cost, (2) accumulated depreciation and impairment losses, and (3) net carrying amount. ·
(b) For the intangible assets and goodwill that Reitmans reports in note 9 and in its balance sheet, identify the following amounts at January 28, 2012: (1) cost, (2) accumulated amortization, and (3) net carrying amount.
(c) Did Reitmans have any impairment losses or reversals of impairment losses in the year ended January 28, 2012? How does Reitmans determine if an impairment loss needs to be recorded?
(d) Depreciation and amortization expense are not disclosed separately on the statement of earnings. Where are they included? What were the amounts for fiscal 2012? (See notes 8 and 9.)
(e) What was the amount of cash used to buy property and equipment and intangible assets during the 2012 fiscal year? (*Hint:* Look at the statement of cash flows to determine this amount.)
(f) What depreciation methods are used by Reitmans for financial reporting purposes? (See note 3 to the financial statements.) What expected useful life does the company use to calculate the depreciation on its property and equipment? On its intangible assets?

Interpreting Financial Statements

BYP9–2   WestJet Airlines Ltd. is one of Canada's leading airlines, offering service to destinations in Canada, the United States, Mexico, and the Caribbean. The following is a partial extract from its December 31, 2011, notes to the financial statements:

Note. 1 (j) Statement of Significant Accounting Policies—Property and Equipment

Property and equipment is stated at cost and depreciated to its estimated residual value.

Asset class	Basis	Rate
Aircraft, net of estimated residual value	Straight-line	20 years
Engine, airframe and landing gear overhaul	Straight-line	8 to 15 years
Buildings	Straight-line	40 years
Leasehold improvements	Straight-line	Term of lease
Assets under finance leases	Straight-line	Term of lease

Major overhaul expenditures are capitalized and depreciated over the expected life between overhauls. All other costs relating to the maintenance of fleet assets are charged to the consolidated statement of earnings on consumption or as incurred.

Instructions

(a) WestJet uses straight-line depreciation for all of its depreciable property and equipment. For which of the assets shown above might WestJet consider using units-of-production instead of straight-line depreciation? Should WestJet use units-of-production for those assets?

(b) According to this note, major overhaul expenditures are treated differently than other fleet maintenance costs. Explain how WestJet records these items. Is this appropriate? Why or why not?

(c) WestJet depreciates the cost of leasehold improvements, and assets under finance leases over the terms of the leases. Is this appropriate? Are these terms the same as the physical lives of these assets?

(d) Does WestJet use component depreciation for any of its property and equipment assets? Should it?

▶ Critical Thinking

Collaborative Learning Activity

Note to instructor: Additional instructions and material for this group activity can be found on the Instructor Resource Site and in *WileyPLUS*.

BYP9–3   In this group activity, you will work in two groups to improve your understanding of the different depreciation methods. First you will work in "expert" groups in which you will ensure that each group member thoroughly understands one method of depreciation. Then you will move to a second group consisting of one student from each of the three expert groups, and take turns teaching each other the different depreciation methods.

Communication Activity

BYP9–4   Long Trucking Corporation is a medium-sized publicly owned trucking company with trucks that are driven across North America. The company owns large garages and equipment to repair and maintain the trucks. Ken Bond, the controller, knows that long-lived assets are reviewed annually for impairment. Ken records an impairment loss of $100,000 and the loss appears on the income statement for the current fiscal year. Jason Long, the company president, reviews the financial statements and wants more information from Ken about the impairment loss.

Instructions

Write an e-mail to Jason Long that explains (1) what might have caused the impairment loss, (2) the journal entry required for the impairment loss, and (3) how this writedown will affect Long Trucking's balance sheet and income statement in future years.

Ethics Case

BYP9–5   Finney Container Company has been seeing sales go down for its main product, non-biodegradable plastic cartons. Although some expenses have also reduced in line with the reduced revenues, there has been a decrease in profit because some expenses, such as depreciation, have not declined. The company uses the straight-line depreciation method.

The president, Philip Shapiro, recalling his college accounting classes, instructs his controller to lengthen the estimated asset lives used for depreciation calculations in order to reduce annual depreciation expense and increase profit. The president's compensation includes an annual bonus based on the amount of net profit reported in the income statement.

A processing line of automated plastic-extruding equipment that was purchased for $2.9 million in January 2012 was originally estimated to have a useful life between five and nine years. Therefore, the company used the middle of that estimate, or seven years, as the useful life, and a residual value of $100,000, to calculate the annual straight-line depreciation for the first two years. However, the president now wants the equipment's estimated useful life to be changed to nine years (total), and to continue using the straight-line method.

The controller is hesitant to make the change, believing it is unethical to increase profit in this way. The president says, "Hey, the useful life is only an estimate. Besides, I've heard that our competition uses a nine-year estimated life on its production equipment. You want the company results to be competitive, don't you? So maybe we were wrong the first time and now we are getting it right. Or you can tell the auditors that we think may be the equipment will last longer now that we are not using it as much."

Instructions

(a) Who are the stakeholders in this situation?
(b) Is the suggested change in asset life unethical, or simply a shrewd business practice by a sharp president?
(c) What would be the impact of the president's proposed change on profit in the year of the change?

"All About You" Activity

BYP9–6 In the "All About You" feature, you learned about actions that have been taken to strengthen Canada's copyright law and the radical changes in technology that are driving the need to update the law. You have recently graduated from a music program and have composed two songs that you believe a recording artist may produce. You are wondering how you can best get copyright protection for your songs.

Instructions

Go to the Canadian Intellectual Property Office website at http://www.cipo.ic.gc.ca and search for its publication "A Guide to Copyrights."

Answer the following questions:

(a) What is a copyright and to what does copyright apply?
(b) How can you obtain a copyright for your songs and what do you have to do to be protected?
(c) What are the benefits to you of getting copyright registration for your songs?
(d) How and where do you register a copyright?
(e) When you register a copyright you are required to pay a fee for the registration. Should the registration fee for the copyright be recorded as an asset or an expense?
(f) Go to the glossary in "A Guide to Copyrights." What is infringement of copyright? Provide a specific example of infringement.
(g) Go to frequently asked questions in "A Guide to Copyrights." Whose responsibility is it for monitoring the use of your songs once you have registered the copyright?

ANSWERS TO CHAPTER QUESTIONS

ANSWERS TO ACCOUNTING IN ACTION INSIGHT QUESTIONS

Business Insight, p. 474

Q: Is the units-of-production method the best depreciation method for Morris Formal Wear to use for its tuxedos or would you recommend another method?

A: Since Morris Formal Wear wants to track wear and tear on each of its tuxedos, the units-of-production depreciation method is the best choice. Rental tuxedos are the type of long-lived asset that will physically wear out with use much faster than they would become obsolete due to changing tuxedo styles. By keeping track of how many times each tuxedo has been used, instead of just how old they are, the company can make better decisions about when to replace the tuxedos.

All About You Insight, p. 490

Q: Why is it important that the copyrights of artists, writers, musicians, and the entertainment industry be protected?

A: Just as it is important that you as an individual be compensated in your career, it is important that individuals in artistic, music, entertainment, and literary careers be compensated fairly for their creativity. Without fair compensation, Canada's creativity and innovation will be discouraged. Without copyright protection, it may be difficult to ensure that appropriate individuals are fairly compensated and companies may not be willing to invest in creative ventures if the work is not protected.

ANSWERS TO SELF-STUDY QUESTIONS

1. c   2. b   3. b   4. c   5. b   6. d   7. c   8. a   9. b   10. c   11. b   12. d

CURRENT LIABILITIES AND PAYROLL

 THE **NAVIGATOR**

- ☐ Understand *Concepts for Review*
- ☐ Read *Feature Story*
- ☐ Scan *Study Objectives*
- ☐ Read *Chapter Preview*
- ☐ Read text and answer *Before You Go On*
- ☐ Review *Comparing IFRS and ASPE*
- ☐ Work *Demonstration Problem*
- ☐ Review *Summary of Study Objectives*
- ☐ Answer *Self-Study Questions*
- ☐ Complete assignments
- ☐ Go to *WileyPLUS* for practice and tutorials

CONCEPTS FOR **REVIEW**

Before studying this chapter, you should understand or, if necessary, review:

a. How to make adjusting entries for unearned revenue (Ch. 3, pp. 120–121) and accrued expenses. (Ch. 3, pp. 124–127)

b. The importance of liquidity in evaluating the financial position of a company. (Ch. 4, pp. 193– 195)

c. How to account for sales discounts. (Ch. 5, p. 246–247)

d. Accounting for notes receivable. (Ch. 8, pp. 427–430)

EVEN SMALL COMPANIES HAVE BIG PAYROLL OBLIGATIONS

TORONTO, Ont.—A big portion of any organization's current liabilities is its payroll obligations: employees' salaries or wages, and any related deductions for things like the Canada Pension Plan (CPP), Employment Insurance (EI), and income taxes. Then there are health care taxes, workers' compensation premiums, and any taxable benefits the employer offers. Depending on the business size and reach, there are more than 190 different pieces of legislation and regulations that a payroll person has to keep up to date with, points out Steven Van Alstine, Vice President, Education, at the Canadian Payroll Association. This includes the federal *Income Tax Act*, *Employment Insurance Act*, and *Canada Pension Plan Act*, along with provincial workers' compensation regulations, employment standards, health tax acts, and so on. "It is difficult, certainly if you're a new small business, being faced with myriad different requirements or legislation," he says. "It is a little daunting when you think, as a new business owner, 'What do I have to do?'"

No doubt, accounting for this liability can be a challenge for smaller businesses. Of the association's 18,000 members, 65% to 70% are organizations with 200 or fewer employees, says Mr. Van Alstine. For about one-third of people working in payroll, it is their sole responsibility, he continues. But for the remaining two-thirds, it's only a part of their responsibilities, which likely include such functions as human resources or accounts payable. The association can help small businesses and people who don't handle payroll full-time. "We are a support for those individuals who may be the sole payroll person within the organization," he says. Consultants are on hand to guide payroll staff through the process by phone.

The association offers a certification program for payroll professionals. In addition, it offers "Learning Payroll" professional development seminars. The association also has a "Setting Up a New Payroll" checklist with various resources and forms an employer may need and where to locate them, including those specific to provinces.

The Canada Revenue Agency also has tools available to help employers with their payroll, including an on-line payroll deduction calculator, which many may think does the job for them. However, as Mr. Van Alstine points out, "The employer needs to know that those are the deductions for the employee." Among other things, employers also have to contribute to CPP and EI for their employees.

Those lacking the necessary qualifications and skills to properly account for payroll may hire a Canadian Payroll Association–certified professional, a bookkeeper, or an accounting firm to take over the paperwork. Or employers may outsource the whole payroll function to a service provider like Ceridian or ADP, which is a growing trend. "Because there is all this legislation to keep up with, they feel that it's better to totally outsource this function," Mr. Van Alstine says. The benefits to employers include reduced costs, partly because they use the service provider's technology rather than setting up their own system.

Payroll is a liability that needs proper administration no matter what the size of the business is. After all, a company's employees are its greatest asset.

THE **NAVIGATOR**

STUDY **OBJECTIVES**

After studying this chapter, you should be able to:

1. Account for determinable or certain current liabilities.

2. Account for estimated liabilities.

3. Account for contingencies.

4. Determine payroll costs and record payroll transactions.

5. Prepare the current liabilities section of the balance sheet.

6. Calculate mandatory payroll deductions (Appendix 10A).

THE **NAVIGATOR**

Whether it is a huge company such as one of Canada's chartered banks, or a small business such as your local convenience store, every company has current liabilities. As explained in Chapter 4, current liabilities are obligations that are expected to be settled within one year from the balance sheet date or in the company's normal operating cycle. Obligations that are expected to be paid after one year or longer are classified as non-current liabilities. We explain current liabilities in this chapter and non-current liabilities in Chapter 15. Payroll creates current liabilities and affects almost every company. It is also explained in this chapter.

The chapter is organized as follows:

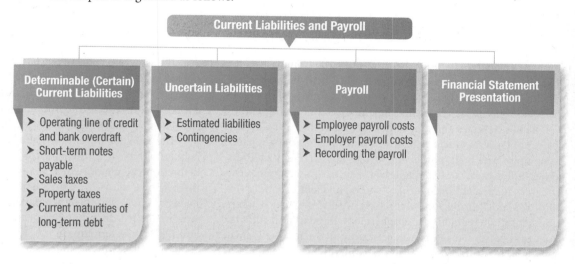

Determinable (Certain) Current Liabilities

Helpful hint Gift cards are an example of an unearned revenue liability where it is necessary to estimate the liability. These are discussed in the next section of this chapter.

Alternative terminology Determinable liabilities are also referred to as *certain liabilities* or *known liabilities*.

In Chapter 1, we defined liabilities as present obligations, arising from past events, to make future payments of assets or services. A future commitment is not considered a liability unless an obligation also exists. For example, a company may have made a commitment to purchase an asset in the future, but the obligation normally arises only when the goods are delivered or if the company has entered into an irrevocable agreement. Thus, an essential characteristic of a liability is the existence of a *present* obligation.

Sometimes there is a great deal of uncertainty regarding whether or not a liability exists. Even if it is certain that the liability exists, sometimes we are not certain as to whom we owe, how much we owe, or when we owe. We will discuss this type of liability in the sections on estimated liabilities and contingencies.

In this section of the chapter, we will discuss liabilities where there is no uncertainty about their existence, amount, or timing. Liabilities with a known amount, payee, and due date are often referred to as **determinable liabilities**.

Examples of determinable current liabilities include bank indebtedness from operating lines of credit, and notes payable, accounts payable, sales taxes payable, unearned revenue, and current maturities of long-term debt. This category also includes accrued liabilities such as property taxes, payroll, and interest payable.

Accounts payable, or trade accounts payable, are often the largest current liability on a company's balance sheet. For example, as shown on Reitmans' balance sheet in Appendix A, its trade and other payables amount to $63,875 thousand, which is almost 72% of its total current liabilities.

The entries for accounts payable and determinable unearned revenues have been explained in previous chapters, and are not included in this section. We will discuss the accounting for other types of current liabilities in this section, including bank indebtedness from an operating line of credit, notes payable, sales taxes payable, property taxes payable, and current maturities of long-term debt. Payroll and employee benefits payable are also examples of determinable liabilities, but as the accounting for payroll is complex, we discuss it in a separate section of this chapter.

OPERATING LINE OF CREDIT AND BANK OVERDRAFT

Operating Line of Credit

Current assets (such as accounts receivable) do not always turn into cash at the exact time that current liabilities (such as accounts payable) must be paid. Consequently, most companies have an **operating line of credit** at their bank to help them manage temporary cash shortfalls. This means that the company has been pre-authorized by the bank to borrow money when it is needed, up to a pre-set limit.

Security, called **collateral**, is usually required by the bank as protection in case the company is unable to repay the loan. Collateral normally includes some, or all, of the company's current assets (e.g., accounts receivable or inventories); investments; or property, plant, and equipment.

Money borrowed through a line of credit is normally borrowed on a short-term basis, and is repayable immediately upon request—that is, on demand—by the bank. In reality, repayment is rarely demanded without notice. A line of credit makes it very easy for a company to borrow money. It does not have to make a call or visit its bank to actually arrange the transaction. The bank simply covers any cheques written in excess of the bank account balance, up to the approved credit limit.

Bank Overdraft

Some companies have a negative (credit), or overdrawn, cash balance at year end. This amount is usually called *bank indebtedness*, *bank overdraft*, or *bank advances*. No special entry or account is required to record the overdrawn amount. The Cash account has a credit balance because the dollar amount of cheques written exceeded the dollar amount of deposits. The credit balance in Cash is reported as a current liability with an appropriate note disclosure.

Interest is usually charged on the overdrawn amount at a floating rate, such as prime plus a specified percentage. The **prime rate** is the interest rate that banks charge their best customers. This rate is usually increased by a specified percentage according to the company's risk profile.

SHORT-TERM NOTES PAYABLE

The line of credit described above is similar to a **note payable**. Notes payable are obligations in the form of written promissory notes. In Chapter 8, we discussed notes receivable and included an illustration of a promissory note. You will recall that the payee has a note receivable and the maker of the note has a note payable.

Notes payable may be used instead of accounts payable. This gives the lender proof of the obligation in case legal action is needed to collect the debt. Accounts and notes payable that result from purchase transactions (i.e., amounts owed to suppliers) are often called **trade payables**. Notes payable are also frequently issued to meet short-term financing needs.

> **Helpful hint** Notes payable are the opposite of notes receivable, and the accounting is similar.

Notes are issued for varying periods. If they are due for payment within one year of the balance sheet date, they are classified as current liabilities. Most notes are interest-bearing, with interest due monthly or at maturity.

To illustrate the accounting for notes payable, assume that Kok Co. borrows $100,000 from the local caisse populaire (credit union) on March 1 for four months, at an interest rate of 6%. The note matures on July 1 and interest, along with the note's principal amount, is payable at maturity.

Kok makes the following journal entry when it signs the note and receives the $100,000:

Mar. 1	Cash	100,000	
	Notes Payable		100,000
	To record issue of four-month, 6% note to		
	Caisse Populaire Dumoulin.		

A = L + OE
+100,000 +100,000

↑ Cash flows: +100,000

Interest accrues over the life of the note; therefore, interest expense must be recorded in the period when the borrowed money is used. Also, at year end, all liabilities (all obligations) must be recorded. If Kok Co. has a March 31 year end, then the interest owing at the end of March must be recorded. An adjusting entry is made to recognize interest expense and interest payable of $500 ($100,000 × 6% × $\frac{1}{12}$)

> **Helpful hint** Interest is normally calculated using the number of days. In this textbook, we use months in order to simplify the calculations.

Helpful hint Interest rates are always expressed as annual rates, not the rate for the duration of the note.

at March 31. Recall from Chapter 3 that interest is calculated by multiplying the principal amount by the annual interest rate by the fraction of the year in the accrual.

The adjusting entry is:

A	=	L	+	OE
		+500		−500

Cash flows: no effect

Mar. 31	Interest Expense	500	
	Interest Payable		500
	To accrue interest to March 31.		

In the March 31 financial statements, the current liabilities section of the balance sheet will show notes payable of $100,000 and interest payable of $500. In addition, interest expense of $500 will be reported as other expenses in the income statement. **Interest payable is shown separately from the note payable.**

At maturity (July 1), Kok Co. must pay the face value of the note ($100,000) plus $2,000 interest ($100,000 × 6% × $^4/_{12}$). One month ($500) of this interest has already been accrued. Interest must also be updated for $1,500 ($100,000 × 6% × $^3/_{12}$) for the three additional months—April through June—since interest was last recorded. This can be done in one compound entry or in separate journal entries as follows:

A	=	L	+	OE
		+1,500		−1,500

Cash flows: no effect

A	=	L	+	OE
−102,000		−100,000		
		−2,000		

↓ Cash flows: −102,000

July 1	Interest Expense	1,500	
	Interest Payable		1,500
	To accrue interest for April, May, and June.		
1	Notes Payable	100,000	
	Interest Payable ($500 + $1,500)	2,000	
	Cash ($100,000 + $2,000)		102,000
	To record payment of Caisse Populaire Dumoulin note and accrued interest.		

SALES TAXES

As a consumer, you are well aware that you pay sales taxes on many products and services. For the business, sales taxes collected from customers are a liability because the company has an obligation to pay the amount collected to the appropriate government body.

Sales taxes are expressed as a percentage of the sales price. As discussed in earlier chapters and in Appendix B, sales taxes usually take the form of the federal Goods and Services Tax (GST) and Provincial Sales Tax (PST). The GST is 5% across Canada. Provincial sales tax rates vary from 0% to 9.975% across the country.

In Ontario, Newfoundland and Labrador, Nova Scotia, and New Brunswick, the PST and GST have been combined into one 13% Harmonized Sales Tax (HST). Prince Edward Island introduced a 14% HST on April 1, 2013, the same day that British Columbia abolished HST and reintroduced PST. When this textbook went to press, Quebec was considering combining its provincial sales tax, the Quebec Sales Tax (QST), and the GST into the HST. Alberta, Yukon, Northwest Territories, and Nunavut do not have PST.

Whether GST, PST, or HST, the business collects the tax from the customer when the sale occurs. The business then pays (remits) the sales taxes collected to the designated federal and provincial collecting authorities. In the case of GST, HST, and QST, collections may be offset against sales taxes paid by the business on its purchases. In such cases, only the net amount owing or recoverable must be paid or refunded. Depending on the size of the business, the sales taxes must be sent to the government monthly, quarterly, or, for very small companies, annually.

The amount of the sale and the amount of the sales tax collected are usually rung up separately on the cash register. The cash register readings are then used to credit sales or services and the correct sales taxes payable accounts. For example, if the March 25 cash register reading for Comeau Company, in New Brunswick, shows sales of $10,000 and Harmonized Sales Tax of $1,300 ($10,000 × 13% HST rate), the entry is as follows:

Mar. 25	Cash	11,300	
	Sales		10,000
	HST Payable		1,300
	To record sales and sales taxes.		

A   =   L   +   OE
+11,300   +1,300   +10,000

↑ Cash flows: +11,300

Comeau Company does not report the sales taxes collected from customers as revenue; sales taxes collected from customers are a liability. Comeau Company serves only as a collection agent for the government. When the company remits (pays) these sales taxes to the appropriate government collecting authorities, the HST Payable account is debited and Cash is credited.

Some businesses include sales taxes in the selling price. They do not separate sales taxes from the price of the goods sold. In these businesses, however, sales taxes must still be recorded separately from sales revenues. To find the sales amount, the total receipts are divided by 100% plus the sales tax percentage.

To illustrate, assume that Comeau Company's total receipts of $11,300 include HST. In this case you divide the total receipts from the sale by 100% plus 13% (which is equal to 1.13) to determine the sales revenue. Thus the sales amount of $10,000 is calculated as follows: $11,300 ÷ 1.13 = $10,000. The HST of $1,300 can be found by multiplying the sales amount by the sales tax rate ($10,000 × 13% = $1,300).

Helpful hint If sales taxes are included in the sales price, then the sales tax collected is equal to the selling price × the sales tax percentage *divided by 100% plus the sales tax percentage.*

PROPERTY TAXES

Businesses that own property pay property taxes. These taxes are charged by the municipal governments, and are calculated at a specified rate for every $100 of assessed value of property (land and buildings). Property taxes generally cover a full calendar year, although bills are not issued until the spring of each year.

To illustrate, assume that Tantramar Management owns land and a building in the city of Regina. Tantramar's year end is December 31 and it makes adjusting entries annually. On March 1, it receives its property tax bill of $6,000 for the calendar year, which is due to be paid on May 31.

In March, when Tantramar receives the property tax bill for the calendar year, two months of that year have passed. The company records the property tax expense for the months of January and February and the liability owed at that point as follows:

Mar. 1	Property Tax Expense ($6,000 × 2/12)	1,000	
	Property Tax Payable		1,000
	To record property tax expense for January and February and amount owing.		

A   =   L   +   OE
+1,000   −1,000

Cash flows: no effect

On May 31, when Tantramar pays the property tax bill, the company records the payment of the liability recorded on March 1. It also records the expense incurred to date for the months of March, April, and May. As at May 31, five months have passed and should be recorded as property tax expense. The remaining seven months of the year are recorded as a prepayment, as shown in the following entry:

May 31	Property Tax Payable	1,000	
	Property Tax Expense ($6,000 × 3/12)	1,500	
	Prepaid Property Tax ($6,000 × 7/12)	3,500	
	Cash		6,000
	To record payment of property tax expense for March through May, and amount prepaid for June through December.		

A   =   L   +   OE
+3,500   −1,000   −1,500
−6,000

↓ Cash flows: −6,000

After the payment of the property tax, Tantramar has a zero balance in its liability account but still has a prepayment. Since Tantramar only makes adjusting entries annually, it would not adjust the prepaid property tax account until year end, December 31. At that time, it would make the following entry:

A	=	L	+	OE
−3,500				−3,500

Cash flows: no effect

Dec. 31	Property Tax Expense	3,500	
	Prepaid Property Tax		3,500
	To record property tax expense for June through December.		

There are other acceptable ways to record and adjust property taxes. Some companies would debit Property Tax Expense when the bill is recorded on March 1 and avoid a later adjusting entry. In addition, companies may prepare monthly or quarterly adjusting entries. Whatever way is used, at year end, the companies would have the same ending balances. In this case, the accounts Prepaid Property Tax and Property Tax Payable should each have a zero balance and Property Tax Expense should have a balance of $6,000.

CURRENT MATURITIES OF LONG-TERM DEBT

Companies often have a portion of long-term debt that will be due in the current year. That amount is considered a current liability. Assume that on January 1, 2014, Cudini Construction issues a $25,000, five-year note payable. Each January 1, starting on January 1, 2015, $5,000 of the note will be repaid. When financial statements are prepared on December 31, 2014, $5,000 should be reported on the balance sheet as a current liability and the remaining $20,000 of the note should be reported as a long-term liability.

It is not necessary to prepare an adjusting entry to recognize the current maturity of long-term debt. The proper statement classification of each liability account is recognized when the balance sheet is prepared. Reitmans reports $1,474 thousand as the "current portion of long-term debt" in the current liabilities section of its balance sheet.

> ### BEFORE YOU GO ON...
>
> ### Do It
>
> **Action Plan**
> - The formula for interest is as follows: principal (face) value × annual interest rate × time.
> - Record sales separately from sales taxes. To calculate sales, divide the total proceeds by 100% plus the sales tax rates. Then calculate HST by multiplying sales by the appropriate rate.
> - Record the property tax expense and the property tax payable for amounts incurred (owed) to date.
>
>
>
> THE NAVIGATOR
>
> Prepare the journal entries to record the following transactions for DiMaria Enterprises. Round any calculations to the nearest dollar.
>
> 1. Accrue interest on January 31 (the company's year end) for a $10,000, 30-month, 8% note payable issued on December 1. Interest is payable the first of each month, beginning January 1.
> 2. The cash register total for sales on April 2 is 282,500. This total includes sales taxes. The HST tax rate is 13%. Record the sales and sales taxes.
> 3. A property tax bill of $12,000 for the calendar year is received on May 1 and is due on June 30. Record the entry on May 1, assuming the company has a January 31 year end.
>
> **Solution**
>
> | Jan. 31 | Interest Expense ($10,000 × 8% × $1/12$) | 67 | |
> |---|---|---|---|
> | | Interest Payable | | 67 |
> | | To accrue interest on note payable. | | |
> | Apr. 2 | Cash | 282,500 | |
> | | Sales ($282,500 ÷ 113%) | | 250,000 |
> | | HST Payable ($250,000 × 13%) | | 32,500 |
> | | To record sales and sales taxes. | | |
> | May 1 | Property Tax Expense ($12,000 × $3/12$) | 3,000 | |
> | | Property Tax Payable | | 3,000 |
> | | To record property tax for February, March, and April. | | |
>
> *Related exercise material:* BE10–1, BE10–2, BE10–3, BE10–4, E10–1, E10–2, E10–3, and E10–4.

Uncertain Liabilities

In the previous section, we discussed current liabilities where there was a high degree of certainty with regard to whom an amount is owed to, when it is owed, and how much is owed. There was no uncertainty about the liability's existence, amount, or timing. In this section, we will discuss liabilities that have a lower degree of certainty but are still likely to occur. We will then discuss situations where there is an even greater degree of uncertainty if an obligation exists, or where the existence of a liability depends on the outcome of a future event.

ESTIMATED LIABILITIES

An **estimated liability** is a liability that is known to exist but whose amount and timing are uncertain. We know we owe someone, but are not necessarily sure how much and when. We may not even know whom we owe. There is a lower degree of certainty than in determinable liabilities, but as long as it is *likely* the company will have to settle the obligation, and the company can reasonably estimate the amount, the liability is recognized. Common estimated liabilities include product warranties, customer loyalty programs, and gift cards. We discuss these three examples in the following sections.

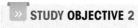

STUDY OBJECTIVE 2

Account for estimated liabilities.

Alternative terminology Estimated liabilities are also known as *provisions*.

Product Warranties

Product warranties are promises made by the seller to a buyer to repair or replace the product if it is defective or does not perform as intended. Warranties (also known as guarantees) are usually issued by manufacturers. For a specified period of time after the item was sold, a manufacturer may promise to repair the item, replace it, or refund the buyer's money under certain conditions. As a buyer, it is important to read all warranty contracts carefully because the promises they make can be quite different.

Warranties will lead to future costs for the manufacturer for the repair or replacement of defective units. At the time of the sale, it is not known which units will become defective, so it is not known in advance whom the company will have to pay, or when it will be paid. But the liability still exists even if the payee and timing are unknown.

There are two possible approaches to accounting for product warranties. Historically, an expense approach has been used to account for the warranty liability. But changes in accounting standards have led some companies to use what is known as a revenue approach. In this chapter, we will illustrate the expense approach. The revenue approach is explained in an intermediate accounting textbook.

Under the expense approach, the warranty liability is measured using the estimated future cost of servicing (honouring) the product's warranty. At the time the product is sold, the costs are not known, but based on their previous experience with a particular product, it is usually not that hard for most companies to estimate it.

This process will also result in the warranty expense being recorded at the same time as the liability. Recognizing both an expense and a liability in the period where the sale occurs also ensures that companies have recognized the full cost of the sale in the period in which the sale occurs. Recall that this is known as matching expenses with revenues. As the actual costs are incurred in subsequent periods, the liability is reduced.

To illustrate the expense approach of accounting for warranty liabilities, assume that Hermann Company sells 10,000 washers and dryers at an average price of $600 in the year ended December 31, 2014. The selling price includes a one-year warranty on parts. Based on past experience, it is expected that 500 units (5%) will be defective, and that warranty repair costs will average $100 per unit.

At December 31, it is necessary to accrue the estimated warranty costs for the 2014 sales. The calculation is as follows:

Number of units sold	10,000
Estimated rate of defective units	× 5%
Total estimated defective units	500
Average warranty repair cost	× $100
Estimated product warranty liability	$50,000

The adjusting entry is:

A = L + OE		Dec. 31	Warranty Expense	50,000	
+50,000 −50,000			Warranty Liability		50,000
Cash flows: no effect			To accrue estimated warranty costs.		

In 2014, warranty contracts were honoured on 300 units at a total cost of $30,000. These costs are recorded when they are incurred, but for our illustration they are being recorded in one summary journal entry for the year:

A = L + OE		Dec. 31	Warranty Liability	30,000	
−30,000 −30,000			Repair Parts Inventory (and/or Wages Payable)		30,000
Cash flows: no effect			To record honouring of 300 warranty contracts on 2014 sales.		

In 2014, a warranty expense of $50,000 is reported as an operating expense in the income statement. The estimated warranty liability of $20,000 ($50,000 − $30,000) is classified as a current liability on the balance sheet.

In 2015, all costs incurred to honour warranty contracts on 2014 sales should be debited to the Warranty Liability account, like what was shown above for the 2014 sales. The Warranty Liability account will be carried forward from year to year—increased by the current year's estimated expense and decreased by the actual warranty costs incurred. It is quite likely that the actual expenses will not exactly equal the estimated liability amount. Every year, as is done with accounts receivable and the allowance for doubtful accounts, the warranty liability is reviewed and adjusted if necessary.

Customer Loyalty Programs

Alternative terminology Customer loyalty programs are also called *promotions* or *incentive programs*.

To attract or keep customers, many companies offer **customer loyalty programs** that result in future savings for the customers on the merchandise or services the company sells. These customer loyalty programs take varying forms. For example, the program may require customers to collect points. A common example of that is airline frequent flyer programs. Or the programs may involve a credit reward that gives a cash discount on future sales. Loyalty programs are designed to increase sales and are important for many businesses.

The most successful loyalty program in Canadian retail history is Canadian Tire "money" (CTM), first introduced in 1958. The "money" resembles real currency (although the bills are considerably smaller than Bank of Canada notes) and is issued with no expiry date. CTM is given out by the cashiers for purchases paid for by cash, debit card, or Canadian Tire Options MasterCard credit card. Customers can use CTM to buy anything at a Canadian Tire store. In fact, some privately owned businesses in Canada also accept CTM as payment since the owners of many of these businesses shop at Canadian Tire.

Customer loyalty programs result in a liability to the business equal to the future savings that customers will receive when they use their points or credit awards. There has been some debate about whether the cost of such programs should be recorded as an expense (similar to the expense approach illustrated earlier in the chapter for warranties) or as a decrease in revenue. While there are a few exceptions, accountants have decided that, when a loyalty program results in a reduced future selling price, it should be accounted for as a decrease in revenue and not as an expense.

The liability for customer loyalty programs must be estimated because at the time of the sale, it is not known if or when customers will redeem the reward. But as long as some redemptions are likely, and can be reasonably estimated based on past experience, the decrease in revenue and a related liability should be recorded in the period when the reward was issued to ensure that liabilities are correctly recognized.

To illustrate, assume that Greenville Co-op has a rewards program whereby Greenville Co-op Gas Bar customers get a redemption reward of 3 cents per litre of gasoline that can be used in Greenville Co-op Food Stores on the purchase of groceries. Assume that during January, the gas bar sells 99,000 litres of gasoline. Greenville Co-op estimates that 90% of the rewards issued will be redeemed. At January 31, Greenville will record the following for the redemption rewards issued during January:

Jan. 31	Sales Discount for Redemption Rewards Issued (99,000 × 90% × $0.03)	2,673	
	Redemption Rewards Liability		2,673
	To record the estimated rewards from January sales that will be redeemed.		

A	=	L	+	OE
		+2,673		−2,673

Cash flows: no effect

The account Sales Discount for Redemption Rewards Issued is a contra sales account, and is deducted from sales to give net sales in the same way that sales returns and allowances are deducted from sales, as we learned in Chapter 5. The company could debit sales, but instead a contra revenue account is used to allow the company to track the redemption rewards. The Redemption Rewards Liability is reported as a current liability on the balance sheet.

Helpful hint Reductions in revenue are recorded in the period in which the reward is issued, not when it is redeemed.

To illustrate what happens when the rewards are redeemed, assume that on February 1, customers redeem $100 of the rewards in the Greenville Co-op Food Store when purchasing $7,500 of groceries. Greenville Co-op makes the following entry that day (ignoring the cost of sales):

Feb. 1	Rewards Redemption Liability	100	
	Cash ($7,500 − $100)	7,400	
	Grocery Sales Revenue		7,500
	To record grocery sales and the redemption of rewards.		

A	=	L	+	OE
+7,400		−100		+7,500

↑ Cash flows: +7,400

Note that when the rewards are redeemed, the amount of cash collected is less than the sales revenue recognized. The liability account is reduced by the difference between the sales revenue and cash collected, which is the amount of the redemption. The liability account should be reviewed periodically and adjusted based on the company's experience with redemption rates.

Gift Cards

Gift cards or gift certificates have become an increasingly popular source of revenue for many companies. They are unearned revenues in that the company receives cash in advance of providing the goods or the services. Thus, when gift cards are issued, the Unearned Revenue account (liability) is recorded. When the gift card is redeemed (used), the company will then record the sales or service revenue and reduce or debit the Unearned Revenue account.

Alternative terminology Unearned revenue is sometimes called *deferred revenue.*

As with customer loyalty programs, the difficulty with gift cards is that it is unknown when and even if the card will be redeemed. Typically, the longer a gift card is outstanding, the less likely it is to be redeemed for merchandise. Similarly, gift cards that have been used but have relatively small remaining balances are less likely to be redeemed than newer, high-balance gift cards.

If it is unlikely that the company will have to settle a portion of the liability, then an obligation no longer exists. As with warranties and customer loyalty programs, a company with a gift card program will need to use past experience to estimate the appropriate balance for the liability.

As shown in Reitmans' financial statements in Appendix A, the company has a deferred liability on its balance sheet for both a customer loyalty program as well as gift cards.

BEFORE YOU GO ON...

Do It

Hockey Gear Company sells hockey skates with a two-year warranty against defects. The company expects that of the units sold each year, 5% will be returned in the first year after they are sold and 2% will be returned in the second year. The average cost to repair or replace a defective unit under warranty is $50. The company reported the following sales and warranty cost information:

	Units Sold	Actual Warranty Costs Incurred
2013	10,000	$20,000
2014	15,000	45,000

Calculate the balance in the Warranty Expense and Warranty Liability accounts at the end of 2014.

Solution

2013: Total defective units = 5% + 2% = 7%
10,000 × 7% = 700 × $50 = $35,000

Warranty Expense		Warranty Liability			
35,000		Actual	20,000	Estimate	35,000
				Bal. Dec. 31, 2013	15,000

2014: 15,000 × 7% = 1,050 × $50 = $52,500

Warranty Expense		Warranty Liability			
52,500		Actual	20,000	Estimate	35,000
				Bal. Dec. 31, 2013	15,000
		Actual	45,000	Estimate	52,500
				Bal. Dec. 31, 2013	22,500

Related exercise material: BE10–5, BE10–6, BE10–7, BE10–8, E10–6, E10–7, and E10–8.

CONTINGENCIES

The current liabilities discussed earlier in this chapter were either definitely determinable or estimable. While it might have been necessary to estimate the timing or amount, in both cases there was no uncertainty about their existence. With contingencies there is much more uncertainty about the timing and the amount and even the existence of a liability.

In general, a **contingency** can be defined as an existing condition or situation that is uncertain, where it cannot be known if a loss (and a related liability) will result from the situation until one or more future events happen or do not happen. In some situations, a gain (and a related asset) may arise from the contingency. But assets that are contingent on the outcome of an event are never recorded, and are not discussed in this textbook.

Lawsuits are good examples of contingencies. The existence of a loss and the related liability depend on the outcome of the lawsuit. The settlement of the lawsuit will confirm the existence of the liability, the amount payable, the payee, and/or the date payable. Under ASPE, a liability for a contingent loss is recorded if **both** of the following conditions are met:

1. The contingency is *likely* (the chance of occurrence is high).
2. The amount of the contingency can be *reasonably estimated*.

Therefore, if it is likely that the company will lose a lawsuit, and if the amount can be reliably estimated, then the company must record the loss and the liability. Under IFRS, a liability is recorded if the chance of occurrence is "probable" as opposed to "likely." Probable events are defined as being "more likely than not." Thus IFRS is generally regarded as having a lower threshold for recognizing these liabilities. Under ASPE, only highly likely contingent losses are recognized.

Under ASPE, these liabilities are called contingent liabilities, and under IFRS, these liabilities are called provisions. Under IFRS, a provision is a liability of uncertain timing or amount. The term "provisions" is often used for other uncertain liabilities, such as warranties, as discussed in the previous section of this chapter.

When a contingent loss is likely, but cannot be reasonably estimated, or if its likelihood of occurrence is not determinable, it is necessary only to disclose the contingency in the notes to the financial statements. In that case, a liability is not recorded.

If a contingency is unlikely—the chance of occurrence is small—it should still be disclosed if the event could have a substantial negative effect on the company's financial position. Otherwise, it does not need to be disclosed. A loan guarantee is an example of a contingency that should be disclosed even if the chance of having to pay is small. General risk contingencies that can affect anyone who is operating a business, such as the possibility of a war, strike, or recession, are not reported in the notes to the financial statements.

ACCOUNTING IN ACTION
BUSINESS INSIGHT

There are many contingencies in the real world. Lawsuits are the most common type of contingency, followed by environmental contingencies. Environmental contingencies generally relate to liabilities that could be incurred in order to clean up environmental problems.

The Canadian National Railway Company discloses the following information in the notes to its consolidated financial statements: "A risk of environmental liability is inherent in railroad and related transportation operations..." the Company goes on to say, "the magnitude of such... liabilities and the costs of complying with future environmental laws and containing or remediating contamination cannot be reasonably estimated... there can thus be no assurance that liabilities or costs related to environmental matters will not be incurred in the future, or will not have a material adverse effect on the Company's financial position or results of operations in a particular quarter or fiscal year, or that the Company's liquidity will not be adversely impacted by such environmental liabilities or costs."

Source: Canadian National Railway Company, 2011 Annual Information Form.

Environmental contingencies are generally considered to be harder to estimate than contingencies from lawsuits. What might be the reason for this difference?

 BEFORE YOU GO ON...

Do It

A list of possible contingencies follows. Identify whether each of the following should be recorded, disclosed, or not reported:

1. A factory risks being damaged by floods. The building is located on a flood plain but has never experienced any damage from flooding in the past.
2. The government may expropriate a company's assets so that a new highway can be built. So far, there have been no discussions about how much the government might pay the company.
3. A public company is being sued for $1 million for unlawful termination of a company executive.
4. A company has guaranteed other companies' loans but the guarantees are unlikely to result in any payments.
5. A private company following ASPE is being sued for negligence and damages by a customer who slipped and broke a leg in the company's store.

Action Plan
- Recall that under ASPE, contingent liabilities are recorded if they are likely and can be reasonably estimated.
- Under IFRS, contingent liabilities (called provisions) are accrued when they are probable (more likely than not) and estimable.
- If the amounts cannot be estimated, they are only disclosed. Contingencies are not disclosed if they are unlikely.

● BEFORE YOU GO ON continued...

Solution

1. No disclosure required.
2. Disclosure required.
3. If it is probable that the company will lose and the amount can be reasonably estimated, then this would be recorded as a provision; otherwise, just disclose.
4. Disclosure required.
5. If it is likely that the company will lose and the amount can be reasonably estimated, then this is recorded as a contingent liability; otherwise, just disclose.

Related exercise material: BE10–9, BE10–10, E10–9, and E10–10.

THE **NAVIGATOR**

Payroll

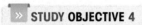

» STUDY OBJECTIVE 4

Determine payroll costs and record payroll transactions.

Payroll accounting involves more than just paying employee salaries and wages. In addition to paying salaries and wages, companies are required by law to have payroll records for each employee, to report and remit payroll deductions, and to respect provincial and federal laws on employee compensation. As mentioned in our feature story, there are up to 190 different pieces of legislation and regulations that employers have to consider when doing payroll. In this section, we will discuss some of the basic issues regarding payroll costs, journalizing payroll, and payroll records. In the appendix to this chapter, we explain calculating mandatory payroll deductions.

There are two types of payroll costs to a company: employee costs and employer costs. The first type, employee costs, involves the gross amount earned by employees. The second type, employer costs, involves amounts paid by the employer on behalf of the employee (employee benefits). We will explore employee and employer payroll costs in the following sections.

EMPLOYEE PAYROLL COSTS

Accounting for employee payroll costs involves calculating (1) gross pay, (2) payroll deductions, and (3) net pay.

Gross Pay

Gross pay, or earnings, is the total compensation earned by an employee. It consists of salaries or wages, plus any bonuses and commissions. The terms "salaries" and "wages" are often used interchangeably and the total amount of salaries or wages earned by the employee is called **gross pay**, or gross earnings.

In addition to the hourly pay rate, most companies are required by law to pay hourly workers for overtime work at the rate of at least one and one-half times the government-regulated minimum hourly wage. The number of hours that need to be worked before overtime becomes payable is based on a standard workweek. A 44-hour standard workweek is fairly common but this will vary by industry and occupation. Most employees in executive, managerial, and administrative positions do not earn overtime pay.

To illustrate gross pay, assume that Mark Jordan works for Academy Company as a shipping clerk. His authorized pay rate is $20 per hour. The calculation of Mark's gross pay for the 48 hours shown on his time card for the weekly pay period ending June 20, 2012, is as follows:

Type of Pay	Hours	×	Rate	=	Gross Pay
Regular	44	×	$20	=	$ 880
Overtime	4	×	30	=	120
Total	48				$1,000

This calculation assumes that Mark receives one and one-half times his regular hourly rate ($20 × 1.5) for any hours worked in excess of 44 hours per week (overtime). Overtime rates can be as much as twice the regular rates.

Payroll Deductions

As anyone who has received a paycheque knows, gross pay is usually very different from the amount that is actually received. The difference is referred to as **payroll deductions**. Payroll deductions are also frequently called "withholdings" because these are the amounts that the employer withholds or holds back from the employee. Payroll deductions may be mandatory or voluntary. Illustration 10-1 shows the types of payroll deductions that most employers usually make.

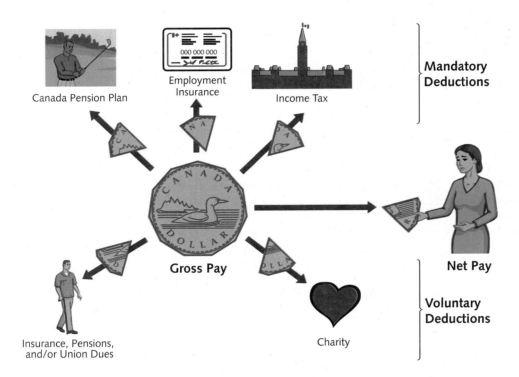

▶ **ILLUSTRATION 10-1**
Employee payroll deductions

Payroll deductions do not result in an expense for the employer. The employer is only a collection agent. The mandatory deductions are later paid to the government (for deductions such as Canada Pension Plan, Employment Insurance, and income tax). The voluntary deductions are later paid to some other agency (such as a union, an insurance company, or the United Way). The designated collection agency for the federal government is the Canada Revenue Agency (CRA), which collects money on behalf of the Receiver General for Canada, the cabinet minister responsible for accepting payments to the Government of Canada.

Mandatory Payroll Deductions. Mandatory deductions are required by law and include Canada Pension Plan contributions, Employment Insurance premiums, and personal income tax. We will discuss these three deductions in the following sections.

Canada Pension Plan. All employees between the ages of 18 and 70, except those employed in the province of Quebec, must contribute to the **Canada Pension Plan (CPP)**. Quebec has its own similar program, the Quebec Pension Plan (QPP). These mandatory plans give disability, retirement, and death benefits to qualifying Canadians.

Contribution rates are set by the federal government and are adjusted every January if there are increases in the cost of living. We will show how to calculate CPP contributions in Appendix 10A. For now, assume that Mark Jordan's CPP contribution for the weekly pay period ending June 20, 2012, is $46.17.

Employment Insurance. The *Employment Insurance Act* requires all Canadian workers who are not self-employed to pay **Employment Insurance (EI)** premiums. Employment insurance is designed to give income protection (in the form of payments representing a portion of one's earnings) for a limited period of time to employees who are temporarily laid off, who are on parental leave, or who lose their jobs. Starting January 2013, self-employed individuals may choose to pay EI to qualify for special benefits such as maternity or parental benefits. But this will not qualify them for employment insurance if they are not able to work.

Each year, the federal government determines the contribution rate and the maximum amount of premiums for the year. We will show how to calculate EI premiums in Appendix 10A. For now, assume that Mark Jordan's EI premium for the weekly pay period ending June 20, 2012, is $18.30.

Personal Income Tax. Under the *Income Tax Act*, employers are required to withhold income tax from employees for each pay period. The amount to be withheld is determined by three variables: (1) the employee's gross pay, (2) the number of credits claimed by the employee, and (3) the length of the pay period. The amount of provincial income taxes also depends on the province in which the employee works. There is no limit on the amount of gross pay that is subject to income tax withholdings. The higher the pay or earnings, the higher the amount of taxes withheld.

The calculation of personal income tax withholdings is complicated and is best done using payroll deduction tables supplied by the CRA. We will show this in Appendix 10A. For now, assume that Mark Jordan's federal income tax is $118.85 and provincial income tax is $60.45, for a total income tax owed of $179.30 on his gross pay of $1,000 for the weekly pay period ending June 20, 2012.

Voluntary Payroll Deductions. Unlike mandatory payroll deductions, which are required by law, voluntary payroll deductions are chosen by the employee.

Employees may choose to authorize withholdings for charitable, retirement, and other purposes. All voluntary deductions from gross pay should be authorized in writing by the employee. The authorization may be made individually or as part of a group plan. Deductions for charitable organizations, such as the United Way, or for financial arrangements, such as Canada Savings Bonds and the repayment of loans from company credit unions, are determined by each employee. In contrast, deductions for union dues, extended health insurance, life insurance, and pension plans are often determined on a group basis. In the calculation of net pay in the next section, we assume that Mark Jordan has voluntary deductions of $10 for the United Way and $5 for union dues.

Net Pay

The difference between an employee's gross pay, or total earnings, less any employee payroll deductions withheld from the earnings is known as **net pay**. This is the amount that the employer must pay to the employee.

Net pay is determined by subtracting payroll deductions from gross pay. For Mark Jordan, net pay for the weekly pay period ending June 20, 2012, is $741.23, as shown in Illustration 10-2.

▶**ILLUSTRATION 10-2**
Employee payroll deductions

Gross pay		$1,000.00
Payroll deductions:		
CPP	$ 46.17	
EI	18.30	
Income tax (federal and provincial)	179.30	
United Way	10.00	
Union dues	5.00	258.77
Net pay		$ 741.23

Before we learn how to record employee payroll costs and deductions, we will turn our attention to *employer* payroll costs. After this discussion, we will record the total employee and employer payroll costs for Academy Company, where Mark Jordan works.

EMPLOYER PAYROLL COSTS

Employer payroll costs are amounts that the federal and provincial governments require employers to pay. The federal government requires CPP and EI contributions from employers. The provincial governments require employers to fund a workplace health, safety, and compensation plan. These contributions, plus such items as paid vacations and pensions, are referred to as **employee benefits**. Employer payroll costs are not debited to the Salaries Expense account, but rather to a separate Employee Benefits Expense account.

Canada Pension Plan

Employers must also contribute to the CPP. For each dollar withheld from the employee's gross pay, the employer must contribute an equal amount. The CPP Payable account is credited for both the employees' and employer's CPP contributions.

Employment Insurance

Employers are required to contribute 1.4 times an employee's EI premiums. The EI Payable account is credited for both the employees' and employer's EI premiums.

Workplace Health, Safety, and Compensation

Each provincial workplace health, safety, and compensation plan gives benefits to workers who are injured or disabled on the job. The cost of this program is paid entirely by the employer; employees do not make contributions to these plans. Employers are assessed a rate—usually between 0.25% and 10% of their gross payroll—based on the risk of injury to employees in their industry and past experience.

Helpful hint CPP contributions and EI premiums are paid by both the employer and the employee. Workers' compensation premiums are paid entirely by the employer.

Additional Employee Benefits

In addition to the three employer payroll costs described above, employers have other employee benefit costs. Two of the most important are paid absences and post-employment benefits. We will describe these briefly here, but leave further details to an intermediate accounting course.

Paid Absences. Employees have the right to receive compensation for absences under certain conditions. The compensation may be for paid vacations, sick pay benefits, and paid statutory holidays. A liability should be estimated and accrued for future paid absences. Ordinarily, vacation pay is the only paid absence that is accrued. Other types of paid absences are disclosed only in notes to the statements.

Post-Employment Benefits. Post-employment benefits are payments by employers to retired or terminated employees. These payments are for (1) pensions, and (2) supplemental health care, dental care, and life insurance. Employers must use the accrual basis in accounting for post-employment benefits. It is important to match the cost of these benefits with the periods where the employer benefits from the services of the employee.

RECORDING THE PAYROLL

Recording the payroll involves maintaining payroll records, recording payroll expenses and liabilities, paying the payroll, and filing and remitting payroll deductions.

Payroll Records

A separate record of an employee's gross pay, payroll deductions, and net pay for the calendar year is kept for each employee and updated after each pay period. It is called the **employee earnings record** and its cumulative payroll data are used by the employer to (1) determine when an employee has reached the maximum earnings subject to CPP and EI premiums, (2) file information returns with the CRA (as explained later in this section), and (3) give each employee a statement of gross pay and withholdings for the year.

An extract from Mark Jordan's employee earnings record for the month of June is shown in Illustration 10-3. This record includes the pay details shown in Illustration 10-2 for the weekly pay period ending June 20, 2012, highlighted in red.

ACADEMY COMPANY
Employee Earnings Record
Year Ending December 31, 2012

Name	Mark Jordan	Address	162 Bowood Avenue
Social Insurance Number	113-114-496		Toronto
Date of Birth	December 24, 1985		Ontario, M4N 1Y6
Date Employed	September 1, 2010	Telephone	416-486-0669
Date Employment Ended		E-mail	jordan@sympatico.ca
Job Title	Shipping Clerk	Claim Code	1

2012 Period Ending	Total Hours	Gross Pay				Deductions						Payment	
		Regular	Overtime	Total	Cumulative	CPP	EI	Income Tax	United Way	Union Dues	Total	Net Amount	Cheque #
June 6	46	880.00	60.00	940.00	19,940.00	43.20	17.20	161.35	10.00	5.00	236.75	703.25	974
13	47	880.00	90.00	970.00	20,910.00	44.68	17.75	169.30	10.00	5.00	246.73	723.27	1028
20	48	880.00	120.00	1,000.00	21,910.00	46.17	18.30	179.30	10.00	5.00	258.77	741.23	1077
27	46	880.00	60.00	940.00	22,850.00	43.20	17.20	161.35	10.00	5.00	236.75	703.25	1133
June Total		3,520.00	330.00	3,850.00		177.25	70.45	671.30	40.00	20.00	979.00	2,871.00	

▶**ILLUSTRATION** **10-3**
Employee earnings record

In addition to employee earnings records, many companies find it useful to prepare a **payroll register**. This record accumulates the gross pay, deductions, and net pay per employee for each pay period and becomes the documentation for preparing paycheques for each employee. Academy Company's payroll register for the weekly pay period ended June 20, 2012, is presented in Illustration 10-4. It shows the data for Mark Jordan in the wages section, highlighted in red. In this example, Academy Company's total payroll is $34,420, as shown in the gross pay column.

ACADEMY COMPANY
Payroll Register
Week Ending June 20, 2012

Employee	Total Hours	Gross Pay			Deductions						Payment	
		Regular	Overtime	Gross	CPP	EI	Income Tax	United Way	Union Dues	Total	Net Pay	Cheque #
Aung, Ng	44	1,276.00		1,276.00	59.83	23.35	266.80	15.00		364.98	911.02	998
Canton, Mathilda	44	1,298.00		1,298.00	60.92	23.75	270.55	20.00		375.22	922.78	999
Caron, William	44	1,166.00		1,166.00	54.39	21.34	229.40	11.00		316.13	849.87	1000
Deol, Réjean	44	880.00	60.00	940.00	43.20	17.20	161.35	10.00	5.00	236.75	703.25	1001
Jordan, Mark	**48**	**880.00**	**120.00**	**1,000.00**	**46.17**	**18.30**	**179.30**	**10.00**	**5.00**	**258.77**	**741.23**	**1077**
Milroy, Lee	47	880.00	90.00	970.00	44.68	17.75	169.30	10.00	5.00	246.73	723.27	1078
Total		32,400.00	2,020.00	34,420.00	1,497.28	629.89	6,722.86	480.00	150.00	9,480.03	24,939.97	

▶**ILLUSTRATION** **10-4**
Payroll register

Note that this record is a listing of each employee's payroll data for the June 20, 2012, pay period. In some companies, the payroll register is a special journal. Postings are made directly to ledger accounts. In other companies, the payroll register is a supplementary record that gives the data for a general journal entry and later posting to the ledger accounts. At Academy Company, the second procedure is used.

Recording Payroll Expenses and Liabilities

Payroll expenses are equal to the employees' gross salaries and wages plus the employer's payroll costs. Typically, as shown in the following entry, employee payroll costs and employer's payroll costs are recorded in separate journal entries.

Employee Payroll Costs. A journal entry is made to record the employee portion of the payroll. For the week ending June 20, the entry for Academy Company, using total amounts from the company's payroll register for the period, as shown in Illustration 10-4, is as follows:

June 20	Salaries Expense	34,420.00	
	CPP Payable		1,497.28
	EI Payable		629.89
	Income Tax Payable		6,722.86
	United Way Payable		480.00
	Union Dues Payable		150.00
	Salaries Payable		24,939.97
	To record payroll for week ending June 20.		

```
A    =    L    +   OE
      +1,497.28 −34,420.00
        +629.89
      +6,722.86
        +480.00
        +150.00
     +24,939.97
Cash flows: no effect
```

The above journal entry records the gross pay of $34,420 in Academy Company's Salaries Expense account. Separate expense accounts may be used for gross pay for office workers, on salary, and other employees, paid an hourly rate. For example, a company may use the account Wages Expense for its hourly workers. The net pay of $24,939.97 that is owed to employees is recorded in the Salaries Payable account. This is equal to the sum of the individual cheques that the employees will receive when the payroll is paid. Academy Company uses separate liability accounts for the amounts that it owes for its employee payroll deductions to the government for CPP, EI, and income tax, and amounts owed to third parties like United Way and for union dues.

Employer Payroll Costs. Employer payroll costs are usually recorded when the payroll is journalized. The entire amount of gross pay is subject to four of the employer payroll costs mentioned earlier: CPP, EI, workers' compensation, and vacation pay. For the June 20 payroll, Academy Company's CPP is $1,497.28 ($1,497.28 × 1). Its EI premium is $881.85 ($629.89 × 1.4).

Assume that Academy Company is also assessed for workers' compensation at a rate of 1%. Its expense for the week would therefore be $344.20 ($34,420 × 1%). For vacation pay, assume that Academy Company employees accrue vacation days at an average rate of 4% of the gross payroll (equivalent to two weeks of vacation). The accrual for vacation benefits in one pay period—one week—is therefore $1,376.80 ($34,420 × 4%).

Some provinces, including the Province of Ontario, require an additional employer payroll cost—an employer health tax to help fund health care. The maximum health tax in the Province of Ontario is 1.95% of payroll, but the tax rate varies by the amount of payroll. For simplicity, we will assume that Academy is exempt from this health tax.

Accordingly, the entry to record the employer payroll costs or employee benefits associated with the June 20 payroll is as follows:

June 20	Employee Benefits Expense	4,100.13	
	CPP Payable		1,497.28
	EI Payable		881.85
	Workers' Compensation Payable		344.20
	Vacation Pay Payable		1,376.80
	To record employer payroll costs on June 20 payroll.		

```
A    =    L    +   OE
      +1,497.28 −4,100.13
        +881.85
        +344.20
      +1,376.80
Cash flows: no effect
```

Employer payroll costs are debited to a separate expense account, normally called Employee Benefits Expense, so the employer can keep track of these costs. It is combined with Salaries Expense on the income statement. The liability accounts are classified as current liabilities since they will be paid within the next year.

Recording Payment of the Payroll

Payment of the payroll by cheque or electronic funds transfer (EFT) is made from either the employer's regular bank account or a payroll bank account. Each paycheque or EFT is usually accompanied by a statement of earnings document. This shows the employee's gross pay, payroll deductions, and net pay for the period and for the year to date.

After the payroll has been paid, the cheque numbers are entered in the payroll register. The entry to record payment of the payroll for Academy Company follows:

A = L + OE			
−24,939.97 −24,939.97	June 20	Salaries Payable	24,939.97
		Cash		24,939.97
↓ Cash flows: −24,939.97		To record payment of payroll.	

Note that Academy Company is only recording payments to its employees in this entry and not its payroll deductions. Employee and employer deductions will be remitted to government authorities or other third parties when they are due later in the month.

Many companies use a separate bank account for payroll. Only the total amount of each period's payroll is transferred, or deposited, into that account before it is distributed. This helps the company determine if there are any unclaimed amounts.

When companies report and remit their payroll deductions, they combine withholdings of CPP, EI, and income tax. Generally, the withholdings must be reported and remitted monthly on a Statement of Account for Current Source Deductions (known by the CRA as the PD7A remittance form), and no later than the 15th day of the month following the month's pay period. Depending on the size of the payroll deductions, however, the employer's payment deadline could be different. For example, large employers must remit more often than once a month, and small employers with perfect payroll deduction remittance records can remit quarterly.

Workplace health, safety, and compensation costs are remitted quarterly to the provincial workers' compensation commission or board. Remittances can be made by mail or through deposits at any Canadian financial institution. When payroll deductions are remitted, payroll liability accounts are debited and Cash is credited.

The entry to record the remittance of payroll deductions by Academy Company in the following month is as follows:

A = L + OE				
−12,203.36 −2,994.56	July 13	CPP Payable ($1,497.28 + $1,497.28)	2,994.56	
−1,511.74		EI Payable ($629.89 + $881.85)	1,511.74	
−6,722.86		Income Tax Payable	6,722.86	
−480.00		United Way Payable	480.00	
−150.00		Union Dues Payable	150.00	
−344.20		Workers' Compensation Payable	344.20	
↓ Cash flows: −12,203.36		Cash		12,203.36
		To record payment of payroll deductions for June 20 payroll.		

Note that the vacation pay liability recorded on June 20 is not debited or "paid" until the employees actually take their vacation.

Other payroll information returns or forms must be filed by the employer with the government by the last day of February each year. In addition, as noted previously, employers must give employees a Statement of Remuneration Paid (called a T4 slip by the CRA) by the same date.

ACCOUNTING IN ACTION
ALL ABOUT YOU INSIGHT

Employers are required by law each month to remit to the CRA mandatory payroll deductions as well as the employer's share of CPP and EI. Failure to do so can lead to interest and stiff penalties.

What happens if you are self-employed and providing consulting services to a company? If you are self-employed, you are required to pay CPP equal to both the employee's and employer's share, and you are also responsible for paying income tax. If you are self-employed, you can choose to pay EI to qualify for special benefits such as maternity or sickness benefits. But this will not qualify you for employment insurance if you are not able to work. If you choose to pay EI, you will not be required to pay the employer's portion of the EI premium.

It may seem beneficial to some companies to hire consultants and avoid paying the employer's share of CPP and EI as well as other benefits. However, the CRA has strict guidelines as to whether an individual is considered an employee or a self-employed consultant. If a company inappropriately treats an individual as self-employed and fails to deduct CPP and EI, the company will be required to pay both the employer's and employee's share of CPP and EI as well as penalties and interest.

Sources: Service Canada website, "Frequently Asked Questions: Employment Insurance (EI) Special Benefits for Self-Employed People," available at http://www.servicecanada.gc.ca/eng/sc/ei/sew/faq.shtml; Canada Revenue Agency website, "Payroll," available at http://www.cra-arc.gc.ca/tx/bsnss/tpcs/pyrll/menu-eng.html; Canada Revenue Agency, "Employee or Self-Employed?", available at http://www.cra-arc.gc.ca/E/pub/tg/rc4110/rc4110-11e.pdf.

If you are providing services to a company, what are the advantages and disadvantages of being a self-employed consultant versus an employee of the company?

 BEFORE YOU GO ON...

Do It

Prepare the journal entries to record the following transactions. Round any calculations to the nearest dollar.

1. A company's gross salaries amount to $10,000 for the week ended July 11. The following amounts are deducted from the employees' wages: CPP of $495; EI of $183; income tax of $3,965; and health insurance of $950. Assume employees are paid in cash on July 11.
2. The company accrues employer's payroll costs on the same day as it records payroll. Assume vacation days are accrued at an average rate of 4% of the gross payroll and that the health insurance is 100% funded by the employees.
3. Record the payment of the mandatory payroll deductions from the July 11 payroll on August 15.

Action Plan

- Record both the employees' portion of the payroll and the benefits owed by the employer.
- Employee deductions are not an expense to the employer.
- The vacation pay liability is not "paid" until the employees actually take their vacation.

Solution

Date	Account	Debit	Credit
July 11	Salaries Expense	10,000	
	CPP Payable		495
	EI Payable		183
	Income Tax Payable		3,965
	Health Insurance Payable		950
	Cash		4,407
	To record payment of wages for week ending July 11.		
July 11	Employee Benefits Expense	1,151	
	CPP Payable		495
	EI Payable ($183 × 1.4)		256
	Vacation Pay Payable ($10,000 × 4%)		400
	To record employer's payroll costs on July 11 payroll.		

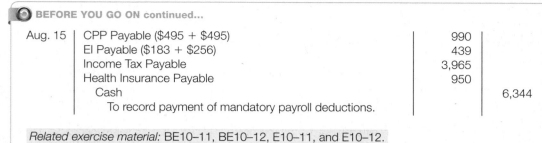

Aug. 15	CPP Payable ($495 + $495)	990	
	EI Payable ($183 + $256)	439	
	Income Tax Payable	3,965	
	Health Insurance Payable	950	
	Cash		6,344
	To record payment of mandatory payroll deductions.		

Related exercise material: BE10–11, BE10–12, E10–11, and E10–12.

THE NAVIGATOR

Financial Statement Presentation

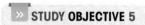

» STUDY OBJECTIVE 5

Prepare the current liabilities section of the balance sheet.

Current liabilities are generally reported as the first category in the liabilities section of the balance sheet. Each of the main types of current liabilities is listed separately. In addition, the terms of operating lines of credit and notes payable and other information about the individual items are disclosed in the notes to the financial statements.

Similar to current assets, current liabilities are generally listed in order of liquidity (by maturity date). However, this is not always possible, because of the varying maturity dates that may exist for specific obligations such as notes payable. Many companies show bank loans, notes payable, and accounts payable first.

As discussed in Chapter 4, international companies often choose to order their current liabilities in order of reverse liquidity. They also often choose to present their current liabilities following the non-current liabilities.

Illustration 10-5 shows how Shoppers Drug Mart presents its current liabilities in traditional order in its balance sheet.

▶**ILLUSTRATION 10-5**
Presentation of current liabilities

SHOPPERS DRUG MART CORPORATION
Balance Sheet (partial)
December 31, 2011
(in thousands)

Current liabilities	
Bank indebtedness	$ 172,262
Accounts payable and accrued liabilities	1,109,444
Income taxes payable	26,538
Dividends payable	53,119
Current portion of long-term debt	249,971
Provisions	12,024
Associate interest	152,880
Total current liabilities	$1,776,238

Income taxes payable and dividends payable are accounts that are used only by corporations and you will learn about these in Chapters 13 and 14. Associate interest is the amount that Shoppers Drug Mart would owe to its associates (owners of the Shoppers Drug Mart stores) if its associate agreements were terminated. Shoppers Drug Mart explains in its notes to its financial statements that it does not expect to pay this amount in the next 12 months, but because it doesn't have the unconditional right to defer settlement of the liability for at least 12 months, under IFRS, the company must report this amount in current liabilities.

Shoppers Drug Mart also discloses information about its provisions and contingencies in the notes to its financial statements, as shown in Illustration 10-6.

▸ ILLUSTRATION 10-6
Disclosure of
provisions and contingent
liabilities

SHOPPERS DRUG MART CORPORATION Notes to Consolidated Financial Statements (partial) December 31, 2011		

Note 22 PROVISIONS

	2011	2010
Balance, beginning of the financial year	$14,414	$12,071
Provisions made	8,980	12,341
Provisions used	(9,907)	(9,817)
Provisions reversed	(192)	(306)
Unwind of discount	430	125
Balance, end of the financial year	$13,725	$14,414
Balance, end of the financial year, presented as follows:		
Current liabilities	$12,024	$12,562
Long-term liabilities	1,701	1,852
	$13,725	$14,414

(a) The Company has been served with a Statement of Claim in a proposed class proceeding that has been filed in the Ontario Superior Court of Justice by two of its licensed Associate-owners, claiming various declarations and damages of $1,000,000 on behalf of a proposed class comprised of all of its current and former licensed Associate-owners resident in Canada, other than in Québec. The claim alleges, among other things, that Shoppers Drug Mart and two of its affiliates breached contractual and other duties to its Associate-owners by collecting, receiving and/or retaining funds and/or benefits that are in excess of those permitted to be collected, received and/or retained by the applicable agreements. The Company believes that the claim is without merit and will vigorously defend the claim. However, there can be no assurance that the outcome of this claim will be favourable to the Company or that it will not have a material adverse impact on the Company's financial position. The amount payable, if any, is not reasonably determinable at this time.

(b) In addition, the Company is involved in certain legal claims arising in the normal course of business. In the opinion of the Company's management, the eventual settlement of such claims will not have a significant effect on the Company's financial position or results of operations. Management has recorded a provision for these claims based on its best estimate of the final settlements.

Notice that Shoppers Drug Mart is following the procedures for contingencies discussed earlier in the chapter. For the lawsuits or statements of claim by two of its licensed associate-members [see (a) in Illustration 10-6], the company is unable to reasonably estimate a probable loss. Therefore, it is only disclosed in this note. For the lawsuits or legal claims [see (b) in Illustration 10-6], where it is probable a loss will be incurred, and where the amount can be reasonably measured, the company has recorded a provision in the amounts shown in the note. In addition, Shoppers Drug Mart explains in Note 19 that it has entered into agreements with banks to guarantee a total of $520,000 thousand of its Associate-owned stores' bank lines of credit.

Companies must carefully monitor the relationship of current liabilities to current assets. This relationship is critical in evaluating a company's short-term ability to pay debt. There is usually concern when a company has more current liabilities than current assets, because it may not be able to make its payments when they become due.

Shoppers Drug Mart has current assets of $2,695,647 at December 31, 2011, which results in a positive current ratio. You will recall from Chapter 4 that the current ratio is calculated by dividing current assets by current liabilities. Shoppers Drug Mart's current ratio is 1.52:1 ($2,695,647 ÷ $1,776,238), which indicates that Shoppers Drug Mart has enough current assets to cover its current liabilities.

Recall also that the current ratio should never be interpreted without also looking at the receivables and inventory turnover ratios to ensure that all of the current assets are indeed liquid. It is also important to look at the acid-test ratio. If we wanted to do a more complete analysis of Shoppers Drug Mart's liquidity, we would need additional information.

BEFORE YOU GO ON...

Do It

The following selected items were included in EastBoat Enterprises' adjusted trial balance at November 30, 2014:

Accounts payable	$52,775
Accounts receivable	30,250
Accrued liabilities	18,350
Bank indebtedness	10,400
Merchandise inventory	85,900
Notes payable	100,000
Prepaid expenses	12,000
Unearned revenue	6,500
Warranty liability	8,825

Additional information:

The $100,000 balance in notes payable consisted of: (1) a six-month, 5%, $25,000 note payable due on March 31, 2015; (2) a two-year, 5.5%, $15,000 note payable due on October 31, 2015; and (3) a three-year, 4.5%, $60,000 note payable due on September 30, 2016.

Prepare the current liabilities section of the balance sheet.

Action Plan

- Determine which items are liabilities.
- Recall that current liabilities are payable within one year of the balance sheet date.

Solution

EASTBOAT ENTERPRISES Balance Sheet (partial) November 30, 2014	
Current liabilities	
Bank indebtedness	$ 10,400
Accounts payable	52,775
Accrued liabilities	18,350
Unearned revenue	6,500
Warranty liability	8,825
Notes payable	40,000
Total current liabilities	136,850

THE NAVIGATOR

Related exercise material: BE10–13, BE10–14, BE10–15, E10–5, E10-13, and E10–14.

APPENDIX 10A | PAYROLL DEDUCTIONS

MANDATORY PAYROLL DEDUCTIONS

>> **STUDY OBJECTIVE 6**

Calculate mandatory payroll deductions.

As discussed in the chapter, payroll deductions may be mandatory or voluntary. Mandatory deductions are required by law and include Canada Pension Plan contributions, Employment Insurance premiums, and income tax. We discuss how to calculate these in the following sections.

Canada Pension Plan (CPP)

CPP contributions are based on a maximum ceiling or limit (called the maximum pensionable earnings) less a basic yearly exemption, and on the contribution rate set each year by the federal government. **Pensionable earnings** are gross earnings less the basic yearly exemption.

As of January 1, 2012, the following amounts were in effect:

Maximum pensionable earnings	$50,100
Basic yearly exemption	$3,500
CPP contribution rate	4.95%
Maximum annual employee CPP contribution	$2,306.70

Illustration 10A-1 shows the formulas and calculations used to determine Mark Jordan's CPP contribution on his gross pay of $1,000 for the weekly pay period ending June 20, 2012.

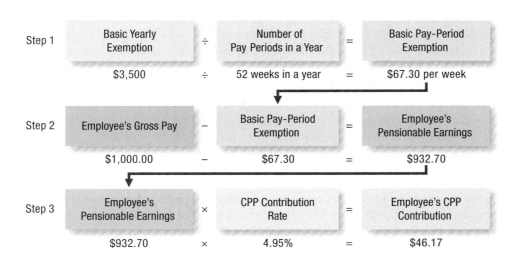

▶ **ILLUSTRATION 10A-1**
Formula for CPP contributions

Note that the basic pay-period exemption of $67.30 is a per-week exemption and is used in this case because Academy Company pays its employees weekly. If a company pays its employees monthly, the basic pay-period exemption would be $291.67 ($3,500 ÷ 12).

An employer stops deducting CPP contributions if and when the employee's earnings are greater than the maximum pensionable earnings. In this way, the employee's CPP contributions will not be greater than the maximum annual CPP contribution. Self-employed individuals pay both the employee and employer share of CPP.

Employment Insurance (EI)

EI calculations are based on a maximum earnings ceiling (called the maximum annual insurable earnings) and the contribution rate set by the federal government each year. Different from CPP, there is no basic yearly exemption. For 2012, the following amounts were in effect:

Maximum insurable earnings	$45,900
EI contribution rate	1.83%
Maximum annual employee EI premium	$839.97

In most cases, **insurable earnings** are gross earnings.

The required EI premium is calculated by multiplying the employee's insurable earnings by the EI contribution rate. Illustration 10A-2 shows the formula and calculations to determine Mark Jordan's EI premium on his gross pay of $1,000 for the pay period ending June 20, 2012.

▶ **ILLUSTRATION 10A-2**
Formula for EI premiums

An employer stops deducting EI premiums if and when the employee's earnings are greater than the maximum insurable earnings. In this way, the employee's EI premiums will not be greater than the maximum annual EI premium. Self-employed individuals who have chosen to pay EI pay only the employee's share of EI.

Personal Income Tax

Income tax deductions are based on income tax rates set by the federal and provincial governments. The federal government uses a progressive tax scheme when calculating income taxes. Basically, this means that the higher the pay or earnings, the higher the income tax percentage, and thus the higher the amount of taxes withheld. For example, effective January 1, 2012, the federal tax rates were:

- 15% **on the first** $42,707 of taxable income, plus
- 22% **on the next** $42,707 of taxable income (on the portion of taxable income between $42,707 and $85,414), plus
- 26% **on the next** $46,992 of taxable income (on the portion of taxable income between $85,414 and $132,406), plus
- 29% of taxable income **over** $132,406.

Taxable income is determined by the employee's gross pay and the amount of personal tax credits claimed by the employee. **Personal tax credits** are amounts deducted from an individual's income taxes and determine the amount of income taxes to be withheld. To indicate to the Canada Revenue Agency (CRA) which credits he or she wants to claim, the employee must complete a Personal Tax Credits Return (known as a TD1 form). In 2012, all individuals were entitled to a minimum personal credit (called the basic personal credit) of $10,822.

In addition, provincial income taxes must be calculated. All provinces, except Alberta, also use a progressive tax scheme. Each province has its own specific tax rates and calculations.

As you can see, the calculation of personal income tax deductions is very complicated. Consequently it is best done using one of the many payroll accounting programs that are available or by using the payroll deduction tools provided by the CRA. These tools include payroll deduction tables and the Payroll Deductions Online Calculator. We will illustrate how to use the payroll deduction tables.

USING PAYROLL DEDUCTION TABLES

Payroll deduction tables are prepared by the CRA and can be easily downloaded from the CRA website (go to www.cra-arc.gc.ca and click on Businesses, then Payroll). There are separate payroll deduction tables for determining federal tax deductions, provincial tax deductions, Canada Pension Plan contributions, and Employment Insurance premiums.

These tables are updated at least once a year on January 1 to reflect the new rates for that year. Income tax tables are also reissued during the year if the federal or provincial governments make changes to income tax rates during the year. It is important to make sure you have the tables that are in effect during the payroll period for which you are calculating deductions.

There are separate sections of the federal and provincial income tax and the CPP tables for weekly, biweekly, semi-monthly, and monthly pay periods. Thus, when determining these amounts, it is important to make sure you are using the table prepared for the company's pay period. The Academy Company would use the weekly tables.

Illustration 10A-3 shows excerpts from the CPP, EI, and federal and Ontario income tax tables effective January 1, 2012. You can use these tables to determine the appropriate deductions for Mark Jordan's gross pay of $1,000 during the pay period ended June 20, 2012.

In the CPP table, under the Pay column, find $1,000. The CPP deduction for the pay range $993.57 to $1,003.56 is $46.10. Earlier in the appendix, we showed how to calculate Mark Jordan's CPP and determined it was $46.17. Why the difference? The amount shown in the table is calculated using the mid-point in the range. As the mid-point is less than $1,000, the amount in the table is less than the calculated amount. Both ways of determining the CPP contribution are correct—the table is just slightly less precise than the calculation. The Academy Company could have used either amount.

In the EI table, under the Insurable Earnings column, find $1,000. The EI deduction in the pay range $999.73 to $1,000.27 is $18.30. This is exactly the same amount we calculated earlier in the appendix because Mark Jordan's pay of $1,000 is the mid-point of this range. As with CPP, companies

Canada Pension Plan Contributions
Weekly (52 pay periods a year)

Cotisations au Régime de pensions du Canada
Hebdomadaire (52 périodes de paie par année)

▶ ILLUSTRATION 10A-3
Excerpts from CPP, EI, and income tax deduction tables prepared by the Canada Revenue Agency, effective January 1, 2012

Pay Rémunération From - De	To - À	CPP RPC	Pay Rémunération From - De	To - À	CPP RPC	Pay Rémunération From - De	To - À	CPP RPC	Pay Rémunération From - De	To - À	CPP RPC
949.02 -	949.21	43.65	963.57 -	973.56	44.61	1683.57 -	1693.56	80.25	2403.57 -	2413.56	115.89
949.22 -	949.42	43.66	973.57 -	983.56	45.11	1693.57 -	1703.56	80.75	2413.57 -	2423.56	116.39
949.43 -	949.62	43.67	983.57 -	993.56	45.60	1703.57 -	1713.56	81.24	2423.57 -	2433.56	116.88
949.63 -	949.82	43.68	993.57 -	1003.56	46.10	1713.57 -	1723.56	81.74	2433.57 -	2443.56	117.38
949.83 -	950.02	43.69	1003.57 -	1013.56	46.59	1723.57 -	1733.56	82.23	2443.57 -	2453.56	117.87
950.03 -	950.22	43.70	1013.57 -	1023.56	47.09	1733.57 -	1743.56	82.73	2453.57 -	2463.56	118.37
950.23 -	950.43	43.71	1023.57 -	1033.56	47.58	1743.57 -	1753.56	83.22	2463.57 -	2473.56	118.86
950.44 -	950.63	43.72	1033.57 -	1043.56	48.08	1753.57 -	1763.56	83.72	2473.57 -	2483.56	119.36
950.64 -	950.83	43.73	1043.57 -	1053.56	48.57	1763.57 -	1773.56	84.21	2483.57 -	2493.56	119.85
950.84 -	951.03	43.74	1053.57 -	1063.56	49.07	1773.57 -	1783.56	84.71	2493.57 -	2503.56	120.35
951.04 -	951.23	43.75	1063.57 -	1073.56	49.56	1783.57 -	1793.56	85.20	2503.57 -	2513.56	120.84
951.24 -	951.44	43.76	1073.57 -	1083.56	50.06	1793.57 -	1803.56	85.70	2513.57 -	2523.56	121.34
951.45 -	951.64	43.77	1083.57 -	1093.56	50.55	1803.57 -	1813.56	86.19	2523.57 -	2533.56	121.83
951.65 -	951.84	43.78	1093.57 -	1103.56	51.05	1813.57 -	1823.56	86.69	2533.57 -	2543.56	122.33
951.85 -	952.04	43.79	1103.57 -	1113.56	51.54	1823.57 -	1833.56	87.18	2543.57 -	2553.56	122.82
952.05 -	952.24	43.80	1113.57 -	1123.56	52.04	1833.57 -	1843.56	87.68	2553.57 -	2563.56	123.32
952.25 -	952.45	43.81	1123.57 -	1133.56	52.53	1843.57 -	1853.56	88.17	2563.57 -	2573.56	123.81
952.46 -	952.65	43.82	1133.57 -	1143.56	53.03	1853.57 -	1863.56	88.67	2573.57 -	2583.56	124.31

Employment Insurance Premiums

Cotisations à l'assurance-emploi

Insurable Earnings Rémunération assurable From - De	To - À	EI premium Cotisation d'AE	Insurable Earnings Rémunération assurable From - De	To - À	EI premium Cotisation d'AE	Insurable Earnings Rémunération assurable From - De	To - À	EI premium Cotisation d'AE	Insurable Earnings Rémunération assurable From - De	To - À	EI premium Cotisation d'AE
949.46 -	949.99	17.38	988.80 -	989.34	18.10	1028.15 -	1028.68	18.82	1067.49 -	1068.03	19.54
950.00 -	950.54	17.39	989.35 -	989.89	18.11	1028.69 -	1029.23	18.83	1068.04 -	1068.57	19.55
950.55 -	951.09	17.40	989.90 -	990.43	18.12	1029.24 -	1029.78	18.84	1068.58 -	1069.12	19.56
951.10 -	951.63	17.41	990.44 -	990.98	18.13	1029.79 -	1030.32	18.85	1069.13 -	1069.67	19.57
951.64 -	952.18	17.42	990.99 -	991.53	18.14	1030.33 -	1030.87	18.86	1069.68 -	1070.21	19.58
952.19 -	952.73	17.43	991.54 -	992.07	18.15	1030.88 -	1031.42	18.87	1070.22 -	1070.76	19.59
952.74 -	953.27	17.44	992.08 -	992.62	18.16	1031.43 -	1031.96	18.88	1070.77 -	1071.31	19.60
953.28 -	953.82	17.45	992.63 -	993.16	18.17	1031.97 -	1032.51	18.89	1071.32 -	1071.85	19.61
953.83 -	954.37	17.46	993.17 -	993.71	18.18	1032.52 -	1033.06	18.90	1071.86 -	1072.40	19.62
954.38 -	954.91	17.47	993.72 -	994.26	18.19	1033.07 -	1033.60	18.91	1072.41 -	1072.95	19.63
954.92 -	955.46	17.48	994.27 -	994.80	18.20	1033.61 -	1034.15	18.92	1072.96 -	1073.49	19.64
955.47 -	956.01	17.49	994.81 -	995.35	18.21	1034.16 -	1034.69	18.93	1073.50 -	1074.04	19.65
956.02 -	956.55	17.50	995.36 -	995.90	18.22	1034.70 -	1035.24	18.94	1074.05 -	1074.59	19.66
956.56 -	957.10	17.51	995.91 -	996.44	18.23	1035.25 -	1035.79	18.95	1074.60 -	1075.13	19.67
957.11 -	957.65	17.52	996.45 -	996.99	18.24	1035.80 -	1036.33	18.96	1075.14 -	1075.68	19.68
957.66 -	958.19	17.53	997.00 -	997.54	18.25	1036.34 -	1036.88	18.97	1075.69 -	1076.22	19.69
958.20 -	958.74	17.54	997.55 -	998.08	18.26	1036.89 -	1037.43	18.98	1076.23 -	1076.77	19.70
958.75 -	959.28	17.55	998.09 -	998.63	18.27	1037.44 -	1037.97	18.99	1076.78 -	1077.32	19.71
959.29 -	959.83	17.56	998.64 -	999.18	18.28	1037.98 -	1038.52	19.00	1077.33 -	1077.86	19.72
959.84 -	960.38	17.57	999.19 -	999.72	18.29	1038.53 -	1039.07	19.01	1077.87 -	1078.41	19.73
960.39 -	960.92	17.58	999.73 -	1000.27	18.30	1039.08 -	1039.61	19.02	1078.42 -	1078.96	19.74
960.93 -	961.47	17.59	1000.28 -	1000.81	18.31	1039.62 -	1040.16	19.03	1078.97 -	1079.50	19.75
961.48 -	962.02	17.60	1000.82 -	1001.36	18.32	1040.17 -	1040.71	19.04	1079.51 -	1080.05	19.76
962.03 -	962.56	17.61	1001.37 -	1001.91	18.33	1040.72 -	1041.25	19.05	1080.06 -	1080.60	19.77
962.57 -	963.11	17.62	1001.92 -	1002.45	18.34	1041.26 -	1041.80	19.06	1080.61 -	1081.14	19.78
963.12 -	963.66	17.63	1002.46 -	1003.00	18.35	1041.81 -	1042.34	19.07	1081.15 -	1081.69	19.79
963.67 -	964.20	17.64	1003.01 -	1003.55	18.36	1042.35 -	1042.89	19.08	1081.70 -	1082.24 -	19.80

Federal tax deductions
Effective January 1, 2012
Weekly (52 pay periods a year)
Also look up the tax deductions
in the provincial table

Retenues d'impôt fédéral
En vigueur le 1er janvier 2012
Hebdomadaire (52 périodes de paie par année)
Cherchez aussi les retenues d'impôt
dans la table provinciale

Pay Rémunération From - De Less than Moins de		0	1	2	3	4	5	6	7	8	9	10
		Deduct from each pay / Retenez sur chaque paie										
931 -	939	136.20	105.00	102.00	96.05	90.05	84.10	78.15	72.15	66.20	60.25	54.25
939 -	947	137.90	106.70	103.70	97.75	91.75	85.80	79.85	73.85	67.90	61.95	55.95
947 -	955	139.60	108.40	105.40	99.45	93.45	87.50	81.55	75.55	69.60	63.65	57.65
955 -	963	141.30	110.10	107.10	101.15	95.15	89.20	83.25	77.25	71.30	65.35	59.35
963 -	971	143.00	111.80	108.80	102.85	96.90	90.95	84.95	79.00	73.05	67.05	61.10
971 -	979	144.80	113.55	110.60	104.60	98.65	92.70	86.70	80.75	74.80	68.85	62.85
979 -	987	146.55	115.35	112.35	106.40	100.40	94.45	88.50	82.50	76.55	70.60	64.60
987 -	995	148.30	117.10	114.10	108.15	102.15	96.20	90.25	84.30	78.30	72.35	66.40
995 -	1003	150.05	118.85	115.85	109.90	103.95	97.95	92.00	86.05	80.05	74.10	68.15
1003 -	1011	151.80	120.60	117.60	111.65	105.70	99.75	93.75	87.80	81.85	75.85	69.90
1011 -	1023	154.00	122.80	119.80	113.85	107.90	101.95	95.95	90.00	84.05	78.05	72.10
1023 -	1035	156.65	125.45	122.45	116.50	110.55	104.55	98.60	92.65	86.65	80.70	74.75
1035 -	1047	159.30	128.10	125.10	119.15	113.15	107.20	101.25	95.30	89.30	83.35	77.40
1047 -	1059	161.95	130.75	127.75	121.80	115.80	109.85	103.90	97.90	91.95	86.00	80.00
1059 -	1071	164.60	133.35	130.40	124.40	118.45	112.50	106.50	100.55	94.60	88.65	82.65
1071 -	1083	167.20	136.00	133.00	127.05	121.10	115.15	109.15	103.20	97.25	91.25	85.30
1083 -	1095	169.85	138.65	135.65	129.70	123.75	117.75	111.80	105.85	99.85	93.90	87.95
1095 -	1107	172.50	141.30	138.30	132.35	126.35	120.40	114.45	108.50	102.50	96.55	90.60
1107 -	1119	175.15	143.95	140.95	135.00	129.00	123.05	117.10	111.10	105.15	99.20	93.20
1119 -	1131	177.80	146.55	143.60	137.60	131.65	125.70	119.70	113.75	107.80	101.85	95.85

Federal claim codes/Codes de demande fédéraux

▶ **ILLUSTRATION 10A-3**

Excerpts from CPP, EI, and income tax deduction tables prepared by the Canada Revenue Agency, effective January 1, 2012 (*continued*)

Ontario provincial tax deductions
Effective January 1, 2012
Weekly (52 pay periods a year)
Also look up the tax deductions in the federal table

Retenues d'impôt provincial de l'Ontario
En vigueur le 1er janvier 2012
Hebdomadaire (52 périodes de paie par année)
Cherchez aussi les retenues d'impôt dans la table fédérale

Pay Rémunération		Provincial claim codes/Codes de demande provinciaux										
		0	1	2	3	4	5	6	7	8	9	10
From De	Less than Moins de	Deduct from each pay Retenez sur chaque paie										
928 -	936	62.40	53.30	52.30	50.35	48.35	46.40	44.45	42.45	40.50	38.55	36.55
936 -	944	63.80	54.65	53.65	51.70	49.75	47.75	45.80	43.85	41.85	39.90	37.90
944 -	952	64.50	55.35	54.40	52.40	50.45	48.45	46.50	44.55	42.55	40.60	38.65
952 -	960	65.20	56.05	55.10	53.10	51.15	49.20	47.20	45.25	43.30	41.30	39.35
960 -	968	65.90	56.80	55.80	53.85	51.85	49.90	47.95	45.95	44.00	42.05	40.05
968 -	976	66.65	57.50	56.55	54.55	52.60	50.65	48.65	46.70	44.75	42.75	40.80
976 -	984	67.40	58.25	57.25	55.30	53.35	51.35	49.40	47.45	45.45	43.50	41.55
984 -	992	68.10	59.00	58.00	56.05	54.05	52.10	50.15	48.15	46.20	44.20	42.25
992 -	1000	68.85	59.70	58.75	56.75	54.80	52.85	50.85	48.90	46.90	44.95	43.00
1000 -	1008	69.60	60.45	59.45	57.50	55.55	53.55	51.60	49.60	47.65	45.70	43.70
1008 -	1016	70.30	61.20	60.20	58.25	56.25	54.30	52.30	50.35	48.40	46.40	44.45
1016 -	1024	71.05	61.90	60.95	58.95	57.00	55.00	53.05	51.10	49.10	47.15	45.20
1024 -	1032	71.80	62.65	61.65	59.70	57.70	55.75	53.80	51.80	49.85	47.90	45.90
1032 -	1040	72.50	63.35	62.40	60.40	58.45	56.50	54.50	52.55	50.60	48.60	46.65
1040 -	1048	73.25	64.10	63.10	61.15	59.20	57.20	55.25	53.30	51.30	49.35	47.40
1048 -	1060	74.15	65.00	64.05	62.05	60.10	58.15	56.15	54.20	52.25	50.25	48.30
1060 -	1072	75.25	66.10	65.15	63.15	61.20	59.25	57.25	55.30	53.35	51.35	49.40
1072 -	1084	76.35	67.20	66.25	64.25	62.30	60.35	58.35	56.40	54.45	52.45	50.50
1084 -	1096	77.45	68.30	67.35	65.35	63.40	61.45	59.45	57.50	55.55	53.55	51.60
1096 -	1108	78.55	69.40	68.45	66.45	64.50	62.55	60.55	58.60	56.60	54.65	52.70
1108 -	1120	79.65	70.50	69.55	67.55	65.60	63.60	61.65	59.70	57.70	55.75	53.80
1120 -	1132	80.75	71.60	70.60	68.65	66.70	64.70	62.75	60.80	58.80	56.85	54.90
1132 -	1144	81.85	72.70	71.70	69.75	67.80	65.80	63.85	61.90	59.90	57.95	56.00
1144 -	1156	82.95	73.80	72.80	70.85	68.90	66.90	64.95	63.00	61.00	59.05	57.10
1156 -	1168	84.05	74.90	73.90	71.95	70.00	68.00	66.05	64.10	62.10	60.15	58.20

Source: T4032 Payroll Deduction Tables, Effective July 1, 2012. Pages: B-15, C-7, E-3, D3-D4; http://www.cra-arc.gc.ca/tx/bsnss/tpcs/pyrll/t4032/jn12/menu-eng.html

can either calculate the EI as shown earlier, or use the tables. Both amounts are correct—the table is just slightly less precise than the calculation.

In the federal tax deduction table, first find $1,000 in the Pay column. Now follow across the table to the Federal Claim Code 1 column. The federal tax deduction in the "from" $995 to "less than" $1,003 range, claim code 1, is $118.85. The same process is used in the Ontario provincial tax deduction table. In the "from" $1,000 to "less than" $1,008 range, provincial claim code 1, the provincial tax deduction is $60.45. The total of these amounts of $179.30 ($118.85 + $60.45) agree with the amounts given for Mark Jordan's income tax deduction earlier in the chapter.

Claim code 1 is used for individuals who qualify for only the basic personal credit on the TD1 form discussed earlier in the appendix. You will notice on the federal and provincial tax deduction tables that the higher the claim code, the lower the income tax deduction. These claim codes can be used for employees who will have more personal tax credits. We have assumed that Mark Jordan will qualify for only the basic personal credit.

As mentioned earlier, employers may also use the payroll software packages or the CRA's Payroll Deductions Online Calculator to determine payroll deductions. All of these methods will provide correct deductions as long as the correct dates, gross pay, pay period, and claim codes are used.

 BEFORE YOU GO ON...

Do It

Highland Company pays salaries on a weekly basis. The payroll for the week ended May 29, 2012, includes three employees as follows:

Employee Name	Weekly Earnings	Claim Code
Hudson, James	$975	4
Randell, Findley	$975	2
Jaegeun, Kim	$1,125	1

Determine the appropriate mandatory payroll deductions and net pay for each employee. Calculate the CPP and EI deductions using the formula provided in Appendix 10A. Use the tables in Illustration 10A-3 to determine federal and provincial income taxes.

Action Plan

- The CPP basic pay-period deduction is the annual basic deduction divided by the number of pay periods in a year.
- CPP deductions are equal to an employee's pensionable earnings times the CPP contribution rate.

Solution

Employee	Gross Pay	Deductions						Net Pay
		CPP	EI	Federal Income Tax	Provincial Income Tax	Total		
Hudson, James	$ 975.00	44.93[1]	17.84[3]	98.65	52.60	214.02		760.98
Randell, Findley	975.00	44.93	17.84	110.60	56.55	229.92		745.08
Jaegeun, Kim	1,125.00	52.36[2]	20.59[4]	146.55	71.60	291.10		833.90

Calculations:
Note: CPP basic pay period deduction = $3,500 ÷ 52 = $67.30
[1] ($975.00 − $67.30) × 4.95% = $44.93
[2] ($1,125.00 − $67.30) × 4.95% = $52.36
[3] $975.00 × 1.83% = $17.84
[4] $1,125.00 × 1.83% = $20.59

Related exercise material: *BE10–16, *BE10–17, *BE10–18, *E10–15, and *E10–16.

THE NAVIGATOR

- EI premiums are equal to an employee's insurable earnings times the EI premium rate.
- The federal tax deduction is the amount in the correct Pay range and Claim Code column on the federal tax deduction table.
- The provincial tax deduction is the amount in the correct Pay range and Claim Code column on the provincial tax deduction table.

Comparing IFRS and ASPE

Key Differences	International Financial Reporting Standards (IFRS)	Accounting Standards for Private Enterprises (ASPE)
Conditions necessary to record a liability for a contingent loss.	Chance of occurrence is "probable" or "more likely than not."	Chance of occurrence is "likely."
Terminology	A liability related to a contingent loss is called a "provision."	A liability related to a contingent loss is called a "contingent liability."

THE NAVIGATOR

Demonstration Problem

Benoit Company has the following selected transactions:

Feb. 1 Signed a $50,000, six-month, 7% note payable to the Central Canadian Bank, receiving $50,000 in cash. Interest is payable at maturity.

10 Cash register receipts totalled $37,565, plus 13% HST.

28 The payroll for the month is salaries of $50,000. CPP contributions and EI premiums withheld are $2,475 and $915, respectively. A total of $15,000 in income taxes is withheld. The salaries are paid on March 1.

The following adjustment data are noted at the end of the month:

1. Interest expense should be accrued on the note.
2. Employer payroll costs are recorded. In addition to mandatory costs, the company also pays $800 a month for a dental plan for all its employees.
3. Some sales were made under warranty. Of the units sold under warranty this month, 350 are expected to become defective. Repair costs are estimated to be $40 per defective unit.

Instructions
(a) Record the February transactions. Round your calculations to the nearest dollar.
(b) Record the adjusting entries at February 28.

ACTION PLAN

- Remember that interest rates are annual rates and must be adjusted for periods of time less than one year.
- Remember that sales taxes collected must be sent to the government and are not part of sales revenue.
- Remember that employee deductions for CPP, EI, and income tax reduce the salaries payable.
- Employer contributions to CPP, EI, and the dental plan create an additional expense.
- Warranty costs are expensed in the period when the sales occur.

THE NAVIGATOR

Solution to Demonstration Problem

(a)

Feb. 1	Cash		50,000	
	Notes Payable			50,000
	Issued six-month, 7% note.			
10	Cash ($37,565 + $4,883)		42,448	
	Sales			37,565
	HST Payable ($37,565 × 13%)			4,883
	To record sales and sales tax payable.			
28	Salaries Expense		50,000	
	Income Taxes Payable			15,000
	CPP Payable			2,475
	EI Payable			915
	Salaries Payable			31,610
	To record February salaries.			

(b)

Feb. 28	Interest Expense ($50,000 × 7% × $1/12$)		292	
	Interest Payable			292
	To record accrued interest for February.			
28	Employee Benefits Expense		4,556	
	CPP Payable ($2,475 × 1)			2,475
	EI Payable ($915 × 1.4)			1,281
	Dental Plan Payable			800
	To record employee benefit costs for February.			
28	Warranty Expense (350 × $40)		14,000	
	Warranty Liability			14,000
	To record estimated product warranty liability.			

▶ Summary of Study Objectives

1. *Account for determinable or certain current liabilities.* Liabilities are present obligations arising from past events, to make future payments of assets or services. Determinable liabilities have certainty about their existence, amount, and timing—in other words, they have a known amount, payee, and due date. Examples of determinable current liabilities include operating lines of credit, notes payable, accounts payable, sales taxes, unearned revenue, current maturities of long-term debt, and accrued liabilities such as property taxes, payroll, and interest.

2. *Account for estimated liabilities.* Estimated liabilities exist, but their amount or timing is uncertain. As long as it is *likely* the company will have to settle the obligation, and the company can reasonably estimate the amount, the liability is recognized. Product warranties, customer loyalty programs, and gift cards result in liabilities that must be estimated. They are recorded either as an expense (or as a decrease in revenue) and a liability in the period when the sales occur. These liabilities are reduced when repairs under warranty or redemptions occur. Gift cards are a type of unearned revenue as they result in a liability until

the gift card is redeemed. As some cards are never redeemed, it is necessary to estimate the liability and make adjustments.

3. *Account for contingencies.* A contingency is an existing condition or situation that is uncertain, where it cannot be known if a loss (and a related liability) will result until a future event happens, or does not happen. Under ASPE, a liability for a contingent loss is recorded if it is it likely a loss will occur and the amount of the contingency can be reasonably estimated. Under IFRS, the threshold for recording the loss is lower. It is recorded if a loss is probable. Under ASPE, these liabilities are called contingent liabilities, and under IFRS, these liabilities are called provisions. If it is not possible to estimate the amount, these liabilities are only disclosed. They are not disclosed if they are unlikely.

4. *Determine payroll costs and record payroll transactions.* Payroll costs consist of employee and employer payroll costs. In recording employee costs, Salaries Expense is debited for the gross pay, individual liability accounts are credited for payroll deductions, and Salaries Payable is

credited for net pay. In recording employer payroll costs, Employee Benefits Expense is debited for the employer's share of CPP, EI, workers' compensation, vacation pay, and any other deductions or benefits provided. Each benefit is credited to its specific current liability account.

5. *Prepare the current liabilities section of the balance sheet.* The nature and amount of each current liability and contingency should be reported in the balance sheet or in the notes accompanying the financial statements. Traditionally, current liabilities are reported first and in order of liquidity. International companies sometimes report current liabilities on the lower section of the balance sheet and in reverse order of liquidity.

6. *Calculate mandatory payroll deductions (Appendix 10A).* Mandatory payroll deductions include CPP, EI, and income taxes. CPP is calculated by multiplying pensionable earnings (gross pay minus the pay period exemption) by the CPP contribution rate. EI is calculated by multiplying insurable earnings by the EI contribution rate. Federal and provincial income taxes are calculated using a progressive tax scheme and are based on taxable earnings and personal tax credits. The calculations are very complex and it is best to use one of the CRA income tax calculation tools such as payroll deduction tables.

THE NAVIGATOR

Flash cards

▶ Glossary

Canada Pension Plan (CPP)   A mandatory federal plan that gives disability, retirement, and death benefits to qualifying Canadians. (p. 537)

Collateral   Property pledged as security for a loan. (p. 527)

Contingency   An existing condition or situation that is uncertain, where it cannot be known if a loss (and a related liability) will result from the situation until one or more future events happen or do not happen. (p. 534)

Contingent liability   A liability whose existence will be confirmed only by the occurrence or non-occurrence of a future event. (p. 535)

Customer loyalty programs   Programs that result in future savings for the customers on the merchandise or services the company sells. (p. 532)

Determinable liability   A liability whose existence, amount, and timing are known with certainty. (p. 526)

Employee benefits   Payments made by an employer, in addition to wages and salaries, to give pension, insurance, medical, or other benefits to its employees. (p. 539)

Employee earnings record   A separate record of an employee's gross pay, payroll deductions, and net pay for the calendar year. (p. 539)

Employment Insurance (EI)   A federal mandatory insurance program designed to give income protection for a limited period of time to employees who are temporarily laid off, who are on parental leave, or who lose their jobs. (p. 538)

Estimated liability   A liability that is known to exist but whose amount or timing is uncertain. (p. 531)

Gross pay   Total compensation earned by an employee. Also known as gross earnings. (p. 536)

Insurable earnings   Gross earnings used to calculate EI deductions. There is a maximum amount of insurable earnings set each year by the government. (p. 547)

Net pay   Gross pay less payroll deductions. (p. 538)

Notes payable   Obligations in the form of written promissory notes. (p. 527)

Operating line of credit   Pre-authorized approval to borrow money at a bank when it is needed, up to a pre-set limit. (p. 527)

Payroll deductions   Deductions from gross pay to determine the amount of a paycheque. (p. 537)

Payroll register   A record that accumulates the gross pay, deductions, and net pay per employee for each pay period and becomes the documentation for preparing a paycheque for each employee. (p. 540)

Pensionable earnings   Gross earnings less the basic yearly exemption. There is a maximum amount of pensionable earnings set each year by the government. (p. 546)

Personal tax credits   Amounts deducted from an individual's income taxes that determine the amount of income taxes to be withheld. (p. 548)

Prime rate   The interest rate banks charge their best customers. (p. 527)

Product warranties   Promises made by the seller to a buyer to repair or replace a product if it is defective or does not perform as intended. (p. 531)

Provisions   Liabilities of uncertain timing or amount. (p. 535)

Trade payables   Accounts and notes payable that result from purchase transactions with suppliers. (p. 527)

Note: All questions, exercises, and problems below with an asterisk (*) relate to material in Appendix 10A.

▶ Self-Study Questions

Answers are at the end of the chapter.

(SO 1) C   1. Which of the following statements is the best description of a liability?
(a) A liability is a commitment to pay an amount in the future.
(b) A liability arises when an expense is incurred.
(c) A liability is an amount that should have been paid in the past.
(d) A liability is a present obligation, arising from past events, to make future payments of assets or services.

(SO 1) AP   2. Gibraltar Company borrows $55,200 on July 31, 2014, from the East Coast Bank by signing a seven-month, 5% note. Interest is payable at maturity. Assuming Gibraltar has a December 31 fiscal year end, how much interest expense will Gibraltar record in 2014 and in 2015?

	2014	2015
(a)	$ 0	$1,610
(b)	$1,150	$ 460
(c)	$1,380	$ 230
(d)	$1,971	$ 789

(SO 1) AP   3. RedEarth Company, located in Ontario, has $5,007 of sales, which included 13% HST. What are the amounts (rounded to the nearest dollar) that should be credited to Sales and to HST Payable?

	Sales	HST Payable
(a)	$5,007	$651
(b)	$4,356	$651
(c)	$4,431	$576
(d)	$5,007	$576

(SO 1) AP   4. On March 1, Swift Current Company receives its property tax assessment of $13,200 for the 2014 calendar year. The property tax bill is due May 1. If Swift Current prepares quarterly financial statements, how much property tax expense should the company report for the quarter ended March 31, 2014?
(a) $3,300
(b) $4,400
(c) $1,100
(d) $13,200

(SO 2) AP   5. Big Al's Appliance Store offers a two-year warranty on all appliances sold. The company estimates that 5% of all appliances sold need to be serviced at an average cost of $100 each. At December 31, 2013, the Warranty Liability account had a balance of $20,000. During 2014, the store spends $14,500 repairing 145 appliances. An additional 4,500 appliances are sold in 2014. On the 2014 income statement, warranty expense will be:
(a) $28,000.
(b) $22,500.
(c) $14,500.
(d) $20,000.

(SO 2) K   6. Friendly Department Store has a customer loyalty program in which customers receive points when they make a purchase. The points can be redeemed on future purchases. The value of the points issued should be recorded as:
(a) a contra revenue when the points are issued.
(b) an expense when the points are issued.
(c) a contra revenue when the points are redeemed.
(d) an expense when the points are redeemed.

(SO 3) K   7. Under IFRS, a contingent loss and the related liability should be recorded in the accounts when:
(a) it is probable the contingency will happen, but the amount cannot be reasonably estimated.
(b) it is probable the contingency will happen, and the amount can be reasonably estimated.
(c) it is highly unlikely the contingency will happen, but the amount can be reasonably estimated.
(d) it is unlikely that the users of the financial statements will read the notes.

(SO 4) AP   8. In a recent pay period, Blue Company employees have gross salaries of $17,250. Total deductions are: CPP $866, EI $316, and income taxes $4,312. What is Blue Company's total payroll expense for this pay period? Ignore vacation benefits and workers' compensation premiums.
(a) $17,250
(b) $18,558
(c) $11,765
(d) $18,432

(SO 5) K   9. On November 1, 2014, SSNL Company borrows $120,000 cash from the bank and issues a two-year, 4% note payable. SSNL must make payments of $5,000 plus interest at the end of each month. On December 31, 2014, what amount will be included in current and in non-current liabilities on the balance sheet?

	Current Liabilities	Non-Current Liabilities
(a)	$60,000	$ 50,000
(b)	$60,000	$ 60,000
(c)	$10,000	$100,000
(d)	$50,000	$ 70,000

(SO 4, 6) *10. During the first week of May 2012, Emily Marquette worked 40 hours at an hourly wage of $25.75 per hour for an employer in Ontario. Using the payroll deduction tables in Appendix 10A, what was her net pay, assuming her only personal tax credit is the basic personal amount?
(a) $1,030.00
(b) $775.47
(c) $841.90
(d) $735.87

▶ Questions

(SO 1) K 1. What is a determinable liability? List some examples.

(SO 1) K 2. Why is a present commitment to purchase an asset in the future not recorded as a liability?

(SO 1) K 3. How is interest calculated on a note payable? How is the amount of interest payable at the fiscal year end calculated?

(SO 1) K 4. What is the difference between an operating line of credit and a bank overdraft?

(SO 1) C 5. A friend is opening a retail store and doesn't understand how to calculate the amount of sales tax collected if the sales tax is included in the selling price. Explain how to do this and provide an example. Assume the company must collect the 13% HST from its customers.

(SO 1) C 6. Your roommate argues that since property taxes are unavoidable, a company should record the full year's worth of property taxes as an expense when it is paid. Is your roommate correct? Explain.

(SO 1) C 7. Laurel Hyatt believes that if a company has a long-term liability, the entire amount should be classified as non-current liabilities. Is Laurel correct? Explain.

(SO 2) C 8. The accountant for Amiable Appliances feels that warranty expense should not be recorded unless an appliance is returned for repair. "Otherwise, how do you know if the appliance will be returned, and if so, how much it will cost to fix?" he says. Do you agree? Explain.

(SO 2) C 9. Why does issuing a customer some form of future savings, when the customer purchases goods or services, result in a liability for the business?

(SO 2) C 10. A restaurant recently started a customer loyalty program. For all bills in excess of $100, the customer receives a 2-for-1 voucher for an appetizer for future meals. How should the restaurant account for the vouchers?

(SO 2) C 11. In what respects are gift cards similar to unearned revenues and why are they classified as a liability? How is a gift card different than an airline's unearned passenger revenue for flights paid in advance?

(SO 1, 2, 3) K 12. What are the differences between determinable, estimated, and contingent liabilities?

(SO 3) C 13. What is a contingency? How is it different from an estimated liability?

(SO 3) C 14. If a company is using ASPE, under what circumstances are a contingent loss and the related liability recorded in the accounts? Under what circumstances are they disclosed only in the notes to the financial statements?

(SO 3) C 15. If a company is using IFRS, under what circumstances are a contingent loss and the related liability recorded in the accounts? How is IFRS different from ASPE in this respect?

(SO 3) C 16. When is it necessary to disclose a contingency even if the chance of occurrence is small?

(SO 4) C 17. What is gross pay? How is it different than net pay? Which amount (gross or net) should a company record as salaries expense?

(SO 4) C 18. Explain the different types of employee and employer payroll deductions, and give examples of each.

(SO 4) K 19. What are an employee earnings record and a payroll register?

(SO 4) C 20. To whom, and how often, are payroll deductions remitted?

(SO 4) K 21. What are some additional employee benefits paid by employers? How are they accounted for?

(SO 5) K 22. In what order are current liabilities generally reported in the balance sheet? Why might this method not always be possible?

(SO 5) K 23. What information about current liabilities should be reported in the notes to the financial statements?

(SO 5) K 24. How can a company determine if its current liabilities are too high?

(SO 6) K *25. Explain how CPP and EI are calculated.

(SO 6) K *26. How is the amount deducted from an employee's wages for income tax determined?

▶ Brief Exercises

BE10–1 Rabbitt Enterprises borrows $10,500 from LowLand Trust Co. on May 1, 2014, signing a 10-month, 4% note payable. Interest is payable the first of each month, starting June 1. Prepare journal entries for Rabbitt Enterprises to record: (a) the receipt of the proceeds of the note; (b) the first interest payment; (c) an adjusting entry, if required, at Rabbitt's year end, August 31, 2014; and (d) the payment of the note at maturity.

Record note payable. (SO 1) AP

BE10–2 Blue Robin Retail has one store in Ottawa, Ontario, and one in Gatineau, Quebec. All sales in Ontario are subject to 13% HST; all sales in Quebec are subject to 5% GST and 9.975% QST. On March 12, 2013, the Ottawa store reports cash sales of $7,200 and the Gatineau store reports cash sales of $8,400. (a) Calculate the sales taxes each store charged for these sales (Note: sales taxes are not included in these amounts.) (b) Prepare a journal entry for each store to record the sales on March 12, 2013.

Calculate sales taxes and record sales. (SO 1) AP

Calculate HST and record sales. (SO 1) AP

BE10–3   Backyard Shed Solutions sells its largest shed for $1,500 plus HST of 13%. On May 10, 2014, it sold 10 of these sheds. In order to increase sales the following weekend, the company offered to sell these sheds for $1,500, sales tax included. On May 17, 2014, the company sold 20 of these sheds. All sales are cash sales. For each day's sales, (a) calculate the HST, and (b) prepare a journal entry to record the sales.

Record property tax. (SO 1) AP

BE10–4   Dresner Company has a December 31 fiscal year end. It receives a $7,860 property tax bill for the 2014 calendar year on March 31, 2014. The bill is payable on June 30. Prepare entries for March 31, June 30, and December 31, assuming the company adjusts its accounts annually.

Record warranty. (SO 2) AP

BE10–5   In 2014, Song Company introduces a new product that includes a two-year warranty on parts. During 2014, 2,500 units are sold for $400 each. The cost of each unit was $175. The company estimates 5% of the units will be defective and that the average warranty cost will be $85 per unit. The company has a December 31 fiscal year end and prepares adjusting entries on an annual basis. (a) Prepare an adjusting entry at December 31, 2014, to accrue the estimated warranty cost. (b) Assume that the warranty contract was honoured on 25 units during 2014 for a total cost of $2,125 to replace defective parts. Prepare an entry dated December 31 to record honouring these warranties. (c) Calculate the profit earned by the company during 2014 on this new product.

Record loyalty rewards issued and redeemed. (SO 2) AP

BE10–6   One-Stop Department Store has a loyalty program where customers are given One-Stop "Money" for cash or debit card purchases. The amount they receive is equal to 2% of the pre-tax sales total. Customers can use the One-Stop Money to pay for part or all of their next purchase at One-Stop Department Store. On July 3, 2014, Judy Wishloff purchases merchandise for $150. She uses $20 of One-Stop Money that she has from earlier purchases, and pays for the rest of the purchase with cash. What entry or entries will One-Stop Department Store record for this transaction? Ignore taxes.

Record estimated liability for cash rebate program. (SO 2) AP

BE10–7   Metropolis Books sold 50,000 copies of a best-selling novel in July for $8 each. Included in each book was a $2 mail-in rebate if the customer sends in proof of purchase with a completed rebate form. Metropolis estimates that 10% of the purchasers will claim the rebate. (a) Calculate the net sales revenue Metropolis earned in July on this book. (b) Prepare an adjusting entry at July 31 to accrue the estimated rebate liability. (c) Assume in August that 1,000 rebate forms are received and processed. Prepare one journal entry to record processing the rebate forms.

Record gift cards issued and redeemed. (SO 2) AP

BE10–8   Rikard's Menswear sells $4,750 of gift cards for cash in December 2014. Rikard's has a December 31 fiscal year end and uses a perpetual inventory system. In January 2015, $2,425 of the gift cards are redeemed for merchandise, with a cost of $1,070. Prepare journal entries for Rikard's for December 2014 and January 2015.

Account for contingencies. (SO 3) C

BE10–9   For each of the following independent situations, indicate whether it should be (1) recorded, (2) disclosed, or (3) neither recorded nor disclosed. Explain your reasoning and indicate if the accounting treatment would be the same or different under IFRS and ASPE.

(a) A customer has sued a company for $1 million. Currently the company is unable to determine if it will win or lose the lawsuit.
(b) A customer has sued a company for $1 million. The company will likely lose the lawsuit.
(c) A competitor has sued a company for $2 million. The lawyers have advised that there is a 55% chance that the company will lose the lawsuit.
(d) A company has guaranteed a $300,000 loan for one of its key suppliers. The supplier has a good credit rating and is not expected to default on the loan.

Discuss contingency. (SO 3) AP

BE10–10   Athabasca Toil & Oil Company, a public company, is a defendant in a lawsuit for improper discharge of pollutants and waste into the Athabasca River. Athabasca's lawyers have advised that it is probable the company will lose this lawsuit and that it could settle out of court for $50,000. Should Athabasca record anything with regard to this lawsuit? Or should it disclose it in the notes to the financial statements? Explain.

Calculate gross, net pay, and employer costs. (SO 4) AP

BE10–11   Becky Sherrick's regular hourly wage rate is $18, and she is paid time and a half for work over 40 hours per week. In the pay period ended March 16, Becky worked 45 hours. Becky's CPP deductions total $38.99, EI deductions total $15.65, and her income tax withholdings are $132.00. (a) Calculate Becky's gross and net pay for the pay period. (b) What are Becky's employer's costs for CPP, EI, and income tax?

Record payroll (SO 4) AP

BE10–12   Bri Company's gross pay for the week ended August 22 totalled $70,000, from which $3,330 was deducted for CPP, $1,281 for EI, and $19,360 for income tax. Prepare the entries to record (a) the employee payroll costs, assuming salaries were paid August 22, and (b) the employer payroll costs, assuming these will not be paid until September.

Identify current liabilities. (SO 1, 2, 3, 4, 5) K

BE10–13   Identify which of the following items should be classified as a current liability. For those that are not current liabilities, identify where they should be classified.

(a) A product warranty
(b) Cash received in advance for airline tickets

(c) HST collected on sales

(d) Bank indebtedness

(e) Interest owing on an overdue account payable

(f) Interest due on an overdue account receivable

(g) A lawsuit pending against a company. The company is not sure of the likely outcome.

(h) Amounts withheld from the employees' weekly pay

(i) Prepaid property tax

(j) A $75,000 mortgage payable, of which $5,000 is due in the next year

BE10–14 Diamond Dealers has two notes payable outstanding on December 31, 2014, as follows:

(a) A five-year, 5.5%, $60,000 note payable issued on August 31, 2014. Diamond Dealers is required to pay $12,000 plus interest on August 31 each year starting in 2015.

(b) A four-year, 4.5%, $96,000 note payable issued on September 30, 2014. Diamond Dealers is required to pay $2,000 plus interest at the end of each month starting on October 31, 2014. All payments are up to date.

Calculate current and non-current portion of notes payable.
(SO 1, 5) AP

Calculate the amount of each note to be included in current and non-current liabilities on Diamond Dealers' December 31, 2014, balance sheet. Ignore interest.

BE10–15 **Suncor Energy Inc.** reported the following current assets and current liabilities (in millions) at December 31, 2011:

Prepare current liabilities section and calculate ratios.
(SO 5) AP

Accounts payable and accrued liabilities	$7,755
Accounts receivable	5,412
Cash and cash equivalents	3,803
Current portion of long-term debt	12
Current portion of provisions	811
Income taxes payable	969
Income taxes receivable	704
Inventories	4,205
Short-term debt	763

(a) Prepare the current liabilities section of the balance sheet.

(b) Calculate the current and acid-test ratios.

*BE10–16 Cecilia Hernandez earned $60,100 in 2012 and was paid monthly. She worked for HillSide Tours for all of 2012. What were her CPP and EI deductions in (a) January 2012 and (b) December 2012?

Calculate CPP and EI deductions. (SO 6) AP

*BE10–17 In 2012, Viktor Petska was paid a gross salary of $1,075 on a weekly basis. For the week ended May 11, 2012: (a) calculate his CPP and EI deductions and (b) use the excerpts in Illustration 10A-3 to determine his income tax deductions assuming his TD1 claim code is 1.

Calculate payroll deductions. (SO 6) AP

*BE10–18 Augustus Jackson earns $860 for a 40-hour week and is paid time and a half for hours above 40. During the week ended April 27, 2012, he worked 48 hours. (a) Calculate his gross pay for the week. (b) Calculate his CPP and EI deductions. (c) Use the excerpts in Illustration 10A-3 to determine his income tax deductions assuming his TD1 claim code is 2. (d) Calculate his net pay.

Calculate gross pay, payroll deductions, and net pay. (SO 4, 6) AP

▶ Exercises

E10–1 On June 1, 2014, Novack Company purchases equipment on account from Moleski Manufacturers for $50,000. Novack is unable to pay its account on July 1, 2014, so Moleski agrees to accept a three-month, 7% note payable from Novack. Interest is payable the first of each month, starting August 1, 2014. Novack has an August 31 fiscal year end. Moleski has a December 31 fiscal year end. Both companies adjust their accounts on an annual basis. Novack honours the note at maturity.

Record note payable and note receivable; interest paid monthly. (SO 1) AP

Instructions

(a) Record all transactions related to the note for Novack Company.

(b) Record all transactions related to the note for Moleski Manufacturers. Assume the cost of the equipment to Moleski was $30,000.

E10–2 On March 1, 2014, Tundra Trees Company purchased equipment from Edworthy Equipment Dealership in exchange for a seven-month, 8%, $30,000 note payable. Interest is due at maturity. Tundra Trees has a July 31 fiscal year end. Edworthy has a May 31 fiscal year end. Both companies adjust their accounts annually. Tundra honours the note at maturity.

Record note payable and note receivable; interest paid at maturity. (SO 1) AP

Instructions

(a) For Tundra Trees, record all transactions related to the note.

(b) For Edworthy Equipment, record all transactions related to the note. Assume the cost of the equipment to Edworthy was $18,000.

Record sales taxes.
(SO 1) AP

E10–3   In providing accounting services to small businesses, you encounter the following independent situations:

1. Sainsbury Company rang up $13,200 of sales, plus HST of 13%, on its cash register on April 10.
2. Hockenstein Company prices its merchandise with sales taxes included. Its register total for April 15 is $35,595, which includes 13% HST.
3. Montgomery Company rang up $30,000 of sales, before sales taxes, on its cash register on April 21. The company charges 5% GST and no PST.
4. Winslow Co. charges 5% GST and 7% PST on all sales. On April 27, the company collected $25,100 sales in cash plus sales taxes.

Instructions

Record the sales transactions and related taxes for each client.

Account for unearned
revenue. (SO 1) AP

E10–4   Charleswood Musical Theatre's season begins in November and ends in April with a different play each month. In October 2014, Charleswood sold 150 season tickets for the 2014–15 season, which sold for $210 each. Charleswood records all season ticket sales as unearned revenue and adjusts its accounts on a monthly basis. The company has a March 31 fiscal year end.

Instructions

(a) Prepare the entry for sale of the season tickets. Date the entry October 31.

(b) Prepare any required adjusting entries on:
   1. November 30, 2014
   2. March 31, 2015
   3. April 30, 2015

(c) Determine the balance (after any required adjustments) in Unearned Revenue on:
   1. November 30, 2014
   2. December 31, 2014
   3. March 31, 2015

Record property tax;
determine financial statement
impact. (SO 1, 5) AP

E10–5   Seaboard Company receives its annual property tax bill of $18,660 for the 2014 calendar year on May 31, 2014, and it is payable on July 31, 2014. Seaboard has a December 31 fiscal year end.

Instructions

(a) Prepare the journal entries for Seaboard on May 31, July 31, and December 31, 2014, assuming that the company makes monthly adjusting entries. (Assume property tax expense in 2013 was $1,475 per month.)

(b) What is recorded on Seaboard's December 31, 2014, balance sheet and income statement for the year ended December 31, 2014, in regard to property taxes?

Record warranty costs.
(SO 2) AP

E10–6   Castellitto Company began selling blenders on November 1, 2014. The company offers a 75-day warranty for defective merchandise. Based on past experience with other similar products, Castellitto estimates that 2.5% of the units sold will become defective in the warranty period, and that the average cost of replacing or repairing a defective unit is $20. In November, Castellitto sold 30,000 units and 450 defective units were returned. In December, Castellitto sold 32,000 units and 630 defective units were returned. The actual cost of replacing the defective units was $21,600.

Instructions

(a) Prepare a journal entry to accrue for the estimated warranty costs for the November and December sales at December 31, 2014.

(b) Prepare one summary journal entry at December 31, 2014, to record the cost of replacing the defective blenders returned during November and December.

(c) What amounts will be included in Castellitto's 2014 income statement and balance sheet at December 31, 2014, with regard to the warranty?

Calculate warranty costs for
multiple years. (SO 2) AP

E10–7   Silver Cloud Company manufactures and sells computers for $2,000 each, with a two-year parts and labour warranty. Based on prior experience, the company expects, on average, to incur warranty costs equal to 5% of sales. The company reports the following sales and warranty cost information:

	Sales (units)	Actual Warranty Costs
2012	500	$30,000
2013	600	46,000
2014	525	53,500

Instructions

(a) Calculate the warranty expense for each year.
(b) Calculate the warranty liability at the end of each year.

E10-8 Steig's Sports Store has a customer loyalty program in which it issues points to customers for every cash purchase that can be applied to future purchases. For every dollar spent, a customer receives three points. Each point is worth one cent. There is no expiry date on the points. Steig's estimates that 35% of the points issued will eventually be redeemed. Steig's has a December 31 year end.

    The program was started in 2014. During 2014, 900,000 points were issued. In 2015, 1.2 million points were issued. Redemptions total 225,000 points in 2014 and 336,000 in 2015.

Calculate customer loyalty program liability. (SO 2) AP

Instructions

(a) What amount should be recorded as contra revenue (sales discounts for redemption rewards issued) in 2014? In 2015?
(b) What was the value of the points redeemed in 2014? In 2015?
(c) What is the redemption rewards liability that should be reported at December 31, 2014? At December 31, 2015?
(d) When the points are redeemed, how is this accounted for? What is the impact of the point redemptions on profit?

E10-9 A list of possible liabilities follows:

Identify type of liability. (SO 1, 2, 3) C

1. An automobile company recalled a particular car model because of a possible problem with the brakes. The company will pay to replace the brakes.
2. A large retail store has a policy of refunding purchases to dissatisfied customers under a widely advertised "money-back, no questions asked" guarantee.
3. A manufacturer offers a three-year warranty at the time of sale.
4. To promote sales, a company offers prizes (such as a chance to win a trip) in return for a specific type of bottle cap.
5. A local community has filed suit against a chemical company for contamination of drinking water. The community is demanding compensation, and the amount is uncertain. The company is vigorously defending itself.

Instructions

(a) State whether you believe each of the above liabilities is determinable, estimable, or contingent, and explain why.
(b) If you identify the liability as contingent in part (a), state what factors should be considered in determining if it should be recorded, disclosed, or neither recorded nor disclosed in the financial statements.

E10-10 Sleep-a-Bye Baby Company, a public company, is the defendant in a lawsuit alleging that its portable baby cribs are unsafe. The company has offered to replace the cribs free of charge for any concerned parent. Nonetheless, it has been sued for damages and distress amounting to $1.5 million. The company plans to vigorously defend its product safety record in court.

Analyze contingency. (SO 3) AP

Instructions

(a) What should the company record or report in its financial statements for this situation? Explain why.
(b) What if Sleep-a-Bye Baby Company's lawyers advise that it is likely the company will have to pay damages of $100,000? Does this change what should be recorded or reported in the financial statements? Explain.
(c) How would your answers to (a) and (b) change if Sleep-a-Bye Baby Company were a private company that had chosen to follow ASPE?

E10-11 Hidden Dragon Restaurant's gross payroll for April is $45,500. The company deducted $2,108 for CPP, $833 for EI, and $8,798 for income taxes from the employees' cheques. Employees are paid monthly at the end of each month.

Record payroll. (SO 4) AP

Instructions

(a) Prepare a journal entry for Hidden Dragon on April 30 to record the payment of the April payroll to employees.
(b) Prepare a journal entry on April 30 to accrue Hidden Dragon's employer payroll costs. Assume that Hidden Dragon is assessed workers' compensation premiums at a rate of 1% per month and accrues for vacation pay at a rate of 4% per month.
(c) On May 15, Hidden Dragon pays the government the correct amounts for April's payroll. Prepare a journal entry to record this remittance.

E10-12 Ahmad Company has the following data for the weekly payroll ending May 31:

Calculate gross pay; prepare payroll register, and record payroll. (SO 4) AP

Employee	\multicolumn{6}{c}{Hours Worked}	Hourly Rate	CPP Deduction	Income Tax Withheld	Health Insurance
	M	Tu	W	Th	F	S				
A. Kassam	9	8	9	8	10	3	$13	$29.17	$ 85.55	$10
H. Faas	8	8	8	8	8	5	14	29.59	87.10	15
G. Labute	9	10	9	10	8	0	15	33.05	102.55	15

Employees are paid 1.5 times the regular hourly rate for all hours worked over 40 hours per week. Ahmad Company must make payments to the workers' compensation plan equal to 2% of the gross payroll. In addition, Ahmad matches the employees' health insurance contributions and accrues vacation pay at a rate of 4%.

Instructions

(a) Prepare the payroll register for the weekly payroll. Calculate each employee's EI deduction at a rate of 1.83% of gross pay.

(b) Record the payroll and Ahmad Company's employee benefits.

Calculate current and non-current portion of notes payable, and interest payable. (SO 1, 5) AP

E10–13 Emerald Enterprises has three notes payable outstanding on December 31, 2014, as follows:

1. A six-year, 6%, $60,000 note payable issued on March 31, 2014. Emerald Enterprises is required to pay $10,000 plus interest on March 31 each year starting in 2015.
2. A seven-month, 4%, $30,000 note payable issued on July 1, 2014. Interest and principal are payable at maturity.
3. A 30-month, 5%, $120,000 note payable issued on September 1, 2014. Emerald Enterprises is required to pay $4,000 plus interest on the first day of each month starting on October 1, 2014. All payments are up to date.

Instructions

(a) Calculate the current portion of each note payable.

(b) Calculate the non-current portion of each note payable.

(c) Calculate any interest payable at December 31, 2014.

Prepare current liabilities section of balance sheet. Calculate current and acid-test ratios. (SO 5) AP

E10–14 The following selected account balances are from LightHouse Distributors' adjusted trial balance at September 30, 2014:

Accounts payable	$ 90,000
Accounts receivable	182,000
Bank overdraft	62,500
CPP payable	7,500
EI payable	3,750
HST payable	15,000
Income tax payable	35,000
Interest payable	10,000
Merchandise inventory	275,000
Mortgage payable	150,000
Notes payable	100,000
Prepaid expenses	12,500
Property taxes payable	10,000
Redemption rewards liability	5,000
Unearned gift card revenue	30,000
Vacation pay payable	13,500
Warranty liability	22,500
Workers' compensation payable	1,250

Additional information:

1. On September 30, 2014, the unused operating line of credit is $75,000.
2. Redemption rewards, warranties, and gift cards are expected to be redeemed within one year.
3. Of the mortgage, $10,000 is due each year.
4. Of the note payable, $1,000 is due at the end of each month.

Instructions

(a) Prepare the current liabilities section of the balance sheet.

(b) Calculate LightHouse's current ratio and acid-test ratio.

(c) Explain why the company did not report any cash as part of its current assets.

Calculate gross pay and payroll deductions; record payroll. (SO 4, 6) AP

*E10–15 Kate Gough's regular hourly wage rate is $22.60, and she receives a wage of 1.5 times the regular hourly rate for work over 40 hours per week. For the weekly pay period ended June 15, 2012, Kate worked 44 hours. Kate lives in Ontario and has a claim code of 1 for tax deductions.

Instructions

(a) Calculate Kate's gross pay, payroll deductions, and net pay. Use Illustration 10A-3 to determine her income tax deductions.

(b) Record Kate's salary on June 15, assuming it was also paid on this date.

(c) Record the employer's related payroll costs on June 15, assuming they were not paid on this date.

*E10–16   In 2012, Donald Green worked for the Green Red Company and earned a gross salary of $57,000 for the year ($4,750 per month). He was paid once a month at the end of each month.

Calculate gross pay and payroll deductions.
(SO 6) AP

Instructions

Calculate Donald's CPP and EI deductions for the following:

(a) September 2012
(b) October 2012
(c) November 2012
(d) December 2012
(e) In total for 2012

⏵ Problems: Set A

P10–1A   Crab Apple Tree Farm has a December 31 fiscal year end. The company has six notes payable outstanding on December 31, 2014, as follows:

Calculate current and non-current portion of notes payable, and interest payable.
(SO 1, 5) AP

1. A 10-month, 5%, $35,000 note payable issued on August 1, 2014. Interest is payable monthly on the first day of each month starting on September 1.
2. A four-month, 4%, $15,000 note payable issued on September 1, 2014. Interest and principal are payable at maturity.
3. A six-month, 4.5%, $26,000 note payable issued on November 1, 2014. Interest and principal are payable at maturity.
4. A five-year, 3.5%, $60,000 note payable issued on March 31, 2014. Crab Apple Tree Farm is required to pay $12,000 plus interest on March 31 each year starting in 2015.
5. A six-year, 5%, $100,000 note payable issued on October 1, 2014. Crab Apple Tree Farm is required to pay $2,000 plus interest on the first day of each month starting on November 1, 2014. All payments are up to date.
6. A four-year, 5%, $40,000 note payable issued on January 31, 2013. Crab Apple Tree Farm is required to pay $10,000 every January 31 starting in 2014. Interest is payable monthly on the last day of each month, starting on February 28, 2013.

Instructions

(a) Calculate the current portion of each note payable.
(b) Calculate the non-current portion of each note payable.
(c) Calculate any interest payable at December 31, 2014.

TAKING IT FURTHER   What are the costs and benefits to the maker and the payee of the note of using a note payable in place of an account payable?

P10–2A   The current liabilities section of the December 31, 2013, balance sheet of Learnstream Company included notes payable of $14,000 and interest payable of $490. The note payable was issued to Tanner Company on June 30, 2013. Interest of 7% is payable at maturity, March 31, 2014.

Record note transactions; show financial statement presentation.
(SO 1, 5) AP

The following selected transactions occurred in the year ended December 31, 2014:

Jan.   12   Purchased merchandise on account from McCoy Company for $20,000, terms n/30. Learnstream uses a perpetual inventory system.
       31   Issued a $20,000, three-month, 5% note to McCoy Company in payment of its account. Interest is payable monthly.
Feb.   28   Paid interest on the McCoy note (see January 31 transaction).
Mar.   31   Paid the Tanner note, plus interest.
       31   Paid interest on the McCoy note (see January 31 transaction).
Apr.   30   Paid the McCoy note, plus one month's interest (see January 31 transaction).
Aug.   1   Purchased equipment from Drouin Equipment by paying $11,000 cash and signing a $30,000, 10-month, 6% note. Interest is payable at maturity.
Sept. 30   Borrowed $100,000 cash from the First Interprovincial Bank by signing a 10-year, 5% note payable. Interest is payable quarterly on December 31, March 31, June 30, and September 30. Of the principal, $10,000 must be paid each September 30.
Dec.   31   Paid interest on the First Interprovincial Bank note (see September 30 transaction).

Instructions

(a) Record the transactions and any adjustments required at December 31.
(b) Show the balance sheet presentation of notes payable and interest payable at December 31.
(c) Show the income statement presentation of interest expense for the year.

TAKING IT FURTHER Why is it important to correctly classify notes payable as either current or non-current in the balance sheet?

Record current liability transactions; prepare current liabilities section.
(SO 1, 2, 4, 5) AP

P10-3A On January 1, 2014, Shumway Software Company's general ledger contained these liability accounts:

Accounts payable	$37,900
Redemption rewards liability	4,500
CPP payable	1,580
EI payable	730
HST payable	9,230
Income tax payable	3,367
Unearned revenue	15,000
Vacation pay payable	9,035

In January, the following selected transactions occurred:

Jan.	2	Issued a $50,000, four-month, 7% note. Interest is payable at maturity.
	5	Sold merchandise for $8,800 cash, plus 13% HST. The cost of this sale was $4,600. Shumway Software uses a perpetual inventory system.
	12	Provided services for customers who had paid $8,500 cash in advance. (*Hint:* Part of this is HST and the remaining amount is Service Revenue.)
	14	Paid the Receiver General (federal government) for sales taxes collected in December 2013.
	15	Paid the Receiver General for amounts owing from the December payroll for CPP, EI, and income tax.
	17	Paid $15,000 to creditors on account.
	20	Sold 500 units of a new product on account for $55 per unit, plus 13% HST. This new product has a one-year warranty. It is estimated that 9% of the units sold will be returned for repair at an average cost of $10 per unit. The cost of this sale was $25 per unit.
	29	During the month, provided $2,300 of services for customers who redeemed their customer loyalty rewards. Assume that HST of 13% is included in $2,300.
	31	Issued 30,000 loyalty rewards points worth $1 each. Based on past experience, 20% of these points are expected to be redeemed.
	31	Recorded and paid the monthly payroll. Gross salaries were $17,500. Amounts withheld included CPP of $809, EI of $320, and income tax of $3,544.

Instructions

(a) Record the transactions.
(b) Record adjusting entries for the following:
  1. Interest on the note payable
  2. The estimated warranty liability
  3. Employee benefits for CPP, EI, and vacation pay (accrued at a rate of 4%)
  4. Estimated property taxes of $8,940 for the 2014 calendar year
(c) Prepare the current liabilities section of the balance sheet at January 31.

TAKING IT FURTHER Explain how and when the Vacation Pay Payable account balance is paid.

Record warranty transactions.
(SO 2) AP

P10-4A On January 1, 2012, Hopewell Company began a warranty program to stimulate sales. It is estimated that 5% of the units sold will be returned for repair at an estimated cost of $30 per unit. Sales and warranty figures for the three years ended December 31 are as follows:

	2012	2013	2014
Sales (units)	1,500	1,700	1,800
Sales price per unit	$150	$120	$125
Units returned for repair under warranty	75	90	105
Actual warranty costs	$2,250	$2,400	$2,640

Instructions

(a) Calculate the warranty expense for each year and warranty liability at the end of each year.
(b) Record the warranty transactions for each year. Credit Repair Parts Inventory for the actual warranty costs.
(c) To date, what percentage of the units sold have been returned for repair under warranty? What has been the average actual warranty cost per unit for the three-year period?

TAKING IT FURTHER   Assume that at December 31, 2014, management reassesses its original estimates and decides that it is more likely that the company will have to service 7% of the units sold in 2014. Management also determines that the average actual cost per unit incurred to date (as calculated in [c] above) is more reasonable than its original estimate. What should be the balance in the warranty liability account at December 31, 2014?

P10–5A   Save-Always Stores started a customer loyalty program at the beginning of 2013 in which customers making cash purchases of gasoline at Save-Always Gas Bars are issued rewards in the form of grocery coupons. For each litre of gasoline purchased, the customer gets a grocery coupon for 3.5 cents that can be redeemed in Save-Always Food Stores. The coupons have no expiry date. Save-Always Stores began selling gift cards in 2014 that do not have expiry dates.

Record customer loyalty program and gift card transactions; determine impact on financial statements. (SO 2) AP

The following are selected transactions in 2013 and 2014:

1. In 2013, the Gas Bars sold 3.5 million litres of gasoline, issuing grocery coupons for these sales.
2. In 2013, customers redeemed $45,000 of the grocery coupons in the Food Stores while purchasing $1.8 million of groceries, paying the balance in cash.
3. In 2014, the Gas Bars sold 4,250,000 litres of gasoline, issuing grocery coupons for these sales.
4. In 2014, customers redeemed $52,500 of the grocery coupons in the Food Stores while purchasing $2,230,000 of groceries, paying for the balance in cash.
5. In 2014, customers purchased $75,000 of gift cards, and $45,400 of the cards were redeemed by the end of the year.

Instructions

(a) Indicate if the following activities will increase, decrease, or have no effect on each of revenues, expenses, and profit:
   1. Issuing grocery coupons
   2. Redeeming grocery coupons
   3. Issuing gift cards
   4. Redeeming gift cards
(b) Record the above transactions.
(c) What balances will be included in current liabilities at December 31, 2013 and 2014, regarding the customer loyalty program and gift cards?

TAKING IT FURTHER   What factors should management consider in determining if current liabilities are correctly valued at December 31, 2014?

P10–6A   Mega Company, a public company, is preparing its financial statements for the year ended December 31, 2014. It is now January 31, 2015, and the following situations are being reviewed to determine the appropriate accounting treatment:

Discuss reporting of contingencies and record provisions. (SO 3, 5) AP

1. Mega Company is being sued for $4 million for a possible malfunction of one of its products. In July 2014, a customer suffered a serious injury while operating the product. The company is vigorously defending itself as it is clear the customer was intoxicated when using the product.
2. In a separate lawsuit, Mega is being sued for $3 million by an employee who was injured on the job in February 2014. It is likely that the company will lose this lawsuit, but a reasonable estimate cannot be made of the amount of the expected settlement.
3. Since June 2012, Mega has guaranteed a $1-million bank loan for one of its main suppliers. In September 2014, the supplier started experiencing financial difficulties, which have continued. On December 16, 2014, the bank called Mega Company to confirm that if the supplier is unable repay the loan in January 2015, the bank will be seeking payment from Mega Company under the guarantee.
4. On December 7, 2014, a potential customer injured himself when he slipped on the floor in the foyer of Mega Company's office building. Mega Company did not have appropriate floor mats in place and melting snow from the customer's boots made the floor very dangerous. Mega has negotiated a potential settlement of $200,000 with the individual's lawyer.

Instructions

For each of the above situations, recommend whether Mega Company should (1) make an accrual in its December 31, 2014, financial statements; (2) disclose the situation in the notes to the financial statements; or (3) not report it. Provide a rationale for your recommendations.

TAKING IT FURTHER   What are the potential benefits and costs of making an accrual for a contingency as opposed to only disclosing it in the notes to the financial statements?

Prepare payroll register and record payroll. (SO 4) AP

P10–7A Sure Value Hardware has four employees who are paid on an hourly basis, plus time and a half for hours worked in excess of 40 hours a week. Payroll data for the week ended March 14, 2014, follow:

Employee	Total Hours	Hourly Rate	CPP	EI	Income Tax	United Way
I. Dahl	37.5	$17.00	$29.22	$11.67	$ 82.25	$ 7.50
F. Gualtieri	42	16.00	30.72	12.59	91.20	8.00
G. Ho	44	15.50	31.96	13.05	97.50	5.00
A. Israeli	46	15.50	34.26	13.90	107.75	10.00

Instructions

(a) Prepare a payroll register for the weekly payroll.
(b) Record the payroll on March 14 and the accrual of employee benefits expense. Assume the company accrues 4% for vacation pay.
(c) Record the payment of the payroll on March 14.
(d) Record the payment of employee benefits on April 15.

TAKING IT FURTHER Does the owner of a proprietorship need to deduct CPP, EI, and income taxes on his or her drawings?

Record payroll transactions and calculate balances in payroll liability accounts. (SO 4) AP

P10–8A On January 31, 2014, Cardston Company had the following payroll liability accounts in its ledger:

Canada Pension Plan payable	$ 7,887	Life insurance payable	$ 855
Disability insurance payable	1,280	Union dues payable	1,450
Employment Insurance payable	3,755	Vacation pay payable	20,520
Income tax payable	16,252	Workers' compensation payable	4,275

In February, the following transactions occurred:

Feb. 4 Sent a cheque to the union treasurer for union dues.
7 Sent a cheque to the insurance company for the disability and life insurance.
13 Issued a cheque to the Receiver General for the amounts due for CPP, EI, and income tax.
20 Paid the amount due to the workers' compensation plan.
28 Completed the monthly payroll register, which shows gross salaries $92,600; CPP withheld $4,281; EI withheld $1,695; income tax withheld $17,595; union dues withheld $1,574; and long-term disability insurance premiums $1,380.
28 Prepared payroll cheques for the February net pay and distributed the cheques to the employees.
28 Recorded an adjusting journal entry to record February employee benefits for CPP, EI, workers' compensation at 5% of gross pay, vacation pay at 4% of gross pay, and life insurance at 1% of gross pay.

Instructions

(a) Journalize the February transactions and adjustments.
(b) Calculate the balances in each of the payroll liability accounts at February 28, 2014.

TAKING IT FURTHER Why do employers need an employee earnings record for each employee as well as a payroll register?

Prepare current liabilities section; calculate and comment on ratios. (SO 5) AP

P10–9A Maple Leaf Foods Inc. reports the following current assets and current liabilities at December 31, 2011 (in thousands):

Accounts payable and accruals	$482,059
Accounts receivable	133,504
Bank indebtedness	36,404
Biological assets	49,265
Current portion of long-term debt	5,618
Income and other taxes recoverable	43,789
Inventories	293,231
Notes receivable	98,545
Other current liabilities	20,409
Prepaid expenses and other assets	24,688
Provisions	44,255

Instructions

(a) Prepare the current liabilities section of the balance sheet.
(b) Calculate the current and acid-test ratios.
(c) At December 31, 2010, Maple Leaf Foods Inc. had current assets of $583,557 thousand, cash, short-term investments plus receivables of $217,751 thousand, and current liabilities of $1,091,960 thousand. Did the current and acid-test ratios improve or weaken in 2011?

TAKING IT FURTHER   What other factors should be considered in assessing Maple Leaf Foods' liquidity?

*P10–10A   Western Electric Company pays its support staff weekly and its electricians on a semi-monthly basis. The following support staff payroll information is available for the week ended June 8, 2012:

Calculate payroll deductions; prepare payroll register. (SO 6) AP

Employee Name	Weekly Earnings	Claim Code
Chris Tanm	$ 945	2
Terry Ng	1,130	4
Olga Stavtech	1,130	1
Alana Mandell	1,067	1

The electricians' salaries are based on their experience in the field, as well as the number of years they have worked for the company. All three electricians have been with the company more than two years. The annual salaries of these employees are as follows:

Employee Name	Annual Salary for 2012
Sam Goodspeed	$43,440
Marino Giancarlo	64,770
Hillary Ridley	76,880

Instructions

(a) Prepare a payroll register for June 8, 2012, weekly payroll for the support staff. Calculate the CPP and EI deductions using the formula provided in Appendix 10A. Use the tables in Illustration 10A-3 to determine federal and provincial income taxes.
(b) Calculate the CPP and EI deductions for each of the electricians for their June 15, 2012, semi-monthly payroll.
(c) In which semi-monthly pay period will each of the electricians reach their maximum CPP and EI payments for 2012?

TAKING IT FURTHER   Why are there separate payroll deduction tables for determining weekly, semi-monthly, and monthly income tax deductions?

▶ Problems: Set B

P10–1B   Juniper Bush Farm has a December 31 fiscal year end. The company has six notes payable outstanding on December 31, 2014, as follows:

Calculate current and non-current portion of notes payable, and interest payable. (SO 1, 5) AP

1. A nine-month, 5%, $25,000 note payable issued on July 1, 2014. Interest is payable monthly on the first day of each month starting on August 1.
2. A six-month, 4%, $10,000 note payable issued on September 1, 2014. Interest and principal are payable at maturity.
3. A seven-month, 4.5%, $40,000 note payable issued on November 1, 2014. Interest and principal are payable at maturity.
4. A five-year, 3.75%, $80,000 note payable issued on May 31, 2014. Juniper Bush Farm is required to pay $16,000 plus interest on May 31 each year starting in 2015.
5. A three-year, 4.25%, $126,000 note payable issued on October 1, 2014. Juniper Bush Farm is required to pay $3,500 plus interest on the first day of each month starting on November 1, 2014. All payments are up to date.
6. A four-year, 5%, $50,000 note payable issued on March 31, 2013. Juniper Bush Farm is required to pay $12,500 every March 31 starting in 2014. Interest is payable monthly at the end of the month, starting on April 30, 2013.

Instructions

(a) Calculate the current portion of each note payable.
(b) Calculate the non-current portion of each note payable.
(c) Calculate any interest payable at December 31, 2014.

Record note transactions; show financial statement presentation. (SO 1, 5) AP

TAKING IT FURTHER What are the costs and benefits to the maker and the payee of the note of using a note payable in place of an account payable?

P10–2B MileHi Mountain Bikes markets mountain-bike tours to clients vacationing in various locations in the mountains of British Columbia. The current liabilities section of the October 31, 2013, balance sheet included notes payable of $15,000 and interest payable of $375 related to a six-month, 6% note payable to Eifert Company on December 1, 2013.

During the year ended October 31, 2014, MileHi had the following transactions related to notes payable:

2013

Dec. 1   Paid the $15,000 Eifert note, plus interest.

2014

Apr. 1   Issued a $75,000, nine-month, 7% note to Mountain Real Estate for the purchase of additional mountain property on which to build bike trails. Interest is payable quarterly on July 1, October 1, and at maturity on January 1, 2015.

30   Purchased Mongoose bikes to use as rentals for $8,000, terms n/30.

May 31   Issued Mongoose an $8,000, three-month, 8% note payable in settlement of its account (see April 30 transaction). Interest is payable at maturity.

July 1   Paid interest on the Mountain Real Estate note (see April 1 transaction).

Aug. 31   Paid the Mongoose note, plus interest (see May 31 transaction).

Oct. 1   Paid interest on the Mountain Real Estate note (see April 1 transaction).

1   Borrowed $90,000 cash from Western Bank by issuing a five-year, 6% note. Interest is payable monthly on the first of the month. Principal payments of $18,000 must be made on the anniversary of the note each year.

Instructions

(a) Record the transactions and any adjustments required at October 31, 2014.
(b) Show the balance sheet presentation of notes payable and interest payable at October 31, 2014.
(c) Show the income statement presentation of interest expense for the year.

TAKING IT FURTHER Why is it important to correctly classify notes payable as either current or non-current in the balance sheet?

Record current liability transactions; prepare current liabilities section. (SO 1, 2, 4, 5) AP

P10–3B On January 1, 2014, Zaur Company's general ledger had these liability accounts:

Accounts payable	$63,700
Redemption rewards liability	2,150
CPP payable	2,152
EI payable	1,019
HST payable	11,390
Income tax payable	4,563
Unearned revenue	16,000
Vacation pay payable	9,120
Warranty liability	5,750

In January, the following selected transactions occurred:

Jan. 5   Sold merchandise for $15,800 cash, plus 13% HST. Zaur uses a periodic inventory system.

12   Provided services for customers who had previously made advance payments of $7,000. (*Hint:* Part of this is HST and the remaining amount is Service Revenue.)

14   Paid the Receiver General (federal government) sales taxes collected in December 2013.

15   Paid the Receiver General for amounts owing from the December payroll for CPP, EI, and income tax.

16   Borrowed $18,000 from Second National Bank on a three-month, 6% note. Interest is payable monthly on the 15th day of the month.

17   Paid $35,000 to creditors on account.

20   Sold 500 units of a new product on account for $60 per unit, plus 13% HST. This new product has a two-year warranty. It is expected that 6% of the units sold will be returned for repair at an average cost of $10 per unit.

30   Customers redeemed $1,750 of loyalty rewards in exchange for services. Assume that HST of 13% is included in this amount.

31   Issued 50,000 loyalty points worth $1 each. Based on past experience, 10% of these points are expected to be redeemed.

31   Determined that the company had used $875 of parts inventory in January to honour warranty contracts.

31   Recorded and paid the monthly payroll. Gross salaries were $25,350. Amounts withheld include CPP of $1,183, EI of $464, and income tax of $4,563.

Instructions

(a) Record the transactions.
(b) Record adjusting entries for the following:
    1. Interest on the note payable for half a month
    2. The estimated warranty liability
    3. Employee benefits, which include CPP, EI, and vacation pay that is accrued at a rate of 4%
(c) Prepare the current liabilities section of the balance sheet at January 31.

TAKING IT FURTHER   Explain how and when the Vacation Pay Payable account balance is paid.

P10–4B On January 1, 2012, Logue Company began a warranty program to stimulate sales. It is estimated that 5% of the units sold will be returned for repair at an estimated cost of $25 per unit. Sales and warranty figures for the three years ended December 31 are as follows:

Record warranty transactions. (SO 2) AP

	2012	2013	2014
Sales (units)	1,200	1,320	1,420
Sales price per unit	$100	$105	$110
Units returned for repair under warranty	60	70	80
Actual warranty costs	$1,275	$1,600	$1,960

Instructions

(a) Calculate the warranty expense for each year and warranty liability at the end of each year.
(b) Record the warranty transactions for each year. Credit Repair Parts Inventory for the actual warranty costs.
(c) To date, what percentage of the units sold have been returned for repair under warranty? What has been the average actual warranty cost per unit for the three-year period?

TAKING IT FURTHER   Suppose at December 31, 2014, management reassesses its original estimates and decides that it is more likely that the company will have to service 7% of the units sold in 2014. Management also determines that the original estimate of the cost per unit is the appropriate cost to use for future repair work. What should be the balance in the warranty liability account at December 31, 2014?

P10–5B Caribou County Service Station started a customer loyalty program at the beginning of 2013 in which customers making cash purchases of gasoline at the gas bar are issued rewards in the form of coupons. For each litre of gasoline purchased, the customer gets a coupon for 2.5 cents that can be redeemed in the service department toward such things as oil changes or repairs. The coupons have no expiry date. Caribou County Service Station began selling gift cards in 2014 that do not have expiry dates.
    The following are selected transactions in 2013 and 2014:

Record customer loyalty program and gift card transactions; determine impact on financial statements. (SO 2) AP

1. In 2013, the gas bar sold 750,000 litres of gasoline, issuing coupons for these sales.
2. In 2013, customers redeemed $5,950 of the coupons in the service department while purchasing $23,800 of repair services for their vehicles, paying the balance in cash.
3. In 2014, the gas bar sold 810,000 litres of gasoline, issuing coupons for these sales.
4. In 2014, customers redeemed $9,500 of the coupons in the service department while purchasing $30,230 of repair services for their vehicles, paying for the balance in cash.
5. In 2014, customers purchased $3,950 of gift cards, and $1,500 of the cards were redeemed by the end of the year.

Instructions

(a) Indicate if the following items will increase, decrease, or have no effect on each of revenues, expenses, and profit:
    1. Issuing coupons
    2. Redeeming coupons
    3. Issuing gift cards
    4. Redeeming gift cards
(b) Record the above transactions.
(c) What balances will be included in current liabilities at December 31, 2013 and 2014, regarding the customer loyalty program and gift cards?

TAKING IT FURTHER   What factors should management consider in determining if current liabilities are correctly valued at December 31, 2014?

P10–6B Big Fork Company, a private company that follows ASPE, is preparing its financial statements for the year ended December 31, 2014. It is now February 15, 2015, and the following situations are being reviewed to determine the appropriate accounting treatment:

Discuss reporting of contingencies and record provisions. (SO 3, 5) AP

1. Since 2007, Big Fork has guaranteed a $250,000 bank loan for one of its main customers, Little Fork. Little Fork has always made all of its payments in a timely fashion.
2. Big Fork is being sued for $3 million for a possible malfunction of one of its products. In March 2014, a customer suffered a serious injury while operating the product. The company is defending itself but it is clear that there was an error in the published operations manual for the product. It is likely that the company will lose this lawsuit, but it is unlikely it will have to pay the full $3 million. At this point, a reasonable estimate cannot be made of the amount of the expected settlement.
3. Big Fork is being sued for $1.5 million by an employee for wrongful dismissal and defamation of character. The employee was fired on August 2, 2014. The company is vigorously defending itself because the employee had a documented history of poor performance at work.
4. On December 16, 2014, a sales representative from one of the company's suppliers injured herself on a visit to Big Fork's offices. She tripped over equipment that had not been properly stored and will be unable to work for several months as a result of her injuries. A $250,000 claim against Big Fork has been filed by the sales representative's insurance company.

Instructions

For each of the above situations, recommend whether Big Fork Company should (1) make an accrual in its December 31, 2014, financial statements; (2) disclose the situation in the notes to the financial statements; or (3) not report it. Provide a rationale for your recommendations.

TAKING IT FURTHER What are the potential benefits and costs of making an accrual for a contingency as opposed to only disclosing it in the notes to the financial statements?

Prepare payroll register and record payroll. (SO 4) AP

P10–7B Scoot Scooters has four employees who are paid on an hourly basis, plus time and a half for hours in excess of 40 hours a week. Payroll data for the week ended February 17, 2012, follow:

Employee	Total Hours	Hourly Rate	CPP	EI	Income Tax	United Way
P. Kilchyk	40	$15.25	$26.86	$11.16	$76.60	$5.00
B. Quon	42	15.00	28.60	11.80	83.70	7.25
C. Pospisil	40	16.25	28.84	11.90	84.10	5.50
B. Verwey	44	14.50	29.68	12.21	87.10	8.25

Instructions

(a) Prepare a payroll register for the weekly payroll.
(b) Record the payroll on February 15 and the accrual of employee benefits expense. Assume the company accrues 4% for vacation pay.
(c) Record the payment of the payroll on February 17.
(d) Record the payment of the employee benefits on March 15.

TAKING IT FURTHER Does the owner of a proprietorship have to deduct CPP, EI, and income taxes from his or her own drawings?

Record payroll transactions and calculate balances in payroll liability accounts. (SO 4) AP

P10–8B On March 31, 2014, Babb Company had the following payroll liability accounts in its ledger:

Canada Pension Plan payable	$ 6,907	Life insurance payable	$ 756
Disability insurance payable	1,134	Union dues payable	1,285
Employment Insurance payable	3,320	Vacation pay payable	3,024
Income tax payable	14,364	Workers' compensation payable	3,780

In April, the following transactions occurred:

Apr.	4	Sent a cheque to the union treasurer for union dues.
	7	Sent a cheque to the insurance company for the disability and life insurance.
	13	Issued a cheque to the Receiver General for the amounts due for CPP, EI, and income tax.
	20	Paid the amount due to the workers' compensation plan.
	28	Completed the monthly payroll register, which shows gross salaries $83,160; CPP withheld $3,799; EI withheld $1,522; income tax withheld $15,800; union dues withheld $1,414; and long-term disability insurance premiums $1,247.
	28	Prepared payroll cheques for the April net pay and distributed the cheques to the employees.
	28	Recorded an adjusting journal entry to record April employee benefits for CPP, EI, workers' compensation at 5% of gross pay, vacation pay at 4% of gross pay, and life insurance at 1% of gross pay.

Instructions

(a) Journalize the April transactions and adjustments.
(b) Calculate the balances in each of the payroll liability accounts at April 30, 2014.

TAKING IT FURTHER   Why do employers need an employee earnings record for each employee as well as a payroll register?

P10-9B   BCE Inc., more commonly known as Bell Canada, reports the following current assets and current liabilities at December 31, 2011 (in millions of dollars):

Cash	$ 130
Cash equivalents	45
Current tax liabilities	47
Debt due within one year	2,106
Dividends payable	415
Interest payable	134
Inventory	427
Other current assets	152
Prepaid expenses	262
Trade and other receivables	3,162
Trade payables and other liabilities	4,056

Prepare current liabilities section; calculate and comment on ratios.
(SO 5) AP

Instructions

(a) Prepare the current liabilities section of the balance sheet.
(b) Calculate the current and the acid-test ratio.
(c) On December 31, 2010, BCE Inc. had current assets of $4,655 million, cash and cash equivalents plus trade and other receivables of $3,795 million, and current liabilities of $6,954 million. Did the current and acid-test ratios improve or weaken in 2011?

TAKING IT FURTHER   What other factors should be considered in assessing BCE Inc.'s liquidity?

*P10-10B   Slovak Plumbing Company pays its support staff weekly and its plumbers on a semi-monthly basis. The following support staff payroll information is available for the week ended May 11, 2012:

Employee Name	Weekly Earnings	Claim Code
Dan Quinn	$ 985	1
Karol Holub	1,037	3
Al Lowhorn	1,080	1
Irina Kostra	950	4

Calculate payroll deductions and prepare payroll register.
(SO 6) AP

The plumbers' salaries are based on their experience in the field, as well as the number of years they have worked for the company. All three plumbers have been with the company more than two years. The annual salary of these employees is as follows:

Employee Name	Annual Salary for 2012
Branislav Dolina	$80,700
Henrietta Koleno	62,500
Aida Krneta	44,120

Instructions

(a) Prepare a payroll register for May 11, 2012, weekly payroll for the support staff. Calculate the CPP and EI deductions using the formula provided in Appendix 10A. Use the tables in Illustration 10A-3 to determine federal and provincial income taxes.
(b) Calculate the CPP and EI deductions for each of the plumbers for their May 15, 2012, semi-monthly payroll.
(c) In which semi-monthly pay period will each of the plumbers reach their maximum CPP and EI payments for 2012?

TAKING IT FURTHER   Why are there separate payroll deduction tables for determining income tax deductions for weekly, semi-monthly, and monthly pay periods?

▶ Continuing Cookie Chronicle

(*Note:* This is a continuation of the Cookie Chronicle from Chapters 1 through 9.)

Natalie has had much success with her cookie-making lessons over the last number of months. A few parents who have attended have shown interest in purchasing gift certificates from Natalie. Natalie is considering a gift certificate that would include a one-hour cookie-making lesson and all of the supplies needed to create two dozen cookies.

Natalie wants to make sure that she has considered all of the risks and rewards of issuing gift certificates. She has come to you with the following questions:

1. From what I understand, if I sell a gift certificate, I need to be recording the money received as "unearned revenue." I am a little confused. How is the use of this account the same as the money that I received from schools that have paid me a deposit for pre-booked cookie-making lessons?
2. What if I record the sale of gift certificates as revenue instead of unearned revenue? Technically, I have made a sale of a gift certificate and therefore should be recording amounts received as revenue for the sale of a gift certificate. What if a gift certificate is never used? Does this not justify a sale being recorded?
3. How do I make sure that the gift certificates that I have sold are in fact used? How do I make sure that the ones that I have sold have not been duplicated and used again?

Instructions

Answer Natalie's questions.

Cumulative Coverage—Chapters 3 to 10

The unadjusted trial balance of LeBrun Company at its year end, July 31, 2014, is as follows:

LEBRUN COMPANY Trial Balance July 31, 2014		
	Debit	Credit
Cash	$ 16,550	
Petty cash	200	
Accounts receivable	38,500	
Allowance for doubtful accounts		$ 2,000
Note receivable (due December 31, 2014)	10,000	
Merchandise inventory	45,900	
Prepaid expenses	16,000	
Land	50,000	
Building	155,000	
Accumulated depreciation—building		10,800
Equipment	25,000	
Accumulated depreciation—equipment		12,200
Patent	75,000	
Accumulated amortization—patent		15,000
Accounts payable		78,900
Warranty liability		6,000
Notes payable (due August 1, 2029)		124,200
S. LeBrun, capital		124,700
S. LeBrun, drawings	54,000	
Sales		750,000
Cost of goods sold	450,000	
Operating expenses	181,220	
Interest revenue		400
Interest expense	6,830	
Totals	$1,124,200	$1,124,200

Adjustment information:

1. The July 31 bank statement reported debit memos for service charges of $50 and a $650 NSF (not sufficient funds) cheque that had been received from a customer for the purchase of merchandise in July.
2. Estimated uncollectible accounts receivable at July 31 are $3,850.
3. The note receivable bears interest of 8% and was issued on December 31, 2013. Interest is payable the first of each month.
4. A physical count of inventory determined that $39,200 of inventory was actually on hand.
5. Prepaid expenses of $5,500 expired in the year (use the account Operating Expenses).
6. Depreciation is calculated on the long-lived assets using the following methods and useful lives:

> Building: straight-line, 25 years, $15,000 residual value
> Equipment: double diminishing-balance, five years, $2,500 residual value
> Patent: straight-line, five years, no residual value

7. The 6% note payable was issued on August 1, 2004. Interest is paid monthly at the beginning of each month for the previous month's interest. Of the note principal, $1,680 is currently due.
8. Estimated warranty costs for July are $1,975 (use Operating Expenses).

Instructions

(a) Prepare the adjusting journal entries required at July 31. (Round your calculations to the nearest dollar.)
(b) Prepare an adjusted trial balance at July 31.
(c) Prepare a multiple-step income statement and statement of owner's equity for the year and a balance sheet at July 31.

BROADENING YOUR PERSPECTIVE | CHAPTER 10

▶ Financial Reporting and Analysis

Financial Reporting Problem

BYP10–1 Refer to the financial statements of **Reitmans (Canada) Limited** and the Notes to the Financial Statements in Appendix A.

Instructions

Answer the following questions about the company's current and contingent liabilities:

(a) What were Reitmans' total current liabilities at January 28, 2012? What was the increase (decrease) in total current liabilities from the previous year?
(b) Which specific current liabilities and in what order did Reitmans present on the January 28, 2012, balance sheet?
(c) Calculate Reitmans' current ratio, acid-test ratio, receivables, and inventory turnover ratios, and operating cycle for 2012 and 2011. Comment on Reitmans' overall liquidity.
(d) Does Reitmans report any contingencies? If so, where are they disclosed? Explain the nature, amount, and significance of Reitmans' contingencies, if any.

Interpreting Financial Statements

BYP10–2 **Canadian Tire Corporation, Limited** reported the following information about contingencies in the notes to its December 31, 2011, financial statements:

CANADIAN TIRE CORPORATION, LIMITED
Notes to the Consolidated Financial Statements
December 31, 2011

23. Contingencies

Legal matters

The Company and certain of its subsidiaries are party to a number of legal proceedings. The Company has determined that each such proceeding constitutes a routine legal matter incidental to the business conducted by the Company and that the ultimate disposition of the proceedings will not have a material effect on its consolidated earnings, cash flows, or financial position.

The Canadian Tire Bank (a wholly-owned subsidiary) is the subject of two class action proceedings regarding allegations that certain fees charged on the Bank issued credit cards are not permitted under the Quebec Consumer Protection Act. The Bank has determined that it has a solid defense to both actions on the basis that banking and cost of borrowing disclosure is a matter of exclusive federal jurisdiction. Accordingly, no provision has been made for amounts, if any, that would be payable in the event of an adverse outcome. If adversely decided, the total aggregate exposure to the Company would have been approximately $24.4 million at December 31, 2011.

Instructions

(a) Why would Canadian Tire disclose information about these legal disputes, including the amount of the potential loss, in the notes to the financial statements instead of accruing an amount for these as liabilities in its accounting records?

(b) Canadian Tire also discloses that it has made "provisions for the cost of legal issues that have not yet been settled. The provisions are based on the Company's best estimate of the expected settlement amount. The amount of the provisions for legal issues is $11.1 million at December 31, 2011 (2010 − $0.3 million)." Why would Canadian Tire accrue for this amount when it hasn't made an accrual for the related legal dispute?

⦿ Critical Thinking

Collaborative Learning Activity

Note to instructor: Additional instructions and material for this group activity can be found on the Instructor Resource Site and in *WileyPLUS*.

BYP10–3 In this group activity, your group must decide on the best accounting treatment for a contingency. Your instructor will provide the class with a scenario and each group will be required to decide if an accrual should be made and, if so, for how much. Groups will simultaneously report to the class and will be required to defend their decisions.

Communication Activity

BYP10–4 The Show Time movie theatre sells thousands of gift certificates every year. The certificates can be redeemed at any time since they have no expiry date. Some of them may never be redeemed (because they are lost or forgotten, for example). The owner of the theatre has raised some questions about the accounting for these gift certificates.

Instructions

Write an e-mail to answer the following questions from the owner:

(a) Why is a liability recorded when these certificates are sold? After all, they bring customers into the theatre, where they spend money on snacks and drinks. Why should something that helps generate additional revenue be treated as a liability?

(b) How should the gift certificates that are never redeemed be treated? At some point in the future, can the liability related to them be eliminated? If so, what type of journal entry would be made?

Ethics Case

BYP10–5 Nice Nuke Corporation, which owns and operates a nuclear plant, recently received notice from the provincial government that it has to find a new disposal site for its radioactive waste. The company was also told that it is responsible for the environmental cleanup of the old site. The vice-president of engineering and the vice-president of finance meet to discuss the situation. The engineer says that it could take many years to clean up the site and that the cost could be considerable—a minimum of $50 million and perhaps as much as $100 million.

The vice-president of finance says that there is no way that the company can afford to record this liability. He says he is not even sure that he wants to disclose the potential liability, because of how this could affect the company's share price.

Instructions

(a) Who are the stakeholders in this situation?

(b) What are the alternative reporting options that the company can use?

(c) What is the likely impact of each alternative on the company's financial position?

(d) Is there anything unethical in what the vice-president of finance suggests doing about this potential liability?

(e) What do you recommend the company do?

"All About You" Activity

BYP10–6 In the "All About You" feature, you learned who is responsible for remitting income tax, CPP, and EI to the CRA if you are an employee or self-employed. You also learned that the CRA has strict guidelines as to whether someone is self-employed or an employee.

Assume that as a new graduate you are accepting a position where you will be providing consulting services to a company. You have agreed to provide the services for $3,000 a month. The company's manager of human resources suggests that you may want to be considered self-employed rather than an employee of the company. Before you make your decision, you need to better understand the CRA's guidelines and the financial implications.

Instructions

(a) Go to the Canada Revenue Agency's website at www.cra-arc.gc.ca and search for document RC4110 "Employee or Self-Employed?" What are the factors that should be considered when determining if a worker is an employee or self-employed?

(b) Assume you are an employee and you are paid monthly and that the following is deducted from your gross earnings: (*Note: The following deductions are based on the 2012 payroll tables for Ontario.*)

CPP	$134.06
EI	54.90
Income tax	407.95

What is the amount of cash you will receive each month? What is the total amount of cash you will receive in a year?

(c) Based on the information in (b), what is the total CPP you will pay in a year? What is the total EI you will pay in a year?

(d) Assume you are self-employed, and you have chosen to pay EI. What is the amount of cash you will receive each month from the company? What is the total CPP you will have to pay in a year? What is the total EI you will have to pay in a year?

(e) Assuming that you will pay the same amount of income tax as you would if you were an employee, calculate the amount of cash you will receive for the year if you are self-employed.

(f) Based on your answers to (c) and (e), do you want to be self-employed or an employee of the company? Explain.

(g) If you had the opportunity to provide consulting services to another company in your spare time, would your answer in (f) be different? Explain.

ANSWERS TO CHAPTER QUESTIONS

ANSWERS TO ACCOUNTING IN ACTION INSIGHT QUESTIONS

Business Insight, p. 535

Q: Environmental contingencies are generally considered to be harder to estimate than contingencies from lawsuits. What might be the reason for this difference?

A: The requirement to account for environmental contingencies is relatively new compared with the requirement to account for contingencies from lawsuits. Although it is difficult to predict whether the company will win or lose a lawsuit and what type of settlement may be involved, there is a vast history of case law that can be used to help a company form an opinion. Environmental regulations, in contrast, are still evolving and there is often no system (e.g., regulatory compliance audits or environmental site assessment data) that would help a company estimate the possible cost, or even the existence, of environmental contingencies for many years.

All About You Insight, p. 543

Q: If you are providing services to a company, what are the advantages and disadvantages of being a self-employed consultant versus an employee of the company?

A: As a self-employed individual, your monthly cash received from the company would be higher as no CPP, EI, and income tax will be deducted. On the other hand, you will have to make quarterly instalment payments of CPP, EI (if you choose to pay it), and income taxes. If you are self-employed, you may be able to deduct certain expenses to reduce your income tax.

However, some individuals may not manage their cash properly and may be unable to make the remittances when required. In addition, you will have to pay twice as much for CPP and you will not qualify for EI benefits. If you are self-employed, you would not qualify for other benefits offered to employees by the company, either.

ANSWERS TO SELF-STUDY QUESTIONS

1. d   2. b   3. c   4. a   5. b   6. a   7. b   8. b   9. a   *10. b

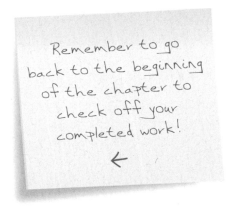

Photo Credits

Chapter 1 Opener: The Canadian Press Images-Mario Beauregard; Page 5: © istockphoto.com/Andreas Rodriguez; Page 26: © istockphoto.com/Jacob Wackerhausen. **Chapter 2** Opener: Courtesy Prestige Dance Academy; Page 63: ©iStockphoto.com/NevinGiesbrecht; Page 76: ©iStockphoto.com/mihalec. **Chapter 3** Opener: Courtesy Seneca College of Applied Arts and Technology; Page 114: ©iStockphoto.com/Ashwin82; Page 122: ©iStockphoto.com/spxChrome. **Chapter 4** Opener: Courtesy Laurel Hyatt; Page 186: Copied with the permission of Canada Post Corporation; Page 187: Adapted and reprinted with the permission of Empire Company Limited; Page 188: BlackBerry®, RIM®, Research In Motion® and related trademarks, names and logos are the property of Research In Motion Limited and are registered and/or used in the U.S. and countries around the world. Used under license from Research In Motion Limited; Page 189: Used with permission of Sears Canada Inc; Page 189: Canadian National Railway Company ("CN"), reproduced by authorization of CN; Page 192: © iStockphoto.com/WillSelarep. **Chapter 5** Opener: Courtesy Moulé; Page 249: © iStockphoto.com/Leah-Anne Thompson. **Chapter 6** Opener: Courtesy Gravitypope/Louise Dirks; Page 304: ©istockphoto.com/SimplyCreativePhotography; Page 319: © istockphoto.com/Lewis Wright. **Chapter 7** Opener: © Barrett & MacKay Photo; Page 365: © istockphoto.com/Peter Garbet; Page 368: © istockphoto.comARICAN. **Chapter 8** Opener: Cindy Wilson/Telegraph-Journal; Page 419: ©iStockphoto.com/Marcus Clackson; Page 434: AP/Charles Krupa/The Canadian Press. **Chapter 9** Opener: Courtesy George Brown College; Page 474: ©istockphoto/DNY59; Page 490: ©istockphoto/Chris Reed. **Chapter 10** Page 524: © istockphoto.com/GRAZVYDAS; Page 535: The Canadian Press/Marcos Townsend; Page 543: istockphoto.com/Morgan Lane Studios. Pages 544 and 555: Shoppers Drug Mart Corporation.

Reitmans (Canada) Limited

In this appendix, we illustrate current financial reporting with a comprehensive set of corporate financial statements that are prepared in accordance with International Financial Reporting Standards (IFRS). We are grateful for permission to use the actual financial statements of Reitmans (Canada) Ltd.—Canada's largest women's specialty clothing retailer.

Reitman's financial statement package features a statement of earnings, statement of comprehensive income, balance sheets, statement of changes in shareholders' equity, statement of cash flows, and notes to the financial statements. The financial statements are preceded by two reports: a statement of management's responsibilities for financial reporting and the independent auditors' report.

We encourage students to use these financial statements in conjunction with the relevant material in the textbook. As well, these statements can be used to solve the Financial Reporting Problem in the Broadening Your Perspective section of the end-of-chapter material.

Annual reports, including the financial statements, are reviewed in detail in *WileyPLUS* and on the companion website to this textbook.

MANAGEMENT'S RESPONSIBILITY FOR FINANCIAL STATEMENTS

The accompanying financial statements and all the information in the annual report are the responsibility of management and have been approved by the Board of Directors of Reitmans (Canada) Limited.

These financial statements have been prepared by management in conformity with International Financial Reporting Standards and include amounts that are based on best estimates and judgments. The financial information used elsewhere in the annual report is consistent with that in the financial statements.

Management of the Company has developed and maintains a system of internal accounting controls. Management believes that this system of internal accounting controls provides reasonable assurances that financial records are reliable and form a proper basis for the preparation of the financial statements and that assets are properly accounted for and safeguarded.

The Board of Directors carries out its responsibility for the financial statements in this annual report principally through its Audit Committee, consisting of all outside directors. The Audit Committee reviews the Company's annual financial statements and recommends their approval to the Board of Directors. The auditors appointed by the shareholders have full access to the Audit Committee, with and without management being present.

These financial statements have been examined by the auditors appointed by the shareholders, KPMG LLP, Chartered Accountants and their report is presented hereafter.

(signed) Jeremy H. Reitman
Chairman and
Chief Executive Officer

(signed) Eric Williams, CA
Vice-President, Finance and
Chief Financial Officer

March 28, 2012

INDEPENDENT AUDITORS' REPORT

To the Shareholders of Reitmans (Canada) Limited

We have audited the accompanying financial statements of Reitmans (Canada) Limited, which comprise the balance sheets as at January 28, 2012, January 29, 2011 and January 31, 2010, the statements of earnings, comprehensive income, changes in shareholders' equity and cash flows for the years ended January 28, 2012 and January 29, 2011, and notes, comprising a summary of significant accounting policies and other explanatory information.

Management's Responsibility for the Financial Statements

Management is responsible for the preparation and fair presentation of these financial statements in accordance with International Financial Reporting Standards, and for such internal control as management determines is necessary to enable the preparation of financial statements that are free from material misstatement, whether due to fraud or error.

Auditors' Responsibility

Our responsibility is to express an opinion on these financial statements based on our audits. We conducted our audits in accordance with Canadian generally accepted auditing standards. Those standards require that we comply with ethical requirements and plan and perform the audit to obtain reasonable assurance about whether the financial statements are free from material misstatement.

An audit involves performing procedures to obtain audit evidence about the amounts and disclosures in the financial statements. The procedures selected depend on our judgment, including the assessment of the risks of material misstatement of the financial statements, whether due to fraud or error. In making those risk assessments, we consider internal control relevant to the entity's preparation and fair presentation of the financial statements in order to design audit procedures that are appropriate in the circumstances, but not for the purpose of expressing an opinion on the effectiveness of the entity's internal control. An audit also includes evaluating the appropriateness of accounting policies used and the reasonableness of accounting estimates made by management, as well as evaluating the overall presentation of the financial statements.

We believe that the audit evidence we have obtained in our audits is sufficient and appropriate to provide a basis for our audit opinion.

Opinion

In our opinion, the financial statements present fairly, in all material respects, the financial position of Reitmans (Canada) Limited as at January 28, 2012, January 29, 2011 and January 31, 2010, and its financial performance and its cash flows for the years ended January 28, 2012 and January 29, 2011 in accordance with International Financial Reporting Standards.

*KPMG LLP**

Chartered Accountants

Montréal, Canada
March 28, 2012

* CA Auditor Permit no. 23443   KPMG LLP is a Canadian limited liability partnership and a member firm of the KPMG network of independent member firms affiliated with KPMG International Cooperative ("KPMG International"), a Swiss entity.
KPMG Canada provides services to KPMG LLP.

REITMANS (CANADA) LIMITED
STATEMENTS OF EARNINGS
(in thousands of Canadian dollars except per share amounts)

	For the years ended	
	January 28, 2012	January 29, 2011
Sales	$ 1,019,397	$ 1,059,000
Cost of goods sold (note 7)	363,333	350,671
Gross profit	656,064	708,329
Selling and distribution expenses	547,367	528,676
Administrative expenses	46,878	55,511
Results from operating activities	61,819	124,142
Finance income (note 19)	5,562	4,505
Finance costs (note 19)	1,509	845
Earnings before income taxes	65,872	127,802
Income taxes (note 11)	18,333	38,817
Net earnings	$ 47,539	$ 88,985
Earnings per share (note 20):		
Basic	$ 0.72	$ 1.33
Diluted	0.72	1.32

The accompanying notes are an integral part of these financial statements.

REITMANS (CANADA) LIMITED
STATEMENTS OF COMPREHENSIVE INCOME
(in thousands of Canadian dollars)

	For the years ended	
	January 28, 2012	January 29, 2011
Net earnings	$ 47,539	$ 88,985
Other comprehensive income:		
Net change in fair value of available-for-sale financial assets (net of tax of $79; 2011 - $427) (note 19)	530	2,866
Reclassification of realized gains on available-for-sale financial assets to net earnings (net of tax of $22) (note 19)	-	(145)
Reclassification of impairment loss on available-for-sale financial assets to net earnings (net of tax of $9; 2011 - $11) (note 19)	64	67
Defined benefit actuarial losses (net of tax of $1,041; 2011 - $272) (note 15)	(2,965)	(777)
Total comprehensive income	$ 45,168	$ 90,996

The accompanying notes are an integral part of these financial statements.

REITMANS (CANADA) LIMITED
BALANCE SHEETS
(in thousands of Canadian dollars)

	January 28, 2012	January 29, 2011	January 31, 2010
ASSETS			
CURRENT ASSETS			
Cash and cash equivalents (note 5)	$ 196,835	$ 230,034	$ 228,577
Marketable securities	71,442	70,413	48,026
Trade and other receivables	3,033	2,866	2,926
Derivative financial asset (note 6)	751	-	-
Income taxes recoverable	4,735	-	-
Inventories (note 7)	78,285	73,201	63,127
Prepaid expenses	11,902	12,491	11,010
Total Current Assets	366,983	389,005	353,666
NON-CURRENT ASSETS			
Property and equipment (note 8)	184,221	193,064	208,362
Intangible assets (note 9)	17,057	13,841	9,964
Goodwill (note 10)	42,426	42,426	42,426
Deferred income taxes (note 11)	23,174	21,021	18,313
Total Non-Current Assets	266,878	270,352	279,065
TOTAL ASSETS	$ 633,861	$ 659,357	$ 632,731
LIABILITIES AND SHAREHOLDERS' EQUITY			
CURRENT LIABILITIES			
Trade and other payables (note 12)	$ 63,875	$ 64,093	$ 54,684
Derivative financial liability (note 6)	1,505	-	-
Deferred revenue (note 13)	22,278	19,834	18,122
Income taxes payable	-	5,998	4,677
Current portion of long-term debt (note 14)	1,474	1,384	1,300
Total Current Liabilities	89,132	91,309	78,783
NON-CURRENT LIABILITIES			
Other payables (note 12)	11,110	10,180	9,105
Deferred revenue (note 13)	-	2,384	2,686
Deferred lease credits	17,317	19,011	20,609
Long-term debt (note 14)	8,573	10,047	11,431
Pension liability (note 15)	14,877	13,626	11,865
Total Non-Current Liabilities	51,877	55,248	55,696
SHAREHOLDERS' EQUITY			
Share capital (note 16)	39,890	29,614	25,888
Contributed surplus	5,158	6,266	5,164
Retained earnings	439,067	468,777	461,845
Accumulated other comprehensive income (note 16)	8,737	8,143	5,355
Total Shareholders' Equity	492,852	512,800	498,252
TOTAL LIABILITIES AND SHAREHOLDERS' EQUITY	$ 633,861	$ 659,357	$ 632,731

Commitments (note 18)

The accompanying notes are an integral part of these financial statements.

On behalf of the Board,

(signed) Jeremy H. Reitman, Director   (signed) Stephen J. Kauser, Director

REITMANS (CANADA) LIMITED
STATEMENTS OF CHANGES IN SHAREHOLDERS' EQUITY
(in thousands of Canadian dollars)

	For the years ended	
	January 28, 2012	January 29, 2011
SHARE CAPITAL		
Balance, beginning of the year	$ 29,614	$ 25,888
Cash consideration on exercise of share options (note 16)	8,828	3,569
Ascribed value credited to share capital from exercise of share options (note 16)	2,228	888
Cancellation of shares pursuant to share repurchase program (note 16)	(780)	(731)
Balance, end of the year	39,890	29,614
CONTRIBUTED SURPLUS		
Balance, beginning of the year	6,266	5,164
Share-based compensation costs (note 17)	1,120	1,990
Ascribed value credited to share capital from exercise of share options (note 16)	(2,228)	(888)
Balance, end of the year	5,158	6,266
RETAINED EARNINGS		
Balance, beginning of the year	468,777	461,845
Net earnings	47,539	88,985
Dividends (note 16)	(52,654)	(51,895)
Premium on repurchase of Class A non-voting shares (note 16)	(21,630)	(29,381)
Defined benefit actuarial losses (net of tax of $1,041; 2011 - $272) (note 15)	(2,965)	(777)
Balance, end of the year	439,067	468,777
ACCUMULATED OTHER COMPREHENSIVE INCOME		
Balance, beginning of the year	8,143	5,355
Net change in fair value of available-for-sale financial assets (net of tax of $79; 2011 - $427) (note 19)	530	2,866
Reclassification of realized gains on available-for-sale financial assets to net earnings (net of tax of $22) (note 19)	-	(145)
Reclassification of impairment loss on available-for-sale financial assets to net earnings (net of tax of $9; 2011 - $11) (note 19)	64	67
Balance, end of the year (note 16)	8,737	8,143
Total Shareholders' Equity	$ 492,852	$ 512,800

The accompanying notes are an integral part of these financial statements.

REITMANS (CANADA) LIMITED
STATEMENTS OF CASH FLOWS
(in thousands of Canadian dollars)

	For the years ended	
	January 28, 2012	January 29, 2011
CASH FLOWS FROM (USED IN) OPERATING ACTIVITIES		
Net earnings	$ 47,539	$ 88,985
Adjustments for:		
Depreciation, amortization and impairment losses	64,990	59,754
Share-based compensation costs	1,120	1,990
Amortization of deferred lease credits	(4,635)	(4,956)
Deferred lease credits	2,941	3,358
Pension contribution	(4,245)	(629)
Pension expense	1,490	1,341
Realized gain on sale of marketable securities	-	(167)
Impairment loss on available-for-sale financial assets	73	78
Net change in fair value of derivatives	754	-
Foreign exchange loss (gain)	2,942	(31)
Interest and dividend income, net	(4,147)	(3,068)
Interest paid	(682)	(797)
Interest received	1,316	1,273
Dividends received	3,460	2,546
Income taxes	18,333	38,817
	131,249	188,494
Changes in:		
Trade and other receivables	(114)	106
Inventories	(5,084)	(10,074)
Prepaid expenses	589	(1,481)
Trade and other payables	504	9,073
Deferred revenue	60	1,410
Cash generated from operating activities	127,204	187,528
Income taxes received	793	6,040
Income taxes paid	(31,060)	(46,388)
Net cash flows from operating activities	96,937	147,180
CASH FLOWS (USED IN) FROM INVESTING ACTIVITIES		
Purchases of marketable securities	(420)	(20,803)
Proceeds on sale of marketable securities	-	1,709
Additions to property and equipment and intangible assets	(59,154)	(46,922)
Cash flows used in investing activities	(59,574)	(66,016)
CASH FLOWS (USED IN) FROM FINANCING ACTIVITIES		
Dividends paid	(52,654)	(51,895)
Purchase of Class A non-voting shares for cancellation	(22,410)	(30,112)
Repayment of long-term debt	(1,384)	(1,300)
Proceeds from exercise of share options	8,828	3,569
Cash flows used in financing activities	(67,620)	(79,738)
FOREIGN EXCHANGE (LOSS) GAIN ON CASH HELD IN FOREIGN CURRENCY	(2,942)	31
NET (DECREASE) INCREASE IN CASH AND CASH EQUIVALENTS	(33,199)	1,457
CASH AND CASH EQUIVALENTS, BEGINNING OF THE YEAR	230,034	228,577
CASH AND CASH EQUIVALENTS, END OF THE YEAR	$ 196,835	$ 230,034

Supplementary cash flow information (note 25)
The accompanying notes are an integral part of these financial statements.

REITMANS (CANADA) LIMITED
NOTES TO THE FINANCIAL STATEMENTS
(all amounts in thousands of Canadian dollars except per share amounts)

1. REPORTING ENTITY

Reitmans (Canada) Limited (the "Company") is a company domiciled in Canada and is incorporated under the Canada Business Corporations Act. The address of the Company's registered office is 3300 Highway #7 West, Suite 702, Vaughan, Ontario L4K 4M3. The principal business activity of the Company is the sale of women's wear at retail.

2. BASIS OF PRESENTATION

a) Statement of Compliance

These financial statements have been prepared in accordance with International Financial Reporting Standards ("IFRS") as issued by the International Accounting Standards Board ("IASB"). These are the Company's first annual financial statements prepared under IFRS in accordance with IFRS 1, *First-time adoption of IFRS*. The first date at which IFRS was applied was January 31, 2010 ("Transition Date"). In accordance with IFRS 1, the Company has:

- Provided comparative financial information

- Applied the same accounting policies throughout all periods presented

- Retroactively applied all effective IFRS standards as at January 28, 2012, as required; and

- Applied certain optional exemptions and certain mandatory exceptions as applicable for first-time IFRS adopters.

The Company's financial statements were previously prepared in accordance with accounting principles generally accepted in Canada ("Canadian GAAP"). An explanation of how the transition from Canadian GAAP to IFRS as at the transition date has affected the reported earnings, balance sheet and cash flows for the Company, including the mandatory exception and optional exemptions under IFRS 1, is provided in note 29.

These financial statements were authorized for issue by the Board of Directors on March 28, 2012.

b) Basis of Measurement

These financial statements have been prepared on the historical cost basis except for the following material items:

- available-for-sale financial assets are measured at fair value through other comprehensive income;

- the pension liability is recognized as the present value of the defined benefit obligation less the total of the fair value of the plan assets and the unrecognized past service cost; and

- derivative financial instruments are measured at fair value.

c) Functional and Presentation Currency

These financial statements are presented in Canadian dollars, which is the Company's functional currency. All financial information presented in Canadian dollars has been rounded to the nearest thousand, except per share amounts.

d) Estimates, Judgments and Assumptions

The preparation of the financial statements in accordance with IFRS requires management to make judgments, estimates and assumptions that affect the application of accounting policies and the reported amounts of assets, liabilities, the disclosure of contingent assets and contingent liabilities at the date of the financial statements and reported amounts of revenues and expenses during the period. These estimates and assumptions are based on historical experience, other relevant factors and expectations of the future and are reviewed regularly. Revisions to accounting estimates are recognized in the period in which the estimates are revised and in any future periods affected. Actual results may differ from these estimates.

The following is a summary of areas involving a higher degree of judgment or complexity, or areas where assumptions and estimates are significant to the financial statements:

Deferred Income Tax Assets

Management is required to make subjective assessments to determine the amount of deferred income tax assets to be recognized. Deferred income tax assets are recorded to the extent that it is probable that there will be adequate taxable income in the future against which they can be utilized.

Pension Plans

The cost of defined benefit pension plans is determined by means of actuarial valuations, which involve making assumptions about discount rates, the expected long-term rate of return on plan assets, future salary increases, mortality rates and the future increases in pensions. Because of the long-term nature of the plans, such estimates are subject to a high degree of uncertainty.

Sales Returns

The Company provides for the possibility that merchandise already sold may be returned by customers. To this end, the Company has made certain assumptions based on the quantity of merchandise returned in the past.

Share-Based Compensation

In computing the compensation cost related to share option awards under the fair value based method, various assumptions are used to determine the expected option life, risk-free interest rate, expected share price volatility and average dividend yield. The use of different assumptions could result in a share compensation expense that differs from that which the Company has recorded.

Gift Cards / Loyalty Points and Awards

Gift cards sold are recorded as deferred revenue and revenue is recognized when the gift cards are redeemed. An estimate is made of gift cards not expected to be redeemed based on the terms of the gift cards and historical redemption patterns. Loyalty points and awards granted under customer loyalty programs are recognized as a separate component of revenue and are deferred at the date of initial sale. Revenue is recognized when the loyalty points and awards are redeemed and the Company has fulfilled its obligation. The amount of revenue deferred is measured based on the fair value of loyalty points and awards granted, taking into consideration the estimated redemption percentage.

Slow-Moving Inventory
The Company has set up provisions for merchandise in inventory that may have to be sold below cost. For this purpose, the Company has developed assumptions regarding the quantity of merchandise sold below cost.

Asset Impairment
The Company must assess the possibility that the carrying amounts of tangible and intangible assets may not be recoverable. Management is required to make significant judgments related to future cash flows to determine the amount of asset impairment that should be recognized.

Fair value of derivative financial instruments
Derivative financial instruments are carried in the balance sheet at fair value estimated by using valuation techniques.

3. SIGNIFICANT ACCOUNTING POLICIES
The accounting policies set out below have been applied consistently to all periods presented in these financial statements.

a) Foreign Currency Translation
Monetary assets and liabilities denominated in foreign currencies at the reporting date are translated into the functional currency at the exchange rate at that date. Other balance sheet items denominated in foreign currencies are translated into Canadian dollars at the exchange rates prevailing at the respective transaction dates. Revenues and expenses denominated in foreign currencies are translated into Canadian dollars at average rates of exchange prevailing during the period. The resulting gains or losses on translation are included in the determination of net earnings.

b) Cash and Cash Equivalents
Cash and cash equivalents consist of cash on hand, bank balances and short-term deposits with original maturities of three months or less.

c) Financial Instruments
All financial instruments are classified into one of the following five categories: financial assets and financial liabilities at fair value through profit or loss, held-to-maturity investments, loans and receivables, available-for-sale financial assets or other financial liabilities. All financial instruments, including derivatives, are included on the balance sheet and are initially measured at fair value. The Company accounts for transaction costs related to financial instruments, other than those classified as fair value through profit or loss and for derivative instruments, in the initial measurement of the instrument. Subsequent measurement depends on their initial classification. Financial instruments and financial liabilities classified as financial assets and liabilities at fair value through profit or loss are subsequently measured at fair value and all gains and losses are included in net earnings in the period in which they arise. Available-for-sale financial instruments are subsequently measured at fair value and changes therein, other than impairment losses, are recognized in other comprehensive income. When an investment is derecognized, the cumulative gain or loss in other comprehensive income is transferred to net earnings. Loans and receivables, held-to-maturity investments and other financial liabilities, are subsequently measured at amortized cost using the effective interest rate method, less impairment losses.

Financial assets and liabilities measured at fair value use a fair value hierarchy to prioritize the inputs used in measuring fair value. Level 1, defined as observable inputs such as quoted prices in active markets; Level 2, defined as inputs other than quoted prices in active markets that are either directly or indirectly observable; and Level 3, defined as unobservable inputs in which little or no market data exists, therefore requiring an entity to develop its own assumptions.

The Company has classified its cash and cash equivalents and its trade and other receivables as loans and receivables and its marketable securities as available-for-sale financial assets. Trade and other payables and long-term debt have been classified as other financial liabilities and are measured at amortized cost.

Financial assets and liabilities are offset and the net amount is presented in the balance sheet when, and only when, the Company has a legal right to offset the amounts and intends either to settle on a net basis or to realize the asset and settle the liability simultaneously.

Derivative instruments are recorded at their fair value except under the own use exemption. Certain derivatives embedded in other contracts must also be measured at fair value. All changes in the fair value of derivatives are recognized in net earnings unless specific hedge criteria are met, which requires that a company must formally document, designate and assess the effectiveness of transactions that receive hedge accounting.

The Company considers the use of foreign currency option contracts, with maturities not exceeding six months, to manage its US dollar exposure. Foreign currency option contracts are not designated as hedges. Derivative financial instruments are not used for trading or speculative purposes.

d) Property and Equipment
Items of property and equipment are measured at cost less accumulated depreciation and accumulated impairment losses. Cost includes expenditures that are directly attributable to the acquisition of the asset, including any costs directly attributable to bringing the asset to a working condition for its intended use. Purchased software that is integral to the functionality of the related equipment is capitalized as part of that equipment.

When parts of an item of property and equipment have different useful lives, they are accounted for as separate items (major components) of property and equipment.

Depreciation is recognized in net earnings on a straight-line basis over the estimated useful lives of each component of an item of property and equipment. Land is not depreciated. Leasehold improvements are depreciated over the lesser of the estimated useful life of the asset and the lease term. Assets not in service include expenditures incurred to-date for equipment not yet available for use. Depreciation of assets not in service begins when they are ready for their intended use. Depreciation is calculated over the depreciable amount, which is the cost of an asset, less its residual value.

The estimated useful lives for the current and comparative periods are as follows:

- Buildings — 10 to 50 years
- Fixtures and equipment — 3 to 20 years
- Leasehold improvements — 6.7 to 10 years

Depreciation methods, useful lives and residual values are reviewed at each annual reporting date and adjusted prospectively, if appropriate.

Gains and losses on disposal of items of property and equipment are recognized in net earnings.

e) Goodwill

Goodwill is measured at the acquisition date as the fair value of the consideration transferred less the net identifiable assets of the acquired company or business activities. Goodwill is not amortized and is carried at cost less accumulated impairment losses.

f) Intangible Assets

Intangible assets that are acquired by the Company and have finite useful lives are measured at cost less accumulated amortization and accumulated impairment losses.

Amortization is calculated over the cost of the asset less its residual value. Amortization is recognized in net earnings on a straight-line basis over the estimated useful lives of the intangible assets. Amortization of intangible assets not in service begins when they are ready for their intended use.

The estimated useful lives for the current and comparative periods are as follows:

Software 3 to 5 years

Amortization methods, useful lives and residual values are reviewed at each annual reporting date and adjusted prospectively, if appropriate.

g) Leased Assets

Leases are classified as either operating or finance, based on the substance of the transaction at inception of the lease. Classification is re-assessed if the terms of the lease are changed.

Leases in which a significant portion of the risks and rewards of ownership are not assumed by the Company are classified as operating leases. The Company carries on its operations in premises under leases of varying terms, which are accounted for as operating leases. Payments under an operating lease are recognized in net earnings on a straight-line basis over the term of the lease. When a lease contains a predetermined fixed escalation of the minimum rent, the Company recognizes the related rent expense on a straight-line basis and, consequently, records the difference between the recognized rental expense and the amounts payable under the lease as deferred rent, which is included in trade and other payables on the balance sheet. Contingent (sales-based) rentals are recognized in net earnings in the period in which they are incurred.

Tenant allowances are recorded as deferred lease credits and amortized as a reduction of rent expense over the term of the related leases.

h) Inventories

Merchandise inventories are measured at the lower of cost, determined on an average basis using the retail inventory method, and net realizable value. Costs include the cost of purchase, transportation costs that are directly incurred to bring inventories to their present location and condition, and certain distribution centre costs related to inventories. The Company estimates net realizable value as the amount that inventories are expected to be sold, in the ordinary course of business, less the

estimated costs necessary to make the sale, taking into consideration fluctuations of retail prices due to seasonality.

i) Impairment

(i) Non-Financial Assets

All non-financial assets are reviewed at each reporting date for indications that the carrying amount may not be recoverable. When there is evidence of impairment, an impairment test is carried out. Goodwill is tested for impairment at least annually at the year-end reporting date, and whenever there is an indication that the asset may be impaired. For the purpose of impairment testing, assets that cannot be tested individually are grouped together into the smallest group of assets that generates cash inflows from continuing use that are largely independent of the cash inflows of other assets or groups of assets (defined as "cash-generating unit" or "CGU"). Impairment losses recognized in respect of CGUs are allocated first to reduce the carrying amount of any goodwill allocated to the CGU, and then to reduce the carrying amount of the other assets in the CGU.

An impairment loss is recognized in net earnings if the carrying amount of an asset or its related CGU exceeds its estimated recoverable amount. The recoverable amount is the higher of the value-in-use and the fair value less costs to sell. The value-in-use is the present value of estimated future cash flows, using a pre-tax discount rate that reflects current market assessments of the time value of money and the risks specific to the asset or CGU. The fair value less costs to sell is the amount for which an asset or CGU can be sold in a transaction under normal market conditions between knowledgeable and willing contracting parties, less costs to sell.

For the purposes of impairment testing, goodwill acquired in a business combination is allocated to the CGUs that are expected to benefit from the synergies of the combination. This allocation reflects the lowest level at which goodwill is monitored for internal reporting purposes.

The Company's corporate assets do not generate separate cash inflows. If there is an indication that a corporate asset may be impaired, then the recoverable amount is determined for the CGUs to which the corporate asset belongs.

An impairment loss in respect of goodwill is not reversed. In respect of other assets, an impairment loss is reversed if there has been a change in the estimates used to determine the recoverable amount. An impairment loss is reversed only to the extent that the asset's carrying amount does not exceed the carrying amount that would have been determined, net of depreciation or amortization, if no impairment loss had been recognized.

(ii) Financial Assets

For an investment in an equity security, a significant or prolonged decline in its fair value below cost is objective evidence of impairment. Impairment losses on available-for-sale financial assets are recognized by reclassifying losses accumulated in accumulated other comprehensive income to net earnings. The cumulative loss that is reclassified from accumulated other comprehensive income is the difference between the acquisition cost and the current fair value, less any impairment losses recognized previously in net earnings.

Any subsequent recovery in the fair value of an impaired available-for-sale equity security is recognized in other comprehensive income.

j) Employee Benefits

(i) Pension Benefit Plans

The Company maintains a contributory defined benefit plan ("Plan") that provides benefits to employees based on length of service and average earnings in the best five consecutive years of employment. The Company also sponsors a Supplemental Executive Retirement Plan ("SERP"), which is neither registered nor pre-funded. The costs of these retirement benefit plans are determined periodically by independent actuaries.

Benefits are also given to employees through defined contribution plans administered by the Federal and Québec governments. Company contributions to these plans are recognized in the periods when the services are rendered.

Pension expense/income is included in the determination of net earnings according to the following policies:

- The present value of the defined benefit obligation is actuarially determined using the projected unit credit method.

- For the purpose of calculating expected return on plan assets, the valuation of those assets is based on quoted market values at the year-end date.

- The discount rate used to value the defined benefit obligation is the yield at the reporting date on AA credit-rated bonds that have maturity dates approximating the terms of the Company's obligations and that are denominated in the same currency in which the benefits are expected to be paid.

- Unrecognized past service costs related to benefits are amortized on a straight-line basis over the average period until vesting. To the extent that the benefits vest immediately, the expense is recognized immediately in net earnings.

The Company recognizes all actuarial gains and losses from the Plan and SERP immediately in other comprehensive income, and reports them in retained earnings. Expenses related to defined contribution plans are recognized in net earnings in the periods in which they occur. The net obligation in respect of the Plan and SERP is the amount of future benefits that members have earned in return for their service in the current and prior periods discounted to its present value, less any unrecognized past service costs and the fair value of the plan assets.

(ii) Short-Term Employee Benefits

Short-term employee benefit obligations, which include wages, salaries, compensated absences and bonuses, are measured on an undiscounted basis and are expensed as the related service is provided.

A liability is recognized for the amount expected to be paid under short-term cash bonus or profit sharing plans if the Company has a present legal or constructive obligation to pay this amount as a result of past service provided by the employee, and the obligation can be estimated reliably.

(iii) Share-Based Compensation

Some employees receive part of their compensation in the form of share-based payments which are recognised as an employee expense, with a corresponding increase in equity, over the period that the employees unconditionally become entitled to the awards. The Company accounts for share-based compensation using the fair value based method. Compensation expense is measured at the fair value at the date of grant and the fair value of each award is recognized over its respective vesting period, which is normally five years. The amount recognized as an expense is adjusted to reflect the number of awards for which the related service conditions are expected to be met.

k) Provisions

A provision is recognized if, as a result of a past event, the Company has a present legal or constructive obligation that can be estimated reliably, and it is probable that an outflow of economic benefits will be required to settle the obligation. If the effect of the time value of money is material, provisions are determined by discounting the expected future cash flows at a pre-tax rate that reflects current market assessments of the time value of money and the risks specific to the liability. Where discounting is used, the unwinding of the discount is recognized as finance cost.

l) Revenue

Revenue is recognized from the sale of merchandise when a customer purchases and takes delivery of the merchandise. Reported sales are net of returns and estimated possible returns and exclude sales taxes.

Gift cards sold are recorded as deferred revenue and revenue is recognized when the gift cards are redeemed. An estimate is made of gift cards not expected to be redeemed based on the terms of the gift cards and historical redemption patterns.

Loyalty points and awards granted under customer loyalty programs are recognized as a separate component of revenue, and are deferred at the date of initial sale. Revenue is recognized when the loyalty points and awards are redeemed and the Company has fulfilled its obligation. The amount of revenue deferred is measured based on the fair value of loyalty points and awards granted, taking into consideration the estimated redemption percentage.

m) Finance Income and Finance Costs

Finance income comprises interest and dividend income, realized gains on sale of marketable securities, changes in the fair value of derivatives as well as foreign exchange gains. Finance costs comprise interest expense, realized losses on sale of marketable securities, changes in the fair value of derivatives as well as foreign exchange losses. Interest income is recognized on an accrual basis and interest expense is recorded using the effective interest method. Dividend income is recognized when the right to receive payment is established. Foreign exchange gains and losses and changes in the fair value of derivatives are reported on a net basis.

n) Income Tax

Income tax expense comprises current and deferred taxes. Current income taxes and deferred income taxes are recognized in net earnings except for items recognized directly in equity or in other comprehensive income.

The Company's income tax expense is based on tax rules and regulations that are subject to interpretation and require estimates and assumptions that may be challenged by taxation authorities. Current income tax is the expected tax payable or receivable on the taxable income or loss for the period, using tax rates enacted or substantively enacted at the reporting date, and any adjustment to taxes payable in respect of previous years. The Company's estimates of current income tax assets and liabilities are periodically reviewed and adjusted as circumstances warrant, such as for changes to tax laws and administrative guidance, and the resolution of uncertainties through either the conclusion of tax audits or expiration of prescribed time limits within the relevant statutes. The final results of government tax audits and other events may vary materially compared to estimates and assumptions used by management in determining the income tax expense and in measuring current income tax assets and liabilities.

Deferred income tax is recognized in respect of temporary differences between the carrying amounts of assets and liabilities for financial reporting purposes and the amounts used for taxation purposes. Deferred income tax assets and liabilities are measured using enacted or substantively enacted income tax rates expected to apply to taxable income in the years in which temporary differences are expected to be recovered or settled. The effect on deferred income tax assets and liabilities of a change in tax rates is included in net earnings in the period that includes the enactment date, except to the extent that it relates to an item recognized either in other comprehensive income or directly in equity in the current or in a previous period.

The Company only offsets income tax assets and liabilities if it has a legally enforceable right to offset the recognized amounts and intends either to settle on a net basis, or to realize the asset and settle the liability simultaneously.

A deferred income tax asset is recognized to the extent that it is probable that future taxable profits will be available against which they can be utilized. Deferred income tax assets are reviewed at each reporting date and are reduced to the extent that it is no longer probable that the related tax benefit will be realized.

Deferred income tax assets and liabilities are recognized on the balance sheet under non-current assets or liabilities, irrespective of the expected date of realization or settlement.

o) Earnings per Share

The Company presents basic and diluted earnings per share ("EPS") data for its shares.

Basic EPS is calculated by dividing the net earnings of the Company by the weighted average number of Class A non-voting and Common shares outstanding during the period.

Diluted EPS is determined by adjusting the weighted average number of shares outstanding to include additional shares issued from the assumed exercise of share options, if dilutive. The number of additional shares is calculated by assuming that the proceeds from such exercises, as well as the amount of unrecognized share-based compensation, are used to purchase Class A non-voting shares at the average market share price during the reporting period.

p) Share Capital

Class A non-voting shares and Common shares are classified as equity. Incremental costs directly attributable to the issue of these shares and share options are recognized as a deduction from equity, net of any tax effects.

When share capital recognized as equity is purchased for cancellation, the amount of the consideration paid, which includes directly attributable costs, net of any tax effects, is recognized as a deduction from equity. The excess of the purchase price over the carrying amount of the shares is charged to retained earnings.

q) New Standards and Interpretations Not Yet Adopted

A number of new standards, and amendments to standards and interpretations, are not yet effective for the year ended January 28, 2012 and have not been applied in preparing these financial statements. New standards and amendments to standards and interpretations that are currently under review include:

IFRS 9 - Financial Instruments

This standard becomes mandatory for the years commencing on or after January 1, 2015 with earlier application permitted. IFRS 9 is a new standard which will ultimately replace IAS 39, *Financial Instruments: Recognition and Measurement*.

IFRS 13 – Fair Value Measurement

This standard provides new guidance on fair value measurement and disclosure requirements, which becomes effective for annual periods commencing on or after January 1, 2013.

IAS 1 - Presentation of Financial Statements

Amendments to IAS 1, *Presentation of Financial Statements* enhance the presentation of Other Comprehensive Income ("OCI") in the financial statements, primarily by requiring the components of OCI to be presented separately for items that may be reclassified to the statement of earnings in the future from those that would never be reclassified to the statement of earnings. The amendments are effective for annual periods beginning on or after July 1, 2012

IAS 19 - Employee Benefits

Amendments to IAS 19, Employee Benefits include the elimination of the option to defer the recognition of gains and losses, enhancing the guidance around measurement of plan assets and defined benefit obligations, streamlining the presentation of changes in assets and liabilities arising from defined benefit plans and the introduction of enhanced disclosures for defined benefit plans. The amendments are effective for annual periods beginning on or after January 1, 2013.

The extent of the impact of adoption of the above noted standards and interpretations on the financial statements of the Company has not yet been determined.

4. DETERMINATION OF FAIR VALUES

A number of the Company's accounting policies and disclosures require the determination of fair value, for both financial and non-financial assets and liabilities. Fair value estimates are made at a specific point in time, using available information about the asset or liability. These estimates are subjective in nature and often cannot be determined with precision. Fair values have been determined for measurement and/or disclosure purposes based on the following methods. When applicable, further information about the assumptions made in determining fair values is disclosed in the notes specific to that asset or liability.

a) Financial Assets

The Company has determined that the carrying amount of its short-term financial assets approximates fair value at the reporting date due to the short-term maturity of these instruments. The fair value of the Company's available-for-sale financial assets is determined by reference to their quoted closing prices in active markets at the reporting date, which is considered Level 1 input in the fair value hierarchy.

b) Non-Derivative Financial Liabilities

The fair value of the Company's long-term debt bearing interest at a fixed rate, which is determined for disclosure purposes, is calculated using the present value of future payments of principal and interest discounted at the current market rates of interest available to the Company for the same or similar debt instruments with the same remaining maturity.

c) Deferred Revenue

The amount of revenue deferred with respect to the Company's customer loyalty reward programs is estimated by reference to the fair value of the merchandise for which the loyalty rewards could be redeemed. The fair value takes into account the expected redemption rate and the timing of such expected redemptions.

d) Derivative Financial Instruments

The fair value of foreign currency option contracts is determined through a standard option valuation technique used by the counterparty based on Level 2 inputs.

e) Share-based Payment Transactions

The fair values of the employee share options are measured based on the Black-Scholes valuation model. Measurement inputs include share price on measurement date, exercise price of the share option, expected volatility (based on weighted average historic volatility adjusted for changes expected due to publicly available information), weighted average expected life of the share option (based on historic experience and general option holder behaviour), expected dividends, and risk-free interest rate (based on government bonds).

5. CASH AND CASH EQUIVALENTS

	January 28, 2012	January 29, 2011	January 31, 2010
Cash on hand and with banks	$ 12,563	$ 4,634	$ 4,677
Short-term deposits, bearing interest at 0.9% (January 29, 2011 - 0.7%; January 31, 2010 - 0.3%)	184,272	225,400	223,900
	$ 196,835	$ 230,034	$ 228,577

6. FINANCIAL INSTRUMENTS

Derivative financial instruments

During the year, the Company entered into transactions with its bank whereby it purchased call options and sold put options, both on the US dollar ("USD"). These option contracts extend over a period of six months. Purchased call options and sold put options expiring on the same date have the same strike price.

Details of the foreign currency option contracts outstanding as at January 28, 2012 are as follow:

	Notional Amount in USD	Derivative Asset	Derivative Liability	Net
Put options sold	$ 44,000	$ 751	$ -	$ 751
Call options purchased	(100,000)	-	(1,505)	(1,505)
	$ (56,000)	$ 751	$ (1,505)	$ (754)

As at January 29, 2011 and January 31, 2010, there were no foreign currency option contracts outstanding.

7. INVENTORIES

During the year ended January 28, 2012, inventories recognized as cost of goods sold amounted to $361,319 (January 29, 2011 - $348,716). In addition, $2,014 (January 29, 2011 - $1,955) of write-downs of inventory as a result of net realizable value being lower than cost was recognized in cost of goods sold, and no inventory write-downs recognized in previous periods were reversed.

8. PROPERTY AND EQUIPMENT

	Land	Buildings	Fixtures and Equipment	Leasehold Improvements	Total
Cost					
Balance at January 31, 2010	$ 5,860	$ 52,411	$ 177,874	$ 194,782	$430,927
Additions	-	400	19,107	21,591	41,098
Disposals	-	(886)	(21,595)	(21,468)	(43,949)
Balance at January 29, 2011	$ 5,860	$ 51,925	$ 175,386	$ 194,905	$428,076
Balance at January 30, 2011	$ 5,860	$ 51,925	$ 175,386	$ 194,905	$428,076
Additions	-	2,291	25,079	24,818	52,188
Disposals	-	(53)	(37,346)	(37,650)	(75,049)
Balance at January 28, 2012	$ 5,860	$ 54,163	$ 163,119	$ 182,073	$405,215
Accumulated depreciation and impairment losses					
Balance at January 31, 2010	$ -	$ 17,946	$ 97,398	$ 107,221	$222,565
Depreciation	-	2,410	26,062	26,708	55,180
Impairment loss	-	-	-	1,724	1,724
Reversal of impairment loss	-	-	-	(779)	(779)
Disposals	-	(886)	(21,580)	(21,212)	(43,678)
Balance at January 29, 2011	$ -	$ 19,470	$ 101,880	$ 113,662	$235,012
Balance at January 30, 2011	$ -	$ 19,470	$ 101,880	$ 113,662	$235,012
Depreciation	-	2,601	25,599	26,699	54,899
Impairment loss	-	-	2,296	4,427	6,723
Reversal of impairment loss	-	-	-	(591)	(591)
Disposals	-	(53)	(37,346)	(37,650)	(75,049)
Balance at January 28, 2012	$ -	$ 22,018	$ 92,429	$ 106,547	$220,994
Net carrying amounts					
At January 31, 2010	$ 5,860	$ 34,465	$ 80,476	$ 87,561	$208,362
At January 29, 2011	$ 5,860	$ 32,455	$ 73,506	$ 81,243	$193,064
At January 28, 2012	$ 5,860	$ 32,145	$ 70,690	$ 75,526	$184,221

During the year, the Company tested for impairment certain items of property and equipment for which there were indications that their carrying amounts may not be recoverable and recognized an impairment loss of $6,723 (January 29, 2011 - $1,724). The recoverable amounts of the CGUs tested for impairment were based on their value-in-use which was determined using a pre-tax discount rate of 11% (January 29, 2011 - 12%). During the year, $591 of impairment losses were reversed following an improvement in the profitability of certain CGUs (January 29, 2011 - $779).

Depreciation expense and net impairment losses for the year have been recorded in selling and distribution expenses and administrative expenses in the statements of earnings.

Property and equipment includes an amount of $8,414 (January 29, 2011 - $3,548) that is not being depreciated. Depreciation will begin when the assets have been available for use.

9. INTANGIBLE ASSETS

	Cost	Accumulated amortization	Net carrying amounts
Balance at January 31, 2010	$ 17,072	$ 7,108	$ 9,964
Additions / amortization	7,506	3,629	3,877
Disposals	(2,394)	(2,394)	-
Balance at January 29, 2011	$ 22,184	$ 8,343	$ 13,841
Balance at January 30, 2011	$ 22,184	$ 8,343	$ 13,841
Additions / amortization	7,175	3,959	3,216
Disposals	(1,105)	(1,105)	-
Balance at January 28, 2012	$ 28,254	$ 11,197	$ 17,057

The amortization of intangibles has been recorded in selling and distribution expenses and administrative expenses in the statements of earnings.

Software includes an amount of $10,846 (January 29, 2011 - $6,930) that is not being amortized. Amortization will begin when the software has been put into service.

10. GOODWILL

Goodwill is tested for impairment as described in note 3(i). For impairment testing purposes the Company uses the value-in-use approach. Value-in-use is determined by discounting the future cash flows generated from the continuing use of the respective CGU.

Management's key assumptions for cash flow projections are based on the most recent annualized operating results, assuming a series of cash flows in perpetuity. Projected cash flows are discounted using a pre-tax rate of 10% (January 29, 2011 - 11%) which reflects the specific risks and weighted average cost of capital for a company of similar size and industry.

Based upon the impairment tests as at January 28, 2012, January 29, 2011 and January 31, 2010, the value-in-use was determined to be higher than the carrying values. As a result, no impairment losses were recognized.

11. INCOME TAX

Income tax expense

The Company's income tax expense is comprised as follows:

	For the years ended	
	January 28, 2012	January 29, 2011
Current tax expense		
Current period	$ 19,840	$ 42,409
Adjustment for prior years	(307)	(740)
Current tax expense	19,533	41,669
Deferred tax expense		
Recognition and reversal of temporary differences	(1,771)	(3,990)
Changes in tax rates	319	494
Adjustment for prior years	252	644
Deferred tax expense	(1,200)	(2,852)
Total income tax expense	$ 18,333	$ 38,817

Income tax recognized in other comprehensive income

	For the year ended January 28, 2012			For the year ended January 29, 2011		
	Before Tax	Tax (expense) benefit	Net of Tax (expense)	Before Tax	Tax (expense) benefit	Net of Tax (expense)
Available-for-sale financial assets	$ 682	$ (88)	$ 594	$ 3,204	$ (416)	$ 2,788
Defined benefit plan actuarial losses	(4,006)	1,041	(2,965)	(1,049)	272	(777)
	$ (3,324)	$ 953	$ (2,371)	$ 2,155	$ (144)	$ 2,011

Reconciliation of effective tax rate

	For the years ended			
	January 28, 2012		January 29, 2011	
Earnings before income taxes	$ 65,872		$ 127,802	
Income tax using the Company's statutory tax rate	18,642	28.30%	38,583	30.19%
Changes in tax rates	319	0.48%	391	0.31%
Non-deductible expenses and other adjustments	393	0.60%	658	0.51%
Tax exempt income	(966)	(1.47%)	(719)	(0.56%)
Over provided in prior periods	(55)	(0.08%)	(96)	(0.08%)
	$ 18,333	27.83%	$ 38,817	30.37%

Recognized deferred tax assets and liabilities

Deferred tax assets and liabilities are attributable to the following:

	Assets		Liabilities		Net	
	January 28, 2012	January 29, 2011	January 28, 2012	January 29, 2011	January 28, 2012	January 29, 2011
Property, equipment and intangible assets	$ 17,364	$ 12,984	$ -	$ -	$ 17,364	$ 12,984
Prepaid expenses	-	214	-	-	-	214
Marketable securities	-	-	379	299	(379)	(299)
Inventories	-	-	1,144	1,082	(1,144)	(1,082)
Trade and other payables	3,461	5,644	-	-	3,461	5,644
Pension liability	3,868	3,534	-	-	3,868	3,534
Other	42	46	38	20	4	26
	$ 24,735	$ 22,422	$ 1,561	$ 1,401	$ 23,174	$ 21,021

Changes in deferred tax balances during the year

	Balance January 31, 2010	Recognized in Net Earnings	Recognized in Other Comprehensive Income	Balance January 29, 2011	Recognized in Net Earnings	Recognized in Other Comprehensive Income	Balance January 28, 2012
Property, equipment and intangible assets	$ 10,626	$ 2,358	$ -	$ 12,984	$ 4,380	$ -	$ 17,364
Prepaid expenses	257	(43)	-	214	(214)	-	-
Marketable securities	121	(4)	(416)	(299)	8	(88)	(379)
Inventories	(1,039)	(43)	-	(1,082)	(62)	-	(1,144)
Trade and other payables	5,260	384	-	5,644	(2,183)	-	3,461
Pension liability	3,076	186	272	3,534	(707)	1,041	3,868
Other	12	14	-	26	(22)	-	4
	$ 18,313	$ 2,852	$ (144)	$ 21,021	$ 1,200	$ 953	$ 23,174

12. TRADE AND OTHER PAYABLES

	January 28, 2012	January 29, 2011	January 31, 2010
Trade payables	$ 26,155	$ 16,457	$ 15,148
Non-trade payables due to related parties	56	66	90
Other non-trade payables	10,553	11,817	4,437
Personnel liabilities	23,053	31,457	30,615
Payables relating to premises	14,398	13,630	12,630
Provision for sales returns	770	846	869
	74,985	74,273	63,789
Less non-current portion	11,110	10,180	9,105
	$ 63,875	$ 64,093	$ 54,684

The non-current portion of trade and other payables, which is included in payables relating to premises, represents the portion of deferred rent to be amortized beyond the next twelve months.

13. DEFERRED REVENUE

Deferred revenue consists of the following:

	January 28, 2012	January 29, 2011	January 31, 2010
Loyalty points and awards granted under loyalty programs	$ 10,979	$ 10,984	$ 10,142
Unredeemed gift cards	11,299	11,234	10,666
	22,278	22,218	20,808
Less amounts expected to be redeemed in the next twelve months	22,278	19,834	18,122
Deferred revenue – non-current	$ -	$ 2,384	$ 2,686

14. LONG-TERM DEBT

	January 28, 2012	January 29, 2011	January 31, 2010
Mortgage payable	$ 10,047	$ 11,431	$ 12,731
Less current portion	1,474	1,384	1,300
	$ 8,573	$ 10,047	$ 11,431

The mortgage, bearing interest at 6.40%, is payable in monthly instalments of principal and interest of $172. It is due November 2017 and is secured by the Company's distribution centre having a carrying value of $18,306 (January 29, 2011 - $19,282; January 31, 2010 - $20,304).

As at January 28, 2012, principal repayments on long-term debt are as follows:

Within 1 year	$ 1,474
Within 2 years	1,570
Within 3 years	1,672
Within 4 years	1,780
Within 5 years	1,896
Subsequent years	1,655
	$ 10,047

As at January 28, 2012, the fair value of long-term debt was $10,882 (January 29, 2011 - $12,247; January 31, 2010 - $13,045) compared to its carrying value of $10,047 (January 29, 2011 - $11,431; January 31, 2010 - $12,731).

15. PENSION LIABILITY

The following tables present reconciliations of the pension obligations, the plan assets and the funded status of the retirement benefit plans:

Funded Status

	Fair value of plan assets	Defined benefit obligation	Funded status	Unamortized non-vested past service cost	Pension asset (liability)
As at January 28, 2012					
Plan	$ 15,727	$ 15,318	$ 409	$ -	$ 409
SERP	-	15,540	(15,540)	254	(15,286)
Total	$ 15,727	$ 30,858	$ (15,131)	$ 254	$ (14,877)
As at January 29, 2011					
Plan	$ 11,936	$ 12,717	$ (781)	$ -	$ (781)
SERP	-	13,184	(13,184)	339	(12,845)
Total	$ 11,936	$ 25,901	$ (13,965)	$ 339	$ (13,626)
As at January 31, 2010					
Plan	$ 10,369	$ 11,399	$ (1,030)	$ -	$ (1,030)
SERP	-	11,259	(11,259)	424	(10,835)
Total	$ 10,369	$ 22,658	$ (12,289)	$ 424	$ (11,865)

The asset allocation of the major asset categories in the Plan for each of the years was as follows:

	January 28, 2012	January 29, 2011	January 31, 2010
Equity securities	60%	62%	61%
Debt securities	38%	36%	37%
Cash and cash equivalents	2%	2%	2%
	100%	100%	100%

The Company's pension expense was as follows:

	For the year ended January 28, 2012			For the year ended January 29, 2011		
	Plan	**SERP**	**Total**	**Plan**	**SERP**	**Total**
Pension costs recognized in net earnings						
Current service cost	$ 596	$ 239	$ 835	$ 480	$ 232	$ 712
Interest cost	684	695	1,379	646	628	1,274
Expected return on plan assets	(808)	-	(808)	(729)	-	(729)
Past service cost	-	84	84	-	84	84
Pension expense	$ 472	$ 1,018	$ 1,490	$ 397	$ 944	$ 1,341

Pension expense is recognized in administration expenses in the statements of earnings.

The following table presents the change in the actuarial gains and losses recognized in other comprehensive income:

	For the year ended January 28, 2012			For the year ended January 29, 2011		
	Plan	**SERP**	**Total**	**Plan**	**SERP**	**Total**
Cumulative amount in retained earnings at the beginning of the year	$ (144)	$ 1,193	$ 1,049	$ -	$ -	$ -
Recognized during the year	2,456	1,550	4,006	(144)	1,193	1,049
Cumulative amount in retained earnings at the end of the year	$ 2,312	$ 2,743	$ 5,055	$ (144)	$ 1,193	$ 1,049
Recognized during the year net of tax			$ 2,965			$ 777

	For the year ended January 28, 2012			For the year ended January 29, 2011		
	Plan	**SERP**	**Total**	**Plan**	**SERP**	**Total**
Movement in the present value of the defined benefit obligation						
Defined benefit obligation, beginning of year	$ 12,717	$ 13,184	$ 25,901	$ 11,399	$ 11,259	$ 22,658
Current service cost	596	239	835	480	232	712
Interest cost	684	695	1,379	646	628	1,274
Employee contributions	144	-	144	140	-	140
Actuarial losses	1,778	1,550	3,328	567	1,193	1,760
Benefits paid	(601)	(128)	(729)	(515)	(128)	(643)
Defined benefit obligation, end of year	$ 15,318	$ 15,540	$ 30,858	$ 12,717	$ 13,184	$ 25,901
Movement in the fair value of plan assets						
Fair value of plan assets, beginning of year	$ 11,936	-	$ 11,936	$ 10,369	$ -	$ 10,369
Expected return on assets	808	-	808	729	-	729
Investment (loss) gain	(677)	-	(677)	712	-	712
Employer contributions	4,117	128	4,245	501	128	629
Employee contributions	144	-	144	140	-	140
Benefits paid	(601)	(128)	(729)	(515)	(128)	(643)
Fair value of plan assets, end of year	$ 15,727	$ -	$ 15,727	$ 11,936	$ -	$ 11,936

The Company has determined that, in accordance with the terms and conditions of the defined benefit plan, and in accordance with statutory requirements (such as minimum funding requirements) of the plans of the respective jurisdictions, the present value of refunds or reductions in the future contributions is not lower than the balance of the total fair value of the plan assets less the total present value of the obligations. As such, no decrease in the defined benefit plan asset is necessary at January 28, 2012 (January 29, 2011 and January 31, 2010 - no decrease in defined benefit asset).

The Common shares and Class A non-voting shares of the Company rank equally and pari passu with respect to the right to receive dividends and upon any distribution of the assets of the Company. However, in the case of share dividends, the holders of Class A non-voting shares shall have the right to receive Class A non-voting shares and the holders of Common shares shall have the right to receive Common shares.

Issuance of Class A Non-Voting Shares

During the year ended January 28, 2012, a total of 722 (January 29, 2011- 292) Class A non-voting shares were issued as a result of the exercise of vested options arising from the Company's share option program. The amounts credited to share capital from the exercise of share options include a cash consideration of $8,828 (January 29, 2011- $3,569), as well as an ascribed value from contributed surplus of $2,228 (January 29, 2011- $888).

Purchase of Shares for Cancellation

For the year ended January 28, 2012, the Company purchased, under the prior year's normal course issuer bid, 1,445 (January 29, 2011 – 1,583) Class A non-voting shares having a book value of $780 (January 29, 2011 - $731) for a total cash consideration of $22,410 (January 29, 2011 - $30,112). The excess of the purchase price over the book value of the shares in the amount of $21,630 (January 29, 2011 - $29,381) was charged to retained earnings.

In November 2011, the Company received approval from the Toronto Stock Exchange to proceed with a normal course issuer bid. Under the bid, the Company may purchase up to 2,580 Class A non-voting shares of the Company, representing 5% of the issued and outstanding Class A non-voting shares as at November 14, 2011. The bid commenced on November 28, 2011 and may continue to November 27, 2012. No Class A non-voting shares were purchased under this new program.

Accumulated Other Comprehensive Income ("AOCI")

AOCI is comprised of the following:

	January 28, 2012	January 29, 2011	January 31, 2010
Net change in fair value of available-for-sale financial assets, net of taxes	$ 8,737	$ 8,143	$ 5,355

Dividends

The following dividends were declared and paid by the Company:

	For the years ended	
	January 28, 2012	January 29, 2011
Common shares and Class A non-voting shares	$ 52,654	$ 51,895

Actuarial assumptions

Principal actuarial assumptions used were as follows:

	For the years ended	
	January 28, 2012	January 29, 2011
Accrued benefit obligation:		
Discount rate	4.30%	5.20%
Salary increase	5.00%	3.00%
Employee benefit expense:		
Discount rate	5.20%	5.50%
Expected return on plan assets	6.50%	7.00%
Salary increase	3.00%	3.00%

Expected rates of return on plan assets are based on external historical and forecast market information.

The Company expects $1,046 in employer contributions to be paid to the Plan and SERP in the year ending February 2, 2013.

The Company measures its accrued benefit obligations and the fair value of plan assets for accounting purposes at year-end. The most recent actuarial valuation for funding purposes was as of December 31, 2010 and the next required valuation will be as of December 31, 2011.

16. SHARE CAPITAL AND OTHER COMPONENTS OF EQUITY

The change in share capital for each of the periods listed was as follows:

	For the years ended			
	January 28, 2012		January 29, 2011	
	Number of shares	Carrying amount	Number of shares	Carrying amount
Common shares				
Balance at beginning and end of the year	13,440	$ 482	13,440	$ 482
Class A non-voting shares				
Balance at beginning of the year	52,869	$29,132	54,160	$25,406
Shares issued pursuant to exercise of share options	722	11,056	292	4,457
Shares purchased under issuer bid	(1,445)	(780)	(1,583)	(731)
Balance at end of the year	52,146	$39,408	52,869	$29,132
Total share capital	65,586	$39,890	66,309	$29,614

Authorized Share Capital

The Company has authorized for issuance an unlimited number of Common shares and Class A non-voting shares. Both Common shares and Class A non-voting shares have no par value. All issued shares are fully paid.

17. SHARE-BASED PAYMENTS

a) Description of the Share-Based Payment Arrangements

The Company has a share option plan that provides that up to 10% of the Class A non-voting shares outstanding, from time to time, may be issued pursuant to the exercise of options granted under the plan to key management and employees. The granting of options and the related vesting period, which is normally up to 5 years, are at the discretion of the Board of Directors and the options have a maximum term of 10 years. The exercise price payable for each Class A non-voting share covered by a share option is determined by the Board of Directors at the date of grant, but may not be less than the closing price of the Company's shares on the trading day immediately preceding the effective date of the grant.

b) Disclosure of Equity-settled Share Option Plan

Changes in outstanding share options were as follows:

| | For the years ended | | | |
| | January 28, 2012 | | January 29, 2011 | |
	Options	Weighted Average Exercise Price	Options	Weighted Average Exercise Price
Outstanding, at beginning of year	3,095	$ 14.58	3,207	$ 14.14
Granted	-	-	215	18.02
Exercised	(722)	12.23	(292)	12.23
Forfeited	(428)	16.33	(35)	14.50
Outstanding, at end of year	1,945	$ 15.07	3,095	$ 14.58
Options exercisable, at end of year	238	$ 18.81	935	$ 13.74

The weighted average share price at the date of exercise for share options exercised in the year was $15.44 (January 29, 2011 - $18.21)

There were no share option awards granted during the year ended January 28, 2012. Compensation cost related to share option awards granted during the year ended January 29, 2011 under the fair value based approach was calculated using the following assumptions:

| | For the year ended January 29, 2011 | | |
	100 Options Granted April 7, 2010	15 Options Granted June 2, 2010	100 Options Granted January 14, 2011
Expected option life	6.5 years	4.9 years	6.5 years
Risk-free interest rate	3.59%	2.44%	2.90%
Expected stock price volatility	47.18%	37.40%	33.52%
Average dividend yield	4.00%	4.38%	4.44%
Weighted average fair value of options granted	$6.22	$4.25	$4.05
Share price at grant date	$18.00	$18.26	$18.00

The following table summarizes information about share options outstanding at January 28, 2012:

| | Options Outstanding | | | Options Exercisable | |
Range of Exercise Prices	Number Outstanding	Weighted Average Remaining Contractual Life	Weighted Average Exercise Price	Number Exercisable	Weighted Average Exercise Price
$14.50	1,675	5.0 years	$ 14.50	-	$ -
$15.90 - $18.26	115	2.4	16.75	83	16.58
$19.23 - $22.02	155	0.7	20.00	155	20.00
	1,945	4.5 years	$ 15.07	238	$ 18.81

c) Employee Expense

For the year ended January 28, 2012, the Company recognized compensation costs of $1,120 relating to share-based payment arrangements ($1,990 for the year ended January 29, 2011), with a corresponding credit to contributed surplus.

18. COMMITMENTS

As at January 28, 2012, financial commitments for minimum lease payments under operating leases for retail stores, offices, automobiles and equipment, as well as amounts pertaining to agreements to purchase goods or services that are enforceable and legally binding on the Company, exclusive of additional amounts based on sales, taxes and other costs are payable as follows:

	Store and Office Operating Leases	Purchases Obligations	Other Operating Leases	Total
Within 1 year	$ 99,202	$102,637	$ 4,498	$ 206,337
Within 2 years	88,467	326	3,723	92,516
Within 3 years	77,563	117	2,672	80,352
Within 4 years	66,012	-	2,477	68,489
Within 5 years	49,802	-	8	49,810
Subsequent years	89,873	-	-	89,873
Total	$ 470,919	$103,080	$ 13,378	$ 587,377

The Company leases retail stores and offices under operating leases. The Company does not sublet any of its leased properties. The leases have varying terms, escalation clauses and renewal rights. Generally, the leases run for a period that does not exceed 10 years, with options to renew that do not exceed 5 years, if at all. The majority of the leases require additional payments for the cost of insurance, taxes, maintenance and utilities. Certain rental agreements include contingent rent, which is generally based on revenue exceeding a minimum amount.

For the year ended January 28, 2012, $181,998 was recognized as an expense in net earnings with respect to operating leases ($181,868 for the year ended January 29, 2011), of which $179,149 ($179,328 for the year ended January 29, 2011) represents minimum lease payments and $2,849 ($2,540 for the year ended January 29, 2011) represents contingent rents.

As at January 28, 2012, a total of 1,945 (January 29, 2011– 398) share options were excluded from the calculation of diluted earnings per share as these options were deemed to be anti-dilutive, because the exercise prices were greater than the average market price of the shares during the period.

The average market value of the Company's shares for purposes of calculating the dilutive effect of share options was based on quoted market prices for the period during which the options were outstanding.

21. RELATED PARTIES

Transactions with Key Management Personnel

Only members of the Board of Directors are deemed to be key management personnel. It is the Board who has the responsibility for planning, directing and controlling the activities of the Company. The Directors participate in the share option plan, as described in note 17. Compensation expense for key management personnel is as follows:

	For the years ended	
	January 28, 2012	January 29, 2011
Salaries and short-term benefits	$ 2,088	$ 2,899
Post-employment benefits	(63)	178
Share-based compensation costs	190	200
	$ 2,215	$ 3,277

Further information about the remuneration of individual Directors is provided in the annual Management Proxy Circular.

Other Related-Party Transactions

The Company leases two retail locations which are owned by companies controlled by the major shareholders of the Company. For the year ended January 28, 2012, the rent expense under these leases was, in the aggregate, approximately $198 (January 29, 2011- $190).

The Company incurred $584 in the year ended January 28, 2012 (January 29, 2011- $606) with professional service firms connected to outside directors of the Company for fees in conjunction with general legal advice and other consultation.

These transactions are recorded at the amount of consideration paid as established and agreed to by the related parties.

19. FINANCE INCOME AND FINANCE COSTS

Recognized in Net Earnings

	For the years ended	
	January 28, 2012	January 29, 2011
Dividend income from available-for-sale financial assets	$ 3,462	$ 2,640
Interest income from loans and receivables	1,367	1,225
Realized gain on disposal of available-for-sale financial assets	-	167
Foreign exchange gain	733	473
Finance income	5,562	4,505
Interest expense - mortgage	682	767
Net change in fair value of derivatives (note 6)	754	-
Impairment loss on available-for-sale financial assets	73	78
Finance costs	1,509	845
Net finance income recognized in net earnings	$ 4,053	$ 3,660

Recognized in Other Comprehensive Income

	For the years ended	
	January 28, 2012	January 29, 2011
Net change in fair value of available-for-sale financial assets arising during the year (net of tax of $ 79; 2011 - $427)	$ 530	$ 2,866
Finance income recognized in other comprehensive income (net of tax)	$ 530	$ 2,866

20. EARNINGS PER SHARE

The calculation of basic and diluted earnings per share is based on net earnings for the year ended January 28, 2012 of $47,539 ($88,985 for the year ended January 29, 2011).

The number of shares used in the earnings per share calculation is as follows:

	For the years ended	
	January 28, 2012	January 29, 2011
Weighted average number of shares per basic earnings per share calculations	65,975	66,771
Effect of dilutive share options outstanding	126	484
Weighted average number of shares per diluted earnings per share calculations	66,101	67,255

22. PERSONNEL EXPENSES

	For the years ended	
	January 28, 2012	**January 29, 2011**
Wages, salaries and employee benefits	$ 248,208	$ 251,702
Expenses related to defined benefit plans	1,490	1,341
Share-based compensation costs	1,120	1,990
	$ 250,818	$ 255,033

23. CREDIT FACILITY

At January 28, 2012, the Company had unsecured operating lines of credit available with Canadian chartered banks to a maximum of $125,000 or its US dollar equivalent. As at January 28, 2012, $52,187 (January 29, 2011 - $60,888) of the operating lines of credit were committed for documentary and standby letters of credit.

24. GUARANTEES

The Company has granted irrevocable standby letters of credit, issued by highly-rated financial institutions, to third parties to indemnify them in the event the Company does not perform its contractual obligations. As at January 28, 2012, the maximum potential liability under these guarantees was $5,083 (January 29, 2011 - $5,060). The standby letters of credit mature at various dates during the year ending February 2, 2013. The contingent portion of the guarantee is recorded when the Company considers it probable that a payment relating to the guarantee has to be made to the other party of the contract or guarantee. The Company has recorded no liability with respect to these guarantees as the Company does not expect to make any payments for these items. Management believes that the fair value of the non-contingent obligations requiring performance under the guarantees in the event that specified triggering events or conditions occur approximates the cost of obtaining the standby letters of credit.

25. SUPPLEMENTARY CASH FLOW INFORMATION

	January 28, 2012	January 29, 2011
Non-cash transactions:		
Additions to property and equipment and intangible assets included in trade and other payables	$ 3,028	$ 2,819
Ascribed value credited to share capital from exercise of share options	$ 2,228	$ 888

26. FINANCIAL RISK MANAGEMENT

The Company's risk management policies are established to identify and analyze the risks faced by the Company, to set appropriate risk limits and controls, and to monitor risks and adherence to limits. Risk management policies and systems are reviewed regularly to reflect changes in market conditions and the Company's activities. Disclosures relating to the Company's exposure to risks, in particular credit risk, liquidity risk, foreign currency risk, interest rate risk and equity price risk are provided below.

Credit Risk

Credit risk is the risk of an unexpected loss if a customer or counterparty to a financial instrument fails to meet its contractual obligations. The Company's financial instruments that are exposed to concentrations of credit risk are primarily cash and cash equivalents, marketable securities, trade and other receivables and foreign currency option contracts. The Company limits its exposure to credit risk with respect to cash and cash equivalents by investing available cash in short-term deposits with Canadian financial institutions and commercial paper with a rating not less than R1. Marketable securities consist primarily of preferred shares of highly-rated Canadian public companies. The Company's trade and other receivables consist primarily of credit card receivables from the last few days of the fiscal year, which are settled within the first days of the next fiscal year.

As at January 28, 2012, the Company's maximum exposure to credit risk for these financial instruments was as follows:

Cash and cash equivalents	$ 196,835
Marketable securities	71,442
Trade and other receivables	3,033
	$ 271,310

Liquidity Risk

Liquidity risk is the risk that the Company will not be able to meet its financial obligations as they fall due. The Company's approach to managing liquidity risk is to ensure, as far as possible, that it will always have sufficient liquidity to meet liabilities when due. The contractual maturity of the majority of trade and other payables is within six months. As at January 28, 2012, the Company had a high degree of liquidity with $268,277 in cash and cash equivalents, and marketable securities. In addition, the Company has unsecured credit facilities of $125,000 subject to annual renewals. The Company has financed its store expansion through internally-generated funds and its unsecured credit facilities are used to finance seasonal working capital requirements for US dollar merchandise purchases. The Company's long-term debt consists of a mortgage bearing interest at 6.40%, due November 2017, which is secured by the Company's distribution centre.

Foreign Currency Risk

The Company purchases a significant amount of its merchandise with US dollars and as such significant volatility in the US dollar vis-à-vis the Canadian dollar can have an adverse impact on the Company's gross margin. The Company has a variety of alternatives that it considers to manage its foreign currency exposure on cash flows related to these purchases. This includes, but is not limited to, various styles of foreign currency option or forward contracts, not to exceed six months, and spot rate purchases. A foreign currency option contract represents an option or obligation to buy a foreign currency from a counterparty. Credit risks exist in the event of failure by a counterparty to fulfill its

Equity Price Risk

Equity price risk arises from available-for-sale equity securities. The Company monitors the mix of equity securities in its investment portfolio based on market expectations. Material investments within the portfolio are managed on an individual basis and all buy and sell decisions are approved by the Chief Executive Officer.

The Company has performed a sensitivity analysis on equity price risk at January 28, 2012, to determine how a change in the market price of the Company's marketable securities would impact equity and other comprehensive income. The Company's equity investments consist principally of preferred shares of Canadian public companies. The Company believes that changes in interest rates influence the market price of these securities. A 5% increase or decrease in the market price of the securities at January 28, 2012, would result in a $3,036 increase or decrease, respectively, in equity and other comprehensive income for the year ended January 28, 2012. The Company's equity securities are subject to market risk and, as a result, the impact on equity and other comprehensive income may ultimately be greater than that indicated above.

27. CAPITAL MANAGEMENT

The Company's objectives in managing capital are:

- to ensure sufficient liquidity to enable the internal financing of capital projects thereby facilitating its expansion;
- to maintain a strong capital base so as to maintain investor, creditor and market confidence;
- to provide an adequate return to shareholders.

The Company's capital is composed of long-term debt, including the current portion and shareholders' equity. The Company's primary uses of capital are to finance increases in non-cash working capital along with capital expenditures for new store additions, existing store renovation projects and office and distribution centre improvements. The Company currently funds these requirements out of its internally-generated cash flows. The Company's long-term debt constitutes a mortgage on the distribution centre facility. The Company maintains unsecured operating lines of credit that it uses to satisfy commitments for US dollar denominated merchandise purchases. The Company does not have any long-term debt, other than the mortgage related to the distribution centre, and therefore net earnings generated from operations are available for reinvestment in the Company or distribution to the Company's shareholders. The Board of Directors does not establish quantitative return on capital criteria for management, but rather promotes year over year sustainable profitable growth. On a quarterly basis, the Board of Directors also reviews the level of dividends paid to the Company's shareholders and monitors the share repurchase program activities. The Company does not have a defined share repurchase plan and decisions are made on a specific transaction basis and depend on market prices and regulatory restrictions. The Company is not subject to any externally imposed capital requirements.

obligations. The Company reduces this risk by dealing only with highly-rated counterparties, normally major Canadian financial institutions. For the year ended January 28, 2012, the Company satisfied its US dollar requirements primarily through spot rate purchases.

The Company has performed a sensitivity analysis on its US dollar denominated financial instruments, which consist principally of cash and cash equivalents of $27,547 and trade payables of $3,840 to determine how a change in the US dollar exchange rate would impact net earnings. On January 28, 2012, a 1% rise or fall in the Canadian dollar against the US dollar, assuming that all other variables, in particular interest rates, had remained the same, would have resulted in a $166 decrease or increase, respectively, in the Company's net earnings for the year ended January 28, 2012.

The Company has performed a sensitivity analysis on its derivative financial instruments, a series of call and put options on US dollars, to determine how a change in the US dollar exchange rate would impact net earnings. On January 28, 2012, a 1% rise or fall in the Canadian dollar against the US dollar, assuming that all other variables had remained the same, would have resulted in a $580 decrease or increase, respectively, in the Company's net earnings for the year ended January 28, 2012.

Interest Rate Risk

Interest rate risk exists in relation to the Company's cash and cash equivalents, defined benefit pension plan and SERP. Market fluctuations in interest rates impacts the Company's earnings with respect to interest earned on cash and cash equivalents that are invested in bank bearer deposit notes and bank term deposits with major Canadian financial institutions and commercial paper with a rating not less than R1. Overall return in the capital markets and the level of interest rates affect the funded status of the Company's pension plans. Adverse changes with respect to pension plan returns and the level of interest rates from the date of the last actuarial valuation may have a material adverse effect on the funded status of the retirement benefit plans and on the Company's results of operations. The Company has unsecured borrowing and working capital credit facilities available up to an amount of $125,000 or its US dollar equivalent that it utilizes for documentary and standby letters of credit, and the Company funds the drawings on these facilities as the payments are due.

The Company has performed a sensitivity analysis on interest rate risk at January 28, 2012 to determine how a change in interest rates would impact equity and net earnings. For the year ended January 28, 2012, the Company earned interest income of $1,367 on its cash and cash equivalents. An increase or decrease of 25 basis points in the average interest rate earned during the year would have increased equity and net earnings by $321 or decreased equity and net earnings by $235, respectively. This analysis assumes that all other variables, in particular foreign currency rates, remain constant.

The Company has performed a sensitivity analysis at January 28, 2012 to determine how a change in interest rates, in relation to the Company's retirement benefit plans, would impact the benefit costs included in other comprehensive income. A one percentage point decrease in the year-end discount rate would have resulted in an increase of approximately $4,300 in benefit costs included in other comprehensive income for the year ended January 28, 2012, whereas a one percentage point increase would have resulted in a decrease of approximately $3,800. The Company's expected long-term rate of return on Plan assets reflects management's view of long-term investment returns. The effect of a 1% variation in such rate of return would have a nominal impact on the total benefit costs included in net earnings and total comprehensive income.

28. COMPARATIVE FIGURES

Certain comparative figures have been reclassified to conform to the current year's presentation.

29. EXPLANATION OF TRANSITION TO IFRS

As stated in note 2 (a), these are the Company's first annual financial statements prepared in accordance with IFRS. The Company has applied IFRS 1 and the accounting policies set out in note 3 have been applied in preparing the financial statements for the year ended January 28, 2012, the comparative information presented in these financial statements for the year ended January 29, 2011 and in the preparation of the opening IFRS balance sheet at January 31, 2010, which is the Company's date of transition.

In preparing these financial statements in accordance with IFRS 1, the Company has adjusted amounts reported previously in the financial statements prepared in accordance with Canadian GAAP. An explanation of how the transition from Canadian GAAP to IFRS has affected the Company's previously published financial statements as at and for the year ended January 29, 2011 and as at January 31, 2010 is set out in the following tables and the notes that accompany the tables.

IFRS 1 requires first-time adopters to retrospectively apply all effective IFRS standards as of the reporting date of its first annual financial statements. However, it also provides for certain optional exemptions and prescribes certain mandatory exceptions for first-time adopters. Set forth below are the IFRS 1 applicable exemptions and exceptions applied in the Company's conversion from Canadian GAAP to IFRS.

a) IFRS Exemption Options

(i) Business Combinations

The Company elected not to retrospectively apply IFRS 3 *Business Combinations* to business combinations that occurred prior to its Transition Date and such business combinations have not been restated. Under the business combinations exemption, the carrying amounts of the assets acquired and liabilities assumed under Canadian GAAP at the date of the acquisition became their deemed carrying amounts under IFRS at that date.

Notwithstanding this exemption, the Company was required at the Transition Date, to evaluate whether the assets acquired and liabilities assumed meet the recognition criteria in the relevant IFRS, and whether there are any assets acquired or liabilities assumed that were not recognized under Canadian GAAP for which recognition would be required under IFRS. The requirements of IFRS were then applied to the assets acquired and liabilities assumed from the date of acquisition to the Transition Date. The application of this exemption did not result in an IFRS transition adjustment to the opening balance sheet at January 31, 2010. In addition, under the business combinations exemption, the Company tested goodwill for impairment at the Transition Date and determined that there was no impairment of the carrying value of goodwill as of that date.

(ii) Employee Benefits

IFRS 1 provides the option to apply IAS 19 *Employee Benefits* paragraph 120A(p), retrospectively or prospectively from the Transition Date. The retrospective basis would require the disclosure of selected information of the defined benefit plans for the current annual period and previous four annual periods. The Company elected to disclose the amounts required by paragraph 120A(p) of IAS 19 as the amounts are determined for each accounting period prospectively from the Transition Date to IFRS.

All companies operating in Canada need to understand how sales taxes apply to their particular business in their province or territory. Sales taxes may take the form of the Goods and Services Tax (GST), Provincial Sales Tax (PST), or Harmonized Sales Tax (HST). GST is levied by the federal government. PST is levied by the provinces, with the exception of Alberta, the Northwest Territories, Nunavut, and Yukon, where no PST is charged. Ontario, Nova Scotia, New Brunswick, Newfoundland and Labrador, and recently Prince Edward Island (effective April 1, 2013) have combined the GST and PST into one Harmonized Sales Tax. At the point of writing this textbook, Quebec announced that it was also considering moving to combining its provincial sales tax, the Quebec Sales Tax (QST), and the GST into the HST.

A business is considered an agent of the federal and provincial governments and is therefore required to collect sales taxes on the sale of certain goods and services. In addition, businesses pay sales taxes on most payments. We will discuss the collection, payment, recording, and remittance of each of these types of sales taxes in the following sections.

Types of Sales Taxes

GOODS AND SERVICES TAX

The GST is a federal sales tax on most goods and services provided in Canada. A business must register for the GST if it provides taxable goods or services in Canada and if it has revenues of more than $30,000 in any year. Businesses that have to or decide to voluntarily register for the GST are called registrants. Registrants can claim a credit—called an input tax credit (ITC)—for the amount of GST they pay or owe on purchases of goods or services against the GST they collect or are owed. GST returns are submitted quarterly for most registrants (monthly for large registrants) to the Canada Revenue Agency. The taxes are payable to the Receiver General, who is the collection agent for the federal government.

For those provinces that have adopted the Harmonized Sales Tax, where the PST and GST have been combined into one tax, the Receiver General is the collection agent for both the federal and provincial governments.

The GST applies at a rate of 5% on most transactions (13%, 14%, or 15% in the case of HST, depending on the province). Transactions subject to GST/HST are called taxable supplies. There are two other categories of goods and services with respect to the GST/HST:

- zero-rated supplies, such as basic groceries and prescription drugs
- exempt supplies, such as educational services, health care services, and financial services

No GST/HST applies to zero-rated or exempt supplies. However, zero-rated suppliers can claim input tax credits.

Illustration B-1 provides the GST/HST status of some typical goods and services.

> » **STUDY OBJECTIVE 1**
>
> Explain the different types of sales tax.

Taxable Supplies	Zero-Rated Supplies	Exempt Supplies
Building materials	Prescription drugs	Used house
Ready-to-eat pizza	Uncooked pizza	Dental services
Two doughnuts	Six or more doughnuts	Insurance policy

▶ ILLUSTRATION **B-1**
Examples of GST/HST status

The reason ready-to-eat pizza and two doughnuts have GST/HST added to the purchase price is because they are considered convenience items, which are taxable, and not basic groceries, which are not taxable.

PROVINCIAL SALES TAX

Provincial sales taxes are charged on retail sales of certain goods and services. As of April 1, 2013, there are only four provinces that charge a separate Provincial Sales Tax: British Columbia, Saskatchewan, Manitoba, and Quebec. For businesses that operate in several provinces, the amount of PST they need to charge will depend on where the goods are being shipped. Consequently, a business could have several PST payable accounts while operating out of a province where only HST applies to sales. Provincial sales taxes are remitted periodically to the Minister of Finance in each province. PST rates vary by province and can change with each provincial budget. Certain goods are exempt, such as children's clothing, textbooks, and residential rent, and may be purchased with no PST. Examples of exempt services that are not taxable include personal services such as dental and medical services. Because rates and exemptions vary by province, it is important, when starting a business, to check with provincial officials for details on how to calculate the provincial tax that must be applied to sales.

HARMONIZED SALES TAX

The provinces of Ontario, Nova Scotia, New Brunswick, Newfoundland and Labrador, and most recently Prince Edward Island charge Harmonized Sales Tax, or HST. Instead of charging GST and PST separately, only the HST is charged at a combined rate. British Columbia also charged HST, but effective April 1, 2013, it reverted from the combined HST to the original separate GST and PST taxes.

To summarize, four provinces—British Columbia, Manitoba, Quebec, and Saskatchewan—apply both PST and GST to the selling price of a taxable good or service. The provincial tax rates used by these four provinces vary but the GST is consistent at the rate of 5%. Five provinces charge a combined HST: New Brunswick, Newfoundland and Labrador, and Ontario charge 13%; Nova Scotia uses 15%; and Prince Edward Island applies 14% HST on the selling price of goods and services. Four provinces and territories charge only the GST: Alberta, the Northwest Territories, Nunavut, and Yukon. The rates of sales tax in each province and territory are shown in Illustration B-2.

▶ ILLUSTRATION **B-2**
Sales tax rates

Province/Territory	GST (HST) Rate	PST Rate	Combined Rate[1]
Alberta	5.0%	0.0%	5.0%
British Columbia	5.0%	7.0%	12.0%
Manitoba	5.0%	7.0%	12.0%
New Brunswick	13.0%	N/A	13.0%
Newfoundland and Labrador	13.0%	N/A	13.0%
Northwest Territories	5.0%	0.0%	5.0%
Nova Scotia	15.0%	N/A	15.0%
Nunavut	5.0%	0.0%	5.0%
Ontario	13.0%	N/A	13.0%
Prince Edward Island	14.0%	N/A	14.0%
Quebec	5.0%	9.975%	14.975%
Saskatchewan	5.0%	5.0%	10.0%
Yukon	5.0%	0.0%	5.0%

[1]These rates are in effect as of April 1, 2013, and are subject to change. Nova Scotia planned to reduce the HST to 14% (from 15%) on July 1, 2014, and to 13% (from 14%) on July 1, 2015.

Similar to GST, HST returns are submitted quarterly for most registrants (monthly for large registrants) to the Receiver General for Canada. The federal government then gives the provincial portion of the tax to the province.

Sales Taxes Collected on Receipts

Sales taxes are collected by businesses from consumers on taxable goods and services. It is important to understand that sales taxes are not a source of revenue for a company. They are collected by a company on behalf of the federal and provincial governments. Consequently, collected sales tax is a current liability to the company until remitted to the respective government at regular intervals.

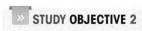

» STUDY OBJECTIVE 2

Record sales taxes collected by businesses on goods and services.

SERVICES

Now let's look at how service companies record sales taxes on the services they provide.

Services with PST

Assume that $250.00 of cleaning services were provided by a company in Manitoba for cash on July 24. These services are subject to both PST (7%) and GST (5%), and would be recorded as follows:

July 24	Cash	280.00	
	Service Revenue		250.00
	PST Payable ($250 × 7%)		17.50
	GST Payable ($250 × 5%)		12.50
	To record cleaning service revenue.		

A	=	L	+	OE
+280.00		+17.50		+250.00
		+12.50		

↑ Cash flows: +280.00

Note that the revenue recorded is $250.00, and not $280.00. The service revenue is exclusive of the GST and PST amounts collected, which are recorded as current liabilities.

Services with HST

Assume now that these same services were provided by a company in New Brunswick, where HST is 13%. The entry would be as follows:

July 24	Cash	282.50	
	Service Revenue		250.00
	HST Payable ($250.00 × 13%)		32.50
	To record cleaning service revenue.		

A	=	L	+	OE
+282.50		+32.50		+250.00

↑ Cash flows: +282.50

MERCHANDISE

Entries are needed to record the sales taxes owed when merchandise inventory (goods) is sold, or to reduce sales taxes payable when merchandise inventory is returned.

Sales with PST

Assume that Staples sells $1,000 of office furniture, on account, in the province of Manitoba, where PST is 7%. GST is 5%. Staples uses a perpetual inventory system and the cost of the furniture to Staples was $800. Staples will make the following two entries to record the sale and the cost of the sale on May 20:

May 20	Accounts Receivable	1,120	
	Sales		1,000
	GST Payable ($1,000 × 5%)		50
	PST Payable ($1,000 × 7%)		70
	To record sale of merchandise on account.		
20	Cost of Goods Sold	800	
	Merchandise Inventory		800
	To record cost of merchandise sold.		

A	=	L	+	OE
+1,120		+50		+1,000
		+70		

Cash flows: no effect

A	=	L	+	OE
−800				−800

Cash flows: no effect

The merchandise inventory does not include any sales taxes that may have been paid when the company purchased the merchandise. We will learn more about that in the next section of this appendix.

Under a periodic inventory system, the second entry would not be recorded.

Sales Returns and Allowances with PST

If a $300 sales return and allowance were granted by Staples on May 25 for returned merchandise from the above sale, Staples' entries to record the sales return would appear as follows:

A	=	L	+	OE
−336		−15		−300
		−21		

Cash flows: no effect

A	=	L	+	OE
+240				+240

Cash flows: no effect

May 25	Sales Returns and Allowances		300	
	GST Payable ($300 × 5%)		15	
	PST Payable ($300 × 7%)		21	
	Accounts Receivable			336
	To record credit for returned merchandise.			
25	Merchandise Inventory ($300 ÷ $1,000 × $800)		240	
	Cost of Goods Sold			240
	To record cost of merchandise returned.			

Note that the GST and PST payable accounts, rather than a receivable account, are debited, to indicate that this is a return of previously collected sales tax. The second entry assumes that the merchandise was in good condition and returned to inventory.

Under a periodic inventory system, the second entry would not be recorded.

Sales with HST

Assume now that Staples sells the same $1,000 of office furniture, on account, in the province of Ontario, where there is no PST and where HST is 13%. Staples uses a perpetual inventory system and the cost of the furniture to Staples was $800. Staples will record the following two entries to record the sale and the cost of the sale on May 20:

A	=	L	+	OE
+1,130		+130		+1,000

Cash flows: no effect

A	=	L	+	OE
−800				−800

Cash flows: no effect

May 20	Accounts Receivable		1,130	
	Sales			1,000
	HST Payable ($1,000 × 13%)			130
	To record sale of merchandise on account.			
20	Cost of Goods Sold		800	
	Merchandise Inventory			800
	To record cost of merchandise sold.			

Under a periodic inventory system, the second entry would not be recorded.

Sales Returns and Allowances with HST

Assume the same $300 sales returns and allowances were granted by Staples on May 25 for returned merchandise from the above sale. Staples' entries to record the sales return would appear as follows:

A	=	L	+	OE
−339		−39		−300

Cash flows: no effect

A	=	L	+	OE
+240				+240

Cash flows: no effect

May 25	Sales Returns and Allowances		300	
	HST Payable ($300 × 13%)		39	
	Accounts Receivable			339
	To record credit for returned merchandise.			
25	Merchandise Inventory ($300 ÷ $1,000 × $800)		240	
	Cost of Goods Sold			240
	To record cost of merchandise returned.			

Under a periodic inventory system, the second entry would not be recorded.

Sales Taxes Paid on Payments

Businesses, similar to consumers, must pay the applicable PST and GST or HST charged by their suppliers on taxable goods and services.

PURCHASE OF MERCHANDISE FOR RESALE

When purchasing merchandise for resale, the treatment of the PST is different than that of the GST. PST is a single-stage tax collected from the final consumers of taxable goods and services. Consequently, wholesalers do not charge provincial sales tax to the retailer, who will in turn resell the merchandise, at a higher price, to the final consumer. By presenting a vendor licence number, retailers are able to buy merchandise for resale, exempt of the PST.

Businesses must pay GST/HST on the purchase of merchandise but can then offset the GST/HST paid against any GST/HST collected. Consequently, when merchandise is purchased, the GST/HST paid by a business is **not** part of the inventory cost. The GST/HST paid on purchases is debited to an account called GST or HST Recoverable and is called an input tax credit.

Purchases with GST

The following is an entry to record the purchase of merchandise for resale in the province of Manitoba on May 4 at a price of $4,000, on account, using a perpetual inventory system:

May 4	Merchandise Inventory	4,000	
	GST Recoverable ($4,000 × 5%)	200	
	Accounts Payable		4,200
	To record merchandise purchased on account.		

A = L + OE
+4,000 +4,200
+200
Cash flows: no effect

As previously discussed, the cost of the merchandise, $4,000, is not affected by the GST, which is recorded as a receivable.

Under a periodic inventory system, the $4,000 debit would have been recorded to the Purchases account.

Purchase Returns and Allowances with GST

The entry to record a $300 return of merchandise on May 8 is as follows:

May 8	Accounts Payable	315	
	GST Recoverable ($300 × 5%)		15
	Merchandise Inventory		300
	To record the return of merchandise.		

A = L + OE
−15 −315
−300
Cash flows: no effect

Note that the GST Recoverable account is credited instead of the GST Payable account because this is a reduction of the previously recorded GST.

Under a periodic inventory system, the credit of $300 would have been recorded to the Purchase Returns and Allowances account.

To summarize, PST is not paid on purchases of merchandise for resale. GST paid on purchases is recoverable and recorded as a current asset in the GST Recoverable account. Purchase returns and allowances require an adjustment of GST only, since PST was not paid on the original purchase.

Purchases with HST

The following is an entry to record the purchase of merchandise for resale in the province of Prince Edward Island, where the HST rate is 14%, on May 4 at a price of $4,000, on account, using a perpetual inventory system:

A	=	L	+	OE
+4,000		+4,560		
+560				

Cash flows: no effect

May 4	Merchandise Inventory	4,000	
	HST Recoverable ($4,000 × 14%)	560	
	Accounts Payable		4,560
	To record merchandise purchased on account.		

The cost of the merchandise, $4,000, is not affected by the HST, which is recorded as a receivable. Under a periodic inventory system, the $4,000 debit would have been recorded to the Purchases account.

Purchase Returns and Allowances with HST

The entry to record a $300 return of merchandise in the province of Prince Edward Island, where the HST rate is 14%, on May 8 is as follows:

A	=	L	+	OE
−42		−342		
−300				

Cash flows: no effect

May 8	Accounts Payable	342	
	HST Recoverable ($300 × 14%)		42
	Merchandise Inventory		300
	To record the return of merchandise.		

Note that the HST Recoverable account is credited instead of the HST Payable account because this is a reduction of the previously recorded HST.

Under a periodic inventory system, the credit of $300 would have been recorded to the Purchase Returns and Allowances account.

To summarize, HST paid on purchases is recoverable and recorded as a current asset in the HST Recoverable account.

OPERATING EXPENSES

The accounting treatment of sales taxes incurred on operating expenses depends on the type of sales taxes that the company is charged.

Operating Expenses with PST

Although PST is not charged on goods purchased for resale, it is charged to businesses that use taxable goods and services in their operations. For example, a business must pay GST and PST when it buys office supplies. As with all purchases made by a business that is a registrant, the GST is recoverable (can be offset as an input tax credit against GST collected). Because the PST is not recoverable, the PST forms part of the cost of the asset or expense that is being acquired.

The following is the entry for a cash purchase of office supplies on May 18 in the amount of $200 in the province of Saskatchewan, where PST is 5% and GST is 5%:

A	=	L	+	OE
+210				
+10				
−220				

↓ Cash flows: −220

May 18	Supplies ($200 + $10* PST)	210	
	GST Recoverable ($200 × 5%)	10	
	Cash		220
	To record purchase of office supplies.		

*$200 × 5% = $10

In this situation, the cost of the supplies includes both the supplies and the PST. Because GST is recoverable, it does not form part of the asset cost.

This same purchase would be recorded as follows if it occurred in the province of Quebec, where PST is 9.975% and GST is 5%:

May 18	Supplies ($200.00 + $19.95* PST)	219.95	
	GST Recoverable ($200.00 × 5%)	10.00	
	Cash		229.95
	To record purchase of office supplies.		

A = L + OE
+219.95
+10.00
−229.95

↓ Cash flows: −229.95

*$200.00 × 9.975% = $19.95

Operating Expenses with HST

When HST is applied, it is treated in the same manner as GST. HST is recoverable and does not form part of the cost of the item purchased. The purchase of office supplies would be recorded as follows if it had occurred in the province of Ontario, where HST is 13%:

May 18	Supplies	200	
	HST Recoverable ($200 × 13%)	26	
	Cash		226
	To record purchase of office supplies.		

A = L + OE
+200
+26
−226

↓ Cash flows: −226

Note that the type and amount of sales tax paid changes the amount recorded as the cost of office supplies in each province: $210.00 in Saskatchewan, $219.95 in Quebec, and $200.00 in Ontario.

PROPERTY, PLANT, AND EQUIPMENT

The PST and GST or HST apply to other purchases, such as the purchase of property, plant, and equipment, in the same manner as described in the operating expenses section above. All GST (or HST) paid is recoverable and is not part of the cost of the asset. The PST, however, is part of the cost of the asset being purchased as it is not recoverable.

Property, Plant, and Equipment with PST

The following is the entry for the purchase of office furniture on May 20 from Staples, on account, for $1,000 plus applicable sales taxes in Manitoba, where PST is 7% and GST is 5%.

May 20	Furniture ($1,000 + $70* PST)	1,070	
	GST Recoverable ($1,000 × 5%)	50	
	Accounts Payable		1,120
	To record purchase of office furniture.		

A = L + OE
+1,070   +1,120
+50

Cash flows: no effect

*$1,000 × 7% = $70

Because the PST is not recoverable, the cost of the furniture is $1,070, inclusive of the PST.

Compare this entry made by the buyer to record the purchase with the entry made by the seller (Staples) to record the sale, shown earlier in this appendix. Both companies record accounts payable and accounts receivable in the same amount, $1,120. However, the seller records both GST and PST payable while the buyer records only GST recoverable. The PST paid by the buyer is not recoverable, so it becomes part of the cost of the office furniture, $1,070.

In Saskatchewan, where PST is 5% and GST is 5%, the same entry would be recorded as follows:

May 20	Furniture ($1,000 + $50* PST)	1,050	
	GST Recoverable ($1,000 × 5%)	50	
	Accounts Payable		1,100
	To record purchase of office furniture.		

A = L + OE
+1,050   +1,100
+50

Cash flows: no effect

*$1,000 × 5% = $50

Property, Plant, and Equipment with HST

In Ontario, where HST is 13%, the entry would be recorded as follows:

A = L + OE
+1,000 +1,130
+130

Cash flows: no effect

May 20	Furniture	1,000	
	HST Recoverable ($1,000 × 13%)	130	
	Accounts Payable		1,130
	To record purchase of office furniture.		

As we have noted before, the type and amount of sales taxes paid change the amount recorded as the cost of the office furniture in each province: $1,070 in Manitoba, $1,050 in Saskatchewan, and $1,000 in Ontario.

Remittance of Sales Taxes

» **STUDY OBJECTIVE 4**

Record the remittance of sales taxes.

As mentioned in the introduction, businesses act as agents of the federal and provincial governments in charging and later remitting taxes charged on sales and services. For example, Staples, the seller of office furniture shown earlier in the appendix, must remit GST or HST to the Receiver General for Canada and PST to the Minister of Finance, where applicable. Notice that even if Staples has not received payment from a customer buying on account before the due date for the remittance, the tax must still be paid to the government authorities. As a registrant, however, Staples will also benefit from claiming input tax credits and recording a reduction in amounts payable from applying GST/HST on sales.

GST (OR HST)

When remitting the amount owed to the federal government at the end of a reporting period for GST (or HST), the amount of GST/HST payable is reduced by any amount in the GST (or HST) Recoverable account. Any difference is remitted, as shown in the following journal entry, using assumed payable and recoverable amounts:

A = L + OE
−2,500 −6,250
−3,750

↓ Cash flows: −3,750

June 30	GST (or HST) Payable	6,250	
	GST (or HST) Recoverable		2,500
	Cash		3,750
	To record remittance of GST (or HST).		

The electronic filing of GST/HST returns requires the registrant to report at specified dates, depending on the business's volume of sales. The amount of the sales and other revenue as well as the amount of GST/HST charged on these sales, whether collected or not, is reported on the return. The amount of the input tax credits claimed is also entered to reduce the amount owing to the Receiver General. If the GST/HST recoverable exceeds the GST/HST payable, the return should be filed as soon as possible in order to ask for a refund. The entry to record the cash receipt from a GST/HST refund will be similar to the entry shown above, except that there will be a debit to Cash, instead of a credit.

The above discussion of the remittance of GST/HST explains why all registrants need two general ledger accounts—a payable account and a recoverable account. The GST (or HST) Payable account is used to keep track of all GST or HST charged on sales and revenues. The second account, GST (or HST) Recoverable, is used to keep track of the GST/HST input tax credits that have been paid on all of the business's purchases. Both amounts must be reported on the return. Failure by a business to capture the proper amounts of input tax credits has a significant impact on income and on cash flows.

PST

The remittance of PST to the Minister of Finance of the applicable province is similar to that of GST/HST except that, since no credit can be claimed, the amount paid at the end of each reporting period is the amount of the balance in the PST Payable account.

Consequently, the entry to record a remittance of PST, using an assumed amount payable, would appear as follows:

June 30	PST Payable	7,400	
	Cash		7,400
	To record remittance of PST.		

A = L + OE
−7,400 −7,400
↓ Cash flows: −7,400

Conclusion

Be careful when you record the amounts of taxes charged or claimed in the business accounts. Numbers must be rounded carefully. If the amount of the tax calculated on a credit sale is less than half a cent, the amount should be rounded down. If the amount of the tax as calculated comes to more than half a cent, the amount should be rounded up. For example, applying 13% HST on an amount of $49.20 would give you $6.396. The tax amount to be recorded must be rounded up to $6.40. On the other hand, if the sale is a cash sale, due to the abolition of the one-cent coin (the penny), the amount of the sale, including all taxes, must be rounded to the nearest five cents. Rounding might seem insignificant, but when a business has many transactions, the amounts can add up and the registrant is responsible to the government authorities for any shortfall created in error.

Sales tax law is intricate. It has added a lot of complexity to the accounting for most transactions flowing through today's businesses. Fortunately, computers that are programmed to automatically determine and record the correct sales tax rate for each good or service provided have simplified matters somewhat. Before recording sales tax transactions, however, it is important to understand all of the relevant sales tax regulations. Check the federal and provincial laws in your jurisdiction.

▶ Brief Exercises

BEB-1 List the various sales taxes in Canada and explain the main differences between the types. In what way are they alike to the consumer?

Explain the different types of sales taxes. (SO 1) AP

BEB-2 Record the sale on account, for $1,600, of merchandise costing $900 in the province of Quebec. Assume the company uses a perpetual inventory system. The QST is 9.975%.

Record sales—perpetual inventory system—Quebec. (SO 2) AP

BEB-3 Half of the shipment described in BEB-2 is returned as the incorrect sizes have been shipped. Record the return of merchandise on the seller's books.

Record sales return—perpetual inventory system—Quebec. (SO 2) AP

BEB-4 Record the sale in BEB-2 and the sales return in BEB-3 assuming the business uses a periodic inventory system.

Record sales and sales return—periodic inventory system—Quebec. (SO 2) AP

BEB-5 Record the billing for $450 of services by D. R. Wong, dentist, in the province of British Columbia. Dental services are exempt from GST and PST.

Record exempt services—British Columbia. (SO 2) AP

BEB-6 Record the billing of accounting services of $700 for the preparation of personal income tax returns in the territory of Nunavut. GST is applicable on this service. Nunavut does not charge PST.

Record fees—Nunavut. (SO 2) AP

BEB-7 Record the purchase on account of $4,100 of merchandise for resale in the province of Manitoba, where the PST is 7%. The company uses a perpetual inventory system and the purchase is PST exempt.

Record inventory purchase—perpetual inventory system—Manitoba. (SO 3) AP

BEB-8 Record the return of $500 of the merchandise purchased in BEB-7.

Record purchase return—perpetual inventory system—Manitoba. (SO 3) AP

Record inventory purchase—perpetual inventory system—New Brunswick. (SO 3) AP

BEB–9 Record the purchase on account of $4,100 of merchandise for resale in the province of New Brunswick, where HST is 13%. The company uses a perpetual inventory system.

Record purchase return—perpetual inventory system—New Brunswick. (SO 3) AP

BEB–10 Record the return of $500 of the merchandise purchased in BEB–9.

Record purchase of supplies—Saskatchewan. (SO 3) AP

BEB–11 Record the cash purchase of $600 of office supplies in the province of Saskatchewan, where PST is 5%.

Record purchase of supplies—Nova Scotia. (SO 3) AP

BEB–12 Record the cash purchase of $600 of office supplies in the province of Nova Scotia, where HST is 15%.

Record purchase of vehicle—Prince Edward Island. (SO 3) AP

BEB–13 Record the purchase on account of a $32,000 delivery truck in the province of Prince Edward Island, where HST is 14%.

Record purchase of vehicle—British Columbia. (SO 3) AP

BEB–14 Record the purchase on account of a $32,000 delivery truck in the province of British Columbia, where the PST is 7%.

Record purchase of supplies and inventory—perpetual inventory system—Manitoba. (SO 3) AP

BEB–15 Record the purchase on account of $300 of office supplies and $5,000 of merchandise for resale in the province of Manitoba. The company uses a perpetual inventory system and the purchase of merchandise is PST exempt. The PST rate is 7%.

Record remittance of GST and PST—British Columbia. (SO 4) AP

BEB–16 Record two payments: one cheque to the Receiver General for GST and one to the Minister of Finance of British Columbia for PST. The balances in the accounts are as follows: GST Payable $6,120, GST Recoverable $940, and PST Payable $8,570.

Record HST refund. (SO 4) AP

BEB–17 Record the deposit of a cheque from the Receiver General for a refund of $690 following the filing of an HST return. The balances in the accounts are as follows: HST Payable $3,920 and HST Recoverable $4,610.

▶ Exercises

Record purchase and sales transactions—perpetual inventory system—Manitoba. (SO 2, 3) AP

EB–1 Wu Limited is a merchant operating in the province of Manitoba, where the PST rate is 7%. Wu uses a perpetual inventory system. Transactions for the business are shown below:

May 1 Paid May rent to the landlord for the rental of a warehouse. The lease calls for monthly payments of $7,300 plus 5% GST.
3 Sold merchandise on account and shipped merchandise to Marvin Ltd. for $25,000, plus applicable sales taxes, terms n/30, FOB shipping point. This merchandise cost Wu $18,600.
5 Granted Marvin Ltd. a sales allowance of $800 for defective merchandise purchased on May 3. No merchandise was returned.
7 Purchased on account from Macphee Ltd. merchandise for resale for $11,000, plus applicable tax.
12 Made a cash purchase at Home Depot of a desk for the shipping clerk. The price of the desk was $600 before applicable taxes.
31 Paid the quarterly remittance of GST to the Receiver General. The balances in the accounts were as follows: GST Payable $7,480 and GST Recoverable $1,917.

Instructions

Prepare the journal entries to record these transactions on the books of Wu Limited.

Record purchase and sales transactions—perpetual inventory system—Alberta. (SO 2, 3) AP

EB–2 Refer to Wu Limited in EB–1. Assume instead that the company operates in the province of Alberta, where PST is not applicable.

Instructions

Prepare the journal entries to record these transactions on the books of Wu.

Record purchase and sales transactions—perpetual inventory system—Ontario. (SO 2, 3) AP

EB–3 Refer to Wu Limited in EB–1. Assume instead that the company operates in the province of Ontario, where HST is 13%.

Instructions

Prepare the journal entries to record these transactions on the books of Wu. Assume that the GST balances on May 31 are the balances in the HST accounts.

EB-4 Using the information for the transactions of Wu Limited in EB-1, assume now that Wu uses a periodic inventory system and operates in the province of Manitoba.

Instructions

Prepare the journal entries to record these transactions on the books of Wu Limited.

Record purchase and sales transactions—periodic inventory system—Manitoba. (SO 2, 3) AP

EB-5 Using the information for the transactions of Wu Limited in EB-1, assume now that Wu uses a periodic inventory system and operates in the province of Alberta, where PST is not applicable.

Instructions

Prepare the journal entries to record these transactions on the books of Wu.

Record purchase and sales transactions—periodic inventory system—Alberta. (SO 2, 3) AP

EB-6 Using the information for the transactions of Wu Limited in EB-1, assume now that Wu uses a periodic inventory system and operates in the province of Ontario, where HST is 13%.

Instructions

Prepare the journal entries to record these transactions on the books of Wu. Assume that the GST balances on May 31 provided in EB-1 are the balances in the HST accounts.

Record purchase and sales transactions—periodic inventory system—Ontario. (SO 2, 3) AP

EB-7 Leon Cheng is a sole proprietor providing accounting services in the province of British Columbia, where PST is charged at the rate of 7% and GST is at the rate of 5%. Transactions for the business are shown below:

Record transactions for services, equipment, and supplies—British Columbia. (SO 2, 3, 4) AP

June	1	Paid cash to a local courier for the delivery of documents to several clients. The invoice was for $200 plus GST and PST.
	5	Paid $800 cash plus GST and PST to have the office painted. Use Repairs Expense.
	10	Purchased photocopy paper for $250 from a local stationery store, on account. The store added the appropriate sales taxes to the purchase price.
	13	Billed a client for accounting services provided. The fee charged was $4,700 and the appropriate sales taxes were added to the fee billed.
	15	Collected $896 on account. This included accounting services of $800, GST of $40, and PST of $56.
	22	Paid $720 cash plus applicable taxes to Air Canada for an airline ticket to Ottawa to meet with a client. Airfare is subject to both PST and GST.
	30	Received invoice from BC Tel. for telephone service for the month of June. The invoice is for $150 plus GST and PST.
	30	Paid the quarterly remittance of GST to the Receiver General. The balances in the accounts were as follows: GST Payable $1,890.50 and GST Recoverable $741.60.
	30	Paid the quarterly remittance of PST to the Minister of Revenue for the province of British Columbia. The balance in the PST Payable account was $2,640.00.

Instructions

Prepare the journal entries to record these transactions on the books of Leon Cheng's accounting business.

EB-8 Ruby Gordon L.L.B. is a sole proprietor providing legal services in the province of Newfoundland and Labrador, where the HST rate is 13%. Transactions for the business are shown below:

Record transactions for services, equipment, and supplies—Newfoundland and Labrador. (SO 2, 3, 4) AP

June	8	Purchased equipment for scanning and printing on account at a cost of $1,500. The appropriate taxes were added to this purchase price.
	10	Purchased toner for the equipment for $100 cash from a local stationery store. The store added the appropriate taxes to the purchase price.
	12	Billed Lee Ltd. for legal services provided. The fee charged was $1,250 plus appropriate taxes.
	18	Paid cash of $220 plus applicable taxes to have a boardroom table repaired.
	22	Collected from Lee Ltd. account billed on June 12.
	30	Paid the quarterly remittance of HST to the Receiver General. The balances in the accounts were as follows: HST Payable $2,520.60 and HST Recoverable $820.45.

Instructions

Prepare the journal entries to record these transactions on the books of Ruby Gordon's legal practice.

EB-9 Refer to the data for Ruby Gordon, L.L.B. in EB-8. Assume instead that Ruby is operating her legal practice in Alberta and that on June 30 she paid a quarterly remittance of GST, as opposed to HST, to the Receiver General. Assume the balances were as follows: GST Payable $970.50 and GST Recoverable $315.55.

Record transactions for services, equipment, and supplies—Alberta. (SO 2, 3, 4) AP

Instructions

Prepare the journal entries to record these transactions on the books of Ruby Gordon's legal practice.

▶ Problems

Record purchase and sales transactions—perpetual inventory system—Ontario. (SO 2, 3) AP

PB-1 Mark's Music is a store that buys and sells musical instruments in Ontario, where the HST rate is 13%. Mark's Music uses a perpetual inventory system. Transactions for the business are shown below:

Nov. 2 Purchased three electric guitars from Fender Supply Limited, on account, at a cost of $900 each.

4 Made a cash sale of two keyboards for a total invoice price of $2,600, plus applicable taxes. The cost of each keyboard was $675.

5 Received a credit memorandum from Western Acoustic Inc. for the return of an acoustic guitar that was defective. The original invoice price before taxes was $700 and the guitar had been purchased on account. Mark's Music intends to return the defective guitar to the original supplier.

7 One of the keyboards from the cash sale of November 4 was returned to the store for a full cash refund because the customer was not satisfied with the instrument. The keyboard was returned to inventory.

8 Purchased supplies from a stationery store. The price of the supplies is $200 before all applicable taxes.

10 Sold one Omega trumpet to Regional Band, on account, for an invoice price of $5,100 before applicable taxes. The trumpet had cost Mark's Music $2,850.

13 Purchased two saxophones from Yamaha Canada Inc. on account. The invoice price was $1,900 for each saxophone, excluding applicable taxes.

14 Collected $4,150 on account. The payment included all applicable taxes.

16 Returned to Yamaha Canada Inc. one of the saxophones purchased on November 13, as it was the wrong model. Received a credit memorandum from Yamaha for the full purchase price.

20 Made a payment on account for the amount owing to Fender Supply Limited for the purchase of November 2.

Instructions

Prepare the journal entries to record the Mark's Music transactions.

Record purchase and sales transactions—perpetual inventory system—British Columbia. (SO 2, 3) AP

PB-2 Transaction data for Mark's Music are available in PB-1. Assume instead that the company operates in the province of British Columbia, where the PST rate is 7% and the GST rate is 5%.

Instructions

Prepare the journal entries to record these transactions on the books of Mark's Music.

Record purchase and sales transactions—periodic inventory system—Ontario. (SO 2, 3) AP

PB-3 Transaction data for Mark's Music are available in PB-1. Assume that the company uses a periodic inventory system instead of a perpetual inventory system and operates in the province of Ontario, where the HST rate is 13%.

Instructions

Prepare the journal entries to record the Mark's Music transactions.

Record purchase and sales transactions—periodic inventory system—British Columbia. (SO 2, 3) AP

PB-4 Transaction data for Mark's Music are available in PB-1. Assume that the company uses a periodic inventory system instead of a perpetual inventory system and operates in the province of British Columbia, where the PST rate is 7% and the GST rate is 5%.

Instructions

Prepare the journal entries to record these transactions on the books of Mark's Music.

Record service transactions—Alberta. (SO 2, 3, 4) AP

PB-5 Manny Lee, L.L.B., is a lawyer operating as a sole proprietor in the province of Alberta. Alberta does not charge provincial sales taxes and the GST rate is 5%. Transactions for the business are shown below:

May 1 Signed a two-year lease for the office space and immediately paid the first and last months' rent. The lease calls for monthly rent of $1,650 plus applicable taxes.

4 Purchased furniture, on account, from George's Furniture at a cost of $4,100. The appropriate sales taxes were added to this purchase price.

5 Returned one chair to George's due to a defect. The cost of the chair before taxes was $800.

6 Billed a client for the preparation of a contract. The client was very pleased with the document and immediately paid Manny's invoice for fees of $2,500 plus taxes.

10 Purchased paper for the photocopier for $300 cash from a local stationery store. The store added the appropriate sales taxes to the purchase price.

13 Billed Manson Ltd. for legal services rendered connected with the purchase of land. The fee charged is $1,100 plus applicable taxes.

18   Paid George's for the furniture purchase of May 4, net of returned items.
19   Paid $22 cash to a local grocery store for coffee for the office coffee machine. Groceries are GST and HST exempt. Use Office Expense.
21   In accordance with the lease agreement with the landlord, Manny must pay for water supplied by the municipality. The water invoice was received and the services amounted to $150. No GST is charged for municipal water.
25   Collected a full payment from Manson Ltd. for the May 13 bill.
27   Completed the preparation of a purchase and sale agreement for Pedneault Inc. and billed fees of $600.

Instructions

(a) Prepare the journal entries to record these transactions on the books of Manny Lee's law practice.
(b) Determine the balances in the GST Payable and GST Recoverable accounts. Determine if the company must make a payment to the Receiver General or if it will apply for a refund. Record the appropriate journal entry.

PB–6   Refer to Manny Lee in PB–5. Assume instead that Mr. Lee operates in the province of Ontario, where the HST rate is 13%.

Record service transactions—
Ontario. (SO 2, 3, 4) AP

Instructions

(a) Prepare the journal entries to record these transactions on the books of Manny Lee's law practice.
(b) Determine the balances in the HST Payable and HST Recoverable accounts. Determine if the business must make a payment to the Receiver General or if it will apply for a refund. Record the appropriate journal entry.

In the textbook, we learned how to record accounting transactions in a general journal. Each journal entry was then individually posted to its respective general ledger account. However, such a practice is only useful in a company where the volume of transactions is low. In most companies, it is necessary to use additional journals (called special journals) and ledgers (called subsidiary ledgers) to record transaction data.

We will look at subsidiary ledgers and special journals in the next sections. Both subsidiary ledgers and special journals can be used in either a manual accounting system or a computerized accounting system.

The illustrations provided in this appendix are taken from a manual accounting system. Computerized accounting systems vary in the way in which the accounting information is captured, processed, and reported. The software nevertheless is programmed to provide the same basic information that is maintained in a manual accounting system. If you can understand how a manual system works, you will be able to follow how a computerized system is capturing, recording, and reporting transactions for a business of any size or type.

Subsidiary Ledgers

Imagine a business that has several thousand customers who purchase merchandise from it on account. It records the transactions with these customers in only one general ledger account—Accounts Receivable. It would be virtually impossible to determine the balance owed by an individual customer at any specific time. Similarly, the amount payable to one creditor would be difficult to locate quickly from a single accounts payable account in the general ledger.

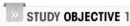

STUDY OBJECTIVE 1

Describe the purposes and advantages of maintaining subsidiary ledgers.

Instead, companies use subsidiary ledgers to keep track of individual balances. A subsidiary ledger is a group of accounts that share a common characteristic (for example, all accounts receivable). The subsidiary ledger frees the general ledger from the details of individual balances. A subsidiary ledger is an addition to, and an expansion of, the general ledger.

Two common subsidiary ledgers are:

1. The accounts receivable (or customers') ledger, which collects transaction data for individual customers
2. The accounts payable (or creditors') ledger, which collects transaction data for individual creditors

Another subsidiary ledger, as described in Chapter 5, is the inventory ledger, which collects transaction data for each inventory item purchased and sold. The inventory ledger may also include information used by the purchasing department, such as the terms negotiated with suppliers. Computerized systems can be programmed to automatically produce purchase orders when the inventory is low to avoid shortages. Some companies also use a payroll ledger, detailing individual employee pay records. Other companies use a long-lived asset ledger to keep track of each item of property, plant, and equipment. In each of these subsidiary ledgers, individual accounts are arranged in alphabetical, numerical, or alphanumerical order.

The detailed data from a subsidiary ledger are summarized in a general ledger account. For example, the detailed data from the accounts receivable subsidiary ledger are summarized in Accounts Receivable in the general ledger. The general ledger account that summarizes subsidiary ledger data is called a control account.

Each general ledger control account balance must equal the total balance of the individual accounts in the related subsidiary ledger. This is an important internal control function.

EXAMPLE

An example of an accounts receivable control account and subsidiary ledger is shown in Illustration C-1 for Mercier Enterprises.

▶ ILLUSTRATION C-1
Accounts receivable
general ledger control
account and subsidiary ledger

GENERAL LEDGER

Accounts Receivable — No. 112

Date	Explanation	Ref.	Debit	Credit	Balance
2014					
Jan. 31			12,000		12,000
31				8,000	4,000

ACCOUNTS RECEIVABLE SUBSIDIARY LEDGER

Aaron Co. — No. 112-172

Date	Explanation	Ref.	Debit	Credit	Balance
2014					
Jan. 11	Invoice 336		6,000		6,000
19	Payment			4,000	2,000

Branden Inc. — No. 112-173

Date	Explanation	Ref.	Debit	Credit	Balance
2014					
Jan. 12	Invoice 337		3,000		3,000
21	Payment			3,000	0

Caron Co. — No. 112-174

Date	Explanation	Ref.	Debit	Credit	Balance
2014					
Jan. 20	Invoice 339		3,000		3,000
29	Payment			1,000	2,000

The example is based on the following transactions:

Credit Sales			Collections on Account		
Jan. 11	Aaron Co.	$ 6,000	Jan. 19	Aaron Co.	$4,000
12	Branden Inc.	3,000	21	Branden Inc.	3,000
20	Caron Co.	3,000	29	Caron Co.	1,000
		$12,000			$8,000

The total debits ($12,000) and credits ($8,000) in Accounts Receivable in the general ledger match the detailed debits and credits in the subsidiary accounts. The balance of $4,000 in the control account agrees with the total of the balances in the individual accounts receivable accounts (Aaron $2,000 + Branden $0 + Caron $2,000) in the subsidiary ledger.

Rather than relying on customer or creditor names in a subsidiary ledger, a computer system expands the account number of the control account. For example, if the general ledger control account Accounts Receivable was numbered 112, the first customer account in the accounts receivable subsidiary ledger might be numbered 112-001, the second 112-002, and so on. Data entry in a computerized system is much faster if account numbers, rather than customer names, are used. Most systems allow inquiries about specific customer accounts in the subsidiary ledger (by account number) or about the control account.

As shown, postings are made monthly to the control account in the general ledger. We will learn, in the next section, how special journals facilitate monthly postings. We will also learn how to fill in the posting references (in the Ref. column) in both the general ledger and subsidiary ledger accounts. Postings to the individual accounts in the subsidiary ledger are made daily. The rationale for posting daily is to ensure that account information is current. This enables Mercier Enterprises to monitor credit limits, send statements to customers, and answer inquiries from customers about their account balances. In a computerized accounting system, transactions are simultaneously recorded in journals and posted to both the general and subsidiary ledgers.

ADVANTAGES OF SUBSIDIARY LEDGERS

Subsidiary ledgers have several advantages:

1. They show transactions that affect one customer or one creditor in a single account. They provide up-to-date information on specific account balances.
2. They free the general ledger from excessive details. A trial balance of the general ledger does not contain vast numbers of individual customer account balances.
3. They make a division of labour possible in posting. One employee can post to the general ledger while different employees post to the subsidiary ledgers. This strengthens internal control, since one employee verifies the work of the other.
4. They help locate errors in individual accounts. The potential for errors is minimized by reducing the number of accounts in one ledger and by using control accounts.

In a computerized accounting system, the internal control achieved by the double-checking of work performed by one employee by another employee, as described in item 3 above, doesn't happen as often. The accounting software is programmed to perform mathematical functions without error and to post entries to the subsidiary and general ledgers simultaneously. Consequently, computerized accounting systems do not make errors such as calculation errors and posting errors. Other errors, such as entry errors, can and do still occur. Internal control must be done using different means in computerized systems since account transactions are posted automatically.

Special Journals

As mentioned earlier, journalizing transactions in a two-column (debit and credit) general journal is satisfactory only when there are few transactions. To help with the journalizing and posting of multiple transactions, most companies use special journals in addition to the general journal.

If a company has large numbers of similar transactions, it is useful to create a special journal for only those transactions. Examples of similar transactions that occur frequently include all sales of merchandise on account, or all cash receipts. The types of special journals a company will use depend largely on the types of transactions that occur frequently for that company.

While the form, type, and number of special journals used will vary among organizations, many merchandising companies use the journals shown in Illustration C-2 to record daily transactions. The letters that appear in parentheses following the journal name represent the posting reference used for each journal.

STUDY OBJECTIVE 2

Record transactions in special journals and post to subsidiary and general ledgers.

Sales Journal (S)	Cash Receipts Journal (CR)	Purchases Journal (P)	Cash Payments Journal (CP)	General Journal (J)
All sales of merchandise on account	All cash received (including cash sales)	All purchases on account	All cash paid (including cash purchases of merchandise)	Transactions that cannot be entered in a special journal, including correcting, adjusting, and closing entries

ILLUSTRATION C-2
Use of special journals and the general journal

If a transaction cannot be recorded in a special journal, it is recorded in the general journal. For example, if you have four special journals, as listed in Illustration C-2, sales and purchase returns and allowances are recorded in the general journal. Similarly, correcting, adjusting, and closing entries are recorded in the general journal. Other types of special journals may sometimes be used in certain situations. For example, if sales returns and allowances are frequent, an additional special journal may be used to record these transactions. A payroll journal is another example of a special journal. It organizes and summarizes payroll details for companies with many employees.

The use of special journals reduces the time needed for the recording and posting process. In addition, special journals permit a greater division of labour. For example, one employee may journalize all cash receipts. Another may journalize credit sales. The division of responsibilities ensures that one person does not have control over related aspects of a transaction. In this instance, recording the sale and account receivable has been separated from recording the collection of cash from that receivable. This may reduce the opportunity for intentional fraud or unintentional error, and is one aspect of good internal control.

For a merchandising company, the same special journals are used whether a company uses the periodic or perpetual system to account for its inventory. The only distinction is the number of, and title for, the columns each journal uses. We will use Karns Wholesale Supply to show the use of special journals in the following sections. Karns uses a perpetual inventory system. The variations between the periodic and perpetual inventory systems are highlighted in helpful hints for your information. In addition, special journals under a periodic inventory system are shown more fully at the end of this appendix.

SALES JOURNAL

The sales journal is used to record sales of merchandise on account. Cash sales of merchandise are entered in the cash receipts journal. Credit sales of assets other than merchandise are entered in the general journal.

Journalizing Credit Sales

Under the perpetual inventory system, each entry in the sales journal results in one entry at selling price and another entry at cost. The entry at selling price is a debit to Accounts Receivable (a control account supported by a subsidiary ledger) and a credit of an equal amount to Sales. The entry at cost is a debit to Cost of Goods Sold and a credit of an equal amount to Merchandise Inventory. Some companies also set up Merchandise Inventory as a control account supported by a subsidiary ledger.

A sales journal with two amount columns can show a sales transaction recognized at both selling price and cost on only one line. The two-column sales journal of Karns Wholesale Supply is shown in Illustration C-3, using assumed credit sales transactions.

▶ILLUSTRATION C-3
Sales journal—
perpetual inventory system

KARNS WHOLESALE SUPPLY
Sales Journal   S1

Date	Account Debited	Invoice No.	Ref.	Accts. Receivable Dr. Sales Cr.	Cost of Goods Sold Dr. Merchandise Inventory Cr.
2014					
May 3	Abbot Sisters	101		10,600	6,360
7	Babson Co.	102		11,350	7,370
14	Carson Bros.	103		7,800	5,070
19	Deli Co.	104		9,300	6,510
21	Abbot Sisters	105		15,400	10,780
24	Deli Co.	106		21,210	15,900
27	Babson Co.	107		14,570	10,200
				90,230	62,190

Helpful hint In a periodic inventory system, the sales journal would have only one column to record the sale at selling price (Accounts Receivable Dr., Sales Cr.). The cost of goods sold is not recorded. It is calculated at the end of the period.

The reference (Ref.) column is not used in journalizing. It is used in posting the sales journal, as explained in the next section. Also, note that, unlike in the general journal, an explanation is not required for each entry in a special journal. Finally, note that each invoice is prenumbered to ensure that all invoices are journalized.

If management wishes to record its sales by department, additional columns may be provided in the sales journal. For example, a department store may have columns for home furnishings, sporting goods, shoes, etc. In addition, the federal government and practically all provinces require that sales taxes be charged on items sold. If sales taxes are collected, it is necessary to add more credit columns to the sales journal for GST Payable and PST Payable (or HST Payable).

Posting the Sales Journal

Postings from the sales journal are made daily to the individual accounts receivable accounts in the subsidiary ledger. Posting the total sales for the month to the general ledger is done monthly. Illustration C-4 shows both the daily postings to the accounts receivable subsidiary ledger and the monthly postings to the general ledger accounts. We have assumed that Karns Wholesale Supply does not maintain an inventory subsidiary ledger. However, if it did, the procedure is similar to that illustrated for the accounts receivable subsidiary ledger.

KARNS WHOLESALE SUPPLY
Sales Journal   S1

Date	Account Debited	Invoice No.	Ref.	Accts. Receivable Dr. Sales Cr.	Cost of Goods Sold Dr. Merchandise Inventory Cr.
2014					
May 3	Abbot Sisters	101	√	10,600	6,360
7	Babson Co.	102	√	11,350	7,370
14	Carson Bros.	103	√	7,800	5,070
19	Deli Co.	104	√	9,300	6,510
21	Abbot Sisters	105	√	15,400	10,780
24	Deli Co.	106	√	21,210	15,900
27	Babson Co.	107	√	14,570	10,200
				90,230	62,190
				(112)/(401)	(505)/(120)

> **ILLUSTRATION C-4**
> Sales journal—perpetual inventory system

Individual amounts are posted daily to the subsidiary ledger.

ACCOUNTS RECEIVABLE SUBSIDIARY LEDGER

Abbot Sisters

Date	Ref.	Debit	Credit	Balance
2014				
May 3	S1	10,600		10,600
21	S1	15,400		26,000

Babson Co.

Date	Ref.	Debit	Credit	Balance
2014				
May 7	S1	11,350		11,350
27	S1	14,570		25,920

Carson Bros.

Date	Ref.	Debit	Credit	Balance
2014				
May 14	S1	7,800		7,800

Deli Co.

Date	Ref.	Debit	Credit	Balance
2014				
May 19	S1	9,300		9,300
24	S1	21,210		30,510

The subsidiary ledger is separate from the general ledger.

Totals are posted at the end of the accounting period to the general ledger.

GENERAL LEDGER

Accounts Receivable   No. 112

Date	Ref.	Debit	Credit	Balance
2014				
May 31	S1	90,230		90,230

Merchandise Inventory   No. 120

Date	Ref.	Debit	Credit	Balance
2014				
May 31	S1		62,190	62,190cr[1]

Sales   No. 401

Date	Ref.	Debit	Credit	Balance
2014				
May 31	S1		90,230	90,230

Cost of Goods Sold   No. 505

Date	Ref.	Debit	Credit	Balance
2014				
May 31	S1	62,190		62,190

Accounts Receivable is a control account.

---

[1]The normal balance for Merchandise Inventory is a debit. But because of the sequence in which we have posted the special journals, with the sales journal first, the credits to Merchandise Inventory are posted before the debits. This posting sequence causes the temporary credit balance in Merchandise Inventory, which exists only until the other journals are posted.

A check mark (√) is inserted in the reference posting column to indicate that the daily posting to the customer's account has been made. A check mark is used when the subsidiary ledger accounts are not individually numbered. If the subsidiary ledger accounts are numbered, the account number is used instead of the check mark in the reference posting column. At the end of the month, the column totals of the sales journal are posted to the general ledger. Here, the column totals are posted as a debit of $90,230 to Accounts Receivable (account no. 112), a credit of $90,230 to Sales (account no. 401), a debit of $62,190 to Cost of Goods Sold (account no. 505), and a credit of $62,190 to Merchandise Inventory (account no. 120). Inserting the account numbers below the column totals indicates that the postings have been made. In both the general ledger and subsidiary ledger accounts, the reference S1 indicates that the posting came from page 1 of the sales journal.

Proving the Ledgers

The next step is to "prove" the ledgers. To do so, we must ensure two things:

1. The sum of the subsidiary ledger balances must equal the balance in the control account.
2. The total of the general ledger debit balances must equal the total of the general ledger credit balances.

The proof of the postings from the sales journal to the general and subsidiary ledgers follows:

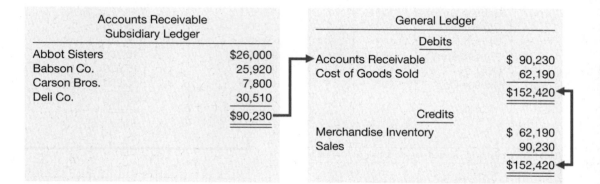

Advantages of the Sales Journal

The use of a special journal to record sales on account has a number of advantages. First, the one-line–two-column entry for each sales transaction saves time. In the sales journal, it is not necessary to write out the four account titles for the two transactions. Second, only totals, rather than individual entries, are posted to the general ledger. This saves posting time and reduces the possibility of errors in posting. Third, the prenumbering of sales invoices helps to ensure that all sales are recorded and that no sale is recorded more than once. Finally, there is a division of labour if the individual responsible for the sales journal is not given responsibility for other journals, such as cash receipts. These last two advantages help internal control.

CASH RECEIPTS JOURNAL

All receipts of cash are recorded in the cash receipts journal. The most common types of cash receipts are cash sales of merchandise and collections of accounts receivable. Many other possibilities exist, such as a receipt of money from a bank loan and cash proceeds from disposals of equipment. A one- or two-column cash receipts journal would not have enough space for all possible cash receipt transactions. A multiple-column cash receipts journal is therefore used.

Generally, a cash receipts journal includes the following columns: a debit column for cash, and credit columns for accounts receivable, sales, and other accounts. The Other Accounts column is used when the cash receipt does not involve a cash sale or a collection of accounts receivable. Under a perpetual inventory system, each sales entry is accompanied by another entry that debits Cost of Goods Sold and credits Merchandise Inventory. A separate column is added for this purpose. A five-column cash receipts journal is shown in Illustration C-5.

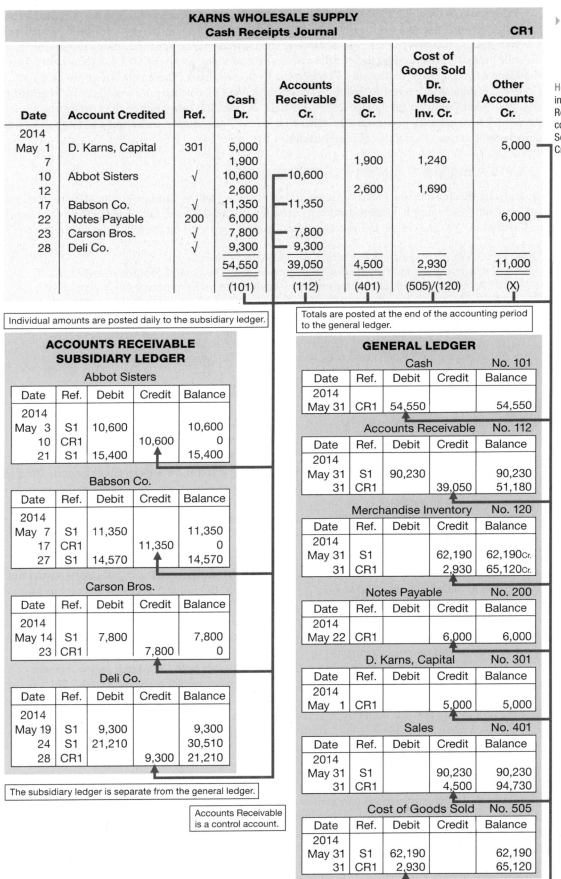

KARNS WHOLESALE SUPPLY
Cash Receipts Journal   CR1

Date	Account Credited	Ref.	Cash Dr.	Accounts Receivable Cr.	Sales Cr.	Cost of Goods Sold Dr. Mdse. Inv. Cr.	Other Accounts Cr.
2014							
May 1	D. Karns, Capital	301	5,000				5,000
7			1,900		1,900	1,240	
10	Abbot Sisters	√	10,600	10,600			
12			2,600		2,600	1,690	
17	Babson Co.	√	11,350	11,350			
22	Notes Payable	200	6,000				6,000
23	Carson Bros.	√	7,800	7,800			
28	Deli Co.	√	9,300	9,300			
			54,550	39,050	4,500	2,930	11,000
			(101)	(112)	(401)	(505)/(120)	(X)

> ▶ **ILLUSTRATION** C-5
> Cash receipts journal—perpetual inventory system
>
> Helpful hint In a periodic inventory system, the Cash Receipts journal would have one column fewer. The Cost of Goods Sold Dr. and Merchandise Inventory Cr. would not be recorded.

Individual amounts are posted daily to the subsidiary ledger.

Totals are posted at the end of the accounting period to the general ledger.

ACCOUNTS RECEIVABLE SUBSIDIARY LEDGER

Abbot Sisters

Date	Ref.	Debit	Credit	Balance
2014				
May 3	S1	10,600		10,600
10	CR1		10,600	0
21	S1	15,400		15,400

Babson Co.

Date	Ref.	Debit	Credit	Balance
2014				
May 7	S1	11,350		11,350
17	CR1		11,350	0
27	S1	14,570		14,570

Carson Bros.

Date	Ref.	Debit	Credit	Balance
2014				
May 14	S1	7,800		7,800
23	CR1		7,800	0

Deli Co.

Date	Ref.	Debit	Credit	Balance
2014				
May 19	S1	9,300		9,300
24	S1	21,210		30,510
28	CR1		9,300	21,210

The subsidiary ledger is separate from the general ledger.

Accounts Receivable is a control account.

GENERAL LEDGER

Cash   No. 101

Date	Ref.	Debit	Credit	Balance
2014				
May 31	CR1	54,550		54,550

Accounts Receivable   No. 112

Date	Ref.	Debit	Credit	Balance
2014				
May 31	S1	90,230		90,230
31	CR1		39,050	51,180

Merchandise Inventory   No. 120

Date	Ref.	Debit	Credit	Balance
2014				
May 31	S1		62,190	62,190cr.
31	CR1		2,930	65,120cr.

Notes Payable   No. 200

Date	Ref.	Debit	Credit	Balance
2014				
May 22	CR1		6,000	6,000

D. Karns, Capital   No. 301

Date	Ref.	Debit	Credit	Balance
2014				
May 1	CR1		5,000	5,000

Sales   No. 401

Date	Ref.	Debit	Credit	Balance
2014				
May 31	S1		90,230	90,230
31	CR1		4,500	94,730

Cost of Goods Sold   No. 505

Date	Ref.	Debit	Credit	Balance
2014				
May 31	S1	62,190		62,190
31	CR1	2,930		65,120

Additional credit columns may be used if they significantly reduce postings to a specific account. For example, cash receipts from cash sales normally include the collection of sales taxes, which are later remitted to the government. Most cash receipts journals have a separate credit column for sales tax collections. Other examples include the cash receipts of a loan company, such as Household Financial Centre, which cover thousands of collections from customers. These collections are credited to Loans Receivable and Interest Revenue. A significant saving in posting time would result from using separate credit columns for Loans Receivable and Interest Revenue, rather than using the Other Accounts credit column. In contrast, a retailer that has only one interest collection a month would not find it useful to have a separate column for Interest Revenue.

Journalizing Cash Receipts Transactions

To illustrate the journalizing of cash receipts transactions, we will continue with the May transactions of Karns Wholesale Supply. Collections from customers are for the entries recorded in the sales journal in Illustration C-3. The entries in the cash receipts journal are based on the following cash receipts:

May	1	D. Karns makes an investment of $5,000 in the business.
	7	Cash receipts for merchandise sales total $1,900. The cost of goods sold is $1,240.
	10	A cheque for $10,600 is received from Abbot Sisters in full payment of invoice No. 101.
	12	Cash receipts for merchandise sales total $2,600. The cost of goods sold is $1,690.
	17	A cheque for $11,350 is received from Babson Co. in full payment of invoice No. 102.
	22	Cash is received by signing a 4% note for $6,000, payable September 22 to the National Bank.
	23	A cheque for $7,800 is received from Carson Bros. in full payment of invoice No. 103.
	28	A cheque for $9,300 is received from Deli Co. in full payment of invoice No. 104.

Further information about the columns in the cash receipts journal follows:

Debit Columns:

1. Cash. The amount of cash actually received in each transaction is entered in this column. The column total indicates the total cash receipts for the month. The total of this column is posted to the cash account in the general ledger.
2. Cost of Goods Sold. The Cost of Goods Sold Dr./Merchandise Inventory Cr. column is used to record the cost of the merchandise sold. (The sales column records the selling price of the merchandise.) The cost of goods sold column is similar to the one found in the sales journal. The amount debited to Cost of Goods Sold is the same amount credited to Merchandise Inventory. One column total is posted to both accounts at the end of the month.

Credit Columns:

3. Accounts Receivable. The Accounts Receivable column is used to record cash collections on account. The amount entered here is the amount to be credited to the individual customer's account in the accounts receivable ledger.
4. Sales. The Sales column is used to record all cash sales of merchandise. Cash sales of other assets (property, plant, and equipment, for example) are not reported in this column. The total of this column is posted to the account Sales.
5. Merchandise Inventory. As noted above, the Cost of Goods Sold Dr./Merchandise Inventory Cr. column is used to record the reduction in the merchandise available for future sale. The amount credited to Merchandise Inventory is the same amount debited to Cost of Goods Sold. One column total is posted to both accounts at the end of the month.
6. Other Accounts. The Other Accounts column is used whenever the credit is not to Accounts Receivable, Sales, or Merchandise Inventory. For example, in the first entry, $5,000 is entered as a credit to D. Karns, Capital. This column is often referred to as the sundry accounts column.

In a multi-column journal, only one line is generally needed for each entry. In some cases, it is useful to add explanatory information, such as the details of the note payable, or to reference supporting documentation, such as invoice numbers if cash sales are invoiced. Note also that the Account Credited column is used to identify both general ledger and subsidiary ledger account titles. The former is shown in the May 1 entry for Karns' investment. The latter is shown in the May 10 entry for the collection from Abbot Sisters.

Debit and credit amounts for each line must be equal. Some accountants use the expression "the journal cross-adds" to describe this feature. When the journalizing has been completed, the amount columns are totalled. The totals are then compared to prove the equality of debits and credits in the cash receipts journal. Don't forget that the Cost of Goods Sold Dr./Merchandise Inventory Cr. column total represents both a debit and a credit amount. Totalling the columns of a journal and proving the equality of the totals is called footing (adding down) and cross-footing (adding across) a journal.

The proof of the equality of Karns' cash receipts journal is as follows:

Debit		Credits	
Cash	$54,550	Accounts Receivable	$39,050
Cost of Goods Sold	2,930	Merchandise Inventory	2,930
	$57,480	Sales	4,500
		Other Accounts	11,000
			$57,480

Posting the Cash Receipts Journal

Posting a multi-column journal involves the following steps:

1. All column totals, except for the Other Accounts total, are posted once at the end of the month to the account title specified in the column heading, such as Cash, Accounts Receivable, Sales, Cost of Goods Sold, and Merchandise Inventory. Account numbers are entered below the column totals to show that the amounts have been posted to the general ledger.
2. The total of the Other Accounts column is not posted. Individual amounts that make up the Other Accounts total are posted separately to the general ledger accounts specified in the Account Credited column. See, for example, the credit posting to D. Karns, Capital. The symbol X is inserted below the total for the Other Accounts column to indicate that the amount has not been posted.
3. The individual amounts in a column (Accounts Receivable, in this case) are posted daily to the subsidiary ledger account name specified in the Account Credited column. See, for example, the credit posting of $10,600 to Abbot Sisters.

The abbreviation CR is used in both the subsidiary and general ledgers to identify postings from the cash receipts journal.

Proving the Ledgers

After the posting of the cash receipts journal is completed, it is necessary to prove the ledgers. As shown below, the sum of the subsidiary ledger account balances equals the control account balance. The general ledger totals of the accounts that have been affected by the entries are also in agreement.

Accounts Receivable Subsidiary Ledger		General Ledger	
Abbot Sisters	$15,400	**Debits**	
Babson Co.	14,570	Cash	$ 54,550
Deli Co.	21,210	Accounts Receivable	51,180
	$51,180	Cost of Goods Sold	65,120
			$170,850
		Credits	
		Merchandise Inventory	$ 65,120
		Notes Payable	6,000
		D. Karns, Capital	5,000
		Sales	94,730
			$170,850

PURCHASES JOURNAL

All purchases on account are recorded in the purchases journal. The most common types of purchases on account are inventory and supplies but there are a variety of other items purchased, or expenses incurred, on account. Each entry in this journal results in a credit to Accounts Payable and a debit to either Inventory, Supplies or other accounts as appropriate. Each business designs its purchases journal based on the types of transactions that occur frequently that involve a credit to Accounts Payable.

The purchases journal for Karns Wholesale Supply includes separate columns for purchases of inventory and for supplies because these are the most common types of transactions on account for Karns. All other purchases on account are recorded in the Other Accounts columns. Karns' purchases journal for May is shown in Illustration C-6, with assumed credit purchases.

▶ **ILLUSTRATION** C-6
Purchases journal—
perpetual inventory system

KARNS WHOLESALE SUPPLY
Purchases Journal P1

Date	Account Credited	Terms	Ref.	Accounts Payable Cr.	Merchandise Inventory Dr.	Supplies Dr.	Other Accounts Account Debited	Ref.	Amount
2014									
May 6	Jasper Manufacturing Inc.	n/20	√	21,000	21,000				
10	Eaton and Howe, Inc.	n/20	√	7,200			Equipment	151	7,200
14	Fabor and Son	n/20	√	6,900	5,000	1,900			
19	Jasper Manufacturing Inc.	n/20	√	17,500	17,500				
26	Fabor and Son	n/20	√	8,700	7,800	900			
28	Eaton and Howe, Inc.	n/20	√	12,600	12,600				
				73,900	63,900	2,800			7,200
				(201)	(120)	(129)			(X)

Individual amounts are posted daily to the subsidiary ledger.

Totals are posted at the end of the accounting period to the general ledger.

Hel pful hint When a periodic inventory system is used, the debit to the Merchandise Inventory account is replaced by a debit to the Purchases account.

ACCOUNTS PAYABLE SUBSIDIARY LEDGER

Eaton & Howe, Inc.

Date	Ref.	Debit	Credit	Balance
2014				
May 10	P1		7,200	7,200
28	P1		12,600	19,800

Fabor and Son

Date	Ref.	Debit	Credit	Balance
2014				
May 14	P1		6,900	6,900
26	P1		8,700	15,600

Jasper Manufacturing Inc.

Date	Ref.	Debit	Credit	Balance
2014				
May 6	P1		21,000	21,000
19	P1		17,500	38,500

The subsidiary ledger is separate from the general ledger.

GENERAL LEDGER

Merchandise Inventory No. 120

Date	Ref.	Debit	Credit	Balance
2014				
May 31	S1		62,190	62,190 Cr.
31	CR1		2,930	65,120 Cr.
31	P1	63,900		1,220 Cr.

Supplies No. 129

Date	Ref.	Debit	Credit	Balance
2014				
May 31	P1	2,800		2,800

Equipment No. 151

Date	Ref.	Debit	Credit	Balance
2014				
May 31	P1	7,200		7,200

Accounts Payable No. 201

Date	Ref.	Debit	Credit	Balance
2014				
May 31	P1		73,900	73,900

Accounts Payable is a control account.

Journalizing Credit Purchases

Entries in the purchases journal are made from purchase invoices. The journalizing procedure for the purchases journal is similar to that for the cash receipts journal. In contrast to the cash receipts journal, there is a column indicating the terms of the purchase to ensure that a purchase discount is not missed.

Posting the Purchases Journal

The procedures for posting the purchases journal are similar to those for the cash receipts journal. In this case, postings are made daily to the accounts payable subsidiary ledger accounts and monthly to the accounts in the general ledger. In both ledgers, P1 is used in the reference column to show that the postings are from page 1 of the purchases journal.

Proof of the equality of the postings from the purchases journal to both ledgers is shown by the following:

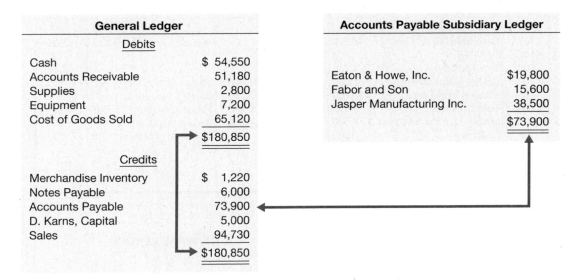

General Ledger		Accounts Payable Subsidiary Ledger	
Debits			
Cash	$ 54,550		
Accounts Receivable	51,180	Eaton & Howe, Inc.	$19,800
Supplies	2,800	Fabor and Son	15,600
Equipment	7,200	Jasper Manufacturing Inc.	38,500
Cost of Goods Sold	65,120		$73,900
	$180,850		
Credits			
Merchandise Inventory	$ 1,220		
Notes Payable	6,000		
Accounts Payable	73,900		
D. Karns, Capital	5,000		
Sales	94,730		
	$180,850		

Note that not all the general ledger accounts listed above have been included in Illustration C-6. You will have to refer to Illustration C-5 to determine the balances for the accounts Cash, Accounts Receivable, Cost of Goods Sold, Notes Payable, D. Karns, Capital, and Sales.

CASH PAYMENTS JOURNAL

All payments of cash are entered in a cash payments journal. Entries are made from prenumbered cheques. Because cash payments are made for various purposes, the cash payments journal has multiple columns. A four-column journal is shown in Illustration C-7.

Alternative terminology The cash payments journal is also called the *cash disbursements journal.*

Journalizing Cash Payments Transactions

The procedures for journalizing transactions in this journal are similar to those described earlier for the cash receipts journal. Each transaction is entered on one line, and for each line there must be equal debit and credit amounts. It is common practice in the cash payments journal to record the name of the company or individual receiving the cheque (the payee), so that later reference to the cheque is possible by name in addition to cheque number. The entries in the cash payments journal shown in Illustration C-7 are based on the following transactions for Karns Wholesale Supply:

May 3   Cheque No. 101 for $1,200 issued for the annual premium on a fire insurance policy from Corporate General Insurance.

3   Cheque No. 102 for $100 issued to CANPAR in payment of freight charges on goods purchased.

7   Cheque No. 103 for $4,400 issued for the cash purchase of merchandise from Zwicker Corp.

10   Cheque No. 104 for $21,000 sent to Jasper Manufacturing Inc. in full payment of the May 6 invoice.

19   Cheque No. 105 for $7,200 mailed to Eaton & Howe, Inc., in full payment of the May 10 invoice.

24   Cheque No. 106 for $6,900 sent to Fabor and Son in full payment of the May 14 invoice.

28   Cheque No. 107 for $7,500 sent to Jasper Manufacturing Inc. in partial payment of the May 19 invoice.

31   Cheque No. 108 for $500 issued to D. Karns as a cash withdrawal for personal use.

▶ILLUSTRATION C-7

Cash payments journal—perpetual inventory system

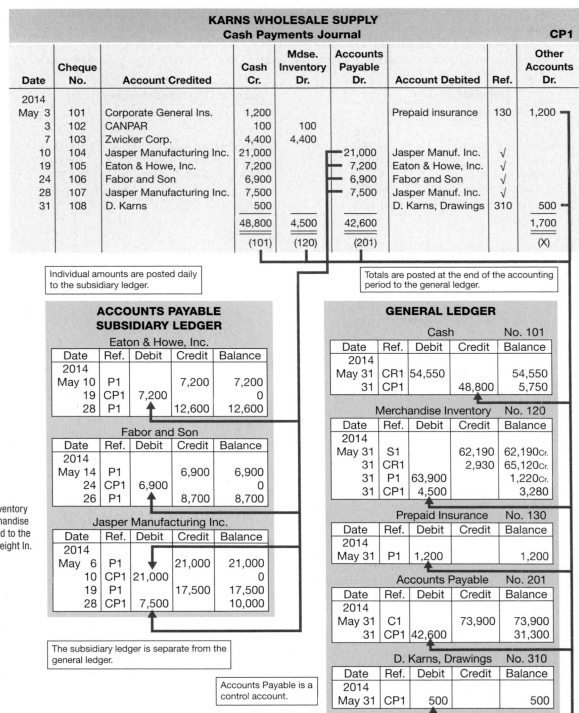

Note that, whenever an amount is entered in the Other Accounts column, a specific general ledger account must be identified in the Account Debited column. The entries for cheque numbers 101 and 108 show this situation. Similarly, a subsidiary account must be identified in the Account Debited column whenever an amount is entered in the Accounts Payable column (as, for example, the entry for cheque no. 104).

After the cash payments journal has been journalized, the columns are totalled. The totals are then balanced to prove the equality of debits and credits. Debits ($4,500 + $42,600 + $1,700 = $48,800) do equal credits ($48,800) in this case.

Posting the Cash Payments Journal

The procedures for posting the cash payments journal are similar to those for the cash receipts journal:

1. Cash and Merchandise Inventory are posted only as a total at the end of the month.
2. The amounts recorded in the Accounts Payable column are posted individually to the subsidiary ledger and in total to the general ledger control account.
3. Transactions in the Other Accounts column are posted individually to the appropriate account(s) noted in the Account Debited column. No totals are posted for the Other Accounts column.

> **Helpful hint** If a company has a subsidiary ledger for merchandise inventory, amounts in the merchandise inventory column would be posted daily in the cash payments journal, as well as in the sales, cash receipts, and purchases journals.

    The posting of the cash payments journal is shown in Illustration C-7. Note that the abbreviation CP is used as the posting reference. After postings are completed, the equality of the debit and credit balances in the general ledger should be determined. The control account balance should also agree with the subsidiary ledger total balance. The agreement of these balances is shown below. Note that not all the general ledger accounts have been included in Illustration C-7. You will also have to refer to Illustration C-5 to determine the balances for the Accounts Receivable, Cost of Goods Sold, Notes Payable, Capital, and Sales accounts.

General Ledger	
Debits	
Cash	$ 5,750
Accounts Receivable	51,180
Merchandise Inventory	3,280
Supplies	2,800
Prepaid Insurance	1,200
Equipment	7,200
D. Karns, Drawings	500
Cost of Goods Sold	65,120
	$137,030
Credits	
Accounts Payable	$ 31,300
Notes Payable	6,000
D. Karns, Capital	5,000
Sales	94,730
	$137,030

Accounts Payable Subsidiary Ledger	
Eaton & Howe, Inc.	$12,600
Fabor and Son	8,700
Jasper Manufacturing Inc.	10,000
	$31,300

EFFECTS OF SPECIAL JOURNALS ON THE GENERAL JOURNAL

Special journals for sales, purchases, and cash greatly reduce the number of entries that are made in the general journal. Only transactions that cannot be entered in a special journal are recorded in the general journal. For example, the general journal may be used to record a transaction granting credit to a customer for a sales return or allowance. It may also be used to record the receipt of a credit from a supplier for purchase returns or allowances, the acceptance of a note receivable from a customer, and the purchase of equipment by issuing a note payable. Correcting, adjusting, and closing entries are also made in the general journal.

    When control and subsidiary accounts are not used, the procedures for journalizing and posting transactions in the general journal are the same as those described in earlier chapters. When control and subsidiary accounts are used, two modifications of earlier procedures are required:

1. In journalizing, both the control and the subsidiary account must be identified.
2. In posting, there must be a dual posting: once to the control account and once to the subsidiary account.

To illustrate, assume that on May 31, Karns Wholesale Supply returns $500 of merchandise for credit to Fabor and Son. The entry in the general journal and the posting of the entry are shown in Illustration C-8. Note that if cash had been received instead of the credit granted on this return, then the transaction would have been recorded in the cash receipts journal.

▶ILLUSTRATION C-8
General journal

Helpful hint In a periodic inventory system, the credit would be to the Purchase Returns and Allowances account rather than to Merchandise Inventory.

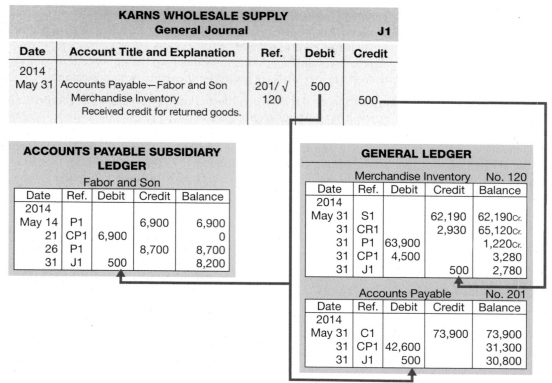

Notice that in the general journal, two accounts are indicated for the debit (the Accounts Payable control account and the Fabor and Son subsidiary account). Two postings (201/√) are indicated in the reference column. One amount is posted to the control account in the general ledger (no. 201) and the other to the creditor's account in the subsidiary ledger (Fabor and Son).

SPECIAL JOURNALS IN A PERIODIC INVENTORY SYSTEM

Recording and posting transactions in special journals is essentially the same whether a perpetual or a periodic inventory system is used. But there are two differences. The first difference relates to the accounts Merchandise Inventory and Cost of Goods Sold in a perpetual inventory system. In this system, an additional column is required to record the cost of each sale in the sales and cash receipts journals, something that is not required in a periodic inventory system.

The second difference concerns the account titles used. In a perpetual inventory system, Merchandise Inventory and Cost of Goods Sold are used to record purchases and the cost of the merchandise sold. In a periodic inventory system, the accounts Purchases and Freight In accumulate the cost of the merchandise purchased until the end of the period. No cost of goods sold is recorded during the period. Cost of goods sold is calculated at the end of the period in a periodic inventory system.

Each of the special journals illustrated in this appendix is shown again here in Illustrations C-9 to C-12. Using the same transactions, we assume that Karns Wholesale Supply uses a periodic inventory system instead of a perpetual inventory system.

▶ ILLUSTRATION C-9
Sales journal—
periodic inventory system

KARNS WHOLESALE SUPPLY
Sales Journal — S1

Date	Account Debited	Invoice No.	Ref.	Accts Receivable Dr. Sales Cr.
2014				
May 3	Abbot Sisters	101	√	10,600
7	Babson Co.	102	√	11,350
14	Carson Bros.	103	√	7,800
19	Deli Co.	104	√	9,300
21	Abbot Sisters	105	√	15,400
24	Deli Co.	106	√	21,210
27	Babson Co.	107	√	14,570
				90,230

Helpful hint Compare this sales journal with the one presented in Illustration C-4.

▶ ILLUSTRATION C-10
Cash receipts journal—
periodic inventory system

KARNS WHOLESALE SUPPLY
Cash Receipts Journal — CR1

Date	Account Credited	Ref.	Cash Dr.	Account Receivable Cr.	Sales Cr.	Other Accounts Cr.
2014						
May 1	D. Karns, Capital	301	5,000			5,000
7			1,900		1,900	
10	Abbot Sisters	√	10,600	10,600		
12			2,600		2,600	
17	Babson Co.	√	11,350	11,350		
22	Notes Payable	200	6,000			6,000
23	Carson Bros.	√	7,800	7,800		
28	Deli Co.	√	9,300	9,300		
			54,550	39,050	4,500	11,000

Helpful hint Compare this cash receipts journal with the one presented in Illustration C-5.

Helpful hint Compare this purchases journal with the one presented in Illustration C-6.

▶ ILLUSTRATION C-11
Purchases journal—
periodic inventory system

KARNS WHOLESALE SUPPLY
Purchases Journal — P1

Date	Account Credited	Terms	Ref.	Accounts Payable Cr.	Purchases Dr.	Supplies Dr.	Account Debited	Ref.	Amount
2014									
May 6	Jasper Manufacturing Inc.	n/20	√	21,000	21,000		Equipment	151	7,200
10	Eaton and Howe, Inc.	n/20	√	7,200					
14	Fabor and Son	n/20	√	6,900	5,000	1,900			
19	Jasper Manufacturing Inc.	n/20	√	17,500	17,500				
26	Fabor and Son	n/20	√	8,700	7,800	900			
28	Eaton and Howe, Inc.	n/20	√	12,600	12,600				
				73,900	63,900	2,800			7,200

> ILLUSTRATION C-12
Cash payments
journal—periodic inventory
system

Helpful hint Compare this cash payments journal with the one presented in Illustration C-7.

					KARNS WHOLESALE SUPPLY Cash Payments Journal			CP1
Date	Cheque No.	Payee	Cash Cr.	Accounts Payable Dr.	Account Debited	Ref.	Other Accounts Dr.
2014							
May 3	101	Corporate General Ins.	1,200		Prepaid Insurance	130	1,200
3	102	CANPAR	100		Freight In	516	100
7	103	Zwicker Corp.	4,400		Purchases	510	4,400
10	104	Jasper Manufacturing Inc.	21,000	21,000	Jasper Manuf. Inc.	√	
19	105	Eaton & Howe, Inc.	7,200	7,200	Eaton & Howe, Inc.	√	
24	106	Fabor and Son	6,900	6,900	Fabor and Son	√	
28	107	Jasper Manufacturing Inc.	7,500	7,500	Jasper Manuf. Inc.	√	
31	108	D. Karns	500		D. Karns, Drawings	310	500
			48,800	42,600			6,200

▶ Brief Exercises

Calculate subsidiary ledger and control account balances. (SO 1) AP

BEC–1 Information related to Bryan Company is presented below for its first month of operations. Calculate (a) the balances that appear in the accounts receivable subsidiary ledger for each customer, and (b) the accounts receivable balance that appears in the general ledger at the end of January.

Credit Sales			Cash Collections		
Jan. 7	Chiu Co.	$1,800	Jan. 17	Chiu Co.	$ 700
15	Elbaz Inc.	6,000	24	Elbaz Inc.	2,000
23	Lewis Co.	3,700	29	Lewis Co.	3,700

Identify general and subsidiary ledger accounts. (SO 1) K

BEC–2 Identify in which ledger (general or subsidiary) each of the following accounts is shown:

1. Rent Expense
2. Accounts Receivable—Chen
3. Bank Loan Payable
4. Service Revenue
5. Salaries Payable
6. Accounts Payable—Dhankar
7. Merchandise Inventory
8. Sales

Identify special journals. (SO 2) K

BEC–3 Chisholm Co. uses special journals and a general journal. Identify the journal in which each of the following transactions is recorded:

1. Sold merchandise on account.
2. Granted a cash refund for a sales return.
3. Received a credit on account for a purchase return.
4. Sold merchandise for cash.
5. Purchased merchandise for cash.
6. Received a collection on account.
7. Recorded depreciation on vehicles.
8. Purchased equipment on account.
9. Purchased merchandise on credit.
10. Paid utility expense in cash.

Identify special journals— perpetual inventory system. (SO 2) K

BEC–4 Swirsky Company uses the cash receipts and cash payments journals illustrated in this appendix for a perpetual inventory system. In October, the following selected cash transactions occurred:

1. Made a refund to a customer for the return of damaged goods that had been purchased on credit.
2. Received payment from a customer.
3. Purchased merchandise for cash.
4. Paid a creditor.
5. Paid freight on merchandise purchased.
6. Paid cash for equipment.
7. Received a cash refund from a supplier for merchandise returned.
8. Withdrew cash for personal use of owner.
9. Made cash sales.

Indicate (a) the journal and (b) the columns in the journal that should be used in recording each transaction.

BEC–5   Identify the journal and the specific column title(s) in which each of the following transactions is recorded. Assume the company uses a periodic inventory system.

1. Cash sale
2. Credit sale
3. Sales return on account
4. Return of merchandise purchased for cash refund
5. Payment of freight on merchandise delivered to a customer
6. Cash purchase of merchandise
7. Credit purchase of supplies
8. Payment of freight on merchandise purchased from a supplier

Identify special journals— periodic inventory system. (SO 2) K

BEC–6   Willis Company has the following year-end account balances on April 30, 2014: Service Revenue $53,800; Rent Revenue $12,000; Salaries Expense $19,400; Depreciation Expense $8,000; Supplies Expense $3,500; B. Willis, Capital $97,000; and B. Willis, Drawings $18,000.
   Prepare the closing entries for Willis Company.

Use general journal for closing entries. (SO 2) AP

BEC–7   As part of the year-end procedures, depreciation for furniture was recorded in the amount of $6,800 for Leelantna Company. Prepare the adjusting entry dated November 30, 2014, using the appropriate journal.

Use general journal for adjusting entry. (SO 2) AP

BEC–8   Following the preparation of the bank reconciliation for Lolitta Services, a correcting journal entry was needed. A cheque issued for the correct amount of $960 for a payment on account was recorded in the amount of $690. Prepare the correcting entry dated February 28, 2014, using the appropriate journal.

Use general journal for correcting errors. (SO 2) AP

▶ Exercises

EC–1   Below are some transactions for Dartmouth Company:

1. Credit received for merchandise returned to a supplier
2. Payment of employee salaries
3. Sale of land for cash
4. Depreciation on equipment
5. Purchase of supplies on account
6. Purchase of merchandise on account
7. Purchase of land for cash
8. Payment on account
9. Return of merchandise sold for credit
10. Collection on account from customers
11. Revenues and expenses closed to income summary
12. Sale of merchandise on account
13. Sale of merchandise for cash

Identify special journals. (SO 2) K

Instructions

For each transaction, indicate whether it would normally be recorded in a cash receipts journal, cash payments journal, sales journal, purchases journal, or general journal.

EC–2   Wong Company, a sole proprietorship owned by V. Wong, uses special journals and a general journal. The company uses a perpetual inventory system and had the following transactions:

Record transactions in sales and purchases journals— perpetual inventory system. (SO 2) AP

Sept.	2	Sold merchandise on account to T. Lu, $2,720, invoice #321, terms n/30. The cost of the merchandise sold was $1,960.
	3	Purchased supplies on account from Berko Co., $175.
	10	Purchased merchandise on account from Leonard Co., $800, FOB shipping point, terms n/30.
	11	Paid freight of $90 to A&F Shippers.
	11	Returned unsatisfactory merchandise to Leonard Co., $200, for credit on account.
	12	Purchased equipment on account from Wells Co., $7,700.
	16	Sold merchandise for cash to L. Maille, for $860. The cost of the merchandise sold was $490.
	18	Purchased merchandise for cash from Leonard Co., $450, FOB destination.
	20	Accepted returned merchandise from customer L. Maille, $860 (see Sept. 16 transaction). Gave full cash refund. Restored the merchandise to inventory.
	24	Paid the correct amount owing for the merchandise purchased from Leonard earlier in the month.
	25	Received payment from T. Lu for Sept. 2 sale.

26 Sold merchandise on account to M. Gafney, $890, invoice #322, terms n/30, FOB destination. The cost of the merchandise was $570. The appropriate party paid $75 to Freight Co. for shipping charges.
30 Paid September salaries, $2,360.
30 Withdrew cash for owner's personal use, $1,250.
30 Paid for supplies purchased on September 3.

Instructions

(a) Draw a sales journal and a purchases journal (see Illustrations C-3 and C-6). Use page 1 for each journal.
(b) Record the transaction(s) for September that should be recorded in the sales journal.
(c) Record the transaction(s) for September that should be recorded in the purchases journal.

Record transactions in cash receipts, cash payments, and general journals—perpetual inventory system. (SO 2) AP

EC–3 Refer to the information provided for Wong Company in EC–2.

Instructions

(a) Draw cash receipts and cash payments journals (see Illustrations C-5 and C-7) and a general journal. Use page 1 for each journal.
(b) Record the transaction(s) provided in EC–2 that should be recorded in the cash receipts journal.
(c) Record the transaction(s) provided in EC–2 that should be recorded in the cash payments journal.
(d) Record the transaction(s) provided in EC–2 that should be recorded in the general journal.

Record transactions in sales and purchases journals—periodic inventory system. (SO 2) AP

EC–4 Refer to the information provided for Wong Company in EC–2.

Instructions

(a) Draw a sales journal and a purchases journal (see Illustrations C-9 and C-11). Use page 1 for each journal.
(b) Record the transaction(s) for September that should be recorded in the sales journal.
(c) Record the transaction(s) for September that should be recorded in the purchases journal.

Record transactions in cash receipts, cash payments, and general journals—periodic inventory system. (SO 2) AP

EC–5 Refer to the information provided for Wong Company in EC–2.

Instructions

(a) Draw cash receipts and cash payments journals (see Illustrations C-10 and C-12) and a general journal. Use page 1 for each journal.
(b) Record the transaction(s) provided in EC–2 that should be recorded in the cash receipts journal.
(c) Record the transaction(s) provided in EC–2 that should be recorded in the cash payments journal.
(d) Record the transaction(s) provided in EC–2 that should be recorded in the general journal.

Record transactions in general journal and explain posting. (SO 1, 2) AP

EC–6 Lee Ltd. has the following selected transactions during October:

Oct. 2 Purchased equipment on account costing $13,200 from Lifelong Inc.
5 Received credit memorandum for $720 from Lyden Company for merchandise returned that had been damaged in shipment to Lee.
7 Issued a credit memorandum for $600 to M. Presti for merchandise the customer returned. The returned merchandise has a cost of $375 and was restored to inventory.

Lee Ltd. uses a purchases journal, a sales journal, two cash journals (receipts and payments), and a general journal. Lee also uses a perpetual inventory system.

Instructions

(a) Record the appropriate transactions in the general journal. If a transaction should be recorded in one of the special journals indicate the name of that journal.
(b) Assume now that Lee Ltd. uses a periodic inventory system. Record the appropriate transactions in the general journal.
(c) In a brief memo to the president of Lee Ltd., explain the postings to the control and subsidiary accounts.

Determine control account balances and explain posting. (SO 1, 2) AP

EC–7 Sven Co. uses both special journals and a general journal. On June 30, after all monthly postings had been completed, the Accounts Receivable control account in the general ledger had a debit balance of $137,800, and the Accounts Payable control account had a credit balance of $144,200.

The July transactions recorded in the special journals are summarized below. Sven Co. maintains a perpetual inventory system. No entries that affected accounts receivable and accounts payable were recorded in the general journal for July.

Sales journal: total sales, $98,670; cost of goods sold, $56,440
Purchases journal: total purchases, $39,700
Cash receipts journal: accounts receivable column total, $79,680
Cash payments journal: accounts payable column total, $42,300

Instructions

(a) What is the balance of the Accounts Receivable control account after the monthly postings on July 31?
(b) What is the balance of the Accounts Payable control account after the monthly postings on July 31?
(c) To what accounts are the column totals for total sales of $98,670 and cost of goods sold of $56,440 in the sales journal posted?
(d) To what account(s) is the accounts receivable column total of $79,680 in the cash receipts journal posted?

EC–8   On September 1, the balance of the Accounts Receivable control account in the general ledger of Mac   Post journals to control
Company was $10,960. The customers' subsidiary ledger contained account balances as follows: Jana, $2,440;   and subsidiary accounts.
London, $2,640; Cavanaugh, $2,060; and Zhang, $3,820. At the end of September, the various journals contained   (SO 1, 2) AP
the following information:

Sales journal: Sales to Zhang, $800; to Jana, $1,260; to Iman, $1,030; and to Cavanaugh, $1,100. The cost of each sale, respectively, was $480, $810, $620, and $660.
Cash receipts journal: Cash received from Cavanaugh, $1,310; from Zhang, $2,300; from Iman, $380; from London, $1,800; and from Jana, $1,240.
General journal: A $190 sales allowance is granted to Zhang on September 30.

Instructions

(a) Set up control and subsidiary accounts, and enter the beginning balances.
(b) Post the various journals to the control and subsidiary accounts. Post the items as individual items or as totals, whichever would be the appropriate procedure. Use page 1 for each journal.
(c) Prepare a list of customers and prove the agreement of the control account with the subsidiary ledger at September 30.

 Problems

PC–1   Selected accounts from the chart of accounts of Jinnah Ltd. are shown below: Record transactions in special
and general journals—
perpetual inventory system.
(SO 2) AP

101	Cash	201	Accounts payable
112	Accounts receivable	401	Sales
120	Merchandise inventory	412	Sales returns and allowances
126	Supplies	505	Cost of goods sold
157	Equipment	729	Salaries expense

The company uses a perpetual inventory system. The cost of all merchandise sold is 60% of the sales price. During January, Jinnah completed the following transactions:

Jan.	3	Purchased merchandise on account from Sun Distributors, $7,800.
	4	Purchased supplies on account from Moon Inc., $480.
	4	Sold merchandise on account to R. Wong, $6,500, invoice no. 371.
	5	Returned $1,450 of damaged goods to Sun Distributors.
	6	Made cash sales for the week totalling $2,650.
	8	Purchased merchandise on account from Irvine Co., $5,400.
	9	Sold merchandise on account to Tops Corp., $2,600, invoice no. 372.
	11	Purchased merchandise on account from Lewis Co., $4,300.
	13	Paid Sun Distributors account in full.
	13	Made cash sales for the week totalling $5,290.
	15	Received payment from Tops Corp. for invoice no. 372.
	15	Paid semi-monthly salaries of $11,300 to employees.
	17	Received payment from R. Wong for invoice no. 371.
	17	Sold merchandise on account to NFQ Co., $7,500, invoice no. 373.
	19	Purchased equipment on account from Mark Corp., $6,600.
	20	Cash sales for the week totalled $1,400.
	20	Paid Irvine Co. account in full.
	23	Purchased merchandise on account from Sun Distributors, $4,800.
	24	Purchased merchandise on account from Levine Corp., $4,690.
	27	Made cash sales for the week totalling $4,370.
	30	Received payment from NFQ Co. for invoice no. 373.
	31	Paid semi-monthly salaries of $11,000 to employees.
	31	Sold merchandise on account to R. Wong, $7,380, invoice no. 374.

Jinnah Ltd. uses a sales journal, a purchases journal, a cash receipts journal, a cash payments journal, and a general journal.

Instructions

(a) Record the January transactions in the appropriate journals.

(b) Foot and cross-foot all special journals.

(c) Show how postings would be made by placing ledger account numbers and check marks as needed in the journals. (Actual posting to ledger accounts is not required.)

Record transactions in special and general journals—perpetual inventory system. (SO 2) AP

PC–2 Selected accounts from the chart of accounts of Zu Company are shown below:

101 Cash
112 Accounts receivable
120 Merchandise inventory
126 Supplies
140 Land
145 Buildings
201 Accounts payable
401 Sales
505 Cost of goods sold
610 Advertising expense

The company uses a perpetual inventory system. The cost of all merchandise sold was 65% of the sales price. During October, Zu Company completed the following transactions:

Oct.	2	Purchased merchandise on account from Madison Co., $5,800.
	4	Sold merchandise on account to Petro Corp., $8,600, invoice no. 204.
	5	Purchased supplies on account from Frey Co., $315.
	7	Made cash sales for the week that totalled $9,610.
	9	Paid the Madison Co. account in full.
	10	Purchased merchandise on account from Chen Corp., $4,900.
	12	Received payment from Petro Corp. for invoice no. 204.
	13	Issued a debit memorandum to Chen Corp. and returned $260 of damaged goods.
	14	Made cash sales for the week that totalled $8,810.
	16	Sold a parcel of land for $45,000 cash, the land's book value.
	17	Sold merchandise on account to Trudeau Co., $5,530, invoice no. 205.
	18	Purchased merchandise for cash, $2,215.
	21	Made cash sales for the week that totalled $8,640.
	23	Paid in full the Chen Corp. account for the goods kept.
	25	Purchased supplies on account from Frey Co., $260.
	25	Sold merchandise on account to Golden Corp., $5,520, invoice no. 206.
	25	Received payment from Trudeau Co. for invoice no. 205.
	26	Purchased for cash a small parcel of land and a building on the land to use as a storage facility. Of the total cost of $45,000, $26,000 was allocated to the land and $19,000 to the building.
	27	Purchased merchandise on account from Schmid Co., $9,000.
	28	Made cash sales for the week that totalled $9,320.
	30	Purchased merchandise on account from Madison Co., $16,200.
	30	Paid advertising bill for the month from The Gazette, $600.
	30	Sold merchandise on account to Trudeau Co., $5,200, invoice no. 207.

Zu Company uses a sales journal, purchases journal, cash receipts journal, cash payments journal, and general journal.

Instructions

(a) Record the October transactions in the appropriate journals.

(b) Foot and cross-foot all special journals.

(c) Show how postings would be made by placing ledger account numbers and check marks as needed in the journals. (Actual posting to ledger accounts is not required.)

PC–3   The post-closing trial balance for Perrault Music Co. follows:

Record transactions in special and general journals—perpetual inventory system. (SO 1, 2) AP

PERRAULT MUSIC CO.
Post-Closing Trial Balance
December 31, 2013

		Debit	Credit
101	Cash	$ 17,900	
112	Accounts receivable	38,000	
115	Notes receivable	45,000	
120	Merchandise inventory	22,600	
140	Land	25,000	
145	Building	75,000	
146	Accumulated depreciation—building		$ 38,800
157	Equipment	6,450	
158	Accumulated depreciation—equipment		1,950
200	Notes payable		–
201	Accounts payable		34,200
275	Mortgage payable		67,400
301	M. Perrault, capital		87,600
310	M. Perrault, drawings	–	
401	Sales	–	
410	Sales returns and allowances	–	
505	Cost of goods sold	–	
725	Salaries expense	–	
		$229,950	$229,950

The subsidiary ledgers contain the following information:

1. Accounts Receivable—S. Armstrong, $6,500; R. Goge, $30,000; B. Lu, $1,500
2. Accounts Payable—Denomme Corp., $4,000; Harms Distributors, $16,000; Watson & Co., $14,200

Perrault Music Co. uses a perpetual inventory system. The transactions for January 2014 are as follows:

Jan.	3	Sold merchandise to B. Rohl, $3,000. The cost of goods sold was $1,250.
	5	Purchased merchandise from Warren Parts, $2,900.
	7	Received a cheque from S. Armstrong, $4,000, in partial payment of its account.
	11	Paid Lindon Co. freight on merchandise purchased, $350.
	13	Received payment of account in full from B. Rohl.
	14	Issued a credit memo to R. Goge for $6,000 as a sales allowance for a previous sale on account.
	15	Sent Harms Distributors a cheque in full payment of account.
	17	Purchased merchandise from Voyer Co., $4,900.
	18	Paid salaries of $3,900.
	20	Gave Watson & Co. a 60-day note for $14,000 as a partial payment of account payable.
	23	Total cash sales amounted to $7,700. The cost of goods sold was $4,840.
	24	Sold merchandise on account to B. Lu, $7,800. The cost of goods sold was $3,300.
	27	Sent Warren Parts a cheque for $1,150 in partial payment of the account.
	29	Received payment on a note receivable of $35,000 from S. Lava.
	30	Returned merchandise costing $400 to Voyer Co. for credit.
	31	Withdrew $1,300 cash for personal use.

Instructions
(a) Open general and subsidiary ledger accounts and record December 31, 2013, balances.
(b) Record the January transactions in a sales journal, a purchases journal, a cash receipts journal, a cash payments journal, and a general journal, as illustrated in this appendix.
(c) Post the appropriate amounts to the subsidiary and general ledger accounts.
(d) Prepare a trial balance at January 31, 2014.
(e) Determine whether the subsidiary ledgers agree with control accounts in the general ledger.

PC–4   The post-closing trial balance for Lee Co. follows. The subsidiary ledgers contain the following information:

Record transactions in special and general journals, post, and prepare trial balance—perpetual inventory system. (SO 1, 2) AP

LEE CO.
Post-Closing Trial Balance
April 30, 2014

		Debit	Credit
101	Cash	$ 36,700	
112	Accounts receivable	15,400	
115	Notes receivable—Cole Company	48,000	
120	Merchandise inventory	22,000	
157	Equipment	8,200	
158	Accumulated depreciation—equipment		$ 1,800
200	Notes payable	–	
201	Accounts payable		43,400
301	C. Lee, capital		85,100
310	C. Lee, drawings	–	
401	Sales		–
410	Sales returns and allowances	–	
505	Cost of goods sold	–	
725	Salaries expense	–	
730	Rent expense	–	
		$130,300	$130,300

The subsidiary ledgers contain the following information:

1. Accounts Receivable—W. Karasch, $3,250; L. Cellars, $7,400; G. Parrish, $4,750
2. Accounts Payable—Summers Corp., $10,500; Cobalt Sports, $15,500; Buttercup Distributors, $17,400

Lee uses a perpetual inventory system. The transactions for May 2014 are as follows:

May	3	Sold merchandise on account to B. Simone, $2,400. The cost of the goods sold was $1,050.
	5	Purchased merchandise from WN Shaw, $2,600, on account.
	7	Received a cheque from G. Parrish, $2,800, in partial payment of account.
	11	Paid freight on merchandise purchased, $318.
	12	Paid rent of $1,500 for May.
	13	Received payment in full from B. Simone.
	14	Issued a credit memo to acknowledge $750 of merchandise returned by W. Karasch. The merchandise (original cost, $325) was restored to inventory.
	15	Sent Buttercup Distributors a cheque in full payment of account.
	17	Purchased merchandise from Lancio Co., $2,100, on account.
	18	Paid salaries of $4,700.
	20	Gave Cobalt Sports a two-month, 10% note for $15,500 in full payment of account payable.
	20	Returned merchandise costing $510 to Lancio for credit.
	23	Total cash sales amounted to $9,500. The cost of goods sold was $4,450.
	27	Sent WN Shaw a cheque for $1,000, in partial payment of account.
	29	Received payment on a note of $40,000 from Cole Company.
	30	Purchased equipment on account from Summers Corp., $4,000.
	31	C. Lee withdrew $1,000 cash for personal use.

Instructions

(a) Open general and subsidiary ledger accounts and record April 30, 2014, balances.
(b) Record the May transactions in a sales journal, a purchases journal, a cash receipts journal, a cash payments journal, and a general journal, as illustrated in this chapter.
(c) Post the appropriate amounts to the subsidiary and general ledger accounts.
(d) Prepare a trial balance at May 31, 2014.
(e) Determine whether the subsidiary ledgers agree with the control accounts in the general ledger.

Record transactions in special and general journals—periodic inventory system. (SO 2) AP

PC–5 Selected accounts from the chart of accounts of Martin Ltd. are shown below:

101	Cash	401	Sales
112	Accounts receivable	412	Sales returns and allowances
126	Supplies	510	Purchases
157	Equipment	512	Purchase returns and allowances
201	Accounts payable	729	Salaries expense

During February, Martin completed the following transactions:

Feb. 3 Purchased merchandise on account from Zears Co., $4,200.
      4 Purchased supplies on account from Green Deer Inc., $290.
      4 Sold merchandise on account to Gilles Co., $5,220, invoice no. 371.
      5 Issued a debit memorandum to Zears Co. and returned $450 worth of goods.
      6 Made cash sales for the week totalling $1,950.
      8 Purchased merchandise on account from Fell Electronics, $7,200.
      9 Sold merchandise on account to Earlton Corp., $2,050, invoice no. 372.
     11 Purchased merchandise on account from Thomas Co., $9,100.
     13 Paid Zears Co. account in full.
     13 Made cash sales for the week totalling $3,850.
     15 Received payment from Earlton Corp. for invoice no. 372.
     15 Paid semi-monthly salaries of $14,100 to employees.
     17 Received payment from Gilles Co. for invoice no. 371.
     17 Sold merchandise on account to Lumber Co., $1,800, invoice no. 373.
     19 Purchased equipment on account from Brown Corp., $16,400.
     20 Cash sales for the week totalled $4,900.
     20 Paid Fell Electronics account in full.
     23 Purchased merchandise on account from Zears Co., $4,800.
     24 Purchased merchandise on account from Lewis Co., $5,130.
     27 Made cash sales for the week totalling $4,560.
     28 Received payment from Lumber Co. for invoice no. 373.
     28 Paid semi-monthly salaries of $14,900 to employees.
     28 Sold merchandise on account to Gilles Co., $9,810, invoice no. 374.

Martin Ltd. uses a sales journal, purchases journal, cash receipts journal, cash payments journal, and general journal. Martin uses a periodic inventory system.

Instructions

(a) Record the February transactions in the appropriate journal.
(b) Foot and cross-foot all special journals.
(c) Show how postings would be made by placing ledger account numbers and check marks as needed in the journals. (Actual posting to ledger accounts is not required.)

Cumulative Coverage—Chapters 2 to 6 and Appendix C

Review the opening account balances in Winter Company's general and subsidiary ledgers on January 1, 2014. All accounts have normal debit and credit balances. Winters uses a perpetual inventory system. The cost of all merchandise sold was 40% of the sales price.

GENERAL LEDGER

Account No.	Account Title	January 1, 2014 Opening Balance
101	Cash	$ 35,050
112	Accounts receivable	14,000
115	Notes receivable	39,000
120	Merchandise inventory	20,000
125	Supplies	1,000
130	Prepaid insurance	2,000
140	Land	50,000
145	Building	100,000
146	Accumulated depreciation—building	25,000
157	Equipment	6,450
158	Accumulated depreciation—equipment	1,500
201	Accounts payable	36,000
275	Mortgage payable	125,000
301	A. Winters, capital	80,000

Accounts Receivable Subsidiary Ledger		Accounts Payable Subsidiary Ledger	
Customer	January 1, 2014 Opening Balance	Creditor	January 1, 2014 Opening Balance
R. Draves	$1,500	Liazuk Co.	$10,000
B. Jacovetti	7,500	Mikush Bros.	15,000
S. Tang	5,000	Nguyen & Son	11,000

Winters' January transactions follow:

Jan. 3 Sold merchandise on credit to B. Sota $3,100, invoice no. 510, and J. Ebel $1,800, invoice no. 511.
5 Purchased merchandise on account from Welz Wares for $3,000 and Laux Supplies for $2,700.
7 Received cheques for $5,000 from S. Tang and $2,000 from B. Jacovetti on accounts.
8 Paid freight on merchandise purchased, $180.
9 Sent cheques to Liazuk Co. for $10,000 and Nguyen & Son for $11,000 in full payment of accounts.
9 Issued credit memo for $400 to J. Ebel for merchandise returned. The merchandise was restored to inventory.
10 Summary cash sales totalled $16,500.
11 Sold merchandise on credit to R. Draves for $1,900, invoice no. 512, and to S. Tang for $900, invoice no. 513.
15 Withdrew $2,000 cash for Winters's personal use.
16 Purchased merchandise on account from Nguyen & Son for $15,000, from Liazuk Co. for $13,900, and from Welz Wares for $1,500.
17 Purchased supplies on account from Laux Supplies, $400.
18 Returned $500 of merchandise to Liazuk and received credit.
20 Summary cash sales totalled $17,500.
21 Issued $15,000 note to Mikush Bros. in payment of balance due. The note bears an interest rate of 10% and is due in three months.
21 Received payment in full from S. Tang.
22 Sold merchandise on credit to B. Soto for $1,700, invoice no. 514, and to R. Draves for $800, invoice no. 515.
23 Sent cheques to Nguyen & Son and Liazuk Co. in full payment of accounts.
25 Sold merchandise on credit to B. Jacovetti for $3,500, invoice no. 516, and to J. Ebel for $6,100, invoice no. 517.
27 Purchased merchandise on account from Nguyen & Son for $14,500, from Laux Supplies for $1,200, and from Welz Wares for $2,800.
28 Purchased supplies on account from Laux Supplies, $800.
31 Summary cash sales totalled $19,920.
31 Paid salaries of $6,900.
31 Received payment in full from B. Soto and J. Ebel on account.

In addition to the accounts identified in the trial balance, the chart of accounts shows the following: No. 200 Notes Payable, No. 230 Interest Payable, No. 300 Income Summary, No. 310 A. Winters, Drawings, No. 401 Sales, No. 410 Sales Returns and Allowances, No. 505 Cost of Goods Sold, No. 711 Depreciation Expense, No. 718 Interest Expense, No. 722 Insurance Expense, No. 725 Salaries Expense, and No. 728 Supplies Expense.

Instructions

(a) Record the January transactions in the appropriate journal—sales, purchases, cash receipts, cash payments, and general.
(b) Enter the opening balances in general and subsidiary ledger accounts. Post the journals to the general and subsidiary ledgers. New accounts should be added and numbered in an orderly fashion as needed.
(c) Prepare an unadjusted trial balance at January 31, 2014. Determine whether the subsidiary ledgers agree with the control accounts in the general ledger.
(d) Prepare and post adjusting journal entries. Prepare an adjusted trial balance, using the following information: (1) Supplies at January 31 total $700 (2) Insurance coverage expires on September 30, 2014 (3) Annual depreciation on the building is $6,000 and on the equipment is $1,500 (4) Interest of $45 has accrued on the note payable (5) A physical count of merchandise inventory has found $44,850 of goods on hand.
(e) Prepare a multiple-step income statement and a statement of owner's equity for January, and a classified balance sheet at the end of January.
(f) Prepare and post the closing entries.
(g) Prepare a post-closing trial balance.

Company Index

Subject Index